ROGUE
REAL ESTATE
INVESTOR
COLLECTION

By Bryan Rundell and Michael Williams

Published by

Mind Like Water®

Overland Park, Kansas

Mind Like Water print edition: Copyright ©2004
First Mind Like Water electronic edition: Copyright ©2003
Mind Like Water hardcover ISBN: 0-9728848-9-0
http://www.rogueinvestor.com

Jacket design by Jeff Fuson
Research, editing by Diane Faile

Mind Like Water, Inc.
7419 Metcalf, # 321
Overland Park, KS 66204
913-381-4520
email: info@mindlikewater.com
website: http://www.mindlikewater.com

Published by

Overland Park, Kansas

ROGUE REAL ESTATE INVESTOR COLLECTION

CONTENTS

ROGUE
REAL ESTATE
INVESTOR

Published by

Mind Like Water®

Overland Park, Kansas

Disclaimer

The *Rogue Real Estate Investor Collection*, and the phone and email support provided with it, are designed to provide accurate information regarding the subject matter covered. However, there are no guarantees in real estate investing and the authors of this book provide no assurances regarding the success of the investing strategies presented.

Be aware that information on the Internet can change quickly. When relying on information provided in this book that is derived from the Internet, be sure to check that the information you have is the most up to date.

This book, the information provided through phone and email support, and information derived from the Internet are not a substitute for legal advice. Please consult a licensed attorney in your State, Province or area.

ROGUE
REAL ESTATE
INVESTOR

CONTENTS

Rogue Real Estate Investor

ONE

The Truth about Real Estate Investing

"Some people handle the truth carelessly;
others never touch it at all." – anonymous

So, you are thinking of investing in real estate or you own a house and would like to buy some rental property. Does the word "caveat emptor" sound familiar? Let the buyer beware! Real estate investing, including owning your own home, is a great way to enjoy a piece of the American Dream, but it comes with a price.

Rarely have I seen a realistic portrayal of both the good and the bad sides of real estate investing. Many late night infomercials and countless books would have you believe that "no money down" and creative financing techniques can take you from rags to riches with little more than the classified advertisements, a phone and a quick appointment to consummate the deal.

On the other hand, friends, family and even the Wall Street gurus will tell you that real estate investing is just not a good idea. It's not a liquid investment. The tax advantages were taken away in 1986. Renters are all low-life, societal rejects who are intent on destroying your property and living in your rental house for free.

As is usually the case, the truth lies somewhere in between. Few people will argue that owning your own home is a bad idea. After all, it is a forced method of investing in a financial instrument that you can see and feel, and the taxes and insurance are even deductible.

What about all the other ways to invest in real estate?

Contrary to what most people think, there are many different ways to invest in real estate:

- If you are a passive investor who desires a low-risk investment with almost no hassles that consistently returns about 15 percent per year, Real Estate Investment Trusts (REITs) might be your ticket.
- If you don't mind doing a little research, making some phone calls and possibly going to an auction, then tax lien certificates might interest you.
- If you are ready to get your hands dirty, but loathe the prospect of dealing with renters, then you might like buying undervalued real estate and fixing it up for a tidy profit.
- Finally, if you have enough courage to deal with renters, consider letting someone else pay down a mortgage and leave you with a handsome nest egg.

As you can see, I've only presented a few options for investing in real estate. It is my opinion that real estate should be an important part of an investor's portfolio. Why? First, land is a precious commodity that is more or less finite during our lifetime. The population of the world is growing and we will need more land to support the voracious demands of the human species. Second, natural resources such as lumber and building supplies are dwindling. With fewer supplies, prices are rising and existing homes are becoming more valuable. Finally, real estate is one of the few investments that you can use a little of your money and a lot of someone else's money (i.e., a mortgage company) to control a large investment.

Now, let's get back to the truth about real estate investing. As a real estate investor, I have read many books on the subject. I have attended seminars and classes, and I have purchased more than one of the infomercial programs. There is a lot of good information to be learned from this material; however, most real estate courses come at a hefty price. In the end, nothing works better than learning it on your own.

What are the benefits of real estate investing?

First, you make money through net cash flow, principal or equity, appreciation, and tax advantages. If you choose to be a landlord, your net cash flow is the difference between what you charge for rent and the monthly mortgage payment, including principal, interest, taxes and insurance. Unless you get the property at well below market value, it is a good rule of thumb to make at least $100 per month to offset the occasional repairs, fix-up costs, and move-in/move-out costs.

Equity is the amount of the original purchase price that you are actually paying off each month. The shorter the mortgage term and the lower the interest rate, the more equity you will accumulate.

Appreciation is by far the best part of real estate investing. Time is your friend. By investing in "bread and butter" houses (a term I picked up from Robert Allen [1990]) in good locations, the value of your house will rise each year. The better the location is, given a good economy, the higher the appreciation. In my area of Johnson County, Kansas (a suburb of Kansas City, Missouri), houses have appreciated over 7 percent per year for several years.

Finally, tax advantages include the following deductible items: depreciation of the property and other equipment, taxes and insurance, repairs and supplies, mileage, and office supplies used for the property.

That sounds pretty good so far. Are there any disadvantages?

You bet! First, if you buy a house using creative financing or if you buy a repossessed home, you are in for some fun times. Get ready for cleaning, painting, replacing carpeting, removing trash, mowing, raking, repairing plumbing, installing fixtures, replacing furnaces or air conditioners, and whatever else is needed to get the property sold or rented.

I recall a Veteran's Administration (VA) repossessed home that my wife and I bought in January 1996. While fixing it up, we heard several loud creaking sounds that eventually were followed by water spewing from broken copper pipes. Had we not been working when the water pipes thawed, the house would have been flooded. Luckily, the VA paid the plumbing bill because the pipes were apparently frozen when we bought the house.

Next, advertising for and securing a decent renter can be expensive and time consuming. The screening process for renters is often an arduous process of phone calls, screening, and crossing your fingers. If you are not nervous about renting your property, I suggest watching the movie *Pacific Heights*. Regardless of what your lease says, renters have inherent rights and, in the unfortunate event of eviction, you often lose.

Repairs are the Achilles heel of the rental game. After purchasing my first rental property, a continuously clogged sewer line led to installing a new line. Thank you very much – there went all of my annual net cash flow (approximately $1,200) in one fell swoop.

Finally, if you think that selling a property is as easy as a classified advertisement and a sign in the yard, you are wrong. Once a property has been labeled a rental house, its inherent value is slightly lower than owner-occupied houses. Even in a good market most buyers use a real estate agent. Why not? It's free after all. The seller has to pay the realtor fees, right? In actuality, the fees come from the real estate transaction and it may appear to be free, but really both the buyer and seller are paying the fees.

If I haven't scared you away, then let's get started with the 10 Steps to Getting in the Game.

TWO

10 Steps to Getting In the Game

"If you fail to plan, you plan to fail." – old saying

Step 1: Goals

What are goals? Goals are plans that we intend to achieve. Goals may change throughout our lives as our values change. Although you may not realize it, everyone has goals. For most people, goals are unwritten. Your daily goals may be to wake up on time, make it through work, and spend time with your family or friends.

Short-term goals for a real estate investor may include calling at least five property owners per week or making at least one offer on a property this month. Long-range goals may be to own and operate 10 rental properties, invest in one REIT mutual fund or attend one foreclosure or tax lien auction. You may aspire to other goals, such as owning a company, writing a book, or traveling around the world. These goals may seem unattainable, but they start by achieving small goals.

Stop for a few minutes and think about your long-range goals. Now write them down in the space provided below. Make sure that your goals are specific and measurable. Notice that a column is provided for a date by which you wish to achieve the goal.

Goal	Date to Complete

Now consider your short-term goals. Are they in alignment with your long-term goals? Each short-term goal should be a brick in the building of a long-term goal.

The most famous example of a study done on goals was completed on the 1954 graduating class at Yale. The study concluded that the 3 percent of the students who had written goals earned more money than the other 97 percent combined, who either lacked goals or had not formalized them (Zig Ziglar, 1995).

Comedy genius Jim Carrey had one huge goal – to become an actor. He was so convinced of this that he wrote his goal as a check to himself in the amount of 1 million dollars. As it turned out, he received his first movie role for that amount just before the date on his check. Now that's a goal you can "take to the bank."

I have read many books that stress the importance of formalized goals; however, very few ever get to the heart of the purpose of goals. Stephen Covey's book *The 7 Habits of Highly Effective People* (1990) has a great discussion on creating a personal mission statement. Many businesses, in fact, have personal mission statements. A personal mission statement simply describes your purpose. Let me share with you part of my personal mission statement.

> My mission is to live a complete and satisfying life, loving others
> and loving myself, inspiring others and challenging myself, giving
> to others and satisfying myself. My hope is that in some small
> way my presence makes a positive difference in the world.

I have also identified personal mission statements for various aspects of my life, such as being a father, husband, friend, professional, etc. My goals should always be in alignment with my personal mission statement.

Step 2: Get Your Personal Finances in Order

If you are thinking about any form of hands-on real estate investing, such as buying a home to fix up or purchasing a rental property, you will quickly find out that you must get your personal finances in order.

Check your credit history

Bank and mortgage companies will check your credit history. Wouldn't it be nice to know yourself what's going on? Even if you have excellent credit, often times the credit bureaus will have mistakes on your credit profile.

According to the Fair Credit Reporting Act, you may be entitled to receive a free copy of your personal credit report if you have been declined credit, employment or housing in the last 60 days, or if adverse action has been taken against you in the last 60 days. Some state laws require free reports or even a reduced fee for consumers in their states.

There are three major credit bureaus to check:

1. Experian (formerly TRW) – http://www.experian.com. For only $14.95 you can check your credit profile online, print it or save it to your computer. I just checked mine again. It is quite interesting to see what you've been up to and what the credit bureaus see. You may be able to receive a free copy, so check that first by calling this number: 866-200-6020. Otherwise, contact Experian by phone at 800-493-1058 or by postal mail at P.O. Box 9556, Allen, Texas 75013.

2. Equifax – http://www.equifax.com. You can order your personal credit profile online for a $12.95 service fee at the following web page: https://www.econsumer.equifax.com/webapp/ConsumerProducts/pgConsumerProducts. Use the following link to see if you qualify for a free credit report (by U.S. mail only): https://www.econsumer.equifax.com/consumer/forward.ehtml?forward=credu_privacyrights. To use Equifax's self-service line, contact them by phone at (800) 685-1111. A request by postal mail can be sent to Equifax Information Services, LLC, P.O. Box 740241, Atlanta, Georgia 30374.

3. Transunion – http://www.transunion.com. Like its competition, you can order a full credit report online for $19.85. To request a copy of your TransUnion Credit Report by phone, call 800-888-4213. You may also order your credit report by mailing your request to Transunion, P.O. Box 2000, Chester, Pennsylvania 19022.

Now, what happens if you find a mistake? Contact the credit bureau by certified letter and explain what the discrepancy is. Be sure to attach a copy of the disputed report. The credit bureau will then respond within approximately 30 days and if the item that you believe is a mistake, then the bureau must remove it from your report.

For legitimate problems that remain on your credit report, prepare a typewritten paragraph response that you can provide when applying for a loan. For example, if you missed a few payments because of a death, divorce, bad business loan, etc., be honest and explain what happened and why it's not a problem now.

Set up a personal filing system

I know this sounds a little obsessive, but you won't believe how much this has helped me maintain my personal finances over the last 10 years. Essentially, what you can do is to buy folders and label each according to major categories of expenses or other important information. Place the folders in a file box or cabinet. You will need a separate folder for each account, such as bank accounts, utilities, mortgages, credit cards, tax information, automobile expenses, loans, warranties, investments, etc. Start fresh each year so you will have your personal financial details by year and category.

Instead of looking in a drawer or box, I can look up my utilities in 1996 if I need to. I can check my Visa account for 1998 if someone has a question. Of course, most importantly you will need access to your tax information.

If you would rather have a personal filing system already designed and set up to maximize tax advantages, visit http://www.incometaxdirectory.com/my_tax_box.html.

Calculate your net worth

You will next need to figure out how much money you have and how much you are in debt. A fancy term for this is called "net worth." Gather your credit reports and your latest statements from banks, creditors and others. The simplest way to think about it is to divide your life into what you have and what you owe:

> **What You Own (Assets) =**
> Personal Property + Cash and Savings + Real Estate
>
> **What You Owe (Debt) =**
> Loans + Credit Card Debt + Real Estate Mortgages
>
> **Net Worth =** What You Own – What You Owe

What you own includes personal property such as available cash on hand, pennies in jars, furniture, jewelry, appliances, electronics, kitchenware, tools, lawnmowers, clothes, blankets, toys, etc. Think about what you have in terms of replacement. In other words, if a fire or natural disaster wiped out your home, what would you lose? You may be surprised. To be fair, you should really use a fair market value or discounted value of what your personal property is worth.

If you have any vehicles, find their "blue book" value. You can visit your public library and ask to see the Kelley Blue Book, or you can check online by using this link: http://www.kbb.com.

Next look at any and all savings accounts, checking accounts, mutual funds, stocks, bonds and other saving instruments. Find your latest statement and record how much you have saved.

Finally, if you own a house, rental properties, time-shares or any interest in real estate, determine a fair market value using one of the methods shown in Chapter 4. If you only own a percentage, be sure to account for that. For married couples, you will usually include both spouses' property and calculate one net worth.

Of course, the sobering truth comes when you calculate what you owe. First, go through all of your personal property, including vehicles, and write down all of your loan balances. Now take all of your credit card debt and other credit lines or loans and jot down all of your latest balances. Finally, find out the payoff balance on your house or any other real estate.

Here is an example of an easy way to calculate your own net worth using a spreadsheet. You can also do this on paper very easily. First write down all of your income and debt items on one column. Find the value (income) of each item and what you owe (debt) on each item. Subtract the income column from the debt column to come up with the net value of each item. Finally, add all of the items in the net value column to come up with your net worth. Notice that some items will be negative (this is especially true with credit card debt).

Net Worth Example
John and Shelly Heineman

Item	Income	Debt	Net Value
Cash	$200	$0	$200
Jewelry	$2,500	$495	$2,005
Furniture	$3,000	$2,450	$550
Tools	$1,000	$0	$1,000
Riding Lawnmower	$2,250	$925	$1,325
Motorcycle (Yamaha 850)	$500	$0	$500
Ford Explorer (2000)	$17,750	$16,950	$800
Honda Civic LX (2002)	$16,690	$17,250	-$560
Dell Pentium Computer	$1,650	$0	$1,650
Kitchenware	$3,000	$0	$3,000
Appliances	$2,500	$0	$2,500
Stereo System	$5,000	$0	$5,000
Visa Account	$0	$3,995	-$3,995
Student Loans	$0	$7,269	-$7,269
MasterCard	$0	$2,125	-$2,125
House	$132,500	$95,000	$37,500
Checking Account	$525	$0	$525
Savings Account	$2,148	$0	$2,148
Company 401k plan	$5,250	$0	$5,250
		Net Worth =	**$50,004**

Just looking over John and Shelly's net worth it is interesting to note that more than half of their net worth is related to real estate. If you are still renting, you might think twice about it now. Owning your own home is one of the best ways to start building a positive net worth. Imagine combining the net worth of your own home with that of other property and real estate investments.

As long as we are getting our personal finances in order, let's talk about debt. I think everyone reading this knows what debt is, but do you know that there are two types of debt – good debt and bad debt? This is open for debate, but I believe that it is important to distinguish between the two.

Real estate is the best example of good debt that I can think of. In fact, if you are not willing to take on some good debt, then your chances of financial independence will be severely limited. Your only other option is frugality and years of patience. Other types of good debt include student loans, home equity credit lines, supplier credit lines and personal signature loans.

Now, let's talk about bad debt. As you can imagine, the worst type of debt is revolving debt or credit card debt. Credit cards are not inherently bad, but how you use them can be devastating to your ability to succeed financially. In addition to their high interest rates (some as high as 24 percent), credit cards often have annual fees, late charges and credit limit fees. If you are seeking ways to become financially free, pay off your credit card debt. If you have equity in a house, consider obtaining a home equity loan to pay off the credit card debt.

Having said that, you should have at least one major credit card. In today's society, it's almost impossible to live without using a credit card. I use a Visa debit card for groceries, hardware, retail shopping, gasoline, restaurants and just about everything I do. Check with your bank about obtaining a debit card. For personal vacations and certain large purchases, I use a different credit card. For business, real estate and business travel, I use another card. As a bonus, the Visa card that I use gives me cash back. I just received a check for $120 cash back on my Visa account.

Why use a credit card? First, as long as you pay the balance off each month and are not late, it is like borrowing money for 30 days. Another reason to use a credit card is to establish your credit profile. Purchasing by credit card is also a great way to keep track of your purchases each month. It is especially valuable during tax season to have a nice record of your expenses. Finally, there is actually power in purchasing through a credit card. For example, if you purchase an item through a credit card and a problem arises and a retailer is not willing to exchange it or give your money back, you can actually call your credit card company and place a dispute. The credit card company will then contact the merchant and they must provide proof to substantiate their claim or you will be given your money back. It's a powerful and free ally.

Auto and personal loans probably rank second on the bad debt list. Automobiles, although necessary, are a depreciating asset and not an investment, except for a few vintage cars. If you are looking to free up cash flow for real estate investing, consider carefully what you are driving. Maybe the SUV is not really necessary for the bad weather that only occurs once or twice a season. Perhaps the extended cab truck is not really necessary to haul lumber once a year, when you can rent a pickup at U-Haul, Home Depot or Lowe's. Remember that the car loan is just one part of the total automobile cost; there are also insurance, inspections, repairs, sales tax and license fees.

Step 3: Consider Your Business Structure

Each and every business has a structure. You have probably seen or heard of businesses that are incorporated. For example, our company is called Mind Like Water, Inc. If you are just starting off, you will be working as a sole proprietor. All that means is that you and the business are the same. If you're married, most likely your household (i.e., husband and wife) and the business are the same.

A sole proprietorship is the easiest business entity available. You really don't need to do much of anything except keep track of your profit and loss so it can be included on your personal income tax return. You can even use your own checking account or set up a separate account and fill out paperwork to use a "doing business as" or DBA name. An example would be JBK Real Estate Investing. Notice that you cannot legally use a designator like Inc., Corp., LLC, etc.

Sole proprietorships have one major drawback. Not only does the money flow back and forth from your personal accounts, the liability or risk also flows back and forth. That is why as a business progresses, it is often set up in another structure to limit the personal liability of the owners.

Some small business structures to consider include the following: Subchapter S Corporations, Limited Liability Companies (LLCs), Limited Liability Partnerships (LLPs), general partnerships, Chapter C Corporations, and other structures.

LLCs

For real estate investors, probably the best option is a Limited Liability Company. LLCs are similar to Chapter S corporations, except they can exist for a defined period of time. Owners receive the tax advantages of a partnership, while also receiving the protection of a corporation. To make it even better, all states except Massachusetts allow an LLC to be formed with one person.

LLCs may be formed for most businesses, except some professional businesses that require licensing for protection of the public. Generally, doctors, lawyers, accountants and other professionals cannot use an LLC to practice. There are some other businesses that are exempt, but as far as real estate investing, you've found the jackpot.

Another reason to set up an LLC is that some states and other government agencies require either a U.S. social security number or a federal tax I.D. number to invest in foreclosed properties. With an LLC, even non-U.S. citizens can apply for a federal tax I.D. number.

Summary of LLC benefits:

- Allows for partnerships with limited liability.
- Protects personal assets of owners or members.
- One owner/member allowed in all states, except Massachusetts.
- Does not require annual shareholder meetings, like Chapter C and S corporations.
- Favorable tax status – can be set up and taxed at owner's tax rate (default) or as a company (requires filing other paperwork).

How does an LLC work?

First, decide on whether you will be setting up the LLC yourself or whether you'll contact an attorney or accountant. If you are planning to do it yourself, then decide where you will set it up. You do not have to set up an LLC in the state that you reside in; however, it may be easier. If you plan on setting it up in another state, you will probably need an agent or representative who lives in that state to act on your behalf. There are companies that will gladly do this for a small fee.

Decide on the structure of the LLC. There are two main types of LLC. One is called a member-managed LLC and the other is called a manager-based LLC. A member-managed LLC essentially says that all owners ("members" in LLC lingo) are equally responsible for management of the LLC. A manager-based LLC says that certain managers are given authority to run the LLC.

The manager-based LLC can get complicated if you offer ownership to others. The U.S. Internal Revenue Service (IRS) and states could perceive the LLC as selling securities, in which case you would fall under U.S. Securities Exchange Commission (SEC) regulations. To avoid this, make sure you only offer membership to a limited group of people, especially people whom you know or have dealt with, and keep the total membership under 35. There are other exemptions, so if you decide to set up a manager-based LLC, you may need to consult with an expert.

Decide on a name. Check your state's requirements. Usually the name must incorporate "LLC," "Limited Liability Company," or some other variation. An example would be Apex Properties, LLC. Check with the state to make sure the name has not been taken, before filling out the paperwork.

Now, what type of paperwork do you have to fill out? You really only need to fill out an Articles of Organization; however, you should also have an Operating Agreement that specifies the details of ownership, compensation, voting rights, etc.

Here is an example of Nebraska's Article of Organization form: http://www.sos.state.ne.us/corps/2606.pdf.

Here is an example of an Operating Agreement for Delaware: http://www.uschamber.com/sb/business/tools/opagree_m.asp.

After you have set up your LLC, don't forget insurance. You will need to obtain commercial liability insurance to cover losses. Please consult with an insurance agent.

To help you find out more information about setting up a business in a particular state, the following table provides relevant phone numbers and website addresses for all of the states:

State	Phone No.	Website Address
Alabama	334-242-5324	http://www.sos.state.al.us/business/corporations.cfm
Alaska	907-465-2530	http://www.dced.state.ak.us/bsc/corps.htm
Arizona	602-542-3135	http://www.cc.state.az.us/corp/index.htm
Arkansas	888-233-0325	http://www.sosweb.state.ar.us/corp_forms.html
California	916-653-3795	http://www.ss.ca.gov/business/business.htm
Colorado	303-894-2251	http://www.sos.state.co.us/pubs/business/main.htm
Connecticut	860-509-6001	http://www.sots.state.ct.us
Delaware	302-739-3073	http://www.state.de.us/corp/
District Columbia	202-442-4400	http://dcra.dc.gov/main.shtm
Florida	850-245-6051	http://www.dos.state.fl.us/doc/index.html
Georgia	404-656-2817	http://www.sos.state.ga.us/corporations
Hawaii	808-586-2727	http://www.businessregistrations.com
Idaho	208-334-2300	http://www.idsos.state.id.us/corp/corindex.htm
Illinois	800-252-8980	http://www.cyberdriveillinois.com/departments/business_services/home.html
Indiana	317-232-6576	http://www.in.gov/sos/business/index.html
Iowa	515-281-5204	http://www.sos.state.ia.us/business
Kansas	913-296-4564	http://www.kssos.org/main.html
Kentucky	502-564-2848	http://www.sos.state.ky.us
Louisiana	504-925-4704	http://www.sos.louisiana.gov/comm/comm-index.htm
Maine	207-624-7740	http://www.state.me.us/sos/cec/cec.htm
Maryland	410-767-1184	http://www.dat.state.md.us/sdatweb/charter.html
Massachusetts	617-727-9640	http://www.state.ma.us/sec/cor
Michigan	517-241-6470	http://www.michigan.gov/cis
Minnesota	877-551-6767	http://www.revisor.leg.state.mn.us/stats/322B
Mississippi	800-256-3494	http://www.sos.state.ms.us
Missouri	573-751-2359	http://www.sos.mo.gov/Default.asp
Montana	406-444-2034	http://sos.state.mt.us/css/BSB/Filing_Forms.asp
Nebraska	402-471-4079	http://www.sos.state.ne.us/corps/corpform.htm
Nevada	775-684-5708	http://sos.state.nv.us/comm_rec/crforms/crforms.htm
New Hampshire	603-271-3244	http://www.state.nh.us/sos/corporate/Forms.html
New Jersey	609-292-9292	http://www.state.nj.us/njbgs/index.html
New Mexico	800-947-4722	http://www.nmprc.state.nm.us
New York	518-473-2492	http://www.nmprc.state.nm.us/corporations/corpsforms.htm
North Carolina	888-246-7636	http://www.secretary.state.nc.us/corporations
North Dakota	701-328-4284	http://www.state.nd.us/sec/businessserv/registrations/index.html
Ohio	877-767-3453	http://www.sos.state.oh.us/sos/busiserv/index.html

Oklahoma	405-522-4560	http://www.sos.state.ok.us/forms/FORMS.HTM
Oregon	503-986-2200	http://www.sos.state.or.us/corporation/forms/index.htm
Pennsylvania	717-787-1057	http://www.dos.state.pa.us/dos/site/default.asp
Rhode Island	401-277-3040	http://www2.corps.state.ri.us/corporations/forms/
South Carolina	803-734-2158	http://www.scsos.com/forms.htm
South Dakota	605-773-4845	http://www.sdsos.gov/forms/
Tennessee	615-741-2286	http://www.state.tn.us/sos/service.htm
Texas	512-463-5583	http://www.sos.state.tx.us/corp/index.shtml
Utah	877-526-3994	http://www.commerce.utah.gov/cor/corpforms.htm
Vermont	802-828-2386	http://www.sec.state.vt.us/tutor/dobiz/llc/llchome.htm
Virginia	804-371-9733	http://www.state.va.us/scc/division/clk/fee_bus.htm
Washington	360-753-7115	http://www.secstate.wa.gov/corps
West Virginia	304-558-8000	http://www.wvsos.com/business/services/formindex.htm
Wisconsin	608-261-7577	http://www.wdfi.org/corporations/default.htm
Wyoming	307-777-7311	http://soswy.state.wy.us/corporat/corporat.htm

Contact your state and find out what forms are necessary. An excellent resource for information on LLCs is the Nolo law guide entitled, *Form Your Own Limited Liability Company* (2000).

Step 4: Purchase Umbrella Liability Insurance

When you first start investing, you may be too busy to deal with a business structure other than a sole proprietorship; therefore, it is important to limit your liability as cheaply as possible. One way is to purchase an umbrella liability policy. Umbrella Liability Insurance is extremely cheap, usually only a few hundred dollars per year for a million dollars worth of coverage.

Most policies will make you bump up your current limits for your automobiles and house before they will issue an umbrella policy. As you purchase rental units you will also need to inform your insurance company so that each one can be added on your policy.

If you haven't already, you should consider consolidating all of your insurance to one company and requesting a discount. That's what I have done. That way you will be dealing with the same company.

Here is why it's important. What if you purchase a property with a current renter and the next day an ice storm causes one of your tenants to fall and break an arm? The tenant may have the right to sue you for not clearing the walkway. A good umbrella policy in combination with your property insurance should cover you. By all means, please speak with an insurance specialist and read your policy in depth.

Step 5: Consider the Tax Implications of Everything You Do

You're a business now so it's time to reap the rewards that Congress has established for business owners. It basically boils down to this. You can offset income by considering all allowable expenses. For some of you, this will be a new way of thinking.

First and foremost, buy one or more blank journal books and keep it in any vehicle that you are going to use to look for, purchase and maintain real estate or rental property. Write down the starting date and mileage of your car. This will be the date that it was "put into service." Now, every trip, and I mean every trip, that is related to your real estate business gets recorded. Why? Because you can take a mileage deduction for all mileage related to your real estate business. There is also an automobile deduction, which can be taken instead of mileage, but for now it is easiest to just use the standard mileage deduction. This changes, but is currently at 37.5 cents per mile. Be sure to record the following trips:

- Looking for property.
- Meeting someone to look at a property.
- Visiting a bank or mortgage company.
- Going to the library or bookstore for research material.
- Visiting the courthouse.
- Buying supplies at a hardware store.
- Buying marketing supplies.
- Buying office supplies.
- Meeting with a partner to discuss a real estate venture.

Do not feel guilty about recording even the most mundane real estate activity.

Next, keep track of all receipts related to your real estate, such as books, office supplies, calculator, computer, hardware, tools, advertising, marketing, professional fees (attorneys, accountants, etc.). An easy way to do this is to set up a separate checking account and use a separate credit card. Be careful, some items may require keeping track of usage, such as a computer used for both personal and business activities. Your tax specialist or accountant will be able to help you or you can learn it as you go.

Step 6: Marketing

Like any business, you will need to spend some time developing or having someone develop business cards, logos, flyers, advertising copy and even magnetic signs for your car. You may even want to develop a website to showcase property that you have for sale.

Real estate investing is a business, so you should treat it like one.

Step 7: Setting Up Your Business at Home

The final step in becoming a business is to set up an office or area in your home or apartment to use for conducting business. Since you will be placing a lot of phone calls and receiving a lot of responses, make sure that you have an answering machine or voice mail. Depending upon the impact of the phone calls on your family, you might consider getting a separate phone line, mobile phone or both. You will have to judge this on your own, but remember the object is to make money not spend it. Try to balance being frugal with being professional.

Most of you reading this already have a computer, but if you don't, most public libraries now offer computers with online access. With the Internet and the World Wide Web, research is just a few clicks away.

Other office equipment to consider as the need arises is a fax machine, a scanner or small copier, file cabinets and a desk. One way around some of the added expenses is to use a local mail and copy shop, such as Mail Boxes Etc. or Kinkos.

Step 8: Buy Your Own Home First

Probably the single most important investment decision you'll ever make is to buy your own home. You've probably heard it before and you may be saying it yourself, "Yeah right, I can barely afford groceries." If you don't buy a house, you'll never feel comfortable enough to use the real estate strategies I'm discussing. If you don't buy a house, you are making someone else rich off of your sweat. If you don't buy a house, you are less likely to build a substantial nest egg. If you don't buy a house, you'll be paying Uncle Sam more in taxes than you have to. I know the most common reason for not buying a house is coming up with the down payment. Believe me, it is possible if you set your goals, save and use some of the information contained in this book. My wife and I were able to buy our first house through a Federal Housing Administration (FHA) first-time homebuyer program with only 3 percent down plus some closing costs. I was then able to borrow against my 401(k) plan at work for the down payment for a near no-money down proposition.

Owning your own home is not a walk through dreamland. There will be maintenance, painting, stopped toilets, water heaters to replace, air conditioners to fix and even the occasional large expense of a new roof or driveway, but it's your property. There is a sense of pride that comes with owning a piece of the world.

If you are thinking about buying a house, I recommend contacting a good real estate agent who works in the area you are interested in. Have the real estate agent act as your "buyer's agent" and she will be highly motivated to find you a property. You do know what areas you are interested in, right? I hate to use this cliché, but I feel compelled to remind you about the three most important things in real estate: (1) location, (2) location and (3) location. What this really means is finding an area where housing is appreciating (going up in value), with good schools, parks and police. Make sure it is not too far from a metropolitan center or area of employment.

As a side benefit of buying your first house, you will get a quick education in the real estate industry. You will encounter numerous real estate agents and brokers. You will learn how to evaluate a house, make an offer and a counter offer. You will get to sign a contract, and work with a title company, as well as structural and mechanical engineers/inspectors. In other words, you will see the whole real estate industry in action. If you plan on building a house, there's even more to consider, such as architectural plans, soil testing, environmental surveys, general contractors, subcontractors, and "a partridge in a pear tree."

Step 9: Learn the Industry

As I have alluded to, real estate is not unlike any other profession. Each profession has its own set of rules and language that you must learn. If you are old enough to have worked in any industry, you know that there are things you do and say that only apply to where you work.

My first job at age 16 was working as busboy. Perhaps you have heard some restaurant lingo, like "86ing" something, which means to get rid of it. More recently, in the environmental field, acronym-speak is so prevalent that you might think another language was being spoken. Here's an example: "In reviewing the Phase I, I noted that most of the BTEX compounds were ND." If you understood that, then you must work in the field. The point is that real estate is the same and you must learn the lingo. I even have a dictionary of real estate terms. Appendix A of this book contains a list of what I believe are some of the most important terms, acronyms and abbreviations.

Spend at least a couple of minutes going through Appendix A. Occasionally we add new real estate definitions on our site at http://www.rogueinvestor.com/definitions/real_estate_investing_definitions.html.

Make sure you are comfortable with the real estate lingo. Here is a quick assignment for you (hint, the answers are given at the end of this chapter):

1. What is the difference between real estate and real property?
2. What is a deed and how does it differ from a mortgage?
3. The difference between what someone owes on a mortgage and what a property is worth is called what?
4. What does FSBO stand for?
5. What is the MLS?
6. The value of most residential property is determined using the CMA process, which is what?
7. Name at least one other method for estimating the value of real estate.
8. Is a fixture, like a ceiling fan, personal property or real property?
9. An agreement between two or more competent and legal parties is called what?
10. A real estate agent who works for a buyer is called what?
11. A real estate agent must work for a _____?
12. Moving a first mortgage to a second mortgage is called what?
13. What is the best type of deed?
14. Oftentimes, one divorcee will use a _____ deed to remove his/her interest in a property.
15. True or false? Contractors are allowed by law to place a lien on a property if the owner fails to pay their fees.
16. Most conventional lenders require at least 20 percent down or PMI must be obtained. What is PMI?
17. What does PITI stand for?
18. What is an ARM?

Step 10: Know Your Investing Options

What are your investing options? First, you have to decide if you want to be a hands-on or hands-off real estate investor. There are obviously benefits and downsides to each one. Many real estate packages focus only on hands-on investing, such as buying and selling houses or investing in rental property. While this is a great way to build a substantial net worth, it may not be what you're looking for. If you're looking for a more passive way to invest in real estate, consider the following options:

Tax lien certificates

Tax liens result when real estate owners fail to pay their property taxes. County and municipal governments rely heavily on tax revenue and rather than fight with property owners in court, they have devised a revenue collection method that allows them to be paid, results in penalties to property owners and enables investors to make some serious money. Every state and county is different, but essentially an investor can bid on a tax lien certificate, which allows him or her to have control of the lien. Property owners must pay off the lien holder (investor) with interest or face possible foreclosure.

To make it even better, the interest rates are often high and it is a safe investment that is backed by a local government entity. What kind of returns can you expect? Here is a sampling:

- Arizona – 16%
- Florida – 18%
- Illinois – 18% for six months
- Iowa – 24%
- New Jersey – 18 to 24%.

Tax deed sales

Some states and Canadian provinces foreclose on the tax liens and take possession of the property's deed. The deeds are then auctioned off and you bid on possession of the property. In many cases, you can pick up real estate for 20 to 30 percent of its value. In essence, you are buying into a lot of instant equity. Tax deeds are one of the most exciting and profitable ways to invest in real estate.

For instance, imagine finding a lake front lot in a prestigious community with a nearby golf course and all the amenities. Now consider that the property values for lake front lots in this area are $90,000 to $125,000. What if I told you that because the owner failed to pay his taxes the county took possession of the property and offered it for sale for around $14,000, which included the minimum bid, taxes and fees? Imagine you have to bid a little bit higher to make sure you win, let's say by roughly $2,000. This hypothetical example is true!

Real estate investment trusts

Briefly, REITs are trusts that pool real estate properties together and allow investors to own a small portion, just like stocks or mutual funds. REITs have some very specific guidelines to follow, such as paying out 95 percent of their profits to their shareholders every year. This often results in high dividend yields, with relatively low risk.

REIT dividend payouts are sometimes huge. I purchased a REIT a few days before the company issued its normal dividend, plus a special dividend. In less than one month the 200 shares I purchased paid out 2.6 percent or $98.50 from my $3,815.95 initial investment. On an annual basis that's over 50 percent return, even taking into account the $12 trading fee. What's even better is that REITs issue dividends four times per year, not just once. The final icing on the cake is that the stock price has gone up about $1 per share, so that's an extra $200 or 5 percent.

Discounted mortgages/notes

Another little known investing option is to invest in mortgages or notes. As you will see in Chapter 5, it is possible to make creative financing arrangements in part by using promissory notes. A promissory note is essentially an IOU or a loan. It has an amount, interest rate and length of term.

A note can be purchased from a homeowner or other investor by simply discounting the note to present value and purchasing the note. This is possible because there is a time value associated with money. In other words, $1,000 is more valuable today than it is in 20 years. That only makes sense, right? In 20 years, $1,000 won't buy as much stuff due to inflation.

The opposite is also true. For example, let's say Betty has a $15,000 note with an interest rate of 9 percent. It is amortized over 10 years. Plugging these numbers into my handy calculator, the present value of the note is $6,119.06. Therefore, you could explain to Betty that she can either wait or have her money now. Betty, who is elderly and wants nothing more than to go on a cruise, may accept your offer. Meanwhile, you have a wonderful, low-risk investment that yields 9 percent interest and is probably secured by real estate. You can even use the purchased note to buy other real estate. Of course, you'll use the full value of the note, or $15,000.

If, however, you are feeling a little more adventurous and would rather see a physical product than a piece of paper, you are ready for hands-on real estate investing. There are essentially three types of property to consider: land, commercial property and residential real estate.

Land

Have you ever caught yourself saying something like, "I should have bought some land there years ago?" This usually happens after you see a new strip mall or housing addition being built on virgin land. Well, it's true that they're not making any more of it, land that is, but be careful if you are thinking about investing in land, especially if you are planning on paying retail prices.

Why? Even if you are good at predictions, you may have to wait 20 to 30 years for land to appreciate to a level that makes it worth your while. In the meantime, you will be paying taxes, assessments and maintenance fees. You also can't depreciate land; therefore, you might miss out on some lucrative tax advantages.

According to Carleton Sheets (1994), the average annual cost of owning vacant land runs between 15 and 20 percent of what you paid for it. Using a common investing trick called the Rule of 76, your land would need to double in value every four to five years to make it worthwhile.

Now having said that, purchasing land at sharp discounts, such as those found in foreclosure or tax sales, can be highly profitable. Imagine paying approximately 10 to 20 percent of the market value of residential lots or acreage. I don't need to imagine. I have done it, and you can too. For more information on buying land, refer to Bonus Gift Number 1.

Commercial property

Commercial property is what I would consider speculative real estate investing. The gains can be substantial and the risks are not for the faint of heart.

Why?

Commercial real estate is tied closely to the business environment. Consider the recent Internet bubble that essentially ended at the turn of the century. At the peak of absurdity, business rents skyrocketed and property owners were smiling all the way to the bank. Now, vacancies have soared again with many companies going out of business. Many commercial property owners are scrambling to find business tenants.

Commercial properties come in all sizes and shapes and if there's one nice thing about owning commercial real estate it's the lease terms, which are usually a minimum of three to five years. Commercial property leases also require much more of the tenant, such as maintenance and repairs.

Having said that, with the recent downturn in the economy, it is also a good time to pick up commercial property for very attractive terms. If you are looking for business space, now is also a great time to negotiate inexpensive leases with good terms.

If you are considering commercial property, be sure to do your homework. Read Chapter 10 on managing environmental risk.

Residential real estate

The real "bread and butter" for most real estate investors, including myself, is residential property. Residential properties include single-family homes, duplexes, x-plexes (x = any number) and apartments.

This is the "bread and butter" of investing because we all need to live somewhere, regardless of where we work or whether we are in school. Young, old, poor and wealthy all live in some dwelling that either they or someone else owns.

First, let's distinguish what I consider the two primary types of residential real estate investments. The first type of property is a growth property, or a property that appreciates in value either due to its wonderful location or your sweat equity or both. The second type of property is an income property. An income property may or may not be located in a good location, but the rents provide you with positive cash flow income, similar to a stock dividend. Again, realize that you don't just sit back and watch the money flow in. You have to work for it occasionally.

You will encounter both types of property. Just like other types of investing, it is a good idea to diversify and own both income and growth properties.

Now, on with the search.

But first, here are the answers to the questions presented earlier in this chapter:

1. Although very similar, real property actually contains a bundle of rights in addition to the real estate. Rights may include mineral, water, air or a number of other things.
2. A deed is a legal document used to transfer real estate. A mortgage is a promise to pay a loan secured by the deed.
3. Equity.
4. For Sale By Owner.
5. The Multiple Listing Service.
6. Competitive Market Analysis uses comparable properties to estimate the value of real estate. It is usually used for single-family homes.
7. Replacement Cost or Income Method.
8. A ceiling fan is personal property until it is attached to the property, at which time it becomes real property.
9. Contract.
10. Buyer's agent.
11. Broker.
12. Subordination.
13. General warranty deed.
14. Quitclaim deed.
15. True. They can place a mechanic's lien on a property.
16. Private mortgage insurance.
17. Principal, Interest, Taxes and Insurance.
18. Adjustable rate mortgage.

THREE

The Search Begins:
Looking for and Evaluating Real Estate

*"The business that we love we rise betime,
and go to it with delight." – Shakespeare*

I consider searching for attractive real estate as fun and you should too. It's almost a game or perhaps a puzzle. Every week new listings can be found in the classified section of your local newspaper and in the Multiple Listing Service (MLS). With the proliferation of the Internet, many of these same listings are available online. With all of these options, you may be asking, "where should I start?"

Search Methods

Newspaper classifieds

The Sunday classified section is still the best place to find real estate. Purchase the Sunday paper each week (save your receipts for tax purposes), get a subscription or wait until it is placed online, if your paper has that capability. Read through the classified advertisements once or twice and circle potential listings. Look for key phrases like any of the following:

- Owner anxious
- Possible owner/seller financing
- Lease option
- Investment property
- Needs TLC
- Fix up and save
- Needs update, carpet and paint
- Investors
- Good investment
- Duplex, triplex, 4-plex, apartment.

Of course, realtors know all of these phrases too, so be a little cautious. For hands-on investing, you are looking for income properties that will produce positive cash flow and that are in an acceptable location. For growth properties, you are looking for properties that are undervalued and that, with a little painting, shrubbery and cleaning, could be resold for a profit or rented for a positive cash flow. Growth properties should be located in an area that is appreciating.

Cut out each ad and use the following phone-screening guide (form on CD for making additional copies). The phone-screening guide suggests those things that I consider important. It is designed to take a little of the stress out of making phone calls. Based upon the classified advertisement, fill out everything you can. Now you're ready for making phone calls.

Real Estate Phone-Screening Guide

_____ (Section in Classifieds) Tape or glue classified advertisement information here, if available. _____ Price	Date: _____ Time: _____ Left Message: Y__N__ Property Name/Address: _____ Directions: _____ _____ _____

Owner's Name: _____ Owner's Phone Number: _____

Real Estate Agent's Name: _____ Company: _____
Agent's Phone Number(s): _____

Property Description: _____
_____
_____

    Roof (type, how old?, does it leak?): _____
    Basement/Structural (any water leakage/damage?): _____
    Plumbing (type water lines, sewer line problems): _____
    HVAC (type and age of furnace and air conditioner): _____
    Termites: _____

Income/Gross Rents: _____

Mortgage (1st) Type (e.g., FHA, VA, conventional, assumable): _____
    Balance/Amount Owed: _____

Other Mortgages/Liens/Judgments on Property (explain): _____
_____

Seller's Equity: _____

Expenses (note if monthly or annual)
    Taxes: _____ Insurance: _____ Water: _____ Sewer: _____
    Electric: _____ Gas: _____ Heating Oil: _____ Propane: _____
    City Fees: _____ Homes Association: _____ Garbage: _____
    Other: _____

Is the Owner Willing to Help with Financing? _____
Why is the Owner Selling? _____

Get a real estate agent working for you

How would you like to call up a professional, like an attorney, and tell him to start working for you and if you like what he comes up with, you'll have the person on the other side of the table pay his services. Sounds great, huh? Well, you can do the same with real estate agents.

Find one or more motivated real estate agents and get them working for you. First of all, they can do searches on the MLS database and, given certain criteria, come up with a list of properties that match what you are looking for. You can even request that they help you evaluate a property's value, but be sure to do your own valuation and understand the process.

Of course, the downside here is that once you locate a property, they will be involved in the process and will be paid a commission. This could limit certain creative financing, but it could also speed up the paperwork. In addition, they can help with showing up for appraisals and inspections if you are too busy.

Run your own classified advertisement

Classified advertising may not be your first choice, but as you grow in the world of real estate investing, you might try it and see what kind of response you get. Of course, the downside here is that classified advertisements (ads) are not free. The other problem is that it might take two or three ads before you have it pulling the potential sellers that you want.

Here is an example for pulling one type of seller:

> I buy all types of houses,
> Any condition considered.
> Call Mike at 555-1212.

Here is a different approach:

> Serious real estate investor has cash,
> Looking for single family homes.
> Call 555-1212.

Remember, access to cash can be through a partner, equity in your house or a good relationship with a bank.

Visit your county courthouse

Your county courthouse may be a treasure of foreclosed properties, upcoming auctions or tax lien properties, depending upon where you live. Make a phone call or two and at least plan on visiting the courthouse, if for no other reason than your own education.

Call banks, savings and loans, and mortgage companies

Banks and lenders are more than happy to send you their list of foreclosed properties, sometimes called REOs (real estate owned). I just got off the phone with a community bank loan officer and he immediately sent me an Excel file showing a list of 13 properties ranging from a $10,000 bungalow to a $2,210,000 apartment complex and everything in between. Treat these properties like any other except that you may be able to negotiate better financing terms directly with the loan officer, who would love nothing more than to get the property off of his balance sheet.

Online resources

With the proliferation of the Internet, the sky is the limit. There are so many resources available that it's amazing. If you are not familiar with using a search engine or directory, open up your computer's browser, which might be Internet Explorer or Netscape Navigator or AOL's own unique browser. Type in the Web address of one of the major search engines or directories. Here are a few:

- http://www.google.com
- http://www.yahoo.com
- http://www.msn.com
- http://www.aol.com
- http://www.alltheweb.com
- http://www.altavista.com
- http://dmoz.org.

There are many others, but start with these. Once you are on the site, use the site directory structure or look for a search box. Type in your request and be as specific as possible. For example, don't expect much out of the term "real estate." Try a more specific term like "bank foreclosures in Missouri."

In the meantime, here are a few of my favorite free online resources for real estate investing.

- http://www.hud.gov – U.S. Department of Housing and Urban Development
- http://www.ginniemae.gov – Government National Mortgage Association
- http://www.freddiemac.com – Federal Home Loan Mortgage Corporation
- http://www.fanniemae.com – Federal National Mortgage Association
- http://www.narei.com – National Association of Real Estate Investors
- http://www.realtor.com – Official Site of National Association of Realtors
- http://www.nareit.com – National Association of Real Estate Investment Trusts.

Financial Analysis

Okay. So you have found a bunch of potential properties. Before spending your valuable time driving all over looking at properties, you should perform a preliminary financial analysis using the following income property screener as a guide (this form is available on the accompanying CD). In other words, make sure that the numbers work out and you can make some money.

Income Property Screener

	Monthly Income/Expenses	Amount
1.	Gross Rents	
2.	Other Property Income	
3.	Subtotal (1+2)	
4.	1st Mortgage Principal and Interest (PI)	
5.	2nd Mortgage PI/Seller Financing	
6.	Other Mortgage/Financing PI	
7.	Subtotal (4+5+6)	
8.	Taxes (ask the property owner/agent)	
9.	Insurance (call your own insurance agent)	
10.	Water	
11.	Gas	
12.	Electricity	
13.	Heating Oil/Propane	
14.	Garbage	
15.	Homes Association	
16.	City Fees	
17.	*Property Management (7 to 10% of income)	
18.	**Repairs (actual amount or assume 5 to 10%)	
19.	Supplies (actual amount or assume 1%)	
20.	Miscellaneous (actual amount or assume 1%)	
21.	Subtotal (8+9+10+11+12+13+14+15+16+17+18+19+20)	
	TOTAL (3-7-21)	

*Optional if you plan on managing the property. Percentages are based upon gross monthly income.
**Assume 5% if you plan on doing most of the repairs and up to 10% if you will hire out.

Using the Income Property Screener, let's take a look at a property that I recently evaluated. It is a 9-plex located in a suburb of Kansas City.

	Monthly Income/Expenses	Amount
1.	Gross Rents (with all units rented)	$3,525.00
2.	Other Property Income	$0.00
3.	Subtotal (1+2)	$3,525.00
4.	1st Mortgage Principal and Interest (PI)	$1,076.12
5.	2nd Mortgage PI/Seller Financing	$308.48
6.	Other Mortgage/Financing PI	$0.00
7.	Subtotal (4+5+6)	$1,384.60
8.	Taxes (ask the property owner/agent)	$185.00
9.	Insurance (call your own insurance agent)	$140.00
10.	Water	$150.00
11.	Gas	$300.00
12.	Electricity	$175.00
13.	Heating Oil/Propane	$0.00
14.	Garbage	$50.00
15.	Homes Association	$0.00
16.	City Fees	$0.00
17.	*Property Management (for now, I will manage it)	$0.00
18.	**Repairs (10%)	$353.00
19.	Supplies (actual amount or assume 1%)	$35.00
20.	Miscellaneous (actual amount or assume 1%)	$35.00
21.	Subtotal (8+9+10+11+12+13+14+15+16+17+18+19+20)	$1,423.00
	TOTAL (3-7-21)	$717.40

As you can see, I am anticipating a positive cash flow of $717.40, even after including repairs, supplies and all associated fees. The numbers look good enough for me to set up a meeting to view the property and discuss it with the current owner in more detail. If I were to hire a property management company, the cash flow would drop to $364.00, which is not quite as enticing, but worthy of consideration.

Now, since this unit is an income producing property with over four units, it is possible to calculate a value based upon the income (this will be discussed in greater detail in Chapter 4). Using the Cap Rate method and knowing the annual net operating income (NOI) and assuming a high cap rate of 14 percent, the value of the property equals the NOI divided by the cap rate:

Value of Property = NOI / Cap Rate

Value of Property = $25,224 / .14 = $180,171

Since the property is priced at $160,000, that's a potential $20,000 in equity. To be fair, the property could use some sprucing up, so I am assuming that the price is in the correct ballpark.

For growth properties, a slightly different tactic is taken. One method is to buy and hold, while the other is to buy low and sell high. Gee that sounds a lot like stock investing. Anyway, the difference here is that you have to learn to look past an ugly exterior or blemishes and find properties that require simple fixes to improve the value.

One thing to consider that I feel is missing in most real estate books and programs is what happens in between purchasing a property, fixing it up, listing it and eventually selling it. Well, I can tell you one thing that happens is that the mortgage loan has to be paid. It is possible, though unlikely, that you could do all of this in a matter of 30 to 45 days and not have to make a mortgage payment.

Here is what I recommend. Even if you are planning on selling the property as soon as possible, rent it out for a year or two or set up a lease option with a potential buyer. The idea is to limit your expenses and fix up the property. Ironically, many renters will help fix up a property for you and the capital gains taxes are much more favorable for long-term investments (investments held more than a year).

The Drive By

For the drive by, make sure you know where you are going. Each city has detailed maps that I recommend you purchase and take with you. Another great alternative is to visit MapQuest at http://www.mapquest.com and type in the property's address – you'll be given a detailed map.

The drive by is more for getting the feel of the location and neighborhood than it is to fully evaluate a property. After all, you will only be able to stop and look at the outside. If it is vacant, you can usually peek inside.

Look at the exterior of the property, the drainage, the roof, the yard, the building's integrity and try to notice any expensive problems.

Now, scrutinize the location, including the neighbors and surrounding community. Know what you are getting into before proceeding.

Follow-up

After visiting a property, new questions will arise. Write down all of your questions and call the owner or real estate agent and say that you are still interested in the property and even drove by it the other day. Say that you have a few more questions and ask away.

If you feel comfortable with the response, set up a time to look inside the place.

On-Site Visit

Come prepared with a property evaluation sheet (this form is available on the accompanying CD):

Property Evaluation Sheet

Property Name/Type/Address: _____

Date/Time: _____ Shown by: _____ Phone No.: _____

General Description: _____
_____

Unit Number __ of __ (Use a separate sheet for each unit, if more than one.)

Tenant's Name: _____

Lease Amount and Terms: _____

Security Deposit: _____ Pet Deposit: _____

Rental History: _____

Other Comments (include owner financing details; let the owner/agent talk): _____
_____

Room/Area/Item	Description	Potential Cost
Front Room		
Kitchen		
Living Room		
Family Room		
Bedroom (1)		
Bedroom (2)		
Bedroom (3)		
Bedroom (4)		
Bathroom (1)		
Bathroom (2)		
Bathroom (3)		
Garage		
Basement/Cellar		
Attic		
HVAC		
Electrical		
Plumbing/Pipes		
Roof		
Exterior/Paint		
Porch/Patio/Deck		

Use the property evaluation sheet as a guide for going through a property and estimating the cost of repairs and what the owner is willing to fix or negotiate with. Be sure to use a separate sheet for each unit if you are evaluating a multi-unit property.

Let's look at a couple of examples: income property investing and growth property investing.

Income property investing example

I am going to walk through a brief financial analysis of a home my wife and I bought in January of 1996 and sold in September of 1998. The property was located in Belton, Missouri, a suburb of Kansas City. The property is a three-bedroom, two-car garage, split level home. It is what I consider a "bread and butter" home. However, it is located in a marginal, though not bad, location. We purchased the house as a closed bid with the Missouri VA. The purchase price was $68,900 and the down payment and fees were only $1,403.

Net Cash Flow

We were able to rent the property for $725 per month, during the rental period, with the exception of the last month. We received a total of $21,750 during the rental period, or approximately $713 per month. During the same period, our expenses (taxes, insurance, interest, repairs, supplies, etc.) totaled $15,983, or approximately $524 per month. Therefore, our net cash flow per month was roughly $189 per month for a total of $5,767.

Appreciation

After fixing it up and renting it for over two years, our tenants could no longer pay and we parted ways. Enlisting the services of a local real estate agent, we were able to sell the property in less than 30 days. The gross sales price was $80,000. If we stop here, like some books would have you do, you would think that we made a fortune on our initial investment of $1,403.

But let's throw in reality. First, I had to pay the real estate agent fee, mechanical fix-up costs, taxes, and other fees. Our actual sales price was $73, 210 and our cash at closing was $6,790. Still, that's not bad. The true appreciation on the house was $4,310 ($73,210 minus 68,900).

Equity

As we diligently paid the mortgage each month, a small fraction went directly to paying off the principal. Remember, our sales price was $68,900 minus the down payment of $700. Our 30-year loan was for $68,200, At closing, the actual payoff of the mortgage was $67,103. Therefore, our equity was $1,097.

Taxes

The rental tax game is quite interesting. We bought a good "bread and butter" income house fully knowing that it would appreciate in value, yet at the end of each year the IRS allowed us to depreciate it over a specified period of time (27.5 years) and using a particular method that they have approved (modified accelerated cost recovery [MACRs]). Wow, what is the catch here? For one thing, land is not a depreciable item, so only the value of the house can be depreciated. Of course, you are free to come up with a value of the land versus the property.

Any improvements, fixtures, appliances, and certain other items can be depreciated. The other catch is that when you sell the property, the government would like its temporary loan back. In other words, you are taxed on the depreciated property at your tax rate. During the rental period we depreciated a total of $5,801 in property, appliances, etc. Certain depreciable items, such as the electric range that we bought, were sold as part of the house and therefore the remaining value was reduced to zero so that these items represented a small tax loss.

The long-term capital gains tax was 20 percent and ordinary gains are taxed at my personal tax rate. After running the numbers through my tax program, the entire sale resulted in a tax burden of $1,768. If we consider the deferred taxes saved over the 30.5-month period ($5,801) and multiply by my tax rate (28 percent), the result is a tax savings of $1,624 over the period of owning the property. Finally, because I paid back $1,768, I nearly broke even, but lost $144.

My advice here is to not rely on tax advantages when evaluating a property. However, once you purchase a property keep all your receipts, monitor your mileage and try to be as tax efficient as possible. Be prepared for April 15th when you sell a rental property.

Labor, Pain and Suffering

The late night programs and books inadvertently, or should I say purposely, forget to tell you about the phone calls on Sunday afternoon complaining about stopped up plumbing or an air conditioner that just went out. The books and programs also fail to mention the late payments, bounced checks, or tenants who purposely lie. The books and programs never talk about the city governments who are now trying to implement fees from landlords. The books and programs also don't mention that my labor is free and not tax deductible.

There is really no way to quantify a number in this category. I'm not including, for example, the extra Rolaids and fast food when working on the properties. I am including labor. Your time and my time are worth something. After all, time is really more precious than money.

To quantify this, I am placing a small value of $10 per hour on my time. I estimate that during the fix-up, management, and selling (fix-up again), my wife and I spent roughly 250 man/woman-hours on the property. Therefore, we lost a potential $2,420.

Summary

Cash flow + Appreciation + Equity +/- Tax benefits – Your labor, pain, and suffering. For our house the equation results in $5,767 + $4,310 + $1,097 – $144 – $2,420 = $8,610. So, with our initial investment of $1,403, we realized a profit of $8,610 over a period of two and one half years. Not bad – that's well over a 200 percent increase per year on our initial investment.

Growth property investing example

I mentioned the buy and hold strategy. I still own a rental house that I bought in 1994. The property is a "bread and butter" single-family house located in a great neighborhood with excellent schools in Roeland Park, Kansas, a suburb of Kansas City, Missouri. Without analyzing this property in depth, I bought the property for $59,110, with only $1,352.97 down.

Although I have been tempted to sell the property, it continues to provide me positive cash flow of nearly $150 per month. The cash flow is secondary to the appreciation and current value. Based upon comparables in the near vicinity, I have determined that the property is worth roughly $105,000. With a current payoff amount of $54,480, I have about $50,520 in equity.

As you can see, the buy and hold strategy works quite well when a property is purchased in a good location.

FOUR

Estimating the Value of Real Property

"Tell me and I'll forget. Show me, and I may not remember.
Involve me, and I'll understand." – Native American saying

As I have alluded to earlier, there are three methods of estimating the value of real property: replacement cost, income method, and competitive market analysis (CMA). These are discussed below.

Replacement Cost

Replacement cost makes use of the cost of real estate on a per square foot basis to estimate the value of real property. Essentially, the cost to build the property, including purchasing the land. Area builders, contractors and architects can be helpful with this type of estimating.

Income Method

A second method of evaluating real estate is based upon its ability to generate income, using the equation below. The income method is best used for multi-family dwellings, such as apartments.

Gross Rent Multiplier = Selling Price / Gross Monthly Rents

Capitalization rate is the rate that other investors would be willing to pay for a similar property.

Cap Rate = Net Operating Income / Value of Property

Value of Property = NOI / Cap Rate

Cap rates vary from location to location and property to property. In general, a low cap rate ranges from 4 to 9, while a high cap rate varies from 11 to 18. Low cap rates are common among properties of higher estimated value. High cap rates are common among higher risk properties with lower estimated values.

Competitive Market Analysis

Competitive market analysis seeks to understand the marketplace and use that knowledge to estimate a value. CMA is most often used for evaluating land, single-family homes, duplexes, triplexes, and 4-plexes. The CMA process works by finding similar properties or comparables near the property in question. It is also possible with some caution to use properties that are currently listed, but have not sold. It is best to use at least three comparables. Here is an example:

Competitive Market Analysis

For: <u>Jack and Tracy Smith</u>   Prepared by: <u>Michael Williams</u>
Property: <u>Single-family home</u>   Date: <u>July 27, 1998</u>

Address	Subject Property	Comparable 1 7601 Maple	Comparable 2 7249 Oak	Comparable 3 7713 Oak
Area (sq ft.)	2135	2200	2100	2300
Living Room	Yes	Yes	Yes	Yes
Dining Room	Yes	Yes	Yes	Yes
Kitchen	Yes	Yes	Yes	Yes
Family Room	Yes	Yes	Yes	Yes
Bedrooms	4	4	4	4
Baths	2.5	2	2	2.5
Basement	Yes	Yes	Yes	Yes
Garage/Carport	2-car attached	1-car attached	2-car attached	2-car attached
Construction	Ranch	Ranch	Split	Split
Lot Size	85' x 105'	80' x 115'	90' x 100'	92' x 105'
Age	5	5.5	4.5	5
Terms of Sale		10% down	20% down	20% down
Days on Market		96	23	38
Date of Sale		11/05/97	05/30/98	06/15/98
Listed Price		$92,500	$98,500	$102,000
Selling Price		$91,000	$97,500	$100,000
Remarks:				
Area Market Conditions: Good				
Estimated Range of Value: $91,000 to $100,000				
Estimated Value of Subject Property: $97,000				

FIVE

Creative Financing: Putting the Deal Together

"A wise man hears one word and understands two."
— Jewish proverb

Well, let's see. You've located a potential property. You conducted a drive by and probably even met with a real estate agent or owner to see the property and discuss any issues that you might have. You're convinced that it's a property to make an offer on. Now what?

It's time to put your "thinking cap" on and come up with some creative financing. Let me say first that there is no right or wrong in creative financing. I've read many books on the subject and I've tried/used several of the methods. The short answer is whatever works best for you.

Having said that, I'll go through some common financing techniques and methods of securing the deal. First, let's review standard financing so you know the difference.

Standard Financing

For those of you who have never purchased property, I'll go through the most common process. Generally, you will contact a mortgage company and tell them who you are and what you are interested in buying. The mortgage company can quote you interest rates and other details, such as points, ARMs, fixed rates, etc. As a homebuyer, you can often choose between three mortgage programs: (1) conventional loans, (2) FHA loans or (3) VA loans.

Conventional loans are the most common type. Conventional loans usually require 20 percent down or a loan to value (LTV) ratio of 80 percent. In other words, the bank will loan you 80 percent of the property's appraised value. Since many people cannot afford 20 percent down, it is possible to finance 90 percent or more using private mortgage insurance (PMI). PMI protects the lender in case you default. Of course, you have to pay a monthly premium for this privilege.

FHA financing was designed by the United States government to make homeowners out of all U.S. citizens. The U.S. government backs FHA mortgages, so banks are completely safe in issuing these loans. FHA loans allow first time homebuyers to get in a property for as little as 3 percent down. Due to the high LTV ratio, these loans also require insurance to protect the lender and the government. In this case, the insurance is called mortgage insurance premium. FHA loans also have funding limits that are based upon where you live.

To find out about the funding limits in your part of the country, visit this link: https://entp.hud.gov/idapp/html/hicostlook.cfm. For example, using the mortgage calculator for Johnson County, Kansas, the current FHA limit is $194,750 for a single-family home.

Finally, VA financing is the ultimate no-money-down proposition for homebuyers. However, there is one catch. You have to have served in the U.S. military. If you did serve in the military, then by all means use this program.

Creative Financing

Now that we have gone through standard financing, let's look at creative financing. As I mentioned, there are endless possibilities here. You will have to experiment and see what works for you and what doesn't. Your success may not only depend upon your financial situation, but also on where you live, the type of properties that you are going after and especially the seller. For more information on creative financing, be sure to refer to the following references:

- *No Down Payment* (Sheets, 1994)
- *Nothing Down for the 90s* (Allen, 1990)
- *Building Wealth* (Whitney, 1994).

Owner carries a second mortgage

Owner financing works with motivated sellers who are willing to help finance their own property. One method of owner financing is to negotiate a second mortgage with the owner and obtain a new first mortgage from a lender. For example, I recently worked with a motivated property owner who is willing to carry back at least $5,000 on a $55,000 tri-plex. I will be obtaining a first mortgage from a lender for 80 percent of the purchase price or $44,000. This leaves $6,000 for me to come up with. If I plan on closing near the first of the month I will be able to receive rents of approximately $1,100 and deposits of approximately $900. In essence, I will only need to come up with $4,000 down, which I can borrow from a signature loan.

Wrap-around mortgage

Certain nonstandard lenders or the seller will accept a wrap-around mortgage. A wrap-around mortgage allows you to pay one mortgage to the seller or lender and the seller/lender continues to pay on the existing mortgage. Usually you will need to pay a higher interest rate for the trouble.

For example, using the scenario above, I might offer the seller $5,000 down plus a wrap-around mortgage for $50,000.

Assume an existing loan

Certain loans, such as owner-financed loans, VA loans and FHA loans, can be assumed. Conventional loans do not qualify for assumption because of a due-on-sale clause. Owner-financed loans are the easiest to assume because individuals are involved, not banks or mortgage companies. VA and FHA loans can be assumed by qualifying with the mortgage holder.

Dig deep in your own pockets

Many times it is necessary to come up with money the old-fashioned way – by digging deep in your own pockets. So how do you come up with money to close the deal? Here are some creative ways:

- Partners: Find a partner and share in the profits. Have your partner provide the needed cash and you find the property, consummate the deal and manage or sell the property. Obviously, you will need to work out the deal with your partner. Be sure to sign an agreement or contract and make it a professional arrangement. Also, be careful not to ruin a relationship with a friend or family member through poor planning or risky ventures.

- Credit unions: Credit unions are a great place to borrow money on easy terms. Many large companies, agencies or even communities offer membership to credit unions. Borrowing money from a credit union will likely require collateral, but in the case of a company credit union you may be able to borrow solely based upon your job. If asked about the purpose of the loan, you can say it will be used for a vacation, to pay off debt or whatever you want to say.

- Signature loans: With good credit comes good terms. Banks and other lenders give signature loans to clients who have excellent credit and other accounts at the institution. For example, I have a signature line of credit at TD Waterhouse, which is both a bank and brokerage company.

- Borrow against personal property: A car, boat, motorcycle or other expensive personal property can be used as collateral for loans at banks, credit unions or even from sellers. You can either offer equity to a seller in the form of a loan, which is secured by the personal property or you can borrow the money from a lender.

- Home equity loans: As discussed earlier, home equity loans are one of the best places to start looking for money. Mortgage companies and banks easily grant home equity loans. In fact, they love these loans. Some home equity lenders will even loan above the appraised value of your house. I have seen advertisements for loan-to-value home equity lines of 125 percent. Be careful not to extend yourself too far. Remember, home equity lines are secured by your personal real estate and if you don't pay them back, a lien can be placed on your property.

Blanket mortgage

A blanket mortgage covers two or more properties. You may be able to use a blanket mortgage if you have existing real estate to fold under the blanket. Suppose you own one rental house and you are looking to buy another one. You may be able to put both mortgages under the same mortgage and use equity in an existing property to help pay for the seller's equity in a new property.

SIX

Presenting the Deal: The Art of Win-Win

"The Devil is in the Details" – anonymous

I'm sorry to say, but there comes a time when you have to do some good old-fashioned selling. Believe me, I'm not a salesman. I'm a scientist by trade. I was the kid in college who was jealous of the business majors, because I was stuck in a laboratory studying for finals on Friday night.

Anyway, real estate is not about greed. It's about making a deal that benefits two different parties and perhaps three if a lender is involved. Whenever possible contact and deal with the seller or homeowner in person. If a real estate agent is involved, request or demand that you be present when the offer is presented. If you can't get access to the seller, you will have to sell the proposal to the agent.

By now, you should have a good idea why the seller is selling. Open up by thanking the owner or agent for allowing you to present the offer. Throw in a few icebreakers if you feel the need. Compliment the owner on the property and what he has done with it. Be honest and explain what your goals are with the property.

Now, break out your written offer and go through it briefly with the seller. You may even want to include more than one offer. Make sure that your offer has a time limit for a response. Allow the seller enough time to evaluate your offer, but not too much time to shop it around. I would recommend between one to three days. If special circumstances dictate longer, you will have to be the judge. Essentially, you want to create some urgency. If you are looking at other properties, you may want to casually mention that, but make sure it's not a snide comment.

Thank the owner and/or agent and say you are looking forward to working with them.

SEVEN

How to Profit from Foreclosures

"Trouble is only opportunity in work clothes."
– Henry J. Kaiser

For any number of reasons, sometimes real estate owners encounter hard times and are forced to relinquish real estate. When this happens, the mortgage holder or lender is forced to take back a property. With VA and FHA loans, the U.S. government is ultimately responsible for purchasing the property back. With conventional loans, a mortgage company or lender is responsible.

The U.S. government and lenders want nothing to do with the properties and would like to resell them as quickly as possible. After all, lenders are in the lending business not real estate investing. That's where you come in. You can help them with their problem and help yourself in the process.

Veterans Affairs (VA) Foreclosures

When I first began investing in real estate, I stumbled across VA properties and didn't quite understand how a non-vet could take advantage of the properties. I was amazed to find that not only does the VA offer foreclosed real estate for sale to homeowners and investors, but in some cases they offer attractive financing with very little down at closing. If you are looking for a way to jump-start your real estate investing career, contact a real estate agent and ask about VA foreclosures or visit their online list of properties available in your state.

VA properties are offered for sale to the public; however, you must contact a VA-registered real estate broker or agent to view the homes. Just like any home, they will open the house/property for you to see. Should you decide that you are interested in a property, you will need to meet the real estate agent and prepare VA-approved loan request and purchase offer paper work.

In purchasing VA properties, the big trick is to quickly view the property and make a decision. Oftentimes the VA will have a short bid time that you have to meet. This makes it nearly impossible to have professionals help you look at plumbing, electrical, roofs and structural elements. All VA homes are sold "as is," so it is important to be as knowledgeable as possible about how much it will cost to fix up a property. You will also need to determine what the interest is in the property. Usually a real estate agent can help you with this or you can see how many agents have come through the property because they will sign a log indicating they showed it to someone.

Furthermore, it is important to recognize that you may have to outbid several other qualified bidders. The bidding process is generally a closed bid. You will instruct your real estate agent on what your bid is and you will need to include an earnest money deposit of at least $500. Your agent will include her fee and submit the paperwork. The winning bid is the net amount from a qualified bidder that results in the most money for the VA.

Why do I mention this? Because it is possible to outbid someone, you might consider talking your agent into dropping her fee slightly. The VA will pay up to 6 percent for real estate brokers. I use a real estate broker who is a one-man show specializing in government foreclosed property. Since he is both a broker and agent, he can reduce his fee and still make a significant commission. In addition, if you are a real estate agent/broker, you can obviously compete much better by doing the paperwork yourself.

The VA used to offer financing to qualified investors; however, recently, with the move to privatization, it is uncertain whether they will be offering financing to investors.

Visit your state VA property link, read the introductory material and find the listings by city. You will then see a form page with various cities. Note that you will not always see the city you are looking for because there may not be any VA foreclosures at that time.

As you should know by now, I live in the Kansas City area, which includes two states: Missouri and Kansas. I check both states. On the Missouri side, I noticed one property worthy of checking. Here is the listing:

Example VA Property

Address	17005 E 44TH STREET, INDEPENDENCE, 64055
Down Payment	$1,500
Listed Price	$160,000
Total Rooms	6
Square Feet	1711
Codes	FR/1/3
Bedrooms/Bathrooms	3/2
Notes 1	
Notes 2	RE Tax 1881.10
List Expires	2002-07-24 before 11:59 p.m.

Notice the codes. The definitions are presented online and below for your convenience. The house has a frame construction ("FR") with no repairs and warranties ("1") and the VA has title to the property ("3").

VA Codes

Disclosure Codes	Description
1	No repairs/warranties
2	Subject to acquisition of title
3	VA has title to property
4	Private sewer or septic
5	Private water
6	Flood insurance required
7	Possible wet basement
8	Purchaser must submit Addendum III
9	10% down payment for non-owner occupants & investors

10	Partial repairs made (no warranty)
11	Occupancy permit required
12	HOA assessments
13	Condominium
14	Driveway easement
15	Defective foundation
16	Duplex
17	Triplex
18	Fourplex
19	"Contractor Special" – in poor condition; may contain lead-based paint
20	House constructed prior to 1978 may contain lead-based paint
21	Property on market 6 months; $500.00 bonus payable
C	Cash only
E	Defective electrical; submit Addendum III
F	VA vendee financing available for less than 30 years – see notes
H	Defective heating/cooling; submit Addendum III
P	Defective plumbing; submit Addendum III
R	Defective roof; submit Addendum III
Feature Codes	**Description**
AD	Adobe
AL	Aluminum siding
AS	Asbestos siding
BR	Brick
BV	Brick veneer
FR	Frame
LG	Log
MA	Masonry
ST	Stucco
VS	Vinyl siding
WF	Wood framing

Special Note: The Department of Veterans' Affairs has awarded the Property Management Services Contract for managing, marketing, and selling VA-acquired properties throughout the United States and its territories to Ocwen Federal Bank FSB. VA began transitioning properties to Ocwen around December 8, 2003, and expects to complete the transition by January 24, 2004. In anticipation of this transition, all properties have been removed from the market. VA expects that Ocwen will begin marketing VA properties in early January 2004.

The following is contact information for Ocwen Federal Bank:

Ocwen Federal Bank, FSB
1675 Palm Beach Lakes Boulevard
The Forum, Suite 1000
West Palm Beach, Florida 33401
Phone: (561) 682-8000; 1-800-33-OCWEN (1-800-336-2936)
Alternative Phone Number: (407) 737-5278
Fax: (561) 681-8177
Email: VAREOSales@ocwen.com
Website: http://www.Ocwen.com

Until the geographic transition is completed, the VA Office of jurisdiction (http://www.homeloans.va.gov/homes.htm) will continue to manage the property. A list of the links to VA Property Management websites can be found by clicking here: http://www.homeloans.va.gov/pmoffice.htm.

Most VA sites listing properties have been discontinued. Ocwen has taken control of VA property listings, but has not yet published a directory listing or search feature showing individual properties. The following table provides state-specific VA property information:

State	VA Regional Office Address	VA & Ocwen Phone Numbers	Ocwen Website Address for VA Property Listings
Alabama	345 Perry Hill Road Montgomery, AL 36109	VA: 800-827-1000 Ocwen: 407-737-5278	http://www.ocwen.com/residential/VA_Properties_sale.cfm
Alaska	Building 65, Fort Roots P.O. Box 1280 Little Rock, AR 72115	VA: 800-827-1000 Ocwen: 407-737-5278	http://www.ocwen.com/residential/VA_Properties_sale.cfm
Arizona	3333 N. Central Avenue Phoenix, AZ 85012-2402	VA: 800-827-1000 Ocwen: 407-737-5278	http://www.ocwen.com/residential/VA_Properties_sale.cfm
Arkansas	P.O. Box 1280 Fort Roots N. Little Rock, AR 72115	VA: 800-827-1000 Ocwen: 407-737-5278	http://www.ocwen.com/residential/VA_Properties_sale.cfm
California – southern, except San Diego area	11000 Wilshire Boulevard Los Angeles, CA 90024	VA: 800-827-1000 Ocwen: 407-737-5278	http://www.ocwen.com/residential/VA_Properties_sale.cfm
California – northern, and northern Nevada	1301 Clay Street, 1300 N. Oakland, CA 94612-5209	VA: 800-827-1000 Ocwen: 407-737-5278	http://www.ocwen.com/residential/VA_Properties_sale.cfm
California – San Diego area	8810 Rio San Diego Drive San Diego, CA 92108	VA: 800-827-1000 Ocwen: 407-737-5278	http://www.ocwen.com/residential/VA_Properties_sale.cfm
Colorado	155 Van Gordon Street Lakewood, CO 80228	VA: 800-827-1000 Ocwen: 407-737-5278	http://www.ocwen.com/residential/VA_Properties_sale.cfm
Connecticut	275 Chestnut Street Manchester, NH 03101	VA: 800-827-1000 Ocwen: 407-737-5278	http://www.ocwen.com/residential/VA_Properties_sale.cfm
Delaware	5000 Wissahickon Avenue Philadelphia, PA 19101	VA: 800-827-1000 Ocwen: 407-737-5278	http://www.ocwen.com/residential/VA_Properties_sale.cfm
D.C., northern VA, Mont. & PG counties in MD	1120 Vermont Ave. NW Washington, D.C. 20421	VA: 800-827-1000 Ocwen: 407-737-5278	http://www.ocwen.com/residential/VA_Properties_sale.cfm
Florida	P.O. Box 1437 St. Petersburg, FL 33731	VA: 800-827-1000 Ocwen: 407-737-5278	http://www.ocwen.com/residential/VA_Properties_sale.cfm
Georgia	1700 Clairmont Road P.O. Box 100023 Decatur, GA 30031-7023	VA: 800-827-1000 Ocwen: 407-737-5278	http://www.ocwen.com/residential/VA_Properties_sale.cfm
Hawaii	459 Patterson Road Honolulu, HI 96819-1522	VA: 800-827-1000 Ocwen: 407-737-5278	http://www.ocwen.com/residential/VA_Properties_sale.cfm
Idaho	805 West Franklin Street Boise, ID 83702-5560	VA: 800-827-1000 Ocwen: 407-737-5278	http://www.ocwen.com/residential/VA_Properties_sale.cfm
Illinois	P.O. Box 8136 Chicago, IL 60680	VA: 800-827-1000 Ocwen: 407-737-5278	http://www.ocwen.com/residential/VA_Properties_sale.cfm
Indiana	575 Pennsylvania Street Indianapolis, IN 46204	VA: 800-827-1000 Ocwen: 407-737-5278	http://www.ocwen.com/residential/VA_Properties_sale.cfm

Iowa	210 Walnut Street Des Moines, IA 50309	VA: 800-827-1000 Ocwen: 407-737-5278	http://www.ocwen.com/residential/VA_Properties_sale.cfm
Kansas	P.O. Box 20077 Wichita, KS 67208-1077	VA: 800-827-1000 Ocwen: 407-737-5278	http://www.ocwen.com/residential/VA_Properties_sale.cfm
Kentucky	545 S. 3rd Street Louisville, KY 40202	VA: 800-827-1000 Ocwen: 407-737-5278	http://www.ocwen.com/residential/VA_Properties_sale.cfm
Louisiana	701 Loyola Avenue New Orleans, LA 70113	VA: 800-827-1000 Ocwen: 407-737-5278	http://www.ocwen.com/residential/VA_Properties_sale.cfm
Maine	275 Chestnut Street Manchester, NH 03101	VA: 800-827-1000 Ocwen: 407-737-5278	http://www.ocwen.com/residential/VA_Properties_sale.cfm
Maryland, except PG and Mont. counties (see D.C.)	31 Hopkins Plaza Baltimore, MD 21201	VA: 800-827-1000 Ocwen: 407-737-5278	http://www.ocwen.com/residential/VA_Properties_sale.cfm
Massachusetts	275 Chestnut Street Manchester, NH 03101	VA: 800-827-1000 Ocwen: 407-737-5278	http://www.ocwen.com/residential/VA_Properties_sale.cfm
Michigan	477 Michigan Avenue Detroit, MI 48226	VA: 800-827-1000 Ocwen: 407-737-5278	http://www.ocwen.com/residential/VA_Properties_sale.cfm
Minnesota	Fort Snelling St. Paul, MN 55111	VA: 800-827-1000 Ocwen: 407-737-5278	http://www.ocwen.com/residential/VA_Properties_sale.cfm
Mississippi	1600 E. Woodrow Wilson Avenue Jackson, MS 39216	VA: 800-827-1000 Ocwen: 407-737-5278	http://www.ocwen.com/residential/VA_Properties_sale.cfm
Missouri	400 S. 18th Street St. Louis, MO 63103-2271	VA: 800-827-1000 Ocwen: 407-737-5278	http://www.ocwen.com/residential/VA_Properties_sale.cfm
Montana	155 Van Gordon Street Lakewood, CO 80228	VA: 800-827-1000 Ocwen: 407-737-5278	http://www.ocwen.com/residential/VA_Properties_sale.cfm
Nebraska	5631 S. 48th Street Lincoln, NE 68516	VA: 800-827-1000 Ocwen: 407-737-5278	http://www.ocwen.com/residential/VA_Properties_sale.cfm
Nevada – northern	1301 Clay Street, 1300 N. Oakland, CA 94612-5209	VA: 800-827-1000 Ocwen: 407-737-5278	http://www.ocwen.com/residential/VA_Properties_sale.cfm
Nevada – southern	3225 N. Central Avenue Phoenix, AZ 85012	VA: 800-827-1000 Ocwen: 407-737-5278	http://www.ocwen.com/residential/VA_Properties_sale.cfm
New England	275 Chestnut Street Manchester, NH 03101	VA: 800-827-1000 Ocwen: 407-737-5278	http://www.ocwen.com/residential/VA_Properties_sale.cfm
New Hampshire	275 Chestnut Street Manchester, NH 03101	VA: 800-827-1000 Ocwen: 407-737-5278	http://www.ocwen.com/residential/VA_Properties_sale.cfm
New Jersey	20 Washington Place Newark, NJ 07102	VA: 800-827-1000 Ocwen: 407-737-5278	http://www.ocwen.com/residential/VA_Properties_sale.cfm

New Mexico	P.O. Box 0968 Albuquerque, NM 87102	VA: 800-827-1000 Ocwen: 407-737-5278	http://www.ocwen.com/residential/VA_Properties_sale.cfm
New York – western	111 West Huron Street Buffalo, NY 14202	VA: 800-827-1000 Ocwen: 407-737-5278	http://www.ocwen.com/residential/VA_Properties_sale.cfm
New York – eastern	245 West Houston Street New York, NY 10014	VA: 800-827-1000 Ocwen: 407-737-5278	http://www.ocwen.com/residential/VA_Properties_sale.cfm
North Carolina	251 North Main Street Winston Salem, NC 27155	VA: 800-827-1000 Ocwen: 407-737-5278	http://www.ocwen.com/residential/VA_Properties_sale.cfm
North Dakota	Fort Snelling St. Paul, MN 55111	VA: 800-827-1000 Ocwen: 407-737-5278	http://www.ocwen.com/residential/VA_Properties_sale.cfm
Oklahoma	125 Main Street Muskogee, OK 74401	VA: 800-827-1000 Ocwen: 407-737-5278	http://www.ocwen.com/residential/VA_Properties_sale.cfm
Ohio	1240 East 9th Street Cleveland, OH 44199	VA: 800-827-1000 Ocwen: 407-737-5278	http://www.ocwen.com/residential/VA_Properties_sale.cfm
Oregon	1220 SW Third Avenue Portland, OR 97204	VA: 800-827-1000 Ocwen: 407-737-5278	http://www.ocwen.com/residential/VA_Properties_sale.cfm
Pennsylvania – western	1000 Liberty Avenue Pittsburgh, PA 15222	VA: 800-827-1000 Ocwen: 407-737-5278	http://www.ocwen.com/residential/VA_Properties_sale.cfm
Pennsylvania – eastern	5000 Wissahickon Avenue Philadelphia, PA 19101	VA: 800-827-1000 Ocwen: 407-737-5278	http://www.ocwen.com/residential/VA_Properties_sale.cfm
Puerto Rico	GPO Box 4867 San Juan, PR 00936	VA: 800-827-1000 Ocwen: 407-737-5278	http://www.ocwen.com/residential/VA_Properties_sale.cfm
Rhode Island	275 Chestnut Street Manchester, NH 03101	VA: 800-827-1000 Ocwen: 407-737-5278	http://www.ocwen.com/residential/VA_Properties_sale.cfm
South Carolina	1801 Assembly Street Columbia, SC 29201	VA: 800-827-1000 Ocwen: 407-737-5278	http://www.ocwen.com/residential/VA_Properties_sale.cfm
South Dakota	Fort Snelling St. Paul, MN 55111	VA: 800-827-1000 Ocwen: 407-737-5278	http://www.ocwen.com/residential/VA_Properties_sale.cfm
Tennessee	110 9th Avenue S. Nashville, TN 37203	VA: 800-827-1000 Ocwen: 407-737-5278	http://www.ocwen.com/residential/VA_Properties_sale.cfm
Texas – southern	6900 Alemeda Road Houston, TX 77030	VA: 800-827-1000 Ocwen: 407-737-5278	http://www.ocwen.com/residential/VA_Properties_sale.cfm
Texas – northern	One Veterans Plaza 701 Clay Street Waco, TX 76799	VA: 800-827-1000 Ocwen: 407-737-5278	http://www.ocwen.com/residential/VA_Properties_sale.cfm
Utah	P.O. Box 11500 Salt Lake City, UT 84147	VA: 800-827-1000 Ocwen: 407-737-5278	http://www.ocwen.com/residential/VA_Properties_sale.cfm
Vermont	275 Chestnut Street Manchester, NH 03101	VA: 800-827-1000 Ocwen: 407-737-5278	http://www.ocwen.com/residential/VA_Properties_sale.cfm

Virginia, except northern VA (see D.C.)	210 Franklin Road, SW Roanoke, VA 24011	VA: 800-827-1000 Ocwen: 407-737-5278	http://www.ocwen.com/residential/VA_Properties_sale.cfm
Washington State	915 Second Avenue Seattle, WA 98174	VA: 800-827-1000 Ocwen: 407-737-5278	http://www.ocwen.com/residential/VA_Properties_sale.cfm
West Virginia	210 Franklin Road, SW Roanoke, VA 24011	VA: 800-827-1000 Ocwen: 407-737-5278	http://www.ocwen.com/residential/VA_Properties_sale.cfm
Wisconsin	5000 National Avenue Milwaukee, WI 53295	VA: 800-827-1000 Ocwen: 407-737-5278	http://www.ocwen.com/residential/VA_Properties_sale.cfm
Wyoming	155 Van Gordon Street Lakewood, CO 80228	VA: 800-827-1000 Ocwen: 407-737-5278	http://www.ocwen.com/residential/VA_Properties_sale.cfm

Housing and Urban Development (HUD) Homes

Most HUD homes are initially offered on a priority basis to owner-occupant purchasers (people who are buying the home as their primary residence). Following the priority period, unsold properties are then available to all buyers, including investors. Use one of the links in the table below for most major cities and U.S. territories. Select cities near where you live or that you are interested in. The HUD database will provide you with the address, type of property, list price, as-is value, listing date, deadline for submitting a bid, and whether it is available to owner-occupants only or all purchasers (including investors). You will also find important notes, such as structural damage, flood zone, settlement, smoke damage, missing electric meter and a host of other things. Finally, be sure to observe the codes, such as LBP, which stands for lead-based paint. The notes and codes are required by disclosure laws and should be looked into, but shouldn't necessarily scare you off. For instance, any house built before 1978 probably contains lead-based paint.

HUD Homes by State
(http://www.hud.org)

State	Phone Number	Website
Alabama	(404) 768-1400	http://bally.towerauction.net/i6/al/index.html
Alaska	(888) 622-7361	http://bally.towerauction.net/ac
Arizona	(714) 241-1096	http://www.hud.org/fp3/az
California – northern	(916) 922-2262	http://www.hud.org/g2/nca
California – southern	(949) 477-6300	http://www.hud.org/g1/sca
Colorado	(972) 788-0026	http://www.hud.org/fp2/co
Connecticut	(860) 244-2783	http://bally.towerauction.net/ne/ct
Delaware	(484) 530-0700	http://www.hud.org/fp5/de
District of Columbia	(888) 673-9356	http://www.hud.org/fp5/dc
Florida	(678) 832-1000	http://www.hud.org/fp4/fl
Georgia	(404) 768-1400	http://bally.towerauction.net/i6/ga/index.html
Hawaii/Guam	(808) 949-0414	http://www.hudpemco.com
Idaho	(916) 922-2262	http://bally.towerauction.net/i7/id
Illinois	(949) 477-6300	http://bally.towerauction.net/i4/il
Indiana	(949) 477-6300	http://bally.towerauction.net/i4/in
Iowa	(972) 788-0026	http://www.hud.org/fp2/ia
Kansas	(303) 830-0777	http://www.hud.org/fp1/ks
Kentucky	(949) 477-6300	http://bally.towerauction.net/i4/ky
Louisiana	(303) 830-0777	http://www.hud.org/fp1/la

Maine	(860) 244-2783	http://bally.towerauction.net/ne/me
Maryland	(410) 772-5800	http://bally.towerauction.net/i3
Massachusetts	(860) 244-2783	http://bally.towerauction.net/ne/ma
Michigan	(248) 273-0041	http://bally.towerauction.net/i1
Minnesota	(972) 788-0026	http://www.hud.org/fp2/mn
Mississippi	(404) 768-1400	http://bally.towerauction.net/i6/ms/index.html
Missouri	(303) 830-0777	http://www.hud.org/fp1/mo
Montana	(972) 788-0026	http://www.hud.org/fp2/mt
Nebraska	(972) 788-0026	http://www.hud.org/fp2/ne
Nevada – northern	(916) 922-2262	http://www.hud.org/g2/nca
Nevada – central/southern	(916) 922-2262	http://www.hud.org/fp3/nv
New Hampshire	(860) 244-2783	http://bally.towerauction.net/ne/nh
New Jersey	(484) 530-0700	http://www.hud.org/fp5/nj
New Mexico	(972) 788-0026	http://www.hud.org/fp2/nm
New York	(484) 530-0700	http://www.hud.org/fp5/ny
North Carolina	(704) 599-1512	http://bally.towerauction.net/i5
North Dakota	(972) 788-0026	http://www.hud.org/fp2/nd
Ohio	(216) 289-1575	http://bally.towerauction.net/i1
Oklahoma	(303) 830-0777	http://www.hud.org/fp1/ok
Oregon	(916) 922-2262	http://bally.towerauction.net/i7/or
Pennsylvania	(916) 922-2262	http://bally.towerauction.net/i7/or
Puerto Rico/U.S. Virgin Islands	(678) 832-1000	http://www.hud.org/fp4/pr
Rhode Island	(860) 244-2783	http://bally.towerauction.net/ne/ri
South Carolina	(803) 996-2944	http://bally.towerauction.net/i5
South Dakota	(972) 788-0026	http://www.hud.org/fp2/sd
Tennessee	(949) 477-6300	http://bally.towerauction.net/i4/tn
Texas	(972) 788-0026	http://www.hud.org/fp2/tx
Utah	(972) 788-0026	http://www.hud.org/fp2/ut
Vermont	(860) 244-2783	http://bally.towerauction.net/ne/vt
Virginia	(888) 673-9356	http://www.hud.org/fp5/va
Washington	(916) 922-2262	http://bally.towerauction.net/i7/wa
West Virginia	(216) 289-1575	http://bally.towerauction.net/i1
Wisconsin	(972) 788-0026	http://www.hud.org/fp2/wi
Wyoming	(972) 788-0026	http://www.hud.org/fp2/wy

Federal Deposit Insurance Corporation (FDIC) Foreclosures

The FDIC was established in 1933 to bolster investor confidence in savings. The FDIC is charged with ensuring the stability of America's financial system. As such, the FDIC ensures most bank deposits up to $100,000.

The FDIC also liquidates a variety of assets including loans and real estate. A list of properties available for sale is updated weekly. Visit this link for more information: http://www2.fdic.gov/drrore.

For more information, contact the FDIC at:

Field Operations Branch
1910 Pacific Avenue
Dallas, TX 75201
(800) 568-9161

Government Services Agency (GSA)/Internal Revenue Service (IRS) Redemption Program

What happens when you don't pay your taxes? The IRS may have a legal right to file a tax lien on your real property. Should a bank or other lender foreclose the property, the IRS can choose to exercise its lien rights and try to recover what it is owed. For this process to work, the IRS must have someone guarantee to purchase the property at a minimum bid price. That's where the GSA comes to the rescue.

The GSA/IRS Redemption Program allows the GSA to assist the IRS in exercising its lien rights and recovering money from the sale of real property.

As an investor, you can obtain a listing of properties to bid on. First, you will need to fill out an application and pay a nominal fee of $5.00. After you've completed the application and submitted the fee, you will be considered a registered bidder.

The GSA sells real property through an auction and, as a guaranteed bidder, you are welcome to bid at or above the minimum price. As a winning bidder, you must purchase the property. For more information, visit this link: http://propertydisposal.gsa.gov/property or contact the GSA at:

GSA Property Disposal Division (9PR)
Attn: IRS Redemption Program
450 Golden Gate Avenue, 4th Floor East
San Francisco, CA 94102-3434
1-800-421-7848

EIGHT

Rental Property Management

"A thick skin is a gift from God."
– Konrad Adenaur

So you negotiated a deal and made it through closing. Now, fear sets in. Can I rent this place? Will I find a good tenant? How much should I ask? You should know most of the answers already, it's just that anxiety often makes us irrational.

Rental property management is not hard if you set the rules ahead of time and follow them.

Advertising

From what I have found, the Sunday classified section is still the best place to run an advertisement. Call your local paper immediately and run an ad. Even if you are fixing up a property, you can still take phone calls and even show the property.

Check out rental property management companies. They often have lists of property that they charge renters for, and are usually more than happy to include your listing for free. Next, buy a for-rent sign at the hardware store and place it in the yard and on the closest busy street.

Making Appointments

Almost immediately you will receive phone calls. I try to be courteous to everyone and return all phone calls. Establish one or two days a week to show the property and no more. For example, you might say, "If you are interested in seeing the property, I will be showing it Friday night between 6:30 p.m. and 8:00 p.m. and Sunday between 2:00 p.m. and 4:00 p.m." You decide, but it is too chaotic to be running over to your unit and showing it every time someone calls.

Showing the Property

Make sure the property is as clean and ready-to-go as possible. Even if you are working on the property, pick it up a little. Be sure to take over rental applications and pens. As each person, couple or family arrives show them the house and spend a few minutes talking to each prospective tenant. You'll be amazed at what you hear.

Ask if they would like to fill out an application or take it with them and fill it out later. I usually indicate that I use a first-come, first serve basis on qualified tenants. In other words, as I receive applications, I number them starting with "1." My prospective tenant is the first qualified applicant. You may choose to charge an application fee, but I don't. I would rather not eliminate a high quality tenant because of an application fee.

Evaluating Tenants

Once you have a pool of tenants to go through, start with the first applicant and apply an impartial screening process. The first thing I use to screen applicants is whether they are employed and how much they earn. I use the 3x rule. My tenants must make at least three times their rent. Employment must be verified with a phone call. I should tell you that incomplete applications do not count. If an employer's number or a previous landlord's number is missing, then the application is held awaiting completion. In other words, it's put on the bottom of the pile.

As you speak with prospective tenants, relatives, employers, etc., you will hear all kinds of stories. I listen and I feel sorry for some applicants, but I also realize that this is my property and a bad tenant is very hard to get rid of.

Finally, sort your top three winning candidates and call to congratulate the winner. Occasionally, you will be surprised to hear that your first candidate has chosen another place or is no longer interested. In this case, move on to your second candidate.

Special Note: As a landlord, you cannot refuse to rent, sell or negotiate with anyone because of race, color, religion, sex, national origin, or mental/physical handicaps. You must abide by the Fair Housing Act requirements. In some states, these requirements only apply to landlords operating a certain number of units (e.g., three or more properties), but to play it safe and do the right thing you should never discriminate in choosing tenants.

Signing the Lease

Set up a time to sign the lease and conduct a walk-through of the property. The walk-through allows both of you to note items that are faulty, missing or broken. Sign two copies of the lease and collect the initial deposits and rent. Always require a money order, cashier's check or cash during the initial signing. Be sure to provide the tenant with a receipt. Inexpensive receipt books are available at office supply stores. After all of this, you are ready to hand over the keys.

Be sure to explain your expectations. Remind the tenant when the rent is due and when it is late. I usually require rents due on the first day of the month and consider them late after the fourth day of the month. Remind the tenant who is responsible for yard maintenance, cleaning gutters, changing furnace filters, etc.

Make sure that you explain your policy on fixing or painting in lieu of rent. I personally don't like to mix the two. In other words, I may allow a tenant to paint or fix something, but I would rather reimburse them for paint or their services instead of taking it off the rent. I know it's the same, but it makes your accounting more difficult to reduce rent and it gives too much incentive for tenants to come up with unique ways to make improvements instead of paying the full rent. Also, it's a good idea to require all improvements to be approved ahead of time and in writing.

Structuring a Lease

You should always require a minimum of one year for every lease, unless you run into serious difficulty in finding suitable tenants. The reason here is that each move takes a toll on your property and you. Even the best tenants create wear and tear that must be fixed before leasing it again. This often means cleaning, painting, fixing, mowing, etc. Remember the phrase, "A bird in the hand is better than two in a bush." It applies here. If possible, sign longer leases (i.e., 2 to 3 years) and offer a discount. For example, if you are leasing a property for $725 a month, consider dropping the price to $700 a month for a 2-year lease. Believe me, it is worth it.

Rental Incentives

You might also consider offering a discount for rent paid on time. Let's say you offer a bonus incentive for your tenants to pay on or before the first day of the month. In exchange, you give them $10 in credit to be redeemed or reimbursed at the end of the year. This is a powerful incentive. You can play it up that it will be extra Christmas money. This is important to you because you want your money on time. Remember the time value of money. Of course, if you decide to use a property management company, they will have their own policies that will help you get your money on time; however, you will be paying a premium for their help.

Security Deposit

You should always require a security or indemnity deposit. The amount may be dictated by the state or local government that you are in. In Kansas, you are not allowed to accept a deposit for more than one month's rent.

I usually require an odd number that is slightly lower than one month's rent. Again, if the monthly rent is $725, I might require $700 for the security deposit. This signals to a tenant that the two are separate, so there is no enticement to skip out the last month and use the last month's rent to pay for it. Some property owners require both a security deposit and the last month's rent or half of the last month's rent. You will have to experiment with this.

Parting Ways/Eviction

If you run into a situation where the tenant's rent is constantly late or they can't pay at all, you may have to part ways. Your first option here should be to work with the tenant and creatively come up with a payment schedule or way to work off the debt. For one of my properties, it became obvious that my tenants could no longer pay the rent. I was patient, but worried that I wouldn't see my money. I met with the tenant and explained that it wasn't working out and the property must be too expensive.

Since the house needed some painting and a few repairs, I suggested that the tenant provide these services and he agreed. They decided to move out in a month and in the mean time, the tenant painted the exterior and fixed the woodwork. Believe me, this is more than I would have received with a hostile attitude.

As an incentive for moving out, you can use the security deposit. It may be possible to entice a tenant to leave with the deposit. For example, you could say that it's not working out and that you'll return part of the security deposit if the tenant moves out in a month.

Sometimes your best efforts won't work and you will have to evict a tenant. To start the eviction process, you must visit the county courthouse and fill out paperwork known as a writ of possession. Each county is different, so you will need to ask a lot of questions and follow their procedures.

NINE

Secrets of Selling Property

"Too much of a good thing is no good."
– overheard somewhere

The Price is Right

Don't even think about selling your property unless it is priced right. Refer back to Chapter 4 on estimating the value of real property. Too many homeowners get greedy here and want every last penny they can get from their property. In the long run what happens is their property stays on the market too long and may even be used by realtors as an example of a property that is overpriced. Remember the time value of money. The time it takes to sell a property is money that you have tied up and could use to make other deals.

Also, I have alluded to the fact that rental property will likely have to be sold at below market value because of the rental stigma. This is especially true for single-family homes.

The Time is Right

Every year something amazing happens, and you can watch it from your car window or while walking down the street. Every spring trees blossom, flowers bloom, birds chirp and there is a sense of wonder and newness in the air. Something amazing happens in the housing market as well. For sale signs begin popping up like rogue weeds.

By far, spring and early summer are the best times to sell a property. I suppose there are a number of reasons for this. Kids are out of school and parents can move easier. The weather is nice and people are in a buying mood. Lawns and landscapes can be made into beautiful arrangements. The best thing about selling in the spring is that demand is high and properties command higher prices. Take advantage of this annual phenomenon.

As you can probably guess, the best time to buy (in most of North America) is in the middle of winter, when it is cold and dreary. Of course, if you live in, or plan on investing in, places like Phoenix, Arizona or Fort Meyers, Florida, then the opposite may be true. Winter may be the best time to sell and summer may be the best time to buy.

The Property is Right

The object here is to make a house sellable by spending the least amount of money. It's amazing what I have seen, and you probably have, too. Homeowners and even investors get caught up in fixing every detail and making a property beautiful when in reality a buyer wants a nice property in a good location and that's about it.

Make small improvements that result in large profits. Here is a quick list of things to do to get your property ready to sell:

- Clean up the inside and outside of your property. Get rid of anything that you don't need. Clean windows, doorknobs, walls and make them bright and shiny. Remove any cobwebs and dust.
- Neatly arrange and reduce the amount of personal property.
- If you are living in the property, get rid of about half of the clothes in your closet and store them somewhere. Closets need to be open and inviting.
- Clean kitchen cupboards and make sure they show plenty of room.
- Clean the basement and garage and remove wetness and mildew. Before applying paint, use a product like Kilz to remove mold.
- Put a fresh coat of paint on the inside and outside. Be sure to use neutral colors (e.g., beige, taupe, off-white, or cream). Depending upon the condition of the paint, you may only need to do a touch up.
- Cut any weeds, tall grass or overgrown shrubs. Plant some inexpensive and blooming flowers.
- Remove stains, odors and dust. Fill your house/property with pleasant odors. If you are living there, a nice home-cooked meal may do the trick; otherwise, use scented candles, incense or find some other pleasing aroma. Be careful here. You are looking for a mild and universally appealing aroma.
- Turn all lights on and use high wattage bulbs. The brighter a house, the cleaner it seems.
- Replace carpeting or steam clean.
- Fix cracks in drywall.
- Fix or install ceiling fans.
- Clean and polish hardwood floors.
- Replace old worn faucets and other inexpensive fixtures.
- Remove old shower curtains and mats.
- Clean or recaulk bathroom tile.

For more information on selling your home, refer to Bruce Hahn's book, *How to Sell Your Home Fast* (1976).

Major improvements are much more risky. The following table, derived from the Chicago Federal Savings and Loan Association (1995), shows what type of cost recovery you can expect from major home expenditures:

Anticipated Cost Recovery of Major Home Expenditures

Improvement	Estimated Cost	Cost Recovery
Deck	$2,000 to $4,000	50% to 60%
Re-siding	$3,000 to $5,000	70%
Add a full bath	$1,500 to $3,000	40% to 70%
Add a garage	$3,000 to $5,000	60% to 100%
3rd Bedroom in existing space	$6,000 to $8,000	Up to 100%
3rd Bedroom house addition	$7,500 and up	Up to 100%
4th Bedroom house addition	$7,500 and up	75% to 100%
Kitchen remodeling	$3,500 to $8,000	80% to 100%
Family room addition	$10,000 to $20,000	80% to 100%
Fireplace	$2,500 to $4,000	Up to 100%
Gutters, soffit, facia	$2,500 to $4,000	30%
Insulation	$600 to $1,700	None
Landscaping	$10 to $2,000	20% to 50%
New heating/air conditioning	$1,000 to $1,500	None (expected)
Patio	$1,500 to $2,500	40% to 50%
Repaint exterior	$1,000 to $2,000	50% to 80%
Roof replacement	$3,000 to $6,000	50%
Storm windows and doors	$6,000 to $10,000	25% to 30%
Swimming pool	$2,500 to $20,000+	Zero to 50%
Home office	$0 to $5,000+	50% to 80%

Source: CNN, July 2002

TEN

Managing Environmental Risk

"A moment's insight is sometimes worth a life's experience."
– Oliver Wendell Holmes

In most cases, real estate is one of the safest ways to make a high return on your money. However, one of the biggest risks you face when purchasing real estate is environmental problems. Purchase a property with environmental contamination and you could lose money or, worse yet, even go bankrupt.

Why?

If you own a property that has known environmental problems, virtually no one will want to buy it. At a minimum, even if the problems are minor, you likely will only be able to sell the property for 10 or 20 percent of what it is really worth. In many cases you will not even be able to give the property away for free. This is because environmental laws are written so the current owner is liable for the contamination, regardless of whether he/she caused the contamination or not.

Therefore, if you purchase a property with environmental problems, you are financially liable for cleaning up the contamination to levels that are acceptable to the United States Environmental Protection Agency (USEPA) and, in many cases, State Environmental Protection Agencies. By law, these agencies can also sue you, the property owner, and make you pay for cleanup. For even minor problems, environmental cleanups can cost hundreds of thousands of dollars. Larger environmental problems can drag on for decades and cost millions of dollars to rectify.

For most situations, any environmental problems should be a deal killer for real estate investors.

For foreclosed properties, understanding and avoiding environmental problems takes on even more significance. This is because you are buying properties from people who are not paying their mortgage or property taxes, in the case of tax liens or tax deeds. A prime reason for letting the property go into default is the creation or discovery of environmental problems. After all, if you bought a property and then discovered that the property had environmental problems and you could not sell it, what would you do?

Commercial vs. Residential Properties

By far, one of the easiest ways to avoid environmental problems is to only purchase residential properties. You will probably avoid 75 to 90 percent of all properties that have environmental problems if you never bid on commercial properties. This is because in most cases, individuals living in residential homes do not have any need to create, store or distribute the type and quantity of hazardous materials that can cause significant environmental contamination.

Also, residential homes are not typically located in industrial areas where nearby commercial businesses are using hazardous substances that could impact the area. Remember how environmental laws are written:

> *Even if your neighbor causes your property to become contaminated, you could still be held liable for the contamination, especially if it cannot be proven who caused the contamination.*

That is one reason why cities and counties have zoning laws and often create areas called industrial parks. In these industrial parks, businesses are kept separate from residential areas so potential environmental impacts to most citizens can be controlled. The environmental laws are also written so levels of contamination in soil, air and water in industrial areas can be higher than residential areas and still be in compliance with the law.

Potential Environmental Problems

Here is a list of areas to be aware of when you start researching properties and looking for potential environmental problems:

Industrial parks

Industrial parks are large tracts of land that have been zoned for commercial operations that are typically involved in manufacturing some type of product. Sometimes, these industrial parks are located in areas that border residential areas, so watch out. Usually you can determine if a property is near an industrial park just by looking at a county map or driving by the property.

Highways

Although you might not expect it, highways can be a place where environmental problems may be present. Asphalt, deicing compounds and lead from automobile exhaust can pollute soils and groundwater. Roadsides along highways can be potential dump sites for just about anyone looking to get rid of something they don't want. And because drainage channels usually border highways, sometimes flooding can be a problem when drainage channels fill up. In addition, remember that it can be difficult to sell properties near major roadways because no one wants traffic in their backyard. If you are looking at property that is near or on a major highway, make sure you inspect the property bordering the highway to look for signs of dumping, flooding, asphalt/tar, soil staining, excessive trash or any other suspicious looking items.

Landfills

Landfills are everywhere. After all, where do you think your garbage goes when the trash truck comes to your door? Landfills range from municipal landfills that are used for disposing of residential garbage to chemical/hazardous waste landfills that are specially designed to dispose of hazardous waste. Property near any landfill almost always gets a big reduction in market value. Property near a chemical/hazardous waste landfill may not even be sellable. You can usually locate landfills by topographic maps or county maps. Also, there is always a lot of truck traffic near a landfill. Unless you have specialized knowledge, never bid on properties near a landfill.

Gas stations

Any property near a gas station should cause alarm. To avoid explosions, gas stations have underground storage tanks where gasoline or diesel fuel is stored. Unfortunately, many of these underground storage tanks leak, often causing environmental contamination in soils and groundwater that can migrate onto adjacent properties. Gasoline and diesel fuels also contain many hazardous chemicals, and some have been proven to cause cancer. Across the United States and the entire world for that matter, billions of dollars a year are spent cleaning up environmental contamination caused by gas stations. Gas stations are also usually very busy and noisy. Avoid any properties near gas stations.

Dry cleaners

Although at the surface dry cleaners may seem harmless, they can be the cause of very serious environmental problems. Dry cleaners use solvents to clean garments that can migrate great distances in the soil or groundwater. It is not uncommon for dry cleaning solvents to migrate several miles from a dry cleaning business. If the solvents are poured down the drain or dumped on the ground, they can migrate below ground and contaminate the groundwater. Once the groundwater is contaminated, it can migrate thousands of feet downgradient of the dry cleaning business and contaminate large areas of groundwater, potentially affecting many property owners. Wells located within the solvent plume become polluted and may no longer be used for drinking water.

Hazardous waste sites and disposal areas

Some companies manufacture, store or transport hazardous chemicals. Federal facilities such as military bases may use large quantities of hazardous wastes to manufacture weapons. When these wastes are improperly handled and released to the environment, the area often becomes what is called a hazardous waste site. Hazardous waste sites can be anywhere, but they are most commonly located near military bases, dump sites, landfills, gas stations, dry cleaners or anywhere where significant quantities of hazardous chemicals may have been used.

Hazardous waste sites that are regulated by the USEPA are called CERCLA (also called Superfund) and RCRA sites. CERCLA stands for Comprehensive Environmental Response, Compensation, and Liability Act and governs most hazardous waste sites that are no longer operating facilities. RCRA stands for Resource Conservation and Recovery Act. This law governs facilities that are still operating. State laws also govern hazardous waste sites such as gas stations and many RCRA facilities. Unless you are an expert in environmental cleanups, never buy a property near a hazardous waste site. You could become liable for cleaning up the contamination. Many people have gone bankrupt after buying land or property on or near a hazardous waste site.

Federal facilities, current and formerly owned military bases

Military bases are notorious for their environmental problems. Some military installations manufacture hazardous materials (e.g., ammunition plants) or store them, other military bases have large maintenance facilities that service aircraft/military equipment or perform weapons testing. Be very careful if you are looking at property near a military base or federal facility. Many of the areas around military bases become Superfund sites that can take decades to clean up. Property values are typically very depressed in these areas.

Airports

Would you want to live near an airport? Probably not. Buy or bid on property near an airport and you might find yourself with something that will be difficult to sell. Also, aircraft maintenance and fueling can cause environmental contamination due to the quantity of fuel used and the toxic compounds in the fuel. Think of an airport as what it really is, a very large gas station, and you will start to understand why it is not somewhere where you would want to invest your money.

Wastewater treatment plants and pump stations

Unless you have a septic tank, when you flush your toilet the water eventually goes to a wastewater treatment plant. These plants are undesirable for neighbors because they often smell and spills/leaks of sewage can occur. Pump stations are areas where the sewage is collected and pumped to the wastewater treatment plant. If you can, avoid properties near all these areas.

Refineries, tank farms, tank cleaners and waste oil storage/handling facilities

Just about any business that manufactures, handles or stores petroleum products should be cause for looking elsewhere. Most forms of petroleum contain hazardous chemicals, and petroleum is very flammable and explosive.

Oil wells, well fields, gas and petroleum pipelines

Even in its raw form, crude oil contains hazardous chemicals. Also, oil drillers can be sloppy in their waste handling practices and may leave large brine pits, open holes and dump sites after they are finished drilling. Many attempted drilling locations also are often abandoned when little or no oil or gas is found.

Electrical substations and power grids

Although no one has been able to definitively prove that living near a large magnetic field causes cancer, there is some pretty good evidence that large electrical substations and power grids can cause serious health problems. Also, PCBs, an environmental contaminate that can be expensive to investigate and clean up, were at one time commonly used in transformer oils. Property located adjacent to an electrical station or beneath a large power transmission grid should therefore be avoided.

Mines and quarries

Abandoned and current mines and quarries should also be avoided. Mines often contain high concentrations of heavy metals, like lead, mercury and arsenic. At most mines, these naturally occurring metals are concentrated, which is the reason the mine was constructed in the first place. Also, explosives are often used at mines to blast away the top rock. Surface water or groundwater passing through a mine can become contaminated with metals and overly acidic (called acid mine drainage). Mines are also usually a liability issue since they can collapse or lure children that can become lost and suffocate. Quarries can have similar problems. Quarries also can have steep cliffs and deep pools of water that can be a hazard to anyone on the property.

Agricultural areas

Agricultural areas, including pig/chicken farms, pesticide/fertilizer manufacturers, agricultural chemical makers and transporters, and grain storage facilities, have the potential for environmental contamination that could migrate to adjacent property. These areas are also usually smelly and may have a lot of truck traffic. Every situation is unique, but if it looks like a major agricultural operation is going on next door, make sure you know what it is and understand that property values may be affected.

Fuel oil tanks

In the Northeast, many homes are heated with fuel oil and properties often have buried fuel oil tanks. While this should not be an immediate cause for alarm, make sure you are familiar enough with the local area to know that their presence could at least be a possibility. A leaking fuel oil tank can be costly to fix or remove. Look for soil staining, oil sheens on nearby streams or standing, oily water. In most cases you will not be able to find the tank. When you go to the county assessor, see if you can find out if the property has a fuel oil tank by looking at the county records available for the property.

Septic tanks

Similar to fuel oil tanks, properties having a septic tank should not necessarily be a cause for alarm. Most rural properties have septic tanks and many operate correctly. However, a faulty septic system is usually easy to spot or, should I say, smell. Look for smells around low spots or in ditches. If you smell sewage and the property is in a rural area, you may have located a septic problem. This may not be a deal killer if the property is a good bargain, but fixing a septic problem can cost thousands of dollars and require approval by the county.

Lead paint

Homes built prior to 1977 may contain lead paint. Due to increased lead levels in children who lived at or near homes containing lead-based paint, lead can no longer be added to paint. However, older homes may have lead-based paint chips around home foundations. This is not usually a problem, but be aware that you may have to disclose this to future buyers of the property, especially if they finance the purchase with an FHA or other government loan.

Asbestos

Asbestos is more common in commercial buildings, but it can be found on older homes or located at dump sites on raw land. Inhaling asbestos fibers has been proven to cause cancer in humans and asbestos cleanups can be very expensive. Look for shingles or insulation that is friable (breaks apart when pulled strongly), old and not flammable. It is rare to find asbestos on a residential property. If you find something that looks suspicious you can have it analyzed for about $100.

Mold

Mold has gotten a lot of attention lately. Insulation or other building materials that get wet and stay damp for a long time can be an incubator for mold. One variety of mold (often called toxic black mold) that appears to grow very well in building materials can cause serious health problems. This environmental problem is sometimes difficult to spot, because even new homes that appear to be properly constructed can develop mold problems that can be hard to rectify. Entire walls may need to be torn out and replaced, and once mold is present in a home it can be difficult to eliminate. Across America, there are many cases of builders being sued for new homes they built that later developed a mold problem. New homes that enter tax delinquency because they could not be sold and show no other environmental problems are possible candidates for mold contamination. However, mold cases are rare, so it is unlikely you will encounter mold problems in most homes.

Radon

Anywhere where property is built directly onto shale, a common type of bedrock, radon may accumulate in crawl spaces, basements and low areas. Radon gas breathed over a lifetime has been shown to cause cancer. A lot has been made about radon and usually the fear is overblown. To fix a radon problem usually only requires better ventilation. Often all that is needed is a fan or better circulation to keep radon levels down. However, like all environmental problems, you should be aware of everything. Radon contamination is most common in the Midwest, where basements are constructed and shale layers in the subsurface are common.

Private wells

Properties with private wells can be a blessing or a curse. If the well is not contaminated, you have a very cheap water supply. If the well has contamination, you probably will not be able to use it and may need to pay to have it abandoned to avoid future problems. Wells that are located in low spots or are near obvious contamination sources like septic tanks or fuel oil tanks are candidates for polluted wells. Also, remember that contamination from other sources like gas stations, dry cleaners, military bases and oil fields can travel many miles underground in what is called a groundwater plume. Groundwater plumes can contaminate all the wells in a large area. Usually, if you avoid buying properties near any of the areas mentioned above, your well should be okay.

Flooding

Flooding is a very common environmental problem that can impair or, in some cases, ruin a real estate investment. In most situations, the government does not allow builders to construct homes in any areas that have been designated a flood plain. However, even these areas are chosen based on educated guesses of how large an area will flood every 50 to 100 years, so if a real deluge occurs, all bets can be off. To find evidence of flooding, look for dark staining on structures that appears to end at the same place. Also, look for debris on small trees, again hanging at roughly the same elevation across an area. Find soils that appear cracked and dry, like they has been through many wet and dry cycles. You can also look at topographic maps and find areas where the contour lines are lower in elevation than anywhere else. These maps may also show dotted areas that are wet during periods of the year.

Settlement

When the ground settles after a structure has been built on it, the structure may fail. Repair of settlement problems can be very expensive. Severely cracked basements and foundations are often easy to spot. Look for concrete structures that are cracked or not level. Clay soils settle a lot more than sand or rock.

Special situations

Earthquake zones, steep cliffs or strongly sloping property, heavy rail traffic, unfavorable soil conditions and polluted groundwater represent situations that may be unique to certain areas. This is why it is very important that you have some understanding of the area before you invest.

Some areas are just not suitable for investment or their market value is at least impaired because of a factor that may be common knowledge to locals but relatively unknown to outsiders. To find most special situations that could impact the property values, learn the area and talk to locals. If many houses in an area are not selling, it is usually a warning sign that something is wrong.

Environmental Assessments

After going through this list of items to consider, you should be familiar with most of the common types of environmental problems.

However, like most subjects, environmental issues can get very complicated. When checking for environmental problems, especially on commercial properties, many real estate attorneys advise their clients to have what is called a Phase I Environmental Site Assessment conducted. During a Phase I Environmental Assessment, an environmental professional will do a property search and often visit the site to check for environmental problems.

During the property search, the environmental professional will review what are called Sanborn maps. These maps are really just historical plat maps that show many of the previous owners and uses of the property. They are dated by year and can be found at the courthouse.

If you are reviewing a property and find potential signs of environmental contamination, or suspect the area was once used for something that could have cause environmental contamination, you should probably consult with an expert or avoid the property.

During a Phase I Environmental Assessment, environmental professionals also review topographic maps, county maps, geologic maps and call state professionals familiar with the area to learn about groundwater in the area, soil conditions and any nearby contaminated sites.

As part of their assessment, they scan for many of the same things discussed above to determine if there is any reason to suspect if the property has current environmental contamination or could become contaminated in the future.

After doing the Phase I Environmental Assessment, a report is prepared and if potential environmental problems are found, the buyer either walks away from the real estate deal or he/she may ask the owner of the property to perform a Phase II Environmental Assessment. During a Phase II Environmental Assessment, samples of soil and possibly groundwater from the site are often collected and the samples are sent to a laboratory to determine if environmental contaminants above regulatory levels are present on the property.

Working as an environmental professional for over 15 years, I have personally done many Phase I and II investigations. In most cases, I have found that common sense prevails during these investigations. Always remember the following:

**If you would not want to live in or near the
property for any reason, do not buy it or bid on it**.

Look on topographic maps and county maps for nearby undesirable neighbors like landfills or waste sites. Drive by the property to see what the neighbors look like. Any nearby commercial or government properties should be scrutinized carefully. Look for obvious signs of contamination on or near the property using the above guidelines.

Tax Implications of Selling Property

*"The point to remember is that what the government
gives it must first take away." – John S. Coleman*

Whether you're buying and selling foreclosures, holding on to rental properties for an extended period, purchasing tax liens or buying notes, Uncle Sam is anxiously awaiting his cut of the profits. If you're like me, you don't mind paying your fair share, right? Well, how about paying more than you're required. In fact, how would you like to pay a lot more than someone else and receive the same benefits? I wouldn't.

The point is to minimize your tax liability. You are not trying to get by without paying taxes; rather, you just want to make sure that you only pay what is required.

Capital Gains and Depreciation Recovery

First, if you buy and sell property and make a profit, you incur capital gains. Long-term capital gains are generally taxed at a rate lower than your personal income tax rate. That is a bonus and another reason to leave your 9 to 5 job and start a career in real estate.

The IRS considers long-term investments as those lasting over a period of one year. Short-term capital gains are taxed at your normal income tax rate, which could be as high as 35 percent for some taxpayers.

Although the capital gains rate and holding periods seem to fluctuate with changing administrations, the recent tendency has been to keep the rate below your ordinary income tax rate. Before May 6, 2003, the rates were 20 percent for most long-term gains and 10 percent for taxpayers in the 15 percent category. Currently, the long-term capital gains rate is 15 percent for most taxpayers. If you fall into the 10 or 15 percent tax brackets, the capital gains rate is only 5 percent.

The incentive is simple. Hold on to real estate longer than a year before selling to reduce your tax liability. For foreclosures and properties that you were planning to resell, it will be necessary to rent out the property for at least one year before selling.

Capital gains occur when you buy a property and sell it for more than what you paid for it or the basis of the property. The basis can be affected by expenses, but for simplicity if you bought a property for $50,000 and sold it a few years later for $65,000, then you have incurred a capital gain of $15,000 and it will be taxed at 15 percent. So, you owe Uncle Sam $2,250.

That's pretty easy so far. Now, how about depreciation? If you depreciate a rental house, then there will come a day of reckoning. In essence, the government has loaned you money and now it's time to pay back your debt. Depreciation recovery is taxed at your tax rate, or 25 percent in most cases.

In our previous example, you may have depreciated the property for a few years and let's say the depreciation taken is $5,000. This $5,000 is recovered and taxed at 25 percent. To summarize, you bought an investment property at $50,000 and sold it for $65,000. You depreciated the property so that its new basis is now $45,000. You owe taxes on $20,000, but at two different rates as shown below:

Investment Property Example
Purchase Price = $50,000

Purchase Price	Sale Price	Tax Rate	Taxes Due
	Appreciation = $15,000	15%	$2,250
Original Basis = $50,000	Depreciation = $5,000	25%	$1,250
	New Basis = $45,000	Not Applicable	$0
		Total	$3,500

So are there any ways around paying these taxes? The simple answer is yes.

Self-Directed Individual Retirement Accounts (IRAs)

Imagine being able to invest in real estate tax free or tax deferred. Well, amazingly you can.

I have to admit that I have only known about true self-directed IRAs for about a year. The problem is that I thought I had a self-directed IRA through my brokerage company. After all, I can buy stocks, mutual funds, bonds and other publicly traded securities. What I didn't realize is that I can also buy any of the following with a true self-directed IRA:

- Real property (i.e., real estate)
- Tax liens
- Tax deeds
- Notes and mortgages
- Businesses
- Partnerships
- LLCs.

So, you can actually buy and sell real estate investments through an IRA. That's right! Maybe I should say that again:

You can buy and sell real estate investments through an IRA.

There are a few items that you can't buy through an IRA and these are included in IRS publication 590 (http://www.irs.gov/publications/p590/index.html). In short, you cannot invest your IRA money in collectibles, antiques, coins, stamps, life insurance contracts, metals, gems and alcoholic beverages. You are also not allowed to buy, sell or exchange property or investments to a disqualified person, such as a spouse, child, father, mother or others who are closely related to you (refer to Publication 590).

Your IRA was designed to give you flexibility; however, it seems that only brokerage companies caught on. They control much of the process and they limit what you can purchase. After all, they don't make any money off of your purchase of a foreclosure or a tax lien certificate.

To make a long story short, you will need to contact another company that is set up to handle a true self-directed IRA. You can find information from these companies on rolling over an existing IRA, qualified retirement plan or setting up a new IRA account. Any purchases or sales will need to be made in the name of the IRA trust account, unless you have the IRA invest in an LLC that you control. Then, you can truly realize flexibility. The following companies are set up to handle true self-directed IRAs:

- Entrust Administration – http://www.entrustadmin.com
- Equity Trust Company (formerly Mid Ohio Securities) – http://www.trustetc.com
- Pensco – http://www.pensco.com
- Sterling Trust Company – http://www.sterling-trust.com

Remember, you can set up a traditional IRA and earnings are deferred until retirement. You can also set up a Roth IRA by paying the taxes upfront. Any earnings in a Roth IRA are tax free. That's right. You do not pay taxes on the earnings. The sky is the limit. If you have children, like I do, consider setting up or rolling over an educational IRA. If you've left an employer and have a 401(k) plan, you can roll it over into an IRA.

For small businesses, you should consider setting up either an SEP Plan or a SIMPLE IRA in addition to your standard or Roth IRA. Then you can truly recognize the power of savings and compound interest.

Like-Kind Exchanges (1031 Exchanges)

Many real estate investors are aware of like-kind or 1031 exchanges. Essentially, you can avoid capital gains taxes (not depreciation recovery), by exchanging one property for another of equal or greater value within a given time frame and by an unbiased third party.

In general, the property exchange must occur by an intermediary. The term like-kind means that just about any investment property that you exchange for another investment property will qualify as a like kind, unless one of the properties is located outside of the United States.

The exchanged property must be identified within 45 days and acquired within 180 days to qualify. The exchange can occur between related parties (e.g., father to son), but certain rules apply. The most notable rule is a two-year holding period.

For more information on like-kind exchanges, visit this web page: http://www4.law.cornell.edu/uscode/26/1031.html.

Owner Financing (Installment Sales)

One simple way to avoid a huge tax bill is to receive payments over time, rather than as a lump sum. This process is referred to as an installment sale. Most real estate investors call it owner financing.

For example, instead of receiving a lump sum payment of $100,000 for a property, you could structure it so that the buyer pays you in installments. In essence, you would be acting as a mortgage company, so you need to balance the tax implications with the risk associated with financing.

For example, you may require a down payment of $10,000, which would be taxable in terms of both recovering depreciation and capital gains taxes. You could then finance the rest over a period of 15 years or any other time frame. You could even create a balloon payment that is due in so many years. An example would be a loan that is amortized of 30 years, but due in 7 years. You may decide that in 7 years, you'll be retired and the lump sum payment will be okay; however, now you are working and the extra income would be devastating.

Remember, if you structure a deal like this you should seek legal advice and have a reputable title company help with the closing. Also, realize that the loan could be paid off early or the buyer could default and you would then have to foreclose, which is not necessarily the easiest process.

Another strategy is to allow the buyer to obtain outside financing and you provide a second mortgage on your equity. This certainly is appealing to the buyer, but you would be in second position for any foreclosure proceedings.

Trusts

Have you ever thought of investing in real estate for your children? A wonderful vehicle by which to do this is a trust, or private annuity trust. These trusts allow you to sell property or deed it to a trust and make your children the trustees and beneficiaries. You then structure the trust so that it pays out in installments. Like IRAs, you must begin receiving payments at age 70 ½. Taxes will then be due only on the installments.

Like most things in life, there are some restrictions that you should be aware of. First, once the trust is established, you are technically not in control. The trust owns and operates the property, and the trustees (presumably, your children) are in charge of it. If you do exert control over the trust, you could be in violation of the trust and lose the tax-deferred status.

Trusts are also not simple to set up and will likely require the services of an attorney. Depending upon the amount of taxes owed, you may want to weigh the attorney fees in the decision process.

Another type of trust, called a Charitable Remainder Trust, can be used in a similar manner to defer taxes. In this case, the qualified non-profit or charity assumes control as the trustee and you receive annuity payments or installments. The installments are taxable, but this may be the perfect way to provide steady income without paying a huge tax bill.

Upon your death, the "remainder" of the trust goes to the charity. What a great way to fund your favorite charity.

For more information on the tax implications of selling your property, Richard Williamson's book, *Selling Real Estate Without Paying Taxes, A Guide to Capital Gains Tax Alternatives* (2003), is an excellent resource.

TWELVE

Summary and Quick Start Guide

"Behold the turtle. He makes progress only
when he sticks his neck out." – James Bryant Conant

Now it's time to get started in real estate investing. Here is a summary of things to remember:

- Real estate investing can and will make you wealthy. The single most important asset that most Americans have is their own home. Why not multiply this effect and own several homes or other types of real estate?

- Only choose houses, condominiums, duplexes, apartments or office buildings that you would be willing to live or work in. If you are investing in residential real estate, think in terms of "bread and butter" houses. A "bread and butter" house is a decent looking, livable house in a good location, with at least three bedrooms. By far, location is more important than the property. Don't kid yourself. You won't make any substantial money on properties bought in neighborhoods in decline.

- There are lucrative methods for investing in real estate other than buying and selling property or rental management. Consider investing in Real Estate Investment Trusts, tax lien certificates, tax deed properties or discounted mortgages.

- Real estate investing is both investing and a small business. Treat it like a small business, not just an investment. Consider your business structure and look into establishing an LLC.

- "No money down" techniques can work, but oftentimes the properties are extremely run down or in bad areas. Most property owners will require some money down or otherwise the risk is on them. Money talks. Sometimes it's better to put some money down to negotiate a better deal. The object is the best deal.

- Get started buying a repossessed home. Contact your local Veteran's Administration. Although each state's VA has its own requirements, there are a few gems that can be acquired for little down, even if you are not a veteran. If you are a veteran, then by all means purchase your own home with a "no money down" VA loan.

- The real estate industry is often wary of anything that strays outside of the norm. In fact, you will know more about real estate investing after reading this book than about 80 percent of the agents you come in contact with.

- There are more or less two types of real estate agents: buyers and sellers. If you are working with an agent to find a house and you have signed a buyer's agency agreement, then you can say anything in confidence and the agent is required by law to work for your best interest. On the other hand, most of the time you will be calling about properties listed with a seller's agent. A seller's agent is not working for you and is not concerned about your best interests. Therefore, be careful of what you say. In certain circumstances, a dual agency situation may arise. My only advice here is to be careful. An agent cannot properly serve two competing interests. For more information on this, call your state real estate commission.

- Agents are required by law to present any offer to the buyer, even if the agent says "he or she won't sell it for that." Agents are also notorious for trying to quash creative financing arrangements.

- If you are renting a property, develop a comprehensive screening system that is fair, non-prejudicial and protective of your investment. For example, use your monthly rent times a multiplier (e.g., 3x) to screen out candidates. If you are asking $700 per month, then make sure that your renter is making at least $2,100 per month. This leaves a portion of their salary for groceries, utilities and other living expenses. Be friendly and respectful to your tenants, but remember that this is a business.

- Always call references, employers and former landlords.

- Remember to think long term. Very few properties will be worth your time or trouble to fix up and sell quickly ("flip," in real estate vernacular). Also, consider that the IRS wants you to hold investments, including real estate, for at least one year. The incentive is a 10 percent decrease in capital gains taxes (from 25 percent to 15 percent for most taxpayers).

- For active participants in real estate (i.e., rental property owners who manage their own properties), lucrative tax advantages are still available.

- Make friends with a handyman or make sure that you can fix plumbing, electrical, heating and air conditioning problems. You want someone who is trustworthy, reasonable with costs, reliable and friendly. Be careful with contractors.

- Make at least $100 per month positive cash flow per unit. Otherwise, it is not worth your time and effort.

- Break out the classified ads and start calling. You'll never learn until you get in the game.

- Avoid properties with environmental problems.

- Before you sell, make sure you understand the tax implications.

Best wishes as you embark on your career in real estate investing. Here is my personal email: geoguy@rogueinvestor.com.

READY…FIRE…AIM

APPENDIX A

Glossary of Real Estate Terms and Definitions

Real Estate Term	Definition
Acre	A unit of area equal to 43,560 square feet used to measure land.
Agent or Real Estate Agent	An individual who works for a real estate broker, but acts as the broker's salesperson to conduct business. A real estate agent helps buy and sell property and in exchange is given a commission from the sale. A real estate agent has a fiduciary responsibility to act in the buyer or seller's best interest depending upon the arrangement.
Amortize	Paying off a loan through a series of equal sized payments. Generally, the initial payments include more interest than principal; toward the end of the amortization period, the payment includes more principal than interest.
ARM	Adjustable Rate Mortgage. A mortgage with an interest rate that fluctuates with the going interest and is based upon a known standard, such as a T-bill.
Assumable	Another individual or entity can acquire the mortgage either with or without qualifying, depending upon the type of loan. Most assumable loans now require the new buyer to qualify. Assumable loans include FHA, VA and owner-financed notes.
Balloon Payment	A mortgage loan under which the final payment is significantly larger than the previous payment. A balloon mortgage is often amortized over a certain number of years (e.g., 15, 20 or 30), but the final payment may be due sooner. For example, it is possible to offer a 7-year balloon mortgage amortized over 20 years.
Blanket Mortgage	A mortgage creating a lien against two or more tracts of real property.
Broker or Real Estate Broker	A real estate broker is an individual who, by law, represents a buyer or seller and has a fiduciary responsibility to act in their best interest. A real estate agent works for a real estate broker. A real estate broker can also be a real estate agent.
Buyer's Agent	A real estate agent who represents the buyer and acts in the buyer's best interest. Generally, the buyer pays nothing for a buyer's agent, but the buyer's agent is paid from the sale. In the case of a buyer and seller's agent, the commission will be split.
Capitalization	In real estate appraisal it is the process of converting income, such as rental income, to a property value.
Capitalization (Cap) Rate	The ratio of income to a property's value.
Cash Flow	The net income from a property or the difference between income and expenses.
CMA	Competitive or Comparable Market Analysis
Commission	The percentage of money earned by a real estate agent/broker. It is negotiable and often depends upon the type of property. Residential homes typically require 7% commission.
Contract	Agreement between competent parties. A real estate contract typically includes an offer, acceptance by the seller and consideration (i.e., earnest money) by the buyer.
Contract For Deed	Also called a Land Contract. A contract under which the seller keeps the title until all payments have been made.
Conventional Mortgage	A mortgage loan that is not backed by a government agency like FHA or VA.

Deed	A legal document used to transfer real estate.
Deed of Trust	A legal document used to transfer real estate to a trustee, like a mortgage. Allows for foreclosure without the necessity of a lawsuit.
Discount Points	A fee charged by lenders that is usually based upon a percentage of the purchase price. For instance, one point is equal to 1% of the purchase price. A point on a $100,000 loan would cost $1,000.
Dual Agent/Agency	A real estate broker representing both the buyer and the seller. Even though two real estate agents are involved, if they work for the same broker, a dual agency situation may arise. The real estate agents should advise you when this is the case.
Due Diligence	A buzzword in real estate for doing your homework and evaluating a property. It is also used in real estate when a buyer is evaluating environmental concerns.
Earnest Money	Usually a deposit to purchase real estate that shows you are serious. If the buyer defaults the seller will receive the earnest money. As an investor, it is important to limit the amount you put down and include contingencies in the contract. For example, a contract can be contingent upon obtaining financing at an interest rate below 9%.
Easement	A right to use or access real estate by another entity. Utility companies usually have easements granted by the city. They have the right to access your property to repair or replace a utility.
Encroachment	Real property that extends onto adjacent land owned by someone else.
Escrow	A neutral or unbiased party used to handle real estate matter. Title companies often act as escrow agents.
Equity	The difference between a property's market value and the loan balance.
Fair Housing Act	Federal Law regulating equal opportunity in the sale and rental of real property.
FHA	Federal Housing Administration. A government agency responsible for ensuring that all qualified Americans are able to purchase real estate. FHA guarantees mortgages and operates a number of other programs designed to encourage home ownership.
Fixture	Personal property that becomes real property by attachment. An example is a ceiling fan that was once personal property. Once attached to the ceiling, it becomes real property.
FSBO	For Sale By Owner. An owner who is attempting to sell real property without a real estate broker.
General Warranty Deed	A deed that contains promises against any other claims to title on the property. It is the most protective of a potential buyer.
HUD	Housing and Urban Development. A U.S. government agency that operates many different housing programs including the FHA program.
Joint Tenant	Two or more parties whom own real property. Upon death, the remaining ownership transfers to the surviving partner(s).
Landlord	A property owner who leases his/her property.
Lease	An agreement to temporarily occupy someone's property.
Legal Description	A means by which others can locate property. It is most often described using the Section, Township and Range method.
Lien	An encumbrance on a property title/deed that must be paid or resolved prior to a sale.
Mechanic's Lien	One of the most common types of liens. It is caused by failure to pay a contractor for services rendered on a property.
MIP	Mortgage Insurance Premium. Insurance required by a lender in case of default. Associated with FHA loans.

MLS	Multiple Listing Service. A database operated by realtors.
Mortgage	A promise to pay that is secured by real estate. It creates a lien against real estate until it is paid.
Personal Property	Property that is not attached to real estate and in the case of a sale is not obligated to remain with the property. Be careful to determine exactly what is personal property and what is real property. For example, a window unit air conditioner is probably not real property, but a central air conditioner is real property.
Phase I	An environmental site assessment for real property that looks for potential environmental hazards, such as lead-based paint, asbestos, radon and nearby chemical plants or gas stations. Phase I environmental site assessments are performed because the owner is liable for environmental cleanups, which can cost thousands to millions of dollars.
PITI	Principal, Interest, Taxes and Insurance.
PMI	Private Mortgage Insurance. Required by most lenders for buyers who put down less than 20% of the purchase price.
Quitclaim Deed	A deed used to release a claim without making any warranties. divorced party will often use a quitclaim deed to release claims on property.
Real Estate	Land plus fixtures on the land. It is also referred to as real property.
Real Property	Real estate that contains the associated rights, such as mineral rights.
REITs	Real Estate Investment Trusts. Securities of companies that invest in real estate.
REO	Real Estate Owned. Property foreclosed by and owned by a banker or lender.
Second/Third Mortgage	Subordinate mortgages that are paid after the primary or first mortgage.
Seller's Agent	A real estate agent who represents the seller in a property transaction. The seller's agent has a fiduciary responsibility to act in the seller's best interest.
Subordination	To move a mortgage to a lower position, as in moving a first mortgage to a second mortgage.
Survey	The process of determining the legal boundaries of real estate.
Tax Lien	A lien against property due to unpaid taxes.
Tax Lien Certificates	Certificates purchased by investors that offer certain rights to property with outstanding tax debt.
Tenant in Common	Two or more tenants that own a certain percentage of property, such as a condominium.
Vendee	A buyer of real estate.
Vendor	A seller of real estate.

Some definitions were modified from Friedman et al. 1987.

References

Robert G. Allen, 1990, *Nothing Down for the 90s*, Simon & Schuster, New York, 362 pp.

Stephen R. Covey, 1990, *The 7 Habits of Highly Effective People*, Simon & Schuster Inc., New York, 360 pp.

Jack P. Friedman et al., 1987, *Dictionary of Real Estate Terms*, Second Edition, Barrons, New York, 329 pp.

Bruce N. Hahn, 1976, *How to Sell Your Home Fast*, The American Homeowners Foundation Press, Arlington, Virginia, 142 pp.

Anthony Mancuso, 2000. *Form Your Own Limited Liability Company*, 3d Edition, Nolo Press, Berkeley, California.

Carleton H. Sheets, 1994, *No Down Payment*, Ninth Edition, The Professional Education Institute.

Russ Whitney, 1994, *Building Wealth*, Simon & Schuster, New York, 283 pp.

Richard T. Williamson, 2003, *Selling Real Estate Without Paying Taxes, A Guide to Capital Gains Tax Alternatives*, Dearborn Trade Publishing, 202 pp.

Zig Ziglar, 1995, *Goals: Setting and Achieving Them on Schedule,* Audiocassette tapes.

BONUS NO. 1

How to Buy Raw Land Without Getting Ripped Off

Buying a piece of rural land is almost a universal dream. Somewhere outside of town or near your favorite vacation spot is 10 acres of land that could become your secret retreat. Find some secluded acreage and you can escape from the crowds, traffic and pollution that are rapidly becoming a part of life.

Unfortunately, something as seemingly simple as buying your dream acreage can actually be fairly complicated. In fact, many real estate experts correctly advise real estate investors to shy away from buying raw land. This is because the factors that create appealing rural land, including limited access, low population density and limited development, often reduce the number of potential buyers should you want to sell. In addition, available amenities such as water, electricity and telephone service may be limited. These factors do make the rural real estate game, especially if the property is raw land without any structures, a more difficult proposition for real estate investors.

However, if your goal is to buy the land for yourself or you intend to be long-term investor, rural real estate can be a good investment. Like anything else in life, if you understand the basic rules of the game and take some steps to reduce the potential risks, you can still find a good deal. Here are the steps and tips you should follow if you are thinking about trying to find some reasonable, rural land.

Defining Your Goal

You will waste a lot of time if you do not define what you are looking for. Unlike most residential properties, rural land can have very wide-ranging characteristics and prices. Here is a checklist of the items you need to focus on when deciding what your dream acreage should be:

- Money available: Unfortunately, this is probably the most important determinant in defining your goal. Over the last 10 to 15 years, the price of rural land in most areas has risen quite a bit due to pressure from development. Unless you are buying hundreds of acres, the days of buying land for $500 or even a $1000 per acre are largely over. Although prices vary a great deal, in most cases the minimum you will pay for small parcels of undeveloped land (less than 20 acres) is $3,000 to $5,000 per acre in the Midwest; $5,000 to $10,000 in mountainous areas; and $10,000 to $20,000 in coastal areas. These are very general ranges. Prices can be much higher in certain areas. For example, secluded land anywhere near Santa Fe, New Mexico, routinely goes for over $1 million dollars per acre, and any type of property with certain features (beach access, incredible views, etc.) will be extremely expensive. Also, generally speaking, the greater the distance from civilization the lower the price, and the greater amount of land being purchased the lower the price.

- Number of acres: Smaller parcels typically command higher prices per acre. Rural landowners usually do not like to break up their land and would rather sell larger tracts to one or two buyers. This reduces the transaction costs and hassles for them and, if they plan to continue living near the area, also the number of neighbors. This means you will have to accept a higher price per acre if you do not plan on buying more than 25 acres. Five- to 10-acre parcels will likely be even more expensive.

- Area: Defining the area is extremely important. You will need to become familiar with the area before you can make an intelligent offer. When you are buying rural property, things like roads, utilities, water rights, access, easements and title issues become extremely important. It will take time to learn the range of land prices and answers to all of the above issues. Define your area to a radius of 100 miles or less, if possible.

- Features: If this is to be your dream property, you should figure out just what you want. You should list the features you desire in their order of importance. For example, waterfront property, old trees, distance from civilization, and gravel road access would be an example of the order of importance.

Overall, the process of defining your goal should be an enjoyable task that you perform with patience. Often defining what is acceptable and what you can afford makes it much more likely that you will be happy with the outcome.

Narrowing Your Search

Once you have defined what you want, you need to narrow your search to potential properties that meet you needs. To accomplish this goal, follow three steps: study, drive by and communicate.

Study

After you have determined the basic area you are interested in, buy some topographical maps (7.5 minute quadrangle maps) of the area from the U.S. Geological Survey. You can go to their website (http://www.usgs.gov) and locate the maps if you want, or sometimes a local bookstore will have quadrangle maps for nearby areas. These maps will give you a general idea of the lay of the land, including the location of drainage ways, roads and often structures that include houses. After you have narrowed your search to areas that look interesting, go the county courthouse and buy a plat book. A plat book is a series of plat maps that show the estimated legal property boundaries of the property and who is the property owner. Use these books to determine where roads and property boundaries are located and what properties deserve a drive through. You will also use the property descriptions later on if you decide to contact the landowners. You can use this time to call local realtors, but don't be disappointed if they are not much help. When buying rural land, realtors may not be helpful because the market for rural land is usually less than residential land. Also, properties that the realtors have for sale may be the most prized and expensive land in the area, since this land may be in more demand making it suitable for development. Remember, often the sole reason you are looking for this land is to find a bargain that will probably not even be listed with a realtor. Your best opportunity may come from a landowner who does not even plan on selling their property until you call them. You can also check the following government websites for surplus land that may be for sale from the government in the area you are looking: Bureau of Land Management (BLM) (http://www.blm.gov) and Government Services Administration (http://www.gsa.gov). There is a lot of BLM land in the western half of the United States.

Drive By

There is no substitute for driving by each piece of property that looks interesting. No map can convey the visual features in the detail that is required to evaluate it. Look for the closest utility hookups, road conditions, potential flooding problems, property slope, and unusual features like trash, sheens or soil stains. Make sure your thoroughly inspect any property you intend to buy, acre by acre.

Communicate

As you spend time in the area, start to communicate with the locals. Find out about landowners who may have property for sale, and visit with officials at the county courthouse to learn about local regulations and customs regarding property deeds. If you see individuals who appear to be locals during your drives, strike up a conversation and ask about local land. This process of chat can be very important to your chances for obtaining the property you want for a fair price. Taking an ad out in several local papers is probably the best way to find sellers. In the ad, define what you want and leave a phone number. For example:

WANTED: 10 to 20 acres of land,
water rights, road access in
Calhoun County, 644-676-8832

Call landowners you have identified from the plat book who have promising sections of land. Be patient, as this process can take a year or more. Unlike residential properties, realtors may not be helpful, causing you to spend a lot of time developing and chasing leads.

Making the Offer

When you are dealing with rural land, it is best to get a lawyer unless the deal has no complications. At a minimum, have a title company research the title and determine that you will have clear title if you purchase the property. If you hire a lawyer they can research the title and draw up the contract. If the property boundaries are not clear, you may need to have a survey of the property performed. The county courthouse will usually tell you if they require a survey of the property. Before you make an offer on the property, make sure you understand the following items: (1) water rights and the costs for getting water to the property, (2) nearest electricity/gas/telephone to the property and the costs for getting utilities to the property, (3) any easements on the property (easements are legal agreements allowing someone else to use portions of the land; e.g., utility easements, road easements), (4) road access and, if no road access is available, the costs for getting a road to the property, (5) taxes and (6) available services. All these factors should go into making a decision regarding the property. Be careful if the costs of bringing utilities, roads and water to the property are more than 25 percent of the total value of the property. Remember, these costs cannot necessarily be recouped if you decide to sell the property.

Things You Should Avoid

Like many real estate deals, there are always more properties that you can buy, so part of your job is to avoid problems to the extent possible. Here are the five main items that you should avoid when buying rural land:

- Price or improvement costs too high: Before you buy, find out the costs that raw land typically sells for in the area you are interested in. The county courthouse will help with this information. Local realtors may also be useful, but their prices may be biased a little high. Unless the property has unique features, don't pay more than approximately two times the local averages for any property. Also, do not buy property where the costs of bringing utilities, water and/or roads exceed more than 25 percent of the total value of the property.

- Water rights: If the property does not have reliable sources of rural water, do not buy it if you cannot obtain the water rights. Also, if groundwater is the source of water, be prepared for drilling expenses and make sure you research if groundwater is available and at what depth. If water appears to be a problem, find a new property. Without a source of water, most raw land has limited value. You can haul water, but it is problematic and usually not what most landowners want.

- Environment problems: Entire books have been written on environmental issues regarding real estate purchases. Generally, avoid any raw land that has even a hint of environmental problems. You can go to the county courthouse and research past owners and uses of the property. Avoid any properties where underground storage tanks were ever present. Avoid properties near gas stations, tank farms, dry cleaners, mines, landfills, power plants, hazardous waste sites and just about any large-scale industrial operation. Inspect any water bodies on the property (creeks, rivers, ponds lakes, seeps) to determine if any seeps, unusual odors or staining are present. How does the water body receive its water? From what appears to be a clean, undeveloped stream or from agricultural runoff? Often, with a little research and a good property inspection, you can spot environmental problems. For more on potential environmental problems, see Chapter 10 of *Rogue Real Estate Investor* in this collection.

- Flooding: To make sure the property does not flood, go the county courthouse and find out how prone the property is to flooding. The U.S. Army Corps of Engineers (http://www.usace.army.mil) publishes floodplain maps that can be used to assess the potential of a property to flooding. If the property is in a floodplain, do not buy it. You can also inspect the property to see if any debris or large trees have been deposited on the property recently.

- Clear title: If you can't get clear title to the property, don't make an offer, period.

BONUS NO. 2

Real Estate Forms

Real estate forms are provided on the CD that is part of your package. Please note that an attorney should review all forms. Every state has unique requirements and you may have individual requirements that differ from the forms presented on the CD. It is often a good idea to contact a local real estate agent, state board of realtors, a title company or an attorney. Many office supply stores sell standard legal form packages for a reasonable price.

As you experiment with real estate, you will find what works best for you.

ROGUE
TAX LIEN
INVESTOR

Published by
Mind Like Water®

Overland Park, Kansas

ROGUE TAX LIEN INVESTOR

CONTENTS

Rogue Tax Lien Investor

ONE

Why Should You Read This Book?

"If a man wants his dreams to come true then he must wake up." – anonymous

What would you say if we told you that there is a safe and virtually guaranteed way to make 16 to 24 percent return per year on your money that few people know about?

What would you say if this investing method could occasionally give you an even greater return on your money, possibly 50 percent to more than 100 percent return on your money per year?

What would you say if we told you that this investing method was sanctioned, encouraged and arranged by the government, and that the government had a very strong motivation to make sure it worked effectively and was as safe as possible?

What would you say if you realized that the safety of this investment was not only monitored by the government, it was actually backed by the most powerful collateral in the world – real property?

Does this sound too good to be true?

It's not.

Tax liens certificates, which are discussed more fully in Chapter 2, are probably the safest, most lucrative and undiscovered investing method in the world. Here are the reasons why:

- Tax lien certificates routinely provide an investment return to investors of 16 to 24 percent per year or more.

- In some states, an investor can earn a flat interest rate of 20 to 25 percent. In Texas, investors can earn 25 percent in less than 6 months for most properties, resulting in a whopping 50 percent or more annual return.

- In some cases, purchasers of tax lien certificates can walk away with an entire property for only the taxes owed (often pennies on the dollar).

- Compared to most investments, tax lien certificates are relatively safe. This is because state governments issue tax liens and monitor tax lien certificate sales, so if you do your homework the investment risk is low. Tax lien certificates are also backed by the property they are issued against, so that if the defaulter does not pay the tax lien certificate investor all the money and interest due, they lose the entire property for only the taxes and penalties owed. People get very motivated to pay up if the alternative is to lose their home.

- Tax lien certificates are an undiscovered investing method. This is because few people have even heard of tax lien certificates and very few books have been written on the subject of tax lien certificate investing. If you don't believe me, go to the library and try to find more than one or two books on tax lien certificate investing. You will be lucky if you find any books at all, and almost all tax lien certificate books are extremely outdated.

We spent the last two years researching tax lien certificates and found most books were 5 to 10 years old and very general. This is because tax lien certificates are handled differently by every state and the procedures change. Also, up until now, it was difficult to decipher all the legal language associated with tax lien certificate investing (almost all the rules and procedures were written by lawyers). However, the Internet changes all that. Many states are beginning to catch on and the information that is publicly available is getting better and better.

When you combine all these factors, tax liens are one of most lucrative and unique investment methods. They are also one of the safest methods of investing. Add the explosive power of the Internet and now is an incredible time to start investing in tax lien certificates.

What would you rather do?

1. Earn 2 to 5 percent per year on your money by buying savings bonds or CDs,

2. Watch your investment dollars go up and down like a yo yo in the stock market and potentially lose money if the economy or an individual company you own does poorly, or the CEO lies about the company's financial numbers, or

3. Earn 16 to 24 percent per year by investing in a government-controlled system that is backed by someone's entire property if they don't repay?

Tax deeds, which also are discussed in Chapter 2, represent a terrific way to buy real estate for 70 to 90 percent off, or literally pennies on the dollar.

In many states, rather than issuing a lien against a property, the county or municipality forecloses on the lien and the deed (ownership) is auctioned off to investors.

If investing in tax lien certificates and tax deeds sounds intriguing, read on.

TWO

What Are Tax Liens and Tax Deeds?

"Don't buy the house; buy the neighborhood." – Russian proverb

County governments are often faced with an interesting problem: some of their property owners do not pay their property tax bills.

Why is this a problem?

County governments depend strongly on tax revenue collected from property owners to operate the county government and pay the county employees. In many counties, over 50 percent of the entire county budget comes from collecting property taxes.

This makes addressing delinquent property taxes a high priority issue for most counties. Fortunately, there is a solution for everyone. This solution provides income for the county, a safe and profitable investment return for the investor, and a little extra time for the person in default to try and come up with the money. It is called a tax lien.

A tax lien is a lien or encumbrance placed on real property for failure to pay taxes. A tax lien is a powerful lien that, in most jurisdictions, takes precedence over mortgage liens or mechanics liens. In essence, a tax lien becomes first priority and, if the property is foreclosed, will eliminate a mortgage lien. Generally, Internal Revenue Service (IRS) liens and local government assessments will still remain and could become the investor's responsibility.

Here is an example of how a tax lien certificate works.

Jerry Latepay gets in some financial trouble and cannot pay his property tax bill. After a few warning letters from the county, he is delinquent. To make Jerry aware of the serious nature of property tax delinquency and start the legal ball rolling, the county places a tax lien on Jerry's property for the amount of the taxes owed. The tax lien becomes a debt on the property and must be paid off before the property can be sold or legally cleared. In most counties, Jerry Latepay is considered in default the day after his property taxes are not paid. This shows Jerry Latepay how serious the county is when it comes to not paying property taxes.

Once a year the county has a tax lien auction. If Jerry Latepay has not paid his property taxes by the time of the auction, the county includes Jerry's property in the tax lien auction. To make the tax lien enticing to investors, a state-mandated interest rate, which varies from state to state but is usually in the range of 10 to 24 percent per year, is added to the tax lien. Some states call this a penalty, while other states just refer to it as the interest rate; however, each state has its own procedures. The state then creates what is called a tax lien certificate (also called a certificate of purchase) to offer to investors at the auction. The tax lien certificate is the physical piece of paper that gives the investor a legal claim to the investment. In most states, the interest rate on the tax lien is what the bidding will start at when investors bid on the tax lien certificate created by Jerry's delinquent tax bill.

At the auction, an investor buys the tax lien certificate issued for Jerry's property. The value of the tax lien certificate is equal to the delinquent taxes owed on the property plus any penalties. When the investor buys the tax lien certificate issued for Jerry's property, he/she is essentially paying off the delinquent property taxes owed to the county. Jerry now owes the tax lien investor all the back taxes owed plus the amount of interest due on the tax lien certificate. Although the rules vary from state to state, in most states interest starts to accrue the day the tax lien certificate is sold. Thus, the longer Jerry waits to pay off the tax lien certificate, the more money the investor earns. In some states, if Jerry waits more than a year to pay, the interest rate increases and the investor makes even more money. After a tax lien certificate is issued, there are two possible outcomes.

In about 95 percent of the cases, Jerry Latepay comes up with the money. This is because Jerry does not want to lose his home. This is why tax lien certificates are an ultra safe investment. When Jerry comes up with the money, he pays the county, the county contracts the tax lien certificate investor, and the investor turns in the tax lien certificate issued at the auction. In exchange for redeeming the tax lien certificate, the investor receives all the money he/she invested in the tax lien certificate plus the accrued interest. This process is called redeeming the tax lien certificate. The county where the tax lien certificate was issued handles the entire process.

In less than 5 percent of the cases, for whatever reason, Jerry cannot come up with the money. In most states this means Jerry will forfeit the entire property to the investor. After following the legal process required by the county, the investor forecloses on Jerry's legal ownership of the property, and in return for paying all remaining liens, taxes and penalties due, the investor receives the entire property, often for a fraction of what it is worth. The period of time that Jerry has to pay back the delinquent taxes is called the redemption period, which can range from as short as six months to as long as five years depending on the state.

Talk about a win/win situation. If Jerry Latepay pays off the tax lien, the investor receives his or her original investment plus a high interest rate. If Jerry does not pay off the tax lien, the investor receives the entire property for nothing more than the property taxes due on the property when Jerry forfeits the property. Are you beginning to see why tax liens are a great, unknown investment?

What is a deed? A deed is a document that transfers ownership to property. A tax deed is a special type of deed resulting from nonpayment of taxes.

In many U.S. states and Canadian provinces, Jerry Latepay is given many opportunities to pay his taxes. Oftentimes, Jerry Latepay is several years delinquent in paying his taxes. After multiple warnings, the county puts his property up for sale to investors for as little as the taxes, penalties and fees that Jerry owes. In some cases, the county is nice and requires a minimum percent of the assessed value. At a tax deed auction, the winning bidder receives the deed to Jerry's property. In some cases, Jerry may still have a short time to redeem; otherwise, the investor becomes the legal owner of the property.

The investor may have to wait a year or so to obtain a marketable title, but the investor may have just bought Jerry's property for a fraction of what it is worth.

THREE

What Every Tax Lien/Tax Deed
Investor Should Know

"Knowledge is Power." – Francis Bacon

Now that you have a basic understanding of what tax liens and tax deeds are, and why they represent unique investment opportunities, it is time to delve into what you should know before you invest.

The Benefits of Tax Lien Certificate Investing

We have already discussed some of the benefits of tax lien investing. They can be summarized as follows:

- Investment return: Although it varies from state to state, a 16 to 24 percent return is common. If the property owner never pays their taxes, the investor may realize profits well in excess of 100 percent by receiving the property for only the amount of the property taxes owed to the county. With interest rates near 50-year lows, tax lien certificates are an incredible bargain.

- Investment risk: The investment risk is very low because (1) state and county governments control the tax lien process, (2) property owners risk losing their property if they do not pay their taxes, (3) in most states the investor receives the property if the delinquent owner does not pay their taxes, and (4) tax lien certificates are not volatile investments. The value of a tax lien certificate does not fluctuate and is not affected by general economic factors like most other investments. In fact, in most cases, the worse the economy performs, the greater the number of tax lien certificates will be issued (more people default on their property taxes and mortgage when the economy does poorly).

- Investment secrecy: Few people have even heard about tax lien certificates. Even fewer people understand how to invest in tax lien certificates. Very little information is available on how to invest in tax lien certificates. Successful investing is almost always about supply and demand. In the United States there are thousands of counties that have tax lien certificate auctions every year. At each auction, hundreds of tax lien certificates are usually available. Many states have so many tax lien certificates that you can buy the ones that didn't sell at auction by mail (also called over-the-counter sales or negotiated sales). No one person can cover more than a few counties in a few states per year. This virtually ensures that for the foreseeable future, the supply of tax lien certificates will be much greater than the demand.

The Drawbacks of Tax Lien Certificate Investing

The drawbacks of tax lien investing can be summarized as follows:

- <u>Liquidity</u>: Tax liens are not liquid investments. In some cases you may have your money tied up for several years before you get the principal plus interest back.

- <u>Complexity</u>: Tax lien laws vary from state to state.

- <u>Time</u>: Tax liens require a time commitment to learn the rules of a state and its counties, research properties and attend auctions.

The Benefits of Tax Deed Investing

We also have already discussed some of the benefits of tax deed investing. They can be summarized as follows:

- <u>Obtain property ownership for 50 to 90 percent below market value</u>: Although it varies from state to state, in certain circumstances you can obtain an entire property for only the taxes and penalties owed. In many cases, you can obtain properties for at least 50 to 90 percent below market value.

- <u>Investment secrecy</u>: If few people have heard about tax lien certificates, even fewer people know anything about tax deed sales. When we started researching tax sales, we found very little information on how to invest in tax lien certificates and no information on how to purchase property at tax deed sales. However, all states have tax deed sales and there are more tax deed sales than tax lien sales. The supply of foreclosed properties almost always exceeds the demand. In the United States there are thousands of counties that have tax deed sales every year. At each auction, hundreds of properties are usually available. Many states have so many properties that they have foreclosure lists based on how many years the property has been in foreclosure.

The Drawbacks of Tax Deed Investing

The drawbacks of tax deed investing can be summarized as follows:

- <u>Liquidity</u>: If tax liens certificates are not liquid investments, then tax deeds are even worse. In some cases you will have your money tied up for several years before you can sell the property, because title companies may not issue title insurance on the property until all liens are cleared and it obvious that clear title can be granted. This process can take more than a year.

- <u>Complexity</u>: Tax deed laws vary from state to state.

- <u>Time</u>: Tax deeds sales require a time commitment to learn the rules of a state and its counties, research properties and attend auctions.

- <u>Risk</u>: Purchasing foreclosed property at a tax deed sale definitely has some risk. You must do your homework. Remember, once you buy a tax deed, you will own the property including all of its potential problems. In addition, title companies sometimes will not issue title insurance for at least the first year on any property bought at a tax deed sale. This means it could be hard to get a loan until it is clear that everything is okay with the property.

- Capital: You definitely will need more capital to buy properties at tax deed sales. Although it varies from property to property and from state to state, you may need a minimum of $5,000 to $10,000 to qualify as a bidder. Check local rules and regulations. A deposit also is usually required. Some states provide financing, in which case you will only need a down payment.

Investment Strategies

Once you have decided to consider investing in tax liens or tax deeds, you will need to make some decisions. Here are the general steps that you will need to take to be prepared to invest.

Identify your investment objective

Your first step is to decide if your primary objective in investing is to obtain a high investment return or to obtain property ownership. This decision will determine in part the state or states you choose to focus on. States with low tax lien interest rates or states that only have delinquent property auctions are suited for individuals with the primary objective of obtaining property ownership. States with high tax lien interest rates are suited for individuals primarily seeking a high investment return with a secondary objective of obtaining property ownership.

If your focus is to obtain properties at tax deed sales, you will need more capital. Because you are buying the entire property at tax deed sales, you will need more money and you must pay careful attention to the condition of the property. At a tax deed sale your potential return could be greater, but your potential liability is also greater.

Select a geographical area in which to invest

Next decide what areas you are going to focus on. It is best if you choose the state you live in or at least a state in the region in which you live. You cannot become an expert in every state or even every county in a single state. Laws vary between states and even within a state because each county has its own method of selling tax lien certificates or delinquent properties. In addition, within each county some areas are usually more desirable for investment than others. In most cases, less populated counties usually have less competition.

Deciding on which areas you are going to focus on is especially important when investing in tax deeds. This is because you need to become familiar with local real estate values, development trends, and what locals consider undesirable property.

To help you decide where to start, Chapter 9 includes detailed profiles of all the states. Study this chapter carefully to decide where and how you want to invest. Once you have chosen several areas to focus on, you will need to study the areas and become familiar with local real estate values and development trends. Chapter 4 provides a general summary of how each state handles tax lien certificates or tax deed sales.

Choose a type of property in which to invest

You will next want to determine what types of properties you are going to focus your efforts on. Tax lien certificate and delinquent property sales include raw land, commercial/industrial properties and residential properties. Generally, raw land and commercial/industrial properties contain the most investment risk and require more expertise. Raw land can sit vacant for years, and may not have water or roads near it. The pool of possible buyers for raw land is also usually small. Commercial/industrial properties may have environmental problems; they also typically require more upfront capital to purchase the tax lien certificate or delinquent property. In addition, commercial/industrial properties require more expertise to determine their potential worth and what improvements may be required to make the property suitable for future use.

Residential properties contain the least investment risk and are usually a good choice for beginning investors. If you own your own home or have a general knowledge of real estate values in the areas you are going to focus your efforts on, you already have some knowledge that will help you understand how to value residential properties that you will bid on.

Decide on a method by which to invest

Your next step is to decide on the primary method by which you want to obtain tax lien certificates or delinquent properties. If you do not mind attending auctions, plan on attending a few tax lien certificate or delinquent property auctions to get your feet wet. Counties typically have one auction period per year. If you do not want to attend auctions, you can call the county treasurer and see if any properties did not sell during the last auction. This can be a good way to get properties if you are patient and willing to accept the fact that the best properties may be sold at the auction. It is also a way to ensure you do not overpay for the tax lien certificate or property since you will not have bidders driving the interest rate down or the price up.

Other important factors to consider if you want to try and buy without attending an auction are establishing a relationship with local officials and trying to buy early in the calendar year. A relationship with local officials can help you get information on properties, so that you can make a better decision on whether the available properties are worth the time and effort to visit and evaluate. Buying earlier in the calendar year can save you money if the property is eventually awarded to you. This is because smaller penalties and interest are owed at the beginning of the year; if you are awarded the property, the less you pay up front, the more profit you make.

Evaluate available properties and determine their market value

When you are bidding at a tax deed sale to take ownership of a property, you need to know a great deal about the property before you can make a reasonable bid. You must assess the risks and determine the fair market value. The county appraiser will already have placed a value on the property, but that is only a start. When you are dealing with foreclosed properties all the time, like a county appraiser often does, you tend to become optimistic. A little water damage, some environmental problems, or legal issues with the title don't look so bad when you see similar real estate problems every day.

Your job is to be as thorough and unemotional as you can be when assessing a property. If you can, find out why the property is in foreclosure and make a list of everything good and bad about it. Use the tips in *Rogue Real Estate Investor* to help you along. If you need a second opinion, get one. Hire an independent appraiser, which usually costs around $300 to $400. Three or four hundred dollars is nothing if you end up getting a property for 50 percent below market value or more. If the property has title problems or other legal issues, hire a real estate attorney familiar with local laws.

Try to become familiar with the bidding process, and find out who typically shows up at the bids in your selected area. Banks may come to these bids and, at a minimum, some experienced investors also will likely attend. This is where striking up a relationship with the local county officials can help a lot.

Compare prices for similar property in the area. If this property was not in foreclosure, what would it sell for? Use everything you can to estimate the market value of the property. As a rough rule of thumb, you can use the property taxes that were due on the property to assess the market value. The amount of property taxes (PT) is usually equal to a county constant (C) multiplied by the market value (MV) multiplied by the mill levy (M): $PT = C \times MV \times M$. This information can be located from the county assessor's office.

If you have information on the property taxes due, you can work backwards using this formula (property taxes divided by the mill levy and the county constant) to find the market value determined by the county. For example, a property that has property taxes of $1,000 per year in a county with a county constant of .10 and a mill levy of .10 has a market value as determined by the county of $100,000.

Narrow your property search and observe the bid process

If you are looking at several properties, you will need to get your list down to a few properties before the tax deed sale occurs. You will not have time to do detailed research on more than a few properties, and you need to focus your time on the best prospects. The more homework you do, the better you will understand the market value of a property and what amount you should bid. Remember, when you walk away from a tax deed sale, the county does not care anymore. With a tax lien certificate, the county is still involved after the sale; but with a foreclosure sale, the county is done after the tax deed is purchased.

Read some of the detailed county profiles in Chapter 9 and you will understand what we are talking about. Most counties that have tax deed sales have all kinds of disclaimers regarding their potential liability if something is wrong with the property. When in doubt, remember the phrase "Buyer Beware."

When you are ready to go to the auction for the first time, make a decision to wait on the sidelines and observe unless you are very confident. Do not get caught up in a bidding war if you do not know what you are doing. A bank or other commercial enterprise may have interest in the property and not care if they pay something near the market value. Bids can even exceed a county's assessment of the property's market value.

The next chapter provides a quick profile of the way each state handles delinquent property taxes. Chapter 7 will take you through the practical steps to investing in tax liens and tax deeds, as well as strategies for bidding.

FOUR

Quick State Profiles

"One man's trash is another man's treasure." – anonymous

This chapter provides a brief introduction to all the states. The first table profiles states that have tax lien certificates sales. For these states, the rating is based on the interest rate, redemption period and general dedication of a state and its counties to the process. States with high interest rates, quick redemption periods, and helpful information to assist investors score high. States with low interest rates, long redemption periods, and limited information to assist investors score low. Five stars is the highest rating for states that offer tax lien certificates.

A few states sell tax deeds with right of redemption. This means that the previous owner or interested party can redeem by paying his/her property taxes. The investor then receives a fee or interest rate, making it look and feel like a tax lien certificate.

The second table profiles states that only have tax deed sales. For these states, the ratings are more reflective of how well sales are advertised and how dedicated a state and its counties appear to be in the overall tax deed sale process. The interest rate and redemption period have no meaning at a tax deed sale. Four stars is the highest rating for states that only have tax deed sales.

This is only an introduction to the states. Chapter 9 provides more detailed state and county information regarding tax lien and tax deed sales, including links to county websites, contact information, bidding procedures, and example requirements.

Tax Lien Certificate and Right of Redemption States

State	Interest Rate	Redemption Period	Rating	Notes
Alabama	12%	3 years	*** Three Stars	Auctions are usually in May.
Arizona	16%	3 years	***** Five Stars	Notice will appear in county newspaper two weeks before sale. Auctions held in February. New laws require the investor to be responsible for foreclosure and hiring an attorney if the tax lien is not redeemed.

State	Interest Rate	Redemption Period	Rating	Notes
Colorado	9% plus federal discount rate; rate is currently about 10%.	3 years	*** Three Stars	Notices will appear in county newspapers in November. Tax lien auctions start on second Monday in December and continue every day until all properties are sold. Highest cash offer wins bid. For most counties you can get on an investors' mailing list by contacting the county.
Connecticut	18%	Varies	**** Four Stars	Municipalities handle the sales, so bidding requirements vary. Great interest rate, but not an easy state in which to track tax lien certificate sales.
Florida	18%	2 years	***** Five Stars	Harder than most states to get property ownership if taxes are not paid. Auctions on or before June 1. At auction you pay 10% of total tax lien; after the tax lien certificate is prepared you must pay the remaining balance within 48 hours.
Georgia	Deed with 20% right of redemption.	1 year	**** Four Stars	Georgia is complicated. In summary, you will bid on a deed, but the owner still has 1 year to redeem, in which case you make a flat interest rate of 20%. The quicker the property is redeemed, the better your annual return. If it is not redeemed, you must be prepared to pay subsequent taxes and foreclose on the property. This state requires more thought and additional research. Hiring a local attorney if you are serious about investing in this state is a good idea. Auctions occur on the first Tuesday of each month.
Illinois	18% the first 6 months; or up to 36% for the full year.	2.5 years	**** Four Stars	May need a lawyer because the court is involved. Two systems exist: one for recently delinquent properties and one for properties delinquent more than 2 years. Under the first system, auctions are held after June 1 and September 1. October or November is when the sales are usually held. Under the second system, auctions are infrequent, usually once every 2 years. Pre-register 1 month in advance of the sale to bid.

State	Interest	Redemption Period	Rating	Notes
Indiana	10% if tax lien is redeemed in less than 6 months; 15% if tax lien is redeemed in more than 6 months, but less than 1 year; and 25% if tax lien is redeemed in more than 1 year.	1 year	***** Five Stars	County requirements can be complicated. Auctions are held on or before August 1 and November 1.
Iowa	24%	1.75 years	***** Five Stars	Auctions occur on the third Monday in June and continue until all properties are offered for sale. Winning bidder offers the total amount due for the smallest percentage of the property, if the property goes to foreclosure.
Kentucky	12%	3 years	*** Three Stars	Kentucky does not seem to emphasis tax certificate sales. Difficult to find information on the Internet.
Louisiana	17%	3 years	**** Four Stars	Tax lien purchaser can ask for immediate possession of the property after 2 years. Auctions held on May 1.
Maryland	10 to 24%.	6 months to 2 years	**** Four Stars	Local variations to tax lien process can be tricky. Each county has its own auction schedule.
Massachusetts	14 to 16%	2.5 years	**** Four Stars	Tax lien sales are rare. Like Iowa, bidding for the property is based on what percentage of the property you would own if the property were foreclosed. Delinquent property owners can pay in installments.
Minnesota	12%	1 year	*** Three Stars	Information on tax lien certificates sales in this state is a little hard to find.
Mississippi	17%	2 years	**** Four Stars	Auctions are the first Monday in April or the third Monday in September. After the 2- year period, obtaining a deed to the property is fairly straightforward.
Missouri	10% on the minimum bid, and 8% over the minimum bid.	2 years	*** Three Stars	Bidders bid on what they would be willing to pay for the property, assuming the owner never redeems.

Montana	10%	2 to 3 years	*** Three Stars	Not a lot of information on tax lien certificate sales.
Nebraska	14%	3 years	*** Three Stars	Public tax sales held once a year on the first Monday in March.
Nevada	12%	120 days for vacant land, 2 years for improved land	*** Three Stars	
New Hampshire	18%	3 years	**** Four Stars	Tax lien sales are not common. Within 45 days of obtaining the tax lien, the tax lien holder is required to notify the holders of the mortgage. Failure to do this will make the tax sale invalid.
New Jersey	18 to 24%	2 years	***** Five Stars	Tax lien sales are called certificates of purchase. Rules are complex. Watch out for environmental problems – New Jersey has many hazardous waste sites.
New York	10 to 14%	2 years	*** Three Stars	Process varies a great deal from county to county. Big investors can take over sales. Often need a lot of capital because property values are high.
North Carolina	9 to 12%	3 years	*** Three Stars	Not much information available on sales.
North Dakota	9 to 12%	3 years	*** Three Stars	Not much information available on sales.
Ohio	18%	1 year	*** Three Stars	Sales are only in counties with a population greater than 200,000 people. Large investors can corner sales.
Oklahoma	8%	2 years	** Two Stars	Not much information available on sales.
Rhode Island	6 to 18%	1 year	*** Three Stars	
South Carolina	8%	1 year	** Two Stars	
South Dakota	8%	3 years	** Two Stars	Sales held the first Tuesday of each month. State now requires a signed form indicating you do not owe taxes. You will need to prepare this ahead of time.
Texas	Right of redemption: 25% in 6 months for most properties.	2 years for agricultural and homestead properties; 6 months for all other properties	**** Four Stars	
Vermont	6 to 12%	1 year	*** Three Stars	

Washington D.C.	12%	6 months	*** Three Stars	
West Virginia	12%	1 year	*** Three Stars	
Wisconsin	18%	2 years	**** Four Stars	
Wyoming	18%	4 years	**** Four Stars	Tax liens are called certificates of purchase. Like Iowa and several other states, you bid for property ownership. The lowest percentage ownership wins the bid. Auctions are in September.

Tax Deed States

State	Rating
Alaska	** Two Stars
Arkansas	**** Four Stars
California*	**** Four Stars
Delaware	** Two Stars
Georgia	**** Four Stars
Hawaii	** Two Stars
Idaho	** Two Stars
Kansas	*** Three Stars
Maine	** Two Stars
Michigan	Unrated: state switching from tax liens to tax deeds
New Mexico	** Two Stars
Oregon	** Two Stars
Pennsylvania	** Two Stars
Tennessee	** Two Stars
Texas	**** Four Stars
Utah	*** Three Stars
Virginia	** Two Stars
Washington	** Two Stars

* California is authorized by law to have tax lien certificates sales (18% interest rate), but no sales have yet been conducted.

These tables provide general information about the states that pay the best interest rates on a tax lien certificate or have good county support for tax deed sales, to help you get started investing. You might also want to spend some time researching the tax laws for the states in which you are interested in investing. The following table provides links to laws and regulations for some states. For each state, links are provided first for laws and then for rules.

State Statutes and Regulations Related to Taxes

Alabama	
Code of AL	http://www.legislature.state.al.us/Search/SearchText.htm
AL Administrative Code	http://www.alabamaadministrativecode.state.al.us/alabama.html
Arizona	
AZ Revised Statutes	http://www.azleg.state.az.us/ArizonaRevisedStatutes.asp
AZ Administrative Code	http://www.sos.state.az.us/public_services/Table_of_Contents.htm
California	
CA Statutes	http://www.leginfo.ca.gov/calaw.html
CA Code of Regulations	http://ccr.oal.ca.gov
Colorado	
CO Revised Statutes	http://www.state.co.us/gov_dir/leg_dir/olls/HTML/colorado_revised_statutes.htm
Code of CO Regulations	http://www.state.co.us/gov_dir/leg_dir/olls/HTML/rules.htm
Florida	
FL Statutes	http://www.flsenate.gov/Statutes/index.cfm?Tab=statutes&submenu=-1&Mode=Main
FL Administrative Code	http://fac.dos.state.fl.us
Georgia	
GA Code	http://www.legis.state.ga.us/cgi-bin/gl_codes_detail.pl?code=1-1-1
GA Rules & Regulations	http://www.state.ga.us/rules
Illinois	
IL Statutes	http://www.legis.state.il.us/legislation/ilcs/chapterlist.html or http://www.legis.state.il.us/search/iga_search.asp?scope=ilcs
IL Administrative Code	http://www.cyberdriveillinois.com/departments/index/home.html
Indiana	
IN Code	http://www.in.gov/legislative/ic/code
IN Administrative Code	http://www.in.gov/legislative/iac
Iowa	
IA Code	http://www.legis.state.ia.us/IACODE/2003
IA Administrative Code	http://www.legis.state.ia.us/IAC.html
Kentucky	
KY Revised Statutes	http://www.lrc.state.ky.us/statrev/frontpg.htm
KY Administrative Regulations	http://www.lrc.state.ky.us/kar/frntpage.htm
Louisiana	
LA Revised Statutes	http://www.legis.state.la.us/tsrs/search.htm
LA Administrative Code	http://www.legis.state.la.us/tsrs/search.htm
Maryland	
MD Code	http://mlis.state.md.us
Code of MD Regulations	http://www.dsd.state.md.us
Massachusetts	
MA General Laws	http://www.state.ma.us/legis/laws/mgl
Code of MA Regulations	http://www.lawlib.state.ma.us/cmr.html
Michigan	
MI Statutes	http://www.michiganlegislature.org/law
MI Administrative Code	http://www.michigan.gov/orr/0,1607,7-142-5698---,00.html
Mississippi	
MS Code	http://library.law.olemiss.edu/library/state/ms.shtml#REGULATIONS
MS Administrative Regulations	http://www.mslawyer.com/statedept/lncmac.htm

Missouri	
MO Revised Statutes	http://www.moga.state.mo.us/homestat.asp
MO Code of State Regulations	http://www.sos.state.mo.us/adrules/csr/csr.asp
Nebraska	
NE Statutes	http://statutes.unicam.state.ne.us
NE Administrative Code	http://www.sos.state.ne.us/local/regsearch
New Hampshire	
NH Revised Statutes	http://www.gencourt.state.nh.us/rsa/html/indexes/default.html
NH Code of Administrative Rules	http://www.gencourt.state.nh.us/rules/listagencies.html
New Jersey	
NJ Statutes	http://lis.njleg.state.nj.us/cgi-bin/om_isapi.dll?clientID=250641591&depth=2&expandheadings=off&headingswithhits=on&infobase=statutes.nfo&softpage=TOC_Frame_Pg42
NJ Administrative Code	http://www.state.nj.us/deptserv.html
New York	
NY State Consolidated Laws	http://assembly.state.ny.us/leg/?sl=0 or http://caselaw.lp.findlaw.com/nycodes/index.html
NY State Rules & Regulations	http://www.gorr.state.ny.us/gorr/Reg_Guide.html
North Dakota	
ND Century Code	http://www.state.nd.us/lr/information/statutes/cent-code.html
ND Administrative Code	http://www.state.nd.us/lr//information/rules/admincode.html
Oklahoma	
OK Statutes	http://www.lsb.state.ok.us
OK Administrative Code	http://www.oar.state.ok.us/oar/codedoc02.nsf/frmMain?OpenFrameSet&Frame=Main&Src=_75tnm2shfcdnm8pb4dthj0chedppmcbq8dtmmak31ctijujrgcln50ob7ckj42tbkdt374obdcli00_
Rhode Island	
General Laws of RI	http://www.rilin.state.ri.us/Statutes/Statutes.html
RI Administrative Code	Not online.
South Carolina	
SC Code of Laws	http://www.scstatehouse.net/code/statmast.htm
SC Code of Regulations	http://www.scstatehouse.net/coderegs/statmast.htm
South Dakota	
SD Statutes	http://legis.state.sd.us/statutes/index.cfm
SD Administrative Rules	http://legis.state.sd.us/rules/index.cfm?FuseAction=List or http://legis.state.sd.us/rules/index.cfm?FuseAction=Search
Vermont	
VT Statutes	http://www.leg.state.vt.us/statutes/statutes2.htm
Code of Vermont Rules	Not online.
West Virginia	
WV Code	http://129.71.164.29/WVCODE/masterfrm3Banner.cfm
WV Code of State Rules	http://www.wvsos.com/csr
Wyoming	
WY Statutes	http://legisweb.state.wy.us/statutes/statutes.htm
WY Rules	http://soswy.state.wy.us/Rule_Search_Main.asp

You will need to search within the state's laws or regulations for those sections dealing with tax sales. Usually the relevant information will be in the areas that cover taxes and/or revenue. If you become too frustrated, send an email to realestate@rogueinvestor.com and we will help.

FIVE

What Can You Expect?

"Eighty percent of success is showing up." – Woody Allen

By now you should a rough idea of how you might want to play the tax lien market (read about investment strategies in Chapter 3). The next section provides a case study of the tax lien investing process.

Tax Lien Investing Case Study

The following two examples show the range of what you can expect from tax lien investing, and are intended to help you become prepared for the process.

Example 1

After visiting the county and deciding that you are interested in real estate in the area, you call the county treasurer or visit the county website to find out what properties are still available after last year's auction. With a little work, you establish a rapport with someone at the county who is knowledgeable about the properties in order to learn more about the location and condition of the properties. One of the properties looks favorable, so you decide to visit it. It is a residential property. The penalties, taxes and interest owed are $1,804.50, which is within your investment range. The state's interest rate is 16 percent. Since the property is not being bought at auction, you automatically get the full interest rate. You send a check to the county treasurer and you receive a tax lien certificate. After 11 months have gone by, you receive a notice from the county treasurer that the owner has paid the debt owed and the property has been redeemed. You mail the tax lien certificate in and you get the full amount you invested plus 11 months of interest at 16 percent.

Example 2

You decide to attend a county auction. To learn about what properties are available, you buy a local newspaper. After checking out the properties, you decide to bid on one of the properties at the auction. At the auction, the bidding in this state starts at 18 percent. The first bid is 18 percent. The next bidder bids 12 percent. Finally, you win the bid at 6 percent. According to state rules you must pay the balance immediately, so you hand a cashier's check to the county treasurer for the full amount right away. After several years go by, you receive a notice in the mail that the county is foreclosing on the property. You celebrate, because you have likely received the property for pennies on the dollar. However, you also recognize the complexity of the foreclosure process. You do the smart thing and hire a local lawyer familiar with the foreclosure process in this area. Like most states, the foreclosure requirements are complex, requiring you to publish a notice of foreclosure in the local newspaper and appear in court. You have already made a killing on the property. By hiring a local lawyer you do not have to deal with the judge at the court appearance and you are confident the paperwork will be done correctly. After the foreclosure process is over, you decide that you do not want to keep the property, so you put the property up for sale right away. Because you got the property so cheap, you can put a bargain price on it, sell it quickly and still make plenty of money.

Tax Lien Investing Process

Earlier chapters of this book have touched on the tax lien investing process. Here are the steps you should follow.

Narrow your search

Narrow your search to one or two states and two to three counties per state. You will not have enough time or knowledge to accomplish much more until you have a lot of experience.

Learn the tax sale specifics

Contact the treasurer's office or the tax collector's office (the specific department varies from state to state) for the county you are interested in, or visit the county website, to find the rules and procedures that govern the county's tax sales, as well as to find a list of the properties available. A few states conduct sales through municipalities, so you will need to contact the county in these states and find out which municipalities handle the tax sales. Chapter 9 provides detailed information for over 100 counties in the country; in addition, the CD that accompanies this book provides links to all the counties in the United States.

Some counties do not post anything about tax sales on their website. County budgets are not always sufficient to keep up, and many counties are just starting to become computer and Internet efficient. You may need to get a copy of the local newspaper to find out about the properties that are available. Many counties have lists of available properties for sale at upcoming tax lien auctions or tax deed sales. You can usually download these lists for free or purchase them for $5 to $50 or more, depending on the county.

You will need to study the local laws and do some research to get ready. Chapter 4 provides links to laws and regulations for many states. These are sometimes difficult to read, but do the best you can. You can also ask the county to tell you what information is important. Once you are familiar with the rules and have a list of properties, narrow your focus to one or two properties.

Arrive early for an auction

If you decide to attend an auction, arrive early. You will have to fill out paperwork. Depending on the rules of the county, you may need a cashier's check or cash to buy tax liens or properties. You may also have to pay a deposit. Some counties and states require that you register 7 to 10 days in advance, so be sure to check your local rules.

Chapter 9 provides detailed county information regarding auctions, rules and procedures. Read this information to get a feel for what is required and how the process works. However, before you go to a sale, make sure you contact the county and find out what the current procedures are and where you need to show up. Although this book is updated frequently, things change rapidly in the tax sale business and county websites are constantly being changed.

**You must become an expert in your area and county
to become proficient and avoid unpleasant surprises!**

Follow the rules after a winning bid

Once you have obtained a tax lien certificate or foreclosed property, follow all the local rules. Failure to do so could cause your entire effort to be wasted, since you could lose your investment. This is where knowledge of the local laws becomes very important. Most counties have strict and often complicated rules on posting notices, foreclosing on properties and clearing title to the property if foreclosure is necessary. You may also have to pay subsequent property taxes to maintain your lien status. Generally, these rules favor the owner of the property so that the owner can pay the back taxes and retain the property if possible.

At tax lien certificate sales, less than five percent of all properties with delinquent taxes generally go to foreclosure. However, if a property you own does go to foreclosure, hire an attorney familiar with the local laws to assist you in the foreclosure process. In states selling foreclosed properties at tax deed sales, be very careful. Here you must follow the foreclosure process and research the property very carefully.

There are several key points that should be emphasized and repeated: (1) if possible, it is wise for you to establish a friendly relationship with the county employees to get more information regarding available properties before you waste your time visiting properties that you do not want, and (2) if the property goes to foreclosure, you should hire a local attorney to settle the foreclosure. Do not do it yourself! It is too complicated. Some states will handle the foreclosure process. Under these circumstances, you may not need a lawyer. However, always err on the side of caution, especially until you have gone through the process a few times and know what to expect.

If you decide to keep the property, use your attorney to make sure you have a clear title to the property and help you legally evict the former owners if they are still on the premises. To make sure you are protected against any future claims to the property, your attorney can quiet the title. To get a court order that will allow you to get the assistance of the local sheriff, if necessary, to remove the former owners, have your attorney file an unlawful detainer action. In most cases, the property will be vacant by this time and your attorney will only need to assist you with the foreclosure process and make sure you have clear title.

SIX

Possible Problems and How to Avoid Them

"Who dares nothing, need hope for nothing." – J.C.F. von Schiller

If you think about it, tax lien certificates and tax deed sales are a symptom of something gone awry with the property owner. Usually the reason is plain negligence (someone goes out of town for an extended period) or a lack of money. When someone has been an owner of the property for a long time and real estate values in the area suddenly rise due to development, the tax burden on a person can double or triple over just 5 or 10 years. Rather than sell the property, the owner procrastinates on the decision until it gets serious.

It is also possible that the property is not worth the amount of taxes owed. Environmental contamination may have been discovered on or near the property or, after years of negligence, the structures on the property may be in disarray. The property may be prone to excessive flooding or have building restrictions. Water rights also might be a issue.

The first step in assessing if there is something truly wrong with the property is to compare the assessment of the property's value to similar properties in the area. For every tax lien certificate or tax deed property, you can find an assessment of the property's value by a government agency. If this assessed value is significantly lower than similar properties in the area, there is probably a problem with the property.

To avoid possible environmental issues, do not buy properties near industrial areas. Do some research in advance and talk to locals to ensure the property is not near any hazardous waste sites. You can also go to the county courthouse and look up of the property on Sanborn Maps, which will show the historical uses, if any, of the property. Avoid any areas that were previously used as commercial or industrial sites. In fact, in most cases where you are looking at buying residential property or raw land, do not buy if the property was ever zoned for anything other than agricultural or residential use.

There are other environmental issues you should consider. Avoid any property near a gas station. Gas stations almost always contain underground storage tanks that can leak, potentially contaminating nearby properties. In general, avoid any property with underground storage tanks. Avoid any property near a dry cleaning facility, which use solvents to clean garments. Many of these solvents are cancer causing and highly mobile, potentially contaminating other properties and groundwater. Other potential problems include asbestos (common in commercial properties more than 20 years old), lead paint (possible in any structures built prior to 1978), and radon (common in areas with basements built in or on top of bedrock). If possible, inspect the property to make sure it is free of debris and does not contain any soil staining, sheens or seeps. Look for water damage and, if possible, survey the local area for drainage ways to determine if the property has the potential for flooding. For residential property, the chances of a serious environmental problem are low. However, that does not mean you should not check for all of the environmental problems just described. Chapter 10 of *Rogue Real Estate Investor* provides a more detailed discussion of potential environmental problems.

Another possible problem is that a property owner could declare bankruptcy while you are holding the tax lien. This will not ultimately affect your investment, because tax lien investors are secured creditors, meaning that you will get your money. However, the receipt of your money could be delayed while the initial portion of the bankruptcy proceeds. If you think the property owner is in danger of declaring bankruptcy, and the best way to tell is how much is due relative to the worth of the property, do not bid on the tax lien.

If you have any uncertainties about a property, do not buy. There are always plenty of tax lien certificates and tax deeds available. Sometimes the best decision is to not get involved.

SEVEN

A Practical Field Guide to Investing
in Tax Liens and Tax Deeds

Lucy: "I never get what I really want [for Christmas]."
Charlie Brown: "What is it you want?"
Lucy: "Real estate."
– A Charlie Brown Christmas, *Charles Schulz*

Introduction

My partner and I attend tax sales nearly every month. This chapter provides a hands-on approach to the art of investing in tax liens and tax deeds.

One of the most important steps in investing in tax liens and tax deeds is to evaluate the real property (land or improvement). Even if you are only investing in tax liens, you should be ready to take ownership and assume that you could acquire the property. Remember, on average, less than 5 percent of tax liens go to foreclosure or deed.

If you are bidding at a tax deed sale, you are actually bidding on the property. Upon winning the bid, the property is yours. As is the case with buying anything, you need to make sure you get what you pay for. This includes your time, energy and effort. After all, you can buy real property through an individual or real estate broker. In fact, if you are not getting a property at a substantial discount to the going rates, then it may not be worth it. There are also larger concerns to consider. In the case of environmental contamination you could get stuck with thousands, if not millions, of dollars of liability if you're not careful. Other problems may not be quite so elaborate, but could result in reducing your return. For example, a land-locked property could require legal costs to force the adjacent owner(s) to provide you with access.

Knowledge is power, so make sure you are prepared ahead of time. This practical guide will help.

Steps to Investing

Step 0: Before you invest, know your goals

Why are you investing? Is it for:

- Income?
- Retirement?
- Building a nest egg?
- Becoming wealthy?
- Freedom?
- Something to do?
- A challenge?

Why do you need to know?

You need to know because your goals will influence the type of deeds or liens that you pursue. For instance, commercial properties may have more risk due to the inherent nature of many businesses, such as improper waste disposal and urban locations. On the other hand, commercial properties may be lucrative if you understand and can manage the risks. If you are only trying to receive a decent return on your money and have no intention of taking ownership of a property, then you will want to orient your investing to tax lien states and properties that will most likely be redeemed.

Be sure to examine your finances closely enough to understand how your tax lien and tax deed investing plays into your overall investing plan. Again, think about how much risk you can handle.

Consider your investing goals in light of the types of properties and locations available. You may be looking for retirement land. If so, ignore all commercial and residential buildings. You may only understand real estate values in a particular region, state or county. If that's the case, bidding outside of your area of expertise will result in higher risk. On the other hand, your county may be too competitive or properties may be scarce and this may force you to become an expert elsewhere.

The point is to know what you want, whether it is land, interest income from a tax lien, or foreclosure potential of residential or commercial properties. All of these factors will influence your potential screening of properties.

Finally, it is highly advisable that you attend at least one tax lien or tax deed auction with no intention of buying. Observe the bidding process and even ask questions after the auction is finished. You will feel much more confident and prepared for your first tax sale.

Step 1: Obtain the list of properties and register

Delinquent property lists are available by contacting the county and finding out how and where they list properties. Some states and counties only work with local newspapers. Other counties publish lists online and even update when properties are redeemed. Some counties will send you a list, but they usually require a fee. The fee is often fairly nominal; however, in some counties like Cooke County, Illinois (Chicago), the fee is a whopping $250.

The best approach is to start with a county website and search for the treasurer's or tax collector's office (see Chapter 9 for detailed county information). If a property list is not available online, you may need to call the county treasurer. Arkansas, for example, provides a free newspaper-type listing that they send out quarterly to anyone who is interested.

We are currently building an online resource with tax sale lists as they become available. For now, this resource is free to customers, so take advantage of it by visiting the following web page: http://www.tax-lien-certificates.com/lists.

Many states only conduct tax sales once a year, so be sure to find out when your state or province is due for its sale. Chapter 9 includes information on the dates of many county sales. You can also refer to the following web page for updated tax sales dates: http://www.tax-lien-certificates.com.

The county treasurer or tax collector will often be responsible for conducting a tax sale, and can inform you about the requirements and what to expect. Spend a few minutes speaking with someone on the phone, or better yet in person.

Find out what requirements are necessary to bid. You may be required to pay in advance. For instance, many counties require a money order or cashier's check for a minimum amount or a percentage of the amount you plan on bidding. The minimum amount may be only $100 or the minimum amount listed in the bid listing. The remaining amount will be required upon successfully winning the bid. If you don't bid, you will be reimbursed. Again, check the rules and see if a personal check is okay. Some counties will not accept a personal check or credit card.

As far as registration, plan ahead. Texas now requires registration in advance and a $10 fee. Some counties, like Coconino in Arizona, require an advanced registration of 7 days. Other counties allow registration even on the day of the bid.

Find out what other requirements are necessary to bid in the state or county. Missouri, for instance, requires that you live in the county or have a representative act as your liaison. In the latter case, you must have a notarized signature from the representative.

Finally, ask a county representative about the sale itself. Here are some questions that you might want to know the answers to:

- Is the bidding held by your office or a professional firm?
- How quickly does the bidding proceed?
- What are the bid increments (e.g., in 1 percent increments or by amounts of $50)?
- What happened during the last sale?
- How long does the sale last?
- How many people usually show up?
- What areas of the county generate the most interest and the least interest, in terms of bidding and why?
- When are payments due (e.g., at the end of the day, immediately, in 24 hours)?
- What happens in the case of ties, as when more than one person bids zero interest on a property?

Step 2: Initial screening

Surprisingly enough, an initial screen can be done by looking through the list of properties and searching for key phrases that might identify where the property is located. An example would be a legal description that contains descriptions of certain areas that you recognize.

The property list will contain the name of the individual or company that is the recorded owner, a legal description, how much taxes are owed and the minimum bid.

Here are two real examples (the names and locations have been altered):

- Example 1
  43. Smith, Betty A. W½ SW¼ NE¼ SW ¼ 9 6N 5W 10.00 Acres Parcel #123-456-789
  1998 Min Bid: $1040.00 Tax Due: $321.21

- Example 2
  51. Parcel # 12-3456-789 Needles, John & Bernice, 1116 NW Maple, Kansas City, MO
  64164 26-53-35 Embassy Harbor Edition Lot 33 Blk 5,
  2001 taxes owed: $675.25
  2002 taxes owed: $711.23
  Printing fee: $50.00
  Total: $1,436.48

Using Example 1, we will take your through everything in the listing so that you understand how to read the tax sale listings.

43

The first number is the bid or listing number. This number is used as the bidding number. Most counties will start with the lowest number and move to the highest or last number on the list. During the auction, the lowest numbers will go first and the higher numbers later. Consecutive numbers may be missing if a property owner redeems or pays his taxes.

> **Special Note:** Sometimes the lower numbers will receive more attention towards the beginning of an auction and the higher numbers will receive less attention later in the bidding because individuals are fatigued or they have exceeded their budget.

Smith, Betty A

The name of the owner is next. This can be significant if you find a landowner or business that you are confident has gone out of business or is financially distraught. You can also look for multiple properties or lots owned by the same individual, which you can use to scoop up adjacent properties. Also, when you are viewing plat maps you may see other landowners with the same name, indicating that a relative might live adjacent to or near a foreclosed property. This is probably not a problem, but you should be aware of it.

W½ SW¼ NE¼ SW ¼ 9 6N 5W

Next, you will usually see what is referred to as a legal description. The most common legal description is based upon the Section and Township demarcation, also referred to as the government rectangular survey. A legal description may also be in metes and bounds or lots and blocks.

A legal description of real property is defined as a method of locating a parcel using an unbiased demarcation that can be used universally to locate real property. The address to a property, such as your house, is not considered a legal description. Thus, 1305 Maple Street is not a legal description for real property.

The system in the U.S. is shown by lines running east, west, north and south in a grid pattern or checkerboard. Each grid or square on, for example, a county plat map is one mile by one mile or 640 acres. There are six grids by six grids or six miles by six miles in a legal township. Numbers starting from a known baseline and running north to south are called Township (T) numbers. Numbers running east to west are called Range (R) numbers. For those of you counting, the total number of grid cells or sections in a legal plat is 36.

Interestingly, the numbers move from the right to the left, down, then left to right and so on until 36 sections are numbered. This is because original surveyors had to traverse the land and it was not practical to return to the starting side. It made much more sense to traverse across, go down and then go back across.

In our example, the numbers shown as 6N and 5W are referred to as Township 6 North (T6N) and Range 5 West (R5W), respectively. The number 9 located immediately in front of the township and range numbers is the section number. In our example, it is Section 9.

R5W

6	5	4	3	2	1
7	8	9	10	11	12
18	17	16	15	14	13
19	20	21	22	23	24
30	29	28	27	26	25
31	32	33	34	35	36

T6N

Find Section 9 and imagine it enlarged as presented below.

A Section of Land
(640 Acres)
1 mile by 1 mile

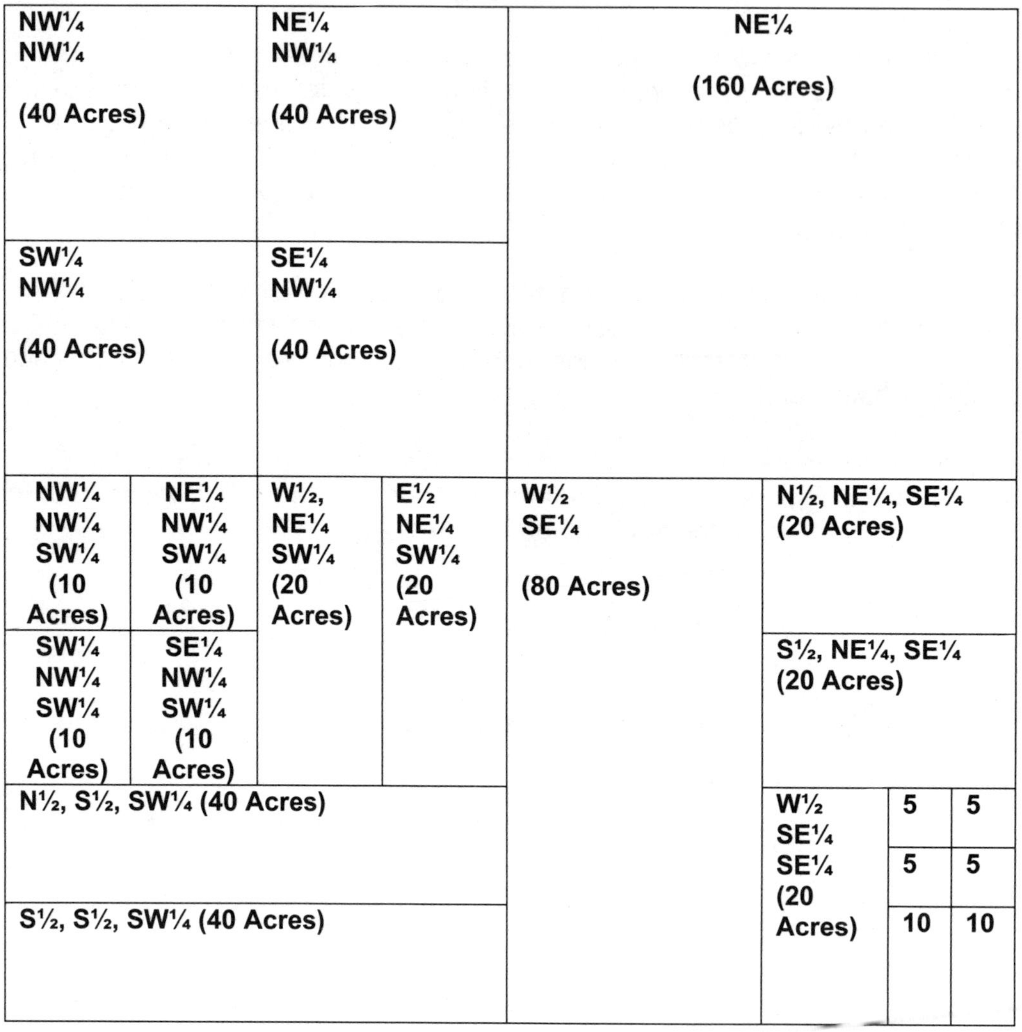

NW¼ NW¼ (40 Acres)	NE¼ NW¼ (40 Acres)	NE¼ (160 Acres)		
SW¼ NW¼ (40 Acres)	SE¼ NW¼ (40 Acres)			

NW¼ NW¼ SW¼ (10 Acres)	NE¼ NW¼ SW¼ (10 Acres)	W½, NE¼ SW¼ (20 Acres)	E½ NE¼ SW¼ (20 Acres)	W½ SE¼ (80 Acres)	N½, NE¼, SE¼ (20 Acres)		
SW¼ NW¼ SW¼ (10 Acres)	SE¼ NW¼ SW¼ (10 Acres)				S½, NE¼, SE¼ (20 Acres)		
N½, S½, SW¼ (40 Acres)					W½ SE¼ SE¼ (20 Acres)	5	5
						5	5
S½, S½, SW¼ (40 Acres)						10	10

When you read a legal description, start from right and work left. For example, when looking at the example legal description, start with the southwest quarter of Section 9 and mark it off.

Section 9

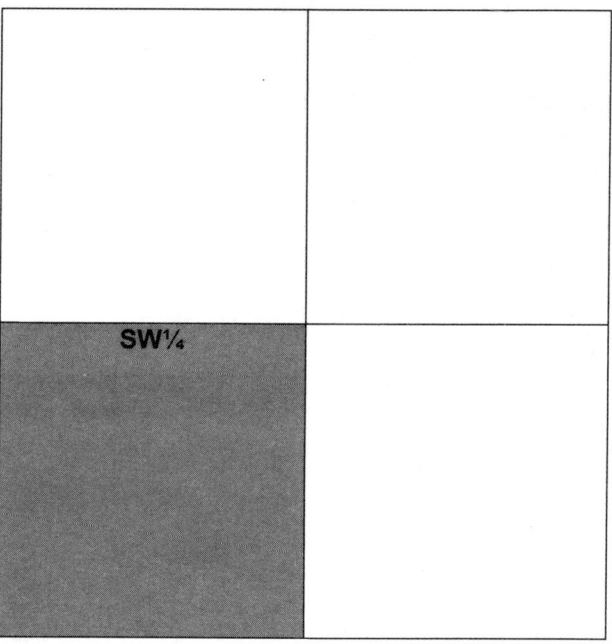

Next, find the northeast quarter of that same quarter, or the northeast quarter of the southwest quarter.

Section 9

Again, find the southwest quarter of the new quarter you've established as shown below, or the southwest quarter of the northeast quarter of the southwest quarter.

Section 9

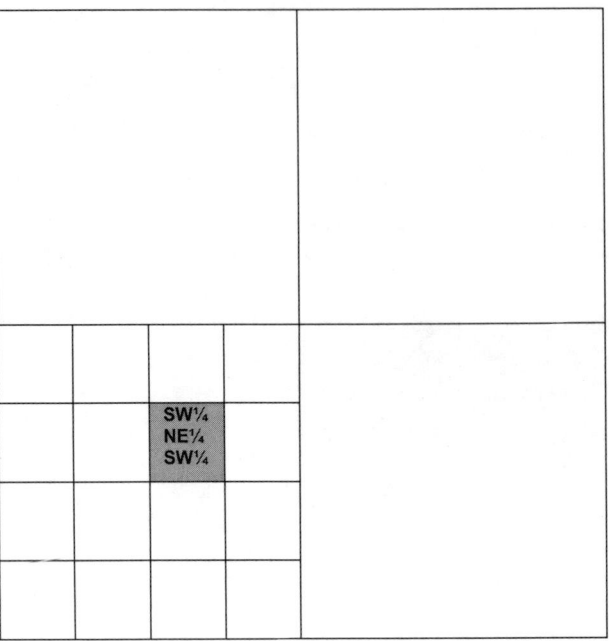

Finally, mark off the west half of the newest quarter that you've established and the location should be located as shown below. Thus, we have located the west half of the southwest quarter of the northeast quarter of the southwest quarter of Section 9 in Township 6 North, Range 5 West.

Section 9

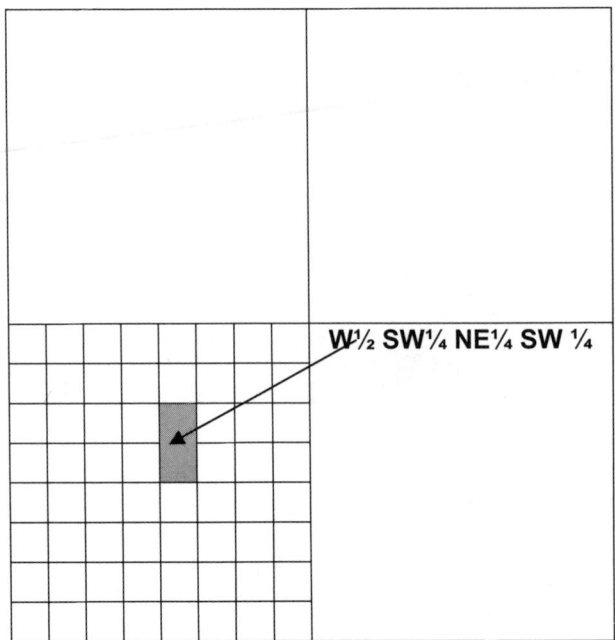

The legal description shows that the parcel is 10 acres, which corresponds with what we calculated. Some legal descriptions will also include additional measurements, such as W150', N60' or a descriptor like "part of." In many cases, the land will not be portioned off as neatly and you may be looking for a parcel that is 12.2 acres or 0.83 acres. In the case of lots, you will be given a legal description that only goes so far as narrowing down the search to a neighborhood or housing addition.

When developers buy land and partition it off, they usually create housing additions with names such as Prairie Fields or Pine Ridge Point. Each addition is then divided into lots. An example would be that your house could be lot 24 of the Prairie Fields Addition. These lots must be approved and recorded with the city, county or local municipality. Therefore, you will need to do research with the county to find the lot and block designation that corresponds to the current property address.

The use of metes and bounds in a legal description involves measurements from a beginning point, such that you could mark it off and create a geometric representation of the property boundary. An example would be "starting at the southwest corner of Main and Highland Street, running south 150 feet, then running west 340 feet, then running north 150 feet and running east 340 feet."

Now, let's get back to our example.

<u>10.00 Acres</u>

The acreage will often be shown immediately following the legal description. For your information, one acre is equal to 43,560 square feet of land or roughly 209 feet by 209 feet. In metric units, one acre is equal to 4,047 square meters or roughly 63 meters by 64 meters.

<u>Parcel #123-456-789</u>

In many cases, a property will have a parcel number, which is used by the state or county as a unique identifier. This number is important to know because it is easier to ask the county assessor for information knowing the parcel number.

<u>1998</u>

Most counties or states will indicate the year(s) the taxes are delinquent. In the case of our example, taxes are delinquent for the year 1998.

<u>Min Bid: $1040.00 Tax Due: $321.21</u>

Be sure to read carefully the rules for bidding for the state and county. In some cases, a total amount will be shown; in other cases, a minimum bid will be shown along with the tax amount due. Although you may only be required to bid the minimum amount, you still may have to pay the winning bid amount plus the taxes due and processing fees.

Step 3: Visit the county assessor and/or treasurer

One of the most important steps in evaluating a property is to visit or call the county assessor's office. From my experience, they are usually helpful and friendly. If you are only interested in one or two properties, a phone call is probably okay. If you are really serious about this type of investing, plan on visiting the county assessor's office and doing some research.

The assessor's office will often have a real estate division or a person responsible for real estate. Find out who that person is. Taking your list of properties that you narrowed down with you, ask them to either show you how to look up information by parcel number, or have them look up properties for you.

Find out if the property has any improvements (e.g., a building, utilities, landscaping, curbs and gutters, etc.) or is just land. Also, find out the assessor's appraised value for both the land and any improvements. Note the taxes due and how much you may be required to pay should you take possession. If the property is located in a development, you may need to look up the original developer's lot description.

Street addresses are not legal descriptions, but oftentimes you will be able to find a street address through the county records. For your purposes a street address is the easiest method of finding a property.

Finally, ask the assessor how you can get a hold of a county plat map or plat booklet. You will need this to do your drive by and locate the property. A street map may also be helpful, and can usually be found at a local gas station, drug store, or retail department store such as Wal-Mart.

> **Special Note:** The county assessor's office is your friend. If you are wondering why a certain development has many properties listed, ask around and you may just find out. Even if you just want to know how to locate a particular area, the assessor's office can usually help.

Step 4: Visit the property

Nothing tells the whole truth better than visiting a property. What you thought was a nice property might be located next to Billy Bob's Flea Market and Junkateria. On the other hand, a lot that you thought was just another worthless developer's mistake may have a breathtaking view and could be considered a hidden gem. Location is everything in real estate.

Using the plat map or developer's drawing that you obtained, mark off the location of each property that you wish to see on the plat map. Next, obtain a county road map (a standard state road map will not be detailed enough). Again, ask the assessor's office or the local department of transportation for information. If you have online access, MapQuest (http://www.mapquest.com) or Yahoo! Maps (http://maps.yahoo.com) can be used. If you have a laptop, you can purchase Microsoft Streets and Trips (check out Amazon at http://www.amazon.com, or another local computer software dealer).

One other map of importance is the topographic map. A topographic map shows contour lines of equal elevation, as well as other features like streams, rivers, lakes and some manmade features. By looking at the topographic map of the area, you can ascertain the lay of the land. Closely spaced contour lines represent steep grades, while widely spaced contours depict gentle slopes or nearly flat terrain.

TopoZone (http://www.topozone.com) has United State Geological Survey (USGS) topographic maps for the entire United States that you can view online for free. TopoZone provides the following USGS scales: 1:100,000, 1:63,360, 1:50,000, 1:30,000, 1:25,000, 1:24,000, and 1:20,000. The scales are unitless, meaning that 1 inch equals 100,000 inches or 1 centimeter equals 100,000 centimeters.

Let's get back to visiting your selected properties. During the site visit or drive by, take note of the following items:

- Overhead utilities or lack thereof
- Underground utilities or lack thereof
- Access to the property or whether it is land locked
- Adjacent property conditions
- Trees, vegetation, landscaping
- Soil/subsurface conditions – sand, clay, shallow bedrock
- Presence of disturbed areas or fill material
- Dead or stressed vegetation
- Discolored soil.

Be sure to drive around the area and note any major industries that might affect the real or perceived value of the property. For example, a nearby landfill, power plant or heavy industrial area could limit the value of the property for residential use.

Next, find similar properties for sale and call the owner or real estate agent/broker and find out the cost and details. Ask him/her about the area and any problems. Ask about the schools, crime, nearby parks, malls and grocery stores.

Special Note: When visiting a property that has a dwelling, remember that the current property owner may still be living there. You will have to show some discretion and not trespass or loiter in front of the property.

Here are some checklists to help assist you with the drive by. These checklists are also presented on the CD that accompanies this book. These guides only serve as a starting point. You will need to use your own judgment and evaluate properties based upon area and the type of property.

Residential Properties
(Houses and Lots)

Parcel Number and Location _____

Tax Assessed Value

	Description	Value
Land		
Improvements		
Other		
Total		

Drive-By Checklist: Residential

Items of Consideration	Excellent	Good	Fair	Poor	Unknown
Neighbors					
Streets					
Curbs/Gutters					
Location					
Fire Department					
Near Hospital					
Near Park					
Near Police					
School System					
Landscaping					
Roof					
Exterior/Paint					
Porch/Deck/Patio					
Structure					
Heating/Air					
Electricity					
Water					
Sewer					
Cable					
Phone					
Trash Service					
Recreational Value					
Property Access					

Competitive Market Analysis: Residential

	Subject Land	Comparable 1	Comparable 2	Comparable 3
Location/Address				
Area (square feet)				
Bedrooms				
Baths				
Basement				
Garage/Carport				
Construction				
Lot Size				
Age				
Listed Price				
Selling Price				
Remarks				
Area Market Conditions:				
Estimated Range of Value of Similar Properties:				
Estimated Value of Subject Property:				

Drive-By Checklist: Land

Items of Consideration	Excellent	Good	Fair	Poor	Unknown
Neighbors					
Location					
Fire Department					
Nearby Town					
Near Hospital					
Near Police					
School System					
Farm Potential					
Mining/Oil Potential					
Timber Potential					
Natural Resources					
Groundwater					
Surface Water					
Soil					
Topography					
Erosion					
Electricity					
Water					
Sewer					
Cable					
Phone					
Trash Service					
Mineral Value					
Recreational Value					
Land Access					

Competitive Market Analysis: Land*

	Subject Land	Comparable 1	Comparable 2	Comparable 3
Location/Address				
Area (acres)				
Lot Size				
Resource Value				
Listed Price				
Selling Price				
Remarks				
Area Market Conditions:				
Estimated Range of Value of Similar Properties:				
Estimated Value of Subject Property:				

* Market values for land are most easily determined by comparing price per area (usually in terms of acreage). Be sure to compare similar property types.

Drive-By Checklist: Commercial or Industrial

Items of Consideration	Excellent	Good	Fair	Poor	Unknown
Business Neighbors					
Location					
Fire Department					
Nearby Town					
Near Hospital					
Near Police					
Deed Restrictions					
Current Owner					
Current Tenant(s)					
Environmental					
Asbestos					
Mold					
Soil Contamination					
Stressed Vegetation					
Groundwater Contamination					
Surface Water Contamination					
Underground Storage Tanks					
Above Ground Storage Tanks					
Chemicals Stored					
Chemicals Used					
Radioactive Signs					
Groundwater					
Surface Water					
Soil					
Topography					
Erosion					
Electricity					
Water					
Sewer					
Cable					
Phone					
Trash Service					
Mineral Value					

Commercial property is often evaluated using the income approach or the replacement value approach. It is often difficult to find comparable properties. You may need to speak with a commercial real estate broker or professional appraiser if you are serious about investing in commercial properties.

Step 5: Check for other liens or problems

After you have narrowed your search to the properties or liens that are worthy of consideration, be sure to visit the county clerk's office or City Hall and ask to see a listing of liens on the properties. Some counties make this process very easy. It may even be computerized so that you can search by the property owner's last name. Other counties are not as sophisticated and you will have to look through books that list liens by either the property owner's name or the name of the individual and/or company placing the liens.

Why are you doing this?

If you are purchasing a tax lien, then you become a lien holder together with the state or county. You are looking for other liens, encumbrances or restrictions that you could be responsible for paying, or that would limit the value of the property.

In most cases, mortgage liens and mechanic's liens are erased or extinguished through the process of tax foreclosure. The tax lien generally has superiority. New Mexico's state law may not erase the other liens, so proceed with caution. In nearly all cases, IRS liens are not removed and will become the deed holder's responsibility.

County, state or local government assessments are usually not released, and therefore become the deed holder's responsibility. An example might be a mandatory assessment for a new sewer line, dredging of a lakefront property, or any number of improvements that the local government makes to the area.

In addition, be sure to check for deed restrictions on the land or property. In other words, find out what can or cannot be done with the property. If it is land, find out what type of improvement (i.e., home or structure) can be built and what cannot be built. If you are looking at commercial property, find out how the property is zoned.

Finally, it is always a good idea, especially for tax deeds, to determine if the previous property owner has filed for bankruptcy. Bankruptcy can slow the tax foreclosure process, leaving many of the decisions to the court. You could become one of many creditors waiting in line.

Step 6: Check for last minute redemptions

One frustrating aspect to investing in tax liens and tax deeds is that property owners can pay their property taxes as late as a few minutes before the auction, depending upon the state. This sets up a system where you can have dedicated a significant amount of time and research only to find out that your property of choice was redeemed.

There is really nothing you can do about this except to plan on bidding on at least four to five properties, knowing that three or four of these properties could be redeemed. For tax deed auctions, last minute redemptions are higher (roughly 40 to 50 percent will be redeemed) because property owners are about to lose their house or land. For tax liens, the rate is lower (roughly 20 percent).

If you can, make sure you review an updated listing of the properties the day before the auction. Some states/counties provide updated lists online. For others, you will just have to call or wait until the auction starts.

Step 7: Attend the auction

With your wish list of properties in hand, it's now "show time." You should plan on arriving about 30 minutes before the auction starts. This will allow you time to sign in, read the rules, and check for property listings that have been redeemed (they may be listed on a dry erase board or elsewhere).

In the case of tax liens and interest rate bids, set a minimum interest rate that you are willing to receive and stick to it. In states like Alabama, the winning bidder will pay the lowest interest rate. Even though the starting bid is 12 percent, the winning bidder may only pay 1 or 2 percent. The reason for this approach could be that there is a high likelihood that the property will go to foreclosure and the winning bidder is betting on that. Otherwise, it would make no sense to bid it down to this level, especially considering all of the work that goes in to preparations.

In Missouri, the winning bidder pays the most for the property and also earns a greater return. However, if the property goes through foreclosure, it is important to make sure that you are buying it at a discount.

> **Special Note:** Set a maximum property bid or a minimum interest rate bid ahead of time for each property. Do not exceed your predetermined bid or you may regret it. Make your bid reasonable in terms of making a decent return on your money for all of your effort, but also realize that the very nature of auctions is not in your favor. Auctions are designed to encourage you to overspend. Be careful. Avoid the bidding frenzy.

The auction will start with a county or state official reading the rules. Pay close attention to details, such as the bid increments or how much you have to increase or decrease your bid. The official may go over the recently redeemed properties or just note the redeemed properties as the auction proceeds.

What will you see at an auction?

First, although the room may be full, only about 30 to 40 percent of those in attendance will actually bid. That's because many people come in pairs or in groups. Others come just to watch. And others are in too much shock to actually bid.

We have noted a few different types of investors, which are described as follows:

Big-Time Investors

At many auctions, you will notice individuals with deep pockets. They probably represent many other investors, a bank, or a large institution. In the case of tax liens, these individuals will bid down to a certain interest rate or up to a predetermined value. In states like Arizona where the interest rate is bid down, these investors will set a predetermined mark and not go below it. That mark may be 6 percent (as in one recent sale) or it could be as low as 1 percent. In most cases, these big-time investors are looking to buy up as many liens as possible, hoping for decent overall yield or a few properties that are not redeemed. In the case of bidding property values up, they may even have hired local real estate agents to tell them what property will sell for.

> **Answer to big-time investors:** Avoid highly populated counties near large cities. Also, look to purchase in areas outside of the popular areas, where the big-time investors may not have done their homework. If you have done your due diligence and you find properties that are valuable and could likely go to foreclosure, bid down to zero in certain cases.

Local Investors

Every auction brings out a group of individuals who live or work near property being auctioned. They are very familiar with the area, and know what is valuable and what is not valuable, at least from a local perspective. Local investors will usually come to bid on a select group of properties, if not one or two properties. Usually they are not as concerned about interest rates as they are about acquiring land or nearby property.

Answer to local investors: You may get in a bidding war on one or two properties, so be prepared with multiple properties or liens. In other words, diversify and don't fall in love with only one property. Oftentimes, locals will have limited investment capital to work with.

High Return Investors

This type of investor is not as concerned about interest rates as it is about acquiring property. High return investors will perform research and select a group of properties that are valuable and that could likely go to foreclosure. In the case of tax deeds, the properties are already in foreclosure, so these investors are looking for marketable properties in either great locations or with features that are unique enough to make them easy to sell. High return investors must do a lot more homework to determine market values as well as to avoid risk from unforeseen expenses.

Answer to high return investors: Most high return investors will have a limited budget. Be patient and wait until the middle to end of the sale if necessary. Some properties will slip through the cracks or, because of other circumstances, high return investors may miss a bid. Also, be sure to diversify. This group of investors can only research a limited number of properties. They may have focused on a few areas of the county because of lack of time.

These investor types are a generalization. There will be many different individuals with varying strategies attending the auctions. Some bidders will immediately annoy you. Other bidders will show their hand very quickly. At least a few bidders will try to cheat, but usually the auctioneer or county official will catch on very quickly.

Take notes. This is excellent classroom training. Note any properties that do not receive a bid. Another strategy is to not even plan on bidding during the auction, and to research the leftovers for any gems that slipped through. We have found some valuable properties this way.

Step 8: Purchase the deed or lien

If you are the winning bidder on a parcel, you will need to be prepared to pay the full bid amount for the deed or lien plus any fees and outstanding taxes (refer to Chapter 9 for specific state and county details). County or state officials will explain what you need to do. Some states may require that you sign an affidavit stating that you are not delinquent on any property taxes.

You will then receive a certificate of purchase. In the case of a tax deed, you still may have to wait until a grace period has passed (e.g., 30 days) before you are issued a Limited Warranty Deed.

In the case of tax liens, you will hold on to your certificate of purchase until it is redeemed by the property owner. At that time, the county or collector's office will provide you with a check for the redeemed amount minus a processing fee.

Step 9: Manage your liens and deeds

If the property is not redeemed during the redemption period, you will then apply for a Collector's Deed. A final notice must usually be sent to the property owner allowing him/her a certain amount of time (e.g., 90 days). Call the county and find out the rules necessary to manage your liens or deeds. For example, you may need to show that there are no other liens on the property.

Many county rules are very strict and you will need to abide by them. Don't miss out on the payoff because of lack of planning or management. Keep track of all of your liens or deeds and the dates to remember.

When a lien is not redeemed during the redemption period, you will likely want to contact a local attorney. He/she can make sure that all procedures are followed, such as notification, clearing the title, eviction or other issues. You may be able to do some of this yourself, but it is best to have it done right until you are intimately familiar with the local process.

For deeds, after any grace periods are over you own the deed, but it is generally not free and clear until a regulatory period has passed. For example, in California there is one-year period during which an interested party (e.g., a previous owner) can challenge the sale. Most states and counties recommend that no major expenditures be done on the property during this period, in case the sale is overturned. This does not prevent you from using the property, renting it, leasing it with an option to buy, owner financing it or employing many other strategies. It does result in the title not being free and clear during this period.

Again, it always best to consult with a local attorney on any legal strategies if you have any questions.

Finally, don't forget to obtain property insurance immediately upon receiving the deed.

Step 10: Sell

If you haven't already, consult the selling strategies in *Rogue Real Estate Investor*. This is real estate you now own, just like your house, rental home, cabin on the lake, or any other type of real property. A few simple selling strategies can pay off handsomely.

EIGHT

Answers to Some of Your
Tax Lien/Tax Deed Questions

*"Great things are not done by impulse, but by a series of
small things brought together." – Vincent van Gogh*

To find answers to your tax lien investing questions, you will need to get familiar with the counties or municipalities where you are going to purchase tax lien certificates or tax deeds. For example, you will need to know where the tax lien sales are held, how much money you may need, if the county will take checks, if you need to pre-register. Review Chapter 9 for more specific information regarding each state, as well as for many of the counties. In the meantime, here are the answers to some of the most commonly asked questions of tax lien/tax deed investors.

Frequently Asked Questions

(1) Can anyone buy tax lien certificates?

Yes, if you have the money you can buy the certificate. The only exceptions to this rule are that if you live in the same state where you are bidding, in many states your own property taxes must be paid in full before you can bid on other properties and, in some cases, especially tax deed sales, large institutions may be the first allowed bidders.

In some states, it may be necessary to have a social security number or federal tax I.D. number.

(2) Will I get ownership of the property?

When you are buying tax lien certificates, less than 5 percent of all delinquent property owners foreclose. So it is rare that you will need to foreclose on a tax lien certificate. However, if you are buying a tax deed, you will be taking possession of the property and you will definitely get ownership of the property.

(3) Is there a limit on the number of tax lien certificates I can buy?

No, in most cases you can buy as many as you can afford. There are a few counties that set limits, but those are rare.

(4) After I buy a tax lien certificate, when do I get my money back plus interest?

You will get your money back when the delinquent property owner pays his/her back taxes. This could take a month or several years. In rare cases, you will not get your money back until you foreclose on the property, and then you will get the property and not your money. The average time to get your money back is around six months to a year. Once the property owner realizes that the clock is ticking and the final bill is growing, something usually happens. After the property owner pays the taxes and penalties owed, you will get your check from the county when you send your tax lien certificate back. This is called redeeming your tax lien certificate.

(5) What do I do with the tax lien certificate?

Put it in a safe deposit box or somewhere else safe. If you lose your certificate, it can be a hassle to get a new one. You will need to verify some information to prove you are the owner of the certificate. It is better to make sure you do not lose it.

(6) What if I want to own property?

If your goal is to take property ownership, attend a tax deed sale instead. Less than 5 percent of all tax lien certificates eventually lead to foreclosure.

(7) What happens if the delinquent taxpayer does not pay and a year goes by?

You can purchase another tax lien certificate on the property the next year if you can pay the back taxes due. Otherwise, another bidder can purchase a tax lien certificate on the property. If foreclosure does occur, you would both be owners of the property. In some states, you lose the certificate if the next year's taxes are not paid.

(8) Can someone else bid for you at the auction?

It depends on the state. In some states, you can have someone else act as an agent for you and bid on properties. In other states, you must be there in person to bid.

(9) Can I buy tax lien certificates without going to the auction?

In many states you can. Tax lien certificates that are not sold at auction can often be purchased by mail. Be a little careful doing this, especially if you've never seen the property.

(10) Can I transfer the tax lien certificate to someone else?

Yes, in most states you can transfer the certificate to anyone you want. There may be a small fee involved.

(11) What is the best type of property to bid on?

Improved land has less risk. In most cases, especially for beginners, it is best to bid on residential property. Unimproved land (vacant land) has more risk. Also, commercial property has more risk.

(12) Can you lose money buying tax lien certificates?

Investing in tax lien certificates is extremely safe. The government handles the sales and owners will lose a huge part of their financial assets if they do not pay their back taxes. However, there are two scenarios where you could lose money:

1. You purchase a tax lien certificate during an auction and the interest rate gets bid down to a very low amount. Then, after you buy the tax lien certificate at a low interest rate, the owner of the property pays their back taxes very quickly and the tax lien certificate gets redeemed in less than a month after the auction. When you combine the fees you paid to buy the certificate and travel costs, you could lose some money. You can avoid this problem if you do not get involved in a bidding war. If there are a lot of bidders, go to another sale or wait until the sale is about over and everyone else has gone home. You can also go to a county where there is less competition; or you can just buy tax lien certificates that are not sold during the auction and then you will have no competition.

2. You must foreclose on the property you bid on because the owner never pays his/her back taxes. You did not do your homework and this property has environmental problems. This situation can be easily avoided if you focus on residential properties and make sure you drive by the property before you bid. Many states do not want you to have a bad experience, so they will often tell you if a property could have problems.

(13) From what I can tell, Fair Market Value (FMV) is determined by the county office and listed in the tax sale list for each property. Is the FMV just the value that it should get on the open market, or are any existing liens/mortgages deducted? I understand that property will usually have a mortgage associated with it – how does that affect the value?

Fair Market Value is the tax assessor's determination of what a property is worth. Depending on how often the appraiser updates the FMV and how advanced the appraiser department is, the FMV may or may not represent true value. For example, a house that has gone into disrepair because of the owner's neglect could be worth less. On the other hand, we have seen properties that would fetch a much higher price than what the county appraised it at. It's a good starting point, but you should do your own research and verify the number.

FMV has nothing to do with mortgages or liens. If the property goes through tax foreclosure (i.e., to deed), you own it subject to a legal period in which the previous owner, mortgage company, lien holder, etc. could challenge the sale. Otherwise, tax foreclosure wipes out the mortgage and most other liens, except IRS liens or county assessments. In New Mexico, mortgage liens may not be extinguished. If you are investing in New Mexico, be sure to do your due diligence. Make sure you check into the liens, find out if there are any deed restrictions, and make sure you know whether or not the previous landowner is going through bankruptcy. Bankruptcy could slow the process down and you'll have to wait until a court finishes the process.

(14) What happens to the original mortgage on the home when you foreclose on it? Let's say the person is $5000 behind on taxes, the property is worth $100,000, and his mortgage is $50,000. You buy the tax lien for 5 grand, and foreclose let's say in 2 years. Will I have to pay off the $50,000 mortgage to take over ownership of the property?

In regard to your question, you are not responsible for the mortgage (but see answer with regards to New Mexico, in previous question). That is a contract between the previous owner and the mortgage company/bank. Once a property goes through tax foreclosure, the mortgage and most other liens are extinguished. In some circumstances the mortgage holder can challenge the sale during the legal period following a sale or they can pay off the taxes and go through their own foreclosure. In any case, you are generally not responsible for the mortgage. You should check for county assessments, deed restrictions, IRS liens and bankruptcy of the owner as a precaution.

(15) Will I be able to rent property during the period in which the deed sale can be legally challenged?

Yes, you will be able to rent the property as long as you are the legal deed holder.

(16) When can I start the eviction process if the owner does not leave the property? Do I also have to wait for one year before I can evict the owner?

Once you have your deed in hand, you can start the eviction process. You do not have to wait one year.

(17) How can I find out how many bedrooms/bathrooms the house has or what the square footage is?

Much of the information that you are seeking is available from the county assessor's office. The assessor has to base real estate taxes on the value of the house, which includes number of bedrooms, square footage, etc. Where we live the county sends out an annual tax appraisal with all of that information, including comparisons to other properties.

(18) Once I get the deed to the property, will I be able to take out a loan on that house, or do I have to clear title before I can get a loan on that property?

You generally will need to clear title before you can take out a loan.

(19) Do some states have you bid by the interest rate percentage and some states by a nominal amount?

In some states you bid the interest rate down on the amount of taxes due (e.g., Illinois, Arizona). In other states (e.g., Missouri), you start bidding at the minimum bid and bid the price up. You usually have to pay the winning bid plus the taxes owed and sometimes recording or other fees. In Missouri you can actually bid up the property value and make money off of the total amount. Tax deed sales are similar to the Missouri example. The winning bidder pays the winning bid plus taxes owed and fees. The difference, of course, is that you get the deed to the property. On tax deeds, you bid the price of the property up. Some states, like Nebraska, have a round robin procedure in which the properties are offered to everyone in turn, and you either accept a property as it comes up or you decline it.

(20) Which state has the shortest time period during which owners can redeem their property?

New Mexico, which is a tax deed state, has a 120-day redemption period (the minimum period required by the federal government). However, New Mexico counties often sell property near the market value. Texas has a 6-month redemption period for most properties.

(21) We are interested in tax deed sales, but only have so much money to invest. We do not want to wait a year or two to see if an owner is going to redeem their property or not. We were thinking that if we bought property over the counter from last year's sale, then a year of the waiting period has already passed, right?

Over-the-counter sales in some states still require the same waiting period even if the property was not sold at the sale. In other words, the redemption clock does not start until you buy the deed (e.g., Arkansas).

(22) Is the mortgage extinguished or can I negotiate with the mortgage company?

The mortgage company is like an owner of the property, so they must redeem to avoid foreclosure. You do not have to negotiate with the mortgage company. As long as they have been notified, then it is up to them to redeem or let the property go. They can challenge a sale if not properly notified.

(23) Does the tax lien sale certificate take precedence over the first mortgage?

Yes.

(24) If you are the successful bidder at a tax deed sale and take title of a tax-defaulted parcel, are you responsible for paying the existing mortgage(s) on the property and/or structures on the property? I am located in California.

No, you are generally not responsible for the existing mortgage (be careful if you are investing in New Mexico). The mortgage holder is like a previous owner. They have an opportunity to redeem or pay the taxes or just let the property go. In California there is a one-year period in which the previous property owner or mortgage company could challenge a tax sale in court. Therefore, you will not be able to sell the property with clear title until after this one-year period. Usually counties/states advise that you not make any major improvements to the property during that time period.

(25) Where should I go to find out about any additional pre-existing liens against a tax-defaulted property subject to the power of sale by the county? Does it usually cost money to do a "lien search"?

You can usually conduct a lien search at the county for free. The information is part of the public record and therefore has to be made available. Visit the county clerk's office and ask to see their recorded liens on real property. Every county is a little different. Some will have computerized information, while others will provide the information in large legal binders.

(26) Are tax liens available in Canada?

Tax liens are not typically offered to investors in Canada. There are tax deed sales. Most sales are held in the most populated municipalities of the various provinces. In a province like Alberta, search for information on, for example, the municipalities of Lethbridge and Edmonton.

(27) Do properties usually bid up to retail levels where I live (California)?

In California, sometimes the properties are bid up to full retail. We can't understand why, but if that's the case you are better off finding a less populated area or even bidding in another state. Also, don't forget that you can buy foreclosed properties through banks, mortgage companies, VA, HUD, IRS, etc.

(28) What if there are three or four properties that you are interested in, but can afford only one or two. The ones that you are less interested in come up for bid first. Should you hold out and wait to bid on the prime property, or bid the first one that comes up?

We usually prioritize all the properties we are interested in. Sometimes it can be a difficult dilemma. One secret that we have noticed is that the bidding is usually more competitive toward the beginning of an auction and it tails off a little later in the sale. You may have a better chance later in the auction than at the beginning. Of course, you never know what type of excitement a particular property will create. You may have to make this judgment on a case-by-case basis.

(29) What should the title search include?

You will want to find out about all liens or any other encumbrances that are on a property. Tax liens take precedence over mortgage liens, mechanic's liens and many others. Tax liens do not take precedence over IRS liens or special county or government assessments. It is also a good idea to check and see if the landowner has filed for bankruptcy.

(30) As a non- U.S. resident (I live in Australia), would I be able to purchase U.S. government tax lien certificates?

Buying tax liens or tax deeds in the U.S. often requires a social security number or a federal tax I.D. number. One way for nonresidents to work around this is to start a small business, such as a limited liability company (LLC) and receive a federal tax I.D. number. Another method is to obtain an Individual Taxpayer Identification Number (ITIN). According to the U.S. Internal Revenue Service, federal law requires individuals with U.S. income, regardless of immigration status, to pay U.S. taxes. The ITIN, a nine-digit number that begins with the number 9, was created for use on tax returns for those taxpayers who do not qualify for a social security number. The IRS has issued 7 million ITINs since 1996.

New updates to the ITIN process were just announced on December 17, 2003. For more information, visit the http://www.irs.gov/newsroom/article/0,,id=112728,00.html.

Any nonresident or U.S. resident alien who is required to file taxes or who can be claimed as an exemption or dependent on a tax return, and who does not qualify for a social security number, can apply for an ITIN. See Publication 501, "Exemptions, Standard Deduction and Filing Information for Exemption Tests" and Publication 519, "U.S. Tax Guide for Aliens" to determine resident status.

You do not need an ITIN if:

- you are a U.S. citizen,
- you were born in the U.S. and do not have diplomatic immunity,
- you have entered the U.S. on a work VISA, or
- you are entitled to a federally funded benefit (stipend/fellowship/grant).

You are eligible for an ITIN if:

- you have entered the U.S. on a non-work VISA,
- you were born in the U.S. and have diplomatic immunity,
- you have applied for and were denied a social security number, or
- you are an undocumented alien.

You can obtain ITIN application forms, W-7/W-7SP, through IRS offices worldwide:

- 1-800-TAX-FORM (1-800-829-3676)
- http://www.irs.gov
- Tax Fax Service at 1-703-368-9694
- IRS kiosks.

Submit your ITIN forms and supporting documentation to:

- IRS Taxpayer Assistance Centers (TACS),
- certain U.S. consular offices abroad,
- a Certified Acceptance Agent, or
- mail to:
  PSPC ITIN Unit
  P.O. Box 447
  Bensalem, PA 19020
  DP N-280

For ITIN Frequently Asked Questions, visit:
http://www.irs.gov/individuals/article/0,,id=96287,00.html.

Download Form W-7, Application for IRS ITIN, at http://www.irs.gov/pub/irs-pdf/fw7.pdf.

(31) I would like to learn more about online tax deed auctions.

Most tax deed auctions are not online. You have to physically go to the county or location of the auction. What we sometimes recommend is to avoid the battles at the auction and call your local county assessor's office and ask if they have any properties for sale by closed bid or through what is called "over-the-counter" or "negotiated" sales lists. You can usually spend more time researching these properties and feel more comfortable about your bid. Many of these properties will not be desirable, but every now and then a gem or two will slip through.

A few progressive counties (e.g., Kern and Alameda counties in California) are starting to offer tax deeds online. Visit http://www.bid4assets.com to find out more information.

(32) With regards to Texas, your book seems to indicate that it is not a tax lien state, but rather a tax deed state. However, I'm confused as to how one can earn 25% in six months by buying tax deeds. Please clarify.

Texas has a unique process. It is a tax deed state, but they still offer a redemption period (2 years for homestead and agricultural property, and 6 months for other property). Should the owner redeem his/her property within this time period, the investor receives a flat 25% interest rate, which is in some ways similar to a tax lien certificate. However, if the property is not redeemed, the investor keeps the deed.

Georgia has a somewhat similar process. The investor receives a deed with the right of redemption for one year. If the property is redeemed, the investor earns 20% on their investment; otherwise, the investor keeps the property.

(33) I contacted my local City Hall and no one seems to know anything about tax sales.

Sometimes it is frustrating trying to find the right person to contact at the city, county or municipality. We have called many times and had to speak with several people before finding someone who knows about tax liens or tax deeds. You just need to be persistent and find someone in the assessor's, treasurer's or collector's office who deals with real estate.

(34) One question about this statement: "...most title companies will not insure the title until one year after the tax sale deed is recorded....Legal action to challenge a tax deed....Therefore it is not advisable to make any improvements during the first year of ownership...." We live in California. Does this mean we cannot turn around and sell the property right away? Do we have to wait a whole year? What happens if the previous owner challenges the sale? Do we lose the investment and property? Does this mean we cannot touch the property for a whole year? We thought these properties were free and clear.

Most tax deed states have a legal period after the sale to challenge the sale. Challenging the sale is usually not an easy matter and doesn't happen as long as all interested parties have been notified by the county. Remember, the owner and lien holders have been given numerous warnings. This legal period is a protection mechanism. It was designed to prevent mishaps, such as one separated spouse defaulting on a property without the other knowing about it, or an individual who is in the military and out of the country defaulting on a property, or a mortgage company who was not notified. A sale can also be challenged if it is not conducted properly and in accordance with state law.

Some states require a legal period that lasts for two years, so California is actually quite good for investors. This does not stop you from renting the property, leasing it with an option to buy, selling it by owner financing, or employing many other strategies. Actually, you can still sell it to anyone who doesn't require clear title. Usually the sticking point is the mortgage company of the buyer.

In the event that a sale is successfully challenged, you will be reimbursed by the county. You also can fight the challenge, and you may have as good of a chance of winning as the challenging party. Legal advice is necessary at this point.

NINE

Detailed State and County Profiles

*"A journey of a thousand miles must begin
with a single step." – Chinese proverb*

This chapter provides detailed information on tax sales for all 50 states. The available information varies widely for each state. Some states are very progressive and have great websites and actively encourage tax lien certificate sales or tax deed sales. In other states, tax sales are not a priority and little information is available. There are also good examples of tax lien certificate sales or tax deed sales procedures. Read these examples and they will start to give you an understanding of what to expect if you were to attend an auction.

Tax sale information for the top 100 counties in the United States by population, as well as some additional counties, are also provided in this chapter. (And we've included information on government, mortgage, etc. foreclosures when available.) County-specific information is derived from county websites, or from our own experience. As with the states, some counties are progressive and provide a great deal of information on tax sales on their websites, while others are just the opposite. If your county is not covered in this book, visit the following web pages for links to county websites throughout the United States:
http://www.naco.org/Template.cfm?Section=Find_a_County&Template=/cffiles/counties/usamap.cfm and http://www.tax-lien-certificates.com. If the county you are interested in does not have a website, or has a website with little or no tax sale information, you will need to contact the county by phone or mail.

Although this book is updated biannually, information on a county (or state) website may have been outdated at the time of our research, or the information may have changed between our updates. Before relying on the county- or state-specific information presented in this chapter, we recommend that you visit the relevant web page source to make sure the information is current. One useful strategy is to read all of the text that you are interested in, and then use the CD that accompanies this book to visit relevant web pages using the active hyperlinks. If you copy a URL into your browser, remember that a URL has no punctuation at the end (e.g., periods, commas).

Be patient. In many cases, county systems are not worked out yet. After you study the information in this chapter, you will need to become familiar with a few counties and their exact procedures as you prepare to bid on properties. To help you with your research, the following website provides general tax lien information: http://www.tax-lien-certificates.com and http://www.tax-deed-sales.com.

Alabama

Tax Lien Sales: Yes

Tax Deed Sales: No

Rating: Three Stars (***)

Interest Rate: 12%

Sale Period: May in most counties.

Redemption Period: 3 years

Bidding Process:
All auctions are by competitive bid. Winning bidder pays lowest interest rate.

State-Specific Information:
Alabama sells tax lien certificates. Although it is not one of the best tax lien states, it does pay an interest rate of 12% per year and the redemption period is 3 years.

Links for All Alabama Counties: Provided on CD

Detailed County-Specific Information:

JEFFERSON COUNTY, ALABAMA
http://www.jeffcointouch.com

TAX COLLECTOR'S OFFICE
http://tc.jeffcointouch.com/taxcollection/HTML/index.asp

Jack Williams, Tax Collector
Phone = (205) 325-5500 for the Birmingham Office or (205) 481-4131 for the Bessemer Office.

(1) Purchase Property from State
http://tc.jeffcointouch.com/taxcollection/HTML/redemption.html?who=state

(2) General Tax Sale Information
http://tc.jeffcointouch.com/taxcollection/HTML/intro_taxsales.html

Code of Alabama, Section 40-10 provides for the disposition of property tax liabilities that are not paid in a timely fashion.

There are two methods by which you may purchase tax interest in Jefferson County properties: Annual Tax Sale, Sold to State Properties.

(2a) Annual Tax Sale
http://tc.jeffcointouch.com/taxcollection/HTML/taxsale_annual.html

As required by Code of Alabama, Section 40-10-15, the Tax Collector conducts a sale (public outcry auction format) in May of each year. For information on the next annual sale, for Birmingham please call (205) 325-5084. For Bessemer cutoff please call (205) 481-4130 or e-mail (boydg@jcc.co.jefferson.al.us) your request between March 1st and May 10th and ask for a *Tax Sale Information Package*. Listings of properties to be included in the annual sale will be available for purchase after the last advertising date in April.

Annual Tax Sale FAQ

How many parcels are normally offered? Approximately 4000 tax certificates are offered annually. The total face amount of certificates offered is usually around $2 million.

How is the sale conducted? Tax certificates are auctioned one at a time, in unit number order. They are sold to the highest bidder with the face amount as the minimum bid.

How long before I get a tax deed? If a certificate that you purchase remains unredeemed on the three-year anniversary of the tax sale, you are entitled to a tax deed.

If I buy a tax certificate, do I ever get clear title? Investors typically buy tax certificates to get a 12% return on their investment and usually do not get "clear title" to the property, although it is possible. Please consult your real estate attorney for legal advice.

How do I participate in the annual sale? You must register at the appropriate time. For information on the next annual sale, for Birmingham please call (205) 325-5084. For Bessemer Cutoff please call (205) 481-4130 or e-mail (boydg@jcc.co.jefferson.al.us) your request between March 1st and May 10th and ask for a *Tax Sale Information Package.*

(2b) Sold to State Properties
http://tc.jeffcointouch.com/taxcollection/HTML/taxsale_soldtostate.html

"Sold to State" properties are parcels that were offered at a past annual tax sale, and were not purchased at that time. As provided by Code Sections 40-10-21 and 40-10-132, the State of Alabama Revenue Department offers for sale tax certificates and tax deeds, which are currently in the possession of the State (usually between 6500 and 8500 items from Jefferson County). You may purchase a complete listing of Jefferson County Sold to State tax parcels via the Internet (http://tc.jeffcointouch.com/taxcollection/HTML/taxsale_buylist.asp) or by calling (205) 325-5084 anytime during business hours (8 to 5, Central Time, M-F). Listings are available in the form of hardcopy, CD or e-mail.

Sold to State Properties FAQ

How many parcels are in a Sold to State status at any given time? Anywhere between 6500 to 8500 Sold to State parcels are available.

How do I purchase certificates from the State of Alabama? You must have the parcel number of the certificate you wish to purchase. Then complete the online State Resale Application (http://tc.jeffcointouch.com/taxcollection/HTML/redemption.html?who=state) (it's free). The completed form will be electronically sent to the State Department of Revenue. The State Revenue Department will respond to your application by mailing directly to you a price quote letter. You will have twenty days to respond to the price quote by sending in a cashier's check for the stated amount.

How do I know if I will get a certificate or tax deed? Tax deeds are issued on properties that have been delinquent for more than three years.

When will I get a document from the State? Once the State receives your payment, they will begin processing either a tax certificate or a tax deed, whichever is appropriate. Upon completion of that document, they will mail it directly to you, in approximately 6 to 8 weeks.

What do I do with my certificate? Keep it in a safe place! If the property is redeemed, you will be notified to return it to us to get your money back plus interest. If the property is not redeemed prior to the three-year anniversary of the original sale, bring the certificate to our office and exchange it for a tax deed ($5.00).

What do I do with my tax deed? Record it immediately in the Judge of Probate Office and consult your legal sources regarding possession and use of the property.

(2bi) Buy List
http://tc.jeffcointouch.com/taxcollection/HTML/taxsale_buylist.asp

Jefferson County Sold To State property listings are available in hard copy or on CD at the Tax Collector's office for $25.00. These can be picked up at our office.

You may purchase an electronic copy of the list on-line using a credit card or check. The list will be attached to an email as a Microsoft Excel spreadsheet (approximate file size is 2.0 MB) and sent to you immediately upon payment.

NOTE: Your e-mail must be able to accommodate file attachments.

The Sold To State List is not available at this time.

The following fees apply to online transactions:

- Credit card $5 per parcel or transaction
- Electronic Check $2 per parcel or transaction.

(3) Contact Information

For Birmingham contact:	*For Bessemer contact:*
Jack Williams, Tax Collector	Grover Dunn, Assistant Tax Collector
Land Redemptions	Attn: Land Redemption Department
Room 160 Courthouse	Room 201 Courthouse
716 Richard Arrington Jr. Blvd	1801 Third Ave. North
Birmingham, AL 35203	Bessemer, AL 35020
Phone: (205) 325-5084	Phone: (205) 481-4130
email: boydg@jcc.co.jefferson.al.us	email: tapleyn@jcc.co.jefferson.al.us

(4) FAQ
http://tc.jeffcointouch.com/taxcollection/HTML/faqs.html

SHERIFF'S OFFICE
http://www.jeffcosheriff.net

(1) Court Services
http://www.jeffcosheriff.net/courtservices.htm

Birmingham Court Service Division is located at 801 Richard Arrington Jr. Blvd, Birmingham, AL 35203. Phone: 205-325-5729; Fax: 205-325-1433

Clerical Support Staff includes Supervisor Cassandra Evans – Executions, Levies, Sheriff Sales, Out of State Civil Papers

Bessemer Court Services is located at 1826 2nd Avenue North, Bessemer, AL 35020. Phone: 205-481-4201; Fax: 205-481-4200

Clerical Support Staff includes Charlotte Lackey – Clerk for Executions, Levies, Sheriff Sales, Levies, Set-Outs.

Tax Lien Sales: No

Tax Deed Sales: Yes

Rating: Two Stars (**)

Interest Rate: No interest rate, state only has tax deed sales.

Sale Period: Depends on the county.

Redemption Period: Properties can be purchased at tax deed sales for immediate ownership.

Bidding Process:
At tax deed sales, all auctions are by competitive bid. Winning bidder pays highest value for property. The minimum bid is set by the Borough and can be as high as the market value of the property.

State-Specific Information:
Counties are also called Boroughs. Municipalities are also authorized to have foreclosure sales.

Links for All Alaska Counties: Provided on CD.

Detailed County-Specific Information:

ANCHORAGE BOROUGH, ALASKA
http://www.muni.org

MUNICIPAL TREASURY'S OFFICE
http://www.muni.org/treasury

Office consists of four sections, including Tax Section (billing, collections).

(1) Tax Section – Real Property Tax Information Web Site
http://www.muni.org/treasury/prop_index.cfm

(2) Tax Section Contact Information
http://www.muni.org/treasury/prop_general.cfm

Phone: (907) 343-6650
Fax: (907) 343-6121

Mailing Address
Municipality of Anchorage
Department of Finance
Treasury Division
P.O. Box 196040
Anchorage, AK 99519-6040

<u>Physical Address</u>
632 West 6th Avenue, Suite 330
Anchorage, AK 99501

(3) Frequently Called Phone Numbers
http://www.muni.org/treasury/prop_freq_num.cfm

Tax Liens/MOA Deeded Property/Tax Deed Auction
907-343-7953
907-343-7986

REAL ESTATE SERVICES OFFICE

4700 S. Bragaw Street, First Floor
Anchorage, AK 99507

THE <u>2003 SEALED BID SALE</u> WAS WEDNESDAY, NOVEMBER 5, 2003.

If you wish to review the 2003 Foreclosed Properties list, please click on the following link:
http://www.muni.org/iceimages/hlb/2003L.pdf.

The next sale of tax-foreclosed properties is tentatively slated for sometime late next fall of 2004. We will post a list on this site approximately six weeks prior to the sealed bid sale date.

Please note: There is no sale without first getting Assembly approval, nor can a list be published until a sale is authorized. For more information, please call us at 907-343-7986 for more information.

Guide to purchasing tax foreclosed property:
http://www.muni.org/iceimages/hlb/20044closedPropGuide.pdf

Arizona

Tax Lien Sales: Yes

Tax Deed Sales: Yes

Rating: Five Stars (*****)

Interest Rate: 16%

Sale Period: February in most counties.

Redemption Period: 3 years

Bidding Process:
All auctions are by competitive bid. Winning bidder pays lowest interest rate. Tax lien sale advertisements usually appear in county newspapers about three weeks prior to the sale. Tax liens certificates are also called certificates of purchase. All bidders must be present to participate in the auction (no bids by telephone or mail). Bidders must fill out a Bidder Information Card (obtained from Client Services Department) and request a Taxpayer Identification Number and Form W-9 (obtained from Client Services Department or IRS). All tax liens must be paid in full (all taxes, interest and fees) by the end of the next day after the tax lien has been purchased.

State-Specific Information:
Arizona is probably one of the most famous tax lien states because the interest rate of 16% per year is favorable.

Many counties have tax liens and full parcels of land for sale throughout the year. Listings of all parcels that are still available after the tax lien sale are available as a printout or on diskette for $50 from the Client Services Department at the Treasurer's Office. Also called assignment purchasing, potential buyers can send a list of the parcels they want to purchase to the Treasurer's Office, along with a certified check/cashier's check/wired money transfer to purchase tax liens that were not sold at auction.

The foreclosure process (going from lien to deed after the redemption period) is a little complicated for investors. You can start foreclosure proceedings three years from the date of the tax sale. Recent changes to the foreclosure process may result in the investor needing to hire an attorney to obtain a judgment deed. Previously, the investor could apply to the court for a deed.

Links for All Arizona Counties: Provided on CD.

Detailed County-Specific Information:

COCHISE COUNTY, ARIZONA
http://www.co.cochise.az.us

TREASURER'S OFFICE
http://www.co.cochise.az.us/treasurer

4 Ledge Avenue, 3rd Floor
P.O. BOX 1778
Bisbee, AZ 85603

Phone: (520) 432-8400; Fax: (520) 432-8438
Email: treasurer@co.cochise.az.us

(1) Tax Lien Sale
http://www.co.cochise.az.us/treasurer/TaxLienSale.htm

(1a) 2004 Tax Lien List
http://www.co.cochise.az.us/treasurer/2004TaxLienList.htm

For February 26, 2004 tax lien sale.

(1b) Bidder Number Application Form
http://www.co.cochise.az.us/treasurer/BidderNumForm.pdf

(1c) Current Back Tax List
http://www.co.cochise.az.us/treasurer/backtax.htm

Certificates purchased during Tax Lien Sales in 1998 and prior must apply for Treasurer Deeds by December 31, 2003. If application is not received by December 31, 2003 these must be foreclosed through Judicial Deed.

Certificates purchased during Tax Lien Sales in 1999 and after must foreclose through Judicial Deeds.

MARICOPA COUNTY, ARIZONA
http://www.maricopa.gov

TREASURER'S OFFICE
http://treasurer.maricopa.gov

Doug Todd, Treasurer
Attention: Correspondence Desk
301 West Jefferson Ste 100
Phoenix, Arizona 85003
phone: (602) 506-8511
TT (602) 506-2348
FAX (602) 506-1102
email: Treasurer@Mail.Maricopa.Gov

(1) Property Tax Calendar
http://treasurer.maricopa.gov/TaxCalendar.asp

(2) Research Material
http://treasurer.maricopa.gov/ResearchMatl.pdf

ROGUE INVESTOR NOTE: Document contains research materials that can be ordered by the general public. Titles include "Tax Sale Advertising List." Document also has a Tax Lien Calendar.

(3) FAQ's
http://treasurer.maricopa.gov/faq.html

(4) Tax Lien Information
http://treasurer.maricopa.gov/lien.html

Related Pages:
- Disclaimer (http://treasurer.maricopa.gov/LienDisclaimer.htm)
- FAQ (http://treasurer.maricopa.gov/TAXLIENSALEFAQ.asp)
- Recommendations (http://treasurer.maricopa.gov/LienRecommendations.htm)
- Lien History Statistics (http://treasurer.maricopa.gov/lienhistory.html)
- Tax Lien Sale Brochure (PDF) (http://treasurer.maricopa.gov/TaxLienSale.pdf)
- Application for Bidder Number (Bidder Information Card) (http://treasurer.maricopa.gov/LienBidder.html)

AUCTION
The Tax Lien Sale provides for the payment of delinquent property taxes by an investor. The tax on the property is auctioned in open competitive bidding based on the least percent of interest to be received by the investor.

Property taxes that are delinquent at the end of December are added to any previously uncollected taxes on a parcel for the Tax Lien Sale. The sale takes place in February of each year. Please read the disclaimer (http://treasurer.maricopa.gov/LienDisclaimer.htm) before deciding to bid, and see our lien FAQ (http://treasurer.maricopa.gov/TAXLIENSALEFAQ.asp) page and lien history page (http://treasurer.maricopa.gov/lienhistory.html).

Parcels whose taxes are subject to sale will be advertised in January, in a Maricopa County newspaper (http://treasurer.maricopa.gov/Newspaper) of general circulation. They are listed by parcel number and have a sequence number for bidding purposes. The advertisement appears about three weeks before the auction and is also posted on the Internet (http://treasurer.maricopa.gov/ListOnWeb). Copies of the newspaper are usually available for purchase at the Treasurer's Office. In addition, a diskette and CD of those parcels can also be purchased.

The investor is responsible for all research on the parcels available for auction. County maps for research may be obtained by visiting the Maricopa County Assessor's Office. Read our Recommendations (http://treasurer.maricopa.gov/LienRecommendations.htm) to all bidders.

PRE-SALE REQUIREMENTS
To be eligible to bid, investors must provide the Treasurer's Office with a completed Bidder Information Card (http://treasurer.maricopa.gov/LienBidder.html) and Request for Taxpayer Identification Number and Certification (IRS Form W-9, http://www.irs.gov). Click the links or contact the Client Services Department for the forms. A number will be assigned to each bidder for use when purchasing tax liens.

BID PROCEDURE
The sequence number and the amount will be read in the order they appear in the newspaper. Visual bids will be recognized as interest rates are called. The lowest interest rate bid on a parcel will be awarded the lien or Certificate of Purchase (CP). Bidders must be present. Bids by telephone or mail are not accepted.

The successful bidder will pay the entire amount of taxes, interest, and fees with guaranteed funds by the end of the next day. If payment has not been made the parcel(s) may be re-offered.

The sale will continue until all liens are sold or the lack of bidding warrants discontinuing the sale.

Each investor will receive an Unmatured Portfolio Report identifying each parcel for which the investor had acquired a tax lien. When making an inquiry on a property, use the parcel number located in the left column of the Portfolio.

BID INTEREST
Bids must be on the basis of interest income to bidder:

1. The maximum bid is 16% simple interest per annum, prorated monthly. The lowest acceptable bid is 0% per annum.
2. The successful (lowest) bid will determine the rate of interest to be paid on the Tax Lien, representing the amount of taxes, interest, fees and charges then due.

REDEMPTION OF LIENS
If the owner and/or agent redeems the property, the investor receives a payment for what they paid for the lien, less the processing fee, plus the prorated monthly rate of interest that was awarded at the sale.

DEEDS
When a property owner fails to redeem the CP prior to the expiration of three years from the date the parcel was first offered at sale, the investor may apply for a court ordered deed to the property (judicial foreclosure). The Treasurer does not participate in judicial foreclosures. A Treasurer's Deed may be applied for after five years from the date of sale. The last day to apply for a Treasurer's Deed is December 31, 2003. After that date all foreclosures must be judicial.

ASSIGNMENTS
Assignments offer the investor an alternative way to purchase liens on parcels at a time other then the Tax Lien sale.

The unsold parcels "struck off to state" (State CPs) at the Tax Lien sale are available to investors by assignment. Assignments will be available upon completion of all Sale Week transactions. Assignment purchases may be made in person or by mail. Payment must accompany the request.

Available parcels are listed as "STATE CP" on a printout located in the Client Services Department of the Treasurer's Office. This listing is available for purchase in two forms, printout or diskette, for $50 each. It lists the tax amount and year involved. The buyer will pay the entire amount of taxes, interest, and fees due at the date of the assignment. The final date for purchasing assignments is January 31. The remaining assignments are prepared for the Tax Lien Sale in February.

NOTE: If a parcel also has current delinquent taxes in addition to "State CP" taxes, the investor may purchase both after June 1, and prevent the parcel from going to the Tax Lien Sale.

ASSIGNMENT PURCHASING
The buyer will submit a list of desired parcels to the Treasurer's Office, along with a cashier's check, money order, certified check, or wire transfer for the approximate total. The submittals will be recorded and processed in the order in which they are received. Should the original payment be in excess of the amount due, a refund will be issued.

The calculations will be made on the assignments up to the amount received. Parcels not covered by funds on hand must remain available to other buyers. The interest earned on an assignment will be the current statutory maximum (16%).

"Assignment" must be specified to prevent an inadvertent processing of a redemption of a Certificate of Purchase.

SUBTAX
Subsequent Tax (Subtax) can be added to an existing lien to protect the investor's fiduciary interest. The subtaxing of the current year's taxes onto existing lien begins June 1 and ends January 31. All remaining taxes go to the Tax Lien Sale in February.

The investor is responsible for the research of the parcel's unpaid taxes. The subtax consists of taxes, interest, and fees dependent on the date the taxes are being paid. There is an additional $5.00 fee for each purchase submitted for subtax to be applied for each year requested.

The payment procedure for a subtax is the same as for assignments. The interest earned on a subtax is the same as that of the original CP.

TRANSFER OF CERTIFICATES OF PURCHASE
If not redeemed, a CP may be transferred by affidavit to another person who has a Bidder Identification Card on file with the Treasurer's Office. There is a $10.00 transfer fee. The Treasurer's Office must be notified of the transfer for it to be valid. The Treasurer pays the redeemed taxes to the last CP holder on record.

MONTHLY ACTIVITY STATEMENT
An Activity Statement will be sent to each CP buyer listing their redemptions, purchases, and surrenders. Statements will not be sent for those accounts that have not had activity.

(4a) Tax Lien Sale Disclaimer
http://treasurer.maricopa.gov/LienDisclaimer.htm

(4b) Tax Sale FAQ
http://treasurer.maricopa.gov/TAXLIENSALEFAQ.asp

(4c) Tax Lien Sale Recommendations
http://treasurer.maricopa.gov/LienRecommendations.htm

You should independently verify legal descriptions of properties before bidding. Otherwise, difficulties, including obtaining title insurance, may occur during foreclosure proceedings.

You should research genealogy and tax status of properties before bidding. Maricopa County and the Maricopa County Treasurer make no title warranties on properties at the sale. Neither the County nor the Treasurer warrant title concerning disclosed or undisclosed title problems including any environmental problems.

You should know that on certain parcels, in addition to the ad valorem taxes offered for a tax lien sale, there may be special assessments due that are unknown to the Maricopa County Treasurer.

You should know that in the event the Board of Supervisors retroactively cancels a property or corrects the valuation or classification of a property by resolution, you may not receive the anticipated interest.

You should know that the tax lien you wish to purchase may be rescinded due to a pre-existing stay order from bankruptcy court. In that case, only your purchase price will be refunded to you at such time as the existence of the stay order affecting a particular property is made known to Maricopa County and the Maricopa County Treasurer.

You should know that in the event of bankruptcy proceedings either before or after the sale of a tax lien, there is no guarantee that the investor of the tax lien will receive the anticipated interest or any interest whatsoever. The United States Bankruptcy Court will make that determination.

You may obtain general tax information by visiting the Treasurer or Assessor Web Sites at http://treasurer.maricopa.gov and http://www.maricopa.gov/assessor. In addition to our web site, the Treasurer's Office offers computer dial-up accounts. For additional information regarding these services, please contact our office at 1-602-506-8511. To obtain copies of Arizona Revised Statutes, you may visit the Maricopa County Law Library at 101 W. Jefferson St, Phoenix AZ (phone: 1-602-506-3461) or check out A.L.I.S. (Arizona Legislative Information Services) at http://www.azleg.state.az.us.

(4d) Tax Lien Statistics
http://treasurer.maricopa.gov/lienhistory.html

(4e) Tax Lien Sale Brochure
http://treasurer.maricopa.gov/TaxLienSale.pdf

(4f) Application for Bidder Number
http://treasurer.maricopa.gov/LienBidder.html

(5) Fee Schedules
http://treasurer.maricopa.gov/FeeSchedule.html

PIMA COUNTY, ARIZONA
http://www.co.pima.az.us

TREASURER'S OFFICE
http://www.to.co.pima.az.us

Beth Ford, Treasurer

Delinquent Real Estate Tax Lien Sale will be February 23 through February 27, 2004, in the Board of Supervisor's Hearing Room, 130 W. Congress, Tucson, Arizona.

(1) Contact Information
http://www.to.co.pima.az.us/contact.html

Pima County Treasurer's Office
115 North Church Ave.
Tucson, AZ 85701-1199
Phone: (520) 740-8341
Fax: (520) 884-4809

(2) Frequently Asked Questions
http://www.to.co.pima.az.us/faq.html

(3) Tax Lien Sale 2004 Information
http://www.to.co.pima.az.us/tax_sale_info.html

(4) Supplemental Tax Lien Information
http://www.to.co.pima.az.us/tools/jsp/bankrupt_parcels.jsp

Parcels flagged as bankruptcy as of January 16, 2004.

CONTACT INFORMATION

Delinquent Tax Fax (520) 740-2743
E-mail: lleikem@exchange.co.pima.az.us
bford@exchange.co.pima.az.us or pdavidson@exchange.co.pima.az.us

SHERIFF'S DEPARTMENT
http://www.pimasheriff.org/index.html

E-mail: pcsd@pimasheriff.net
Sheriff Clarence Dupnik

(1) Phone Numbers
http://www.pimasheriff.org/phone.html

Tax Collection
32 N. Stone Avenue, 8th Floor
phone: 520-740-5515

(2) Organizational Chart
http://www.pimasheriff.org/adminorgchart.html

Administrative Bureau
Technical Services Division
Court Enforcement, Ken Maurer, Manager

YUMA COUNTY, ARIZONA
http://www.co.yuma.az.us

TREASURER'S OFFICE
http://www.co.yuma.az.us/treas/index.htm

410 Maiden Lane, Suite C, Yuma, Arizona 85364
phone: (928) 539-7781; FAX (928) 539-7793; E-Mail: treasinfo@admin.co.yuma.az.us

(1) Tax Lien FAQ
http://www.co.yuma.az.us/treas/faq.htm

1. What is the date, time and location of your tax lien sale? Date: Last Wednesday in February of each year. Time: Sign In at 8:00 a.m., Auction at 9:00 a.m. Location: Yuma County Board of Supervisor's Auditorium. 198 S. Main Street, Yuma, Arizona.

2. How often do you hold tax lien sales? Once a year.

3. Does your county hold a tax deeded property sale? Yes. The Board of Supervisors are responsible for holding this sale. For more information contact Dunia Federico at (928) 329-2104 or go to their website at www.co.yuma.az.us/bos/auctions.htm.

4. When and where will the tax lien sale list be advertised? When: Beginning of February (usually on the second Monday of the month). Where: The Sun, 2055 S. Arizona Ave., Yuma, AZ 85364, phone: (928) 783-3333. MUST HAVE ADVERTISEMENT DATE BEFORE CALLING FOR A LIST. Also on our website at: http://www.co.yuma.az.us/treas/delinquentlist.htm and www.publicnoticeads.com/az.

5. How and when do I register for the tax sale? We provide a bidder information sheet along with a W-9 form, which is filled out the morning of the auction by the bidder.

6. What are the payment requirements at the sale? Is there a deposit required before the sale? Cashier's check, money order, cash or direct wire are the methods of payments we accept. We do not require any deposit.

7. What is the bidding process? The bidding is on the interest percentage rate that you would earn on your initial investment starting at 16% per year and bidding down from that rate.

8. What type of document is issued at the sale? After the tax lien sale is over you will receive a Bid Report with a list of parcel numbers you purchased and amounts due.

9. Are there any other expenses in addition to the cost of the lien? Yes, there is a $20.00 fee on the day of the sale ($10.00 Non-refundable processing fee, $10.00 C.P Fee). For parcels that have old years on them the fee is $15.00 ($10.00 Non-refundable processing fee, $5.00 Endorsement Fee).

10. What is the foreclosure process and will the county handle the foreclosure process for a fee? There are two kinds of foreclosures, Judicial and Treasurer's deed. The Judicial foreclosure is handled by an attorney through the courts after three years from the original date of sale, making the taxes a total of five years delinquent. The fee for Judicial foreclosures is up to the attorney and the courts. The Treasurer's deed is handled through our office after five years from the original date of sale, making the taxes a total of seven year's delinquent; the fee is approximately $324.00-$424.00 (subject to change at any time). A.R.S. 42-18251 states tax liens purchased on a 1997 or later year must be foreclosed through the judicial system only. Treasurer's deed will not apply to 1997 or later delinquent taxes. Tax Liens on 1996 and prior must be applied for by December 31, 2003.

11. What happens to the liens that are not sold at the tax lien auction? Can they be purchased over-the-counter directly from the county? Can I purchase them now? Tax liens can be purchased over-the-counter directly from our office every month except for February, October, November 1-8 and April 23 – May 8.

12. Do you allow investors to invest in tax lien certificates without attending the auction via mail or telephone or fax? Can I send a representative to the sale to bid for me? You must be present at the auction in order to purchase from the auction. A representative can bid for you at the auction, but must have a completed W-9 Form. We do sell tax liens by mail, telephone or fax during the year as listed above in question 11.

13. Would you please send me a current list of tax lien certificates available and place me on your mailing list if you have one. If there is a charge for the list please notify me and I will be happy to send the proper fee. The list we have is $30.00. It must be paid for in advance by cashier's check or money order before we will mail it out. The list includes a parcel number, the owner's name and the approximate amount of taxes due on the property. We do not have a mailing list. You may also view the list on the Internet at two different locations: www.publicnoticeads.com/az and www.co.yuma.az.us/treas/delinquent.htm.

14. Would you please forward me a copy of the statutes regarding tax sales in your jurisdiction? The Arizona Revised Statutes can be found at www.azleg.state.az.us. The link to the statutes is in the upper right hand corner of the homepage.

(2) Tax Lien List
http://www.co.yuma.az.us/treas/delinquentlist.htm

Tax lien list as of February 20, 2004.

YUMA COUNTY AUCTIONS
http://www.co.yuma.az.us/bos/auctions.htm

For More Information Contact:
Dunia Federico
Administrative Assistant
Yuma County
Board of Supervisors
198 S Main Street, Yuma, AZ 85364
Tel: 928-373-1102
FAX: 928-373-1120
Internet: dufe@admin.co.yuma.az.us
Webmaster: cijo@admin.co.yuma.az.us

ARIZONA NEWSPAPERS
http://www.publicnoticeads.com/az

The newspapers of Arizona, through its Arizona Newspapers Association, joined together to post the public notices from each edition to this central Internet database at the same time they are published.

Tax Lien Sales: No

Tax Deed Sales: Yes

Rating: Four Stars (****) – probably one of the best states for tax deed sales.

Interest Rate: No interest rate; state only has tax deed sales.

Sale Period:
Depends on the county. Tax deed sales can be as often as three times per year. Call 1-501-324-9222 to find out when sales will be held. Anyone can be placed on a mailing list that displays list of available properties by contacting the Commissioner of State Lands. Catalog is free. Catalog lists properties for sale, and minimum bid amounts (equal to assessed land value, taxes due and any other fees).

Redemption Period: Properties can be purchased at tax deed sales for immediate ownership.

Bidding Process:
At tax deed sales, all auctions are by competitive bid. Winning bidder pays highest value for property. Bids can be in person at auction or by mail. If bidding by mail, Commissioner of Lands must receive entire bid amount seven days prior to the auction. Properties not sold at auction are offered for 90 days after the sale. Properties that did not sell are broken into three categories: S-2 Land Sales (only up for one year), S-3 Land Sales (offered for more than one year) and S-4 Land Sales (more than two years has elapsed since first offered at auction) S-4 Land Sales are negotiable, since the county wants to get rid of these properties. The minimum bid is generally set at 20 percent of the assessed value. The bidder is also responsible for back taxes and fees.

State-Specific Information:

Laws Governing the Redemption and Sale of Tax Delinquent Land

§26-37-101. Transfer of tax-delinquent lands.
(a) (1) All lands upon which the taxes have not been paid for two (1) years following the date the taxes were due, October 10, shall be forfeited to the State of Arkansas and transmitted by certification to the Commissioner of State Lands for collection or sale.
(2) No tax-delinquent lands shall be sold at the county level.
(b) The county collector shall hold all tax delinquent lands in the county for two (2) years after the date of delinquency, and if not redeemed by the certification date, which shall be no later than July 1 of the following year, the collector shall transmit it to the state after notice as provided in this chapter indicating all, taxes, penalties, interest, and costs due and the name and last known address of the owner of record of the tax-delinquent land.
(c) Upon receipt of the certification, title to the tax delinquent lands shall vest in the State of Arkansas in care of the Commissioner of State Lands.

Publisher's Notes. Acts 1983, No. 626, § 2, as amended by Acts 1987, No. 814, § 5, provided that on December 31, 1985, the delinquent real property tax records of the county clerks should be transferred to the collectors, unless the clerks and collectors, by agreement, transferred such duties and responsibilities prior to that date, and that it would be the responsibility of the clerks to maintain said tax records until their duties and responsibilities are transferred to their respective collectors.

Acts 1983, No. 626, § 7, as amended by Acts 1985, No. 179, § 5, and Acts 1987, No. 814, § 6, provided that "(a) except as provided in subsection (b) of this section [Acts 1987, No. 814, § 6(b)], all tax delinquent land then held by the Commissioner of State Lands should be disposed of according to the provisions of Act 626 of 1983, as amended. For the purposes of Act 626 of 1983, as amended, the word 'taxes' should mean ad valorem taxes on real estate and the annual installments of the assessments of benefits levied by municipal improvements districts formed in second class cities under Act 84 of 1981, as amended, § 14-88-101 et seq., or Act 64 of 1929, as amended, § 14-88-203 et seq., for the sole purpose of acquiring, constructing, operating, or maintaining a recreational facility. The term 'tax delinquent land' when used in Act 626 of 1983, as amended, should mean all land upon which the ad valorem property taxes have not been paid and the term should also include land subject to a lien for nonpayment of annual installments of the assessments of benefits levied by municipal recreation improvement districts created pursuant to §14-88-201 et seq., or § 14-88-203 et seq.

"(b) All tax delinquent land which has been or will be forfeited to the State and conveyed to the Commissioner of State Lands by certification but which remains neither sold nor redeemed two (2) years from the date of the applicable public auction conducted in accordance with the provisions of Act 626 of 1983, as amended, may not be subject to the provisions of Act 626 of 1983, as amended, or any other Act relating to the sale of land by the Commissioner at public sales or by negotiation for whatever price the Commissioner determines to be in the best interest of the State and its local taxing units."

"(c) The Commissioner of State Lands shall have the authority to promulgate such rules and regulations as may be necessary to effectively carry out the provisions of Act 626 of 1983, as amended, [and,] upon adoption, such rules and regulations shall have the full force and effect of law."

§26-37-102. Publication of notice – Fee.
(a) The county collector in each county shall, not less than thirty (30) days nor more than forty (40) days prior to the certification of the land, cause to be published in a newspaper of general circulation in the county:
(1) A list of real property not previously redeemed;
(2) The names of the owners of record;
(3) The amount of the taxes, penalties, interest, and cost necessary to be paid to redeem the property;
(4) The date upon which such period of redemption expires; and
(5) Notice that unless the property is redeemed prior to the expiration of the period of redemption, the lands will be forfeited to the state.
(b) Fees for the publication shall be the same as set forth in § 26-37-108.

§26-37-103. Verification by county assessor.
(a) Prior to certification to the Commissioner of State Lands, the county assessor shall:
(1) Verify the assessment to establish value on all parcels to be certified;
(2) Verify the name and last known address of the owner of record of the tax-delinquent land; and
(3) Determine whether the tax-delinquent land exists;
(b) If the land is found to be nonexistent, the county assessor shall remove the delinquent entry from the assessment rolls.
(c) No tax-delinquent lands shall be certified to the Commissioner of State Lands without the assessor's verification.

§26-37-104. Cost of notices.
All costs of notice shall be added to the costs to be collected from the purchaser or redeemer.

§26-37-105. Collection fee.
The Commissioner shall charge a twenty-five dollar ($25.00) collection fee against each parcel of tax delinquent land which has been certified to his office.

§26-37-201. Publication of notice – Fee.
(a) The Commissioner of State Lands shall publish a notice of sale of land upon which the ad valorem property taxes have not been paid in a newspaper having general circulation in the county wherein the land is located. The publication fee for the notice shall be the same as set forth in § 26-37-108.
(b) The notice shall:
(1) Contain the assessed value of the land;
(2) Contain the amount of taxes, interest, penalties, and other costs due on the land;
(3) Contain the legal description of the land;
(4) Contain a list of all recorded liens against the land that are known to the Commissioner of State Lands; and
(5) Indicate that the land will be sold to the highest bidder if the bid is equal to at least the assessed value of the land as certified to the Commissioner of State Lands.
(c) The highest bidder shall pay all taxes, interest, penalties, and other costs. Thereafter, all interested parties known to the Commissioner and not previously notified shall receive notice by mail of the sale from the Commissioner.

§26-37-202. Procedure to sell.
(a) Bidders may bid at the sale or mail their bid to the office of the Commissioner of State Lands. Bids shall be delivered at the appropriate place before the deadline established in the notice of sale.
(b) If no one bids at least the assessed value, the Commissioner may negotiate a sale. All negotiated sales shall have approval of the Attorney General of the State of Arkansas.
(c) The Commissioner shall conduct tax-delinquent sales in the county wherein the land is located, unless the Commissioner determines there are not enough parcels of land to justify a sale in one (1) county only. In that case, the Commissioner may hold a tax-delinquent land sale in one (1) location and thereat sell land located in more than one (1) county if the counties wherein the lands are located are adjoining counties.
(d) The sales shall be conducted on the dates specified in the notices required by this subchapter.
(e) Unless the owners of record tender all taxes, penalties, interest, and costs due within thirty (30) days after the date of sale, a limited warranty deed will be issued by the Commissioner to the purchaser.

§26-37-203. Conveyance to purchaser – Contest.
(a) If the tax-delinquent land is not redeemed within the thirty-day period, the Commissioner of State Lands shall issue a limited warranty deed to the land.
(b)(1) All actions to contest the validity of the conveyance shall be brought within two (2) years after the date of the conveyance or thereafter be barred, except as to causes of actions by persons suffering a mental incapacity, minority, or serving in the United States armed forces during time of war during the two-year period.
(2) Those persons shall not be allowed to contest the validity of the conveyance after the expiration of two (2) years after the disability is removed or the person reaches majority or the person is released from active duty with the armed forces.
(c) No deed issued after January 1, 1987, by the Commissioner of State Lands shall be void or voidable on the ground that the county did not strictly comply with the laws governing tax-

delinquent land, provided that prior to the issuance of the deed, the Commissioner of State Lands complied with the laws governing the disposition of tax-delinquent land.

(d) Nothing in this section shall prevent any taxpayer from attacking a deed issued by the Commissioner of State Lands on the ground that taxes have actually been paid.

§26-37-204. Sales set aside.

(a) In the event the sale is set aside by legal action or if the land is proven to be nonexistent or double assessed, the purchaser shall be entitled to reimbursement of moneys paid.

(b) The Commissioner of State Lands shall have the authority to set aside any sale. In the event the Commissioner determines that a sale shall be set aside, the purchaser may be entitled to reimbursement of moneys paid to the Commissioner of State Lands.

(c) In cases where the sales may be set aside by the Commissioner of State Lands or by legal action by the record owner or the heirs or assigns of the record owner, the record owner or the heirs or assigns of the record owner shall pay all back taxes, penalties, interest, and costs charged against the land.

§26-37-205. Distribution of funds.

(a) All moneys collected by the Commissioner of State Lands from the sale or redemption of tax delinquent lands shall be distributed as follows:

(1) First, to the Commissioner of State Lands, the penalties, the collection fees, sale costs, and other costs as prescribed by law;

(2) Second, an amount to each county equal to the taxes due plus interest and costs to the county as certified by the county tax collector, which amount shall be held in an escrow fund administered by the Commissioner and remitted to the counties within one calendar year of their receipt by the Commissioner;

(3) Third, the remainder, if any, shall be placed in another escrow fund administered by the Commissioner.

(b) If no actions are brought within two (2) years after the date of conveyance as provided in 26-37-202, the remaining funds, if any, shall be distributed by the Commissioner as follows:

(1) To former owners of the tax delinquent land. Such former owners must file an application with the Commissioner requesting the release of any remaining funds. The application shall be provided by the Commissioner of State Lands and shall require proof of ownership. In addition, the application may require other information the Commissioner may deem necessary to obtain prior to the release of said funds. In the event of multiple claims of ownership or controversy regarding the release of such funds, it shall be the responsibility of the parties seeking release of the funds to resolve such controversy.

(2) The funds shall be held in escrow for five (5) more years and at the end of such five (5) year period, If the funds have not been distributed, the escrow funds shall escheat to the county wherein the property is located.

(c) All funds distributed to each county by the Commissioner of State Lands from the redemption or sale of tax-delinquent lands, including any interest and costs, are to be distributed to the applicable taxing units where the delinquent land is located within the county in the manner and proportion that the taxes would have been distributed if they had been collected in the year due.

(d) All funds received by a county from the redemption of tax-delinquent land at the county level, including any penalty, interest, and costs, are to be distributed to the applicable taxing units where the delinquent land is located within the county in the manner and proportion that the taxes would have been distributed if they had been collected in the year due.

§26-37-301. Notice to owner.

(a) Subsequent to receiving tax delinquent land, the Commissioner of State Lands shall notify the owner at the owner's last known address by certified mail of the owner's right to redeem by paying all taxes, penalties, interest and costs, including the cost of the notice. Further, all interested parties known to the Commission shall receive notice of the sale in like manner from the Commissioner of State Lands.

(b) The notice to the owner/interested party shall also indicate that the tax delinquent land will be sold if not redeemed prior to the date of sale. The notice shall also indicate the sale date, and that date shall be no earlier than two (2) years after the land is certified to the Commissioner.

(c) For the purposes of this section, the terms "owner" and "interested parties" shall mean any person, firm, corporation, or partnership holding title to or interest in the property by virtue of a recorded instrument at the time of certification to the Commissioner of State Lands.

(d) The Commissioner of State Lands shall not be required to notify, by certified mail or by any other means, any person, firm, corporation, or partnership whose title to or interest in the property is obtained subsequent to certification to the Commissioner of State Lands.

§26-37-302. Payment required.

(a) In order to redeem, whether with the county collector or the Commissioner of State Lands, and in order to purchase at the Commissioner's sale, the redeemer/purchaser of tax-delinquent land shall pay all delinquent taxes, plus:

(1) ten percent (10%) simple interest for each year of delinquency;

(2) A ten percent (10%) penalty for each year of the delinquency; and

(3) The costs incurred by the county and the Commissioner of State Lands.

(b) The penalties and interest shall accrue beginning on October 11 in the year of delinquency.

§26-37-303. Redemption deed.

(a) If the owner redeems the tax-delinquent land, the Commissioner of State Lands shall issue a redemption deed and record it in the county wherein the land is located.

(b) The fee for the redemption deed and the fee for recording the deed shall be borne by the owner.

More Arkansas Information

Arkansas is possibly the best tax deed state. Sales occur in all counties once per year, but the sales are staggered so that every quarter at least 5 or 10 counties have a tax deed sale. The state is also heavily involved in the sales, and their website (http://www.state.ar.us/land/land.html) is excellent. You can either get a list of the properties available at the sale from the website, or write/call using the contact information below to get a hard copy mailed to you free of charge:

Mark Wilcox, Commissioner of State Lands
109 State Capitol, Little Rock, AR 72201-1003
Phone: (501) 324-9222, Fax: (501) 324-9421, Email: land@aristotle.net

The properties are divided into three categories based on how long they have been in delinquency:

- Class 1 properties have been in delinquency for 4 years and the owner has 2 years left to redeem.
- Class 2 properties have been in delinquency for 5 years and the owner has 1 year left to redeem.
- Class 3 properties have been in delinquency for 6 years and the owner has no time left to redeem these properties. The sale prices for these properties are negotiable, because the state wants to start collecting taxes on these properties as soon as possible.

Links for All Arkansas Counties: Provided on CD.

Tax Lien Sales: Yes – authorized to conduct tax lien sales, but no sales yet.

Tax Deed Sales: Yes

Rating: Four Stars (****)

Interest Rate: 18% (authorized, but no tax lien sales yet)

Sale Period: Tax deed sales occur year round.

Redemption Period: No counties have elected to have tax lien sales yet.

Bidding Process:
For tax deed sales, the process varies by county. Most counties offer maps showing properties that can be obtained from the county treasurer. In most counties, payment can be made by cashier's check or credit card.

State-Specific Information:
Although California is authorized to have tax lien sales, no county has had a sale yet. California does conduct a great number of tax deed sales (more than 10,000 individual parcels are sold at tax deed sales every year). California is probably one of the best tax deed sale states. However, in most cases you will need substantial capital to bid on properties since property values are so high.

Links for All California Counties: Provided on CD.

Detailed County-Specific Information:

County Assessors

County	Phone & FAX Numbers	County Assessor	Office Address	Board Member
Alameda	(510) 272-3755, FAX (510) 272-3803	Ron Thomson	1221 Oak Street Room 145 Oakland 94612-4288	Migden
Alpine	(530) 694-2283, FAX (530) 694-2491	Dave Peets	Courthouse, 99 Water Street P.O. Box 155 Markleeville 96120-0155	Leonard
Amador	(209) 223-6351, FAX (209) 223-6721	James Rooney	500 Argonaut Lane Jackson 95642	Leonard
Butte	(530) 538-7721, FAX (530) 538-7991	Kenneth Reimers	25 County Center Drive Oroville 95965-3382	Leonard
Calaveras	(209) 754-6356, FAX (209) 754-6739	Grant Metzger, Jr.	Government Center 891 Mountain Ranch Road San Andreas 95249-9709	Leonard
Colusa	(530) 458-0450, FAX (530) 458-0461	E. Dan O'Connell	Courthouse 547 Market Street Colusa 95932-2452	Migden

Contra Costa	(925) 313-7500, **FAX** (925) 313-7660	Gus Kramer	2530 Arnold Drive Suite 400 Martinez 94553-4359	Migden
Del Norte	(707) 464-7200, **FAX** (707) 464-3115	Gerald Cochran	981 H Street Suite 120 Crescent City 95531-3415	Migden
El Dorado	(530) 621-5719, **FAX** (530) 642-8148	Tim Holcomb	360 Fair Lane Placerville 95667-4103	Leonard
Fresno	(559) 488-3514, **FAX** (559) 488-6774	Robert Werner	2281 Tulare Street Suite 201 P.O. Box 1146 Fresno 93715-1146	Leonard
Glenn	(530) 934-6402, **FAX** (530) 934-6571	Vince Minto	516 West Sycamore Street 2nd Floor Willows 95988	Leonard
Humboldt	(707) 445-7276, **FAX** (707) 445-7410	Linda Hill	Courthouse 825 Fifth Street, Room 300 Eureka 95501-1153	Migden
Imperial	(760) 482-4244, **FAX** (760) 482-4243	Jose Rodriguez, Jr.	940 West Main Street Suite 115 El Centro 92243-2874	Parrish
Inyo	(760) 878-0302, **FAX** (760) 878-0307	Thomas Lanshaw	Courthouse 168 North Edwards P.O. Box J Independence 93526-0609	Leonard
Kern	(661) 868-3485, **FAX** (661) 868-3209	James Fitch	1115 Truxtun Avenue 3rd Floor Bakersfield 93301-4617	Leonard
Kings	(559) 582-3211, **FAX** (559) 582-2794	George Misner	County Government Center 1400 West Lacey Boulevard Hanford 93230-5997	Leonard
Lake	(707) 263-2302, **FAX** (707) 263-3703	Doug Wacker	255 North Forbes Street Lakeport 95453-5997	Migden
Lassen	(530) 251-8241, **FAX** (530) 251-8245	Kenneth Bunch	220 South Lassen Street Suite 4 Susanville 96130-4324	Leonard
Los Angeles	(213) 974-3211, **FAX** (213) 617-2348	Rick Auerbach	500 West Temple Street Room 320 Los Angeles 90012-2770	Chiang/ Leonard/ Parrish
Madera	(559) 675-7710, **FAX** (559) 675-7654	Thomas Kidwell	209 West Yosemite Avenue Madera 93637-3534	Leonard
Marin	(415) 499-7215, **FAX** (415) 499-6542	Joan Thayer	3501 Civic Center Drive Room 208 P.O. Box C San Rafael 94913-3902	Migden
Mariposa	(209) 966-2332, **FAX** (209) 966-6496	Robert Lowrimore	4982 10th Street P.O. Box 35 Mariposa 95338-0035	Leonard
Mendocino	(707) 463-4311, **FAX** (707) 463-6597	Marsha Wharff	501 Low Gap Road Room 1040 Ukiah 95482	Migden
Merced	(209) 385-7631, **FAX** (209) 725-3956	David Cardella	2222 M Street Merced 95340-3780	Leonard

Modoc	(530) 233-6218, **FAX** (530) 233-6237	Josephine Johnson	204 South Court Street Room 106 Alturas 96101-4064	Leonard
Mono	(760) 932-5510, **FAX** (760) 932-5511	R. Glenn Barnes	25 Bryant Street P.O. Box 456 Bridgeport 93517-0456	Leonard
Monterey	(831) 755-5035, **FAX** (831) 755-5435	Stephen Vagnini	240 Church Street Room 202 P.O. Box 570 Salinas 93902-0570	Migden
Napa	(707) 253-4467, **FAX** (707) 253-6171	John Tuteur	1127 First Street Room 128 Napa 94559-2931	Migden
Nevada	(530) 265-1232, **FAX** (530) 470-2532	Dale Flippin	950 Maidu Avenue Nevada City 95959-8600	Leonard
Orange	(714) 834-2727, **FAX** (714) 558-0681	Webster Guillory	12 Civic Center Plaza 630 N. Broadway, Room 142 Santa Ana 92702-0149	Parrish
Placer	(530) 889-4300, **FAX** (530) 889-4305	Bruce Dear	DeWitt Center 2980 Richardson Drive Auburn 95603-2640	Leonard
Plumas	(530) 283-6380, **FAX** (530) 283-0946	Charles Leonhardt	520 Main Street Room 205 Quincy 95971-9114	Leonard
Riverside	(909) 955-6250, **FAX** (909) 955-6238	Gary Orso	4080 Lemon Street P.O. Box 12004 Riverside 92502-2204	Parrish
Sacramento	(916) 875-0760, **FAX** (916) 875-0765	Kenneth Stieger	3701 Power Inn Road Suite 3000 Sacramento 95826-4329	Leonard
San Benito	(831) 636-4030, **FAX** (831) 636-4033	Arnold Fontes	440 Fifth Street Room 108 Hollister 95023-3893	Migden
San Bernardino	(909) 387-6730, **FAX** (909) 387-6781	Donald Williamson	172 West Third Street San Bernardino 92415-0310	Leonard/Parrish
San Diego	(619) 531-5507, **FAX** (619) 557-4056	Gregory Smith	1600 Pacific Highway Room 110 San Diego 92101-2480	Parrish
San Francisco	(415) 531-5596, **FAX** (415) 554-7151	Mabel Teng	1 Drive Carlton B. Goodlett Place Room 190 San Francisco 94102-4698	Migden
San Joaquin	(209) 468-2630, **FAX** (209) 468-0422	Gary Freeman	24 South Hunter Street Room 303 Stockton 95202-3273	Leonard
San Luis Obispo	(805) 781-5643, **FAX** (805) 781-5641	Tom Bordonaro	County Government Center 1050 Monterey Street Room 100 San Luis Obispo 93408-2070	Migden
San Mateo	(650) 363-4500, **FAX** (650) 363-1903	Warren Slocum	555 County Center 1st Floor Redwood City 94063-1654	Migden
Santa Barbara	(805) 568-2550, **FAX** (805) 568-3247	Joseph Holland	105 East Anapamu Street Room 204 P.O. Box 159 Santa Barbara 93101-0159	Leonard/Migden

Santa Clara	(408) 299-5570, **FAX** (408) 297-9526	Lawrence Stone	70 West Hedding Street East Wing San Jose 95110-1705	Migden
Santa Cruz	(831) 454-2002, **FAX** (831) 454-2495	Gary Hazelton	Courthouse 701 Ocean Street Room 130 Santa Cruz 95060-4073	Migden
Shasta	(530) 225-3600, **FAX** (530) 225-5673	Cris Andrews	Courthouse 1500 Court Street Room 115 Redding 96001-1694	Leonard
Sierra	(530) 289-3283, **FAX** (530) 289-2801	William Copren	100 Courthouse Square P.O. Box 8 Downieville 95936-0008	Leonard
Siskiyou	(530) 842-8036, **FAX** (530) 842-8059	Mike Mallory	311 Fourth Street Room 108 Yreka 96097-2984	Leonard
Solano	(707) 421-6200, **FAX** (707) 421-6209	Skip Thomson	600 Texas Street Fairfield 94533-6386	Migden
Sonoma	(707) 565-1888, **FAX** (707) 565-1364	Eeve Lewis	585 Fiscal Drive Room 104F Santa Rosa 95403-2872	Migden
Stanislaus	(209) 525-6461, **FAX** (209) 525-6586	Doug Harms	1010 10th Street Suite 2400 Modesto 95354-0847	Leonard
Sutter	(530) 822-7160, **FAX** (530) 822-7198	Michael Strong	212 Bridge Street P.O. Box 1555 Yuba City 95992-1555	Leonard
Tehama	(530) 527-5931, **FAX** (530) 529-4019	Mark Colombo	444 Oak Street, # B P.O. Box 428 Red Bluff 96080-0428	Leonard
Trinity	(530) 623-1257, **FAX** (530) 623-8398	Dero Forslund	101 Court Street P.O. Box 1255 Weaverville 96093-1255	Migden
Tulare	(559) 733-6361, **FAX** (559) 737-4468	Gregory Hardcastle	221 S. Mooney Boulevard Room 102-E Visalia 93291-4593	Leonard
Tuolumne	(209) 533-5535, **FAX** (209) 533-5674	David Wynne	2 South Green Street Sonora 95370	Leonard
Ventura	(805) 654-2181, **FAX** (805) 645-1305	Dan Goodwin	800 South Victoria Avenue Ventura 93009-1270	Leonard
Yolo	(530) 666-8135, **FAX** (530) 666-8213	Dick Fisher	625 Court Street Room 104 Woodland 95695-3448	Migden
Yuba	(530) 741-6221, **FAX** (530) 741-6051	David Brown	935 14th Street Marysville 95901-4188	Leonard

ALAMEDA COUNTY, CALIFORNIA
http://www.co.alameda.ca.us

TREASURER – TAX COLLECTOR'S OFFICE
http://www.co.alameda.ca.us/treasurer

Treasurer Donald White

(1) Property Taxes, Frequently Asked Questions
http://www.co.alameda.ca.us/treasurer/faqprop.shtml

Property delinquent for the first year shall be declared defaulted for non-payment of taxes. After 5 years, the Tax Collector has the power to sell tax-defaulted property that is not redeemed.

(2) Tax Collection
http://www.co.alameda.ca.us/treasurer/taxcoll.shtml

Prior Year Secured Tax Defaulted Property

The Tax Collector may offer Tax-Defaulted property, where the taxes remain unpaid for five years or more, for sale through a public auction. This unit provides the following prior year tax services:

- publication of tax defaulted property
- auction sales of tax defaulted property
- sales of tax defaulted property to public agencies
- sealed bid sales of tax defaulted property.

(3) Contact Information
http://www.co.alameda.ca.us/treasurer/taxphone.shtml

1221 Oak Street, Room 131
Oakland, California 94612-4685
phone = 510-272-6800, Fax = 510-272-3856

Treasurer-Tax Collector - Donald R. White
Phone = 510-272-6803, Fax = 510-272-3856

Prior Year Secured Tax Defaulted Property
Phone = 510-272-6800, Fax = 510-272-6807

CONTRA COSTA COUNTY, CALIFORNIA
http://www.co.contra-costa.ca.us

TREASURER-TAX COLLECTOR'S OFFICE
From http://www.co.contra-costa.ca.us, click on "Departments" at top of page, and then on "Treasurer-Tax Collector"

William Pollacek, Treasurer-Tax Collector
County Finance Building
625 Court Street, Rooms 100 and 102
P.O. Box 631
Martinez, CA 94553
Email: Taxinfo@tax.co.contra-costa.ca.us

Tax Defaulted Land Auction is Scheduled for Wednesday, February 25, 2004.

(1) Public Auction

from Treasurer-Tax Collector home page, click on "Services" and then on "Public Auction"

(1a) Public Auction General Information

from Treasurer-Tax Collector home page, click on "Services," then on "Public Auction" and then on "General Information"

The sale of "Tax Defaulted Property Subject to Power of Sale" is conducted by the Contra Costa County Treasurer-Tax Collector pursuant to the provisions of the Revenue and Taxation Code and written authorization of the Board of Supervisors.

(1b) Public Auction Frequently Asked Questions

from Treasurer-Tax Collector home page, click on "Services," then on "Public Auction" and then on "FAQ's"

How can I obtain a list of properties to be offered at the tax sale? A list of properties to be offered for sale is available from the Office of the Treasurer Tax Collector at the beginning of January. Remember, because property owners have the right to redeem their property prior to the sale, the final list of parcels to be offered for sale will not be available until the day of the sale. **AUCTION LIST SALES ARE FINAL.** Updated information on properties that remain in the sale is available at the Tax Collector's office or by visiting our web site at (TBD).

Can I mail in or submit a sealed bid for a property in the public auction sale? No. This is an oral public auction requiring your presence, or that of your representative, to verbally bid upon the properties.

Can I obtain a property available at the public auction tax sale by paying the delinquent taxes thereon prior to the tentative tax sale date? No. Legal title to tax-defaulted property subject to power of sale can be obtained through the Treasurer and Tax Collector only by being the successful bidder at the tax sale.

How do I find or see a property I'd like to bid on at the tax sale? Vacant ("unimproved") land (which accounts for most property offered at our tax sales) usually has no address and therefore its approximate geographic location can be determined through the use of County Assessor plat maps. Exact boundary lines of a property can be determined only by a survey of the property initiated at the purchaser's expense. "Improved" properties frequently (but not always) will bear a "situs" (street) address, making it quite simple to assess the location. A "situs" (street) address does not mean there are improvements on the property or that the improvements are on the sale.

Do all properties with an address have a home on them? No! An address does not mean there is or was a structure on the property. It does not guarantee that the address shown in the tax sale list is correct or that the structure is part of the sale.

How soon can I take possession of a property after my purchase at the tax sale? The successful bidder may take possession of a property after the Tax Deed to Purchaser has been recorded.

How is the minimum bid on a tax sale property determined? State law dictates that the minimum bid for property offered at a public auction tax sale be an amount not less than the total amount necessary to redeem the tax default, plus cost. Except pursuant to Section 3698.5(c) of the California Revenue and Taxation Code, when property interests have been offered at a previous sale and no acceptable bids were received, the Tax Collector may offer that property or property interest at a minimum bid that is less than the amount of the tax default, plus cost.

Is a tax sale publicly advertised? Yes. State law dictates that the event of a tax sale must be published three (3) times in successive seven (7) day intervals before the tax sale date in a newspaper, or newspapers of general circulation within Contra Costa County. All parcels in the next tax sale will be advertised in various local newspapers, the first publication date being not less than twenty-one (21) days prior to the date of the sale.

When does the right of redemption on a tax-defaulted parcel subject to the power to sell cease?
The right of redemption on a tax-defaulted parcel subject to the Tax Collector's power to sell ceases at the close of business on the last business day prior to the date of sale. There is no extended right of redemption in the State of California as does exist in some others states.

How soon may I begin improvement of the property after my purchase? There is a one (1) year period of time, after the date the tax deed is executed, that a proceeding based on alleged invalidity or irregularity can be commenced, pursuant to Section 3725 of the California Revenue and Taxation Code.

What happens to the properties that do not sell at the auction? Can tax sale properties be purchased directly from the County? If no acceptable bids are received for a property, it will be offered again at intervals of no more than six years until the property is sold, pursuant to Section 3692 of the California Revenue and Taxation Code. Legal title to tax-defaulted property subject to power of sale can be obtained through the Treasurer-Tax Collector only by being the successful bidder at the tax sale. Additionally, pursuant to Section 3698.5(c) of said code, the Tax Collector may re-offer the property at any time for a minimum bid that is set at the discretion of the Tax Collector and approved by the County Board of Supervisors.

Do liens or encumbrances on Tax Sale properties transfer to the new owner through a Tax sale property purchase? Chapter 7, Section 3712 of the California Revenue and Taxation Code states: "The deed conveys title to the purchaser free of all encumbrances of any kind existing before the sale, except:

(a) Any lien for installments of taxes and special assessments, which installments will become payable upon the secured roll after the time of sale.
(b) The lien for taxes or assessments or other rights of any taxing agency which does not consent to the sale under this chapter.
(c) Liens for special assessments levied upon the property conveyed which were, at the time of the sale under this chapter, not included in the amount necessary to redeem the tax-defaulted property, and, where a taxing agency which collects its own taxes has consented to the sale under this chapter, not included in the amount required to redeem from sale to the taxing agency.
(d) Easements constituting servitude upon or burdens to the property; water rights, the record title to which is held separately from the title to the property; and restrictions of record.
(e) Unaccepted, recorded, irrevocable offers of dedication of the property to the public or a public entity for a public purpose, and recorded options of any taxing agency to purchase the property or any interest therein for a public purpose.
(f) Unpaid assessments under the Improvement Bond Act of 1915 (Division 10 [commencing with Section 8500] of the Streets and Highways Code) which are not satisfied as a result of the sale proceeds being applied pursuant to Chapter 1.3 (commencing with Section 4671) Part 8.
(g) Any federal Internal Revenue Service liens which, pursuant to provisions of federal law, are not discharged by the sale, even though the tax collector has provided proper notice to the Internal Revenue Service before that date.
(h) Unpaid special taxes under the Mello-Roos Community Facilities Act of 1982 (Chapter 2.5 [commencing with Section 53311] of Part 1 of Division 2 of Title 5 of the Government Code) that are not satisfied as a result of the sale proceeds being applied pursuant to Chapter 1.3 (commencing with Section 4671) of Part 8.

Note: A title search initiated at the prospective purchaser(s)' expense should reveal any liens or encumbrances on a property in the tax sale.

What guarantees do I have that the property is in good condition and can be used for my purposes? The sale of these properties should not, in any way, be equated to real estate sales by licensed salespeople, brokers or realtors. The Treasurer-Tax Collector cannot guarantee the condition of the property nor assume any responsibility for conformance to codes, permits or zoning ordinances. The burden is on the purchaser to thoroughly research, before the sale, any matters relevant to his or her decision to purchase, rather than on the county, whose sole interest is the recovery of back taxes. It is also recommended that bidders consult with the zoning and planning departments of any city within which a particular parcel lies.

What are the conditions of payment for property at the Tax Sale? Property purchased for less than $50,000 must be PAID FOR IN FULL at the tax sale. The minimum bid must be tendered at time of sale in CASH, CASHIER'S CHECK OR BANK MONEY ORDERS payable to the Contra Costa County Tax Collector. Cash and personal checks will be accepted for amounts over the minimum bid.

If the purchase price is $50,000.00 or greater, a credit transaction will be accepted. The purchaser must deposit $5,000.00 or ten percent (10%) of the purchase price, whichever is greater; the $5,000.00 or ten percent payment must be in cash, cashier's check, or money order, the remainder may be paid with a personal check.

The transaction MUST be completed with 90 days. Failure to complete the transaction in full and on time will result in forfeiture of all deposits.

Purchasers of property within the cities of Richmond and San Pablo must also pay a City Transfer Tax in addition to the Documentary Transfer Tax. The rate for this city tax is $7.00 per $1,000.00 of the purchase price.

Purchasers of property within the cities of Richmond, San Pablo, and El Cerrito must also pay a City Transfer Tax in addition to the Documentary Transfer Tax. The rate for this city tax is $7.00 per $1,000.00 of the purchase price.

How can I determine what use I can make of a Tax Sale property before I purchase it? Consult the zoning and planning departments of any city within which a property lies or the County's Building Inspection Department for property in unincorporated areas regarding use of the parcel. The County Recorder's records should be consulted for any recorded easements on a property.

How do I obtain information on Tax Lien Certificate Sales? The Contra Costa County Treasurer-Tax Collector does NOT offer tax lien certificates.

How can I get parcel maps of the properties? Copies of the parcel maps can be purchased from the county Assessor. The Tax Collector has a limited number of sets of maps for public viewing at the office. Please remember to investigate before you purchase. All sales are final.

Should the successful purchaser desire a survey of the property, it will be at the purchaser's own initiative and expense. No warranty is made by the County, either expressed or implied, relative to the usability, the ground location, or property lines of the properties. The exact location, desirability, and usefulness of the properties must be determined by the prospective purchaser.

The County assumes no liability for any other possible liens, encumbrances or easements, recorded or not recorded. When property is sold at a tax sale on which the IRS holds a tax lien, the United States has the right of redemption for 120 days from the date of such sale (26 USC Sec. 3712[g] and 7425[d]). The IRS will pay the actual amount paid for the property by the bidder, plus interest at 6% per annum from the date of sale, plus the expenses of sale that exceed any income received from the property.

(1c) Public Auction Bidder Registration Information and Form
from Treasurer-Tax Collector home page, click on "Services," then on "Public Auction" and then on "Registration Form (pdf)"
(http://www.co.contra-costa.ca.us/depart/tax/BidderRegistration.pdf)

(1d) Public Auction – Remaining Items
from Treasurer-Tax Collector home page, click on "Services," then on "Public Auction" and then on "Remaining Items"

ROGUE INVESTOR NOTE: public auction remaining items list saved on CD:
USA Tax Lien Info/California/contra_costa_co_CA/sale_list.htm

(1e) Notice of Power to Sell
from Treasurer-Tax Collector home page, click on "Services," then on "Public Auction" and then on "Notice of Power to Sell"

(2) Contact Information
from Treasurer-Tax Collector home page, click on "About" and then on "Contact Information"

County Finance Building
625 Court Street, Room 100
Martinez, CA

Mailing Address
P.O. Box 631
Martinez, CA 94553-0063

Phone: (925) 646-4122 for all secured, unsecured and supplemental taxes

---

DEL NORTE COUNTY, CALIFORNIA
http://www.co.del-norte.ca.us

TREASURER/TAX COLLECTOR'S OFFICE
from http://www.co.del-norte.ca.us, click on "Departments" and then on "Treasurer-Tax Collector"

Dawn Langston, Treasurer/Tax Collector (dlangston@co.del-norte.ca.us)
Lynn Mitchell, Assistant Treasurer/Tax Collector (lmitchell@co.del-norte.ca.us)

981 H Street, Suite 150
Crescent City, CA 95531
Phone: (707) 464-7283; FAX: (707) 464-7247

(1) PUBLIC INTERNET AUCTION INFORMATION FOR 2004
from the Treasurer/Tax Collector's home page, click on "Tax Sale"

The Del Norte County Tax Collector will hold a public Internet auction of Tax-Defaulted Properties on May 5-6, 2004. The auction will be held on the Internet over a two-day period giving more people the opportunity to bid. Properties to be sold may include residential, commercial, and undeveloped land in various locations throughout Del Norte County.

Those interested in finding out more about the auction are encouraged to review the information links below:

- List of Parcels for Sale with Parcel Maps
- Research Information (pdf)
- Frequently Asked Questions (pdf)
- Additional Terms of Sale (pdf)
- Offline Bid Form (pdf)
- Property Spreadsheet (pdf)

Potential bidders may register April 1st through May 4, 2004 at http://www.bid4assets.com. Bidders are responsible for understanding the Additional Terms of Sale issued by the Del Norte County Tax Collector as well as Bid4Assets' Terms of Service.

If you are not able to access the Internet, information packets and "Off-Line" bid forms will be available in the Tax Collector's Office. Parcel Map Booklets will also be available for a nominal fee.

(1a) List of Parcels for Sale with Parcel Maps
from the Treasurer/Tax Collector's home page, click on "Tax Sale" and then on "List of Parcels for Sale with Parcel Maps"

ROGUE INVESTOR NOTE: list of parcels for sale saved on CD:
USA Tax Lien Info/California/del_norte_co_CA/sales_list.htm

(1b) Research Information

from the Treasurer/Tax Collector's home page, click on "Tax Sale" and then on "Research Information"

(1c) Frequently Asked Questions

from the Treasurer/Tax Collector's home page, click on "Tax Sale" and then on "Frequently Asked Questions"

(1d) Additional Terms of Sale

from the Treasurer/Tax Collector's home page, click on "Tax Sale" and then on "Additional Terms of Sale"

TERMS OF SALE

ALL POTENTIAL BIDDERS ARE REQUIRED TO READ AND UNDERSTAND THESE TERMS.

(1) The auction will begin at 6:00 a.m. PST (9:00 a.m. EST) on May 5, 2004 and the auction will close at the time shown on each auction item on May 6, 2004.

(2) The asset information is being updated daily and will not be finalized until the day of the sale. Please read all due diligence materials and check the spreadsheets for updates.

(3) The descriptions provided are based on the Official Records of the County Recorder's Office and are presumed to be correct. The property to be sold may be approximately located from maps provided in the property information section on each auction item on Bid4Assets.com.

(4) The right of the former owner to redeem any parcel is forfeited as of 5:00 p.m. PST. On May 4, 2004. Properties removed from the sale will be so indicated on the Asset Page listing for a specific county.

(5) Prospective purchasers are urged to examine the title, location and desirability of the properties available to their own satisfaction prior to the sale. ALL PROPERTIES ARE SOLD AS IS. The County makes no guarantee, expressed or implied, relative to the title, location or condition of the properties for sale. The County assumes no liability for any other possible liens, encumbrances or easements, recorded or not recorded.

(6) Prospective purchasers are advised that some bonds or other assessments which are levied by agencies or offices other than the Treasurer-Tax Collector may still be outstanding after the tax sale; in addition, the IRS has the option of redeeming, up until 120 days after the sale, any property on which there is an IRS lien recorded.

(7) Some properties in some counties may have 1911, 1913 and/or 1915 Improvement Act Bonds, or Mello Roos Bonds, which are noted on the Asset Page listing of the property.

(8) When property is sold at public auction on which the IRS holds a tax lien, the United States has the right of redemption for 120 days from the date of such sale (26 USC Sec. 3712[g] and 7425[d]). The IRS will pay the actual amount paid for the property by the bidder, plus interest at 6% per annum from the date of sale, plus the expenses of sale that exceed any income received from the property.

(9) The County assumes no liability for any other possible liens, encumbrances or easements, recorded or not recorded.

(10) If the successful purchaser desires a survey of the property, it will be at the purchaser's own initiative and expense. The County makes no warranty, either expressed or implied, relative to the usability, the ground location, or property lines of the properties. The prospective purchaser must determine the exact location, desirability, and usefulness of the properties.

(11) The sale of these properties should not, in any way, be equated to real estate sales by licensed salesmen, brokers and realtors. The County Tax Collector cannot guarantee the condition of the property nor assume any responsibility for conformance to codes, permits or zoning ordinances. You should inspect the property before investing. The burden is on the purchaser to thoroughly research, before the sale, any matters relevant to his or her decision to purchase, rather than on the county, whose sole interest is the recovery of back taxes.

(12) Your bid is an irrevocable offer to purchase the asset.

(13) Successful bidders will be asked to complete a deed information form showing how they want the title to the property to be held (vesting). The Deed Information form will be provided to the winning bidders and must be completed within 48 hours following the close of the auction. The copy of the deed will be mailed to the purchaser after recording, and the County Recorder will send the original deed usually within four to six weeks. This deed conveys all right, title, and interest to the property in accordance with the provisions of Revenue and Taxation Code section 3712.

(14) A California documentary transfer tax will be added to, and collected with, the full purchase price. This tax is calculated at the rate of $.55 for each $500.00 or fractional part thereof, if the purchase price exceeds $100.00.

(15) The notification of winning bid will include the total purchase price, including documentary transfer tax, with instructions concerning the various payment methods.

(16) Unless otherwise noted, payment in full by wire transfer, electronic funds transfer or cashier's check will be required by May 11, 2004 at 5:00 p.m. (PST) or three (3) business days after a subsequent sale closes. No personal checks or credit card payments will be accepted. Payments in excess of the total purchase price will be refunded by mail within 30 days. To ensure that a cashier check payment is received timely, Express Mail, UPS and Federal Express are recommended as reliable delivery services. If payment policy is not adhered to, the successful bidder may be banned from future sales.

(17) Properties identified on an asset description page as being eligible for a credit sale will require a deposit of $5,000 or 10% of winning bid, whichever is greater, by May 11, 2004 at 5:00 p.m. (PST) or three (3) business days after a subsequent sale closes. The balance will be due, meaning good funds in the Tax Collector's office, within 30 days.

(18) Only a successful bidder has the opportunity to purchase County assets. If the successful bidder defaults, under California State Law, the County cannot resort to the second highest bidder, and will be required to take appropriate legal action against the bidder who defaults. Failure on the part of the successful bidder to consummate the sale within the specified time shall result in the forfeiture of the deposit made and all rights that the purchaser may have had with respect to the property.

(19) The successful bidder may take possession of the property after the tax deed to purchase has been recorded. Most title companies will not insure title on properties sold at public auction for at least one (1) year after the tax deed has been recorded. Legal action to challenge a tax sale must be commenced within one (1) year of the tax recording date.

(20) ALL SALES ARE FINAL. THERE ARE ABSOLUTELY NO REFUNDS. RULES ARE SUBJECT TO MODIFICATION BETWEEN NOW AND COMMENCEMENT OF SALE

(1e) Offline Bid Form
from the Treasurer/Tax Collector's home page, click on "Tax Sale" and then on "Offline Bid Form"

(1f) Property Spreadsheet
from the Treasurer/Tax Collector's home page, click on "Tax Sale" and then on "Property Spreadsheet"

ROGUE INVESTOR NOTE: property spreadsheet saved on CD:
USA Tax Lien Info/California/del_norte_co_CA/Property Spreadsheet.pdf

BID4ASSETS
http://www.bid4assets.com/storefront/?sfID=120

Treasurer/Tax Collector Office tax-defaulted auction storefront.

ROGUE INVESTOR NOTE: Information had not been updated for 2004.

FRESNO COUNTY, CALIFORNIA
http://www.co.fresno.ca.us

AUDITOR-CONTROLLER/TREASURER-TAX COLLECTOR OFFICE
http://www.fresno.ca.gov/0410/default.htm

Vicki Crow, C.P.A.
Fresno County Treasurer
2281 Tulare Street (at M Street)
Hall of Records, Room 105
Fresno, California 93721
P.O. Box 1247
Fresno, California 93715

Phone: (559) 488-3496
Fax: (559) 488-3493
Email: TaxCollectorWebMail@co.fresno.ca.us

Bill Casarez, C.P.A. Deputy Auditor-Controller
Balbina (Bobbie) Ormonde, C.P.A. Deputy Treasurer-Tax Collector
Frances Leon, Administrative Secretary

TAX COLLECTION UNIT
(Auditor-Controller/Treasurer-Tax Collector's Office)
http://www.fresno.ca.gov/0410/tax.htm

phone: (559) 488-3482
FAX: (559) 488-3487
email: TaxCollectorWebMail@Fresno.Ca.Gov

Tax Defaulted Property

The Tax Collector is responsible for maintaining tax-defaulted property (secured delinquent) tax records. This includes preparing all required notices of payment due, courtesy notices and required publications, preparing and recording Notices of Power to Sell and releases, and scheduling the actual sale of tax defaulted property and maintaining the appropriate records.

Public Service Information

The Tax Collector is responsible for providing property tax information to the public, governmental agencies and other county departments. This includes preparing correspondence and reports, mobile home tax clearances and vessel registration clearances, tax status letters, certifications of taxes paid, certificates of lien and lien releases, and certifications of subdivision and parcel maps.

Rolein Hiatt, C.P.A., Chief Accountant-Tax Manager
Eliz Manoukian, Senior Accountant
Cathy Lilly, Tax Supervisor

(1) Tax Sales
http://www.fresno.ca.gov/0410/TaxSales.htm

Our next Tax Sale is scheduled for March 1 - 3, 2004. The list of properties will be available approximately one month prior to the sale.

The Fresno County Auditor-Controller/Treasurer-Tax Collector is not allowed, by law, to sell properties by any means other than at a public auction. Fresno County does not sell tax liens for tax-defaulted properties nor do we maintain a list of contacts for tax sales. The sale of "Tax Defaulted Property Subject to Power to Sell" is conducted pursuant to the provisions of the Revenue and Taxation Code and the written authorization of the Board of Supervisors.

Research Before You Invest

The sale of these properties should not, in any way, be equated to real estate sales by licensed salesmen, brokers and realtors. The Fresno County Auditor-Controller/Treasurer-Tax Collector cannot guarantee the condition of the property nor assume any responsibility for conformance to codes, permits or zoning ordinances. You should inspect the property before investing. The burden is on the purchaser to thoroughly research, before the sale, any matters relevant to his or her decision to purchase, rather than on the county, whose sole interest is the recovery of back taxes.

It is recommended that bidders consult with the Zoning Department of any city within which a particular parcel lies. Tax-defaulted property will be sold on an "as is" basis.

Should the successful purchaser desire a survey of the property, it will be at the purchaser's own initiative and expense. No warranty is made by the County, either expressed or implied, relative to the usability, the ground location, or property lines of the properties. The exact location, desirability, and usefulness of the properties must be determined by the prospective purchaser.

The County assumes no liability for any other possible liens, encumbrances or easements, recorded or not recorded.

When property is sold at public auction on which the IRS holds a tax lien, the United States has the right of redemption for 120 days from the date of such sale (26 USC Sec. 3712[g] and 7425[d]). The IRS will pay the actual amount paid for the property by the bidder, plus interest at 6% per annum from the date of sale, plus the expenses of sale that exceed any income received from the property.

ALL SALES ARE FINAL, INVESTIGATE BEFORE BIDDING

(1a) Tax Sales – Questions and Answers
http://www.fresno.ca.gov/0410/taxsalesQA.htm

Internet Auction
http://www.bid4assets.com/fresno
Offline Bidding Instructions: call toll free 1-877-427-7387

Who can place a bid? Only registered bid4assets.com members. You must register to bid.

What is an autobid? An autobid (or proxy) saves you time and money. An autobid authorizes Bid4Assets to bid $100 above any competing bid, up to, but not exceeding the maximum dollar amount that you are willing to pay. In other words, your bid will automatically increase ONLY as other bidders participate, up to your specified maximum amount. This enables you to continually bid without having to constantly monitor the auction.

Can I change or cancel a bid? Your bid is an irrevocable offer to purchase the asset.

What is the minimum bid price? That is the minimum dollar amount we are willing to accept for an item to be sold at the auction.

What happens when the auction ends? The winning bidder will receive an Asset Alert stating that the auction has closed, including the asset description and closing bid price. If you are the winning bidder, you will need to either wire funds to us or FedEx a cashier's check made payable to Fresno County Tax Collector. Our address is 2281 Tulare Street, Room 105, Fresno, CA 93721. It is your responsibility to complete the sale in accordance with the Terms of Sale in the online Asset Listing.

How do I bid offline? You must contact bid4assets.com's Client Services Department at 1-877-427-7387. You will be registered to bid and will then receive the Offline Bid Form, either faxed or mailed to you. You will also receive Terms of Service and Additional Terms of Service information.

(1b) General Tax Sale Information
http://www.fresno.ca.gov/0410/taxsalesGeneralInfo.htm

Fresno County's Tax Sale, scheduled for March 1-3, 2004, will be held on the Internet!

The Fresno County Auditor-Controller/Treasurer-Tax Collector does not maintain a permanent tax sale mailing list. If you wish to view our list of tax-defaulted properties, please call Bid4Assets.com at 1-877-427-7387 or visit their website (http://www.bid4assets.com/fresno).

Prospective purchasers will be asked to register via the Internet. Each registered bidder will receive an identification number, which the bidder must have in order to participate. All parcels will be sold by item number and in the order listed. Minimum bids will be as stated per parcel and each raise will be in increments of at least $100 until sold.

The descriptions given are based on the official records of the Fresno County Assessor-Recorder's Office and are presumed to be correct. The property to be sold may be approximately located from maps available for viewing at the Internet Auction Advertising Service Provider's website address.

The right of the former owner to redeem any parcel is forfeited as of 5:00 p.m. on the last business day prior to the sale.

Prospective purchasers are urged to examine the title, location and desirability of the properties available to their own satisfaction prior to the sale. ALL PROPERTIES ARE SOLD AS IS. Fresno County makes no guarantee, expressed or implied, relative to the title, location or condition of the properties for sale. All property taxes currently due will be paid from the proceeds of the sale.

PLEASE NOTE: PROSPECTIVE PURCHASERS ARE ADVISED THAT SOME BONDS OR OTHER ASSESSMENTS WHICH ARE LEVIED BY AGENCIES OR OFFICES OTHER THAN THE AUDITOR-CONTROLLER/TREASURER-TAX COLLECTOR MAY STILL BE OUTSTANDING AFTER THE TAX SALE; IN ADDITION, THE I.R.S. HAS THE OPTION OF REDEEMING, UP UNTIL 120 DAYS AFTER THE SALE, ANY PROPERTY ON WHICH THERE IS AN I.R.S. LIEN RECORDED.

The successful bidder may take possession of the property after the tax deed to purchaser has been recorded. Most title companies will not insure title on properties sold at public auction for at least one (1) year after the tax deed has been recorded. Legal action to challenge a tax sale must be commenced within one (1) year of the tax recording date.
ALL SALES ARE FINAL.

Prior to payment, successful bidders will be asked to complete a "deed slip" showing how they want the property purchased to be conveyed. The deed will be mailed to the purchaser after recording, usually within six to eight weeks. This deed conveys all right, title, and interest to the property in accordance with the provisions of Revenue and Taxation Code section 3712.

A California documentary transfer tax will be added to, and collected with, the full purchase price. This tax is calculated at the rate of $.55 for each $500.00 or fractional part thereof, if the purchase price exceeds $100.00.

Payment in full by wire transfer or cashier's check (made payable to Fresno County Tax Collector) will be required by March 9, 2004 (within 4 business days of the close of the auction). No business checks, personal checks or credit cards will be accepted. Payments in excess of the purchase price will be refunded by mail within 30 days.

(1c) Tax Sale List Available February 3, 2004
http://www.bid4assets.com/storefront/?sfID=155

The Treasurer-Tax Collector's Office of Fresno County, California, is offering 197 tax defaulted properties for auction online.

Auctions Start: March 1, 2004 at 11:00 a.m. ET (8:00 a.m. PT)
Auctions End: March 3, 2004

*Closing times vary; check listings below for details.

Bids Start as low as $850.
These are all NO RESERVE auctions!

Preview Now!

For asset specific questions, please contact the county at (559) 488-3482.

To search for property by APN number, please use our search feature located on the right hand side of this page.

Prospective purchasers are urged to examine the title, location and desirability of the properties available to their own satisfaction prior to the sale. ALL PROPERTIES ARE SOLD AS IS. The County of Fresno makes no guarantee, expressed or implied, relative to the title, location or condition of the properties for sale. All property taxes currently due will be paid from the proceeds of the sale. PLEASE NOTE: PROSPECTIVE PURCHASERS ARE ADVISED THAT SOME BONDS OR OTHER ASSESSMENTS WHICH ARE LEVIED BY AGENCIES OR OFFICES OTHER THAN THE TREASURER-TAX COLLECTOR MAY STILL BE OUTSTANDING AFTER THE TAX SALE; IN ADDITION, THE I.R.S. HAS THE OPTION OF REDEEMING, UP UNTIL 120 DAYS AFTER THE SALE, ANY PROPERTY ON WHICH THERE IS AN I.R.S. LIEN RECORDED.

- Fresno County Terms of Sale: http://www.bid4assets.com/info/sfid155/40517.pdf?auctionid=0;
- Offline Bid Form: http://www.bid4assets.com/info/sfid155/40527.pdf?auctionid=0; and
- Download Property Spreadsheet: http://www.bid4assets.com/info/sfid155/40526.pdf?auctionid=0.

ROGUE INVESTOR NOTE: property spreadsheet saved on CD:
USA Tax Lien Info/California/fresno_co_CA/property_spreadsheet.xls.

(2) Important Dates
http://www.fresno.ca.gov/0410/ImportantDates.htm

KERN COUNTY, CALIFORNIA
http://www.co.kern.ca.us

TREASURER AND TAX COLLECTOR
http://www.kcttc.co.kern.ca.us/gentaxes.asp

Phil Franey, Kern County Treasurer and Tax Collector
1115 Truxtun Avenue
Bakersfield, CA 93301
Phone = 661-868-3490, Toll-free = 800-552-KERN
FAX = 661-868-3409

(1) General Tax Information, Important Dates to Remember
http://www.kcttc.co.kern.ca.us/ttc2.asp

(2) Tax Sales
http://www.kcttc.co.kern.ca.us/taxsales.asp

Our next Tax Sale is scheduled for March 8-10, 2004 and will feature property located primarily in the California City, Mojave, Ridgecrest and North Edwards areas of Kern County.

The list of properties is now available.

The Treasurer-Tax Collector is not allowed, by law, to sell properties by any means other than at a public auction. Kern County does not sell tax liens for tax-defaulted properties nor do we maintain a list of contacts for tax sales.

Research Before You Invest!

The sale of these properties should not, in any way, be equated to real estate sales by licensed salesmen, brokers and realtors. The County Treasurer-Tax Collector cannot guarantee the condition of the property nor assume any responsibility for conformance to codes, permits or zoning ordinances. You should inspect the property before investing. The burden is on the purchaser to thoroughly research, before the sale, any matters relevant to his or her decision to purchase, rather than on the county, whose sole interest is the recovery of back taxes.

It is recommended that bidders consult with the Zoning Department of any city within which a particular parcel lies. Tax-defaulted property will be sold on an "as is" basis.

Should the successful purchaser desire a survey of the property, it will be at the purchaser's own initiative and expense. No warranty is made by the County, either expressed or implied, relative to the usability, the ground location, or property lines of the properties. The exact location, desirability, and usefulness of the properties must be determined by the prospective purchaser.

The County assumes no liability for any other possible liens, encumbrances or easements, recorded or not recorded. When property is sold at public auction on which the IRS holds a tax lien, the United States has the right of redemption for 120 days from the date of such sale (26 USC Sec. 3712[g] and 7425[d]). The IRS will pay the actual amount paid for the property by the bidder, plus interest at 6% per annum from the date of sale, plus the expenses of sale that exceed any income received from the property.

(2a) Tax Sale Questions and Answers
http://www.kcttc.co.kern.ca.us/salefaq.asp

Internet Auctions
http://www.bid4assets.com
Offline Bidding Instructions: call toll free 1-877-427-7387

Who can place a bid? Only registered bid4assets.com members. You must register to bid.

What is an autobid? An auto bid (or proxy) saves you time and money. An auto bid authorizes Bid4Assets to bid $100 above any competing bid, up to, but not exceeding the maximum dollar amount that you are willing to pay. In other words, your bid will automatically increase ONLY as other bidders participate, up to your specified maximum amount. This enables you to continually bid without having to constantly monitor the auction.

Can I change or cancel a bid? Your bid is an irrevocable offer to purchase the asset.

What is the minimum bid price? That is the minimum dollar amount we are willing to accept for an item to be sold at the auction.

What happens when the auction ends? The winning bidder will receive an Asset Alert stating that the auction has closed including the asset description and closing bid price. If you are the winning bidder, you will need to either wire funds to us or FedEx a cashier's check made payable to Phil Franey-KCTTC. Our address is: 1115 Truxtun Avenue, Bakersfield, CA 93301. It is your responsibility to complete the sale in accordance with the Terms of Sale in the online Asset Listing.

How do I bid offline? You must contact bid4assets.com's Client Services Department at 1-877-427-7387. You will be registered to bid and will then receive the Offline Bid Form, either faxed or mailed to you. You will also receive Terms of Service and Additional Terms of Service information.

(3b) General Tax Sale Information
http://www.kcttc.co.kern.ca.us/taxdeflt.asp

NOTE: The Treasurer-Tax Collector does not maintain a permanent tax sale mailing list. If you wish to view our list of tax-defaulted properties, please call Bid4Assets.com at 1-877-427-7387 or visit their website at http://www.bid4assets.com.

- Prospective purchasers will be asked to register via the Internet. Each registered bidder will receive an identification number, which the bidder must have in order to participate. All parcels will be sold by item number and in the order listed. Minimum bids will be as stated per parcel and each raise will be in increments of at least $100 until sold.

- The descriptions given are based on the official records of the Kern County Assessor-Recorder's Office and are presumed to be correct. The property to be sold may be approximately located from maps available for viewing at the Internet Auction Advertising Service Provider's website address.

- The right of the former owner to redeem any parcel is forfeited as of 5:00 p.m. on the last business day prior to the sale.

- Prospective purchasers are urged to examine the title, location and desirability of the properties available to their own satisfaction prior to the sale. ALL PROPERTIES ARE SOLD AS IS. The County of Kern makes no guarantee, expressed or implied, relative to the title, location or condition of the properties for sale. All property taxes currently due will be paid from the proceeds of the sale. PLEASE NOTE: PROSPECTIVE PURCHASERS ARE ADVISED THAT SOME BONDS OR OTHER ASSESSMENTS WHICH ARE LEVIED BY AGENCIES OR OFFICES OTHER THAN THE TREASURER-TAX COLLECTOR MAY STILL BE OUTSTANDING AFTER THE TAX SALE; IN ADDITION, THE I.R.S. HAS THE OPTION OF REDEEMING, UP UNTIL 120 DAYS AFTER THE SALE, ANY PROPERTY ON WHICH THERE IS AN I.R.S. LIEN RECORDED.

- The successful bidder may take possession of the property after the tax deed to purchaser has been recorded. Most title companies will not insure title on properties sold at public auction for at least one (1) year after the tax deed has been recorded. Legal action to challenge a tax sale must be commenced within one (1) year of the tax recording date.

- ALL SALES ARE FINAL.

- Prior to payment, successful bidders will be asked to complete a "deed slip" showing how they want the property purchased to be conveyed. The deed will be mailed to the purchaser after recording, usually within four to six weeks. This deed conveys all right, title, and interest to the property in accordance with the provisions of Revenue and Taxation Code section 3712.

- A California documentary transfer tax will be added to, and collected with, the full purchase price. This tax is calculated at the rate of $.55 for each $500.00 or fractional part thereof, if the purchase price exceeds $100.00.

Payment in full by cash or cashier's check (made payable to Phil Franey, KCTTC) within 5 business days after the conclusion of the online auction. *No personal checks will be accepted*. Payments in excess of the purchase price will be refunded by mail within 30 days.

(2c) Tax Sale Comparison
http://www.kcttc.co.kern.ca.us/salestat.asp

(2d) Entire List of Tax-Defaulted Properties Subject to Power to Sell
http://www.kcttc.co.kern.ca.us/ptslist.asp

SUBJECT TO POWER TO SELL

After 5 years of tax-defaulted status, defaulted properties become subject to the "Power to Sell." These properties may be sold at future Internet auctions, unless redeemed for the full taxes, penalties, and other associated costs. Occasionally, other factors such as a bankruptcy may delay the offering of a property for sale. The listing of tax-defaulted properties displays the owner name of record, the ATN (Assessor Tax Number), and the Amount Owed (approximation).

Dated as of December 30, 2003

(3) Contact Information
http://www.kcttc.co.kern.ca.us/contact.asp

For Property Taxes
KCTTC Taxpayer Service Center
P.O. Box 580
Bakersfield, CA 93302-0580

Other
KCTTC
1115 Truxtun Avenue
Bakersfield, CA 93301
phone: (661) 868-3490 or 800 552- KERN
FAX: (661) 868-3409
email: 2servu@co.kern.ca.us

BID4ASSETS – KERN COUNTY STOREFRONT
http://www.bid4assets.com/storefront/?sfid=164

The Treasurer-Tax Collector's Office of Kern County, California is offering 1134 tax defaulted properties for auction online. The properties are zoned as agriculture, commercial, residential, estate as well as many others.

Auctions Start: March 8, 2004 at 9:00 PM ET (6:00 PM PT)
Auctions End: March 10, 2004

*Closing times vary; check listings for details.

Bids Start as low as $ 100.00
These are all NO RESERVE auctions!

Preview Now!

For asset specific questions, please contact the county at (661) 868-3490.

To search for property by ATN number, please use our search feature located on the right hand side of this page.

Prospective purchasers are urged to examine the title, location and desirability of the properties available to their own satisfaction prior to the sale. ALL PROPERTIES ARE SOLD AS IS. The County of Kern makes no guarantee, expressed or implied, relative to the title, location or condition of the properties for sale. All property taxes currently due will be paid from the proceeds of the sale. PLEASE NOTE: PROSPECTIVE PURCHASERS ARE ADVISED THAT SOME BONDS OR OTHER ASSESSMENTS WHICH ARE LEVIED BY AGENCIES OR OFFICES OTHER THAN THE TREASURER-TAX COLLECTOR MAY STILL BE OUTSTANDING AFTER THE TAX SALE; IN ADDITION, THE I.R.S. HAS THE OPTION OF REDEEMING, UP UNTIL 120 DAYS AFTER THE SALE, ANY PROPERTY ON WHICH THERE IS AN I.R.S. LIEN RECORDED.

- Additional Terms of Sale: http://www.bid4assets.com/info/sfid164/40800.pdf?auctionid=0
- Offline Bid Form: http://www.bid4assets.com/info/sfid164/40801.pdf?auctionid=0
- Downloadable Property Sheet: http://www.bid4assets.com/info/sfid164/40808.pdf?auctionid=0

ROGUE INVESTOR NOTE: property sheet saved on CD:
USA Tax Lien Info/California/kern_co_CA/property_sheet.xls

LOS ANGELES COUNTY, CALIFORNIA
http://www.co.la.ca.us

TREASURER AND TAX COLLECTOR
http://ttax.co.la.ca.us/main.htm

Mark Saladino, Treasurer and Tax Collector

(1) Public Auction
From http://ttax.co.la.ca.us/main.htm, click on "Services" and then on "Public Auction"

(1a) 2004 Tax Sale – General Information
http://ttax.co.la.ca.us/auction_intro.htm

Auction Information
Date: March 1 and 2, 2004, 9 a.m.
Place: Los Angeles County Fairgrounds, 1101 W. McKinley Avenue, Building 7, Pomona, CA, 91768

Information on Sale Items: (213) 974-2045
Email: http://ttax.co.la.ca.us

Registration Information
Date of Registration: January 26 to February 13, 2004, 8:00 a.m. to 5:00 p.m.

Place to Register: Treasurer-Tax Collector, 225 N. Hill Street, Room 130, Los Angeles, CA 90012

Registration Information: (213) 974-2040
Email: http://ttax.co.la.ca.us
Prospective bidders are required to pre-register IN PERSON with a $1,000 deposit in the form of cash, cashier's check or bank issued money order. Other money orders and personal or business checks will not be accepted. For other requirements contact the Tax Defaulted Land Unit at 225 N. Hill Street, Room 130, Los Angeles, CA.

There will be NO REGISTRATION AT THE AUCTION SITE.

Auction Book
How to purchase an Auction Book:

- By mail: Orders by mail should be addressed to the Los Angeles County Tax Collector, 500 W. Temple Street, Room 114, Los Angeles, CA 90012. Only cashier's check or bank issued money order made payable to the Los Angeles County Tax Collector will be accepted. Personal or business checks will NOT be accepted.

- By telephone: Orders by telephone must be directed to (213) 974-2646 or (213) 974-2647 between the hours of 8:00 a.m. and 4:00 p.m., Monday through Friday, and paid by using Visa, MasterCard or Discover Card. Callers must have their credit card number ready when calling.

- In person: Purchases in person are to be directed to the Cashier Windows located on the First Floor Lobby area of the Kenneth Hahn Hall of Administration, 225 N. Hill Street, Los Angeles, CA. between the hours of 8:00 a.m. and 5:00 p.m., Monday through Friday. Only cash, cashier's check, bank issued money orders, Visa, MasterCard and Discover Card will be accepted. Personal or business checks will NOT be accepted.

Cost of Auction Book:

- Purchase at cashier's window = $16.24
- Purchase by mail and telephone = $20.99

THE LAST DATE TO REDEEM TAX SALE PROPERTIES IS 5:00 P.M., FEBRUARY 27, 2004.

Properties Subject to Weed Abatement Charges
(http://ttax.co.la.ca.us/Flier_for_tax_del._sale.pdf)

LOS ANGELES COUNTY AGRICULTURAL COMMISSIONER/WEIGHTS AND MEASURES PROPERTIES SUBJECT TO WEED ABATEMENT CHARGES. INVESTIGATE BEFORE YOU BUY!!!!

Following is a list of parcels that may have weed abatement charges resulting in liens that are not extinguished by a tax sale. Please be advised that there may be other parcels that are not listed as the Tax Collector is not always aware of the charges accrued from July 1, 2003, until the time of sale. Parcels are sold on an "as" is basis and the County in no way assumes any responsibility, implied or otherwise as to the condition of the properties or of any other liens that may exist.

IRS Liens
(http://ttax.co.la.ca.us/2004A%20IRS%20LIEN%20INFO.pdf)

The attached list indicates properties with Internal Revenue Service (IRS) Liens. Please be aware that some properties may have been redeemed or removed from the 2004A tax sale scheduled March 1 and 2, 2004, and may no longer be offered for auction. Please check the updated list of properties remaining in this tax sale to verify if a particular property is still eligible for public auction. Also, please be advised that there may be other parcels that are not listed as the Tax Collector is not always aware of the charges accrued after the list has been compiled. Investigate before you buy!

(1b) Bid Registration and Information Form
http://ttax.co.la.ca.us/BidderRegistration.pdf

(1c) Frequently Asked Questions
http://ttax.co.la.ca.us/auction_faq.htm

How can I obtain a list of properties to be offered at the tax sale? A list of properties to be offered for sale is available from the Office of the Treasurer and Tax Collector.

AUCTION LIST SALES ARE FINAL. The auction list is also available for public inspection during regular business hours at Regional Offices of the County Assessor, District Offices of members of the Board of Supervisors, and certain Los Angeles County Public Libraries. Updated information on properties which remain in the sale is available at the Tax Collector's office or by visiting our website at http://ttax.co.la.ca.us/Main.htm.

Please remember to investigate before you purchase. All sales are final.

ROGUE INVESTOR NOTE: Additional questions and answers on web page.

(1d) Remaining Items as of February 2, 2004
http://ttax.co.la.ca.us/RemainingItems.asp

ROGUE INVESTOR NOTE: remaining items list saved on CD:
USA Tax Lien Info/California/kern_co_CA/Remaing Items.htm

(1e) List of Sold Parcels
http://ttax.co.la.ca.us/ListofSoldParcels.pdf

(1f) Terms and Conditions
http://ttax.co.la.ca.us/2002A%20Auction%20Book%20Preamble.pdf

Official terms and conditions of the sale of tax defaulted property 2004A Tax Sale March 1 and 2, 2004.

(7) Contact Information
http://ttax.co.la.ca.us/contact_Information.htm

General Information
Kenneth Hahn, Hall of Administration
500 W. Temple Street
Los Angeles, CA 90012
Email submittal form = http://ttax.co.la.ca.us/General_form.htm

Secured Property Tax Office
Kenneth Hahn Hall of Administration
225 North Hill Street
Los Angeles, CA 90012
phone = (213) 974-2111 or
toll-free = (888)-807-2111

ORANGE COUNTY, CALIFORNIA
http://www.oc.ca.gov

ASSESSOR DEPARTMENT
http://www.oc.ca.gov/assessor

(1) Lien Dates to Remember
http://www.oc.ca.gov/ac/newpage/dateremb.asp

January 1 = Lien Date for Secured and Unsecured Properties

OFFICE OF THE TREASURER- TAX COLLECTOR
http://www.oc.ca.gov/treas

John M. W. Moorlach, Treasurer-Tax Collector

This office is responsible for the sale of property subject to the "power to sell," formerly known as delinquent tax deeded property.

TAX COLLECTOR'S OFFICE
(Office of the Treasurer-Tax Collector)
http://www.oc.ca.gov/treas/tax_page.htm

The Tax Collector's Office is responsible for collecting taxes on all secured and unsecured property in Orange County. This office is also responsible for the sale of property subject to the "power to sell," formerly known as delinquent tax deeded property.

(1) Treasurer-Tax Collector's Auction
http://www.ocgov.com/treas/Auction/intro.htm

The next tax sale will be held on March 25, 2004. For additional information, please call our Tax Sale Division at (714) 834-5701.

(1a) Tax Sale FAQs
http://www.ocgov.com/treas/auction/taxsaleinformation.htm

Q. How can I obtain a list of properties to be offered at the next tax sale? There is a fee of $1.20 to have your name added to our mailing list for the fiscal year. This fee may be paid in person or mailed to O.C. Tax Collector, P.O. Box 1438, Santa Ana, CA 92702. Approximately four (4) weeks prior to the sale, the list will be available for purchase. Customers who have already paid their $1.20 will receive the list through the mail and we will also be selling the list in room G-58 of the Tax Collector's office. The auction list will be available for public viewing in our office, free of charge, two weeks prior to the auction. It will also be published on our website at: http://www.oc.ca.gov/treas/auction/intro.htm.

Parcel maps will not be supplied; you may purchase copies from the Orange County Assessor. You can contact the Assessor's Office at (714) 834-2727 for more information.

ROGUE INVESTOR NOTE: Additional questions and answers on web page.

(1b) General Information and Bidder's Instructions on the Auction Sale of Tax Delinquent Real Property in the County of Orange
http://www.ocgov.com/treas/auction/webquestions.htm

(2) Contact Information
http://www.oc.ca.gov/treas/contact_us.htm

The Treasurer-Tax Collector
12 Civic Center Plaza
Santa Ana, CA 92701
Phone: (714) 834-3411

Mailing Address for General Inquiries
P.O. Box 4515
Santa Ana, CA 92702

The Tax Collector conducts tax sales (email: ttcinfo@ttc.ocgov.com).

(3) Tax Calendar
http://www.oc.ca.gov/treas/impdates.htm

PLACER COUNTY, CALIFORNIA
http://www.placer.ca.gov

TREASURER-TAX COLLECTOR'S OFFICE
http://www.placer.ca.gov/tax/tax.htm

Jenine Windeshausen, Treasurer-Tax Collector
Finance Administration Building
2976 Richardson Drive, 2nd Floor
Auburn, CA 95603
email: taxcollector@placer.ca.gov

(1) Tax Defaulted Land Sales
http://www.placer.ca.gov/tax/tax-sale.htm

Everything You Ever Wanted To Know About Tax Defaulted Land Sales
Prospective purchasers will be asked to register on the morning of the sale. Registration will include name and mailing address and may require identification as deemed necessary for the processing of auction documents. A $500.00 refundable deposit is required when you register (cash or cashier's check). If you are a successful bidder, payment must be made in full, either by cash, certified check, and in some cases, approved credit. Personal checks will not be accepted. Unsuccessful bidders will be refunded their deposit at the conclusion of the sale.

Each registered bidder will receive an identification number, which the bidder must have in order to participate. All parcels will be sold by item number and in the order listed. Minimum bids will be as stated per parcel and each raise will be in increments of at least $100 until sold.

The descriptions given are based on the official records of the Placer County Assessor's Office and are presumed to be correct. The property to be sold may be approximately located from maps available for viewing in the Treasurer-Tax Collector's Office at 2976 Richardson Drive, 2nd Floor, Auburn, CA 95603. Please contact the Assessor's Office at 2980 Richardson Drive, 2nd Floor, Auburn, CA 95603 (phone: 530-889-4300), if assistance is needed in locating the properties on these maps.

The right of the former owner to redeem any parcel is forfeited on the last business day prior to the sale. Properties removed from the sale may be obtained by calling (530) 889-4120. In addition, properties removed from the sale will be announced at the beginning of the sale.

Prospective purchasers are urged to examine the title, location and desirability of the properties available to their own satisfaction prior to the sale. ALL PROPERTIES ARE SOLD AS IS. The County of Placer makes no guarantee, expressed or implied, relative to the title, location or condition of the properties for sale. All property taxes currently due will be paid from the proceeds of the sale.

PLEASE NOTE: PROSPECTIVE PURCHASERS ARE ADVISED THAT SOME BONDS OR OTHER ASSESSMENTS WHICH ARE LEVIED BY AGENCIES OR OFFICES OTHER THAN THE TREASURER-TAX COLLECTOR MAY STILL BE OUTSTANDING AFTER THE TAX SALE; IN ADDITION, THE I.R.S. HAS THE OPTION OF REDEEMING, UP UNTIL 120 DAYS AFTER THE SALE, ANY PROPERTY ON WHICH THERE IS AN I.R.S. LIEN RECORDED.

The successful bidder may take possession of the property after the tax deed to purchaser has been recorded. Most title companies will not insure title on properties sold at public auction for at least one (1) year after the tax deed has been recorded. Legal action to challenge a tax sale must be commenced within one (1) year of the tax recording date.

ALL SALES ARE FINAL.

Prior to payment, successful bidders will be asked to complete a "deed slip" showing how they want the property purchased to be conveyed. The deed will be mailed to the purchaser after recording, usually within four to six weeks. This deed conveys all rights, title, and interest to the property in accordance with the provisions of Revenue and Taxation Code section 3712.
A California documentary transfer tax will be added to, and collected with, the full purchase price. This tax is calculated at the rate of $.55 for each $500.00 or fractional part thereof, if the purchase price exceeds $100.00.

Payment in full by cash or cashier's check will be required at the time of sale. No personal checks will be accepted. Payments in excess of the purchase price will be refunded by mail within 30 days.

On the day of the sale, for each parcel bid in excess of $5000.00, the successful bidder may choose to deposit $5000.00 or 10% of the purchase price, whichever is greater, by cash or cashier's check. The balance of the purchase price must be paid by cash or cashier's check within 90 days of the date of sale. Transfer of title will not be completed until full payment is received.

FAILURE ON THE PART OF THE SUCCESSFUL BIDDER TO CONSUMMATE THE SALE WITHIN THE SPECIFIED TIME SHALL RESULT IN THE FORFEITURE OF THE DEPOSIT MADE AND ALL RIGHTS THAT THE PURCHASER MAY HAVE HAD WITH RESPECT TO THE PROPERTY.

The Treasurer-Tax Collector is pleased to offer a "Public Auction Information Packet" including a complete set of maps to all properties being sold. These assessor maps have been marked with the item number being sold and show an approximate size and location of that item. The packets are normally available 6-8 weeks before the scheduled date of the next land sale. Please check the web site for updates on availability and cost. When available, the packet may be obtained by sending your name, address and payment to the following address:

Placer County Treasurer-Tax Collector
P.O. Box 7790
Auburn, CA 95604-7790
Attention: Ann Dondro

The Treasurer-Tax Collector maintains a tax sale mailing list. If you wish to be notified of the next sale, please send a large, self-addressed, stamped envelope with your request to:

Placer County Treasurer-Tax Collector
Redemption Section
P.O. Box 7790
Auburn, CA 95604-7790

Frequently Asked Questions

The following are typical questions and answers and may assist you in understanding our procedures. If you have additional questions, please feel free to call Land Sale Coordinator Ann Dondro at (530) 889-4120.

(1) What is the date and location of the sale? The next Tax Land Sale has not yet been determined.

DIRECTIONS

Tax Collector's Office:

From Sacramento, take Interstate 80 East to Auburn, exit Bell Road, turn left onto Bell Road. Follow Bell Road approximately 3 miles, go through the intersection with Highway 49 and past the Sheriff's Department. The next street (on the left side of the street) is Richardson Drive, make a left. The Tax Collector is in the 2-story brick building on the left side of the street. Our physical address is 2976 Richardson Drive; we are located on the second floor.

Board of Supervisor's Chambers:

From Sacramento, take Interstate 80 East to Auburn. Exit I-80 at 49/Grass Valley Highway. Turn left onto Highway 49, follow to second signal light, Fulweiler/Elm Avenue. Turn left on Fulweiler, follow approximately 1/4 mile to Placer County Administrative Center (http://www.placer.ca.gov/maps/domes.htm), located on the right.

COUNTY DEPARTMENTS

The addresses and phone numbers of frequently requested County Departments have been provided below for your convenience.

Assessor 2980 Richardson Drive, 2nd Floor Auburn, CA 95603-2640 (530) 889-4300	Planning Department 11414 B. Avenue Auburn, CA 95603 (530) 889-7470
Building Department 11424 B. Avenue Auburn, CA 95603 (530) 889-7487	Public Works 11444 B. Avenue Auburn, CA 95603 (530) 889-7500
County Clerk-Recorder-Registrar 2954 Richardson Drive, 1st Floor Auburn, CA 95603 (530) 886-5600	Treasurer-Tax Collector 2976 Richardson Drive, 2nd Floor Auburn, CA 95603 (530) 889-4120
Environmental Health 11454 B Avenue Auburn, CA 95603 (530) 889-7335	Tahoe Regional Planning Agency 308 Dorla Court Zephyr Cove, NV 89448 (775) 588-4527

2. When and where is the sale advertised? The sale is advertised in a newspaper published in the county seat (Auburn) approximately three weeks before the sale.

3. How and when do I register for the tax sale? Registration normally begins at 8:00 A.M. the day of the sale.

4. What are the payment requirements at the sale? Generally, a $500.00 non-refundable deposit is required when you register (cash or cashier's check). If you are a successful bidder, payment must be made in full, either by cash, certified check and, in some cases, approved credit. Personal checks will not be accepted. Unsuccessful bidders will be refunded their deposit at the conclusion of the sale.

5. What is the bidding process? Public auction. You must be present to bid.

6. What type of document is issued at the sale? Receipt at time of sale. A tax deed is forwarded to the successful bidder approximately four weeks after the sale.

7. Are there any other expenses in addition to the cost of the lien? Normally, recording fees and transfer tax.

8. What is the foreclosure process and will the county handle the foreclosure process for a fee? No, the county does not handle the foreclosure process.

9. What happens to the properties that are not sold at the Tax Land Sale? The property will be offered at a subsequent sale if not redeemed sooner.

10. Do you allow individuals to purchase Tax Lien Certificates? The county does not currently sell tax lien certificates.

11. Do you allow individuals to purchase property at the Tax-Defaulted Land Sale without attending the auction via mail, phone or fax? Can I send a representative to the sale to bid for me? No. The public auction requires your presence, or that of your notarized representative, to orally bid on the properties.

12. Would you please send me a current list of Tax-defaulted properties subject to sale and place me on your mailing list? Please send a self-addressed, stamped envelope to the address listed previously in this page and the list will be mailed approximately six weeks before the sale. Up-to-date information can also be viewed on this website by clicking on this link: http://www.placer.ca.gov/tax/taxsaleprop.htm

13. Would you please forward me a copy of the statues regarding tax sales in your jurisdiction? The California State statues are available at your public library or on the Internet at http://www.leginfo.ca.gov/calaw.html.

14. Do liens or encumbrances on a tax-defaulted property transfer to the new owner after purchase of the property at a tax sale? A tax deed to the purchaser conveys title free of most encumbrances existing before the sale (e.g. Deed of Trust, mechanics liens, judgments, as well as all prior delinquent taxes). Those encumbrances which continue, primarily liens of special assessments and easements, are described in Section No. 3712 of the Revenue & Taxation Code.

PARCELS ARE SOLD ON AN "AS IS" BASIS AND PLACER COUNTY ASSUMES NO RESPONSIBILITY, IMPLIED OR OTHERWISE, THAT THE PROPERTIES ARE IN COMPLIANCE WITH ZONING ORDINANCES, CONFORM TO BUILDING CODES AND PERMITS OR THE SITUS ADDRESS. NO GOVERNMENT ENTITY IS LIABLE FOR DAMAGES SUSTAINED TO PROPERTY PURCHASED AT PUBLIC AUCTION, INCLUDING FROM THE TIME OF THE SALE UNTIL THE RECORDATION OF THE TAX DEED TO THE PURCHASER. RULES SUBJECT TO CHANGE BETWEEN NOW AND COMMENCEMENT OF SALE.

If you have any questions regarding the sale of tax defaulted property, please call (530) 889-4120.

RIVERSIDE COUNTY, CALIFORNIA
http://www.co.riverside.ca.us

OFFICE OF THE TREASURER-TAX COLLECTOR
http://www.co.riverside.ca.us/depts/treasure

Treasurer Paul McDonnell

(1) News and Information
http://www.co.riverside.ca.us/depts/treasure/news.html

Tax Defaulted Auction
Although this office does not sell tax liens, we do sell tax defaulted property at auction. Check out the Tax Sale Information page (http://www.co.riverside.ca.us/depts/treasure/tax_sale_information.html) for more

information. We will be posting additional information on the sale and properties being offered as it becomes available.

(2) Tax Sale Information
http://www.co.riverside.ca.us/depts/treasure/tax_sale_information.html

The Treasurer-Tax Collector regularly offers tax defaulted parcels for sale pursuant to State law.

Information On Our Next Sale
Annual Live Auction, March 15-16, 2004, 9:00 a.m.
(Must be present to bid)
Riverside Convention Center
3443 Orange Street, Riverside, CA

Bidder Registration by mail until March 4, 2004
Bidder Registration in person March 11, 2004

NOTE: We will not be registering bidders at the sale. More information will be posted as it becomes available.

Bidder Instructions: http://www.co.riverside.ca.us/depts/treasure/tsinfo-170.pdf
Bidder Registration Card:
http://www.co.riverside.ca.us/depts/treasure/BIDDER%20REGISTRATION%20FORM%20TC170.pdf

View the List of Properties to be Offered: http://www.co.riverside.ca.us/depts/treasure/Int170.txt
Properties No Longer on Sale: http://www.co.riverside.ca.us/depts/treasure/170Parcels.htm
Parcel Maps for Properties to be Offered: http://www.co.riverside.ca.us/depts/treasure/maps170.html

Please note that the maps are also available for purchase in our office for $26.50. Please contact our office for additional information.

Previous Sales

ROGUE INVESTOR NOTE: See web page for links to previous sales.

Parcel Inventory

This is the entire inventory of parcels subject to the Tax Collectors Power of Sale as of July 1, 2003. If you are interested in having any of these properties offered at auction, please contact us at taxsale@co.riverside.ca.us. Be sure to include the assessment number(s) you are interested in and how we can contact you in your message including your name, address and phone number. Any requests received by September 30, 2003, will be considered for the March 2004 sale.

Inventory of Parcels Subject to the Power of Sale: http://www.co.riverside.ca.us/depts/treasure/pts-int.pdf (Updated 8/27/03)
Inventory of Parcels Subject to the Power of Sale – http://www.co.riverside.ca.us/depts/treasure/PTS-INVENTORY.xls (Updated 8/27/03)
Please note: If you request a parcel, or multiple parcels, to be placed on our tax sale and you do not bid the minimum bid price on each parcel requested, you will may barred from registering for future sales.

ROGUE INVESTOR NOTE: inventory of parcels subject to the power of sale saved on CD:
USA Tax Lien Info/California/riverside_co_CA/power_of_sale_parcels.xls

(2a) Bidder Instructions
http://www.co.riverside.ca.us/depts/treasure/tsinfo-170.pdf

(2b) Bidder Registration Card
http://www.co.riverside.ca.us/depts/treasure/BIDDER%20REGISTRATION%20FORM%20TC170.pdf

(2c) List of Properties to be Offered
http://www.co.riverside.ca.us/depts/treasure/Int170.txt

ROGUE INVESTOR NOTE: list of properties saved on CD:
USA Tax Lien Info/California/riverside_co_CA/sales_list.txt

(2d) Properties No Longer On Sale
http://www.co.riverside.ca.us/depts/treasure/170Parcels.htm

Parcels that have been redeemed or otherwise removed from the March 15-16, 2004 tax sale.

ROGUE INVESTOR NOTE: property list saved on CD:
USA Tax Lien Info/California/riverside_co_CA/redeemed_parcels.htm

(2e) Parcel Maps for Properties to Be Offered
http://www.co.riverside.ca.us/depts/treasure/maps170.html

(3) Contact
http://www.co.riverside.ca.us/depts/treasure/contact_us.html

Phone: (909) 955-3900
FAX: (909) 955-3906
Mailing address: P.O. Box 12005, Riverside, CA 92502-2205
Email: ttc@co.riverside.ca.us

SHERIFF'S DEPARTMENT
http://www.co.riverside.ca.us/sheriff/

(1) Contact Information
http://www.co.riverside.ca.us/sheriff/main/contact.htm
http://www.co.riverside.ca.us/sheriff/department/directory.htm

email: SHill@rc-lawnet.org

Administration
Sheriff Bob Doyle
4095 Lemon Street
Riverside, CA 92501
(909) 955-2400

COURT SERVICES DIVISION
(Sheriff's Department)
http://www.co.riverside.ca.us/sheriff/crtsrvs/ServInfo.htm

Services include real property sales.

SAN BERNARDINO COUNTY, CALIFORNIA
http://www.co.san-bernardino.ca.us

TREASURER-TAX COLLECTOR OFFICE, TAX COLLECTOR DIVISION
http://www.co.san-bernardino.ca.us/ttc/tr/default.asp

Richard (Dick) Larsen, Treasurer-Tax Collector
172 West Third Street, First Floor
San Bernardino, CA 92415-0360
phone: (909) 387-8308

(1) FAQ
http://www.co.san-bernardino.ca.us/ttc/tr/PublicFAQ.asp

What is a Tax Sale? Property that has been in default of tax payment(s) for a period of greater than five years becomes subject to a tax sale. The property(s) will be offered for sale at a public auction for a minimum bid. The minimum bid is the amount of taxes owed plus all penalties, interest and costs that have applied to the property(s).

(2) Tax Sales

(2a) Terms and Conditions
http://www.co.san-bernardino.ca.us/ttc/tr/TaxsaleFramePage.htm

Please read the terms and conditions before continuing!
The next sale is scheduled for May 17-28, 2004.

ROGUE INVESTOR NOTE: See web page for tax sale terms and conditions.

(2b) Items Currently Eligible for Sale
from http://www.co.san-bernardino.ca.us/ttc/tr/taxsaleFramePage.htm, click on "Current Sale Items"

Tax Sale - 031354
The list of properties for the next sale will be posted here when available.

(2c) Results of Previous Tax Sales
from http://www.co.san-bernardino.ca.us/ttc/tr/taxsaleFramePage.htm, click on "Previous Sales Results"

(2d) Brochures/Map Order Information
from http://www.co.san-bernardino.ca.us/ttc/tr/taxsaleFramePage.htm, click on "Brochures and CDs"

Brochures for the next auction will be available approximately 6 to 8 weeks before the next auction.

SHERIFF'S DEPARTMENT
http://www.co.san-bernardino.ca.us/sheriff/

Sheriff Gary Penrod

COURT SERVICES BUREAU, CIVIL DIVISION
(Sheriff's Department)
http://www.co.san-bernardino.ca.us/sheriff/courtsvs/civil.asp

Captain Richard Diggs oversees the Court Services Civil Division
email: csregion2@sbcsd.org

The Sheriff serves all processes and notices, including summons, complaints, subpoenas, claims, orders, warrant of arrest, levies for garnishments or attached earnings, personal property, real property, evictions and Sheriff's sales.

(1) FAQ
http://www.co.san-bernardino.ca.us/Sheriff/CourtSvs/FAQ.asp

How can I find information on pending Sheriff sales? There are no mailing lists for real or personal property sales. Information pertaining to a pending sale may be obtained in the following ways:

Sales of Real Property
The sale notices are posted in one public place in the city in which the sale is to be held; if not a city area, in the judicial district. A second posting of the property is be made in a conspicuous place on the property to be sold. Additionally, the sale is published in a newspaper of general circulation, published in the city where the property is located if in a city; if not, in the judicial district.

(2) Contact Information
http://www.co.san-bernardino.ca.us/Sheriff/CourtSvs/CSOffices.asp

351 North Arrowhead Avenue, First Floor
San Bernardino, CA 92415-0225
phone: (909) 387-3250

SAN DIEGO COUNTY, CALIFORNIA
http://www.co.san-diego.ca.us

TREASURER-TAX COLLECTOR DEPARTMENT
http://www.co.san-diego.ca.us/cnty/cntydepts/general/treastax

(1) Contact Information
http://www.co.san-diego.ca.us/cnty/cntydepts/general/treastax/contactus.html

Dan McAllister, Treasurer-Tax Collector
Main Office – County Administration Center
1600 Pacific Highway, Room 162
San Diego, CA 92101
phone Number: (619) 236-2424
Fax: (619) 531-6056
email: taxmantr@co.san-diego.ca.us

(2) Treasurer-Tax Collector Facts
http://www.co.san-diego.ca.us/cnty/cntydepts/general/treastax/pdfs/091803A.pdf

(3) Tax Sale
http://www.co.san-diego.ca.us/cnty/cntydepts/general/treastax/taxsale.html

Scheduled to be held Friday, February 27, 2004 at 9:00 a.m. at:
The San Diego Concourse
202 'C' Street, Rooms 227 & 228 (Copper Room)
San Diego, CA 92101

(3a) Current Year Tax Sale Parcel List
http://www2.sdcounty.ca.gov/treastax/taxsale/taxsale.asp

Click on a map area below to display Tax Sale Properties Scheduled for Sale at Public Auction Tax Sale for that area OR use the input fields on the forms below the map to search for specific records.

ROGUE INVESTOR NOTE: parcel list saved on CD:
USA Tax Lien Info/CA/san_diego_co_CA/parcel_list.htm

(4) Tax Sale General Information
http://www.co.san-diego.ca.us/cnty/cntydepts/general/treastax/taxsaleinfo.html

DEED INFORMATION

A "Deed Information Sheet" must be completed prior to the purchase of property at the auction (http://www.co.san-diego.ca.us/cnty/cntydepts/general/treastax/pdfs/DeedInfo.pdf). Extra forms will be available at our information table at the tax sale. The information required is necessary for the proper completion of a Tax Deed to Purchaser. Completion of forms beforehand will help speed up the sale.

The San Diego County Treasurer-Tax Collector is encouraging bidders to pre-register for the Public Auction Tax Sale No. 6999 to be held Friday, February 27, 2004 at 9:00 a.m. Bidders wishing to pre-register should have their "Deed Information Sheet" filed in our office no later than 5:00 p.m., Thursday, February 26, 2004.

The successful bidder may take possession of a property after the Tax Deed to Purchaser has been recorded. However, most title companies will not insure the title until one year after the tax sale deed is recorded. Legal action to challenge a tax sale must be brought within one year of the tax sale deed recording date. Therefore, it is not advisable to make any improvements to the property during the first year of ownership.

NOTE: In the event that a sale is canceled all payments made will be returned without interest. Any costs incurred by the purchaser during the process will be borne by the purchaser.

PROPERTY MAPS

Plat maps on the properties are available in the Assessor's Office, Room 103. The maps show the approximate dimensions and general geographical location of the properties. Copies of maps are also offered for sale by the Assessor in Room 103 and on this web site by selecting "detail Map" for desired parcel(s) and clicking "show Detail Map".

A representative from the Assessor's Office will be available at the Tax Sale to answer questions pertaining to assessment and ownership. Thank you for your interest in participating in the San Diego County's Public Auction Tax Sale.

ZONING LINKS

City	Phone	Address
Carlsbad	(760) 602-4600	1635 Faraday Avenue Carlsbad CA 92008
Chula Vista	(619) 691-5101	276 Fourth Avenue Chula Vista, CA 91910
Coronado	(619) 522-7326	1825 Strand Way Coronado, CA 92118
Del Mar	(858) 755-9313	1050 Camino Del Mar Del Mar CA 92014
El Cajon	(619) 441-1726	200 East Main St, 3rd Floor El Cajon, CA 92020
Encinitas	(760) 622-2710	505 South Vulcan Avenue Encinitas, CA 92024
Escondido	(760) 839-4671	201 North Broadway Escondido, CA 92025
Imperial Beach	(619) 628-1356	825 Imperial Beach Boulevard Imperial Beach, CA 91932
La Mesa	(619) 667-1177	8130 Allison Avenue La Mesa, CA 91941
Lemon Grove	(619) 825-3805	3232 Main Street Lemon Grove, CA 91945
National City	(619) 336-4310	1243 National City Boulevard National City, CA 91950
Oceanside	(760) 435-3520	300 North Coast Highway Oceanside, CA 92054
Poway	(858) 679-4290	13202 Poway Road Poway, CA 92064
San Diego	(619) 236-6598	202 C Street, 5th Floor San Diego, CA 92101
San Marcos	(760) 744-1050 x3204	1 Civic Center Drive San Marcos, CA 92069

Santee	(619) 258-4100 x152	10601 Magnolia Avenue Santee, CA 92071
Solana Beach	(858) 720-2400	635 South Highway 101 Solana Beach CA 92075
Vista	(760) 639-6100	600 Eucalyptus Avenue Vista, CA 92084
County of SD	(858) 694-2960	5201 Ruffin Road, Suite B San Diego, CA 92123

ROGUE INVESTOR NOTE: Additional information on web page.

(5) INFORMATION ON SAN DIEGO COUNTY'S ANNUAL PUBLIC AUCTION (ORAL) TAX SALE
http://www.co.san-diego.ca.us/cnty/cntydepts/general/treastax/taxsalefaqs.html

Where and when will the next Public Auction Tax Sale for San Diego County be held? At a location and tentative date and time indicated in our next Public Auction Tax Sale Brochure, this website, and Information line (619) 531-4862. Typically our sales are held at the end of February at a downtown location.

How can I obtain a list of properties to be offered at the next Tax Sale? By completing a Tax Sale Mailing List card available through this office for our Public Auction Tax Sale brochure, which is published approximately six to eight weeks prior to a tentative sale date. The cost is $12.00 for the brochure, if mailed to you, or $10.00 if purchased at one of our office locations (http://www.co.san-diego.ca.us/cnty/cntydepts/general/treastax/contactus.html). The computer diskette is $10.00 if mailed to you, or $8.00 if purchased after December at one of our office locations. Also, the information will be available at our web site address, which is http://www.sdtreastax.com. Copies of the County Assessor's plat maps of the tax sale properties are available for perusal in the Assessor's Office, Room 103, approximately six to eight weeks prior to the tentative tax sale date. Individual maps are also available on a self-serve basis.

ROGUE INVESTOR NOTE: Additional questions and answers on web page.

(5a) Office Locations
http://www.co.san-diego.ca.us/cnty/cntydepts/general/treastax/contactus.html

Main Office – County Administrative Center
1600 Pacific Highway, Room 162
San Diego, CA 92101
phone Number: (619) 236-2424
Fax: (619) 531-6056
Office Hours: 8:00 am - 5:00 pm

ROGUE INVESTOR NOTE: Other office locations listed.

(6) Tax Sale Forms
http://www.co.san-diego.ca.us/cnty/cntydepts/general/treastax/taxsaleforms.html

Form Fill-in Feature. These forms can be filled in online and printed out for mailing to the Treasurer Tax-Collector. Click here for instructions on how to complete fill-in forms: http://www.co.san-diego.ca.us/cnty/cntydepts/general/treastax/fillins2.html.

- Deed Information:
  http://www.co.san-diego.ca.us/cnty/cntydepts/general/treastax/pdfs/DeedInfo.pdf
- Tax Sale Mailing List Card:
  http://www.co.san-diego.ca.us/cnty/cntydepts/general/treastax/pdfs/mailinglistcard.pdf

(7) Legal Advertising: NOTICE OF DIVIDED PUBLICATION OF THE PROPERTY TAX DEFAULT (DELINQUENT) LIST
http://www.co.san-diego.ca.us/cnty/cntydepts/general/treastax/pdfs/legaladvertising.pdf

---

San Francisco County, California
http://www.ci.sf.ca.us

OFFICE OF THE TREASURER-TAX COLLECTOR
http://www.sfgov.org/site/treasurer_index.asp

Susan Leal, Treasurer

(1) Overview
http://www.sfgov.org/site/treasurer_page.asp?id=13387

The Office of the Treasurer-Tax Collector is responsible for conducting the sale of tax defaulted properties.

(2) Contact Information
http://www.sfgov.org/site/treasurer_page.asp?id=13433
http://www.sfgov.org/site/treasurer_page.asp?id=13434

For questions regarding property tax, business tax, collection notices, and/or for general assistance, please contact Taxpayer Assistance.

Taxpayer Assistance (415) 554-4400
Treasurer (415) 554-4478

Office Location
City Hall, Room 140
1 Drive Carlton B. Goodlett Place
San Francisco, CA 94102

Business inquiries and payment, please mail to:
San Francisco Tax Collector
P.O. Box 7425
San Francisco, CA 94120
Email: Treasurer.TaxCollector@sfgov.org

(3) Delinquent Property Tax – FAQ
http://www.sfgov.org/site/treasurer_page.asp?id=8110

What happens if I fail to pay my delinquent taxes? Your taxes can remain unpaid for a maximum of five years following their tax default, at which time your property becomes subject to the power of sale. This means that your property will be sold at a public auction or acquired by a public agency if you do not pay the taxes before the date on which the property is offered for sale or acquisition.

SHERIFF'S DEPARTMENT
http://sfgov.org/sheriff/home.htm

Michael Hennessey, Sheriff
Email:sheriff@sfgov.org

CIVIL DIVISION
(Sheriff's Department)
http://sfgov.org/sheriff/civil.htm

The Civil Division is responsible for carrying out all judgments of the civil courts, including selling real property.

(1) Contact Information
http://sfgov.org/sheriff/directory.htm#Civil

City Hall, Room 456
1 Carlton Goodlett Place
San Francisco, CA 94102
phone = (415) 554-7235

SAN JOAQUIN COUNTY, CALIFORNIA
http://www.co.san-joaquin.ca.us

TREASURER-TAX COLLECTOR'S OFFICE
http://www.co.san-joaquin.ca.us/Treasurer

Shabbir A. Khan
Treasurer/Tax Collector
44 North San Joaquin Street
Stockton, CA 95202
phone: (209) 468-2133
Fax: (209) 468-2158
email: Treasury@co.san-joaquin.ca.us

(1) Property Tax Default Information
http://www.co.san-joaquin.ca.us/Treasurer/DefaultedPropInfo.htm

PROPERTY TAX DEFAULT (DELINQUENT) LIST

Made pursuant to Section 3371, Revenue and Taxation Code

I, SHABBIR A. KHAN, San Joaquin County Tax Collector, State of California, certify that:

Notice is hereby given that the real properties listed below were declared to be in tax default at 12:01 a.m. on July 1, 2002, by operation of law. The declaration of default was due to non-payment of the total amount due for the taxes, assessments and other charges levied in 2001-2002 that were a lien on the listed real property. The name of the assessee and the total, which was due June 28, 2002, is shown opposite the parcel number, which describes the property. Tax-defaulted real property may be redeemed by payment of all unpaid taxes and assessments, together with the additional penalties and fees, as prescribed by law, or it may be redeemed under an installment plan of redemption. If the taxes remain unpaid after June 30, 2007 the property will be subject to sale at public auction. All information concerning redemption of tax-defaulted property will be furnished, upon request, by SHABBIR A. KHAN, San Joaquin County Tax Collector, 44 N. San Joaquin Street, Stockton, California 95202, (209) 468-2133.

"I declare under penalty of perjury that the foregoing is true and correct."

SHABBIR A. KHAN
San Joaquin County Tax Collector
Executed at Stockton, California
San Joaquin County, August 25, 2003

PARCEL NUMBERING SYSTEM EXPLANATION

The Assessor's Parcel Number (APN), when used to describe property in this list, refers to the assessor's map book, the map page, the block on the map, if applicable, and to the individual parcel numbers on the map page or in the block.

A parcel number such as 016-105-04 would be analyzed as follows:

- 016 would be the map book number; 105 would be the map page 10 and block 5 (if the "5" were a "0", that page would not contain a block); 04 is the parcel number.
- A parcel number with the suffixes 90, 80, 70 or 60 (such as 016-104-04-90) indicates a segregation of the original parcel.

The maps referred to are available for inspection in the office of the Assessor.

PROPERTY TAX DEFAULTED IN THE YEAR 2002, FOR THE TAXES, ASSESSMENTS AND OTHER CHARGES FOR THE FISCAL YEAR 2001-2002:

CLICK HERE for List of Properties: http://www.co.san-joaquin.ca.us/Treasurer/DefaultedProp2003.htm

Date: October 1, 2003

(1a) List of Properties
http://www.co.san-joaquin.ca.us/Treasurer/DefaultedProp2003.htm

ROGUE INVESTOR NOTE: list saved on CD:
USA Tax Lien Info/California/san_joaquin_co_CA/delinquent_property_list.htm

(2) Tax Collection Division Services
http://www.co.san-joaquin.ca.us/Treasurer/serv.htm

Auction of Power to Sell Property

(3) Auction
from http://www.co.san-joaquin.ca.us/Treasurer, click on "Auction" under Program/Services header

Public Auction…How It Works

The following explains the sale of tax-defaulted land by public auction. When secured real property remains tax-defaulted for five years, it becomes subject to the Tax Collector's Power to Sell, and may be sold at public auction. The purpose of offering tax-defaulted property at auction is to collect the unpaid taxes.

San Joaquin holds "In-Person" Public Auctions.

How often are public auctions held? The law requires that a sale be held at least once every four years. San Joaquin County strives to hold auctions once a year.

Are tax sales publicly advertised? Yes. State law dictates that notice of a tax sale must be published once a week for three successive weeks in a newspaper of general circulation published in the county.

How can I obtain a list of properties that will be offered for sale at public auction? The list of available properties can be requested by sending $5.00 to San Joaquin County Treasurer-Tax Collector, P.O. Box 2169, Stockton, CA 95201-2169. For further information please call the County Tax Collector's Office, Redemption Division, at (209) 468-2133.

Can I obtain property available at the tax sale by paying the delinquent taxes prior to the tax sale date? No. Legal title to a tax-defaulted property subject to the Tax Collector's Power to Sell can be obtained only by becoming the successful bidder at the public auction. Paying the taxes prior to the auction will redeem the property for the assessed owner.

When is the last day the property owner may redeem the tax-defaulted property to prevent its sale at public auction? The right to redeem tax-defaulted property subject to the Power to Sell ceases at the close of business on the last business day prior to the sale. The right to redeem revives if the property does not sell at the public auction.

How do I find or see property on which I want to bid at the tax sale? Improved properties frequently will have a "situs" (street) address, making it easier to determine its general location. However, vacant land, which accounts for most properties offered at auction, usually has no address. Parcel maps, obtainable through the County Assessor's Office by phoning (209) 468-2658, can determine the approximate location of any parcel. Exact boundary lines of a property can be determined only by a survey of the property, initiated at the prospective purchaser's expense.

How can I determine what use I can make of a tax sale property before I purchase it? Buyer Beware! It is your responsibility as a bidder to have investigated any parcels that you wish to bid on. No statements are made nor implied as to what you may use the parcel for if you are the successful bidder. It is recommended you physically look at the property to determine its use

The Tax Collector does not guarantee access or use of any parcel. Prospective purchasers should conduct an appropriate review to determine property use and value before bidding. This review may include, but is not limited to, (1) consulting with the zoning department of the city or the zoning section of the County Department of Planning and Building, (2) examining the County Recorder's records for any recorded easements on the property, (3) viewing the property.

Who qualifies as a potential bidder at public auction? All bidders must be at least 18 years of age. Bidders must register and receive their Bidder's Packet and Registration Number prior to placing any bids. A picture identification must be presented when registering to bid. If you will be acting as an agent, a notarized letter from the individual for whom you will be bidding, stating the manner in which title is to be vested, is required.

Can I mail in or submit a sealed bid for a property in the auction? No. The public auction requires your presence, or that of your representative, to verbally bid upon the properties.

How is the minimum bid amount determined? When a property first becomes eligible for public auction, the minimum bid cannot be less than the total amount to redeem the property, plus costs associated with offering the parcel for sale. If any property is not sold due to lack of interested bidders, the minimum bid for those particular properties may be reduced at subsequent sales.

How and when does the successful bidder pay for a property at the tax sale? Cash, cashiers check or money order. Personal checks will be accepted if accompanied with a letter of credit from your bank. The letter of credit needs to state that the funds are available the day of the sale and at least 10 days after the auction. Payment must be made immediately following the final bid for each parcel. Only those payment types listed above are authorized. No other method of payment will be accepted.

Do liens or encumbrances on tax-defaulted property transfer to the new owner after the purchase of the property at public auction? Section 3712 of the California Revenue and Taxation Code states in relevant part:
Title conveyed. The deed conveys title to the purchaser free of all encumbrances of any kind existing before the sale, except:

(a) Any lien for installments of taxes and special assessments, which installments will become payable upon the secured roll after the time of the sale.

(b) The lien for taxes or assessments or other rights of any taxing agency which does not consent to the sale under this chapter.

(c) Liens for special assessments levied upon the property conveyed which were, at the time of the sale under this chapter, not included in the amount necessary to redeem the tax-defaulted property . . ..

(d) Easements constituting servitudes upon or burdens to the property; water rights, the record title to which is held separately from the title to the property; and restrictions of record.

(e) Unaccepted, recorded, irrevocable offers of dedication of the property to the public or a public entity for a public purpose, and recorded options of any taxing agency to purchase the property or any interest therein for a public purpose.

(f) Unpaid assessments under the Improvement Bond Act of 1915 (Division 10 [commencing with Section 8500] of the Streets and Highways Code) which are not satisfied as a result of the sale of proceeds being applied pursuant to Chapter 1.3 (commencing with Section 4671) of Part 8.

(g) Any federal Internal Revenue Service liens which, pursuant to provisions of federal law, are not discharged by the sale, even though the tax collector has provided proper notice to the Internal Revenue Service before that date.

(h) Unpaid special taxes under the Mello-Roos Community Facilities Act of 1982 that are not satisfied as a result of the sale proceeds being applied pursuant to Chapter 1.3 (commencing with Section 4671) of Part 8.

Are there any guarantees that accompany property acquired at public auction? No. All parcels sold at public auction are sold "as is." No warranty is expressed or implied in any manner regarding property sold at the public auction, including, but not limited to, the following example: no claims are made to guarantee access to, or building permits for, any of the parcels involved in the sale. Prior to bidding, it is the bidder's responsibility to adequately research properties to know what is being purchased. Lack of adequate research may result in the purchase of unusable property, with no entitlement to a refund.

ALL SALES ARE FINAL

How will title to the property be vested? Title will be vested in the name of the actual purchaser present at the sale. If you are acting as an agent, and title is to be vested differently, a letter is required from the individual for whom you are acting as agent, stating the manner in which title is to be vested. A Notary according to California law must acknowledge the signature of the individual.

How soon can I take possession of a property after my purchase at the public auction? The successful bidder may take possession of a property immediately after making payment in full. A tax deed will be issued to the purchaser within 60 days of the auction. However, the validity of the Tax Collector's deed to the purchaser may be challenged within one year after the execution of the deed. In addition, if the property purchased has an IRS lien on it, the Internal Revenue Service has the right to redeem the property from the purchaser, up to 120 days from the date of the sale.

If you have any questions or comments regarding any of the brochures, please write to the San Joaquin County Treasurer-Tax Collector, P.O. Box 2169, Stockton, California 95201-2169.

ROGUE INVESTOR NOTE: Information on web page is dated May 10, 2002 and includes information for a 2002 public auction.

SHERIFF'S OFFICE
from http://www.co.san-joaquin.ca.us/TopLevelPages/departmentsCat.htm, click on "Sheriff-Coroner-Public Administrator's Office" under header Law & Justice

Sheriff Baxter Dunn
phone: (209) 468-4562,4565

CIVIL DIVISION
(Sheriff's Office)
from Sheriff's home page, click on "Civil Division"

phone: (209) 468-4475
Fax: (209) 468-5516
Sgt. Sam Malcolm, email = smalcolm@co.san-joaquin.ca.us

(1) Other Services
from Civil Division home page, click on "Other Services"

Real property sales. For further information, please contact Margie at (209) 468-4478 or send an email to miturraran@co.san-joaquin.ca.us.

SAN MATEO COUNTY, CALIFORNIA
http://www.co.sanmateo.ca.us

TAX COLLECTOR-TREASURER'S OFFICE
http://www.co.sanmateo.ca.us/smc/department/tax/home/0,,65031_65077,00.html

555 County Center, 1st Floor
Redwood City, California 94063
phone: (650) 363-4142
email: Taxmaster@co.sanmateo.ca.us

(1) Secured Property Taxes, FAQ

http://www.co.sanmateo.ca.us/smc/department/tax/home/0,2242,65031_36012595,00.html

What are "secured" property taxes? The term "Secured" simply means taxes that are assessed against real property (e.g., land or structures). The tax is a lien that is "secured" by the land/structure even though no document was officially recorded. This means that if the taxes remain unpaid after a period of 5 years, the property may be sold to cover the taxes owed.

(2) Some Important Dates

http://www.co.sanmateo.ca.us/smc/department/tax/home/0,2242,65031_36016709,00.html

January 1, Tax Lien Date

SHERIFF'S OFFICE
http://www.smcsheriff.com

(1) Contact Information

from http://www.smcsheriff.com, click on "General Information"

San Mateo County Sheriff's Office
400 County Center
Redwood City, CA 94063
email: gbalkus@co.sanmateo.ca.us

(2) Civil Bureau

from http://www.smcsheriff.com, click on "Divisions/Units" and then on "Civil Division" under Support Services Division header

400 County Center, 3rd Floor
Redwood City, CA, 94063
phone: (650) 363-4497
fax: (650) 363-4833

SALES
Notices of Sheriff's Sales are posted on the public bulletin board, First Floor, Hall of Justice and Records, 400 County Center, Redwood City. Real Property sales are also published in the San Mateo County Times and posted in the Redwood City Main Library. The Sheriff's Office does not maintain a mailing list for auctions.

Prospective bidders should refer to Section 701.510 to 701.680, inclusive, of the Civil Code of Procedure for provisions governing the terms, conditions, and effect of the sale and the liability of defaulting bidders. (701.547 CCP)

SANTA CLARA COUNTY, CALIFORNIA
http://claraweb.co.santa-clara.ca.us

FINANCE AGENCY, TAX COLLECTOR'S OFFICE
http://www.sccgov.org/site/0,4760,sid%253D13768,00.html

The Finance Agency's Tax Collector's Office bills and collects current and delinquent taxes under the authority of the State Revenue and Taxation Code, administers tax-defaulted property until disposition, and processes all tax roll changes.

Cheryl Johnson, Tax Collector
Tax Collector's Office
70 West Hedding Street
East Wing, 6th Floor
San Jose, CA 95110
Phone: (408) 808-7900
Email: scctax@tax.co.scl.ca.us

(1) Frequently Asked Questions Glossary
http://www.sccgov.org/content/0,4745,chid%253D125404%2526ccid%253D26977,00.html

Certificate of Tax Lien
- Lien: A form of encumbrance which usually makes specific property security for the payment of a debt. Usually a recorded document. Example: judgments, taxes, mortgages, deeds of trust, etc.
- Lien Date: The time when taxes for any fiscal year become an encumbrance on property, January 1.

OFFICE OF THE SHERIFF
http://www.sccsheriff.org

(1) Contact Information
http://www.sccgov.org/channel/0,4770,chid%3D335613%26sid%3D12655,00.html

Santa Clara County
Office of the Sheriff, Laurie Smith
Headquarters
55 West Younger Avenue
San Jose, California 95110-1721

Toll Free: (800) 211-2220
Phone: (408) 808-4900
FAX: (408)283-0562
e-mail: so.website@sho.co.scl.ca.us

(2) Civil Division
http://www.sccgov.org/channel/0,4770,chid%253D16067%2526sid%253D12655,00.html

55 West Younger Avenue
San Jose, CA 95110-1722
Phone: (408) 808-4800 / Fax (408) 998-0636

SANTA CRUZ COUNTY, CALIFORNIA
http://www.co.santa-cruz.ca.us

TREASURER -TAX COLLECTOR'S OFFICE
http://www.santa-cruzcountyca.us/ttc

Richard Bedal, Treasurer-Tax Collector
Room 150, County Government Center
Santa Cruz, California 95060
Phone: (831)454-2510
Fax: (831)454-2257
Email: ttc001@co.santa-cruz.ca.us

(1) Public Auction of Tax Defaulted Properties
http://www.co.santa-cruz.ca.us/ttc/auction.htm

Public Auction... How It Works
When secured real property remains tax-defaulted for five years, it becomes subject to the Tax Collector's Power to Sell, and may be sold at public auction. The purpose of offering tax-defaulted property at auction is to collect the unpaid taxes and to convey title of the property to a responsible owner.

Next Auction – 2005. Unscheduled as of yet.
Our next auction will be in 2005. At this time no exact date has been set. It will be on our web site at that time. If you want us to mail you the list when available, please send us a stamped, self-addressed envelope to:

County Tax Collector
P.O. Box 1817
Santa Cruz, CA 95061-1817

ROGUE INVESTOR NOTE: See web page for additional information.

(2) Auction Results from March 2003
http://www.co.santa-cruz.ca.us/ttc/auction2003.htm

VENTURA COUNTY, CALIFORNIA
http://www.ventura.org

TREASURER-TAX COLLECTOR'S OFFICE
http://www.ventura.org/taxcollector

Lawrence Matheney, Treasurer, Tax Collector, Public Administrator

(1) Contact Information
http://www.ventura.org/taxcollector/PhoneNum.html

Ventura CountyTax Collector
800 South Victoria Avenue
Ventura, CA 93009-1290

- Public Auction Tax Sales
  phone: 805-654-3741
- Personal Property Tax Liens & Releases
  phone: 805-654-3727
- Real Estate Property Tax
  phone: 805-654-3744

(2) Public Auction of Tax-Defaulted Properties
http://www.ventura.org/taxcollector/auction.htm

The next auction will be held on March 26, 2004 at 9:00 a.m. The auction will be held at the Ventura County Government Center, Administration Building, Lower Plaza Assembly Room, 800 South Victoria Avenue, Ventura, CA 93009-1290.

An Auction Book containing a List of Properties for Sale (http://www.ventura.org/taxcollector/list.htm) and a complete package of parcel maps is available now.

It also includes information regarding Auction requirements and the Terms of Sale (http://www.ventura.org/taxcollector/saleterm.htm).

If you would like to purchase an Auction Booklet, you may either buy one at the front counter of the Ventura County Tax Collector's Office for a cost of $10.00, or you may send a check for $12.50 (includes postage and handling) along with your name and mailing address to: Tax Collector, Attention Auction Booklet, 800 S. Victoria Avenue, Ventura, CA 93009-1290.

(2a) List of Properties for Sale
http://www.ventura.org/taxcollector/list.htm

Public Auction Property Listing: March 26, 2004
Last updated: Wednesday, February 4, 2004, at 11:48:29 PST

ROGUE INVESTOR NOTE: sales list saved on CD:
USA Tax Lien Info/California/ventura_co_CA/sales_list.htm

(2b) Terms of Sale
http://www.ventura.org/taxcollector/saleterm.htm

Colorado

Tax Lien Sales: Yes

Tax Deed Sales: No

Rating: Three Stars (***)

Interest Rate: 9% + Federal Discount Rate

Sale Period: October or November in most counties.

Redemption Period: 3 years

Bidding Process:
Some auctions are by competitive bid, while others are through a round-robin process. The bidding process is highly county dependent. The winning bidder pays the total advertised price consisting of tax, interest to the date of sale and an advertising fee. The winning bidder also pays a certificate fee plus any premium bid. A premium bid is the amount paid above the total advertised tax lien fee, which essentially results in a lower interest rate on your earnings.

Most counties require cash or certified funds to be placed on the deposit before you bid. During bidding, you cannot exceed your deposit amount. Each buyer must complete a W-9, which can be obtained from the IRS.

Tax lien sale advertisements usually appear in county newspapers about three weeks prior to the sale. Bidders must fill out a Bidder Information Card.

State-Specific Information:
Colorado is a decent state for tax sales. Property ownership because of non-redemption, although rare, can be lucrative because land is often valuable.

Links for All Colorado Counties: Provided on CD.

Detailed County-Specific Information:

DENVER COUNTY, COLORADO
http://www.denvergov.org

TREASURY DIVISION
http://198.202.202.66/Treasury

(1) FAQ
http://198.202.202.66/Treasury/410faq800.asp

(2) Property Tax Info (Tax Lien Sales)
http://198.202.202.66/Treasury/4109248template1jump.asp

(2a) General Property Tax Information
http://198.202.202.66/Treasury/template110468.asp

Research of records for tax status should be addressed to Taxpayer Service Unit, Treasury Division, Annex III, 144 West Colfax Avenue, Denver, CO 80202. There is a $15.00 per hour charge for research payable in advance.

If you have any further questions, contact us at (720) 865-7070. If you have questions concerning valuation, call the Assessor's Office at (720) 913-4162.

ROGUE INVESTOR NOTE: Additional information on web page.

(2b) Rules for the Treasure's Annual Sale of Real Estate Tax Liens
http://198.202.202.66/Treasury/template110488.asp

Any questions regarding the Annual Tax Lien Sale should be directed to the Treasury Division, Taxpayer Service Section, 144 West Colfax Avenue, Denver Colorado 80202, phone: (720) 865-7070.

ROGUE INVESTOR NOTE: Information on web page is regarding registration/deposits, seating, tax lists and bidding on web page (information is for a 2003 sale).

(2c) Information on the Sale of Delinquent Real Property Tax Liens
http://198.202.202.66/Treasury/template110470.asp

The Tax Lien Sale is usually held around the first part of November. Buyers pay the total advertised price consisting of tax, interest to the date of sale and an advertising fee. They also pay a $4.00 certificate fee plus any premium bid. The person paying the highest amount is issued a Certificate of Purchase. This is a negotiable document representing a recorded lien on the property. It is valid for 15 years. The buyer does not recover the premium paid over the starting amount. The certificate earns interest at the rate stated on the certificate with portions of calendar months considered as whole months.

A buyer list showing certificate numbers, schedule numbers and total paid will be provided to the Taxpayer. Buyers are responsible for keeping adequate records. The Treasury Division is responsible for the sale of the tax lien, immediate notification to buyers of redemptions and payment upon surrender of the redeemed certificate. (We will hold your certificate if you wish and provide copies to you.)

The redemption amount paid is the certificate amount (tax, interest, advertising, and fees), plus redemption interest. The annual redemption interest rate for each year's sale is established by adding 9% to the September 1st Federal Reserve discount rate. One twelfth of this rate accrues for each month or portion thereof. The September 1, 2002 discount rate was 1.25%. The redemption rate for certificates sold in November of 2002 will be 10% or .833% per month. Upon redemption, we notify the buyer to return their certificate for payment of the certificate face value plus accrued interest. If we are holding your certificate, a check will be mailed immediately.

Buyers may after July 1st pay the subsequent year's unpaid taxes for endorsement onto their certificates. These payments earn the same rate of interest as does the original sale.

If the property has not been redeemed after three years, the buyer can apply for and receive a Treasurer's Deed to the property. Buyers return their certificates to us and deposit expense money. After a title search, advertising, and notification of all interested parties, a Treasurer's Tax Deed is issued if there has been no redemption.

Erroneous sales are paid interest at the rate of 2% above the discount rate rounded to the nearest full percent but no lower than 8%. The lower redemption interest rate is applicable to discoveries made after May 23, 1988 and can be applied to the entire certificate regardless of when the certificate was purchased.

If you wish to participate in our sale, please notify us that you need a copy of the rules showing the date of the sale and any details. Information will be mailed to you after September 1st. We furnish a copy of the list of parcels for sale at the time of the sale.

The subject of Tax Lien Sales, Deeds, Redemptions, etc., which are administered by County Treasurers, is covered by Colorado Revised Statutes, Title 39, Articles 11, and 12. Any questions should be referred to the Taxpayer Service Unit at (720) 865-7070.

(2d) Tax Lien Sale Announcements
http://198.202.202.66/Treasury/template110472.asp

(4e) Payment of Subsequent Years' Taxes
http://198.202.202.66/Treasury/template110481.asp

(5) Contact Information
http://198.202.202.66/Treasury/410contact.asp

Steve Hutt, Treasurer
phone: 720-865-7202

City and County of Denver
Treasury Division
McNichols Civic Center Building
144 W. Colfax Avenue
Denver, CO 80202-5391

General email address for Treasury: treasinfo@ci.denver.co.us

Property Tax Information
Taxpayer Service Unit
phone: 720-865-7070

DOUGLAS COUNTY, COLORADO
http://www.douglas.co.us

TREASURER'S OFFICE
from http://www.douglas.co.us/Orgchart_top.htm, click on "Treasurer"

Sharon Jones, Treasurer
Douglas County Treasurer
100 Third Street
Castle Rock, CO 80104
Email: dctreasurer@douglas.co.us

Office prepares and conducts the annual tax lien sale.

(1) Investor's Guide to the Annual Tax Sale
from Treasurer's Office home page, click on "Investor's Guide to Annual Tax Sale" in left column

Tax Lien Registration
100 Third Street
Philip S. Miller Building
Computer Registration Treasurer's Office, 1st Floor

(1) If you are pre-registered, go to pre-registered check-in station in Treasurer's Office.

(2) If you are not pre-registered, go to the Treasurer's office to pick up the registration forms; these can be filled out in Conference Rooms A and B. Once completed, take the forms back to the Treasurer's office for computer registration AT OPEN REGISTRATION STATIONS.

When you have completed registration and received your bidder's number card, proceed to the Sale Room (Commissioner's Hearing Room). Coffee and doughnuts will be available in Conference Rooms A & B.

Tax Lien Auction

100 Third Street, Commissioners' Hearing Room. Sale Begins at 9:00 a.m.

Purchases include all taxes, advertising, penalty, and any premiums bid. Please monitor your purchase so you don't purchase more liens than you are prepared to pay for. Inability to pay for purchase will result in loss of bidder status and liens purchased. Liens not paid for will be re-offered to eligible bidders.

Check-Out: Treasurer's Office, where you registered.

All registered buyers must return bidder number card to a check-out clerk. Present your bidder number to check-out clerk. You will receive a print-out of your purchases and account balance. Please review carefully, and make payment for said purchases. REMEMBER: Your bidder number card is your i.d. as a registered buyer.

(2) Rules for Annual Tax Sale
from Treasurer's home page, click on "Rules for Annual Tax Sale" in left column

Payment of taxes: Taxes must be paid by 4:30 p.m. November 5, 2003. No payments will be accepted on the day of the sale. If tax lien has already been sold, 1 month's tax lien interest will be charged in addition to fees and advertising. Payment must be in cash or certified funds. Taxes, interest, and penalties must be paid by November 5 to avoid taxes going to tax lien sale. Once delinquent taxes have been advertised, they must be paid in certified funds.

Form W-9: The IRS now requires County Treasurers to report, on form 1099, interest income earned through tax lien investments. W-9 forms are available, and should be completed prior to registration. If a W-9 is not on file with the Treasurer's office, the Treasurer will withhold 30% of interest earned at the time the tax lien certificate is redeemed.

Deposits: We will no longer require funds on deposit to purchase liens at our Tax Lien Sale. All bids must be covered by certified funds, or personal checks. Buyers are responsible for ensuring that the information on the registration form is legible and correct, and that the name given to the registration clerks is the same as that on the registration form since the certificates of purchase are prepared from this information. Each bidder will bid in the names on the registration forms held by them.

Refunds: Deposited funds in excess of purchases, if any, will be refunded after all post-sale balancing completes or within three business days.

Registration: 7:30 A.M. Treasurer's Office, 100 Third Street, Philip S. Miller Executive Building. For a printable Registration form, please click here: http://www.douglas.co.us/Treasurer/2003%20Tax%20Sale%20Registration%20Form.pdf.

Seating: Seating will be on the basis of arrival with no reserved seats. The doors of the sale room (first floor Hearing Room) will open at 7:30 a.m.

Sale: A complimentary, updated currently deleted listing will be available in book form the day of the sale. This list will be followed in numerical order as closely as possible during the sale. A currently deleted copy of the newspaper publication will be posted near the entrance to the sale room.

The sale will be conducted as rapidly as possible consistent with the objectives of the sale and fair play to all bidders.

As is expected at auctions, premiums are allowed. Rules of other persons and/or counties will not apply in Douglas County.

A parcel will be subject to open bidding and the taxes will be sold to that person "who shall further pay the largest amount in cash in excess of said taxes, penalty, interest and costs." On taxes of $500 or less, premium bids will be in $5.00 increments. On taxes of $501 and up, premium bids must be in increments of $10 or more.

The auctioning will fairly provide all bidders present and qualified the opportunity to compete in an open bidding procedure. No parcel will be passed until after further bidding has been refused twice. Parcels not bid on during the sale will be struck off to the County at the conclusion of the Tax Lien Sale. (C.R.S. 39-11-108[III]).

The sale position number, tax schedule (parcel) number, and total dollar amount of each parcel will be read only once by the auctioneer. All successful bids are final. No changes in, or cancellations of, parcels will be made after the parcel has been sold.

Pursuant to Colorado state statutes, all Special and Local Improvement District assessments will be listed and sold with any applicable ad valorem taxes.

Once a bidder ceases to purchase – i.e., closes out their account and pays for their purchases, should he/she wish to purchase additional tax liens, they must re-register, using the same bidder number from their original registration to reactivate their account.

Insofar as possible, the day will be used entirely to conduct the Tax Lien Sale. There will be a 15-minute break in the morning and, if necessary, a 45-minute lunch break and 15-minute afternoon break. Should it be necessary, the Tax Lien Sale will be reconvened the following business day.

Anyone desiring to bid on specific parcels other than through the bid process must apply at the Treasurer's office no later than November 5 and must provide proof of legal interest in such property.

Disclaimer: Purchase of a tax lien should be considered, first and foremost, as a loan to the property owner at the specified annual rate of interest with the property as collateral for that loan! IT IS NOT WITHIN THE INVESTOR'S PURVIEW TO NOTIFY THE PROPERTY OWNER OF THE LIEN OR TO TRY TO ENCOURAGE THE PROPERTY OWNER TO REDEEM THE TAX LIEN.

It is the purchaser's responsibility to determine the status of any property offered at tax lien sale. Any purchase of a tax lien is done at the purchaser's own risk. Particular attention should be given to those properties in bankruptcy; under the control of the Resolution Trust Corporation (RTC), the Federal Deposit Insurance Corporation (FDIC); those affected by the Drug Enforcement Agency (DEA); and any properties which may have a special improvement assessment or may be located in a special district which may be in financial distress. The purchase of a tax lien on these properties could result in a loss of interest. Any applicable federal laws or regulations and/or special concerns regarding any special assessments take precedence over the rights of a tax lien purchaser.

If you have any questions regarding your rights as a purchaser of a tax lien, you should consult an attorney.

Every effort has been made to determine which properties are in conservatorship or receivership of RTC or FDIC. Any properties discovered subsequent to sale which are so owned will be considered an erroneous sale by this office, if prior permission to include in sale has not been received from RTC or FDIC.

In the event of an abatement or tax roll correction on any parcel subsequent to its sale, redemption interest will be based on the reduced statutory rate (C.R.S. 39-12-111).

Douglas County Department of Planning and Community Development encourages potential purchasers to research the status of land, as it may or may not be suitable for development due to zoning restrictions, natural or man-made hazards.

Certificates: The Certificate to be issued on a successful bid will be in the statutory form, showing the lawful rates of interest (for the life of the certificate), the legal description, purchase amount, and buyer's name (as entered on the registration form), and the date of the Tax Lien Sale. Certificates will not be issued in a name other than the name or names on the registration form. THE NAMES ON THE REGISTRATION FORMS CANNOT EXCEED 26 CHARACTERS TOTAL.

The holder of original tax lien certificates may, if they wish, endorse, i.e., pay taxes for subsequent years, until the certificate is redeemed. Information on subsequent endorsements will be sent out from the Douglas County Treasurer's office in August. Original Certificates will be held at the Douglas County Treasurer's office unless otherwise requested by purchaser. Original certificates not retained by us must be returned to the Douglas County Treasurer's office for endorsement or redemption.

Interest: Interest begins on the date of sale in October/November and, June 16th thereafter. The per annum rate of interest for 2002 Tax Liens will be set by the State Banking Commissioner on September 1, 2003 and that per annum rate will remain fixed at that rate for the life of the Certificate. Premiums on bids are not refundable nor do they earn interest.

(3) Tax Lien Sale Information
from Treasurer's home page, click on "Tax Lien Sale Information" in left column

(3a) Treasurer's Deed Application
http://www.douglas.co.us/Treasurer/Applica1.pdf

(3b) Tax Sale Date Listing
http://www.douglas.co.us/Treasurer/Tax%20Lien%20Sale%20Dates%202003.pdf

(4) County Held Lien Listing
from Treasurer's home page, click on "County Held Lien Listing" in left column

ROGUE INVESTOR NOTE: listing saved on CD:
USA Tax Lien Info/Colorado/douglas_co_CO/County Held Lien Listing.pdf

(5) Tax Lien Investment Informational Presentation
http://www.douglas.co.us/Treasurer/PresentationFile101503.pdf

(6) Public Notice: Delinquent Real Property
http://www.douglas.co.us/Treasurer/Delinq%20Real%20Property.pdf

(7) Public Notice: Delinquent Minerals and Mineral Rights Property
http://www.douglas.co.us/Treasurer/Delinq%20Minerals%20&%20Min%20Rights%20Property.pdf

(8) Public Notice: Delinquent Real Property with SIDS
http://www.douglas.co.us/Treasurer/Delinq%20Real%20Property%20with%20SIDS.pdf

---

EL PASO COUNTY, COLORADO
http://www.elpasoco.com

TREASURER'S OFFICE
http://trs.elpasoco.com/default.asp

Real property and manufactured home unpaid taxes are enforced through the annual tax lien sale with the Treasurer becoming the agent through which the lien is paid.

Sandra J. Damron, Treasurer
27 E. Vermijo Avenue
Colorado Springs, CO 80903
Phone: (719) 520-6666, email: trsweb@elpasoco.com

(1) County Held Tax Lien Sales
http://trs.elpasoco.com/countyheldtaxliens.asp

The El Paso County held tax lien list consists of tax liens not purchased by investors at the public auction. These liens are available for assignment by submitting a written request to the El Paso County Treasurer's office. You are advised to research, and if possible, accomplish a site inspection of any parcel(s) prior to submitting an assignment request. It is your responsibility to determine if the property you are requesting the tax lien assignment on is worth your investment.

Parcel numbers beginning with 99000 or 99001 are for severed mineral interests.
Public record property information and parcel maps are available on the Assessor's website at http://land.elpasoco.com.

If you have additional questions, you may contact our office at (719) 520-6670.

(1a) List of El Paso County Held Tax Liens
http://trs.elpasoco.com/countyheldtaxliens.txt

Dated December 3, 2003

ROGUE INVESTOR NOTE: list saved on CD:
USA Tax Lien Info/Colorado/denver_co_CO/countyheldtaxliens.txt

(2) Tax Lien Sale Procedures
http://trs.elpasoco.com/saleproc.asp

Real property and mobile home delinquent taxes are enforced through the annual tax lien sale.

Date, Time, Location
The sale of El Paso County's unpaid taxes and special assessment liens will be held on October 27, 2004. The sale will be conducted at 9:00 a.m. at the following location:

El Paso County Office Building
27 East Vermijo Avenue, 3rd Floor
Colorado Springs, CO 80903

Deposits
All bids must be covered by cash, certified checks, or personal checks guaranteed by irrevocable letters of credit from the bank on which the check is drawn and deposited with the Treasurer prior to opening of the sale. Bidders' deposits are made in the Office of the County Treasurer, 27 East Vermijo Avenue, First Floor, Colorado Springs, Colorado. Deposits will be accepted up to one week before sale day and the office will be open at 8:00 a.m. on the sale day.

Deposits must be made in the name which will appear on the tax lien sale certificate and no transfers of deposits from one account to another are permitted during the sale. When the deposit of a buyer equals the total consideration (taxes, interest, costs, and bonus bids) stricken off to him/her, he/she shall no longer be recognized as a buyer unless an additional deposit in compliance with original deposit criteria is made. Unused deposits will be returned as quickly as possible after the close of the sale.

Seating
Seating is limited and reserved for registered participants. Those who want to observe may do so from the back of the room or outer corridor.

Buyer Data
Only one bidder card will be issued per buyer. Each buyer must be present and registered to participate in the sale. Each buyer is required to complete an Internal Revenue Service Form W-9 with name, address, and social security number or federal tax identification number and a buyer registration form. After the forms have been completed and the buyer has provided proof of deposit, he/she will be assigned a bidder number and given a bidder's card.

IRS Form W-9 (http://www.irs.gov/pub/irs-pdf/fw9.pdf)
Buyer's Registration Form (http://trs.elpasoco.com/BuyerRegistrationForm.pdf)

Buyers are responsible to assure that the information is correct. Tax lien sale certificates, refund checks, redemption checks, and 1099 interest forms are prepared from this information.

Buyer's Responsibility
It is the buyers' responsibility to know the quality of the property on which they are paying the taxes and receiving a lien. Buyers must rely entirely on their own information, judgment, and inspection of the property records. Particular attention should be given to the impact of a bankruptcy filing which could place a cloud on the tax lien sale certificate. The recommendation of the Treasurer is that you consult with private legal counsel prior to participation in the tax lien sale.

Sale Procedures
Each parcel will be offered in compliance with Title 39, Article 11, of the Colorado Revised Statutes. To facilitate the sale procedure, parcels which are contiguous or contained within one subdivision may be combined and sold as a group.

The base (minimum) amount for each tax lien will be comprised of the unpaid ad valorem tax, special assessment, late payment interest, advertising cost, and fees.

The tax liens will be separated into categories to facilitate the sale.

- <u>Category One</u> will contain the liens where the total amount of the lien is less than or equal to $100.00. These liens will be offered for general (open) bidding and will be sold to the buyer who pays the largest amount (bonus bid) in excess of the minimum amount.
- <u>Category Two</u> will contain the liens for a single property or multiple properties where the total amount of the lien is greater than $100.00 and less than or equal to $2,000.00. These tax liens will be offered for rotation bidding. Rotation bidding will be in buyer number order. Each buyer has the right of refusal and the lien will be offered to the next buyer until sold. The next lien will be offered to the buyer whose number follows the purchaser of the previous lien. If no buyer elects to purchase a lien offered in rotation, the lien will be offered for general (open) bidding at the end of the sale.
- <u>Category Three</u> will contain the liens for a single property or multiple properties where the total lien is greater than $2,000.00. These tax liens will be offered for general (open) bidding and will be sold to the buyer who pays the largest amount (bonus bid) in excess of the minimum amount.
- <u>Category Four</u> will contain the liens for properties with alert information. The alert information is a good faith effort to share known information with prospective tax lien sale buyers. It is not all inclusive. The Treasurer and the County are unable to warrant the alert information or lack of alert information. The tax lien sale buyer participates at his or her own risk. These liens will be offered for general (open) bidding.

The sale process is subject to change depending on the number of tax liens available.

The sequence index number and the base (minimal) amount of each parcel or unit will be read only once. All successful bids are final (assuming the buyer has sufficient monies on deposit). No changes in, or cancellation of, parcels purchased can be made after the lien is sold.

The sale will be conducted as rapidly as possible, consistent with the objectives of the sale and in fairness to all buyers. We will have a lunch break at approximately 12:00 noon or may choose to continue until the sale is completed.

If a continuance of the tax lien sale is necessary, the sale will be reconvened on the succeeding business day. Any announcement of adjournment or reconvening will be made at the sale.

Rules for General (Open) Bidding
Tax liens will be sold to the person who shall pay in addition to the lien amount a bonus (premium) bid. Bonus (premium) bids are not returned or recovered when a tax lien is redeemed (cured).

Bonus Bids

Bonus (premium) bids will not be less than $1.00 and, after reaching $5.00, will be increased by increments of $5.00 to $20.00. After reaching a bonus bid of $20.00, the amount will be increased by increments of $10.00. After reaching a bonus bid of $100.00, the amount will be increased by increments of $50.00.

Record of Purchase

A tax lien sale certificate of purchase will be issued for each property and will be in the statutory form stating the property description, purchase amount, rate of interest, buyer's name, and the date of sale. Certificates will not be issued in a name other than the name of the buyer. If delinquent taxes occur in the future, the certificate holder may endorse the amount of delinquent taxes and lawful charges onto his/her certificate until redemption.

Redemption Interest

Interest begins to accrue from the month the certificate is issued. The interest earned is calculated based on the interest rate and the number of months up to and including the month of redemption. There is no compounding. The interest rate for tax lien sale certificates of purchase in 2003 is eleven percent. (The rate of interest is nine percentage points above the discount rate on September 1, 2003 rounded to the nearest full percent.) The interest rate for the 2004 sale will be known after September 1, 2004.

Prohibited Buyers

No El Paso County official or employee may purchase a tax lien at this sale. This also applies to the immediate family or any agent of an El Paso County official or employee.

General Information

It must be understood that the sale and purchase of the tax or special assessment lien at a tax lien sale does not, as it might under simple sales and purchase agreements, convey the right of possession, use, improvement, or access to the property. The buyer is issued a tax lien sale certificate of purchase on which he/she is entitled to interest. The lien may be redeemed by the property owner, recorded lienholder or by the agent of either party at any time prior to the issuance of a Treasurer's tax deed. A Treasurer's tax deed cannot be issued prior to the third anniversary of the tax lien.

The certificate holder has the right of paying subsequent years delinquent taxes (sub-taxing). Sub-taxing occurs after June 16 each year, since redemption interest accrues only after the taxes become delinquent.

If the lien remains unredeemed (not cured) and becomes eligible for a tax deed, the certificate holder must make application to the Treasurer in order to initiate the process. The procedural process requirements normally take nine to twelve months to accomplish. An extension of the time period may occur when there are complex problems related to the property. Deed applications may be made four calendar months prior to the third anniversary date of the certificate. When application is made, monies must be deposited to pay all related deed expenses. The deed application processing costs are recoverable if the property is redeemed; however, no redemption interest is earned on the deed expense deposit. Prior to receiving a Treasurer's tax deed, all subsequent taxes, special assessment liens, and current taxes must be paid. El Paso County makes no guarantee for the condition or marketability of any property which is acquired through a Treasurer's tax deed.

WRONGFULLY SOLD LIEN: a lien is wrongfully sold and the County must pay the certificate holder the redemption interest, the rate will be calculated as set forth in Section 39-12-111, Colorado Revised Statutes.

Publication Information

The real estate list of unpaid taxes will be published for three consecutive weeks on September 28, October 6 and October 13, 2004. The publisher will be known after September 1, 2004. The list of unpaid taxes for the 2004 tax sale and parcel maps will be available beginning October 2004 on our website: http://trs.elpasoco.com/TaxSale.asp. The list will be updated periodically for accounts that are paid.

Contact Information

If there are further questions, contact the El Paso County Treasurer at the following:

P.O. Box 2007
Colorado Springs, CO 80901-2007
Telephone (719) 520-6666
E-mail: trsweb@elpasoco.com
Web Site: http://trs.elpasoco.com

(3) Frequently Asked Questions: Real Property Tax Lien Sale Information
http://trs.elpasoco.com/faqlien.asp

(3a) Real Estate Tax Lien Sale of 2002 Taxes Payable in 2003
http://trs.elpasoco.com/TaxSale.asp

Tax lien sale information for 2003 taxes payable in 2003 is no longer available. Please visit us again in October 2004 for information on 2003 taxes payable in 2004.

(3b) Buyer Registration Form
http://trs.elpasoco/BuyerRegistrationForm.pdf

(4) Redemption Statistics
http://trs.elpasoco/Redmstats.asp

JEFFERSON COUNTY, COLORADO
http://co.jefferson.co.us

TREASURER'S OFFICE
http://co.jefferson.co.us/ext/dpt/officials/treas/index.htm

100 Jefferson County Parkway
Golden, CO 80419
303-271-8330

(1) Contact the Treasurer
http://co.jefferson.co.us/ext/dpt/officials/treas/contact_treasurer.htm

(2) Tax Lien Sale Information
http://co.jefferson.co.us/ext/dpt/officials/treas/saleinfo.htm

(3) Tax Lien Seminar
http://co.jefferson.co.us/ext/dpt/officials/treas/saleseminar.htm

(4) View Maps of Tax Lien Properties
http://co.jefferson.co.us/ext/dpt/officials/treas/maplink.htm

(5) County Held Certificates
http://co.jefferson.co.us/ext/dpt/officials/treas/countyheld.htm

(6) Register for the Tax Lien Sale
http://co.jefferson.co.us/ext/dpt/officials/treas/saleregistration.htm

(7) List of Properties
http://co.jefferson.co.us/ext/dpt/officials/treas/salepropdownload.htm

(7a) Delinquent Properties Update List
http://co.jefferson.co.us/ext/dpt/officials/treas/salepropupdates.htm

(8) Tax Sale Procedures
http://co.jefferson.co.us/ext/dpt/officials/treas/saleprocedures.htm

Advertisement of Sale
The list of tax liens available to purchase is advertised for three consecutive weeks prior to the sale in the local newspaper. A "condensed list" is issued the day of the sale. This is the advertised list minus the tax liens that have bee paid after the list was published.

Registration
All buyers are strongly encouraged to pre-register prior to the actual tax sale date. Click here for information regarding registration: http://co.jefferson.co.us/ext/dpt/officials/treas/saleregistration.htm.

The Bidding Process
You must be present and registered to participate in the bidding process. Jefferson County holds an open bid. Each buyer is issued a paddle with a number on it. When the taxes you wish to purchase are auctioned, you raise your paddle. The investor offering the highest premium (the amount above the tax due) may purchase the tax lien. Please note that the premium you bid will not be refunded to you at the time the taxes are redeemed.

Every parcel will be offered in compliance with Chapter 39, Article 11, of the Colorado Revised Statutes. To facilitate the bidding procedure, each parcel will be subject to general biding and will be sold to the person who pays the highest amount in excess of said taxes, penalty, interest, and costs. No bids of less than one dollar ($1.00) will be accepted.

All parcels listed as "unbuildable strips" will be sold separately after the other parcels have been offered for sale.

The auctioning will provided all bidders with an opportunity to compete for each parcel. No property will be struck off until after the bidding has been refused twice. The County Treasurer may change the method of sale at his discretion prior to commencement of the sale.

All successful bids are final. No changes in, or cancellation of a purchased parcel will be made after the parcel is pronounced sold.

Liens not sold at the sale
Any tax liens not sold at the sale are held by the county and are, in most cases, available to buy through the treasurer's office. Click here for more information regarding county held certificates: http://co.jefferson.co.us/ext/dpt/officials/treas/countyheld.htm.

ROGUE INVESTOR NOTE: Web page contains additional information.

Tax Lien Sales: Yes

Tax Deed Sales: No

Rating: Four Stars (****)

Interest Rate: 18% per year

Sale Period: Varies, handled by municipalities.

Redemption Period: Varies, handled by municipalities. Generally one year.

Bidding Process:
All auctions are by competitive bid. Winning bidder pays lowest interest rate. Bidding process can be complicated because municipalities within counties handle tax lien sales. After you find a county that interests you, find the specific town within that county to get more information on tax lien sales in that municipality.

State-Specific Information:

Example Statute Information

Sec. 12-173. Certificate continuing lien. Discharge. Valid notice.
(a) The collector of each municipality, by pursuing the method authorized by either section 12-174 or 12-175, may continue any tax lien existing against any item of real estate to secure the payment of the tax assessed by such municipality thereon or of any obligation to make a payment in lieu of any such tax, as defined in section 12-171, as such tax has been increased by legal interest, fees and charges, by making out and filing, within the time limited by section 12-174 or 12-175, in the office of the town clerk of the town wherein such real estate is situated, a certificate containing the following information: (1) The name of the person against whom such tax appears in the rate bill; (2) a description of such real estate; (3) the principal of such tax due thereon, the amount of which, with interest, if any, and fees and other charges, is secured by such lien; (4) the date or dates when the principal of such tax became due; and (5) a statement giving notice of his intention to file a lien pursuant to sections 12-172 and 49-73a to 49-73i, inclusive, against the proceeds of any policy of insurance providing coverage for loss or damage caused by fire, if a loss or damage has occurred. The town clerk shall record such certificate in the land records. Any tax lien so continued, when the tax has been paid with interest, fees and charges as provided by law, shall be discharged by a certificate of the then collector of taxes. Such certificate of release shall be delivered by such collector to the town clerk, who shall record it in the land records.

(b) A certificate continuing a tax lien under this section, filed in a timely manner, provides valid notice of the continuance of the lien to a subsequent purchaser or encumbrancer if the recorded certificate is sufficient to place a subsequent purchaser or encumbrancer on notice of the existence and extent of that lien, notwithstanding any error, irregularity or omission in that certificate. A certificate that erroneously states the amount due provides valid notice to a subsequent purchaser or encumbrancer up to the amount stated or the amount actually due, whichever is less.

Links for All Connecticut Counties: Provided on CD.

Detailed County-Specific Information:

Link to contact information for all Connecticut tax collectors, by city:
http://www.opm.state.ct.us/igp/TAXCOLL/Taxcoll03.doc

HARTFORD COUNTY, CONNECTICUT
http://www.hartford.gov

OFFICE OF THE TAX COLLECTOR
http://www.hartford.gov/tax/Default.htm

550 Main Street, Room 103
Hartford, CT 06103
phone: (860) 543-8565, FAX: (860) 543-8549

Donald Lefevre, Tax Collector

One of the office's initiatives is real property tax sales and liens.

(1) City of Hartford Tax Sale
http://www.hartford.gov/tax/PublicInfo/Default.htm

The City of Hartford will conduct its 14th Tax Sale in June 2004. For more information on the sale and details of the properties, please call the Tax Collector's Office at 860-543-8565, or email dmeggett@ci.hartford.ct.us.

AARON POSNIK & CO
http://www.posnik.com

Auctioneers and appraisers.

(1) 2003 Guide to the City of Hartford Tax Collector's Sale
http://www.posnik.com/html03/061403htfd/061403_gd1.htm

(2) City of Hartford Tax Sale Parcel Identification Listing
http://www.posnik.com/html03/061403htfd/061403htfd.htm

Tax Lien Sales: No

Tax Deed Sales: Yes

Rating: Two Stars (**)

Interest Rate: Counties have tax deed sales and cities have deed sales with a right of redemption. The City of Dover, Kent County offers an interest rate of 15% if redeemed in 60 days.

Sale Period: Sale dates vary depending on county rules.

Redemption Period:
Properties can be purchased at tax deed sales for immediate ownership. Cities have specific redemption periods. The City of Dover's redemption period is 60 days.

Bidding Process:
At tax deed sales, all auctions are by competitive bid. Winning bidder pays highest value for property.

State-Specific Information:
Delaware only has three counties. Each county handles tax deed sales differently. Cities or towns also can have tax sales.

Links for All Delaware Counties: Provided on CD.

Detailed County-Specific Information:

KENT COUNTY, DELAWARE
http://www.co.kent.de.us

SHERIFF'S OFFICE

Kent County Courthouse
38 The Green
Room 125
Dover, DE 19901
phone: 302-736-2161, FAX: 302-736-2164

(1) Sheriff's Sales
http://www.co.kent.de.us/sheriff_na.htm

(1a) Procedures for Sheriff's Sales
http://www.co.kent.de.us/ssprocedures.htm

1. COUNTY TAX SALES: PROPERTIES ARE BEING SOLD FOR NONPAYMENT OF COUNTY TAXES AND OR COUNTY WATER AND SEWER FEES FOR NO LESS THAN A TWO YEAR PERIOD. THESE SALES ARE HELD APPROXIMATELY EVERY THREE MONTHS.

2. CITY OR TOWN TAX SALES: PROPERTIES ARE BEING SOLD FOR NON- PAYMENT OF TOWN TAXES. ALL PROPERTIES ARE LOCATED WITHIN A TOWN OR CITY LIMITS AND TAXES HAVE

NOT BEEN PAID FOR NO LESS THAN A TWO YEAR PERIOD. THESE SALES ARE VERBAL BIDDING, PROPERTY GOING TO THE HIGHEST BIDDER.

NO MATTER WHAT IS OWED IN TAXES, THE PROPERTY IS GOING TO THE HIGHEST BIDDER.

THE FULL AMOUNT OF THE BID PRICE IS DUE DAY OF THE SALE. CASH, CERTIFIED CHECK AND CASHIER'S CHECK IS THE ONLY FORM OF PAYMENT THAT WILL BE ACCEPTED. YOU WILL BE GIVEN A COUPLE OF HOURS TO GO TO THE BANK TO SECURE FUNDS. THE ORIGINAL OWNER OF THE PROPERTY HAS APPROXIMATELY 60 DAYS TO PAY THEIR DELINQUENT TAXES PLUS 15% OF THE HIGHEST BID TO REDEEM THEIR PROPERTY.

IF FOR SOME REASON THE SALE IS OVERTURNED BY THE COURT, THE HIGHEST BIDDER WILL ONLY RECEIVE BACK THEIR BID, BUT NO 15%.

WITHIN THIS 60 DAY PERIOD, YOU WILL ONLY HEAR FROM THIS OFFICE IF THE PROPERTY IS REDEEMED OR IF THE SALE HAS BEEN OVERTURNED BY THE COURT. IF YOU DO NOT HEAR FROM THIS OFFICE, PROCEED TO YOUR ATTORNEY'S OFFICE TO HAVE YOUR DEED PREPARED. YOUR DEED WILL BE SENT OVER TO THIS OFFICE FOR THE SHERIFF'S SIGNATURE. AT THIS TIME A CHECK WILL BE MADE OUT FOR OUR 1 1/2% OF THE TRANSFER FEE.

THE SIGNED DEED AND CHECKS WILL BE RETURNED TO YOUR ATTORNEY FOR RECORDING.

3. MORTGAGE FORECLOSURES: MORTGAGE FORECLOSURES ARE USUALLY HELD THE FIRST TUESDAY OR THURSDAY OF EVERY MONTH. PROPERTIES ARE BEING SOLD FOR NONPAYMENT OF MORTGAGE. THIS SALE IS ALSO VERBAL BIDDING. PROPERTY GOING TO THE HIGHEST BIDDER. THE ATTORNEY FOR THE MORTGAGE COMPANY GIVES THE OPENING BID AND THE BIDDING STARTS FROM THERE. PRIOR TO THE SALE, WE HAVE NO IDEA WHERE THE BIDDING IS GOING TO START OR STOP. THERE IS NO REDEMPTION PERIOD FOR THIS TYPE OF SALE. IF YOU ARE THE SUCCESSFUL BIDDER, WE REQUIRE 20% OF YOUR BID PRICE THAT DAY. PAYMENT AGAIN IS CASH, CASHIER OR CERTIFIED CHECK. YOU WILL BE GIVEN A COUPLE OF HOURS TO GO TO THE BANK TO SECURE FUNDS. THE BALANCE OF YOUR BID IS DUE IN APPROXIMATELY 30 DAYS, IN THE SAME TYPE OF FORM. AFTER THE SALE IS CONFIRMED BY SUPERIOR COURT, YOU THEN GO TO YOUR ATTORNEY TO HAVE A DEED DRAWN UP. THE DEED IS SENT TO THE SHERIFF'S OFFICE TO BE SIGNED BY THE SHERIFF, AT WHICH TIME A CHECK IS CUT FOR 1 1/2% OF THE TRANSFER FEE. THE DEED ALONG WITH THE CHECK FOR THE TRANSFER FEE IS RETURNED TO YOUR ATTORNEY TO BE RECORDED. IF FOR SOME REASON THE SALE IS NOT CONFIRMED BY THE COURT, YOU WILL BE NOTIFIED. IT IS VERY IMPORTANT FOR YOU, THE BUYER, TO RESEARCH THESE PROPERTIES AS TO WHETHER THERE ARE ANY OTHER MORTGAGES OR LIENS AGAINST THE PROPERTY THAT YOU COULD BE RESPONSIBLE FOR IF YOU ARE THE SUCCESSFUL BIDDER.

THIS OFFICE DOES NOT GUARANTEE CLEAR TITLES.....

RESEARCH CAN BE DONE AT THE RECORDER OF DEEDS OFFICE, WHICH IS LOCATED IN THE O'BRIEN BUILDING ON FEDERAL STREET, DOVER, ALSO AT THE PROTHONOTARY'S OFFICE, WHICH IS LOCATED IN THE COURTHOUSE ON THE GREEN.

IF YOU PAY YOUR 20% ON THE DAY OF SALE, AND DO NOT COME BACK WITH THE BALANCE OF THE MONIES ON THE ASSIGNED DATE, YOU WILL FORFEIT YOUR 20% DOWN PAYMENT. IF YOU ARE THE SUCCESSFUL BIDDER AND YOU DO NOT COME BACK WITH THE 20% DOWN PAYMENT, OR YOU FOR SOME REASON CHANGE YOUR MIND ABOUT PURCHASING THE PROPERTY, YOU WILL BE BARRED FROM ALL FUTURE SALES.

ALL SALES ARE ADVERTISED IN THE DOVER POST AND THE DELAWARE STATE NEWS ON WEDNESDAYS. WE HAVE SALE PACKETS IN THIS OFFICE FOR THE PUBLIC TO COME BY AND PICK UP. THERE IS ALSO A COUNTY WEB SITE, WHERE SALES ARE LISTED: http://www.co.kent.de.us/sheriff_na.htm.

AS OF OCTOBER 1, 2003, A $2,000 CERTIFIED CHECK IS REQUIRED AT THE TIME YOUR WINNING BID IS ACCEPTED. THE BALANCE OF YOUR 20% MAY BE PAID WITH A PERSONAL CHECK.

(2) Future Sales
http://www.co.kent.de.us/sheriff_na.htm

(2a) February 5, 2004 Sale
http://www.co.kent.de.us/shfeb2004.htm

ROGUE INVESTOR NOTE: sale list saved on CD:
USA Tax Lien Info/Delaware/kent_co_DE/Feb2004_salelist.htm

(2b) March 4, 2004 Sale
http://www.co.kent.de.us/ss200403.htm

ROGUE INVESTOR NOTE: sale list saved on CD:
USA Tax Lien Info/Delaware/kent_co_DE/March2004_salelist.htm

NEW CASTLE COUNTY, DELAWARE
http://www.co.new-castle.de.us

OFFICE OF FINANCE
http://www.co.new-castle.de.us/Finance/Finance1.htm

Treasury
87 Reads Way
New Castle, DE 19720
Phone: (302) 323-2600

Tax Lien Sales: Yes

Tax Deed Sales: Yes

Rating: Five Stars (*****)

Interest Rate: 18% per year (minimum mandatory fee of 5%, even if redeemed early).

Sale Period: April and May in most counties.

Redemption Period: 2 years

Bidding Process:
All auctions are by competitive bid. Winning bidder pays lowest interest rate. Bids go in quarter percentage increments; for example, 17 ¾% followed by 17 ½%. Tax lien sale advertisements usually appear in county newspapers about three weeks prior to the sale. Tax deeds are offered through competitive bid to the highest bidder.

State-Specific Information:
Florida is probably one of the most famous tax lien states because the interest rate of 18% per year is favorable and, if the property goes to foreclosure, the redemption period of 2 years is short.

If the tax certificate is not redeemed, the certificate holder cannot institute foreclosure and receive the deed; rather, a public deed sale must occur. The winning bidder pays enough to redeem the tax certificate(s) plus fees for the cost of the sale and interest at 1.5% per month from the time of application of deed to the time of sale. Florida also has specific sales requirements for homestead properties. Homestead properties are sold for a minimum bid of one half of their assessed value.

Links for All Florida Counties: Provided on CD.

Detailed County-Specific Information:

BROWARD COUNTY, FLORIDA
http://www.co.broward.fl.us

REVENUE COLLECTION DIVISION
http://www.co.broward.fl.us/revenue

(1) Tax Sale Information
http://www.co.broward.fl.us/revenue/rvi00309.htm

ROGUE INVESTOR NOTE: Information not updated since September 2003 sale; additional information on web page.

The sale of Tax Certificates on Delinquent 2002 Real Estate Taxes will be held in room 422, County Commission meeting room, Governmental Center, 115 South Andrews Avenue, Fort Lauderdale, Florida, commencing Friday, September 26, 2003 at 9:30 a.m. Any additions/deletions to the following schedule will be announced Friday September 26, 2003 9:30 a.m.

Sale Notice
To be advertised in the Broward Daily Business Review: Tuesdays, September 9, 16, 23, 2003.

Deposit
A $1,000 deposit is required for each Tax Certificate buyer prior to participation in the sale. This deposit will be applied to the purchase of Tax Certificates. If no Tax Certificates are purchased, the deposit will be refunded approximately one month after the end of the tax sale.

Payment
Payments of not less than ten percent (10%) of the total bid made daily by the bidder are required. This ten percent (10%) may include the original $1,000.00 cash deposit. Only cash, certified check, bank draft or money order is acceptable (no exceptions). All checks are made payable to Broward County Revenue Collection. Personal checks, business checks, trust account checks or money market checks will not be accepted.

This payment must be made each day on the amount of certificates purchased the prior day. Non-sale days excluded. This procedure is necessary to ensure the purchaser will pay for the certificates when delivered. If a timely deposit is not made, continued participation in the tax sale will not be authorized until the amount is settled.

All bidders are responsible for researching items prior to bidding. No bids will be voided or changed. Any person neglecting or refusing to pay a bid made by himself, or on his behalf, shall not be entitled to have any other bids accepted and will forfeit the deposit.

Pick-Up Notice
Upon completion of the Tax Certificate sale, the revenue collector will notify each purchaser when the tax sale electronic listings are ready. The notification will include the balance due and the location where the purchaser can obtain the listing. The balance due must be paid within forty-eight hours of the mailing of the notice (exclusive of holidays, Saturdays and Sundays) and must be in the form of cash, money order, certified check or bank draft. Wire transfers must be received by the Revenue Collection prior to the deadlines.

Tax Certificate Information
Buyers of Tax Certificates do not bid on the property, but bid on the percentage of interest their money earns, starting at eighteen (18) percent and bidding down.

When a Certificate has been redeemed, the holder is entitled to the face value plus whatever interest it has earned at the time of the redemption. The redemption is handled through the division of revenue collection. The proceeds are remitted to the Certificate holder.

The life of a Certificate is seven (7) years from the date of issuance. However, the holder of a Tax Certificate may, at any time after two (2) years have elapsed since April 1 of the year of issuance and before the expiration date of seven (7) years, file an application for a Tax Deed. Upon application, costs of a title search, all outstanding back taxes, advertising costs, interest, sheriff costs, etc., must be paid and this amount will be the opening bid. The property would then be offered at a public auction and the holder of the Certificate could bid along with other interested persons if so desired. Failure to pay all fees within the required time could result in cancellation of the Tax Deed application and loss of all fee payments made by applicant.

The holder of a Tax Certificate may not directly, through an agent or otherwise, initiate contact with the owner of property upon which he or she holds a Tax Certificate to encourage or demand payment.

(2) Contact Information
http://www.co.broward.fl.us/revenue/rvi00310.htm

Broward County Revenue Collection Division
115 S. Andrews Avenue, Room 218
Fort Lauderdale, Florida 33301
Phone: 954-765-4697
email: revenue@broward.org

CHARLOTTE COUNTY, FLORIDA
http://www.charlottecountyfl.com

TAX COLLECTOR'S OFFICE
http://www.cctaxcol.com

Vickie Potts, Tax Collector

(1) Delinquent Real Estate Taxes
http://www.cctaxcol.com/advalorem.htm#Delinquent

Real estate taxes become delinquent on April 1st each year. Florida Statutes require the Tax Collector to advertise the delinquent parcels in a local newspaper once a week for three consecutive weeks following the payment deadline. Advertising and collection fees are added to the delinquent taxpayer's bill.

Beginning on or before June 1st, the Tax Collector is required by law to hold a Tax Certificate Sale. The certificates represent liens on all unpaid real estate properties. The sale allows citizens to buy certificates by paying off the owed tax debt. The sale is conducted in reverse auction style with participants bidding downward on interest rates starting at 18%. The certificate is awarded to the lowest bidder.

A tax certificate, when purchased, becomes an enforceable first lien against the real estate. The certificate holder is actually paying the taxes for a property owner in exchange for a competitive bid rate of return on his investment. In order to remove the lien, the property owner must pay the Tax Collector all delinquent taxes plus accrued interest, penalties and advertising fees. The Tax Collector then notifies the certificate holder of any certificates redeemed and a refund check is then issued to the certificate holder.

A tax certificate is valid for seven years from the date of issuance. The holder may apply for a tax deed when two or more years have elapsed since the date of delinquency. If the property owner fails to pay the tax debt, the property tax deed is sold at public auction.

Tax certificate sale brochure: http://www.cctaxcol.com/images/certsale.pdf

---

DADE COUNTY, FLORIDA
http://miamidade.gov

CLERK OF COURTS
http://www.miami-dadeclerk.com/dadecoc

Miami-Dade County Courthouse
73 West Flagler Street, Suite # 242
Miami, Florida 33130
Telephone: (305) 275-1155
email: recording@miamidade.gov
Harvey Ruvin, Clerk

(1) Tax Deeds Sales
http://www.miami-dadeclerk.com/tax-deeds/home.asp

Tax-Deeds Sales
140 W. Flagler Street, Room 908, Miami, Florida 33130

Effective October 1, 2001, at time of sale a $200.00 Non Refundable cash deposit will be required from the successful bidder pursuant to FLORIDA STATUE NO. 197.542 (2). The deposit shall be applied to the sale price at time of full payment. Full payment will continue to be due, as described in the STATUE, within 24 hours from time of sale.

DISCLAIMER: By using this service, in any form, the user agrees to indemnify and hold harmless the Miami-Dade Clerk of Courts and anyone involved in storing, retrieving or displaying this information for any damages of any type that may be caused by retrieving this information over the Internet. To review the complete Miami-Dade County Disclaimer, follow this link: http://co.miami-dade.fl.us/disclaimer.htm.

Tax deed sales lists:

March 3, 2004: http://www.miami-dadeclerk.com/tax-deeds/Td0303.asp
March 4, 2004: http://www.miami-dadeclerk.com/tax-deeds/Td0304.asp
March 10, 2004: http://www.miami-dadeclerk.com/tax-deeds/Td0310.asp
March 11, 2004: http://www.miami-dadeclerk.com/tax-deeds/Td0311.asp
March 17, 2004: http://www.miami-dadeclerk.com/tax-deeds/Td0317.asp
March 18, 2004: http://www.miami-dadeclerk.com/tax-deeds/Td0318.asp
March 24, 2004: http://www.miami-dadeclerk.com/tax-deeds/Td0324.asp
March 25, 2004: http://www.miami-dadeclerk.com/tax-deeds/Td0325.asp
April 7, 2004: http://www.miami-dadeclerk.com/Tax-Deeds/Td0407.asp
April 8, 2004: http://www.miami-dadeclerk.com/Tax-Deeds/Td0408.asp
April 14, 2004: http://www.miami-dadeclerk.com/Tax-Deeds/Td0414.asp
April 15, 2004: http://www.miami-dadeclerk.com/Tax-Deeds/Td0415.asp

ROGUE INVESTOR NOTE: sales lists saved on CD:
USA Tax Lien Info/Florida/dade_co_FL/March3_04_saleslist.htm, /March4_04_saleslist.htm, etc.

(2) Foreclosure Sales
http://www.miami-dadeclerk.com/foreclosure-sales/home.asp

Mortgage foreclosure sales lists:

February 25, 2004: http://www.miami-dadeclerk.com/foreclosure-sales/FC022504.asp
February 26, 2004: http://www.miami-dadeclerk.com/foreclosure-sales/FC022604.asp
February 27, 2004: http://www.miami-dadeclerk.com/foreclosure-sales/FC022704.asp
March 3, 2004: http://www.miami-dadeclerk.com/foreclosure-sales/FC030304.asp
March 4, 2004: http://www.miami-dadeclerk.com/foreclosure-sales/FC030404.asp
March 5, 2004: http://www.miami-dadeclerk.com/foreclosure-sales/FC030504.asp
March 10, 2004: http://www.miami-dadeclerk.com/foreclosure-sales/FC031004.asp
March 11, 2004: http://www.miami-dadeclerk.com/foreclosure-sales/FC031104.asp
March 12, 2004: http://www.miami-dadeclerk.com/foreclosure-sales/FC031204.asp
March 17, 2004: http://www.miami-dadeclerk.com/foreclosure-sales/FC031704.asp
March 18, 2004: http://www.miami-dadeclerk.com/foreclosure-sales/FC031804.asp
March 19, 2004: http://www.miami-dadeclerk.com/foreclosure-sales/Fc031904.asp

ROGUE INVESTOR NOTE: sales lists saved on CD:
USA Tax Lien Info/Florida/dade_co_FL/Feb25_04_mortgforelist.htm, /Feb26_04_mortgforelist.htm, etc.

(3) Mortgage Foreclosure
http://www.miami-dadeclerk.com/dadecoc/Mortgage.asp

(4) Contact Information
http://www.miami-dadeclerk.com/dadecoc/Contact_Us.asp

Mortgage/Foreclosure
Metro-Dade Flagler Building
140 West Flagler Street, Suite 1502
Miami, Florida 33130
Telephone: (305) 275-1155

MIAMI-DADE POLICE DEPARTMENT
http://www.mdpd.com

(1) Court Services Bureau Civil Process Section
http://www.mdpd.com/CSB/Default.htm

140 West Flagler Street, Room #801
Miami, FL 33130-1561
Phone: (305) 375-5100
Fax: (305) 375-5517

(1a) Sheriff's Sale Conditions
http://www.mdpd.com/CSB/Sheriff-sale01.htm

DUVAL COUNTY, FLORIDA
http://www.ci.jax.fl.us

TAX COLLECTOR'S OFFICE
http://www.coj.net/tc

Mike Hogan, Tax Collector
Tax Department, Room 130
231 E. Forsyth Street, Jacksonville, FL 32202-3380
email: taxjax@coj.net

(1) Dates to Remember
http://www.coj.net/Departments/Tax+Collector/Dates+to+Remember.htm

May
- Tax warrant processing begins on delinquent tangible personal property taxes May 1st.
- List of delinquent taxes advertised in local newspaper one time.
- List of delinquent real estate taxes advertised once per week for three consecutive weeks prior to tax certificate sale in a local newspaper.

June
- Tax certificate sale for delinquent real estate taxes begins on or before June 1st.

(2) Delinquent Real Estate Taxes
http://www.coj.net/Departments/Tax+Collector/Delinquent+Real+Estate+Taxes.htm

(2a) Advertising List Download
http://www.coj.net/Departments/Tax+Collector/Advertising+List.htm

The download file lists those properties that remain unpaid as of April 1st of the current tax year and are advertised in accordance with Florida Statutes. This file contains Real Estate Numbers, Property Descriptions and Tax Amounts (See file layout below).

This file, containing the advertising file, has been compressed using PKZIP. It was created on April 23, 2003 and will not change until it is replaced in April of 2004. This file has 29,161 records and is 1.8 MB in size. When unzipped, it will be 5.5 MB in size.

ROGUE INVESTOR NOTE: advertising list saved on CD:
USA Tax Lien Info/Florida/duval_co_FA/advlist.zip

(2b) Delinquent File Download
http://www.coj.net/Departments/Tax+Collector/Delinquent+File+Download.htm

On April 1st of each year the current year Real Estate taxes become delinquent. If the taxes remain unpaid after the advertising period has expired, a certificate for the unpaid taxes can be sold at auction. This sale takes place on or before June 1st of the year they become delinquent. Those certificates not sold at auction are transferred to the City of Jacksonville where they may accrue interest until paid. Certificates can be purchased by individual buyers from the city according to the rules and laws governing delinquent taxes. Please refer to the Delinquent Tax section (http://www.coj.net/Departments/Tax+Collector/Delinquent+Real+Estate+Taxes.htm) for further information.

The first file, Unpaid Certificates City Held Certificates, list those certificates, held by the City of Jacksonville, which remain unpaid as of the last day of the previous month. This file contains certificates from the past seven tax years. Click here for the record layout: http://www.coj.net/Departments/Tax+Collector/Unpaid+Certificates+File+Layout.htm. This file will be updated on the first working day of the month. (A working day is Monday thru Friday, non-holiday.) This file has 8,600 records and is 5 MB in size.

The second file, Delinquent Tax File, is a complete list of all delinquent certificates, City held and those held by individuals and companies. This file contains more information than the first and is considerably larger in size. This file is updated weekly. Click here for the record layout: http://www.coj.net/Departments/Tax+Collector/Delinquent+Certificates+File+Layout.htm.This file contains a list all unpaid delinquent tax certificates. It has been compressed using PKZIP. It is created weekly. This file contains approximately 33,100 records and is 4 MB in size. When unzipped, it will be 33 MB in size.

Please note that those certificates with a status of Deferred or Bankruptcy are not available for purchase.

ROGUE INVESTOR NOTE: both files saved on CD:
USA Tax Lien Info/Florida/duval_co_FL/unpd_city_held_certificate_file.dat and /delinquent_tax_file.ZIP

(2c) Duval County Tax Deed Application Listing
http://tc.coj.net/deed

The Real Estate Department for the Duval County Tax Collector is implementing a new procedure for certificate holders that are filing tax deed applications. Effective immediately, certificate holders will do their own research for delinquent taxes. This information is provided on the Internet at http://www.coj.net/tc. This will show how many tax certificates are outstanding, the certificate holder's name and the amount due. The web site will also show if the property is homesteaded or not. Certificate holders may apply on 50 properties per TIN/SSN at one time. Once the certificate holder decides which certificates are going to be applied on, you can start here to fill in certificate/real estate numbers to get the amount to apply for tax deed. The list, certified check, and all applications must be received in our office by the 1st of the month. If received after the 1st of the month the figures and certified check will have to be resubmitted for the following month. Each application must be complete with the legal description, no exception. If the certificate holder does not have the complete legal for each property, a listing of all certificates can be purchased at the cost of $5.00 per TIN/SSN. This list will provide the legal for each certificate. Homestead properties must be listed on a separate sheet than properties that are not homesteaded. Properties that are homesteaded should not be included in the 50 properties that are being applied on.

(3) Delinquent Real Estate Summary Search
http://tc.coj.net/delinquent

(4) Tax Certificate Sale Information
http://www.coj.net/Departments/Tax+Collector/Tax+Sale+FAQ.htm

The following is a list of general information regarding the tax certificate sale for Duval County.

Tax Certificate Sales are held once a year and last approximately 5 to 6 days.

The number of bidders is usually around 100 to 150.

The total dollar amount for the tax sale is around $21,000,000.00 for approximately 18,000 parcels (http://www.coj.net/Departments/Tax+Collector/Advertising+List.htm). Information is not available on the number of certificates not redeemed within the last two years.

Interest rate starts at 18%, down bidding is permissible, and the average is around 7%.

The Tax Certificate Sale is advertised in the Financial News (http://www.jaxdailyrecord.com), 10 North Newnan Street, Jacksonville, Florida 32202, Phone (904) 356-2466. The dates of advertising vary, but are usually the first three weeks of May. Florida Statutes require we advertise 3 consecutive weeks in May before our sale begins.

The Tax Collector's office does not maintain a mailing list for notification of Tax Certificate Sales.

The tax sale begins usually around the 29th of May 9:00 A.M., in Room 505 of the Duval County Courthouse, located at 330 East Bay Street. We suggest that you contact this office around the first of May for the beginning date and location of the sale. The day's bidding usually ends around 4:30 P.M. A 10% deposit is required by Cash or Cashier's Check before participating in the tax sale, at which time you will be given a bidder number. If your daily purchase amount exceeds your 10% deposit you may make an additional deposit. The deposits are made in the Tax Collector's Office located in the Claude Yates Building, 231 East Forsyth Street, Room 130, Phone (904) 630-1916. Information on properties can also be obtain from our website (http://www.coj.net/Departments/Tax+Collector/Real+Estate+Taxes.htm).

Once the tax sale has ended and has been balanced, each bidder will receive a letter stating their balance due and the length of time to respond. The balance will need to be remitted to the office by the time specified and payable in Cash or Cashier's Check.

Additional information is available in our online pamphlet:

http://www.coj.net/NR/rdonlyres/etdh5km7xf2sj43exsavke73tmu7di4usl6ai5rw0zyyjqxi7cghahxsorbocbtrb wd5wv66nar3twwiybo3fkmsyjc.pdf

(5) Contact Information
http://www.coj.net/Departments/Tax+Collector/Contact+Us.htm
http://www.coj.net/Departments/Tax+Collector/Mailing+Addresses+and+Phone+Numbers.htm

Administration
Mike Hogan, Tax Collector
phone: 904-630-1464
email: taxjax@coj.net

Tax Collector Call Center
Tags, Taxes and Licenses
General Information
phone: 904-630-1916
email: taxjax@coj.net

HERNANDO COUNTY, FLORIDA
http://www.co.hernando.fl.us

TAX COLLECTOR
http://www.co.hernando.fl.us/tc

Juanita B. Sikes, Tax Collector
email: tc@co.hernando.fl.us

Hernando County Government Center
20 North Main Street, Room 112
Brooksville, FL 34601
phone: (352) 754-4180, Fax: (352) 754-4189

(1) Tax Sale General Information
http://www.co.hernando.fl.us/tc/taxsale.htm

The Hernando County Tax Sale is held annually on or before June 1. Normally the sale is the third or fourth week in May and usually lasts 2 1/2 to 3 days. The exact date, time and location vary each year.

Tax Deed Sales (actual sale of real estate) are handled by the Clerk of Circuit Court (http://www.clerk.co.hernando.fl.us), Recording Department, 20 N. Main Street, Room 215, Brooksville, FL 34601, phone: (352) 754-4201.

The Tax Sale is advertised one time each week for three weeks prior to the sale. The paper is determined annually, usually in February.

Registration for the Tax Sale can be done in person or by mail with the Tax Collector's office, 20 N. Main Street, Room 112, Brooksville, FL 34601, phone: (352) 754-4180. All persons or entities registering for the Tax Sale must complete Internal Revenue Service form W-9 (http://www.irs.gov/forms_pubs/forms.html) showing the name, address and social security number or employer identification number of the certificate purchaser. This form must be signed by the person registering. All interest is reported to the IRS annually. All certificates will be issued to the name(s) as shown on the W-9. Any changes will be charged a transfer fee on each certificate.

A deposit in the amount of the estimated amount to be purchased must be submitted prior to the commencement of bidding. Anyone going over his or her deposit will be notified during the Sale. No credit cards or out of state checks will be accepted.

The bidding is done at a public auction at the time and location as advertised in the listing of the delinquent taxes in the St. Petersburg Times newspaper. Bidding starts at 18% and the bidding is done inversely and will continue until the lowest possible bid is received. Bidding is done with bidder cards that are issued to the registrants the day of the Tax Sale, and the amount of interest being bid is called out. This bidder number remains the same year to year. At the close of bidding, the certificate purchaser is issued a receipt for the certificates purchased, showing the account number and the amount paid. No other documents will be issued. No other expenses will be incurred by the certificate purchaser at the time of purchase. If the certificate holder chooses to apply for Tax Deed after the certificate is two years old, then he would pay all outstanding taxes and assessments and the cost of application.

Any certificates not sold to individuals are struck off to the County. After the Tax Sale is closed and balanced, these certificates can be purchased in the Tax Collector's office. A listing of the County certificates can be purchased from the Tax Collector's office for a minimum of $10. The price will vary. Certificates struck off to the county will not be available for individual purchase until 8/1/2003.

Anyone wishing to bid at the Tax Sale must be present at the Sale, or a representative may bid for them, providing the necessary deposit and paper work is completed.

For further information, please read Chapter 197, Florida Statutes.

(2) How Tax Certificates Work
http://www.co.hernando.fl.us/tc/taxcert.htm

Property taxes are due November 1, 200_, and become delinquent on April 1, 200_. If taxes are not paid by April 1, the county adds a 3% penalty.

Sometime after April 1, the county place advertisements of unpaid taxes in the newspaper to publicize an auction of tax certificates.

By June 1, the county auctions a tax certificate, giving the certificate buyer a claim against the property for delinquent taxes, interest, cost, and advertising fee. The auction determines the interest rate investors will receive on the certificate. Instead of bidding in dollars, investors bid interest rates at the auction starting at 18% and going down. The bidder who is willing to accept the lowest return is issued the tax certificate.

Once the certificate is sold, the bidder must pay to the county the face amount (gross tax, 3% penalty, 5% commission and advertising fee) of the certificate.

For a certificate to be redeemed, the Tax Collector must collect the face amount, plus all accrued interest, plus a $6.25 Tax Collector's redemption fee.

The holder of the certificate can force a public auction of the property after two years. Bidders may include anyone. To acquire the property, the certificate holder must make the highest bid. Once the property is transferred, all other liens against the property, including mortgages, are wiped out with the exceptions of government liens. If no action is taken after seven years, the tax certificate will be cancelled.

CLERK OF THE CIRCUIT COURT
http://www.clerk.co.hernando.fl.us

Karen Nicolai, County Clerk
Hernando County Courthouse
20 N. Main Street
Brooksville, Florida 34601

(1) Tax Deed Sale List
http://www.clerk.co.hernando.fl.us/other/TaxDeedSaleList.html

Link to website containing DR219 form: http://sun6.dms.state.fl.us/dor
March 3, 2004 tax deed sale list: http://www.clerk.co.hernando.fl.us/reports/MAR3SALE.pdf
April 7, 2004 tax deed sale list: http://www.clerk.co.hernando.fl.us/reports/APR7SALE.pdf
April 8, 2004 tax deed sale list: http://www.clerk.co.hernando.fl.us/reports/APR8SALE.pdf

ROGUE INVESTOR NOTE: sales lists saved on CD:
USA Tax Lien Info/Florida/hernando_co_FL/MAR3SALE.pdf, /APR7SALE.pdf, and /APR8SALE.pdf

(2) Tax Deed Division FAQ
http://www.clerk.co.hernando.fl.us/other/RecordingFAQ.html#taxdeed

What are the date, time and location of the next tax deed sale? The tax deed sale is held by the Clerk of Circuit Court at the courthouse door that faces Main Street (weather permitting; otherwise, it is held inside the entrance, in the hallway), on the first Wednesday of the month (unless it falls on a holiday, then it would be the following Wednesday) at 11:00 a.m.

When and where do you advertise the sale? The property is advertised for four consecutive weeks prior to the Tax Deed sale. Currently we are advertising in the Hernando Section of the St. Petersburg Times.

Can you send me a "sale list" of properties that will be available? Records stored at the facility continue to belong to the department that generated them. Each time a Tax Deed Sale is scheduled, the Tax Deed Clerk prepares a "Sale List." The list includes information pertaining to the minimum starting bid, the assessed value of the property, the legal description and the last known titleholder of record. To receive a copy of any "Tax Deed Sale List," a fee of $.15 per page (plus postage) must be paid in advance. To receive a copy of each sale list on a regular basis, interested parties can be placed on our mailing list by establishing an escrow account.

What form of payment do you accept? Purchase price is payable at the Clerk's Office upon completion of the sale, payable by cashier's check, money order or cash. If full payment is not received upon completion of the sale, a non-refundable deposit of $200.00 is required. The remaining balance must be received within 24 hours of the sale. If the purchaser does not return within the 24-hour period, the $200.00 deposit is forfeited.

Can I bid without attending? No, the Tax Deed Sale is open to the public and is auctioned (a public outcry) to the highest bidder. You MUST be present at the sale in order to bid.

If I end up with a property, who handles the quiet title process? Tax Deeds are not clear titles. Quiet title suits to clear the title of properties are Civil lawsuits and are not handled by the Tax Deed Clerk. Information on this procedure and costs would be available from an Attorney that handles these types of legal proceedings.

What happens to the properties that are not sold at the auction? A property that does not sell at the Tax Deed Sale is placed on the "List of Lands Available for Taxes." After 90 (ninety) days from the sale date, anyone can purchase property off the "List of Lands Available for Taxes." This applies only if it is a Hernando County held Certificate. If not a Hernando County held Certificate, and there are no bids, it is sold to Applicant/Certificate holder.

What happens to liens that are against the property when sold at tax deed sale? Governmental liens and judgments survive the issuance of the Tax Deed and may be fully or partially satisfied with any overbid monies from the sale. Liens of government units, not satisfied in full, survive the issuance of the Tax Deed. Should you have any questions concerning other types of liens and judgments that survive the Tax Deed Sale, consult an attorney. We cannot advise you.

HILLSBOROUGH COUNTY, FLORIDA
http://www.hillsboroughcounty.org

TAX COLLECTOR'S OFFICE
http://www.hillstax.org

Main Branch
601 East Kennedy Boulevard
County Center, 14th Floor
Tampa, Florida 33602
Phone: (813) 635-5200

(1) Contact Information
http://www.hillstax.org/ContactUs/EmailInformation.htm
http://www.hillstax.org/ContactUs/PhoneNumbers.htm
http://www.hillstax.org/ContactUs/MailingAddresses.htm

Real Estate Taxes
phone: (813) 635-5200
email: taxes@hillstax.org

Tax & License
Doug Belden, Tax Collector
P.O. Box 172920
Tampa, Florida 33672-0920

Locations – Downtown Main Office = http://www.hillstax.org/Locations/DowntownBranch1.htm
Email Information = http://www.hillstax.org/ContactUs/EmailInformation.htm
Phone Numbers = http://www.hillstax.org/ContactUs/PhoneNumbers.htm
Mailing Addresses = http://www.hillstax.org/ContactUs/MailingAddresses.htm

(2) Tax Certificate Sale Information and Search
http://www.hillstax.org/tax/tax_certificate_sale.asp

ROGUE INVESTOR NOTE: Web page also contains links to information regarding 2003 tax certificate sale.

(2a) 2004 Tax Certificate Sale Buyer Information
http://www.hillstax.org/tax/Forms/2004BuyerInformation.pdf

Date, Time, and Location
Sale begins May 28th, 2004 at 3:30 p.m. The sale will continue Monday through Friday from 8:30 a.m. to 4:30 p.m. each business day, until all certificates have been sold. The sale will be conducted on the 26th Floor of the County Center, which is located at 601 E. Kennedy Boulevard, Tampa, FL 33602.

ROGUE INVESTOR NOTE: Additional information available on web page.

(2b) Current Certificate Search by Buyer
http://www.hillstax.org/taxapp/search_by_buyernum.asp

As of 01/01/04, the tax deed application fee will increase to $75.00.

ROGUE INVESTOR NOTE: Search form on web page allows delinquent property search by buyer number.

(2c) Advertising File Layout
http://www.hillstax.org/tax/Advertising_File.pdf

(2d) Key Information on the Delinquent Advertisement
http://www.hillstax.org/tax/Forms/Adv_Sample_2003%20Seminar2.pdf

(2e) Understanding a Section-Township-Range Map
http://www.hillstax.org/tax/Forms/Understanding_Section_Map.pdf

CLERK OF THE CIRCUIT COURT
http://www.hillsclerk.com

TAX DEED SALES DEPARTMENT, FINANCIALS SECTION
(Clerk of the Circuit Court)
http://www.hillsclerk.com/content/financials/tax_deeds/tax_deed_sales.htm

The Clerk of the Circuit Court is statutorily responsible for conducting Tax Deed Sales and issuing a tax deed in the name of the county to the successful bidder at a sale. Tax Deed Sales and the issuance of tax deeds are governed by Chapter 197, Florida Statutes.

The procedure involves a Tax Certificate Holder (tax certificates are sold to collect delinquent taxes) applying for a tax deed through the Tax Collector.

There is no case filed in court and no court order issued for the Clerk to conduct a tax deed sale.

(1a) Tax Deeds Sales – List by Date
http://www.hillsclerk.com/content/financials/tax_deeds/td_sales_list.asp

These lists contain only the folio numbers for the properties being offered at sale. We do not have information regarding structures (home, office building, warehouse) located on the property. You must do the research to find out what is on the land and also the condition of the land.

You may visit the Property Appraiser's web site (http://www.hcpafl.org) or the Tax Collector's web site (http://www.hillstax.org) for basic information regarding the listed properties. Be sure to make note of the folio numbers you want to research before leaving our site.

The lists are subject to change. Properties are redeemed daily. Redeemed properties are no longer available for sale by tax deed auction. To hear a listing of redeemed properties by file number and auction date, please call (813) 276-8100, extension 7246, then press 1. You may also contact the Tax Deed Department to determine which properties may have been redeemed prior to the listed auction dates and are no longer available for sale by a tax deed auction.

ROGUE INVESTOR NOTE: tax deeds lists saved on CD:
USA Tax Lien Info/Florida/hillsborough_co_FA/Feb04_taxdeedslist.htm and /Mar04_taxdeedslist.htm

(1b) List of Lands Available
http://www.hillsclerk.com/content/financials/tax_deeds/td_lol.asp

Lands Available for Taxes: Listing of delinquent tax real estate property that did not sell at auction and is available to be sold for taxes and applicable fees.

Properties for which no bids are received at the auction are placed on our "Lands Available for Taxes" list. Florida Statutes Chapter 197.502 states that the County may, at any time within the first 90 days from the day the property is placed on the list, purchase the property for the opening base bid. After the ninety-day period is over, anyone can come and purchase the property for the base bid, accrued interest, and any taxes due, plus documentary stamps, recording and indexing fees.

This list is subject to change. You may contact the Tax Deed Department for updated information regarding this list.

You may visit the Property Appraiser's web site (http://www.hcpafl.org) or the Tax Collector's web site (http://www.hillstax.org) for basic information regarding the listed properties. Be sure to make note of the folio numbers you want to research before leaving our site.

To view the List of Lands Available report, please click on this link:
http://www.hillsclerk.com/content/financials/tax_deeds/td_lol_detail.asp?Status=List%20Of%20Lands

ROGUE INVESTOR NOTE: list of lands available saved on CD:
USA Tax Lien Info/Florida/hillsborough_co_FA/List of Lands.htm

(1c) Tax Deed Sale Fees
http://www.hillsclerk.com/content/fees/fee_schedule.htm#f20

(1d) Tax Deed Sales FAQs
http://www.hillsclerk.com/content/financials/tax_deeds/tax_deed_sales_faq.htm

This information is provided only as a helpful guide to assist you. It is not meant to be all encompassing of everything you need to know about the Tax Deed Sales processes. Contact the Tax Deed Sales Department (taxdeeds@hillsclerk.com) if you have any further questions.

Q. Where can I get more information about tax deed research? All of the procedures followed for Tax Deed Sales are governed by the Florida Statutes (http://www.flsenate.gov/statutes/index.cfm?Mode=ViewStatutes&Submenu=1) and the Florida Administrative Code. You can also get more information from the following offices:

Tax Deed Sales Department
http://www.hillsclerk.com/content/financials/tax_deeds/tax_deed_sales_contact_information.htm
Main Courthouse
419 Pierce Street
Tampa, FL 33602
phone: (813) 276-8100 Ext. 7246

Property Appraiser's Office
http://www.hcpafl.org
County Center, 16th Floor
601 E. Kennedy Boulevard
Tampa, FL 33602
phone: (813) 272-6100

Tax Collector's Office
http://www.hillstax.org
County Center, 14th Floor
601 E. Kennedy Boulevard
Tampa, FL 33602
phone: (813) 307-6536

ROGUE INVESTOR NOTE: Additional questions and answers on web page.

(1e) Tax Deed Sales Contact Information
http://www.hillsclerk.com/content/financials/tax_deeds/tax_deed_sales_contact_information.htm

Clerk of Circuit Court
Tax Deed Sales
Main Courthouse
419 Pierce Street, Room 114
Tampa, FL 33602
taxdeeds@hillsclerk.com

ORANGE COUNTY, FLORIDA
http://www.citizens-first.co.orange.fl.us

TAX COLLECTOR'S OFFICE
http://www.octaxcol.com

(1) General Information Real Estate Taxes
http://www.octaxcol.com/real_estate_taxes.htm

Taxes become delinquent April 1st of each year, at which time a 3% penalty is added to the bill. Advertising costs are also added before the Tax Certificate Sale.

DELINQUENT PROPERTY TAXES
Real Estate taxes become delinquent on April 1st of each year. After real estate taxes have become delinquent, they are advertised in a local newspaper once a week for three consecutive weeks. The advertising and collection cost is added to the delinquent tax bill. On or before June 1st, the Tax Collector must conduct a tax certificate sale for unpaid taxes on each parcel of property. The sale is operated on a competitive bid basis with interest bids beginning at 18% and progressing downward. When a certificate

is sold against a piece of property, the successful bidder pays the delinquent taxes on that property and holds a certificate that constitutes a first lien against the property.

To redeem the certificate, the owner of the property must pay the Tax Collector all delinquent taxes plus accrued interest, and advertising cost. The Tax Collector will reimburse the certificate holder all monies due and the property will be free of that tax lien.

If the tax certificate is not redeemed within two years, the certificate holder may file a tax deed application with the Tax Collector. The property owner is notified of this action and, if the taxes are not paid, the Clerk of the Circuit Courts conducts a public auction and sells the property to the highest bidder. In Orange County only Tax Deed Sales are processed through the Orange County Comptroller Office.

(2) Contact Information
http://www.octaxcol.com/Contact%20Us.htm

Real Estate Taxes, email = Taxes@octaxcol.com

(3) Office Locations
http://www.octaxcol.com/OfficeLocations.htm#Main%20Office

Main Office:
The SunTrust Center
200 South Orange Avenue, Suite 1600
Orlando, Florida 32801
407-836-2709
407-836-2700

PALM BEACH COUNTY, FLORIDA
http://www.co.palm-beach.fl.us

TAX COLLECTOR'S OFFICE
http://www.co.palm-beach.fl.us/tax/index1.htm

email: taxcol@co.palm-beach.fl.us

(1) Office Location
http://www.co.palm-beach.fl.us/tax/office_hours.htm

Governmental Center
Administration/Occupational License/Real Estate
301 North Olive Avenue, 3rd Floor
West Palm Beach, FL 33401
Mailing address:
P. O. Box 3715, West Palm Beach, FL 33402

(2) Phone
http://www.co.palm-beach.fl.us/tax/phone.htm

Automatic Phone System: 561-355-2264
web page includes a phone menu

(3) Tax Deeds
http://www.co.palm-beach.fl.us/tax/services/property_tax/taxdeeds.htm

The holder of a tax certificate may apply for a tax deed when two (2) years or more have elapsed since April 1st of the year the certificate was issued. Application for a tax deed is made to the Tax Collector's Office. The application allows the property to be sold at public auction. However, the owner may retain the property by paying the taxes any time before the tax deed is issued.

(4) Delinquent Real Estate/Tax Certificates
http://www.co.palm-beach.fl.us/tax/services/property_tax/delinquent_real_estate_tax.htm

Payment of delinquent taxes must be paid by cash, cashier's check, money order, certified check, or bank draft. Payments must be received by the Tax Collector's Office on or before the last working day of the month to be considered paid in that month. The postmark date of the payment will not be considered. A tax certificate is a tax lien on property created by payment of the taxes due. *It is not a purchase of the property.*

The face amount of the certificate is the sum of the unpaid real estate tax and non-ad valorem assessment, 3% interest (for April and May), 5% Tax Collector's commission and advertising costs. Sale of tax certificates begins on or before June 1 for the preceding year's delinquent real estate tax parcels. Prior to the sale, the Tax Collector advertises the delinquent taxes for three (3) consecutive weeks.

To participate in the sale, a bidder must register with the Tax Collector's office. Bidding on interest starts at 18% and is bid down until the certificate is sold. A certificate of ownership and listing of certificates purchased is provided to each buyer. Individual certificates may be transferred by completing a form and filing it with the Tax Collector.

Tax certificates are dated as of the first day of the sale and expire after seven (7) years. Tax certificates can be canceled or reduced if errors, omissions, or double assessments are made. Canceled or reduced certificates receive 8% interest or the rate of interest bid at the tax certificate sale, whichever is less. When a tax certificate is redeemed, interest is paid at the rate of the "winning" bid. When interest earned on the face amount is less than 5%, mandatory interest of 5% is paid.

Tax certificates not sold to private bidders at the annual sale are "sold" to Palm Beach County, but they are available for purchase by private investors. The amount due on all County held certificates (status/unpur) is subject to change because the certificate may be purchased. The prospective purchaser must identify the property by the property control and certificate numbers to complete the transaction. A list of available tax certificates may be purchased in person or requested by mail. Advance payment of $25 is required. For more information, call 561 355-2269.

All unpaid taxes are eligible for tax deed application two years after the date of delinquency. For example, a 1998 tax goes delinquent April 1, 1999. Therefore, the property is in jeopardy of a tax deed application April 1, 2001. The tax deed application begins a process that may result in the property being offered for sale at public auction due to non-payment of taxes. The certificate holder may file an application for tax deed two years after the date of delinquency and up to seven years from the date the certificate was issued. The tax certificate expires seven years after the date of issuance.

The Tax Collector provides free access for citizens to obtain information on specific parcels. To access delinquent real estate tax records from your web browser, click this link to the Public Access: http://www.co.palm-beach.fl.us/tc_pubaccess/default.asp. Public access terminals are also available at the Tax Collector's Office in the Governmental Center, 301 North Olive Avenue, 3rd Floor, West Palm Beach.

The *Property Appraiser's Public Access System (PAPA)* (http://www.co.palm-beach.fl.us/papa) can provide background information about any property in Palm Beach County, including the most recent year's taxes and parcel identification information (e.g., name and address of owner, legal description and property control number).

(5) Public Information Access
http://www.co.palm-beach.fl.us/tc_pubaccess/default.asp

Click on "Delinquent Property Tax (Certificates)" to do a delinquent real estate search. For further information, call (561) 355-2266 or email taxcol@co.palm-beach.fl.us.

(6) Glossary
http://www.co.palm-beach.fl.us/tax/services/property_tax/glossary.htm

Tax Certificate – A first-lien instrument offered for sale by the Tax Collector through competitive bid to pay delinquent taxed. A tax certificate expires seven (7) years from the date issued.

Tax Deed Application – A legal document filed with the Tax Collector by the holder of a tax certificate to demand payment. The tax deed may be applied for two (2) years from April 1 of the year of issuance. If the taxes are not paid by the date set for the tax deed sale, the property is sold by the Clerk of Courts' Office to the highest bidder.

Tax Lien – A lien for property taxes effective January 1 of the tax year. Taxes are due November 1 and are payable prior to April 1 of the next year.

PINELLAS COUNTY, FLORIDA
http://www.co.pinellas.fl.us/bcc

TAX COLLECTOR'S OFFICE
http://www.taxcollect.com

Diane Nelson, Tax Collector
email: taxcollector@taxcollect.com

(1) About the Office
http://www.taxcollect.com/Content.aspx?ContentID=67&CommandID=2&DeptID=1

The Florida statutes authorize county tax collectors to collect delinquent taxes by the sale of tax certificates and, later, processing of tax deed applications for the sale of real property.

(2) Taxpayer's Calendar
http://www.taxcollect.com/Content.aspx?ContentID=86&CommandID=2&DeptID=17

ROGUE INVESTOR NOTE: Web page last updated March 26, 2003.

(3) Office Locations
http://www.taxcollect.com/Content.aspx?ContentID=6&CommandID=2&DeptID=18

Main office located in Clearwater Courthouse
315 Court Street, 3rd Floor
P.O. Box 1729
Clearwater, FL 33757
Phone: 727-562-3262

(4) Delinquent Real Estate Taxes
http://www.taxcollect.com/Content.aspx?ContentID=97&CommandID=2&DeptID=3

Real estate taxes become delinquent on April 1 of the year following the year of assessment. A 3% mandatory interest is added to the amount due at that time. If the taxes remain unpaid, the delinquent property will be advertised once a week for three consecutive weeks prior to the Tax Certificate Sale and the advertising fee will be added to the tax bill. The Tax Collector is required by law to hold a Tax Certificate Sale on or before June 1 each year. If payment is not received by 5:00 p.m. on the day immediately preceding the date the tax certificate sale has been advertised to begin, a certificate will be issued and additional charges will accrue.

A tax certificate is an enforceable first lien against the property for unpaid real estate taxes. The sale allows investors to purchase certificates by paying the tax debt. The sale is conducted in a reverse auction style with participants bidding downward on interest rates starting at 18%. The certificate is awarded to the bidder who will pay the taxes, interest and costs and accept the lowest rate of interest. If there are no bidders, the certificate is issued to the County at 18% annual interest.

To redeem the certificate, the property owner or his representative must pay the Tax Collector the delinquent taxes plus accrued interest, advertising costs and collection fees. Payment of delinquent taxes must be made with a cashier's check, money order, cash or credit card. The amount due for delinquent taxes is determined by the date received by the Tax Collector and not the postmark. After payment is received and validated, the certificate holder is reimbursed the cost of the certificate plus interest and the lien against the property is removed.

If taxes remain unpaid, the certificate holder may file a tax deed application with the Tax Collector two years after the date of delinquency. The property will be sold at a public auction conducted by the Clerk of the Circuit Court should the property owner fail to pay the tax debt.

For more information about delinquent taxes you may contact us at 727-562-3262.

RESULTS OF THE 2003 TAX CERTIFICATE SALE
Tax Certificate Sale started: May 30, 2003
Duration of Sale: 5 days
Average interest rate: 3.0458%
Number of parcels advertised: 19,904
Advertised Value: $42,955,758.23
Number of certificates issued: 14,465
Value of certificates issued: $29,423,046.39

CLERK OF THE CIRCUIT COURT
http://www.pinellasclerk.org/aspInclude2/ASPInclude.asp?pageName=index.htm

Karleen De Blaker, Clerk of the Circuit Court

(1) Tax Deed Sales
http://www.pinellasclerk.org/aspInclude2/ASPInclude.asp?pageName=taxdeed.htm

Where is the tax deed sale held? Tax deed sales are conducted in the main lobby of the Clearwater Courthouse located at 315 Court Street, Clearwater, Florida, beginning at 11:00 A.M. The deputy clerk will read the notice of sale and will offer the lands described in the advertised notice for sale to the highest bidder for cash at public auction.

What action must I take if I am the successful bidder at the sale? You must report to the Tax Deed Department, Room 163 of the Clearwater Courthouse, immediately after the sale. The deputy clerk will calculate the documentary stamps and recording fees that are due in addition to the bid amount.

When is a cash deposit required? If there were other bids, the high bidder is required to post a $200 nonrefundable cash deposit with the Clerk at the time of the sale. If full payment of the final bid amount, the documentary stamp tax and recording fees is not made within 24 hours of the sale, excluding weekends and holidays, the Clerk will pay all re-advertising costs and costs of the sale from the deposit. If full payment is made in accordance with the requirements, the deposit will be applied to the sale price.

What type of payment must be made if I am the successful bidder? Payment in the form of cash, cashier's check or money order is acceptable. Payment for the documentary stamps and recording fees should be separate from the payment for the bid amount. All sales are final. No refunds will be issued.

How long do I have to make payment? The bid amount plus applicable documentary stamp taxes and recording fees are required to be paid in full to the Clerk of the Circuit Court within twenty four (24) hours after the advertised time of sale.

Does a tax deed provide a marketable title? You may wish to research or seek advice on any property you are considering bidding for before the tax deed sale. Generally, when any lands are sold for the nonpayment of taxes, the title may not be a marketable title.

Where can I find information regarding the sale of "tax certificates"? Tax Certificate information can be obtained from the Tax Collector's Office located on the 3rd Floor of the Main Courthouse at 315 Court Street, Clearwater, Florida. Telephone: (727) 562-3262.

Where can structural information or the physical address of the property be obtained? Information on the property subject to a tax deed sale is available in the Property Appraiser's Office located on the 2nd Floor of the Main Courthouse at 315 Court Street, Clearwater, Florida. Telephone: (727) 464-3207.

What if I need additional information regarding a tax deed sale? Additional information is available from the Tax Deed Office located in Room 163, 1st Floor of the Main Courthouse at 315 Court Street, Clearwater, Florida.

ROGUE INVESTOR NOTE: Additional questions and answers available on web page.

(2) Tax Deed Sales – Online Listing
http://pubtitlet.co.pinellas.fl.us/servlet/taxdeed.saledates.DM79

ROGUE INVESTOR NOTE: Web page includes property listings by sale date, in three report formats (comprehensive, post-ad date, sale date), plus instructions and an explanation of terms.

(3) After the Sale – Tax Deed Status
http://pubtitlet.co.pinellas.fl.us/clerk/taxdeed/certificatelist/DM49Input.jsp

ROGUE INVESTOR NOTE: Browse tax deed certificates by date of certificate.

(4) Lands Available for Taxes – Online Listing
http://pubtitlet.co.pinellas.fl.us/clerk/taxdeed/landsavailable/DM68Input.jsp

ROGUE INVESTOR NOTE: Browse the "Lands Available for Taxes" listing by parcel.

(5) Lands Available for Taxes – More Information
http://www.pinellasclerk.org/aspInclude2/ASPInclude.asp?pageName=landsavailable.htm

ROGUE INVESTOR NOTE: See web page for questions and answers.

Tax Lien Sales: No, but similar process.

Tax Deed Sales: Yes, actually a deed with right of redemption for one year.

Rating: Four Stars (****)

Interest Rate:
20% interest rate or fee (not an annual rate), regardless of when the property is redeemed within the one-year period. If redeemed within one month, the investor still receives 20%, which results in an outstanding annual return of 240%.

Sale Period: Sales occur on the first Tuesday on any month, by determination of the county treasurer.

Redemption Period: 1 year

Bidding Process: All auctions are by competitive bid.

State-Specific Information:
Georgia is a complicated tax lien state because the auctions happen often and, although the redemption period is quick, the foreclosure process is not easy.

Links for All Georgia Counties: Provided on CD.

Detailed County-Specific Information

COBB COUNTY, GEORGIA
http://www.co.cobb.ga.us

TAX COMMISSIONER'S OFFICE
http://www.cobbtax.org/Home.asp?cmd=Home&mnu=Home

Gail Downing, Tax Commissioner
Tori Steele, Chief Clerk

The main office for the Property Tax Division is located at:
100 Cherokee Street, Suite 250
Marietta, GA 30090
phone: 770-528-8600
fax: 770-528-8679

(1) Delinquent Taxes
http://www.cobbtax.org/template.asp?page=Delinquent_Taxes.htm&mnu=PropertyTaxes&submnu=TaxesGeneralInfo&lftmnu=DelinquentTaxes

Any taxes remaining unpaid at this time are subject to levy and tax sale. A listing of all delinquent taxes may be found in the Cobb County Tax Commissioner's Tax Vault located on the 2nd floor at 100 Cherokee Street in Marietta. This listing is updated monthly. Terminals are also available for public use in checking unpaid taxes.

The Cobb County Tax Commissioner's Office follows legal procedures prescribed by the Official Code of Georgia Annotated (OCGA) when levying property. We strongly suggest you read those sections of Georgia law that pertain to tax executions and tax sales. OCGA Title 48 - Revenue and Taxation, Chapter 3 - "Tax Executions," and Chapter 4 - "Tax Sales," contain important information that you must be aware of. If you need further information contact the Delinquent Tax Department at (770) 528-8623 or request a copy of our booklet "Real Property Tax Sales."

Tax Sales

Tax sales are held on the first Tuesday of each month, between the hours of 10 a.m. and 4 p.m. on the steps of the Superior Court building (except when the first Tuesday of the month falls on a legal holiday, in which case the sale is held the next business day). Properties up for tax sale may be reviewed in the Levy Department of the Tax Commissioner's Office. A listing of the properties may also be found in the Friday edition of the Marietta Daily Journal for a four-week period prior to the sale.

Starting bid lists may be picked up after 12 noon the Friday before the sale in the Levy Department. You do not need to pre-register to bid at the tax sale; however, you must be present in order to bid. We do not accept mail, phone, or fax bids. The opening bid for a particular property is the amount of tax due, plus penalties, interest, fi. fa. costs, levy costs, administrative levy fee, certified mail cost, advertising cost, and tax deed recording fee. The property is sold to the highest bidder. We require payment in full upon conclusion of the tax sale. Payment must be in the form of cash, certified check, cashier's check, or money order. If there are any excess funds after paying taxes, accrued costs, and all expenses of a tax sale, they shall be paid to the person authorized to receive them (OCGA 48-4-5). Any properties not receiving a bid may be reauctioned that afternoon at 3:00 p.m.

The tax sale purchaser receives a tax deed to the property. However, they cannot take immediate possession of the property, make any improvements to the property, evict any tenants, or move onto the property. Georgia law allows the property owner, or anyone with any right, title or interest in the property to repurchase (redeem) the property. Until the right of redemption has been foreclosed or the title has ripened by prescription, a tax deed has the same force and effect as a lien.

Right of Redemption

When real property is sold at a tax sale, the owner, creditor, or any person having an interest in the property may redeem (repurchase) the property from the holder of the tax deed within 12 months.

The redemption price is the bid amount, plus any taxes paid by the purchaser after the tax sale, plus any special assessments on the property, plus a 20% premium of the amount for the first year or fraction of a year which has elapsed since the date of sale, plus a 10% premium for each additional year or fraction of a year thereafter, plus the sheriff and advertisement costs. The tax sale purchaser is responsible for determining the amount payable for redemption.

Redemption of the property puts the title conveyed by the tax sale back to the owner of record subject to all liens that existed at the time of the tax sale.

Notice of Foreclosure of Right to Redeem

After 12 months from the date of the tax sale, the purchaser at the tax sale may terminate or foreclose on the owner's right to redeem the property by causing a notice(s) of the foreclosure to be served by certified mail to the owner of record and to all interest holders that appear on the public record. In addition, the notice of foreclosure is to be published in the newspaper in the county in which the property is located once a week for four consecutive weeks.

(2) Tax Sales
http://www.cobbtax.org/pdffiles/taxsales.pdf

This brief publication is designed to answer tax sales questions and provide an insight into the legal framework that gives the authority for conducting a real estate tax sale in the state of Georgia.

ROGUE INVESTOR NOTE: See web page for additional information.

DEKALB COUNTY, GEORGIA
http://www.co.dekalb.ga.us

TAX COMMISSIONER'S OFFICE
https://dklbweb.dekalbga.org/taxcommissioner/index8.htm

Tom Scott, DeKalb County Tax Commissioner
4380 Memorial Drive, Suite 100
Decatur, GA 30032
phone: 404-298-4000
email: motorveh@co.dekalb.ga.us
email address for DeKalb County: dekalb@co.dekalb.ga.us

(1) Tax Sale General Information
from https://dklbweb.dekalbga.org/taxcommissioner/PropertyTaxMain2.htm, click on "Tax Sales"

(For specific information consult your attorney.)

A tax lien attaches to the property at its valuation (January 1st; O.C.G.A. 48-2-56). A tax lien against real property is superior to all other liens. The lien is released by paying the tax charged against it. On December 31st (O.C.G.A. 48-3-3) of each year the Tax Commissioner must issue an execution (FiFa.) against all delinquent taxpayers. Executions direct the levying officer to levy on the property. It is the duty of that person to enforce an execution by either collection or levy and sale.

Tax sales are held each month, generally from April through December. Sales are scheduled on the first Tuesday of any given month on the Courthouse steps at 11:00 a.m. Notice of the sale is published once a week for four weeks immediately preceding the sale in the legal organ (newspaper) for the county, which is presently *The Champion Newspaper*. We do not have a mailing list for our tax sales; however, if you are interested in what properties are being sold, you should contact *The Champion Newspaper* at 404-373-7779, or by mail at Legal Advertising, *The Champion Newspaper*, P.O. Box 361500, Decatur, GA 30036-1500.

Tax sale bidding commences with the total of taxes and costs (levy, recording, advertising and commissions) on each parcel, with the property being sold to the highest bidder. If there are no bidders, the County may enter a bid on the property equal to the starting bid.

While the successful bidder receives a tax deed, he has no immediate control over the property. The taxpayer or any other person having a right, title, interest in, or lien upon the property may redeem it at any time within twelve (12) months from the date of the sale by paying the redemption price. The purchaser is not entitled to rents and/or profits arising from the property during the redemption period. The redemption price is the amount paid for the tax deed at the tax sale plus any taxes subsequently paid by the tax deed purchaser plus 20% of that amount for the first year or fraction of a year elapsing between the date of the sale and the date of redemption. After the first year following the conclusion of the tax sale the tax deed purchaser is entitled to an additional 10% for each subsequent year or fraction of a year until redemption.

Twelve months after the date of the sale the purchaser may begin to forever bar the right of redemption by having proper notice served upon the taxpayer, occupant (if any) and upon all persons having recorded any right, title, interest in, or lien on the property in the county where the property is located in accordance with O.C.G.A. 48-4-45 through 48-4-48. Additional fees may be charged for sheriff's service and advertising 30 days after service of notice. Thus a minimum time of one year and forty-five days elapses between acquisition of a tax deed and the right to physical control of the property.

Even though the purchaser receives defeasible title before the redemption period expires, he or she acquires sufficient interest in the property to make a return on the property after January 1st the following year (if still unredeemed) and also to be liable for taxes due on the property the year in which it is sold and subsequent years until redeemed. Current year tax information is available through the DeKalb County Tax Commissioner website at https://dklbweb.dekalbga.org/taxcommissioner/index8.htm.

A recent Georgia Supreme Court Decision (Blizzard v. Moniz, 271 Ga. 50, 518 S.E.2d 407 [1999]) has rendered "ripening by prescription" (O.C.G.A. 48-4-48) inapplicable to tax sale purchases in most cases. The Court determined that actual possession of the property is necessary for a tax deed to convey fee simple title to the property absent the process of barring or foreclosing the right of redemption.

(2) Conditions of Sale
from Tax Sale General Information page, click on "Conditions of Sale"

(3) Basic Property Description
from Tax Sale General Information page, click on "Basic Property Description"

No Tax Sales are currently scheduled.

ROGUE INVESTOR NOTE: No tax sales scheduled as of February 4, 2004.

FULTON COUNTY, GEORGIA
http://www.co.fulton.ga.us

TAX COMMISSIONER'S OFFICE
http://www.co.fulton.ga.us/departments/tax_comm.html

Phone: 404-730-6100

Responsibilities include the collection of real taxes for the City of Atlanta and Fulton County.

(1) Taxes/Liens – Judicial In-Rem Tax Foreclosure
http://www.co.fulton.ga.us/services/services_detail_T27_R68.html

Properties exposed to sale under the Judicial In Rem Foreclosure Process shall be sold by the Fulton County Tax Commissioner at auction for cash on the first each month on the Fulton County Courthouse steps, 136 Pryor Street, Atlanta, Georgia 30303 at 10:00 A.M. All bidders must be prepared to pay immediately upon conclusion of the auction by cash, certified bank check, bank cashier's check or other collected funds. Personal checks shall not be accepted. If the successful bidder fails to produce payment immediately upon conclusion of the auction by cash, certified bank check, bank cashier's check or other collected funds, the property shall be immediately re-auctioned. The minimum bid listed for each property consists of delinquent tax years 2000 and prior, plus accrued interest and fees through date of sale. Outstanding current ad valorem taxes which include the 2001 and 2002 tax years must be paid at the same time the successful bid is paid.

Please Note:
All properties sold at the Judicial In Rem Tax Foreclosure sale are under the "Caveat Emptor" (Buyer Beware) principle. Pursuant to state law, tendering bids at public sales or outcries, bidders become personally liable and responsible for such bids. We strongly recommend proper due diligence is performed on each property listed above prior to appearing and attempting to purchase a property at the tax sale. Please govern yourself accordingly.

If you have any questions, please feel to free to call Cory Calloway (cory.calloway@co.fulton.ga.us) at (404) 730-6220, Dahlia Davila (dahlia.davila@co.fulton.ga.us) at (404) 730-6224, Courtney Ross (courtney.ross@co.fulton.ga.us) at (404) 730-6223, or Troi Smith (troi.smith@co.fulton.ga.us) at (404) 730-6237 at the Fulton County Tax Commissioner's Office.

(1a) In-Rem Tax Sale Letter Sample
http://www.co.fulton.ga.us/Fulton_County/departments/In_Rem_Tax_Sale_Letter_Sample.pdf

(2) Taxes/Liens – Non-Judicial Tax Sales
http://www.co.fulton.ga.us/services/services_detail_T27_R215.html

Rules of Sale

Properties Exposed to Sale (http://www.co.fulton.ga.us/departments/tax_comm_reports_T316_R3.html) under the Non-Judicial Process shall be sold by the Fulton County Tax Commissioner at auction for CASH on the first Tuesday of each month on the Fulton County Courthouse steps, 136 Pryor Street, Atlanta, Georgia 30303 at 10:00 A.M. All bidders must be prepared to pay immediately upon conclusion of the auction by Cash, Certified Bank Check, Bank Cashier's Check or other collected funds. Personal checks shall not be accepted. If the successful bidder fails to produce payment immediately upon conclusion of the auction by Cash, Certified Bank Check, Bank Cashier's Check or other collected funds, the property shall be immediately re-auctioned.

The minimum bid listed for each property consists of delinquent tax years 2001 and prior, plus accrued interest and fees through date of sale. In order to protect your interest and maximize the return on your investment you should pay the current (2002) ad valorem taxes after receipt of the tax deed. If you have any questions, please feel free to call Janet Fletcher at (404) 730-6221 or Gerald Hunt at (404) 730-6234, who are located at the Fulton County Tax Commissioner's Office.

(2a) Properties Exposed to Sale
http://www.co.fulton.ga.us/departments/tax_comm_reports_T316_R3.html

March Courtesy List
March Non-Judicial Tax Sale Courtesy List
Date Posted: February 12, 2004
http://www.co.fulton.ga.us/Fulton_County/departments/MARCH_COURTESY_LIST___RULES_OF_SALE.pdf

February Courtesy List and Rules of Sale
February Non-Judicial Tax Sale Courtesy List
Date Posted: January 22, 2004
http://www.co.fulton.ga.us/Fulton_County/departments/FEBRUARY_COURTESYLIST___RULES_OF_SALE.pdf

February 2004 Tax Sale List, Revised
February Judicial Tax Sale Courtesy List
Date Posted: January 22, 2004
http://www.co.fulton.ga.us/Fulton_County/departments/february_2004_tax_sale_list___revised.pdf

January Courtesy List
January Non-Judicial Tax Sale Courtesy List
Date Posted: December 11, 2003
http://www.co.fulton.ga.us/Fulton_County/departments/View_Documet.pdf

January Courtesy List
January Judicial Tax Sale Courtesy List
Date Posted: December 11, 2003
http://www.co.fulton.ga.us/Fulton_County/departments/View_This_Document.pdf

ROGUE INVESTOR NOTE: lists saved on CD:
USA Tax Lien Info/Georgia/fulton_co_GA/Mar04_nonjud_taxlist.pdf, /Feb04_nonjud_taxlist.pdf, /Feb04_jud_taxlist.pdf, /Jan04_nonjud_taxlist.pdf and /Jan04_jud_taxlist.pdf

(3) Rules for Selling Property Under the Non-Judicial Process
http://www.co.fulton.ga.us/departments/tax_comm_forms_T317_R2.html
http://www.co.fulton.ga.us/Fulton_County/departments/RULES_OF_SALE.pdf

(4) Contact Information
http://www.co.fulton.ga.us/departments/tax_comm_contact_T312_R1.html

No information available.

SHERIFF'S DEPARTMENT
http://www.co.fulton.ga.us/departments/sheriff.html
http://www.fultonsheriff.org/

(1) Contact Information
http://www.co.fulton.ga.us/departments/sheriff_contact_T242_R2.html
http://www.fultonsheriff.org/misc/address_book.asp

Fulton County Courthouse
185 Central Avenue, SW, 9th Floor
Atlanta, GA 30303
Phone: (404) 730-5100
Fax: (404) 730-6947
Email: jhbarrett@fultonsheriff.org
Sheriff Jacquelyn H. Barrett

Property Taxes
Lt. Earl Glenn
Email: Earl.Glenn@co.fulton.ga.us
Phone: 404-730-6595

GWINNETT COUNTY, GEORGIA
http://www.co.gwinnett.ga.us

TAX COMMISSIONER'S OFFICE
from http://www.co.gwinnett.ga.us, click on "departments" and then on "Tax Commissioner"
(http://www.co.gwinnett.ga.us/cgi-bin/bvgwin/egov/page.jsp?aolFX=y&pm=Departments&sm=Tax+Commissioner)

PROPERTY TAX DIRECTOR
(Tax Commissioner's Office)
from Tax Commissioner page, click on "Property Tax"
(http://www.co.gwinnett.ga.us/cgi-bin/bvgwin/egov/page.jsp?aolFX=y&pm=Departments%7CTax+Commissioner&sm=Property+Tax)

Property Tax Director, Robert Higdon
75 Langley Drive
Lawrenceville, GA 30045
Phone: (770) 822-8800
Email: Property_Tax@co.gwinnett.ga.us
FAX: (770) 822-7292

(1) Tax Lien and Tax Sale General Information
from Property Tax page, click on "Tax Sales"

Upcoming Tax Sales
The next tax sale is scheduled for March 2, 2004 at 10:00 a.m. in front of the Gwinnett Justice and Administration Building at 75 Langley Drive, Lawrenceville, Georgia. For more information call 770-822-8800.

Properties Scheduled for Tax Sale as of January 26, 2004
http://www.co.gwinnett.ga.us/departments/taxcomm/excel/website_bid_table.xls

ROGUE INVESTOR NOTE: tax sale list saved on CD:
USA Tax Lien Info/Georgia/gwinnett_co_GA/tax_sale_list.xls

Tax Lien and Tax Sale General Information

The Tax Commissioner, Gwinnett County, Georgia is responsible for collection of real and personal property taxes. The Tax Commissioner must issue a tax lien (commonly known as an execution or FIFA) against all delinquent taxpayers. A tax lien is released only when the delinquent taxes are satisfied in full. Georgia Law under code section 9-13-36 requires the Tax Commissioner to sell these FIFAs to any third party. The Tax Commissioner will either collect the tax from the taxpayer, sell the lien to a third party for the amount of delinquent taxes, or levy the property and auction it at a tax sale.

The Tax Commissioner occasionally auctions property at a tax sale for the collection of delinquent taxes. Tax sale proceedings are held according to the official code of Georgia sections 48-4-45 through 48-4-48. Sales are scheduled the first Tuesday of any given month in front of the courthouse. The bidding commences with the total taxes, fees, and interest on each parcel. The tax deed is then sold to the highest bidder. Tax sales are advertised in Thursday's legal advertisement section of the Gwinnett Daily Post. The newspaper ad is run once a week for four weeks prior to the sale. We also advertise on the cable government TV channel. We do not have a mailing list for tax sale information.

Tax Sale Guide

The following information is for the first time buyers. It is generic information on how to select properties and the rights associated with the tax deed.

Research Properties before the Tax Sale

One of the first things to consider before investing in tax sale properties is to research the property that you are interested in purchasing. Before a property is advertised to be sold, the Tax Commissioner or other firm must conduct a diligent title search on the property. Following the search we must notify all interested parties or lien holders. This process eliminates much of the burden of the tax sale purchaser. Keep in mind, when a property is sold at a tax sale, all liens are erased once foreclosure is completed; this includes mortgages, liens, and federal tax liens. However, these interest holders are entitled to redeem the property within 12 months of the tax sale (sale of property). It is strongly suggested that all buyers go to see the property in person, review the warranty deed, and review the mapping located in the Tax Assessor's Office.

Redemption Rights

It is your responsibility as a purchaser of a tax sale property to foreclose the right of redemption on that property. Georgia Code Sections 48-4-40 through 48-4-48 outlines the complete process. The following is a condensed version of these codes:

When real property is sold under a tax execution (sold at tax sale), the original taxpayer or any persons having a right, title, interest in, or lien upon the property may redeem the property at anytime within 12 months from the date of the purchase at tax sale by paying the redemption price. The property may be redeemed at anytime during this period until the tax sale purchaser terminates the right to do so by giving proper legal notice. The 12-month limit does not begin, however, until the tax purchaser pays the amount that he or she bid. The tax purchaser is not prohibited from consenting to redemption after the statutory period has expired, and as a matter of grace granting such a privilege.

Redemption Price

The redemption price to be paid to you, if the original debtor chooses to redeem, is the amount paid for the property at the tax sale, plus 20% of the amount for the first year, or fraction of a year thereafter, elapsing between the sale date and the date the redemption is made and 10% for each year or fraction of the year thereafter, plus any tax paid on the property during this period by the tax purchaser after the sale. If redemption is not made within the 30 days, and after the notice terminating the right to redeem has been properly issued and advertised, there must be added to the redemption price the sheriff's cost of serving notice and the cost of publishing the notice. All amounts comprising the redemption price are paid to you, the tax sale purchaser.

<u>After redemption period has expired</u>
The tax sale purchaser is to make original notice in accordance with a form shown in the statutes and provide a copy for each person to be served. The purchaser is to deliver these, together with a list of persons to be served, to the sheriff of the county in which the land is located, not less than 45 days before the date set in the notice for termination of the right of redemption. Within 15 days, the sheriff must serve a copy of the notice upon all persons on the list residing in the county and make an entry of such service on the original notice. Leaving a copy of the notice at the residence of any person required to be served is considered sufficient service. If the sheriff makes an entry that he or she has been unable to serve the notice on any person, the purchaser must immediately have it published in the official county newspaper once a week for two consecutive weeks. This constitutes service.

Upon payment of the sheriff's cost, the original notice must be returned to the tax sale purchaser. The notice and entries on it may be recorded on the deed records in the Clerk of Superior Court's Office in the county in which the land is located.

In the event that the property is redeemed by the original debtor or interested parties (mortgage companies, banks, or lien holders, etc.), the tax sale purchaser must make a quitclaim deed (Release of Claim) to the original delinquent taxpayer, reciting, among other things, who paid the redemption money. The redemption of the property gives back to the original delinquent taxpayer the title conveyed by the tax sale, subject to all liens existing at the time of sale.

If the redemption is made by a creditor of the original delinquent taxpayer or other persons having interest in the property, the amount expended by either constitutes a first lien and must be paid prior to any other claims on the property. However, it is necessary that the quitclaim deed have been properly recorded in the Clerk of Superior Court's Office.

The purchaser of a tax sale property may sell the property before the redemption period has expired. However, the person buying from the tax sale purchaser acquires the defeasible (i.e., can be annulled) title of the tax sale purchaser, subject to the right of the original delinquent taxpayer to redeem it within the period prescribed by law (12 months).

As noted above, the purchaser receives only a defeasible title before the redemption period expires. However, the purchaser acquires sufficient interest in the property to render him or her liable for the taxes that become due on it.

No tax sale purchaser is entitled to rents and profits arising from the property during the redemption period. A tax sale purchaser may obtain a court order to enable them to make improvements upon the property in the event the improvement is aimed at the preservation of the value of said property (i.e., a leaking roof that is causing water to damage a home).

A title under a tax deed shall ripen by prescription after a period of four years from the date of execution. However, see your local real estate attorney to inquire about a quiet title action. Notice of foreclosure of the right to redeem property sold at the tax sale shall not be required to have been provided, in order for the title to such property to have ripened.

The information contained within this website is only a broad overview of the tax lien, transfer, and sale procedures and is being provided solely as a public service to the members of the general public. If you need specific information, we suggest you seek legal counsel specializing in real estate transactions. Also, you may visit the State of Georgia website (http://www.state.ga.us/Departments/DOR/ptd) to view the actual code section (48-4-40 through 48-4-48).

SHERIFF'S DEPARTMENT
http://www.gwinnettcountysheriff.com

Sheriff R.L. (Butch) Conway
email: blacksy@co.gwinnett.ga.us

(1) Civil Division
http://www.gwinnettcountysheriff.com/Civil%20Division.htm

75 Langley Drive
Lawrenceville, Georgia 30045
phone: (770) 822-8200

The Civil Division is responsible for serving all civil process papers, including evictions and property seizures.

Tax Lien Sales: No

Tax Deed Sales: Yes

Rating: Two Stars (**)

Interest Rate: Deed with a right of redemption. State law allows for a 12% per year fee to the investor if redeemed.

Sale Period: Each county handles tax deed sales differently.

Redemption Period: Properties can be purchased at tax deed sales for immediate ownership.

Bidding Process:
At tax deed sales, all auctions are by competitive bid. Winning bidder pays highest value for property.

State-Specific Information:
Hawaii only has five counties. In contrast to the other four counties, Kalawao County's tax sales are handled by the state, through the State Department of Taxation located in Honolulu, Hawaii.

Links for All Hawaii Counties: Provided on CD.

Detailed County-Specific Information

HONOLULU COUNTY, HAWAII
http://www.co.honolulu.hi.us

FINANCE OFFICE

(1) Revised Ordinances of Honolulu
http://www.co.honolulu.hi.us/rpa/chapter8.pdf

Article 5.Liens – Foreclosures. References to "director" are to Director of Finance of the City and County of Honolulu.

BUDGET & FISCAL SERVICES DEPARTMENT
http://www.co.honolulu.hi.us/budget/index.htm

530 S. King Street (Honolulu Hale)
Honolulu, HI 96813
Ivan Lui-Kwan, Director, pending City Council approval
real property tax delinquencies phone = 808-523-4972

SHERIFF'S OFFICE

Keith Kamita
Department of Public Safety
3375 Kaopaka Street, Suite D100
Honolulu, HI 96819
phone: 808-594-0150, 808-538-5660; Fax: 808-594-0156

Tax Lien Sales: No

Tax Deed Sales: Yes

Rating: Two Stars (**)

Interest Rate: No interest rate, state only sells tax deeds.

Sale Period:
No scheduled sales. Each county handles tax deed sales differently and usually holds delinquent properties until an interested buyer shows up.

Redemption Period:
Properties can be purchased from county commissioners for immediate ownership. Properties where the taxes are not paid up within three years are deeded to the county.

Bidding Process:
Property is sold to the highest bidder. Contact the county commissioner to find out what properties are available. Financing is allowed through a contract with the county not to exceed 10 years.

State-Specific Information:
In Idaho, the Tax Collector is generally the County Treasurer.

Links for All Idaho Counties: Provided on CD.

Detailed County-Specific Information:

CASSIA COUNTY, IDAHO
http://www.cassiacounty.org

TREASURER'S OFFICE
http://www.cassiacounty.org/treasurer/index.htm

Gayle Erekson, Cassia County Treasurer
email: gerekson@cassiacounty.org

Treasurer's Office
1459 Overland Avenue
Burley, ID 83318
Phone: (208) 878-7202
Fax: (208) 878-1012

BOARD OF COUNTY COMMISSIONERS
http://www.cassiacounty.org/commissioners/index.htm

(1) Real Property Tax Sales
http://www.cassiacounty.org/commissioners/rpts.htm

Board of County Commissioners (BoCC) review real property list, and determine what to sell at public auction.

BoCC have Notice of Auction prepared and published in South Idaho Press in accordance with Idaho Code § 60-106. The notice shall comply with the following:

- Publish not less than ten (10) days prior to auction.
- Shall contain legal description of property, and next to such description shall place name of delinquent taxpayer.
- Shall contain street address of property.
- If located outside of city limits and does not have a street address, then the description shall also contain the distance and direction of the location of the real property from the closest city.

PROPERTY SHALL BE SOLD TO THE HIGHEST BIDDER

- BoCC may reserve right to reject any and all bids.
- BoCC have discretionary authority to reject or accept any bid made for an amount less than total amount of delinquent taxes, late charges, costs and interest.

PURCHASE PROCESS

- Can be purchased on contract with County.
  (i) Contract must be recorded.
  (ii) Term cannot exceed ten (10) years.
  (iii) Interest rate not to exceed rate specified by I.C. Section 28-22-104(1).
  (iv) BoCC have authority to cancel contract if purchaser fails to comply with contract terms and County retains all payments made on contract.
  (v) Title to all property sold on contract is retained in name of Cassia County until full payment is made by purchaser.
  (vi) Purchaser shall be responsible for payment of all property taxes during period of contract.
- Sale of property vests all right, title and interest, which was held by Cassia County in the subject property, in the purchaser. (Including all delinquent taxes which become a lien on the property.)
- In addition to the purchase price, the purchaser shall pay all fees required by law for transfer of property.
- If property is not sold, or is not bid upon, at public auction, then county may sell, without further notice, at public or private sale.

REDEMPTION OF TAX DEEDED PROPERTY (I.C. Section 63-1007)

- After issuance of tax deed to County, may be redeemed only by record owner or party in interest, up to the time BoCC have entered into a contract of sale or the property has been transferred by County deed.
- To redeem, have to pay any delinquency including late charges, accrued interest and costs.
- Once payments are made, then County will issue a Redemption Deed.
- Right of Redemption shall expire, if property not earlier sold by County, three (3) years from the date of issuance of the tax deed to the County.

MISCELLANEOUS INFORMATION

- Payment may be made by cash, cashier's check or personal check, bankable the day of sale. If payment does not clear on the first attempt, the bid will be disqualified and the property may be awarded to the next highest, responsible bidder.
- Bids may be submitted by mail. The bidder is responsible to assure that a mailed bid is received by the county prior to commencement of the public auction.

Tax Lien Sales: Yes

Tax Deed Sales: No

Rating: Four Stars (****)

Interest Rate: 18% every six months or 36% per year. On farmland, the interest rate is 12% every six months or 24% per year, and the interest rate is considered a penalty, not interest.

Sale Period: October or November in most counties.

Redemption Period: 2 years

Bidding Process:
You must register one month in advance in most counties or you cannot bid on properties. All auctions are by competitive bid. Winning bidder pays lowest interest rate. Tax lien sale advertisements usually appear in county newspapers about three weeks prior to the sale.

State-Specific Information:
Illinois is an excellent tax lien state because the interest rate of 36% per year is very favorable. Some of the larger counties are highly competitive and big-time investors will bid rates down to as low as 1%. If you are looking to acquire a property that is not likely to be redeemed, one strategy is to bid down to zero and shut out the "big-time" investors.

Links for All Illinois Counties: Provided on CD.

Detailed County-Specific Information:

CHAMPAIGN COUNTY, ILLINOIS
http://www.co.champaign.il.us

OFFICE OF THE SUPERVISOR OF ASSESSMENTS
http://www.co.champaign.il.us/soaoff/soaoff.htm

The Office of the Supervisor of Assessments is located in Pod 100 of the Champaign County Brookens Administrative Center, 1776 E. Washington Street, Urbana, IL 61802.

The phone number is (217) 384-3760 and the fax number is (217) 384-3896.

The Chief County Assessment Officer for Champaign County, Illinois, is Bonnie J. Vaughn.

(1) Tax Sale
from http://www.co.champaign.il.us/soaoff/soaoff.htm, click on "Tax Sale"

Champaign County's Annual Tax Sale of delinquent property taxes is generally held on the last Monday in October, with registration for tax buyers occurring 10 business days prior. For further information regarding qualifications for tax buyers and the exact dates, please contact the County Treasurer (http://www.co.champaign.il.us/deptlist/depts.htm). Listings of the delinquent property taxes may be purchased from the County Treasurer preceding the Tax Sale.

In addition to the Annual Tax Sale, the Champaign County Board has authorized direct sale of some tax certificates. To participate in the Champaign County Delinquent Tax Program, please contact any of the following:

Champaign County Delinquent Tax Agent
141 St. Andrews Avenue
P.O. Box 96
Edwardsville, IL 62025
(800) 248-2850
(618) 656-5744 (Direct)

Tax Certificate Information: Martin Saville, Title Department
Purchasing or Sale Information: Jack Butler, Auction Department

---

COOK COUNTY, ILLINOIS
http://www.co.cook.il.us

TREASURER'S OFFICE
http://www.cookcountytreasurer.com/main.wu

(1) How the Cook County Treasurer's Office Operates
http://www.cookcountytreasurer.com/Pamphlets/About%20the%20Office.wu

After second installment property taxes have been collected, an Annual Tax Sale of unpaid taxes is held. Every other year, a Scavenger Sale on properties with two or more years of tax delinquency is held.

(2) Annual Tax Sale Background Information
http://www.cookcountytreasurer.com/taxdates/taxsale

Under Illinois law, the Treasurer's Office is required to conduct two types of real estate tax sales in which delinquent property taxes are sold.

The first is the Annual Tax Sale, held once a year, sometime after the second installment. If property taxes for the immediately preceding tax year are delinquent on a parcel, they are offered for sale to tax purchasers at the Annual Tax Sale. The sale might be held any time from the Fall of that year to the Spring of the following year.

All annual tax sale participants must meet a set of qualifications to participate in the annual tax sale. They must complete registration materials and provide collateral or a bond. The registration materials include rules for the conduct of a tax sale.

The 2002 Annual Tax Sale will be held in April of 2004. Check back at this site for updates.

The biennial Scavenger Sale (conducted in odd-numbered years) offers taxes on properties that have delinquencies on two or more years that were not purchased at the annual tax sales. In Cook County, the sale has traditionally taken place in the fall or early winter months.

For a complete understanding of the distinctions between these sales and how to proceed to tax deed, read 35 ILCS (Illinois Compiled Statutes) 200/1-1, et seq. This information can be found in any law library.

(3) Scavenger Tax Sale
http://www.cookcountytreasurer.com/taxdates/scavenger

The biennial Scavenger Sale (conducted in odd-numbered years) offers taxes on properties that have delinquencies on two or more years that were not purchased at the annual tax sales. In Cook County, the sale has traditionally taken place in the fall or early winter months.

The next Scavenger Tax Sale will be held in 2005.

(4) Tax Bill Schedule
http://www.cookcountytreasurer.com/taxdates/schedule

(5) Contact Information
http://www.cookcountytreasurer.com/contact
http://www.cookcountytreasurer.com/contact/phone

Maria Pappas, Cook County Treasurer
118 North Clark, Room 212
Chicago, Illinois 60602
phone: (312) 443-5100
email: info@cookcountytreasurer.com

Call the Office of the Cook County Clerk at (312) 603-5645 for information on the 2000 tax year (due in 2001) or any prior tax year: prior tax year forfeitures, prior tax year open items, and prior tax year tax-sale redemptions.

Cook County Clerk's Office
118 North Clark Street, Room 434
Chicago, IL 60602
312-603-5645

DUPAGE COUNTY, ILLINOIS
http://www.co.dupage.il.us

SHERIFF'S OFFICE
http://www.co.dupage.il.us/sheriff

sheriff@dupageco.org: inquiry will be forwarded to the Sheriff or appropriate division head

CIVIL DIVISION OF SHERIFF'S OFFICE
from http://www.co.dupage.il.us/sheriff, click on "About the Office" and then on "Civil Division & Fees"

Auctions relating to the foreclosure of real estate are conducted by the Civil Division. The phone number for Evictions & Foreclosures is (630) 682-7251.

(1) February 2004 Foreclosure Sale
http://www.co.dupage.il.us/sheriff/Civil/FORECLOSURE%20SALES%20LIST.pdf

ROGUE INVESTOR NOTE: information saved on CD:
USA Tax Lien Info/Illinois/dupage_co_IL/Feb04_foreclosure_saleslist.pdf

(2) Foreclosure Research/Information Sheet
from http://www.co.dupage.il.us/sheriff/, click on "About the Office," then on "Civil Division & Fees," and then on "Foreclosure Research"

TREASURER'S OFFICE
http://www.dupageco.org/treasurer/index.cfm

County Treasurer, John Novak (Phone: 630-682-7005)

(1) Paying Your Taxes
http://www.dupageco.org/treasurer/generic.cfm?doc_id=130

The annual real estate tax sale will begin on Monday, November 22, 2004. To avoid tax sale, payment must be received by 4:30 p.m. Friday, November 19, 2004.

LAKE COUNTY, ILLINOIS
http://www.co.lake.il.us

TREASURER'S OFFICE
http://www.co.lake.il.us/treasurer/default.asp

The staff holds the annual tax sale.

(1) Real Estate Taxes
http://www.co.lake.il.us/treasurer/realestate.asp

Those interested in participating in the tax sale must register 10 business days prior to the sale.

(2) Tax Sale Instructions
http://www.co.lake.il.us/treasurer/taxsale.asp

The sale will be held at 9:00 AM on the 10th floor in the Assembly Room of the County Administration Building. The tax sale usually starts on the first or second Monday in December with the delinquent lists becoming available 2 or 3 weeks prior to the sale. Listed below is some important information for those attending the sale:

1. Fees involved prior to the tax sale:
   I. Registration begins October 1st
   II. $50 registration fee (applies to each buyer number to be used at the sale)
   III. $500 tax sale list ($50 for the actual list and $450 will be applied toward any items purchased at the sale)
2. Application and fees must be received in the Lake County Treasurer's Office 10 business days prior to the beginning of the sale.
3. If you would like the Treasurer's Office to mail you a paper copy, there will be an additional charge of $20 per list.
4. There will be no refunds on the registration fee or tax sale list.
5. The tax sale list provided for you should be used for the sole purpose of the delinquent property tax sale. Use of this information for any other purpose is strictly prohibited. The County Treasurer reserves the right to deny sale of the list to anyone violating this rule. Newspaper listings of each township will be available in our office (approximately the third week in November).
6. Anyone interested in buying only one or two parcels will need to register 10 business days prior to the start of the sale. There will be no registration fee involved. These will take place each day prior to the sale. Payment for those parcels will be required that day.
7. Buyers purchasing fewer than 10 parcels must pay the total amount due on the day of the sale or those sales will be voided.
8. Buyers purchasing more than 10 parcels will be notified the following morning of the amount due. That amount must be paid on the following business day after notification (i.e., Monday's sales must be paid on Wednesday, Tuesday's sales must be paid on Thursday, etc.).
9. A list will be available to tax buyers purchasing more than 10 parcels on the morning following completion of the sale. Any corrections must be made by 5:00 PM on the date of the sale.
10. All tax buyers will be notified when certificates are ready. Certificates must be picked up in person. THEY WILL NOT BE MAILED.

Publication Dates: October 21st & 23rd (papers will be available in our office October 27th)
$500.00 Tax Sale List, available the 2nd week in November
Last Day to Register: November 13th at 5:00pm
Tax Sale: December 1st & 2nd

If you should have any further questions, please contact the Treasurer's Office at 847-377-2323 or online at treasurer@co.lake.il.us.

(3) Contact the Treasurer
http://www.co.lake.il.us/treasurer/contact.asp

Robert Skidmore, Treasurer
18 N. County Street
Waukegan, IL 60085
phone: 847-377-2323
email: Treasurer@co.lake.il.us

MADISON COUNTY, ILLINOIS
http://www.co.madison.il.us

TREASURER'S OFFICE
from http://www.co.madison.il.us, click on "Treasurer" under list of Departments

Fred Bathon, Treasurer
Phone: (618) 692-6260

(1) Contact Information
from Treasurer's Office home page, click on "Contacting Madison County" and "Office Hours and Location"

Treasurer's Office
157 North Main Street
Edwardsville, IL 62025

For information on Tax Rates, Tax Levies, or Delinquent Taxes, contact the County Clerk:
phone = (618) 692-6290
email: dlboda@co.madison.il.us

(2) Madison County Annual Real Estate Tax Sale General Information
from Treasurer's Office home page, click on "Tax Sale Information" and then on "Real Estate Tax Sale"

Sale Procedures
The format of the tax sale is an oral auction. You or a representative must attend the sale to participate. The order of the sale is by township, by parcel ID. The Treasurer's Office reads the alternate ID number and judgment amount for each parcel. Bids may begin as high as 18% (semi-annual rate) with the sale going to the lowest bidder. If no bid is received, the parcel is sold to the County's trustee. For dates and information, contact the office of Joseph E. Meyer, 141 Street Andrews Avenue, P.O. Box 96, Edwardsville, IL 62025, Tel: (800) 248-2850, Fax: (618) 656-5094.

Date of Sale
The approximate official start date of the sale will be Wednesday, November 12, 2003. Only one parcel is sold on the first day. The remainder of the sale will be held on November 13th and 14th. The sale will begin at 9:00 a.m. each day. The sale will be held in the Administration Building at 157 North Main Street, in Edwardsville, Illinois, in the County Board Room on the second floor.

Registration
There is no fee to register. You must register in writing at least 10 business days before the sale by sending a letter to the Madison County Treasurer's Office, P.O. Box 729, Edwardsville, IL 62025. Please include your address, telephone number, and the name of the person attending. Each person or business attending is required to fill out a W-9 form (http://www.co.madison.il.us/Treas/W-9.pdf), Request for Taxpayer Identification Number and Certification when registering. Forms are available in the County Treasurer's or County Clerk's offices.

List of Properties

A tentative listing of available properties (printed report or on disk) is available approximately 2 weeks before the sale for a fee of $250. This fee includes daily updates that are available to pick up in the Treasurer's Office, identifying additional parcels that have been paid and removed from the sale. A "final" listing of available properties will be available on the Wednesday morning of the sale, for an additional $250 fee. This list will be final with the exception of any final adjustments that need to be made at the last minute by our office. You must notify the Treasurer's Office by 5 p.m. on the previous Monday if you want to purchase this "final" listing.

Payment

Payment must be made immediately following the sale at the end of each day for the judgment amount (taxes plus penalties and interest) plus fees of $95 per parcel purchased. Payment is preferred by check. Credit cards are not accepted.

Advertisement

The Treasurer's Office does not advertise for the sale. Listings of delinquent properties by township, by owner name, are published in area newspapers approximately 2-3 weeks before the sale.

ROGUE INVESTOR NOTE: Tax sale date not updated for 2004.

(3) Request for Taxpayer Identification Number and Certification (W-9)
http://www.co.madison.il.us/Treas/W-9.pdf

(4) Madison County Annual Mobile Home Tax Sale General Information
from Treasurer's Office home page, click on "Tax Sale Information" and then on "Mobile Home Tax Sale"

Tax Lien Sales: Yes

Tax Deed Sales: No

Rating: Five Stars (*****)

Interest Rate: Varies, but the rate can be as high as 25% per year: 10% if tax lien is redeemed in less than six months, 15% if tax lien is redeemed in more than six months but less than one year, and 25% if tax lien is redeemed in more than one year.

Interest on the overbid amount is 1%. Interest on any taxes or assessments paid by the investor after the sale is 10%. If the sale is declared invalid before the deed, the investor receives 6%. If the sale is declared invalid after the deed, the investor receives 10%.

Sale Period: August in most counties.

Redemption Period: 1 year

Bidding Process:
All auctions are by competitive bid. Winning bidder pays the most for the property lien. Tax lien sale advertisements usually appear in county newspapers about three weeks prior to the sale.

State-Specific Information:
Indiana is an excellent tax lien state because the interest rate of up to 25% per year is very favorable and the redemption period of one year is extremely short.

Links for All Indiana Counties: Provided on CD.

Detailed County-Specific Information:

MARION COUNTY, INDIANA
http://www.indygov.org

TREASURER'S OFFICE
http://www.indygov.org/treas

Gregory N. Jordan
200 E. Washington Street, Suite 1001
Indianapolis, IN 46204-3356

Customer Service
phone = 317-327-4444
TDD = 317-327-5186
Fax = 317-327-4440

(1) 2003 Tax Sale Information and Procedures
http://www.indygov.org/treas/taxsale/proptax_2003.htm

Marion County, Indiana, 2003 TAX SALE Information and Procedures

The information and procedures listed in this guide pertain to Marion County's 2003 Tax Sale. Exact information for the 2004 Tax Sale will not be available until early summer 2004. However, you may use this as a guide to understand, generally, how Marion County's Tax Sale is conducted.

The 2004 Tax Sale will be held on October 7, 8, and 13, 2004.

PLEASE REVIEW THE ENTIRE CONTENTS OF THIS GUIDE!

NOTE: The Tax Sale item list will be available on the Treasurer's web page. More information about this feature can be found on page 3 of this guide.

Notice: The Marion County Tax Sale List will be available online through the last day of the Tax Sale. This list will be updated on a regular basis (normally once each day) during the course of the sale.

(1a) Introduction
http://www6.indygov.org/treas/taxsale/proptax_2003introduction.htm

(1b) General Instructions
http://www6.indygov.org/treas/taxsale/proptax_2003general.htm

(1c) Instructions for Buyers
http://www6.indygov.org/treas/taxsale/proptax_2003buyers.htm

(2) County-Owned Surplus Sale
http://www6.indygov.org/treas/surplus/surplusmain.htm

Auction Dates for 2004: January 6, April 22, June 17, August 12

ROGUE INVESTOR NOTE: Additional information is available on web page.

SHERIFF'S DEPARTMENT
http://www.indygov.org/mcsd

40 South Alabama Street
Indianapolis, Indiana 46204
Administrative phone number: 317-231-8200

CIVIL DIVISION OF THE SHERIFF'S DEPARTMENT
http://www.indygov.org/mcsd/civil/civil.htm

Marion County Sheriff's Department
Civil Division
200 East Washington Street, Suite # 1122
Indianapolis, Indiana 46204
general information telephone number is (317) 231-8430

(1) Real Estate Forms
http://www.indygov.org/mcsd/civil/real-estate-forms.htm

(1a) Real Estate Sale Rules
http://www6.indygov.org/mcsd/forms/Sale%20Rules.pdf

(1b) Clerk Return
http://www6.indygov.org/mcsd/forms/Clerk%20Return.pdf

(1c) Sheriff's Deed Form
http://www6.indygov.org/mcsd/forms/Sheriff%20Deed.pdf

(1d) Notice of Sheriff's Sale Form
http://www6.indygov.org/mcsd/forms/Sheriff%20Notice.pdf

(3) Real Estate List Information
http://www6.indygov.org/mcsd/civil/real-estate-list.htm

The Marion County Sheriff's Department Civil Office maintains two Real Estate Lists. The first is the "short" one listing the property's address, sale number and township. There is also a "full" list that shows the address of the property, sale number, township, plaintiff, judgment amount and any additional charges or fees. There is a charge for either list and it varies from month to month. For information about the Real Estate List including prices, availability, and updates, please call the Civil Office at (317) 231-8427 for a recorded message containing the most current information.

The listings of real estate in Marion County are available for purchase on-line through CivicNet, the business-oriented web site of the Indianapolis/Marion County Government. The list is available for purchase with a credit card or as a paid subscription service. The real estate listings are also available for purchase in person at the Marion County Sheriff's Department Civil Office. The Civil Office is located in room 1122 on the 11th floor of the center tower of the City County Building at 200 East Washington Street. It is open 8:00 AM to 4:00 PM, Monday through Friday, except for county holidays.

Questions? Please call our Civil Office Real Estate Office at (317) 231-8425.

(4) Monthly Real Estate Listings
https://www.civicnet.net/apps/police/realestate

Real Estate Lists Available Online
Short List:
Subscription users $3.00. Credit card users $5.50.
Includes: address of the property sale number township

Full List:
Subscription users $13.00. Credit card users $15.50.
Includes: address of the property sale number township plaintiff judgment amount

The MCSD Civil Office maintains a 24-hour recorded message with up-to-the-minute list prices, availability and updated information on the Real Estate Lists at (317) 231-8427.

(5) Real Estate Sales Dates
http://www.indygov.org/mcsd/civil/sale-dates.htm

Attention: Buyers
The Sheriff's Sale Date and Advertising dates are the significant dates. Approximately three weeks prior to the Sheriff's Sale Date, we will have a listing of properties scheduled for that sale. List availability can be obtained by calling 316-231-8427.

ROGUE INVESTOR NOTE: Information on web page is for 2003.

Tax Lien Sales: Yes

Tax Deed Sales: No

Rating: Five Stars (*****)

Interest Rate: 24% per year

Sale Period: Third week in June

Redemption Period: As quick as 21 months

Bidding Process:
All auctions are by competitive bid. Bidders bid on the percentage of the property they will own. Thus, when two bidders bid on the same property, they can both end up owning a percentage of the property. The bidding process can also be by random round robin. Tax lien sale advertisements usually appear in county newspapers about three weeks prior to the sale.

State-Specific Information:
Iowa is an excellent tax lien state because the interest rate of up to 24% per year is very favorable, the redemption period of 21 months is extremely short, and unsold certificates can be purchased by mail.

Links for All Iowa Counties: Provided on CD.

Detailed County-Specific Information:

POLK COUNTY, IOWA
http://www.co.polk.ia.us:8080

TREASURER'S OFFICE
http://www.co.polk.ia.us:8080/modules.php?name=Departments&deptnum=17

Mary Maloney, Treasurer
Polk County Administration Building
111 Court Avenue, Room #140
Des Moines IA, 50309
Phone: 515 / 286-2036
Fax: 515 / 286-2225

(1) Property Tax Division
http://www.co.polk.ia.us:8080/modules.php?name=Sections&sop=viewarticle&artid=8

Polk County Administration Building
111 Court Avenue, Room 154
Des Moines IA, 50309
Phone: 515-286-3060
Fax: 515-323-5202
Property Tax Email: propertytax@co.polk.ia.us

The Treasurer is also responsible for conducting the tax sale; processing tax sale redemptions; issuing tax sale deeds.

(2) Tax Sale Buyer Information
http://www.co.polk.ia.us:8080/modules.php?name=Sections&sop=viewarticle&artid=225

Tax Sale Redemption Funds
http://www2.co.polk.ia.us/breq.php
Tax sale buyer request for available redemption funds.

Below is the 2003 Tax Sale information in a pdf file, provided for reference purposes only.

2003 Tax Sale Information http://www.co.polk.ia.us:8080/downloads/treasurer/TaxSale2003.pdf

The Polk County Treasurer is responsible for the administration of the Annual Tax Sale and must offer for sale, in an open competitive bidding process (Iowa Code Chapter 446, http://www.legis.state.ia.us/IowaLaw.html), parcels in which taxes have become delinquent. The purpose of the tax sale is to collect unpaid taxes. The Annual Tax Sale takes place in June of each year at the Polk County Convention Complex (http://www.conventioncomplex.com).

Delinquent taxes on a parcel subject to sale will be advertised in June in a Polk County newspaper of general circulation. Properties are listed in parcel number order and have a sequence number for bidding purposes. Copies of the newspaper are available for purchase at the Polk County Treasurer's Office.

In addition, computer reports of delinquent items are available in three formats:

1. Paper report: Paper reports can be picked up in room 155 or mailed through the U.S. Postal Service or UPS regular delivery.

2. Electronic Report Via Treasurer's Web Site (view only) – No Charge: Customers may view the computer report from the Treasurer's Office Web Site beginning May 1, 2001, at no cost by selecting one of the links below:

   - Real Estate Public Bidder Sale (http://www2.co.polk.ia.us/TSPublic.php)
   - Real Estate Regular Sale (http://www2.co.polk.ia.us/TSRegular.php)
   - Mobile Home Public Bidder Sale (http://www2.co.polk.ia.us/MHPublic.php)
   - Mobile Home Regular Sale (http://www2.co.polk.ia.us/MHRegular.php)

3. Electronic Download Report Via Treasurer's Web Site – Password Access: Customers may download the computer report from the Treasurer's web site in a format compatible with most spreadsheet and database programs for a fee. The fee includes unlimited download capability. The Treasurer's Office will assign a user name and password to you upon receipt of your payment. The user name and password number is valid only for the tax sale(s) listed in the table below.

To place an order in one or more of the previously mentioned formats, complete the "Delinquent Tax List Order Form" (http://www.co.polk.ia.us:8080/downloads/Treasurer/TaxListOrderFm.pdf) and return it with your check for the appropriate fee to the Polk County Treasurer's Office.

You will receive a user ID, password and the Internet website address from the Treasurer's Office once you have paid for the report.

Format	Method of Delivery	Effective Dates	Cost
Paper Report	Pick Up	2003 June Tax Sale	$40.00 ea.
Paper Report	U.S. Mail / UPS	2003 June Tax Sale	$50.00 ea.
Paper Report	Pick Up	All 2003 Adjourned Tax Sales	$10.00 ea.
Paper Report	U.S. Mail / UPS	All 2003 Adjourned Tax Sales	$10.00 ea.
Electronic Report (view only)	Internet	All 2003 Tax Sales	Free
Electronic Download Report	Internet	2003 June Tax Sale & Adjourned Tax Sales	$50.00

Submit the request and payment for paper reports or electronic downloadable files to:

Polk County Treasurer
Attn: Tax Administrative Supervisor
111 Court Avenue
Des Moines, IA 50309-2298
Fax: (515)323-5202
E-mail: propertytax@co.polk.ia.us

Copying, distributing, or selling the tax sale computer report is prohibited.

The investor is responsible for all research on parcels available for auction.

The following sites are available that may help an investor research parcels for the tax sale.

- Assessor Link (http://207.108.41.49/)
- Auditor GIMS Link (http://www.gis.co.polk.ia.us)

Please contact the Cash Management Division of the Polk County Treasurer's Office at 515-286-3035 for information concerning tax sale redemption funds.

Tax Lien Sales: No

Tax Deed Sales: Yes

Rating: Three Stars (***)

Interest Rate: No interest rate, state only sells tax deeds.

Sale Period: Some auctions are not regularly scheduled.

Redemption Period:
Properties can be purchased from county sheriffs for immediate ownership.

Bidding Process:
The local sheriffs hold auctions with the opening bid starting at the amount of taxes owed on the property. The minimum bid is equal to back taxes plus interest, fees and costs of the sale. You may have a buyer's agent buy properties for you. Highest bidder wins the property. Contact the county sheriffs to find out what properties are available.

Links for All Kansas Counties: Provided on CD.

Detailed County-Specific Information:

JOHNSON COUNTY, KANSAS
http://www.jocoks.com

TREASURER'S OFFICE
from http://www.jocoks.com/agencies.htm, click on "Treasurer's Office"

Dennis Wilson, Treasurer
111 S. Cherry Street, Suite 1500
Olathe, KS 66061

(1) Delinquent Taxes
http://treasurer.jocogov.org/delinquent_taxes.htm

Publication of Delinquent Real Estate Taxes

Delinquent real estate taxes not paid within 3 years are referred to the Legal Department for foreclosure action, thus putting the property in jeopardy of being sold at auction.

Details of Tax Foreclosure Sales may be obtained by requesting a brochure entitled "Johnson County, Kansas, Tax Foreclosure Sale" from the Johnson County Legal Department, or go to Tax Foreclosure Sale: http://www.jocogov.org/countyclerk/taxsale/tax_sale.htm.

Real Estate taxes that are unpaid August 1st of the current year are published in the official county newspaper (as designated by the Board of County Commissioners) for 3 consecutive weeks in August in accordance with the provisions of K.S.A. 79-2301 to 79-2323a.

LEGAL DEPARTMENT
http://legal.jocogov.org

Johnson County Legal Department
111 S. Cherry Street, Suite 3200
Olathe, KS 66061-3486
Phone: (913) 715-1900
FAX: (913) 715-1873

(1) Tax Foreclosure Sale
http://www.jocoks.com/countyclerk/taxsale/tax_sale.htm

The County does not sell tax lien certificates.

A list of the properties, as well as the date, time and location of the auction and registration requirements, will be published prior to the sale in the *Johnson County Sun* and the *Olathe Daily News* once a week for three weeks. You may also view a list of properties at this web site; the list follows this message.

Also, for a nominal fee, you may obtain a list of the properties at the Johnson County Legal Department. Properties are listed by parcel identification number and by legal description; approximate addresses are listed where available but are not warranted. You may view maps of the properties at this web site; the maps follow the list of properties.

Booklets containing lists and maps of the properties are also available at the Johnson County Legal Department for $5.00 each. Booklets may be purchased in person or by mail. To order the booklet by mail, send your name, address, and money order or cashier's check in the total amount of $7.00 (which includes postage) to Johnson County Legal Department, 111 S. Cherry Street, Suite 3200, Olathe, KS 66061-3441.

The amount of tax listed for each property in the sale ad is the amount of delinquent taxes owed, plus interest, not the assessed value. Ownership of the property remains with the current owner(s) until the sale. Therefore, you may not enter the property without the permission of the owner(s). The current owner(s) may redeem the property at any time prior to the time of sale.

The Auction
Properties are sold at public auction to the highest qualified bidder. The county may bid on properties up to the amount of taxes and interest it is owed. Some properties may sell for less than the taxes owed; some may sell for more. Registration prior to the sale is required.

Registration will be held the morning of the sale, as advertised. Generally, state law prohibits the following people from buying at the auction:

> Those who owe delinquent taxes in Johnson County; those who have an interest in the property, such as the owners, mortgagees, relatives, or officers of a corporation which owns the property; and those who buy the property with the intent to transfer it to someone who is prohibited from buying at the auction. All bidders must execute an affidavit, under oath, that they meet the statutory qualifications for bidding on tax sale property. Properties will be sold by legal description and by county parcel identification number.

PROPERTIES ARE SOLD "AS IS." THERE ARE NO WARRANTIES.
All the properties must be paid for by the stated time on the day of the sale. Only cash, a cashier's check, or a money order will be accepted. Personal checks are not accepted. The buyer must pay the fee for filing the deed with the register of deeds at the time of the sale. The buyer will receive a receipt for payment on the day of the sale.

<u>After the Auction</u>
The court will hold a hearing approximately three weeks after the auction to determine whether to confirm the sales. Some properties sold at the auction are subject to a federal lien. A deed will be issued for those properties after the expiration of the applicable federal redemption period, if the federal agency chooses not to redeem the property.

For properties not subject to a federal lien, the Sheriff will issue a Sheriff's Deed after the court confirms the sale. All other liens which were of record will be extinguished upon confirmation of the sale; however, covenants, and restrictions and easements of record are not extinguished, and the buyer takes the property subject to those encumbrances.

The buyer is responsible for any taxes and assessments, which are not included in the judgment, including the full amount of taxes assessed against the property <u>for the calendar year in which the auction is held.</u> The buyer is responsible for taking any necessary legal action to obtain possession of the property, such as by filing an eviction proceeding.

For twelve months after the deed is recorded, a legal challenge may still be made to question the procedures that the county followed. If such a challenge is successful, the property could revert to the original owner, in which case the court would order the purchase price refunded to the buyer.

Johnson County does not discriminate on the basis of race, color, national origin, gender, religion, age, and/or disabled status in employment or the provision of services.

<u>Upcoming Auctions</u>
A date for the next tax foreclosure sale has not been determined. There will be no property lists or maps available until a new sale is being prepared. Please check again at a later date.

You may leave the building to obtain the cash, money order, or certified check for payment, but you must return to pay for the property by 4:00 p.m. that day. Payments will be accepted until noon at the auction site. Payments will be accepted from noon to 4:00 p.m. at the Johnson County Sheriff's Civil Division, 125 North Cherry Street, Room 122, Olathe, Kansas. Sale list is subject to change if property is redeemed.

<u>FREQUENTLY ASKED QUESTIONS</u>
Q: What is the date, time, and location of your tax auctions?
A: Auctions are scheduled when all other tax auction procedures required by law and County policy have been completed. Auction dates, times, and location will be posted on this site as they are set.

Q: When and how are your tax auctions advertised? How can I obtain a list of properties for upcoming auctions?
A: A list of the properties, as well as the date, time and location of the auction and registration requirements, will be published prior to the auction in the *Johnson County Sun* and the *Olathe Daily News* once a week for three weeks. A list of the properties and maps for the properties are available for viewing on this web site. Also, for a nominal fee, you may obtain a list of the properties and maps at the Johnson County Legal Department. Maps and lists may be purchased in person or by mail. To order the maps and list by mail, send your name, address, and cashier's check or money order in the amount of $15 to Johnson County Legal Department, 111 S. Cherry Street, Suite 3200, Olathe, KS 66061-3486.

Q: What payment requirements do you have at the auction?
A: Only cash, a cashier's check, or a money order will be accepted. Personal checks will not be accepted.

Q: Is payment in full required on the day of the auction?
A: Yes. All properties must be paid for by the stated time on the day of the auction.

Q: Does Johnson County offer a financing program?
A: No.

Q: What type of ownership document is issued at the auction?
A: The buyer will receive a receipt for payment on the day of the auction. The court will hold a hearing approximately three weeks after the auction to determine whether to confirm the auctions. For properties not subject to a federal lien, the Sheriff will issue a Sheriff's Deed after the court confirms the auction. Some properties sold at the auctions are subject to a federal lien. A Sheriff's Deed will be issued for those properties upon the expiration of the applicable federal redemption period, if the federal agency chooses not to redeem the property. If the federal agency redeems the property, no deed will be issued and the person with the winning bid at the auction will receive a refund.

Q: Once a property is acquired through a tax auction, is there a redemption period before the purchaser may take possession?
A: No, except for properties subject to federal lien. The federal agency may redeem the property during the applicable federal redemption period. A deed will not be issued by the Sheriff until expiration of the federal redemption period and only if the federal agency does not redeem the property.

Q: Does Johnson County allow investors to purchase at tax auctions without attending the tax auction?
A: Yes, but the investor's agent must register prior to the auction and must attend and bid at the auction. Further, if the investor is the successful bidder, the investor must execute the required affidavit in the allotted time, generally within 48 hours after the auction. All bidders must register prior to the auction. Registration will be held the morning of the auction. The successful buyers must execute an affidavit, under oath, that they meet the statutory qualifications for bidding on tax auction property. Generally, Kansas law prohibits the following people from buying at the auction: (1) those who owe delinquent taxes in Johnson County; (2) those who have an interest in the property (for example, owners, mortgagees, relatives, or officers of a corporation that owns the property); and (3) those who buy the property with the intent to transfer it to someone who is prohibited from buying.

Q: What happens to properties that do not sell at the auction? May they be purchased directly from Johnson County?
A: In the event all the properties are not sold at an auction, Johnson County will consider all available options and procedures allowed by state law for addressing the unsold properties, including offering those properties again, at the next auction.

Q: Do you have a mailing list?
A: No.

Q: Does Johnson County sell tax liens?
A: No. Kansas law does not provide for the auction of tax liens.

Q: Will there be a minimum bid?
A: The County may choose to bid in at an amount up to the amount of its lien, thereby setting a minimum bid. However, the County is not required to do so.

Q: Will the properties sell for the amount of taxes owed?
A: They may sell for more; they may sell for less.

Q: What types of properties are in the auctions?
A: All types. Some have buildings or houses; some are vacant; some are very small strips of land. It is the buyer's responsibility to research the property to determine whether it is suitable for the buyer.

SEDGWICK COUNTY, KANSAS
http://www.sedgwick.ks.us

TREASURER'S OFFICE
http://www.sedgwick.ks.us/Treasurer

Jan Kennedy, Sedgwick County Treasurer
525 N. Main
Wichita, KS 67203
phone: (316) 660-9110
Fax: (316) 383-7113

Sign up to receive an electronic Tax Foreclosure Auction notification from the County Treasurer.

(1) Feedback Form
http://www.sedgwick.ks.us/Treasurer/feedback.html

Use this feedback form to send suggestions, questions, comments and/or inquiries to us or you may e-mail Jan Kennedy (jkennedy@sedgwick.gov), CPA/Sedgwick County Treasurer or Anne Smarsh (asmarsh@sedgwick.gov), Chief Deputy Treasurer directly.

(2) Frequently Asked Questions
http://www.sedgwick.ks.us/Treasurer/faq.html

How does the tax foreclosure process work? Properties with delinquent taxes of 3 1/2 years are eligible to be sold at a public auction to the highest bidder. A sale date will be determined at least 30 days prior to any sale. There are usually three sales each year; the sale dates and listings of properties to be sold will be published in a daily newspaper designated by Sedgwick County. Currently, that publication is the Derby Daily Reporter. Listings will also be available in the Treasurer's Office after publication.

(3) General Information
http://www.sedgwick.ks.us/Treasurer/general_information.pdf

Foreclosure
When a property remains unpaid for a certain length of time, it is selected for foreclosure (sale of property by County to pay back taxes) and is noted on the AB02 screen in the County's mainframe computer system. There is no set date for any property to enter foreclosure.

When a key number is in foreclosure status 0, it means the property has started the foreclosure process and at this stage we can accept payment of the oldest year in full to take the property out of foreclosure. In foreclosure status 1, abstractor's fees have been added and we can still accept payment of the oldest year in full to take the property out of foreclosure. In foreclosure status 2, attorney fees have been added and we can accept payment of the oldest year in full to take the property out of foreclosure. In foreclosure status 3, court costs are added, the foreclosure case is filed and within several months, the foreclosure sale date is set. In status 3 foreclosure, the Treasurer's Office can only accept certified funds (cash, cashier's check, or money order) for all years due up to 5 PM the day before the sale from the taxpayer, lien-holder or other vested interest party.

The foreclosure sales are published thirty days before the sale date in the official paper (when a sale date is set, it is in the Derby Daily Reporter, which is available in limited supply on a first come, first served basis in this office) and on the Treasurer's website (http://www.sedgwickcounty.org/treasurer). Foreclosure sales are properties sold in an "as is" basis and buyers should research the properties very thoroughly before buying (some basic information on this is available in the Treasurer's Office and is published on the Treasurer's website when a sale is scheduled). There are usually four to six sales per year, and they usually occur between May and October, but there is no established or scheduled time until the Foreclosure Attorney sets a sale date.

ROGUE INVESTOR NOTE: See document for additional information.

(4) Delinquent Tax Listing
http://www.sedgwick.ks.us/Treasurer/DelinquentTax/index.html

Welcome to the Sedgwick County Treasurer's Office delinquent tax listing application. The purpose of this application is to allow you to view a list of all delinquent properties in Sedgwick County.

To search for delinquent property, enter a name, choose a property type and click on the Search button. You will be taken to an alphabetical list of properties starting with the name that is greater than or equal to the name entered below. You then can click on "Forward" and "Backward" to page through the listing.

Tax Lien Sales: Yes

Tax Deed Sales: No

Rating: Three Stars (***)

Interest Rate: 12% per year

Sale Period: Varies, depending on the county.

Redemption Period: 3 years

Bidding Process:
All auctions are by competitive bid. Tax lien sale advertisements usually appear in county newspapers about three weeks prior to the sale.

State-Specific Information:
Kentucky is an average tax lien state. The interest rate of 12% is not great and the 3-year redemption period is fairly long.

Links for All Kentucky Counties: Provided on CD.

Detailed County-Specific Information:

JEFFERSON COUNTY, KENTUCKY
http://www.loukymetro.org

SHERIFF'S OFFICE
http://www.jcsoky.org

Sheriff Colonel John Aubrey
email: sheriff@jcsoky.org

531 Court Place, Suite 604
6th Floor, Fiscal Court Building
Louisville, KY 40202
Phone: 502-574-5400
General email: info@jcsoky.org

Real Estate taxes are collected by the Sheriff's Office based on the Assessed Value given to us each September-October by the Property Valuation Administrator (http://www.pvalouky.org).

Delinquent Property Bills are turned over to the County Clerk (http://www.countyclerk.jefferson.ky.us/vip).

COUNTY CLERK'S OFFICE
http://www.countyclerk.jefferson.ky.us/vip

Bobbie Holsclaw, County Clerk

(1) Delinquent Real Estate Taxes
http://www.countyclerk.jefferson.ky.us/vip/drtaxes.htm

Professional License Department handles the collection of delinquent real estate taxes. Pursuant to KRS 134.480, third parties (any person) may purchase tax payers' delinquent tax bills. This purchase can occur at anytime each year after the Sheriff's "Tax Sale."

(2) Contact Information
http://www.countyclerk.jefferson.ky.us/vip/drcontacts.htm

Delinquent Tax Department
527 W. Jefferson Street, Room 100A
Louisville, KY 40202
(502) 574-6016

Tax Lien Sales: Yes

Tax Deed Sales: No

Rating: Four Stars (****)

Interest Rate: 12% plus a 5% penalty per year, for a total of 17%

Sale Period: Varies, depending on the county.

Redemption Period: 3 years

Bidding Process:
All auctions are by competitive bid. Tax lien sale advertisements usually appear in county newspapers about three weeks prior to the sale.

State-Specific Information:
Louisiana is a decent tax lien state. The interest rate of 17% is good, but the 3-year redemption period is fairly long.

Links for All Louisiana Counties: Provided on CD.

Detailed County-Specific Information:

CADDO PARISH, LOUISIANA

ASSESSOR'S OFFICE
http://www.caddoassessor.org

The Caddo Parish Tax Collector, which is the Caddo Parish Sheriff, is responsible for sending tax bills and collecting taxes based on the assessments and the millage rates.

(1) Contact Information
http://www.caddoassessor.org/contact_us.html

Charles Henington, Jr., Assessor
phone: 318-226-6711
email: Assessor@caddoassessor.org

Real Estate Division
email: Realestate@caddoassessor.org
Department Director, Greg Johnson, phone: 318-226-6725
Residential, phone: 318-226-6725
Commercial, phone: 318-226-6728
Land Use Value, phone: 318-226-6710
Mobile Homes, phone: 318-226-6728

PARISH SHERIFF'S OFFICE
http://www.caddosheriff.org/index.php3

Sheriff Steve Prator

SHERIFF'S OFFICE TAX DIVISION
http://www.caddosheriff.org/departments/tax.php3

phone: (318) 681-0638
FAX: (318) 429-7670
Email: cpsotax@caddosheriff.org

Tell me a little about the tax sale. The Tax Sale is held in Room G18 at the Caddo Parish Courthouse, 501 Texas Street, Shreveport, LA 71101. The first day of the Tax Sale, all the unsettled properties that appeared in the newspaper advertising are read aloud. People in the room are considered Tax Buyers. These buyers have pre-registered with the Sheriff's Office. (Tax Buyer registration begins before the Tax Sale. Anyone can register up to the start of and during the sale.)

After the reading of a property, Buyers bid for a portion of ownership on the property. By law, the Sheriff continues accepting bids until the lowest bid is received in the interest of the actual property owner, which gives the Buyer who bid that amount the right to purchase it.

What happens if a property is not sold at the Tax Sale (Adjudicated)? Any unsold property will be adjudicated to Caddo Parish. The Parish then becomes owner of the property.

What if my property is bought by a Buyer and I want to get it back? The original owner has up to three years from the date the deed is filed in the Clerk of Court's Office to redeem the property. A redemption is calculated by the Tax Collector. The amount of redemption will include a redemption fee, tax sale fee, interest due the tax buyer, the base taxes and monthly interest accrued on the account after December 31 of the delinquent year.

EAST BATON ROUGE PARISH, LOUISIANA
http://brgov.com

SHERIFF'S OFFICE
http://www.ebrso.org

Elmer B. Litchfield, Sheriff
300 North Boulevard, Baton Rouge, LA 70801
P.O. Box 3277, Baton Rouge, LA 70821
phone: (225) 389-5000
email: webmaster@ebrso.org

(1) Contact Information
http://www.ebrso.org/contact.htm

Civil Division, Foreclosures
Phone: 389-4818, Fax: 389-4822

(2) Civil Foreclosure Department
http://www.ebrso.org/civil.htm

Processes all 19th Judicial District Civil Papers, and executes all Writs that are issued due to non-payment of mortgage on real estate and moveable and money judgments. This is action taken following the failed efforts of debt collection agencies, financial institutions, etc.

They conduct the Sheriff's Auctions every Wednesday, 10:00 a.m., in the lobby of the Governmental Building, 222 St. Louis Street, Baton Rouge, LA. This alternates each week between real estate and moveable properties. They also type the deeds after the auctions and record them in the Clerk of Court's Office.

ORLEANS PARISH, LOUISIANA
http://www.new-orleans.la.us/home

OFFICE OF THE CIVIL SHERIFF
http://www.civilsheriff.com
http://www.civilsheriff.com/default.asp

Paul Valteau, Jr. Civil Sheriff

Ownership of property, either real estate or movables, can be jeopardized by a money judgment or by a delinquent payment on a loan. When the interests of a borrower and/or other defendants in a property are foreclosed, the property is sold to satisfy the debt at a sale called a public auction. The Office of the Civil Sheriff is the official auctioneer for Civil Court ordered sales in Orleans Parish.

Office of the Civil Sheriff
403 Civil Courts Building
421 Loyola Avenue
New Orleans, Louisiana 70112
Phone: 504-523-6143

(1) Contact Information
http://www.civilsheriff.com/ContactUs.htm

real estate: 504-523-6380
immoveable seizures: douglab@civilsheriff.com

(2) Auctions of Real Estate
http://www.civilsheriff.com/realestate.htm

The Sheriff Sale Information Sheet (formally called the "Pink Sheet") is now available for download: http://www.civilsheriff.com/pinksheet.pdf.

What is Real Estate? It is land with its improvements and the right to own and use it.

Where is the Real Estate auction held? In the lobby of the Civil District Courthouse located at 421 Loyola Avenue at Poydras Street.

When is the auction held? Every Thursday at noon unless otherwise advertised. Each property and its auction date is advertised in the Times Picayune, the official newspaper of record, thirty (30) days before the auction and again on Monday, the week of the auction. Properties are also advertised in a second publication like The Louisiana Weekly newspaper to run concurrently with those ads run in the Times Picayune. Upcoming lists of properties for sale are available in the Real Estate Division of the Sheriff's Office three (3) weeks prior to the actual auction of a piece of property and on this website under the heading, "Real Estate Sales Lists."

How many days does it take before a foreclosed property goes to auction? It takes a minimum of forty-five (45) days from receipt of the writ to advertisement for the auction. During this time the foreclosure may be stopped for reasons such as bankruptcy or payment of the balance owed.

What are the usual costs of foreclosure? Advertising, appraisals, mortgage, conveyance and tax certificates, curator's fees, deed, docket and a three (3) percent sales commission on the sales price to the Office of the Civil Sheriff. These costs and fees are not paid by a successful bidder. A successful bidder only pays the amount of his or her bid.

What is the minimum opening bid? There are two categories for the minimum opening bid:

When the sale is with appraisal the bid must open at two thirds (2/3) of the appraisal and must satisfy any superior claims. If 2/3 of the appraisal results in an opening bid insufficient to cover the costs and commission, then the opening bid will be raised to reflect those expenses.

When the sale is "without" appraisal the bid must cover any superior claims plus the costs and commission. Usually this is a relatively low amount between two and five thousand dollars.

Can I enter the property before I bid? No access is allowed prior to the auction. The sale is not officially completed until the entire purchase price is paid in full. Therefore, it is only then that access to the property is legally permissible. All property is sold "As Is Where Is" and the deeds are not warranted.

Must I bring the entire cash amount to the auction? Upon successfully bidding on the property, the successful bidder must immediately provide the Sheriff ten percent (10%) of the purchase price paid in cash, money order, official, cashier's or certified check (no personal checks are accepted), plus their name, address, phone number, marital status and social security number. With some properties the entire amount must be paid in cash and this will be specified in the advertisement prior to the auction.

When must I pay the balance due? The balance must be paid within thirty (30) days after the sale unless the terms of the sale require the full purchase price at the time of the successful bid. Failure to meet this deadline may result in the property being reset for a second auction. Should the second auction result in a lesser sales price, the first bidder may lose all or part of his deposit.

When will I receive the property deed? Not less than fifteen (15) days after paying the balance of the purchase price. Payment of the balance by certified funds results in delivery of the deed sooner.

Why are pictures shown on some properties and not on others? In order to avoid confusion, pictures are not taken of condominium units, time share units, or vacant lots. Since condominium buildings consist of many units in various buildings, and since usually only the individual units are being sold, it would be impossible to properly depict in a photograph the specific premises being sold. Vacant lots bear no defined municipal number; therefore, it is most difficult to depict the property to be sold in a photograph. Certain properties that are otherwise suitable for pictures are not photographed for a number of reasons, including but not limited to time constraints, weather conditions, remoteness of locale, and the availability of personnel to perform the service. The Sheriff reserves the right to make determinations relative to the publication of photographs of properties to be sold. No inferences should be drawn relative to the value or condition of property based upon the presence or absence of a photograph.

What does it mean when a property is sold with appraisal? Under the law, both the plaintiff (the creditor) and the defendant (the debtor) have the right to appoint an appraiser to value the property that is being foreclosed upon, if that right was not previously waived by the defendant. Each party who names an appraiser shall deliver the appraisal to the sheriff at least two days, exclusive of holidays, prior to the time of the sale. If the parties do not appoint an appraiser the Sheriff appoints the appraisers. Appraisals are posted on the Internet, but because of the 48-hour opportunity to appraise, the amounts are usually posted immediately before the sale.

In a Sheriff's Sale can I rely on the appraisal supplied by the plaintiff, defendant or the Sheriff?
There is no substitute for viewing and appraising property oneself. All appraisals are nothing more than a reflection of an individual's opinion of the value of a property. The parties to the litigation have varying interests with respect to appraisal amounts. Ordinarily, a plaintiff hopes for a low appraisal and a defendant hopes for a high appraisal. Since there are varying interests involved, prospective bidders should be aware that appraisals might reflect those interests. In almost all Sheriff's Sales appraisers do not have access to the inside of the premises to be sold. The bottom line here is the top and the bottom line of this answer. There is no substitute for viewing and appraising property oneself.

(3) Real Estate Sales List
http://www.civilsheriff.com/RealEstateSales.asp

ROGUE INVESTOR NOTE: sales list saved on CD:
USA Tax Lien Info/Louisiana/orleans_parish_LA/RealEstateSales.htm

HOUSING LAW UNIT

Housing Law Unit
1340 Poydras Street, Suite 1115
New Orleans, Louisiana 70112
Phone (504) 299-4850

If ad valorem property taxes are not paid on a piece of property, the City of New Orleans can put the property up at public sale for the taxes. If the property is sold to a private individual or entity, it is said that the property was "sold" for taxes or was sold at "tax sale". If no private individual or entity bids at the public sale, the assessor bids the property in for the City, and it is said that the property was "adjudicated to the City" for taxes or was sold at "tax adjudication". In the case of a tax sale, the owner has three years, or if the property has been declared "blighted" or is "abandoned" as defined by R.S. 33:4720.12(1), 18 months, from the date that the tax sale is recorded with the Register of Conveyances to redeem the property from the tax sale. La. Const. Art. 7, §25. In the case of a tax adjudication, the owner may redeem the property at any time prior to the City's determining that the property is needed for a public use or the City's donating or selling the property (see, e.g., the section on "Donation of Abandoned and Blighted Property to Non-Profits").

Upon redemption, the tax sale purchaser is entitled to receive from the owner "the value of the improvements made upon such real estate by the purchaser thereof at the sale", La. R.S. 47:2222, and "the cost of any repairs, rehabilitation, maintenance, removal, or demolition made or done thereon by said purchaser to the extent not otherwise included in the value of the improvements for which payment is required under R.S. 47:2222, when required by an order of [the City] for the purpose of enforcing a property standards ordinance. The reimbursement for costs set forth in this Section shall be limited to the minimum amount reasonably necessary to comply with the order of [the City] and the property standards ordinance....", La. R.S. 47:2222.1. After the period of redemption has passed, the purchaser at a tax sale files a proceeding to quiet the tax title.

Tax Lien Sales: No

Tax Deed Sales: Yes

Rating: Two Stars (**)

Interest Rate: No interest rate, state only sells tax deeds.

Sale Period: Varies, depending on municipality and county regulations.

Redemption Period: Varies. Failure to pay property taxes results in the municipality filing a tax lien mortgage, which must be paid within 18 months or the property is foreclosed with no redemption available.

Bidding Process:
Process can be complicated, and it varies from county to county and municipality to municipality. Municipalities have the right to take ownership of properties, and they can accept or reject public auction bids. Real estate can sometimes be purchased for only the taxes owed.

State-Specific Information:
Sales are sometimes called Maine Land Sales or Maine Property Tax Sales.

The Maine Revenue Services, Property Tax Division (14 Edison Drive, Augusta, Maine 04332, http://www.state.me.us/revenue/propertytax) is the state agency for property tax administration in Maine. The Property Tax Division consists of two sections: Municipal Services and Unorganized Territory. Property taxes in Maine are assessed at the local level; however, municipal assessors are governed by state statutes. The Property Tax Division administers the annual State Valuation program, administers the property tax for the Unorganized Territory and provides technical support services to assessors, taxpayers, legislators and other governmental agencies.

The Unorganized Territory section is responsible for assessing and collecting property and excise taxes for those parts of Maine with no municipal government:

Unorganized Territory Section
http://www.state.me.us/revenue/propertytax/Unorganized%20Page/Unorganized%20Territory%20Page.htm

Phone: (207) 287-4785
Fax: (207) 287-6396

Time line (dates reflect calendar year 2003):
- January: Lien Notices mailed out for 2002 delinquent Real Estate Accounts.
- February: Final Notice of Foreclosure mailed out for 2001 year delinquent Real Estate Accounts.
- March: Liens recorded prior to March 15th for 2002 delinquent Real Estate Accounts. Liens for 2001 unpaid taxes mature March 30th and State takes title to property.
- July: Tax Acquired property can be redeemed by prior owner.
- December: Bid list for 2001 Tax acquired property is available.

(1) Tax-acquired bidding instructions
http://www.state.me.us/revenue/propertytax/Unorganized%20Page/Tax%20Acquired%20Instructions.htm

Annually, Maine Revenue Services has a few tax-acquired parcels that are sold via a sealed bid process. Interested parties may receive a listing of the parcels to be sold and details on how to bid, by mailing a letter to:

Property Tax Division – Unorganized Territory
Maine Revenue Services
P.O. Box 9106
Augusta, ME 04332-9106

The requesting envelope should have L.S. written on it in the lower right hand corner. Inside this envelope should be a self-addressed, stamped 9' X 11' envelope with 3, 37 cent stamps on it. Nothing else is required.

This envelope will be used to return information to you on the parcels being offered for bid that year and an explanation of the process and timeframe. Typically, the bid period timeframe varies from December to January in terms of bids being accepted.

(2) List of Tax-Acquired Property
http://www.state.me.us/revenue/propertytax/Unorganized%20Page/Tax%20Acquired.htm

(3) Bid Sheet
http://www.state.me.us/revenue/propertytax/Unorganized%20Page/BID%20SHEET.htm

Links for All Maine Counties: Provided on CD.

Tax Lien Sales: Yes

Tax Deed Sales: No

Rating: Four Stars (****)

Interest Rate: Depending on the county, the interest rate usually ranges from 10% to 24%.

Sale Period: June in most counties

Redemption Period:
Redemption period can be as quick as six months or as long as two years.

Bidding Process:
All auctions are by competitive bid. Tax lien sale advertisements usually appear in county newspapers about three weeks prior to the sale.

State-Specific Information:
Maryland is a decent tax lien state. The interest rate of up to 24% is good, and the short redemption period (as quick as 6 months) is favorable. However, each county is different, making the process a little more complicated.

Links for All Counties in Maryland: Provided on CD.

Detailed County-Specific Information:

BALTIMORE COUNTY, MARYLAND
http://www.co.ba.md.us

OFFICE OF BUDGET AND FINANCE
http://www.baltimorecountyonline.info/Agencies/budfin

Fred Homan, Director
Office of Budget and Finance
400 Washington Avenue, Suite 200, Mail stop 2109
Towson, MD 21204
phone: 410-887-3313
fax: 410-887-3097
email: financeinfo@co.ba.md.us

(1) Tax Sale FAQ
http://www.co.ba.md.us/FAQ/taxes.html#Sale

Q. When does Baltimore County conduct the Real Property Tax Sale?
A. The annual tax sale is held in May or June (specific date to be determined).

Q. Are there tax sale penalties in addition to the monthly interest charged on delinquent accounts?
A. Yes. Currently a postage and handling fee of $25.00 per account is assessed in March. A $50.00 advertising fee is assessed in April. A $15.00 legal fee is charged on the day of the sale.

Q. Where can I find a list of the properties that will be sold at tax sale?
A. Baltimore County will advertise in the Jeffersonian newspaper four weeks prior to the sale or you can visit our web site at http://www.co.ba.md.us/taxsale. A list of properties will be available on the web site around the middle of May.

Q. Can I bid on tax sale properties without attending the sale?
A. Yes. Your authorized agent who will be attending the sale can bid for you. Agents must pre-register.

Q. Does the County handle the foreclosure process on tax sale properties?
A. No. The tax lien holder is responsible for the foreclosure process. The foreclosure process cannot begin until after six months from the date of the sale. Four months from the date of tax sale, the purchaser may add any expenses to which he/she is entitled under Section 14-843 of the Maryland Annotated Code to the redemption amount. These expenses, composed of attorney's fees and title search charges, average $650 in today's market.

Q. What number can I call to get more information about Tax Sales?
A. Call 410-887-5616 for information and redemption amount or call 410-887-2403 from any touch tone phone and select option 3 to redeem via credit card.

Q. What form of payment do you accept at the tax sale?
A. Payment by cash or personal check for properties purchased must be made the day of the sale. Purchasers are required to remit the full amount of taxes due on the property, whether in arrears or not, together with interest and penalties on the taxes, expenses incurred in the making of the sale and the high bid premium, if applicable.

Q. How do I register for the tax sale and is there a fee?
A. If you are interested in participating as a bidder at the tax sale, you must register and agree to the "Collectors Terms and Registration Form for the Tax Sale" before bidding. Individuals are allowed to register at the sale or they may register in advance. There is no fee to register. A registration form is available on our web site at http://www.co.ba.md.us/taxsale around the middle of May.

Q. If my property has been sold at a tax sale auction, do I have the right to redeem my property?
A. Yes. All property owners have the right of redemption for six months after the date of the sale. To redeem, all taxes, charges and fees must be paid by cash, certified check, money order, or by using the "Fast Track" automated phone system's credit card option (MasterCard/Discover).

(2) Tax Sale
http://www.baltimorecountyonline.info/go/taxsale

Baltimore County conducts an annual Real Property Tax Sale in May or June. The County will post information about the sale on this page during the month prior to the sale.

For more information about the Tax Sale, see:

- Frequently Asked Questions
  http://www.baltimorecountyonline.info/Agencies/budfin/finance/taxesfaq.html#Sale
- Taxpayer's Brochure
  http://www.co.ba.md.us/Agencies/budfin/finance/taxpayerbrochure.html#anchor452986
- Or check back in April or May.

MONTGOMERY COUNTY, MARYLAND
http://www.co.mo.md.us

DEPARTMENT OF FINANCE
http://www.montgomerycountymd.gov/govtmpl.asp?url=/content/finance/index.asp

(1) Tax Facts 2003
http://www.montgomerycountymd.gov/govtmpl.asp?url=/content/finance/CountyTaxes/Info%20Taxes/county%20taxes.ASP

Delinquent taxes will result in the sale of the property tax lien through a public tax sale on the second Monday of June of the subsequent calendar year. Accounts eligible for tax sale are listed for four consecutive weeks in a Montgomery County newspaper and are subject to a $25 advertising fee. Property tax accounts taken to "tax sale" are subject to additional legal costs incurred by the new certificate holder.

(2) Tax Lien Sale Information and Procedures
http://www.montgomerycountymd.gov/govtmpl.asp?url=/content/finance/CountyTaxes/Info%20Taxes/reviews.ASP

The Montgomery County tax sale program enables the County to collect all unpaid and delinquent property taxes as required by statute. Legal references for this program are provided in the Tax Property Article of the Annotated Code of Maryland, 2001 Replacement Volume, as amended. All unpaid taxes on real property constitute a lien on the real property from the date they become due until paid (Section 14-804 [a], Section 14-805 [a]). It is mandatory that the Collector sell any property on which taxes are in arrears (Section 14-808). There may be properties sold for which taxes were paid prior to the sale date or other circumstances which render the sale invalid and void. In the event the tax sale is invalid and void the County will, as the exclusive remedy available to the bidder/purchaser, reimburse the bidder/purchaser the tax sale purchase price paid, without interest, and any applicable high bid premium paid, without interest. The tax sale bidder/purchaser assumes all risks of any irregularity of the sale and has no other remedy against the County. The County is not liable for and will not pay the bidder/purchaser any interest, costs, expenses or attorney fees associated with the invalid and void sale. There is no warranty, expressed or implied, that a property has a marketable title or that it contains the area of land which it is said to contain; therefore, the purchaser assumes all risks in that regard. At the tax sale, a property tax lien is offered for sale to the highest bidder. Once sold and the total amount due is paid by the bidder/purchaser to the County, the County's lien on the property passes to the bidder/purchaser. The public sealed bid sale is conducted annually on the second Monday of June of each Levy Year. For Levy Year 2002, the sale will commence on Monday, June 9, 2003, from 8:00 a.m. to 2:00 p.m. in the Division of Treasury, Department of Finance, located at 255 Rockville Pike, Rockville, Maryland 20850. These tax sale procedures are unique to Montgomery County and may differ from those used in other Maryland counties. This document provides information and procedures relative to the June 9, 2003 tax sale. Tax sales are complex proceedings and the County recommends that you seek legal advice prior to participation in the annual tax sale.

(3) Contact Information
http://www.montgomerycountymd.gov/govtmpl.asp?url=/content/finance/About%20Finance/contact.ASP

Montgomery County Tax Section
Division of Treasury
255 Rockville Pike
Rockville, MD 20850
Phone: (240) 777-8950
Email: treasury@montgomerycountymd.gov

SHERIFF'S OFFICE
http://www.montgomerycountymd.gov/mc/judicial/sheriff/sheriff.html

Rockville, Maryland
Phone: (240) 777-7000
FAX: (240) 777-7145
Sheriff, Raymond M. Kight

The Sheriff's Office conducts sales of seized or attached items.

PRINCE GEORGE'S COUNTY, MARYLAND
http://www.co.pg.md.us

OFFICE OF FINANCE
J. Michael Dougherty, Jr., Director
14741 Governor Oden Bowie Drive
Room 3200
Upper Marlboro, MD 20772
Phone: 301-952-5025
Fax: 301-952-3148
email: bkhumphreys@co.pg.md.us

TREASURY DIVISION, OFFICE OF FINANCE
http://www.co.pg.md.us/Government/AgencyIndex/Finance/treasury.asp?h=20&s=40&n=30

The Treasury Division is responsible for selling properties at tax sale for delinquent taxes.

(1) Real Property Tax Information
http://www.co.pg.md.us/Government/AgencyIndex/Finance/real_property.asp?h=20&s=40&n=30&n1=20

2004 Tax Sale
To review current Tax Sale listing and for additional information go to: http://www.tlcol.com (Tax Lien Certificates On-Line).

March 16 – Tax payments must be by certified check, cashier's check, money order or cash.
April 1 – Advertising fee due May 7. All payments must be IN THE OFFICE AND POSTED by 4:30 p.m. to avoid Tax Sale.
May 10 – 8:00 a.m. to 1:00 p.m., Tax Sale Sealed Bid Auction
May 17 – For redemption information, call 301-952-3948.

Contact information
Prince George's County Treasury Division
P.O. Box 1700
Upper Marlboro, MD 20773-1700

Prince George's County Treasury Division
14741 Gov. Oden Bowie Drive, Room 1090
Upper Marlboro, MD 20772

TAX LIEN CERTIFICATES ON-LINE
http://www.tlcol.com

Tax Lien Certificates On-Line, a service of 21st Century Solutions LLC, provides investors and other interested parties with all the information needed to participate in tax lien sales across the country (where available).

Massachusetts

Tax Lien Sales: Yes

Tax Deed Sales: No

Rating: Four Stars (****)

Interest Rate: 16%

Sale Period: Sales are handled by municipalities; therefore, sales dates vary across the state.

Redemption Period: Redemption period can be as quick as six months.

Bidding Process:
All auctions are by competitive bid. Tax lien sale advertisements usually appear in city or county newspapers about three weeks prior to the sale. Municipalities handle the sale; therefore, some sales are handled by cities and some are handled by counties. For example, tax lien sales involving rural property are handled by the county.

State-Specific Information:
Massachusetts is a decent tax lien state. The interest rate of 16% is acceptable and the short redemption period (as quick as 6 months) is favorable. However, the fact that municipalities, which can include cities or counties, handle the sales can complicate the process. Tax lien sales are also called tax title sales in Massachusetts.

Links for All Massachusetts Counties: Provided on CD.

Detailed County-Specific Information:

NORFOLK COUNTY, MASSACHUSETTS
http://www.norfolkcounty.org

TREASURER'S OFFICE
http://www.norfolkcounty.org/treasurer.html

Norfolk County Treasurer's Office
614 High Street
P.O. Box 346
Dedham, MA 02026
Telephone: 781-461-6110
Fax: 781-326-4527
email: jconnolly@norfolkcounty.org

SHERIFF'S OFFICE
http://www.norfolkcounty.org/housecorrection.html

Norfolk County Sheriff's Office and Correctional Center
200 West Street
Dedham, MA 02026
Telephone: 781-329-3705 / email: dfalcone@norfolksheriffma.org

---

SUFFOLK COUNTY, MASSACHUSETTS
http://www.cityofboston.gov

TAXPAYER REFERRAL AND ASSISTANCE CENTER
http://www.cityofboston.gov/trac

On July 1, 1998, the Assessing and Collector/Treasury Departments combined the taxpayers services provided by each organization into a new Taxpayer Referral & Assistance Center, known as TRAC. The new TRAC office was created to provide "one-stop" service to Boston taxpayers on tax related matters.

Provides Municipal Lien certificate fee schedule; and provides referral to "expert" assistance in either the Assessing Department or Collector's office, for the issuing and processing of Municipal Lien Certificates.

(1) Contact Information
http://www.cityofboston.gov/contact/default.asp?ID=50

Room M-5
1 City Hall Plaza
Boston, MA 02201
Telephone: 617-635-4287
Email: TRAC@ci.boston.ma.us

(2) FAQ – Municipal Lien Certificate
from http://www.cityofboston.gov/trac/faq03.asp, click on "Municipal Lien Certificate"

How do I get a municipal lien certificate?
If you wish to obtain a Municipal Lien Certificate, the following are required:

- Ward, parcel, sub-parcel number
- Self-addressed stamped envelope if you wish the municipal lien certificate mailed to you
- Acceptable forms of payment: attorney's check, certified or registered check, and cash (if in person)
- Allow ten (10) business days for processing
- Mail to:
  Collector of Taxes, City of Boston
  P.O. Box 1911
  Boston, MA 02105
  Attn: MLC - Window M-32

SHERIFF'S DEPARTMENT
http://www.scsdma.org

(1) Civil Process Division
http://www.scsdma.org/deptOverview/civilProcessDivision.html

This division performs Sheriff's sales.

45 Bromfield Street
5th Floor
Boston, MA 02108
Phone: 617-989-6999
Fax: 617-695-0740

WORCESTER COUNTY, MASSACHUSETTS
http://www.ci.worcester.ma.us

OFFICE OF TREASURER AND COLLECTOR
from http://www.ci.worcester.ma.us, click on "City Services" and then on "City Hall Offices" and then on "Treasurer and Collector of Taxes"

Thomas F. Zidelis, Treasurer
Treasurer: Room 209, phone: (508) 799-1095
Collector: Room 203, phone: (508) 799-1075
treasurer@ci.worcester.ma.us

(1) Real Estate FAQ
from home page of Office of Treasurer and Collector, click on "Frequently Asked Questions – Real Estate"

(2) Tax Foreclosure Listing
from home page of Office of Treasurer and Collector, click on "Tax Foreclosure – Tax Foreclosure Listing"

The following is a list of tax foreclosures in which title has been vested in the name of the City by a decree of the Land Court. These properties are under the care, custody and control of the Tax Title Custodian. The sale (disposition) of these properties are through public auction as allowed by statute. If you are interested in any of the properties you may contact the Treasurer's Office and request that it be offered at its next foreclosure auction.

(2a) Tax Foreclosure List
http://www.ci.worcester.ma.us/trs/properties/foreclosure_list.htm

ROGUE INVESTOR NOTE: information saved on CD:
USA Tax Lien Info/Massachusetts/worcester_co_MA/foreclosure_list.htm

(3) Next Auction
http://www.ci.worcester.ma.us/trs/properties/nextauction.pdf

Tax Lien Sales: No.

Tax Deed Sales: Yes

Rating: Unrated

Interest Rate: None, state only sells tax deeds.

Sale Period: Tax deed sales are held throughout the state at anytime.

Redemption Period: Redemption period can be as quick as 1 year.

Bidding Process:
All auctions are by competitive bid. Tax deed sale advertisements usually appear in city or county newspapers about three weeks prior to the sale. For tax deed sales, the minimum bid will be back taxes, fees and costs associated with the tax sale.

State-Specific Information:
Michigan's tax sale process is currently in transition from a tax lien certificate/tax deed state to a tax deed state only, following passage of Public Act 123 of 1999. The process is not completely worked out and is very new to the counties, so be patient.

The following is a summary of the information regarding the new law governing Michigan's tax sale process, also called tax-reversion process.

Tax reversion is the process by which delinquent property taxes are collected, or in lieu of collection, the process that governs the disposition of real and tangible personal property upon which property taxes remain unpaid. On July 22, 1999, Governor Engler signed into law significant changes to the Michigan tax-reversion process.

The former process had often been criticized as both cumbersome and detrimental to economic development, due to the amount of time taken to return tax-reverted property to productive use. The new legislation will greatly simplify and expedite the tax-reversion process, ensure that the process produces marketable title to tax-reverted property, and permit counties to exercise significant control over the handling of tax-reverted property within their boundaries with minimal involvement by the State.

The new legislation establishes a three-year tax-reversion process compared to the former six-year process. Annual tax-lien sales were eliminated in favor of an annual forfeiture and judicial foreclosure process. Due process and notification procedures were significantly strengthened. In addition, changes were made to expedite the handling of abandoned tax reverted property. As under the former process, county treasurers will be responsible for collecting delinquent taxes and for sending notices prior to forfeiture. County treasurers also will be responsible for the foreclosure and sale of tax-reverted property, unless a county elects to "opt out" of those portions of the tax-reversion process. Non-participation by a county will require a resolution to that effect adopted by the county board of commissioners, together with the written concurrence of the county treasurer, and of the county executive if any, by December 1, 1999. If a county elects not to participate in the foreclosure and sale of tax-reverted property, the State will be responsible for those portions of the tax-reversion in that county.

The new legislation will take effect on October 1. The repeal of certain obsolete statutory provisions will take effect in 2003 and 2006. The new process will apply to property taxes levied after December 31, 1998. For transitional purposes, the former system will remain in effect through December 2006 for property taxes levied before January 1, 1999.

In summary, Public Act 123 shortens the amount of time property owners have to pay their delinquent taxes before losing their property from six years to three years. Property owners with taxes that are three years delinquent will be foreclosed and the property will be sold at public auction. For example, people who fail to pay their 2000 delinquent taxes will lose their property to foreclosure in March 2003. With this new act, the amount of time to pay taxes has been reduced from approximately five years to approximately two years. Property owners who have multiple tax years owing will have to pay several years to avoid losing their property.

Property owners face higher interest and fees for not paying their taxes. Taxes that are more than one year old will have a substantially higher interest rate (1.5% per month, as opposed to the current 1%). After one year, taxes will also have a $175.00 forfeiture fee and additional administrative fees added to them.

A copy of Public Act 123 is available at: http://www.michiganlegislature.org/documents/1999-2000/publicact/pdf/1999-PA-0123.pdf

Tax Reversion and Land Records Public Auction Site
http://www.michigan.gov/dnr/1%2C1607%2C7-153-10368_11797-23142--%2C00.html

Please note that all auctions for 2003 have been completed, and no auctions are planned for any time in the near future. As of November 2003, it appears that the Michigan Department of Natural Resources will not conduct further auctions of tax delinquent property until September 2004.

Under the 1999 Public Act 123 amendment to Public Act 206, the State only forecloses on parcels for 51 counties. Addresses and phone numbers for "Opt In" Counties, which have opted to handle their own tax foreclosed parcel auctions, are listed here: http://www.michigan.gov/documents/Opt_In_Counties_Addresses_37448_7.pdf. Please note that many of the Opt In counties have hired Title Check (http://www.title-check.com) to conduct their land auctions.

Links for All Michigan Counties: Provided on CD.

Detailed County-Specific Information:

KENT COUNTY, MICHIGAN
http://www.co.kent.mi.us

TREASURER'S OFFICE
http://www.co.kent.mi.us/government/treasurer

Kenneth D. Parrish, CPA, Treasurer
County Administration Building
300 Monroe Avenue NW
Grand Rapids, MI 49503-2287
Phone: (616) 336-3641
Fax: (616) 336-2010

SHERIFF'S OFFICE
http://www.co.kent.mi.us/government/departments/sheriff_index.htm

Sheriff Lawrence Stelma
701 Ball Avenue NE
Grand Rapids, MI 49503
General Information: (616) 632-6100

BID4ASSETS
http://www.bid4assets.com/storefront/?sfid=139

(1) Kent County, Michigan, Treasurer-Tax Collector, Tax Defaulted Properties Auction
http://www.bid4assets.com/storefront/?sfid=139

(2) Buyer's Guide
http://www.bid4assets.com/Help/BidderGuide.cfm?ct=InsideTopNavBidderGuide

Information on how to register, how to bid and other frequently asked questions.

(3) Terms and Conditions for Sale
http://www.bid4assets.com/info/sfid139/34577.pdf?auctionid=0

ROGUE INVESTOR NOTE: Information is for a 2003 sale, but contain useful information.

(4) Offline Bid Form
http://www.bid4assets.com/info/sfid139/34489.pdf?auctionid=0

(5) Contact Information for Bid4Assets
http://www.bid4assets.com/newsroom/index.cfm?ct=InsideTopNavNewsroom

Bid4Assets, Inc.
Jenny Monroe Lynch
1010 Wayne Avenue, Suite 505
Silver Spring, Maryland 20910
Toll Free: (877) 427-7387
Local: (301) 650-9193
Fax: (301) 650-9194
Email: jmonroe@bid4assets.com

MACOMB COUNTY, MICHIGAN
http://www.co.macomb.mi.us

TREASURER'S OFFICE
http://www.co.macomb.mi.us/treasurer/index.htm

Macomb County Treasurer – Ted B. Wahby
Macomb County Administration Building
1 South Main Street, 2nd Floor
Mount Clemens, Michigan 48043
Phone: (586) 469-5190
Fax: (586) 469-6770

(1) Notice of Show Cause Hearing and Judicial Foreclosure Hearing Non-Payment of Property Taxes
http://macombcountymi.gov/TREASURER//Notice%20of%20SHOWCAUSE%20HEARING%20and%20JUDICIAL%20FORECLOSURE%20HEARING2.doc

(2) Forfeiture Rules and Regulations
http://www.co.macomb.mi.us/treasurer/images/REVISEDRulesRegulations.doc

ROGUE INVESTOR NOTE: Revised as of October 7, 2003.

SHERIFF'S OFFICE
http://www.macomb-sheriff.com

(1) Contact Information
http://www.macomb-sheriff.com/information.htm

Main phone number = (586) 469-5151
43565 Elizabeth Road
Mt. Clemens, MI 48043
Sheriff Mark Hackel

OAKLAND COUNTY, MICHIGAN
http://www.co.oakland.mi.us

TREASURER'S OFFICE
http://www.co.oakland.mi.us/treasure

The Oakland County Treasurer's Office is responsible for the collection of delinquent property taxes. Patrick Dohany is the Treasurer.

(1) About Us
http://www.co.oakland.mi.us/treasure/about

Under new legislation, taxes not paid within 24 months are sold at a County land sale.

(2) Contact Information
http://www.co.oakland.mi.us/treasure/contact

Oakland County Treasurer's Office
1200 North Telegraph Road, Building 12 East
Pontiac, Michigan 48341
Telephone: 248-858-0611 / Toll-free: 888-350-0900

(3) Property Tax Administration Division
http://www.co.oakland.mi.us/treasure/divisions/pt_administration.html

One of the Division's specific functions is the collection of all real property taxes returned delinquent by the County's 61 cities, villages and townships; and the sale at public auction of any land for which taxes were not paid within 24 months of delinquency.

(4) Delinquent Property
http://www.co.oakland.mi.us/treasure/del_prop

Phone: 248-858-0611
Delinquent tax collections (toll-free): 888-600-3773

(4a) @ccess Oakland
http://ea2.co.oakland.mi.us/eap/index.cfm?Ua_Id=6VZOb14D&Token_Id=CVRcY1bY

The products available at @ccess Oakland provide the public with the ability to view and analyze specially packaged public records information via the Internet for a fee, including delinquent tax information and many city, village and township current tax information.

(4b) Foreclosed Properties
link currently inactive

The Foreclosed Properties section is active from May until the end of the County land sale(s) in December. This section displays properties that have been foreclosed, are owned by the County Treasurer, and may be available at one or more of the County's land sales.

(4c) Oakland County Land Sale Rules and Regulations
http://www.co.oakland.mi.us/treasure/del_prop/rules.pdf

(4d) Forfeited Properties
http://www.co.oakland.mi.us/fcloser/fmain?cmd=fcvt

The Forfeited Properties section is *active from December to March*. This section displays properties that are in jeopardy of pending foreclosure.

SHERIFF'S OFFICE
http://www.co.oakland.mi.us/sheriff

Sheriff Michael Bouchard

(1) Contact Information
http://www.co.oakland.mi.us/sheriff/contact/index.html

Oakland County Sheriff's Office
1201 North Telegraph Road
Pontiac Michigan 48341-1044
phone: 248-858-5000
email: ocsd@co.oakland.mi.us

INGHAM COUNTY, MICHIGAN
http://www.ingham.org

TREASURER'S OFFICE
http://www.ingham.org/TR/TRINDEX.HTM

Eric Schertzing, Treasurer, email: eschertzing@ingham.org
Mary Ruttan, Chief Deputy, email: mruttan@ingham.org

Ingham County Courthouse, P.O. Box 215, Mason, MI 48854
Phone: (517) 676-7220 / Fax: (517) 676-7242

(1) Public Auction of Tax-Foreclosed Lands
http://www.michigan.gov/dnr/1%2C1607%2C7-153-10368_11797-23142--%2C00.html

Welcome to the Tax Reversion and Land Records Public Auction site. Please note that all auctions for 2003 have been completed, and no auctions are planned for any time in the near future. As of November 2003, it appears that the Michigan Department of Natural Resources (DNR) will not conduct further auctions of tax delinquent property until September 2004.

You may view a copy of Public Act 123, here: http://www.michiganlegislature.org/documents/1999-2000/publicact/pdf/1999-PA-0123.pdf.

Under the 1999 PA 123 amendment to PA 206, the State only forecloses on parcels for 51 counties. Addresses and phone numbers for "Opt In" Counties, which have opted to handle their own tax foreclosed parcel auctions, are listed here:

http://www.michigan.gov/documents/Opt_In_Counties_Addresses_37448_7.pdf. Please note that many of the Opt In counties have hired Title Check (http://www.title-check.com) to conduct their land auctions.

(2) Sale of State-Owned Lands
http://www.michigan.gov/dnr/0,1607,7-153-10368_11797-32607--,00.html

2004 SEALED BID AUCTION SCHEDULE OF PUBLIC LANDS

Auction 1: Bid notices available April 23, 2004. All Bids must be postmarked by May 28, 2004. Bid opening is on June 9, 2004.

Auction 2: Bid notices available June 25, 2004. All Bids must be postmarked by July 30, 2004. Bid opening is on August 11, 2004.

Auction 3: Bid notices available August 13, 2004. All Bids must be postmarked by September 3, 2004. Bid opening is on September 15, 2004.

Auction 4: Bid notices available October 29, 2004. All Bids must be postmarked by November 29, 2004. Bid opening is on December 15, 2004.

PLEASE NOTE
If you are looking for "Public Auctions of Tax-Foreclosed Land," please call (517) 373-1250. If you have questions regarding the "Sealed Bid Auction" and/or "Public Land for Direct Purchase" information listed on this page, you may call (517) 373-1240.

ROGUE INVESTOR NOTE: list of state-owned land available for "Direct Purchase" from the Department of Natural Resources saved on CD:
USA Tax Lien Info/Michigan/ingham_county_MI/Sale_State_Owned_Lands.htm

(2) Form – Offer to Purchase State-Owned Land
http://www.michigan.gov/documents/FormOffertoPurchasePR6345-6_78261_7.pdf

---

WASHTENAW COUNTY, MICHIGAN
http://www.ewashtenaw.org

TREASURER'S OFFICE
http://www.ewashtenaw.org/government/treasurer/index_html

Catherine McClary, Treasurer
200 N. Main Street, Suite 200
P.O. Box 8645
Ann Arbor, MI 48107
Phone: 734-222-6600
Fax: 734-222-6632
email: taxes@ewashtenaw.org

New legislation passed in the summer of 1999 has changed the delinquent property tax sale process. To see a copy of the new law (Public Act 123 of 1999, as amended 2001), click here:
http://www.ewashtenaw.org/content/pa123.pdf.

Under provisions of the General Property Tax Act (MCL 211.78m [2]), Washtenaw County Treasurer Catherine McClary announces the time and location for the sale to the highest bidder of property for non-payment of taxes.

Washtenaw County tax foreclosured property sales held by Bid4Assets at:
http://www.bid4assets.com/washtenaw

(1) Public Act 123 of 1999, as amended 2001
http://www.ewashtenaw.org/content/pa123.pdf

BID4ASSETS
http://www.bid4assets.com/storefront/?sfID=132

Notice provided for a 2003 sale:

These properties were foreclosed for delinquent real property taxes as required by The General Property Tax Act, Public Act 206 of 1893, as amended, MCL 211.1 TO 211.157. Pursuant to the act and by order of the Washtenaw County Circuit Court in Case No. 02-708-CZ, all rights of redemption by any former owner expired on February 26, 2003. All liens against these properties under Michigan Law, except future installments of special assessments and liens recorded under the Natural Resources and Environmental Protection Act, Public Act 451 of 1994, as amended, MCL 324.101 to 324.90106, were extinguished. All existing recorded and unrecorded interests in these properties were extinguished, except visible or recorded easements or rights-of-way, private deed restrictions, or restrictions or other governmental interests in these properties imposed pursuant to the Natural Resources and Environmental Protection Act, Public Act 451 of 1994, as amended, MCL 324.101 to 324.90106. Subject to these exceptions, fee simple title to these properties has vested in the Washtenaw County Treasurer as the foreclosing governmental unit for Washtenaw County. As the foreclosing governmental unit, the Washtenaw County Treasurer now offers these properties for sale to the highest bidder.

(1) Terms and Conditions of Sale
http://www.bid4assets.com/info/sfid132/36673.pdf?auctionid=0

ROGUE INVESTOR NOTE: Terms and conditions are for a November 2003 sale.

(2) Offline Bid Form
http://www.bid4assets.com/info/sfid132/36642.pdf?auctionid=0

WAYNE COUNTY, MICHIGAN
http://www.waynecounty.com

TREASURER'S OFFICE
From http://www.waynecounty.com, click on "Elected Officials" and then on "Treasurer"

Raymond J. Wojtowicz
Treasurer of Wayne County
400 International Center Building, Monroe Street
5th Floor, Detroit, Michigan 48226
Telephone: 313-224-5990

(1) Michigan Tax-Reversion Revisions, Q&A
from Treasurer's Office home page, click on "Tax Revision Summary"

What is Tax Reversion? Tax reversion is the process by which delinquent property taxes are collected, or in lieu of collection, the process which governs the disposition of real and tangible personal property upon which property taxes remain unpaid. On July 22, 1999, Governor Engler signed into law significant changes to the Michigan tax-reversion process.

Why were changes made to the Tax-Reversion Process? The former process had often been criticized as both cumbersome and detrimental to economic development, due to the amount of time taken to return tax-reverted property to productive use. The new legislation will greatly simplify and expedite the tax-reversion process, ensure that the process produces marketable title to tax-reverted property, and permit counties to exercise significant control over the handling of tax-reverted property within their boundaries with minimal involvement by the State.

What were some of the significant changes? The new legislation establishes a three-year tax-reversion process compared to the former six-year process. Annual tax-liens sales were eliminated in favor of an annual forfeiture and judicial foreclosure process. Due process and notification procedures were significantly strengthened. In addition, changes were made to expedite the handling of abandoned tax-reverted property.

Who will operate the new Tax-Reversion Process? As under the former process, county treasurers will be responsible for collecting delinquent taxes and for sending notices prior to forfeiture. County treasurers also will be responsible for the foreclosure and sale of tax-reverted property unless a county elects to "opt out" of those portions of the tax-reversion process. Non-participation by a county will require a resolution to that effect adopted by the county board of commissioners, together with the written concurrence of the county treasurer, and of the county executive if any, by December 1, 1999. If a county elects not to participate in the foreclosure and sale of tax-reverted property, the State will be responsible for those portions of the tax-revision in that county.

When will the new legislation take effect? The new legislation will take effect on October 1. The repeal of certain obsolete statutory provisions will take effect in 2003 and 2006. The new process will apply to property taxes levied after December 31, 1998. For transitional purposes, the former system will remain in effect through December 2006 for property taxes levied before January 1, 1999.

(2) Comparison of Old vs. New Processes
from Treasurer's Office home page, click on "Comparison of Old vs. New Processes"

(3) Delinquent Property Listing
http://www.waynecounty.com/pta

(3a) Delinquent Property Listing Disclaimer
http://www.waynecounty.com/pta/Disclaimer.asp

Welcome to the Delinquent Property Listing (DPL) maintained by the Office of the Wayne County Treasurer. The DPL is provided to the user for the sole and limited purpose of providing access to information to identify real and personal property located in Wayne County whose taxes appear to be delinquent based on information used to compile the DPL. The DPL merely provides key information taken from tax records on delinquent property and may not include all special assessments or taxes that have been assessed against a particular piece of property. The Office of the Wayne County Treasurer does not, therefore, guarantee or assure the accuracy of the information contained in this web site listing and disavows the use of the DPL for any purpose other than as stated herein.

The information listed in the DPL is neither a certified copy of the Wayne County Treasurer's tax records nor an official tax record of the Office of the Wayne County Treasurer. The information is not to be used or relied on as an official statement of the tax liability, if any, relating to any property identified in the DPL.

Official delinquent Wayne County Treasurer tax records, tax statements and other information regarding any property referenced in the DPL may be obtained in person at the Wayne County Treasurer Office, 400 Monroe, 5th Floor, Detroit, Michigan 48226. For further information regarding delinquent taxes, call The Wayne County Treasurer tax information line at 313-224-5990, or send a letter at the address shown above.

(3b) Delinquent Property Listing Search Form
http://www.waynecounty.com/pta/Default.asp

(4) Property Foreclosure Information
from Treasurer's Office home page, click on "Property Foreclosure Information"

(4a) Properties Identified for Foreclosure
from Treasurer's Office home page, click on "Property Foreclosure Information" and then on "Properties Identifed for Foreclosure"

Properties are identified by community.

PROSECUTOR'S OFFICE
from http://www.waynecounty.com, click on "Elected Officials" and then "Prosecutor"

Kym Worthy, Prosecutor
1200 Frank Murphy Hall of Justice
1441 Street Antoine
Detroit, MI 48226
phone: (313) 224-5777 / Fax: (313) 224-0974

(1) Property Auctions
from http://www.waynecounty.com/property/default.htm, click on "Prosecutor's Auctions"

The Prosecutor's Auction contains houses that have been abandoned or seized in drug raids.

(1a) Current Properties for Auction
from http://www.waynecounty.com/property/default.htm, click on "Prosecutor's Auctions" and then on "See Listings"

ROGUE INVESTOR NOTE: auction listing saved on CD:
USA Tax Lien Info/Michigan/wayne_co_MI/prosecutor_auction_listing.htm

(1b) Information
from http://www.waynecounty.com/property/default.htm, click on "Prosecutor's Auctions" and then on "Information"

Homes for Sale!
Auction and Bidding Information
Questions and Answers
Definitions
Forms (Purchase Agreement Form)
(1c) Contact
from http://www.waynecounty.com/property/default.htm, click on "Prosecutor's Auctions" and then on "Contact Us"

General Assistance: (313) 224-5799
online email submittal form

HOUSING DIVISION

(1) Housing Division Auctions
from http://www.waynecounty.com/property/default.htm, click on "Housing Division Auctions"

The Housing Division auction includes homes claimed by the County for non-payment of taxes.

(1a) Current Properties for Auction
from http://www.waynecounty.com/property/default.htm, click on "Housing Division Auctions" and then on "See Listings"

Currently there is no property for bid.

(1b) Information
from http://www.waynecounty.com/property/default.htm, click on "Housing Division Auctions" and then on "Information"

(1c) Contact
from http://www.waynecounty.com/property/default.htm, click on "Housing Division Auctions" and then on "Contact Us"

Online email submittal form

Minnesota

Tax Lien Sales: Yes

Tax Deed Sales: Yes

Rating: Three Stars (***)

Interest Rate: 12% per year

Sale Period: Tax lien sales are held in May. Tax deed sales are also held.

Redemption Period: Redemption period can be as quick as 1 year.

Bidding Process:
All auctions are by competitive bid. Tax lien sale advertisements usually appear in city or county newspapers about three weeks prior to the sale. Tax deed sales are sold for the minimum bid of the appraised value.

State-Specific Information:
Minnesota is average for tax lien sales. The interest rate of 12% is decent, and the redemption period of one year is fairly quick. Properties sold for appraised value will limit the investor's potential for profit.

Links for All Minnesota Counties: Provided on CD.

Detailed County-Specific Information:

HENNEPIN COUNTY, MINNESOTA
http://www.co.hennepin.mn.us

TAXPAYER SERVICES DEPARTMENT
http://www.co.hennepin.mn.us/taxsvcs/gstxmain.htm

A600 Government Center
Minneapolis, Minnesota 55487-0060
phone: 612-348-3734
Fax: 612-348-9616
email: jeff.strand@co.hennepin.mn.us

PROPERTY TAX DIVISION
(Taxpayer Services Department)
http://www.co.hennepin.mn.us/taxsvcs/gstxmain.htm#Tax

Marie Kunze, Manager
email: Marie.Kunze@co.hennepin.mn.us
Fax: 612-348-9677
TDD: 612-348-3461

Land Sales: Please check back for more information about a Spring 2004 Public Auction or call 612-348-3734.

Delinquent Tax and Tax Forfeited Land Information: 612-348-3734

(1) Notice to Tax Lien and Forfeited Land Investors
http://www.co.hennepin.mn.us/taxsvcs/TFL/taxliens.htm

General Information About Frequently Asked Questions Concerning Tax Liens/Tax Forfeited Lands/Public Auctions

(2) Redevelopment Sites
http://www.co.hennepin.mn.us/taxsvcs/redevelopment/cover.htm

The material contained herein is provided for purposes of public information as to Hennepin County tax-forfeited land sites which are known and/or suspected to be environmentally impaired parcels. The subject properties are involved in the Taxpayer Services Department segment of the Hennepin County Board "Contaminated Lands Restoration Program" approved August 20, 1996.

The subject properties may or may not be available for public or private sale from Hennepin County, and may be subject to specific legal requirements pertaining to site investigation and remediation, and may be subject to specific terms and conditions of sale if and when they become available for sale by Hennepin County. For more detailed information or if you have specific questions, please contact the Taxpayer Services Department staff referenced herein.

(3) Tax-Forfeited Land Auctions
http://www.co.hennepin.mn.us/taxsvcs/gstxtfla.htm

Please check back for more information about a Spring 2004 Public Auction or call 612-348-3734.

(3a) Tax-Forfeited Land, Terms of Sale
http://www.co.hennepin.mn.us/taxsvcs/TFL/TermsofSale/TOS_11.htm

ROGUE INVESTOR NOTE: Terms of sale are for a 2003 public auction.

(3b) Supplemental Information
http://www.co.hennepin.mn.us/taxsvcs/TFL/auction11/supplemental.htm

ROGUE INVESTOR NOTE: Supplemental information is for a 2003 public auction.

(3c) Sample Sales Transactions
http://www.co.hennepin.mn.us/taxsvcs/TFL/samplesales.htm

(4) Tax-Forfeited Land Repurchase Policy
http://www.co.hennepin.mn.us/taxsvcs/TFL/TFLForms/rba974194.pdf

(5) BUYER PURCHASING "AS IS" ADDENDUM / CODE COMPLIANCE (RES. 87-2-126) ADDENDUM / SOIL CONDITIONS VACANT LAND "AS IS" ADDENDUM
http://www.co.hennepin.mn.us/taxsvcs/TFL/as-is.htm

If you have questions, contact the Tax-Forfeit & Property Revenue Office at (612) 348-3734, visit A-600 Government Center, Minneapolis, MN between 8:00 a.m. and 4:00 p.m., or send an e-mail to Ray.Ball@co.hennepin.mn.us or Rory.Lucas@co.hennepin.mn.us.

(6) Phone Numbers for Municipalities Located in Hennepin County
http://www.co.hennepin.mn.us/taxsvcs/TFL/cities.htm

SHERIFF'S OFFICE
http://www.co.hennepin.mn.us/sheriff/sheriff2.htm

Sheriff Patrick D. McGowan
350 South 5th Street
Courthouse, Room 6
Minneapolis, MN 55415
phone: 612.348.3744
email: Roseann.Campagnoli@co.hennepin.mn.us

(1) List of Sales
http://www.co.hennepin.mn.us/sheriff/divisions/civil/manual/listsofsales.htm

The Hennepin County Sheriff's Office does not provide a list of sales. Mortgage Foreclosure sales are advertised in legal newspapers. Most sales are published in *Finance and Commerce*, but notices are also published in the *Star Tribune* and, occasionally, the *Sun Newspaper*. To qualify as a legal newspaper, the publication must have a paid subscription of over 500 subscribers. Sales are listed in the real estate section.

If the Sheriff's Office is conducting a sale pursuant to Judgment & Decree or as part of an Execution action, the sale notice will be posted in three public display cases located at:

- Minneapolis City Hall, Main Level – 4th Avenue, south side of the building near the Father of Waters Statue.
- Minneapolis City Hall, 2nd Floor – 5th Avenue, south side of the building near the elevators.
- Hennepin County Government Center – Public Service Level (PSL).

Mechanic's Lien sales, which the Sheriff's Office may conduct as an auctioneer, generally are published in the same mentioned papers. Notices of these sales are also displayed in the three public display cases mentioned.

(2) Mortgage Foreclosures
http://www.co.hennepin.mn.us/sheriff/divisions/civil/manual/mortgageforeclosures.htm

Mortgage Foreclosures are legal actions taken to foreclose upon real estate, as opposed to personal property. These are covered by Minnesota Statutes Chapters 580 – 582.

ROGUE INVESTOR NOTE: More information is available on web page.

(3) Redemption of Mortgage Foreclosed Property
http://www.co.hennepin.mn.us/sheriff/divisions/civil/manual/redemptionmortgage.htm

Pursuant to Minnesota Statutes, *most* properties sold in a Mortgage Foreclosure action can be redeemed by the mortgagor. The published Notice of Mortgage Foreclosure Sale usually contains a paragraph indicating the length of the redemption period. In most cases, this is six months. Minnesota Statutes Chapters 580 – 582 regulate these redemptions. However, some Mortgage Foreclosures are subject to federal regulations, in which case there is no redemption period.

A Certificate of Redemption can be obtained from the Sheriff's Office of the county in which the foreclosure occurred or from the Mortgagee (lending institution).

ROGUE INVESTOR NOTE: More information is available on web page.

(4) Sales
http://www.co.hennepin.mn.us/sheriff/divisions/civil/manual/sales.htm

The Sheriff's Office conducts various types of sales under the appropriate statutes. In most cases the Sheriff's Office is simply an auctioneer for the person who needs the sale performed. These sales include, but are not limited to the following:

- Mortgage Foreclosure Sales (see section on Mortgage Foreclosures)
- Execution Sales (see section on Writs of Execution)
- Sales pursuant to Court Orders, Tax Warrants, etc.
- Miscellaneous sales pursuant to various statutes (applying to specific circumstances)
- Mechanic Lien Sales.

ROGUE INVESTOR NOTE: More information is available on web page.

Tax Lien Sales: Yes

Tax Deed Sales: Yes

Rating: Four Stars (****)

Interest Rate: 17% per year

Sale Period: In most cases, last Monday in August

Redemption Period: 2 years

Bidding Process:
All auctions are by competitive bid. Tax lien sale advertisements usually appear in city or county newspapers about three weeks prior to the sale. Tax deed sales also occur.

State-Specific Information:
Mississippi is decent for tax lien sales. The interest rate of 17% is good and the redemption period of 2 years is not bad.

The following information is from the Secretary of State's Office, Public Land Division.

Mississippi Law provides that the ownership of real property be forfeited to the State after (1) default occurs in the payment of taxes and (2) the property is not redeemed during the subsequent two-year period, referred to as "the period of redemption." The process by which real property is forfeited to the state, simply stated, is as follows.

Default in the annual payment of tax assessment results in the property being included on a list of properties advertised for sale by the County Tax Collector of the county wherein the land is situated. All such lands and improvements, if any, are thereafter sold at public sale to the highest bidder for payment of taxes due and unpaid, together with all fees, penalties and damages provided by law. These "tax sales" occur annually in each county, beginning on the last Monday of August, and, at the option of the tax collector (infrequently exercised), on the first Monday of April. If no buyer is found, the property is removed from the sale list and placed on a list of properties that will be forfeited or "matured" to the state if not redeemed by the payment of taxes due and other amounts due during the aforementioned two-year redemption period. (If a property is not sold to a private buyer at the annual tax sale, it is described as "sold to the State for taxes" although the State does not pay out monies to the county tax assessor.) Within thirty days of the expiration of the period of redemption, each chancery clerk, on forms prescribed by the Secretary of State, certifies to the Secretary of State a list of all lands "struck off to the state for taxes, which have not been redeemed." Miss. Code Ann. § 27-45-21. These rules govern the procedures of the Secretary of State from the time he receives the certified lists through the patent of lands back into private ownership (and rescission of patent, if necessary), or to any other state agency, county, municipality or political subdivision of the state.

The following are *ineligible* to purchase tax-forfeited lands:

1. Corporations (except a banking corporation holding a mortgage or deed of trust on the tax-forfeited parcel at the time it matured to the state, which mortgage is still in force and effect).

2. Nonresident aliens may not purchase more than three hundred twenty (320) acres for industrial purposes and five (5) acres for residential purposes.
3. Associations composed in whole or in part of nonresident aliens.
4. Persons who have purchased one hundred and sixty (160) acres of tax-forfeited lands in the year in which the current application is made. (See Rule IV B. 2 for exceptions to this restriction.)

Application to purchase tax-forfeited lands shall be made on forms prescribed by the Secretary of State and available from his office, county tax assessors and chancery clerks. (See application form at http://www.sos.state.ms.us/PublicLands/TaxForfeited/0901_MISSWHITEFORM.PDF) The application shall request the following information:

a. A description of the land to be purchased.
b. Name and address of record owner of land at the time of forfeiture to the state.
c. Name and address of person(s) to whom land was assessed at time of forfeiture to the state.
d. Whether the land is occupied, and if so, by whom and for what purpose.
e. The value of the land and the nature and value of improvements to the land.
f. Approximate quantity and value of marketable timber on the land.
g. The price the applicant is willing to pay for the property.
h. Any other information required by the Secretary of State with the approval of the Governor.
i. The name, address, and telephone number of the applicant.

The completed application must be signed by the applicant, notarized and returned to the Secretary of State with a two dollars and fifty cents ($2.50) application fee. Payment must be by certified check or money order.

Applications will be accepted after the date the property certifies to the State. Applications received before that date will be returned.

How does a property become available for purchase? Every year each county chancery clerk sends the Secretary of State a list of property on which taxes have not been paid and the former owner has not redeemed by the statutory deadline. The properties on these lists are entered into the state's tax forfeited inventory and offered for sale.

How do I obtain a listing of lands available for purchase in a particular county? This web page provides access to the properties available for sale or you may contact the Public Lands Division in the Secretary of State's Office: http://www.sos.state.ms.us/msos/Script/ctylst.idc.

Approximately how long does the process take? The process normally takes about 90 to 120 days from receipt of the application to the issuance of the patent.

What are the major steps in the process? The applicant must first file an application with all of the necessary information complete and the filing fee included. The Secretary of State's Office then contacts the county tax assessor for a current market value of the property and makes an investigation of the title. Once the tax assessor value is received, a recommendation of the offer price is made to the Governor's Office. Upon receipt of the Governor's approval, an offer letter is sent to the applicant. If the purchase money is paid by the applicant, a patent (or deed) is prepared, signed by the Governor and the Secretary of State, and sent to the applicant for filing in the chancery clerk's office.

How is the value for the property determined? The county tax assessor certifies the current market value of the property. In some instances, the Public Lands Division may commission an independent appraisal of the current market value of the property. The purchase price is then normally set at 50% of the market value or the amount of back taxes owed on the property, <u>whichever is greater</u>.

If I have any questions about the process, how do I contact your office? You may contact the Public Lands Division by telephone at (601) 359-6373; by fax at (601) 359-1461; by mail at Post Office Box 136, Jackson, MS, 39205; or by E-mail at the address on this web page.

How do I obtain another copy of a land patent? Contact the Public Lands Division for copies of patent records. If you are the patentee, there will be a charge of $25.00 to issue a duplicate patent.

If you have any questions or comments relative to these tax forfeited lands, please contact our office at

Phone: (601) 359-6373
Voice: (601) 359-1350
In State Toll Free: (866) TFLANDS, (866) 835-2637
Fax: (601) 359-1461
email: publiclands@sos.state.ms.us

Gerald McWhorter
Assistant Secretary of State
Director of the Public Lands Division

This link provides more information: http://www.sos.state.ms.us/PublicLands/TaxForfeited.

Links for All Mississippi Counties: Provided on CD.

Tax Lien Sales: Yes

Tax Deed Sales: No

Rating: Three Stars (***)

Interest Rate: 10% per year

Sale Period: Most sales are in August.

Redemption Period: 2 years

Bidding Process:

All auctions are by competitive bid. Tax lien sale advertisements usually appear in city or county newspapers about three weeks prior to the sale.

State-Specific Information

Missouri is average for tax lien sales. The interest rate of 10% is decent, as is the redemption period of 2 years.

Missouri adds an interesting twist to the tax lien certificate process. When you bid on the tax lien certificate, you are actually bidding on what you would be willing to pay for the property assuming the owner never redeems the certificate. For example, if the tax lien certificate was for $1,456 dollars, then when you are at the auction, this would be the minimum bid, and bidders would then bid on what they believed the property was worth, with the highest bidder winning the tax lien certificate. The state then pays the bidder a 10 percent per year interest rate on the tax lien certificate up to the amount of the certificate, and then 8 percent bid on any amount bid over the minimum bid. If the property owner does not redeem the certificate, the bidder gets the property for the total bid made. If the property owner does redeem the certificate, the bidder gets his or her money back plus interest (10 percent up to the minimum bid and 8 percent for all additional monies bid), no matter what amount was bid.

This means the tax lien certificate sale is actually more like a combination of a tax lien certificate sale and a tax deed sale. Because bids can be accepted well above the minimum bid, it is more likely delinquent owners may not be able to redeem the property. Therefore, the chance of obtaining the deed can be much higher than in most states using a more traditional tax lien certificate sales procedure.

What does this mean for you, the tax lien certificate investor?

You need to research the properties, assuming you could take ownership. You also can bid a little higher than some states because you still get your money back plus interest if the owner doesn't redeem, and a higher bid by you could actually keep the owner from redeeming. Certainly, never bid above what you perceive to be the market value, but if you really want to take possession, a bid well above the minimum bid but below market value could be okay.

In Missouri, properties became delinquent after one year of not paying taxes. The owner is then given three years to redeem the certificate. Therefore, some properties in the sale may go to deed in only 90 days, if the property owner has not paid their taxes for three years. These late properties are very likely to go to deed; so, depending on what you bid on, in Missouri you can actually be a tax lien certificate investor and a tax deed investor at the same sale.

During the sale, the properties are listed as 1st, 2nd, 3rd, and 4th offerings, based on the length of time the property has been in delinquency. With 1st offerings, the owner has two years left to redeem; with 2nd offerings, the owner has one year left to redeem; with 3rd offerings, the owner has 90 days to redeem; and with 4th offerings, the investor gets the deed and the owner has no chance to redeem.

I want to give you two words of caution about Missouri tax lien certificate sales:

1. If you are not a resident of the State of Missouri, then you will need to find a resident of the county you want to bid in and have them notarize a form that indicates they will essentially be responsible for your actions during the sale. This form must be submitted and approved by the County Clerk prior to the sale.
2. In Missouri, all sales are on the same day at the same time. You must pick a county and focus on the sales only in that county, because you can only be in one place at a time.

Here is an example of a recent tax lien certificate auction in Platte County, Missouri:

Tax Lien Certificate Sale
Platte County, Missouri
Platte County Courthouse
August 25, 2003

The Platte County Clerk started the sale at approximately 10:00 a.m. About 100 properties were offered, ranging from commercial buildings with land, raw land, residential homes and building lots. About 10 properties were never purchased. The bidding focused on several commercial buildings, some with substantial amounts of land. The sale lasted about one hour. On average, properties were bought for 3 to 5 times the minimum bid. In my opinion, based on my knowledge of real estate values in this area, bids were 75 percent to 90 percent below market value in most cases. Here is an example of an actual property sale:

A lot of the bidding focused on a commercial building with 80 acres of land. The minimum bid for this property was $315.91, basically the amount of taxes and penalties owed by the owner. The property had been in delinquency for about one year. The winning bid was $7,000 dollars. In my opinion, this may have been one of the best deals at the sale. When I drove by the property, it was obvious that the property needed some cleaning and repair, but it could be worth $100,000 to $200,000 or more, with some work. The listing looked like this:

Parcel #
12-3.0-06-000-000-006-000
Name and Address:
Engineering and Testing Company, 3200 NW Vivion Rd, Riverside, MO 64150
Legal Description: 6-53-34
W ½ of SE ¼ Less Rd R/W 80AC
Minimum bid: $315.91

Links for All Missouri Counties: Provided on CD.

Detailed County-Specific Information:

BOONE COUNTY, MISSOURI
http://www.showmeboone.com

COLLECTOR'S OFFICE
http://www.showmeboone.com/COLLECTOR

Collector, Patricia Lensmeyer

Roger B. Wilson Boone County Government Center
Boone County Collector
801 E. Walnut, Room 118
Columbia, MO 65201-4890
Phone: (573) 886-4285
Fax: (573) 886-4294

(1) Delinquent Tax Certificate Sale
from http://www.showmeboone.com/COLLECTOR/, click on "Delinquent Tax Certificate Sale"

Effective August 28, 2003, legislation changed some requirements relating to the delinquent tax certificate sale, property redemption and the collector's deed. Those changes have been incorporated into the following information. Property sold or purchased at a tax sale prior to August 28, 2003, is governed under the laws in effect before August 28, 2003. If you have any questions regarding the new requirements, please contact our office.

All lands and lots on which taxes are delinquent and unpaid are subject to sale at public auction. The tax sale is held annually on the fourth Monday in August commencing at 10:00 a.m. at the Boone County Courthouse.

Delinquent taxes with penalty, interest and costs may be paid to the County Collector at any time before the property is sold.

The list of properties subject to sale is published in a local newspaper for three consecutive weeks prior to the tax sale.

Non-residents of Missouri *may not bid* unless special arrangements have been made with the Collector prior to the sale.

The sale is conducted by the Collector with the help of an auctioneer. Bidding begins for the amount of taxes, penalties and sales costs.

Buyers *must be present to bid*.

Each parcel offered for sale is individually identified by brief legal description.

Buyer must sign an affidavit stating that he/she is not currently delinquent on any tax payments on any property. Failure to sign such affidavit, as well as signing a false affidavit, may invalidate the property purchase. Affidavits are available at the Collector's office or the sale site immediately prior to the tax sale.

The successful bidder receives a sale sheet identifying the parcel and bid price at the auction. The total purchase price must be paid to the Collector's Office *immediately* at the close of the sale. Cashier's check, personal check, bank draft, cash and/or Novus/Discover, American Express, MasterCard or Visa credit cards are accepted.

- If the bid is not paid, a penalty of 25% of the bid amount plus a prosecuting attorney's fee may be assessed against the bidder.
- The Collector issues and mails a Certificate of Purchase to the purchaser. The Certificate of Purchase is retained for one year or until the property is redeemed except Certificates issued prior to August 28, 2003 are retained for two years or until property is redeemed.
- The original property owner may redeem the property anytime within one year from the sale date except property owners whose property was sold prior to August 28, 2003 may redeem anytime within two years from the sale date.
- The purchaser may assign ownership of the Certificate of Purchase by completing the assignment portion on the Certificate. The assignee must be a resident of Missouri. The Certificate cannot be assigned to anyone owing delinquent taxes. Such assignment must be notarized and presented to the Collector's office to be recorded. The Collector's office normally has a notary public available.
- Liens are not extinguished at the time of sale or during any period of redemption.

(2) Property Redemption
from http://www.showmeboone.com/COLLECTOR, click on "Redeeming Tax Sales Property"

Property sold at tax certificate sale for delinquent taxes may be redeemed within one year from the issuance of a Certificate of Purchase except property sold prior to August 28, 2003 may be redeemed within two years from the issuance of a Certificate of Purchase as follows:

1. Please advise the Collector's office at least 24 hours prior to the date you will be redeeming. We recommend scheduling an appointment and allowing twenty minutes to process;
2. Pay the Collector the amount on the Certificate of Purchase plus 10% annual interest;
3. Pay the Collector the amount of any subsequent years' taxes paid, if applicable, plus 8% annual interest; and
4. Pay Collector a redemption charge of twenty-five cents.

Property may be redeemed by the owner of record, or on the owner's behalf.

Any tax sale bid amount which resulted in a surplus amount above the delinquent taxes and sales costs paid by the Certificate of Purchase holder is available for the owner of record. The Collector remits the surplus amount to the owner of record when possible. Otherwise, the surplus amount is deposited in a separate fund and held for the owner. If undisputed, the surplus amount may be obtained from the Boone County Treasurer. Disputed claims are determined at a public hearing before the Boone County Commission.

The Collector's office notifies the Certificate of Purchase holder when the property has been redeemed. The Certificate of Purchase must be surrendered to the Collector before the holder will be reimbursed the bid amount plus interest. The Collector will provide a check to the Certificate of Purchase holder for the redeemed amount less the twenty-five cents redemption fee.

A Certificate of Redemption will be issued to the owner of record when property is redeemed. The Certificate of Purchase holder will receive a copy of the Certificate of Redemption.

(3) Collector's Deed
from http://www.showmeboone.com/COLLECTOR, click on "Collector's Deed"

If the property has not been redeemed during the one-year redemption period or the two-year redemption period on property sold prior to August 28, 2003, the holder of the Certificate of Purchase may apply for and receive a Collector's Deed to the property. A Collector's Deed can be issued to the Certificate of Purchase holder provided the following has occurred:

- The legal holder of the Certificate of Purchase is named as the original tax sale purchaser or the assignee on the original Certificate of Purchase;
- A title search on the property has been made by the purchaser and verification furnished to the Collector;
- At least ninety days before requesting a Collector's Deed, the Certificate of Purchase holder has notified any person who holds a publicly recorded deed of trust, mortgage, lease, lien, or claim upon that real estate of their right to redeem such person's publicly recorded security or claim by certified mail and verification of such mailing furnished to the Collector;
- If the search revealed no lien holders, the Certificate of Purchase holder has notified the Collector by affidavit that no publicly recorded deed of trust, mortgage, lease, lien, or claim exists;
- At least ninety days prior to requesting a Collector's Deed, the Certificate of Purchase holder has notified the publicly recorded owner at the last known available address and the notification must have been by certified mail, stating the purchaser's intent to obtain a Collector's Deed;
- Property liens, with the possible exception of a federal tax lien, are extinguished once a Collector's Deed is issued assuming compliance with notification(s) to lienholder(s) is proven;
- The Certificate of Purchase has been surrendered to the Collector; and
- Appropriate fees have been paid to the Collector including recording and collection fees.

Failure of the purchaser to obtain a Collector's Deed within two years from the date on the Certificate of Purchase, or four years from the date on the Certificate of Purchase for property sold prior to August 28, 2003, results in the loss of the purchaser's lien on the property.

The Collector's office makes every attempt to notify the interested parties; however, failure to receive notice(s) does not affect the legal time constraints for redeeming property or obtaining a Collector's Deed.

JACKSON COUNTY, MISSOURI
http://www.jacksongov.org

COLLECTIONS DEPARTMENT
http://www.jacksongov.org/gov_de_co.shtml

Director Mike Pendergast

The Delinquent Tax Unit pursues collection of property taxes on approximately 50,000 delinquent accounts, prepares the annual delinquent tax suit and coordinates the subsequent sale.

Jackson County Courthouse
415 E. 12th Street, 1st floor
Kansas City, MO 64106
phone: (816) 881-3232

Independence Courthouse Annex
308 W. Kansas, 1st floor
Independence, MO 64050
phone: (816) 881-4403
email: Collections@jacksongov.org

ST. LOUIS COUNTY, MISSOURI
http://www.co.st-louis.mo.us

DEPARTMENT OF REVENUE
http://revenue.stlouisco.com

Robert H. Peterson, Acting Director of Revenue
41 South Central Avenue, Fourth Floor
Clayton, MO 63105
Located in the Lawrence K. Roos County Government Building.

Customer Service
phone: (314) 615-5500
TTY: (314) 615-3746

COLLECTION DIVISION
(Department of Revenue)
http://revenue.stlouisco.com/Collection/Default.aspx

Collection Division
41 South Central Avenue
Clayton, MO 63105
Located on the street level floor of the Lawrence K. Roos County Government Building.
phone: (314) 615-5500
email: collector@stlouisco.com

SHERIFF'S OFFICE
http://www.stlouisco.com/circuitcourt/sheriff.html

Gene Overall, Sheriff
5th Floor, 7900 Carondelet Avenue
Clayton, MO 63105
General Information Telephone Number: 314-615-4724
Fax: 314-615-2548

Montana

Tax Lien Sales: Yes

Tax Deed Sales: No

Rating: Three Stars (***)

Interest Rate: 10% per year

Sale Period: Varies, depending on the county

Redemption Period: 2 – 3 years

Bidding Process:
All auctions are by competitive bid. Tax lien sale advertisements usually appear in city or county newspapers about three weeks prior to the sale. Be careful in this state. Tax liens pay approximately 1% per month; and if you bid against someone, your actual interest rate can be even lower. This means you can actually lose money if the tax lien is redeemed too quickly.

State-Specific Information
Montana is average for tax lien sales. The interest rate of 10 percent is okay, and the redemption period of 2 to 3 years is average.

Links for All Montana Counties: Provided on CD.

Detailed County-Specific Information:

Some Web Site Addresses and
Phone Numbers for Montana Counties

Lake County http://www.lakecounty-mt.org/treasurer/taxes.html phone: (406) 883-7224	Flathead County Tax Department http://www.co.flathead.mt.us phone: (406) 758-5680
Ravalli County Treasurer's Office http://www.co.ravalli.mt.us phone: (406) 375-6300	Jefferson County Assessor http://www.co.jefferson.mt.us phone: (406) 225-4020
Cascade County Treasurer http://www.co.cascade.mt.us phone: (406) 454-6850	Gallatin County Assessor http://www.co.gallatin.mt.us phone: (406) 582-3400
Yellowstone County Treasurer http://www.co.yellowstone.mt.us phone: (406) 256-2802	Teton County Treasurer http://www.tetoncomt.org phone: (406) 466-2694
Sanders County Department of Revenue http://www.co.sanders.mt.us phone: (406) 827-6932	Lincoln County Treasurer http://www.libby.org phone: (406) 293-8577
Lewis and Clark County http://www.co.lewis-clark.mt.us phone: (406) 447-8329	Butte-Silver Bow County http://www.co.silverbow.mt.us phone: (406) 497-6290
Pandera County Department of Revenue phone: (406) 271-4015	

Tax Lien Sales: Yes

Tax Deeds Sales: No

Rating: Three Stars (***)

Interest Rate: 14%

Sale Period: Public tax sales are held once a year. Liens not sold at the tax sale are offered at private tax sales over the counter at the Treasurer's office throughout the year. A foreclosure sale by the County Attorney may be offered.

Redemption Period: 3 years

Bidding Process:
Auctions are conducted in the round robin format. The first available parcel is offered in parcel number order, and the first bidder will have the option of purchasing the tax lien for all delinquent back taxes and fees on that parcel. If the first bidder chooses not to purchase the tax lien, then the second bidder has the option, and so on. If you pass on your turn you are done for the round of sale until they have gone through all other bidders.

A person may bid without attending the sale. This can be done by mail or fax if (1) he/she has obtained a permanent bid number prior to the sale and has submitted payment for the amount of the bid to the Treasurer's Office; or (2) he/she has obtained a permanent bidder's number prior to the sale and a representative attends the tax sale on his/her behalf using his/her bidder's number.

State-Specific Information:
Real estate acquired by the county which is not redeemed within the time provided for redemption can be offered for sale at public auction at the discretion of the board of county commissioners.

Links for All Nebraska Counties: Provided on CD.

Detailed County-Specific Information:

DOUGLAS COUNTY, NEBRASKA
http://www.co.douglas.ne.us

TREASURER'S OFFICE
http://www.co.douglas.ne.us/dept/treasurer

Julie Haney, County Treasurer
Treasurer's Office
Civic Center, 1819 Farnam Street
Omaha, NE 68183
Telephone: 402-444-7866

(1) Contact Information
http://www.co.douglas.ne.us/dept/treasurer/Admin.htm

Administration phone: (402) 444-7082
Information phone: (402) 444-7103
Julie Haney, Douglas County Treasurer, email: Treas@co.douglas.ne.us
George Ireland, Chief Deputy/Operations & Personnel, email: gireland@co.douglas.ne.us

(2) Tax Sale FAQ
http://www.co.douglas.ne.us/dept/treasurer/PT_TaxSale.htm

What is a Tax Sale? In Douglas County delinquent property taxes are advertised in the February following the date they became delinquent. If taxes are unpaid by April 1 or August 1 and are still unpaid by February of the following year, they are delinquent and will be advertised at that time. A tax sale is a delinquent tax "auction" held by the county, which allows investors to pay delinquent taxes and thus places a tax lien against the property.

If the taxes are redeemed (paid by the homeowner) the investor will earn 14% interest on the lien (14% is the interest rate Douglas County charges on ALL delinquent taxes). If the homeowner does not redeem the property within three (3) years of the purchase of the lien the investor may foreclose on the property.

When and where is the tax sale held? The First Monday of March, 8:00 AM, Civic Center, 1819 Farnam LC-Legislative Chambers, Omaha, NE. Please arrive early, we will begin at exactly 8:00 AM. The Civic Center doors will be open at 7:00 AM.

How often are public tax sales held? Public tax sales are held once a year on the first Monday in March; next sale: March 1, 2004.

Is there a deed sale in addition to a lien sale? Douglas County does not have a deed sale. Douglas County has a Foreclosure Sale through the County Attorney's Office after the public tax sale is completed. The Foreclosure Sale is held randomly throughout the year. If no redemption is made a deed will be issued two years after the sale. For further information contact the County Attorney for time and location of foreclosure sales (402-444-7866).

When and where is the tax sale advertised? It is advertised in the "Daily Record" for three consecutive weeks in February prior to the March sale. You may purchase a delinquent property list from the "Daily Record" located at 3323 Leavenworth Street, Omaha, NE 68102 (their phone number is 402-345-1303).

A diskette or CD listing all liens to be sold may be purchased through the Douglas County Treasurer's Office for $25.00. The disc does contain additional information not included in the "Daily Record". In February, contact the Treasurer's Office at (402) 444-7272 to purchase a diskette/CD. All disc sales are final. This delinquent tax information is provided solely as part of the Douglas County Tax Sale process; it is NOT intended for use as a marketing tool.

How and when to register for the tax sale? Bidders are required to furnish name, address, telephone number, fax number (if applicable), and social security number or Federal ID number to the Treasurer's Office.

The information may be furnished by mail or in person at the Douglas County Treasurer's Office, 1819 Farnam Street, Room H-02, Omaha, NE 68183-0003 or by fax: (402) 444-7699. There is no charge to register but you must register before the sale.

What types of payments are accepted at the sale? Personal checks, cashier's checks, money orders or convenience checks (NO credit cards). Payment must be made by close of business on the day of the sale.

Is there a deposit required before the sale? No deposit is required.

How does the bidding process work? Our sale is conducted as a round robin. The definitions of a round robin and a standard auction are listed below:

In a round robin, the investors agree to buy the liens for the delinquent tax amount including interest and advertising fees. The properties are offered one by one to the investors in a specific order. If an investor accepts an offer then the following property will be offered to the next investor in line. If an investor passes up a property they forfeit that bid and the parcel is offered to the next investor in line (the investor that passed will not get another opportunity for a parcel until the bid works full circle back to them).

In a standard auction, the winning bid amount plus the amount of taxes, plus interest, plus $5.00 advertising. In the case of duplicate bids on any parcel, the parcel will first be offered to the bidder who bids the smallest portion (undivided interest), of the same. If no person bids for less quantity than the whole, the sale will be decided by an acceptable method of lottery.

What type of document is issued at the sale? A Certificate of Tax Sale is issued. A copy of the certificate will be mailed approximately 2 weeks after the sale.

Are there any other expenses in addition to the cost of the lien? Yes, a ten dollar ($10.00) fee for the Certificate (which will be included in the redemption amount), and an additional ten dollar ($10.00) fee per Certificate, if you choose to re-assign a Certificate (this re-assignment fee is non-refundable).

Does the county handle the foreclosure procedure? The Douglas County Treasurer does NOT handle foreclosure or deed application procedures. It is up to the individual bidder to follow through with the foreclosure if necessary.

What happens to the liens that are not sold at the Tax Lien Certificate auction? Liens not sold at the Tax Sale are offered at a private tax sale over the counter at the Treasurer's Office on the first Monday in May. A foreclosure sale by the County Attorney may be offered. Contact the County Attorney's Office at (402) 444-7866 for dates and times of the foreclosure sales.

Can a person bid on Tax Lien Certificates without attending the auction? A bidder or a bidder's representative MUST attend the sale to obtain a lien. When a representative attends the tax sale on behalf of a bidder they will use the bidder's permanent number. Only one bidder is permitted to participate in the sale per company or investor.

LANCASTER COUNTY, NEBRASKA
http://www.ci.lincoln.ne.us

TREASURER'S OFFICE
http://www.ci.lincoln.ne.us/cnty/treas/index.htm

Richard Nuernberger, County Treasurer
555 S. 10th Street, 102
Lincoln, Nebraska 68508

(1) Tax Delinquency Listing
http://www.ci.lincoln.ne.us/cnty/treas/taxdel.htm

This listing shows only those properties that have delinquencies as of. Properties that have delinquent Tax Sale Certificates already for prior years are listed with an "X" in the tax sales column. The "Tax Owing Column" does not include all penalties and cost on this property.

Should these taxes remain unpaid for five years, the property will be declared "Subject to Tax Auction" and offered for sale. This listing will be updated once a week with a "Y" in the paid column if paid.

Although all effort has been made to maintain absolute accuracy for this online listing there may be errors. This listing is mandated by Nebraska State Law to be published in the newspaper of general circulation within the county and that listing be on file in the County Treasurer's Office. This online listing is provided as a courtesy only!

(1a) Listing
http://www.ci.lincoln.ne.us/cnty/treas/adlist/adlist.htm

ROGUE INVESTOR NOTE: list saved on CD:
USA Tax Lien Info/Nebraska/lancaster_co_NE/adlist.htm

(2) Frequently Asked Questions
http://www.ci.lincoln.ne.us/cnty/treas/faq.htm

Real Estate, Personal Taxes, & Special Assessments
555 South 10th Street, Room 101
Lincoln, Nebraska 68508

(3) Contact Information
http://www.ci.lincoln.ne.us/cnty/treas/tele.htm

County Treasurer
Phone: 441-7425
Fax: 441-8841
Email: cotreas@ci.lincoln.ne.us

Tax Lien Sales: Yes

Tax Deed Sales: Yes (also called trustee sales)

Rating: Three Stars (***)

Interest Rate: 12%

Sale Period: Varies, depending on the county.

Redemption Period:
The redemption period for vacant land is 120 days; for improved property the redemption period is 2 years. After 2 years or more, the property will be sold at a tax sale for unpaid taxes.

Bidding Process:
Tax lien certificates are sold at public sale and you must be present to make a purchase. All interested parties must register to receive a bidder number. A random number will be drawn to select the winning bidder. A first and second alternate will also be selected for the parcel from the number selection. The sale will then continue with all bidders eligible for each parcel on the sale list.

State-Specific Information:
Nevada has 17 counties. Tax certificates are issued at the annual tax sale in each county, but the county acquires all such certificates. They are not available to individuals. The county treasurer holds the tax certificates for two years, during which time the delinquent taxpayers have a right of redemption. After the period of redemption has expired, tax deeds are issued to the county and held in trust for the state. The board of county commissioners can order a tax sale of property acquired by the county due to nonpayment of taxes on tax certificates held for two years or more.

Nevada Revised Statutes: http://www.leg.state.nv.us/NRS/SEARCH/NRSQuery.cfm

Links for All Nevada Counties: Provided on CD.

Detailed County-Specific Information:

CLARK COUNTY, NEVADA
http://www.co.clark.nv.us

TREASURER'S OFFICE
www.accessclarkcounty.com/treasurer

Laura Fitzpatrick, Treasurer
500 South Grand Central Parkway
P.O. Box 551220
Las Vegas, Nevada 89155-1220
phone: 702-455-4323 (Information)

(1) Delinquent Property Sales
http://www.co.clark.nv.us/TREASURER/delinq.htm

Next Trustee Auction: April 15 & 16, 2004

(1a) Trustee Sales
http://www.co.clark.nv.us/TREASURER/trs2003.htm

If you are the owner of any of the parcels listed, you may reconvey your property by paying the delinquent taxes in full (certified funds only) before 5:00 p.m. on March 19, 2004.

Revised, January 23, 2004

ROGUE INVESTOR NOTE: information saved on CD:
USA Tax Lien Info/Nevada/clark_co_NV/trustee_parcels.htm

(1b) Real Property Tax Trustee Sale – Frequently Asked Questions
http://www.co.clark.nv.us/TREASURER/trusfaq.htm

When are real property tax trustee sales held? The Clark County Treasurer's Office conducts one tax sale per year, usually in late winter or early spring. Information regarding the date, time and location will be posted to our website, http://www.accessclarkcounty.com/treasurer/delinq.htm, as soon as it is available.

Where can I get a listing of the properties eligible for the upcoming sale? A list of all properties deeded to the Clark County Treasurer as Trustee is available on our website, http://www.accessclarkcounty.com/treasurer/delinq.htm. All properties on the list are subject to sale; however, a person having the right to reconvey the property (paying all amounts due) may do so up to the date of publication of the sale in the newspaper.

Where can I obtain a copy of the sale rules? The sale rules/guidelines will be made available at the Treasurer's Office and on our website, http://www.accessclarkcounty.com/treasurer/rulesofauction.htm, prior to the sale.

When and where are the tax sales advertised? The tax sale will be advertised for 20 consecutive days prior to the sale date. The list of properties is published in a newspaper of local circulation, usually the Las Vegas Review Journal. The list will also be posted to the Clark County Treasurer's website, http://www.accessclarkcounty.com/treasurer/delinq.htm.

How and when do I register for the tax sales? Pre-registration will begin 3 weeks prior to the sale date. You may register by coming into the Clark County Treasurer's office at 500 S. Grand Central Parkway, Las Vegas, Nevada, or by mailing your registration form and fee to the Clark County Treasurer, Attention: Delinquent Tax Division, P.O. Box 551220, Las Vegas, Nevada 89155-1220 (89106, if by express mail). The registration form may be obtained from the Treasurer's Office or from our website, http://www.accessclarkcounty.com/treasurer/regform.htm.

Is there a fee to register for the tax sale? There is a $500.00 registration fee to participate in the tax sale. The registration fee must be in the form of certified funds – cash, cashier's check or money order, made payable to Clark County Treasurer. The registration fee must accompany the registration form. (Do not send cash through the mail.) The registration fee will be credited against the amount of the successful bid, or refunded to unsuccessful bidders, approximately 15 days after the sale date. *Should a successful bidder default on a purchase the deposit will be forfeited.*

What type of bidding process will be used? The tax sale will be conducted as an auction with minimum bids for each property.

Where can I research the sale parcels? Ownership and lien information may be researched through the Clark County Assessor and Recorder offices. Both offices are located at the Clark County Government Center, 500 S. Grand Central Parkway, Second Floor, Las Vegas, NV. The Assessor maps are also available from the following website addresses: http://www.accessclarkcounty.com/assessor and http://www.accessclarkcounty.com/recorder/recindex.htm.

How is the minimum bid determined on a parcel? The minimum bid consists of all delinquent property taxes, penalties, interest and legally chargeable costs. It may also include items such as special assessments, sanitation liens, abatements, etc. The property will be sold to the highest bidder.

Is payment in full required on the day of the sale? Payment in full is required on the day of the sale by the time set in the rules/guidelines for the sale.

What payment requirements do you have at the sale (cashier's check, etc.)? Payment must be made in the form of certified funds, cash, cashier's check or money order, made payable to Clark County Treasurer.

What type of ownership document is issued when the sale is completed? The County Treasurer will record an *absolute deed* to the property within 30 days of the sale date. The Recorder's office will mail the deed to the buyer. Your rights of ownership do not begin until you have received the recorded deed. Please refer to Nevada Revised Statute 361.595 for information on an absolute deed.

Once the property is acquired through the tax sale, is there a redemption period before you can take possession? There is no redemption period on property acquired through the tax sale. Once you *receive* the recorded absolute deed the property is yours. However, there is a 2-year period after the deed is recorded during which the previous owner (or other legal party of interest) may protest the sale. Title companies will not usually issue title insurance during this 2-year period.

Are investors permitted to make purchases at the tax sales without attending the tax sale (i.e., absentee bidding)? No, all interested bidders must attend the sale. If a bidder is representing a company, a letter of authorization must accompany the bidder.

What happens to the properties that do not sell at the tax sale? Properties that do not sell at the tax sale will be placed on the list for the next Trustee sale or conveyed in a manner as prescribed in NRS 361.603 or NRS 361.604.

ROGUE INVESTOR NOTE: Additional questions and answers available on web page.

(1c) Auction Pre-registration Form
http://www.co.clark.nv.us/TREASURER/regform.htm

There is a $500.00 registration fee to participate in the auction. The registration fee must be in the form of certified funds: cash, cashier's check or money order made payable to Clark County Treasurer. The registration fee must accompany the registration form. (Do not send cash through the mail.) The registration fee will be refunded to bidders approximately 15 days after the sale date. *NOTE: Should a successful bidder default on a purchase the deposit will be forfeited.*

The registration form and fee may be mailed to the office prior to the sale. (Postmark deadline April 9, 2004.) You may also register at the Clark County Treasurer's Office April 12, 2004.

Type in your responses below. Then print the screen and mail it to Clark County Treasurer – Delinquent Property Sales: P.O. Box 551220, Las Vegas, NV 89155-1220. Please call the Clark County Treasurer's Office at (702) 455-3087, (702) 455-0142, or (702) 455-3682 if you have any questions.

(1d) Notice of Trustee Auction
http://www.co.clark.nv.us/TREASURER/auction.htm

(1e) Rules/Guidelines of Trustee Auction
http://www.co.clark.nv.us/TREASURER/rulesofauction.htm

All properties listed on the Trustee Auction List were previously deeded to the Clark County Treasurer as trustee for the state and county and will be sold at public auction.

The sale will be held at the Clark County Government Center, Commission Chambers located at 500 S. Grand Central Parkway, Las Vegas, Nevada 89155. Registration begins at 7:30 a.m. Auction begins at 9:00 a.m. You may also register at the Clark County Treasurer's Office from March 15, 2004 thru April 15, 2004.

A valid picture ID is required to register. If bidding for a company, a signed letter of authorization on company letterhead is required and must be presented prior to the sale or at the time of registration. The minimum bid amount for each property is the total amount of taxes, penalties, interest and fees legally chargeable against the property and is subject to change prior to the sale date. (The Auction properties and respective minimum bid amounts are located at http://www.accessclarkcounty.com/treasurer/auction.htm.)

The successful bidder must pay in full (*certified funds only*) on the date of the sale by 2:00 p.m. The $500 registration fee is forfeited if the bid amount is not paid by 2:00 p.m. The properties will be re-auctioned at 3:00 p.m. with payment (*certified funds only*) due by 5:00 p.m. on the same day of sale. *CAUTION: INVESTIGATE BEFORE YOU BID.* Properties are sold "*AS IS*." It is recommended that bidders conduct any research of due diligence they wish to conduct prior to submitting a bid. Maps are available in the Clark County Assessors Office to review, or may be purchased for $25.00. *There may be other government liens that remain on this property after this sale.*

The Clark County Treasurer makes no representation or claims as to fitness for purpose, ingress/egress, conditions, covenants, or restrictions. There are no warranties, express or implied, regarding properties offered.

The County Treasurer assumes no liability for any other possible liens, encumbrances, or easement, recorded or not recorded, which were not canceled by the foreclosure of the property under Nevada Revised Statues.

These properties are subject to any applicable state, county or local zoning or building ordinance. The County Treasurer does not guarantee the usability or access to any of these properties. It is the responsibility of the prospective purchaser to do their own research as to the use of the properties for their intended purpose and to inspect the property personally to determine if it will be suitable for the purposes for which it is purchased.

AUCTION PRE-REGISTRATION: There is a $500 registration fee to participate in the Trustee auction. The fee must be in the form of certified funds only, made payable to "Clark County Treasurer," and must accompany the registration form. (Do not send cash through the mail). Registration forms are available on the Treasurer's website at http://www.co.clark.nv.us/TREASURER/regform.htm. You may also view the rules of the Trustee auction at http://www.co.clark.nv.us/TREASURER/rulesofauction.htm). You may also register at the Clark County Treasuror's Office, April 15, 2004.

A valid picture ID will be required when registering for your bidder card on the day of the auction. Pre-Registration begins March 15, 2004. You may register through the mail, with a postmark deadline of April 2, 2004. Prior to the sale, the registration form and fee may be mailed to the Clark County Treasurer, 500 S. Grand Central Parkway, P.O. Box 551220, Las Vegas, Nevada 89155, Attn: Trustee Sale.

The registration fee will be refunded to unsuccessful bidders approximately fifteen (15) days after the sale date. If a successful bidder fails to pay, the registration fee will be forfeited.

The name of the bidder will go on the Absolute deed and will be recorded within 30 days of the sale date. The original recorded document will be mailed by the Clark County Recorders Office. Only registered bidders will be permitted inside the chambers and all others may view from the monitors in the hallway outside the Commission Chambers.

If you have any questions, please call the Clark County Treasurer's Office at (702) 455-4323.

(1f) Remainderment Available on Parcels Sold at Trustee Auction
http://www.co.clark.nv.us/TREASURER/rem0403.htm

REMAINDERMENT AVAILABLE ON PARCELS SOLD AT TRUSTEE AUCTION. Last date to claim remainderment: APRIL 29, 2005

ROGUE INVESTOR NOTE: information saved on CD:
USA Tax Lien Info/Nevada/clark_co_NV/remainderment_available.doc

(1g) Documents Required to Claim Excess Proceeds
http://www.co.clark.nv.us/TREASURER/remins.htm

(1h) Request for Release of Funds, Treasurer's Trustee Sale
http://www.co.clark.nv.us/TREASURER/PDF/Delinquent/remapp.PDF

(2) Special Assessments
http://www.co.clark.nv.us/TREASURER/sa_cont.htm

(2a) What is a Special Assessment?
http://www.co.clark.nv.us/TREASURER/sa_what.htm

(2b) Special Assessment Sale Parcel
http://www.co.clark.nv.us/TREASURER/sa_sale.htm

Notice is hereby given that the County Treasurer of Clark County, Nevada will, at the hour of 11:00 a.m. on January 27, 2004 at the Clark County Commission Chambers (500 S. Grand Central Parkway), sell certificates of sale for the following parcels which are delinquent in the payment of assessments owing to the County:

For Parcel Listing: http://www.amgnv.com (Assessment Management Group)
For additional information, please call (702) 455-6478.

(2c) Special Assessment – Frequently Asked Questions, Tax Lien Certificates
http://www.co.clark.nv.us/TREASURER/sa_faq.htm

(2d) Special Assessment Information For Certificate of Sale Purchasers and Notification Requirements
http://www.co.clark.nv.us/TREASURER/sa_certbuyers.htm

DOCUMENTATION TO TURN INTO TREASURER
Certificate of Sale (original)
Notarized Statement (steps taken to notify property owner)
Copy of Notice to Property Owner Affidavit of Notice (proof of service on property owner)
Affidavit of Search (if unable to locate, what did you do to locate the property owner)
Affidavit of Publication (proof of publication)

ROGUE INVESTOR NOTE: Additional information is available on web page.

(3) Contact Information
http://www.accessclarkcounty.com/treasurer/content.htm

Laura B. Fitzpatrick, Clark County Treasurer
500 South Grand Central Parkway
P.O. Box 551220
Las Vegas, Nevada 89155-1220
phone: 702-455-4323 (Information) / Toll Free: 1-800-492-3177
Fax: (702) 455-5969
email: trinfo1@co.clark.nv.us

DOUGLAS COUNTY, NEVADA
http://www.co.douglas.nv.us

TREASURER'S OFFICE
http://cltr.co.douglas.nv.us/treasurer.htm

Douglas County Treasurer
1616 8th Street
P.O. Box 3000
Minden, NV 89423
Telephone: 775-782-9018
Fax: 775-782-9888
email: tlundergreen@co.douglas.nv.us

(1) Tax Lien Sale Information
http://cltr.co.douglas.nv.us/taxsalesmain.htm

There are no tax sales or assessment sales scheduled at this time.

(1a) Sign Up for Tax Sale List
http://cltr.co.douglas.nv.us/DCTAXSALELIST.htm

The $5.00 fee will allow you to be on our list for the next five years. If you have any questions please feel free to contact our office at 775-782-9017.

(1b) FAQs on Delinquent Property Tax: Trustee Auction
http://cltr.co.douglas.nv.us/TaxsaleFAQ.htm

(1c) FAQs on Delinquent Special Assessments: Tax Lien Certificates
http://cltr.co.douglas.nv.us/salefaqassess.htm

Q. What is a tax lien certificate? A tax lien certificate is a Certificate of Sale note issued on a property that is sold for non-payment of a special assessment.

Q. How often does Douglas County conduct sales on delinquent special assessments? Douglas County conducts sales on delinquent assessment parcels as they are required.

Q. How do you determine the amount of the Certificate of Sale note? The note is sold for the principal amount of a delinquent assessment plus accrued interest, penalties and costs.

Q. If I purchase a Certificate of Sale note, do I own the property? No. You own a note on the property, for a specified redemption period, and earn interest for each month the note remains outstanding. At the end of the redemption period you may request the deed to the property. The buyer has no legal claim or obligations during the redemption period.

Q. How long before I can move into the home? You must wait until after the redemption period when you request a deed from the Treasurer's office. The buyer has no legal claim or obligations during the redemption period.

Q. Does the buyer retain the right of refusal during the sale? If the buyer chooses not to purchase the property, then the bidder number is left out and another number is drawn.

Q. Who can redeem the Certificate of Sale note? The property owner and other major lien holders (i.e., the mortgage company) may redeem the certificate of sale at any time during the redemption period. Payment must be in the form of cash, cashiers check, or money order.

Q. If the Certificate of Sale is redeemed, do I get my money back? Yes. The Certificate of Sale is redeemed with interest at a rate of 1% per month.

Q. Is the Certificate of Sale a public document? The Certificate of Sale note is recorded with the Douglas County Recorder's office. The original note will be mailed to the buyer after it is recorded.

Q. Where are the sales held? The Douglas County Commission Chambers at 1616 8th Street, Minden, Nevada. (The Old Courthouse.)

Q. Do I have to be present to purchase a tax lien or may I do it by mail? Tax lien certificates are sold at public sale and you must be present.

Q. How do I find out what parcels are available for the sale? The available parcels will be posted to the Douglas County Treasurer website, http://cltr.co.douglas.nv.us/treasurer, at the beginning of the sale month. They will also be published in the Record Courier, one time each week, for the three consecutive weeks prior to the sale date. It should be noted that property owners, or their mortgage company, may bring the parcel current up to the day of the sale. On the sale date they may pay the assessment off before the time of the sale.

Q. How do I purchase a Certificate of Sale note? All interested parties must register to receive a bidder number. A random number will be drawn to select the winning bidder. A first and second alternate will also be selected for the parcel from the number selection. The sale will then continue with all bidders eligible for each parcel on the sale list.

Q. What do I need to register to bid? Registration begins one hour before the scheduled sale (9:00 a.m.), at the front counter of the Treasurer's office. You must fill out the registration form presented to you and show a valid picture identification (driver's license) with your current address. From this you will be assigned a bidder number.

Q. Do I need to be present to register or may a friend register for me? You must be present to register. We will not allow a friend or family member to register for you.

Q. What happens if there are back taxes? The buyer is not required to pay any delinquent property taxes at the time of the sale. Should the buyer wish to protect their interest in the property, they may pay the delinquent tax and have the amount added to the Certificate of Sale. Delinquent taxes must be paid before a deed will be issued on the property.

Q. If I win the purchase of a Certificate of Sale, how long do I have to pay the purchase price? Payment must be received by 10:00 a.m. the day following the sale. Payment must be in the form of cash, cashier's check, or money order made payable to the Douglas County Treasurer.

Q. What happens to the parcels that do not sell, or for which payment is not received, by the following day? The buyer has until 10:00 a.m. the day following the sale to make payment on their purchase. Parcels that have not been paid for will be offered to the first alternate at 10:01 a.m. Payment must be made by 5:00 p.m. on that date. If the first alternate declines or does not make payment, the second alternate is called. Payment must be made by 5:00 p.m. that day. If the property has not been paid for or there is no interest in the property, the Certificate of Sale will be issued in the name of Douglas County. Douglas County may then sell the note, over the counter, to any interested party for the sale amount plus 1% interest for each month that Douglas County holds the note to the property.

Q. Where do I find out information on other liens that may be on the parcels? We advise you to research the Douglas County Assessor and Douglas County Recorder records for information on the properties. Your research should be completed prior to the sale date.

Q. What is the length of the redemption period I must hold the note? The redemption period for vacant land is 120 days and for improved property the redemption period is 2 years.

Q. What is the interest rate I will earn on the note? The interest rate is 1% per month (12% per annum) for each month the note remains outstanding.

Q. Is the monthly interest ever pro-rated? No. The monthly interest is a full month.

Q. What type of deed will I receive at the end of the redemption period? Douglas County will issue you a <u>deed</u>, upon your request, at the end of the redemption period. Refer to Nevada Revised Statutes 271.420 and 271.600 for information on deeds.

Q. What happens if the property owner files bankruptcy? Douglas County will not sell a parcel that has a stay in bankruptcy. We recommend that you contact your attorney for any recourse you would have should the property owner file bankruptcy after you have purchased the note.

Q. Will there be additional costs to the buyer? There are costs associated with the notification procedures to request the deed to the property. However, the County cannot determine what, if any, additional costs the buyer may incur. Reasonable costs may be added to the note (i.e., publication, process server, etc.) prior to the date of redemption, and will earn 1% interest from that date forward. It is the buyer's responsibility to provide the Treasurer's office with receipts of the costs.

New Hampshire

Tax Lien Sales: Yes

Tax Deed Sales: No

Rating: Four Stars (****)

Interest Rate: 18%

Sale Period: Varies depending on the municipality

Redemption Period: 2 years

Bidding Process: Varies depending on the municipality

State-Specific Information:
This is a state where the majority of assessments and sales are conducted by the municipalities, such as towns and cities. However, the State Department of Revenue and Administration handles the assessment and collection of taxes and the sale of property for nonpayment of taxes in all of the unorganized areas of the state, on behalf of the 11 counties of New Hampshire.

Links for All New Hampshire Counties: Provided on CD.

Detailed County-Specific Information:

City of Manchester
http://www.manchesternh.gov/index.asp
1 City Hall Plaza, West Wing
Manchester, NH 03101
Tax Collector's Office
http://www.manchesternh.gov/CityGov/TAX/Home.html
Tax Collector Jan Porter, phone: 603-624-6575

Cheshire County
http://www.co.cheshire.nh.us
33 West Street
Keene, NH 03431
County Treasurer Finance Department
http://www.co.cheshire.nh.us/Finance/index.html
Treasurer Ellen DeYoung, phone: (603) 355-0154

City of Goffstown
http://www.ci.goffstown.nh.us
16 Main Street
Goffstown, NH 03045
Tax Collector's Office
http://www.town.goffstown.nh.us/townhall/tax.shtml
Tax Collector Gail Lavallee, phone: 603-497-3614, ext. 110

City of Greenfield
http://www.greenfieldnh.org
P.O. Box 256
Greenfield, NH 03047
Tax Collector Robert Geisel, 603-547-2782

Rockingham County
http://co.rockingham.nh.us
119 North Road
Brentwood, NH 03833
Treasurer Sandy Buck, phone: 603-679-5335

City of Claremont
http://www.claremontnh.com
Tremont Square
Claremont, NH 03743
Treasurer Jeannine Perry: 603-542-7000

Grafton County
RR 1 Box 67
North Haverhill, NH 03774
Treasurer Kathleen Ward: 603-787-6941

City of Hanover
http://www.hanovernh.org
P.O. Box 483
Hanover, NH 03755
Tax Collector Sallie Johnson, phone: 603-643-0742, ext. 105

Hillsborough County
http://www.hillsboroughcountynh.org
300 Chestnut Street
Manchester, NH 03101
Treasurer's Office
http://www.hillsboroughcountynh.org/ct/ct.html
Treasurer David Fredette: 603-627-5602

Merrimack County
163 North Main Street, Suite 4
Concord, NH 03301-5091
Treasurer Charles Carroll, phone: 603-228-0331

Strafford County
P.O. Box 799
Dover, NH 03821-0799
Treasurer Charles Crocco, phone: 603-742-1458

CITY OF MANCHESTER
http://www.manchesternh.gov

TAX COLLECTOR'S OFFICE
http://www.manchesternh.gov/CityGov/TAX/Home.html

(1) Contact Information
http://www.manchesternh.gov/CityGov/TAX/ContactUs.html

Joan A Porter, Tax Collector
City of Manchester
Tax Collector's Office
One City Hall Plaza – West Wing
Manchester, NH 03101
Phone: (603) 624-6575
Fax: (603) 628-6162
Email: taxcollector@ci.manchester.nh.us

(2) Real Estate Tax
http://www.manchesternh.gov/CityGov/TAX/RealEstate.html

Tax Liens

After the due date on the Notice of Arrearage, the Tax Collector's office begins the lien process. At least thirty days prior to the execution of the lien, a Notice of Impending Lien, (RSA 80:60) (http://www.gencourt.state.nh.us/rsa/html/v/80/80-60.htm) is sent to the last known owner of the property via certified mail, return receipt requested. This notice includes principal, interest and costs up to the date of the lien. The returned receipt or the unclaimed notice serves as evidence that the City mailed the Notice of Impending Lien and has met all of the requirements of the law. The cost of the certified mailing is also added to the delinquent account.

If the taxes remain unpaid after the date and time given for final payment on the Notice of Impending Lien, the Tax Collector's office places a lien on the property. All principal, interest and costs are combined to form the principal amount of the lien and the cost of the execution of the lien (RSA 80:81) (http://www.gencourt.state.nh.us/rsa/html/v/80/80-81.htm) is added to the total amount due. Interest begins at eighteen percent interest (RSA 80:69) (http://www.gencourt.state.nh.us/rsa/html/v/80/80-69.htm) on the unpaid balance until the lien is paid in full. The lien is recorded at the Registry of Deeds and a title search is done. A Certified letter is sent to each lien holder notifying him or her of the lien. An administrative cost (RSA 80:67) (http://www.gencourt.state.nh.us/rsa/html/v/80/80-67.htm) of $10.00 as well as any additional expenses incurred as a result of the title search are added to the cost of notifying mortgagees. Taxpayers should also be aware that if the City places a lien on their property, it becomes part of their credit report and remains there for seven years after it is paid.

When full payment of a Lien is made, the Release Of Lien will automatically be sent within thirty days to the Hillsborough County Register Of Deeds (http://www.nhdeeds.com/hils/web/start.htm). For example: If the Lien is paid in full on March 14th, the Lien Release will be sent to the Hillsborough County Register Of Deeds by April 21st, located at 19 Temple Street Nashua, NH, phone: (603) 882-6933.

If you are looking for a copy of your Lien Release (http://www.manchesternh.gov/CityGov/TAX/InformationRequestForms.html), please visit our Information Request Forms page.

Tax Deeds

After two years from the execution of the tax lien, the Tax Collector shall Deed (RSA 80:76) (http://www.gencourt.state.nh.us/rsa/html/V/80/80-76.htm) the property to the City. At least thirty day prior to deeding, another title search is completed and a notice of impending deed is sent to the current owner (RSA 80:77) (http://www.gencourt.state.nh.us/rsa/html/V/80/80-77.htm) and all mortgagees (RSA 80:77-a) (http://www.gencourt.state.nh.us/rsa/html/V/80/80-77-a.htm) with an interest in the property. Once the property is deeded, you, as well as anyone holding a mortgage, lose all interest in the property. If you are living on the premises, you will be charged rent and eventually evicted from the property. Once the City has deeded the property, it has the authority to sell the property at public auction.

Click here for more information on the Real Estate Laws (Chapters 71-90):
http://www.gencourt.state.nh.us/rsa/html/indexes/V.html

Tax Lien Sales: Yes

Tax Deed Sales: Yes (actually Sheriff's sales of foreclosed properties)

Rating: Five Stars (*****)

Interest Rate: 18%. There can be penalties added to the interest depending on the amount paid for the tax certificate.

Sale Period: Varies, depending on the municipality

Redemption Period: 2 years

Bidding Process: Varies, depending on the municipality

State-Specific Information:
Tax certificates are offered and sold to bidders by the tax collectors of the various municipalities in the state of New Jersey. Click on this link for information about New Jersey municipalities: http://www.state.nj.us/localgov.htm.

Links for All New Jersey Counties: Provided on CD.

Detailed County-Specific Information:

BERGEN COUNTY, NEW JERSEY
http://www.co.ba.md.us

BOARD OF TAXATION
http://www.co.bergen.nj.us/taxboard/index.html

Bergen County Board of Taxation
Administration Building
One Bergen County Plaza
Room 370
Hackensack, NJ 07601-7000
phone: (201) 336-6300
Fax: (201) 336-6310

SHERIFF'S DEPARTMENT
http://www.co.bergen.nj.us/constitutional/sheriff.html

Sheriff Joel Trella

The Bergen County Sheriff's Department is responsible for the foreclosures.

CAMDEN COUNTY, NEW JERSEY
http://www.co.camden.nj.us

Camden County is comprised of 37 municipalities (see
http://www.co.camden.nj.us/government/municip.html). Cherry Hill Township (http://www.cherryhill-nj.com) is provided as an example of tax sales in this county.

TAX OFFICES
http://www.cherryhill-nj.com/government/departments/tax-offices/tax-offices.asp

Property taxes are actually four different taxes, all collected by the Tax Collector, but established by and paid to four different governments, each elected by the voters. Camden County is one of the four governments. Questions about county taxes can be addressed to: Jeffrey Nash, Freeholder Director, 520 Market Street, Camden, New Jersey, 08102-1375. The phone number is (856) 225-5431.

TAX COLLECTION DEPARTMENT
(Tax Offices)
http://www.cherryhill-nj.com/government/departments/tax-offices/overview.asp

The Tax Collection Department handles the billing and collection of property taxes.
Phone: 856-488-7880

CAMDEN COUNTY OFFICE OF THE SHERIFF
http://www.camdencounty.com/sheriff/index.html

Michael McLaughlin, Sheriff
Camden County
Office of the Sheriff
Mailing Address: P.O. Box 769
Room 100 – Courthouse
520 Market Street
Camden, New Jersey 08101
phone: (856) 225-5470
Fax: (856) 225-5578
email: sheriff@camdencounty.com or sheriff@co.camden.nj.us

(1) Sheriff's Sales
http://www.camdencounty.com/sheriff/Sales/indexsales.htm

To confirm a sale date please contact the Camden County Sheriff's Office Civil Division Foreclosure Unit at 856-225-5531. You must have the Sheriff's Docket Number or the Defendant's name for inquiries. Or you can email us at Sheriffsales@camdencounty.com.

Sale date is March 2, 2004. Links to Sheriff's Sales Lists for Camden County municipalities, including Cherry Hill Township.

ROGUE INVESTOR NOTE: information saved on CD:
USA Tax Lien Info/New_Jersey/camden_co_NJ/Sheriff's_Sales.htm

(2) Foreclosure Sale Information Bulletin
from http://www.camdencounty.com/sheriff/Sales/indexsales.htm, click on "Foreclosure Sales"

One of the functions of the Sheriff's Office is to conduct the sale of real property after foreclosure proceedings have been completed.

We hope this information is beneficial to those who would like to bid on properties but are unfamiliar with the conditions and manner of sale.

Foreclosure sales are for real property only; the Sheriff's Office does not know if any structures are on the property. Further, we cannot give permission for prospective bidders to enter and inspect any structure that may be located on the property to be sold.

All properties sold at auction at the Sheriff's Office are advertised Thursday in the Courier Post and local weekly newspapers. Advertisements appear once a week for four consecutive weeks prior to the initial date of sale.

In addition to the newspaper advertising, notices of sale are posted for public viewing at the Sheriff's Office, on the second floor, Room 202 of City Hall, 520 Market Street, Camden.

The Sheriff's Office does not have a list, for general distribution, of the properties to be sold. Persons interested in properties can make their own lists from newspaper legal advertisements.

Sales of property are "open-type" auction sales (no sealed bids). A minimum of $100 is bid on the first round by the plaintiff. All subsequent bids are for a minimum of $100 each. The property is sold to the highest bidder. The successful bidder, upon full payment of the bid, will receive a Sheriff's Deed. This deed does not give clear title to the property. In order to obtain a clear title, one must satisfy all outstanding liens and encumbrances. If a purchaser does not complete the sale he can be held liable for his deposit.

If you are interested in a particular piece of property, we recommend a title search before you actually bid. Title searches are conducted by private firms. Their telephone numbers may be found in the yellow pages of the telephone directory. A fee is charged. You may also do your own title search.

If you are the successful bidder on a piece of property, you are required to post a deposit of 20% on the total bid price. It must be paid by certified check, treasurer's check, or cash. It must be paid immediately following the signing of the Conditions of Sale.

The balance of the bid is payable and due on the 30th day from the date of sale. Lawful interest is charged on the balance due from the 11th to the 30th day. If the balance is not paid on the 30th day, purchasers lose their deposit and are held responsible for all losses and expenses, but receive no benefits from the second sale.

If the property you purchased is occupied, it is your responsibility to have the occupants removed.

Deed recording fees must be paid by the purchaser to the County Clerk's office when the deed is recorded.

Rights of Defendants

In most cases, the property, even after the sale, can be redeemed by the owner for a period of 10 calendar days from the date of sale.

The Sheriff has the discretionary right to make two adjournments of the sale, and no more, not exceeding two weeks for each adjournment. A written letter and fee of $20 is required by the defendant or his attorney requesting the first adjournment for a just cause.

All fees and commissions that are collected by the Sheriff's Office are turned over to the General Treasury of the County of Camden.

To speed your inquiry on a specific piece of property, it is helpful if you refer to the property by its file number or plaintiff and defendant, which appears in the legal advertisement. Please feel free to contact the Sheriff's Sales Office of the Office of the Sheriff at (856) 225-5531 or 225-5551, if we can be of further assistance.

SALES ARE CONDUCTED WEDNESDAY AT 12:00 PM

This is a public service Information bulletin. If you have any further questions, consult your attorney.

(3) Civil Division

from http://www.camdencounty.com/sheriff/Sales/indexsales.htm, click on "Civil Division"

The Civil Division is also involved with weekly Sheriff's sales.

(4) Sheriff Sale Procedures

from http://www.camdencounty.com/sheriff/Sales/indexsales.htm, click on "Sheriff's Sales Procedures"

All Foreclosures are sold subject to special conditions. The Sheriff's conditions are as follows:

1. Any person bidding upon the said premises shall be considered by the act of such bidding to have accepted these conditions of sale.

2. The highest bidder shall be the purchaser and immediately upon the property being struck off to him shall sign his name to these conditions; should he refuse to do so, the Sheriff may sign the same as his agent.

3. TWENTY PERCENT of the bid shall be paid by the purchaser in cash or certified check as soon as the property is struck off to him.

4. In cases where no confirmation is required by law, the deed shall be delivered to the purchaser thirty days from the date of sale, at the sales office of the Sheriff in City Hall, Room 202, Camden, New Jersey. In cases where the sale is required by law to be confirmed by the Court, the deed shall be delivered to the purchaser thirty days from the date of sale.

5. The Sheriff is not required to send any notice to the purchaser. If the deed is ready for delivery at such time and place and the purchaser neglects to attend and make settlement at said time and place, the Sheriff may, at his option, either charge legal interest on the whole amount of the bid until settlement is made, or treat such failure on part of the purchaser as a breach of these conditions of sale.

6. The purchaser shall be liable for payment of the purchase money, whether he attends and receives his deed at such time and place or not; in case he neglects to receive his deed and pay the balance of the purchase money as aforesaid the Sheriff will have the option of either re-advertising the property and selling it again or of proceeding to compel the purchaser to complete his purchase. In the event of a resale, if property should produce a lesser sum than the former bid, interest and expenses, the purchaser will be held liable for the difference. If it should produce a larger sum than the former bid, interest and expenses, the purchaser shall not receiving any benefit thereby.

7. The bidding will be kept open after the property is struck off. In the event that the purchaser fails to comply with any of the above conditions of sale, the Sheriff, at his option, may again immediately put up the premises for sale, subject to these same conditions, and the original purchaser shall be held liable for any deficiency and shall not receive any benefits from any increased bid.

8. The reference to "he," "his" or "him," relating to the purchaser shall be held to apply to one or more individuals, male or female, or a corporation or corporations.

9. Sheriff's fee and commissions are taken from the struck off purchase price.

All Sheriff's Sales are sold subject to a first mortgage, if any, and any Municipal, State or Federal liens, if any.

The attorney representing the Plaintiff will have his own conditions of sale. He will read these conditions prior to his sale. If he would like to know ahead of time what the conditions are, he should contact the office.

We strongly urge anyone who is not familiar with Sheriff's Sale Procedures to seek legal advice and to have a Title Search run on the property BEFORE HE BIDS on any property. The Search will reveal if there are out standing liens, which the bidder would assume if he is the highest bidder.

Sheriff's Sales are held as an open auction. The Attorney for the Plaintiff will start the bidding at $100.00. The bidding will continue until the highest bid is reached, and the highest bidder will be the purchaser. The Plaintiff's attorney normally does not allow the bid to go for less than the Judgment amount due his client. He will bid until he has reached his Upset Price. An Upset Price is the total of the Judgment due, interest, attorney's costs, Sheriff's fees, advertising costs and commissions. Once the attorney has reached his Upset Price he may stop bidding and the highest bidder, thereafter, will be the successful bidder.

The Sheriff's Sales are held on Wednesday, at 12:00 p.m., in the Sheriff's Office, 2nd floor, Room 202, City Hall, 600 Market Street, Camden, New Jersey.

The Sheriff's Sales are advertised for four weeks every Tuesday in the Courier Post prior to sale. The sales are also advertised for four consecutive weeks in a second newspaper: (1) Journal, (2) Retrospect, (3) Record Breeze, (4) Camden County Record, (5) Gloucester City News, (6) Camden Weekly Journal. On the fourth and final week of advertising, the property is sold on that Wednesday if the sale has not been adjourned. The Plaintiff's attorney may adjourn as many times as is necessary for any reason.

A person planning to attend a Sheriff's Sale should call our office or check the Sale Notices posted in our office before or on the sale date, to be sure the sale has not been adjourned, placed in Bankruptcy stay or cancelled.

Our office will post a notice of sale on the property during the week of the first advertising. Our office does not enter the premises being sold for any other reason. Until the sale is final, the defendant (owner) has all his rights and privileges of privacy to his property. A bidder wishing to approach the owner to see the property before the sale is advised that he is on his own.

The owner of the property may at anytime, prior to sale, try to save his home and/or property in several ways. He may try to reinstate his delinquent amount owed, pay the judgment in full, obtain another loan, etc. He may also try to sell the property in order to pay the Judgment and at the same time profit from any proceeds. The defendant has a 10-day Redemption Period after the sale during which time he may object to the sale through the courts or redeem the property. The bidder, in this case, would receive his 20 percent deposit back.

The Sheriff's sale deed will be prepared and ready in approximately 11 days after the sale. The balance due on the sale must be paid no later than 30 days after sale, in accordance with the conditions of sale. It's the responsibility of the purchaser to record the deed in the Register of Deeds office. It is the sole responsibility of the purchaser to notify the owner he has purchased the property and now holds the deed to the property. If the defendant does not voluntarily leave the property, the purchaser must apply to the court for a Writ of Possession. Our office will serve the Writ upon the defendant which will advise him to vacate the premises within a particular period of time. If the defendant has not vacated by the stated tentative date, the Sheriff's Office will set a final date to have a moving van sent to the property and have the defendant's personal belongings removed and stored in a place of safe keeping. The costs of the moving and storage is the responsibility of the purchaser. A Writ of Possession is not necessary if the property is vacant before, during or after the sale.

Additional inquiries may be made by calling (856) 225-5531 or 225-5551 between the hours of 8:30 a.m. and 4:30 p.m. Monday through Friday.

ESSEX COUNTY, NEW JERSEY
http://www.co.essex.nj.us

SHERIFF'S OFFICE
http://www.essexsheriff.com

Essex County Sheriff's Office
50 Nelson Place
Newark, New Jersey 07102
Sheriff Armando Fontoura

(1) Civil Process Division
http://www.essexsheriff.com/ecs04.htm

Once real property is seized, the Sheriff's Office, at the direction of the court, coordinates a sale and/or forwards the property to the party adjudicated to be entitled to the property under the judgment.

HUDSON COUNTY, NEW JERSEY
http://www.hudsoncountynj.org

Hudson County's Internet Directory:
http://www.hudsoncountynj.org/directory/municipal.asp?rec=13&title=Board+And+Agencies

BOARD OF TAXATION
567 Pavonia Avenue
Jersey City, NJ 07306
Phone: (201) 795-6588
Fax: (201) 659-9128

SHERIFF'S OFFICE
http://www.hudsonsheriff.com

Sheriff Joseph Cassidy
Administration Building
595 Newark Avenue
Jersey City, NJ 07306
Phone: (201) 795-6000
Fax: (201) 216-0802

(1) Sheriff Sales
from http://www.hudsonsheriff.com/welcome.html, click on "Sales" in left-hand frame.

All properties sold at auction at the Sheriff's Office are advertised on Mondays and Tuesdays in The Jersey Journal and in The Star Ledger. Advertisements appear each of the four weeks prior to the initial date of sale.

In addition to the newspaper advertising, notices of sale are posted for public viewing at the Sheriff's Office, Jersey City, New Jersey.

The Sheriff's Office does not have a list of properties to be sold for general distribution. Persons interested in following up on these properties must make their own lists by checking the legal advertisements in the newspapers.

Sales of property are "open-type" auction sales (no sealed bids). A minimum bid of $100.00 is bid on the first round by the Plaintiff. The successful bidder - upon full payment of the bid - will receive a Sheriff's Deed.

To determine what funds you may need as a deposit, you must ascertain what your highest bid will be and then make out the certified check for 20% of that amount. Cash deposits would be the same. Certified checks should be made payable to yourself, and if you are the highest bidder, you would then endorse the check to the Office of the Sheriff

If the property you purchase is occupied, it is your responsibility to have the occupants removed.

<u>SALES ARE CONDUCTED THURSDAYS</u>

In most cases the property, even after the sale, can be redeemed by the owner for a period of 10 calendar days from the date of sale. By law the owner can declare bankruptcy within that same period. In certain cases, the redemption is extended beyond the 10 days; an announcement to that effect will be made prior to the sale of the property.

There are times when the sale of property is not completed on the date advertised because of adjournments, settlements or bankruptcies. We recommend you call the Sheriff's Business Office on the scheduled date of the sale to determine the status of the sale.

To speed your inquiry on a specific piece of property, it is helpful if you refer to the property by its "S" number which appears in the legal advertisement. Further assistance is available through the Foreclosure Unit of the Sheriff's Office, 201-795-6321.

<u>ROGUE INVESTOR NOTE</u>: Additional information is available on web page.

(2) Contact Information
from http://www.hudsonsheriff.com/welcome.html, click on "Contact Info." in left-hand frame.

Sheriff Joseph Cassidy
phone: 201-795-6373
Fax: 201-714-7830
email: webmaster@hudsonsheriff.com

MIDDLESEX COUNTY, NEW JERSEY
http://co.middlesex.nj.us

TAX BOARD
http://co.middlesex.nj.us/taxboard/index.asp

Freeholder Liaison: Christopher D. Rafano
Tax Administrator: Irving Verosloff

Functions include: File printed list of all current sales within the County.

(1) Contact
http://co.middlesex.nj.us/taxboard/contact.asp

Celeste Florek, Office Supervisor
Phone: (732) 745-3350

Irving Verosloff, Administrator
Phone: (732) 745-3350

SHERIFF'S OFFICE
http://co.middlesex.nj.us/sheriff/index.asp

Department Head: Joseph C. Spicuzzo, Sheriff

A large responsibility of the Sheriff's Department is enforcing court orders, many of which relate to collecting judgments on behalf of a plaintiff. These orders include foreclosures on real property.

CIVIL PROCESS/BUSINESS OFFICE
(Sheriff's Office)
http://co.middlesex.nj.us/sheriff/civil-process.asp

Foreclosure Execution: This writ commands the Sheriff to sell the mortgaged premises of a defendant and use the proceeds from that sale to satisfy the mortgage. In a typical year, there are an estimated 400 foreclosures completed.

(1) Contact Information
http://co.middlesex.nj.us/sheriff/contact.asp

Donna Gaglione, Foreclosures
phone = (732) 745-3383

RoseMarie Gentile, Supervisor, Foreclosures
phone = (732) 745-3646

MONMOUTH COUNTY, NEW JERSEY
http://www.visitmonmouth.com

COUNTY BOARD OF TAXATION
http://tax.co.monmouth.nj.us

Matthew Clark, Tax Administrator
email: mclark@co.monmouth.nj.us

UNION COUNTY, NEW JERSEY
http://www.unioncountynj.org

SHERIFF'S OFFICE
from http://www.unioncountynj.org, click on "Constitutional Offices" and then on "Sheriff".

Sheriff Ralph Froehlich
phone: (908) 527-4450
Foreclosures, phone: (908) 527-4478

(1) Sheriff's Sales Information
http://www.unioncountynj.org/sheriff/sales.htm

THE SHERIFF IS AN OFFICER OF THE COURT. HE CONDUCTS OR ADJOURNS SALES IN ACCORDANCE WITH STATE STATUTES OR COURT RULES. IT IS RECOMMENDED THAT YOU TALK TO AN ATTORNEY BEFORE BIDDING ON PROPERTIES AT THE SHERIFF'S FORECLOSURE SALE.

The Sheriff's Office also offers printed listings of sale properties at a cost of $1.00 a page. Persons interested in properties may copy from the master list, which is available at our business office, or they should save advertisements printed in the "Star Ledger" or local newspapers.

We recommend calling the sheriff's foreclosure unit the afternoon of the sale at 908-527-4478 or 527-4479 to determine if the sale will be held. Adjournments, settlements or bankruptcies may cause a sale to be canceled. This may occur at any time prior to the sale. In most cases, property will not be re-advertised. To speed your inquiry, refer to the "ch" number that appears in the legal notice or newspaper advertisement.

Sheriffs' sales of property are open type auction sales (sealed or mailed bids are not accepted). The plaintiff opens with a bid of $100.00 and all subsequent bids are in multiples of at least $100.00. Property is sold to the highest bidder. Interest will accrue until the balance is paid.

The successful bidder must post a deposit of at least 20% of the total bid price at the close of the sales. The balance, and a deed preparation cost of $35.00, is due within 30 days from the date of the sale.

If the balance is not paid within 30 days, the buyer may lose his or her deposit. Additional time is not granted to the buyer to obtain a mortgage.

The purchaser will receive a sheriff's deed when full payment of the purchase price is received by the sheriff's office.

In most cases, the property can be redeemed by the former owner within ten days of the sale. In some cases, the owner can also declare bankruptcy within this same time period. If this is done, the sale is put on hold until the court makes its decision.

Sheriffs' foreclosure sales are held every Wednesday at 2:00 p.m. at the Union County Sheriff's Office, Union County Administration Building, Elizabethtown Plaza, Elizabeth, NJ.

ROGUE INVESTOR NOTE: Additional information is available on web page.

DEPARTMENT OF FINANCE, DIVISION OF TREASURER
from http://www.unioncountynj.org, click on "Union County Government and Services," and then on "Finance"

Department of Finance
Union County Administration Building
Elizabethtown Plaza
Elizabeth, NJ 07207

Division of Treasurer
Director, Joseph Bowe
908-527-4099
(908) 527-4050

BOARD OF TAXATION
from http://www.unioncountynj.org, click on "Union County Government and Services," then on "Boards & Agencies," and then on "Board of Taxation"

271 North Broad Street, 3d Floor
Elizabeth, NJ 07207
phone: 908-527-4775
Christopher R. Duryee, County Tax Administrator

Tax Lien Sales: No

Tax Deed Sales: Yes

Rating: Two Stars (**)

Interest Rate: No interest rate, state only has tax deed sales

Sale Period:
Tax deed sales are held whenever properties become available. There is no set schedule for public auction sales; sales are set as research and field checks are completed in each county. For information as to when a sale may be conducted in a given county that is not listed on the New Mexico Current Sale Schedule, please refer to the Tentative Sale Schedule or contact the New Mexico Property Tax Division office (see below). Properties are auctioned at the county seat (courthouse) or such place as is designated by the department, in the county where the properties are located

New Mexico Taxation & Revenue Department
Property Tax Division
Delinquent Property Tax Bureau
Web site address: http://www.state.nm.us/tax
phone: (505) 827-0883

Redemption Period:
The state of New Mexico has no right of redemption for former owners. However, there is a two-year period allowed in which the former owner has the right to challenge the sale through court. The only redemption period in New Mexico is a 120-day Federal IRS redemption period.

Bidding Process:
Bidding is on an oral basis. Bidders must be physically present or be represented by an agent. In the event an agent is representing a bidder, the agent must present to the Property Tax Division, prior to the sale, a document authorizing him to act as an agent for the party he will represent.

State-Specific Information:
There are 32 counties in New Mexico. Tax certificates are not offered to the public or acquired by the counties. Tax lien auction sales are conducted by the Department of Revenue and Taxation of the State of New Mexico. These sales are conducted at varying times during the year. During almost every month there is one or more tax sales in this state. Some counties have 3, 4, or even 5 sales per year. The minimum bid is set by the Department of Taxation and Revenue, but is normally less than 10% of the fair market value of the property.

DELINQUENT PROPERTY TAX BUREAU
http://www.state.nm.us/tax/ptd/delhmpg.htm

The Delinquent Property Tax Bureau's main responsibility is to collect delinquent property taxes on real property and to conduct public auction sales of these properties if all other collection efforts are not successful.

Other duties of the bureau are to (1) ensure that all delinquent taxpayers are allowed every opportunity to satisfy the lien for delinquent property taxes in order to prevent the sale of the property, (2) assist taxpayers with information pertaining to the collection process and the Property Tax Statutes, and (3) provide information pertaining to Tax Deeds.

(1) Current Sales
http://www.state.nm.us/tax/ptd/saleint.htm

(1a) Sale List
http://www.state.nm.us/tax/ptd/salesche.htm

Sale dates are tentative and can be changed without notice.

ROGUE INVESTOR NOTE: sales list saved on CD:
USA Tax Lien Info/New Mexico/salesdwm.htm

(2) Terms of Sales
http://www.state.nm.us/tax/ptd/aucterms.htm

The Terms of the Sale Are As Follows:

All persons intending to bid upon property are required to register and obtain a bidder's number from the auctioneer and to provide the auctioneer with their full name, mailing address, telephone number and social security number. Deeds will be issued to registered names only. Conveyances to other parties will be the responsibility of the buyer at auction. Persons acting as "agents" for other persons will register accordingly and must provide documented proof as being a bona fide agent at time of registration. REGISTRATION WILL CLOSE PROMPTLY AT START OF SALE. CONTACT PROPERTY TAX DIVISION OR COUNTY TREASURER FOR EXACT LOCATION WHERE AUCTION WILL BE CONDUCTED.

2. A sale properly made under provisions of Section 7-38-67 constitutes full payment of all delinquent taxes, penalties, and interest that are a lien against the property at the time of the sale, and the sale extinguishes the lien. The property is sold subject to lien for the property taxes for the year of the sale, provided those taxes are not delinquent. The buyer at public auction or his successor in interest will be liable for those taxes when they become due.

3. The description of the real property is required by Section 7-38-67 to be sufficient to permit its identification and location by potential purchasers. Prospective buyers shall not trespass onto any listed property nor contact (disturb) occupants, if any, for the purpose of gathering information about any listed property. The State of New Mexico warrants no title to property purchased at public auction sale.

4. Section 7-38-74, NMSA 1978, prohibits officers or employees of the State or any of its political subdivisions engaged in the administration of the Property Tax Code from directly or indirectly acquiring an interest in, buying, or profiting from any property sold by the Property Tax Division for delinquent taxes, except that an officer or employee may purchase property offered for sale if he is and was the owner at the time the taxes became delinquent. Any officer or employee violating Section 7-38-74 is guilty of a fourth degree felony and shall be fined not more than $5000.00 or imprisoned for not less than one year nor more than five years or both and he shall be removed from office or have his employment terminated upon conviction. A real property sale in violation of Section 7-38-74 is void.

5. Successful bidders are required to make payment in full of the amount bid before leaving the premises on the day of the sale. Payment is required to be by money order, certified check,

cashier's check, or a personal check which is accompanied by a bank letter of credit which guarantees payment in the amount of or in excess of the amount of the personal check drawn to the order of the Property Tax Division of the Taxation and Revenue Department. No bids will be accepted at future auctions from a bidder who fails to make payment on the day of the sale. The bidder shall be responsible for all costs, expenses, and attorney fees expended in the collection of accepted bids.

6. Upon receiving payment for the real property sold for delinquent taxes, the Property Tax Division shall execute and deliver a deed to the purchaser. Until a deed, which consummates the sale, is received from the Division, a successful bidder has no right of entry to property purchased. The deed conveys all the former property owner's interest in the real property as of the date the state's lien for real property taxes arose in accordance with the Property Tax Code, subject only to perfected interests in the real property existing before the date the property tax lien arose. The property tax lien against real property arises on January 1, of the tax year for which the taxes are imposed.

7. Property sold at public auction may be subject to a 120-day Federal (IRS) Redemption period.

8. In the event a sale is rescinded, only the amount paid for the property at the sale can be refunded. Neither expenses incurred by the buyer in connection with the sale nor interest on the purchase amount will be paid to the buyer, regardless of the basis for the rescission.

9. The sale price of real property at this public auction sale is not to be taken or considered as being the value of that property for property taxation purposes.

10. The auctioneer reserves the right to withdraw from sale any of the properties listed below, to sell any of the property listed below together, or to sell only a portion of any of the properties listed below. If any dispute arises between or among the bidders, the auctioneer's decision with respect to the dispute is final, and the auctioneer may auction the property again, in his discretion. The auctioneer reserves the right to reject any and all bids. The real property listed below may not be sold for less than the listed minimum bid.

IMPORTANT ROGUE INVESTOR NOTE: According to New Mexico State law, the tax lien does not have priority over other liens filed before it. **Be careful here.** This is one of the few cases where a tax lien may not have superiority over a mortgage lien or other lien. Check with the county or have a title search performed.

Links for All New Mexico Counties: Provided on CD.

Detailed County-Specific Information:

BERNALILLO COUNTY
http://www.bernco.gov
Treasurer's Office: http://www.bernco.gov/treasurer/index.html
contact information (http://www.bernco.gov/treasurer/contact.htm):
County Treasurer, Alex Abeyta Jr.
Albuquerque Bernalillo County Government Center
Bernalillo County Treasurer
P.O. Box 627
Albuquerque, New Mexico 87103-0627
Phone: (505) 768-4031
Fax: (505) 768-4023
Email: treas@bernco.gov

DONA ANA COUNTY
http://www.co.dona-ana.nm.us
Treasurer's Office: http://www.co.dona-ana.nm.us/treas/welcome.html
David Gutierrez, Treasurer
email: davidg@co.dona-ana.nm.us
251 W. Amador
Las Cruces, New Mexico 88001
phone: (505) 647-7433 / TDD: (505) 647-7285
Fax: (505) 647-7224

Tax Lien Sales: Yes. Some counties do not have tax lien certificate sales, only tax deed sales. Some counties offer both.

Tax Deed Sales: Yes, but only some counties.

Rating: Three Stars (***)

Interest Rate: 14%

Sale Period:
Sales are usually in April or August, but there are no real rules in New York State. The New York City Department of Finance is authorized by statute to conduct individual and bulk tax lien sales.

Redemption Period:
Legal age requirements, which differ for different classes of properties, refer to the age of the oldest tax lien on an individual property's balance. For Class 2 (multiple dwellings, excluding cooperatives and condominiums), Class 3 (utility properties), and Class 4 (commercial, industrial) properties, a property's entire balance of delinquent charges is eligible for sale once the oldest tax lien remains unpaid for at least one year.

For Class 1 (one thru five family homes) and Class 2 (residential condos and co-ops) properties, a property's entire balance of delinquent charges is eligible for sale once the oldest tax lien remains unpaid for at least three years.

Bidding Process: Many of these auctions can have no minimum bid.

State-Specific Information
There are 62 counties in the state of New York. Tax collections are handled at the county level and by the cities and municipalities that have charters and provisions for the collection of taxes. Tax lien certificates can be sold, as in the case in New York City. Both counties and cities authorize public auctions.

Special Note: In some municipalities, individual investors are not allowed to bid. Check the rules in your area.

Links for All New York Counties: Provided on CD.

Detailed County-Specific Information:

ERIE COUNTY, NEW YORK
http://www.erie.gov

ERIE COUNTY GOVERNMENT

(1) FAQ
http://www.erie.gov/faq.phtml

For property tax information, call 716-858-8333.
For information on foreclosures, call 716-858-6230.

FINANCE DEPARTMENT
http://www.erie.gov/depts/finance

We are located on the 1st floor, Room 100, of 95 Franklin Street, Buffalo, NY, 14202. The Erie County Finance Department is a unit of the Division of Budget Management and Finance. The Erie County Office of Real Property Tax Services is also in the Finance Department.

Joseph L. Maciejewski serves as the Acting Deputy Commissioner of Finance and is also the Director of Real Property Tax Services.

(1) Auction of County Owned Property
http://www.erie.gov/depts/finance/auction2003.phtml

ROGUE INVESTOR NOTE: Information has not been updated for 2004.

SHERIFF'S OFFICE
http://www.erie.gov/sheriff/from_sheriff.asp

Sheriff Patrick Gallivan
10 Delaware Avenue
Buffalo, New York, 14202
phone: (716) 858-7608
Fax: (716) 662-5554

(1) Civil Process Division
http://www.erie.gov/sheriff/civil_division.asp

134 West Eagle Street
Buffalo, New York, 14202
phone: (716) 858-7606

(1a) Sheriff's Sales
http://www.erie.gov/sheriff/civil_division_feeschedule.asp#section5 (scroll to Section 5)

1. What is a Sheriff's sale? The Sheriff seizes or levies upon property for the purpose of satisfying a money judgment. This is done by liquidating the asset (that is, converting the asset into cash). This is accomplished by a "Sheriff's Sale," which is a public auction. The highest bidder pays his bid price to the Sheriff and takes custody and ownership (see # 7 below) of the auctioned property. The Sheriff pays any service providers or vendors who assisted in the seizure (like towing and storage), from the sale proceeds, deducts the various fees and expenses associated with the levy and sale from the proceeds and applies the balance to the judgment. Note that these types of sales are not like the public auctions held by police departments where the property sold is usually property recovered from a crime, or simply lost but unclaimed by the true owner. The proceeds from those sales are turned over to the municipality.

2. When are Sheriff's sales conducted? Another difference between a Sheriff's sale and a police auction is that police auctions are usually held approximately once a year and Sheriff's sales are held throughout the year, at no set schedule. When the Sheriff conducts a sale depends upon when he seizes property; it is not the case where the Sheriff would seize property in connection with several or many cases and hold the property for one big sale. Sales are held "as needed." We might have three different sales in one week and then go four months without another.

3. Where are Sheriff's sales conducted? All real estate execution sales are conducted at our office located on the 4th floor at 134 West Eagle Street in downtown Buffalo.

4. Who can bid at a Sheriff's sale? Sheriff's sales are public auctions, so anyone can bid. The only exception is that members of the Erie County Sheriff's Office may not bid. A person acting as agent for a company or corporation may bid on behalf of the company or corporation he represents. There are no sealed bids or phone bids. A party may bid on behalf of/as agent for, a party not present as long as the agent is present at the sale and the bidder has provided his authority to the Sheriff for such arrangement, in writing, prior to the sale.

Additionally, while anyone may attend and participate in the bidding, only those bidders who have registered to bid will be allowed to do so. This simply involves the bidder signing and printing his name, address and phone number on a ledger sheet provided at the sale.

5. What is the sale format? A standard auction format is used and there is usually no reserve, opening bid, minimum bid, or buyer's premium. Bidding must be in dollar increments. A judgment creditor or execution creditor cannot use his judgment as credit for bidding unless a court order granted and entered prior to the sale is delivered to the Sheriff prior to the sale.

6. What are the terms of the sale? All property is sold "as is, where is." No guarantees or warrantees are made, expressed or implied, for anything sold at any sale, with respect to condition, value, use, operation, safety, marketability, re-sale, sufficiency or accuracy of description, authenticity, or any other matter not consistent with the obligations or duties of the Sheriff.

All sales are for cash only, U.S. currency. A minimum of 10% is due and payable at the conclusion of bidding. Cash is always required for a down payment. If the bid is unusually high, the balance might be paid with a bank cashier's check, certified funds or money order. Any other potential exceptions must be cleared prior to the sale.

If the full bid price is paid at the time of sale, the bidder should discuss with the deputy the release procedure to be able to take immediate possession of the property.

If a down payment is made, the remaining balance is due by 4:00 P.M. of that same day. Alternate arrangements must be pre-approved. The bidder cannot take possession of the property until he receives a written release from the deputy and the release will not be issued until the bid price is fully paid.

Nothing is added to the bid price except for sales tax at the prevailing rate. Those exempt from sales tax must provide, before a release or certificate of sale is issued by the Sheriff, a properly completed tax exemption form no. ST-120 or other form as required by any law. The expenses of the levy and sale will be deducted from the sale proceeds, if any. Where storage has accrued, it will be paid up to and including the day of sale. Thereafter, the purchaser is responsible for any charges. The purchaser is also responsible for making arrangements for the removal, transportation, security, safety, etc. of the purchased property.

When real property is sold, the purchaser must pay to the Sheriff a $22.00 deed fee at the time the deed and associated documents are delivered. The Sheriff does not charge or collect any taxes, fees or charges that may be due or assessed with respect to the sale, transfer or recordation.

Any other terms or requirements as may be expressed or implied by any rule or law are operational as long as such is not inconsistent with the Sheriff's duties and responsibilities as stated here or by law, at the time of sale, or other time. The preceding policies and procedures are subject to modification based upon innumerable variations and factors related to the property, court directions, etc.

7. What exactly is the high bidder purchasing? The purchaser at a sheriff's sale is acquiring the interest of the judgment debtor in the property levied upon. If, for example, the interest of the judgment debtor in a motor vehicle is subject to a lien, then that is what the bidder is buying. For real property, if the debtor's interest is governed by a joint tenancy, for example, or other deed restriction, or is subject to a superior lien or encumbrance, then that is what the bidder is purchasing. The purchaser is acquiring the judgment debtor's "right, title and interest" in or to the property, whatever that may be. The Sheriff does not research such things nor make opinions or assertions relative to such matters.

8. What documents will the purchaser receive from the Sheriff? When real property is sold, the purchaser will receive a receipt for the payment of the bid price, a Sheriff's Deed and the several documents attesting to procedure.

9. How does one find out if and when a sale is scheduled? A printed notice of sale is usually posted in three public places in the City of Buffalo, typically at our office at 134 West Eagle Street, at the foreclosure alcove at the County Clerk's Office at 25 Delaware Avenue, and in the Buffalo City Court Building.

For real property sales, the law requires a notice of sale to be posted at three public places in the town or city where the parcel is situated, at least 56 days before the sale. Such postings are typically done at the local town hall and other government buildings. Additionally, the real property notice of sale will be published in a local newspaper on four different occasions.

The Sheriff does not maintain a mailing list. We will, however, post notices on this website.

MONROE COUNTY, NEW YORK
http://www.co.monroe.ny.us

SHERIFF'S OFFICE
http://www.monroecountysheriff.info

Sheriff Patrick O'Flynn

CIVIL BUREAU OF SHERIFF'S OFFICE
http://www.monroecountysheriff.info/bureaus/civil.html

The Civil Bureau is authorized, by statute, to act as the enforcement officer for all courts within the County of Monroe. Responsibilities delegated to this bureau are in two distinct areas. One of these areas is enforcement, which includes the sale of levied property. personal property, sale of levied property, orders and warrants of arrest for civil contempt.

65 West Broad Street, Suite 300
Rochester, New York 14614-2210
Telephone Number: (585) 428-2320
Fax: (585) 428-2288

(1) Auctions
http://www.monroecountysheriff.info/bureaus/civil/civil_auction.html

Auction Items
To be added in the future.

NASSAU COUNTY, NEW YORK
http://www.co.nassau.ny.us

TREASURER'S OFFICE
http://www.co.nassau.ny.us/treasurer/index.html

240 Old Country Road
Mineola, NY 11501-4248
Henry M. Dachowitz, Treasurer
email: treasurer@mail.co.nassau.ny.us

(1) Annual Tax Lien Sale
http://www.co.nassau.ny.us/treasurer/html/taxlien.html

The 2003 Annual Tax Lien Sale will be held beginning Tuesday February 17, 2004 and run through Friday February 20, 2004. The sale will take place at the Nassau County Police Headquarters located at

1490 Franklin Avenue, Mineola, NY. The sale will begin promptly at 9:00 a.m. for daily registrations. Pre-auction registration information is available on this site or by calling the Tax Sale Department at 516-571-5023.

Any prospective bidder wishing to purchase a listing of Liens to be sold can purchase said list for $150. All checks should be made payable to the Nassau County Treasurer and mailed to the attention of Greg Faling at Nassau County Treasurer, 240 Old Country Road, Mineola, NY 11501. The listing will be made available approximately six (6) weeks prior to the scheduled lien sale.

(2) Notice to Tax Lien Purchasers
http://www.co.nassau.ny.us/treasurer/html/Lien-notice.html

Purchase of Lien
The lien you have purchased must be fully paid for within sixty days of the date of the lien sale. You will be notified by the County Treasurer's Office by regular first class mail within 10 days of the due date. Failure to pay the ninety percent when due will result in automatic loss of the lien plus your total down payment, which consists of the required ten percent down payment (rounded up to the nearest dollar) together with any additional sum provided with that required down payment. Requests for extensions of time to pay the ninety- percent balance will not be considered.

Redemption
All liens purchased at this sale may be redeemed by the property owner or interested party at any time prior to either the Treasurer's issuance of a tax deed or the commencement of a foreclosure action in court. Neither of these events can occur before February 17, 2006 at the earliest. All redemption payments will be charged the total interest rate due at the time of payment. The County Treasurer will pay you the appropriate interest for your lien paid by the property owner or interested party. The interest collected will be in accordance with the provisions of the Nassau County Administrative Code, which call for the same rate as bid at sale for the first twenty-four month period calculated at six-month intervals beginning February 17, 2004. In cases of one-year hardship extensions, interest on the lien for the 25th month through the 36th month will be at five percent per six-month period of time.

Notice to Redeem
When serving Notices to Redeem, the Office of the County Treasurer will insist on strict compliance with all applicable sections of the Nassau County Administrative Code. Copies of the Code and the recent amendments thereto are available at the Office of the Clerk of the County Legislature, located on the first floor of the County Executive Building, One West Street, Mineola, New York.

(3) Annual Tax Lien Sale: Terms of Sale
http://www.co.nassau.ny.us/treasurer/html/Termsofsale.html

(4) Pre-registration Forms
http://www.co.nassau.ny.us/treasurer/html/adobe.html

Request for Unpaid Tax Journal
http://www.co.nassau.ny.us/treasurer/pdf/two-forms.pdf

(5) Annual Tax Lien Sale Listing
http://www.co.nassau.ny.us/treasurer/html/sale-off.html

The Annual Tax Lien Sale Listing for the 2003 Sale will not be available until January 2004.

(6) Forms Download
http://www.co.nassau.ny.us/treasurer/html/formsdownload.html

Affidavit In Lieu Of Lost Certificate:
http://www.co.nassau.ny.us/treasurer/pdf/affid_in_lieu_of_lostcert.pdf

Tax Deed Application:
http://www.co.nassau.ny.us/treasurer/pdf/taxdeedapp.pdf

Tax Lien Surrender Form – Individual:
http://www.co.nassau.ny.us/treasurer/pdf/liensurrenderindv.pdf

Assignment Of Tax Liens:
http://www.co.nassau.ny.us/treasurer/pdf/lienassign.pdf

Freedom Of Information-Application for Public Access to Records:
http://www.co.nassau.ny.us/treasurer/pdf/FOIL.pdf

(7) Contact Information
http://www.co.nassau.ny.us/treasurer/html/contacts.html

Tax Sale
Gregory Faling
phone: 516-571-5023

(8) Office Description
http://www.co.nassau.ny.us/treasurer/html/description.html

Annually the office has conducted a Tax Lien Sale to recoup the funds owed to the county as unpaid taxes. The Treasury Office is organized into four broad units, one of which is Tax Sale and Records.

NEW YORK CITY COUNTY, NEW YORK
http://home.nyc.gov

New York City County includes the Bronx Borough and Queens Borough. Kings County is now coterminous with the borough of Brooklyn in New York City County.

DEPARTMENT OF FINANCE
http://home.nyc.gov/html/dof

REAL ESTATE TAX INFORMATION PORTAL
(Department of Finance)
http://home.nyc.gov/html/dof/html/realprop.html

The Department of Finance sets assessments and collects Real Property taxes and related charges, maintains title records and tax maps, sells tax liens, and administers the City and State transfer and mortgage recording taxes.

(1) NYC Real Estate Tax Lien Sales
http://home.nyc.gov/html/dof/html/liensale2.html

The New York City Department of Finance is authorized by law to conduct regular tax lien sales. A "tax lien" is a legal claim against real property for unpaid real estate taxes and other property charges and interest due to the City of New York. Once certain unpaid amounts have been delinquent for a specified period of time and after we notify the owner, the City can sell its right to collect these amounts to a third party, also known as the lienholder.

The sale of a tax lien on a parcel does NOT mean that the property has been sold. It does NOT mean that the City or new lienholder has taken title to the property. However, after the City sells the lien, the taxpayer must pay the lienholder the entire amount of the lien sold, plus additional fees and interest directly. The taxpayer can no longer pay these charges to the City of New York. If the taxpayer does not pay the full amount due, the lienholder can ultimately foreclose on a property and sell the property to someone else. Finally, a property owner must still pay all new taxes and charges to the City even if a lien for old taxes and charges has been sold.

Customer Assistance

If you have questions or would like more information about the City's lien sale:

- Call the Tax Lien Ombudsperson's Office at (718) 694-0424.
- Senior citizens who need special assistance related to tax lien sales can call the Senior Citizen Tax Lien Ombudsperson at (718) 694-8260.
- E-mail Tax Lien Customer Assistance (http://home.nyc.gov/html/dof/html/emailtaxlien.html).
- Visit the NYC Department of Finance's Tax Lien Ombudsperson's Office in Brooklyn at 25 Elm Place (between Livingston and Fulton Streets), Fourth Floor. Alternately, you can ask to meet with the Ombudsperson at any of Finance's Payment Centers (except Brooklyn) listed below.
- For questions relating to liens for unpaid water and sewer charges, call the NYC Department of Environmental Protection, Bureau of Customer Service, at (718) 595-7000.

Finance Payment Centers

Bronx: 1932 Arthur Avenue, 1st Floor
Brooklyn: 210 Joralemon Street, 1st Floor
Manhattan: 66 John Street, 2nd Floor
Queens: 144-06 94 Avenue, 1st Floor
Staten Island: 350 St. Marks Place, 1st Floor

The Offices of the City Register are located at the same addresses as the Finance Payment Centers shown above, except in Staten Island. Real property documents in Staten Island are filed at the Richmond County Clerk's Office located at 130 Stuyvesant Place.

Tax Lien Sale Information and Outreach Sessions
Download 2003 Tax Lien Sale Brochure for Common Questions and Answers on the City's Lien Sale Process: http://home.nyc.gov/html/dof/pdf/01pdf/liensale.pdf

Update: 2003 Tax Liens Sold
The Department of Finance is in the process of posting all payments made by the close of business on Monday, May 12th to taxpayer accounts. Finance will post a final list of all liens sold in the 2003 Tax Lien Sale as soon as it is available. If you have questions or need further information about the status of a lien, please contact the Tax Lien Ombudsperson's Unit at (718) 694-0424 or the Senior Citizen Tax Lien Ombudsperson at (718) 694-8260.

ROGUE INVESTOR NOTE: Additional information on web page.

(2) 2003 Tax Lien Sale: Understanding the City's Lien Sale Process
http://home.nyc.gov/html/dof/pdf/01pdf/liensale.pdf

(3) 2003 Business, Excise, and Real Estate Tax Calendar
http://home.nyc.gov/html/dof/html/taxcal2003.html

(4) Contact Information
http://home.nyc.gov/html/dof/html/emailtaxlien.html

Contact the Tax Lien Ombudsman using the online form.

SUFFOLK COUNTY, NEW YORK
http://www.co.suffolk.ny.us

TREASURER'S OFFICE
http://www.co.suffolk.ny.us/webtemp5.cfm?dept=37&ID=2018

John C. Cochrane, Treasurer
Riverhead County Center
330 Center Drive
Riverhead, New York 11901-3311
phone: (631) 852-1500
FAX: (631) 852-1507

H. Lee Dennison Building
100 Veterans Memorial Highway, 2nd Floor
Hauppauge, New York 11788-0099
phone: (631) 853-4641
FAX: (631) 853-4642

(1) Information for Taxpayers
http://www.co.suffolk.ny.us/webtemp3.cfm?dept=37&id=2016

Taxes Payable to County Treasurer. After May 31st of each year all taxes are due and payable to the County Treasurer. In addition to the flat amount of the tax, a 5% penalty is added together with interest at the rate of 1% per month calculated from February 1st. Interest is calculated on the total of flat tax and penalty. Interest rates are 5% for June, 6% for July, 7% for August, 8% for September, 9% for October, 10% for November, 11% for December. Any taxes remaining unpaid after August 31st will also be charged a tax sale advertising fee. If taxes have not been paid prior to the date of tax sale, a tax lien will be sold for such unpaid taxes and accrued charges.

Tax Lien Sale. If taxes have not been paid by the date of the tax lien sale, which is usually held in November or December, the County Treasurer will sell a lien to the County of Suffolk on the property to cover delinquent taxes for the current year. A list of tax liens is published in the Official Newspapers for a period of six weeks, and in one newspaper in each of the ten Towns in which the property is located, for a period of two weeks prior to the sale of the unpaid tax liens.

Right to Redeem from Tax Sale. The owner or any person having an interest in the property may redeem the property sold at tax sale within twelve months from the date of the sale, except property assessed as a one-, two-, or three-family residence, which may be redeemed within thirty-six months from the date of the sale, by paying the amount of the lien, plus interest accrued and any subsequent taxes due to the County, upon application to the County Treasurer. Redemptions must be made within the twelve or thirty-six month period from the date of the sale and not thereafter. Redemption statements covering all outstanding tax liens can be furnished upon request to the County Treasurer.

Tax Deeds. A tax deed will be issued to the County of Suffolk at the expiration of the one- or three-year redemption period, provided prior redemption has not been made.

(2) Taxpayer Information Brochure
http://www.co.suffolk.ny.us/Treasurer/brochure.pdf

Redemption of Property Taken by Tax Deed
phone number: 631-853-5900
Email: Treasurer@co.suffolk.ny.us

(3) FAQ
http://www.co.suffolk.ny.us/webtemp3.cfm?dept=37&id=2210

What happens after the lien has been sold to the county? The owner or any person having an interest in the property may redeem the property sold at tax sale within twelve months from the date of the sale, except property assessed as a one-, two-, or three-family residence, which may be redeemed within thirty-six months from the date of the sale, by paying the amount of the lien, plus interest accrued and any subsequent taxes due to the County, upon application to the County Treasurer. Redemptions must be made within the twelve or thirty-six month period from the date of sale and not thereafter.

If payment has not been made within the twelve or thirty-six month period, the County of Suffolk will issue a tax deed for the property. An application to redeem the property must then be made to the Department of Planning, Division of Real Estate (631-853-5900).

ROGUE INVESTOR NOTE: Additional FAQs on web page.

(4) Contact Information
http://www.co.suffolk.ny.us/webtemp3.cfm?dept=37&id=2209

Redemption of Property Taken by Deed
phone: 631-853-5900
email: Treasurer@co.suffolk.ny.us

WESTCHESTER COUNTY, NEW YORK
http://www.co.westchester.ny.us

TAX COMMISSION
http://www.westchestergov.com/taxcommission

The Tax Commission does not establish individual property assessments or collect property taxes. These functions are carried out individually by towns, cities and villages throughout the county.

Westchester County Tax Commission
110 Dr. Martin Luther King Jr. Boulevard, Room L-222
White Plains, New York 10601
Telephone: (914) 995-4325
Fax: (914) 995-4333
Email: dbj1@westchestergov.com

(1) General Tax Information
from http://www.westchestergov.com/taxcommission, click on "General Tax Information"

For questions about liens, judgments or New York State Tax Warrants, contact:

Westchester County Clerk
http://www.westchesterclerk.com
Legal Division
(914) 995-3070

(2) Municipal Officials Contact Information
from http://www.westchestergov.com/taxcommission, click on "Contact Your Municipal Officials"

Tax Lien Sales: Yes

Tax Deed Sales: Yes

Rating: Three Stars (***)

Interest Rate: 9 to 12%

Sale Period: Sales are in December

Redemption Period: 3 years

Bidding Process: Varies, depending on the county

State-Specific Information:
Tax collections and sales are the responsibility of the county tax collector or the municipal tax collector, as the case may be. Judicial foreclosures sales are held in North Carolina.

Links for All North Carolina Counties: Provided on CD.

Detailed County-Specific Information:

MECKLENBURG COUNTY, NORTH CAROLINA
http://www.charmeck.nc.us

OFFICE OF THE TAX COLLECTOR
http://www.charmeck.nc.us/Departments/Tax+Collections/Home.htm

Tax Customer Service Center
Phone: 704-336-4600
Fax: 704-336-6879
Email: mecktax@co.mecklenburg.nc.us

(1) Important Tax Dates
http://www.charmeck.nc.us/Departments/Tax+Collections/Tax+101/Important+Tax+Dates.htm

The tax lien or assessment date each year is January 1st.
Delinquent taxpayers are advertised in the Charlotte Observer in April.

(2) General Tax Lien/Foreclosure Questions and Answers
http://www.charmeck.nc.us/Departments/Tax+Collections/Frequently+Asked+Questions/
Tax+Liens+and+Foreclosures.htm

Q. Does Mecklenburg County sell tax liens?
A. No. The requirement to sell tax liens was abolished by the legislature in 1983. The sale of a tax lien is different from the sale of the property by way of a tax foreclosure action for failure to pay taxes.

Q. Does Mecklenburg County advertise tax liens on real property?
A. Yes. Each year, the Office of the Tax Collector advertises in *The Charlotte Observer* the names of all persons who have not paid Real Estate and Personal Property taxes for the previous year. This is simply a reminder to the specific taxpayers and to the public of the unpaid taxes for the previous year.

Q. Does Mecklenburg County sell property for failure to pay taxes?
A. Yes. At any time after taxes become delinquent, the Tax Collector has the authority to file a tax foreclosure action to have the property sold for collection of the delinquent taxes. All persons who have an interest in the property have to be named in the action and served with notice of the pending sale of the property. The taxpayer or any other person can pay the taxes and costs of the action at any time prior to the sale of the property. This procedure takes from four to six months to complete.

Q. How can the public find out about pending tax foreclosure action?
A. All sales are advertised in *The Mecklenburg Times* and posted at the County Courthouse. The *Times* is published twice weekly and can be purchased on the newsstands or by subscription. The mailing address for *The Mecklenburg Times* is Post Office Box 36306, Charlotte, North Carolina, 28236. The telephone number is 704-377-6221.

Q. Can prospective purchasers be placed on a list to be notified when sales are to be held?
A. No. We receive requests from many people to be notified when sales are to be conducted. From a logistical standpoint, it is impractical to notify a long list of persons when property is to be sold. Persons who are interested in tax sales or any other distressed sales (such as mortgage foreclosures, sheriff sales, etc.) should subscribe to *The Mecklenburg Times* or check the County Courthouse Bulletin Board.

Q. If a person is interested in a specific property on which there are delinquent taxes, will the Tax Collector file a foreclosure action to have the property sold?
A. Yes. There are hundreds of properties on which taxes remain unpaid and often the amount of taxes outstanding is relatively small. There are significant costs in bringing a foreclosure action including court costs, advertising costs, commissioner's fee, auctioneer's fee, guardian ad litem fee, and legal fees. The balance of unpaid taxes and interest are also included. In addition, there is the time factor involved in bringing each suit to a conclusion. Most of the outstanding taxes (approximately 98%) are collected by personnel in the Tax Collector's Office without the necessity of a foreclosure action. However, some taxes cannot be collected in this manner and the only avenue for collection would be through a tax foreclosure action.

Q. If a property is sold for nonpayment of delinquent taxes, what is the bidding process?
A. All sales are public, and usually conducted on Mondays at 12:00 noon in the Courthouse. The property is sold to the highest bidder. There is a ten (10) day upset period after the sale during which time anyone can pay off the taxes and costs, or can trigger a resale by raising the bid by the greater of five percent (5%) of the previous bid or $750. If a raised bid is filed, the property will be advertised again and resold at public sale.

Q. Can any person pay the taxes and obtain title to the property?
A. No. Any person can pay the taxes but payment of the taxes does not entitle the person to any interest in the property. Unless the person is an owner of the property, he/she should not pay the taxes with the expectation of acquiring title to the property.

Q. What kind of title does the purchaser of tax lien foreclosed property obtain?
A. A commissioner is appointed by the Court to sell the property. When the property is sold, the commissioner will deliver a deed to the purchaser but the deed has no warranties.

Q. How does a person obtain a list of properties on which taxes are delinquent?
A. Tax records are public information. If a person has a specific tax parcel in mind, personnel in the Tax Customer Service Center (email at mecktax@co.mecklenburg.nc.us or fax at 704-336-6879) will assist in determining the status of the taxes. There is a specific scroll that contains a list of delinquent taxpayers and there is a fee involved. The Tax Collector's Office does not have sufficient personnel to assist a person in scrolling through the tax records to find properties on which taxes are delinquent.

(3) Contact Information
http://www.charmeck.nc.us/Departments/Tax+Collections/Tax+101/Contact+Us.htm

Office Location
Bob Walton Plaza – First Floor
700 E. Stonewall Street
Charlotte, NC 28202

Mailing Address for Correspondence
City-County Tax Collector
P.O. Box 31457
Charlotte, NC 28231-1457

SHERIFF'S OFFICE
http://www.charmeck.nc.us/Departments/MCSO/Home.htm

Mecklenburg County Sheriff's Office
700 East Fourth Street
Charlotte, NC 28202
phone: 704-336-2543
Fax: 704-336-6118

SPECIAL SERVICES DIVISION
(Sheriff's Office)
http://www.charmeck.nc.us/Departments/MCSO/Divisions/Special+Services/specservexec.htm

Executions
The Sheriff of Mecklenburg County is required to enforce and carry out orders of the court that are directed to him per North Carolina General Statute. An execution is a post-judgment remedy; it is a judicial order issued by the court that has rendered the judgment. An order or writ from the court is directed to a particular officer/sheriff and requires the seizure and/or sale of sufficient property owned by the judgment debtor, to pay in full or satisfy the judgment of the court.

The Executions Division is supervised by Sgt. D.L. Jakeman
phone: 704-432-0847
Fax: 704-336-6118
email: jakemdl@co.mecklenburg.nc.us

RANDOLPH COUNTY
http://www.co.randolph.nc.us

TAX DEPARTMENT
http://www.co.randolph.nc.us/tax

Tax Administrator/Collector, Ben Chavis
Email: btchavis@co.randolph.nc.us

Randolph County Tax Department
Randolph County Office Building
725 McDowell Road
Asheboro, North Carolina 27205

Tax Department Section
Delinquent Collections, phone: 318-6508 or 318-6510

(1) Foreclosure Sales 2004, Legal Division
http://www.co.randolph.nc.us/tax/ForeclosureSales/Foreclosure.htm

Information Outline for Randolph County Tax Foreclosure Sales

Tax foreclosure sales are held on the average of 3-4 times per year. An advertisement runs in the Asheboro Courier-Tribune, Sunday edition, for two consecutive Sundays prior to the sale date. This ad will give the following information: the name of the township in which the property is located, the listing taxpayer, the years in which the judgment covers, the parcel identification number (PIN), a deed description of the property, the place and time of the auction, and the amount the bidding will start at (this amount includes: tax amounts under judgment [additional taxes may be owed over this amount], advertising fees, and sheriff's fees).

It is important to note that the deed description of the property contained in this ad <u>may or may not be the exact description</u> of what is actually being sold. The property to be sold is that property contained in the deed description SAVE AND EXCEPT ANY CONVEYANCES OF RECORD. In other words, the deed description may include portions of land that have been sold off by the current owner, portions that are NOT subject to the sale.

IT IS YOUR RESPONSIBILITY TO RESEARCH AND OBTAIN INFORMATION REGARDING THE PROPERTY, PRIOR TO THE SALE!!

The PIN number contained in the advertisement can be used to access a tax map of the property, along with the parcel information. This can be done in the Public Access Room of the Randolph County Tax Department or via the Internet at http://www.co.randolph.nc.us (Click on *Department*, Click on *Tax*, Choose *Foreclosure Sales* option at top of page and follow further instructions). While this will not provide complete information concerning this property, it is a good place to start.

The Auction Sale Process

(1) The Sheriff will open the bidding at the advertised amount, and then the bidding will be raised by anyone interested in the property. (The Sheriff will not raise the bid, as would an auctioneer.)

(2) When the highest bidder is determined, he must then go to the Clerk of Superior Court and fill out some paperwork: name, address, social security number, etc.

(3) The entire amount of the bid (cash, money order or certified bank check) is due by <u>4:00 p.m.</u> on the day of the sale. NO PERSONAL CHECKS.

(4) The sale is held open for upset bids for 10 calendar days, should that day fall on a Sunday or a Holiday, the following day at 5:00 will be the closing time of the sale.

(5) Upset bids: anyone may upset the highest bidder in the 10-day waiting period. To upset a bid, you must bid the original highest bid amount plus a minimum of 5% but not less than $750.00, and pay the entire amount at the same time (cash or certified bank check).

(6) Confirmation of sale is filed when no upset bid or no further upset bid is filed within 10 days of prior report of sale or upset bid.

(7) If you were the highest bidder, you may pick up your Sheriff's Deed at the Sheriff's Office, 727 McDowell Road, Asheboro anytime after the 10 days has expired. You may call Jo Ann White at (336) 318-6507 or Lt. Jerry Brower at (336) 318-6684 for information regarding the time and pick-up of your Deed.

Please click to see a list of sale properties: 2004 Tax Foreclosure Sale:
http://www.co.randolph.nc.us/tax/ForeclosureSales/TaxForeclosureSale.htm

Next Sale Date: Please watch this page for future postings of sale dates.

(2) List of Foreclosure Sale Properties
http://www.co.randolph.nc.us/tax/ForeclosureSales/TaxForeclosureSale.htm

Next Sale Date:
February 5, 2004
10:00 a.m.

Sale location:
Randolph County Courthouse
First Floor Public Lounge
176 East Salisbury Street
Asheboro, NC 27203

ROGUE INVESTOR NOTE: list of foreclosed properties saved on CD:
USA Tax Lien Info/North_Carolina/randolph_co_NC/foreclosure_properties.htm

---

WAKE COUNTY, NORTH CAROLINA
http://www.co.wake.nc.us

REVENUE DEPARTMENT
http://www.wakegov.com/general/tax/revenue.htm

Charged with the duty of collecting all current and delinquent taxes.
Phone: 919-856-5400
email: revhelp@co.wake.nc.us

(1) Real Estate
http://www.wakegov.com/general/tax/realestate/default.htm

Wake County does not sell tax lien certificates on real estate. Foreclosure proceedings are initiated on real estate parcels only after all other methods of collection have been exhausted. Notification of pending judgment and scheduled dates for sale by auction are published in the classified section of the News & Observer.

(2) Foreclosures
http://www.wakegov.com/general/tax/realestate/foreclosures.htm

Execution sales are held approximately five to six months after a judgment is docketed. Notice of sale by auction is advertised in the News & Observer and posted at the entrance of the Wake County Courthouse twenty days prior to the auction date.

Sales are conducted at the Salisbury Street entrance of the Wake County Courthouse on the scheduled day of the auction at noon, unless otherwise noted. The successful bidder at this sale is required to make a cash deposit of 10% of the bid. The successful bid lays open for 10 days to allow for upset bids. The minimum amount of an upset bid is 5% of the original bid or $750, whichever is greater. Upset bids are made at the Clerk of Court office, located on the 1st floor of the Wake County Courthouse. In the event the successful bidder refuses to accept the deed and honor the bid, the deposit will be forfeited and applied toward defraying the costs and expenses. This in no way restricts or limits any other remedies that may be available against a defaulting bidder.

The Clerk of Court, Special Proceedings Division, also maintains a listing of all properties scheduled for foreclosure by Deed of Trust holders. This listing can be reviewed at their office located on the 12th floor of the Wake County Courthouse.

Please visit http://web.co.wake.nc.us/courts/foreclosure.html for more information.

CLERK OF SUPERIOR COURT
http://web.co.wake.nc.us/courts/index.html

Janet I. Pueschel, Clerk of Superior Court

(1) Contact Information
http://web.co.wake.nc.us/courts/directory.html

Wake County Clerk of Superior Court
P.O. Box 351
Raleigh, NC 27602-0351

Special Proceedings
12th Floor
919-835-3114

SPECIAL PROCEEDINGS DIVISION, FORECLOSURES
(Clerk of Supreme Court)
http://web.co.wake.nc.us/courts/foreclosure.html

Foreclosures
The following is the general process for the conduct of foreclosures and upset bids. This information is not intended as legal advice; as with any judicial proceeding, it is strongly recommended that you seek competent legal counsel to help you.

Sale of Foreclosed Properties
1. An Order of Sale assigns a date for the property to be sold at public auction.
2. A Notice of Hearing is issued and posted by the Substitute Trustee on the Courthouse bulletin boards located on the Ground Floor (Parking/Salisbury Street level) of the Courthouse.
3. Auctions are conducted in front of the bulletin boards on the Ground Floor.
4. Upon completion of any particular auction, a Notice of Sale is posted on the bulletin boards on the Ground Floor and a Report of Sale is filed with the Special Proceedings Division.
5. A ten (10) day period is provided by law for the filing of upset bids; if that ten (10) day period elapses and no upset bids have been filed, the property is considered legally sold.

Filing Upset Bids
1. After a property is sold at public auction but before the ten (10) day upset bidding period elapses, any interested party may file an upset bid with the Special Proceedings Division.
2. To file an upset bid, the bid must be raised by at least 5% and either $750.00 or 5% of the new bid (whichever is greater) must be deposited with the Clerk of Superior Court.
3. Once an upset bid is filed, a new ten (10) day upset bidding period begins. Once this upset bidding period elapses and no new upset bids have been filed, the property will be considered legally sold to the highest bidding party.
4. If the highest bidding party defaults on their bid, they lose their deposit and a new sale process will begin.

For more information about foreclosure proceedings, you may visit the Special Proceedings Division on the 12th floor of the Wake County Courthouse. Please see directions (http://web.co.wake.nc.us/courts/directions.html) for our location and directions.

Tax Lien Sales: Yes

Tax Deed Sales: No

Rating: Three Stars (***)

Interest Rate: 9 to 12%. Purchasers of tax lien certificates receive 9% interest on their investment provided no other bidder offers to accept the certificates for a lessor percentage.

Sale Period: Sales are in December.

Redemption Period:
The owner of the property has a minimum of three years in which to redeem, and can redeem anytime within 60 days after receiving a notice of the expiration of the right to redeem.

Bidding Process: Varies, depending on the county.

State-Specific Information:
There are 53 counties in the state of North Dakota. The county auditor of each county is the official primarily responsible for the collection of delinquent taxes and the sale of property for nonpayment of taxes.

Links for All North Dakota Counties: Provided on CD.

Detailed County-Specific Information:

CASS COUNTY
http://www.casscountygov.com

AUDITOR'S OFFICE
http://www.co.cass.nd.us/departments/Auditor/index.htm

As Property Tax Administrator, the county auditor's oversight includes the collection of delinquent taxes.

County Auditor is Michael Montplaisir.

(1) Contact Information
http://www.co.cass.nd.us/departments/Auditor/contact.htm

In Person
The County Auditor's office is located on the first floor of the Cass County Courthouse.
211 9th Street South
Fargo, North Dakota 58103

By Phone or Fax
Phone: 701-241-5600
Fax: 701-297-5736

By Email
auditor@co.cass.nd.us

By Mail
Cass County Auditor
P.O. Box 2806
Fargo, North Dakota 58108-2806

TREASURER'S OFFICE
http://www.casscountygov.com/Departments/Treasurer

Charlotte Sandvik, Cass County Treasurer

Questions the office answers include those related to delinquent property taxes.

(1) Contact Information
http://www.casscountygov.com/Departments/Treasurer/contact.htm

In Person
The County Treasurer's office is located on the first floor of the Cass County Courthouse.
211 9th Street South
Fargo, North Dakota 58103

By Phone or Fax
Phone: 701-241-5611
Fax: 701-241-5728

By Email
treasurer@co.cass.nd.us

By Mail
Cass County Treasurer
P.O. Box 2806
Fargo, North Dakota 58103

OHIO

Tax Lien Sales: Yes

Tax Deed Sales: Yes

Rating: Three Stars (***)

Interest Rate: 18% (only for counties with populations of at least 200,000)

Sale Period: Varies by county. Can be as often as weekly, but usually scheduled in June.

Redemption Period: Can be as short as 1 year.

Bidding Process:
Varies, depending on the county. At tax deed sales, bids are competitive and winning bid goes to highest dollar amount bid. At tax lien sales, bidding starts at 18% and is bid down in quarter point increments. Also, liens must be purchased in blocks.

State-Specific Information:
There are 88 counties in the State of Ohio. Each county auditor is responsible for the sale of property for nonpayment of taxes. Recent changes in the statutes do not allow counties with populations of 200,000 or less to issue tax lien certificates. However, Ohio does have tax deed sales.

In each of the 88 counties, tax sales are held only after following a judicial foreclosure procedure.

Links for All Ohio Counties: Provided on CD.

Detailed County-Specific Information:

CUYAHOGA COUNTY, OHIO
http://www.cuyahoga.oh.us

SHERIFF'S OFFICE
http://www.cuyahoga.oh.us/sheriff/default.htm

1215 W. 3d Street
Cleveland, OH 44113
email: shcuy@www.cuyahoga.oh.us
Sheriff Gerald McFaul

(1) Terms of Sales
http://www.cuyahoga.oh.us/sheriff/foreclosures/terms.htm

Foreclosure sales are conducted every Monday at 10:00 a.m. unless Monday is a holiday, and then the sale will be conducted on Tuesday morning. The sales are held in the Justice Center, 1215 West 3rd Street, Cleveland, Ohio 44113.

A DEPOSIT OF 10% OF THE SUCCESSFUL BID MUST BE MADE IMMEDIATELY AT THE TIME OF SALE OF THAT PARCEL OF PROPERTY.

FOR ADDITIONAL FORECLOSURE INFORMATION, PLEASE CONTACT THE DOCKET DIVISION OF THE CUYAHOGA COUNTY CLERK'S OFFICE LOCATED ON THE 1ST FLOOR OF THE JUSTICE CENTER. YOU WILL NEED THE CASE NUMBER OF THE PROPERTY FOR REFERENCE. FLOOR CLERKS WILL ASSIST YOU IN FINDING THE BOOK VOLUME AND PAGE NUMBER. INFORMATION MAY ALSO BE OBTAINED WITH THE BUILDING CARD DEPARTMENT, LOCATED ON THE 3RD FLOOR IN THE COUNTY ADMINISTRATION BUILDING, 1219 ONTARIO, CLEVELAND, OHIO 44113. YOU WILL NEED THE PARCEL NUMBER AND / OR THE ADDRESS OF THE PROPERTY. ANY MEMBER OF THE PUBLIC MAY REQUEST A COPY OF THE BUILDING CARD. PLEASE NOTE THAT A FEE WILL BE CHARGED FOR THE REQUEST.

PLEASE CONTACT THE DAILY LEGAL NEWS AT (216) 696-3322 FOR SUBSCRIPTION INFORMATION

ROGUE INVESTOR NOTE: Additional information on web page.

(2) FYI Warning
http://www.cuyahoga.oh.us/sheriff/foreclosures/warning.htm

(3) Foreclosure Sales Property Search
http://www.cuyahoga.oh.us/sheriff/foreclosures/default.asp

(4) Civil Division
http://www.cuyahoga.oh.us/sheriff/civil.htm

The function of the Civil Division of the Sheriff's Office is to carry out court orders. Presently, there are six departments, including one for land sales.

Land Sales Department sets up foreclosures and tax delinquent sales.
Phone: (216) 443-6018
FAX: (216) 443-6259

FRANKLIN COUNTY, OHIO
http://www.co.franklin.oh.us

TREASURER'S OFFICE
http://www.co.franklin.oh.us/treasurer

Richard Cordray
Franklin County Treasurer's Office
373 South High Street, 17th Floor
Columbus, Ohio 43215-6306
Phone: (614) 462-3053
FAX: (614) 221-8124

(1) Tax Lien Information
http://www.co.franklin.oh.us/treasurer/content/taxlien.shtml

(1a) Information for Taxpayers
http://www.co.franklin.oh.us/treasurer/content/taxlienTaxpayer.shtml

(1b) Information for Tax Lien Buyers
http://www.co.franklin.oh.us/treasurer/content/taxlienBuyer.shtml

Revised Overview of the Tax Lien Sale
Bidder Registration Form
Questions or comments, email Ed Leonard at taxlien@co.franklin.oh.us

Overview of the Franklin County Tax Lien Sale
http://www.co.franklin.oh.us/treasurer/content/taxlienSale.shtml

Franklin County Treasurer Richard Cordray would like to thank you for your interest in our first tax lien certificate sale. This document is designed to give you a general description of how the sale works in Ohio and some specific information about the Franklin County tax lien certificate sale. You are strongly encouraged to familiarize yourself with the Ohio Revised Code as it pertains to the sale of tax lien certificates.

Registration

Bidders seeking to participate in the auction of tax lien certificates must complete an IRS Form W-9 Request for Taxpayer Identification Number and Certification and submit the completed Form W-9 with a refundable deposit of $500. Registration deposit must be in the form of a cashier check, money order or certified check made payable to "[Your Company's Name] OR Franklin County Treasurer Richard Cordray." By making the payment payable to yourself OR the County Treasurer, the check can be returned to you on the day of sale if you are not the successful bidder.

The deposit will be returned to all unsuccessful bidders at the conclusion of the auction. The deposit of the successful bidder will be applied to the purchase price of the liens.

Conduct of the Auction

The bidders are purchasing a large group or portfolio of lien certificates for the full value of the liens. The portfolio of lien certificates is not sold at a discount. Individual lien certificates will not be sold. This auction will be an auction of blocks lien certificates.

The bidding will be based upon the interest rate to be charged to the block(s) of liens in the auction. The bidding on a portfolio of lien certificates will begin at the statutory maximum interest rate of 18% simple interest annually. Bidding continues downward in quarter point (¼) increments until the lowest interest rate bid is reached.

Form and Timing of Payment of the Purchase Price

On the date of the auction, the successful bidder must be prepared to pay not less than 10% of the total value of the tax lien certificate portfolio purchased. Payment must be made in the form of a cashier or certified check made payable to Franklin County Treasurer Richard Cordray. Payment of the balance of the portfolio value plus fees must be made via wire transfer. On the auction date, successful bidder(s) will be given all necessary details for the wire transfer of the balance of the portfolio purchase price.

Value of the Lien & Life of the Lien

The successful bidder will be purchasing a group or portfolio of tax lien certificates from the Franklin County Treasurer. The purchase price for a group or portfolio of lien certificates is the total of all taxes and administrative fees due for each lien in a portfolio at the time of the sale. Taxes include all penalties, interest and special assessments then due to the County Treasurer at the time of sale. The value of each lien certificate purchased includes an administrative fee of $200 per lien. The bid interest rate of the successful bid applies to the entire amount of each lien, including the administrative fee.

The lien certificates purchased by the successful bidders are valid for a period of three years from the date of purchase. The date of purchase for purposes of the lien certificate expiration date shall be the auction date.

List of Properties

A list of properties to be included in the tax lien certificate sale will be made available in electronic format via email free of charge. By emailing Ed Leonard at ejleonar@co.franklin.oh.us, you may obtain an email listing of properties included in the tax lien certificate sale. A printed form of the listing or an electronic form on disc is available for the cost of the media ($.05 per page or $1 per disc). Such public record requests may be directed to Ed Leonard, Office of Franklin County Treasurer Richard Cordray, 373 S. High Street, Columbus, Ohio 43215, phone: (614) 462-3430.

Owners of prospective tax lien properties may pay the tax due at any time up to the day before the auction. Consequently, the Franklin County Treasurer's Office will provide an updated list of properties periodically during the weeks leading up to the auction date. The final updated list of properties will be made available via email on the evening prior to the auction.

Updates to the tax lien properties list will be provided via email to prospective bidders who have submitted such email address information to the Treasurer's Office. Prospective bidders seeking such updates in an alternative format must contact Ed Leonard, Franklin County Treasurer's Office, phone: (614) 462-3430 to arrange for any alternative format. Once again, the final updated list of properties will be made available via email on the evening prior to the auction. Finalized list(s) of the properties in tax lien certificate portfolios will be available on the morning of the auction.

Auditor Information

The Office of Franklin County Auditor Joe Testa has an outstanding website that will provide additional information regarding the properties listed. The website can be found at http://www.franklincountyauditor.com. To query parcel information, you will need to use the District and Parcel Number (for example, 010-003214-00).

Recording of the Tax Liens

Lien Certificate Holders will be provided a printed copy of all tax lien certificates purchased. The Treasurer's Office will record the tax certificate in the Office of the Franklin County Recorder.

Tax lien certificate information is noted on the electronic tax records of the Franklin County Treasurer's Office.

Buyers' Right of Redemption

For the period of one year from the date of sale, the property owner has the right to pay the tax certificate lien in full with interest. Pursuant to the Ohio Revised Code, partial payments made by the taxpayer will be retained by the Treasurer's Office and disbursed to the lien certificate holder when payment is made in full.

Calculation of Interest

As mentioned previously, the bid interest rate of the successful bid applies to the entire amount of each lion, including the $200 administrative fee. Interest will be calculated on a simple interest basis using a base of 365 days per year.

"Certificate interest period" means, with respect to a tax certificate sold under section 5721.32 of the Revised Code, the period beginning on the date the certificate is purchased and … ending on one of the following dates:

(1) In the case of foreclosure proceedings instituted under section 5721.37 of the Revised Code, the date the certificate holder submits a payment to the treasurer under division (B) of that section;

(2) In the case of a certificate parcel redeemed under division (A) or (C) of section 5721.38 of the Revised Code, the date the owner of record of the certificate parcel, or any other person entitled to redeem that parcel, pays to the county treasurer or to the certificate holder, as applicable, the full amount determined under that section.

Foreclosure Process

Foreclosure of the tax lien certificate parcels is governed by Ohio Revised Code § 5721.37. Foreclosure cannot commence until one year from the date of sale of the tax lien certificate. Currently, Ohio law dictates that the County Prosecuting Attorney shall prosecute the foreclosure actions initiated at the request of tax certificate holders.

The prosecuting attorney may charge the tax lien certificate holder a fee to cover the cost of prosecuting the foreclosure action. Other Ohio counties conducting tax lien certificate sales have charged foreclosure fees of $2,000 per action. At this time, the Franklin County Prosecuting Attorney's Office has not determine the fee to be charged for handling the tax lien foreclosure actions.

Purchase of Subsequent Delinquent Taxes (Sub-Buys)

The purchaser of a tax lien certificate shall have the right to purchase the lien on all subsequent delinquent taxes on any parcel for which the purchaser holds a tax lien certificate. The interest rate on a tax certificate for subsequent delinquent taxes is 18% simple interest.

Communications with the Taxpayers

The relationship between the tax lien certificate holder and the Treasurer's Office is very important to the success of this tax lien sale program. It is the Treasurer's goal that this program be executed with the highest standards of professionalism and integrity. To ensure that all Franklin County taxpayer's are treated with respect, the Treasurer has established a policy that prohibits the tax lien certificate holder from contacting taxpayers without written prior approval by the Treasurer's Office.

ROGUE INVESTOR NOTE: More information available on web page.

PROSECUTING ATTORNEY'S OFFICE
http://www.co.franklin.oh.us/Prosecuting_Attorney

Rob O'Brien, Prosecuting Attorney

The six major programs comprising the Office of the Franklin County Prosecuting Attorney include Delinquent Tax and Asset Recovery Program.

Tax Division
373 South High Street
17th Floor
Columbus, Ohio 43215
Phone: (614) 462-3500
FAX: (614) 462-2530

SHERIFF'S OFFICE
http://www.sheriff.franklin.oh.us

Sheriff Jim Karnes
email: elwheele@co.franklin.oh.us

(1) Real Estate Sale Information
from http://www.sheriff.franklin.oh.us, click on "Civil Real Estate Sales" in left-hand frame

All sales are pursuant to the provisions of the Ohio Revised Code. The sale is held every Friday morning at 10:00 a.m. in the first floor Press Room, Franklin County Court House, 373 S. High Street, Columbus, Ohio 43215. There are no Sheriff's Sales on Federal Holidays. The official listing of upcoming property to be sold can be found in The Daily Reporter (five weeks in advance of the sale). Additionally, a list is posted in the lobby of 369 S. High Street, Columbus, Ohio 43215 and in the Real Estate office second floor, 369 S. High Street, Columbus, Ohio 43215. The list on this Web Site is for informational purposes only and does not contain any withdrawals. A complete list of withdrawals is read at the beginning of each Sheriff's Sale.

Conditions of the Sale

All bids begin at 2/3 of the appraised value of the property unless dictated otherwise by the Court. If you purchase a property, you will need a cashier's check in the amount of the required deposit. Balance will be due according to the terms of the sale. All sales stipulate *"buyer beware"*. If you are the successful bidder, a deed will be prepared by the Sheriff's Office once a copy of the confirmation is received from the Clerk of Courts. Deed preparation takes approximately 2 to 4 weeks after confirmation.

Properties may be withdrawn from a sale with a court order. For an updated listing of this week's withdrawals, please contact the Real Estate Division at 614-462-4231. Deed preparation takes approximately 2 to 4 weeks after confirmation. A searchable database is available on their website. This Database currently contains 1709 records. Please send Civil Sale comments to: Deputy Wheeler, elwheele@co.franklin.oh.us

(1a) Frequently Asked Questions – Real Estate Sale Information

from http://www.sheriff.franklin.oh.us, click on "Civil Real Estate Sales" in left-hand frame, then on "Frequently Asked Questions"

THE SHERIFF DOES NOT GUARANTEE CLEAR TITLE. A TITLE SEARCH IS RECOMMENDED. SHERIFF SALE INFORMATION IS AVAILABLE IN OUR OFFICE AT 369 SOUTH HIGH STREET, SECOND FLOOR, OUR WEBSITE http://www.sheriff.franklin.oh.us OR IN THE TUESDAY EDITION OF THE DAILY REPORTER NEWSPAPER. THE PROMPTS ON OUR PHONE LINE (614) 462-4231 WILL DIRECT YOU TO THE WITHDRAWAL LIST FOR THE CURRENT WEEK'S SALE. (THIS LINE IS UPDATED MONDAY MORNING AND THURSDAY AFTERNOON.) THE SHERIFF'S OFFICE MAKES EVERY EFFORT TO PROVIDE INFORMATION TO THE PUBLIC, BUT DUE TO THE CURRENT VOLUME, LIMITED INFORMATION IS AVAILABLE OVER THE PHONE. FOR QUESTIONS OF A LEGAL NATURE, CONTACT A LEGAL ADVISOR.

Understand that the Sheriff's Office acts in the capacity as an agent for the sale of real estate (properties) in compliance with a court order. Properties are appraised by independent appraisers, advertised, and sold at public auction. Properties are advertised in the Tuesday Edition of the Daily Reporter Newspaper (614) 224-4835, which is available at most newsstands. Public libraries with a newspaper file may also carry this publication for your review. Information is also provided on both the Sheriff's website and on the counter in the Sheriff's Real Estate Office, 2nd floor, 369 South High Street. The ad from the Daily Reporter will provide you with the same information that the Sheriff 's Office has on any given property. The Daily Reporter also has the terms of sale, which include how long you have after the sale before the balance of the purchase price is due to the Sheriff's Office.

Tax Sales

Tax sales are foreclosures filed by the Treasurer's Office for delinquent taxes. They are intermingled with the regular weekly foreclosure sales. The amount of delinquent taxes is the amount where bidding begins and is also the deposit amount required. Properties sold for taxes are not appraised. Franklin County does not have so called "Over the Counter" Tax Sales. Consideration is given to defendants in these cases and a much higher percentage of these properties are redeemed. A title search is recommended. On Tax Sales you may be required to pay more than the purchase price at the time of sale since the purchaser is responsible for all taxes due and owed on a particular parcel, up to the point of confirmation. Tax sales are advertised for three consecutive weeks prior to sale. If they are not sold the first time offered, they are set for sale again three weeks later, but are not re-advertised. Properties unsold after two attempts fall into one of two categories: (1) properties requested by the City of Columbus under ORC 5722 are deeded to the City of Columbus for the land bank, and (2) properties not sold under ORC 5722 are forfeited to the State of Ohio and are sold by the County Auditor at an Auditor's Sale. For further information on Auditor Sales, contact the Auditor's Office.

ROGUE INVESTOR NOTE: Additional information available on web page.

(1b) Real Estate Sale Results

from http://www.sheriff.franklin.oh.us, click on "Civil Real Estate Sales" in left-hand frame, then on "Real Estate Sale Results"

HAMILTON COUNTY, OHIO
http://www.hamilton-co.org

TREASURER'S OFFICE
http://www.hamilton-co.org/treasurer/default.asp?NavBar=42

Email: county.treasurer@treasurer.hamilton-co.org
Phone: (513) 946-4800/4820, Real Estate
Phone: (513) 946-4780, Delinquent Personal Property
Fax: (513) 946-4818/4837, Real Estate
Fax: (513) 946-4844, Delinquent Personal Property

Robert A. Goering, Hamilton County Treasurer
County Administration
Building 138 East Court Street
Cincinnati, Ohio 45202

AUDITOR'S OFFICE
http://www.hamiltoncountyauditor.org

Dusty Rhodes
dusty.rhodes@fuse.net
138 East Court Street, Room 304
Cincinnati, Ohio 45202
phone: 513-946-4000

phone number for real estate/delinquent taxes: 513-946-4133

(1) Foreclosures Questions and Answers
http://www.hamiltoncountyauditor.org/tax_delinquent.asp

What are the date, time, and location of your tax sales? Delinquent properties are offered for sale every Thursday at 11:00 A.M. in the Sheriff's Office located in the Hamilton County Courthouse, Room 260. Mr. Rick Snow is in charge of the sale and can be reached at 513-946-5340.

When and where are your tax sales advertised? Properties being foreclosed either due to delinquent taxes or mortgage foreclosures are advertised in the Monday edition of the Court Index. Copies of the Court Index are sold in the Hamilton County Courthouse or you can call or write to:

Cincinnati Court Index Press, Inc.
119 W. Central Parkway
Cincinnati, OH 45202
Phone: 513-241-1450
FAX: 513-684-7821

What happens to the properties that do not sell at the auction? There are two attempts to sell each property at a Sheriff's sale. Properties not sold at the weekly sales are offered for a third time at the Forfeited Land Sale. This sale is held every June. All of the property to be sold is advertised in the Cincinnati Enquirer in May.

(2) Advertising of Delinquencies
http://www.hamiltoncountyauditor.org/auditor_duties22.asp

- Prepare Advertisements for Delinquent Lands: §315.18
- Advertise Delinquent Personal Property Taxes: §5719.04
- Advertise Delinquent Real Estate Taxes: §5721.03
- Advertise Forfeited Lands: §5723.05

After the Treasurer has unsuccessfully tried twice to sell at public auction any foreclosed real property, the land is forfeited to the State of Ohio. The Auditor, as agent of the State, must then advertise the sale of forfeited lands. The advertising requirements are substantially the same as for Delinquent Real Estate as far as notices and frequency.

Want More Information On Ohio's Revised Code?
http://onlinedocs.andersonpublishing.com/oh/lpExt.dll?f=templates&fn=main-h.htm&cp=PORC

ROGUE INVESTOR NOTE: Additional information on web page.

(2) Other Delinquent Tax Duties
http://www.hamiltoncountyauditor.org/auditor_duties23.asp

At the same time the Delinquent Personal Property Tax List is prepared, the Auditor also prepares a list of every delinquent taxpayer who owes more than $100. This list is then filed with the Recorder's office, which enters it onto the Lien Record. These liens accrue against both personal property of the delinquent taxpayer and any real property the delinquent taxpayer may own. The Auditor also prepares the Abstract of Delinquent Property Tax Lists for Personal Property and for Real Estate. These abstracts summarize the total amount of delinquencies by taxing district and type.

SHERIFF'S OFFICE
http://www.hcso.org

Sheriff Simon L. Leis, Jr.

COURT SERVICES DIVISION
(Sheriff's Office)
http://www.hcso.org/Divisions/CTS/CTS_Main.shtm

Division is commanded by Major Dale Menkhaus.
email: dmenkhaus@sheriff.hamilton-co.org

Execution Section represents the Sheriff's Office in the areas of property foreclosures (http://www.hcso.org/Divisions/CTS/propertysales.shtm), Sheriff sales, and various court orders relative to property possession and/or seizure as determined by the court.

(1) Contact
http://www.hcso.org/ContactUs.shtm

Court Services
1000 Main Street, Room 260
Cincinnati, OH 45202
General Information phone: (513) 946-5320
Court Services Section phone: (513) 946-5320
Execution Section phone: (513) 946-5340

(2) Property Sales
http://www.hcso.org/Divisions/CTS/propertysales.shtm

Weekly Property Sales Information
The weekly Sheriff's sale is conducted every Thursday at 11:00 a.m. outside of Room 260 at the Hamilton County Court House. The Court House is located at 1000 Main Street, Cincinnati, OH 45202.

There are two types of property offered for sale: (1) those for non-payment of the property taxes, and (2) those for mortgage foreclosure.

Payment in full is required for the majority of the purchases. This does not mean a letter of pre-approval or letter of commitment. A check must be issued at the time of the auction. The properties are bought "buyer beware" without any warranty or guarantee.

We recommend consulting a Real Estate attorney before attempting any purchase.

A list of sale properties can be obtained by contacting The Cincinnati Court Index at 513-241-1450, or at http://www.courtindex.com. Any questions regarding sale procedures can be directed to the Hamilton County Sheriff's Office Execution Section at 513-946-5340.

MONTGOMERY COUNTY, OHIO
http://www.co.montgomery.oh.us

TREASURER'S OFFICE
http://www.montcnty.org/Departments/Treasurer/index.htm

451 W. Third Street
Dayton, OH 45422-1475
Phone: (937) 225-4010
Fax: (937) 496-7122
Hugh Quill, Montgomery County Treasurer

(1) Treasurer's Sales
http://www.montcnty.org/Sheriff/Dispatch_Records/Sheriff_Sale.htm

Tax sale list, updated as of January 26, 2004. Next update is February 2, 2004.

ROGUE INVESTOR NOTE: information saved on CD:
USA Tax Lien Info/Ohio/montgomery_co_OH/Sheriff_Sale.htm

(2) Treasurer's Sale Photos
http://www.montcnty.org/Departments/Treasurer/salephotos.htm

(3) General Property Questions
http://www.mcohio.org/Departments/Treasurer/faq.htm#9

SHERIFF'S OFFICE
http://www.montcnty.org/Sheriff

Sheriff Dave Vore
330 W. Second Street
(P.O. Box 972)
Dayton, Ohio 45422
phone: (937) 225-4357
fax: (937) 496-7986
email: vored@mcohio.org

(1) Real Estate Foreclosure Sales
http://www.mcohio.org/Sheriff/Dispatch_Records/Real_Estate.html

email: WrightL@mcohio.org

Real estate foreclosure sales are held in the Lower Level Auditorium, Montgomery County Administration Building, 451 West Third Street, Dayton, Ohio, and the sale begin promptly at 10:00 A.M. Check the list of properties for sale for the exact sale date. The list is updated weekly.

Click here to view the list: http://www.montcnty.org/Sheriff/Dispatch_Records/Sheriff_Sale.htm. Sales are advertised in the *Daily Court Reporter*. The ads run once per week for a minimum of three consecutive weeks. If you want to find out more information about the property, please buy the *Daily Court Reporter*. You can send a check to the newspaper office, and the paper will be mailed to you on a daily basis. Their telephone number is (937) 222-6000. The newspaper may be purchased at 120 W. Second Street, lower level smoke shop called the Picnic Basket. The Sheriff's Office does not mail or give away a list of properties or information about purchasing foreclosed property.

The property is not available for tour or inspection. The buyer gets the property "as is," *caveat emptor* (let the buyer beware). The Sheriff's Office does not have information on liens or taxes. Real estate tax information can be found on the Treasurer's web site, http://www.mctreas.org. You can view the entire case file, which lists the liens against the property, by going to the Clerk of Court's web site at http://www.clerk.co.montgomery.oh.us.

Terms of sale are not the same on mortgage foreclosures and real estate tax foreclosures. Check the web site list of properties for exact terms of sale.

All revenue generated from Sheriff's real estate sales goes to the County's general fund.

(2) Real Estate Foreclosure Sales List
http://www.mcohio.org/Sheriff/Dispatch_Records/Sheriff_Sale.htm

ROGUE INVESTOR NOTE: information saved on CD:
USA Tax Lien Info/Ohio/montgomery_co_OH/Sheriff_Sale.htm

SUMMIT COUNTY, OHIO
http://www.co.summit.oh.us

FISCAL OFFICE
http://www.co.summit.oh.us/fiscaloffice/index.htm

As a result of a Charter Amendment passed by the voters of Summit County in November 2001, the county auditor's office has merged with the county treasurer's office into a new office. The treasurer's office has been renamed the fiscal office and John A. Donofrio is the Fiscal Officer.

(1) Real Estate Taxes FAQ
from http://www.co.summit.oh.us/fiscaloffice/index.htm, click on "Treasurer Division" in the left-hand column, and then on "Real Estate Taxes FAQ"

Q: When are Tax Certificate Lien Sales held? Tax Certificate Lien Sales are held in late October of each year.

(2) Real Estate Tax Certificate Liens
from http://www.co.summit.oh.us/fiscaloffice/index.htm, click on "Treasurer Division" in the left-hand column, and then on "Real Estate Tax Certificate Liens"

To learn more about Tax Certificate Liens, click here:
http://www.co.summit.oh.us/fiscaloffice/pdfs/tax%20certificate%20info%20new.pdf

(2a) Real Estate Tax Certificate Liens (House Bill 371)
http://www.co.summit.oh.us/fiscaloffice/pdfs/tax%20certificate%20info%20new.pdf

House Bill 371 provides an optional procedure under which county treasurers of counties having a population of 200,000 or more can collect delinquent property taxes by selling tax certificates on delinquent properties to private parties by public auction. Twelve of Ohio's eighty-eight counties qualify to hold the sales.

ROGUE INVESTOR NOTE: More information available on web page.

(3) Office Divisions
from http://www.co.summit.oh.us/fiscaloffice/index.htm, click on "Treasurer Division" in the left-hand column, and then on "Office Divisions"

(4) Contact Fiscal Officer
from http://www.co.summit.oh.us/fiscaloffice/index.htm, click on "Contact Fiscal Officer"

email address for Fiscal Officer: summittreas@summitoh.net

(5) Fiscal Office News Releases
from http://www.co.summit.oh.us/fiscaloffice/index.htm, click on "Press Information"

Click on "January 12, 2004, Fiscal Officer provides data on revenues generated from Tax Certificate Lien Sale"

Fiscal Officer John A. Donofrio has announced that his recent Tax Certificate Lien Sale, held on October 25, 2003, has brought in over $3.9 million delinquent tax dollars from 2351 parcels consisting of residential, commercial and industrial properties. Donofrio stated that over $12.1 million in delinquent taxes has been collected from August 2003 through early December 2003. That includes $1.5 million collected in delinquent special assessments.

ROGUE INVESTOR NOTE: More information available on web page.

(6) Phone Numbers
http://www.co.summit.oh.us/phonebook/PhoneBookPage04.html#Auditor

John A. Donofrio, Fiscal Officer
Ohio Building, Room 400
175 S. Main Street
Akron, Ohio 44308-1306
FAX: (330) 643-2622
General Information: 330- 643-2630
John Donofrio, Fiscal Officer: 330-643-7934
Melinda Gullace, Assistant to Fiscal Officer: 330-643-7934
Nikki Sipe, Support Services Administrator: 330-643-2718

SHERIFF'S OFFICE
http://www.co.summit.oh.us/sheriff/index.htm

(1) Contact
http://www.co.summit.oh.us/sheriff/contact.htm

Phone: (330) 643-2181
Fax: (330) 434-3513
Email: drewalexander@summitsheriff.com

(2) FAQ
http://www.co.summit.oh.us/sheriff/faqsheriff.htm

How does one bid on a foreclosed property? Foreclosure sales are held every Friday at 10:00 a.m. on the first floor of the Summit County Court House, located at 209 S. High Street, Akron, Ohio. The bidding process is competitive and the highest bidder purchases the property. Once bidding is completed, the winning bid purchases must submit 5% of the purchase price with the remaining balance to be paid within thirty days.

May I view the property prior to the sale? There is no formal process to view the property prior to the sale. Some purchasers inquire about the property with the neighbors and others contact the utility companies about rates and usage prior to bidding.

Is cash required in order to purchase or bid? The terms of payment: cash, money order, and cashier's check. Letters of credit or personal checks are not accepted.

How long does it take to obtain the deed after the purchase? Usually all paper work and confirmations take between 6 and 8 weeks; once that is completed, the deed is signed over.

What if I can't produce the balance in thirty days? If the balance is not received within thirty days the purchase is considered a loan with a 10% interest rate on the yearly balance. Also, the person may be charged with contempt of court for failing to abide by the agreement.

(3) Sheriff Sales
http://www.co.summit.oh.us/sheriff/sales.htm

The Sheriff Sales are held on the first floor of the Summit County Courthouse at 209 South High Street, Akron, OH 44308 at 10:00 a.m.

For more information please call: (330) 643-2278
Email: lcampbell@sheriff.summitoh.net

ROGUE INVESTOR NOTE: Web page includes links to Sheriff sales lists.

(3a) Rules Regarding Sheriff Sales
http://www.co.summit.oh.us/sheriff/sheriffsales/rules.htm

(3b) Information Sheet/Instructions Regarding Mortgage Foreclosure Sales
http://www.co.summit.oh.us/sheriff/salesinfo.htm

(3c) Information Sheet/Instructions Regarding Delinquent Tax Sales
http://www.co.summit.oh.us/sheriff/salesinfo-TAX.htm

(3d) Past Sheriff Sales Results
http://www.co.summit.oh.us/sheriff/salesresults.htm

January 23, 2004 http://www.co.summit.oh.us/sheriff/sheriffsales/RESULTS/01-23-04results.htm
January 16, 2004: http://www.co.summit.oh.us/sheriff/sheriffsales/RESULTS/01-16-04results.htm
January 9, 2004: http://www.co.summit.oh.us/sheriff/sheriffsales/RESULTS/01-09-04results.htm
January 2, 2004: http://www.co.summit.oh.us/sheriff/sheriffsales/RESULTS/01-02-04results.htm

ROGUE INVESTOR NOTE: sheriff sale results saved on CD:
USA Tax Lien Info/Ohio/summit_co_OH/[date]_saleresults.htm

(3e) Sheriff Sales Lists

March 5, 2004 Sheriff Sale
http://www.co.summit.oh.us/sheriff/sheriffsales/03-05-04.htm

February 27, 2004 Sheriff Sale
http://www.co.summit.oh.us/sheriff/sheriffsales/02-27-04.htm

February 20, 2004 Sheriff Sale
http://www.co.summit.oh.us/sheriff/sheriffsales/02-20-04.htm

February 13, 2004 Sheriff Sale (100 properties)
http://www.co.summit.oh.us/sheriff/sheriffsales/02-13-04.htm

February 6, 2004 Sheriff Sale
http://www.co.summit.oh.us/sheriff/sheriffsales/02-06-04.htm

January 30, 2004 Sheriff Sale
http://www.co.summit.oh.us/sheriff/sheriffsales/01-30-04.htm

January 23, 2004 Sheriff Sale
http://www.co.summit.oh.us/sheriff/sheriffsales/01-23-04.htm

January 16, 2004 Sheriff Sale
http://www.co.summit.oh.us/sheriff/sheriffsales/01-16-04.htm

January 9, 2004 Sheriff Sale
http://www.co.summit.oh.us/sheriff/sheriffsales/01-09-04.htm

January 2, 2004 Sheriff Sale
http://www.co.summit.oh.us/sheriff/sheriffsales/01-02-04.htm

ROGUE INVESTOR NOTE: Sheriff's sales lists saved on CD:
USA Tax Lien Info/Ohio/summit_co_OH/[date]_saleslist.htm

Tax Lien Sales: Yes

Tax Deed Sales: Yes

Rating: Two Stars (**)

Interest Rate: 8% per year

Sale Period:
Tax lien certificate sales are held the first Monday in October. Tax deed sales are held the second Monday in June and unsold parcels are available over the counter. Oklahoma also has over the counter tax sales if tax certificates are not sold for 2 years.

Redemption Period: 2 years

Bidding Process:
On properties where there are no bidders the county buys the tax lien certificates. These certificates are assignable to any person provided application for assignment is applied for on or before the first day of the advertisement of the tax "resale." If more than one bidder is interested in a tax certificate on a property, then a drawing is held.

State-Specific Information:
There are 77 counties in Oklahoma. Oklahoma has what is titled a "resale" when the county acquires tax certificates not redeemed within the time provided by law. At this tax resale it is possible to actually acquire the property for the total amount of taxes, penalties, and costs due at the time of the tax resale. The minimum bid is the amount of taxes, penalties, interest and costs due at that time.

Links for All Oklahoma Counties: Provided on CD.

Detailed County-Specific Information:

OKLAHOMA COUNTY, OKLAHOMA
http://www.oklahomacounty.org

TREASURER'S OFFICE
http://www.oklahomacounty.org/Treasurer

Downtown Office Location:
320 Robert S. Kerr
Room 307
Oklahoma City OK 73102
Phone: (405) 713-1300
Fax: (405) 713-7158
County Treasurer, Forrest "Butch" Freeman

The Treasurer's office also manages County-owned property acquired at annual sales of real estate for delinquent taxes. The Treasurer also may sell these pieces of property, upon approval of the Board of County Commissioners.

Some Important Dates Related to Tax Sales

The first Monday in October: Tax Lien Sale for previous year tax that is delinquent.

September 3 and 10: Publications for the Lien Sale for current delinquent Real Estate taxes to be held the first Monday in October.

(1) Brief Tax Lien Sale Information

http://www.oklahomacounty.org/Treasurer/LeinSales/BriefTaxLienSaleInformation2.htm

Under mandatory statutes the County Treasurer must advertise and offer for "Sale" all real estate tax liens which are delinquent in a local newspaper. A mailing list is not available. The information is on request only. Although designated as a "Sale," it is merely a sale of the tax lien of the County, acquired by virtue of the delinquent taxes. It is not an actual "Sale" of the property, at this time. The "Sale" is conducted the first Monday in October. The amount received for the tax lien can only be for the same amount of the delinquent taxes plus interest, advertising and costs. At this time the County Treasurer will issue to the purchaser of the tax lien a "Tax Certificate" which evidences the payment. The certificate will bear eight per cent interest per annum until redeemed by the record owner of the property, or someone with a legal or equitable interest in the property. At the end of two years, from the date of the lien sale certificate, the certificate holder may then apply for a tax deed to the property. Sixty days after application for tax deed is applied for, if no redemption has been made, a tax deed will be issued to the certificate holder. We do not check for other liens and encumbrances. That is the responsibility of the certificate holder.

If a lien is not sold, it is retained by the County and subject to a later sale, designated as a "Resale." If no redemption has been made of property liens still held by the County, an actual sale of the property is held approximately two and one-half years from the date of the Original October Tax Lien Sale. According to State Statutes this sale is to be held the Second Monday in June, after the publication of properties involved for four consecutive weeks prior to the Resale in a newspaper in the County. This sale is an actual auction for cash. If no one buys the Property at the "Resale," actual deeds are issued to the County, and the property is removed for the list of taxable properties in the County.

According to State Statutes, the County Treasurer may sell any property acquired by the County at Resale. This is subject to approval of the Board of County Commissioners at its discretion. The Board of County Commissioners has the power to reject any and all bids. Bids must first be presented in writing to the County Treasurer's Office.

There is a list available of all of the County Owned properties in the Treasurer's Office for a cost of $20.00, plus postage.

(2) Lien Sale Instructions

http://www.oklahomacounty.org/Treasurer/LeinSales/LIENSALEINSTRUCTIONS2.htm

The amount of interest earned by the certificate holder is an annual eight per cent (8%) per year. Cost for issuance of the certificate is $10.50. Bidders will be required to pay for any bids made with certified funds or cash. Certificates will be issued only in the name of the original bidder. If more than one person is interested in the same property, those bidders numbers are placed in a box and one drawn to determine who receives the tax certificate. Property will be offered on a first come first serve basis. Current taxes should be endorsed to your certificate, as soon as possible after January 15, 2004 and must be endorsed prior to the next year's publication.

In the event a bankruptcy is filed on any property on which a certificate has been issued, the Certificate Holder will be given the following two choices:

SURRENDER YOUR TAX SALE CERTIFICATE AND BE REFUNDED THE AMOUNT OF MONEY THAT YOU PAID FOR THE CERTIFICATE WITHOUT ANY INTEREST. THERE IS NO STATUTORY AUTHORITY TO PAY INTEREST IN THESE SITUATIONS.

KEEP THE TAX SALE CERTIFICATE AND PURSUE YOUR RIGHT TO FILE YOUR CLAIM FOR PAYMENT THROUGH THE BANKRUPTCY COURT. PLEASE BE ADVISED IF YOU CHOOSE THIS OPTION YOU DO SO AT YOUR OWN RISK AND IT IS POSSIBLE THAT ALL OR A PORTION OF

YOUR BANKRUPTCY CLAIM COULD BE DENIED BY THE BANKRUPTCY COURT. IF THAT SHOULD HAPPEN TO OCCUR THE COUNTY WILL NOT BE RESPONSIBLE FOR YOUR LOSS.

ROGUE INVESTOR NOTE: Web page includes additional information.

(3) Lien Sale Publication
http://www.oklahomacounty.org/Treasurer/LeinSales/leinsale2.htm

ROGUE INVESTOR NOTE: Information is for October 2003 sale.

(4) Resale Instructions
http://www.oklahomacounty.org/Treasurer/Resales/RESALEINSTRUCTIONS2.htm

THIS IS FOR INFORMATION ONLY AND SUBJECT TO CHANGE WITHOUT NOTICE

To Whom It May Concern:

The Oklahoma County Treasurer's Office has changed the procedures on the June resale of property sold for delinquent taxes. Due to the high volume of returned items, on the day of the sale all bids must be paid in cash. We will allow cash deposits to be made and put on trust with our office any time before the date of sale. If you would like to put check or money orders on trust you must present these items to our office in time to clear your bank. (Allow at least ten days.) You must present our office proof that your check has cleared your bank five days before the sale.

If you need any more details regarding these changes, please contact our office at 405-713-1300.

ALL RESALE BIDDERS MUST BE 18 YEARS OR OLDER IN ORDER TO BID ON PROPERTY.

All Successful Bids include the amount bid and any other taxes, cost, abstract fee, and Resale advertising. Once property is auctioned off, sale will stop. The bidder then pays for property by cash. The sale of property will continue once all transactions are complete.

Deeds on Property sold will be sent to the successful bidder after the same has been filed with the Registrar of Deeds in the County Clerk's Office. The Treasurer shall collect $10.00 for each deed issued and an additional filing fee of $15.00. Receipt must be submitted to the County Treasurer's Office before the recorded deed will be given.

If any person is bidding for someone else or in the name of any firm or corporation, it should be so reported to the Clerk of the Resale as the deed form prescribed by state statutes require such information.

All property must be sold for a sum not less than two-thirds of the assessed value of such real estate as fixed for the current fiscal year, or for the total amount of taxes, penalties, interest and cost due on such property, whichever is the lesser. However, all statutory fees, costs due to advertising, abstracting and treasurer's cost will be due in addition to the final bid. If there is no bid, a deed will be issued to the County, but the County cannot bid.

**In accordance with court decisions, and not Statutory Law, Tax Deeds only affect satisfaction of the taxes as listed in the official Resale Advertising publications. Other classes of Taxes are not affected and all Taxes of every nature are to be paid in addition to the amount bid for any properties in the Resale. We will attempt to advise you of all types of Taxes that the Treasurer's Office knows is delinquent and payable at this time, but we will not guarantee the amount. A Resale Deed will not affect future installments as they become due on special assessments; such as paving, sewer, water, or any other lawful tax.

ROGUE INVESTOR NOTE: Web page includes additional information.

(6) Instructions for Bidding on County-Owned Property
http://www.oklahomacounty.org/Treasurer/INSTFORBIDSONCOUNTYOWNEDPROP2.htm

SHERIFF'S OFFICE
http://www.oklahomacounty.org/sheriff/default.htm

Sheriff John Whetsel
201 N. Shartel
Oklahoma City, OK 73102
Phone: 405-713-1000

(1) Sheriff's Foreclosure Sales
http://www.oklahomacounty.org/sheriff/SheriffSales/SaleNotice.htm

NOTICE OF SHERIFF'S FORECLOSURE SALES, OKLAHOMA COUNTY

Publication of Sales
Published one time each week, for two consecutive weeks, at least thirty days prior to date of sale.
Published in area newspapers in which property is located.

Location of Sales
Oklahoma County Courthouse Annex Building
320 Robert S. Kerr, Room 103
Oklahoma City, Oklahoma

Time of Sales
Tuesdays, 2:00 p.m.

Requirements to Purchase
Minimum Bid must be at least 2/3 of the appraised price of the property.
Down payment of at least ten percent (10%) of purchase price due within 24 hours of sale.
Certified funds are required, made payable to Patricia Presley, Court Clerk.
Any Sale is subject to cancellation by the plaintiff.

For Further Information Contact
Carolyn Price
Oklahoma County Sheriff's Office
Phone: 405-713-1056
Email: carpri@oklahomacounty.org

Sheriff Sales January 2004: http://www.oklahomacounty.org/sheriff/SheriffSales/Jan2004.htm
Sheriff Sales February 2004: http://www.oklahomacounty.org/sheriff/SheriffSales/Feb2004.htm
Sheriff Sales March 2004: http://www.oklahomacounty.org/sheriff/SheriffSales/Mar2004.htm
Sheriff Sales April 2004: http://www.oklahomacounty.org/sheriff/SheriffSales/Apr2004.htm
Sheriff Sales May 2004: http://www.oklahomacounty.org/sheriff/SheriffSales/May2004.htm
Sheriff Sales June 2004: http://www.oklahomacounty.org/sheriff/SheriffSales/Jun2004.htm
Sheriff Sales July 2004: http://www.oklahomacounty.org/sheriff/SheriffSales/Jul2004.htm
Sheriff Sales August 2004: http://www.oklahomacounty.org/sheriff/SheriffSales/Aug2004.htm
Sheriff Sales September 2004: http://www.oklahomacounty.org/sheriff/SheriffSales/Sep2004.htm
Sheriff Sales October 2004: http://www.oklahomacounty.org/sheriff/SheriffSales/Oct2004.htm
Sheriff Sales November 2004: http://www.oklahomacounty.org/sheriff/SheriffSales/Nov2004.htm
Sheriff Sales December 2004: http://www.oklahomacounty.org/sheriff/SheriffSales/Dec2004.htm

---

TULSA COUNTY, OKLAHOMA
http://www.tulsacounty.org

TREASURER
from http://www.tulsacounty.org, click on "Departments/Divisions" in left-hand column, and then on "Treasurer"

Treasurer Dennis Semler
Phone: (918) 596-5071
Fax: (918) 596-5029

Tulsa County Administration Building
500 S. Denver, 3rd Floor
Tulsa, Oklahoma 74103-3840

Property Auction
The Treasurer's Office conducts a public auction on the second Monday of each June. The auction is for the sale of real estate for non-payment of ad valorem property taxes or non-payment of special assessments such as cleaning and mowing. On an average year, Tulsa County will auction 150 to 200 such properties. The sale is open to the public and all properties are sold to the highest bidder. Lists of these properties become available from our office in May preceding the June auction.

Properties for Sale

(1) Message to Buyers
from http://www.tulsacounty.org, click on "Properties for Sale" in left-hand column, and then on "Message to Buyers"

Delinquent Tax Department
phone: (918) 596-5080 or 596-5070

(2) General Information
from http://www.tulsacounty.org, click on "Properties for Sale" in left-hand column and then on "General Information"

COMMISSIONERS' SALE OF TULSA COUNTY PROPERTIES ACQUIRED AT RESALES

PLACE BID ALONG WITH A DEPOSIT IN THE AMOUNT OF $126.00 PER PARCEL.
A. Bid amount. (Can be any amount.)
B. $126.00 for costs and fees as follows:
- $110.00, legal publication*
- $15.00, County Clerk's filing fee
- $1.00, Treasurer's deed fee
- $126.00, TOTAL

*The costs for publication will be paid from an invoice from the publisher. The costs may be less, but not more than, the amount collected. Any balance will be refunded. If you are bidding on multiple parcels, you may request to have the advertising costs combined.

A PUBLIC AUCTION WILL BE SCHEDULED APPROXIMATELY SIXTY (60) DAYS FROM THE DATE OF THE PROPOSED BID.
- A. Thirty (30) days for Commissioners to inspect property, and accept or deny bid.
- B. If accepted, the bid will be published for three (3) consecutive weeks.
- C. The auction will be held on the fourth week.

IF THE SALE IS APPROVED, A DEED IN FEE SIMPLE TITLE WILL BE ISSUED WHEN SIGNED BY THE CHAIRMAN OF THE BOARD OF COUNTY COMMISSIONERS.

FOR FURTHER INFORMATION CALL THE TULSA COUNTY TREASURER'S OFFICE - DELINQUENT TAX DEPARTMENT AT: 596-5070, 596-5078, 596-5080 or 596-5047.

(3) Request to Bid
from http://www.tulsacounty.org, click on "Properties for Sale" in left-hand column and then on "Request to Bid"

(4) List of Properties
from http://www.tulsacounty.org, click on "Properties for Sale" in left-hand column and then on "List of Properties"

The attached list represents properties which have been acquired by Tulsa County through prior tax resales. Pursuant to Title 68, § 3135 of the Oklahoma Statutes, all property acquired by Tulsa County at resale may be sold by the County Treasurer after notice by publication for three (3) consecutive weeks, stating a bid has been received and setting a date for the sale. The sale takes the form of an auction with the subject property being sold to the highest bidder. The Board of County Commissioners then either accept or reject the successful bid. If accepted, a deed conveying the title to the successful bidder will be executed.

Please be advised that this list of properties is only provided as a guide for prospective bidders.

THE TULSA COUNTY TREASURER DOES NOT GUARANTEE THE ACCURACY OF ANY STREET ADDRESS, LEGAL DESCRIPTION, OR OTHER INFORMATION HEREIN.

***** BUYER BEWARE *****

Some of the properties acquired by Tulsa County at resales, beginning with the resale held June of 1998, may have taxes or other assessments which were not advertised prior to the resale. The Tulsa County District Attorney's Office has advised that these taxes or assessments were not extinguished as a result of the resale, and are still due. Before placing a bid on these properties, it is recommended that you inquire about any unadvertised taxes or assessments that may remain unpaid.

These properties are subject to being sold again at a future county sale if these taxes or assessments remain unpaid.

(4a) Property Listings
from http://www.tulsacounty.org/ click on "Properties for Sale" in left-hand column, and then "List of Properties" and then "Browse Property Listings"

ROGUE INVESTOR NOTE: List revised as of August 1, 2003.

SHERIFF'S OFFICE
http://www.tcso.org

Sheriff Stanley Glanz
Email: sglanz@tcso.org

The Sheriff's Office currently has two locations:

Courthouse
500 S. Denver, Tulsa, Oklahoma 74103
phone: 918-596-5601
Fax: 918-596-5697

Faulkner Building
303 W. 1st
Tulsa, Oklahoma 74103
phone: 918-596-5701

(1) Auction Foreclosure Sales Instruction Sheet
http://www.tcso.org/auctionsale/prod01.htm

The Tulsa County Sheriff is ordered to sell foreclosed properties. The foreclosed property sales are held Tuesdays and Thursdays at 10:00 A.M. in Room 119 of the Tulsa County Courthouse Administration Building. The properties are not sold in any particular order. The foreclosed property sale list is updated on Thursday afternoon. Recalls must be filed with the Sheriff Office before the start of the sale to prevent the sale of a property. When the courthouse is unexpectedly closed (weather, etc.), all sales for that date will be re-scheduled at a later date. The Sale of foreclosed properties is open auctions and anyone can bid. Bidding will begin at two-thirds of the appraised value, and the plaintiff gets the first bid. The successful bidder will be asked to provide identification and a phone number at the time of sale. The successful bidder must have a cashier's check payable to Tulsa County Court Clerk for 10% of the bid price in the Sheriff's Office by 11:00 A.M. the following day. The remaining 90% is due upon confirmation of the sale (approximately 3 weeks after the date of sale). Foreclosed properties may be occupied. For information about the property you may contact the plaintiff's attorney listed on the foreclosed property sale list.

For additional Information:
Sheriff's Office, Civil Desk: phone: 918-596-5663 / email: civil@TCSO.org
County Court Clerk, Civil Court Clerk: phone: 918-596-5430

(2) Auction Page
http://www.tcso.org/auctionsale/AuctionOptionsPage.htm

Welcome to the Auction Page. This page will allow you to decide your very own option of viewing the Auction Sales List. There are 4 different formats and 5 different options:

If you have any problems viewing or downloading the list, call 918-596-5661 or email cbyers@tcso.org.

ROGUE INVESTOR NOTE: See web page to download auction sales lists.

(3) Auction listing for January 2004
http://www.tcso.org/auctionsale/Public%20Auction%20Report.html

ROGUE INVESTOR NOTE: information saved on CD:
USA Tax Lien Info/oklahoma/Tulsa_co_OK/Jan04_auction_listing.htm

Tax Lien Sales: No

Tax Deed Sales: Yes

Rating: Two Stars (**)

Interest Rate: None, only has tax deed sales.

Sale Period:
County Sheriffs conduct the sales, which are known as Sheriff's Sale of Surplus County-Owned Real Property. Registration before sales is required in every county. Lists of properties are available from county Property Management Departments.

Redemption Period:
Oregon statutes refer to the two-year time frame of the county hold as a redemption period. The property owner no longer has any redemption rights after the property is deeded to the county.

Bidding Process:
Minimum bids are usually set at 80% of the Assessed Value, not the fair market value, and are set by the County Board of Commissioners for sale. The sales are held in an oral, open, and competitive format. Payment for successful bids is expected in certified funds. Some counties provide financing for properties for which the minimum bid exceeds a certain dollar amount. This amount varies from county to county.

State-Specific Information:
Oregon has a total of 36 counties. Foreclosure of tax liens and the sale of properties foreclosed on are handled slightly different in Oregon than any other state.

Taxes become delinquent if not paid by August l6 of each year. After they are delinquent for a period of 2 years they become subject to foreclosure. Tax liens are foreclosed by the county and the county receives a deed to the property. The property owner no longer has any redemption rights after the property is deeded to the county. Thereafter, the county can sell the property at public auction or in some cases at a private sale.

Taxes on real property shall be a lien from there on and including July 1 of the year in which they are levied until paid.

Subsequently, real property taxes are due in three equal installments on or before November 15th of that year, and February 15th and May 15th of the following year for each year levied. Delinquent interest begins to accrue at one and one third percent per month (16% per annum) after these dates.

Real property is subject to foreclosure for delinquent taxes whenever three years have elapsed from the earliest date of delinquency of taxes levied. At that time, the tax collector with the assistance of the district attorney shall institute proceedings in a court of competent jurisdiction to foreclose the liens for all delinquent taxes.

The court shall give judgment that the liens of such taxes be foreclosed. The court shall order that the properties be sold directly to the county. All real properties sold to the county shall be held by the county for a period of two years from and after the date of judgment unless redeemed. The properties not redeemed in this two-year time frame are deeded to the county by the tax collector. All rights of redemption terminate on the execution of the deed to the county.

Basically it takes approximately six years from the original date of delinquency to get a property to auction. However, counties do have the authority to accelerate the redemption period and offer for sale properties under certain conditions.

Oregon statutes do refer to the two-year time frame of county hold as a redemption period.

When a county acquires real property by foreclosure for delinquent taxes, the conveyance vests in the county title to the property, free from all liens and encumbrances except assessments levied by a municipality for local improvements to the property.

Some Oregon counties are even willing to provide title insurance for properties for which the sale price exceeds a certain dollar amount.

Links for All Oregon Counties: Provided on CD.

Detailed County-Specific Information:

MULTNOMAH COUNTY, OREGON
http://www.co.multnomah.or.us

DIVISION OF ASSESSMENT AND TAXATION
http://www.co.multnomah.or.us/dbcs/assess_tax

Tax Information Line: (503) 988-3326
FAX: (503) 988-3330
Address
501 SE Hawthorne Boulevard
Portland, OR 97214
Mailing Address
Multnomah County Oregon
Assessment & Taxation
P.O. Box 2716
Portland OR 97208-2716

(1) Delinquent Taxes and Lien Dates
http://www.co.multnomah.or.us/dbcs/assess_tax/delinq.shtml

The fiscal year (or tax year) for all property is July 1 through June 30. The assessment date for the tax year is January 1. Personal and real property taxes are a lien from July 1.

Real property taxes become delinquent if not paid by May 15. Foreclosure proceedings will begin on real property after three years from the date taxes become delinquent.

(2) Real Property Foreclosure
http://www.dor.state.or.us/infoc/310-671.html

Telephone, Salem: 503-945-8293
Toll-free within Oregon: 1-800-356-4222

(3) Disposition/Sale of Foreclosed Properties

http://www.co.multnomah.or.us/dbcs/assess_tax/taxtitle.shtml

A public auction of foreclosed properties is typically held once a year. All auctions are oral and open to the public. All successful bidders must post 20% of the minimum advertised price for any property they purchase at the time of the auction. The remainder of the purchase price must be paid within 3 business days of the auction. The only acceptable forms of payment are cash or cashier's check. The property is sold to the highest bidder who meets or exceeds the minimum price. There is no assignment purchasing allowed and no tax certificates are issued. All properties are sold "as is". Properties that do not sell at the public auction are placed on a future public auction or disposed of as otherwise provided by law.

The County may enter into a private sale of certain tax-foreclosed properties if (1) the property is valued at less than $5,000 and (2) the local planning and zoning jurisdiction determines that the parcel is not suitable for the construction or placement of a dwelling. The County's policy with respect to properties that qualify for private sales is to first offer them to adjacent property owners.

Notification of properties to be sold at auction

If you are interested in being notified of the next scheduled auction, please send your name, address, and a self-addressed envelope (minimum 6.5" x 9.5") with 0.74 cents postage to:

Multnomah County Tax Title
Auction List
P.O. Box 2716
Portland, OR 97208

For more information *write* to Gary Thomas or Becky Grace at the above listed P.O. Box number or telephone 503-988-3590 or fax 503-988-3085.

ROGUE INVESTOR NOTE: Web page includes additional information.

(4) Oral Public Auction Rules

http://www.co.multnomah.or.us/dbcs/assess_tax/auction/rules.shtml

The day of the Auction all participants should bring funds equal to 20% of the minimum advertised price for each property they wish to acquire. Successful bidders must make a 20% down payment of the minimum bid for each property at the time the bidding for that property is closed. The individual payment for that property must be in the form of cash or certified funds. Cashier's checks should be made out to Multnomah County Tax Title. Personal checks and business checks will not be accepted.

If a purchaser fails to complete the purchase of the property within 3 business days of the auction, Multnomah County will retain 1% of the minimum purchase price or $1000, whichever is greater.

If a purchaser fails to complete the purchase after 3 business days, the entire 20% deposit will be non-refundable.

The property shall be sold to the highest bidder who meets or exceeds the minimum advertised price.

ROGUE INVESTOR NOTE: Web page includes additional information.

(5) Terms of Cash Sale

http://www.co.multnomah.or.us/dbcs/assess_tax/auction/terms.shtml

SHERIFF'S OFFICE
http://www.co.multnomah.or.us/sheriff

phone: (503) 988-4300
Fax: (503) 988-4320

Administrative Office located at:
501 SE Hawthorne Boulevard, Suite 350
Portland, OR 97214

Sheriff Bernie Giusto
Email: webmaster@mcso.us

(1) Auctions
http://www.co.multnomah.or.us/sheriff/auctions.htm

We no longer hold general public auctions for seized property. The Sheriff's Civil Unit conducts auctions of real property on a case-by-case basis and we advertise these sales in the *Daily Journal of Commerce* newspaper. Sorry, we do not maintain a mailing list.

(2) Civil Process Unit
http://www.co.multnomah.or.us/sheriff/civil.htm

Civil Process Unit
phone: 503 251-2412
Manager, Captain Garr Nielsen
phone: 503 251-2514

Pennsylvania

Tax Lien Sales: No

Tax Deed Sales: Yes

Rating: Two Stars (**)

Interest Rate: None, state only has tax deed sales.

Sale Period :
Normally, tax sales are held in September of each year after the property taxes have been delinquent for two years. In the event property is not sold at the tax sale auction for the upset price, the property is held over for three months for private sale. If the property still doesn't sell in that three-month span, the court then decides whether to free the property of all liens against it.

Redemption Period: 2 years

Bidding Process: It depends on the county. Usually the minimum bid is back taxes, penalties and fees; however, additional state liens can be assessed.

State-Specific Information: There are 67 counties in Pennsylvania.

Links for All Pennsylvania Counties: Provided on CD.

Detailed County-Specific Information:

ALLEGHENY COUNTY, PENNSYLVANIA
http://www.county.allegheny.pa.us/index.asp

TREASURER'S OFFICE
http://www.county.allegheny.pa.us/treasure/index.asp

John Weinstein, County Treasurer
Courthouse Room 108
436 Grant Street
Pittsburgh, PA 15219-2497
email: webmaster.treasurer@county.allegheny.pa.us
Lien Tax Payments or Information: 412-350-3847
Real Estate Tax Information or Toll Free (1-866-282-TAXS): 412-350-4100, 412-350-4101, 412-350-4105

(1) Real Estate and Tax Information
http://www.county.allegheny.pa.us/treasure/tax.asp

SHERIFF'S OFFICE
http://trfn.clpgh.org/acsd/welcome.shtml

Sheriff Peter DeFazio
Phone: 412-350-4700
Fax: 412-350-6388

(1) County Calendar
http://www.county.allegheny.pa.us/calendar

Click on "Sheriff's Sale" (e.g., Monday, February 2nd) to get information on Sheriff's Sales.

ROGUE INVESTOR NOTE: 2004 sheriff's sales are scheduled for January 5, 2004, and February 2, 2004.

(2) Sheriff Sales
http://trfn.clpgh.org/acsd/shersale.html

Where are the Sheriff Sales held?
The Sheriff Sales are held in the Gold Room on the 4th floor of the Allegheny County Courthouse, 436 Grant Street, Pittsburgh, Pennsylvania 15219.

When do the Sheriff's Sales take place?
The Sheriff's Sale is the first Monday of every month from 9:00 a.m. to 4:30 p.m. In the event of a holiday, the sale will fall on Tuesday.

Where are the Sheriff Sales advertised?
The Sheriff Sales are advertised in alternating newspapers, the Tribune Review and the Pittsburgh Post Gazette. The sales are always advertised in the Legal Journal as well. The Sheriff sales are advertised for three Mondays prior to the sale.

What methods of payment are accepted?
The Sheriff's Office accepts cash, cashier's checks and money orders. The cashier's checks and money orders should be made payable to the Sheriff of Allegheny County.

How much money is required at the time of the Sheriff's Sale?
At the time of sale, you must bring 10% of the bid price. The balance is due the Friday following the sale before 10:00 a.m.

Is any property research required before the Sheriff's Sale?
The Sheriff's Office strongly recommends doing a complete title search. Please visit the following offices: Register of Wills, Prothonotary, Recorder of Deeds, Federal Clerk of Courts, and the County Treasurer. Also take time to contact the local taxing body where the property is located. This will also help you to decide whether to buy the property or not.

2004 Sale Dates: January 5, February 2

ROGUE INVESTOR NOTE: Web page also includes General Announcements.

BUCKS COUNTY, PENNSYLVANIA
http://www.buckscounty.org

TAX CLAIM BUREAU
http://www.buckscounty.org/departments/tax_claim_bureau/index.html

The Tax Claim Bureau provides for the efficient collection of delinquent real estate taxes and the return of properties to the tax rolls.

The Bureau receives over 10,000 liens each year. Over 8,000 liens are settled either through receipt of payment or an agreement to stay sale of property. The Bureau also remains in constant contact with the public and their financial problems regarding these liens.

(1) Request for Tax Lien Certificate
http://www.buckscounty.org/departments/tax_claim_bureau/Tax_Lien_Cert.htm

(2) Contact Information
http://www.buckscounty.org/departments/tax_claim_bureau/index.html

Tax Claim Bureau
55 East Court Street
Third Floor, Administration Building
Doylestown, PA 18901
Phone: 215-348-6274

SHERIFF'S DEPARTMENT
http://www.buckscounty.org/departments/sheriff/index.html

The Sheriff's Department handles foreclosures on delinquent mortgages and final sale of real estate, approximately 100 per month.

Sheriff's Department
Bucks County Court House
55 E. Court Street, 1st Floor
Doylestown, PA 18901
Phone: 215-348-6124

DELAWARE COUNTY, PENNSYLVANIA
http://www.co.delaware.pa.us

TAX CLAIM BUREAU OF TREASURER'S OFFICE
http://www.co.delaware.pa.us/treasurer/taxclaim.html

Director Josephine Rizzo
Government Center, Ground Floor
201 W. Front Street
Media, PA 19063
Phone: 610-891-4293
Fax: 610-891-4115

Properties are auctioned for sale annually in the fall in what is known as the Upset price sale. Unsold properties from the Upset Price Sale are auctioned again in the spring, free and clear of liens, by permission of the Court in what is known as the Judicial Sale. Properties failing a successful sale here are held by the County on a Repository List. These properties can be purchased at any time, save the weeks immediately following the auction sales, by visiting the Tax Claim Bureau.

Managed by the Tax Claim Bureau, for non-payment of taxes: (1) Upset Price Sale, (2) Judicial Sale, (3) Repository Sale.

Managed by the Sheriff's Office (610-891-430) for non-payment of mortgages: Sheriff's Sale.

(1) Upset Sales

(1a) Upset Price Sale
http://www.co.delaware.pa.us/judicalsale/upsetpricesale.html

Director John A. Dowd
Government Center, Ground Floor
210 W. Front Street
Media, PA 19063
Phone: 610-891-4284
Fax: 610-891-4115

Instructions and Procedures for Upset Sale:
http://www.co.delaware.pa.us/judicalsale/instructupsetsale.html

For more information, please contact the Upset Sale Coordinator at 610-891-4284.

Disclaimer:
Note that action taken by a property owner, the Courts, Government Agencies and/or the Tax Claim Bureau may result in deleting a listed property from the UPSET PRICE SALE at any time.

(2) Judicial Sales
http://www.co.delaware.pa.us/judicalsale/judicialsale.html

Director John A. Dowd
Government Center, Ground Floor
210 W. Front Street
Media, PA 19063
Phone: 610-891-4399
Fax: 610-891-7257

The 2003 Sale has taken place. Properties for sale (Spring 2004) will be listed at this web site and various publications 30 days prior to a yet to be determined 2004 sale date.

The Tax Claim Bureau of Delaware County will conduct a public sale of properties, to be determined. If need be, because of the volume of properties, the sale may be continued on to be determined. The sale will be held in the County Council meeting room on the first floor of the Government Center Building, 201 W. Front Street, Media, PA.

The purpose of the sale is to offer the properties to the highest bidder free and clear of all tax and municipal claims, mortgages, judgments, charges and estates of whatsoever (due at the time of sale) except ground rents separately taxed.

A registration fee of $600.00 will be required for admittance into the public sale. The registration fee is payable to the Tax Claim Bureau. Registration fee must be paid by treasurer/cashier checks or money orders made out to the Tax Claim Bureau. The registration will admit 2 (two). Fee will be applied towards the purchase of property/properties; it is non-refundable if the sale is not finalized. If no purchase is made the fee will be refunded. The registration to be determined at a future date in the spring of 2004. No registration on the day of the sale.

The initial bid shall start at $ 600.00 plus state and local transfer tax and all recording costs. The Bid price must be paid by treasurer/cashier check or money orders payable to the Tax Claim Bureau. Separate treasurer/cashier checks or money orders will be required for the state and local transfer tax and costs. All payments must be paid no later than 1 (one) hour before the close of business on the day the sale is held or at such other date and time designated by the Bureau.

Prior advertisement of the properties can be found in issues of the Delaware County Legal Journal, Daily Times, Chester Times, Upper Darby Press, Marcus Hook Press, Yeadon Courier and the News of Delaware County. Issues dates are 1930 thru 2002 depending on date of Treasurer sale, Commissioner sale, or Upset Price sale. Please call for dates if needed.

Judicial Sale Coordinator
Delaware County Tax Claim Bureau
Government Center Building
Media, Pennsylvania

Instructions and Procedures for Judicial Sale:
http://www.co.delaware.pa.us/judicalsale/instructionsandprocedures.html

Disclaimer:
Note that action taken by a property owner, the Courts, Government Agencies and/or the Tax Claim Bureau may result in deleting a listed property from the JUDICIAL SALE at any time.

(3) Repository Sales
http://www.co.delaware.pa.us/judicalsale/repossale.html

Director John A. Dowd
Government Center, Ground Floor
210 W. Front Street
Media, PA 19063
Phone: 610-891-4824
Fax: 610-891-4115

Current Repository Sale List: http://www.co.delaware.pa.us/judicalsale/repossale.pdf

For more information, please contact the Repository Sales Coordinator at 610-891-4294.

Disclaimer:
Note that action taken by a property owner, the Courts, Government Agencies and/or the Tax Claim Bureau may result in deleting a listed property from the JUDICIAL SALE at any time.

ROGUE INVESTOR NOTE: information saved on CD:
USA Tax Lien Info/Pennsylvania/delaware_co_PA/current_repos_sales_list.pdf

OFFICE OF THE SHERIFF
http://www.co.delaware.pa.us/sheriff

Sheriff: Joseph McGinn
Courthouse, Room 101201
W. Front Street
Media, PA 19063
Phone: 610-891-4296
Fax: 610-891-1765

Real Estate Administrator, phone: 610-891-4305
Real Estate Clerk, phone: 610-891-4875

http://www.co.delaware.pa.us/sheriff/phoneguide.html = phone guide to Sheriff's Office

(1) Real Estate
http://www.co.delaware.pa.us/sheriff/realestate.html

List of Current Properties up for Sheriff Sales
List of Properties Continued from Prior Months
Other Property Sale Information

Sheriff's Sale Disclaimer: This is the sale list for this month. Changes in the status of each property may occur during the month. For updated information, you can call 610-891-4305 or email the Sheriff's Office at the numbers provided herein. A new list of properties is posted each month.

Frequently Asked Questions

When do the Sheriff's Sales take place? Sales take place on the third Friday of each Month at 11:00 A.M. If the third Friday is a holiday, the sale will be held on Thursday

Where are the Sheriff's Sales held? Sales are held in the County Council Meeting Room on the first floor of the Government Center Building, Delaware County Court House, Front Street & Veterans Square, Media, PA.

Can I obtain a list of the properties to be sold? Yes. For each property to be sold there is a handbill posted in the Sheriff's Office at the Delaware County Court House and an advertisement in the local newspaper where the property is situated will appear once a week for the three weeks before the sale. In addition, there is a desk copy of the list for each month's sale available for reference in the Sheriff's Office. Copies of the list may also be purchased for $5.00.

If I see a property I want to buy, can I inspect it before the sale? No, the properties are not available for inspection.

How do I buy a property at Sheriff's Sale? You need to attend the sale at the date and time advertised. The sale is a public auction and you will have to bid for the property.

What is hand money? Hand money is the deposit you have to pay in cash or by certified check at the time of the sale.

When do I have to pay the rest of the money? The balance of your bid is payable within ten calendar days to the Sheriff in cash or by certified check. If you do not pay the balance of your bid, you lose your hand money.

Why does the Sheriff's Office highly recommend that you consult your own attorney for advice about how to purchase property at Sheriff's Sale? Just for one example, you may buy a property with numerous liens requiring you to pay a lot more money than what you bid for the property, that you must under the law pay to these lien holders to clear what is now YOUR Title (read your problem).

Do Sheriff's Sales differ from Tax Sales or Judicial Sales? Yes, there are significant differences. For information about Tax Sales or Judicial Sales, contact the Delaware County Tax Claim Bureau in the Government Center Building at the Courthouse in Media or call 610-891-4281.

(1a) List of Current Properties up for Sheriff Sales
http://www.co.delaware.pa.us/sheriff/list1.pdf

Real Estate Sale for February 20, 2004

ROGUE INVESTOR NOTE: information saved on CD:
USA Tax Lien Info/Pennsylvania/delaware_co_PA/current_sales_list.pdf

(1b) List of Properties Continued from Prior Months
http://www.co.delaware.pa.us/sheriff/list2.pdf

Continued List for February 20, 2004

ROGUE INVESTOR NOTE: information saved on CD:
USA Tax Lien Info/Pennsylvania/delaware_co_PA/continued_sales_list.pdf

---

MONTGOMERY COUNTY, PENNSYLVANIA
http://www.montcopa.org

TAX CLAIM BUREAU
http://www.montcopa.org/taxclaim

One Montgomery Plaza
Swede and Airy Streets
P.O. Box 311
Norristown, PA 19404
Phone: 610-278-3570
Fax Number: 610-278-3869

Commissioners
Michael D. Marino, Esq.
Chairman
James R. Matthews
Ruth S. Damsker
Garrett D. Page, Treasurer and Director
M. Elizabeth McBride, Deputy Treasurer

The Tax Claim Bureau is responsible for the collection of past due real estate taxes. The Tax Claim Bureau also conducts tax sales (http://www.montcopa.org/taxclaim/default.asp) on those parcels whose taxes remain delinquent. The Tax Claim Bureau acts as the agent for all taxing districts in the County.

(1) Tax Sales
http://www.montcopa.org/taxclaim/default.asp

The Montgomery County Tax Claim Bureau uses, as its guide, the Pennsylvania Real Estate Tax Sale Law, Act 542 of 1947, as amended through the 1999-2000 Legislative Sessions.

In accordance with the Tax Sale law, the Tax Claim Bureau is able to sell parcels in one of four ways: (1) Upset Sale, (2) Private Sale, (3) Judicial Sale, and (4) Repository Sale.

(1) The **Upset Sale** is scheduled each September and includes those parcels (http://www.montcopa.org/taxclaim/properties.asp) whose taxes, from two years earlier, remain unpaid or other specified conditions exist. Properties scheduled to be presented for Upset Sale (http://www.montcopa.org/taxclaim/properties.asp) are advertised in two newspapers and the Montgomery Bar Association journal within two months of the sale. Purchasers of property at the Upset Sale assume responsibility for all liens on the property. To read conditions of Upset Sales click here: http://www.montcopa.org/taxclaim/upsetsalesconditions.htm.

(2) A **Private Sale** can occur after a property has been exposed but not sold at an Upset Sale. An interested buyer submits a written bid to the Tax Claim Bureau. The Bureau decides whether to accept the bid. If accepted, the bid is advertised in a newspaper and the Montgomery Bar Association journal. Any one objecting to the sale must petition the court within 45 days to disprove the sale. As in the Upset Sale, purchasers of property via Private Sale assume responsibility for all liens on the property.

(3) A **Judicial Sale** is held at least once each year and can include only those properties that have been exposed but not sold at an Upset Sale (http://www.montcopa.org/taxclaim/judicialproperties.asp). After advertisement, notice to owners and lienholders, etc., the parcels are presented free and clear of all liens.

(4) Properties that are exposed but not sold at a Judicial Sale are placed in a **Repository** for unsold properties (http://www.montcopa.org/taxclaim/repoproperties.asp). Any bid on a Repository Property must be approved by all taxing districts where the property is located (i.e., township borough, county, school).

(1a) Upset Sale Properties
http://www.montcopa.org/taxclaim/properties.asp

ROGUE INVESTOR NOTE: Zero properties listed as of January 28, 2004.

(1b) Conditions of Upset Sales
http://www.montcopa.org/taxclaim/upsetsalesconditions.htm

(1c) Judicial Sale Properties
http://www.montcopa.org/taxclaim/judicialproperties.asp

52 properties listed as of January 28, 2004

ROGUE INVESTOR NOTE: information saved on CD:
USA Tax Lien Info/Pennsylvania/montgomery_co_PA/judicial_properties.htm

(1d) Repository Properties
http://www.montcopa.org/taxclaim/repoproperties.asp

98 properties listed as of January 28, 2004

ROGUE INVESTOR NOTE: information saved on CD:
USA Tax Lien Info/Pennsylvania/montgomery_co_PA/repository_properties.htm

SHERIFF'S DEPARTMENT
http://www.montcopa.org/countyoffices/Sheriff/default.htm

John P. Durante, Sheriff
Montgomery County Sheriff's Office
Court House, 1st Floor
P.O. Box 311 Norristown, PA 19404-0268
phone: (610) 278-3331

The Sheriff conducts sale of real property at the request of litigants, including the city, county and state.

(1) Sheriff Sales on Real Estate
http://www.montcopa.org/sherreal/sheriffsales.htm

Sheriff Sale property information sheets are available in the Sheriff's Office, Court House 1st floor, Norristown, PA (please no phone calls). For directions to the Courthouse click here:
http://www.montcopa.org/montco/direction.htm.

ROGUE INVESTOR NOTE: 2002/2003/2004 dates for sheriff sales on real estate and conditions of sale. Click on a date for a list of properties.

(2) Real Estate Sales Q&A Booklet
http://www.montcopa.org/countyoffices/Sheriff/sheriff_sales__real%20estate_q&a_.htm

---

PHILADELPHIA COUNTY, PENNSYLVANIA
http://www.phila.gov

DEPARTMENT OF REVENUE
http://www.phila.gov/revenue

phone: (215) 686-6600
email address: revenue@phila.gov

(1) Contact Information
http://www.phila.gov/revenue/pdfs/mission_statement.pdf

Nancy Kammerdeiner, Commissioner
Phone: 215-686-6400

For further information about current or delinquent Real Estate taxes, call (215) 686-6442.

Center City Office
Municipal Services Building
1401 John F. Kennedy Boulevard
Philadelphia, PA 19102
Taxpayer service – Public Concourse level

(2) Taxes FAQ
from http://www.phila.gov/faqs/index.html, click on "Taxes"

OFFICE OF THE SHERIFF
http://www.phillysheriff.com

John D. Green, Sheriff
100 South Broad Street, 5th Floor
Philadelphia, PA 19110
Phone: 215-686-3530 / Fax: 215-686-3971
Email: JohnGreen@PhillySheriff.com

(1) View Lien Holder Information on Mortgage Foreclosure Properties
http://www.phillysheriff.com/3129/3129book178.htm

Affidavit Pursuant to Rule 3129

(2) Real Estate Division
http://www.phillysheriff.com/homerealestate.html

The Real Estate Division is responsible for processing court-ordered tax delinquency and mortgage foreclosure sales, most commonly known as Sheriff's Sales. Properties listed for tax and foreclosure sale are not attached by the Sheriff's Office, but rather placed there by order of the court. By law, the Sheriff's Office is mandated to enforce the court-ordered sales.

Nearly every property exposed to Sheriff's Sale is sold, with the exception of those that are stayed or postponed. If the property's legal owner makes arrangements to settle the outstanding debt, the property is stayed, or withheld from sale. If the owner remains in default, the property is scheduled for Sheriff's Sale. Properties that are postponed are done so by a legal motion from the attorney representing the lien holder, namely the City Solicitor's Office in the case of Sheriff's Sales; a tax delinquent lien is presented to the Sheriff's Office by the Law Department. On average, a third of the properties at Sheriff's Sales are sold, a third are stayed, and a third are postponed. Sheriff Green places radio ads to advertise the properties available at the Sheriff's Sales in his effort to open up the Sheriff's Sale process to first-time home buyers who may not have the financial resources required for traditional real estate transactions. These ads are an extension of Sheriff Green's HOPE program.

(3) Conditions of Sheriff's Sales
http://www.phillysheriff.com/homesales.html

Conditions for (1) Judicial/Foreclosure Sale, (2) Tax Delinquent Sale, and (3) Tax Lien Sale.

(3a) Advertising Schedule
from http://www.phillysheriff.com/homesales.html, click on "Advertising Schedule"

Judicial Mortgage Foreclosure Sales Dates

Sale	News Publication	Advertising Dates
January 6, 2004	Philadelphia Daily News	December 15, 22, 39 [2003]
February 3, 2004	Philadelphia Tribune	January 13, 20, 27 [2004]
March 2, 2004	Philadelphia Inquirer	February 9, 16, 23
**April 13, 2004	Philadelphia Daily News	March 22, 29, April 5
May 4, 2004	Philadelphia Tribune	April 13, 20, 27
**June 8, 2004	Philadelphia Inquirer	May 17, 24, 31
July 6 2004	Philadelphia Daily News	June 14, 21, 28
August 3, 2004	Philadelphia Tribune	July 13, 20, 27
**September 14, 2004	Philadelphia Inquirer	August 23, 30, - September 6
October 5, 2004	Philadelphia Daily News	September 13, 20, 27
**November 9, 2004	Philadelphia Tribune	October 19, 26, November 2
December 7, 2004	Philadelphia Inquirer	November 15, 22, 29
January 4, 2005	Philadelphia Daily News	December 13, 20, 27
** denotes 2nd Tuesday of the Month		

Tax Lien Sales Dates

Sale Date	News Publication	Advertising Dates
Jan. 22, 2004	Philadelphia Tribune	Dec. 30, [2003] - Jan. 6, 13 [2004]
Feb. 26, 2004	Philadelphia Daily News	Feb. 2, 9, 16 [2004]
March 25, 2004	Philadelphia Tribune	March 2, 9, 16
April 22, 2004	Philadelphia Daily News	March 29, April 5, 12
May 27, 2004	Philadelphia Tribune	May 4, 11, 18
June 24, 2004	Philadelphia Daily News	May 31, June 7, 14
July 22, 2004	Philadelphia Tribune	June 29 - July 6, 13
August 26, 2004	Philadelphia Daily News	August 2, 9, 16
Sept. 23, 2004	Philadelphia Tribune	August 31, September 7, 14
Oct. 28, 2004	Philadelphia Daily News	October 4, 11, 18
**Nov. 18, 2004	Philadelphia Tribune	October 26, November 2, 9
**Dec. 16, 2004	Philadelphia Daily News	November 22, 29, December 6
Jan. 27, 2005	Philadelphia Tribune	January 4, 11, 18 [2005]

** denotes 3rd Thursday of the Month

Tax Delinquent Sales Dates will be posted soon!

(3b) Mortgage Foreclosure Listings
from http://www.phillysheriff.com/homesales.html, click on "Mortgage Foreclosure Listings"

SHERIFF'S SALE FEBRUARY 3, 2004
194-301 to 194-1121
Properties to be sold by John D. Green
February 3, 2004 10:00 a.m.
The First District Plaza
3801 Market Street, 3rd Floor, Philadelphia, PA
Judicial Mortgage Foreclosure Sale

ROGUE INVESTOR NOTE: information saved on CD:
USA Tax Lien Info/Pennsylvania/philadelphia_co_PA/mortgage_foreclosure_listings.doc

(3c) Tax Lien Listings
from http://www.phillysheriff.com/homesales.html, click on "Tax Lien Listings"

SHERIFF'S SALE FOR February 26, 2004
194-2001 TO 194-2200
Properties to be sold by John D. Green, Sheriff
Thursday, February 26, 2004, 10:00 a.m. at The First District Plaza
3801 Market Street, 3rd Floor, Philadelphia, PA
Tax Lien Sale

ROGUE INVESTOR NOTE: information saved on CD:
USA Tax Lien Info/Pennsylvania/philadelphia_co_PA/tax_lien_listings.doc

(4) Frequently Asked Questions
http://www.phillysheriff.com/answers.html

Tax Lien Sales: Yes

Tax Deed Sales: No

Rating: Three Stars (***)

Interest Rate: 10% penalty for the first six months, plus 1% each additional month up to a total of 16% (one year).

Sale Period: The tax collector of each municipality holds a tax sale once a year, but at no set time.

Redemption Period: 1 year

Bidding Process: Varies, depending on the tax collector of each municipality.

State-Specific Information:
There are 5 counties in Rhode Island. The state of Rhode Island is made up of 39 cities and towns, each of which has its own administration.

After one year the investor is automatically responsible for the property, even before foreclosure. This could create a potential for environmental or other liability that the investor should be aware of. Should the property owner redeem within the one-year redemption period, the holder of the tax deed receives, in additional to the total amount he paid for the deed, a penalty of 10% if redeemed anytime with six months following the tax sale plus 1% for each month after six months. This can provide an extremely high rate of yield to investors in tax certificates.

Rhode Island Division of Compliance and Collections
Phone: 401-222-2957
URL: http://www.tax.ri.gov/lien/xlien.pdf

Links for All Rhode Island Counties: Provided on CD

Tax Lien Sales: Yes

Tax Deed Sales: No

Rating: Two Stars (**)

Interest Rate:
The tax title holder receives only 7% interest unless the alternate method of tax collection is used, in which case the interest amounts to a penalty of 8% if redeemed during the first year of delinquency plus 4% additional penalty if redeemed during the second year.

Sale Period: October

Redemption Period:
The owner of the property has 1 year in which to redeem, unless the alternative method is used as provided by SCRS 12-51-10, in which case the redemption period is 18 months.

Bidding Process: All tax lien auctions are by competitive bid. Money must be paid by the end of the day or you can be fined up to $300 dollars.

State-Specific Information:
There are 46 counties in South Carolina. Tax sales are handled at the county level even though it is done on behalf of the state. Tax titles are sold at the first tax sale.

Links for All South Carolina Counties: Provided on CD.

Detailed County-Specific Information:

CHARLESTON COUNTY, SOUTH CAROLINA
http://www.charlestoncounty.org

DELINQUENT TAX DEPARTMENT
http://www.charlestoncounty.org/index2.asp?p=/departments/d-deltax.htm

Functions include planning, conducting and managing tax sales.

Frequently Asked Questions
Q: How can I purchase properties seized for non-payment of taxes?
A: Attend the tax sales held periodically throughout the year. The dates of delinquent tax sales are advertised in local newspapers before each sale.

Q: If my property is sold at a delinquent tax sale, can I get it back?
A: When real property or mobile homes are sold at a delinquent tax sale, the defaulting taxpayer has one year from the date of the sale to redeem the property. In order to redeem property before it is conveyed to a new owner, the defaulting taxpayer must pay the redemption amount. This consists of the taxes, interest on the bid amount (the amount for which the property was sold at the tax sale) plus penalties.

Q: If my property is sold at a delinquent tax sale, what happens to any leftover money after the taxes, penalties, levy costs and interest are paid?

A: The Delinquent Tax Department creates a "balance-in-trust" when the bid amount exceeds the delinquent taxes, penalties, levy costs and current year's taxes. If the property is conveyed to the bidder, the defaulting taxpayer is entitled to the balance-in-trust. If the delinquent taxpayer redeems the property, the bid amount plus interest is returned to the bidder.

History

Originally, the Delinquent Tax Department was under the jurisdiction of the Charleston County Sheriff. In November 1991, the Department was brought under the control of the County Administrator. In 2001, the Delinquent Tax Department began reporting to the Chief Financial Officer (http://www.charlestoncounty.org/index2.asp?p=/departments/D-Chieffinoff.htm).

Interesting Facts

Each year, this department sells approximately 1,500 to 2,000 properties and generates approximately 300 to 400 quitclaim deeds to new owners.

Contact Information

O.T. Wallace County Office Building
2 Courthouse Square, Room 102
Charleston, SC 29401
Phone: (843) 958-4570
Fax: (843) 958-4577

(1) Information and Instructions – Delinquent Tax Sale

http://www.charlestoncounty.org/index2.asp?p=/departments/del_tax_sale.htm

ROGUE INVESTOR NOTE: This information is for the October 6, 2003 tax sale.

BY VIRTUE OF EXECUTIONS issued by the Treasurer of the County of Charleston, the Delinquent Tax Collector has levied upon and will sell certain pieces and parcels of real property in order to collect delinquent taxes, assessments, penalties and costs. The auction is being held in the Charleston County Council Chambers in the Charleston County Public Service Building at 4045 Bridge View Drive, Charleston, SC beginning at 10 a.m., October 6, 2003 and ending at 4 p.m. that day. If additional days are necessary to complete the auction an announcement will be made to that effect before the close of business each day. The sale on subsequent days (if necessary) will begin promptly at 9:30 a.m. and end at 4:00 p.m.

Bidder Registration

Anyone interested in bidding on property should register with the Delinquent Tax Collector beginning June 20, 2003. Prospective bidders are required to show a valid driver's license or other acceptable identification and will be required to complete an IRS Form W-9.

Bidding Procedure

Property will be auctioned in tax map number order to the highest bidder and must be paid for with cash, money order or certified check by the close of business on the day of the sale. Should the bid amount not be paid by that time, the defaulting bidder is liable for not more than three hundred dollars damages, which may be collected by the Delinquent Tax Collector. The property may then be offered for sale again. If there is no bid, the property will be considered purchased by the county's Forfeited Land Commission for the amount of the taxes, penalties and costs.

Assignment of Bids

Assignment of bids, either in whole or in part, will be accepted beginning October 20, 2003 until August 27, 2004. Questions concerning assignment of bids by the Forfeited Land Commission should be directed to its chairman.

This amendment is in effect for all tax sales held after the signing by the Governor on June 6, 2000.

Once property is redeemed the bidder will be notified by mail and must return the original sale receipt to the delinquent tax collector before a refund check is issued. The bidder should allow at least thirty days for the processing of the refund.

IMPORTANT NOTE: THE PURCHASER OF PROPERTY AT A TAX SALE ACQUIRES THE TITLE WITHOUT WARRANTY AND BUYS AT HIS OWN RISK. THE COUNTY IS NOT LIABLE FOR THE QUALITY OR QUANTITY OF THE PROPERTY SOLD.

For the bidder's own protection, it is recommended that professional advice be sought if there are any legal questions pertaining to a delinquent tax sale.

James M. Farris, Director

(2) Tax Sale Listings
http://www.charlestoncounty.org/index2.asp?p=/departments/del_tax_sale.htm

ROGUE INVESTOR NOTE: Information was last updated October 4, 2003.

South Dakota

Tax Lien Sales: Yes

Tax Deed Sales: No

Rating: Two Stars (**)

Interest Rate: Tax certificates are offered at the first tax sale bearing interest at the rate of 12% per annum.

Sale Period: Any properties with delinquent taxes are offered at public sale on the third Monday of December.

Redemption Period:
A tax deed to the property may not be issued any sooner than three years for property within corporate limits, or any sooner than four years for property located outside a municipality. The property owner has four years in which to redeem, otherwise the certificate holder is entitled to a deed to the property.

Bidding Process: If no bidder, the tax certificate is issued in the name of the county. These may be purchased during the year.

State-Specific Information:
There are 66 counties in South Dakota. Tax sales in each of the counties in South Dakota are handled by the county treasurer or auditor.

Sample Problem: Each year "certificates" are sold on properties with delinquent taxes. The certificate is purchased by person(s) who bid on the property. The bid includes the amount of taxes, interest and costs due on the property. It also states the interest per year the person would require for redemption from the certificate.

Buyer A purchases a certificate on Property X, paying taxes, interest and cost. The next year, the owner of the same Property X is delinquent in paying his taxes. Buyer B purchases the tax certificate. Within four years, Buyer A may start proceedings to obtain a tax deed to Property X.

Buyer A would not have clear title to Property X as Buyer B still holds a certificate. It would be in Buyer A's best interest to redeem the certificate held by Buyer B, as the following year Buyer B may start tax deed proceedings on Property X.

Links for All South Dakota Counties: Provided on CD

Detailed County-Specific Information:

MINNEHAHA COUNTY, SOUTH DAKOTA
http://www.minnehahacounty.org

TREASURER'S OFFICE
http://www.minnehahacounty.org/depts/treasurer/treasurer.asp

Department Head: Billy Jo Waara
415 N. Dakota Ave.
Sioux Falls, SD 57104-2465
Phone: (605) 367-4211
Fax: 605-367-6091
Email: treasurer@minnehahacounty.org

SHERIFF'S OFFICE
http://www.minnehahacounty.org/depts/sheriff/sheriff.asp

Sheriff Mike Milstead
Minnehaha County Sheriff
320 W. 4th St.
Sioux Falls, SD 57104
Phone: 605-367-4300
Fax: 605-367-7319
Email: mmilstead@minnehahacounty.org

(1) Mortgage Foreclosures
http://www.minnehahacounty.org/depts/sheriff/foreclosures/foreclosures.asp

Mortgage foreclosures sales are held every Wednesday starting at 11:00 AM and are held inside the front door of the Minnehaha County Courthouse, 425 N. Dakota Avenue.

ROGUE INVESTOR NOTE: Web page contains current listings.

(2) Mortgage Foreclosure Results
http://www.minnehahacounty.org/depts/sheriff/foreclosures/foreclosures_results.asp

ROGUE INVESTOR NOTE: Web page contains current listings.

Tax Lien Sales: No

Tax Deed Sales: Yes

Rating: Two Stars (**)

Interest Rate: State only has tax deed sales.

Sale Period: The Clerk and Master of the Chancery Court conduct the tax sales. They hold annual auctions.

Redemption Period: 1 year

Bidding Process:
The opening bid at the sale is the total amount of delinquent taxes due on the parcel of property, plus the total amount of accrued penalties, interest and court costs. The specific amount of money owed on each parcel to be sold may be obtained by contacting the Delinquent Tax Office. The Metropolitan Government will institute legal action against any purchaser who fails to comply with their bid.

State-Specific Information:
There are 95 counties in Tennessee. The county trustee, the county executive, the back-tax collector, the back-tax attorney, the district attorney general, and agents of the commissioner of revenue all have one or more functions with respect to the collection of delinquent taxes and the sale of property for nonpayment of taxes.

Links for All Tennessee Counties: Provided on CD.

Detailed County-Specific Information:

DAVIDSON COUNTY, TENNESSEE
http://www.nashville.gov

SHERIFF'S OFFICE
http://www.nashville-sheriff.net

Sheriff Daron Hall
506 2nd Avenue North
Nashville, TN 37201-1085
Phone: 615-862-8170
Fax: 615-862-8188
Email: sheriff@dcso.nashville.org

(1) Sheriff's Sales

Upon orders from the Court, the Sheriff's Office sells seized property to satisfy civil judgments against defendants.

When such sales are scheduled, the Sheriff's Office posts notices in public places, announcing the dates, times, and locations of the sales, and including brief descriptions of the items involved. We are now publishing similar notices on this page of our website to provide another opportunity for citizens to learn of these sales.

IMPORTANT!
- NO ADDITIONAL INFORMATION IS AVAILABLE ABOUT ANY ITEM LISTED, AND PHONED OR E-MAILED INQUIRES FOR FURTHER INFORMATION CANNOT BE ANSWERED. Interested parties are responsible for attending the sale if they wish to learn more.
- Registration may only be done just prior to the sale, and only at its published location.
- Payment must be made in full at the time of purchase.
- Only cash, cashier's checks, and certified checks are accepted for payment.
- Items purchased must be removed from the site at the time of sale. Removal is the purchaser's responsibility.
- The Sheriff's Office makes no guarantee or warranty regarding the condition, value, or functionality of any item sold. Every item is sold as-is.

SHELBY COUNTY, TENNESSEE
http://www.co.shelby.tn.us

TRUSTEE'S OFFICE
http://www.shelbycountytrustee.com

Bob Patterson
160 N. Main St., 2nd Floor, Suite 250
Memphis, TN 38103
phone: (901) 521-1829
Email: CustomerService@shelbycountytrustee.com

(1) Tax Sale
From http://www.shelbycountytrustee.com, click on "Tax Sale" in left-hand column

The County Trustee's office holds tax sales throughout the year to sell property for delinquent taxes. The delinquent properties appear in a Notice of Tax Sale in a designated local paper. This listing of properties includes parcel number, names of all owners, amount due and a brief description, along with the time and location of the sale.

A notice of the tax sale is also sent by certified mail to the last known address of the present owner. The tax sale is conducted in the Shelby County Commissioners' Chambers located at 160 N. Main Street, Memphis, TN 38103, and is open to anyone. Tax sales are not held on weekends or non-judicial days. The court orders the sale of the property for cash, subject to one year of redemption, whereby the property owner/lien holder has the right to pay taxes, interest, penalties and costs, and terminate the sale proceeding.

For the tax sales service center click here: http://www.shelbycountytrustee.com/TaxsaleInformation.htm. For additional information on tax sales, please contact the Tax Sale Department at (901) 545-4819.

(2) Tax Sale FAQ
From http://www.shelbycountytrustee.com, click on "FAQs" in left-hand column, and then on "Tax Sale" link

How do I purchase property from Shelby County? Individuals interested in purchasing Shelby County owned properties should contact the Shelby County Real Estate Office at (901) 387-5704.

How can I obtain a list of properties being sold in Tax Sale? A listing of properties being sold in each tax sale is published approximately 30 days prior to the sale date.

For tax sale dates and related information click here:
http://www.shelbycountytrustee.com/TaxsaleSchedule.htm

Upcoming tax sales dates: March 16, 2004 (tax sale list available February 13, 2004) and May 17, 2004 (tax sale list available April 15, 2004).

(3) Tax Sale Service Center

From http://www.shelbycountytrustee.com, click on "Tax Sale" in left-hand column and then on link for "tax sales service center"

In general, the amount(s) required are:

- The full minimum bid plus 10% of the final bid at tax sale.
- $20.00 filing fee.
- The court may require additional compensation to the purchaser for maintenance of the property.

How do I purchase property at tax sale? Tax sales are conducted in the Shelby County Commissioner's Chambers and are open to anyone. On the date of the sale, anyone wishing to bid will need to arrive early for registration. Registration begins at 8:00 a.m. and each tax sale begins at 10:00 a.m. You will complete a bidder information form and receive a bidder card. If you are the highest bidder on a property, you will need to remain after the sale so that Chancery Court can verify your bid amount. There is no deposit required. Payment is to be made in the form of cashier's check, money order, or cash, on the day following the tax sale. Payment is made at Chancery Court located at 140 Adams Street, Memphis, TN 38103

* Note: You must make full payment within 24 hours if you are the high bidder. Failure to make full payment could result in legal action.

What does the minimum bid represent? The minimum bid at a tax sale is the total amount of city and county taxes owed, along with any fees associated with tax sale. These fees may include court costs, attorney fees, and service costs.

When do I take title to the property? Once the sale is confirmed, you may request a deed from the Chancery Court Clerk Master.

When is the sale confirmed? The confirmation date is typically 30-45 days after the date of sale. The court files a final list of property sold at tax sale.

What if someone redeems the property I purchased at tax sale? The court will be returning your bid amount, along with 10% per annum on your bid. (Calculated from the date of confirmation until the petition to redeem is filed.) In addition to this amount, the court may award reimbursement for costs of maintaining the property during your ownership.

* Note: We do not recommend spending money to improve property bought at tax sale until after the 1-year redemption period expires. Such expenditures may or may not be reimbursed by the court.

View list of properties available for tax sale.
From http://www.shelbycountytrustee.com, click on "Tax Sale" in left-hand column and then on link for "tax sales service center"

Use search form.

(4) View list of properties removed from tax sale
From http://www.shelbycountytrustee.com, click on "Tax Sale" in left-hand column and then on link for "tax sales service center"

Use search form.

(5) View schedule of tax sales
From http://www.shelbycountytrustee.com, click on "Tax Sale" in left-hand column and then on link for "tax sales service center"

REAL ESTATE OFFICE
From http://www.shelbycountytrustee.com, click on "Tax Sale" in left-hand column, then on link for "tax sales service center" and then on "View list of properties owned by Shelby County Real Estate Office"

Bill Goss, Manager
160 N. Main Street, Suite 350
Memphis, TN 38103
phone: (901) 545-4320
email: goss-w@co.shelby.tn.us

If you are interested in buying some land at reasonable prices, check out the Surplus or Tax Lien property lists. They can be found by clicking on the links located at the top of this page. If you are interested in buying one of the parcels listed, have the "WRD BLK PCL" number ready and call the Real Estate office at (901) 545-4900 or email Mike Blackwell at blackw-m@co.shelby.tn.us. New property lists are posted at the beginning of each month.

You can also look up the specific property information at the Shelby County Assessor's web site. *You will need to convert the "ward/block/parcel" number.* To do so, simply add a "0" to the first set of digits and three "0's" to the third set of digits found in the "WRD BLK PCL" column (Ex. 12-062-18 = 01206200018).

Click here for the Shelby County Assessor's web site: http://www.assessor.shelby.tn.us.

For more information, contact Mike Blackwell, Real Estate Specialist, at blackw-m@co.shelby.tn.us.

(1) Delinquent Tax Parcels for Sale
from Real Estate Office page, click on "Delinquent Tax Parcels for Sale"

SHERIFF'S OFFICE
http://www.shelby-sheriff.org

Mark Luttrell, Sheriff
201 Poplar Avenue, 9th Floor
Memphis, TN 38103
phone: (901) 545-5500

Tax Lien Sales: No, but similar process.

Tax Deed Sales: Yes, with right of redemption.

Rating: Four Stars (****)

Interest Rate: 25% (not an annual rate)

Sale Period: First Tuesday of each month at the courthouse of each county.

Redemption Period:
Can be as soon as one year but can also go on for years if no one decides to force the process. Texas' system allows the investor with the winning bid to receive the deed; however, the deed may be redeemed within 6 months for a flat fee of 25 percent. The investor essentially purchases what is similar to a tax lien certificate, except that the interest rate is not an annual rate, but a flat 25 percent. Therefore, if the owner redeems within one month, the investor earns a 300 percent annual rate.

Bidding Process:
Amazingly, private law firms handle the tax deed sales for each county in Texas. Sheriffs or Constables actually conduct the auctions.

State-Specific Information:
Even though there are probably more tax delinquent accounts in Texas than in any other state, there are many cases in which taxes have been delinquent for 20, 30, 40, and even more years without ever being sold for taxes at a tax foreclosure sale.

Texas statutes provide that any taxing jurisdiction can foreclose real property tax liens. This means that every independent school district, which number in the hundreds, can foreclose tax liens. Every city or town can foreclose tax liens and sell the property. These facts create literally thousands of opportunities in Texas to acquire real property for non-payment of taxes or to receive an extremely high rate of return on your investment.

Special Note: House Bill 335, passed in September 2003, requires a written statement and a $10 fee to show that you are not delinquent on taxes in each county. The Request for the Assessor's Written Statement must by filled out, notarized and delivered to the County Tax Assessor *at least 10 days prior to the sale*. Be sure to plan ahead!

Links for All Texas Counties: Provided on CD.

Detailed County-Specific Information:

BEXAR COUNTY, TEXAS
http://www.co.bexar.tx.us

TAX ASSESSOR-COLLECTOR'S OFFICE
http://www.co.bexar.tx.us/links/taxoffice/taxoffice.htm

(1) Tax FAQ
http://www.co.bexar.tx.us/links/TaxOffice/Tax-About/TAX_-_Property/TAXFAQ-1/taxfaq-1.htm

(2) Real and Personal Property Calendar
http://www.co.bexar.tx.us/links/TaxOffice/Tax-About/TAX_-_Property/TAXCAL1/taxcal1.htm

(3) Contact Information
http://www.co.bexar.tx.us/links/TaxOffice/Tax-Hours/tax-hours.htm

Sylvia S. Romo, Tax Assessor-Collector
Bexar County
P.O. Box 839950
San Antonio, TX 78283-3950
Phone, General Information: 210-335-2251
Phone, Property Tax: 210-335-6628
Email: taxoffice@co.bexar.tx.us

COLLIN COUNTY, TEXAS
http://www.co.collin.tx.us/index.jsp

TAX ASSESSOR AND COLLECTOR DEPARTMENT
http://www.co.collin.tx.us/tax_assessor/index.jsp

Kenneth Maun, Tax Assessor and Collector
University Drive Courts Facility
1800 N. Graves Street
McKinney, TX 75069
Phone: 972-547-5020 (Property Taxes)
Email: taxassessor@collincountytx.gov

SHERIFF'S OFFICE
http://www.co.collin.tx.us/sheriff/index.jsp

Terry Box, Sheriff

(1) Sheriff's Sales
http://www.co.collin.tx.us/sheriff/sales.jsp

The listed sales are for the Sheriff's Office only and do not include sales by the Constable's Offices or other Collin County Departments.

(2) Contact Information
http://www.co.collin.tx.us/sheriff/email.jsp

Captain Pam Palmisano: For information on Support Services including Dispatch, Civil, Warrants or Records (ppalmisano@collincountytx.gov=subject=Weblink)
Sheriff Box: sheriff@collincountytx.gov=subject=Weblink

CONSTABLES
http://www.co.collin.tx.us/constables/index.jsp

Elected Officials
Jerry Kunkle, Constable 1
Collin County Government Center
Annex A
200 S. McDonald Street
Suite 220
McKinney, TX 75069
const1@collincountytx.gov
972-548-4419 (McKinney)
972-424-1460 ext. 4419 (Metro)

Joe Barton, Constable 2
Collin County Sub-Courthouse
406 A Raymond Street
Farmersville, TX 75442
const2@collincountytx.gov
972-782-7211 (Farmersville)
972-424-1460 ext. 4480 (Metro)

Bob Bell, Constable 3
Collin County Sub-Courthouse
920 E. Park Boulevard
Plano, TX 75074
const3@collincountytx.gov
972-881-3070 (Plano)
972-424-1460 ext. 3070 (Metro)

Frank Svoboda, Constable 4
Collin County SubCourthouse
8585 John Wesley Drive
Frisco, TX 75034
const4@collincountytx.gov
972-731-7320 (Frisco)
972-424-1460 ext. 7320 (Metro)

DALLAS COUNTY, TEXAS
http://www.dallascounty.org

PUBLIC WORKS DEPARTMENT, PROPERTY DIVISION
http://www.dallascounty.org/html/citizen-serv/pubwks/div-prop.html

Dallas County Public Works
Administration Building
411 Elm Street, 4th Floor
Dallas, Texas 75202

An additional responsibility of the Property Division is to maintain an inventory of County owned property. Under this responsibility the Property Management section manages and coordinates disposition of tax foreclosure properties struck off to Dallas County at the Sheriff's Sale. Based on the number and nature of the properties within the inventory, a sale via a sealed bid procedure may be scheduled each quarter of the fiscal year. These tax resales are conducted in conformance with the Dallas County Tax Foreclosure Resale Policy (http://www.dallascounty.org/html/citizen-serv/pubwks/media/div-prop-resalepolicy.pdf) and the Property Tax Code, Section 34.05.

If you have any questions about tax resales, please check our FAQ section (http://www.dallascounty.org/html/citizen-serv/pubwks/div-prop-faq.htm) for answers. For additional information, please contact Pam Easterling at peasterling@dallascounty.org.

The Property Division is headed by the Assistant Director of Public Works, Selas Camarillo, who can be reached at 214-653-6400 or scamarillo@dallascounty.org. The support staff is divided into four sections, one of which includes property management.

(1a) Dallas County Tax Foreclosure Resale Policy
http://www.dallascounty.org/html/citizen-serv/pubwks/media/div-prop-resalepolicy.pdf

(2) Dallas County Tax Foreclosure Resales FAQ
http://www.dallascounty.org/html/citizen-serv/pubwks/div-prop-faq.htm

(3) County of Dallas Offer and Purchase Agreement
http://www.dallascounty.org/html/citizen-serv/pubwks/media/PurAgrPrivateRev2003.pdf

(4) Dallas County Tax Foreclosed Properties
http://www.dallascounty.org/html/citizen-serv/pubwks/strucklist.pdf

(5) Property Tax FAQ

Deadlines & Delinquency
http://www.dallascounty.org/html/citizen-serv/tax/taxoffice_propertyFAQ-4.html#faqnav

Other Questions
http://www.dallascounty.org/html/citizen-serv/tax/taxoffice_propertyFAQ-5.html#faqnav

SHERIFF'S OFFICE
http://www.dallascounty.org/html/citizen-serv/DCSD/sheriff.html

Sheriff Jim Bowles
Frank Crowley Courts Building
133 N. Industrial Boulevard, LB 31 – 1st Floor
Dallas, Texas 75207
(214) 653-3450, Office
(214) 653-3420, FAX

DENTON COUNTY, TEXAS
http://www.co.denton.tx.us

TAX ASSESSOR/COLLECTOR'S OFFICE
http://tax.dentoncounty.com/main.asp?Dept=55

Steve Mossman, Tax Assessor/Collector
email: Steve.Mossman@dentoncounty.com

(1) Contact Information
http://tax.dentoncounty.com/main.asp?Dept=55&Link=206

300 E. McKinney
Denton, TX 76201-4232

Mailing Address
P. O. Box 1249
Denton, TX 76202-1249

Tax Department Fax
(940) 349-3500 (Metro)
(972) 434-8835 (Metro)
(940) 349-3501(Metro)

(2) Property Tax FAQ
http://tax.dentoncounty.com/main.asp?Parent=556&Link=211

State law automatically places a tax lien on property on January 1 of each year to ensure that taxes are paid. The person who owned the property on January 1 of the tax year is personally liable for the tax, even if he/she sold the property during the year.

SHERIFF'S OFFICE
http://sheriff.dentoncounty.com/main.asp?Dept=54

Law Enforcement Center
127 N. Woodrow Lane
Denton, Texas 76205-6397
phone: (940) 898-5601/ Metro (972) 434-5001
fax: (940) 898-5604/ Metro (972) 434-5020
Weldon Lucas, County Sheriff

(1) Sheriff's Sales
http://sheriff.dentoncounty.com/main.asp?Dept=54&Link=517

The Sheriff's Sale is conducted on the first Tuesday of each month at the Denton County Courts Building (http://dentoncounty.com/locations/crt.asp), 1450 E. McKinney, in the City of Denton, Texas, at 10:00 a.m. Denton County will sell said below described Real Estate at public venue, for cash, to the highest bidder.

For further information please email Janie.Coleman@dentoncounty.com or Jon.Royea@dentoncounty.com.

Page contains Sheriff's sales for February 2004.

Note: Opening bids will be added when all figures are received from each agency involved.

Foreclosure sales are not conducted by the Sheriff's office. Contact the lender for that information.

(1a) FAQ About Tax Sales
http://sheriff.dentoncounty.com/main.asp?Parent=517&Link=534

How often does the Sheriff's Department hold Tax Sales? Tax Sales are only held when Orders of Sale are issued from the District Courts in reference to tax judgments for delinquent taxes. Sales are not always scheduled each month. Real property is required by Texas law to be sold on the first Tuesday of the month. All counties have sales on the same day.

When and where will the tax sales be advertised*?* We advertise the sales in the Denton Record Chronicle on the three Wednesdays prior to the first Tuesday of the month if there is a sale set.

Do you have to register for the sales*?* There is no formal registration process. You or your representative have to be present in person for the sale.

What are the payment requirements*? Is there a deposit required before the sale?* Denton County require payment in the form of cash or a cashier's check for the total amount that was bid. Payment plans are not accepted. Payment is not required at the time of purchase, but the total amount must be paid by 4:00 PM on the day of sale unless special arrangements are made with the Sheriff's Department at the time of sale. (Special arrangements are sometimes made if the buyer banks out of state.) No deposit is required before the sale.

What is the type of bidding process? It is an open/oral bid process.

What type of document is issued after the sale? A Sheriff's Deed is issued to the purchaser.

Are there any other expenses in addition to the opening bid amount? All the expenses are included in the opening bid; however there may be additional taxes due on the property that have accrued since the judgment was rendered.

What happens to any property that is not sold to the public at the auction? All the property is sold, either to the public or to the taxing entity who received the judgment. If a property goes to the taxing entity, contact can be made with the attorney who represents that entity for purchase information.

Where are the sales posted? The sale notices are posted at the Denton County Courts Building (http://dentoncounty.com/locations/crt.asp) at 1450 E. McKinney in Denton, at the Courthouse Annex in Lewisville (http://dentoncounty.com/locations/lgc.asp) at 190 N. Valley Parkway, and at the Denton County Sheriff's Office (http://dentoncounty.com/locations/lec.asp) (visible 24 hours a day).

Does the Sheriff's Department conduct the foreclosure Sales? No, these are conducted by the trustees or attorneys for the lending institutions involved with the loans. These types of sales are also held on the first Tuesday of the month and are posted at the Denton County Courts Building. Additional information is available Monday through Friday from 8:00 a.m. to 5:00 p.m. by calling (940) 898-5694 or Metro (972) 434-5004, or e-mail Janie.coleman@dentoncounty.com.

(1b) Sheriff Sale Information
http://sheriff.dentoncounty.com/main.asp?Parent=517&Link=533

The Sheriff Sale is held the first Tuesday of each month at 10:00 A.M. at the Denton County Courts Building at 1450 E. McKinney St., Denton, Texas.

All properties going to the Sheriff Sale are published in the Denton Record Chronicle on the third Wednesday prior to the first Tuesday of the month. Notice is posted at the Courthouse, Sheriff's Department front entrance and the Lee Walker Government Center in Lewisville.
Payment in full is required on your purchase by cash or cashier's check and is due by 4 p.m. the day of the sale.

The minimum bid represents the taxes and cost due plus interest, Sheriff's fees and ad fees.
If the property is not sold it will be struck off to the city, county or school district that offered it for sale. They will hold the deed until after the redemption period expires and then they may attempt to sell it. The redemption period is six months; for a homestead or agriculture property it is two years. If the owner redeems the property from the purchaser they must pay the purchase price plus 25% interest on the six months. The redemption for a homestead or agriculture property is 25% the first year and 50% if redeemed the second year.

You or a representative must be present to bid on the properties. This is not a Tax Lien Certificate sale. The real property is sold. You will receive a Sheriff's Deed to the property. All sales are as is, to the highest bidder and for cash on a "BUYER BEWARE BASIS." Any and all questions concerning the properties offered for sale should be directed to your attorney. If purchaser fails to pay, legal action may be taken.

EL PASO COUNTY, TEXAS
http://www.co.el-paso.tx.us

COUNTY OF EL PASO TAX OFFICE
http://www.epcounty.com/TaxOffice .

Victor Flores
County Tax Assessor-Collector
500 E. Overland Suite 101
El Paso, TX 79901
Phone: (915) 546-2140
Fax: (915) 546-8100
E-Mail: VFlores@co.el-paso.tx.us

(1) Property Tax
http://www.epcounty.com/TaxOffice/npropertytax.htm

Property Taxes for The County of El Paso are handled by the City of El Paso's Tax Office located at #2 Civic Center Plaza, El Paso, Texas 79901. An interlocal agreement between the County of El Paso, The City of El Paso, and 24 other taxing entities was formed back in 1986 to better serve the citizens of El Paso, County.

CITY OF EL PASO TAX OFFICE
http://www.ci.el-paso.tx.us./tax/tax.htm

The City of El Paso collects property taxes on behalf of all the 26 units of government that levy a tax within El Paso County. We are one of the few large urban offices in Texas fully consolidated for purposes of property tax collection.

City of El Paso
Tax Office
City Hall, Two Civic Center Plaza
El Paso, TX 79901
Phone: (915) 541-4054
Inquiry form: citytaxoffice@ci.el-paso.tx.us
FAX: (915) 541-4116

(1) Property Tax Sales
http://63.113.174.35/pls/sales/property_inquire$.startup

The law firm of Linebarger Goggan Blair & Sampson, LLP places tax sale property listings online for the benefit of the public. Listings will be available from the 15th of each month until the next sale date, the first Tuesday of the next month (e.g., from January 15 - February 1 for the February 1, 2000 sale). Please check back to see the listings for the next sale.

If you have questions about property tax sales, please check our FAQ (http://www.publicans.com/FAQ.htm) section for answers.

LINEBARGER GOGGAN BLAIR & SAMPSON, LLP
http://www.publicans.com

(1) Commonly Asked Questions and Answers Regarding Tax Sales
from http://www.publicans.com, click on "Tax Sale Properties" in left-hand column

(2) Property Tax Sales
from http://www.publicans.com, click on "Tax Sale Properties" in left-hand column and then "Go to Tax Sale Property Listings"

HARRIS COUNTY, TEXAS
http://www.co.harris.tx.us

TAX OFFICE
http://www.tax.co.harris.tx.us
(or http://www.hctax.net)

phone: (713) 368-2000
1001 Preston
Houston, Texas 77002
tax_office@co.harris.tx.us (Tax questions)

Paul Bettencourt
Tax Assessor-Collector
P.O. Box 3547
Houston, Texas 77253-3547

(1) New Tax Sale Procedures – HB 335 Compliance
http://www.tax.co.harris.tx.us/hb335/default.asp

Obtain the Request for Written Statement:

This online program will allow you to create a user account for yourself, enter the account numbers for your properties, and print the Request for Written Statement form. *Before you begin, it would be advantageous to have all of the Harris County tax account numbers for your currently owned properties, and, if applicable, previously owned properties, available for input into the system.* (A link is provided to our web site if you need to research an account by name or address.) By inputting all of these account numbers into your "portfolio" of properties, you will not need to physically list these same properties on your request form. These properties will automatically display on your request form for you when you print.

Please include all property located within Harris County, including property in any school district or city that is only partially located within Harris County.

For a bidder who needs to register, please go to STEP ONE:
https://www.hctax.net/salesportfolio/step1.asp.

If you are already registered but need to access your account information, please login here:
https://www.hctax.net/salesportfolio/login.asp.

NOTE: Please do not create multiple user accounts for the same individual or company. If you discover that you made an error entering your contact information, you will have an opportunity later to make changes from a link on your portfolio page. Creating another account will delay the processing of your request form.

Download the Request for Written Statement form and manually complete it:
http://www.tax.co.harris.tx.us/hb335/hb335reqform.pdf.

Please print this form, and complete all blanks. Please remember to have your Request for Written Statement form notarized before you send it to our office. There is a $10 service fee for preparation of the Statement of Taxes due with your request. Please make sure you enclose your $10 payment with your request form, as your request will not be processed until the fee is paid. Make your check payable to Paul Bettencourt, TAC. Mail your request form and payment to:

Paul Bettencourt, TAC
P.O. Box 3746
Houston, TX. 77253-3746

You can also hand-deliver your request form and payment to our downtown office in Houston at 1001 Preston Street, between Main and Fannin.

Register for a Constable's Sale Online:

Register for a constable's sale online (https://www.hctax.net/salesportfolio/bidders/default.asp) instead of waiting until the morning of the sale.

If you are already registered for the constable's sales, you can make changes to your bidder contact information if needed (https://www.hctax.net/salesportfolio/bidders/reviewcontactinfo.asp).

Printing the Request for Written Statement
Here are some basic printing tips (http://www.tax.co.harris.tx.us/hb335/printing.htm) for printing your Request for Written Statement.

Need Help?
For questions concerning HB 335 procedures, please call our Special Tax Services Department at 713-368-2727.

Download a PowerPoint presentation about HB 335 and its impact on Harris County Public Auctions (25 MB – right click the link and save to your computer)
http://www.tax.co.harris.tx.us/hb335/hb335seminar.ppt

(2a) HB 335 Compliance - Step 1
https://www.hctax.net/salesportfolio/step1.asp

(2b) PowerPoint presentation on HB 335 and its impact on Harris County public auctions
http://www.tax.co.harris.tx.us/hb335/hb335seminar.ppt

(3) Property Tax Frequently Asked Questions
from http://www.tax.co.harris.tx.us, click on "Tax" in upper left-hand corner, then on "Property Tax," and then on "Frequently Asked Questions"

(4) 2001 Texas Property Tax Code
http://www.hcad.org/TaxCode/Default.htm

LINEBARGER GOGGAN BLAIR & SAMPSON, L.L.P.
http://www.publicans.com

(1) Commonly Asked Questions and Answers Regarding Tax Sales
from http://www.publicans.com, click on "Tax Sale Properties" in left-hand column

(2) Property Tax Sales
from http://www.publicans.com, click on "Tax Sale Properties" in left-hand column and then "Go to Tax Sale Property Listings"

HIDALGO COUNTY, TEXAS
http://www.co.hidalgo.tx.us

OFFICE OF THE COUNTY CLERK
http://www.hidalgocountyclerk.com

Honorable J.D. Salinas, County Clerk

(1) Location
http://www.hidalgocountyclerk.com/LocationHours.htm

Hidalgo County Courthouse
100 North Closner
Edinburg, Texas 78539

mailing address
Hidalgo County Courthouse
100 North Closner
P.O. Box 58
Edinburg, Texas 78539

Phone: (956) 318-2100
Toll Free: 888-318-2811
Fax: (956) 318-2105

(2) Foreclosures Sales
http://www.hidalgocountyclerk.com

Check "Upcoming Events" for notice of foreclosures sale.

LANDTITLE USA
http://www.landtitleusa.com

Receive a list of foreclosures, appraisals or tax records.

TAX ASSESSOR'S OFFICE
http://www.hidalgocountytax.org

Armando Barrera, Tax Assessor
Administration Building
100 E. Cano, 1st floor
Edinburg, TX 78539
phone: 956-318-2157
fax: 956-318-2733

SHERIFF'S DEPARTMENT
http://www.hidalgoso.org

Sheriff Enrique "Henry" Escalon
Hidalgo County Sheriff's Department
P.O. Box 1228
Edinburg, TX 78540
Phone: (956) 383-8114 or 393-6000
email: hcso_webmaster@despammed.com

ADMINISTRATION DEPARTMENT
(Sheriff's Department)
http://www.hidalgoso.org/administration.htm

head of Department = Captain Quintanilha
email: capt_quintanilha@hidalgoso.org

(1) Civil Process
http://www.hidalgoso.org/civil_process_photos.htm

email for Specialized Tax Unit: taxes@hidalgoso.org

JEFFERSON COUNTY, TEXAS
http://www.co.jefferson.tx.us

TAX OFFICE
http://co.jefferson.tx.us/taxoffice/main.htm

Miriam Johnson, Tax Assessor-Collector

The main duties of the Tax Assessor-Collector include issuing tax certificates, and conducting Sheriff Sales for real property in Jefferson County.

(1) Contact Information
http://co.jefferson.tx.us/taxoffice/contact_us.htm

Beaumont Tax Office
Jefferson County Courthouse
1149 Pearl Street
Beaumont, TX 77701
Mailing address:
P.O. Box 2112
Beaumont, TX 77704
Property Tax Section:
Phone: 409-835-8516
FAX: 409-835-8589
sjames@co.jefferson.tx.us

Port Arthur Tax Office
Jefferson County Sub-Courthouse
525 Lakeshore Drive
Port Arthur, TX 77640
Mailing Address:
P.O. Box 309
Port Arthur, TX 77641
Property Tax Section:
Phone: 409-983-8316
FAX: 409-983-8388

Mid-County Tax Office
4605 Jerry Ware Drive
Beaumont, TX 77705
Phone: 409-727-8578
FAX: 409-727-3370

PROPERTY TAX SECTION
(Tax Office)
http://co.jefferson.tx.us/taxoffice/property_tax.htm

(1) New State Law Applicable to Sheriff's Sales: House Bill 335
http://co.jefferson.tx.us/taxoffice/house_bill_335.htm

(2) General Information Regarding Delinquent Tax Sales
http://co.jefferson.tx.us/taxoffice/house_bill_335.htm

The following is important information regarding the property for sale. You must carefully read this information and evaluate these facts in light of your anticipated use of the property.

(1) The property will be sold at public auction and will be sold for cash to the highest bidder, based on oral bids. The rules covering auctions generally will apply. Purchasers must pay for their property with cash or a cashier's check payable to the Jefferson County Sheriff's Department.

(2a) Original Sale. The amount of the opening bid is set out next to each tract, and the bidding must start at that figure or higher, and sums less than the given figure cannot be accepted.

(2b) Absolute Sale. The amount of the suggested opening bid is set out next to each tract or will be stated by the auctioneer at the time the property is offered for sale. Bidding may start at that figure. Bids less than the suggested starting bid may be accepted at the discretion of the tax assessor-collector. The tax assessor reserves the right to set the minimum bid on any property. Properties so designated will be noted orally and in writing.

(3) Any successful bidder who fails to make payment shall be held liable for twenty percent of the value of the property plus costs incurred as a result of the bidder's default pursuant to Rule 652 of the Texas Rules of Civil Procedure. If the property is later sold at another absolute auction, but the bid does not meet the minimum required to cover taxes and cost due, then you will be held liable for the difference.

(4) Purchasers at this tax foreclosure sale will receive an ordinary type of sheriff's deed which is without warranty, express or implied. The property is being sold "as is."

(5) All property purchased at this sale may be subject to a statutory right of redemption. This redemption period commences to run from the date the original sheriff sale deed was filed for record in the County Clerk's office. There is a two-year right of redemption for homestead property and property appraised as agricultural land. There is a six-month right of redemption for all other property. It is the bidder's responsibility to determine the redemption period.

(6) Anyone having a legal interest in the property at the time of the original Sheriff's Sale may redeem the property from the purchaser during the redemption period. The redemption price is set by the Property Tax Code.

(7) Anyone redeeming the property is required to reimburse the purchaser for any costs paid by the purchaser described in paragraph 34.21 (q)(2) of the State Property Tax code: "Costs include the amount reasonably spent by the purchaser for the maintenance, preservation, and safekeeping of the property . . . "

(8) Since purchasers will only have a sheriff's deed to the property, a policy of title insurance may be difficult to obtain.

(9) This sale includes taxes through all tax years which were delinquent at the date of judgment. This may or may not include the most recent tax year. You must inquire as to which tax years are included on the property you are interested in purchasing. You will be required to pay the taxes for the tax years that became due since the date of judgment.

(10) It will be necessary for the bidders to satisfy themselves concerning location of the property on the ground prior to the sale. Maps and plats of these properties are on file in the office of the County Clerk, and all papers in the lawsuit(s) on which this sale is based are on file in the office of the District Clerk. The approximate property address reflected herein is the address on the tax records and may or may not be completely accurate. The Tax Office suggests that you do not purchase any property based on any slides shown at the sale unless you have personally viewed the property and the associated maps or plats in the office of the Jefferson County Tax Assessor-Collector.

(11) Prior to the day of the sale, a bidder must request a Statement of No Delinquent Taxes Owed, from the Jefferson County Tax Office.

(12) A bidder at the sale must be registered, at the time the sale begins, with the person conducting the sale. The bidder must submit a Statement of No Delinquent Taxes Owed to the person conducting the sale, in order to register.

(3) Request for Statement of No Delinquent Taxes Owed
http://co.jefferson.tx.us/taxoffice/pdf/Request_Statement_No_Taxes.pdf

---

MONTGOMERY COUNTY, TEXAS
http://www.co.montgomery.tx.us

TAX ASSESSOR-COLLECTOR'S OFFICE
http://www.co.montgomery.tx.us/mctax

JR. Moore, JR., Tax Assessor-Collector
Office email: rnusz@co.montgomery.tx.us

(1) Contact Information
http://www.co.montgomery.tx.us/mctax/faq.htm

Tax Office
400 N. San Jacinto
Conroe, Texas 77301
phone: (936) 539-7897
fax: (936) 538-8129
e-mail: tax@co.montgomery.tx.us

CONSTABLES
http://www.co.montgomery.tx.us/consts/index.shtml

Constable Precinct 1 (http://www.co.montgomery.tx.us/const1/index.shtml)
Don Chumley
300 S. Danville, Willis, Texas 77378
Phone: 936-856-6329
Fax: 936-856-9408

Constable Precinct 2 (http://www.co.montgomery.tx.us/const2/index.shtml)
Gene DeForest
130 North Main, Conroe, Texas 77301
Phone: 936-539-7854
Fax: 936-539-7935
email: const2@co.montgomery.tx.us

Constable Precinct 3 (http://www.co.montgomery.tx.us/const3/index.shtml)
Tim Holifield
9909 Grogan's Mill Road, The Woodlands, Texas 77380
Phone: 281-363-1161 or 936-539-7813
Fax: 936-788-8337

Constable Precinct 4 (http://www.co.montgomery.tx.us/const4/index.shtml)
Travis Bishop
21130 U.S. Highway 59 #C, New Caney, Texas 77357
Phone: 281-577-8985 or 936-521-8985
Fax: 281-577-8984 or 936-521-8984
email: const4@co.montgomery.tx.us

Constable Precinct 5 (http://www.co.montgomery.tx.us/const5/index.shtml)
David Hill
31350 Industrial Lane, Magnolia, Texas 77355
Phone: 281-356-3883 or 936-539-7807
Fax: 281-356-5152

TAX FORECLOSURE SALES INFORMATION
http://www.co.montgomery.tx.us/taxf.shtml

Tax Foreclosure Sales occur the first Tuesday of every month on the west side Courthouse steps in downtown Conroe beginning at 10 a.m.

Below is a list of the Tax Attorneys who submit their lists to Constable Precinct 2 Gene DeForest's office. Two of them have links to the foreclosure listings as they are posted to their individual websites. Please note that some of the properties may not have a minimum bid listed, so you would need to contact Constable DeForest's office at (936) 539-7854 prior to the sale to obtain the minimum bids. Minimum bid information on Tax Foreclosures for the Willis Independent School District can be made to Constable Precinct 1 Don Chumley's office at (936) 539-7821.

- Perdue, Brandon, Fielder, Collins & Mott, L.L.P. (http://www.pbfcm.com/Houston_Tax_Sales.htm) County tax sale lists for Brazoria, Chambers, Fort Bend, Galveston, Harris County, Harris County Precint 4, Harris County Precinct 5, Montgomery, Waller.

  ROGUE INVESTOR NOTE: information saved on CD:
  USA Tax Lien Info/texas/montgomery_co_TX/purdue_brandon_tax_sale_lists.htm

- Linebarger, Goggan, Blair, Pena & Sampson, L.L.P. (http://www.publicans.com/home.htm) click on "Tax Sale Properties"

- Ray, Wood & Bonilla, L.L.P. (http://www.rwblaw.net/clientlist.htm) List of properties that are to be sold on the courthouse steps in Conroe, Montgomery County, Texas, at 10:00 AM on February 3, 2004

  ROGUE INVESTOR NOTE: information saved on CD:
  USA Tax Lien Info/texas/montgomery_co_TX/ray_wood_tax_sale_lists.htm

---

TARRANT COUNTY, TEXAS
http://www.tarrantcounty.com

TAX ASSESSOR/COLLECTOR'S OFFICE
http://www.tarrantcounty.com/taxweb/site/default.asp

Betsy Price, Tax Assessor/Collector
Tax Office email: taxoffice@tarrantcounty.com

(1) Locations
http://www.tarrantcounty.com/taxweb/cwp/browse.asp?a=13&bc=0&c=41024&taxwebNav=|

Main Office Building
100 East Weatherford Street
Fort Worth, Texas 76196
Phone: 817-884-1100

(2) Auctions
http://www.tarrantcounty.com/taxweb/cwp/browse.asp?a=13&bc=0&c=43136&taxwebNav=|

Forms: Delinquent Tax Sales - Request for Written Statement
http://www.tarrantcounty.com/taxweb/lib/taxweb/Request34015.pdf

Attorneys: Linebarger Goggan Blair & Sampson, LLP (http://www.publicans.com) and Perdue, Brandon, Fielder, Collins and Mott, LLP (http://www.pbfcm.com/about_us.htm)

(3) Linebarger Goggan Blair & Sampson, Property Tax Sales
http://www.publicans.com

(3a) Property Tax Sales
from http://www.publicans.com, click on "Tax Sale Properties" in left-hand column and then "Go to Tax Sale Property Listings"

The law firm of Linebarger Goggan Blair & Sampson, LLP places tax sale property listings online for the benefit of the public. You can search for current listings by completing the following form.

Do Your Own Search form available.

(4) Perdue, Brandon, Fielder, Collins & Mott, L.L.P.
http://www.pbfcm.com

Attorneys at Law providing property tax services for cities, schools, counties and special districts throughout Texas since 1970.

(4a) Tax Sales
http://www.pbfcm.com/tax_sales.htm

IMPORTANT: New Statewide Bidding Requirements: http://www.pbfcm.com/bidding_requirements.htm

The Texas Property Tax Code now requires that:

(1) An individual may not bid on or purchase property in the name of another.
(2) The officer conducting the sale will not deliver a deed to a purchaser, unless the purchaser exhibits an unexpired written statement from the County Tax Collector showing the purchaser does not owe delinquent taxes to any taxing jurisdiction in the county.
(3) A request to the County Tax Collector for a statement of no delinquent taxes must be made in writing. A request form is available at the County Tax Office.

For important information about tax sales please click here: http://www.pbfcm.com/tax_sale_%20info.htm

Tax foreclosure sales are conducted by the Sheriff or a constable of the county where the property is located. These sales are required to be held on the first Tuesday of the month between the hours of 10:00 a.m. and 4:00 p.m. on the courthouse steps at a place designated by the commissioners' court. All sales are for cash. The officer conducting the sale will adjourn the sale to allow the successful bidder a short time to pay the cash price. However, if the cash price is not paid within that time, the sale will be reconvened in time to complete the sale before 4:00 p.m.

All sales are without warranty and subject to the owner's right of redemption. The redemption period is two years for homestead property and agriculture use property and six months for all other property. Purchasers receive a Sheriff or Constable's deed that is without warranty. Bidders should satisfy themselves concerning title and location of the property and improvements on the property including any encroachments prior to bidding.

To receive an email notice of future updates to our sale pages, click here: http://lb.bcentral.com/ex/manage/subscriberprefs.aspx?customerid=37721

Sales lists provided by county.

FAQ: http://www.pbfcm.com/faq.htm#Answer%20to%204:

Re-Sales by county: http://www.pbfcm.com/Resales.htm

(4b) Legislative Updates
http://www.pbfcm.com/Legislative_Update.htm

(4c) Office Locations
http://www.pbfcm.com/office_locations.htm

Amarillo Larry Brandon, Partner 1616 S. Kentucky, Bldg. D Amarillo, Texas 79105 (800) 692-4053 mailto:lbrandon.pbfcm.com	Lubbock Jim Collins, Partner 2005 Broadway Lubbock, Texas 79401 (800) 624-5329 mailto:jcollins@pbfcm.com
Arlington C. David Fielder, Partner 4025 Woodland Park Blvd. #300 Arlington, Texas 76013 (800) 772-5490 mailto:dfielder@pbfcm.com	Midland W. Tracy Crites, Jr. 24 Smith Road, Tgaar Tower, Suite 304 Midland, Texas 79701 (432) 522-2427 mailto:tcrites@pbfcm.com
Austin John Banks 6300 La Calma, Suite 450 Austin, Texas 78752 (800) 290-8391 mailto:jbanks@pbfcm.com	Tyler Tab Beall, Partner 102 N. College, Suite 610 Tyler, Texas 75702 (800) 262-5404 mailto:tbeall@pbfcm.com
Houston Michael J. Darlow, Partner 1235 N. Loop W., Suite 600 Houston, Texas 77008 (800) 833-5886 mailto:mdarlow@pbfcm.com	Wichita Falls Harold Lerew, Partner 900 Eighth Street, Suite 1100 Wichita Falls, Texas 76301 (800) 525-2481 mailto:hlerew@pbfcm.com

CONSTABLES
http://www.tarrantcounty.com/constable/site/default.asp

Constables are constitutionally authorized peace officers elected by precinct. There are eight Constables in Tarrant County. The Constables of Tarrant County are also responsible for the Delinquent Tax Sales.

Constable, Precinct 1	Constable, Precinct 2
Jerry Crowder	David Harris
Courthouse 100 Weatherford	Southeast Sub-Courthouse 724 E. Border - Suite 202
Fort Worth, Texas 76196-0203	Arlington, Texas 76010
817-884-1385	817-548-3910
Constable, Precinct 3	Constable, Precinct 4
Zane Hilger	Jack Allen
Northeast Sub-Courthouse 645 Grapevine Hwy.	Northwest Sub-Courthouse 6713 Telephone Road
Hurst, Texas 76054	Fort Worth, Texas 76135
817-581-3610	817-238-4411
Constable, Precinct 5	Constable, Precinct 6
Sergio Deleon	Joe Kubes
Criminal Courts Building 300 W. Belknap	Southwest Sub-Courthouse 6551 Granbury Rd.
Fort Worth, Texas 76196-0207	Fort Worth, Texas 76133
817-884-1892	817-370-4510
Constable, Precinct 7	Constable, Precinct 8
Mike Honeycutt	Chester Luckett
1100 East Broad Street, Suite 201	Poly Sub-Courthouse 3212 Miller Avenue
Mansfield, Texas 76063	Fort Worth, Texas 76119
817-473-5110	817-531-5610
fax 817-473-5109	

(1) Delinquent Tax Sales
http://www.tarrantcounty.com/constable/cwp/browse.asp?a=4&bc=0&c=41884

(1a) October 7, 2003 Constable's Sale
http://www.tarrantcounty.com/constable/cwp/view.asp?A=4&Q=423314

ROGUE INVESTOR NOTE: information saved on CD:
USA Tax Lien Info/Texas/tarrant_co_TX/Constable February 3, 2003 Sale.htm

(2) Delinquent Tax Sales Questions
http://www.tarrantcounty.com/constable/cwp/browse.asp?a=15&bc=0&c=42121&constableNav=|

When is the tax deed auction scheduled? We do not conduct tax deed auctions. The type of sale that we conduct is a "Delinquent Tax Auction." We sell real property for the back taxes (county, school, city, etc.). Pursuant to Texas law, all sales are held on the first Tuesday of each month.

Where is the auction held and what time does it begin? All property sales are held on the Courthouse steps between the hours of 10:00 a.m. and 4:00 p.m. Tax Sales begin at 10:00 a.m. The Tarrant County Courthouse is located at 100 W. Weatherford Street, Fort Worth, Texas (at the intersection of Main Street and Weatherford Street).

What newspaper is the sale advertised in? We use the Fort Worth Commercial Recorder. Their telephone number is (817) 926-5351. Their newsstands are located at the Tarrant County Subcourthouses. You may also subscribe. This is the most convenient way to get a complete listing of the upcoming sale notices. We do not have a mailing list due to the lack of manpower. The sale notices are published once each week (usually on Tuesday) three weeks prior to the sale.

What form of payment is accepted? We only accept cash, cashier's check or money order made payable to Constable Zane Hilger. However, at the time of the sale we will hold a personal check for the full amount of your bid until 11:00 a.m. the following day. You must then come to our office located on the Grapevine Highway to replace that check with either cash, a cashier's check or money order for the full amount. We do not accept wire transfers, credit cards, traveler's checks or letters of credit. We also do not have a financing plan.

Does the county require payment in full at the end of the sale?
Yes. (See "What form of payment is accepted?")

How do I register for the sale? You do not have to register for our sale.

Can I bid from my home or office, by mail, fax or telephone? No. The bidder or his agent must be there in person.

If I am the successful bidder, what type of document is issued? The Constable's Office will issue a document entitled "Constable's Deed to Individual in Delinquent Tax Suits." This deed must be filed by the winning bidder with the Tarrant County Clerk's Office as soon as possible.

TRAVIS COUNTY, TEXAS
http://www.co.travis.tx.us

TAX ASSESSOR-COLLECTOR'S OFFICE
http://www.co.travis.tx.us/tax_assessor/default.asp

Nelda Well Spears, Tax Assessor-Collector

(1) Contact Information
http://www.co.travis.tx.us/tax_assessor/reach_us.asp

5501 Airport Boulevard
Austin, TX 78701
Phone: (512) 854-9473
Fax: (512) 854-9056
Mailing Address
P.O. Box 1748
Austin, TX 78767
e-mail Public Information Officer Tina Morton at tina.morton@co.travis.tx.us.

(2) Tax Sales
http://www.co.travis.tx.us/tax_assessor/foreclosure/default.asp

Important Changes

The Texas Legislature has instituted new requirements for participating in a tax sale. Travis County is implementing those requirements effective beginning with the October 7, 2003 tax sale. Get more information: http://www.co.travis.tx.us/tax_assessor/foreclosure/new_reqs.asp.

Tax sales are the final remedy to collect delinquent taxes and sales include properties located throughout the county. Conducted by a deputy constable, tax sales are always held on the first Tuesday of the month (unless it is a holiday) on the west steps of the Travis County Courthouse. Find out more: http://www.co.travis.tx.us/tax_assessor/foreclosure/tax_sale_info.asp.

Resales
Properties that do not sell at a tax sale become part of the resale inventory offered by the Travis County Tax Office and they are for sale at any time. Find out more: http://www.co.travis.tx.us/tax_assessor/foreclosure/resale_info.asp.

Disclaimer
Tax Sale and Resale Properties may have other liens against them. It is the responsibility of the bidder or purchaser to determine the liabilities that exist in each property before and after the sale.

There are no warranties, expressed or implied, including but not limited to the implied warranties of merchantability and fitness for a particular purpose. You buy the property "as is." No ad valorem taxes with related penalties, interests, costs, and expenses that have accrued subsequent to the judgment are waived and may be currently due. If you have any questions, you need to consult legal counsel of your choice.

Research Right of Redemption
To know about owner's rights, review Sec 34.21, Texas Property Tax Code
(http://www.taxnetusa.com/98code/chapter34.htm#34.21).

(3) Bidder's Guide to Tax Sales
http://www.co.travis.tx.us/tax_assessor/foreclosure/tax_sale_info.asp

What is a Tax Sale?
Tax Sales are the final remedy to collect delinquent taxes and sales include properties located throughout the county. Conducted by a deputy constable, tax sales are always held on the first Tuesday of the month at 10:00 a.m. on the west steps of the Travis County Courthouse, 1000 Guadalupe Street, in Austin, Texas.

To participate in a tax sale, bring the Statement for Person Eligible to Purchase Real Property at a Tax Sale (http://www.co.travis.tx.us/tax_assessor/foreclosure/new_reqs.asp) and arrive before 10:00 a.m. You will be assigned a number in order to bid. Full payment is due at the time of sale and can be made by check, money order, cashier's check, or credit card (add vendor fee of 3%).

Buyer Beware
It is your responsibility to determine the liabilities that exist on each property before and after the sale. You buy the property "as is." If you have any questions, you may wish to consult legal counsel of your choice.

Find Sale Data
Tax sale postings appear in the classified sections of local newspapers three weeks before the sale. At the same time, postings are available on a paper list (call 512-854-9473) or interested persons may access the list online at http://www.co.travis.tx.us/tax_assessor/foreclosure/tax_sales.asp.

A minimum bid is set for each property at the time of posting. The bid consists of the amount of taxes and fees due. If you purchase a property, you receive a receipt in the mail within a few days. Deeds are mailed within four to five weeks.

Right of Redemption
All properties sold at a tax sale are subject to the previous owner's right of redemption. Properties that do not have a homestead exemption or agricultural land use designation may be redeemed by the previous owner within six months of the date the deed was filed for all taxes and fees paid plus 25% is paid to the buyer. Properties with a homestead exemption or special land use designation have a two-year redemption period in which 25% is paid to the buyer in the first year and 50% in the second.

Properties that do not sell at the scheduled foreclosure sale may be included in the listing of resales (http://www.co.travis.tx.us/tax_assessor/foreclosure/resales.asp) found on this site.

(3a) List of Tax Sales
http://www.co.travis.tx.us/tax_assessor/foreclosure/tax_sales.asp

Before researching property sales information, here are some helpful definitions:

- Struck Off – Property did not sell on the original sale date and may be available for resale (http://www.co.travis.tx.us/tax_assessor/foreclosure/resale_info.asp).
- Pulled – Property was retrieved by original owner before the sale date.

The most recent tax sale information is for Tuesday, February 03, 2004 (http://www.co.travis.tx.us/tax_assessor/foreclosure/Feb). Deadline to request a statement of eligibility (http://www.co.travis.tx.us/tax_assessor/foreclosure/new_reqs.asp) to participate in this sale: Tuesday, January 27, 2004.

A list of properties to be auctioned is made available in the Austin American Statesman 21 days prior to the auction. Look for the online posting of properties for sale approximately 19 days before the sale date. Auctions are held at 10:00 a.m. on the west steps of the county courthouse at 1000 Guadalupe Street, Austin, Texas, on the first Tuesday of the month.

Methods of payment include cash, check, cashier's check, money order and major credit card. Payment made with credit cards will be subject to a service fee of 3%.

ROGUE INVESTOR NOTE: tax foreclosure sale list for February 3, 2004, sale saved on CD: USA Tax Lien Info/Texas/travis_co_TX/Tax Foreclosure Sale.htm

Buyer's Guide:
http://www.co.travis.tx.us/tax_assessor/foreclosure/tax_buyer_guide.asp

Tax Sale Bidder's Worksheet:
A print-friendly version of the worksheet is available at
http://www.co.travis.tx.us/tax_assessor/pdffiles/BiddersGuideWrksht.pdf

Part I: Property Identification

Where to find the information:
- The Travis Central Appraisal District (http://www.traviscad.org)
- Travis County Tax Sales property listings (http://www.co.travis.tx.us/tax_assessor/foreclosure/tax_sales.asp)
- Travis County Tax Office online property tax statements (http://www.traviscountytax.org/property/index.htm)
- Travis County Tax Office: phone 512-854-9473, or visit the Compliance Public Research area at 5501 Airport Boulevard, Austin, TX.

What to make note of:
- Parcel and billing number
- Control and cause number
- Property type and characteristics
- Owner name and mailing address. You'll need the owner's name to research the deed index.
- Property location (address)
- Legal description. This is needed to research liens.
- Is there a homestead exemption?
- Is it designated for agricultural use?
- Approximate minimum bid
- Approximate annual taxes
- Additional taxes
- Years and amount due

Part II: Property Ownership Record

Where to find the information
- County Clerk, Room 222, Travis County Courthouse, 1000 Guadalupe Street, 512-854-9188
- The County Clerk's Deed Index

What to make note of:
- Deed number
- Liens other than delinquent taxes
- Details of those liens
- Were liens released? If not, go to the District Clerk.

Part III: Lawsuits

Where to find the information:
- District Clerk, Room 301, Travis County Courthouse, 1000 Guadalupe Street, 512-854-9457

What to make note of:
- Defendants or lien holders to contact (for example, IRS)
- Judge's comments
- Lien status: extinguished?

Part IV: Property Summary

What to make note of:
- Visual inspection comments
- Minimum bid
- Status of other liens, if any
- Estimated annual taxes
- Additional taxes, if any
- Redemption period: 6 months or 2 years
- Total cost at tax sale plus applicable fees

(4) Title 1. Property Tax Code, Subtitle E. Collections and Delinquency, Chapter 34. Tax Sales and Redemption
http://www.taxnetusa.com/98code/chapter34.htm

(5) New Requirements for Participation in a Tax Sale
http://www.co.travis.tx.us/tax_assessor/foreclosure/new_reqs.asp

Starting October 7, 2003, two new legislative mandates take effect:

- First, in order to bid at a tax sale, an individual must first obtain a statement from the tax assessor-collector indicating they do not owe delinquent taxes in Travis County, or in a school district or municipality having territory in Travis County. The request for statement requires the individual to list all properties currently or previously owned, and the names as listed on the deed to each property. Owners of property with delinquent taxes due will not be permitted to bid at a tax sale.

  The fee is $10, and the qualified bidder will receive three copies of the statement. This statement will be good for 90 days from issuance date. This document is issued pursuant to the requirements of Texas Tax Code sections 34.0445 and 34.015 and is not a tax certificate issued per Texas Tax Code section 31.08.

  Call or visit the Tax Office at least 5 days before the sale to request this statement. You may download an application for the statement from this web site (http://www.co.travis.tx.us/tax_assessor/foreclosure/request_for_statement.pdf). This application can be mailed or brought in.

- The second part of the new law states that the bidder at a tax sale shall be listed as grantee of the tax deed. This means a bidder may no longer bid on behalf of another; however, the law does not apply to corporations, partnerships, charities, or agencies.

(5a) Request for Statement to be Eligible to Purchase Real Property At a Tax Sale
http://www.co.travis.tx.us/tax_assessor/foreclosure/request_for_statement.pdf

(6) Resales Buyer's Guide
http://www.co.travis.tx.us/tax_assessor/foreclosure/resales_buyer_guide.asp

Minimum Bids: A minimum bid is set for each property at the time of posting. The bid consists of the amount of taxes and fees due. Find bid information listed with each property.

Buyer's Guide to Resales

1. **Check property sale listings:** Check the Travis County website (http://www.co.travis.tx.us/tax_assessor/foreclosure/resales.asp) or contact the tax office by email (tax_office@co.travis.tx.us).
2. **Visit or call the Tax Office:** Contact the Tax Office (http://www.co.travis.tx.us/tax_assessor/reach_us.asp) to obtain property information on the property worksheet below or check property records at http://www.traviscountytax.org or http://www.traviscad.org.
3. **Inspect the property:** Decide if this is a property you wish to own.
4. **Visit the County Clerk:** Using the legal description, research the Property Ownership Record in the county clerk's office (http://www.co.travis.tx.us/county_clerk/default.asp) for liens and note those that have not been released. You must have the owner's name to research the deed index. Since the owner of record is no longer listed with this property after foreclosure of the tax lien, locate his/her name for research by contacting the tax office at (512) 854-9473. A cause number may also be used to identify the owner at the district clerk's office.
5. **Visit the District Clerk:** If there are liens that remain, research the lawsuit (including the judge's remarks) in the district clerk's office (http://www.co.travis.tx.us/district_clerk/default.asp) to determine if the lien will be released or not when the property is sold.
6. **MAIL BIDS ONLY:** WALK IN BIDS WILL NOT BE ACCEPTED. MAIL YOUR WRITTEN PROPOSAL WITH PROPERTY IDENTIFICATION TO Elliott Beck, Assistant Travis County Attorney, Resale, P.O. Box 1748, Austin, TX 78767. You can pay by check, money order, cashier's check or Novus Discover credit card. The buyer who submits the first payment (minimum bid*) that is honored receives the property. Subsequent bids will be returned. Those who purchase a property receive a receipt in the mail within a few days. Deeds are mailed within 4-5 weeks.

*PLEASE NOTE: If the minimum bid showing is 0, please contact the tax office (512 854-9473) for further information.

Sample Bid Submission Form: http://www.co.travis.tx.us/tax_assessor/pdffiles/bidform1.pdf. Directions: Print this form, enter the appropriate information, enclose payment, and MAIL to the address on the form. This form will not be accepted in person.

Property Worksheet

- Property Identification:
  Access the website, call the Tax Office at 512-854-9473, or visit 1010 Lavaca, Compliance Public Research area for this information.

- Property Ownership Record:
  Research this information in the county clerk's office: http://www.co.travis.tx.us/county_clerk/default.asp. You must have the property owner's name.

- If there is a lien which has not been released, proceed to the district clerk's office: http://www.co.travis.tx.us/district_clerk/default.asp.

- Lawsuit:
  Research this information in the district clerk's office: http://www.co.travis.tx.us/district_clerk/default.asp.

(6a) Sample Bid Submission Form
http://www.co.travis.tx.us/tax_assessor/pdffiles/bidform1.pdf

---

WILLIAMSON COUNTY, TEXAS
http://www.wilco.org/index.html

TAX ASSESSOR/COLLECTOR'S OFFICE
http://www.wilco.org/Assessor/Tax.html

Deborah Hunt, Tax Assess/Collector
710 S. Main Street, S-102
Georgetown, Texas 78626
Property Tax phone: 512-943-1603

Delinquent property tax sales are handled by the Law Firm of McCreary, Veselka, Bragg, and Allen. Sales will be held on the first Tuesday of the month on the south side of the main courthouse, when there is property to be sold.

(1) Tax Foreclosure Sales
http://www.wilco.org/Assessor/propertytax.html

Auctions are scheduled for 10:00 a.m. the first Tuesday of the month on the south steps of the County Courthouse.

Direct link to existing Delinquent Property Tax Sales list.
http://www.wilco.org/Assessor/tax%20sales/Feb2004/feb.pdf

(2) Tax Foreclosure Sales Rules
http://www.wilco.org/Assessor/tax%20sales/Main/rules.pdf

Tax Lien Sales: No

Tax Deed Sales: Yes

Rating: Three Stars (***)

Interest Rate: None, state law only allows for tax deed sales.

Sale Period:
The statute sets the date of January 16th as the date when all real estate subject to a lien for any taxes which are then delinquent is considered to have been sold to the county at a preliminary tax sale (this is not an actual sale, rather an operation of law) to pay the taxes, penalty, and costs for which the real estate is liable.

All property sold to the county through the above described mechanism, and that is not redeemed by March 31 following the lapse of four years from the date of the preliminary tax sale (January 16), is listed with the county auditor for final sale in May. This is known as the Final May Tax Sale Listing.

Redemption Period:
Owners of record have 4 years to redeem their property from the date of the preliminary tax sale.

Bidding Process:
The county governing bodies are afforded by statute several methods by which to accept bids during the final May sale. The most widely used method would be that of accepting the highest bid offered for an entire parcel of property. There are nine other options allowed by statute for disposing of delinquencies at sale. However, no bid may be accepted for less than the taxes, interest, penalties and costs due.

State-Specific Information:
Utah has 29 counties. Tax certificates are sold at the preliminary tax sale on all real property delinquent for nonpayment of taxes as of November 30. The county acquires all such tax certificates.

Links for All Utah Counties: Provided on CD.

Detailed County-Specific Information:

SALT LAKE COUNTY, UTAH
http://www.co.slc.ut.us

TREASURER'S OFFICE
http://www.treasurer.slco.org

Larry Richardson, Treasurer

Salt Lake County Treasurer
2001 S. State Street N1200
Salt Lake City, UT 84190-1250
phone: (801) 468-3400
Email: slcoTreasurer@co.slc.ut.us

(1) Some Important Property Tax Dates
http://www.treasurer.slco.org/cfml/tr_ti_dates.cfm?subnav=tinfo%2Ecfm

May, June: During May and/or June, the Auditor conducts the final tax sale(s) of properties for which the redemption period has expired. Public notice of the final tax sale is published in a newspaper of general circulation once each week for four consecutive weeks immediately preceeding the scheduled sale. Notice is also provided by certified and first class mail to the recorded owner, the occupant, and all other interests of record. Properties may be redeemed on behalf of the recorded owner at any time prior to the tax sale.

(2) Property Tax FAQ
http://www.treasurer.slco.org/cfml/tr_fq_ptax.cfm?subnav=div%2Ecfm

Does the County sell property for back taxes? How do I find out about the tax sale?
Each May, the Salt Lake County Auditor conducts a sale of properties that have a delinquent tax which is at least 5 years delinquent. The properties to be sold are advertised in a newspaper approximately four weeks prior to the sale. Utah State law does not permit the sale of tax liens or tax lien certificates. For more information about the Tax Sale, please contact the Tax Division of the Salt Lake County Auditor's Office (http://www.slpropertyinfo.org).

AUDITOR'S OFFICE
http://www.slcountyauditor.org

Craig B. Sorensen, Auditor

(1) About/Contact
http://www.slcoaud.org/docs/site/aboutus.html

Salt Lake County Auditor's Office
2001 South State Street #N3300
Salt Lake City, Utah 84190-1100
Main Reception Desk: (801) 468-3381
Fax: 468-3296
email: Audinter@aud.co.slc.ut.us

Mike Reed, Director, Tax Administration Division, phone: 801-468-3256
Mike Grobstein, Associate Director, Tax Administration Division, phone: 801-468-3262

Vermont

Tax Lien Sales: Yes

Tax Deed Sales: No

Rating: Three Stars (***)

Interest Rate: 12%

Sale Period: Varies, but sometimes in December.

Redemption Period: 1 year

Bidding Process: Varies, handled by municipalities.

State-Specific Information:
There are 14 counties in Vermont. The collection of taxes and the disposition of real property for nonpayment of taxes are handled by the town and city administrations in Vermont.

5136. Interest on over-due taxes
(a) When a municipality votes under an article in the warning to collect interest on over-due taxes, such taxes, however collected, shall be due and payable not later than December 1, and shall bear interest at the rate of not more than one percent per month or fraction thereof for the first three months and thereafter one and one-half percent per month or fraction thereof from the due date of such tax. A municipality having so voted to collect interest as hereinbefore provided, and the amount thereof, shall thereafter collect such interest each year until the municipality shall vote otherwise at a meeting duly warned for the purposes of voting on such question.

Links for All Vermont Counties: Provided on CD.

Detailed County-Specific Information:

WINDSOR COUNTY, VERMONT

FINANCE/TREASURER'S OFFICE
City of Hartford, Vermont

Hartford Municipal Building, 1st floor
171 Bridge Street, White River Junction, VT 05001
Telephone: (802) 295-3002 / Fax: (802) 295-6382

The tax sale is conducted in a manner similar to an auction. The delinquent tax collector identifies the property, and specifies the minimum amount that must be paid to satisfy the delinquent taxes, penalties, and fees outstanding. The property is sold to the highest bidder, so long as the highest bid equals or exceeds the minimum amount specified. In cases where there are no other bids, the Town will be acquiring the liens and shall thus be entitled to tax deeds for these properties as allowed by statute. After property has been sold at tax sale, the owner has up to one year from the date of sale to redeem or repay the taxes, penalties, and fees, along with interest at the rate of 1% per month. At the end of the year, if the property has not been redeemed, the Town will issue to the person purchasing the tax lien a Tax Deed, which is the equivalent of a Quit Claim Deed. Persons receiving such a Tax Deed are responsible for the payment of the balance of any taxes that may be unpaid on the property at that time, as well as the payment of any applicable Vermont Property Transfer Taxes.

Tax Lien Sales: No

Tax Deed Sales: Yes

Rating: Two Stars (**)

Interest Rate: None, state only has tax deed sales.

Sale Period: Sales occur approximately four times per year.

Redemption Period: None, state only has tax deed sales.

Bidding Process:
Properties are sold to the highest bidder. There is no minimum bid, other than the back taxes, penalties, fees and liens. The court must approve the sale by hearing arguments, if any.

State-Specific Information:
There are 95 counties in Virginia and 40 independent cities.

Links for All Virginia Counties: Provided on CD.

Detailed County-Specific Information:

FAIRFAX COUNTY, VIRGINIA
http://www.co.fairfax.va.us

DEPARTMENT OF TAX ADMINISTRATION
http://www.co.fairfax.va.us/living/taxes

(1) How to Contact
http://www.co.fairfax.va.us/dta/contact.htm

Department of Tax Administration (DTA)
Fairfax County Government Center, Suite 223
12000 Government Center Parkway
Fairfax, Virginia 22035

DTA Director, Kevin Greenlief
email: kevin.greenlief@fairfaxcounty.gov

Real Estate Division Director, Janet Coldsmith
janet.coldsmith@fairfaxcounty.gov or jcolds@fairfaxcounty.gov
http://www.co.fairfax.va.us/dta/re_home.htm

Personal assistance, phone: 703-222-8234

(2) Properties to be Auctioned
http://www.co.fairfax.va.us/dta/auction.htm

In accordance with <u>Section 58.1 of the Code of Virginia</u>, Fairfax County will be auctioning the following property for the payment of delinquent taxes at the time and location designated below. For more information, contact the Fairfax County Sheriff's Department at 703-246-3227.

There are currently no properties up for auction. Please check back often. This page is updated as sales are scheduled.

(3) Revenue Collection Division
http://www.co.fairfax.va.us/dta/delinquent_collections.htm

The Delinquent Collection section has several enforcement and collection methods to aid in the collection of past due taxes that do not require court intervention. These methods include the following:

<u>Seizure of Property or Assets</u>: In extreme cases, the Department of Tax Administration may work with the Office of the Sheriff to seize property and/or assets that can be used to satisfy or can be sold to satisfy delinquent taxes. These properties are sold through auctions (http://www.co.fairfax.va.us/dta/auction.htm) that are open to the public.

If you have any questions regarding the collection of delinquent taxes, call us at 703-222-8234 (TTY: 703-222-7594).

SHERIFF'S OFFICE
http://www.co.fairfax.va.us/ps/sheriff

Public Safety Complex
4110 Chain Bridge Road
Fairfax, VA 22030

Tax Lien Sales: No

Tax Deed Sales: Yes

Rating: Two Stars (**)

Interest Rate: None, state only has tax deed sales.

Sale Period: Varies

Redemption Period: Varies

Bidding Process: Varies

State-Specific Information:
There are 39 counties in Washington. Tax collections and the sale of property for nonpayment of taxes are handled at the county level by the county treasurer.

Links for All Washington Counties: Provided on CD.

Detailed County-Specific Information:

KING COUNTY, WASHINGTON
http://www.metrokc.gov

TREASURY OPERATIONS
http://www.metrokc.gov/finance/treasury.htm

Finance and Business Operations Division
Department of Executive Services
King County
email: DOFweb.finance@metrokc.gov

Manager Garry Holmes
500 Fourth Avenue
Seattle, WA 98104
Mail Stop: ADM-FI-611
Phone: 206-296-7326
Fax: 206-205-0776
TTY: 206-296-4184

(1) Frequently Asked Questions About Property Tax
http://www.metrokc.gov/finance/treasury/kctaxinfo/TaxInfo_FAQ.htm

When does foreclosure begin and what does it involve? Real property with a tax that is three or more years delinquent is subject to foreclosure after April 30. To redeem the property after foreclosure proceedings begin, all years' taxes, interest, penalties and administrative costs must be paid. For further information, please call (206) 296-4184. Senior citizen and disabled property owners may qualify for deferral from foreclosure. (RCW 84.64)

(2) 2004 King County Tax Foreclosure Information
http://www.metrokc.gov/finance/treasury/foreclosure

Date: December 17, 2004 at 9:00 a.m.
Location: Washington State Convention & Trade Center, Rooms 2A & 2B, 800 Convention Place, Seattle, WA 98101
Publication Date: Unknown

1. In 2004, the properties subject to foreclosure are those on which the 2001 full year tax is delinquent. In some cases, 2000 or earlier taxes may also be delinquent. The grace period is 3 years and the full year 2001 taxes will be 3 years past due on May 1, 2004. NOTE: It does not matter if the 2002, 2003 or 2004 taxes are paid. It is not when there are 3 years of taxes past due but when 1 year's tax is 3 years past due that foreclosure begins.

2. *We do not maintain a mailing list to notify people of each year's tax foreclosure.* The great majority of people who ask for information never attend the auction or do any research once they find out what is required and what is involved. Further, people move without telling us and it is a waste of county resources when the list is returned. After we file in court in late May, a list of property in foreclosure may be found at http://www.metrokc.gov/finance/treasury/foreclosure. The Summons and Notice, which includes a list of the properties, will be published in the Seattle Times classified (legal) section sometime in late October after all our title reports are completed. After we publish this notice, a paper copy computer list may be purchased for $5.00 ($8.00 if mailed).

3. We do not sell "tax certificates" or "deeds" of any nature. In some states you may purchase a certificate of some kind showing that you paid the delinquent taxes, but we don't have any information on this procedure because there is no provision for it in Washington State law.

4. If you obtain a list from us for research purposes, remember that you will need to come into our office or visit our web site periodically to delete those accounts that were paid since your list was printed. The web site list will normally be updated once a week on Monday. Due to the volume of work this information will not be provided by telephone. Parcels may be redeemed from foreclosure at any time up to the day before the auction; thus, we do not know what will be in the sale until the morning of the auction.

5. There is no redemption period after the sale except in cases where the owner on the day of the sale was either a minor child or a person adjudicated to be legally incompetent. In those cases, there is a 3-year redemption period.

6. As real estate taxes are in the first lien position, the tax foreclosure extinguishes all other encumbrances including but not limited to Deeds of Trust, mortgages, contracts, liens, judgments and any similar items. However, any Local Improvement Assessments (LID's) remain and become the obligation of the buyer. Also, Internal Revenue liens remain.

7. Parcels are sold in the same order as they appeared in the newspaper and in the computer list mentioned in #2. Parcels are in numerical order by tax account number which, in turn, derives from the alphabetical order of the plat name or from the Section, Township & Range if the property is unplatted.

8. **ALL SALES ARE FINAL. PROPERTIES ARE SOLD ON A "WHERE IS" AND "AS IS" BASIS.**

All research must be done by the interested party. Normally this would include checking maps in the Assessor's Office and doing research through the public computer terminals in the Assessor's Office. An on-site inspection should also be made. Just because a property looks desirable on the map does not mean it is in actuality. The map does not show the topography such as ravines, hill, slopes, etc., nor does the map show what is on the property (dense growth, swamp, boulders, etc.). Some properties may be private roads covered by easements for ingress and egress. Easements are not extinguished by the foreclosure sale but remain with the land. You may not block the easement to try to extort money out of the users.

Similarly, when you see that a property lies near or under a transmission line easement, there will likely be restrictions against building anything on the land. Transmission line easements do appear on the Assessor's maps but private easements do not.

Some properties may be subject to use restrictions and covenants set up in the original plat. Some of these may be labeled Open Space, Open Area, Greenbelt or similar. Their use is often strictly limited. The King County Department of Developmental & Environmental Services has ruled it will not issue building permits on any such lots. You should also be aware of properties where the legal description contains the term "Drainage Easement" or Retention Pond" or similar terms.

It is up to you to know exactly what you are bidding on. We cannot stress this too strongly. Every year people who have done little or no research or who do not know how to read a legal description buy properties that, to them, are totally useless. Knowledgeable parties who have done the proper research will avoid these properties. We do not overturn a sale and refund the purchase price because a bidder didn't know what they were bidding on, nor because they didn't understand the legal description.

9. Do not count on buying a house at the foreclosure auction. Normally, owners of improved properties subject to tax foreclosure will raise the money to redeem the property before the sale, often at the last minute. Most houses that are foreclosed on have delinquent loans held by banks, mortgage companies or other lenders. There is no department within the county that has information on these lending agency foreclosures.

10. Properties not sold to the public at the auction are sold to King County. These parcels are thereafter called "Tax Title Properties." Most of these parcels are of little value, which is why they didn't sell at the auction in the first place. Many of these properties are "dangling strips" or "isolated triangles." The former are usually narrow strips anywhere from a few inches to a few feet wide that were left over because of an error in a legal description, a survey or platting error, or a mismeasurement by the Assessor's office. The triangles generally are created when a street or highway cuts through a lot leaving a small isolated triangle cut off from the rest of the lot or block.

11. The County may try to sell the Tax Title Properties at some future date after the foreclosure sale, but only those properties that may have some value to an adjacent owner. Tax Title sale information may be obtained by calling the Property Services Division at 206-296-7470.

12. THE TAX FORECLOSURE AUCTION

No King County Employee or officer, or person who is an immediate family member of and residing with a King County employee, may bid at the sale, nor may such person bid as an agent or allow any agent to bid on their behalf. (RCW 84.64.080)

We do not have a bidder registration requirement.

The minimum bid includes the amount due to the County for the tax, interest, penalties and foreclosure costs. Bidding must be done in person, not by phone or mail. This is an open oral auction, not a sealed bid auction.

Payment by the successful bidder must be made immediately upon winning the bid. Payment must be made by cashier's check, money order, certified check, or cash. NO OTHER FORM OF PAYMENT WILL BE ACCEPTED INCLUDING PERSONAL CHECKS, BUSINESS, CHECKS, CREDIT CARD CHECKS, TRAVELER'S CHECKS, LETTERS OF CREDIT OR SIMILAR. There are no exceptions to this policy. Checks are made payable to the King County Treasury.

Most people bring a cashier's check for the maximum amount they are willing to spend, whether they intend to buy just one parcel or bid on several. If the check is for too much, we refund the difference, but if it's not enough you won't have time to run to the bank for more.

Foreclosure section phone number: 206-296-4184.

THE FOLLOWING IS THE 2003 FORECLOSURE AUCTION "TERMS OF SALE". THE "TERMS OF SALE" ARE PROVIDED FOR INFORMATIONAL PURPOSES ONLY AND MAY BE DIFFERENT FOR THE 2004 SALE.

KING COUNTY TREASURY OPERATIONS – KING COUNTY, WASHINGTON
TAX FORECLOSURE SALE, DECEMBER 12, 2003

TERMS OF SALE

1. The opening bid as announced by the auctioneer includes all unpaid general real property taxes, all unpaid deferred real property taxes, all personal property and gambling taxes which have been certified to real property, all delinquent compensating use taxes, all demolition assessments which have been certified to the King County Treasury Operations, all special taxes (but NOT Special Assessments), interest to and including December 12, 2003, penalties, and foreclosure costs, surface water management charges, King Conservation District Fees, Fire Protection Fees, noxious weed fees, and principal & interest due King County on unpaid Tax Title Contracts, if any.

2. Properties are sold subject to special assessments. We will announce, prior to the bidding on a parcel, if a parcel is encumbered by liens for delinquent special assessments if that fact was reported to us by Pacific Northwest Title Company of Washington, Inc. Whether or not such an announcement is made, however, parcels are sold subject to any special assessments that may have been placed on such property.

3. We will also announce prior to bidding on certain parcels that they were encumbered by Internal Revenue Service liens if that fact was reported to us by Pacific Northwest Title Company of Washington, Inc. Whether or not we make such an announcement, however, parcels sold that were encumbered by an Internal Revenue Service lien are subject to redemption within 120 days of this sale.

4. Bids must be made in increments of no less than $10, in even dollar amounts.

5. The sale will be made by auction to the highest and best bidder for cash. This is a cash sale for the full amount of the final bid plus other fees described in paragraph 8 below. Only cash, certified or cashier's checks and money orders will be accepted and the bidder must pay in full at the time of the successful bid. Personal checks will not be accepted, nor any other form of payment not specified above.

6. If a winning bid is accepted and the bidder defaults by not rendering payment before the completion of the next sale, the parcel shall be immediately rebid. Rebidding shall start at the original minimum bid. A bidder defaulting more than once shall be excluded from further bidding on any parcel at this auction.

7. The sale of each parcel shall be considered final and closed upon acceptance of the winning bid. Unsold properties will be offered a second time at the end of the sale and if there are again no bids, the property will be sold to King County.

8. The successful bidder will be responsible for payment to King County of $26.00 for the deed and recording fee. The payment for the deed and recording fees must be made at the same time as payment of the amount of the final bid price. A receipt for payment of the bid price and fees for the deed and recording is given at the time of payment.

9. The parcels are offered on a "where is" and "as is" basis, and King County makes no representation of warranty, expressed or implied, nor any guaranty of warranty, expressed or implied, as to the condition of title to any property nor the physical condition of any property or its fitness for any use or purpose. Bidders are further advised that certain properties may be subject to easements or use restrictions set forth in the Covenants, Rights, and Restrictions of certain plats, as well as in zoning and other land use controls. Certain parcels may be designated as "Open Space", "open area", "permanent open area", "common area", "drainage" or similar designations, and are subject to open space restrictions which include, but are not limited to, prohibitions on placing improvements on such parcels. Bidders are further advised that King County does not warrant or make any express or implied representations regarding the physical condition of any parcel including, but not limited to, whether the parcel is contaminated with hazardous waste or contamination from any source, or whether the parcel is subject to restrictions based

on the King County sensitive areas ordinance or other applicable land use laws or regulations. For any property purchased, it shall be the buyer's sole responsibility to make a determination whether any such contamination exists or whether the property is restricted in any manner.

10. If you are a successful bidder, a Tax Deed will be issued for the parcel in about 45 days and forwarded to the King County Records, Elections and Licensing Services Division for recording. If you are a successful bidder, your name and address as given to us for issuance of the Tax Deed will be available by law as a public record. Because of the volume of paperwork which needs to be accomplished following the auction, we will not be able to make records from the foreclosure sale available for inspection by the public until January 7, 2004.

11. No King County employee or officer, or person who is an immediate family member of and residing with a King County employee, may bid at the sale, nor may such person bid as an agent or allow any agent to bid on their behalf.

12. No one claiming any right, title, interest or estate in the property may redeem at this time or hereafter; EXCEPT, the real property of any minor or person adjudicated as legally incompetent may be redeemed at any time within three years after the date of the Tax Deed.

13. It is possible that a parcel may be registered under the Torrens System. The King County Treasury Division cannot advise you if it is. If this is the case, the purchaser will be required to register certain portions of the foreclosure proceedings themselves and at additional expense.

14. 2004 first half taxes are due on April 30, 2004. You will be mailed a current 2004 tax statement on February 14, 2004 for any parcels you purchase at the name and address provided for the Tax Deed in paragraph 8 above. If you have not received a 2004 statement by March 5, 2004, contact our office at 206-296-0923.

15. If necessary, we will take a lunch break at 12:00 noon and resume the sale at 12:45 p.m.

Foreclosure section phone number: 206-296-4184.

Continue to King County Property Tax Foreclosure List:
http://www.metrokc.gov/finance/treasury/foreclosure/Disclaimer.asp

(2a) Property Tax Foreclosure List Disclaimer
http://www.metrokc.gov/finance/treasury/foreclosure/Disclaimer.asp

(2b) Property Tax Foreclosure List
http://www.metrokc.gov/finance/treasury/foreclosure/ShowMessage.asp

There are currently no property tax foreclosure properties listed in King County, Washington.

The 2004 property tax foreclosure list will be available the second week of June 2004.

ASSESSOR-TREASURER'S OFFICE
http://www.co.pierce.wa.us/PC/abtus/ourorg/at/at.htm

(1) Contact Information
http://www.co.pierce.wa.us/pc/abtus/ourorg/at/email2.htm

Real Property and/or ULID Foreclosure:
Sandy Moore at smoore@co.pierce.wa.us or 253-798-7133
Ken Madsen, Assessor-Treasurer, at pcatr@co.pierce.wa.us or 253-798-2775

2401 South 35th Street, Room 142
Tacoma, Washington 98409
Customer Service Hotline: (253) 798-6111

(2) Property Tax Information
http://www.co.pierce.wa.us/pc/abtus/ourorg/at/property_info.htm

(3) General Foreclosure Information
http://www.co.pierce.wa.us/pc/abtus/ourorg/at/bulletin/foreclosure.htm

Real property with a tax that is three (3) or more years delinquent is subject to foreclosure. To redeem the property after foreclosure proceedings begin, all years' taxes, interest, penalties, and foreclosure costs must be paid (RCW 84.64).

The only way to purchase a parcel from foreclosure is to attend the annual auction held in December of each year. A minimum bid will be solicited for each parcel. This bid must include all taxes, interest, penalties and foreclosure costs. The auction is verbal and full payment is due at the time of successful bid. Acceptable forms of payment are cash or cashier's check only, made payable to Pierce County. If you present a cashier's check that is greater than the amount of your bid, a refund of the difference will be available on the next business day.

The successful bidder will receive a Treasurer's Deed without any expressed or implied warranty. Pierce County does not warrant any property suitable for any use, nor do they make any claims regarding easements, covenants or restrictions. All parcels are sold "as is" and all sales are final. Potential purchasers should seek the advice of a real estate attorney if additional information is needed. Pierce County does NOT issue Tax Lien Certificates as Washington state Is NOT a Tax Lien state.

2004 Foreclosure Sale will be held in December.

How to Prepare for Auction

- A list of properties subject to foreclosure is not available until after the amended *Certificate of Delinquency* is filed each year. In September this list will be available online and will also be printed in the classified section of *The Eatonville Dispatch,* the Official County Newspaper, under "Legal Notices." This ad will list the parcels in foreclosure at that time. The number of parcels listed will change dramatically by the date of the sale in December. An updated list is kept at the Assessor-Treasurer's public counter so individuals can determine which properties have been redeemed. Anyone desiring information please call the Foreclosure Department (253) 798-7133 or e-mail smoore@co.pierce.wa.us.
- Research is the key to purchasing a parcel to meet your needs. The Assessor-Treasurer's office has computers, maps and other research tools available for your use at the public service counter. There is a self-service area as well as trained counter personnel to assist you. Self-service classes are available. Please call this office at (253) 798-6111 for days and times of classes. Also, due to limited staff, research assistance is not available by mail or phone.

Parcels that do not receive the minimum bid will be announced as "sold to Pierce County." This means they are now a *Tax Title* property and may be sold at auction at another date and time. For information regarding these parcels, please call Real Property Management at (253) 798-7223, or email shedlu1@co.pierce.wa.us.

Utility Local Improvement District (ULID) foreclosure begins after one annual installment is two years delinquent. There is a two-year right of redemption and a Certificate of Sale will be issued to the successful bidder. After the redemption time has expired, a Utility Local Improvement Deed will be issued to the previously successful bidder. Please call 253-798-3704, or email kculber@co.pierce.wa.us with further questions or concerns regarding ULID foreclosures.

(4) How to Foreclosure Information
from http://www.co.pierce.wa.us/pc/abtus/ourorg/at/bulletin/foreclosure.htm, mouse over "Foreclosure" in left column and click on "How to Foreclosure Information"

Any parcel may be redeemed (paid) in advance of the sale date, and removed from the foreclosure list. Only parties with a recorded interest in a parcel may pay the delinquent taxes. If you are paying taxes on behalf of a taxpayer whose real property is in foreclosure, state law requires that you provide notarized documentation of the relationship between you and the taxpayer. The Pierce County Authorization to Pay Property Tax as Agent form is available on-line. Please have your documentation completed and notarized before coming in to pay taxes. The Assessor-Treasurer's office does not have a notary available. To determine the current amount owing, obtain the ten-digit parcel number and call Sandy Moore at (253) 798-7133 or Kim Culbertson at (253) 798-3704.

All payments must be in full and paid by cash or cashier's check only.

Legal descriptions listed are for tax purposes only.

Please Note: All parcels are sold "where is" and "as is" without any representation or warranty, expressed or implied.

Pierce County would like you, as a potential buyer, to be aware that any parcel of property subject to foreclosure could have environmental issues. We encourage all potential buyers to research all parcels fully. If you have questions or concerns regarding environmental issues, please contact the Tacoma/ Pierce County Health Department at (253) 798-6470 or (253) 798-6566. The Assessor-Treasurer's Office recommends that potential bidders visit a parcel to ascertain its' merits before bidding at auction.

Generally, if a parcel has a street address it also has a structure, but there are many exceptions to this rule.

(5) Foreclosure Form: Authorization to Pay Property Tax as Agent
from http://www.co.pierce.wa.us/pc/abtus/ourorg/at/bulletin/foreclosure.htm, click on "Forms On-Line" in left column, scroll down page to "Foreclosure" header, and click on "Authorization to Pay Property Tax as Agent"

SHERIFF'S OFFICE
http://www.co.pierce.wa.us/PC/Abtus/ourorg/sheriff

Sheriff Paul Pastor
Headquarters:
930 Tacoma Avenue South (1st Floor of the County-City Building)
Tacoma, Washington 98402
Phone: (253) 798-7530

(1) Contact Information
http://www.co.pierce.wa.us/pc/Abtus/ourorg/sheriff/locfone/pcphone.htm

Civil Unit, phone: 253-798-7520

SNOHOMISH COUNTY, WASHINGTON
http://www.co.snohomish.wa.us

TREASURER'S OFFICE
http://www.co.snohomish.wa.us/treasurer/index.asp

Bob Dantini, Treasurer

(1) Contact Information
http://www.co.snohomish.wa.us/treasurer/Trs02-ContactUs.asp

3000 Rockefeller, M/S 501
Everett, WA 98201
phone: 425-388-3366
email inquiry: http://www.co.snohomish.wa.us/treasurer/Trs02-ContactForm.asp
phone: 425-388-3606 – Foreclosures
phone: 425-388-3366 – Real estate taxes

(2) Treasurer FAQ
http://www.co.snohomish.wa.us/treasurer/Trs02-FAQ.asp

(3) Snohomish County Tax Foreclosure Information
http://www.co.snohomish.wa.us/treasurer/Trs02-Foreclosure_Info.asp

Information per RCW Chapter 84.64: Lien Foreclosure

January 12, 2004: The Tax Foreclosure Sale for this year has been completed!
The Snohomish County Treasurer conducts an annual Tax Foreclosure Sale.

The 2004 sale is tentatively scheduled for January 2005.

More information on the exact date, time, and location of the Sale will be posted as they become available. This information is complied in the 4th quarter of the calendar year and is usually made public in the month of December.

Please view the information linked below, if you wish to become involved in the Tax Auction.

Tax Foreclosure Sale Instructions and FAQ:
http://www.co.snohomish.wa.us/treasurer/foreclosure/docs/general_foreclosure_info.pdf

Main Phone: 425-388-3606
Email: treasurer@co.snohomish.wa.us

(3a) Tax Foreclosure Sale Instructions and FAQ
http://www.co.snohomish.wa.us/treasurer/foreclosure/docs/general_foreclosure_info.pdf

Please Note: The following information is valid as of January 1, 2003. The information is provided as general background material and is subject to change as the laws governing the Tax Foreclosure Sale are modified. Specific information regarding the 2003 Tax Foreclosure Sale (to be held in early 2004) will be posted here as soon as it becomes available.

The Snohomish County Treasurer conducts an annual tax foreclosure sale.

THE SALE

The tax foreclosure sale is a voice auction, starting with a minimum bid. Minimum bid includes the amount owed for all unpaid taxes, interest, penalties and costs. Minimum bid may also include delinquent personal property taxes that have been attached, as well as any delinquent assessments normally collected by the treasurer.

To place a bid, you or your representative must attend in person. Parcels cannot be purchased via the mail.

Bids are to be made in increments of no less than $25.00 or more. Each parcel must be paid in full by CASH, CASHIER'S OR CERTIFIED CHECK ONLY – PAYABLE AT THE TIME OF SUCCESSFUL BID. Absolutely no personal checks or business checks will be accepted.

If you bring a cashier's or certified check, you will be asked to come to the Treasurer's office at the end of the sale and a refund check will be prepared for any overage due you.

The successful bidder will be responsible for payment of a five-dollar deed fee together with proper recording and excise fees. These costs are payable at the time of the successful bid.

No person who is a County employee or officer may bid at the sale, nor may any such person bid as an agent or allow any agent to bid on their behalf.

If you are going to attend the sale and bid on parcels, we would appreciate your being at the sale early (9:30 or so), as you will have to complete a bid card to participate in the sale.

GENERAL INFORMATION

Anyone considering buying property at a tax foreclosure sale should be aware that THERE ARE RISKS. When selling parcels, the county conveys the entirety of the interest which it is legally capable of transferring, unless otherwise noted. HOWEVER, THE COUNTY DOES NOT GUARANTEE OR PROVIDE WARRANTY AS TO THE EXTENT OF THAT INTEREST. The county makes NO guarantees whatsoever on parcels sold at a tax sale.

This is a *BUYER BEWARE* sale. All parcels are sold on a "where is" and "as is" basis. The County makes no representation of warranty, nor any guarantee of warranty, express or implied, as to the condition of title to any property, nor the physical condition of any property or its fitness for any use or purpose.

The foreclosure properties can be redeemed up through closing the day *BEFORE* the sale. There is no right of redemption by owners or lienholders the day of the sale.

County tax foreclosures fall under different laws than other types of foreclosure sales. Once a property has gone through tax foreclosure, the prior owners have no rights to the property, *UNLESS* they were a minor or adjudicated to be legally incompetent.

Minors and legal incompetents have the right to redeem anytime within three years from the date of the foreclosure sale. If they do so, they must pay the amount for which the property was sold, plus interest on the tax amount from and after the date of sale, plus the reasonable value of all improvements made in good faith, less the value of use thereof.

DO YOUR RESEARCH!

Thorough research on all potential purchases is essential. It is important you complete this research prior to the day of sale. Buying property without doing complete research can result in unwanted and costly surprises. Be aware that even the most diligent research efforts may not uncover all difficulties or unexpected problems.

To help you get started, the Snohomish County Assessor's office makes available information about each foreclosure parcel for viewing in their lobby. Among other things, this information includes parcel maps on which the location of each parcel will be highlighted.

Other resources: Questions about buildability, zoning, use restrictions and controls, are just a few things that should be checked out prior to purchase. City and county departments of engineering, building and codes, and planning are places for you to get information.

Title Insurance: Check with a title company to make sure your parcel is insurable.

Assessments: Parcels may have local improvements, special assessments or utility liens for which payment will be due. You need to check into this information. Only a few assessments are collected by the County Treasurer.

Local Ordinances: Parcels may be subject to easements or use restrictions, as well as zoning and other land use controls. All properties are sold subject to applicable city and county ordinances. The existence of these are the buyer's responsibility to determine.

Community Association Dues: All properties are sold subject to restrictive covenants of record which may allow for the imposition of community association fees.

Improvements: If there are improvements on the parcel, you should find out if they go with the land and how they are currently being used.

Physical Inspection of Property: It is strongly recommended that you visit all the property sites you are interested in purchasing. Is there access to the parcel; can you accurately identify property boundaries; is the parcel being used in some way by adjoining owners; is the parcel affected by water in some way?

LIENS

Some government liens, such as the Internal Revenue Service, have a redemption period of six months in which they can decide to take action. After that time, the lien is extinguished.

Parcels are sold subject to special assessment liens, if any; liens of other taxing districts; and easements of record per RCW 36.35.290. LID liens and utility liens, where known, will be announced.

Generally, other liens are extinguished. However, the county can make no guarantees that prior lienholders will honor this extinguishment. If prior lienholders attempt to collect on their liens after the property has been sold at a tax sale, it is entirely up to the new owner to defend against these claims.

EXCEPTION: When the *RECORD OWNER* purchases property at tax sale, *ALL LIENS REMAIN.*

AFTER THE TAX SALE

A Tax Deed will be issued approximately thirty (30) days from the date of sale. The deeds will be forwarded to the auditor's office for recording and will then be mailed to the purchaser.

Tax Deeds do not warrant clear title and provide the purchaser no guarantees. There may be clouded titles or other problems that the county is neither aware of nor responsible for.

Any proceeds from the sale in excess of minimum bid will be held by the County Treasurer up to three (3) years from the date of sale, to be refunded following payment of all water and sewer district liens, upon proper application by the record owner of the property. The record owner of the property is the person who held title on the date of the issuance of the certificate of delinquency.

This information is designed to assist you and in no way encompasses the entirety of information regarding tax foreclosure sales. Some or all of this information is subject to change. Circumstances may differ from sale to sale and/or require special exceptions.

This is not intended to provide legal advice – anyone with questions is advised to seek the advice of their attorney.

If you have further questions regarding the tax foreclosure sale, please telephone (425) 388-3606 or telephone toll free within Washington State 1-800-562-4367 extension 3606.

Our e-mail address is: treasurer@co.snohomish.wa.us.

(3b) Current List of Properties Scheduled for Auction
http://www.co.snohomish.wa.us/treasurer/foreclosure/docs/foreclosure_info-2003.htm

Snohomish County Property Foreclosure List
Updated: September 30, 2003 (Note: This page is automatically refreshed every 10 minutes)

These figures are not current amounts. Please call 425-388-3606 for current amounts.

ROGUE INVESTOR NOTE: information saved on CD:
USA Tax Lien Info/Washington/snohomish_co_WA/PROPERTY_INFORMATION.htm

---

SPOKANE COUNTY, WASHINGTON
http://www.spokanecounty.org

TREASURER'S OFFICE
http://www.spokanecounty.org/treasurer

Mailing Address (Taxes)
Spokane County Treasurer
P.O. Box 199
Spokane, WA 99210-0199

Treasurer's Office
1116 West Broadway Avenue
Second Floor, Spokane County Courthouse
Spokane, WA, 99260
Phone: (509) 477-4713
Fax: (509) 477-3674
Email: treasurer@spokanecounty.org

(1) Contact Information
http://www.spokanecounty.org/treasurer/contactus.asp

Foreclosures
Phone: (509) 477-6446
Email: foreclosure@spokanecounty.org

(2) Foreclosures
http://www.spokanecounty.org/treasurer/foreclosure/default.asp

Real property foreclosure proceedings will start if any one tax, assessment or lien is three full years delinquent. For more information on property in foreclosure related to an improvement district assessment, please contact (509) 477-6041.

If personal property and/or mobile homes on leased land become delinquent, the Treasurer can start the foreclosure process at any time. If the first half is not paid, the full amount is delinquent and must be paid in full with all interest, costs, and penalties.

For questions or comments regarding foreclosures, send email to foreclosure@spokanecounty.org or call (509) 477-6446 for real estate or (509) 477-5746 for personal property and mobile homes.

To get more information on the how the foreclosure process works, please download the 2003 Tax Foreclosure Information: http://www.spokanecounty.org/treasurer/pdf/2003ForeclosureInformation.pdf.

Current Parcels In Foreclosure
This document is available for viewing and printing in a PDF format:
http://www.spokanecounty.org/treasurer/pdf/ForeclosureList.pdf

Tax Lien Sales: Yes

Tax Deed Sales: Yes

Rating: Three Stars (***)

Interest Rate: 12% (1% per month)

Sale Period: Annual real property tax sale is held on the third Tuesday in July at the office of the Collector of Taxes.

Redemption Period: 6 months

The time period for redemption of properties brought to tax sale under Section 47-1205 (b) shall be 6 months. The time period for redemption of properties brought to tax sale under Section 6-2907 (f) shall be 6 months. The time period for redemption of property brought to tax sale under Section 43-1529, Section 43-1609, or Section 43-1610 shall be 180 days.

At the time of the auction, the buyer must pay a deposit of 20 percent of the amount he/she plans on bidding or $100, whichever is greater.

Bidding Process:
In case no other person bids the amount due, together with penalties and costs, on any lot, the Collector of Taxes shall bid the amount due, together with penalties and costs, and purchase it for the District.

Detailed Information:

OFFICE OF THE CHIEF FINANCIAL OFFICER
http://cfo.washingtondc.gov/main.asp

(1) Contact Information
http://cfo.washingtondc.gov/atd/ci_main.asp

Office of the Chief Financial Officer
Government of the District of Columbia
John A. Wilson Building
1350 Pennsylvania Avenue NW
Suite 203
Washington, DC 20004
phone: (202) 727-2476
ocfo@dc.gov

(2) Real Property Tax Sale
http://cfo.washingtondc.gov/services/tax/delinquent/index.shtm

As required by DC statute, the Office of Tax and Revenue (OTR) holds a public auction each July to sell real property tax liens - both commercial and residential - for which property taxes were unpaid during the previous tax year. Property owners have until the date of this Tax Sale to pay their taxes in full, including penalties and interest, to prevent their property from being auctioned.

A list of all Tax Sale properties, sorted by parcel, square, suffix and lot number with the name of the owner of record and the unpaid tax amount, is advertised in local newspapers the month prior to the auction. The advertised list is also made available for download on this website.

Property owners wishing to settle their tax obligations prior to the Tax Sale should pay their outstanding tax liabilities reflected in their final bill. Anyone with questions about the status of their property should call OTR's customer service representatives at (202) 727-4TAX (727-4829).

Tax Sale 2003 Information

- 2003 Tax Sale List: http://cfo.washingtondc.gov/services/tax/property/taxsale_list.shtm
- Tax Sale Begins July 14 for District Properties with Unpaid Taxes: http://cfo.washingtondc.gov/services/tax/news/2003/june/06_06_03.shtm
- Delinquent Property Taxpayers Get Final Warning Before Tax Sale: http://cfo.washingtondc.gov/services/tax/news/2003/may/05_01_03.shtm
- Notice of Delinquency and Final Bill Prior to Tax Sale: http://cfo.washingtondc.gov/services/tax/property/taxsale_final_notice2002.shtm
- Tax Sale Workbook: http://cfo.washingtondc.gov/services/tax/property/taxsale_workbook.shtm

Rules and Procedures

- Annual Tax Sale Process and Procedures: http://cfo.washingtondc.gov/services/tax/property/tax_sale_process_p2.shtm
- Notice of Final Rulemaking Regarding Real Property Tax Sales: http://cfo.washingtondc.gov/services/tax/property/taxsale_rulemaking.shtm
- Notice of Redemption Requirements: http://cfo.washingtondc.gov/services/tax/property/redempt_tsale2001.shtm
- Notice to Tax Sale Purchasers Concerning Redemptions: http://cfo.washingtondc.gov/services/tax/property/tax_sale_chapter13a.shtm

West Virginia

Tax Lien Sales: Yes

Tax Deed Sales: No

Rating: Three Stars (***)

Interest Rate: 12%

Sale Period: Sale dates vary by county, and are scheduled in October and November for some counties.

Redemption Period:
Property owners have approximately eighteen months to redeem property before it is sold on the auction block

Bidding Process:
Tax certificates are sold to individuals by public auction to the highest bidder. In many cases the bid can be higher than the total amount of taxes, penalties, and costs due. In such cases the excess over the total amount due is payable to the delinquent taxpayer.

State-Specific Information:
West Virginia has a total of 55 counties. Tax collections and sales are handled by the county sheriff and the tax commissioner at the county level.

West Virginia State Auditor's Office
http://www.wvauditor.com

County Collections
http://www.wvauditor.com/county_collections/cc.aspx
Email: Russ Rollyson russr@wvauditor.com
State Capitol Building 1, Room W-100
Charleston, WV
Phone: 877-982-9148 or 304-558-2251
Fax: 304-558-5200

- search delinquent land properties:
    http://www.wvauditor.com/county_collections/delinquent_land2.asp
- land sales: http://www.wvauditor.com/county_collections/land_sales2.asp
- county collections staff: http://www.wvauditor.com/staff/staffdir.aspx#A5

Links for All West Virginia Counties: Provided on CD.

Detailed County-Specific Information:

KANAWHA COUNTY, WEST VIRGINIA
http://www.kanawha.us

Contact Information
from http://www.kanawha.us, click on "Contact information – Kanawha County"

Sheriff's Tax
Kathy Burdell, email: kathyburdell@kanawha.us
Shirley Cottrill, email: shirleycottrill@kanawha.us

Assessor
Phyllis Gatson, email: assessor@kanawha.us

SHERIFF'S DEPARTMENT
from http://www.kanawha.us, click on "Government" and then on "Sheriff"
(http://www.kanawhasheriff.us)

Dave Tucker, Sheriff
407 Virginia Street East
Charleston, WV 25301
Phone: 304-357-0200

Tax Division
phone: 304-357-0210

ASSESSOR'S OFFICE
from http://www.kanawha.us, click on "Government" and then on "Assessor"

Phyllis Gatson, Assessor
Charleston, WV 25301
Phone: 304-357-0250
Fax: 304-357-0551
email: assessor@kanawha.us

Real Estate
Steve Duffield, Supervisor
email: steveduffield@kanawha.us

Tax Lien Sales: Yes

Tax Deed Sales: Yes

Rating: Four Stars (****)

Interest Rate: 15% plus 3% penalty

The interest rate on delinquent general property taxes, special charges, special assessments and special taxes included in the tax roll for collection is 1% per month (12% per annum) or fraction of a month.

In addition, any county board and/or the common council of any city may by ordinance impose a penalty of up to 0.5% per month or fraction of a month, in addition to the interest on any delinquent general property taxes, special assessments, special charges and special taxes included in the tax roll.

A person who holds a mortgage or other lien on real property and pays real property taxes, special assessments, special charges or special taxes levied against the property or any interest or penalty increases the amount of his or her most senior lien against the property by the amount paid, plus interest at the rate of 1.0% per month or fraction of a month.

Sale Period: September

Redemption Period: 2 years

Bidding Process:
Varies by municipalities, which handle the tax sales. Tax sale properties are sold for the appraised value.

State-Specific Information:
Municipalities handle the tax sales. Wisconsin has 72 counties, plus numerous cities and towns authorized to collect taxes, issue tax sale certificates, and sell property acquired by the governing body for nonpayment of taxes.

Tax certificates bid in the name of the governing body are not assignable. These tax certificates bear a minimum of 15% annual interest plus a 3% penalty

Links for All Wisconsin Counties: Provided on CD.

Detailed County-Specific Information:

MILWAUKEE COUNTY, WISCONSIN
http://www.co.milwaukee.wi.us

OFFICE OF THE TREASURER
http://www.milwaukeecounty.org/Service/OrganizationDetail.asp?org=3090&audience=5

Dorothy K. Dean, Treasurer
Courthouse, Room 102
901 N. 9th Street
Milwaukee, WI 53233-1462
Phone: 414-278-4033
FAX: 414-223-1383
Email: ddean@milwcnty.com

(1) Tax Collection
http://www.milwaukeecounty.org/Service/serviceDetail.asp?service=1406&audience=5

(2) Delinquent Property Tax Collection
http://www.milwaukeecounty.org/Service/serviceDetail.asp?service=42&audience=5

The Treasurer's office arranges collection of back taxes through foreclosures, through suing the individual personally for the taxes, or through monthly payments.

(3) Tax Deeds, Auctions and Sales
http://www.milwaukeecounty.org/Service/serviceDetail.asp?service=1474&audience=5

Wisconsin State Law provides for the transferring of title to land when taxes are delinquent. The delinquency must be more than one year in Milwaukee County and Milwaukee City (in other Wisconsin Counties it is two years). Milwaukee County has chosen to use the "in rem" foreclosure process. Milwaukee County does not sell foreclosed properties for back taxes. **All foreclosed property is sold for fair market value;** the way any other piece of property is sold. If you wish to inquire about any tax foreclosure properties that are currently on the market, you can call 414-278-4045 (8 a.m. - 5 p.m. Central Time). The Milwaukee County Sheriff holds real estate auctions every Monday morning on properties that are lender foreclosures. This means for non-payment of the mortgage. More information is available by calling 414-278-4907 (8 a.m. - 5 p.m. Central Time). If you are interested in a property that is in one of the Sheriff's auctions, be sure to check for delinquent taxes. Most of the Sheriff sale properties are located in the City of Milwaukee. Contact the City of Milwaukee at 414-286-2240.

Contact: Helen Nett
Courthouse, Room 102
901 N. 9th Street, Room 102
Milwaukee, WI 53233-1462
Phone: 414-278-4045
FAX: 414-223-1383
Email: hnett@milwcnty.com

(4) What is Foreclosure?
http://www.milwaukeecounty.org/Service/serviceDetail.asp?id=1475

Foreclosure is a legal process by which a local government takes title to a property. In Wisconsin this is done when all attempts to collect property taxes on the property have failed. The Sheriff handles sales of properties that have been foreclosed for non-payment of mortgage. For information on Sheriff sales call 414-278-4907 (8 p.m. - 5p.m. Central Time).

SHERIFF'S OFFICE
http://www.milwaukeecounty.org/frameSet.asp?url=http://www.mkesheriff.org

(1) Contact Information
http://www.milwaukeecounty.org/frameSet.asp?url=http://www.mkesheriff.org
click on "Contact Us" link, and "About Us" link (and then "Phone Directory" link)

Sheriff David Clarke, Jr.
821 W. State Street, Room 107
Milwaukee, WI 53233
phone: 414-278-4766
Fax: 223-1386

Sheriff's Sales
Email: mcsosheriffsales@milwcnty.com
phone: 278-4907

Wyoming

Tax Lien Sales: Yes

Tax Deed Sales: No

Rating: Four Stars (****)

Interest Rate: 18% per year. 3% minimum plus 15% for the first year; 18% for subsequent years.

Sale Period: Sale dates vary by county, ranging from July through October for most counties.

Redemption Period: 4 years

Bidding Process: All tax lien auctions are by competitive bid.

State-Specific Information:
There are 23 counties in Wyoming. Tax certificate liens are offered for sale by the county treasurer at public auction after the property is delinquent.

Links for All Wyoming Counties: Provided on CD.

Detailed County-Specific Information:

Albany County (Laramie) (307) 721-2502	Pinedale County (Sublette) (307) 367-4373
Buffalo County (Johnson) (307) 684-7302	Sheridan County (Sheridan) (307) 674-6522
Hot Springs County (Thermopolis) (307) 864-3616	Sundance County (Crook) (307) 283-1244
Lander County (Fremont) (307) 332-1105	Teton County (Jackson) (307) 733-4770

SWEETWATER COUNTY, WYOMING
http://www.co.sweet.wy.us

TREASURER'S OFFICE
http://www.co.sweet.wy.us/treas/propertytaxes/index.html

(1) Contact Information

Robb Slaughter, County Treasurer
80 West Flaming Gorge Way, Suite 139
Green River, WY 82935

Property Taxes
Green River Phone: 307-872-6392
Rock Springs Phone: 307-352-6705
Fax: 307-872-6393

(2) Tax Sales/Redemptions
http://www.co.sweet.wy.us/treas/propertytaxes/page5.html

Tax Sales
The county recovers the loss of uncollected property tax revenue at the annual tax sale. The county sells its tax lien on the property to attending purchasers for the amount of taxes, interest, and costs associated with the sale. The notice of sale must be published for three consecutive weeks in a legal newspaper within the county. As a general rule, this office publishes the notice every Thursday for three weeks and then holds the sale either the last Thursday in July or the first Thursday in August. State statute provides a tax lien purchaser interest at 15% per annum in addition to a 3% penalty the day of the purchase. Subsequent year taxes may also be paid by the purchaser and earn 15% interest.

Redemptions
The legal owner of the property may redeem taxes sold at the annual tax sale. To redeem, the owner must pay to the Treasurer's Office the amount of tax sold at the tax sale, a 3% penalty, 15% simple interest, and a redemption fee. Any subsequent year taxes paid by the purchaser must also be paid with interest, at the time of the redemption. The purchaser can obtain a Tax Deed for the property owner within four years of the date of sale.

CONVERSE COUNTY, WYOMING
http://www.conversecounty.org

TREASURER'S OFFICE
http://www.conversecounty.org/treasurer

Ernest Orrell, Treasurer

(1) Contact Information
http://www.conversecounty.org/treasurer/contact.htm

107 North 5th Street, Suite 129
Douglas, WY 82633
Phone
Douglas Area: 307-358-3120
Glenrock Area, Monday, Tuesday, Wednesday, Friday: 307-436-8650
Glenrock Office, Thursday: 307-259-5888
Fax: 307-358-6883
Email: jament@coffey.com

(2) Tax Sale
http://www.conversecounty.org/treasurer/taxsalehow.htm

The Treasurer is required to conduct a tax sale every year to offer CERTIFICATES OF PURCHASE on properties with unpaid taxes.

Investors attend the tax sale to take advantage of the interest rate of return on the taxes they pay (18%). Other taxpayers attend the sale to try and gain interest in specific parcels of land around the county.

- How does the tax sale work? http://www.conversecounty.org/treasurer/taxsalehow.htm
- When will the tax sale take place? http://www.conversecounty.org/treasurer/taxsalewhen.htm
- What is sold at a tax sale? http://www.conversecounty.org/treasurer/taxsalewhat.htm
- How do I find out what's for sale and where it is?
  http://www.conversecounty.org/treasurer/taxsalewhere.htm
- How much does it cost to purchase a certificate at the sale?
  http://www.conversecounty.org/treasurer/taxsalecost.htm
- What rights to the property does the certificate holder have?
  http://www.conversecounty.org/treasurer/taxsaleright.htm

- Once I receive a certificate of purchase, what do I have to do?
  http://www.conversecounty.org/treasurer/taxsaledo.htm
- If the landowner pays the taxes, what do I get back?
  http://www.conversecounty.org/treasurer/taxsalecr.htm
- How do tax deeds work? http://www.conversecounty.org/treasurer/taxsaledeed.htm
- How do I apply for a Tax Deed? http://www.conversecounty.org/treasurer/taxsaledeed2.htm

ROGUE INVESTOR NOTE: Highlights from the above tax sale FAQ pages:

- Interest Rate = 18% per year (3% minimum penalty plus 15% the first year; subsequent tax years paid by the same investor are a flat 18% per year).
- The Treasurer's Office advertises the land for 3 weeks in the newspaper, along with a notice giving the time and place for the sale.
- People show up at the sale and sign up to become a purchaser.
- The names of all purchasers are mixed and random names are drawn in succession, beginning at 9:00 a.m.
- The purchaser can choose up to 5 of the available parcels.
- The purchaser pays the amount of the taxes due on the land, plus interest to the date of the sale, plus advertising and certificate fees.
- The county issues the purchaser a Certificate of Purchase, entitling the purchaser to a lien on the land.
- The landowner has 4 years from the date of the sale to pay the purchaser back his money, including all fees and 18% interest, or the purchaser may apply for a Tax Deed on the land.
- Usually, Converse County holds its tax sale on the first Monday in August, at 9:00 a.m. in the Treasurer's Office. Although technically the sale continues until 5:00 p.m., all properties are usually sold by 11:00 a.m.
- The Converse County Treasurer's Office advertises in both the Douglas Budget and the Glenrock Independent.
- $20.00 advertising fee.
- $20.00 Certificate of Purchase Fee.

Once 4 years have passed for the original purchaser, he/she applies for a Tax Deed. But, in order to get a clear Tax Deed, the purchaser now has to redeem the property from the second Certificate of Purchaser (CP) Holder, or as many as there were in the 4 years. That means the original CP Holder must pay any subsequent CP Holders the taxes plus interest, fees and 18% interest. That's why most CP Holders pay taxes for subsequent years, even though it's not required.

TEN

Detailed Canadian Province Profiles

"Who dares nothing, need hope for nothing." – J.C.F. von Schiller

If you are looking for tax deed sales, Canada is worth considering. Virtually all provinces in Canada have some sort of tax deed sale. However, in Canada tax lien certificates are not typically sold to investors, so you must focus on property ownership by purchasing tax deeds. In total, there are approximately 10 provinces in Canada where most tax sales are held. These provinces include Ontario, Quebec, British Columbia, Alberta, Manitoba, Saskatchewan, Nova Scotia, New Brunswick, Newfoundland and Prince Edward Island.

Overall, the rules for each sale are specific to the province or municipality. To prepare for the sale, you need to be familiar with the rules and regulations particular to each province and municipality. At the end of this section, you will find a summary of the common sale procedures for each province. Use this section as a starting guide for deciding where and how you will bid, but make sure you contact the municipality prior to the sale to get a list of properties and learn the local rules and procedures. Tax sale dates and rules change, and some provinces and municipalities do not have regular sales.

There are some similarities between provinces and municipalities governing why, how and where sales occur. General terminology is also similar in most cases. Here is a summary of the general tax sale process for Canada.

If after two years a property owner fails to pay his property taxes, the municipal treasurer, following the rules of the municipality and the province, may prepare what is called a tax arrears certificate. This tax arrears certificate is registered with the Registry of Land Titles Office. The certificate includes, among other things, a legal description of the property and acknowledgement that the property will be offered for public sale within one year if the taxes are not paid. Also included is the cancellation price, equal to primarily the taxes owed, interest, any penalties incurred and other costs such as legal fees, survey fees and advertising expenses.

After this tax arrears certificate is issued, the municipal treasurer is required to send a notice to the property owner within 60 days telling them that if they do not "buy" the tax arrears certificate from the county and cancel the process, the property will be offered for sale. The municipal treasurer must attempt to contact both the actual property owner and immediate relatives. A spouse of the owner must receive a separate letter. Current tenants, if the owner does not occupy the property, will also receive a letter.

For one year after the tax arrears certificate is issued, anyone can cancel the property sale by paying the amount included on the certificate. The current property owner then retains ownership and the property is not offered for sale. In some provinces, the municipality may make arrangements with the owner for an alternative payment schedule. In addition, in some Provinces the municipality is allowed to purchase the tax arrears certificate and take possession if it can demonstrate that the municipality has a specified use for the property.

If the tax arrears certificate is not redeemed, a final notice is sent approximately 90 days from the date of the property sale to give the owner one more chance. Then the property is offered for sale either at a public tax sale auction or by a public tender offer.

At public auction, the property is offered for sale via a bidding process. The opening bid usually starts for the amount of the tax arrears certificate. In most cases, the winning bidder pays the highest amount bid.

If the bid procedure is public tender offer, sealed bids are sent in and on the day of the sale, the offers are opened and the winning bidder is usually the highest bidder based on the written tender offer.

In Canada, most tax sales are advertised in Provincial gazettes and municipality newspapers. Some municipalities are also starting to list sales information on the Internet, but to date this information is limited and is no substitute for what can be learned by getting municipality newspapers and talking to local officials.

For unorganized territories, delinquent properties are turned over to the Crown. These properties then become available through the Crown Land Marketing Program. Here is the address and phone number for getting a list of properties available from the Crown:

Crown Publications
521 Fort Street
Victoria, British Columbia V8W 1E7
Canada
1-250-386-4636

The following is a summary of tax sale procedures for provinces that handle their own sales.

Tax Lien Sales: No

Tax Deed Sales: Yes

Rating: Three Stars (***)

Interest Rate: No interest rate, only tax deeds are sold.

Sale Period: Varies depending on the municipality, but sales are usually held once per year.

Redemption Period: 1 year

Bidding Process:
Sales are by public auction. Minimum bids are set by municipalities. According to Alberta law, the minimum bid is set near the market value.

Province-Specific Information:

Alberta is a decent Province for tax deed sales; however, the presence of a high minimum bid could limit an investor's potential profit. Sales information appears in the Alberta Gazette and the largest newspaper in the municipality holding the sale.

Detailed Municipality-Specific Information:

EDMONTON, ALBERTA
http://www.gov.edmonton.ab.ca

LAND SALES
http://www.gov.edmonton.ab.ca/portal/server.pt/gateway/PTARGS_0_2_273_215_0_43/http://CMSServer/COEWeb/for+business/buying+from+the+city/land+sales/default.htm

(1) Catalog of Land for Sale

New Offerings, updated February 25, 2004
http://www.edmonton.ca/landsales/ici_catalogue/ICI_Feature_Properties.pdf

- Feature Properties & First Time Offerings:
- North West Industrial Land:
  http://www.edmonton.ca/landsales/ici_catalogue/ICI_Northwest_Industrial.pdf
- North East Industrial Land:
  http://www.edmonton.ca/landsales/ici_catalogue/ICI_Northeast_Industrial.pdf
- South Side Industrial Land:
  http://www.edmonton.ca/landsales/ici_catalogue/ICI_Southside_Industrial.pdf
- Commercial Land: http://www.edmonton.ca/landsales/ici_catalogue/ICI_Commercial_Land.pdf
- Multi Family Land: http://www.edmonton.ca/landsales/ici_catalogue/ICI_Multi_Family_Land.pdf
- Single Family Houses:
  http://www.edmonton.ca/landsales/ici_catalogue/ICI_Single_Family_Houses.pdf
- Residential Infill: http://www.edmonton.ca/landsales/ici_catalogue/ICI_Residential_Infill.pdf

This Catalogue is always changing as properties are sold and new properties are added.

Purchasing Land From the City of Edmonton (Interactive Form):
http://www.gov.edmonton.ab.ca/portal/server.pt/gateway/PTARGS_0_2_273_215_0_43/http:/CMSServer/COEWeb/for+business/buying+from+the+city/land+sales/iForm_Buy+Land.htm

Buyers Information Form in a PDF format:
http://www.edmonton.ca/landsales/ici_catalogue/buyers_app.pdf

City Map: http://www.edmonton.ca/landsales/ici_catalogue/City_Map.pdf

Email notification service. If you want to be notified by email of our "New Offerings," please send a blank email to propertysales@edmonton.ca with SUBSCRIBE in the subject line.

(2) Additional Information

We're Open for Business; Terms and Conditions; Pricing of City Lands; All Lands is for Sale or Lease; Standard Terms and Conditions of Sale; Current Sales Policies, Procedures and Timelines; Development Requirements; Servicing Costs and Hook Up Charges; Roadway Access; Taxes and Local Improvement Charges; Forms You Need; Where to Start; Disclaimers; How Are We Doing?

ROGUE INVESTOR NOTE: See web page for additional information.

LETHBRIDGE, ALBERTA
http://www.city.lethbridge.ab.ca

City Hall
910 – 4th Avenue South
Lethbridge, Alberta
T1J 0P6, Canada
Phone: (403) 320-3950
Fax: (403) 320-4956
Email: ahodge@city.lethbridge.ab.ca

Tax Lien Sales: No

Tax Deed Sales: Yes

Rating: Three Stars (***)

Interest Rate: No interest rate, only tax deeds are sold.

Sale Period: Vancouver has sales in November; all remaining municipalities have tax sales on the same day, usually in September or October. Crown Land Property sales are held twice per year.

Redemption Period: 1 year

Bidding Process: Sales are usually by public auction.

Province-Specific Information:
British Columbia is generally a good province for tax deed sales. Sales procedures for Vancouver are based on the Vancouver Charter; sales procedures for other, smaller municipalities are based on the Municipal Act; and sales procedures for organized territories are based on the Taxation Act. Sales are published in the British Columbia Gazette and municipal papers holding the sale. The Property Tax Office provides the property-specific information. For unorganized territories, delinquent properties are turned over to the Crown. These properties then become available through the Crown Land Marketing Program. Here is the address and phone number for getting a list of properties available from the Crown: Crown Publications, 521 Fort Street, Victoria, British Columbia, V8W 1E7, Canada, phone: 50-386-4636.

Detailed Municipality-Specific Information:

VANCOUVER, BRITISH COLUMBIA
http://www.city.vancouver.bc.ca

Corporate Services Group
453 West 12th Avenue
Vancouver, British Columbia, V5Y 1V4, Canada
Phone: (604) 873-7633 / Fax: (604) 873-7051

Tax Sale
http://www.city.vancouver.bc.ca/corpsvcs/treasury/tax/taxsale.htm

The Tax Sale is a public auction. Any property with taxes unpaid at the end of three years will be sold at the City's annual tax sale. In 2003, the tax sale date was November 12, 2003, at 10:00 a.m. Location: City Hall, 453 West 12th Avenue. Tax Sale List pick up at City Hall only, available in November

General procedures: Property bidding begins with the Upset Price and continues to the highest bid. This price is the total of the oldest years' taxes, interest to the date of sale and some additional charges. Successful bidders must secure their bid by payment (certified cheque, money order, cash or debit card) of the Upset Price by noon of the day following the sale. In the event of redemption, the purchaser will receive interest on the monies invested to the date of redemption.

Tax Lien Sales: No

Tax Deed Sales: Yes

Rating: Two Stars (**)

Interest Rate: No interest rate, only tax deeds are sold.

Sale Period: Varies depending on the municipality, but sales are usually once per year.

Redemption Period: 1 year

Bidding Process: Sales are by public auction.

Province-Specific Information:
Manitoba is a decent province for tax deed sales. Sales information appears in the Manitoba Gazette and the largest newspaper in the municipality holding the sale. The City of Winnipeg Act governs the sales in Winnipeg and the Municipalities Act governs the sales in the smaller municipalities. However, sometimes municipalities keep the tax delinquent properties and the tax sales are not always open to the public. Check with each municipality to determine rules and if the sales are open to the public.

Detailed Municipality-Specific Information:

WINNIPEG, MANITOBA

For land within the City of Winnipeg, contact the Minister of Finance: 204-945-2262.

For land outside the City of Winnipeg, contact the town or municipality concerned.

New Brunswick and Prince Edward Island

Tax Lien Sales: No

Tax Deed Sales: Yes

Rating: Three Stars (***)

Interest Rate: No interest rate, only tax deeds are sold. New Brunswick has a 15% right of redemption fee if redeemed within 90 days.

Sale Period: Usually February, June and October.

Redemption Period: 1 year. In New Brunswick, a 90-day right of redemption occurs after the purchase.

Bidding Process:
Sales are by public auction. In New Brunswick, the minimum bid is not posted until the day of the sale. The minimum bid is the back taxes, fees and other expenses.

Province-Specific Information:

New Brunswick and Prince Edward Island use the central government (Provincial Department of Finance) to handle the tax sales. Sales information appears in the Royal Gazette and the largest newspaper in the municipality holding the sale. Here is the address for the Royal Gazette: Royal Gazette, Queen's Printer, P.O. Box 6000, Fredericton, N.B., E3B 5H1.

Tax Lien Sales: No

Tax Deed Sales: Yes

Rating: Two Stars (**)

Interest Rate: No interest rate, only tax deeds are sold.

Sale Period: Sales are infrequent, depending on the municipality.

Redemption Period: No redemption, the winning bidder gets clear title at the auction.

Bidding Process: Sales are by public auction.

Province-Specific Information:

Newfoundland is a decent province for tax deed sales. The winning bidder get clear title, but the sales are infrequent due to the small total population of this Province and the fact that properties that are owner-occupied cannot be sold. Also, few owners default because the province turns off the water at residences with delinquent taxes. Sales information is included in local newspapers four weeks prior to the sale.

Nova Scotia

Tax Lien Sales: No

Tax Deed Sales: Yes

Rating: Three Stars (***)

Interest Rate: No interest rate, only tax deeds are sold.

Sale Period: Varies depending on the municipality, but sales are held once per year.

Redemption Period: 1 year

Bidding Process: Sales are by public auction.

Province-Specific Information:
Nova Scotia is a decent province for tax deed sales. Sales information appears in the largest newspaper in the municipality holding the sale.

Tax Lien Sales: No

Tax Deed Sales: Yes

Rating: Three Stars (***)

Interest Rate: No interest rate, only tax deeds are sold.

Sale Period: Varies, but sales can occur throughout the year.

Redemption Period: 1 year

Bidding Process:
Sales can be either public tender or public auction depending on the municipality. Public tender sales are essentially sealed bid sales. Usually a small deposit is required with the tender bid. The minimum bid is the back taxes, interest, fees and costs associated with the sale. The winning bidder is the highest qualified bidder.

Province-Specific Information: Ontario is generally a good province for tax deed sales. Sales information appears in the Ontario Gazette and the largest newspaper in the municipality holding the sale.

Detailed Municipality-Specific Information:

TORONTO, ONTARIO
http://www.city.toronto.on.ca

City of Toronto, Finance Department
General Correspondence
5100 Yonge Street
Toronto, Ontario M2N 5V7, Canada
Telephone: 416-338-4829
TDD: 416-392-0719
Fax: 416-392-0363

With the filing of Municipal Tax Sales Rules on May 5, 2003 by Ontario Regulation 181/03, which prescribes the information to be included, documents can now be registered electronically.

Tax Lien Sales: No

Tax Deed Sales: Yes

Rating: Three Stars (***)

Interest Rate: No interest rate, only tax deeds are sold.

Sale Period: In Montreal, sales are usually the first or second day in December.

Redemption Period: 1 year

Bidding Process:
Sales are usually conducted by public auction and in Montreal the sheriff handles the sales. In smaller municipalities, sales are handled by the secretary treasurer's office. In Montreal, the minimum bid must be at least equal to 25 percent of the assessed value of the property.

Province-Specific Information:
Quebec is a decent province for tax deed sales. Sales information appears in French in the Ontario Gazette officielle du Quebec and the largest newspaper in the municipality holding the sale. Here is the address and phone number for the Gazette officielle du Quebec:

Gazette officielle du Quebec
Minister of Culture and Communications
4380 Rue Garrand, Ville St-Laurent
Montreal, H4R 2A9, Canada
1-888-272-1373 (or) 1-514-333-9606

Detailed Municipality-Specific Information:

MONTREAL, QUÉBEC
http://www2.ville.montreal.qc.ca

Ville de Montréal
Service des finances
C.P. 11043, succ. Centre-Ville
Montréal (Québec)
H3C 4X8
Phone: 514-872-2305
Email: taxes@ville.montreal.qc.ca
http://www2.ville.montreal.qc.ca/finances/actualites/index-a.shtm

Various Borough Offices:
http://www2.ville.montreal.qc.ca/finances/infogen/lieux_infopai-a.shtm

Tax Lien Sales: No

Tax Deed Sales: Yes

Rating: Four Stars (****)

Interest Rate: No interest rate, only tax deeds are sold.

Sale Period: Varies depending on the municipality, but sales are usually held once per year.

Redemption Period: No redemption period, successful bidder gets clear title immediately following the sale.

Bidding Process: Sales are by public auction.

Province-Specific Information:
Saskatchewan is a good province for tax deed sales. The successful bidder receives a clear title directly after the sale without having to wait for a year as with most provinces. Sales appear in the largest newspaper in the municipality holding the sale.

Sales are governed by the tax enforcement act.

ELEVEN

Summary

"Without courage, all other virtues lose their meaning." – Winston Churchhill

Tax liens and tax deeds represent a largely undiscovered and potentially highly profitable investment vehicle. If you are willing to do a little research and focus on a few areas, you can gain the knowledge you will need to make wise investment decisions. However, tax lien and tax deed laws can be complicated and vary a great deal from state to state. Becoming familiar with a few areas and establishing a relationship with county officials are critical components of successful tax sale investing.

If the property goes to foreclosure, hire a local attorney to assist you in the foreclosure process so you do not make any mistakes and lose the property. Avoid properties with potential environmental problems and never purchase a tax lien certificate or a tax deed on any property that does not meet your comfort level.

Reading List

J. S. Moskowitz, 1994, *The 16 Percent Solution, How to Get High Interest Rates in a Low Interest World with Tax Lien Certificates*, Andrews and McMeel.

Prime Directive Management, Ltd., 2000, *The Complete Guide To Investing In Tax Lien Certificates.*

BONUS NO. 1

Best Tax Lien States

The best tax lien states achieve a balance of excellent returns, quick redemption periods, strong state support and some Internet support. If you live near any one of these states and you want to buy tax liens and achieve a high rate of return, then look no further.

Arizona (sales are in February)	
16 percent interest rate	Excellent state support and interest
3-year redemption period	Excellent Internet support for many counties
Tips: Arrive at sales early, as some counties are very popular.	Link: http://treasurer.maricopa.gov/lien.html

Florida (sales are in April or May)	
18 percent interest rate	Excellent state support and interest
2-year redemption period	Excellent Internet support for many counties
Tips: Arrive at sales early, as some counties are very popular.	Links: http://www.cctaxcol.com/advalorem.htm#Delinquent http://www.co.hernando.fl.us/tc/taxsale.htm
At the auction you pay 10 percent of the total lien amount and the remaining balance within 48 hours. Florida can also be a good tax deed state.	

Illinois (sales are in November)	
18 to 36 percent interest rate	Good state support
2.5-year redemption period	Good Internet support for some counties
Tips: You must pre-register one month in advance. This may require two trips to the state.	Link: http://www.co.lake.il.us/treasurer/taxsale.asp
Courts handle system, which can increase legal complexity.	

Indiana (sales are in August)	
10 to 25 percent interest rate	Good state support
1-year redemption period	Good Internet support for some counties
Tips: Less known in some counties, good choice for a state with less competition.	Link: http://www.indygov.org/treas/taxsale/index.htm
Very quick redemption period, so ownership is possible.	

Iowa (sales are in May)

24 percent interest rate is excellent	Good state support
1.75-year redemption period	Good Internet support for some counties
Tips: Arrive early at sales. You bid on the percentage of the property you would own if the tax lien goes to foreclosure, so be careful how you bid.	Link: http://www.co.polk.ia.us:8080/modules.php?name=Sections&sop=viewarticle&artid=225
You can buy tax liens over the counter after the sale	

Missouri (sales are in August)

10 percent and 8 percent over the minimum bid.	Although it appears that the interest rate is not favorable, in Missouri you earn 10 percent on the minimum bid and 8 percent on anything you bid over the minimum. You bid the price up, not the interest rate down. In some states and counties, the winning bids are often much lower than Missouri's guaranteed rate. Be careful not to bid more than the property is worth in case it is not redeemed.
2-year redemption period	
Tips: Register in advance.	
You may need a notarized document from someone who lives in the county to act as your representative.	

New Jersey (sales vary by municipality)

18 to 24 percent	
2-year redemption period	
Tips: Watch for environmental problems. Rules can be complex.	Link: http://www.state.nj.us/localgov.htm
Tax liens also called certificates of purchase.	

Best Tax Deed States

The best tax deed states achieve a balance of strong state support, available properties and Internet information so you can research properties. If you live near any one of these states and you want to buy tax deeds (become a property owner), then look no further.

Arkansas (sales can be every month)	
Many properties available	Strong state support
Tips: Use the county websites to get on their mailing lists – they will send you tax deed sales information for free. Properties can be inexpensive in some areas.	Excellent Internet support for many counties
	Link: http://www.state.ar.us/land/land.html

California (sales vary by county, but generally held once per year)	
Almost all counties have sales	Strong state support
Tips: Arrive at sales early, as some counties are very popular. Properties are generally expensive because land values are high; therefore, you will need substantial capital.	Excellent Internet support
	Links: http://www.co.riverside.ca.us/depts/treasure/tax_sale_information.html http://www.sfgov.org/site/treasurer_index.asp http://www.co.santa-cruz.ca.us/ttc/auction.htm http://www.co.solano.ca.us/SubSection/SubSection.asp?NavID=533 http://www.co.stanislaus.ca.us/Taxtr/Auction/ http://www.ventura.org/taxcollector/auction.htm

Georgia (sales occur once a month)	
Right of redemption state.	If redeemed within one year, investor receives a 20% fee.
Tips: The foreclosure process can be tricky and may require help.	

Texas (sales occur once a month)	
Right of redemption state. Large state with many properties.	Deed can be redeemed in 6 months for most properties, and the investor earns a 25% fee.
Strong state support	Links:
Good Internet support	http://www.co.travis.tx.us/tax_assessor/foreclosure/default.asp
Tips: Laws and procedures are a little different.	http://www.co.travis.tx.us/tax_assessor/foreclosure/resales.asp

ROGUE
REIT
INVESTOR

Published by
Mind Like Water®

Overland Park, Kansas

Disclaimer

The *Rogue Real Estate Investor Collection*, and the phone and email support provided with it, are designed to provide accurate information regarding the subject matter covered. However, there are no guarantees in real estate investing and the authors of this book provide no assurances regarding the success of the investing strategies presented.

Be aware that information on the Internet can change quickly. When relying on information provided in this book that is derived from the Internet, be sure to check that the information you have is the most up to date.

This book, the information provided through phone and email support, and information derived from the Internet are not a substitute for legal advice. Please consult a licensed attorney in your State, Province or area.

ROGUE
REIT
INVESTOR

CONTENTS

Rogue REIT Investor

ONE

Why Should I Read This Book?

"The life which is unexamined is not worth living." – Plato

The last several years have proven that the stock market can be very volatile. However, if you want a more stable investment that provides a good rate of return, your choices seem limited. Certificates of deposit are safe if you don't mind earning 3 to 5 percent per year on your money. Bonds aren't much better, earning about 4 to 6 percent on average per year. Real estate has been the shining star, averaging about 7 to 10 percent per year over the last several years. But if you already own your own home and do not have the time to be a landlord or attend a lot of public auctions, your options for additional real estate investing may seem limited.

What would you say if I told you that there is a very easy way to own just about any type of real estate in any market with minimal effort? What would you say if told you that this method of investing in real estate has returned, on average, 15 percent per year for the last 30 years with almost 50 percent less risk than the stock market? What would you say if I told you that this method of investing in real estate does not make you wait 1 year, 5 years or 10 years for your money to appreciate like many investments, but instead pays you part of the profits every three months?

Does this sound too good to be true?

It's not.

Real estate investment trusts, or REITs as they are commonly called, are one of the best-kept investment secrets. Since 1960, REITs have returned almost 15 percent per year on average (includes capital appreciation and dividends). This investment return beats the Dow, the S&P 500 and even small capitalization stocks. More amazing, REITs achieved this high investment return with much less risk than almost any other stock market investment, and by law REITs are required to pay 95 percent of their profits back to the shareholders.

If earning 15 percent per year with minimal risk, time and money sounds intriguing, read on.

TWO

What Are REITs?

*"The REIT business is shifting from being a cottage industry
to a mainstream investment choice." – Bernard Winograd*

REITs were born in 1960, when Congress passed the Real Estate Investment Trust Act. Similar to stock ownership in companies, Congress wanted to make it possible for anyone with limited capital to become part owner of residential subdivisions, shopping malls, apartment complexes, office buildings, hotels, mortgages and many other types of real estate. By pooling real estate properties together and following some fairly strict guidelines, real estate developers could create a trust of real estate properties that individuals could purchase ownership on the major stock exchanges. Viewed in this manner, REITs are essentially real estate mutual funds. However, unlike most stock mutual funds that you may be familiar with, REITs have some unique characteristics.

**First, REITs do not have to pay taxes on any profits
they earn as long as they pay out at least 95 percent
of their profits to their shareholders every year.**

These means REITs often have high dividend yields and commonly pay their shareholders a 5 to 8 percent return on their money every year. In this way, REITs are more like bonds and other fixed yield investments (e.g., certificates of deposit). However, unlike bonds and other fixed yield investments, REITs typically increase their dividend payments every year, as the REIT continues to grow by purchasing new properties or expanding existing properties. In this way, REITs are more like high yielding stocks (e.g., utility stocks and energy stocks). But unlike other high yielding stocks, REITs do not have to pay any taxes on their dividends as long as they pay out 95 percent of their profits to shareholders.

This makes REITs a very compelling investment choice for investors seeking a balance of growth and income with limited risk.

**Second, the majority of the shares in a REIT
cannot be owned by 5 individuals or less and
every REIT must have at least 100 shareholders.**

This means it is uncommon for REITs to be controlled by a few individuals that may not have the best interests of the other shareholders in mind.

Third, REITs cannot speculate.

This means REITs cannot purchase or sell properties with the intention of making a short-term gain. This often forces the managers of a REIT to maintain a long-term focus that delivers steady dividends and steady dividend growth.

**Fourth, REITs can only raise additional
capital by equity or debt financing.**

This means REITs can only raise additional funds by issuing more stock or by borrowing money. Profit that is created by the REIT cannot be used to expand the business because the REIT must pay out this money to the shareholders. Profit can be used to pay back debt.

What does all this mean?

REITs are unique in the investment world. They can avoid taxes if they reward shareholders. They must maintain a long-term focus. The management cannot hoard profits or use the profits to invest in other business ventures.

Overall, this combination of stability, prohibition from speculation, growth potential and incentive to pay shareholders so taxes are avoided can create a great investment opportunity. Since 1960, REITs have outperformed every major stock market average with 50 percent less investing risk. In fact, when you look at stock charts for most REITs, they show a steady uptrend with limited price fluctuation. Here is the 10-year stock chart for Hospitality Properties Trust (HPT), a REIT that invests in hotels:

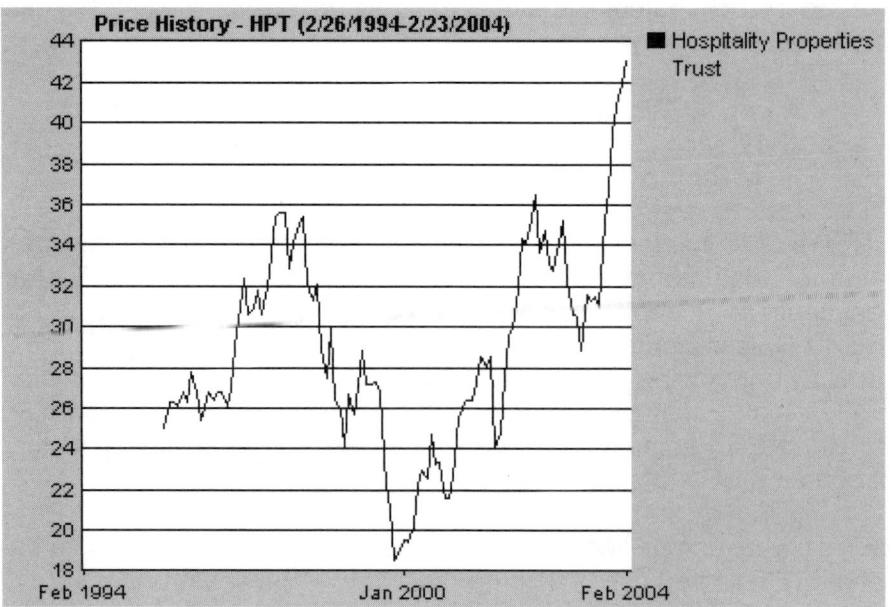

Are you beginning to see why REITs are a hidden investment opportunity?

THREE

What Every REIT Investor Should Know

"Knowledge is Power." – Francis Bacon

Now that you have a basic understanding of what a REIT is and why REITs represent a unique investment opportunity, it is time to take the gloves off and really delve into what you should know before you decide to invest in REITs.

The Benefits of REIT Investing

We have already discussed some of the benefits of REIT investing. The benefits of REIT investing can be summarized in the following bullets:

- Investment return: Since 1960, REITs have averaged a 15 percent return per year. This rate of return has outperformed all major stock market averages.

- Investment risk: REITs have been able to achieve a 15 percent return per year with almost 50 percent less risk than the most popular stock market average, the S&P 500.

- Dividend payments: REITs, by law, must pay out 95 percent of their profits to shareholders in order to avoid taxes. This means you do not have to wait for years to see your profits grow; instead you will receive a quarterly dividend payment every three months. Summed over a year, these dividend payments will typically equal approximately 5 to 8 percent of your total investment.

- Dividend growth: Unlike bonds, REITs typically increase their dividend payments every year.

- Diversification: REITs must own multiple properties or mortgages to properties, diversifying your risk.

- Liquidity: Unlike individual real estate ownership, REITs are highly liquid and can be bought or sold at any time on major stock exchanges for minimal cost.

- Speculation: By law, REITs cannot speculate for the purpose of making a short-term gain.

- Ownership: REITs cannot be controlled by less than 5 individuals and require a total of a least 100 separate owners.

The Drawbacks of REIT Investing

The drawbacks of REIT investing can be summarized in the following bullets:

- Capital: REITs cannot accumulate income. By law, REITs can only raise capital by issuing more stock or by borrowing money.

- Investment return: Because REITs must pay out 95 percent of their profits to shareholders, REITs typically have a cap on how much they can appreciate in a year. For example, REITs are great investments because they appreciate by 15 percent a year on average, but REITs almost never double in value over one or two years.

- Dividend payments: Unless your REIT investments are tax deferred, you must pay taxes on the dividend payments you receive every year.

- Interest rate changes: Because REITs pay out most of their profits in dividend payments, when interest rates rise, the value of REITs typically falls. It is also more difficult for REITs to borrow money and still make a profit if interest rates are too high.

- Market risk: Real estate values do fluctuate. However, on average real estate values fluctuate less than the stock market.

- Debt: Because REITs commonly use debt to expand, too much debt can magnify investment returns but also increase risk to shareholders.

The Types of REITs

REITs are typically divided into two main categories: Equity REITs and Mortgage REITs. Hybrid REITs (a combination of both equity and mortgage REITs) used to be popular, but are no longer allowed by Congress because they were complicated to manage and understand, making it difficult for investors to evaluate their worth.

Equity REITs maintain direct ownership in real estate properties and typically focus on one main type of real estate. Mortgage REITs do not directly own real estate but make money by holding mortgages to real estate. Overall, investing in Equity REITs is less risky and more straightforward. Equity REITs are also much less sensitive to interest rate changes. With these factors in mind, this book focuses on Equity REITs. Equity REITs come in all shapes and sizes. Here is a list of the main types of real estate equity REITs to invest in:

- Hotels
- Residential homes
- Manufactured homes
- Self-storage facilities
- Industrial properties
- Apartment buildings
- Office buildings
- Health care facilities
- Shopping malls
- Specialty properties
- Diversified properties
- Free standing retail properties.

Each Equity REIT specializes in one of the above property types. At the end of 2003, over 200 equity REITs were listed on the New York, Nasdaq and American Stock Exchange. Here is a list of the REITs traded on the major stock exchanges:

REITs Traded on Major United States Stock Exchanges

Symbol	Company Name	Industry	Market Cap	Dividend Yield	Debt to Equity
HCP	Health Care Property Investors Inc.	REIT - Healthcare Facilities	3,412,157,350	6.4	1.09
HCN	Health Care REIT, Inc.	REIT - Healthcare Facilities	1,793,776,785	6.4	0.78
HR	Healthcare Realty Trust	REIT - Healthcare Facilities	1,625,495,752	6.6	0.63
LTC	LTC Properties, Inc.	REIT - Healthcare Facilities	259,789,543	4.4	0.95
NHI	National Health Investors	REIT - Healthcare Facilities	678,340,660	1.6	0.44
NHR	National Health Realty	REIT - Healthcare Facilities	190,949,333	6.8	0.67
NHP	Nationwide Health Properties Inc.	REIT - Healthcare Facilities	1,187,699,445	7.4	1.44
OHI	Omega Healthcare Investor	REIT - Healthcare Facilities	372,482,119	1.5	0.49
UHT	Universal Health Realty	REIT - Healthcare Facilities	352,516,541	6.7	0.27
VTR	Ventas, Inc.	REIT - Healthcare Facilities	1,920,941,843	4.6	NA
WRS	Windrose Medical Properties Trust	REIT - Healthcare Facilities	71,150,000	5.6	1.49
AFR	American Financial Realty Trust	REIT - Diversified	1,990,919,213	2.7	0.86
AQQ	American Spectrum Realty, Inc.	REIT - Diversified	19,947,940	0	7.59
AMV	AmeriVest Properties Inc.	REIT - Diversified	127,916,802	7.1	1.82
ANH	Anworth Mortgage Asset	REIT - Diversified	539,646,318	9.6	0
AZL	Arizona Land Income Corp.	REIT - Diversified	8,977,350	8.2	0
AHT	Ashford Hospitality Trust, Inc.	REIT - Diversified	238,811,513	0	NA
BNP	BNP Residential Properties, Inc.	REIT - Diversified	69,066,237	8.5	7.67
BRE	BRE Properties, Inc.	REIT - Diversified	1,612,273,763	5.9	1.39
CARS	Capital Automotive REIT	REIT - Diversified	1,105,262,535	4.9	2.27
CT	Capital Trust, Inc.	REIT - Diversified	149,707,000	4.6	1.63
CDR	Cedar Shopping Centers Inc.	REIT - Diversified	2,920,260	0	49.79
CNVLZ	City Investing Company Liquidating Trust	REIT - Diversified	77,217,397	0	0
CLP	Colonial Properties Trust	REIT - Diversified	1,032,606,852	6.8	1.93
CUZ	Cousins Properties Inc.	REIT - Diversified	1,427,854,340	5	0.98
CEI	Crescent R.E. Equities Co.	REIT - Diversified	1,740,450,974	8.5	2.88
CMM	CRIIMI MAE Inc.	REIT - Diversified	172,980,403	0	1.05
DDR	Developers Diversified Realty	REIT - Diversified	2,806,713,775	5.7	2.04
DRE	Duke Realty Corp.	REIT - Diversified	4,178,788,258	5.9	1.07
EGP	EastGroup Properties Inc.	REIT - Diversified	668,966,565	5.7	1.14
EPR	Entertainment Properties Trust	REIT - Diversified	685,055,018	5.9	1.04
FPO	First Potomac Realty Trust	REIT - Diversified	146,951,128	0	NA
FUR	First Union RE Investment	REIT - Diversified	57,850,981	0	0.87
GLB	Glenborough Realty Trust	REIT - Diversified	522,828,844	8.2	1.15
GTA	Golf Trust of America, Inc.	REIT - Diversified	18,135,500	0	0
HTG	Heritage Property Invest. Trust Inc.	REIT - Diversified	1,166,724,032	7.6	1.24
HIW	Highwoods Properties, Inc.	REIT - Diversified	1,404,199,486	7.1	1.44
HMG	HMG/Courtland Properties	REIT - Diversified	9,964,350	0	0.48
IMH	IMPAC Mortgage Holdings, Inc.	REIT - Diversified	1,027,175,420	11.6	16.88
IOT	Income Opportunity Realty	REIT - Diversified	22,505,960	0	0.88

KRC	Kilroy Realty Corporation	REIT - Diversified	900,092,414	6.3	1.65
KRT	Kramont Realty Trust	REIT - Diversified	437,908,750	7.2	1.99
LQI	La Quinta Corporation	REIT - Diversified	1,134,204,334	0	0.58
LXP	Lexington Corp. Prop. Trust	REIT - Diversified	840,154,532	6.5	1.22
LBI	Liberte Investors Inc.	REIT - Diversified	174,800,605	0	0
MRTI	Maxus Realty Trust, Inc.	REIT - Diversified	14,869,240	8	2.22
MPQ	Meredith Enterprises, Inc.	REIT - Diversified	14,820,000	7.6	2.44
MFA	MFA Mortgage Investments	REIT - Diversified	587,903,742	11.1	0.04
MAA	Mid-America Apartment	REIT - Diversified	658,026,215	6.8	2.57
MNRTA	Monmouth R.E. Inv. Corp.	REIT - Diversified	136,997,694	6.5	1.32
NCT	Newcastle Investment Corp.	REIT - Diversified	726,126,511	7.5	4.83
OLP	One Liberty Properties, Inc.	REIT - Diversified	195,945,750	6.1	1.51
PEI	Pennsylvania R.E.I.T.	REIT - Diversified	833,856,582	7.3	1.14
PW	Pittsburgh & WV Railroad	REIT - Diversified	13,590,000	5.9	0
PP	Prentiss Properties Trust	REIT - Diversified	1,371,973,826	6.9	1.3
PDL.A	President Realty A	REIT - Diversified	3,687,000	8.3	NA
PDL.B	Presidential Realty Corp.	REIT - Diversified	25,207,000	8.4	1.33
RPT	Ramco-Gershenson Properties Trust	REIT - Diversified	403,808,442	6.6	2.13
RA	Reckson Associates Realty	REIT - Diversified	1,166,987,000	7	1.8
RWT	Redwood Trust, Inc.	REIT - Diversified	1,024,385,150	5.1	24.35
BFS	Saul Centers, Inc.	REIT - Diversified	440,301,364	5.6	NA
HXD	Shelbourne Properties I, Inc.	REIT - Diversified	13,667,311	391.5	1.75
HXE	Shelbourne Properties II, Inc.	REIT - Diversified	17,900,000	326.3	0.96
HXF	Shelbourne Properties III, Inc.	REIT - Diversified	8,126,700	518	2.1
SIZ	Sizeler Property Investors	REIT - Diversified	141,459,665	8.4	1.78
TARR	Tarragon Realty Investors	REIT - Diversified	245,048,364	0	5.82
TMA	Thornburg Mortgage, Inc.	REIT - Diversified	1,956,389,109	9.5	14.37
TCI	Transcontinental Realty	REIT - Diversified	137,241,000	0	2.71
UBP	Urstadt Biddle Properties	REIT - Diversified	93,778,000	5.5	0.48
VNO	Vornado Realty Trust	REIT - Diversified	6,198,976,098	5.5	1.56
WRE	Washington Real Estate Investment Trust	REIT - Diversified	1,128,279,183	5.1	1.57
ARE	Alexandria RE Equities	REIT - Office	1,117,719,495	3.9	1.62
BDN	Brandywine Realty Trust	REIT - Office	1,058,595,500	6.6	1.3
BED	Bedford Property Investors, Inc.	REIT - Office	466,172,973	7	1.37
CLI	Mack-Cali Realty Corp.	REIT - Office	2,287,921,750	6.3	1.1
CRE	CarrAmerica Realty Corp.	REIT - Office	1,536,385,500	6.8	2.12
EOP	Equity Office Properties	REIT - Office	11,193,364,000	7.1	1.2
HRP	HRPT Properties Trust	REIT - Office	1,442,017,454	8.1	0.9
KE	Koger Equity, Inc.	REIT - Office	461,976,178	6.5	0.97
KTR	Keystone Property Trust	REIT - Office	566,734,208	6.1	1.67
LRY	Liberty Property Trust	REIT - Office	2,970,085,446	6.5	1.34
OFC	Corporate Office Properties Trust	REIT - Office	624,802,100	4.5	1.88
PCC	PMC Commercial Trust	REIT - Office	99,766,032	10	0.73
PGE	Prime Group Realty Trust	REIT - Office	145,564,352	0	1.99
BOY	Boykin Lodging Company	REIT - Hotel/Motel	166,502,407	7.5	1.12
ENN	Equity Inns, Inc.	REIT - Hotel/Motel	390,256,863	5.8	1.25
FCH	FelCor Lodging Trust Inc.	REIT - Hotel/Motel	717,870,577	0	1.81

HMT	Host Marriott Corporation	REIT - Hotel/Motel	3,823,620,900	0	4.04
HOT	Starwood Hotels & Resorts Worldwide, Inc.	REIT - Hotel/Motel	7,489,169,133	9.2	1.02
HPT	Hospitality Properties Trust	REIT - Hotel/Motel	2,577,958,444	8.8	0.5
HT	Hersha Hospitality Trust	REIT - Hotel/Motel	128,358,064	7	5.76
HUMP	Humphrey Hospitality Trust	REIT - Hotel/Motel	53,738,540	3.9	1.9
IHT	InnSuites Hospitality Trust	REIT - Hotel/Motel	3,483,090	0	NA
JAMS	Jameson Inns, Inc.	REIT - Hotel/Motel	34,430,401	7.4	2.39
KPA	Innkeepers USA Trust	REIT - Hotel/Motel	358,726,657	1.8	0.79
MHX	MeriStar Hospitality Corporation	REIT - Hotel/Motel	440,573,000	0	2.55
SNH	Senior Housing Properties	REIT - Hotel/Motel	1,061,506,471	6.8	0.62
WXH	Winston Hotels, Inc.	REIT - Hotel/Motel	270,713,529	5.7	0.51
AMB	AMB Property Corporation	REIT - Industrial	2,782,667,955	4.9	1.41
CNT	CenterPoint Properties	REIT - Industrial	1,749,006,265	3.5	1.73
FR	First Industrial Realty, Inc.	REIT - Industrial	1,359,362,580	8.1	1.64
PLD	ProLogis	REIT - Industrial	5,588,377,224	4.6	1.2
PSA	Public Storage, Inc.	REIT - Industrial	5,661,334,000	4	0.03
PSA.A	Public Storage CL A	REIT - Industrial	397,390,000	8.2	NA
PSB	PS Business Parks, Inc.	REIT - Industrial	923,024,784	2.7	0.14
SHU	Shurgard Storage Centers, Inc.	REIT - Industrial	1,724,203,584	5.7	1.08
SSS	Sovran Self Storage, Inc.	REIT - Industrial	498,757,573	6.7	0.96
AEC	Associated Estates Realty	REIT - Residential	150,962,250	8.9	7.87
AIV	Apartment Investment and Management Co.	REIT - Residential	3,165,455,856	9.1	3.01
AMC	American Mortgage Acceptance Company	REIT - Residential	137,743,764	9.6	0
AML	AMLI Residential Properties Trust	REIT - Residential	520,821,017	7.5	1.51
ANL	American Land Lease, Inc.	REIT - Residential	140,205,250	5	1.18
ASN	Archstone-Smith Trust	REIT - Residential	5,128,815,362	6.4	0.97
AVB	AvalonBay Communities	REIT - Residential	3,316,627,408	6	1.08
BRT	BRT Realty Trust	REIT - Residential	171,857,418	6.1	0.06
CMO	Capstead Mortgage Corporation	REIT - Residential	238,148,827	25.6	3.5
CPT	Camden Property Trust	REIT - Residential	1,643,939,500	6.1	1.87
DX	Dynex Capital, Inc.	REIT - Residential	77,422,879	0	15.65
EQR	Equity Residential	REIT - Residential	7,836,865,660	6.1	1.3
EQY	Equity One, Inc.	REIT - Residential	1,238,905,142	6.4	0.93
ESS	Essex Property Trust, Inc.	REIT - Residential	1,396,054,102	5.1	1.38
GBP	Gables Residential Trust	REIT - Residential	972,716,863	7.1	2.1
HME	Home Properties, Inc.	REIT - Residential	1,193,634,000	6.3	2.25
IRETS	Investors Real Estate Trust	REIT - Residential	422,644,434	6.1	2.33
MHC	Manufactured Home Communities	REIT - Residential	671,043,794	6.7	4.06
PPS	Post Properties, Inc.	REIT - Residential	1,062,563,845	6.4	1.58
RPI	Roberts Realty Investors, Inc.	REIT - Residential	36,230,349	0	5.57
SMT	Summit Properties Inc.	REIT - Residential	681,573,750	5.8	1.85
SUI	Sun Communities, Inc.	REIT - Residential	732,767,132	6.4	2.04
TCR	Cornerstone Realty Income Trust, Inc.	REIT - Residential	524,555,033	8.7	2.7
TCT	Town & Country Trust	REIT - Residential	395,909,380	6.8	52.28
UBA	Urstadt Biddle Properties Inc.	REIT - Residential	269,771,000	5.8	NA
UDR	United Dominion Realty	REIT - Residential	2,183,774,711	6.3	2.41

UMH	United Mobile Homes, Inc.	REIT - Residential	137,840,761	5.3	1.23
WRP	Wellsford Real Properties, Inc.	REIT - Residential	124,213,439	0	0.61
ADC	Agree Realty Corporation	REIT - Retail	183,240,317	6.9	0.87
AKR	Acadia Realty Trust	REIT - Retail	339,066,016	4.8	1.15
ATLRS	Atlantic Realty Trust	REIT - Retail	60,440,017	2.7	NA
CBL	CBL & Associates Properties, Inc.	REIT - Retail	1,709,181,500	5.1	3.04
CPG	Chelsea Property Group	REIT - Retail	2,335,090,833	4	2.31
FRT	Federal Realty Investment Trust	REIT - Retail	1,917,396,000	5	2.06
GGP	General Growth Properties	REIT - Retail	6,000,369,218	3.9	3.79
GRT	Glimcher Realty Trust	REIT - Retail	810,061,959	8.3	4.95
KIM	Kimco Realty Corp.	REIT - Retail	4,891,295,816	5	0.75
MAC	The Macerich Company	REIT - Retail	2,614,987,756	5.2	2.78
MAL	Malan Realty Investors	REIT - Retail	25,553,789	16.4	5.33
MLS	The Mills Corporation	REIT - Retail	2,176,922,437	5.1	6.44
NNN	Commercial Net Lease Realty	REIT - Retail	823,356,765	7.2	0.79
NXL	New Plan Excel Realty Trust	REIT - Retail	2,392,136,595	6.7	1.07
O	Realty Income Corp.	REIT - Retail	1,530,765,460	5.9	0.54
PNP	Pan Pacific Retail Properties, Inc.	REIT - Retail	2,014,450,000	4.1	1.03
REG	Regency Centers Corp.	REIT - Retail	2,383,426,591	5.2	1.26
SKT	Tanger Factory Outlet Center	REIT - Retail	437,887,816	5.9	3.61
SPG	Simon Property Group, Inc.	REIT - Retail	9,345,004,708	4.9	3.95
TCO	Taubman Centers, Inc.	REIT - Retail	1,128,485,819	4.8	4.95
TRZ	Trizec Properties, Inc.	REIT - Retail	2,355,919,643	5.1	1.6
WRI	Weingarten Realty Investors	REIT - Retail	2,492,773,718	5	1.79
ABFI	American Business Financial Services	Mortgage Investment	11,905,880	7.8	67.54
AHH	American Home Mortgage Holdings	Mortgage Investment	389,670,393	10.1	0.29
AHR	Anthracite Capital Inc.	Mortgage Investment	536,128,324	10.2	5.66
AIA	American Insured Mortgage Investors	Mortgage Investment	15,300,000	5.3	0
AII	American Insured Mortgage Investors - 85	Mortgage Investment	57,742,403	7.6	0
AIJ	American Insured Mortgage Inv. L.P. 86	Mortgage Investment	11,970,000	192.6	0
AIK	American Insured Mortgage Inv. 88	Mortgage Investment	13,379,040	73.6	0.93
APRO	America Firot Apartment	Mortgage Investment	57,702,749	8.8	1.7
ATAXZ	Amer. 1st Tax Exempt Inv.	Mortgage Investment	71,325,500	7.5	0.86
CAA	Capital Alliance Income	Mortgage Investment	6,031,590	9.5	1.65
CFC	Countrywide Financial Corp.	Mortgage Investment	14,788,518,344	0.8	4.54
CHC	CharterMac	Mortgage Investment	936,723,070	6.7	1.23
DFC	Delta Financial Corporation	Mortgage Investment	156,987,459	0	1.26
DRL	Doral Financial Corp.	Mortgage Investment	3,603,235,074	1.5	2.11
FNM	Fannie Mae	Mortgage Investment	73,526,040,111	2.5	35.73
FRE	Freddie Mac	Mortgage Investment	43,839,990,175	1.7	22.34
HCM	Hanover Capital Mortgage Holdings, Inc.	Mortgage Investment	103,548,297	10.6	0.73
INV	American Residential Invest. Trust, Inc.	Mortgage Investment	64,419,199	0	1.73
LEND	Accredited Home Lenders Holding Co.	Mortgage Investment	775,993,968	0	16
MTXC	Matrix Bancorp, Inc.	Mortgage Investment	59,465,848	0	1.66
NCEN	New Century Financial	Mortgage Investment	1,618,665,208	1.4	8.18
SAXN	Saxon Capital, Inc.	Mortgage Investment	765,268,184	0	0.08
TFN	Transnational Financial Network, Inc.	Mortgage Investment	8,860,800	0	1.05

UFM	United Financial Mortgage Corporation	Mortgage Investment	29,986,999	0	9.38
UPFC	United PanAm Financial	Mortgage Investment	240,468,478	0	0.1
VSTN	Vestin Group, Inc.	Mortgage Investment	11,948,000	19.6	0.34
ACP	American Real Estate Partners, L.P.	Property Management	803,939,722	0	0.16
AFREZ	America First Real Estate Investment	Property Management	62,872,250	7.7	1.09
ALX	Alexander's Inc.	Property Management	737,647,500	0	12.23
AMY	AmREIT	Property Management	36,497,269	5.4	0.95
APSA	Alto Palermo S.A. (ADR)	Property Management	108,716,997	3.2	0.37
ARI	Arden Realty, Inc.	Property Management	1,888,714,775	6.9	0.98
ARL	American Realty Investors	Property Management	92,463,598	0	12.25
BEI	Boardwalk Equities Inc.	Property Management	667,863,607	1	4.48
BFEN	BF Enterprises, Inc.	Property Management	29,836,061	0	0
BNN	Brascan Corporation	Property Management	5,454,561,166	2.3	2.94
BPO	Brookfield Properties Corporation	Property Management	4,483,915,919	2.1	2.57
BXP	Boston Properties, Inc.	Property Management	4,597,391,025	5.3	2.07
CDX	Catellus Development Corp. (REIT)	Property Management	2,307,849,837	2.3	2.09
CPI	Capital Properties, Inc.	Property Management	39,566,999	1	0
CPV	Correctional Properties Trust	Property Management	326,627,048	6.1	0.29
CXW	Corrections Corp. of America	Property Management	1,028,598,261	6.8	1.51
ETT	ElderTrust	Property Management	97,844,878	5.1	2.31
FCE.A	Forest City Enterprises, Inc.	Property Management	1,797,531,000	0.7	5.36
FCE.B	Forest City Enterprises B	Property Management	677,570,000	0.7	NA
GL	Great Lakes REIT, Inc.	Property Management	257,070,253	10.2	1.8
GNI	Great Northern Iron Ore	Property Management	138,375,000	7.1	0
GOOD	Gladstone Commercial Corp.	Property Management	129,531,906	0.1	0
GTY	Getty Realty Corp.	Property Management	641,030,000	6.5	0
GYRO	Gyrodyne Co. of America	Property Management	31,948,000	0	0
HRY	Hallwood Realty Partners	Property Management	207,140,295	0	3.56
INTG	The InterGroup Corporation	Property Management	30,992,500	0	4.65
JLL	Jones Lang LaSalle Inc.	Property Management	663,514,883	0	0.54
JOE	The St. Joe Company	Property Management	2,927,577,716	0.8	0.77
KWIC	Kennedy-Wilson, Inc.	Property Management	53,975,671	0	0.88
LHO	LaSalle Hotel Properties	Property Management	410,774,294	4.3	0.66
LNR	LNR Property Corp.	Property Management	1,478,017,944	0.1	1.37
MAYS	J.W. Mays, Inc.	Property Management	27,216,000	0	0.16
MIM	MI Developments Inc.	Property Management	1,252,088,132	0	NA
MONM	Monmouth Capital Corporation	Property Management	22,042,640	6.3	1.74
MPG	Maguire Properties, Inc.	Property Management	1,001,328,060	3.5	2.82
MSW	Mission West Properties	Property Management	232,590,507	7.4	2.77
NEN	New England Realty Assoc.	Property Management	8,996,000	2.5	8.29
PKY	Parkway Properties, Inc.	Property Management	474,848,000	5.9	0.8
RCG	RCG Companies Incorporated	Property Management	32,100,640	0	0.07
RDI.A	Reading International Inc.	Property Management	133,108,000	0	0.53
RDI.B	Reading Int'l Inc. B	Property Management	12,703,000	0	NA
RSE	The Rouse Company	Property Management	4,255,991,000	3.7	3.4
SCC	Security Capital Corp.	Property Management	51,285,449	0	0.35
SLG	SL Green Realty Corp.	Property Management	1,477,852,762	4.8	1.01

SNRR	Sunterra Corporation	Property Management	214,735,493	0	0.02
TCC	Trammell Crow Company	Property Management	515,452,000	0	0.11
USV	U.S. Restaurant Props.	Property Management	386,357,397	7.7	1.93
WPC	W.P. Carey & Co. LLC	Property Management	1,118,245,828	5.8	0.35
XLG	Price Legacy Corporation	Property Management	139,969,967	0	3.16
APO	American Community Properties Trust	Real Estate Development	43,301,281	0	2.65
AVTR	Avatar Holdings Inc.	Real Estate Development	346,620,313	0	0.18
BXG	Bluegreen Corporation	Real Estate Development	224,523,000	0	1.37
CALC	California Coastal Communities, Inc.	Real Estate Development	107,710,470	0	0
CTO	Consolidated-Tomoka Land	Real Estate Development	179,654,854	0.8	0
HTL	Heartland Partners, LP	Real Estate Development	14,121,000	34.1	0.31
IRS	IRSA Inversiones Representaciones (ADR)	Real Estate Development	235,944,158	0	0.73
MXM	MAXXAM Inc.	Real Estate Development	139,010,405	0	NA
STRS	Stratus Properties, Inc.	Real Estate Development	86,188,303	0	0.5

Several of the REITs in this table are highlighted. These REITs look promising based on their dividend yield, price to earnings ratio (P/E ratio), and debt. The next chapter will profile some of the indicators that can be used to evaluate if a REIT is a good investment.

FOUR

When Do REITS Become a Bargain?

"One man's trash is another man's treasure." – Anonymous

If you have been a stock market investor over the last decade you are probably getting seasick, watching your investments go up and down like a yo yo. Also, after all the financial scandals, you are probably wondering if any stock market investment is safe.

Usually, the best investing medicine boils down to three factors: knowledge, patience and diversification.

Always remember that over the long haul, stocks have outperformed almost every asset class. However, stocks do not appreciate along a straight line. The probability that stocks will go up or down by more than 20 percent in a given year is greater than 50 percent. The more you know and understand your investments, the better you can usually stomach price declines and learn to recognize bargains.

When I wrote my first book, *Rogue Investor*, in 1994, I spent considerable effort trying to explain how, based on extensive research, creating wealth depended on the following five important concepts:

- Always save a portion of what you earn.

- Invest a portion of this money in quality investments.

- Diversify this money in at least 10 to 12 different, quality investments.

- Avoid speculation, or if you must speculate do it with a very small percentage of the money you save.

- Be very patient, as investment success is often measured in decades, not years.

Certainly this investment advice has not changed. Investors who saved money and avoided speculation by maintaining ownership in quality companies have survived every major stock market decline. Others who ignored this advice got wiped out or turned sour on investing in the stock market forever. This is what happens during every bear market.

However, something else also happens during every bear market. The sectors of the market that under performed, over perform. If you look at what bull and bear markets really are, they are nothing more than definitions. During a bull market, the stocks that represent the most widely recognized stock market averages go up on average. In contrast, less well-recognized markets that are often ignored by the vast majority, including small stocks, REITs, and energy/commodity stocks, usually do not participate as strongly during a bull market. These markets often do well when more popular stocks are declining or moving sideways.

This is where we are today. As the major stock market averages bounce around, REITs, small stocks and energy stocks have held up fairly well. In fact, REITs have been one of the star performers over the last several years. With interest rates at 40-year lows, stable real estate values and high dividend yields, REITs represent one of the most promising investments over the next decade. In fact, as baby boomers enter their retirement years, REITs offer something most other stock market investments cannot: growth and high income.

So if now is an excellent time to invest in REITs, how do you decide which REITs represent the best investment?

If you are lazy, in a hurry, pressed for time or have limited money to invest, consider investing in a REIT mutual fund. REIT mutual funds buy multiple REITs, automatically diversifying your risk. Here are names, mutual fund symbols and phone numbers for six REIT mutual funds that look promising:

- Cohen & Steers Reality Shares (CSRSX)   800-437-9912
- Fidelity Real Estate (FRESX)   800-544-8888
- Vanguard REIT Index (VGSIX)   800-662-7447
- CGM Reality (CGMRX)   800-345-4048
- Third Avenue Real Estate Value (TAREX)   800-443-1021
- Alpine Reality Income and Growth (AIGYX)   888-785-5578.

If you are patient and willing to do some research, here are the most important items to consider when determining which real estate investment trusts represent the best value:

- Debt: Remember, real estate trusts can only expand business by borrowing more money or issuing more shares. High debt can artificially inflate the profits of a REIT and increase investing risk, but some debt is healthy. Avoid any REIT with a debt to equity ratio greater than 2 or an interest to debt ratio coverage less than 2.

- Dividend yield: Look for REITs with a dividend yield in the range of 5 to 8 percent. A dividend yield that is too high usually means something is wrong, while a low dividend yield means the REIT is overpriced or focused more on growing the business.

- Payout ratio: The ratio of the dividend yield to the total amount of cash flow, or funds from operations (FFO) as it is commonly called in the REIT industry, is called the payout ratio. The payout ratio can range from less than 50 percent to greater than 100 percent. REITs that have ample room to raise dividend payments and increase their profits typically have lower payout ratios. REITs with high payout ratios typically offer a higher dividend yield but may not increase dividend payments or grow profits. Avoid REITs with a payout ratio greater than 200 percent, especially if you want the REIT to increase dividend payments each year.

- Insider ownership: Look for REITs where the insiders control at least 10 to 15 percent of the total shares of the REIT. This means the insiders will have a vested interest in the success of the REIT, motivating them to help the other shareholders.

- Avoid REIT IPOs: In other words, REITS that recently had their initial public offering. Anyone who invested in most Internet IPOs over the last few years should understand the risk of investing in an IPO. Although REIT IPOs are usually more stable than typical stock IPOs, a new, or extremely young company often does not have a proven management team. Unless you have direct knowledge of the management team or the REIT has existed successfully in the private real estate market for more than 5 or 10 years, wait until the REIT has been a public company for at least 5 years before you invest.

To find all of this information, do the following:

1. Go to http://www.msn.com and type in the stock symbol in the Get Quote lookup field. If you do not know the stock symbol, you can type in the company name instead and the lookup feature will help you find the stock symbol. A web page with company information will appear.
2. Click on the Detailed Quote link. A web page with lots of company information and links will appear.
3. Click on the Company Report link under the header "Research."
4. Scroll around the web page that appears. You should be able to find a description of the company, the dividend yield, the dividend growth rate and the debt to equity.
5. After you are satisfied with this page, click on the Ownership link under the header "Research." The web page that appears will provide information on the percentage of ownership insiders have (look at insider ownership).
6. Now click on the Financial Results link under the header "Research." The web page that appears will give you the payout ratio along with a lot of other financial information.
7. There will also be new links under the Financial Results link on this page. Click on the one called Key Ratios. On the web page that appears, you will be given a new list of links. Click on the one called Financial Condition. The web page that appears will give you the interest rate coverage (called interest coverage).

To assist you in your quest for good REIT investments, I have already performed some screens for promising REITs.

Promising REITs With Limited Debt and Consistent Dividend Growth

Symbol	Company Name	Industry	Current Dividend Yield	P/E Ratio	Debt to Equity	Interest Coverage	5-Year Dividend Growth
CUZ	Cousins Properties Inc.	REIT - Diversified	5.1	5.9	0.98	5.3	20.06
VNO	Vornado Realty Trust	REIT - Diversified	5.4	21.7	1.56	2.3	11.32
DRE	Duke Realty Corp.	REIT - Diversified	5.9	30.3	1.07	2.3	7.67
BRE	BRE Properties, Inc.	REIT - Diversified	6	16.8	1.39	2	6.73
EPR	Entertainment Properties Trust	REIT - Diversified	5.8	19.9	1.04	2.2	6.29
WRE	Washington Real Estate Investment	REIT - Diversified	5.2	24.5	1.57	2.6	5.34
KRC	Kilroy Realty Corporation	REIT - Diversified	6.1	15.3	1.65	2.4	4.64
BED	Bedford Property Investors, Inc.	REIT - Office	7.1	16	1.37	2.3	9.64
LRY	Liberty Property Trust	REIT - Office	6.5	18.3	1.34	2.2	7.47
ARE	Alexandria RE Equities	REIT – Office	4	18.3	1.62	2.8	4.97
CLI	Mack-Cali Realty Corp.	REIT - Office	6.4	16	1.1	2.2	4.27
HCP	Health Care Property Investors Inc.	REIT - Healthcare Facilities	6.1	32.1	1.09	2.6	4.97
HR	Healthcare Realty Trust	REIT - Healthcare Facilities	6.6	26	0.63	2.8	3.37
HCN	Health Care REIT, Inc.	REIT - Healthcare Facilities	6.4	23.1	0.78	2.5	2.61

HPT	Hospitality Properties Trust	REIT - Hotel/Motel	8.6	21.9	0.5	4.1	2.16
PSA	Public Storage, Inc.	REIT - Industrial	4	35.1	0.03	198.2	23.05
PLD	ProLogis	REIT - Industrial	4.6	36	1.2	2.4	3.08
SSS	Sovran Self Storage, Inc.	REIT - Industrial	6.7	24.5	0.96	2.9	2.16
EQY	Equity One, Inc.	REIT - Residential	6.1	18.5	0.93	2.4	18.14
ESS	Essex Property Trust, Inc.	REIT - Residential	5.1	31.7	1.38	2	10.89
ANL	American Land Lease, Inc.	REIT - Residential	5	16.9	1.18	2.6	4.27
UMH	United Mobile Homes, Inc.	REIT - Residential	5.3	17.4	1.23	3.4	3.77
HCM	Hanover Capital Mortgage Holdings	Mortgage Investment	10.4	8.2	0.73	2.8	16.57
CHC	CharterMac	Mortgage Investment	6.6	16.7	1.23	3.8	8.36
MONM	Monmouth Capital Corporation	Property Management	6.2	14.3	1.74	2.6	67.07
GTY	Getty Realty Corp.	Property Management	6.4	18.2	0	282.8	48.42
PKY	Parkway Properties, Inc.	Property Management	5.9	16.6	0.8	3	10.78
WPC	W.P. Carey & Co. LLC	Property Management	5.7	28.6	0.35	5.4	7.89
SLG	SL Green Realty Corp.	Property Management	4.8	15.7	1.01	2.7	6.41

In the next chapter, I profile two REITs that look like good, long-term investments.

FIVE

Two REITs That Could Do Well Over the Next Decade

"Before everything else, getting ready
is the secret of success." – Henry Ford

Hospitality Properties Trust (HPT)

The U.S. hotel business has largely been a solid performer during a difficult economic environment. The trend is away from planes and back into car travel. People need a place to stay and hotel REITs have been rewarding shareholders. Hospitality Properties Trust (HPT) serves the middle to upper class traveler with ownership of Wyndham Garden, Courtyard (Marriott) and Residence Inn hotels. Most of HPT's properties are in the New England area, and management has recently been acquiring more properties during the recent economic downturn. This is a sign of interest rates at 40-year lows and a company that is doing well. Typically when interest rates are below 7 to 8 percent, a sustainable long-term growth rate for well-managed REITs, a good management team will be able to continue to make money and grow the business.

HPT has limited debt (50 percent of total equity), ample interest rate coverage (4 times) and a long-term growth rate in dividends of over 2 percent. Recent acquisitions should boost the dividend growth rate over the next 5 years. Insiders have a substantial interest (13 percent), making them accountable. The dividend rate of over 8 percent is generous and the payout ratio is a little high (131), but since the company has so little debt it is acceptable.

Public Storage, Inc. (PSA)

Ever wonder what company owns all of the storage facilities that you see throughout America? Public Storage, Inc., owns a large number of them. Over the next several decades' growth, trends in the public storage market look very favorable. Public storage facilities do not require the high maintenance costs typically associated with other real estate properties. In addition, as people continue to move frequently and acquire more and more stuff, they will need somewhere to store their excess belongings. The scarcity of land is also starting to drive up storage costs.

PSA has very limited debt (less than 1 percent of total equity), incredible interest rate coverage (200 times) and an excellent long-term growth rate in dividends of over 20 percent. Insiders have a substantial interest (45 percent), making them accountable. The dividend rate of 4 percent is a little stingy and the payout ratio is a little high (141), but since the company has so little debt and the dividend growth rate is exceptional, these numbers are acceptable.

SIX

The Future of REITs

"Our favorite holding period is forever." – Warren Buffett

REITs currently have a lot going for them. Investment stability, no tax on profits, high insider ownership and big dividend yields in an otherwise uncertain market. But how will REITS perform over the next several decades?

Surprisingly, some favorable demographic and investment trends indicate that REITs may be a superior investment choice for the next 25 years. Here is a list of some of the major factors that could make REITs outperform most other stock investments over the next several decades:

- Scarcity of land: Over the last two decades, the United States has been in a high real estate growth mode. This pace of growth, especially into previously undeveloped rural areas, has shown no sign of letting up, even during the recent recession. All this development has caused the price of land to double (on average) over the past decade. Higher real estate prices in combination with less available land will cause the value of REITs to increase over the next several decades.

- Current REIT property ownership is low: In most developed countries, the percentage of publicly traded real estate as a percentage of the total available real estate is high. For example, in the United Kingdom, approximately 50 percent of the total market value of the countries' real estate is publicly traded. In contrast, only 10 to 15 percent of the total market value of U.S. real estate is publicly traded. If the U.S. real estate market follows the trends of other developed countries, the current REIT market could grow by a factor of 5 without even accounting for any possible appreciation in real estate prices.

- Need for income: As the large number of baby boomers begin to approach retirement, they will likely need some investment income to live on. With high quality bonds yielding only 4 to 5 percent and most stocks having tiny dividend yields of 1 percent or less, the 5 to 8 percent dividend yields offered by REITs look very attractive. These high dividend yields in combination with the general investment stability of REITs should create many new REIT investors over the next several decades, pushing REIT prices higher.

- Low interest rates: Currently, interest rates are at 40-year lows. This means REITs can borrow money at very low interest rates and use this money to buy new properties or expand existing properties. A common rule of thumb is that REITs can easily grow earnings if interest rates are below 8 percent. With current interest rates well below 8 percent, well-managed REITs will be able to consistently grow earnings.

SEVEN

Summary

"The best bet is to bet on yourself." – Arnold Glasow

REITs represent a largely unknown investment opportunity that has consistently returned 15 percent per year with minimal risk. By law, REITs do not have to pay taxes if they pay out 95 percent of their profits to shareholders, giving REIT managers a strong incentive to reward shareholders. Providing dividend yields of 5 to 8 percent and strong stability in an uncertain investing environment, REITs should be compelling to any savvy investor. Future trends look even more favorable as baby boomers retire but still want current income, and land becomes scarcer. REITs with limited debt, high insider ownership and a demonstrated ability to grow earning and consistently increase dividend payments usually represent the best investments. Investors can also obtain ownership in REITs by purchasing REIT mutual funds. With these factors in mind, REITs should become part of every investor's portfolio.

Reading List

H. L. Block, 1998, *Investing in REITs (Real Estate Investment Trusts)*, Bloomberg Personal Bookshelf, 367 pp.

F. Cappiello and K. McClellan, 1988, *From Main Street to Wall Street, Making Money in Real Estate*, John Wiley & Sons, Inc., 209 pp.

G. T. Haight and D. A. Ford, 1987, *REITs, New Opportunities in Real Estate Investment Trust Securities,* Probus Publishing Company, 227 pp.

ROGUE INVESTOR

Take Control of Your Financial Future, Become a Rogue Investor!

What Is Rogue Investing?

Rogue Investing is about taking control of your financial future by making your own intelligent investment decisions.

In the **Rogue Stock Investor Collection**, you'll learn how to use simple investment principles to find the best stock investments without relying on expensive professional advice.

In the **Rogue Real Estate Investor Collection**, you'll learn how to find real estate bargains using little known techniques, including tax lien certificates, tax deeds, REITs and government foreclosures. Real estate has always been one of the safest methods of becoming wealthy.

To make sure you have the most up-to-date information, we are constantly updating the **Rogue Investor Series**. We are dedicated to helping you make the best financial decisions for your personal situation. We are always glad to help. Visit us at: www.rogueinvestor.com

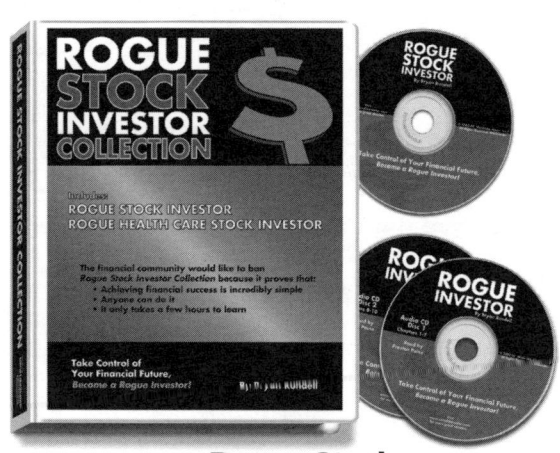

Rogue Stock Investor Collection

Online Tax Lien Course

Rogue Investor Audio CDs

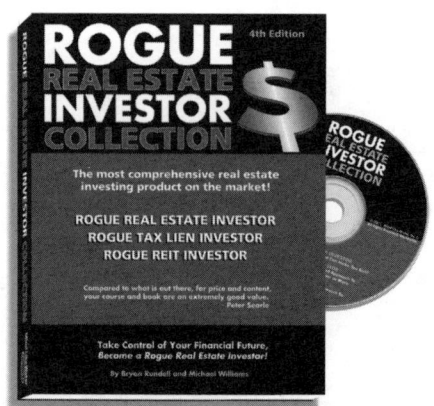

Rogue Real Estate Investor Collection

See all the great Rogue Investor products at:

www.rogueinvestor.com

ROGUE STOCK INVESTOR COLLECTION

How do people get rich in America?

The truth is that wealthy people use very simple investment strategies to make money. Regardless of your prior financial training, making your own financial decisions is the only sure way to achieve financial independence.

Fortunately, you don't have to spend 15 years researching how to achieve financial independence like I did. Instead, I have created a unique investment package called *Rogue Stock Investor Collection* that explains the **7 Investment Principles** used by the world's greatest investors in a format that can be read and understood by anyone in a few hours.

To ensure you have immediate access to the investing concepts, the *Rogue Stock Investor Collection* includes four separate products:

1. A hard cover notebook
2. A CD-ROM
3. Two audio CDs (over 2 hours)
4. An electronic book that you can download and read immediately.

The *Rogue Stock Investor Collection* also includes personal phone and email support to make sure that you can understand and apply these investing concepts plus seven separate stock screens that are updated every two months.

These stock screens include:

- Two screens profiling large cap and small cap companies with heavy insider buying.
- Two screens highlighting some of the most promising and rapidly growing public companies in the world.
- Three screens of dirt cheap companies selling for less than book value, less than yearly revenues and for little or no debt.

Special Bonus Material

How would you like to get in a time machine and go back to 1983 and buy Intel before it went up a thousand fold?

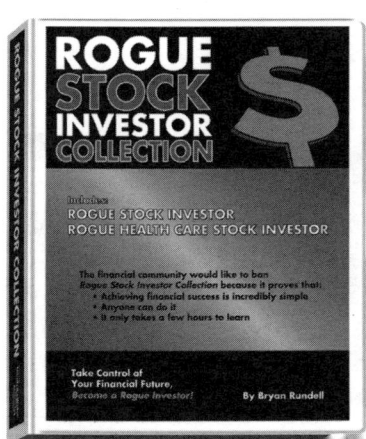 

Over the next 20 years there will be an explosion in health care spending. Some health care companies will go up by a factor of 100 to 1000 times as the baby boom generation turns 60 years old.

As part of the *Rogue Stock Investor Collection*, you will receive *Rogue Health Care Investor*. This brand new book in the **Rogue Investor Series** profiles the incredible investing opportunities in the health care market over the next 20 years.

Find out more about this and the other great **Rogue Investor** products at:
www.rogueinvestor.com

www.rogueinvestor.com

ROGUE TAX LIEN INVESTOR

ONLINE TAX LIEN COURSE

This 100 percent hands-on, tax lien/tax deed field course shows you how to find, research and buy tax liens and tax deeds for yourself. With our help you will start at the beginning and learn how to find, value, legally research and bid on tax lien certificates and tax deeds.

What will you learn in this hands-on class?

- The tools you will need to do your research.
- How to look at a tax sale list and determine what properties are worth researching.
- How to find properties using topographic maps and plat maps.
- How to quickly assess what a property is worth.
- How to research outstanding liens and other potential legal problems with a property.
- How to bid at an auction.
- How to find, research and buy properties over the counter without going to any sales.

As an added bonus, we will go over how to determine if a property has environmental problems.

Other companies are charging $2,000 to $4,000 for classroom tax sale seminars. In our opinion, these prices are excessive.

We want to give you the opportunity to participate in an affordable online tax sale course that you can start using immediately to make your own deals. Throughout the course, you will have phone and email access if you have any questions. You can go through the course at your own pace.

To sign up, visit: http://www.rogueinvestor.com/tax_lien_course.html

Take Control of Your Financial Future, Become a Rogue Investor!

See all the great Rogue Investor products at:

www.rogueinvestor.com

Bretton Woods '44, '45 ⌐ Gold 356
                                   358
                                   359

10 QE/
6- Secret grain sale   10?, 113 FF   123, 136 >   charts ⊗
7- Paul Volker   5-11   History ⊗
10- Debt ceiling crisis, US downgrade   ↳
11- QE₃ ⌐ Govt shutdown, Taper   ⊕ 106
                                        22

                                                      ✓ stock

106 - UST 10yr 1960   ...ter Sector ⊗
112 - FF %   ...tory - Savings ⊗
116 - UST 2yr %
126 - ✓ 30 yr

Oil ⊕ 72 - 1973 Yom Kippur War
 CPI   74 - 1979 Iran crisis
         1930 > QE

prime flat 5 on — 136 - Prime/Discount 1972 >
              — 138 - CPI - 1972 >
                 142 Unemployment ✓
                 148 - hourly wages
              — 150 - US GDP - 1930 -
              — 151 - ✓ Gross Debt ⌐ —
    ⊕ 1930 > 152 - Fed Surplus/Deficit
                 153 - Retail Sales
                 155 - US Housing Starts 1972 -

         ⊗ 197 - Russia Secret grain buys 1972
                      + CPI

    ⊘ 272 - Equities - History
    ↘ 276 - DJIA - 1888
        284 - VIX
        288 - NASDAQ
        291 - SP500 1922 -
        294 - ✓ midcap
        298 - Russell 2000

        356 - Gold

              FDR vs Hoover 1932
       272 - Stocks < 96% > 1929 - 1932 - bottom!
       277 ✓ DJIA   ↳   ↳
       291 - SP500   ↳

The CRB Encyclopedia of Commodity and Financial Charts and Prices
2014

Commodity Research Bureau

www.crbencyclopedia.com

For general information on our other products and services or for technical support, please contact our Customer Support Department within the United States at (800) 621-5271, outside the United States at (312) 554-8456 or fax (312) 939-4135.

ISBN 978-0-910418-30-0

Printed in the United States of America

10   9   8   7   6   5   4   3   2   1

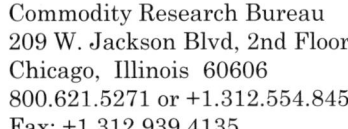

Commodity Research Bureau
209 W. Jackson Blvd, 2nd Floor
Chicago, Illinois 60606
800.621.5271 or +1.312.554.8456
Fax: +1.312.939.4135
Website: www.crbtrader.com
Email: info@crbtrader.com

Table of Contents

Introduction

The purpose of this book is to present the "big picture" for the commodity and financial markets by providing a (1) a complete array of long-term price charts, (2) a brief written history and outlook for each commodity and financial sector, and (3) comprehensive supporting data.

The long-term charts in this book are difficult to find anywhere else. Commodity Research Bureau (CRB) has been in business since 1934 and CRB has developed the most complete database of commodity and financial price history available in the industry. Many of the chart services that are available on the web, and even the more expensive terminal-based chart services, have limited price histories and a limited graphical ability to display long-term charts. This book fills that gap by providing a handy reference guide with easy-to-access long-term price charts. This book also includes inflation-adjusted charts for a variety of commodity markets, which provide an interesting perspective on long-term prices.

The brief written histories of the key commodity and financial sectors give market participants an easy way to get up to speed on the main events that have moved the markets in the post-war period. Understanding what has happened in the past is critical for forecasting the markets looking ahead. In just a few pages, readers can quickly gain an overview of what has been happening in each major commodity and financial sector and also gain an important understanding of the key factors that are likely to drive each market in the future.

In the historical commentary, we often use data from the *CRB Commodity Yearbook* to explain the supply/demand factors that have moved the markets. The *CRB Commodity Yearbook 2014* is the companion book for this publication since it contains a host of fundamental data on the commodity and financial markets. This data provides an important means to gain a deeper understanding of the fundamental supply/demand factors that move the markets.

———

The world economy has yet to fully recover from the global financial crisis and the Great Recession of 2007/09. The world economy is still seeing sub-par growth and disinflationary pressure.

The U.S. housing melt-down was the event that kicked off the 2007/09 global credit crisis. However, the crisis erupted into a severe global event because of the high degree of leverage in the global financial system and because of increased counterparty risks in the huge derivatives market. The Lehman bankruptcy in September 2008 quickly kicked off a dramatic chain of events including a plunge in global stock markets, soaring credit spreads, a near collapse of the U.S. and European banking systems, and a plunge in commodity prices.

The U.S. Federal Reserve and Treasury rode to the rescue with a wide variety of programs including liquidity injections and guarantees for the banking system. Yet U.S. GDP during the 2007/09 recession fell by a total of -4.1% from peak to trough, easily making it the worst U.S. economic slump since the Great Depression. U.S. GDP then showed positive growth for four straight years from 2010 through 2013. However, U.S. GDP growth in 2013 was weak at about 1.7% and is expected to improve to only +2.6% in 2014, still below the post-war average of +3.3%.

The European economy was hit by the global financial crisis in 2007/09 but also experienced the severe Eurozone debt crisis starting in 2010. Eurozone countries such as Greece, Portugal, Ireland, and Cyprus all required bailouts for various reasons that included massive government budget deficits, housing slumps, and banking collapses. Spain and Italy just narrowly averted the need for government bailouts.

The European Central Bank in late 2012 finally put its foot down and announced a rescue program in which it would use its unlimited balance sheet to support troubled countries. The ECB's rescue program finally alleviated market concern that the Eurozone might be spinning apart and the bond yields of troubled countries therefore dropped sharply. Still, the Eurozone economy saw negative growth in 2012-13 and is expected to eke out only a marginally positive growth rate in 2014.

When the global financial crisis exploded in 2008, the Chinese government implemented an aggressive stimulus program that helped boost Chinese GDP growth to +10.4% by 2010. However, Chinese GDP growth then sagged on weak global export demand with the Eurozone recession, sub-par U.S. economic growth, and weaker growth in the emerging countries. In addition, China is facing a difficult transition period for its economic model of switching away from an economy that is mainly driven by investment and exports to an economy that relies more upon domestic consumer spending. The market is expecting Chinese GDP growth to be relatively stable near +7.5% over the next several years.

The main risk for the global economy going into 2014 is the Federal Reserve's action to slowly end its third securities purchase program (quantitative easing). The U.S. and global economy would be at risk if long-term U.S. Treasury yields move sharply higher in 2014.

Commodity price indexes saw a run-up to record highs in early 2011 thanks to fears of inflation with the Federal Reserve's heavy liquidity injections. However, the commodity price indexes then fell into a correction from 2011 through 2013 due to disinflation and poor physical demand for commodities caused by sub-par global economic growth. Commodity prices could revive going into 2014, however, if the global economy picks up traction and inflation moves higher.

Richard Asplund, CRB Chief Economist

Key World and Market Events

12/23/13

Federal Reserve Established—1913—Congress creates the modern Federal Reserve after a series of runs on national banks makes clear the need for a centralized monetary authority to manage the money supply and act as the lender of last resort to commercial banks.

World War I begins—1914-1918—First World War lasts from August 1914 to November 1918.

1929 Stock Market Crash—October 28-29, 1929—Dow Jones Industrial Average plunges 23.6% in just two days and then plunges by an overall 90% to the low in 1932. *11/ Election*

Smoot-Hawley Act—1930—Congress passes the protectionist Smoot-Hawley Act which helps cause the 1929 Stock Market Crash and deepens the Great Depression by causing a sharp drop in US trade. *– after Depression*

Glass-Steagall?

Great Depression—1929-33—The Great Depression lasts nearly 4 years (Aug 1929 to March 1933) and devastates the US economy and social structure. The Great Depression is later shown to result in part from an inadvertent deflationary monetary policy by the Federal Reserve. *1/3 reduction in money supply 1929-32*

← FDR cap on % rates!   D Day: June 6, 1944

US & Gold Illegal to own

Bretton Woods Conference—July 22, 1944—US and UK, looking ahead to the end of World War II, meet in Bretton Woods, New Hampshire and create a post-war monetary system based on fixed exchange rates and the fixed convertibility of the dollar into gold. The Bretton Woods conference also sets the stage for the creation of the World Bank, the International Monetary Fund (IMF), and the General Agreement on Tariffs and Trade (GATT). The Bretton Woods currency system is highly successful for over two decades but finally breaks down in 1971 under stress from US inflation and trade deficit and the need for more global flexibility. *Greedy UK, Germ, Eur*

$35   *No 1964 –*

– Potsdam

World War II ends—1945—World War II ends in Europe on May 8, 1945, with the surrender of Germany and Italy. World War II ends in the Pacific with Japan's surrender on August 15, 1945.

Korean War—1950-53—Korean War lasts from 1950-1953 as US fights communism.

William McChesney Martin becomes Fed Chairman—April 2, 1951—William McChesney Martin Jr. begins his long 19-year term as Fed Chairman (through Jan 31, 1970). *End of Govt / Fed Res cap on % rates*

OPEC is formed—September 1960—OPEC is formed among several Middle East Arab countries to gain negotiating leverage with the major oil companies.

Berlin Wall is built—1961—Soviet Union builds Berlin Wall as Cold War emerges between the Soviet Union and the US and its allies.

Cuban Missile Crisis—October 16, 1962—Cold War reaches its peak with the Cuban Missile Crisis which ends with the Soviet Union removing its missiles from Cuba. *Nuclear*

Kennedy assassination—November 22, 1963—President Kennedy is assassinated in Dallas by Lee Harvey Oswald. Vice President Lyndon Johnson becomes President. *?*

Gulf of Tonkin incident—August 1964—US military involvement in Vietnam starts to escalate into an all-out war after a North Vietnamese gunboat fires on an American destroyer. Major US involvement in the Vietnam War finally ends 9 years later in 1973 with the Paris Peace Accords.

1967 Arab-Israeli War—June 5-10, 1967—Israel launches a pre-emptive attack in a war with Egypt, Syria and Jordan, and takes control of Sinai Peninsula, the West Bank, and about half of the Golan Heights. Sinai is returned to Egypt when Israel and Egypt declare peace in the Camp David Accords, signed on September 17, 1978. *defense*

1968 UK close London Gold Pool

Arthur Burns becomes Fed Chairman—February 1, 1970—Arthur Burns begins his 8-year term as Fed Chairman (through Jan 31, 1978).

Brent oil field is discovered—1971—The Brent oil field in the North Sea is discovered by Shell-Esso.

Nixon closes the gold window, ending Bretton Woods—August 15, 1971—President Nixon announces that the US government will no longer exchange gold for dollars. That effectively ends the Bretton Woods monetary system that had been in place since 1945. Major currencies are freely floating by 1973. Along with the gold announcement, Nixon also announces 90-day wage and price controls and a 10% import surcharge in an attempt to curb inflation and the US trade deficit. *CB*

Nixon travels to China—February 21-28, 1972—Nixon travels to China to seek rapprochement with the Communist nation. US and China announce they will work toward full diplomatic relations. China's long isolation starts to thaw.

Soviet Grain Purchases—Summer 1972—The Soviet Union during the summer of 1972 purchases a huge amount of corn, wheat, soybeans and soybean meal from the US in response to poor domestic crops, thus causing grain and soybean prices to soar in late 1972 and early 1973. *Secret*   *CYB 1997 – Grain prices ⊗ + p 197.*

Yom Kippur War—October 6, 1973—Israel barely wins the war that started with a surprise attack on Yom Kippur by Egypt and Syria in an attempt to win back Sinai and Golan Heights, respectively.

Arab Oil Embargo—October 17, 1973—Arab members of OPEC halt exports of oil to the US in retaliation for supporting Israel during the Yom Kippur War. Oil prices triple from $3.50 to the $10-11 per barrel range by 1974-75. The embargo lasts only 5 months (until March 1974) but the long-term impact is severe.

1973-75 US recession and stock bear market—Serious US stock bear market emerges in response to the Arab Oil Embargo and the major US economic recession from Nov-1973 to March-1975.

President Nixon resigns—August 4, 1974—President Nixon resigns due to the Watergate scandal. Vice President Gerald Ford becomes President.

US citizens can legally own gold—1975—US allows its citizens to own gold bullion. Owning gold was illegal from 1933-1974 except for jewelry and coin collecting.

Lead in gasoline is phased out—1975—The U.S. begins to phase out lead in gasoline. MTBE initially replaces lead but MTBE is then banned in almost all states by 2004-06 due to groundwater contamination and health risks. Ethanol becomes the new oxygenate additive for gasoline.

SPR is established—1975—The U.S. Department of Energy establishes the Strategic Petroleum Reserve in response to the 1973-74 oil embargo as a means to stockpile crude oil for emergencies.

China begins economic liberalization—1978—The People's Republic of China starts reforming its economy from a centrally-planned economy to a market-oriented economy, but retains communist political structure. Rapid Chinese economic growth begins (average annual Chinese GDP growth is +9.7% from 1978-2005).

C. William Miller becomes Fed Chairman—March 8, 1978—C. William Miller is appointed Fed Chairman by President Jimmy Carter and begins his short 1-year term.

Paul Volcker becomes Fed Chairman—August 6, 1979—Paul Volcker is appointed Federal Reserve Chairman by President Jimmy Carter and begins his 8-year term. Volcker cracks down on money supply to force inflation lower, causing double dip recessions in 1980 and 1981-82. The federal funds rate target peaks at 20% in March 1980 and again in May 1981.

Shah is deposed by Iranian Revolution—January 16, 1979—Shah of Iran is deposed by popular protest and is replaced by an Islamic theocracy headed by Ayatollah Khomeini, who arrives in Iran on February 1, 1979, two weeks after the Shah fled on January 16, 1979. Oil prices surge as Iran's oil production is devastated by the revolution.

Iranian hostage crisis begins—November 1979—Iranian militants take hostages at the U.S. embassy, causing President Jimmy Carter to order a halt to all petroleum imports into the U.S. from Iran.

1979 Oil Crisis—Crude oil prices more than double from about $15 to $40 per barrel on oil supply disruptions caused initially by the Iranian revolution, which severely cut Iranian oil production. Americans experience long lines at the gas pumps as shortages are worsened by President Carter's gasoline price controls.

Soviet Grain Embargo—January 4, 1980—President Carter announces an embargo on grain exports to the Soviet Union in retaliation for the Soviet Union's invasion of Afghanistan.

Gold and silver hit record highs—January 1980—Gold reaches a record high of $850.00 (London PM gold fix on Jan 21, 1980) and silver in New York reaches a record high of $48.00 (NY daily close) due to inflationary 1970s, but precious metals prices then plunge as Volcker cracks down on inflation.

1980 US Recession—US recession (January 1980 to July 1980) is caused by Fed's crack-down on money supply and inflation and the surge in oil prices tied to the Iranian revolution. First dip of the "double-dip" recession.

Iran-Iraq War begins—September 22, 1980—The Iran-Iraq War lasts from 1980-1988 and causes sharp cutbacks in Iranian and Iraqi oil production and puts new upward pressure on oil prices. A ceasefire is finally declared on August 20, 1988.

1981-82 US Recession—US economy enters another recession (the second dip of the "double-dip recession") from July 1981 to November 1982 as the US economy continues to suffer from high oil prices and the Fed's crack-down on inflation.

Latin American Debt Crisis—Early-1980s—Latin America countries (Brazil, Argentina and Mexico in particular) are unable to pay large debts owed to global banks due to world recession and oil price spike.

President Reagan's first term begins—January 20, 1981—Ronald Reagan's 8-year term as President begins with his mission of "supply side economics." Reagan terminates oil price controls and forces a 25% tax cut through Congress, which eventually produces a huge federal budget deficit but also stimulates the economy.

US stocks begin bull market—1982—After plunging on an inflation-adjusted basis from 1973-1982, the US stock market finally enters a long-term bull market that lasts until 2000, with corrections in 1987 and 1990.

KEY WORLD AND MARKET EVENTS

Continental Bank failure—May 1984—Continental Illinois National Bank and Trust Company, at the time the seventh largest bank in the U.S., becomes the largest bank failure in U.S. history until Washington Mutual's failure in 2008.

Plaza Accord—September 1985—G5 nations agree on plan to drive the dollar lower via currency market intervention.

Chernobyl nuclear power plant disaster—April 1986—The world's worst nuclear accident occurs with an explosion and fire that spread large amounts of radioactive particles over much of Europe and western Soviet Union.

Louvre Accord—February 21-22, 1987—G5 nations agreed to stabilize currencies and halt the dollar's decline.

Greenspan becomes Fed Chairman—August 11, 1987—Alan Greenspan is appointed as Federal Reserve Chairman by President Reagan and begins his long 18-1/2 year term (through January 31, 2006).

1987 "Black Monday" Stock Market Crash — October 19, 1987—US stock market crashes 20.5% but recovers its losses within just 9 months as Fed successfully manages the crisis by flooding the banking system with liquidity.

Iran-Iraq ceasefire—March 1988—After a long and brutal war, Iran and Iraq declare a ceasefire and oil production starts to recover in both countries.

Berlin Wall Falls—November 9, 1989—Berlin Wall, which was originally built in 1961 by the Soviets to separate East and West Germany, falls. Unification of East and West Germany follows in 1990, creating economic dislocations for Germany.

Nikkei index peaks and Japan's bubble later bursts—December 1980—Japan's stock market peaks and the stock and property bubble starts to burst. Japan suffers more than a decade of deflation and sub-par economic growth. The Nikkei index plunges by three-quarters and Tokyo land prices fall by one-half.

Iraq invades Kuwait—August 2, 1990—Iraqi dictator Saddam Hussein invades Kuwait to take control of oil fields, with likely intention to move on to Saudi Arabia.

"Desert Storm" Gulf War—January 17, 1991—US and coalition forces go to war against Iraq to force Iraq out of Kuwait. US stops short of Baghdad and leaves Saddam Hussein in power.

1990-91 US Recession—US economy is in recession from July 1990 to March 1991 due mainly to the oil price spike caused by Iraq's invasion of Kuwait and the subsequent US-Coalition war against Iraq.

Soviet Union dissolves—December 26, 1991—The Supreme Soviet, the highest governmental body of the Soviet Union, dissolves itself and Russia and other republics later become independent nations.

S&L Bailout—1991—Congress bails out the US savings and loan banking sector which is insolvent due to high short-term rates and rampant speculation. Bailout costs some $350 billion but is disposed of fairly quickly by the Resolution Trust Corporation.

NAFTA—1993—US Congress approves North American Free Trade Zone among the US, Mexico and Canada.

Mexican Peso Crisis—1994—Mexican peso collapses by 40% in two weeks. President Clinton bails out Mexico with a $50 billion loan and the fall-out is contained.

Uruguay Round is completed—April 1994—After 7-1/2 years, the Uruguay Round of world trade talks finally concludes successfully with agreement among 125 countries, creating the World Trade Organization (replacing the General Agreement on Tariffs and Trade, or GATT) and promoting a major expansion in world trade. Previous world trade agreements include the Tokyo Round (1979), the Kennedy Round (1967), and five others.

Asian financial crisis—July 1997—Run starts on East Asian Tiger currencies causing a collapse in the East Asian stock markets and an economic recession. Countries most affected were Thailand, South Korea and the Philippines.

Russian debt default—August 17, 1998—Russia defaults on its foreign sovereign debt and devalues the ruble due to high debt from Soviet era, limited success with market reforms, high inflation, and low currency reserves due in part to spending $6 billion to defend the ruble during the Asian currency crisis in 1997. The ruble is floated in the wake of the crisis.

LTCM hedge fund bailout—September 1998—Federal Reserve orchestrates bailout of Long-Term Capital Management hedge fund in order to prevent systemic financial system crisis.

European Monetary Union—January 1, 1999—European Monetary Union is completed and the Euro comes into existence to replace individual currencies such as the mark, franc and lira. The European Central Bank takes over responsibility for Euro-Zone monetary policy.

US stock market hits record high but bubble subsequently bursts—March 2000—The S&P 500, the Nasdaq Composite and other key stock market indices hit record highs in March 2000 but subsequently enter a bear market.

2001 US Recession—US economy enters recession from March 2001 to November 2001 due to bursting of equity bubble and post-Y2K technology spending bust.

9/11 terrorist attacks on US—September 11, 2001—Al-Qaeda attacks US with airplanes crashing into World Trade Center and the Pentagon. As a result, US enters two wars (Afghanistan and Iraq) and military spending, along with the US budget deficit, soar.

US invades Afghanistan—October 7, 2001—US invades Afghanistan to oust Taliban government and deny safe haven to al-Qaeda.

Doha Round begins—November 2001—In an attempt to extend Uruguay Round success, the Doha Round of world trade talks begins but little progress is made through early 2006 due to objections by Brazil and others about G7 government agricultural subsidies to local farmers.

Enron declares bankruptcy—December 2001—Enron declares a record-sized bankruptcy with $63 billion in assets, until WorldCom's even larger bankruptcy occurs in 2002. *July 21 -*

Congress passes Sarbanes-Oxley—July 30, 2002—Congress passes Sarbanes-Oxley Act which creates corporate governance reforms and enhanced financial disclosure in response to the string of corporate frauds that developed during the stock bubble, including Enron (bankruptcy Dec 2001), Worldcom (bankruptcy July 2002), Tyco, and others.

SARS outbreak begins—February 2003—SARS, a new and deadly type of pneumonia, is first reported in Asia in February 2003 and quickly spreads to various locations around the world, hurting economic growth in Asia, Canada and elsewhere. The disease is contained, however, and no cases are reported after late- 2004.

US launches war against Iraq's Saddam Hussein—March 20, 2003—US and UK begin "Operation Iraqi Freedom" against Iraq and topple Saddam Hussein, who is captured by US forces on December 13, 2003, and hung after a trial in an Iraqi court.

First case of Mad Cow is found in US—December 2003—The US first case of Mad Cow disease (BSE) is found in a Canadian-born dairy cow in Washington state. More than 50 countries suspend imports of US cattle and beef products. *China until 2017 +? Japan?*

Avian flu emerges—August 2004—Sporadic outbreaks of avian flu are seen in August-October 2004 in Vietnam and Thailand. Avian flu progressively spreads into other parts of Asia and then to Africa and Europe by early 2006.

de dern? ⊕ ne 1994 - 50%

China revalues Yuan and moves to crawling peg—July 21, 2005—China announces a one-time revaluation in the yuan by 2.1%, and then allows the yuan to crawl higher in a nod to international demands that China allow its currency to rise to help curb its soaring trade surplus.

Hurricane Katrina—August 29, 2005—Hurricane Katrina makes landfall near New Orleans and causes widespread devastation including the flooding and shutdown of New Orleans.

U.S. home sales peak—September 2005—U.S. existing home sales reach a record high of 7.25 million units in September 2005 but then proceed to plunge by 52% to a post-crisis low of 3.45 million units in July 2010.

U.S. boosts ethanol mandates—2005—The U.S. Energy Policy Act of 2005 increases the amount of biofuel (usually ethanol) that must be mixed with gasoline sold in the United States.

Bernanke becomes Fed Chairman—February 1, 2006—Economist, former Fed Governor and Bush-advisor, Ben Bernanke, is appointed Fed Chairman by President George W. Bush, taking over from Alan Greenspan, who retired after an 18-1/2 year term.

> 2/07 HSBC - create huge Reserve on RE Loan

U.S. home prices peak—April 2007—The U.S. home price index from the Federal Housing Financing Agency peaks in April 2007 and proceeds to plunge by 20% to its post-crisis trough in March 2011.

Two Bear Stearns hedge funds are insolvent—June 2007—The U.S. mortgage crisis accelerates after two Bear Stearns mortgage-backed hedge funds become insolvent, requiring a $3.2 billion loan from the Bear Stearns parent company. The funds nevertheless end up filing bankruptcy in August 2007.

BNP Paribas freezes hedge fund redemptions—August 10, 2007—BNP Paribas freezes redemptions from three mortgage security hedge funds, sparking a run on other hedge funds by institutional investors.

US officially enters recession in December 2007—In a decision announced a year later in December 2008, the National Bureau of Economic Research declares that a U.S. recession began in December 2007.

First fiscal stimulus plan—February 8, 2008—Congress approves and President Bush signs a $168 billion fiscal stimulus program. *QE ?*

Bear Stearns bailout—March 14, 2008—Bear Stearns, under distress, is acquired by JPMorgan Chase for $1.4 billion with support from US government.

QE - 1× 2/2008 ?

KEY WORLD AND MARKET EVENTS

Fannie Mae and Freddie Mac are seized--September 8, 2008—The US government effectively nationalizes Fannie Mae and Freddie Mac due to insolvency and funding problems.

Lehman Brothers declares bankruptcy—September 15, 2008—Lehman Brothers declares bankruptcy, causing the US mortgage crisis to balloon into a financial crisis of global proportions. Barclays later buys the bulk of Lehman for $1.75 billion. On the same day, Merrill Lynch, under distress, is acquired by Bank of America for $50 billion.

AIG receives support—September 17, 2008—Insurance-giant AIG, facing bankruptcy, receives a federal bailout.

Goldman Sachs and Morgan Stanley convert to commercial bank status—September 22, 2008—Goldman Sachs and Morgan Stanley convert to commercial bank status to gain direct access to Federal Reserve funding, sounding the death knell for the Wall Street investment bank model.

$700 billion TARP bank bailout—October 4, 2008—President Bush signs into law the $700 billion Troubled Asset Relief Program (TARP), which is subsequently used to inject capital into banks.

Fed money market rescue—October 22, 2008—Federal Reserve announces a $540 billion program to backstop the U.S. money market industry to prevent a larger run by investors.

Obama elected president—November 2008—Barack Obama is elected to the first of his two terms as president.

Fed announces QE1 rescue package—November 26, 2008—The Federal Reserve announces a rescue program that eventually evolves into its first quantitative easing program (QE1), which involves the purchase of $1.425 trillion in Treasury securities, mortgage-backed securities, and agency debt from November 2008 through March 2010.

GDP plunges –8.3%—Q4-2008—In the worst quarter of the recession, U.S. GDP plunges by –8.3% (quarter-on-quarter annualized).

Barack Obama becomes President—January 20, 2009—Barack Obama takes office as the 44th President of the United States, winning the election with his promise of change.

Obama stimulus plan—February 2009—Congress approves and President Obama signs a $787 billion fiscal stimulus bill to revive the U.S. economy.

U.S. recession ends—June 2009—The end of what comes to be known as the "Great Recession" is declared as of June 2009 by the National Bureau of Economic Research, the official arbiter of recession dating, although the recovery will be long and painful.

U.S. unemployment rate peaks—October 2009—The U.S. unemployment rate peaks at a three-decade high of 10.1%. The U.S. economy loses nearly 9 million payroll jobs during the recession.

Eurozone sovereign debt crisis begins—December 8, 2009—Fitch cuts Greece's debt rating to BBB+ from A1, a day after S&P warned of a downgrade.

U.S. foreclosures peak—March 2010—U.S. home foreclosure filings peak at 367,056 in Q1-2010, according to Realty Trac.

BP Gulf oil spill—April 2010—The BP-operated Deepwater Horizon causes the world's largest marine oil spill in the Gulf of Mexico.

EFSF bailout facility is announced—May 9, 2010—Eurozone bailout capacity of 750 billion euros is announced with 440 billion euros from the Eurozone nations (European Financial Stability Facility), 60 billion euros from an EU emergency fund, and 250 billion euros from the IMF. ECB starts program of buying Greek, Portuguese and Irish bonds.

Dodd-Frank Act—July 2010—President Obama signs the Dodd-Frank Wall Street Reform and Consumer Protection Act, which has far-reaching effects in stepping up regulation on banks and consumer finance.

Fed's QE2 program—November 3, 2010—Fed announces its second quantitative easing program (QE2) that involves the purchase of $600 billion of Treasury securities from November 2010 through June 2011.

U.S. home prices bottom out and turn higher—March 2011—The U.S. home price index from the Federal Housing Financing Agency posts a 9-year low and proceeds to recover by 14% through late 2013.

Permanent ESM bailout facility is created—July 11, 2011—Eurozone finance ministers sign the treaty establishing the permanent European Stability Mechanism (ESM).

U.S. debt ceiling crisis—August 5, 2011—After Congress nearly fails to agree on a debt ceiling increase and nearly causes a Treasury default, S&P downgrades U.S debt to AA+ from AAA. The debt ceiling crisis includes an agreement for $1.2 trillion of sequester spending cuts over 10 years.

Fed's "Operation Twist" program—September 2011—The Fed in September 2011 began its "Operation Twist" program where it sold short-term Treasury securities from its portfolio in order to buy long-term Treasury securities, thus attempting to keep long-term Treasury yields low.

Severe drought hits the U.S.—Summer 2012—A drought during the summer of 2012 is the worst since 1956 and the fifth worst in U.S. recorded history going back to 1895, affecting 57.2% of the lower 48 states, according to NOAA.

ECB announces definitive rescue plan—September 6, 2012—The ECB announces its "Outright Monetary Transactions" program in which the ECB can buy an uncapped amount of 1-3 year bonds of troubled countries that agree to an austerity and reform program supervised by Eurozone and IMF officials. The rescue plan is largely successful in restoring market confidence and bringing down bond yields of troubled countries.

Fed's QE3 program—September 2012—The Fed in September 2012 began its third quantitative easing program (QE3) which by December 2012 evolved into the open-ended commitment to purchase $85 billion per month of securities consisting of $45 billion of Treasury securities and $40 billion of mortgage securities.

Hurricane Sandy—October 2012—Hurricane Sandy blasts the northeastern U.S. and forces a 2-day shutdown of the NYSE on Oct 29-30, 2012.

"Fiscal cliff" is averted—December 31, 2012—Congress and the White House reach a "fiscal cliff" deal that involves an increase in tax rates on joint income above $450,000, the expiration of the 2 percent payroll tax holiday, and a 2-month deferral of sequester automatic spending cuts.

Sequester spending cuts—March 1, 2012—As a result of the summer 2011 debt ceiling agreement, $1.2 trillion in automatic spending cuts (sequester) over 10 years start taking effect.

Abenomics starts in Japan—December 2012—Prime Minister Shinzo Abe, leader of the LDP party, wins a landslide victory in parliamentary elections and begins his program of forcing the Bank of Japan to expand its quantitative easing program in a direct attempt to push inflation higher to shock Japan out of its two decades of deflation and lackluster GDP growth.

Seaway Pipeline is reversed—May 2013—The Seaway Pipeline is reversed so that bottlenecked U.S. oil supplies at the hub in Cushing, Oklahoma starts flowing from Cushing to the Gulf Coast.

U.S. government shutdown—October 1-16, 2013—The U.S. government is forced to shut down nonessential services for more than two weeks as House Republicans tried in vain to use the need for a continuing resolution and a debt ceiling hike to either defund or delay Obamacare.

U.S. debt rises above $17 trillion—October 2013—The U.S. public debt subject to the debt ceiling crosses above $17 trillion to a fresh record high, tripling since the end of 2000.

ECB rate cut to 0.25%—November 7, 2013—The European Central Bank cuts its refinancing rate by 25 basis points to 0.25% in an attempt to stimulate the Eurozone economy and address disinflation.

EPA proposes lower ethanol mandate—November 2013—The Environmental Protection Agency issues a proposal to cut the U.S. corn-based ethanol mandate in 2014 to 13.0 billion gallons from 13.8 billion gallons in 2013.

First-stage Iranian nuclear agreement is reached—November 24, 2013—World powers reached a first-stage 6-month agreement for Iran to curb its nuclear program in exchange for a modest rollback of sanctions.

Federal Reserve begins tapering QE3—December 18, 2013—The Federal Reserve reduces the size of its third quantitative easing program (QE3) by $10 billion to $75 billion per month. The market expects the Fed to incrementally reduce the size of QE3 to end the securities-purchase program by late 2014.

"Volcker Rule" is approved—December 2013—U.S. regulatory agencies finally approve implementation of the "Volcker Rule" effective in 2014. The Volcker Rule bans proprietary trading by commercial banks that take deposits from the public and that receive FDIC insurance.

Congressional budget agreement—December 2013—Congress approves a 2-year budget agreement for fiscal 2014 and 2015, which should avert the risk of another government shutdown.

Janet Yellen—February 1, 2014—Janet Yellen is appointed by President Obama to become the new Fed Chairperson to succeed Ben Bernanke.

Learn to Analyze the COT

The first Commitment of Traders (COT) report was published for 13 agricultural commodities as of June 30, 1962. At the time, this report was proclaimed as another step forward in the policy of providing the public with current and basic data on futures market operations. Those original reports were compiled on an end-of-month basis and were published on the 11ᵗʰ or 12ᵗʰ calendar day of the following month (think about technology back then).

The purpose of the COT was to differentiate between Commercial and Non-Commercial traders.

The COT gradually became known as a tool that commodity traders used in an attempt to see the "thinking" of the large speculators and the commercials. It was a given that the commercials and large speculators enjoy an enormous advantage and are more knowledgeable about the markets than the "small speculator" (my group). The COT levels the playing field by exposing the players behind the trades. Trading without reference to it would be like buying a used car at night in the dark.

Commercials (aka hedgers) are companies or traders that deal with actual commodities as part of doing business. Commercials are exempt from position limits and post smaller margins than speculators. Large speculators are traders whose trading levels are high enough that they require reporting to the Commodity Futures Trading Commission (CFTC). Small speculators are the traders remaining after the commercials and large speculators have been subtracted from the total open interests. The CFTC releases the COT report once per week, each Friday. It summarizes changes in futures positions in all major commodities by all major players. While tremendously useful, the COT seems by most to be so complex. Because of this belief, not many retail traders, novice or experienced use this vital information. If you look at open interest, not knowing who the players are could cost you. The following pages will help you understand the COT and show you exactly how to utilize this information in your trading and help you catch the big market moves we are all searching for. It is more of a compass, showing a direction of the markets pushed along by increased buying and selling, than a timing tool.

$ peak ?

GC - Gold - Weekly Nearest Candlestick Chart

*Though there are no hard and fast rules about the success of each group, Small Speculators are often looked at as the example of what **NOT** to do in futures trading.*

The Commitments of Traders Report
Why it is Important

Rising open interest tells us new buyers are entering a market, and for every new buyer, there must be a new seller for open interest to increase. If you take anything away from this book realize "who are the traders selling in an up-trending market"?

There is a tool that can help you see exactly how all major trends start in any market-increased buying and selling buy big money. It is called the Commitment of Traders report (COT). Every Friday the Commodity Futures Trading Commission (CFTC) releases the COT. The first report separated Commercials, Large Speculators, and Small Speculators (my category). You cannot make an intelligent analysis of open interest without analyzing the COT. This report is essential, without it you have no idea how "big money" is posturing in a market. (For the best views and analysis of the COT report visit www. TrendsinFutures.com)

As large cash merchants in the business, commercials maintain their own intelligence-gathering networks and analysis. In fact, in some markets-such as softs, grains, and meats commercial trade houses are the primary source of fundamental supply and demand statistics available to the trading public. Assuming these numbers are accurately reported, you can be sure they already have been acted on in the market before the data is released to the public. The COT report detects these actual market manipulations. Besides a decided informational advantage,

large commercials by definition trade in sizes large enough to move markets. Given these advantages, their futures trading prowess is not surprising.

So how do you use this?

Although each COT report contains many statistics, of primary concern to futures and options traders are the actual positions and the changes from the prior report. Some try to work directly from the raw numbers, but the data are most easily analyzed when graphed as net positions opposite a weekly price chart. (The best place to view this is on the weekly charts at Trends in Futures.) To derive the net positions for each trade category, simply subtract the short contracts from the long. A positive result indicates a net long position (more long than short contracts), and a negative difference indicates a net short position (more shorts than longs).

Whether a particular trader group is net long or short is not important to the analysis-net positions relative to historical levels are. Therefore a simple net position is meaningless; it is imperative to compare the current net position with the recent historical levels in the respective market. The relative bullishness/bearishness of the commercial net position is easier to see when you can view the current net position with both the highest net commercial position and the lowest net commercial position over a selected period of time. (See the Commercial Tracker under Resources at Trends in Futures for the quickest view covering all of the markets for the past 52-weeks.)

Commercial Net Positions - Legacy Report

12-mo hi 12-mo low Commodity	Net - to + 12-mo low	12-mo hi	6-Dec	2-Dec	22-Nov	15-Nov	8-Nov	1-Nov	25-Oct	18-Oct
Cattle (feed)	425	3,181	1,537	1,535	1,865	1,154	1,671	425	473	838
Cattle (live)	-57,090	20,296	-54,044	-46,874	-52,397	-56,711	-57,090	-53,521	-51,592	-48,975
Hogs	-83,822	17,425	-47,720	-52,048	-58,943	-69,869	-73,533	-75,049	-73,573	-71,675
Corn	-255,021	226,561	189,502	202,989	158,110	159,637	212,278	226,561	222,908	216,765
Oats	-5,583	4,712	-3,300	-3,021	-2,062	-2,008	-2,406	-2,737	-2,518	-1,760
Soybeans	-148,068	-16,836	-129,451	-128,789	-114,518	-109,016	-86,299	-104,918	-116,220	-108,885
Soybean Meal	-9,746	-27,754	-74,498	-69,712	-53,455	-57,967	-42,422	-63,899	-61,617	-55,374
Soybean Oil	-3,252	67,101	33,703	21,886	22,619	9,022	6,202	14,291	15,780	29,521
Wheat	3,998	77,984	73,074	76,163	73,991	71,632	48,810	19,264	3,998	8,710
Orange Juice	-14,621	454	-3,207	-2,939	-2,212	-1,736	211	454	-171	-2,357
Coffee	-5,968	22,870	16,486	18,879	19,980	22,568	22,870	21,318	16,015	11,672
Cocoa	-93,039	-18,314	-89,455	-87,086	-85,647	-83,910	-93,039	-81,013	-81,185	-80,055
Sugar	-242,529	35,138	-114,040	-152,811	-185,463	-206,270	-228,394	-236,940	-242,529	-227,220
Cotton	-99,052	763	-2,847	-1,517	763	-1,051	-7,357	-13,010	-39,835	-48,827
British Pound	-62,763	103,998	-35,420	-12,044	-8,095	1,432	-8,373	-21,936	-27,976	-22,978
Canadian Dollar	-101,824	85,843	56,430	41,002	23,221	23,532	25,167	21,521	5,526	16,299
Euro FX	-70,600	110,578	10,569	20,998	9,890	4,005	-31,653	-68,878	-70,600	-54,358
Japanese Yen	86,803	176,689	176,689	168,579	155,322	138,065	108,905	91,517	98,564	87,475
Swiss Franc	-28,922	44,234	-12,602	-8,588	-6,895	-7,412	-19,813	-25,952	-24,069	-23,264
US Dollar Index	-59,735	13,383	-17,043	-20,936	-19,791	-19,156	-11,582	-5,602	-6,754	-5,720
Mexican Peso	-161,163	8,816	-10,691	-15,246	-13,608	-8,755	-8,788	-9,349	-11,271	-10,916
Australian Dollar	-120,319	102,236	60,536	44,843	44,478	43,227	27,927	20,962	24,160	36,248
S&P 500	-48,742	19,123	-31,739	-36,809	-32,945	-35,281	-29,664	-29,736	-29,126	-21,980
T-note, 10yr	-141,135	38,347	383,247	318,038	338,392	336,799	323,635	245,881	272,696	285,071

Source: Commodity Research Bureau

THE "NEW" REPORT

The Commodity Futures Trading Commission (Commission) began publishing a Disaggregated Commitments of Traders (Disaggregated COT) report on September 4, 2009. The first iteration of the report covered 22 major physical commodity markets; on December 4, 2009, the remaining physical commodity markets were included.

The Disaggregated COT report increases transparency from the legacy COT reports by separating traders into the following four categories of traders: Producer/Merchant/Processor/User; Swap Dealers; Managed Money; and Other Reportables. The legacy COT report separates reportable traders only into "commercial" and "non-commercial" categories.

All of the COT reports provide a breakdown of each Tuesday's open interest for markets in which 20 or more traders hold positions equal to or above the reporting levels established by the CFTC. The reports are published in futures-only formats as well as futures-and-options combined formats. The data are available in both a short format and a long format.

The Disaggregated COT report is being published side-by-side with the legacy COT formats. The Commission is soliciting comment on the new report and will review whether to continue to publish both side-by-side or to replace the legacy report with the new report.

This initiative for providing market transparency arises from the recommendation to disaggregate the existing "commercial" category in the Commission's September 2008 Staff Report on Commodity Swap Dealers & Index Traders. Specifically, that report recommended:

Remove Swap Dealer from Commercial Category and Create New Swap Dealer Classification for Reporting Purposes: In order to provide for increased transparency of the exchange traded futures and options markets, the Commission has instructed the staff to develop a proposal to enhance and improve the CFTC's weekly Commitments of Traders Report by including more delineated trader classification categories beyond commercial and non-commercial, which may include at a minimum the addition of a separate category identifying the trading of swap dealers.

The new categories are as follows:
Producer/Merchant/Processor/User

A "producer/merchant/processor/user" is an entity that predominantly engages in the production, processing, packing or handling of a physical commodity and uses the futures markets to manage or hedge risks associated with those activities.

Swap Dealer

A "swap dealer" is an entity that deals primarily in swaps for a commodity and uses the futures markets to manage or hedge the risk associated with those swaps transactions. The swap dealer's counterparties may be speculative traders, like hedge funds, or traditional commercial clients that are managing risk arising from their dealings in the physical commodity. (See next chapter on Swap Dealers)

Money Manager

A "money manager," for the purpose of this report, is a registered commodity trading advisor (CTA); a registered commodity pool operator (CPO); or an unregistered fund identified by CFTC. these traders are engaged in managing and conducting organized futures trading on behalf of clients.

Other Reportables

Every other reportable trader that is not placed into one of the other three categories is placed into the "other reportables" category.

To get immediate access and see how I analyze the COT everyday on the trades recommended at Trends in Futures take the 30-day trial.

SWAPS DEALERS

Unlike most standardized futures contracts, swaps are not exchange traded instruments. Instead, swaps are customized contracts that are traded in the over-the-counter (OTC) market between private parties. Firms and financial institutions dominate the swaps market, with (if any) individuals ever participating.

In 1987, the International Swaps and Derivatives Association (ISDA) reported that the swaps market had a total notional value of $865.5 billion. By mid-2006, this figure was just over $250 trillion, according to the Bank for International Settlements (BIS). Back then that was more than 15-times the size of the US public equities market. As of the second half of 2013 reported by BIS the total notional value is over $692 trillion (see table on next page).

Amounts outstanding of over-the-counter (OTC) derivatives
By risk category and instrument
In billions of US Dollars

Risk Category / Instrument	Notional amounts outstanding					Gross market values				
	Jun 2011	Dec 2011	Jun 2012	Dec 2012	Jun 2013	Jun 2011	Dec 2011	Jun 2012	Dec 2012	Jun 2013
Total contracts	**706,884**	**647,811**	**639,396**	**632,579**	**692,908**	**19,518**	**27,307**	**25,417**	**24,740**	**20,158**
Foreign exchange contracts	**64,698**	**63,381**	**66,672**	**67,358**	**73,121**	**2,336**	**2,582**	**2,240**	**2,304**	**2,424**
Forwards and forex swaps	31,113	30,526	31,395	31,718	34,421	777	919	771	803	953
Currency swaps	22,228	22,791	24,156	25,420	24,654	1,227	1,318	1,184	1,247	1,131
Options	11,358	10,065	11,122	10,220	14,046	332	345	285	254	339
Interest rate contracts	**553,240**	**504,117**	**494,427**	**489,703**	**561,299**	**13,244**	**20,001**	**19,113**	**18,833**	**15,155**
Forwards rate agreements	55,747	50,596	64,711	71,353	86,334	59	67	51	47	168
Interest rate swaps	441,201	402,611	379,401	369,999	425,569	11,861	18,046	17,214	17,080	13,663
Options	56,291	50,911	50,314	48,351	49,396	1,324	1,888	1,848	1,706	1,325
Equity-linked contracts	**6,841**	**5,982**	**6,313**	**6,251**	**6,821**	**708**	**679**	**645**	**605**	**693**
Forwards and swaps	2,029	1,738	1,880	2,045	2,321	176	156	147	157	206
Options	4,813	4,244	4,434	4,207	4,501	532	523	497	448	487
Commodity contracts	**3,197**	**3,091**	**2,994**	**2,587**	**2,458**	**471**	**481**	**390**	**358**	**386**
Gold	468	521	523	486	461	50	75	61	53	80
Other commodities	2,729	2,570	2,471	2,101	1,997	421	405	328	306	306
Forwards and swaps	1,846	1,745	1,659	1,363	1,327					
Options	883	824	812	739	670					
Credit default swaps	**32,409**	**28,626**	**26,931**	**25,069**	**24,349**	**1,345**	**1,586**	**1,187**	**848**	**725**
Single-name instruments	18,105	16,865	15,566	14,309	13,135	854	958	715	527	430
Multi-name instruments	14,305	11,761	11,364	10,760	11,214	490	628	472	321	295
of which index products	12,473	10,514	9,731	9,663	10,170					
Unallocated	**46,498**	**42,613**	**42,059**	**41,611**	**24,860**	**1,414**	**1,978**	**1,842**	**1,792**	**775**
Memorandum Item:										
Gross Credit Exposure						2,971	3,939	3,691	3,609	3,900

Source: Bank for International Settlements (www.bis.org)

Keep in mind the ISDA made numerous attempts to stop the Swap Dealers positions from being removed from the Commercial category. Luckily for the small retail speculator that did not work. Looking at the old report together with the new report you will see why this was so important. The charts on the following pages will give you the perfect pictures to see for yourself. The charts I am using can be found at www.TrendsinFutures.com. If you need any assistance in using this vital information please email me at Gary@TrendsinFutures.com.

So who are the Swap Dealers?

As of June 30, 2013 based on notional amounts of derivative contracts held for trading the following 4 financial institutions are the top swap dealers.

1. JPMorgan Chase
2. Citibank
3. Goldman Sachs
4. Bank Of America

No surprises here. See the table below for confirmation (provided by the Comptroller of the Currency.)

Notional Amounts of Derivative Contracts Held for Trading
Top 4 Commercial Banks, Savings Associations and Trust Companies in Derivatives
June 30, 2013, $ Millions

Rank	Bank Name	State	Total Assets	Total Derivatives	Total Held for Trading & MTM	% Held for Trading & MTM	Total Not for Trading MTM	% Not for Trading MTM
1	JP Morgan Chase Bank NA	OH	$1,947,794	$64,998,125	$64,189,073	98.8	$809,052	1.2
2	CitiBank National Assn	SD	1,319,359	57,220,377	57,121,671	99.8	98,706	0.2
3	Goldman Sachs Bank USA	NY	113,064	42,761,165	42,741,421	100.0	19,744	0.0
4	Bank of America NA	NC	1,429,737	39,630,089	37,040,232	93.5	2,589,857	6.5
	Top 4 Commercial Banks, SAs & TCs with Derivatives		$4,809,954	$204,609,756	$201,092,397	98.3	$3,517,359	1.7
	Other Commercial Banks, SAs & TCs with Derivatives		7,867,235	15,860,956	14,603,380	92.1	1,257,576	7.9
	Total Amount for Commercial Banks, SAs & TCs with Derivatives		12,677,189	220,470,712	215,695,777	97.8	4,774,935	2.2

Note: Currently, the Call Report does not differentiate between traded and not-traded credit derivatoves. Credit derivatives have been excluded from the sum of total derivatives here.
Note: Numbers may not add due to rounding.
Data Source: Call Reports, schedule RC-L

A PICTURE IS WORTH 1,000 WORDS

On the following pages you will find weekly charts with both the old legacy report and the new disaggregated report. You will see why I now use the new report over the old report.

You will find that the financial markets like the currencies and stock indices do not have a disaggregated report. On these charts you will only see the legacy report. You will find this is very helpful in watching big money move through the financial markets. (charts provided by www.trendsinfutures.com)

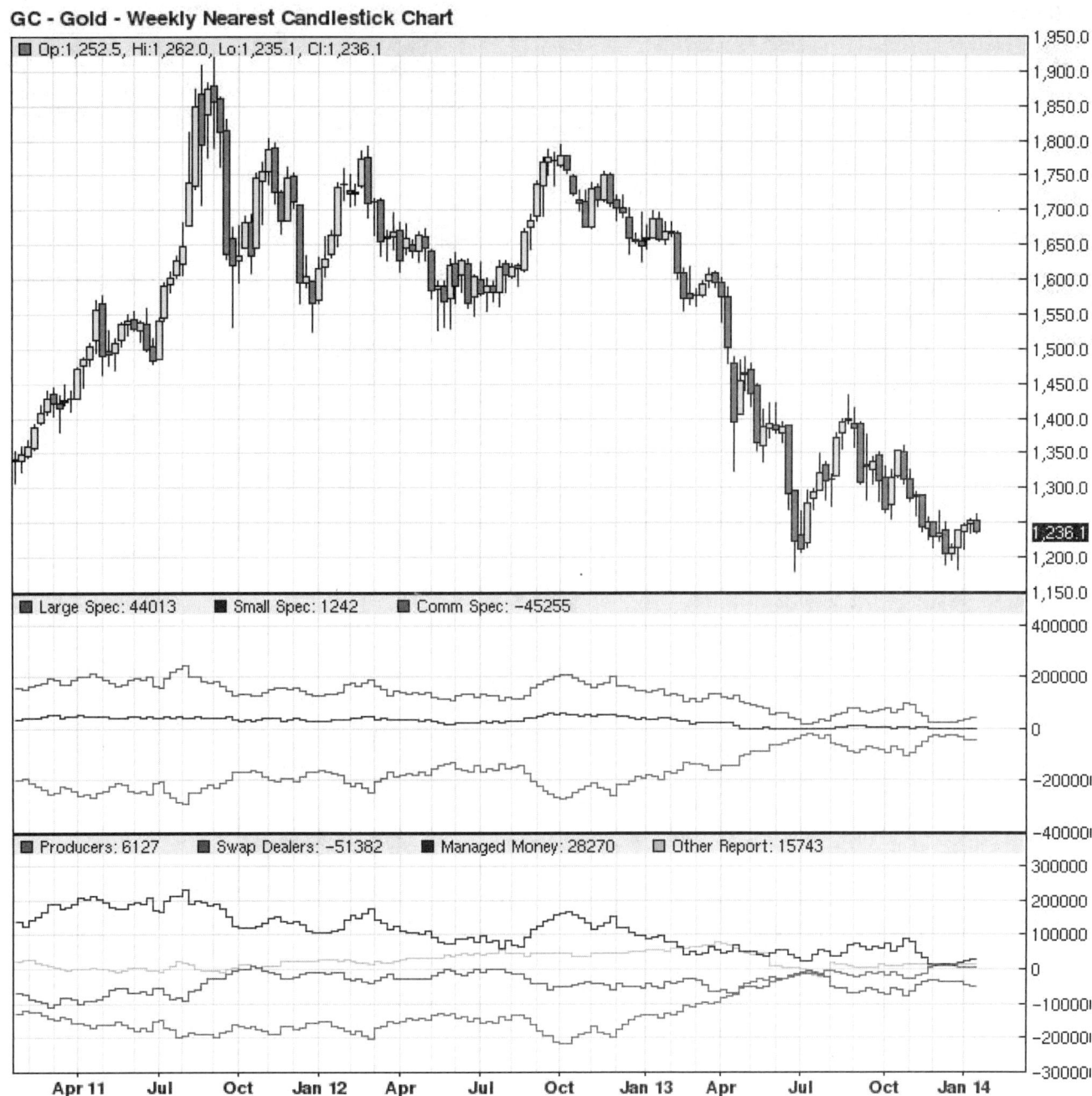

GC - Gold - Weekly Nearest Candlestick Chart

Op:1,252.5, Hi:1,262.0, Lo:1,235.1, Cl:1,236.1

Large Spec: 44013   Small Spec: 1242   Comm Spec: −45255

Producers: 6127   Swap Dealers: −51382   Managed Money: 28270   Other Report: 15743

Looking at the gold chart now with the new report you can see the change that occurred in 2013. Swap Dealers became the larger sell side of gold. You can see in the older report Commercials are net short -45,255 contracts. The newer more transparent report shows Producers net long for the first time 6,127 contracts and Swap Dealers are net short -51,382 contracts. See how Managed Money is adding to net longs now 28,270 contracts. You read it here-big money has just started a bullish posture in gold. Onward and upward unless they stop their bullish posturing.

ZC - Corn - Weekly Nearest Candlestick Chart

Op:424-0, Hi:429-0, Lo:421-0, Cl:425-6

Large Spec: -66214   Small Spec: -109308   Comm Spec: 175522

Producers: -122768   Swap Dealers: 298290   Managed Money: -48939   Other Report: -17275

On the chart above for Corn provided by TrendsinFutures.com you can see that the Commercials in the older 3-line legacy report have a net long position of 175,522 contracts. In fact Producers (true commercials) have a net short position of -122,768 contracts, as seen on the disaggregated 4-line report. The difference being the Swap Dealers are net long 298,290 contracts. Look at the price action when Managed Money starts adding to net longs and Producers add to net shorts. Take a good look at the "Drought of 2012". Without increased selling by producers and increased buying by Managed Money the price action in corn climbing to above $8.00 would not have happened.

Looking at the Live Cattle chart above you can see that in the 3-line report Commercials are net short -83,631 contracts. In fact Producers are net short -159,500 contracts and Swap Dealers are net long 75,869 contracts. Managed Money is net long 112,928 contracts. Look at the price action when Managed Money and Producers are moving away from each other. Make sure you look up the livestock ETF (ticker COW). Currently with approximately $73 million in assets, you will never guess what those assets are compromised of? If you said futures contracts you are correct. As long as we see increased selling and buying by big money Live Cattle prices will continue to rise further into historical highs.

CL - Crude Oil WTI - Weekly Nearest Candlestick Chart

Looking at Crude above you see that Commercials are net short -337,308 contracts. But look closely at what group is the true sell side of crude at this time. Producers are once again net short -16,487 contracts, Swap Dealers (sell side) are net short -320,821 contracts, and Managed Money is net long 147,448 contracts. Look at mid-January 2012.

That is when Producers crossed up over Swap Dealers, strange times. Now look at the rally up in April 2013. What exactly were Swap Dealers doing in crude? Why are Swap Dealers the sell side of crude today? One reason could be USO the crude oil ETF with $1,340,000,000.00 in assets. What are these assets? Long only futures contracts.

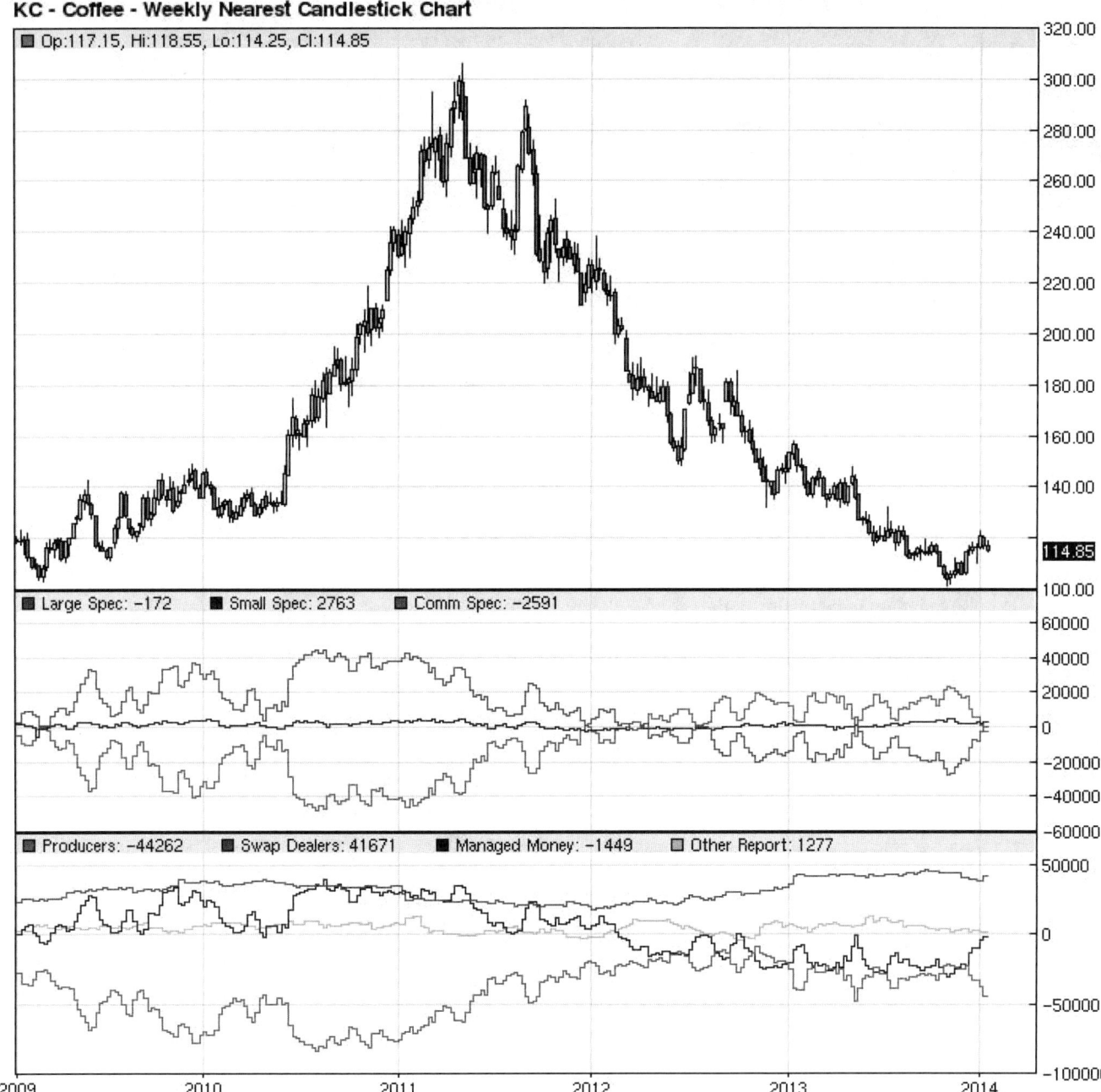

KC - Coffee - Weekly Nearest Candlestick Chart
Op:117.15, Hi:118.55, Lo:114.25, Cl:114.85

Large Spec: -172   Small Spec: 2763   Comm Spec: -2591

Producers: -44262   Swap Dealers: 41671   Managed Money: -1449   Other Report: 1277

Yes your morning cup of coffee is affected by big money. See the chart above where you see Commercials net short -2,591 contracts. Looking at the new report you see Producers actually net short -44,262. The difference here is Swap Dealers are net long 41,671 contracts. While Managed Money comes in at -1,449 contracts net short. See the major trends you would have caught knowing how big money was posturing? Any idea how much money you would catching the ride up in 2010 when coffee rallied from 140.00 to 300.00 and then reversed from there and headed down to 100.00. Increased buying and selling buy big money in 2010 and liquidation starting in 2011 into the end of 2013. All along through the drop look at Swap Dealers, interesting isn't it.

Currencies

Current Dollar Outlook

The outlook for the dollar index going into 2014 looks supportive. The markets are expecting the Federal Reserve to progressively wind down its third quantitative easing program (QE3) during 2014. The dollar should see support from the end of the Fed's QE programs, which injected a massive $3 trillion of excess dollar liquidity in the global financial system from 2008-13. *> 2017 548↑↓*

The dollar should also see support from the market's expectations for the U.S. economy to perform much better than the Eurozone and Japanese economies. Moreover, the markets currently expect the Federal Reserve to start raising its key federal funds rate in 2015, beating the European Central Bank and the Bank of Japan to the punch on raising interest rates. The dollar may also see support going into 2014 from a slowly declining U.S. current account deficit tied to (1) the possibility of an increased savings rate among U.S. consumers chastised by the 2008/09 financial crisis, and (2) reduced U.S. oil imports due to a continued surge in U.S. oil production, which soared by +45% during 2011-13.

Potential bearish factors for the dollar include (1) reduced safe-haven demand for the dollar if the global economy normalizes, and (2) the possibility that the Fed under new Fed Chairwoman Janet Yellen may continue its extraordinarily easy monetary policy much longer than the markets currently expect.

Dollar History

Modern floating rate currency era begins in 1973

NO

Exchange rates from 1945 to 1971 were fixed by the Bretton Woods agreement. Major world currencies were fixed in terms of the dollar, which was the system's "reserve currency." The dollar in turn was fixed and convertible into gold by the U.S. government at $35 per ounce. The Bretton Woods era of fixed exchange rates effectively ended on August 15, 1971, when President Nixon announced that the U.S. government would close the gold window and no longer exchange gold for dollars. With the gold convertibility of the system removed, the system of fixed exchange rates slowly broke down and by 1973 the major world currencies were trading in a floating-rate currency system where the market, rather than a government, determines the value of a currency.

1960s!

The Bretton Woods system broke down mainly because the U.S. by the early 1970s was seeing increased inflation and a balance of payments deficit. When currencies started floating freely in 1973, the U.S. dollar depreciated through most of the rest of the 1970s due to the relatively high U.S. inflation rate seen during the 1970s, which averaged +7.1% annually, up sharply from an average +2.2% in the 1950s and 1960s.

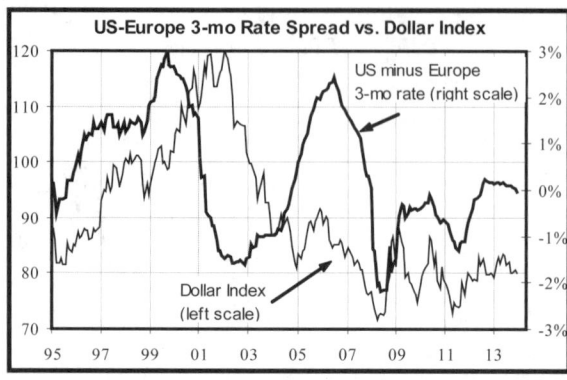

US-Europe 3-mo Rate Spread vs. Dollar Index

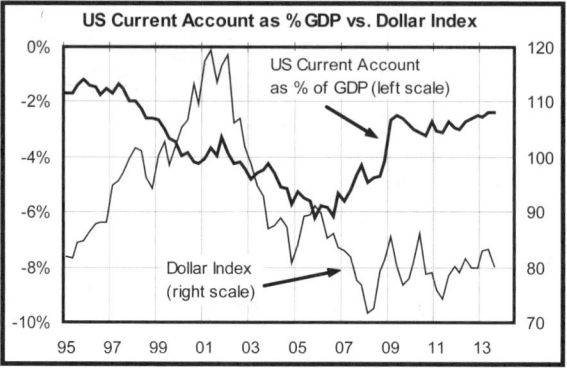

US Current Account as % GDP vs. Dollar Index

Dollar strength during the Volcker Era

Paul Volcker was appointed Federal Reserve Chairman in August 1979 and he raised interest rates sharply to crack down on money supply growth and to halt runaway inflation. Sharply higher U.S. interest rates quickly allowed the dollar to stabilize in the 1979-1980 period. The dollar then rallied sharply starting in mid-1980 as U.S. inflation started to fall and as investors bought dollars to take advantage of high U.S. yields.

Plaza Accord of 1985

The dollar index nearly doubled in value from mid-1981 to the record high in 1985, driven higher by (1) declining U.S. inflation, (2) a stimulative fiscal policy caused by the Reagan tax cuts and budget deficits, and (3) the sharp rally in the U.S. stock market which attracted foreign capital into the U.S.. The Reagan administration took a lassie-faire attitude to the surge in the dollar and made little effort to curb the dollar's gains.

By 1985, however, U.S. manufacturers and the U.S. auto industry in particular were screaming because their export goods were no longer competitive in the world market. U.S. exports plunged and imports rose, thus causing the U.S. current account deficit to soar to a then-record high of 3.2% of GDP by the end of 1985.

The Reagan administration finally arranged the Plaza Accord in September 1985 where the G5 countries (U.S., UK, West Germany, France and Canada) agreed to force a depreciation in the dollar, mainly through $10 billion of currency market intervention. The outcome was very successful and the dollar fell sharply, giving back all of its 1981-85 rally.

The sharp decline became alarming, however, as some market commentators started spinning doomsday scenarios involving a dollar melt-down. In order to halt the plunge in the dollar seen in 1985-87, the G5 nations signed the Louvre Accord in February 1987, in which they agreed to halt the decline in the dollar. The Louvre Accord was largely successful in halting the plunge in the dollar. However, the dollar from 1987 through 1995 continued to trade on a weak note, undercut by the declining trend in U.S. interest rates and the generally high U.S. current account deficit.

1995-2002 rally and the introduction of the Euro

The dollar then rallied sharply during the 1995-2002 period after the Fed raised its funds rate target to the 6% area in 1994, thus giving the dollar a strong advantage on interest rate differentials. In addition, foreign demand for dollars was strong as foreign investors scrambled to buy internet and technology stocks during the U.S. stock market boom.

The euro was introduced January 1, 1999 as part of the European Economic and Monetary Union (EMU). Eleven European countries initially participated in the common currency, which replaced each nation's individual currencies. The idea was to create a common economic area with a free flow of trade and to eliminate the inefficiencies caused by individual currencies. The European Central Bank took over the duty of setting monetary policy for the Eurozone countries. The euro has largely been a success and has become a critical component of the global financial system.

2002-08 plunge in the Dollar

The dollar index from early 2002 through early 2008 plunged by a total of 41%. The early part of that sell-off was due to: (1) the bursting of the U.S. equity bubble and the weak U.S. economy from 2001-03, (2) the Fed's sharp cut in the federal funds rate target to an extraordinarily low 1.00% by June 2003, and (3) the sharp increase in the U.S. current account deficit from about 4% of GDP in 2002 to 6.3% by the end 2004.

The U.S. current account deficit was driven higher by a variety of long-term structural factors including (1) the huge U.S. appetite for foreign imported oil, (2) the improved comparative advantage of nations such as China and India, which have cheap labor and the resources to use that labor to create export powerhouses, and (3) the poor U.S. household savings rate and the massive U.S.

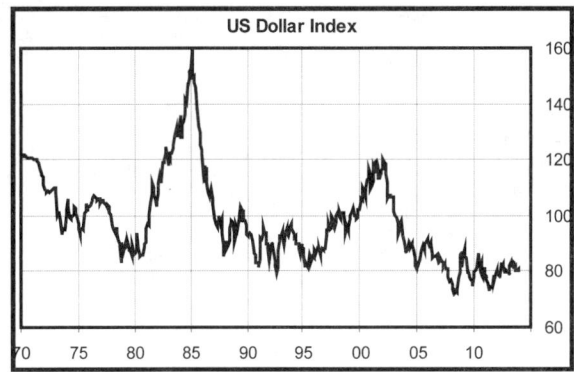

federal budget deficit, which meant the U.S. had to import a huge amount of capital to cover its capital needs (boosting the capital account surplus and the U.S. current account deficit). The U.S. current account deficit finally started stabilizing in 2006 due to strong overseas economic growth and strong demand for U.S. exports.

2008 crisis recovery in the dollar

The dollar in the latter half of 2008 staged a sharp rally sparked by the U.S. banking crisis that finally exploded with the Lehman Brother bankruptcy in mid-September. During the global financial crisis, investors and financial institutions around the world scrambled for liquidity in dollars. With a complete lack of trust among investors and financial institutions, there was a run towards the depth and safety of the world's reserve currency. The U.S. Federal Reserve was forced to provide huge quantities of dollars, both within the U.S. and also in Europe and Asia through swap lines set up with overseas central banks. The dollar was also pushed higher in late 2008 by U.S. investors who scrambled to sell their overseas stock investments during the crisis and then had to convert foreign currencies back into dollars into order to repatriate their cash.

After the initial run-up in 2008, the dollar index in 2009 then fell back and traded basically sideways in a choppy range from 2009-2013. The dollar during the 2009-2013 timeframe saw support from (1) continued safe-haven demand with traumatized investors still looking for safety in the post-crisis period, (2) the stronger performance of the U.S. economy relative to the Eurozone and Japanese economies, (3) the reduced U.S. trade deficit tied to strength in U.S. exports and a decline in petroleum imports due to the sharp increase in U.S. oil production, and (4) the Eurozone sovereign debt crisis that raged from 2010-12 and caused global investors to avoid Euros.

Despite these bullish factors, the dollar was held in check during 2009-13 by the offsetting bearish factor of the Fed's $3 trillion purchase of securities from 2008-2013 (quantitative easing), which injected an extraordinary amount of excess dollar liquidity into the global financial system.

U.S. DOLLAR INDEX

Nearby Futures through Last Trading Day.   Index (close): 01/1967 to 12/1970; Index: 01/04/1971 to 11/19/1985; Futures: 11/20/1985 to date.
The U.S. Dollar Index® in computed using a trade-weighted geometric average of six currencies. The six currencies and their trade weights are: Euro (57.6%), Japanese Yen (13.6%), British Pound (11.9%), Canadian Dollar (9.1%,)Swedish Krona (4.2%), and Swiss Franc (3.6%)

Annual High, Low and Settle of U.S. Dollar Index Futures   Index Value

Year	High	Low	Settle	Year	High	Low	Settle	Year	High	Low	Settle
1972	111.27	107.76	110.14	1986	125.62	104.20	104.24	2000	118.90	99.40	109.28
1973	110.31	90.54	102.39	1987	105.02	85.55	85.66	2001	121.29	108.04	117.21
1974	109.50	96.86	97.29	1988	99.70	86.07	92.29	2002	120.80	102.26	102.26
1975	104.81	92.82	103.51	1989	106.52	91.75	93.93	2003	103.67	86.70	87.26
1976	107.60	102.91	104.56	1990	95.44	81.46	83.89	2004	92.50	80.48	81.00
1977	106.01	96.44	96.44	1991	98.23	80.60	84.69	2005	92.53	81.11	90.96
1978	97.87	82.07	86.50	1992	94.20	78.43	93.87	2006	91.18	82.18	83.43
1979	91.02	85.43	85.82	1993	97.69	88.92	97.63	2007	85.25	74.65	76.70
1980	94.88	84.12	90.39	1994	97.85	84.95	88.69	2008	89.25	70.81	82.15
1981	114.88	88.95	104.69	1995	89.79	80.14	84.83	2009	89.71	74.27	78.22
1982	126.02	104.62	117.91	1996	89.20	84.51	87.86	2010	88.80	75.24	79.29
1983	134.05	115.43	131.79	1997	101.68	88.01	99.57	2011	81.64	72.86	80.52
1984	151.47	126.18	151.47	1998	102.82	90.74	93.96	2012	84.25	78.12	79.87
1985	164.72	123.24	123.55	1999	104.60	93.12	101.42	2013	84.97	78.92	80.19

Futures begin trading 11/20/1985.   *Source: ICE Futures U.S.*

U.S. DOLLAR INDEX
Monthly Cash as of 12/31/2013

Date	Open	High	Low	Close
08/30/13	81.671	82.494	80.754	82.087
09/30/13	82.118	82.671	80.030	80.221
10/31/13	80.259	80.754	78.998	80.195
11/29/13	80.261	81.482	80.254	80.680
12/31/13	80.661	80.993	79.686	80.035

MONTHLY CASH
As of 12/31/2013
Chart High 164.720 on 02/25/1985
Chart Low 70.698 on 03/17/2008

Index (close): 01/1967 to 12/1970; Index: 01/04/1971 to date.
The U.S. Dollar Index® in computed using a trade-weighted geometric average of six currencies. The six currencies and their trade weights are: Euro (57.6%), Japanese Yen (13.6%), British Pound (11.9%), Canadian Dollar (9.1%,)Swedish Krona (4.2%), and Swiss Franc (3.6%).

Annual High, Low and Settle of U.S. Dollar Index   Index Value

Year	High	Low	Settle	Year	High	Low	Settle	Year	High	Low	Settle
1972	111.27	107.76	110.14	1986	125.21	103.55	103.58	2000	119.07	99.71	109.56
1973	110.31	90.54	102.39	1987	104.35	85.33	85.42	2001	121.02	108.09	116.82
1974	109.50	96.86	97.29	1988	99.61	85.87	92.50	2002	120.51	101.80	101.85
1975	104.81	92.82	103.51	1989	106.56	91.77	93.21	2003	103.20	86.36	86.92
1976	107.60	102.91	104.56	1990	94.72	81.27	83.07	2004	92.29	80.39	80.85
1977	106.01	96.44	96.44	1991	97.32	80.34	83.52	2005	92.63	80.77	91.17
1978	97.87	82.07	86.50	1992	92.52	78.19	92.36	2006	91.16	82.24	83.72
1979	91.02	85.43	85.82	1993	96.85	88.37	96.84	2007	85.43	74.48	76.70
1980	94.88	84.12	90.39	1994	97.10	84.91	88.73	2008	88.46	70.70	81.31
1981	114.88	88.95	104.69	1995	89.63	80.05	84.76	2009	89.62	74.17	77.86
1982	126.02	104.62	117.91	1996	89.14	84.48	88.18	2010	88.71	75.63	79.03
1983	134.05	115.43	131.79	1997	101.79	88.15	99.65	2011	81.31	72.70	80.18
1984	151.47	126.18	151.47	1998	102.88	90.57	94.17	2012	84.10	78.10	79.77
1985	164.72	123.24	123.46	1999	104.88	93.05	101.87	2013	84.75	78.92	80.04

Source: ICE Futures U.S.

U.S. DOLLAR INDEX

U.S. DOLLAR INDEX - ICE
Weekly Nearest Futures as of 01/03/2014

Date	Open	High	Low	Close
12/06/13	80.685	81.015	80.220	80.315
12/13/13	80.230	80.420	79.755	80.220
12/20/13	80.165	81.005	79.500	80.750
12/27/13	80.750	80.780	79.820	80.538
01/03/14	80.415	81.060	80.055	80.955

WEEKLY NEAREST FUTURES
As of 01/03/2014

Chart High 92.530	on 11/16/2005
Chart Low 70.805	on 03/17/2008
CONTRACT SIZE	1,000 USD x Index
MIN TICK VALUE	.005 points / 5 USD/CONTRACT
EACH GRID VALUE	0.5 points / 500 USD/CONTRACT
DAILY LIMIT VALUE	NONE
TRADING HOURS	7:00p-10:00p / 3:00a-3:00p ET

Commercial = 28
NonCommercial = -4345
NonReportable = 4317

Nearby Futures through Last Trading Day.   The U.S. Dollar Index® in computed using a trade-weighted geometric average of six currencies. The six currencies and their trade weights are: Euro (57.6%), Japanese Yen (13.6%), British Pound (11.9%), Canadian Dollar (9.1%,)Swedish Krona (4.2%), and Swiss Franc (3.6%)

Quarterly High, Low and Settle of U.S. Dollar Index Futures   Index Value

Quarter	High	Low	Settle	Quarter	High	Low	Settle	Quarter	High	Low	Settle
03/2005	85.46	81.11	84.05	03/2008	77.49	70.81	72.17	03/2011	81.64	75.51	76.07
06/2005	89.35	83.31	88.98	06/2008	74.50	71.05	72.80	06/2011	76.87	72.86	74.64
09/2005	90.66	86.02	89.35	09/2008	80.40	71.56	79.36	09/2011	79.65	73.52	79.08
12/2005	92.53	88.35	90.96	12/2008	89.25	78.78	82.15	12/2011	81.31	74.86	80.52
03/2006	91.18	87.69	89.39	03/2009	89.71	81.99	85.90	03/2012	82.05	78.12	79.14
06/2006	90.03	83.41	84.90	06/2009	87.22	78.38	80.43	06/2012	83.67	78.67	81.75
09/2006	87.05	84.17	85.68	09/2009	81.17	76.05	76.86	09/2012	84.25	78.60	80.03
12/2006	87.08	82.18	83.43	12/2009	78.77	74.27	78.22	12/2012	81.52	78.97	79.87
03/2007	85.25	82.38	82.66	03/2010	82.52	76.74	81.29	03/2013	83.52	78.92	83.18
06/2007	83.26	81.10	81.69	06/2010	88.80	80.14	86.28	06/2013	84.60	80.51	83.38
09/2007	82.00	77.58	77.63	09/2010	86.55	78.62	78.94	09/2013	84.97	80.12	80.32
12/2007	78.80	74.65	76.70	12/2010	81.53	75.24	79.29	12/2013	81.58	79.06	80.19

Source: ICE Futures U.S.

U.S. DOLLAR INDEX
Weekly Cash as of 01/03/2014

WEEKLY CASH
As of 01/03/2014

Chart High 102.150   on 03/21/2003
Chart Low   70.698   on 03/17/2008

Index Value

Date	Open	High	Low	Close
12/06/13	80.661	80.993	80.223	80.315
12/13/13	80.303	80.419	79.757	80.214
12/20/13	80.215	80.827	79.810	80.575
12/27/13	80.534	80.617	79.686	80.392
01/03/14	80.327	80.895	79.929	80.791

The U.S. Dollar Index® in computed using a trade-weighted geometric average of six currencies. The six currencies and their trade weights are: Euro (57.6%), Japanese Yen (13.6%), British Pound (11.9%), Canadian Dollar (9.1%,)Swedish Krona (4.2%), and Swiss Franc (3.6%).

Quarterly High, Low and Settle of U.S. Dollar Index   Index Value

Quarter	High	Low	Settle	Quarter	High	Low	Settle	Quarter	High	Low	Settle
03/2005	85.44	80.77	84.06	03/2008	77.35	70.70	71.80	03/2011	81.31	75.25	75.86
06/2005	89.48	83.36	89.11	06/2008	74.31	71.19	72.46	06/2011	76.61	72.70	74.30
09/2005	90.77	85.99	89.52	09/2008	80.38	71.31	79.45	09/2011	78.86	73.42	78.55
12/2005	92.63	88.53	91.17	12/2008	88.46	77.69	81.31	12/2011	80.85	74.72	80.18
03/2006	91.16	87.83	89.73	03/2009	89.62	78.88	85.43	03/2012	81.78	78.10	79.00
06/2006	90.40	83.60	85.22	06/2009	86.87	78.33	80.13	06/2012	83.54	78.60	81.63
09/2006	87.33	84.39	85.97	09/2009	80.89	75.83	76.65	09/2012	84.10	78.60	79.94
12/2006	87.30	82.24	83.72	12/2009	78.45	74.17	77.86	12/2012	81.46	78.94	79.77
03/2007	85.43	82.64	82.93	03/2010	82.24	76.60	81.07	03/2013	83.30	78.92	82.98
06/2007	83.27	81.25	81.92	06/2010	88.71	80.03	86.02	06/2013	84.50	80.50	83.14
09/2007	82.13	77.67	77.72	09/2010	86.26	78.41	78.72	09/2013	84.75	80.03	80.22
12/2007	78.89	74.48	76.70	12/2010	81.44	75.63	79.03	12/2013	81.48	79.00	80.04

Source: ICE Futures U.S.

AUSTRALIAN DOLLAR

AUSTRALIAN DOLLAR - IMM
Monthly Nearest Futures as of 12/31/2013

Date	Open	High	Low	Close
08/31/13	.8924	.9217	.8823	.8892
09/30/13	.8923	.9476	.8892	.9279
10/31/13	.9278	.9725	.9242	.9431
11/30/13	.9433	.9518	.9045	.9092
12/31/13	.9110	.9164	.8772	.8882

MONTHLY NEAREST FUTURES
As of 12/31/2013

Chart High 1.4885	on 12/07/1973
Chart Low .4774	on 04/02/2001
CONTRACT SIZE	100,000 AUD
MIN TICK VALUE	.0001 USD
EACH GRID VALUE	10 USD/CONTRACT
	0.005 USD
	500 USD/CONTRACT
DAILY LIMIT VALUE	None
TRADING HOURS	5:00p-4:00p / 7:20a-2:00p CT

01/13/1987: Futures begin trading.

Nearby Futures through Last Trading Day.   FRB: to 12/31/1981; IMM: 01/04/1982 to 02/11/1986; Forex: 02/14/1986 to 01/12/1987; Futures: 01/13/1987 to date.

Annual High, Low and Settle of Australian Dollar Futures   In USD per AUD

Year	High	Low	Settle	Year	High	Low	Settle	Year	High	Low	Settle
1972	1.2732	1.1880	1.2732	1986	.7490	.5715	.6650	2000	.6693	.5075	.5590
1973	1.4885	1.2710	1.4825	1987	.7395	.6288	.7170	2001	.5725	.4774	.5074
1974	1.4875	1.3025	1.3245	1988	.8810	.6940	.8450	2002	.5773	.5033	.5548
1975	1.3655	1.2518	1.2545	1989	.8880	.7315	.7760	2003	.7475	.5578	.7455
1976	1.2610	1.0054	1.0890	1990	.8335	.7330	.7656	2004	.7980	.6730	.7790
1977	1.1410	1.0822	1.1380	1991	.7985	.7493	.7565	2005	.7992	.7214	.7325
1978	1.1860	1.1230	1.1500	1992	.7670	.6775	.6869	2006	.7931	.7006	.7866
1979	1.1518	1.0902	1.1057	1993	.7242	.6392	.6770	2007	.9382	.7665	.8726
1980	1.1814	1.0670	1.1814	1994	.7795	.6762	.7730	2008	.9770	.5975	.6997
1981	1.1890	1.1225	1.1280	1995	.7725	.7055	.7401	2009	.9382	.6231	.8917
1982	1.1308	.9339	.9801	1996	.8210	.7276	.7936	2010	1.0168	.8049	1.0141
1983	.9910	.8542	.8985	1997	.8005	.6475	.6518	2011	1.1005	.9302	1.0171
1984	.9668	.8187	.8258	1998	.7005	.5465	.6085	2012	1.0833	.9564	1.0325
1985	.8230	.6350	.6822	1999	.6743	.6123	.6583	2013	1.0547	.8772	.8882

Futures begin trading 01/13/1987.   *Source: CME Group; Chicago Mercantile Exchange*

AUSTRALIAN DOLLAR / U.S. DOLLAR
Monthly Cash as of 12/31/2013

Date	Open	High	Low	Close
08/30/13	.8982	.9234	.8848	.8903
09/30/13	.8941	.9529	.8926	.9326
10/31/13	.9320	.9757	.9293	.9453
11/29/13	.9455	.9543	.9056	.9109
12/31/13	.9112	.9171	.8820	.8930

MONTHLY CASH
As of 12/31/2013
Chart High 1.4885 on 12/07/1973
Chart Low .4778 on 04/02/2001

Free Market Pound (avg): to 01/1966; Free Market Dollar (avg): 02/1966 to 12/1970; FRB: 01/04/1971 to 13/31/1981; IMM: 01/04/1982 to 02/11/1986; Forex: 02/14/1986 to date.

Annual High, Low and Settle of Australian Dollar   In USD per AUD

Year	High	Low	Settle	Year	High	Low	Settle	Year	High	Low	Settle
1972	1.2732	1.1880	1.2732	1986	.7490	.5715	.6650	2000	.6685	.5075	.5585
1973	1.4885	1.2710	1.4825	1987	.7395	.6380	.7215	2001	.5725	.4778	.5106
1974	1.4875	1.3025	1.3245	1988	.8833	.6955	.8540	2002	.5796	.5052	.5615
1975	1.3655	1.2518	1.2545	1989	.8967	.7270	.7880	2003	.7537	.5614	.7521
1976	1.2610	1.0054	1.0890	1990	.8480	.7392	.7718	2004	.8003	.6777	.7825
1977	1.1410	1.0822	1.1380	1991	.8038	.7500	.7595	2005	.7990	.7234	.7335
1978	1.1860	1.1230	1.1500	1992	.7705	.6783	.6885	2006	.7930	.7016	.7894
1979	1.1518	1.0902	1.1057	1993	.7253	.6413	.6793	2007	.9398	.7681	.8748
1980	1.1814	1.0670	1.1814	1994	.7789	.6773	.7764	2008	.9849	.6010	.7029
1981	1.1890	1.1225	1.1280	1995	.7764	.7077	.7437	2009	.9406	.6249	.8972
1982	1.1308	.9339	.9801	1996	.8211	.7313	.7943	2010	1.0256	.8068	1.0232
1983	.9910	.8542	.8985	1997	.8012	.6463	.6515	2011	1.1080	.9387	1.0220
1984	.9668	.8187	.8258	1998	.6880	.5503	.6101	2012	1.0857	.9582	1.0396
1985	.8230	.6350	.6822	1999	.6745	.6106	.6568	2013	1.0601	.8820	.8930

Data continued from page 32.   *Source: Forex*

AUSTRALIAN DOLLAR

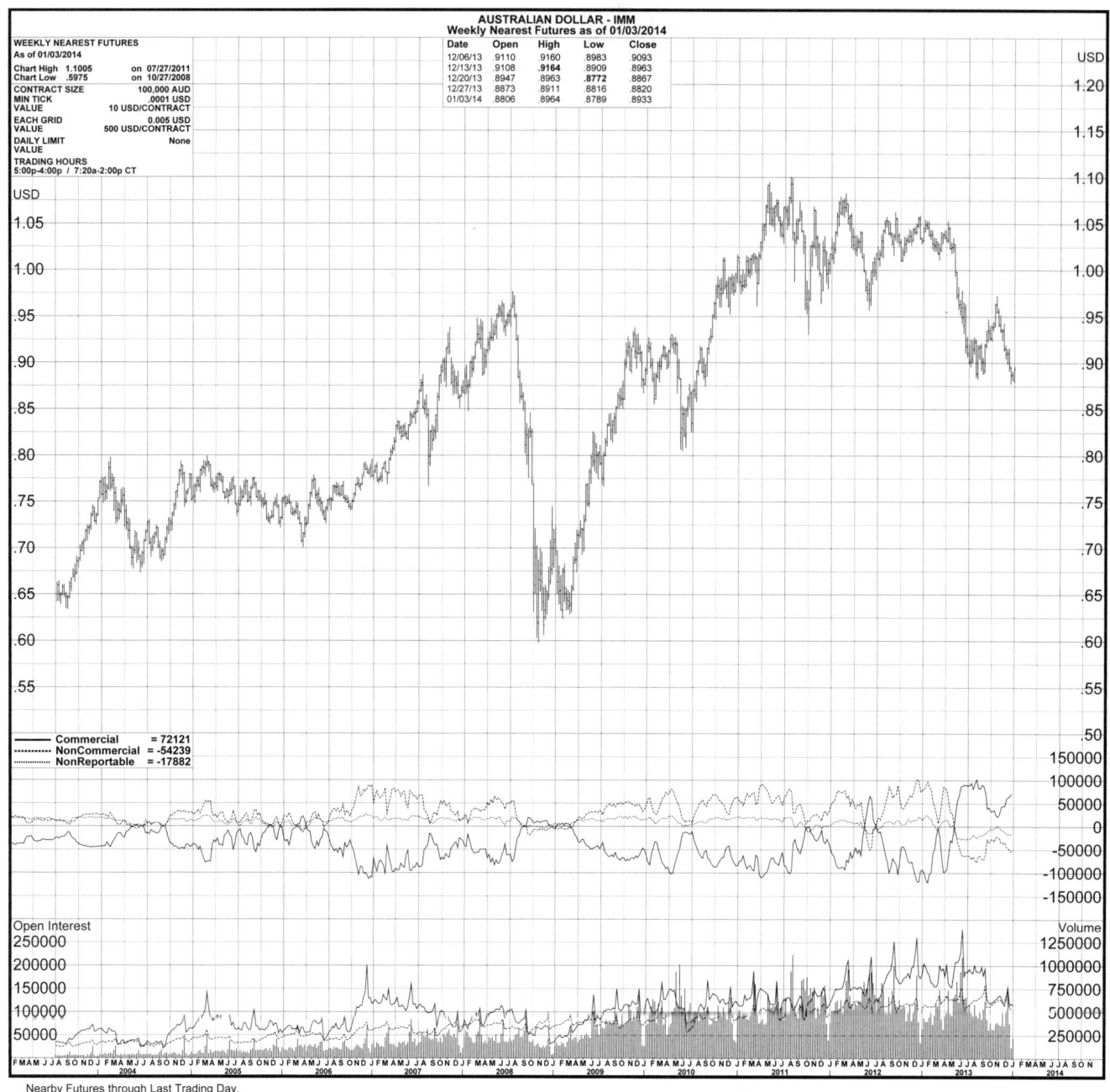

AUSTRALIAN DOLLAR - IMM
Weekly Nearest Futures as of 01/03/2014

Date	Open	High	Low	Close
12/06/13	.9110	.9160	.8983	.9093
12/13/13	.9108	.9164	.8909	.8963
12/20/13	.8947	.8963	.8772	.8867
12/27/13	.8873	.8911	.8816	.8820
01/03/14	.8806	.8964	.8789	.8933

WEEKLY NEAREST FUTURES
As of 01/03/2014

Chart High 1.1005 on 07/27/2011
Chart Low .5975 on 10/27/2008
CONTRACT SIZE 100,000 AUD
MIN TICK VALUE .0001 USD / 10 USD/CONTRACT
EACH GRID VALUE 0.005 USD / 500 USD/CONTRACT
DAILY LIMIT VALUE None
TRADING HOURS 5:00p-4:00p / 7:20a-2:00p CT

Commercial = 72121
NonCommercial = -54239
NonReportable = -17882

Nearby Futures through Last Trading Day.

Quarterly High, Low and Settle of Australian Dollar Futures   In USD per AUD

Quarter	High	Low	Settle	Quarter	High	Low	Settle	Quarter	High	Low	Settle
03/2005	.7992	.7475	.7685	03/2008	.9481	.8469	.9041	03/2011	1.0281	.9606	1.0273
06/2005	.7819	.7469	.7564	06/2008	.9670	.8938	.9493	06/2011	1.0954	1.0200	1.0626
09/2005	.7761	.7336	.7601	09/2008	.9770	.7748	.7886	09/2011	1.1005	.9524	.9611
12/2005	.7622	.7214	.7325	12/2008	.7990	.5975	.6997	12/2011	1.0687	.9302	1.0171
03/2006	.7579	.7006	.7157	03/2009	.7230	.6231	.6924	03/2012	1.0833	1.0065	1.0269
06/2006	.7789	.7107	.7428	06/2009	.8259	.6822	.8029	06/2012	1.0422	.9564	1.0169
09/2006	.7718	.7393	.7444	09/2009	.8794	.7663	.8774	09/2012	1.0625	1.0040	1.0303
12/2006	.7931	.7404	.7866	12/2009	.9382	.8500	.8917	12/2012	1.0592	1.0089	1.0325
03/2007	.8108	.7678	.8072	03/2010	.9275	.8547	.9097	03/2013	1.0547	1.0104	1.0353
06/2007	.8504	.8048	.8460	06/2010	.9308	.8049	.8374	06/2013	1.0531	.9062	.9107
09/2007	.8871	.7665	.8857	09/2010	.9650	.8247	.9586	09/2013	.9476	.8823	.9279
12/2007	.9382	.8508	.8726	12/2010	1.0168	.9464	1.0141	12/2013	.9725	.8772	.8882

Source: CME Group; Chicago Mercantile Exchange

AUSTRALIAN DOLLAR / U.S. DOLLAR
Weekly Cash as of 01/03/2014

WEEKLY CASH
As of 01/03/2014

Chart High 1.1080 on 07/27/2011
Chart Low .5826 on 02/03/2003

Date	Open	High	Low	Close
12/06/13	.9112	.9171	.8987	.9105
12/13/13	.9129	.9166	.8909	.8957
12/20/13	.8964	.8971	.8820	.8925
12/27/13	.8925	.8958	.8863	.8872
01/03/14	.8872	.9003	.8834	.8943

Forex.

Quarterly High, Low and Settle of Australian Dollar   In USD per AUD

Quarter	High	Low	Settle	Quarter	High	Low	Settle	Quarter	High	Low	Settle
03/2005	.7990	.7507	.7731	03/2008	.9497	.8527	.9134	03/2011	1.0372	.9705	1.0325
06/2005	.7841	.7477	.7605	06/2008	.9668	.9032	.9585	06/2011	1.1012	1.0289	1.0718
09/2005	.7765	.7370	.7629	09/2008	.9849	.7804	.7916	09/2011	1.1080	.9625	.9671
12/2005	.7646	.7234	.7335	12/2008	.8020	.6010	.7029	12/2011	1.0756	.9387	1.0220
03/2006	.7586	.7016	.7157	03/2009	.7266	.6249	.6916	03/2012	1.0857	1.0145	1.0351
06/2006	.7792	.7117	.7428	06/2009	.8261	.6856	.8064	06/2012	1.0474	.9582	1.0239
09/2006	.7720	.7402	.7455	09/2009	.8847	.7707	.8825	09/2012	1.0625	1.0102	1.0381
12/2006	.7930	.7414	.7894	12/2009	.9406	.8568	.8972	12/2012	1.0585	1.0150	1.0396
03/2007	.8127	.7681	.8086	03/2010	.9328	.8579	.9173	03/2013	1.0601	1.0115	1.0412
06/2007	.8521	.8067	.8480	06/2010	.9390	.8068	.8405	06/2013	1.0582	.9117	.9144
09/2007	.8886	.7683	.8876	09/2010	.9734	.8316	.9669	09/2013	.9529	.8848	.9326
12/2007	.9398	.8556	.8748	12/2010	1.0256	.9537	1.0232	12/2013	.9757	.8820	.8930

Source: Forex

31

AUSTRALIAN DOLLAR

AUSTRALIAN DOLLAR / U.S. DOLLAR
Quarterly Cash as of 03/31/2014

Date	Open	High	Low	Close
12/31/12	1.0361	1.0585	1.0150	1.0396
03/29/13	1.0397	**1.0601**	1.0115	1.0412
06/28/13	1.0414	1.0582	.9117	.9144
09/30/13	.9127	.9529	.8848	.9326
12/31/13	.9320	.9757	**.8820**	.8930

QUARTERLY CASH
As of 03/31/2014

Chart High 2.2930 on 12/31/1930
Chart Low .4778 on 04/02/2001

Free Market Pound (avg): 1928 to 1930; Free Market Pound (avg): 08/1931 to 01/1966; Free Market Dollar (avg): 02/1966 to 12/1970; FRB: 01/04/1971 to 13/31/1981; IMM: 01/04/1982 to 02/11/1986; Forex: 02/14/1986 to date.

Annual High, Low and Settle of Australian Dollar   In USD per AUD

Year	High	Low	Settle	Year	High	Low	Settle	Year	High	Low	Settle
1930	2.2930	2.2930	2.2930	1944	----	----	----	1958	1.1224	1.1169	1.1171
1931	1.8648	1.3425	1.3425	1945	1.6071	1.6035	1.6071	1959	1.1221	1.1149	1.1149
1932	1.4970	1.3075	1.3089	1946	1.6071	1.6054	1.6054	1960	1.1209	1.1155	1.1185
1933	2.0488	1.3360	2.0375	1947	1.6061	1.6045	1.6061	1961	1.1217	1.1105	1.1194
1934	2.0527	1.9576	1.9614	1948	1.6062	1.6058	1.6062	1962	1.1216	1.1159	1.1169
1935	1.9726	1.8928	1.9564	1949	1.6062	1.1158	1.1158	1963	1.1175	1.1142	1.1142
1936	2.0053	1.9477	1.9550	1950	1.1158	1.1155	1.1155	1964	1.1153	1.1090	1.1118
1937	1.9908	1.9463	1.9905	1951	1.1158	1.1131	1.1131	1965	1.1170	1.1119	1.1164
1938	1.9991	1.8603	1.8603	1952	1.1205	1.1087	1.1179	1966	1.1171	1.1111	1.1116
1939	1.8667	1.5633	1.5657	1953	1.1231	1.1167	1.1197	1967	1.1185	1.1088	1.1185
1940	1.6079	1.3040	1.6075	1954	1.1229	1.1105	1.1105	1968	1.1198	1.1084	1.1089
1941	1.6085	1.6056	1.6075	1955	1.1166	1.1090	1.1166	1969	1.1143	1.1081	1.1143
1942	1.6075	1.6075	1.6075	1956	1.1186	1.1086	1.1096	1970	1.1184	1.1087	1.1112
1943	1.6075	1.6075	1.6075	1957	1.1179	1.1087	1.1179	1971	1.1888	1.1124	1.1887

Data through 02/14/1966 is theoretical based on AUP / 2.   Data continued on page 29.   *Source: Forex*

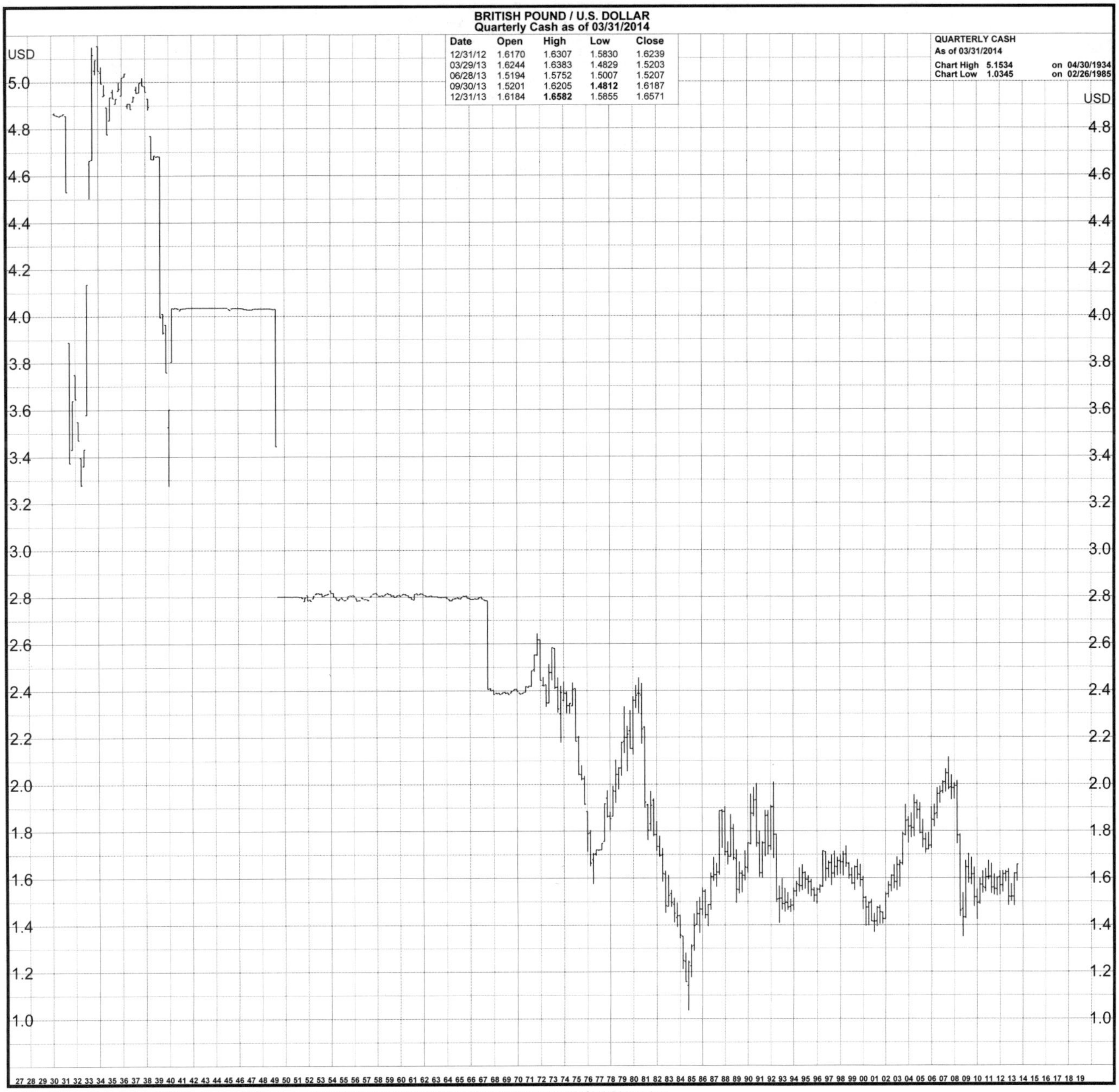

BRITISH POUND / U.S. DOLLAR
Quarterly Cash as of 03/31/2014

Date	Open	High	Low	Close
12/31/12	1.6170	1.6307	1.5830	1.6239
03/29/13	1.6244	1.6383	1.4829	1.5203
06/28/13	1.5194	1.5752	1.5007	1.5207
09/30/13	1.5201	1.6205	1.4812	1.6187
12/31/13	1.6184	1.6582	1.5855	1.6571

QUARTERLY CASH
As of 03/31/2014

Chart High 5.1534 on 04/30/1934
Chart Low 1.0345 on 02/26/1985

Black Market (close): to 12/1970; FRB: 01/04/1971 to 03/30/1972; IMM: 04/03/1972 to 02/11/1986; Forex: 02/14/1986 to date.

Annual High, Low and Settle of British Pound   In USD per GBP

Year	High	Low	Settle	Year	High	Low	Settle	Year	High	Low	Settle
1930	4.8707	4.8564	4.8566	1944	4.0350	4.0350	4.0350	1958	2.8171	2.8033	2.8034
1931	4.8649	3.3737	3.3737	1945	4.0350	4.0249	4.0337	1959	2.8165	2.7984	2.7984
1932	3.7500	3.2753	3.2787	1946	4.0338	4.0294	4.0294	1960	2.8135	2.7997	2.8073
1933	5.1497	3.3614	5.1159	1947	4.0313	4.0271	4.0313	1961	2.8154	2.7874	2.8096
1934	5.1534	4.9408	4.9458	1948	4.0315	4.0307	4.0315	1962	2.8153	2.8009	2.8033
1935	4.9699	4.7762	4.9288	1949	4.0314	2.8007	2.8007	1963	2.8048	2.7965	2.7965
1936	5.0363	4.8880	4.9078	1950	2.8007	2.8000	2.8000	1964	2.7994	2.7834	2.7906
1937	4.9964	4.8851	4.9964	1951	2.8007	2.7949	2.7949	1965	2.8037	2.7908	2.8021
1938	5.0180	4.6703	4.6703	1952	2.8079	2.7812	2.8059	1966	2.8039	2.7888	2.7901
1939	4.6857	3.9247	3.9301	1953	2.8190	2.8028	2.8103	1967	2.7992	2.4063	2.4063
1940	4.0356	3.2736	4.0350	1954	2.8281	2.7874	2.7874	1968	2.4092	2.3842	2.3842
1941	4.0350	4.0248	4.0350	1955	2.8026	2.7836	2.8026	1969	2.3973	2.3840	2.3973
1942	4.0350	4.0348	4.0350	1956	2.8077	2.7825	2.7850	1970	2.4061	2.3853	2.3906
1943	4.0350	4.0350	4.0350	1957	2.8058	2.7827	2.8058	1971	2.5538	2.3938	2.5520

Data continued on page 35.   *Source: Forex*

33

BRITISH POUND

BRITISH POUND - IMM
Monthly Nearest Futures as of 12/31/2013

Date	Open	High	Low	Close
08/31/13	1.5198	1.5716	1.5098	1.5493
09/30/13	1.5516	1.6194	1.5493	1.6177
10/31/13	1.6175	1.6252	1.5886	1.6048
11/30/13	1.6037	1.6383	1.5850	1.6360
12/31/13	1.6370	**1.6572**	1.6203	1.6558

MONTHLY NEAREST FUTURES
As of 12/31/2013

Chart High 2.6440 on 03/09/1972
Chart Low 1.0345 on 02/26/1985
CONTRACT SIZE 62,500 GBP
MIN TICK VALUE .0001 USD
VALUE 6.25 USD / contract
EACH GRID VALUE 0.01 USD
VALUE 625 USD / contract
DAILY LIMIT VALUE None
TRADING HOURS
5:00p-4:00p / 7:20a-2:00p CT

Nearby Futures through Last Trading Day.   Black Market (close): to 12/1970; FRB: 01/04/1971 to 05/15/1972; Futures: 05/16/1972 to date.

Annual High, Low and Settle of British Pound Futures   In USD per GBP

Year	High	Low	Settle	Year	High	Low	Settle	Year	High	Low	Settle
1972	2.6440	2.3270	2.3342	1986	1.5525	1.3600	1.4720	2000	1.6578	1.3952	1.4948
1973	2.5880	2.2550	2.2940	1987	1.8845	1.4530	1.8825	2001	1.5700	1.3652	1.4486
1974	2.4270	2.1340	2.2910	1988	1.9045	1.6456	1.7992	2002	1.6052	1.4004	1.6022
1975	2.4300	1.9920	2.0040	1989	1.8180	1.4940	1.5888	2003	1.7843	1.5390	1.7739
1976	2.0255	1.5290	1.6640	1990	1.9740	1.5640	1.9094	2004	1.9500	1.7436	1.9071
1977	1.9250	1.6670	1.9195	1991	1.9898	1.5824	1.8448	2005	1.9318	1.7046	1.7187
1978	2.0985	1.7960	2.0410	1992	2.0088	1.4780	1.4986	2006	1.9853	1.7186	1.9572
1979	2.3245	1.9685	2.2015	1993	1.5904	1.4050	1.4684	2007	2.1138	1.9183	1.9785
1980	2.4485	2.1280	2.4185	1994	1.6436	1.4522	1.5670	2008	2.0397	1.4329	1.4557
1981	2.4475	1.7645	1.9040	1995	1.6570	1.5200	1.5514	2009	1.7043	1.3492	1.6146
1982	1.9340	1.5820	1.6295	1996	1.7128	1.4880	1.7124	2010	1.6454	1.4227	1.5581
1983	1.6310	1.4105	1.4625	1997	1.7114	1.5650	1.6466	2011	1.6738	1.5179	1.5500
1984	1.4975	1.1525	1.1540	1998	1.7300	1.6042	1.6568	2012	1.6304	1.5222	1.6240
1985	1.4975	1.0345	1.4390	1999	1.6798	1.5476	1.6190	2013	1.6572	1.4806	1.6558

Futures begin trading 05/16/1972.   *Source: CME Group; Chicago Mercantile Exchange*

BRITISH POUND / U.S. DOLLAR
Monthly Cash as of 12/31/2013

MONTHLY CASH
As of 12/31/2013

Chart High 2.6440   on 03/09/1972
Chart Low   1.0345   on 02/26/1985

Date	Open	High	Low	Close
08/30/13	1.5211	1.5717	**1.5096**	1.5491
09/30/13	1.5508	1.6205	1.5504	1.6187
10/31/13	1.6184	1.6260	1.5894	1.6032
11/29/13	1.6041	1.6383	1.5855	1.6359
12/31/13	1.6371	**1.6582**	1.6218	1.6571

Black Market (close): to 02/1966 to 12/1970; FRB: 01/04/1971 to 03/30/1972; IMM: 04/03/1972 to 02/11/1986; Forex: 02/14/1986 to date.

Annual High, Low and Settle of British Pound   In USD per GBP

Year	High	Low	Settle	Year	High	Low	Settle	Year	High	Low	Settle
1972	2.6440	2.3312	2.3478	1986	1.5590	1.3660	1.4865	2000	1.6581	1.3955	1.4926
1973	2.5843	2.3055	2.3222	1987	1.8875	1.4640	1.8870	2001	1.5100	1.3688	1.4555
1974	2.4370	2.1780	2.3460	1988	1.9055	1.6565	1.8115	2002	1.6133	1.4044	1.6100
1975	2.4343	2.0173	2.0237	1989	1.8305	1.4935	1.6110	2003	1.7944	1.5463	1.7860
1976	2.0358	1.5745	1.7006	1990	1.9875	1.5885	1.9320	2004	1.9553	1.7482	1.9188
1977	1.9195	1.6950	1.9170	1991	2.0040	1.5995	1.8655	2005	1.9326	1.7047	1.7208
1978	2.1050	1.8040	2.0420	1992	2.0100	1.4965	1.5095	2006	1.9847	1.7191	1.9578
1979	2.3325	1.9780	2.2130	1993	1.5971	1.4082	1.4760	2007	2.1161	1.9186	1.9848
1980	2.4555	2.1255	2.3875	1994	1.6440	1.4545	1.5660	2008	2.0394	1.4354	1.4612
1981	2.4320	1.7610	1.9100	1995	1.6570	1.5213	1.5507	2009	1.7042	1.3504	1.6149
1982	1.9390	1.5840	1.6180	1996	1.7163	1.4898	1.7140	2010	1.6459	1.4232	1.5608
1983	1.6310	1.4105	1.4500	1997	1.7145	1.5678	1.6480	2011	1.6747	1.5271	1.5535
1984	1.4950	1.1560	1.1575	1998	1.7365	1.6085	1.6628	2012	1.6309	1.5234	1.6239
1985	1.5015	1.0345	1.4475	1999	1.6791	1.5475	1.6150	2013	1.6582	1.4812	1.6571

Data continued from page 33.   *Source: Forex*

BRITISH POUND

BRITISH POUND - IMM
Weekly Nearest Futures as of 01/03/2014

WEEKLY NEAREST FUTURES
As of 01/03/2014

Chart High	2.1138	on 11/09/2007
Chart Low	1.3492	on 01/23/2009
CONTRACT SIZE	62,500 GBP	
MIN TICK	.0001 USD	
VALUE	6.25 USD / contract	
EACH GRID	0.005 USD	
VALUE	312.5 USD / contract	
DAILY LIMIT	None	
VALUE		
TRADING HOURS		
5:00p-4:00p / 7:20a-2:00p CT		

Date	Open	High	Low	Close
12/06/13	1.6370	1.6442	1.6292	1.6342
12/13/13	1.6344	1.6465	1.6263	1.6291
12/20/13	1.6297	1.6476	1.6203	1.6324
12/27/13	1.6322	1.6570	1.6314	1.6453
01/03/14	1.6480	1.6572	1.6387	1.6413

Commercial = -34332
NonCommercial = 14420
NonReportable = 19912

Nearby Futures through Last Trading Day.

Quarterly High, Low and Settle of British Pound Futures   In USD per GBP

Quarter	High	Low	Settle	Quarter	High	Low	Settle	Quarter	High	Low	Settle
03/2005	1.9318	1.8456	1.8826	03/2008	2.0397	1.9280	1.9712	03/2011	1.6385	1.5397	1.6052
06/2005	1.9168	1.7829	1.7863	06/2008	1.9966	1.9313	1.9819	06/2011	1.6738	1.5894	1.6051
09/2005	1.8492	1.7242	1.7603	09/2008	2.0074	1.7442	1.7840	09/2011	1.6615	1.5316	1.5609
12/2005	1.7894	1.7046	1.7187	12/2008	1.7921	1.4329	1.4557	12/2011	1.6158	1.5179	1.5500
03/2006	1.7938	1.7186	1.7380	03/2009	1.5356	1.3492	1.4348	03/2012	1.6030	1.5222	1.5988
06/2006	1.9035	1.7265	1.8508	06/2009	1.6742	1.4275	1.6463	06/2012	1.6298	1.5267	1.5677
09/2006	1.9161	1.8200	1.8730	09/2009	1.7043	1.5766	1.6002	09/2012	1.6304	1.5390	1.6136
12/2006	1.9853	1.8529	1.9572	12/2009	1.6876	1.5702	1.6146	12/2012	1.6304	1.5822	1.6240
03/2007	1.9914	1.9183	1.9669	03/2010	1.6454	1.4778	1.5174	03/2013	1.6314	1.4831	1.5165
06/2007	2.0128	1.9584	2.0055	06/2010	1.5520	1.4227	1.4956	06/2013	1.5750	1.5006	1.5204
09/2007	2.0636	1.9638	2.0419	09/2010	1.5997	1.4873	1.5707	09/2013	1.6194	1.4806	1.6177
12/2007	2.1138	1.9712	1.9785	12/2010	1.6295	1.5335	1.5581	12/2013	1.6572	1.5850	1.6558

Source: CME Group; Chicago Mercantile Exchange

BRITISH POUND / U.S. DOLLAR
Weekly Cash as of 01/03/2014

WEEKLY CASH
As of 01/03/2014

Chart High 2.1161 on 11/09/2007
Chart Low 1.3504 on 01/23/2009

Date	Open	High	Low	Close
12/06/13	1.6371	1.6443	1.6294	1.6345
12/13/13	1.6356	1.6467	1.6265	1.6295
12/20/13	1.6295	1.6489	1.6218	1.6327
12/27/13	1.6330	1.6579	1.6323	1.6479
01/03/14	1.6480	1.6597	1.6394	1.6414

Forex.

Quarterly High, Low and Settle of British Pound   In USD per GBP

Quarter	High	Low	Settle	Quarter	High	Low	Settle	Quarter	High	Low	Settle
03/2005	1.9326	1.8509	1.8901	03/2008	2.0394	1.9339	1.9840	03/2011	1.6400	1.5407	1.6026
06/2005	1.9218	1.7872	1.7914	06/2008	2.0045	1.9364	1.9924	06/2011	1.6747	1.5912	1.6047
09/2005	1.8500	1.7272	1.7639	09/2008	2.0155	1.7446	1.7810	09/2011	1.6619	1.5329	1.5587
12/2005	1.7903	1.7047	1.7208	12/2008	1.7874	1.4354	1.4612	12/2011	1.6168	1.5271	1.5535
03/2006	1.7935	1.7191	1.7365	03/2009	1.5375	1.3504	1.4325	03/2012	1.6037	1.5234	1.6006
06/2006	1.9024	1.7251	1.8483	06/2009	1.6744	1.4274	1.6462	06/2012	1.6302	1.5270	1.5687
09/2006	1.9144	1.8178	1.8716	09/2009	1.7042	1.5771	1.5985	09/2012	1.6309	1.5395	1.6146
12/2006	1.9847	1.8518	1.9578	12/2009	1.6876	1.5708	1.6149	12/2012	1.6307	1.5830	1.6239
03/2007	1.9917	1.9186	1.9676	03/2010	1.6459	1.4785	1.5181	03/2013	1.6383	1.4829	1.5203
06/2007	2.0133	1.9592	2.0077	06/2010	1.5525	1.4232	1.4941	06/2013	1.5752	1.5007	1.5207
09/2007	2.0654	1.9656	2.0461	09/2010	1.6000	1.4875	1.5715	09/2013	1.6205	1.4812	1.6187
12/2007	2.1161	1.9758	1.9848	12/2010	1.6298	1.5345	1.5608	12/2013	1.6582	1.5855	1.6571

Source: Forex

CANADIAN DOLLAR

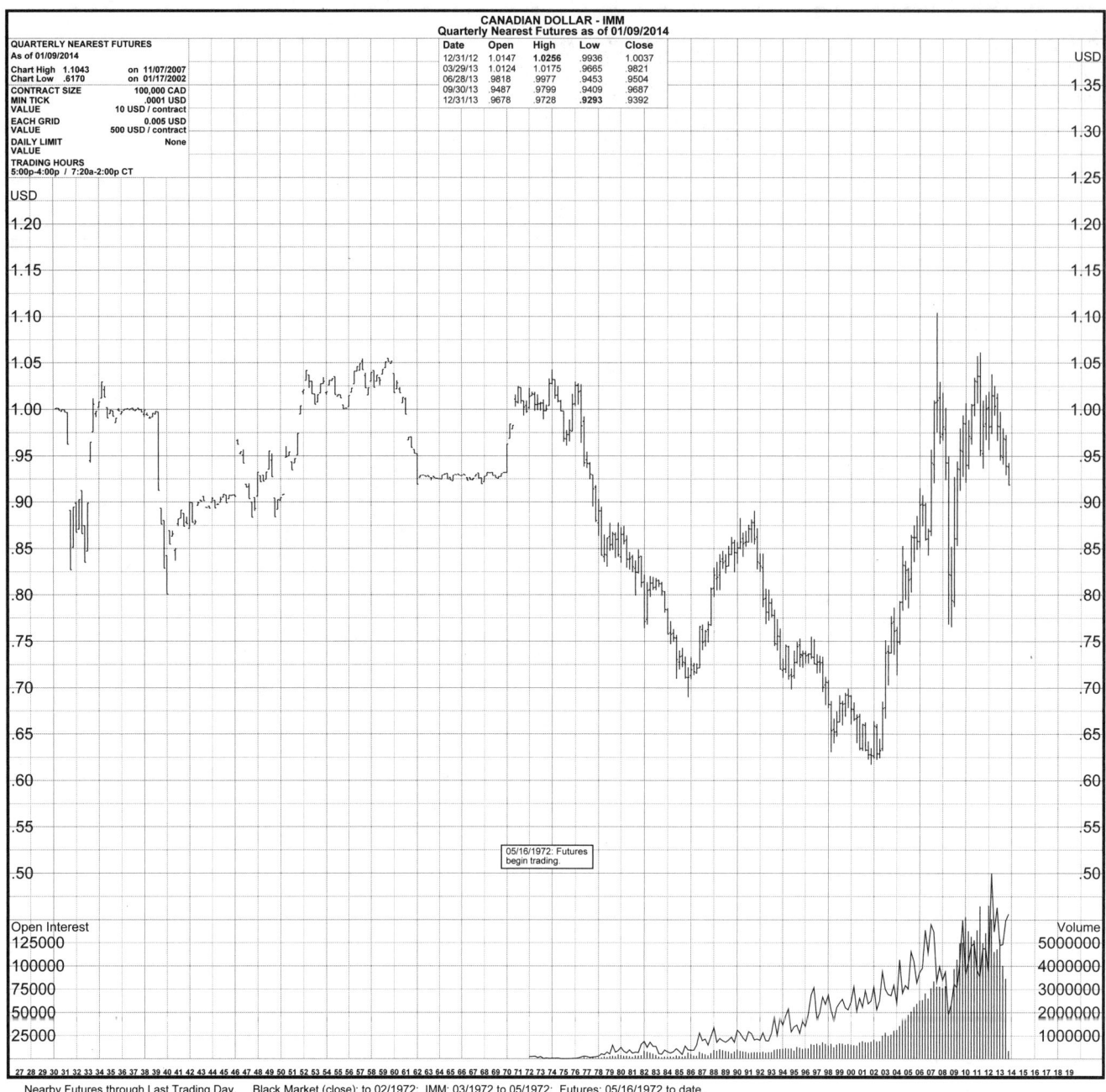

CANADIAN DOLLAR - IMM
Quarterly Nearest Futures as of 01/09/2014

Date	Open	High	Low	Close
12/31/12	1.0147	**1.0256**	.9936	1.0037
03/29/13	1.0124	1.0175	.9665	.9821
06/28/13	.9818	.9977	.9453	.9504
09/30/13	.9487	.9799	.9409	.9687
12/31/13	.9678	.9728	**.9293**	.9392

QUARTERLY NEAREST FUTURES
As of 01/09/2014

Chart High 1.1043 on 11/07/2007
Chart Low .6170 on 01/17/2002
CONTRACT SIZE 100,000 CAD
MIN TICK VALUE .0001 USD / 10 USD / contract
EACH GRID VALUE 0.005 USD / 500 USD / contract
DAILY LIMIT VALUE None
TRADING HOURS 5:00p-4:00p / 7:20a-2:00p CT

05/16/1972: Futures begin trading.

Open Interest: 125000, 100000, 75000, 50000, 25000
Volume: 5000000, 4000000, 3000000, 2000000, 1000000

Nearby Futures through Last Trading Day.   Black Market (close): to 02/1972; IMM: 03/1972 to 05/1972; Futures: 05/16/1972 to date.

Annual High, Low and Settle of Canadian Dollar   In USD per CAD

Year	High	Low	Settle	Year	High	Low	Settle	Year	High	Low	Settle
1930	1.0012	.9889	.9990	1944	.9051	.8933	.8975	1958	1.0416	1.0154	1.0366
1931	.9998	.8271	.8271	1945	.9083	.8991	.9073	1959	1.0551	1.0258	1.0512
1932	.9123	.8513	.8660	1946	.9678	.9060	.9544	1960	1.0515	1.0178	1.0178
1933	1.0118	.8351	1.0055	1947	.9569	.8836	.8836	1961	1.0127	.9589	.9589
1934	1.0294	.9917	1.0131	1948	.9323	.8906	.9225	1962	.9568	.9191	.9292
1935	1.0018	.9858	.9905	1949	.9552	.8841	.8841	1963	.9285	.9233	.9262
1936	1.0012	.9950	1.0006	1950	.9604	.8921	.9491	1964	.9310	.9247	.9304
1937	1.0015	.9986	.9995	1951	.9741	.9348	.9741	1965	.9311	.9228	.9294
1938	1.0002	.9906	.9906	1952	1.0417	.9949	1.0300	1966	.9304	.9232	.9232
1939	.9977	.8762	.8762	1953	1.0301	1.0055	1.0275	1967	.9315	.9238	.9256
1940	.8802	.8007	.8656	1954	1.0344	1.0157	1.0329	1968	.9321	.9196	.9318
1941	.8913	.8369	.8739	1955	1.0350	1.0005	1.0005	1969	.9321	.9253	.9308
1942	.8996	.8717	.8788	1956	1.0409	1.0008	1.0409	1970	.9842	.9318	.9828
1943	.9064	.8940	.8940	1957	1.0547	1.0230	1.0230	1971	1.0248	.9933	1.0024

Data continued on page 40.   *Source: Forex*

U.S. DOLLAR - CANADIAN DOLLAR
Quarterly Cash as of 03/31/2014

QUARTERLY CASH
As of 03/31/2014

Chart High 1.61930 on 01/21/2002
Chart Low .90600 on 11/07/2007

Date	Open	High	Low	Close
12/31/12	.98300	1.00580	.97350	.99240
03/29/13	.99300	1.03420	.98150	1.01730
06/28/13	1.01770	1.05570	1.00150	1.05150
09/30/13	1.05150	1.06080	1.01840	1.03030
12/31/13	1.03080	1.07370	1.02700	1.06200

Black Market (close): to 02/1972; IMM: 03/1972 to 02/1986; Forex: 02/14/1986 to date.

Annual High, Low and Settle of Canadian Dollar   In CAD per USD

Year	High	Low	Settle	Year	High	Low	Settle	Year	High	Low	Settle
1930	1.0112	.9988	1.0010	1944	1.1194	1.1049	1.1142	1958	.9848	.9601	.9647
1931	1.2090	1.0002	1.2090	1945	1.1122	1.1010	1.1022	1959	.9748	.9478	.9513
1932	1.1747	1.0961	1.1547	1946	1.1038	1.0333	1.0478	1960	.9825	.9510	.9825
1933	1.1975	.9883	.9945	1947	1.1317	1.0450	1.1317	1961	1.0429	.9875	1.0429
1934	1.0084	.9714	.9871	1948	1.1228	1.0726	1.0840	1962	1.0880	1.0452	1.0762
1935	1.0144	.9982	1.0096	1949	1.1311	1.0469	1.1311	1963	1.0831	1.0770	1.0797
1936	1.0050	.9988	.9994	1950	1.1210	1.0412	1.0536	1964	1.0814	1.0741	1.0748
1937	1.0014	.9985	1.0005	1951	1.0697	1.0266	1.0266	1965	1.0837	1.0740	1.0760
1938	1.0095	.9998	1.0095	1952	1.0051	.9600	.9709	1966	1.0832	1.0748	1.0832
1939	1.1413	1.0023	1.1413	1953	.9945	.9708	.9732	1967	1.0825	1.0735	1.0804
1940	1.2489	1.1361	1.1553	1954	.9845	.9667	.9681	1968	1.0874	1.0728	1.0732
1941	1.1949	1.1220	1.1443	1955	.9995	.9662	.9995	1969	1.0807	1.0728	1.0743
1942	1.1472	1.1116	1.1379	1956	.9992	.9607	.9607	1970	1.0732	1.0161	1.0175
1943	1.1186	1.1033	1.1186	1957	.9775	.9481	.9775	1971	.9990	.9785	.9990

Data continued on page 41.   *Source: Forex*

CANADIAN DOLLAR

CANADIAN DOLLAR - IMM
Monthly Nearest Futures as of 12/31/2013

Date	Open	High	Low	Close
08/31/13	.9718	.9745	.9455	.9492
09/30/13	.9492	.9799	.9461	.9687
10/31/13	.9678	.9728	.9514	.9585
11/30/13	.9574	.9607	.9404	.9407
12/31/13	.9411	.9467	.9293	.9392

MONTHLY NEAREST FUTURES
As of 12/31/2013

Chart High 1.1043 on 11/07/2007
Chart Low .6170 on 01/17/2002
CONTRACT SIZE 100,000 CAD
MIN TICK .0001 USD
VALUE 10 USD / contract
EACH GRID 0.005 USD
VALUE 500 USD / contract
DAILY LIMIT None
VALUE
TRADING HOURS
5:00p-4:00p / 7:20a-2:00p CT

Nearby Futures through Last Trading Day.   Black Market (close): to 02/1972; IMM: 03/1972 to 05/1972; Futures: 05/16/1972 to date.

Annual High, Low and Settle of Canadian Dollar Futures   In USD per CAD

Year	High	Low	Settle	Year	High	Low	Settle	Year	High	Low	Settle
1972	1.0260	.9961	1.0051	1986	.7328	.6898	.7210	2000	.6992	.6403	.6679
1973	1.0160	.9892	1.0001	1987	.7715	.7213	.7679	2001	.6719	.6225	.6276
1974	1.0427	1.0040	1.0090	1988	.8440	.7667	.8362	2002	.6640	.6170	.6322
1975	1.0100	.9610	.9775	1989	.8625	.8233	.8561	2003	.7772	.6318	.7694
1976	1.0296	.9640	.9822	1990	.8828	.8246	.8555	2004	.8530	.7135	.8322
1977	.9924	.8951	.9141	1991	.8906	.8520	.8602	2005	.8753	.7855	.8620
1978	.9181	.8355	.8437	1992	.8718	.7685	.7815	2006	.9152	.8489	.8602
1979	.8777	.8305	.8597	1993	.8060	.7401	.7557	2007	1.1043	.8427	1.0099
1980	.8780	.8294	.8385	1994	.7638	.7088	.7128	2008	1.0298	.7682	.8224
1981	.8490	.7992	.8406	1995	.7530	.6983	.7331	2009	.9798	.7653	.9562
1982	.8420	.7641	.8128	1996	.7551	.7216	.7332	2010	1.0069	.9213	1.0044
1983	.8196	.7990	.8043	1997	.7524	.6954	.7007	2011	1.0617	.9367	.9821
1984	.8042	.7469	.7538	1998	.7120	.6305	.6520	2012	1.0380	.9568	1.0037
1985	.7569	.7097	.7114	1999	.6947	.6473	.6922	2013	1.0175	.9293	.9392

Futures begin trading 05/16/1972.   Data continued from page 38.   *Source: CME Group; Chicago Mercantile Exchange*

U.S. DOLLAR - CANADIAN DOLLAR Monthly Cash as of 12/31/2013				
Date	Open	High	Low	Close
08/30/13	1.02790	1.05700	1.02670	1.05330
09/30/13	1.05340	1.05600	1.01840	1.03030
10/31/13	1.03080	1.04980	1.02700	1.04300
11/29/13	1.04310	1.06290	1.03979	1.06190
12/31/13	1.06150	1.07370	1.05590	1.06200

MONTHLY CASH
As of 12/31/2013
Chart High 1.61930   on 01/21/2002
Chart Low .90600   on 11/07/2007

Black Market (close): to 02/1972; IMM: 03/1972 to 02/1986; Forex: 02/14/1986 to date.

Annual High, Low and Settle of Canadian Dollar   In CAD per USD

Year	High	Low	Settle	Year	High	Low	Settle	Year	High	Low	Settle
1972	1.0014	.9747	.9953	1986	1.4475	1.3625	1.3808	2000	1.5627	1.4318	1.4987
1973	1.0112	.9747	.9963	1987	1.3805	1.2945	1.2990	2001	1.6052	1.4901	1.5918
1974	.9947	.9587	.9911	1988	1.3010	1.1830	1.1922	2002	1.6193	1.5035	1.5730
1975	1.0393	.9910	1.0167	1989	1.2118	1.1560	1.1585	2003	1.5776	1.2840	1.2956
1976	1.0368	.9648	1.0101	1990	1.2097	1.1273	1.1600	2004	1.4002	1.1719	1.1997
1977	1.1151	1.0022	1.0942	1991	1.1661	1.1195	1.1556	2005	1.2734	1.1429	1.1626
1978	1.1959	1.0905	1.1862	1992	1.2936	1.1405	1.2708	2006	1.1797	1.0931	1.1663
1979	1.2021	1.1392	1.1667	1993	1.3481	1.2408	1.3218	2007	1.1876	.9060	.9986
1980	1.2127	1.1409	1.1946	1994	1.4088	1.3078	1.4017	2008	1.3016	.9712	1.2219
1981	1.2453	1.1753	1.1860	1995	1.4268	1.3276	1.3641	2009	1.3066	1.0207	1.0525
1982	1.3017	1.1844	1.2291	1996	1.3865	1.3265	1.3703	2010	1.0854	.9925	.9980
1983	1.2517	1.2180	1.2444	1997	1.4415	1.3346	1.4289	2011	1.0657	.9407	1.0196
1984	1.3397	1.2442	1.3218	1998	1.5848	1.4048	1.5349	2012	1.0447	.9633	.9924
1985	1.4086	1.3180	1.3986	1999	1.5468	1.4428	1.4458	2013	1.0737	.9815	1.0620

Data continued from page 39.   *Source: Forex*

CANADIAN DOLLAR

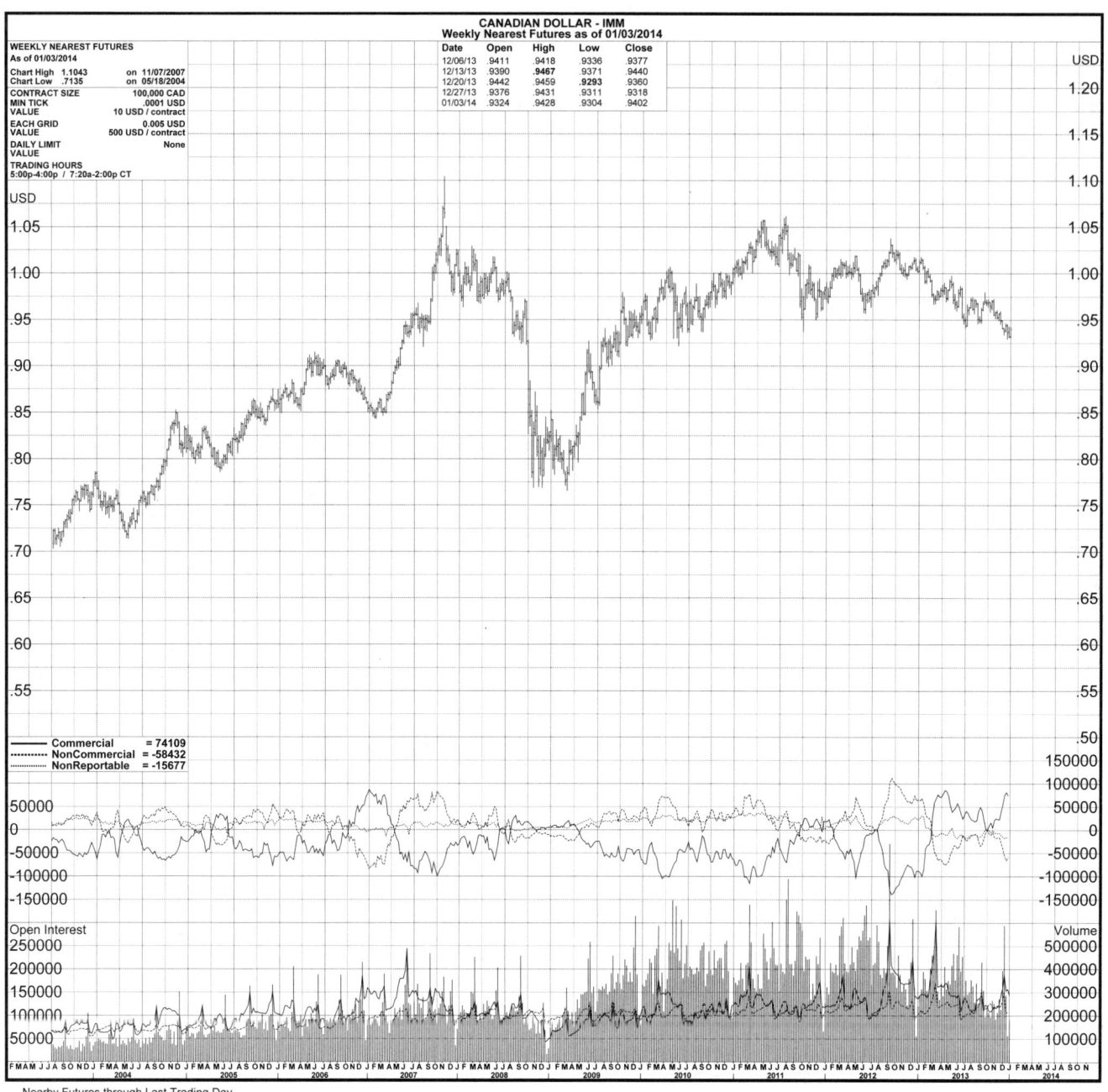

CANADIAN DOLLAR - IMM
Weekly Nearest Futures as of 01/03/2014

Date	Open	High	Low	Close
12/06/13	.9411	.9418	.9336	.9377
12/13/13	.9390	.9467	.9371	.9440
12/20/13	.9442	.9459	.9293	.9360
12/27/13	.9376	.9431	.9311	.9318
01/03/14	.9324	.9428	.9304	.9402

WEEKLY NEAREST FUTURES
As of 01/03/2014

Chart High	1.1043	on 11/07/2007
Chart Low	.7135	on 05/18/2004
CONTRACT SIZE	100,000 CAD	
MIN TICK	.0001 USD	
VALUE	10 USD / contract	
EACH GRID	0.005 USD	
VALUE	500 USD / contract	
DAILY LIMIT VALUE	None	
TRADING HOURS		
5:00p-4:00p / 7:20a-2:00p CT		

Commercial = 74109
NonCommercial = -58432
NonReportable = -15677

Nearby Futures through Last Trading Day.

Quarterly High, Low and Settle of Canadian Dollar Futures   In USD per CAD

Quarter	High	Low	Settle	Quarter	High	Low	Settle	Quarter	High	Low	Settle
03/2005	.8370	.7945	.8269	03/2008	1.0298	.9631	.9709	03/2011	1.0342	.9932	1.0306
06/2005	.8295	.7855	.8163	06/2008	1.0180	.9668	.9816	06/2011	1.0578	1.0067	1.0358
09/2005	.8650	.8027	.8624	09/2008	1.0018	.9239	.9427	09/2011	1.0617	.9504	.9561
12/2005	.8753	.8357	.8620	12/2008	.9498	.7682	.8224	12/2011	1.0097	.9367	.9821
03/2006	.8854	.8489	.8579	03/2009	.8523	.7653	.7941	03/2012	1.0157	.9675	1.0010
06/2006	.9152	.8513	.8971	06/2009	.9273	.7871	.8610	06/2012	1.0192	.9568	.9816
09/2006	.9076	.8742	.8967	09/2009	.9444	.8530	.9364	09/2012	1.0380	.9740	1.0149
12/2006	.8993	.8587	.8602	12/2009	.9798	.9124	.9562	12/2012	1.0256	.9936	1.0037
03/2007	.8717	.8427	.8691	03/2010	.9938	.9274	.9851	03/2013	1.0175	.9665	.9821
06/2007	.9570	.8638	.9426	06/2010	1.0069	.9213	.9402	06/2013	.9977	.9453	.9504
09/2007	1.0098	.9205	1.0072	09/2010	.9889	.9360	.9713	09/2013	.9799	.9409	.9687
12/2007	1.1043	.9757	1.0099	12/2010	1.0061	.9625	1.0044	12/2013	.9728	.9293	.9392

Source: CME Group; Chicago Mercantile Exchange

WEEKLY CASH
As of 01/03/2014

Chart High 1.53830 on 01/21/2003
Chart Low .90600 on 11/07/2007

CAD

U.S. DOLLAR - CANADIAN DOLLAR
Weekly Cash as of 01/03/2014

Date	Open	High	Low	Close
12/06/13	1.06150	1.07070	1.06120	1.06490
12/13/13	1.06360	1.06710	1.05590	1.05870
12/20/13	1.05930	1.07370	1.05730	1.06300
12/27/13	1.06460	1.07170	1.05820	1.07090
01/03/14	1.07000	1.07280	1.05890	1.06330

Forex.

Quarterly High, Low and Settle of Canadian Dollar   In CAD per USD

Quarter	High	Low	Settle	Quarter	High	Low	Settle	Quarter	High	Low	Settle
03/2005	.8370	.7946	.8268	03/2008	1.0296	.9635	.9742	03/2011	1.0344	.9942	1.0303
06/2005	.8286	.7853	.8158	06/2008	1.0183	.9683	.9791	06/2011	1.0585	1.0088	1.0372
09/2005	.8629	.8013	.8608	09/2008	1.0023	.9240	.9394	09/2011	1.0630	.9525	.9525
12/2005	.8750	.8349	.8601	12/2008	.9481	.7683	.8184	12/2011	1.0108	.9384	.9808
03/2006	.8850	.8477	.8562	03/2009	.8501	.7654	.7935	03/2012	1.0161	.9690	1.0020
06/2006	.9148	.8495	.8962	06/2009	.9273	.7865	.8605	06/2012	1.0205	.9572	.9831
09/2006	.9065	.8726	.8945	09/2009	.9441	.8528	.9354	09/2012	1.0381	.9755	1.0173
12/2006	.8972	.8570	.8574	12/2009	.9797	.9126	.9501	12/2012	1.0272	.9942	1.0077
03/2007	.8694	.8420	.8663	03/2010	.9938	.9276	.9847	03/2013	1.0189	.9669	.9830
06/2007	.9551	.8621	.9401	06/2010	1.0070	.9213	.9395	06/2013	.9985	.9472	.9510
09/2007	1.0085	.9204	1.0055	09/2010	.9894	.9366	.9720	09/2013	.9819	.9427	.9706
12/2007	1.1038	.9758	1.0014	12/2010	1.0076	.9640	1.0020	12/2013	.9737	.9314	.9416

Source: Forex

43

EURO FX

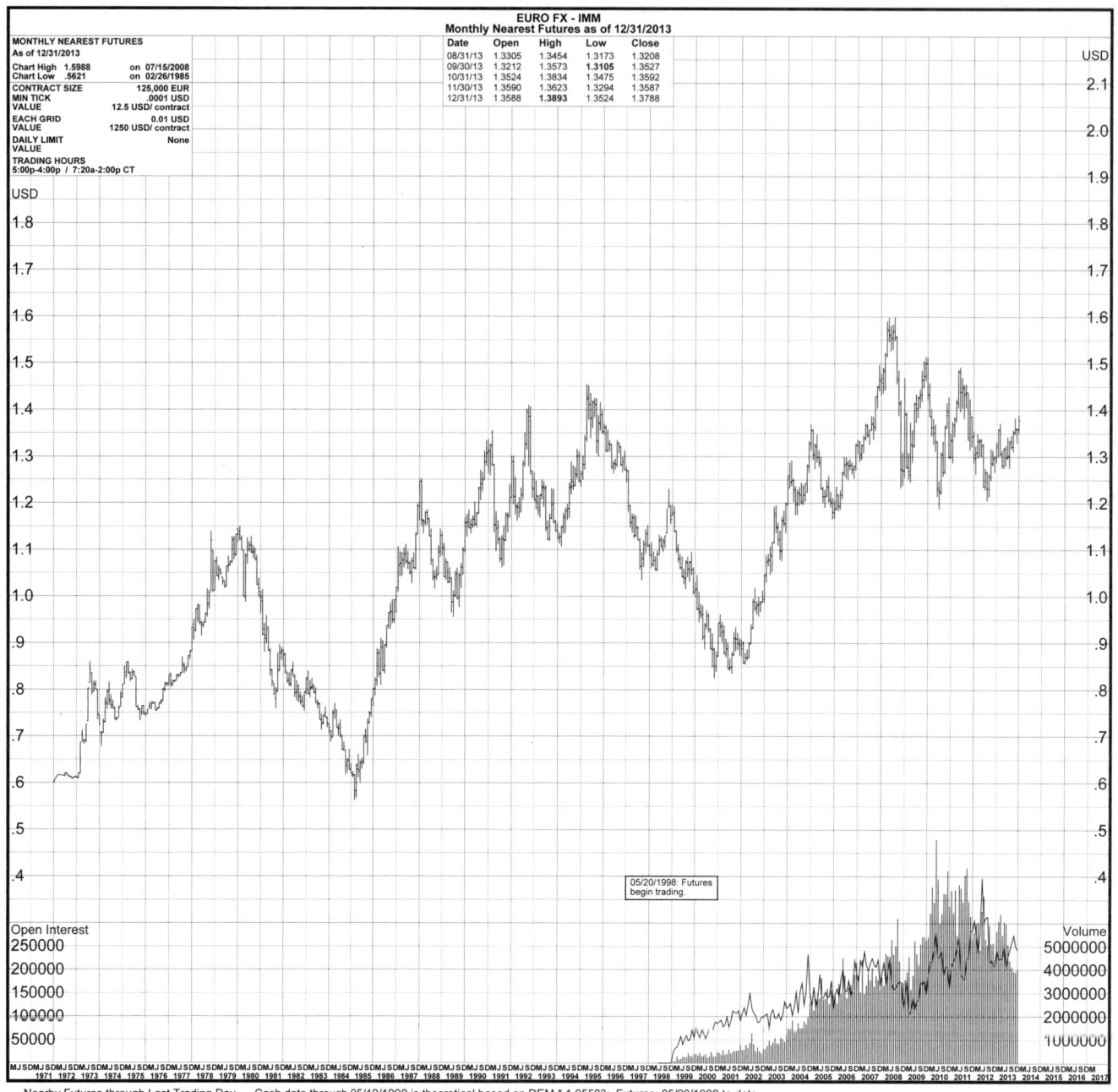

EURO FX - IMM
Monthly Nearest Futures as of 12/31/2013

Date	Open	High	Low	Close
08/31/13	1.3305	1.3454	1.3173	1.3208
09/30/13	1.3212	1.3573	1.3105	1.3527
10/31/13	1.3524	1.3834	1.3475	1.3592
11/30/13	1.3590	1.3623	1.3294	1.3587
12/31/13	1.3588	1.3893	1.3524	1.3788

MONTHLY NEAREST FUTURES
As of 12/31/2013
Chart High 1.5988 on 07/15/2008
Chart Low .5621 on 02/26/1985
CONTRACT SIZE 125,000 EUR
MIN TICK .0001 USD
VALUE 12.5 USD/ contract
EACH GRID 0.01 USD
VALUE 1250 USD/ contract
DAILY LIMIT None
VALUE
TRADING HOURS
5:00p-4:00p / 7:20a-2:00p CT

05/20/1998: Futures begin trading.

Nearby Futures through Last Trading Day.   Cash data through 05/19/1998 is theoretical based on DEM * 1.95583; Futures: 05/20/1998 to date.

Annual High, Low and Settle of Euro FX Futures   In USD per EUR

Year	High	Low	Settle	Year	High	Low	Settle	Year	High	Low	Settle
1972	.6219	.6085	.6110	1986	1.0195	.7863	1.0187	2000	1.0464	.8245	.9428
1973	.8606	.6087	.7233	1987	1.2469	1.0084	1.2454	2001	.9615	.8342	.8878
1974	.8166	.6773	.8107	1988	1.2521	1.0160	1.1044	2002	1.0473	.8549	1.0471
1975	.8592	.7329	.7467	1989	1.1677	.9550	1.1566	2003	1.2623	1.0302	1.2534
1976	.8304	.7467	.8297	1990	1.3369	1.1270	1.3109	2004	1.3687	1.1745	1.3558
1977	.9330	.8050	.9320	1991	1.3559	1.0617	1.2885	2005	1.3593	1.1661	1.1880
1978	1.1395	.9062	1.0749	1992	1.4101	1.1614	1.2073	2006	1.3373	1.1835	1.3236
1979	1.1448	1.0167	1.1328	1993	1.2493	1.1189	1.1245	2007	1.4977	1.2901	1.4590
1980	1.1495	.9625	.9965	1994	1.3160	1.1067	1.2624	2008	1.5988	1.2326	1.3921
1981	1.0149	.7583	.8735	1995	1.4549	1.2496	1.3620	2009	1.5144	1.2456	1.4334
1982	.8770	.7528	.8221	1996	1.3670	1.2431	1.2690	2010	1.4577	1.1874	1.3364
1983	.8397	.7037	.7170	1997	1.2712	1.0345	1.0874	2011	1.4925	1.2869	1.2968
1984	.7712	.6171	.6196	1998	1.2320	1.0537	1.1768	2012	1.3488	1.2051	1.3208
1985	.8031	.5621	.8015	1999	1.1925	1.0000	1.0160	2013	1.3893	1.2751	1.3788

Cash data through 05/19/1998 is theoretical based on DEM * 1.95583.   Futures begin trading 05/20/1998.   *Source: CME Group; Chicago Mercantile Exchange*

EURO / U.S. DOLLAR
Monthly Cash as of 12/31/2013

Date	Open	High	Low	Close
08/30/13	1.3299	1.3449	1.3175	1.3218
09/30/13	1.3226	1.3569	1.3105	1.3528
10/31/13	1.3529	1.3831	1.3474	1.3581
11/29/13	1.3582	1.3621	1.3301	1.3588
12/31/13	1.3597	**1.3895**	1.3524	1.3754

MONTHLY CASH
As of 12/31/2013
Chart High 1.6038 on 07/15/2008
Chart Low .5621 on 02/26/1985

Cash data through 12/31/1998 is theoretical based on DEM * 1.95583; Forex: 01/04/1999 to date.

Annual High, Low and Settle of Euro FX   In USD per EUR

Year	High	Low	Settle	Year	High	Low	Settle	Year	High	Low	Settle
1972	.6219	.6085	.6110	1986	1.0195	.7863	1.0187	2000	1.0413	.8230	.9422
1973	.8606	.6087	.7233	1987	1.2469	1.0084	1.2454	2001	.9592	.8352	.8912
1974	.8166	.6773	.8107	1988	1.2521	1.0160	1.1044	2002	1.0505	.8565	1.0493
1975	.8592	.7329	.7467	1989	1.1677	.9550	1.1566	2003	1.2649	1.0336	1.2588
1976	.8304	.7467	.8297	1990	1.3369	1.1270	1.3109	2004	1.3666	1.1760	1.3567
1977	.9330	.8050	.9320	1991	1.3559	1.0617	1.2885	2005	1.3581	1.1641	1.1837
1978	1.1395	.9062	1.0749	1992	1.4101	1.1614	1.2073	2006	1.3367	1.1802	1.3197
1979	1.1448	1.0167	1.1328	1993	1.2493	1.1189	1.1245	2007	1.4967	1.2868	1.4587
1980	1.1495	.9625	.9965	1994	1.3160	1.1067	1.2624	2008	1.6038	1.2333	1.3977
1981	1.0149	.7583	.8735	1995	1.4549	1.2496	1.3620	2009	1.5144	1.2456	1.4325
1982	.8770	.7528	.8221	1996	1.3670	1.2431	1.2690	2010	1.4580	1.1877	1.3389
1983	.8397	.7037	.7170	1997	1.2712	1.0345	1.0874	2011	1.4940	1.2858	1.2943
1984	.7712	.6171	.6196	1998	1.2320	1.0537	1.1717	2012	1.3487	1.2043	1.3187
1985	.8031	.5621	.8015	1999	1.1890	.9992	1.0088	2013	1.3895	1.2747	1.3754

Data through 12/31/1998 is theoretical based on DEM * 1.95583.   *Source: Forex*

EURO FX

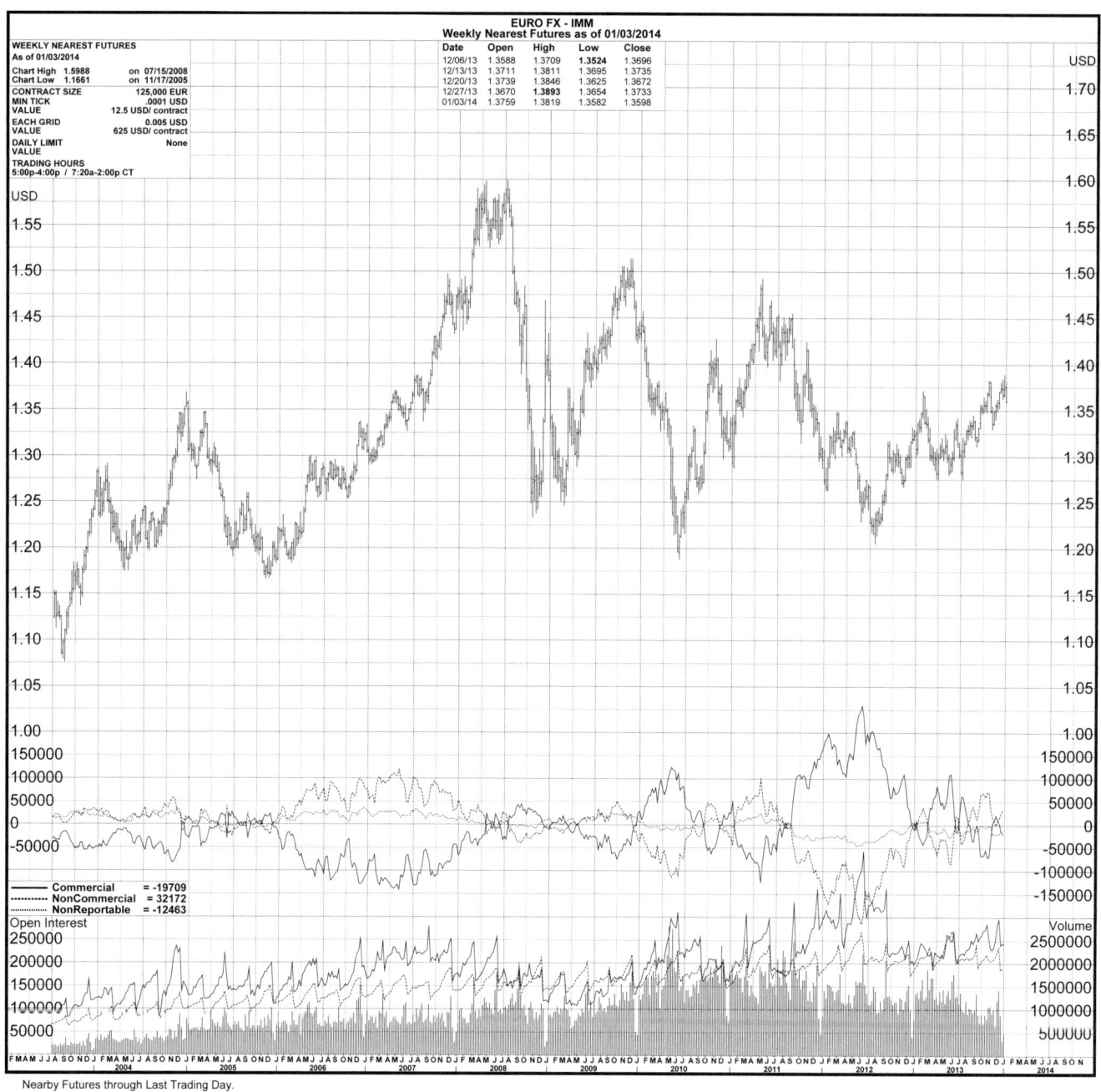

EURO FX - IMM
Weekly Nearest Futures as of 01/03/2014

Date	Open	High	Low	Close
12/06/13	1.3588	1.3709	**1.3524**	1.3696
12/13/13	1.3711	1.3811	1.3695	1.3735
12/20/13	1.3739	1.3846	1.3625	1.3672
12/27/13	1.3670	**1.3893**	1.3654	1.3733
01/03/14	1.3759	1.3819	1.3582	1.3598

WEEKLY NEAREST FUTURES
As of 01/03/2014

Chart High 1.5988 on 07/15/2008
Chart Low 1.1661 on 11/17/2005
CONTRACT SIZE 125,000 EUR
MIN TICK .0001 USD
VALUE 12.5 USD/ contract
EACH GRID 0.005 USD
VALUE 625 USD/ contract
DAILY LIMIT None
VALUE
TRADING HOURS
5:00p-4:00p / 7:20a-2:00p CT

Commercial = -19709
NonCommercial = 32172
NonReportable = -12463

Nearby Futures through Last Trading Day.

Quarterly High, Low and Settle of Euro FX Futures   In USD per EUR

Quarter	High	Low	Settle	Quarter	High	Low	Settle	Quarter	High	Low	Settle
03/2005	1.3593	1.2735	1.2982	03/2008	1.5907	1.4355	1.5729	03/2011	1.4229	1.2870	1.4181
06/2005	1.3143	1.2012	1.2137	06/2008	1.5985	1.5255	1.5690	06/2011	1.4925	1.3963	1.4488
09/2005	1.2598	1.1900	1.2059	09/2008	1.5988	1.3880	1.4134	09/2011	1.4553	1.3357	1.3415
12/2005	1.2249	1.1661	1.1880	12/2008	1.4687	1.2326	1.3921	12/2011	1.4241	1.2869	1.2968
03/2006	1.2359	1.1835	1.2179	03/2009	1.3956	1.2456	1.3283	03/2012	1.3488	1.2627	1.3339
06/2006	1.3003	1.2089	1.2850	06/2009	1.4338	1.2878	1.4040	06/2012	1.3387	1.2288	1.2668
09/2006	1.2961	1.2503	1.2739	09/2009	1.4844	1.3831	1.4645	09/2012	1.3172	1.2051	1.2862
12/2006	1.3373	1.2525	1.3236	12/2009	1.5144	1.4215	1.4334	12/2012	1.3321	1.2665	1.3208
03/2007	1.3458	1.2901	1.3394	03/2010	1.4577	1.3266	1.3510	03/2013	1.3715	1.2758	1.2823
06/2007	1.3715	1.3266	1.3568	06/2010	1.3694	1.1874	1.2248	06/2013	1.3424	1.2751	1.3023
09/2007	1.4300	1.3370	1.4293	09/2010	1.3678	1.2197	1.3634	09/2013	1.3573	1.2755	1.3527
12/2007	1.4977	1.4033	1.4590	12/2010	1.4276	1.2968	1.3364	12/2013	1.3893	1.3294	1.3788

Source: CME Group; Chicago Mercantile Exchange

EURO / U.S. DOLLAR
Weekly Cash as of 01/03/2014

Date	Open	High	Low	Close
12/06/13	1.3597	1.3708	**1.3524**	1.3699
12/13/13	1.3706	1.3812	1.3693	1.3739
12/20/13	1.3739	1.3811	1.3624	1.3674
12/27/13	1.3675	**1.3895**	1.3656	1.3737
01/03/14	1.3753	1.3821	1.3585	1.3592

WEEKLY CASH
As of 01/03/2014
Chart High 1.6038 on 07/15/2008
Chart Low 1.0504 on 03/21/2003

Forex.

Quarterly High, Low and Settle of Euro FX   In USD per EUR

Quarter	High	Low	Settle	Quarter	High	Low	Settle	Quarter	High	Low	Settle
03/2005	1.3581	1.2732	1.2958	03/2008	1.5897	1.4368	1.5781	03/2011	1.4249	1.2868	1.4156
06/2005	1.3125	1.1981	1.2102	06/2008	1.6017	1.5286	1.5748	06/2011	1.4940	1.3971	1.4502
09/2005	1.2589	1.1868	1.2029	09/2008	1.6038	1.3884	1.4099	09/2011	1.4578	1.3363	1.3391
12/2005	1.2205	1.1641	1.1837	12/2008	1.4722	1.2333	1.3977	12/2011	1.4248	1.2858	1.2943
03/2006	1.2324	1.1802	1.2116	03/2009	1.4057	1.2456	1.3251	03/2012	1.3487	1.2622	1.3341
06/2006	1.2980	1.2035	1.2788	06/2009	1.4339	1.2887	1.4034	06/2012	1.3381	1.2288	1.2653
09/2006	1.2939	1.2457	1.2681	09/2009	1.4844	1.3832	1.4639	09/2012	1.3173	1.2043	1.2846
12/2006	1.3367	1.2484	1.3197	12/2009	1.5144	1.4218	1.4325	12/2012	1.3308	1.2661	1.3187
03/2007	1.3411	1.2868	1.3356	03/2010	1.4580	1.3267	1.3510	03/2013	1.3713	1.2748	1.2822
06/2007	1.3680	1.3264	1.3535	06/2010	1.3692	1.1877	1.2229	06/2013	1.3417	1.2747	1.3016
09/2007	1.4278	1.3360	1.4259	09/2010	1.3683	1.2195	1.3634	09/2013	1.3569	1.2759	1.3528
12/2007	1.4967	1.4016	1.4587	12/2010	1.4283	1.2969	1.3389	12/2013	1.3895	1.3301	1.3754

Source: Forex

JAPANESE YEN

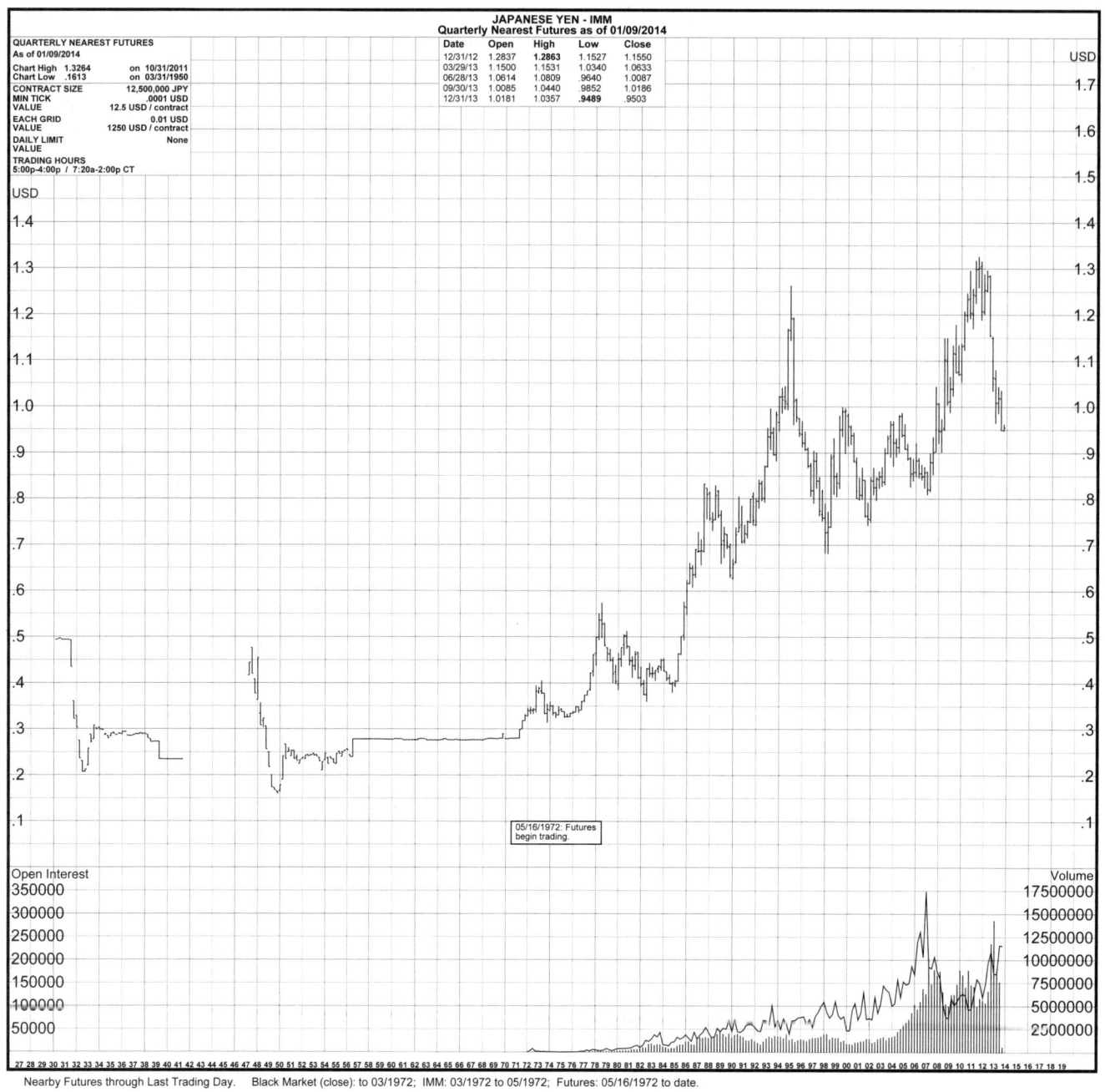

JAPANESE YEN - IMM
Quarterly Nearest Futures as of 01/09/2014

Date	Open	High	Low	Close
12/31/12	1.2837	**1.2863**	1.1527	1.1550
03/29/13	1.1500	1.1531	1.0340	1.0633
06/28/13	1.0614	1.0809	.9640	1.0087
09/30/13	1.0085	1.0440	.9852	1.0186
12/31/13	1.0181	1.0357	**.9489**	.9503

QUARTERLY NEAREST FUTURES
As of 01/09/2014

Chart High 1.3264	on 10/31/2011
Chart Low .1613	on 03/31/1950
CONTRACT SIZE	12,500,000 JPY
MIN TICK	.0001 USD
VALUE	12.5 USD / contract
EACH GRID	0.01 USD
VALUE	1250 USD / contract
DAILY LIMIT	None
VALUE	
TRADING HOURS	
5:00p-4:00p / 7:20a-2:00p CT	

05/16/1972: Futures begin trading.

Nearby Futures through Last Trading Day.   Black Market (close): to 03/1972; IMM: 03/1972 to 05/1972; Futures: 05/16/1972 to date.

Annual High, Low and Settle of Japanese Yen   In USD per JPY

Year	High	Low	Settle	Year	High	Low	Settle	Year	High	Low	Settle
1930	.4962	.4909	.4962	1944	----	----	----	1958	.2779	.2779	.2779
1931	.4944	.4346	.4346	1945	----	----	----	1959	.2779	.2776	.2776
1932	.3599	.2062	.2073	1946	----	----	----	1960	.2787	.2768	.2781
1933	.3074	.2074	.3074	1947	.4762	.4167	.4202	1961	.2786	.2762	.2762
1934	.3031	.2868	.2882	1948	.4545	.3030	.3226	1962	.2790	.2762	.2790
1935	.2932	.2798	.2874	1949	.3058	.1681	.1681	1963	.2789	.2755	.2756
1936	.2941	.2851	.2851	1950	.2667	.1613	.2353	1964	.2784	.2757	.2784
1937	.2909	.2849	.2908	1951	.2597	.2312	.2312	1965	.2786	.2759	.2769
1938	.2905	.2721	.2721	1952	.2439	.2247	.2410	1966	.2770	.2757	.2758
1939	.2730	.2344	.2344	1953	.2469	.2299	.2299	1967	.2763	.2758	.2763
1940	.2344	.2343	.2344	1954	.2469	.2105	.2358	1968	.2794	.2760	.2794
1941	.2344	.2344	.2344	1955	.2513	.2247	.2494	1969	.2795	.2781	.2795
1942	----	----	----	1956	.2779	.2392	.2779	1970	.2896	.2783	.2796
1943	----	----	----	1957	.2779	.2779	.2779	1971	.3175	.2790	.3175

Data continued on page 50.   *Source: Forex*

U.S. DOLLAR - JAPANESE YEN
Quarterly Cash as of 03/31/2014

Date	Open	High	Low	Close
12/31/12	77.930	86.780	**77.800**	86.780
03/29/13	86.680	96.730	86.560	94.220
06/28/13	94.200	103.700	92.590	99.150
09/30/13	99.230	101.540	95.790	98.210
12/31/13	98.290	**105.410**	96.560	105.330

QUARTERLY CASH
As of 03/31/2014

Chart High 620.000   on 03/31/1950
Chart Low   75.310   on 10/31/2011

Black Market (close): to 02/1972; IMM: 03/1972 to 02/1986; Forex: 02/14/1986 to date.

Annual High, Low and Settle of Japanese Yen   In JPY per USD

Year	High	Low	Settle	Year	High	Low	Settle	Year	High	Low	Settle
1930	203.71	201.53	201.53	1944	----	----	----	1958	359.84	359.84	359.84
1931	230.10	202.27	230.10	1945	365?	----	----	1959	360.23	359.84	360.23
1932	484.97	277.85	482.39	1946	----	----	----	1960	361.27	358.81	359.58
1933	482.16	325.31	325.31	1947	240.00	210.00	238.00	1961	362.06	358.94	362.06
1934	348.68	329.92	346.98	1948	330.00	220.00	310.00	1962	362.06	358.42	358.42
1935	357.40	341.06	347.95	1949	595.00	327.00	595.00	1963	362.98	358.55	362.84
1936	350.75	340.02	350.75	1950	620.00	375.00	425.00	1964	362.71	359.20	359.20
1937	351.00	343.76	343.88	1951	432.50	385.00	432.50	1965	362.45	358.94	361.14
1938	367.51	344.23	367.51	1952	445.00	410.00	415.00	1966	362.71	361.01	362.58
1939	426.62	366.30	426.62	1953	435.00	405.00	435.00	1967	362.58	361.93	361.93
1940	426.80	426.62	426.62	1954	475.00	405.00	424.00	1968	362.32	357.91	357.91
1941	426.62	426.62	426.62	1955	445.00	398.00	401.00	1969	359.58	357.78	357.78
1942	----	----	----	1956	418.00	359.84	359.84	1970	359.32	345.30	357.65
1943	----	----	----	1957	359.84	359.84	359.84	1971	379.00	313.00	313.00

Data continued on page 51.   *Source: Forex*

JAPANESE YEN

Nearby Futures through Last Trading Day.   Black Market (close): to 03/1972; IMM: 03/1972 to 05/1972; Futures: 05/16/1972 to date.

Annual High, Low and Settle of Japanese Yen Futures   In USD per JPY

Year	High	Low	Settle	Year	High	Low	Settle	Year	High	Low	Settle
1972	.3480	.3175	.3410	1986	.6608	.4922	.6354	2000	.9974	.8794	.8827
1973	.4055	.3320	.3329	1987	.8320	.6283	.8316	2001	.8907	.7600	.7629
1974	.3600	.3130	.3310	1988	.8288	.7296	.8069	2002	.8685	.7415	.8447
1975	.3503	.3240	.3260	1989	.8187	.6588	.6968	2003	.9384	.8220	.9318
1976	.3500	.3260	.3407	1990	.8046	.6254	.7384	2004	.9825	.8710	.9797
1977	.4228	.3406	.4216	1991	.7993	.7031	.7991	2005	.9873	.8252	.8551
1978	.5735	.4140	.5270	1992	.8419	.7402	.8004	2006	.9217	.8390	.8484
1979	.5306	.3995	.4197	1993	.9959	.7915	.8959	2007	.9350	.8087	.9013
1980	.5056	.3847	.5025	1994	1.0442	.8818	1.0108	2008	1.1492	.9013	1.1029
1981	.5128	.4115	.4624	1995	1.2625	.9601	.9773	2009	1.1790	.9867	1.0740
1982	.4669	.3596	.4315	1996	.9755	.8676	.8713	2010	1.2466	1.0532	1.2328
1983	.4438	.4048	.4371	1997	.9050	.7623	.7736	2011	1.3264	1.1697	1.3010
1984	.4543	.3984	.3987	1998	.8974	.6807	.8884	2012	1.3160	1.1527	1.1550
1985	.5018	.3794	.5004	1999	.9990	.8040	.9892	2013	1.1531	.9489	.9503

Futures begin trading 05/16/1972.   Data continued from page 48.   *Source: CME Group; Chicago Mercantile Exchange*

U.S. DOLLAR - JAPANESE YEN
Monthly Cash as of 12/31/2013

Date	Open	High	Low	Close
08/30/13	97.900	99.940	**95.790**	98.160
09/30/13	98.320	100.630	97.530	98.210
10/31/13	98.290	99.030	96.560	98.350
11/29/13	98.340	102.600	97.610	102.420
12/31/13	102.430	**105.410**	101.630	105.330

MONTHLY CASH
As of 12/31/2013
Chart High 321.000 on 01/31/1972
Chart Low 75.310 on 10/31/2011

Black Market (close): to 02/1972; IMM: 03/1972 to 02/1986; Forex: 02/14/1986 to date.

Annual High, Low and Settle of Japanese Yen   In JPY per USD

Year	High	Low	Settle	Year	High	Low	Settle	Year	High	Low	Settle
1972	321.00	294.12	301.75	1986	203.58	151.85	158.10	2000	115.05	101.36	114.34
1973	302.39	254.45	280.27	1987	159.75	120.90	121.10	2001	132.08	113.57	131.56
1974	304.88	273.97	301.11	1988	137.30	120.30	125.00	2002	135.14	115.54	118.79
1975	306.84	284.58	305.16	1989	151.90	123.20	143.95	2003	121.88	106.74	107.38
1976	306.00	285.96	292.83	1990	160.40	123.75	135.45	2004	114.89	101.83	102.43
1977	292.83	237.47	240.10	1991	142.10	124.79	124.84	2005	121.40	101.69	117.96
1978	243.90	176.30	194.14	1992	134.95	118.65	124.80	2006	119.87	108.98	119.03
1979	251.19	193.12	240.73	1993	126.21	100.40	111.83	2007	124.14	107.22	111.69
1980	261.85	201.98	203.00	1994	113.58	96.15	99.71	2008	112.04	87.14	90.66
1981	246.36	198.60	219.92	1995	104.65	79.78	103.46	2009	101.45	84.84	93.01
1982	278.70	217.20	234.85	1996	116.43	103.18	115.93	2010	94.99	80.21	81.20
1983	247.64	226.50	231.74	1997	131.58	110.63	130.20	2011	85.52	75.31	76.95
1984	251.95	221.04	251.95	1998	147.62	111.73	113.88	2012	86.78	76.03	86.78
1985	263.85	199.92	200.08	1999	124.78	101.30	102.18	2013	105.41	86.56	105.33

Data continued from page 49.   *Source: Forex*

JAPANESE YEN

JAPANESE YEN - IMM Weekly Nearest Futures as of 01/03/2014				
Date	Open	High	Low	Close
12/06/13	.9756	.9841	.9674	.9717
12/13/13	.9700	.9791	.9623	.9691
12/20/13	.9695	.9793	.9560	.9616
12/27/13	.9612	.9641	.9508	.9515
01/03/14	.9502	.9612	.9486	.9558

WEEKLY NEAREST FUTURES
As of 01/03/2014
Chart High 1.3264 on 10/31/2011
Chart Low .8087 on 06/15/2007
CONTRACT SIZE 12,500,000 JPY
MIN TICK .0001 USD
VALUE 12.5 USD / contract
EACH GRID 0.005 USD
VALUE 625 USD / contract
DAILY LIMIT None
VALUE
TRADING HOURS
5:00p-4:00p / 7:20a-2:00p CT

Commercial = 185186
NonCommercial= -143822
NonReportable = -41364

Nearby Futures through Last Trading Day.

Quarterly High, Low and Settle of Japanese Yen Futures   In USD per JPY

Quarter	High	Low	Settle	Quarter	High	Low	Settle	Quarter	High	Low	Settle
03/2005	.9873	.9343	.9383	03/2008	1.0440	.9022	1.0071	03/2011	1.2957	1.1909	1.2040
06/2005	.9629	.9074	.9092	06/2008	1.0086	.9209	.9471	06/2011	1.2570	1.1697	1.2433
09/2005	.9208	.8844	.8877	09/2008	.9740	.9013	.9498	09/2011	1.3173	1.2243	1.2987
12/2005	.8920	.8252	.8551	12/2008	1.1492	.9484	1.1029	12/2011	1.3264	1.2582	1.3010
03/2006	.8880	.8390	.8585	03/2009	1.1496	1.0032	1.0104	03/2012	1.3160	1.1879	1.2078
06/2006	.9217	.8487	.8832	06/2009	1.0657	.9867	1.0388	06/2012	1.2881	1.2011	1.2535
09/2006	.8901	.8454	.8559	09/2009	1.1341	1.0228	1.1162	09/2012	1.2967	1.2492	1.2832
12/2006	.8754	.8412	.8484	12/2009	1.1790	1.0738	1.0740	12/2012	1.2863	1.1527	1.1550
03/2007	.8701	.8229	.8575	03/2010	1.1346	1.0679	1.0703	03/2013	1.1531	1.0340	1.0633
06/2007	.8599	.8087	.8201	06/2010	1.1375	1.0532	1.1315	06/2013	1.0809	.9640	1.0087
09/2007	.8995	.8158	.8797	09/2010	1.2077	1.1225	1.2001	09/2013	1.0440	.9852	1.0186
12/2007	.9350	.8529	.9013	12/2010	1.2466	1.1838	1.2328	12/2013	1.0357	.9489	.9503

Source: CME Group; Chicago Mercantile Exchange

				US. DOLLAR - JAPANESE YEN				
				Weekly Cash as of 01/03/2014				
WEEKLY CASH				Date	Open	High	Low	Close
As of 01/03/2014				12/06/13	102.430	103.400	101.630	102.910
Chart High 124.140	on 06/22/2007			12/13/13	102.590	103.950	102.140	103.160
Chart Low 75.310	on 10/31/2011			12/20/13	103.220	104.620	102.500	104.040
				12/27/13	104.100	105.190	103.770	105.190
				01/03/14	105.130	105.410	104.100	104.800

Forex.

Quarterly High, Low and Settle of Japanese Yen   In JPY per USD

Quarter	High	Low	Settle	Quarter	High	Low	Settle	Quarter	High	Low	Settle
03/2005	107.70	101.69	107.22	03/2008	112.04	96.67	99.70	03/2011	83.98	76.26	83.16
06/2005	110.99	104.20	110.90	06/2008	108.59	99.60	106.19	06/2011	85.52	79.57	80.56
09/2005	113.72	108.78	113.47	09/2008	110.66	103.56	106.21	09/2011	81.49	75.95	77.11
12/2005	121.40	113.02	117.96	12/2008	106.54	87.14	90.66	12/2011	79.52	75.31	76.95
03/2006	119.40	113.44	117.69	03/2009	99.69	87.11	99.01	03/2012	84.17	76.03	82.85
06/2006	118.90	108.98	114.42	06/2009	101.45	93.86	96.35	06/2012	83.30	77.66	79.93
09/2006	118.28	113.47	118.15	09/2009	97.80	88.24	89.68	09/2012	80.10	77.13	78.01
12/2006	119.87	114.45	119.03	12/2009	93.15	84.84	93.01	12/2012	86.78	77.80	86.78
03/2007	122.19	115.16	117.85	03/2010	93.78	88.14	93.44	03/2013	96.73	86.56	94.22
06/2007	124.14	117.46	123.07	06/2010	94.99	88.25	88.43	06/2013	103.70	92.59	99.15
09/2007	123.68	111.64	114.87	09/2010	89.16	82.89	83.49	09/2013	101.54	95.79	98.21
12/2007	117.95	107.22	111.69	12/2010	84.51	80.21	81.20	12/2013	105.41	96.56	105.33

Source: Forex

MEXICAN PESO

MEXICAN PESO - IMM
Monthly Selected Futures as of 12/31/2013

MONTHLY SELECTED FUTURES
As of 12/31/2013

Chart High 32.2373   on 11/22/1993
Chart Low   6.3900   on 03/09/2009

Date	Open	High	Low	Close
08/31/13	7.8150	7.9450	7.4550	7.4700
09/30/13	7.4875	7.8925	7.4175	7.5675
10/31/13	7.5975	7.8100	7.4500	7.6600
11/30/13	7.6500	7.7625	7.4775	7.6100
12/31/13	7.6150	7.8075	7.5300	7.5925

CONTRACT SIZE 500,000 MXN
MIN TICK .0025 USD
VALUE 12.5 USD/CONTRACT
EACH GRID 0.2 USD
VALUE 1000 USD/CONTRACT
DAILY LIMIT None
VALUE
TRADING HOURS
5:00p-4:00p / 7:20a-2:00p CT

04/25/1995: Futures begin trading.

Nearby Futures through Last Trading Day.   Forex: 07/1994 to 03/1995; Futures: 04/25/1995 to date.

Annual High, Low and Settle of Mexican Peso Futures   In USD per MXN

Year	High	Low	Settle	Year	High	Low	Settle	Year	High	Low	Settle
1972	----	----	----	1986	----	----	----	2000	10.8600	9.5700	10.1275
1973	----	----	----	1987	----	----	----	2001	11.1400	9.7400	10.7825
1974	----	----	----	1988	----	----	----	2002	11.0300	9.3600	9.4925
1975	----	----	----	1989	----	----	----	2003	9.8800	8.6650	8.8300
1976	----	----	----	1990	----	----	----	2004	9.2350	8.4600	8.8575
1977	----	----	----	1991	----	----	----	2005	9.6025	8.6425	9.3475
1978	----	----	----	1992	----	----	----	2006	9.5775	8.6300	9.2200
1979	----	----	----	1993	32.2373	30.8642	32.1750	2007	9.3750	8.8075	9.1075
1980	----	----	----	1994	32.2061	17.4978	20.4708	2008	10.0950	6.8500	7.0300
1981	----	----	----	1995	20.0803	11.4000	11.9800	2009	8.0050	6.3900	7.5775
1982	----	----	----	1996	13.4000	11.9100	12.1350	2010	8.2000	7.0675	8.0575
1983	----	----	----	1997	12.8800	10.3000	12.0600	2011	8.6750	6.9725	7.1350
1984	----	----	----	1998	12.1400	8.7500	9.6100	2012	7.9650	6.8375	7.6825
1985	----	----	----	1999	10.7400	7.5000	10.2900	2013	8.3525	7.3725	7.5925

Futures begin trading 04/25/1995.   *Source: CME Group; Chicago Mercantile Exchange*

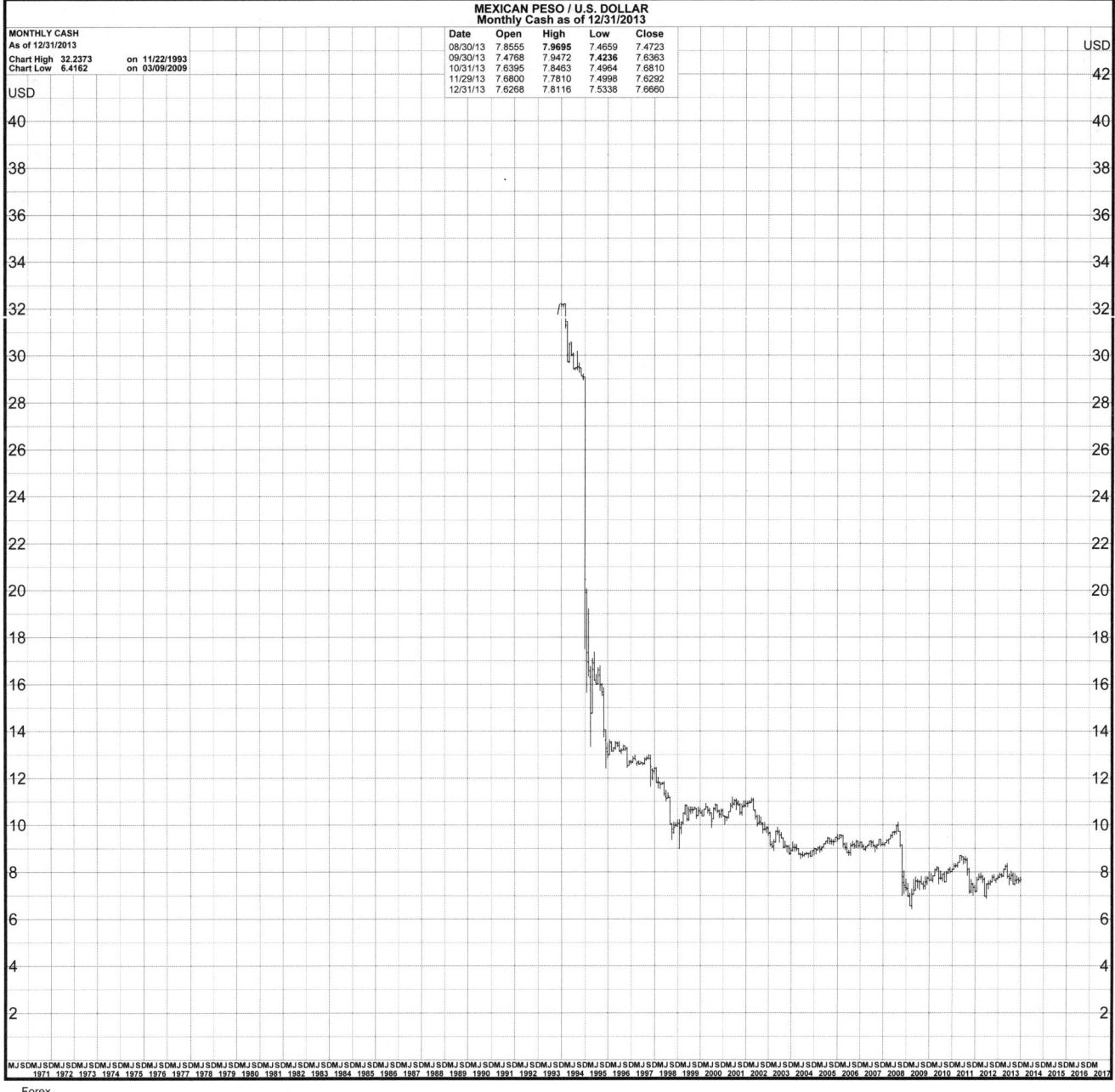

MEXICAN PESO / U.S. DOLLAR Monthly Cash as of 12/31/2013				
Date	Open	High	Low	Close
08/30/13	7.8555	7.9695	7.4659	7.4723
09/30/13	7.4768	7.9472	7.4236	7.6363
10/31/13	7.6395	7.8463	7.4964	7.6810
11/29/13	7.6800	7.7810	7.4998	7.6292
12/31/13	7.6268	7.8116	7.5338	7.6660

MONTHLY CASH
As of 12/31/2013
Chart High 32.2373 on 11/22/1993
Chart Low 6.4162 on 03/09/2009

Forex.

Annual High, Low and Settle of Mexican Peso   In USD per MXN

Year	High	Low	Settle	Year	High	Low	Settle	Year	High	Low	Settle
1972	----	----	----	1986	----	----	----	2000	10.9390	9.8570	10.3950
1973	----	----	----	1987	----	----	----	2001	11.2110	10.0050	10.9200
1974	----	----	----	1988	----	----	----	2002	11.1669	9.5279	9.6339
1975	----	----	----	1989	----	----	----	2003	9.9162	8.7276	8.9049
1976	----	----	----	1990	----	----	----	2004	9.2878	8.5417	8.9804
1977	----	----	----	1991	----	----	----	2005	9.6167	8.7443	9.4091
1978	----	----	----	1992		----	----	2006	9.5938	8.6818	9.2535
1979	----	----	----	1993	32.2373	30.8642	32.1750	2007	9.3995	8.8276	9.1651
1980	----	----	----	1994	32.2061	17.4978	20.4708	2008	10.1451	6.9959	7.3125
1981	----	----	----	1995	20.0803	12.4069	13.0039	2009	8.0081	6.4162	7.6400
1982	----	----	----	1996	13.6426	12.4224	12.6968	2010	8.2440	7.4714	8.1050
1983	----	----	----	1997	12.9870	11.6279	12.4069	2011	8.7107	6.9890	7.1698
1984	----	----	----	1998	12.4688	9.3589	10.0650	2012	7.9675	6.8485	7.7787
1985	----	----	----	1999	10.8640	8.9710	10.5290	2013	8.3783	7.4236	7.6660

Source: Forex

MEXICAN PESO

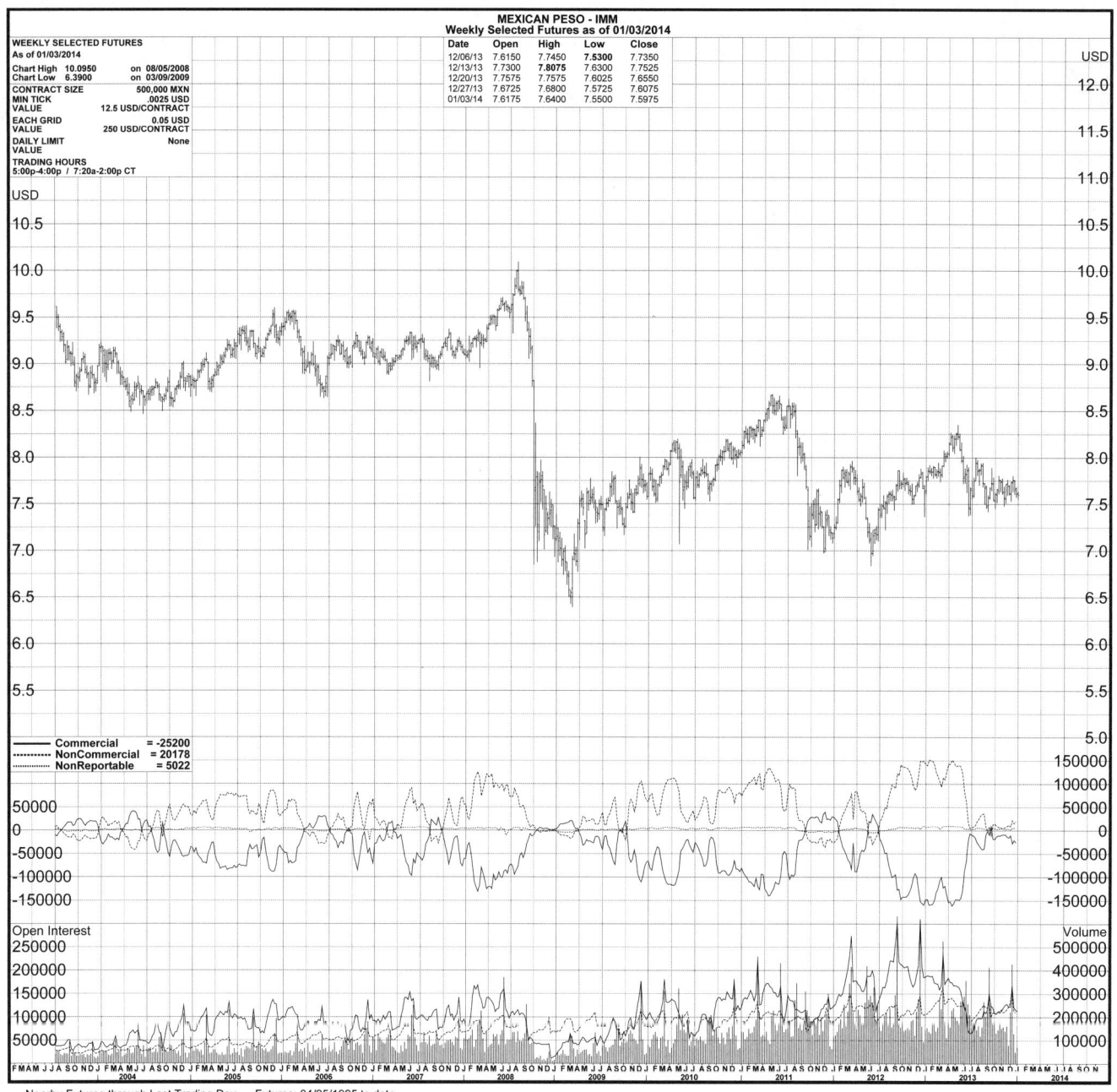

Nearby Futures through Last Trading Day.   Futures: 04/25/1995 to date.

Quarterly High, Low and Settle of Mexican Peso Futures   In USD per MXN

Quarter	High	Low	Settle	Quarter	High	Low	Settle	Quarter	High	Low	Settle
03/2005	9.1200	8.6425	8.8300	03/2008	9.3725	8.9500	9.3050	03/2011	8.4075	8.0375	8.3575
06/2005	9.2650	8.7400	9.1700	06/2008	9.7150	9.3050	9.5950	06/2011	8.6750	8.2475	8.4825
09/2005	9.4125	9.0450	9.1850	09/2008	10.0950	8.9500	9.0775	09/2011	8.6250	7.0100	7.1600
12/2005	9.6025	9.0150	9.3475	12/2008	9.0925	6.8500	7.0300	12/2011	7.6650	6.9725	7.1350
03/2006	9.5775	8.8900	9.1225	03/2009	7.3925	6.3900	6.9775	03/2012	7.9650	7.1350	7.7500
06/2006	9.2400	8.6300	8.7900	06/2009	7.7725	6.9525	7.5225	06/2012	7.8200	6.8375	7.4375
09/2006	9.3050	8.6375	9.0700	09/2009	7.8500	7.1550	7.3275	09/2012	7.8650	7.2175	7.7150
12/2006	9.3425	8.9525	9.2200	12/2009	8.0050	7.1650	7.5775	12/2012	7.8825	7.3625	7.6825
03/2007	9.2750	8.8775	9.0225	03/2010	8.0800	7.5100	8.0350	03/2013	8.0800	7.7325	8.0400
06/2007	9.3450	9.0125	9.2175	06/2010	8.2000	7.0675	7.6900	06/2013	8.3525	7.3725	7.6675
09/2007	9.3200	8.8075	9.1000	09/2010	7.9900	7.5275	7.8925	09/2013	8.0050	7.4175	7.5675
12/2007	9.3750	9.0525	9.1075	12/2010	8.2000	7.8675	8.0575	12/2013	7.8100	7.4500	7.5925

Source: CME Group; Chicago Mercantile Exchange

MEXICAN PESO / U.S. DOLLAR
Weekly Cash as of 01/03/2014

Date	Open	High	Low	Close
12/06/13	7.6268	7.7538	7.5338	7.7278
12/13/13	7.7377	7.8116	7.6328	7.7605
12/20/13	7.7669	7.7934	7.6474	7.7072
12/27/13	7.7169	7.7229	7.6135	7.6625
01/03/14	7.6689	7.6840	7.5947	7.6301

WEEKLY CASH
As of 01/03/2014

Chart High 10.1451 on 08/04/2008
Chart Low 6.4162 on 03/09/2009

Forex.

Quarterly High, Low and Settle of Mexican Peso   In USD per MXN

Quarter	High	Low	Settle	Quarter	High	Low	Settle	Quarter	High	Low	Settle
03/2005	9.1226	8.7443	8.9526	03/2008	9.4082	9.0742	9.3960	03/2011	8.4251	8.0794	8.4011
06/2005	9.3190	8.8684	9.3046	06/2008	9.7477	9.3942	9.6989	06/2011	8.7107	8.3215	8.5350
09/2005	9.4882	9.1611	9.2920	09/2008	10.1451	9.0481	9.1418	09/2011	8.6758	7.0722	7.1956
12/2005	9.6167	9.1124	9.4091	12/2008	9.1728	6.9959	7.3125	12/2011	7.6943	6.9890	7.1698
03/2006	9.5938	9.0342	9.1896	03/2009	7.5286	6.4162	7.0528	03/2012	7.9675	7.1454	7.8077
06/2006	9.2561	8.6818	8.8183	06/2009	7.7993	7.0439	7.5789	06/2012	7.8749	6.8485	7.4758
09/2006	9.3165	8.6843	9.1027	09/2009	7.8317	7.2228	7.4015	09/2012	7.8681	7.2581	7.7698
12/2006	9.3615	8.9931	9.2535	12/2009	8.0081	7.2395	7.6400	12/2012	7.8981	7.5202	7.7787
03/2007	9.2985	8.8840	9.0564	03/2010	8.1356	7.5456	8.0871	03/2013	8.1256	7.7401	8.1206
06/2007	9.3489	9.0381	9.2527	06/2010	8.2440	7.4714	7.7331	06/2013	8.3783	7.4290	7.7182
09/2007	9.3475	8.8276	9.1443	09/2010	8.0394	7.5405	7.9445	09/2013	8.0458	7.4236	7.6363
12/2007	9.3995	9.0659	9.1651	12/2010	8.2153	7.9191	8.1050	12/2013	7.8463	7.4964	7.6660

Source: Forex

SWISS FRANC

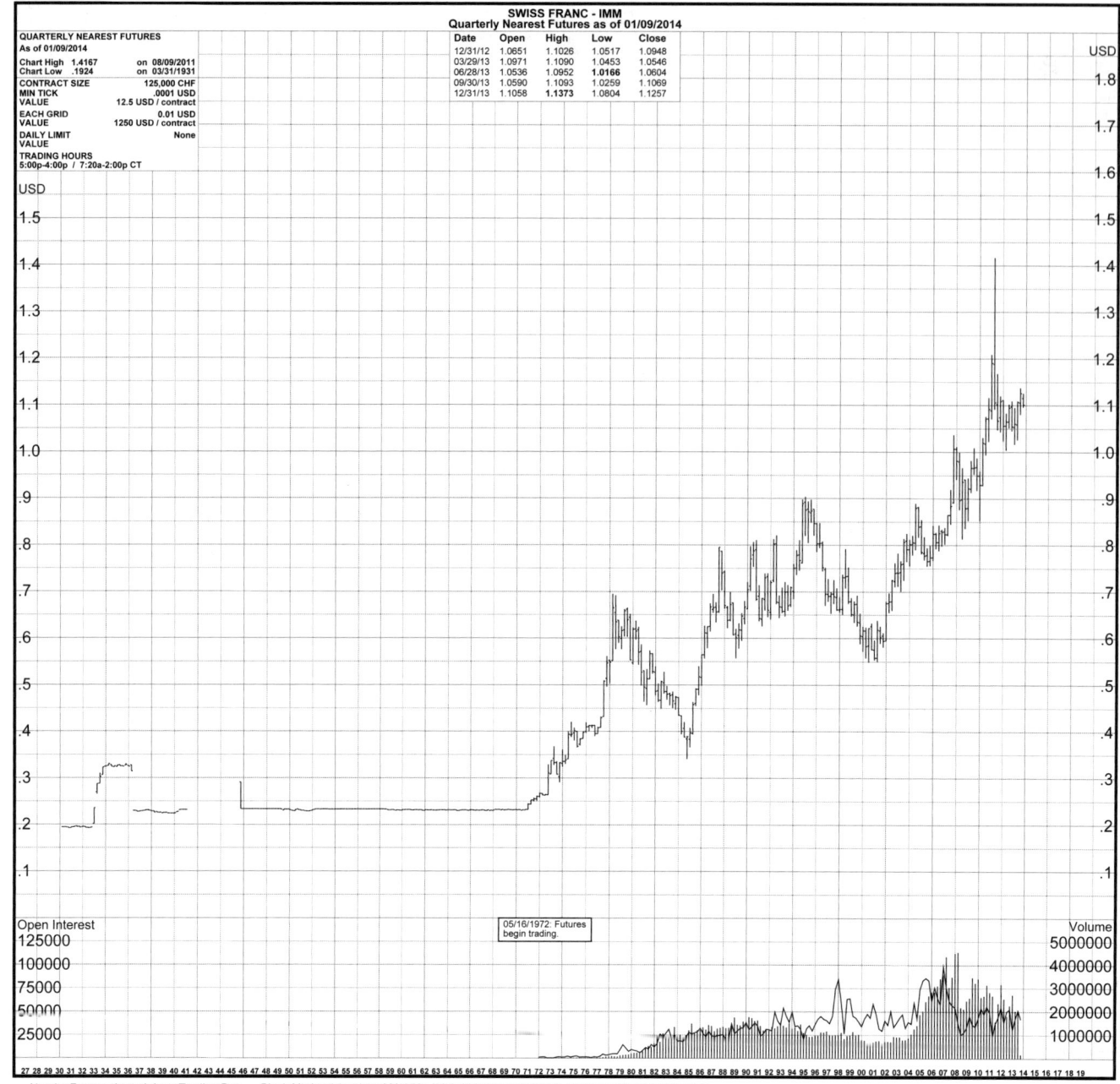

Annual High, Low and Settle of Swiss Franc   In USD per CHF

Year	High	Low	Settle	Year	High	Low	Settle	Year	High	Low	Settle
1930	.1944	.1929	.1940	1944	----	----	----	1958	.2334	.2330	.2332
1931	.1960	.1924	.1948	1945	----	----	----	1959	.2320	.2304	.2313
1932	.1951	.1924	.1924	1946	.2907	.2336	.2336	1960	.2323	.2305	.2323
1933	.3102	.1928	.3025	1947	.2336	.2336	.2336	1961	.2322	.2310	.2317
1934	.3302	.3064	.3241	1948	.2336	.2336	.2336	1962	.2317	.2301	.2317
1935	.3275	.3231	.3243	1949	.2336	.2308	.2329	1963	.2317	.2310	.2317
1936	.3303	.2298	.2298	1950	.2329	.2294	.2320	1964	.2317	.2311	.2317
1937	.2315	.2279	.2312	1951	.2330	.2288	.2290	1965	.2316	.2300	.2316
1938	.2323	.2260	.2261	1952	.2333	.2288	.2333	1966	.2317	.2304	.2313
1939	.2267	.2242	.2242	1953	.2333	.2325	.2329	1967	.2317	.2303	.2316
1940	.2320	.2225	.2320	1954	.2333	.2331	.2333	1968	.2327	.2299	.2326
1941	.2322	.2320	.2321	1955	.2334	.2332	.2334	1969	.2327	.2312	.2320
1942	----	----	----	1956	.2334	.2333	.2334	1970	.2326	.2309	.2319
1943	----	----	----	1957	.2334	.2331	.2334	1971	.2580	.2316	.2554

Data continued on page 60.   *Source: Forex*

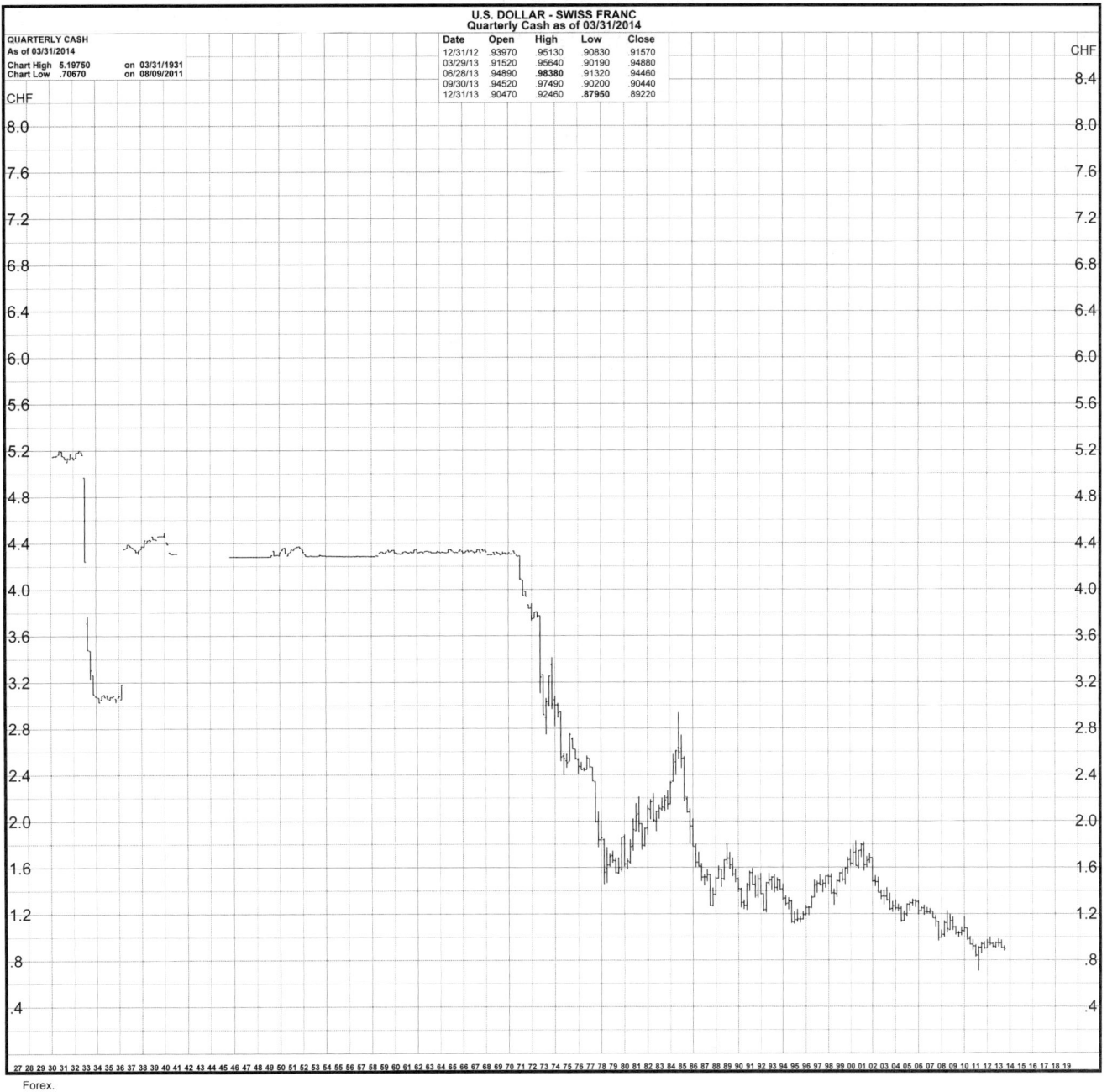

U.S. DOLLAR - SWISS FRANC Quarterly Cash as of 03/31/2014				
Date	Open	High	Low	Close
12/31/12	.93970	.95130	.90830	.91570
03/29/13	.91520	.95640	.90190	.94880
06/28/13	.94890	.98380	.91320	.94460
09/30/13	.94520	.97490	.90200	.90440
12/31/13	.90470	.92460	.87950	.89220

QUARTERLY CASH
As of 03/31/2014
Chart High 5.19750   on 03/31/1931
Chart Low   .70670   on 08/09/2011

Forex.

Annual High, Low and Settle of Swiss Franc   In CHF per USD

Year	High	Low	Settle	Year	High	Low	Settle	Year	High	Low	Settle
1930	5.1840	5.1440	5.1546	1944	----	----	----	1958	4.2918	4.2845	4.2882
1931	5.1975	5.1020	5.1335	1945	----	----	----	1959	4.3403	4.3103	4.3234
1932	5.1975	5.1256	5.1975	1946	4.2808	3.4400	4.2808	1960	4.3384	4.3048	4.3048
1933	5.1867	3.2237	3.3058	1947	4.2808	4.2808	4.2808	1961	4.3290	4.3066	4.3159
1934	3.2637	3.0285	3.0855	1948	4.2808	4.2808	4.2808	1962	4.3459	4.3159	4.3159
1935	3.0950	3.0534	3.0836	1949	4.3328	4.2808	4.2937	1963	4.3290	4.3159	4.3159
1936	4.3516	3.0276	4.3516	1950	4.3592	4.2937	4.3103	1964	4.3271	4.3159	4.3159
1937	4.3879	4.3197	4.3253	1951	4.3706	4.2918	4.3668	1965	4.3478	4.3178	4.3178
1938	4.4248	4.3048	4.4228	1952	4.3706	4.2863	4.2863	1966	4.3403	4.3159	4.3234
1939	4.4603	4.4111	4.4603	1953	4.3011	4.2863	4.2937	1967	4.3422	4.3159	4.3178
1940	4.4944	4.3103	4.3103	1954	4.2900	4.2863	4.2863	1968	4.3497	4.2974	4.2992
1941	4.3103	4.3066	4.3085	1955	4.2882	4.2845	4.2845	1969	4.3253	4.2974	4.3103
1942	----	----	----	1956	4.2863	4.2845	4.2845	1970	4.3309	4.2992	4.3122
1943	----	----	----	1957	4.2900	4.2845	4.2845	1971	4.2950	3.9400	3.9400

Data continued on page 61.   *Source: Forex*

SWISS FRANC

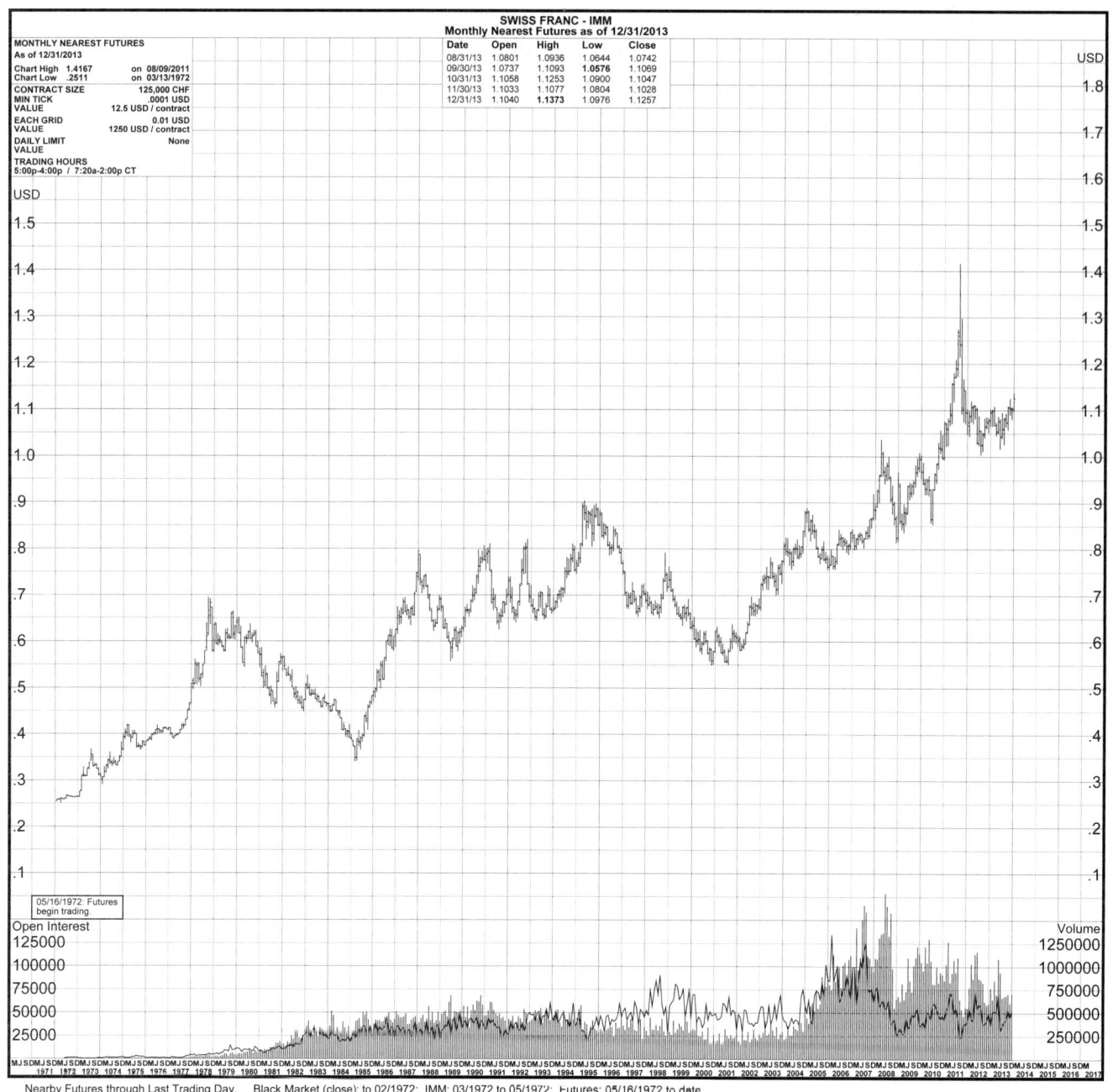

SWISS FRANC - IMM
Monthly Nearest Futures as of 12/31/2013

Date	Open	High	Low	Close
08/31/13	1.0801	1.0936	1.0644	1.0742
09/30/13	1.0737	1.1093	1.0576	1.1069
10/31/13	1.1058	1.1253	1.0900	1.1047
11/30/13	1.1033	1.1077	1.0804	1.1028
12/31/13	1.1040	**1.1373**	1.0976	1.1257

MONTHLY NEAREST FUTURES
As of 12/31/2013

Chart High 1.4167 on 08/09/2011
Chart Low .2511 on 03/13/1972

CONTRACT SIZE 125,000 CHF
MIN TICK .0001 USD
VALUE 12.5 USD / contract
EACH GRID 0.01 USD
VALUE 1250 USD / contract
DAILY LIMIT None
VALUE
TRADING HOURS
5:00p-4:00p / 7:20a-2:00p CT

05/16/1972: Futures begin trading.

Nearby Futures through Last Trading Day.   Black Market (close): to 02/1972; IMM: 03/1972 to 05/1972; Futures: 05/16/1972 to date.

Annual High, Low and Settle of Swiss Franc Futures   In USD per CHF

Year	High	Low	Settle	Year	High	Low	Settle	Year	High	Low	Settle
1972	.2685	.2511	.2644	1986	.6268	.4779	.6247	2000	.6536	.5488	.6217
1973	.3676	.2642	.3078	1987	.7955	.6144	.7950	2001	.6382	.5492	.6020
1974	.3993	.2908	.3935	1988	.7877	.6215	.6728	2002	.7265	.5808	.7249
1975	.4202	.3652	.3838	1989	.6773	.5569	.6474	2003	.8138	.7010	.8066
1976	.4189	.3843	.4122	1990	.8068	.6296	.7875	2004	.8892	.7554	.8796
1977	.5094	.3895	.5079	1991	.8108	.6254	.7300	2005	.8826	.7548	.7656
1978	.6951	.4961	.6347	1992	.8209	.6405	.6781	2006	.8428	.7560	.8254
1979	.6648	.5764	.6394	1993	.7212	.6436	.6702	2007	.9200	.7979	.8838
1980	.6516	.5430	.5697	1994	.8108	.6680	.7673	2008	1.0367	.8134	.9364
1981	.5865	.4566	.5668	1995	.9038	.7616	.8731	2009	1.0090	.8356	.9669
1982	.5675	.4486	.5070	1996	.8772	.7439	.7520	2010	1.0762	.8527	1.0714
1983	.5280	.4507	.4658	1997	.7520	.6529	.6897	2011	1.4167	1.0225	1.0670
1984	.4763	.3870	.3879	1998	.7920	.6503	.7331	2012	1.1200	1.0040	1.0948
1985	.4928	.3408	.4908	1999	.7525	.6258	.6347	2013	1.1373	1.0166	1.1257

Futures begin trading 05/16/1972.   Data continued from page 58.   *Source: CME Group; Chicago Mercantile Exchange*

U.S. DOLLAR - SWISS FRANC Monthly Cash as of 12/31/2013				
Date	Open	High	Low	Close
08/30/13	.92590	.93990	.91500	.93070
09/30/13	.93160	.94570	.90200	.90440
10/31/13	.90470	.91770	.88910	.90670
11/29/13	.90700	.92460	.90240	.90640
12/31/13	.90520	.91120	.87950	.89220

MONTHLY CASH
As of 12/31/2013
Chart High 3.94000 on 12/31/1971
Chart Low .70670 on 08/09/2011

Black Market (close): to 02/1972; IMM: 03/1972 to 02/1986; Forex: 02/14/1986 to date.

Annual High, Low and Settle of Swiss Franc   In CHF per USD

Year	High	Low	Settle	Year	High	Low	Settle	Year	High	Low	Settle
1972	3.8775	3.7286	3.7693	1986	2.1097	1.6025	1.6090	2000	1.8300	1.5427	1.6140
1973	3.7707	2.7473	3.2531	1987	1.6360	1.2695	1.2700	2001	1.8219	1.5680	1.6585
1974	3.4153	2.5157	2.5523	1988	1.6155	1.2630	1.5010	2002	1.7225	1.3810	1.3835
1975	2.7563	2.3981	2.6212	1989	1.8090	1.4870	1.5410	2003	1.4274	1.2310	1.2398
1976	2.6192	2.4050	2.4456	1990	1.5895	1.2395	1.2720	2004	1.3227	1.1285	1.1398
1977	2.5654	1.9861	1.9940	1991	1.5936	1.2319	1.3585	2005	1.3286	1.1369	1.3139
1978	2.0833	1.4550	1.6200	1992	1.5496	1.2105	1.4665	2006	1.3239	1.1881	1.2192
1979	1.7437	1.5451	1.5987	1993	1.5520	1.3823	1.4883	2007	1.2572	1.0889	1.1338
1980	1.8801	1.5637	1.7771	1994	1.4950	1.2363	1.3088	2008	1.2297	.9647	1.0708
1981	2.2123	1.7421	1.7901	1995	1.3188	1.1123	1.1534	2009	1.1965	.9919	1.0356
1982	2.2416	1.7790	2.0092	1996	1.3538	1.1490	1.3413	2010	1.1730	.9302	.9346
1983	2.2212	1.9113	2.1815	1997	1.5387	1.3398	1.4616	2011	.9785	.7067	.9379
1984	2.6102	2.1003	2.6068	1998	1.5470	1.2747	1.3751	2012	.9973	.8931	.9157
1985	2.9385	2.0712	2.0777	1999	1.6021	1.3404	1.5913	2013	.9838	.8795	.8922

Data continued from page 59.   Source: Forex

SWISS FRANC

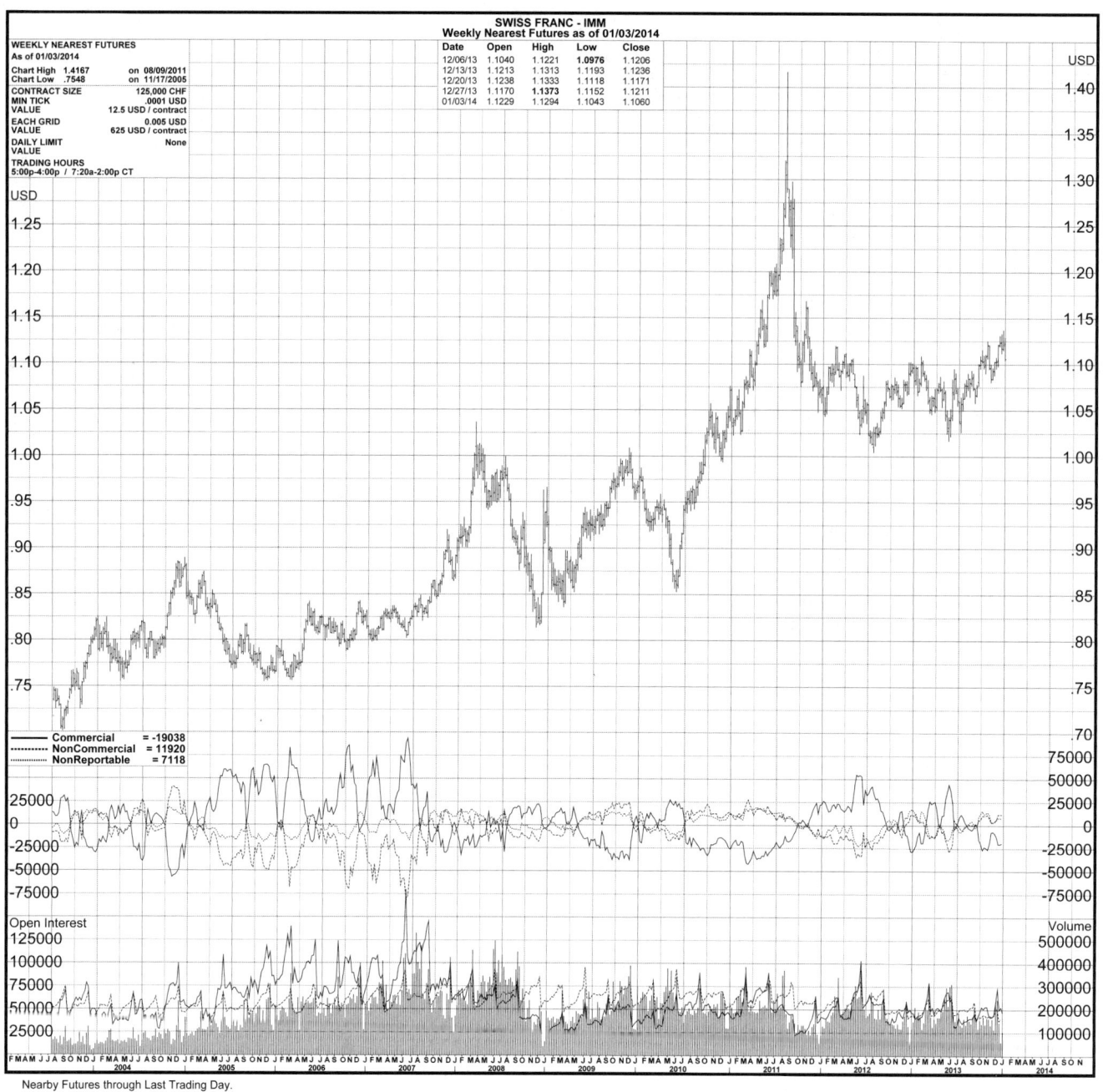

Nearby Futures through Last Trading Day.

Quarterly High, Low and Settle of Swiss Franc Futures   In USD per CHF

Quarter	High	Low	Settle	Quarter	High	Low	Settle	Quarter	High	Low	Settle
03/2005	.8826	.8169	.8395	03/2008	1.0367	.8902	1.0066	03/2011	1.1163	1.0225	1.0918
06/2005	.8543	.7813	.7850	06/2008	1.0116	.9410	.9810	06/2011	1.2091	1.0710	1.1907
09/2005	.8178	.7680	.7772	09/2008	.9993	.8758	.8963	09/2011	1.4167	1.0916	1.1061
12/2005	.7943	.7548	.7656	12/2008	.9665	.8134	.9364	12/2011	1.1682	1.0474	1.0670
03/2006	.8001	.7560	.7735	03/2009	.9420	.8356	.8789	03/2012	1.1200	1.0431	1.1086
06/2006	.8421	.7672	.8241	06/2009	.9443	.8523	.9220	06/2012	1.1119	1.0235	1.0561
09/2006	.8270	.7923	.8060	09/2009	.9819	.9135	.9660	09/2012	1.0831	1.0040	1.0649
12/2006	.8428	.7879	.8254	12/2009	1.0090	.9522	.9669	12/2012	1.1026	1.0517	1.0948
03/2007	.8340	.7979	.8283	03/2010	.9875	.9176	.9493	03/2013	1.1090	1.0453	1.0546
06/2007	.8375	.8020	.8232	06/2010	.9590	.8527	.9295	06/2013	1.0952	1.0166	1.0604
09/2007	.8650	.8205	.8645	09/2010	1.0309	.9281	1.0195	09/2013	1.1093	1.0259	1.1069
12/2007	.9200	.8447	.8838	12/2010	1.0762	.9935	1.0714	12/2013	1.1373	1.0804	1.1257

Source: CME Group; Chicago Mercantile Exchange

U.S. DOLLAR - SWISS FRANC
Weekly Cash as of 01/03/2014

Date	Open	High	Low	Close
12/06/13	.90520	.91120	.89150	.89330
12/13/13	.89210	.89330	.88410	.88980
12/20/13	.88940	.90020	.88320	.89560
12/27/13	.89600	.89720	.87950	.89230
01/03/14	.89170	.90560	.88590	.90510

WEEKLY CASH
As of 01/03/2014
Chart High 1.42740 on 08/26/2003
Chart Low .70670 on 08/09/2011

Forex.

Quarterly High, Low and Settle of Swiss Franc   In CHF per USD

Quarter	High	Low	Settle	Quarter	High	Low	Settle	Quarter	High	Low	Settle
03/2005	1.2262	1.1369	1.1966	03/2008	1.1333	.9647	.9937	03/2011	.9785	.8851	.9195
06/2005	1.2877	1.1739	1.2815	06/2008	1.0622	.9889	1.0215	06/2011	.9339	.8276	.8403
09/2005	1.3081	1.2241	1.2936	09/2008	1.1417	1.0015	1.1224	09/2011	.9185	.7067	.9069
12/2005	1.3286	1.2674	1.3139	12/2008	1.2297	1.0369	1.0708	12/2011	.9549	.8570	.9379
03/2006	1.3239	1.2558	1.3043	03/2009	1.1965	1.0609	1.1394	03/2012	.9596	.8931	.9026
06/2006	1.3137	1.1921	1.2233	06/2009	1.1743	1.0592	1.0861	06/2012	.9772	.9002	.9496
09/2006	1.2622	1.2184	1.2506	09/2009	1.0955	1.0189	1.0363	09/2012	.9973	.9239	.9409
12/2006	1.2770	1.1881	1.2192	12/2009	1.0508	.9919	1.0356	12/2012	.9513	.9083	.9157
03/2007	1.2572	1.2031	1.2152	03/2010	1.0899	1.0132	1.0541	03/2013	.9564	.9019	.9488
06/2007	1.2469	1.1996	1.2214	06/2010	1.1730	1.0435	1.0780	06/2013	.9838	.9132	.9446
09/2007	1.2233	1.1627	1.1638	09/2010	1.0791	.9709	.9827	09/2013	.9749	.9020	.9044
12/2007	1.1894	1.0889	1.1338	12/2010	1.0067	.9302	.9346	12/2013	.9246	.8795	.8922

Source: Forex

EURO / SWISS FRANC

EURO / SWISS FRANC
Monthly Cash as of 12/31/2013

MONTHLY CASH
As of 12/31/2013

Chart High 2.4801 on 10/31/1973
Chart Low 1.0074 on 08/09/2011

Date	Open	High	Low	Close
08/30/13	1.2320	**1.2432**	1.2267	1.2301
09/30/13	1.2313	1.2416	1.2215	1.2235
10/31/13	1.2239	1.2376	1.2217	1.2318
11/29/13	1.2318	1.2352	1.2283	1.2316
12/31/13	1.2315	1.2324	**1.2168**	1.2276

Black Market (close): to 02/1972; IMM: 03/1972 to 02/1986; Forex: 02/14/1986 to date.

Annual High, Low and Settle of Euro / Swiss Franc   In CHF per EUR

Year	High	Low	Settle	Year	High	Low	Settle	Year	High	Low	Settle
1972	2.3775	2.2919	2.3030	1986	1.7041	1.5353	1.6390	2000	1.6174	1.4942	1.5210
1973	2.4801	2.1494	2.3530	1987	1.7174	1.5582	1.5816	2001	1.5480	1.4399	1.4780
1974	2.3744	2.0359	2.0691	1988	1.6870	1.5381	1.6576	2002	1.4882	1.4442	1.4503
1975	2.1221	1.9545	1.9573	1989	1.8126	1.6274	1.7823	2003	1.5748	1.4484	1.5605
1976	2.0326	1.8155	2.0291	1990	1.8535	1.5685	1.6674	2004	1.5867	1.5037	1.5463
1977	2.0994	1.8386	1.8584	1991	1.7820	1.5959	1.7504	2005	1.5661	1.5295	1.5555
1978	1.9746	1.4547	1.7413	1992	1.8398	1.6420	1.7705	2006	1.6105	1.5407	1.6090
1979	1.8566	1.7212	1.8110	1993	1.8547	1.6264	1.6736	2007	1.6828	1.5933	1.6538
1980	1.8928	1.6928	1.7709	1994	1.6997	1.5963	1.6522	2008	1.6557	1.4314	1.4947
1981	1.8404	1.5261	1.5636	1995	1.7085	1.5086	1.5709	2009	1.5449	1.4578	1.4832
1982	1.7023	1.5244	1.6517	1996	1.7098	1.5518	1.7080	2010	1.4890	1.2401	1.2509
1983	1.7130	1.5440	1.5642	1997	1.7258	1.5795	1.5966	2011	1.3243	1.0074	1.2153
1984	1.6891	1.5323	1.6152	1998	1.6675	1.5489	1.6218	2012	1.2199	1.1996	1.2079
1985	1.7072	1.5590	1.6425	1999	1.6302	1.5783	1.5998	2013	1.2647	1.2070	1.2276

Source: Forex

EURO / SWISS FRANC

Forex.

Quarterly High, Low and Settle of Euro / Swiss Franc   In CHF per EUR

Quarter	High	Low	Settle	Quarter	High	Low	Settle	Quarter	High	Low	Settle
03/2005	1.5634	1.5344	1.5504	03/2008	1.6557	1.5333	1.5684	03/2011	1.3204	1.2415	1.3017
06/2005	1.5574	1.5295	1.5509	06/2008	1.6377	1.5665	1.6087	06/2011	1.3243	1.1811	1.2188
09/2005	1.5661	1.5400	1.5559	09/2008	1.6369	1.5666	1.5819	09/2011	1.2345	1.0074	1.2144
12/2005	1.5653	1.5354	1.5555	12/2008	1.5881	1.4314	1.4947	12/2011	1.2474	1.2123	1.2153
03/2006	1.5821	1.5407	1.5803	03/2009	1.5449	1.4578	1.5102	03/2012	1.2199	1.2032	1.2042
06/2006	1.5858	1.5452	1.5645	06/2009	1.5378	1.5008	1.5243	06/2012	1.2076	1.1996	1.2013
09/2006	1.5967	1.5591	1.5859	09/2009	1.5365	1.5077	1.5169	09/2012	1.2185	1.2005	1.2084
12/2006	1.6105	1.5811	1.6090	12/2009	1.5204	1.4820	1.4832	12/2012	1.2169	1.2030	1.2079
03/2007	1.6290	1.5933	1.6230	03/2010	1.4890	1.4210	1.4239	03/2013	1.2573	1.2070	1.2168
06/2007	1.6673	1.6210	1.6533	06/2010	1.4588	1.3165	1.3185	06/2013	1.2647	1.2129	1.2295
09/2007	1.6689	1.6179	1.6598	09/2010	1.3923	1.2767	1.3399	09/2013	1.2464	1.2215	1.2235
12/2007	1.6828	1.6300	1.6538	12/2010	1.3834	1.2401	1.2509	12/2013	1.2376	1.2168	1.2276

Source: Forex

65

EURO / BRITISH POUND

EURO / BRITISH POUND Monthly Cash as of 12/31/2013				
Date	Open	High	Low	Close
08/30/13	.87481	.87699	.85040	.85325
09/30/13	.85292	.85311	.83390	.83557
10/31/13	.83564	.85864	.83324	.84745
11/29/13	.84686	.84770	.82965	.83056
12/31/13	.83087	.84698	.82516	.83033

MONTHLY CASH
As of 12/31/2013
Chart High .98020   on 12/29/2008
Chart Low   .23465   on 04/19/1972

Black Market (close): to 02/1972; IMM: 03/1972 to 02/1986; Forex: 02/14/1986 to date.

Annual High, Low and Settle of Euro / British Pound   In GBP per EUR

Year	High	Low	Settle	Year	High	Low	Settle	Year	High	Low	Settle
1972	.2619	.2347	.2602	1986	.6934	.5478	.6853	2000	.6415	.5685	.6309
1973	.3446	.2587	.3115	1987	.7130	.6487	.6600	2001	.6444	.5953	.6123
1974	.3462	.3041	.3456	1988	.6602	.6034	.6097	2002	.6543	.6072	.6517
1975	.3797	.3448	.3690	1989	.7233	.5946	.7179	2003	.7254	.6470	.7049
1976	.5180	.3690	.4879	1990	.7193	.6426	.6785	2004	.7108	.6545	.7071
1977	.5062	.4683	.4862	1991	.6907	.6526	.6907	2005	.7095	.6611	.6879
1978	.5418	.4742	.5264	1992	.8163	.6645	.7998	2006	.7022	.6671	.6741
1979	.5309	.4609	.5119	1993	.8416	.7552	.7619	2007	.7389	.6536	.7348
1980	.5114	.4117	.4174	1994	.8230	.7463	.8061	2008	.9802	.7344	.9563
1981	.4794	.3856	.4573	1995	.9012	.8034	.8783	2009	.9649	.8401	.8870
1982	.5127	.4447	.5081	1996	.8820	.7420	.7420	2010	.9150	.8067	.8576
1983	.5546	.4804	.4945	1997	.7557	.6371	.6630	2011	.9083	.8285	.8331
1984	.5399	.4916	.5353	1998	.7164	.6303	.7104	2012	.8506	.7755	.8124
1985	.5576	.4801	.5537	1999	.7183	.6199	.6253	2013	.8816	.8085	.8303

Source: Forex

Date	Open	High	Low	Close
12/06/13	.83087	.83882	.82516	.83805
12/13/13	.83809	.84413	.83515	.84305
12/20/13	.84288	.84698	.83300	.83755
12/27/13	.83684	.83924	.83298	.83403
01/03/14	.83493	.83738	.82713	.82789

EURO / BRITISH POUND
Weekly Cash as of 01/03/2014

WEEKLY CASH
As of 01/03/2014
Chart High .98020 on 12/29/2008
Chart Low .65160 on 02/03/2003

Forex.

Quarterly High, Low and Settle of Euro / British Pound   In GBP per EUR

Quarter	High	Low	Settle	Quarter	High	Low	Settle	Quarter	High	Low	Settle
03/2005	.7095	.6849	.6856	03/2008	.7981	.7344	.7954	03/2011	.8853	.8285	.8833
06/2005	.6904	.6611	.6756	06/2008	.8098	.7767	.7904	06/2011	.9070	.8611	.9037
09/2005	.6989	.6713	.6819	09/2008	.8188	.7795	.7915	09/2011	.9083	.8529	.8592
12/2005	.6908	.6707	.6879	12/2008	.9802	.7695	.9563	12/2011	.8830	.8303	.8331
03/2006	.6985	.6784	.6978	03/2009	.9649	.8639	.9251	03/2012	.8506	.8222	.8336
06/2006	.7022	.6753	.6918	06/2009	.9257	.8401	.8526	06/2012	.8358	.7950	.8064
09/2006	.6962	.6685	.6776	09/2009	.9301	.8456	.9157	09/2012	.8116	.7755	.7957
12/2006	.6795	.6671	.6741	12/2009	.9412	.8834	.8870	12/2012	.8226	.7943	.8124
03/2007	.6868	.6536	.6788	03/2010	.9150	.8603	.8899	03/2013	.8816	.8085	.8432
06/2007	.6858	.6709	.6743	06/2010	.8904	.8067	.8185	06/2013	.8638	.8398	.8559
09/2007	.7028	.6679	.6971	09/2010	.8685	.8142	.8674	09/2013	.8770	.8339	.8356
12/2007	.7389	.6895	.7348	12/2010	.8942	.8336	.8576	12/2013	.8586	.8252	.8303

Source: Forex

BRITISH POUND / JAPANESE YEN

BRITISH POUND / JAPANESE YEN
Monthly Cash as of 12/31/2013

Date	Open	High	Low	Close
08/30/13	148.853	154.693	**147.817**	152.119
09/30/13	152.439	160.015	152.439	159.083
10/31/13	159.129	159.969	154.803	157.728
11/29/13	157.753	167.928	156.715	167.591
12/31/13	167.712	**174.608**	165.958	174.547

MONTHLY CASH
As of 12/31/2013
Chart High 832.260 on 01/31/1972
Chart Low 116.868 on 09/22/2011

Black Market (close): to 02/1972; IMM: 03/1972 to 02/1986; Forex: 02/14/1986 to date.

Annual High, Low and Settle of British Pound / Japanese Yen   In JPY per GBP

Year	High	Low	Settle	Year	High	Low	Settle	Year	High	Low	Settle
1972	832.26	701.75	708.45	1986	298.53	218.36	235.02	2000	179.76	148.28	170.71
1973	717.92	627.23	650.84	1987	249.24	225.18	228.52	2001	191.61	165.45	191.43
1974	718.14	641.89	706.41	1988	241.90	220.83	226.56	2002	197.23	179.23	191.35
1975	713.43	612.80	617.55	1989	233.14	216.37	231.82	2003	199.50	179.48	191.77
1976	621.45	462.27	497.98	1990	286.94	232.81	262.16	2004	208.05	190.15	196.51
1977	500.67	435.58	460.26	1991	264.46	220.62	232.66	2005	213.02	189.60	202.95
1978	472.50	358.29	396.43	1992	249.19	186.70	188.46	2006	234.78	200.59	233.05
1979	550.35	393.06	532.74	1993	195.37	147.29	165.10	2007	251.09	219.45	221.68
1980	573.72	481.32	484.66	1994	169.63	149.13	156.18	2008	222.75	129.90	132.50
1981	494.40	401.18	420.05	1995	164.52	128.33	160.48	2009	163.08	118.84	150.20
1982	468.62	375.34	379.99	1996	198.89	156.47	198.75	2010	150.72	125.51	126.75
1983	387.18	331.17	336.02	1997	218.95	181.36	215.20	2011	140.03	116.87	119.54
1984	354.56	288.01	291.63	1998	240.91	186.54	189.40	2012	141.12	117.31	140.96
1985	341.77	268.91	289.62	1999	201.89	161.05	165.05	2013	174.61	137.97	174.55

Source: Forex

BRITISH POUND / JAPANESE YEN

BRITISH POUND / JAPANESE YEN
Weekly Cash as of 01/03/2014

Date	Open	High	Low	Close
12/06/13	167.712	169.199	**165.958**	168.293
12/13/13	167.796	170.111	167.653	168.157
12/20/13	168.268	171.347	166.661	169.935
12/27/13	170.010	173.982	169.796	173.349
01/03/14	173.331	**174.962**	171.130	172.072

WEEKLY CASH
As of 01/03/2014
Chart High 251.092 on 07/20/2007
Chart Low 116.868 on 09/22/2011

Forex.

Quarterly High, Low and Settle of British Pound / Japanese Yen   In JPY per GBP

Quarter	High	Low	Settle	Quarter	High	Low	Settle	Quarter	High	Low	Settle
03/2005	202.72	189.60	202.61	03/2008	222.75	192.85	197.73	03/2011	135.53	122.72	133.29
06/2005	205.35	194.20	198.68	06/2008	213.92	197.24	211.62	06/2011	140.03	128.18	129.28
09/2005	203.47	192.80	200.12	09/2008	215.87	184.58	189.18	09/2011	130.87	116.87	120.22
12/2005	213.02	199.21	202.95	12/2008	189.93	129.90	132.50	12/2011	127.34	117.00	119.54
03/2006	211.16	200.59	204.34	03/2009	145.12	118.84	141.87	03/2012	133.50	117.31	132.62
06/2006	213.72	203.94	211.49	06/2009	162.60	139.05	158.60	06/2012	133.26	118.84	125.40
09/2006	223.85	209.56	221.12	09/2009	163.08	139.80	143.36	09/2012	128.85	120.86	125.95
12/2006	234.78	220.48	233.05	12/2009	153.24	139.34	150.20	12/2012	141.12	124.79	140.96
03/2007	241.47	221.11	231.85	03/2010	150.72	132.14	141.89	03/2013	148.01	137.97	143.27
06/2007	247.94	231.28	247.13	06/2010	145.98	126.82	132.15	06/2013	156.80	140.50	150.85
09/2007	251.09	219.45	235.03	09/2010	137.79	127.69	131.23	09/2013	160.02	147.82	159.08
12/2007	241.38	220.98	221.68	12/2010	134.25	125.51	126.75	12/2013	174.61	154.80	174.55

Source: Forex

EURO / JAPANESE YEN

EURO / JAPANESE YEN
Monthly Cash as of 12/31/2013

MONTHLY CASH
As of 12/31/2013
Chart High 285.34 on 12/03/1979
Chart Low 88.97 on 10/26/2000

Date	Open	High	Low	Close
08/30/13	130.15	132.42	**127.97**	129.73
09/30/13	129.78	135.01	129.75	132.89
10/31/13	132.96	135.48	131.16	133.59
11/29/13	133.58	139.70	131.25	139.16
12/31/13	139.25	**145.75**	138.41	144.90

MJSDMJSDMJSDMJSDMJSDMJSDMJSDMJSDMJSDMJSDMJSDMJSDMJSDMJSDMJSDMJSDMJSDMJSDMJSDMJSDMJSDMJSDMJSDMJSDMJSDMJSDMJSDMJSDMJSDMJSDMJSDMJSDMJSDMJSDMJSDMJSDMJSDMJSDMJSDMJSDMJSDMJSDMJSDM
1971 1972 1973 1974 1975 1976 1977 1978 1979 1980 1981 1982 1983 1984 1985 1986 1987 1988 1989 1990 1991 1992 1993 1994 1995 1996 1997 1998 1999 2000 2001 2002 2003 2004 2005 2006 2007 2008 2009 2010 2011 2012 2013 2014 2015 2016 2017

Black Market (close): to 02/1972; IMM: 03/1972 to 02/1986; Forex: 02/14/1986 to date.

Annual High, Low and Settle of Euro / Japanese Yen   In JPY per EUR

Year	High	Low	Settle	Year	High	Low	Settle	Year	High	Low	Settle
1972	195.55	182.91	184.37	1986	163.59	140.66	161.05	2000	111.96	88.97	107.75
1973	228.58	174.63	202.72	1987	169.45	148.39	150.81	2001	117.30	99.98	117.23
1974	244.11	198.71	244.11	1988	158.75	134.13	138.05	2002	125.60	111.30	124.64
1975	251.20	221.37	227.86	1989	168.32	132.30	166.49	2003	140.96	124.13	135.17
1976	242.96	221.89	242.96	1990	188.93	159.76	177.56	2004	141.63	125.83	138.98
1977	243.99	209.72	223.77	1991	179.11	144.59	160.86	2005	143.61	130.61	139.62
1978	233.94	177.43	208.68	1992	175.41	148.60	150.67	2006	157.18	137.11	157.09
1979	285.34	205.94	272.70	1993	155.73	115.15	125.75	2007	168.95	149.26	162.88
1980	278.06	201.11	202.29	1994	128.94	112.99	125.87	2008	169.96	113.65	126.75
1981	205.21	175.92	192.10	1995	144.37	110.60	140.91	2009	139.21	112.09	133.24
1982	213.63	188.51	193.06	1996	149.11	132.46	147.63	2010	134.37	105.42	108.69
1983	197.66	164.93	166.16	1997	148.01	121.75	142.62	2011	123.33	99.53	99.59
1984	181.35	149.67	156.11	1998	162.57	132.36	135.10	2012	114.69	94.12	114.47
1985	169.36	146.12	160.36	1999	135.16	102.10	103.25	2013	145.75	113.58	144.90

Source: Forex

Date	Open	High	Low	Close
12/06/13	139.25	140.96	138.41	140.93
12/13/13	140.75	142.79	140.70	141.69
12/20/13	141.74	142.90	140.96	142.31
12/27/13	142.23	145.75	142.08	144.52
01/03/14	144.68	145.17	141.97	142.41

Forex.

Quarterly High, Low and Settle of Euro / Japanese Yen   In JPY per EUR

Quarter	High	Low	Settle	Quarter	High	Low	Settle	Quarter	High	Low	Settle
03/2005	140.72	133.00	138.91	03/2008	164.05	151.72	157.33	03/2011	118.00	106.60	117.72
06/2005	140.49	130.61	134.23	06/2008	169.46	156.34	167.22	06/2011	123.33	113.42	116.84
09/2005	138.85	132.54	136.48	09/2008	169.96	147.05	149.71	09/2011	117.74	101.93	103.27
12/2005	143.61	135.86	139.62	12/2008	150.59	113.65	126.75	12/2011	111.56	99.53	99.59
03/2006	143.42	137.11	142.59	03/2009	134.49	112.09	131.21	03/2012	111.45	97.04	110.52
06/2006	146.65	140.21	146.33	06/2009	139.21	124.37	135.23	06/2012	111.15	95.60	101.10
09/2006	150.74	145.03	149.82	09/2009	138.71	127.01	131.29	09/2012	103.85	94.12	100.20
12/2006	157.18	148.50	157.09	12/2009	138.49	126.94	133.24	12/2012	114.69	99.78	114.47
03/2007	159.65	150.76	157.39	03/2010	134.37	119.64	126.22	03/2013	127.74	113.58	120.79
06/2007	166.95	156.94	166.58	06/2010	127.92	107.33	108.17	06/2013	133.80	119.08	129.05
09/2007	168.95	149.26	163.82	09/2010	114.73	105.42	113.82	09/2013	135.01	127.97	132.89
12/2007	167.74	158.74	162.88	12/2010	115.67	107.61	108.69	12/2013	145.75	131.16	144.90

Source: Forex

Energy

Crude Oil Market Outlook

The oil market over the last few years has seen game-changing technology with the development of fracking and horizontal drilling. This has led to a 45% surge in U.S. oil production during 2011-13. As the technology spreads, other countries will be able to boost their production as well. The surge in world oil production is likely to keep a cap on oil prices in coming years even though demand should slowly continue to rise with the ongoing global economic recovery. OPEC will continue to be a major player since it still has the cheapest oil-extraction costs. Nevertheless, the rise of non-OPEC production will likely keep downward pressure on world oil prices and should reduce the incidence of oil price spikes that have caused recessions in recent decades. In addition, oil demand is likely to be curtailed in coming years by higher gas-mileage automobiles and by increased reliance on alternative energy technologies. The world powers in late 2013 reached a first-step agreement with Iran to curb its nuclear program. If a final agreement is reached with Iran to halt its nuclear program and relations with Iran are normalized, then OPEC will have a major challenge trying to offset a sharp increase in Iranian oil exports.

Crude Oil Price History

1973 oil crisis

The world oil market from the 1930s through the early 1970s was tightly controlled by the major oil companies, which were referred to as the "Seven Sisters." However, in the early 1970s, Middle East countries started to nationalize oil facilities and take control of their own oil production destiny. This gave the Arab countries the leverage to announce an oil embargo against the U.S. in 1973 in retaliation for U.S. support for Israel during the Yom Kippur War when Israel suffered a surprise military attack by Egypt and Syria.

In the space of a few months, prices for West Texas Intermediate (WTI) oil spiked higher and roughly tripled from $3.56 per barrel in mid-1973 to $10.11 in early 1974. The shock to U.S. consumers came not only from higher gasoline prices but also from shortages and long lines at the gas pumps. Shortages quickly arose because of ill-conceived U.S. oil price controls and rationing that were imposed by President Nixon and Congress in the early 1970s. Those price controls discouraged exploration and production and reduced the supply of gasoline available to U.S. consumers at the gas pump (President Reagan finally dismantled oil price controls in 1981).

OPEC was initially formed in 1960 in order to present a united front in negotiations with the major oil companies. OPEC currently has 12 members (Saudi Arabia, Iran, Venezuela, Iraq, UAE, Kuwait, Nigeria, Libya, Indonesia, Algeria, Qatar, Angola). OPEC members together account for some two-thirds of world oil reserves. Although OPEC is not a true cartel since it does not account for 100% of oil production, OPEC seeks to influence world oil prices by

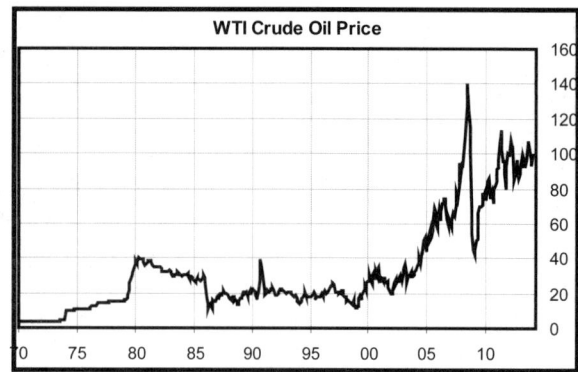

WTI Crude Oil Price

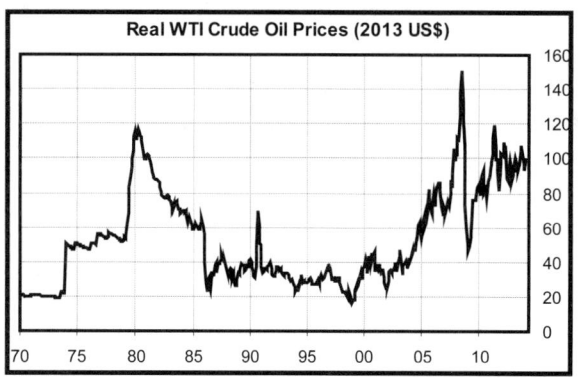

Real WTI Crude Oil Prices (2013 US$)

acting as the "swing producer," increasing or decreasing production in order to control oil prices. OPEC wants to maximize its long-term oil revenues, but OPEC does not want to push oil prices too high because a price spike would (1) cause oil demand to plunge from a world recession, (2) cause non-OPEC oil production to become economical in higher-cost areas, and (3) encourage the development of alternative sources of energy.

1979 oil crisis

After the 1973 Arab Oil Embargo was over, oil prices did not fall back but instead rose steadily through the latter half of the 1970s as OPEC enforced its newly-found pricing power and as oil demand grew. Oil prices then spiked higher in 1979 on the Iranian revolution against the Shah of Iran in January 1979, which devastated Iranian oil production. The Iran-Iraq war, which began in September 1980, then caused a sharp reduction in both Iranian and Iraqi oil output. OPEC production plunged by half, from 30 million barrels per day (bpd) in 1978 to only 15 million bpd by 1984. In response to those events, oil prices spiked higher in 1979 from about $15 per barrel in late-1978 to $38 per barrel at the end of 1979 and to a then-record of $39.50 in June 1980 (which is equivalent to $112 per barrel in current dollars). After peaking in 1980, oil prices then moved steadily lower through 1985 as the world adjusted to the Iranian-Iraqi oil production disruptions and as other sources of supply came on line. In addition, oil prices were undercut by the double-dip U.S. recessions seen in 1980 and 1981-82.

1986 oil price collapse

Oil prices then plunged in 1986 to $10 per barrel as Iranian and Iraqi oil production started to come back on line even though the Iraq-Iraq war did not officially end until 1988. Iranian oil production started rising sharply in 1986 from about 2.0 mln bpd in 1985 to 3.2 mln bpd by early 1989. Iraqi production nearly doubled from 1.5 mln bpd in 1984 to 2.7 mln bpd by early 1987. Other OPEC members failed to cut production fast enough to accommodate rising Iran-Iraq production, thus causing a collapse in oil prices. Oil prices finally recovered in 1987 back to the $20 area after OPEC reinstated some pro-duction discipline.

1990 spike on first Gulf war

Oil prices were relatively steady and averaged $19 per barrel from the late-1980s through 1996. There was a brief upward spike to nearly $40 per barrel seen in 1990 when the U.S. and coalition forces went to war against Iraq to push Saddam Hussein out of Kuwait and to protect Saudi Arabia and its oil fields.

1998 oil price collapse and 1999-2000 recovery

After moving sideways near $20 per barrel during much of the 1990s, oil prices in 1997-99 plunged due to (1) reduced Asian oil demand tied to the 1997 Asian currency crisis, (2) a four-fold increase in Iraqi production (from 500,000 bpd at the end of 1996 to 2 million bpd in mid-1998) as the UN oil-for-food program allowed for a restoration of Iraq's oil production, and (3) the failure of OPEC to cut production fast enough to accommodate increased Iraqi production. OPEC finally agreed to new production discipline and oil prices then more than tripled from $10 to over $30 by 2000. However, oil prices then fell sharply in 2000-01 from the $30 area to a low of $16.70 in November 2001 due to reduced oil demand caused by the U.S. recession in 2001 and the soft global economy that followed the bursting of the equity bubble.

2002-06 supply/demand squeeze

From the low of $16.17 per barrel seen in November 2001, oil prices then more than quadrupled to a then-record high of $70 per barrel in August 2005. That rally was driven by (1) stronger worldwide demand with the global economic recovery and particularly strong oil import demand from China (China's oil imports doubled from 60 million tons in mid-2002 to over 120 million tons in early 2005), (2) various temporary supply disruptions including Hurricane Ivan in 2004 and Hurricanes Katrina and Rita in 2005, and (3) the lack of any significant world excess capacity that could be quickly ramped up to meet new demand.

2007-08 spike up to $147

The crude oil price rally accelerated into high gear in 2007 and 2008 on speculative fever and reached a record

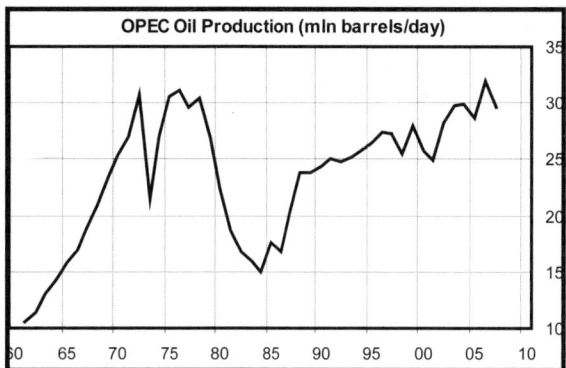

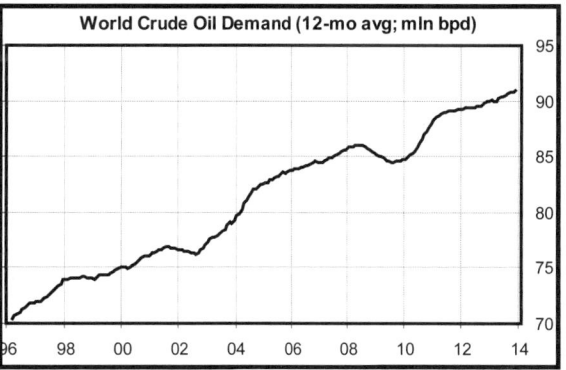

high of $147.27 in July 2008. In response to the surge in oil prices, OPEC sharply boosted production by 15% from 26.4 million bpd in May 2007 to a record high of 30.305 million bpd in August 2008.

When the global recession and financial crisis emerged in mid-2008, oil prices plunged as speculators bailed out of their long positions and as world oil demand plunged. OPEC in late-2008 and early-2009 responded to the plunge in oil prices with a production cut-back to the 26 million bpd area. Oil prices from 2009-2011 then recovered as the global economy emerged from recession and as OPEC kept its production in check.

2011-13 range-trading

Oil prices remained in the relatively narrow range of $75 to $115 during 2011-13 as supply roughly matched demand. Oil demand slowly recovered after the 2007-09 recession, but there was plenty of world oil supply especially due to the surge in U.S. oil production. U.S. oil production during 2011-13 surged by 45% to a 25-year high of 8 million barrels per day in late 2013 thanks to the new oil extraction technologies. Higher production by Saudi Arabia helped offset supply disruptions caused by tighter sanctions on Iran and the temporary drop in Libyan oil production tied to the revolution against Colonel Qaddafi.

CRUDE OIL

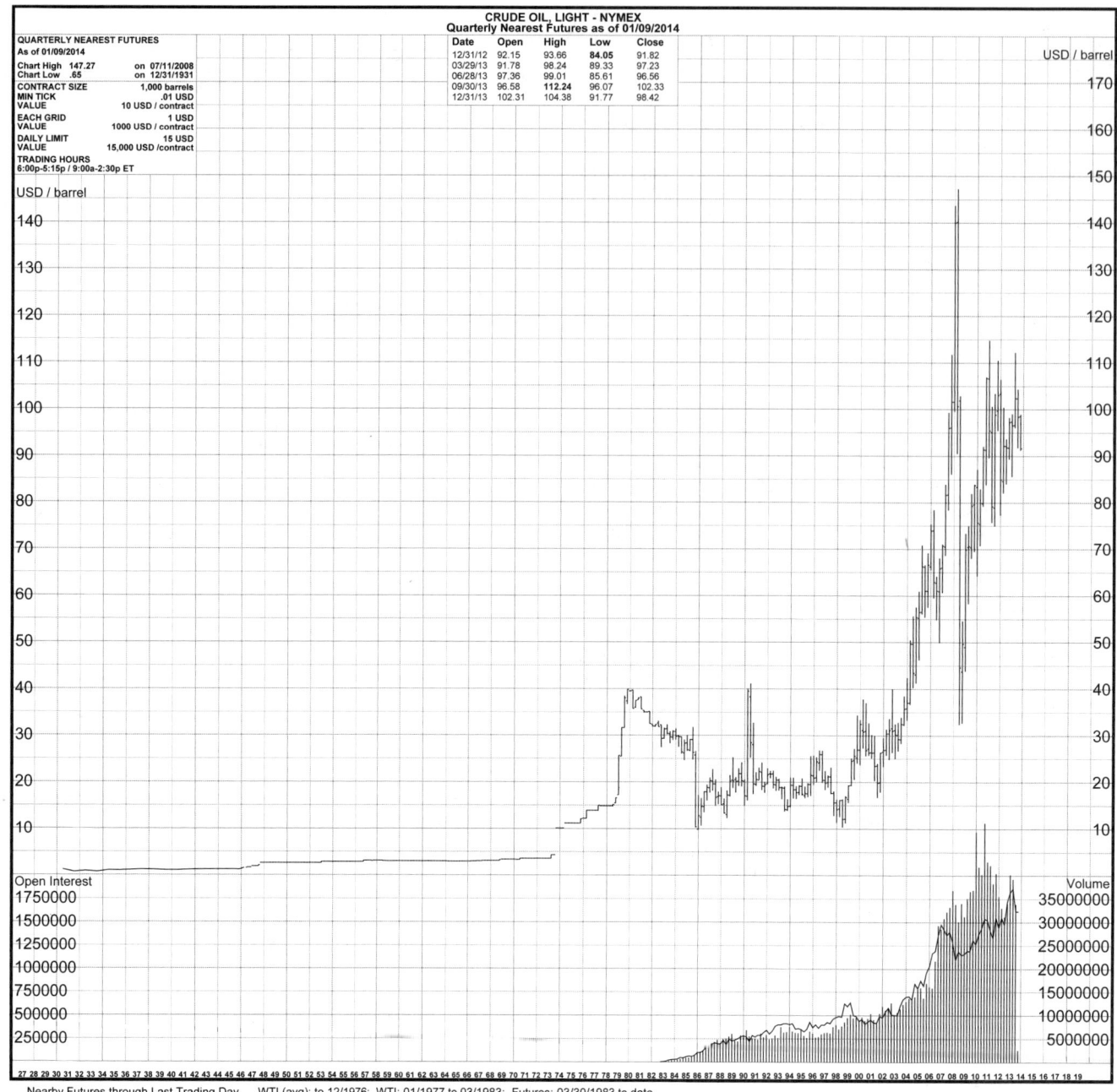

QUARTERLY NEAREST FUTURES
As of 01/09/2014

Chart High 147.27	on 07/11/2008	
Chart Low .65	on 12/31/1931	
CONTRACT SIZE	1,000 barrels	
MIN TICK	.01 USD	
VALUE	10 USD / contract	
EACH GRID	1 USD	
VALUE	1000 USD / contract	
DAILY LIMIT	15 USD	
VALUE	15,000 USD /contract	
TRADING HOURS		
6:00p-5:15p / 9:00a-2:30p ET		

Nearby Futures through Last Trading Day.   WTI (avg): to 12/1976; WTI: 01/1977 to 03/1983; Futures: 03/30/1983 to date.

Annual High, Low and Settle of Crude Oil   In USD per Barrel

Year	High	Low	Settle	Year	High	Low	Settle	Year	High	Low	Settle
1930	1.19	1.19	1.19	1944	1.21	1.21	1.21	1958	3.07	3.00	3.00
1931	0.65	0.65	0.65	1945	1.22	1.22	1.22	1959	3.00	2.97	2.97
1932	0.87	0.87	0.87	1946	1.62	1.17	1.62	1960	2.97	2.97	2.97
1933	0.67	0.67	0.67	1947	2.07	1.62	2.07	1961	2.97	2.97	2.97
1934	1.00	1.00	1.00	1948	2.57	2.57	2.57	1962	2.97	2.97	2.97
1935	0.97	0.97	0.97	1949	2.57	2.57	2.57	1963	2.97	2.97	2.97
1936	1.09	1.09	1.09	1950	2.57	2.57	2.57	1964	2.97	2.92	2.92
1937	1.18	1.18	1.18	1951	2.57	2.57	2.57	1965	2.92	2.92	2.92
1938	1.13	1.13	1.13	1952	2.57	2.57	2.57	1966	2.97	2.92	2.97
1939	1.02	1.02	1.02	1953	2.82	2.57	2.82	1967	3.07	2.97	3.07
1940	1.02	1.02	1.02	1954	2.82	2.82	2.82	1968	3.07	3.07	3.07
1941	1.14	1.14	1.14	1955	2.82	2.82	2.82	1969	3.35	3.07	3.35
1942	1.19	1.19	1.19	1956	2.82	2.82	2.82	1970	3.56	3.31	3.56
1943	1.20	1.20	1.20	1957	3.07	2.82	3.00	1971	3.56	3.56	3.56

Data continued on page 76.   Source: CME Group; New York Mercantile Exchange

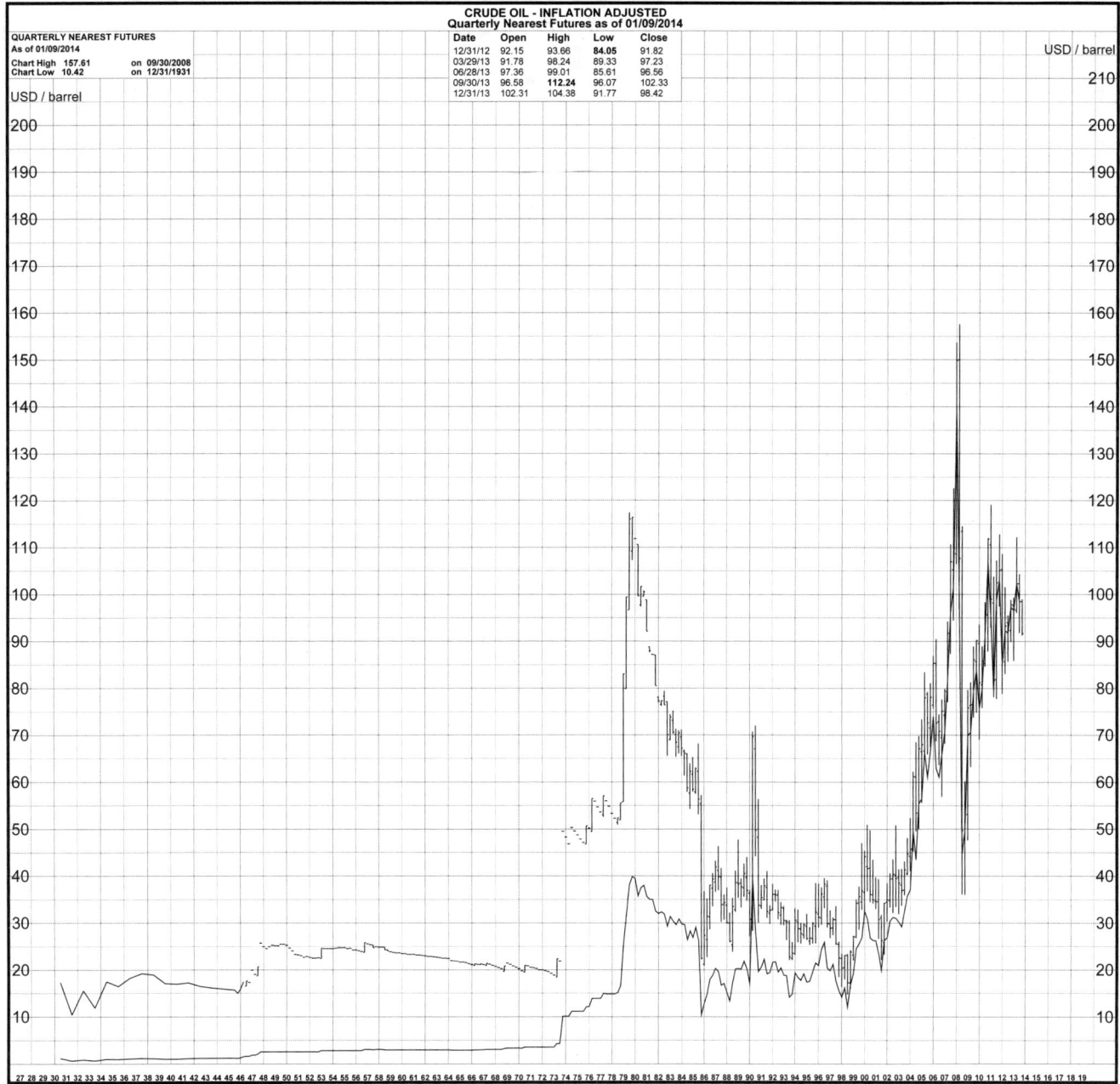

CRUDE OIL - INFLATION ADJUSTED
Quarterly Nearest Futures as of 01/09/2014

Date	Open	High	Low	Close
12/31/12	92.15	93.66	**84.05**	91.82
03/29/13	91.78	98.24	89.33	97.23
06/28/13	97.36	99.01	85.61	96.56
09/30/13	96.58	**112.24**	96.07	102.33
12/31/13	102.31	104.38	91.77	98.42

QUARTERLY NEAREST FUTURES
As of 01/09/2014
Chart High 157.61   on 09/30/2008
Chart Low   10.42   on 12/31/1931
USD / barrel

Nearby Futures through Last Trading Day.   WTI (avg): to 12/1976; WTI: 01/1977 to 03/1983; Futures: 03/30/1983 to date.

Annual High, Low and Settle of Crude Oil   In USD per Barrel

Year	High	Low	Settle	Year	High	Low	Settle	Year	High	Low	Settle
1930	1.19	1.19	1.19	1944	1.21	1.21	1.21	1958	3.07	3.00	3.00
1931	0.65	0.65	0.65	1945	1.22	1.22	1.22	1959	3.00	2.97	2.97
1932	0.87	0.87	0.87	1946	1.62	1.17	1.62	1960	2.97	2.97	2.97
1933	0.67	0.67	0.67	1947	2.07	1.62	2.07	1961	2.97	2.97	2.97
1934	1.00	1.00	1.00	1948	2.57	2.57	2.57	1962	2.97	2.97	2.97
1935	0.97	0.97	0.97	1949	2.57	2.57	2.57	1963	2.97	2.97	2.97
1936	1.09	1.09	1.09	1950	2.57	2.57	2.57	1964	2.97	2.92	2.92
1937	1.18	1.18	1.18	1951	2.57	2.57	2.57	1965	2.92	2.92	2.92
1938	1.13	1.13	1.13	1952	2.57	2.57	2.57	1966	2.97	2.92	2.97
1939	1.02	1.02	1.02	1953	2.82	2.57	2.82	1967	3.07	2.97	3.07
1940	1.02	1.02	1.02	1954	2.82	2.82	2.82	1968	3.07	3.07	3.07
1941	1.14	1.14	1.14	1955	2.82	2.82	2.82	1969	3.35	3.07	3.35
1942	1.19	1.19	1.19	1956	2.82	2.82	2.82	1970	3.56	3.31	3.56
1943	1.20	1.20	1.20	1957	3.07	2.82	3.00	1971	3.56	3.56	3.56

Data continued on page 77.   *Source: CME Group; New York Mercantile Exchange*

CRUDE OIL

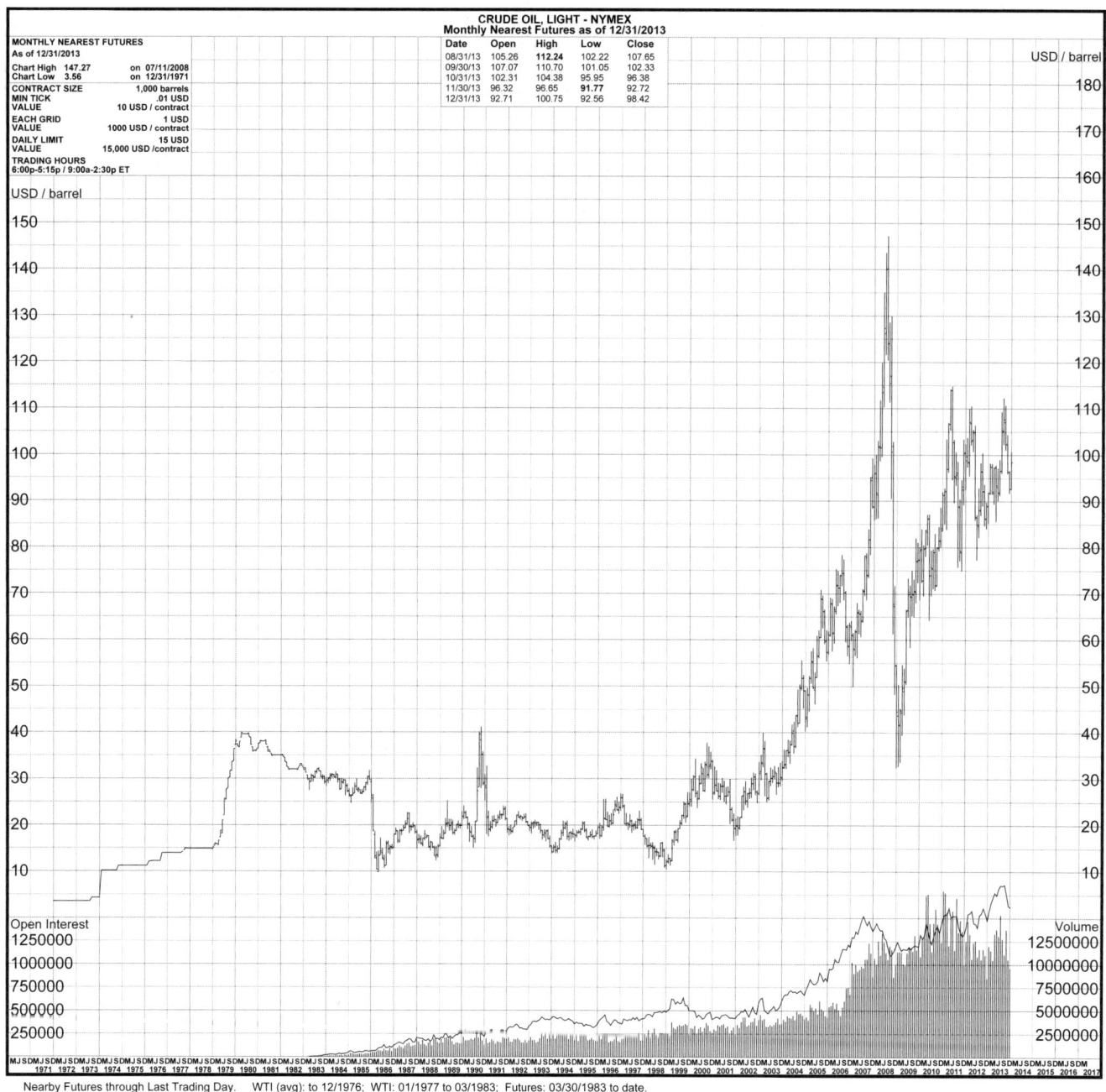

CRUDE OIL, LIGHT - NYMEX
Monthly Nearest Futures as of 12/31/2013

Date	Open	High	Low	Close
08/31/13	105.26	112.24	102.22	107.65
09/30/13	107.07	110.70	101.05	102.33
10/31/13	102.31	104.38	95.95	96.38
11/30/13	96.32	96.65	91.77	92.72
12/31/13	92.71	100.75	92.56	98.42

MONTHLY NEAREST FUTURES
As of 12/31/2013

Chart High 147.27   on 07/11/2008
Chart Low   3.56   on 12/31/1971
CONTRACT SIZE   1,000 barrels
MIN TICK   .01 USD
VALUE   10 USD / contract
EACH GRID   1 USD
VALUE   1000 USD / contract
DAILY LIMIT   15 USD
VALUE   15,000 USD /contract
TRADING HOURS
6:00p-5:15p / 9:00a-2:30p ET

Nearby Futures through Last Trading Day.   WTI (avg): to 12/1976; WTI: 01/1977 to 03/1983; Futures: 03/30/1983 to date.

Annual High, Low and Settle of Crude Oil Futures   In USD per Barrel

Year	High	Low	Settle	Year	High	Low	Settle	Year	High	Low	Settle
1972	3.56	3.56	3.56	1986	26.60	9.75	17.94	2000	37.80	23.70	26.80
1973	4.31	3.56	4.31	1987	22.76	14.90	16.70	2001	32.70	16.70	19.84
1974	11.16	10.11	11.16	1988	18.92	12.28	17.24	2002	33.65	17.85	31.20
1975	11.16	11.16	11.16	1989	25.30	16.91	21.82	2003	39.99	25.04	32.52
1976	13.90	11.16	13.90	1990	41.15	15.06	28.44	2004	55.67	32.20	43.45
1977	14.97	13.78	14.85	1991	32.75	17.45	19.12	2005	70.85	41.25	61.04
1978	15.14	14.72	15.14	1992	22.95	17.72	19.50	2006	78.40	54.86	61.05
1979	38.47	15.48	38.01	1993	21.14	13.75	14.17	2007	99.29	49.90	95.98
1980	39.81	35.75	37.48	1994	20.98	13.88	17.76	2008	147.27	32.40	44.60
1981	38.25	34.87	35.00	1995	20.82	16.60	19.55	2009	82.00	32.70	79.36
1982	35.12	31.87	31.87	1996	26.80	17.08	25.92	2010	92.06	64.24	91.38
1983	32.35	27.40	29.60	1997	26.74	17.50	17.64	2011	114.83	74.95	98.83
1984	31.50	26.04	26.41	1998	18.06	10.35	12.05	2012	110.55	77.28	91.82
1985	31.82	24.66	26.30	1999	27.15	11.26	25.60	2013	112.24	85.61	98.42

Data continued from page 74.   Futures begin trading 03/30/1983.   *Source: CME Group; New York Mercantile Exchange*

Crude Oil, WTI Spot
Monthly Cash as of 12/31/2013

MONTHLY CASH
As of 12/31/2013

Chart High 145.66 on 07/11/2008
Chart Low 3.56 on 12/31/1971

USD / barrel

USD / barrel

Date	Open	High	Low	Close
08/30/13	107.93	110.17	103.45	107.98
09/30/13	108.67	110.62	102.36	102.36
10/31/13	102.09	104.15	96.29	96.29
11/29/13	94.56	95.35	92.05	92.55
12/31/13	93.61	99.94	93.61	98.17

WTI (avg): to 12/1976; WTI: 01/1977 to date.

Annual High, Low and Settle of Crude Oil   In USD per Barrel

Year	High	Low	Settle	Year	High	Low	Settle	Year	High	Low	Settle
1972	3.56	3.56	3.56	1986	26.55	10.40	17.95	2000	37.00	23.84	25.76
1973	4.31	3.56	4.31	1987	22.40	15.15	16.70	2001	32.30	17.48	19.78
1974	11.16	10.11	11.16	1988	18.60	12.60	17.25	2002	32.73	17.98	31.23
1975	11.16	11.16	11.16	1989	24.65	17.05	21.80	2003	37.83	25.23	32.55
1976	13.90	11.16	13.90	1990	40.40	15.30	28.45	2004	55.23	32.48	43.46
1977	14.97	13.78	14.85	1991	32.00	17.85	19.10	2005	69.82	42.13	61.04
1978	15.14	14.72	15.14	1992	22.89	17.85	19.48	2006	77.03	56.27	61.06
1979	38.47	15.48	38.01	1993	21.43	13.79	14.13	2007	98.83	50.49	96.01
1980	39.81	35.75	37.48	1994	20.87	13.86	17.78	2008	145.66	30.81	44.60
1981	38.25	34.87	35.00	1995	20.71	16.67	19.47	2009	81.37	33.98	79.36
1982	35.12	31.87	31.87	1996	26.56	17.26	25.91	2010	92.21	66.88	89.84
1983	32.25	27.40	29.60	1997	26.61	17.53	17.63	2011	113.93	75.67	98.83
1984	31.00	26.05	26.40	1998	17.81	10.80	11.66	2012	109.77	77.69	91.82
1985	31.80	25.20	26.30	1999	26.94	11.36	26.92	2013	110.62	86.68	98.17

Data continued from page 75.   *Source: Energy Information Administration, U.S. Department of Energy (EIA-DOE)*

CRUDE OIL

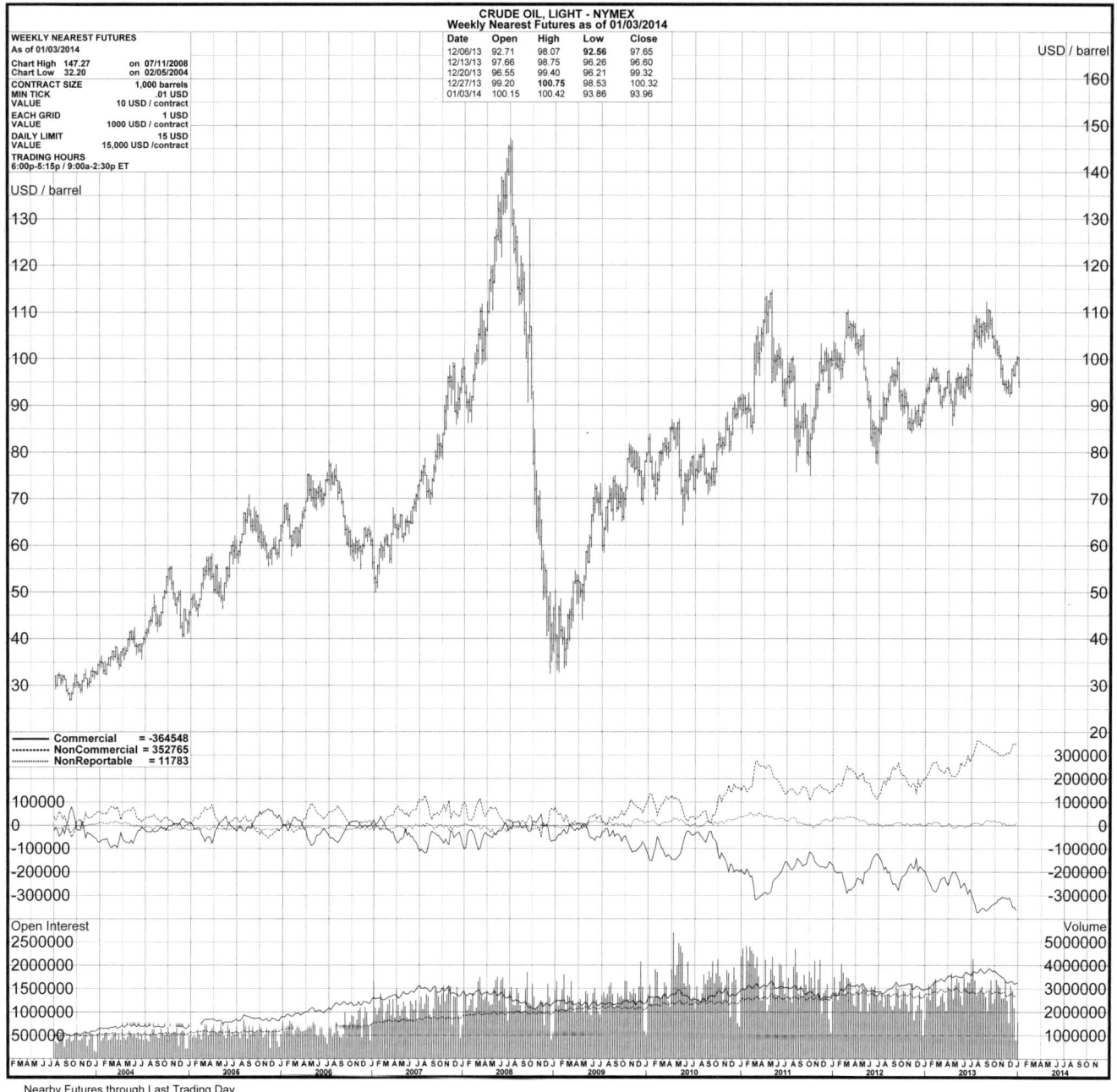

Date	Open	High	Low	Close
12/06/13	92.71	98.07	92.56	97.65
12/13/13	97.66	98.75	96.26	96.60
12/20/13	96.55	99.40	96.21	99.32
12/27/13	99.20	100.75	98.53	100.32
01/03/14	100.15	100.42	93.86	93.96

WEEKLY NEAREST FUTURES
As of 01/03/2014

Chart High 147.27 on 07/11/2008
Chart Low 32.20 on 02/05/2004
CONTRACT SIZE 1,000 barrels
MIN TICK .01 USD
VALUE 10 USD / contract
EACH GRID 1 USD
VALUE 1000 USD / contract
DAILY LIMIT 15 USD
VALUE 15,000 USD /contract
TRADING HOURS
6:00p-5:15p / 9:00a-2:30p ET

Commercial = -364548
NonCommercial = 352765
NonReportable = 11783

Nearby Futures through Last Trading Day.

Quarterly High, Low and Settle of Crude Oil Futures In USD per Barrel

Quarter	High	Low	Settle	Quarter	High	Low	Settle	Quarter	High	Low	Settle
03/2005	57.60	41.25	55.40	03/2008	111.80	86.11	101.58	03/2011	106.95	83.85	106.72
06/2005	60.95	46.20	56.50	06/2008	143.67	99.55	140.00	06/2011	114.83	89.61	95.42
09/2005	70.85	56.10	66.24	09/2008	147.27	90.51	100.64	09/2011	100.62	75.71	79.20
12/2005	66.62	55.40	61.04	12/2008	102.84	32.40	44.60	12/2011	103.37	74.95	98.83
03/2006	69.20	57.55	66.63	03/2009	54.66	32.70	49.66	03/2012	110.55	95.44	103.02
06/2006	75.35	65.60	73.93	06/2009	73.38	43.83	69.89	06/2012	106.43	77.28	84.96
09/2006	78.40	59.52	62.91	09/2009	75.00	58.32	70.61	09/2012	100.42	82.10	92.19
12/2006	64.15	54.86	61.05	12/2009	82.00	68.05	79.36	12/2012	93.66	84.05	91.82
03/2007	68.09	49.90	65.87	03/2010	83.95	69.50	83.76	03/2013	98.24	89.33	97.23
06/2007	71.06	60.68	70.68	06/2010	87.15	64.24	75.63	06/2013	99.01	85.61	96.56
09/2007	83.90	68.63	81.66	09/2010	82.97	70.76	79.97	09/2013	112.24	96.07	102.33
12/2007	99.29	78.35	95.98	12/2010	92.06	79.25	91.38	12/2013	104.38	91.77	98.42

Source: CME Group; New York Mercantile Exchange

Crude Oil, WTI Spot
Weekly Cash as of 01/03/2014

Date	Open	High	Low	Close
12/06/13	93.61	97.48	**93.61**	97.48
12/13/13	97.10	98.32	96.27	96.27
12/20/13	97.18	99.11	96.99	99.11
12/27/13	98.62	**99.94**	98.62	99.94
01/03/14	98.90	98.90	93.66	93.66

WEEKLY CASH
As of 01/03/2014
Chart High 145.66   on 07/11/2008
Chart Low 25.23   on 04/29/2003

USD / barrel

WTI: to date.

Quarterly High, Low and Settle of Crude Oil In USD per Barrel

Quarter	High	Low	Settle	Quarter	High	Low	Settle	Quarter	High	Low	Settle
03/2005	56.62	42.13	55.41	03/2008	110.33	87.15	101.59	03/2011	106.72	84.32	106.72
06/2005	59.65	46.81	56.50	06/2008	140.21	100.98	140.00	06/2011	113.93	90.61	95.42
09/2005	69.82	55.49	66.25	09/2008	145.66	91.15	100.64	09/2011	99.59	79.20	79.20
12/2005	65.48	56.15	61.04	12/2008	98.53	30.81	44.60	12/2011	102.59	75.67	98.83
03/2006	68.36	57.66	66.66	03/2009	54.34	33.98	49.66	03/2012	109.77	96.36	103.02
06/2006	74.62	66.24	73.98	06/2009	72.68	45.88	69.89	06/2012	106.16	77.69	84.96
09/2006	77.03	60.11	62.92	09/2009	73.82	59.52	70.61	09/2012	99.00	83.75	92.19
12/2006	63.44	56.27	61.06	12/2009	81.37	69.51	79.36	12/2012	92.48	84.44	91.82
03/2007	66.04	50.49	65.88	03/2010	83.76	71.19	83.76	03/2013	97.94	90.12	97.23
06/2007	70.69	61.48	70.69	06/2010	86.84	66.88	75.63	06/2013	98.44	86.68	96.56
09/2007	83.36	69.32	81.67	09/2010	82.55	71.21	79.97	09/2013	110.62	96.07	102.36
12/2007	98.83	79.03	96.01	12/2010	92.21	79.49	89.84	12/2013	104.15	92.05	98.17

Source: Energy Information Administration, U.S. Department of Energy (EIA-DOE)

CRUDE OIL, BRENT

CRUDE OIL, BRENT - ICE
Monthly Nearest Futures as of 12/31/2013

Date	Open	High	Low	Close
08/31/13	107.81	**117.34**	105.85	114.01
09/30/13	114.00	116.56	107.22	108.37
10/31/13	108.38	112.00	106.27	108.84
11/30/13	109.05	111.66	**102.98**	109.69
12/31/13	109.60	113.02	107.80	110.80

MONTHLY NEAREST FUTURES
As of 12/31/2013

Chart High 147.50	on 07/11/2008
Chart Low 8.55	on 07/23/1986
CONTRACT SIZE	1,000 BARRELS
MIN TICK	.01 USD
VALUE	10 USD/CONTRACT
EACH GRID	1 USD
VALUE	1000 USD/CONTRACT
DAILY LIMIT	NONE
VALUE	
TRADING HOURS	
10:02a - 8:15p	

USD / barrel

Nearby Futures through Last Trading Day.   Futures: 07/24/1989 to date.

Annual High, Low and Settle of Crude Oil, Brent Futures   In USD per Barrel

Year	High	Low	Settle	Year	High	Low	Settle	Year	High	Low	Settle
1972	----	----	----	1986	26.45	8.55	18.15	2000	35.30	21.30	23.87
1973	----	----	----	1987	20.80	15.20	18.00	2001	31.05	16.65	19.90
1974	----	----	----	1988	18.65	11.10	15.80	2002	31.02	18.23	28.66
1975	----	----	----	1989	21.35	16.28	20.28	2003	34.55	22.97	30.17
1976	----	----	----	1990	40.95	15.33	28.27	2004	51.95	28.45	40.46
1977	----	----	----	1991	31.20	16.00	17.61	2005	68.89	38.81	58.98
1978	----	----	----	1992	21.61	16.68	18.29	2006	78.65	57.39	60.86
1979	42.00	18.95	40.50	1993	19.68	13.20	13.20	2007	96.65	50.75	93.85
1980	40.85	33.40	40.15	1994	19.41	12.90	16.50	2008	147.50	36.20	45.59
1981	40.30	33.25	36.70	1995	19.38	15.41	18.33	2009	80.26	39.35	77.93
1982	35.85	29.30	31.75	1996	25.06	15.93	23.81	2010	95.20	67.87	94.75
1983	31.10	28.20	28.95	1997	24.91	16.50	16.52	2011	127.02	92.37	107.38
1984	30.13	26.98	26.98	1998	16.80	9.55	10.53	2012	128.40	88.49	111.11
1985	30.75	25.20	26.30	1999	26.15	9.90	25.08	2013	119.17	96.75	110.80

Futures begin trading 07/24/1989.   *Source: ICE Futures Europe*

CRUDE OIL, BRENT - ICE
Weekly Nearest Futures as of 01/03/2014

Date	Open	High	Low	Close
12/06/13	109.60	113.02	109.28	111.61
12/13/13	111.69	111.79	108.02	108.83
12/20/13	109.15	111.89	107.80	111.77
12/27/13	111.55	112.80	111.27	112.18
01/03/14	112.20	112.64	106.79	106.89

WEEKLY NEAREST FUTURES
As of 01/03/2014

Chart High 147.50 on 07/11/2008
Chart Low 36.20 on 12/24/2008
CONTRACT SIZE 1,000 BARRELS
MIN TICK .01 USD
VALUE 10 USD/CONTRACT
EACH GRID 1 USD
VALUE 1000 USD/CONTRACT
DAILY LIMIT NONE
VALUE
TRADING HOURS
10:02a - 8:15p

Nearby Futures through Last Trading Day.

Quarterly High, Low and Settle of Crude Oil, Brent Futures   In USD per Barrel

Quarter	High	Low	Settle	Quarter	High	Low	Settle	Quarter	High	Low	Settle
03/2005	56.15	38.81	54.29	03/2008	108.02	85.00	100.30	03/2011	119.79	92.37	117.36
06/2005	59.59	47.47	55.58	06/2008	143.91	98.99	139.83	06/2011	127.02	102.28	112.48
09/2005	68.89	55.25	63.48	09/2008	147.50	88.90	98.17	09/2011	120.40	98.74	102.76
12/2005	63.96	53.75	58.98	12/2008	100.31	36.20	45.59	12/2011	116.48	99.11	107.38
03/2006	69.03	57.90	65.91	03/2009	53.86	39.35	49.23	03/2012	128.40	108.35	122.88
06/2006	74.97	65.73	72.88	06/2009	73.50	47.26	69.30	06/2012	125.97	88.49	97.80
09/2006	78.65	59.32	62.48	09/2009	76.00	59.49	69.07	09/2012	117.95	95.30	112.39
12/2006	64.92	57.39	60.86	12/2009	80.26	65.90	77.93	12/2012	116.20	104.76	111.11
03/2007	69.14	50.75	68.10	03/2010	82.82	67.87	82.70	03/2013	119.17	106.80	110.02
06/2007	72.25	63.80	71.41	06/2010	89.58	68.15	75.01	06/2013	111.79	96.75	102.16
09/2007	81.05	68.14	79.17	09/2010	82.86	70.77	82.31	09/2013	117.34	101.63	108.37
12/2007	96.65	75.64	93.85	12/2010	95.20	80.75	94.75	12/2013	113.02	102.98	110.80

Source: ICE Futures Europe

GASOIL

GAS-OIL-PETROLEUM - ICE
Monthly Nearest Futures as of 12/31/2013

Date	Open	High	Low	Close
08/31/13	918.75	**985.75**	891.50	969.50
09/30/13	957.00	971.75	900.00	913.00
10/31/13	915.00	948.75	903.50	932.50
11/30/13	934.25	948.25	**885.00**	943.00
12/31/13	938.25	957.25	915.00	944.25

Nearby Futures through Last Trading Day.   Futures: 06/03/1986 to date.

Annual High, Low and Settle of Gasoil Futures   In USD per Metric Ton

Year	High	Low	Settle	Year	High	Low	Settle	Year	High	Low	Settle
1972	----	----	----	1986	150.00	86.50	150.00	2000	350.00	194.00	245.00
1973	----	----	----	1987	177.00	123.00	150.75	2001	272.75	145.00	168.50
1974	----	----	----	1988	157.00	101.75	150.50	2002	267.50	155.00	253.75
1975	----	----	----	1989	230.00	133.00	221.75	2003	360.00	202.00	272.00
1976	----	----	----	1990	363.00	137.50	272.50	2004	508.00	245.50	368.00
1977	----	----	----	1991	352.00	153.04	158.00	2005	663.50	354.50	510.75
1978	----	----	----	1992	201.00	152.25	174.00	2006	675.25	506.50	516.50
1979	----	----	----	1993	185.50	138.00	139.25	2007	861.50	461.50	839.25
1980	----	----	----	1994	168.50	135.25	147.75	2008	1,339.25	390.00	418.50
1981	----	----	----	1995	183.50	139.75	179.75	2009	664.25	351.50	635.50
1982	----	----	----	1996	250.00	152.50	223.75	2010	788.00	551.50	762.50
1983	----	----	----	1997	235.25	149.75	150.00	2011	1,064.50	757.25	924.00
1984	----	----	----	1998	151.25	89.25	95.50	2012	1,045.25	805.75	927.00
1985	----	----	----	1999	222.50	90.75	222.25	2013	1,031.75	815.50	944.25

Futures begin trading 06/03/1986.   *Source: ICE Futures Europe*

GAS-OIL-PETROLEUM - ICE
Weekly Nearest Futures as of 01/03/2014

WEEKLY NEAREST FUTURES
As of 01/03/2014

Chart High 1339.25 on 07/11/2008
Chart Low 351.50 on 03/12/2009
CONTRACT SIZE 100 METRIC TONS
MIN TICK .25 USD
VALUE 25 USD/CONTRACT
EACH GRID 10 USD
VALUE 1000 USD/CONTRACT
DAILY LIMIT NONE
VALUE
TRADING HOURS
9:15a - 5:27p

USD / metric ton

Date	Open	High	Low	Close
12/06/13	938.25	952.75	932.75	940.75
12/13/13	943.25	944.75	916.75	917.75
12/20/13	922.50	949.00	915.00	945.25
12/27/13	946.75	957.25	941.00	955.75
01/03/14	951.25	955.75	905.75	910.25

USD / metric ton

Nearby Futures through Last Trading Day. Futures: 06/03/1986 to date.

Quarterly High, Low and Settle of Gasoil Futures   In USD per Metric Ton

Quarter	High	Low	Settle	Quarter	High	Low	Settle	Quarter	High	Low	Settle
03/2005	515.00	354.50	514.50	03/2008	1,001.25	753.25	969.00	03/2011	999.50	757.25	993.00
06/2005	542.00	424.25	525.25	06/2008	1,304.00	915.25	1,262.50	06/2011	1,064.50	857.00	926.50
09/2005	663.50	503.25	626.75	09/2008	1,339.25	867.25	914.50	09/2011	1,000.00	851.75	883.50
12/2005	641.50	487.50	510.75	12/2008	954.00	390.00	418.50	12/2011	1,002.25	849.25	924.00
03/2006	590.00	506.50	582.00	03/2009	527.00	351.50	420.00	03/2012	1,045.25	931.00	1,014.25
06/2006	655.75	574.50	643.25	06/2009	595.50	410.75	557.00	06/2012	1,037.25	805.75	848.50
09/2006	675.25	525.25	546.25	09/2009	618.00	481.75	552.00	09/2012	1,019.25	846.50	980.75
12/2006	571.25	511.50	516.50	12/2009	664.25	541.50	635.50	12/2012	1,030.00	897.00	927.00
03/2007	597.00	461.50	591.75	03/2010	692.75	551.50	683.75	03/2013	1,031.75	892.75	915.50
06/2007	636.25	562.00	626.00	06/2010	747.50	585.75	644.75	06/2013	935.00	815.50	883.25
09/2007	716.50	607.00	712.50	09/2010	716.25	607.00	706.75	09/2013	985.75	875.50	913.00
12/2007	861.50	667.75	839.25	12/2010	788.00	691.75	762.50	12/2013	957.25	885.00	944.25

Source: ICE Futures Europe

GASOLINE, RBOB

MONTHLY NEAREST FUTURES
As of 12/31/2013

Chart High	3.6310	on 07/11/2008
Chart Low	.3025	on 07/31/1986
CONTRACT SIZE	42,000 gallons	
MIN TICK VALUE	.0001 USD / 4.2 USD / contract	
EACH GRID VALUE	0.02 USD / 840 USD / contract	
DAILY LIMIT VALUE	.4 USD / 16,800 USD /contract	
TRADING HOURS	6:00p-5:15p / 9:00a-2:30p ET	

USD / Gallon

Nearby Futures through Last Trading Day.   Unleaded: to 11/1984; Futures: 12/03/1984 to date.

Annual High, Low and Settle of Gasoline, RBOB Futures   In USD per Gallon

Year	High	Low	Settle	Year	High	Low	Settle	Year	High	Low	Settle
1972	----	----	----	1986	.7085	.3025	.4790	2000	1.0960	.6540	.7858
1973	----	----	----	1987	.5785	.3950	.4367	2001	1.1750	.4780	.5725
1974	----	----	----	1988	.5450	.3895	.4788	2002	.9400	.5310	.8648
1975	----	----	----	1989	.7920	.4660	.6322	2003	1.1630	.7630	.9492
1976	.4300	.3920	.4260	1990	1.1100	.5350	.7092	2004	1.4700	.9290	1.0887
1977	.4670	.4270	.4650	1991	.8600	.5175	.5487	2005	2.9200	1.0980	1.7400
1978	.5700	.4470	.5375	1992	.6775	.5025	.5404	2006	2.5050	1.4100	1.6021
1979	1.2900	.5250	1.1800	1993	.6250	.3670	.3877	2007	2.5175	1.3351	2.4758
1980	1.1750	.8500	.9725	1994	.6105	.4010	.5590	2008	3.6310	.7850	1.0082
1981	1.0750	.9550	.9550	1995	.6740	.4870	.5886	2009	2.1124	.9669	2.0525
1982	1.0400	.8325	.8325	1996	.7810	.5150	.7067	2010	2.4555	1.8241	2.4303
1983	.9275	.7475	.7600	1997	.7290	.5250	.5281	2011	3.4800	2.3414	2.6863
1984	.7290	.6605	.6810	1998	.5600	.3160	.3570	2012	3.4455	2.5376	2.8120
1985	.8650	.6560	.7140	1999	.7720	.3240	.6910	2013	3.2672	2.4945	2.7858

Futures begin trading 12/03/1984; through December 2005 contract "Unleaded"; January 2006 contract to date "RBOB".
Source: CME Group; New York Mercantile Exchange

RBOB REGULAR NON-OXY, N.Y.
Monthly Cash as of 12/31/2013

Date	Open	High	Low	Close
08/30/13	2.9420	2.9420	2.7030	2.8750
09/30/13	2.9100	3.2470	2.7220	2.7220
10/31/13	2.7070	2.8620	2.6490	2.6970
11/29/13	2.6510	2.7120	2.5830	2.6400
12/31/13	2.6550	2.8680	2.5140	2.8490

MONTHLY CASH
As of 12/31/2013
Chart High 3.5930   on 06/06/2008
Chart Low   .2907   on 12/04/1998

USD / Gallon

Unleaded: to 12/2006; RBOB: 01/2007 to date.

Annual High, Low and Settle of Gasoline, RBOB   In USD per Gallon

Year	High	Low	Settle	Year	High	Low	Settle	Year	High	Low	Settle
1972	----	----	----	1986	.7260	.3050	.4625	2000	1.1093	.6380	.7553
1973	----	----	----	1987	.5800	.4130	.4360	2001	1.0120	.4622	.5478
1974	----	----	----	1988	.5900	.4270	.4850	2002	.9328	.5010	.8468
1975	----	----	----	1989	.7575	.4675	.6350	2003	1.1231	.6831	.9580
1976	.4300	.3920	.4260	1990	1.1075	.5225	.7035	2004	1.4240	.9297	1.0885
1977	.4670	.4270	.4650	1991	.8420	.5300	.5525	2005	3.1340	1.0965	1.7700
1978	.5700	.4470	.5375	1992	.6655	.4950	.5400	2006	2.4199	1.3812	1.6446
1979	1.2900	.5250	1.1800	1993	.6160	.3499	.3855	2007	2.5216	1.3078	2.4708
1980	1.1750	.8500	.9725	1994	.6155	.3970	.5115	2008	3.5930	.7552	.9744
1981	1.0750	.9550	.9550	1995	.6663	.4605	.5251	2009	2.1205	1.0075	2.0291
1982	1.0400	.8325	.8325	1996	.7464	.4755	.6915	2010	2.4701	1.8331	2.3993
1983	.9275	.7475	.7600	1997	.7639	.4924	.4924	2011	3.4947	2.3264	2.9217
1984	.8575	.6525	.6575	1998	.5167	.2907	.3408	2012	3.4000	2.6131	2.8287
1985	.9000	.6575	.7125	1999	.7788	.2930	.6755	2013	3.2470	2.5140	2.8490

Source: Energy Information Administration, U.S. Department of Energy (EIA-DOE)

GASOLINE, RBOB

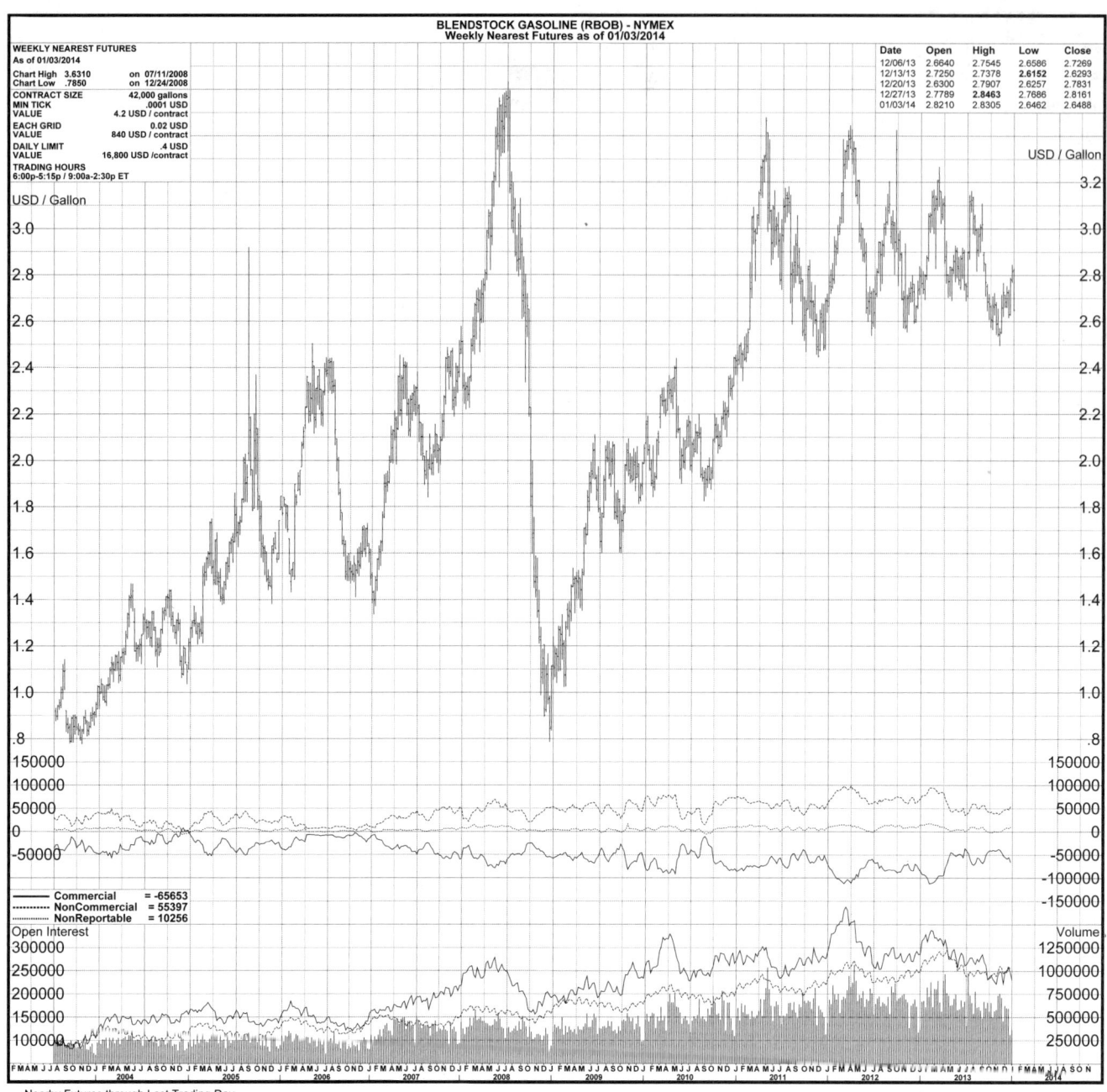

BLENDSTOCK GASOLINE (RBOB) - NYMEX
Weekly Nearest Futures as of 01/03/2014

WEEKLY NEAREST FUTURES
As of 01/03/2014

Chart High	3.6310 on 07/11/2008
Chart Low	.7850 on 12/24/2008
CONTRACT SIZE	42,000 gallons
MIN TICK VALUE	.0001 USD / 4.2 USD / contract
EACH GRID VALUE	0.02 USD / 840 USD / contract
DAILY LIMIT VALUE	.4 USD / 16,800 USD /contract
TRADING HOURS	6:00p-5:15p / 9:00a-2:30p ET

Date	Open	High	Low	Close
12/06/13	2.6640	2.7545	2.6586	2.7269
12/13/13	2.7250	2.7378	2.6152	2.6293
12/20/13	2.6300	2.7907	2.6257	2.7831
12/27/13	2.7789	2.8463	2.7686	2.8161
01/03/14	2.8210	2.8305	2.6462	2.6488

Commercial = -65653
NonCommercial = 55397
NonReportable = 10256

Nearby Futures through Last Trading Day.

Quarterly High, Low and Settle of Gasoline, RBOB Futures   In USD per Gallon

Quarter	High	Low	Settle	Quarter	High	Low	Settle	Quarter	High	Low	Settle
03/2005	1.6750	1.0980	1.6549	03/2008	2.7752	2.2183	2.6163	03/2011	3.1250	2.3414	3.1076
06/2005	1.7491	1.3770	1.5721	06/2008	3.5850	2.5920	3.5015	06/2011	3.4800	2.7348	3.0316
09/2005	2.9200	1.5700	2.1381	09/2008	3.6310	2.3348	2.4847	09/2011	3.1816	2.5150	2.6260
12/2005	2.1390	1.3805	1.7400	12/2008	2.5040	.7850	1.0082	12/2011	2.8667	2.4440	2.6863
03/2006	2.0805	1.4310	2.0645	03/2009	1.5372	.9669	1.4000	03/2012	3.4455	2.6647	3.3899
06/2006	2.5050	2.0500	2.3931	06/2009	2.1124	1.3411	1.8972	06/2012	3.4278	2.5376	2.7272
09/2006	2.4450	1.4800	1.5632	09/2009	2.0855	1.6010	1.7259	09/2012	3.4258	2.5700	3.3420
12/2006	1.7300	1.4100	1.6021	12/2009	2.0953	1.6885	2.0525	12/2012	2.9929	2.5524	2.8120
03/2007	2.1488	1.3351	2.1115	03/2010	2.3212	1.8419	2.3100	03/2013	3.2672	2.6915	3.1054
06/2007	2.4550	1.9820	2.2942	06/2010	2.4411	1.9008	2.0606	06/2013	3.1425	2.6870	2.7520
09/2007	2.3836	1.8400	2.0683	09/2010	2.1993	1.8241	2.0448	09/2013	3.1632	2.6066	2.6347
12/2007	2.5175	1.9450	2.4758	12/2010	2.4555	2.0301	2.4303	12/2013	2.8463	2.4945	2.7858

Through December 2005 contract "Unleaded"; January 2006 contract to date "RBOB".   *Source: CME Group; New York Mercantile Exchange*

RBOB REGULAR NON-OXY, N.Y.
Weekly Cash as of 01/03/2014

Date	Open	High	Low	Close
12/06/13	2.6550	2.7220	2.6500	2.7220
12/13/13	2.6390	2.6610	2.5140	2.5140
12/20/13	2.5270	2.7200	2.5270	2.7200
12/27/13	2.7350	2.8680	2.7350	2.8680
01/03/14	2.8490	2.8490	2.6958	2.7080

WEEKLY CASH
As of 01/03/2014
Chart High 3.5930 on 06/06/2008
Chart Low .6831 on 05/02/2003

USD / Gallon

Unleaded: to 12/2006; RBOB: 01/2007 to date.

Quarterly High, Low and Settle of Gasoline, RBOB   In USD per Gallon

Quarter	High	Low	Settle	Quarter	High	Low	Settle	Quarter	High	Low	Settle
03/2005	1.5313	1.0965	1.5313	03/2008	2.5986	2.1586	2.3863	03/2011	3.1177	2.3264	3.1177
06/2005	1.6048	1.3223	1.4731	06/2008	3.5930	2.4392	3.4916	06/2011	3.4947	2.8341	3.0642
09/2005	3.1340	1.5001	2.1231	09/2008	3.5372	2.3920	2.5016	09/2011	3.2968	2.5688	2.6331
12/2005	2.1047	1.4119	1.7700	12/2008	2.4075	.7552	.9744	12/2011	2.9251	2.4552	2.9217
03/2006	1.9807	1.3812	1.8718	03/2009	1.4745	1.0075	1.2934	03/2012	3.3550	2.7263	3.2299
06/2006	2.3519	1.9157	2.1826	06/2009	2.0898	1.3298	1.9057	06/2012	3.3155	2.6804	2.6842
09/2006	2.4199	1.4729	1.5632	09/2009	2.1205	1.6055	1.7303	09/2012	3.4000	2.7489	3.3920
12/2006	1.7894	1.4590	1.6446	12/2009	2.0767	1.7103	2.0291	12/2012	3.3751	2.6131	2.8287
03/2007	2.0655	1.3078	2.0155	03/2010	2.1975	1.8650	2.1975	03/2013	3.1095	2.6879	2.8554
06/2007	2.5216	2.0277	2.3179	06/2010	2.3575	1.9345	2.0629	06/2013	2.9057	2.5690	2.7558
09/2007	2.4046	1.8937	2.0670	09/2010	2.1785	1.8331	2.0536	09/2013	3.2470	2.7030	2.7220
12/2007	2.5020	1.9813	2.4708	12/2010	2.4701	2.0810	2.3993	12/2013	2.8680	2.5140	2.8490

Source: Energy Information Administration, U.S. Department of Energy (EIA-DOE)

GASOLINE, RBOB

UNLEADED GAS - INFLATION ADJUSTED
Monthly Nearest Futures as of 12/31/2013

MONTHLY NEAREST FUTURES
As of 12/31/2013

Chart High 4.2050   on 05/31/1979
Chart Low   .4491   on 11/30/1998

USD / Gallon

USD / Gallon

Date	Open	High	Low	Close
08/31/13	2.9963	**3.1095**	2.8161	3.0183
09/30/13	2.8875	2.9000	2.6066	2.6347
10/31/13	2.6234	2.7240	2.5418	2.6337
11/30/13	2.5970	2.7676	**2.4945**	2.6841
12/31/13	2.6640	2.8463	2.6152	2.7858

MJSDMJSDMJSDMJSDMJSDMJSDMJSDMJSDMJSDMJSDMJSDMJSDMJSDMJSDMJSDMJSDMJSDMJSDMJSDMJSDMJSDMJSDMJSDMJSDMJSDMJSDMJSDMJSDMJSDMJSDMJSDMJSDMJSDMJSDMJSDMJSDMJSDMJSDMJSDMJSDMJSDMJSDMJSDMJSDMJSDMJSDMJSDM
1971 1972 1973 1974 1975 1976 1977 1978 1979 1980 1981 1982 1983 1984 1985 1986 1987 1988 1989 1990 1991 1992 1993 1994 1995 1996 1997 1998 1999 2000 2001 2002 2003 2004 2005 2006 2007 2008 2009 2010 2011 2012 2013 2014 2015 2016 2017

Nearby Futures through Last Trading Day.   Unleaded: to 11/1904; Futures: 12/03/1984 to date.

HEATING OIL #2 - INFLATION ADJUSTED
Monthly Nearest Futures as of 12/31/2013

Date	Open	High	Low	Close
08/31/13	3.0565	**3.2254**	2.9193	3.1396
09/30/13	3.1275	3.1756	2.9300	2.9710
10/31/13	2.9692	3.0806	2.8930	2.9678
11/30/13	2.9553	3.0710	**2.8285**	3.0478
12/31/13	3.0302	3.1416	2.9533	3.0772

MONTHLY NEAREST FUTURES
As of 12/31/2013
Chart High 4.4064 on 07/31/2008
Chart Low .4137 on 02/28/1999

USD / Gallon

USD / Gallon

Nearby Futures through Last Trading Day.   #2 Fuel Oil to 11/1978; Futures: 11/14/1978 to date.

Annual High, Low and Settle of Heating Oil   In USD per Gallon

Year	High	Low	Settle	Year	High	Low	Settle	Year	High	Low	Settle
1930	----	----	----	1944	----	----	----	1958	----	----	----
1931	----	----	----	1945	----	----	----	1959	----	----	----
1932	----	----	----	1946	----	----	----	1960	----	----	----
1933	----	----	----	1947	----	----	----	1961	----	----	----
1934	----	----	----	1948	----	----	----	1962	----	----	----
1935	----	----	----	1949	----	----	----	1963	----	----	----
1936	----	----	----	1950	----	----	----	1964	----	----	----
1937	----	----	----	1951	----	----	----	1965	----	----	----
1938	----	----	----	1952	----	----	----	1966	----	----	----
1939	----	----	----	1953	----	----	----	1967	.1080	.1044	.1080
1940	----	----	----	1954	----	----	----	1968	.1120	.1080	.1100
1941	----	----	----	1955	----	----	----	1969	.1100	.1100	.1100
1942	----	----	----	1956	----	----	----	1970	.1160	.1100	.1160
1943	----	----	----	1957	----	----	----	1971	.1200	.1185	.1185

Data continued on page 91.   *Source: Energy Information Administration, U.S. Department of Energy (EIA-DOE)*

HEATING OIL

HEATING OIL #2 - NYMEX
Monthly Nearest Futures as of 12/31/2013

Date	Open	High	Low	Close
08/31/13	3.0565	**3.2254**	2.9193	3.1396
09/30/13	3.1275	3.1756	2.9300	2.9710
10/31/13	2.9692	3.0806	2.8930	2.9678
11/30/13	2.9553	3.0710	**2.8285**	3.0478
12/31/13	3.0302	3.1416	2.9533	3.0772

MONTHLY NEAREST FUTURES
As of 12/31/2013

Chart High 4.1586 on 07/11/2008
Chart Low .1185 on 12/31/1971
CONTRACT SIZE 42,000 gallons
MIN TICK .0001 USD
VALUE 4.2 USD / contract
EACH GRID 0.02 USD
VALUE 840 USD / contract
DAILY LIMIT .4 USD
VALUE 16,800 USD /contract
TRADING HOURS
6:00p-5:15p / 9:00a-2:30p ET

Nearby Futures through Last Trading Day.   #2 Fuel Oil: to 11/1978; Futures: 11/14/1978 to date.

Annual High, Low and Settle of Heating Oil #2 Futures   In USD per Gallon

Year	High	Low	Settle	Year	High	Low	Settle	Year	High	Low	Settle
1972	.1185	.1185	.1185	1986	.7680	.2995	.4890	2000	1.1100	.6275	.9066
1973	.2270	.1209	.2270	1987	.5870	.4260	.5144	2001	.8979	.4930	.5507
1974	.2895	.2450	.2754	1988	.5440	.3700	.5348	2002	.9255	.4990	.8655
1975	.3137	.2739	.3137	1989	1.1000	.4440	1.0187	2003	1.3100	.6690	.9127
1976	.3383	.2954	.3383	1990	1.0780	.4630	.8131	2004	1.6030	.8150	1.2297
1977	.3670	.3430	.3660	1991	.9300	.4660	.4829	2005	2.2100	1.1680	1.7280
1978	.4540	.3550	.4300	1992	.6615	.4915	.5640	2006	2.1700	1.5700	1.5979
1979	1.0450	.4300	.8275	1993	.6005	.4325	.4416	2007	2.7272	1.4530	2.6444
1980	.9736	.7170	.9690	1994	.5540	.4260	.5131	2008	4.1586	1.1914	1.4057
1981	1.0530	.8945	.9710	1995	.6265	.4405	.5863	2009	2.1380	1.1252	2.1188
1982	1.0420	.7001	.8281	1996	.7675	.4890	.7284	2010	2.5669	1.8272	2.5424
1983	.8630	.6850	.8424	1997	.7450	.4890	.4908	2011	3.3300	2.4678	2.9350
1984	1.0530	.7185	.7240	1998	.4985	.3080	.3400	2012	3.3176	2.5100	3.0451
1985	.9015	.6685	.8055	1999	.7150	.2920	.6903	2013	3.2575	2.7255	3.0772

Futures begin trading 11/14/1978.   *Source: CME Group; New York Mercantile Exchange*

FUEL OIL #2, N.Y.
Monthly Cash as of 12/31/2013

Date	Open	High	Low	Close
08/30/13	2.9430	3.0920	2.8410	3.0260
09/30/13	3.0440	3.0600	2.8720	2.8970
10/31/13	2.8630	3.0352	2.8590	2.9380
11/29/13	2.8780	3.0400	2.8300	3.0210
12/31/13	3.0420	3.1240	2.9440	3.0820

MONTHLY CASH
As of 12/31/2013

Chart High 4.0785 on 07/03/2008
Chart Low .1185 on 12/31/1971

USD / Gallon

#2 Fuel Oil

Annual High, Low and Settle of Heating Oil   In USD per Gallon

Year	High	Low	Settle	Year	High	Low	Settle	Year	High	Low	Settle
1972	.1185	.1185	.1185	1986	.7835	.3175	.4675	2000	1.6878	.6595	.9074
1973	.2270	.1209	.2270	1987	.5800	.4275	.5125	2001	.8983	.4691	.5495
1974	.2895	.2450	.2754	1988	.5585	.3700	.5385	2002	.9017	.5049	.8648
1975	.3137	.2739	.3137	1989	1.1500	.4520	1.1300	2003	1.2847	.6898	.9027
1976	.3383	.2954	.3383	1990	1.0535	.4725	.8095	2004	1.5758	.8405	1.2165
1977	.3670	.3430	.3660	1991	.9510	.4595	.4615	2005	2.1585	1.1740	1.7243
1978	.4275	.3550	.4100	1992	.6555	.4670	.5610	2006	2.0944	1.5400	1.5829
1979	1.1400	.3620	.8500	1993	.5975	.4172	.4440	2007	2.6941	1.4432	2.6531
1980	.9500	.7250	.9500	1994	.6375	.4530	.5140	2008	4.0785	1.1920	1.4032
1981	1.0375	.8950	.9875	1995	.6221	.4410	.5853	2009	2.1081	1.1193	2.1081
1982	1.0300	.8000	.8325	1996	.7990	.5024	.7282	2010	2.5333	1.8650	2.4804
1983	.8550	.7225	.8400	1997	.7409	.4906	.4906	2011	3.3072	2.4825	2.9088
1984	1.0500	.7175	.7175	1998	.4921	.3008	.3355	2012	3.2874	2.5387	3.0498
1985	.8875	.6800	.8075	1999	.7350	.2842	.7055	2013	3.2622	2.5621	3.0820

Data continued from page 89.   *Source: Energy Information Administration, U.S. Department of Energy (EIA-DOE)*

HEATING OIL

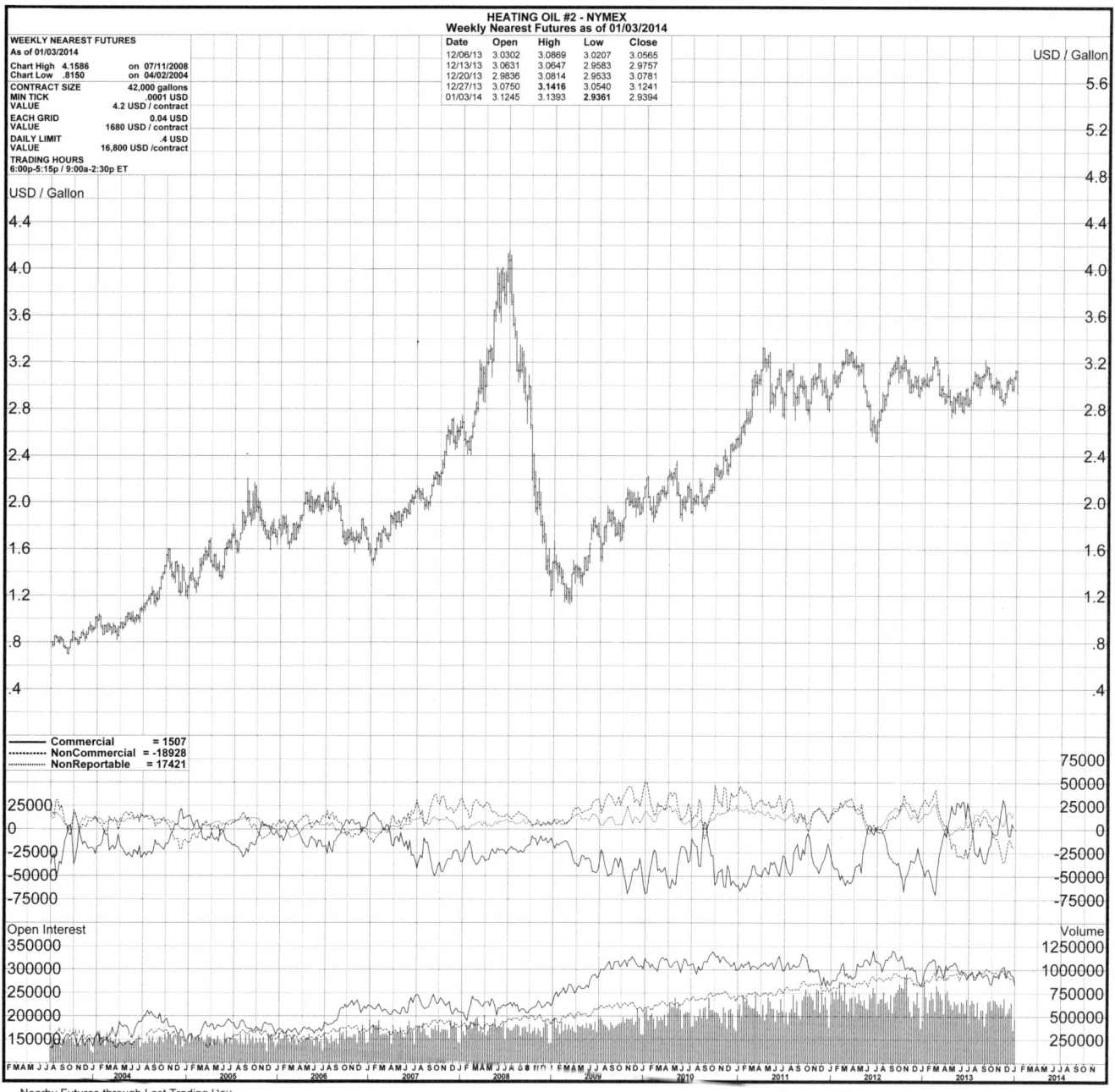

Nearby Futures through Last Trading Day.

Quarterly High, Low and Settle of Heating Oil #2 Futures   In USD per Gallon

Quarter	High	Low	Settle	Quarter	High	Low	Settle	Quarter	High	Low	Settle
03/2005	1.6700	1.1680	1.6576	03/2008	3.2220	2.4042	3.0492	03/2011	3.1372	2.4678	3.0898
06/2005	1.6950	1.3340	1.6191	06/2008	4.0153	2.8489	3.9029	06/2011	3.3300	2.7150	2.9327
09/2005	2.2100	1.5560	2.0673	09/2008	4.1586	2.6712	2.8636	09/2011	3.1955	2.7020	2.7948
12/2005	2.1470	1.5875	1.7280	12/2008	2.9500	1.1914	1.4057	12/2011	3.2004	2.6975	2.9350
03/2006	1.8920	1.5970	1.8618	03/2009	1.6688	1.1252	1.3438	03/2012	3.3176	2.9267	3.1684
06/2006	2.1080	1.8338	1.9642	06/2009	1.8805	1.2785	1.7180	06/2012	3.2610	2.5100	2.6960
09/2006	2.1700	1.6249	1.6846	09/2009	1.9738	1.4871	1.7960	09/2012	3.2633	2.6488	3.1694
12/2006	1.8611	1.5700	1.5979	12/2009	2.1380	1.7377	2.1188	12/2012	3.2668	2.8936	3.0451
03/2007	1.9055	1.4530	1.8794	03/2010	2.2272	1.8272	2.1646	03/2013	3.2575	2.8430	2.9152
06/2007	2.0710	1.7638	2.0319	06/2010	2.3574	1.8368	1.9817	06/2013	3.1044	2.7255	2.8798
09/2007	2.2640	1.9290	2.2379	09/2010	2.2525	1.8968	2.2440	09/2013	3.2254	2.8500	2.9710
12/2007	2.7272	2.1415	2.6444	12/2010	2.5669	2.1862	2.5424	12/2013	3.1416	2.8285	3.0772

Source: CME Group; New York Mercantile Exchange

FUEL OIL #2, N.Y.
Weekly Cash as of 01/03/2014

WEEKLY CASH
As of 01/03/2014

Chart High 4.0785   on 07/03/2008
Chart Low   .6898   on 09/19/2003

USD / Gallon

Date	Open	High	Low	Close
12/06/13	3.0420	3.0550	3.0370	3.0430
12/13/13	2.9980	3.0120	2.9560	2.9560
12/20/13	2.9690	3.0680	2.9440	3.0680
12/27/13	3.0590	3.1240	3.0590	3.1240
01/03/14	3.0880	3.0880	2.9670	2.9670

#2 Fuel Oil

Quarterly High, Low and Settle of Heating Oil   In USD per Gallon

Quarter	High	Low	Settle	Quarter	High	Low	Settle	Quarter	High	Low	Settle
03/2005	1.6579	1.1740	1.6579	03/2008	3.2345	2.4103	3.0592	03/2011	3.0987	2.4825	3.0987
06/2005	1.6760	1.3491	1.6124	06/2008	3.9602	2.9772	3.9100	06/2011	3.3072	2.7378	2.9363
09/2005	2.1585	1.5227	2.0486	09/2008	4.0785	2.6947	2.8597	09/2011	3.1205	2.7548	2.7718
12/2005	2.0334	1.5872	1.7243	12/2008	2.8144	1.1920	1.4032	12/2011	3.1641	2.7234	2.9088
03/2006	1.8856	1.5400	1.8641	03/2009	1.6175	1.1193	1.3313	03/2012	3.2874	2.9909	3.1567
06/2006	2.0792	1.8124	1.9575	06/2009	1.8180	1.3047	1.7055	06/2012	3.2421	2.5387	2.7010
09/2006	2.0944	1.5797	1.6471	09/2009	1.9331	1.4700	1.8074	09/2012	3.2057	2.6784	3.1694
12/2006	1.7952	1.5739	1.5829	12/2009	2.1081	1.7586	2.1081	12/2012	3.2609	2.8875	3.0498
03/2007	1.8745	1.4432	1.8742	03/2010	2.1917	1.8650	2.1608	03/2013	3.2622	2.8797	2.9202
06/2007	2.1496	1.8015	2.0331	06/2010	2.3100	1.8679	1.9654	06/2013	2.9787	2.5621	2.7598
09/2007	2.2421	1.9193	2.2316	09/2010	2.2360	1.8767	2.2360	09/2013	3.0920	2.7336	2.8970
12/2007	2.6941	2.1408	2.6531	12/2010	2.5333	2.1693	2.4804	12/2013	3.1240	2.8300	3.0820

Source: Energy Information Administration, U.S. Department of Energy (EIA-DOE)

NATURAL GAS

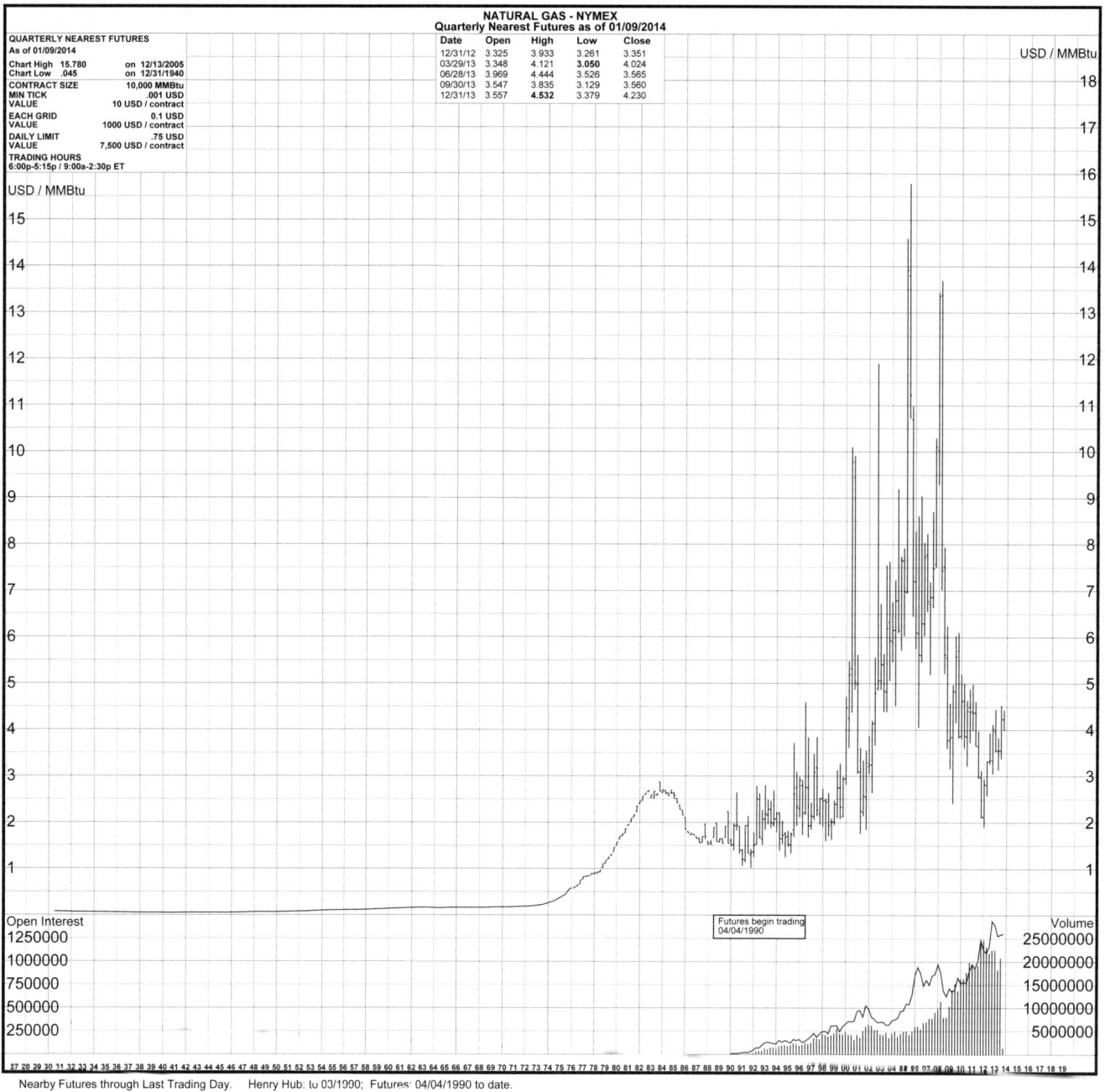

NATURAL GAS - NYMEX
Quarterly Nearest Futures as of 01/09/2014

Date	Open	High	Low	Close
12/31/12	3.325	3.933	3.261	3.351
03/29/13	3.348	4.121	3.050	4.024
06/28/13	3.969	4.444	3.526	3.565
09/30/13	3.547	3.835	3.129	3.560
12/31/13	3.557	4.532	3.379	4.230

USD / MMBtu

QUARTERLY NEAREST FUTURES
As of 01/09/2014

Chart High 15.780	on 12/13/2005
Chart Low .045	on 12/31/1940
CONTRACT SIZE	10,000 MMBtu
MIN TICK	.001 USD
VALUE	10 USD / contract
EACH GRID VALUE	0.1 USD
	1000 USD / contract
DAILY LIMIT	.75 USD
VALUE	7,500 USD / contract
TRADING HOURS	
6:00p-5:15p / 9:00a-2:30p ET	

Futures begin trading 04/04/1990

Open Interest
1250000
1000000
750000
500000
250000

Volume
25000000
20000000
15000000
10000000
5000000

Nearby Futures through Last Trading Day.   Henry Hub: to 03/1990; Futures: 04/04/1990 to date.

Annual High, Low and Settle of Natural Gas   In USD per MMBtu

Year	High	Low	Settle	Year	High	Low	Settle	Year	High	Low	Settle
1930	.076	.076	.076	1944	.051	.051	.051	1958	.120	.120	.120
1931	.070	.070	.070	1945	.049	.049	.049	1959	.130	.130	.130
1932	.064	.064	.064	1946	.053	.053	.053	1960	.140	.140	.140
1933	.062	.062	.062	1947	.060	.060	.060	1961	.150	.150	.150
1934	.060	.060	.060	1948	.065	.065	.065	1962	.160	.160	.160
1935	.058	.058	.058	1949	.063	.063	.063	1963	.160	.160	.160
1936	.055	.055	.055	1950	.065	.065	.065	1964	.150	.150	.150
1937	.051	.051	.051	1951	.073	.073	.073	1965	.160	.160	.160
1938	.049	.049	.049	1952	.078	.078	.078	1966	.160	.160	.160
1939	.049	.049	.049	1953	.092	.092	.092	1967	.160	.160	.160
1940	.045	.045	.045	1954	.101	.101	.101	1968	.160	.160	.160
1941	.049	.049	.049	1955	.104	.104	.104	1969	.170	.170	.170
1942	.051	.051	.051	1956	.108	.108	.108	1970	.170	.170	.170
1943	.052	.052	.052	1957	.110	.110	.110	1971	.180	.180	.180

Henry Hub.   Data continued on page 96.   *Source: CME Group; New York Mercantile Exchange*

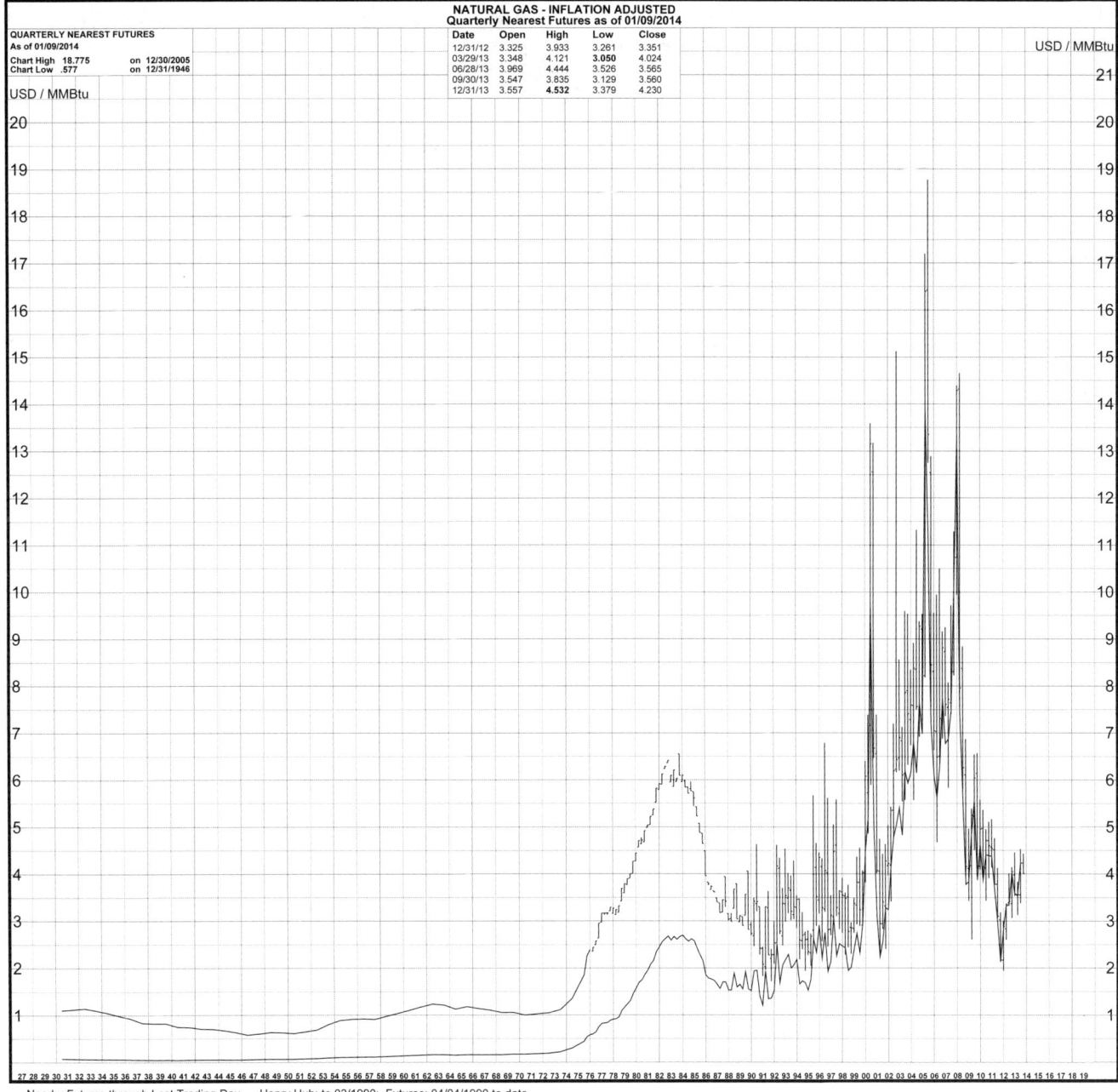

Date	Open	High	Low	Close
12/31/12	3.325	3.933	3.261	3.351
03/29/13	3.348	4.121	**3.050**	4.024
06/28/13	3.969	4.444	3.526	3.565
09/30/13	3.547	3.835	3.129	3.560
12/31/13	3.557	**4.532**	3.379	4.230

QUARTERLY NEAREST FUTURES
As of 01/09/2014

Chart High 18.775   on 12/30/2005
Chart Low .577   on 12/31/1946

USD / MMBtu

USD / MMBtu

Nearby Futures through Last Trading Day.   Henry Hub: to 03/1990; Futures: 04/04/1990 to date.

Annual High, Low and Settle of Natural Gas   In USD per MMBtu

Year	High	Low	Settle	Year	High	Low	Settle	Year	High	Low	Settle
1930	.076	.076	.076	1944	.051	.051	.051	1958	.120	.120	.120
1931	.070	.070	.070	1945	.049	.049	.049	1959	.130	.130	.130
1932	.064	.064	.064	1946	.053	.053	.053	1960	.140	.140	.140
1933	.062	.062	.062	1947	.060	.060	.060	1961	.150	.150	.150
1934	.060	.060	.060	1948	.065	.065	.065	1962	.160	.160	.160
1935	.058	.058	.058	1949	.063	.063	.063	1963	.160	.160	.160
1936	.055	.055	.055	1950	.065	.065	.065	1964	.150	.150	.150
1937	.051	.051	.051	1951	.073	.073	.073	1965	.160	.160	.160
1938	.049	.049	.049	1952	.078	.078	.078	1966	.160	.160	.160
1939	.049	.049	.049	1953	.092	.092	.092	1967	.160	.160	.160
1940	.045	.045	.045	1954	.101	.101	.101	1968	.160	.160	.160
1941	.049	.049	.049	1955	.104	.104	.104	1969	.170	.170	.170
1942	.051	.051	.051	1956	.108	.108	.108	1970	.170	.170	.170
1943	.052	.052	.052	1957	.110	.110	.110	1971	.180	.180	.180

Henry Hub.   Data continued on page 97.   *Source: CME Group; New York Mercantile Exchange*

NATURAL GAS

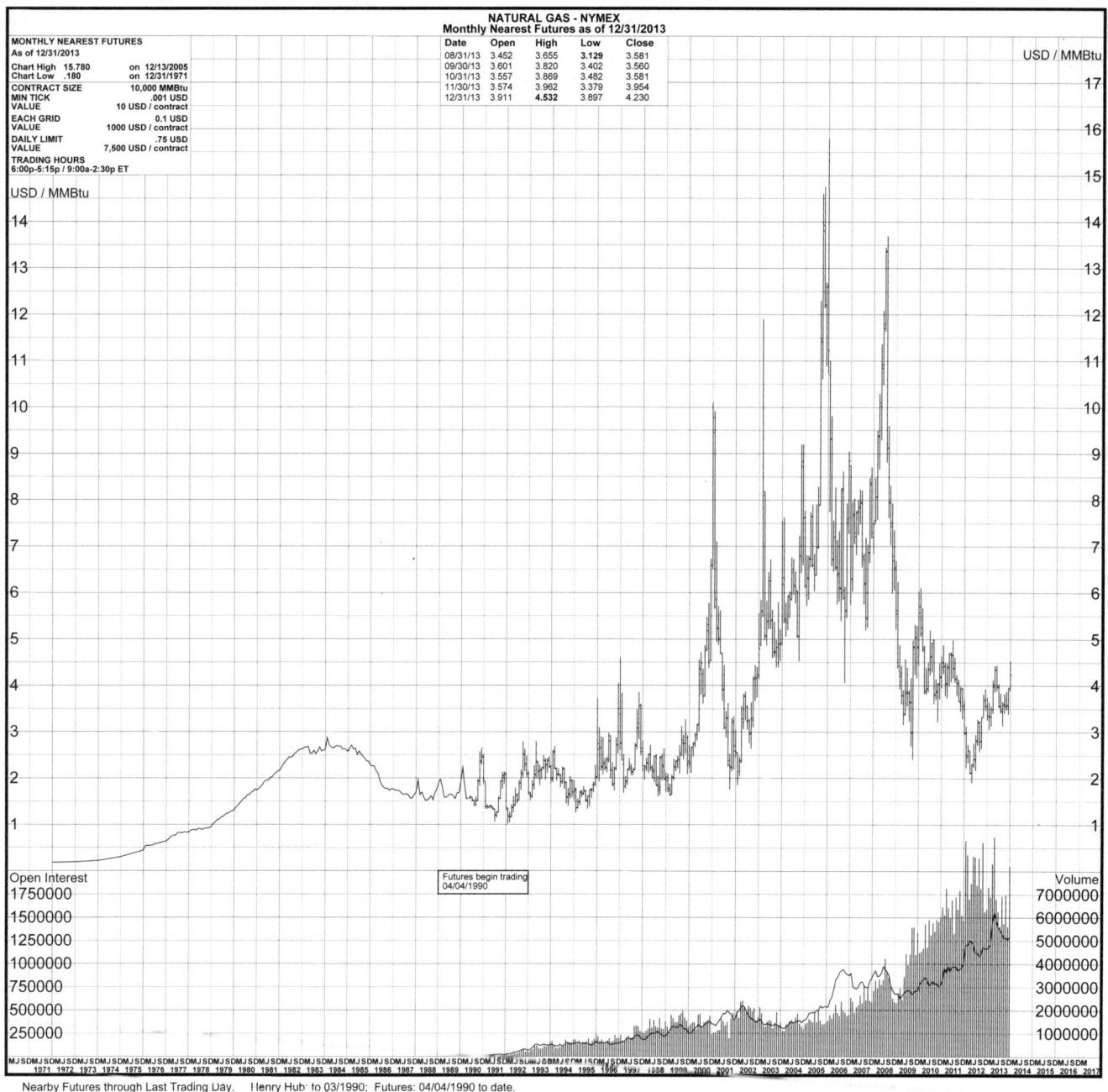

NATURAL GAS - NYMEX
Monthly Nearest Futures as of 12/31/2013

Date	Open	High	Low	Close
08/31/13	3.452	3.655	3.129	3.581
09/30/13	3.601	3.820	3.402	3.560
10/31/13	3.557	3.869	3.482	3.581
11/30/13	3.574	3.962	3.379	3.954
12/31/13	3.911	**4.532**	3.897	4.230

MONTHLY NEAREST FUTURES
As of 12/31/2013

Chart High	15.780	on	12/13/2005
Chart Low	.180	on	12/31/1971
CONTRACT SIZE	10,000 MMBtu		
MIN TICK VALUE	.001 USD 10 USD / contract		
EACH GRID VALUE	0.1 USD 1000 USD / contract		
DAILY LIMIT VALUE	.75 USD 7,500 USD / contract		
TRADING HOURS	6:00p-5:15p / 9:00a-2:30p ET		

USD / MMBtu

Open Interest
Volume

Futures begin trading 04/04/1990

Nearby Futures through Last Trading Day.   Henry Hub to 03/1990; Futures: 04/04/1990 to date.

Annual High, Low and Settle of Natural Gas Futures   In USD per MMBtu

Year	High	Low	Settle	Year	High	Low	Settle	Year	High	Low	Settle
1972	.190	.190	.190	1986	2.260	1.730	1.760	2000	10.100	2.125	9.775
1973	.220	.220	.220	1987	1.740	1.560	1.700	2001	9.916	1.760	2.570
1974	.300	.300	.300	1988	1.960	1.520	1.890	2002	5.560	1.850	4.789
1975	.440	.440	.440	1989	1.980	1.550	1.920	2003	11.899	4.390	6.189
1976	.640	.540	.640	1990	2.650	1.396	1.950	2004	9.200	4.520	6.149
1977	.840	.670	.840	1991	2.140	1.060	1.343	2005	15.780	5.710	11.225
1978	.960	.870	.960	1992	2.790	1.020	1.687	2006	11.000	4.050	6.299
1979	1.310	1.020	1.310	1993	2.800	1.521	1.997	2007	8.712	5.192	7.483
1980	1.760	1.370	1.740	1994	2.690	1.395	1.725	2008	13.694	5.210	5.622
1981	2.160	1.770	2.160	1995	3.720	1.250	2.619	2009	6.240	2.409	5.572
1982	2.620	2.230	2.620	1996	4.600	1.735	2.757	2010	6.108	3.212	4.405
1983	2.680	2.520	2.610	1997	3.850	1.680	2.264	2011	4.983	2.957	2.989
1984	2.870	2.570	2.570	1998	2.725	1.600	1.945	2012	3.933	1.902	3.351
1985	2.710	2.280	2.280	1999	3.275	1.625	2.329	2013	4.532	3.050	4.230

Futures begin trading 04/04/1990.   Data continued from page 94.   *Source: CME Group; New York Mercantile Exchange*

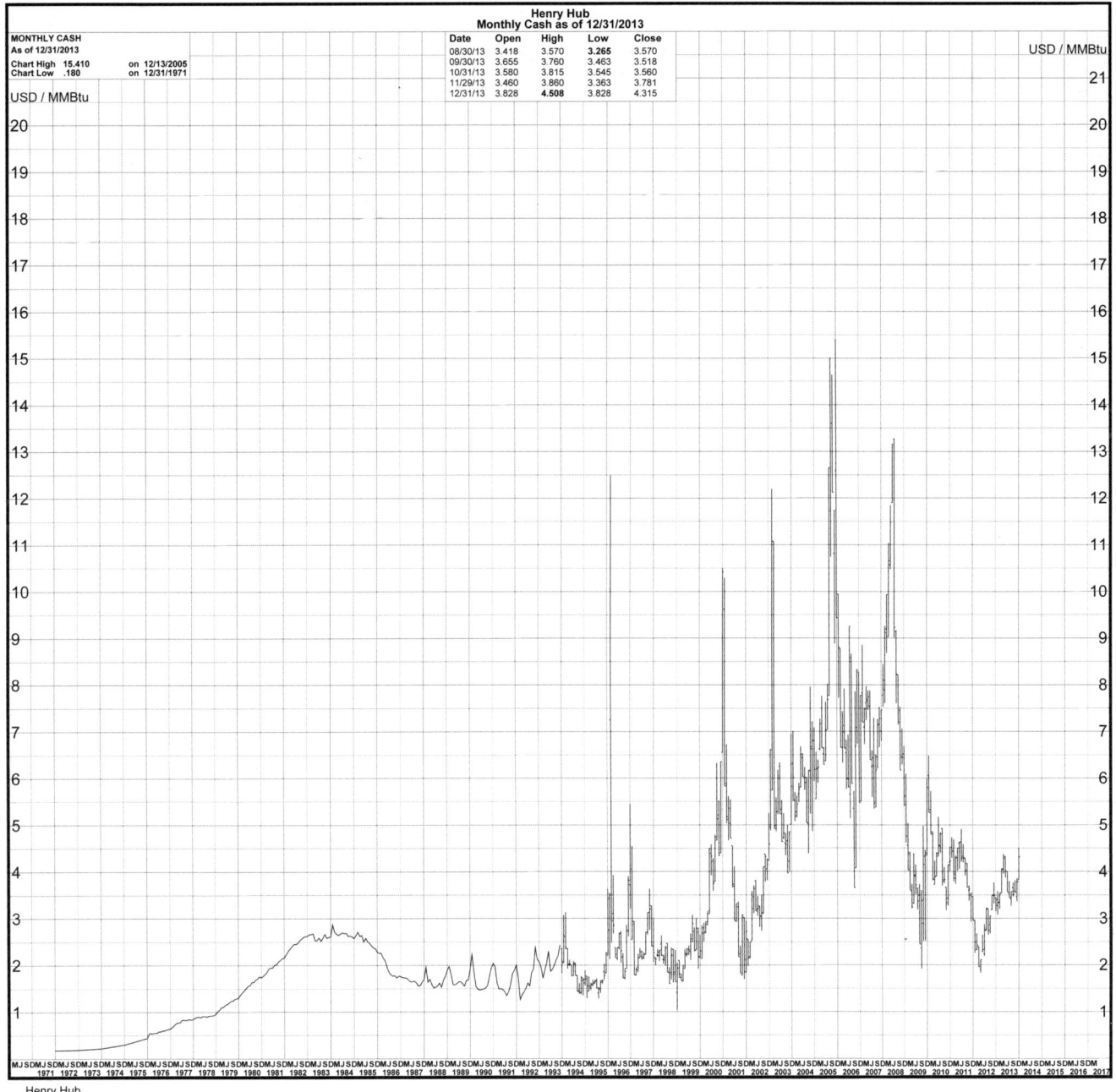

MONTHLY CASH
As of 12/31/2013

Chart High 15.410   on 12/13/2005
Chart Low   .180   on 12/31/1971

USD / MMBtu

Henry Hub Monthly Cash as of 12/31/2013				
Date	Open	High	Low	Close
08/30/13	3.418	3.570	3.265	3.570
09/30/13	3.655	3.760	3.463	3.518
10/31/13	3.580	3.815	3.545	3.560
11/29/13	3.460	3.860	3.363	3.781
12/31/13	3.828	4.508	3.828	4.315

Henry Hub

Annual High, Low and Settle of Natural Gas In USD per MMBtu

Year	High	Low	Settle	Year	High	Low	Settle	Year	High	Low	Settle
1972	.190	.190	.190	1986	2.260	1.730	1.760	2000	10.500	2.140	10.415
1973	.220	.220	.220	1987	1.740	1.560	1.700	2001	10.295	1.695	2.720
1974	.300	.300	.300	1988	1.960	1.520	1.890	2002	5.250	1.980	4.585
1975	.440	.440	.440	1989	1.980	1.550	1.920	2003	12.200	3.965	5.825
1976	.640	.540	.640	1990	2.230	1.470	2.040	2004	7.960	4.385	6.185
1977	.840	.670	.840	1991	2.000	1.340	2.000	2005	15.410	5.560	9.435
1978	.960	.870	.960	1992	2.380	1.260	2.070	2006	9.945	3.655	5.475
1979	1.310	1.020	1.310	1993	2.430	1.720	2.080	2007	8.860	5.350	7.465
1980	1.760	1.370	1.740	1994	3.130	1.345	1.705	2008	13.275	5.400	5.620
1981	2.160	1.770	2.160	1995	3.625	1.280	2.750	2009	6.095	1.920	5.805
1982	2.620	2.230	2.620	1996	12.500	1.695	4.050	2010	6.480	3.170	4.225
1983	2.680	2.520	2.610	1997	4.550	1.785	2.265	2011	4.915	2.925	2.963
1984	2.870	2.570	2.570	1998	2.635	1.035	1.935	2012	3.765	1.831	3.404
1985	2.710	2.280	2.280	1999	3.075	1.645	2.305	2013	4.508	3.074	4.315

Henry Hub.   Data continued from page 95.   *Source: Energy Information Administration, U.S. Department of Energy (EIA-DOE)*

NATURAL GAS

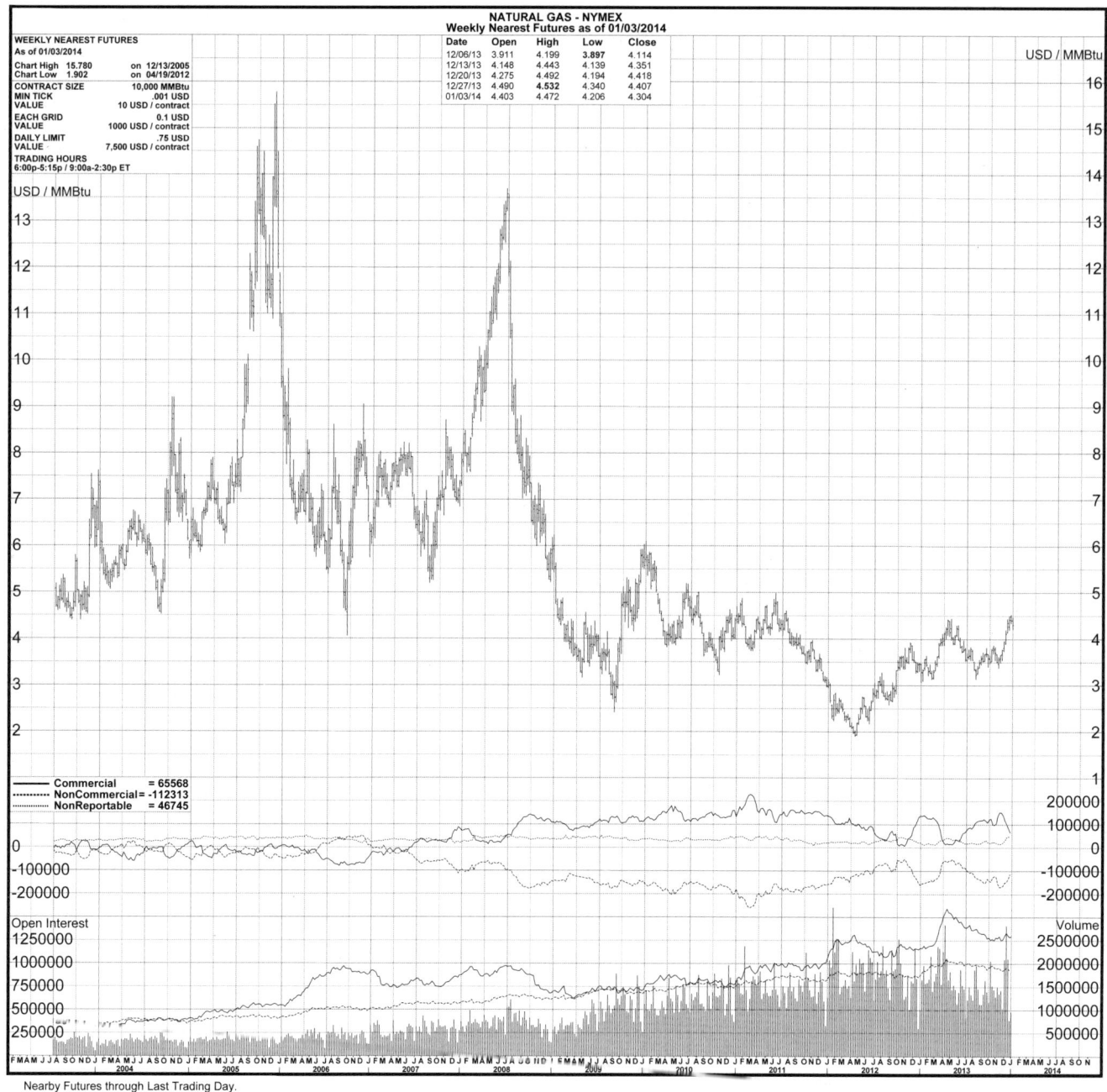

Source: CME Group; New York Mercantile Exchange

Quarterly High, Low and Settle of Natural Gas Futures   In USD per Gallon

Quarter	High	Low	Settle	Quarter	High	Low	Settle	Quarter	High	Low	Settle
03/2005	7.740	5.710	7.653	03/2008	10.294	7.500	10.101	03/2011	4.879	3.731	4.389
06/2005	7.915	6.030	6.981	06/2008	13.448	9.290	13.353	06/2011	4.983	3.990	4.374
09/2005	14.600	6.949	13.921	09/2008	13.694	7.023	7.438	09/2011	4.612	3.662	3.666
12/2005	15.780	10.720	11.225	12/2008	7.938	5.210	5.622	12/2011	3.978	2.957	2.989
03/2006	11.000	6.450	7.210	03/2009	6.240	3.600	3.776	03/2012	3.123	2.101	2.126
06/2006	8.280	5.750	6.104	06/2009	4.575	3.155	3.835	06/2012	2.946	1.902	2.824
09/2006	8.619	4.050	5.620	09/2009	4.975	2.409	4.841	09/2012	3.330	2.575	3.320
12/2006	9.050	5.460	6.299	12/2009	6.035	4.157	5.572	12/2012	3.933	3.261	3.351
03/2007	8.035	6.030	7.730	03/2010	6.108	3.820	3.869	03/2013	4.121	3.050	4.024
06/2007	8.230	6.551	6.773	06/2010	5.196	3.810	4.616	06/2013	4.444	3.526	3.565
09/2007	7.192	5.192	6.870	09/2010	5.007	3.610	3.872	09/2013	3.835	3.129	3.560
12/2007	8.712	6.640	7.483	12/2010	4.637	3.212	4.405	12/2013	4.532	3.379	4.230

Source: CME Group; New York Mercantile Exchange

Henry Hub
Weekly Cash as of 01/03/2014

Date	Open	High	Low	Close
12/06/13	3.828	4.138	3.828	4.138
12/13/13	4.228	4.398	4.225	4.376
12/20/13	4.248	4.345	4.211	4.345
12/27/13	4.508	4.508	4.330	4.330
01/03/14	4.403	4.403	4.315	4.340

WEEKLY CASH
As of 01/03/2014
Chart High 15.410 on 12/13/2005
Chart Low 1.831 on 04/19/2012

USD / MMBtu

Henry Hub

Quarterly High, Low and Settle of Natural Gas   In USD per Gallon ⁷

Quarter	High	Low	Settle	Quarter	High	Low	Settle	Quarter	High	Low	Settle
03/2005	7.275	5.560	7.170	03/2008	9.935	7.530	9.935	03/2011	4.730	3.735	4.295
06/2005	7.760	6.290	7.025	06/2008	13.155	9.030	13.155	06/2011	4.915	4.018	4.283
09/2005	15.000	7.035	15.000	09/2008	13.275	7.140	7.205	09/2011	4.585	3.663	3.663
12/2005	15.410	8.880	9.435	12/2008	7.535	5.400	5.620	12/2011	3.703	2.925	2.963
03/2006	9.945	6.325	6.985	03/2009	6.095	3.605	3.605	03/2012	2.965	1.959	1.959
06/2006	7.920	5.765	5.805	06/2009	4.390	3.205	3.710	06/2012	2.880	1.831	2.738
09/2006	9.250	3.655	3.655	09/2009	3.735	1.920	3.380	09/2012	3.220	2.650	3.051
12/2006	8.325	4.075	5.475	12/2009	5.985	2.515	5.805	12/2012	3.765	3.153	3.404
03/2007	8.860	5.500	7.480	03/2010	6.480	3.810	3.835	03/2013	4.068	3.074	4.055
06/2007	7.970	6.395	6.395	06/2010	5.175	3.725	4.555	06/2013	4.374	3.560	3.560
09/2007	7.295	5.350	6.180	09/2010	4.925	3.700	3.825	09/2013	3.794	3.265	3.518
12/2007	7.525	6.205	7.465	12/2010	4.523	3.170	4.225	12/2013	4.508	3.363	4.315

Henry Hub.   Source: Energy Information Administration, U.S. Department of Energy (EIA-DOE)

PROPANE / MONT BELVIEU, TEXAS
Monthly Cash as of 12/31/2013

Date	Open	High	Low	Close
08/30/13	.9645	1.1794	.9577	1.1794
09/30/13	1.1912	1.1912	1.0311	1.0510
10/31/13	1.0726	1.1715	1.0726	1.1713
11/29/13	1.1657	1.2018	1.1562	1.1562
12/31/13	1.1900	1.3244	1.1900	1.2609

MONTHLY CASH
As of 12/31/2013
Chart High 1.9794 on 07/14/2008
Chart Low .0573 on 12/31/1971

USD / gallon

Baton Rouge (annual close): to 1976; Wholesale (close): 01/1977 to 12/1982; Mont Belvieu, TX (close) 01/1983 to date.

Annual High, Low and Settle of Propane   In USD per Gallon

Year	High	Low	Settle	Year	High	Low	Settle	Year	High	Low	Settle
1972	.0621	.0573	.0621	1986	.4000	.1850	.1900	2000	.8375	.4288	.8338
1973	.1328	.0621	.1328	1987	.2775	.2150	.2375	2001	.8875	.2675	.3200
1974	.1928	.1348	.1664	1988	.2525	.1875	.2200	2002	.5650	.2775	.5400
1975	.2075	.1662	.2075	1989	.7100	.1900	.7100	2003	1.0625	.4725	.6675
1976	.2213	.1975	.2213	1990	.7400	.2163	.4425	2004	.9688	.5550	.7463
1977	.2680	.2290	.2670	1991	.4750	.2410	.2735	2005	1.1932	.7000	1.0275
1978	.2700	.2210	.2210	1992	.3890	.2510	.3250	2006	1.1850	.8575	.9150
1979	.4040	.2120	.4040	1993	.3790	.2312	.2535	2007	1.6054	.8500	1.6019
1980	.4650	.4060	.4650	1994	.3585	.2500	.3325	2008	1.9794	.5633	.6150
1981	.4930	.4550	.4550	1995	.4013	.3025	.3825	2009	1.3210	.6025	1.3210
1982	.5320	.3490	.5320	1996	.7050	.3225	.5025	2010	1.4461	.9613	1.3156
1983	.5500	.4075	.4550	1997	.5525	.3188	.3263	2011	1.6269	1.3113	1.3980
1984	.4925	.3625	.3625	1998	.3298	.2025	.2025	2012	1.4056	.7054	.8858
1985	.4825	.3150	.4275	1999	.4869	.2025	.4575	2013	1.3244	.7890	1.2609

Source: Energy Information Administration, U.S. Department of Energy (EIA-DOE)

PROPANE / MONT BELVIEU, TEXAS
Weekly Cash as of 01/03/2014

Date	Open	High	Low	Close
12/06/13	1.1900	1.2698	1.1900	1.2698
12/13/13	1.2851	1.3244	1.2851	1.3073
12/20/13	1.3073	1.3073	1.2503	1.2503
12/27/13	1.2511	1.2758	1.2511	1.2758
01/03/14	1.2746	1.2746	1.2444	1.2444

WEEKLY CASH
As of 01/03/2014
Chart High 1.9794 on 07/14/2008
Chart Low .4725 on 04/04/2003
USD / gallon

Mont Belvieu, TX

Quarterly High, Low and Settle of Propane   In USD per Gallon

Quarter	High	Low	Settle	Quarter	High	Low	Settle	Quarter	High	Low	Settle
03/2005	.9500	.7000	.8907	03/2008	1.6338	1.3313	1.4650	03/2011	1.5512	1.3113	1.3668
06/2005	.9225	.7788	.8257	06/2008	1.9075	1.4367	1.9075	06/2011	1.6198	1.3830	1.4867
09/2005	1.1932	.8113	1.1750	09/2008	1.9794	1.4125	1.4125	09/2011	1.6269	1.4519	1.5148
12/2005	1.1738	.9525	1.0275	12/2008	1.6218	.5633	.6150	12/2011	1.5410	1.3260	1.3980
03/2006	1.0639	.8575	.9600	03/2009	.7705	.6025	.6400	03/2012	1.4056	1.1717	1.2375
06/2006	1.1600	.9519	1.1600	06/2009	.8875	.6162	.8375	06/2012	1.2185	.7054	.8175
09/2006	1.1850	.9350	.9481	09/2009	.9788	.6593	.8761	09/2012	.9904	.7784	.9140
12/2006	1.0200	.8875	.9150	12/2009	1.3210	.8967	1.3210	12/2012	1.0014	.7210	.8858
03/2007	1.0875	.8500	1.0875	03/2010	1.4461	1.0900	1.1130	03/2013	.9671	.7890	.9574
06/2007	1.1750	1.0450	1.1475	06/2010	1.1609	.9800	.9897	06/2013	.9696	.8067	.8461
09/2007	1.3383	1.1491	1.3383	09/2010	1.2009	.9613	1.2009	09/2013	1.1912	.8565	1.0510
12/2007	1.6054	1.3075	1.6019	12/2010	1.3400	1.1663	1.3156	12/2013	1.3244	1.0726	1.2609

Source: Energy Information Administration, U.S. Department of Energy (EIA-DOE)

ETHANOL

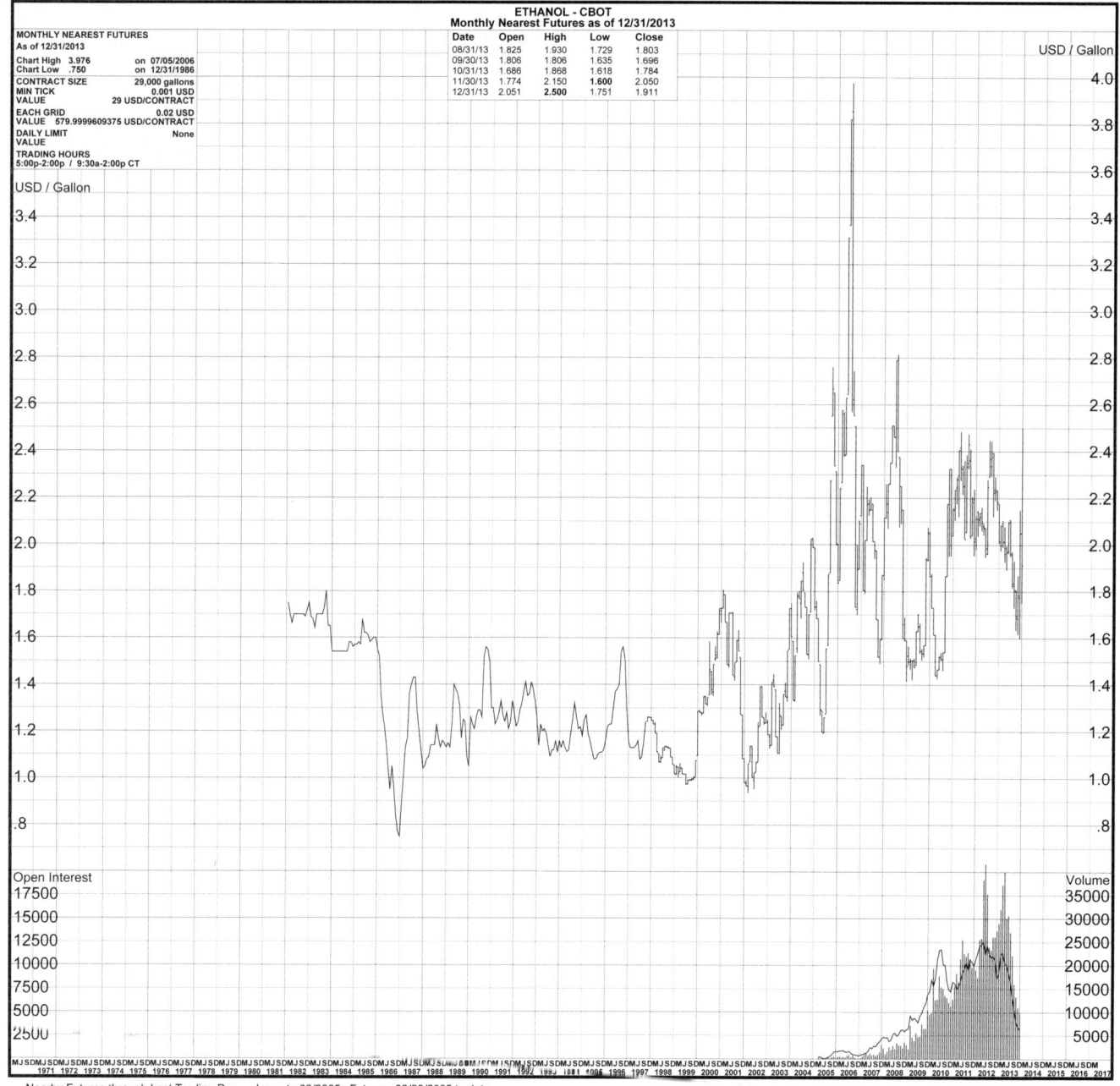

ETHANOL - CBOT
Monthly Nearest Futures as of 12/31/2013

Date	Open	High	Low	Close
08/31/13	1.825	1.930	1.729	1.803
09/30/13	1.806	1.806	1.635	1.696
10/31/13	1.686	1.868	1.618	1.784
11/30/13	1.774	2.150	1.600	2.050
12/31/13	2.051	2.500	1.751	1.911

MONTHLY NEAREST FUTURES
As of 12/31/2013
Chart High 3.976 on 07/05/2006
Chart Low .750 on 12/31/1986
CONTRACT SIZE 29,000 gallons
MIN TICK 0.001 USD
VALUE 29 USD/CONTRACT
EACH GRID 0.02 USD
VALUE 579.9999609375 USD/CONTRACT
DAILY LIMIT None
VALUE
TRADING HOURS
5:00p-2:00p / 9:30a-2:00p CT

Nearby Futures through Last Trading Day.   Iowa: to 02/2005; Futures: 03/23/2005 to date.

Annual High, Low and Settle of Ethanol Futures   In USD per Gallon

Year	High	Low	Settle	Year	High	Low	Settle	Year	High	Low	Settle
1972	----	----	----	1986	1.520	0.750	0.750	2000	1.728	1.267	1.727
1973	----	----	----	1987	1.430	0.890	1.040	2001	1.807	0.979	0.980
1974	----	----	----	1988	1.230	1.050	1.130	2002	1.393	0.936	1.186
1975	----	----	----	1989	1.400	1.050	1.050	2003	1.749	1.107	1.607
1976	----	----	----	1990	1.560	1.210	1.300	2004	2.029	1.330	1.734
1977	----	----	----	1991	1.330	1.210	1.280	2005	2.700	1.150	2.090
1978	----	----	----	1992	1.410	1.220	1.260	2006	4.330	1.680	2.493
1979	----	----	----	1993	1.230	1.090	1.160	2007	2.490	1.510	2.368
1980	----	----	----	1994	1.320	1.112	1.180	2008	2.955	1.370	1.620
1981	----	----	----	1995	1.270	1.080	1.160	2009	2.165	1.455	1.950
1982	1.750	1.660	1.750	1996	1.560	1.160	1.160	2010	2.395	1.465	2.378
1983	1.800	1.540	1.540	1997	1.261	1.080	1.247	2011	3.070	2.055	2.203
1984	1.580	1.540	1.570	1998	1.248	1.017	1.017	2012	2.760	1.970	2.190
1985	1.680	1.550	1.550	1999	1.286	0.971	1.286	2013	2.755	1.600	1.911

Iowa through 02/2005.   Futures begin trading 03/23/2005.   *Source: CME Group; Chicago Board of Trade*

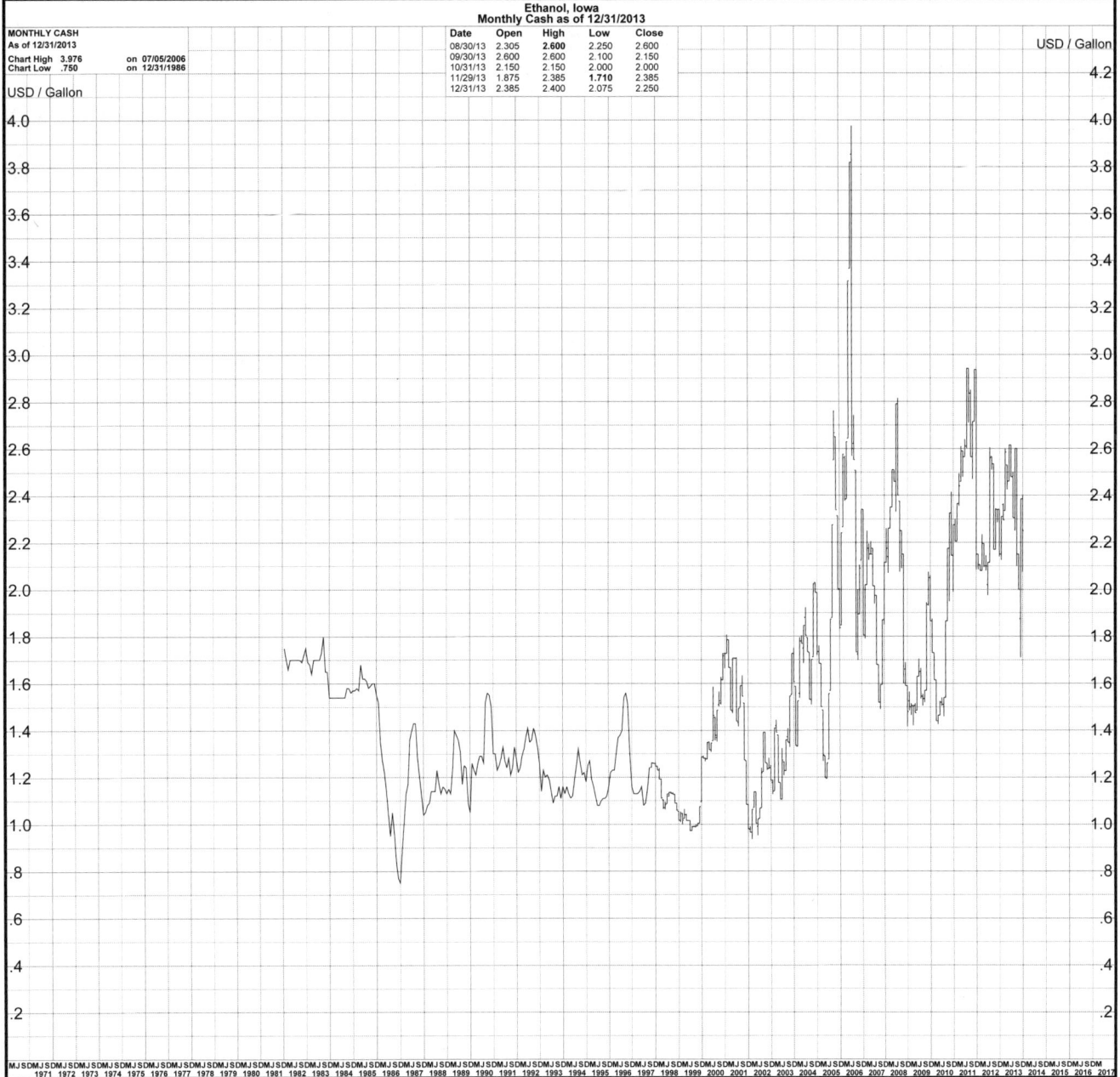

Ethanol, Iowa
Monthly Cash as of 12/31/2013

Date	Open	High	Low	Close
08/30/13	2.305	**2.600**	2.250	2.600
09/30/13	2.600	2.600	2.100	2.150
10/31/13	2.150	2.150	2.000	2.000
11/29/13	1.875	2.385	**1.710**	2.385
12/31/13	2.385	2.400	2.075	2.250

MONTHLY CASH
As of 12/31/2013

Chart High 3.976 on 07/05/2006
Chart Low .750 on 12/31/1986

USD / Gallon

Iowa

Annual High, Low and Settle of Ethanol   In USD per Gallon

Year	High	Low	Settle	Year	High	Low	Settle	Year	High	Low	Settle
1972	----	----	----	1986	1.520	0.750	0.750	2000	1.728	1.267	1.727
1973	----	----	----	1987	1.430	0.890	1.040	2001	1.807	0.979	0.980
1974	----	----	----	1988	1.230	1.050	1.130	2002	1.393	0.936	1.186
1975	----	----	----	1989	1.400	1.050	1.050	2003	1.749	1.107	1.607
1976	----	----	----	1990	1.560	1.210	1.300	2004	2.029	1.330	1.734
1977	----	----	----	1991	1.330	1.210	1.280	2005	2.761	1.194	1.836
1978	----	----	----	1992	1.410	1.220	1.260	2006	3.976	1.700	2.340
1979	----	----	----	1993	1.230	1.090	1.160	2007	2.340	1.490	2.115
1980	----	----	----	1994	1.320	1.112	1.180	2008	2.815	1.415	1.480
1981	----	----	----	1995	1.270	1.080	1.160	2009	2.075	1.420	1.865
1982	1.750	1.660	1.750	1996	1.560	1.160	1.160	2010	2.415	1.425	2.275
1983	1.800	1.540	1.540	1997	1.261	1.080	1.247	2011	2.940	2.085	2.150
1984	1.580	1.540	1.570	1998	1.248	1.017	1.017	2012	2.605	1.975	2.150
1985	1.680	1.550	1.550	1999	1.286	0.971	1.286	2013	2.615	1.710	2.250

Source: U.S. Department of Agriculture (USDA)

ETHANOL

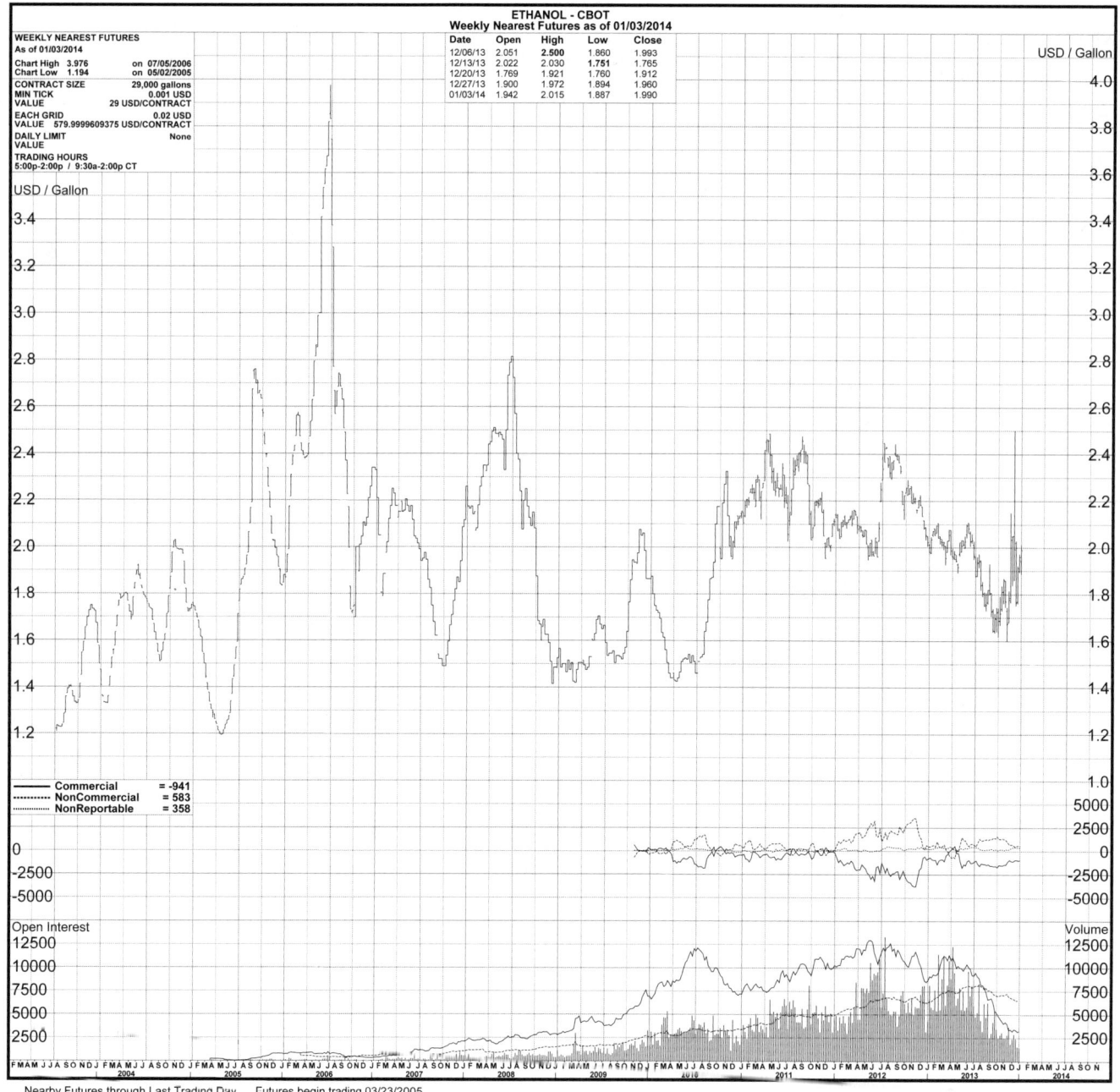

ETHANOL - CBOT
Weekly Nearest Futures as of 01/03/2014

Date	Open	High	Low	Close
12/06/13	2.051	2.500	1.860	1.993
12/13/13	2.022	2.030	1.751	1.765
12/20/13	1.769	1.921	1.760	1.912
12/27/13	1.900	1.972	1.894	1.960
01/03/14	1.942	2.015	1.887	1.990

WEEKLY NEAREST FUTURES
As of 01/03/2014

Chart High	3.976	on 07/05/2006
Chart Low	1.194	on 05/02/2005
CONTRACT SIZE	29,000 gallons	
MIN TICK VALUE	0.001 USD 29 USD/CONTRACT	
EACH GRID VALUE	0.02 USD 579.9999609375 USD/CONTRACT	
DAILY LIMIT VALUE	None	
TRADING HOURS	5:00p-2:00p / 9:30a-2:00p CT	

Commercial = -941
NonCommercial = 583
NonReportable = 358

Nearby Futures through Last Trading Day.   Futures begin trading 03/23/2005.

Quarterly High, Low and Settle of Ethanol Futures   In USD per Gallon

Quarter	High	Low	Settle	Quarter	High	Low	Settle	Quarter	High	Low	Settle
03/2005	1.250	1.185	1.230	03/2008	2.510	2.080	2.450	03/2011	2.665	2.228	2.656
06/2005	1.490	1.150	1.470	06/2008	2.955	2.300	2.847	06/2011	2.787	2.460	2.555
09/2005	2.700	1.490	2.430	09/2008	2.883	2.040	2.185	09/2011	3.070	2.435	2.485
12/2005	2.550	1.900	2.090	12/2008	2.098	1.370	1.620	12/2011	2.845	2.055	2.203
03/2006	2.730	2.100	2.565	03/2009	1.695	1.475	1.598	03/2012	2.360	2.107	2.265
06/2006	4.330	2.550	3.400	06/2009	1.803	1.536	1.635	06/2012	2.294	1.970	2.233
09/2006	3.605	1.680	1.765	09/2009	1.785	1.455	1.783	09/2012	2.760	2.210	2.344
12/2006	2.493	1.795	2.493	12/2009	2.165	1.781	1.950	12/2012	2.472	2.180	2.190
03/2007	2.490	1.870	2.195	03/2010	1.984	1.525	1.547	03/2013	2.645	2.170	2.451
06/2007	2.280	1.920	1.950	06/2010	1.649	1.465	1.529	06/2013	2.755	2.340	2.453
09/2007	2.040	1.510	1.550	09/2010	2.170	1.533	1.994	09/2013	2.605	1.764	1.950
12/2007	2.380	1.520	2.368	12/2010	2.395	1.910	2.378	12/2013	2.500	1.600	1.911

Source: CME Group; Chicago Board of Trade

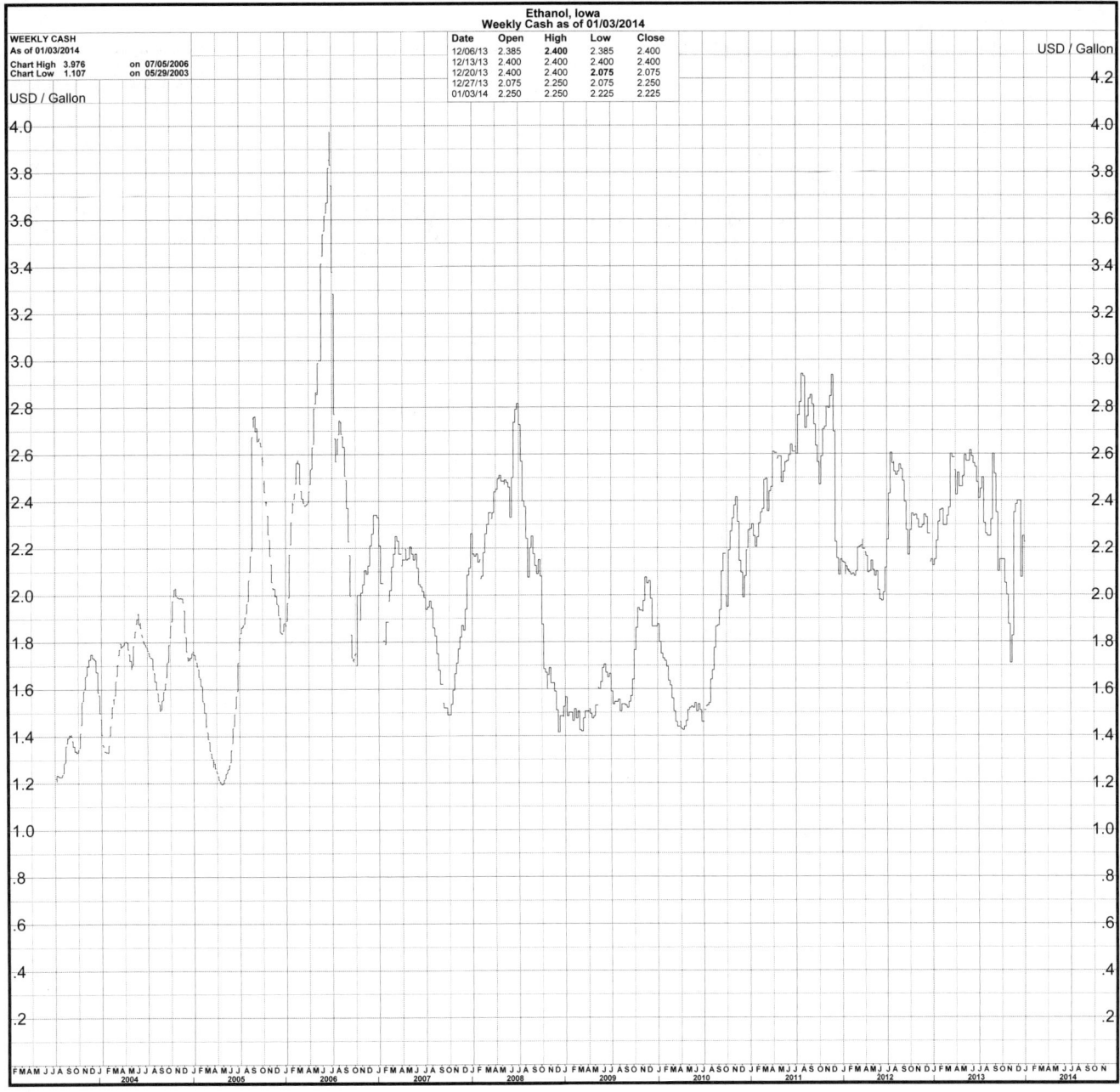

Ethanol, Iowa
Weekly Cash as of 01/03/2014

Date	Open	High	Low	Close
12/06/13	2.385	2.400	2.385	2.400
12/13/13	2.400	2.400	2.400	2.400
12/20/13	2.400	2.400	2.075	2.075
12/27/13	2.075	2.250	2.075	2.250
01/03/14	2.250	2.250	2.225	2.225

Iowa

Quarterly High, Low and Settle of Ethanol   In USD per Gallon

Quarter	High	Low	Settle	Quarter	High	Low	Settle	Quarter	High	Low	Settle
03/2005	1.760	1.268	1.294	03/2008	2.350	2.070	2.350	03/2011	2.495	2.205	2.440
06/2005	1.556	1.194	1.556	06/2008	2.790	2.330	2.790	06/2011	2.640	2.460	2.610
09/2005	2.761	1.569	2.667	09/2008	2.815	2.075	2.150	09/2011	2.940	2.565	2.565
12/2005	2.650	1.833	1.836	12/2008	2.150	1.415	1.480	12/2011	2.935	2.085	2.150
03/2006	2.576	1.847	2.383	03/2009	1.565	1.420	1.505	03/2012	2.235	2.080	2.195
06/2006	3.819	2.385	3.819	06/2009	1.705	1.475	1.650	06/2012	2.195	1.975	2.115
09/2006	3.976	1.733	1.733	09/2009	1.665	1.505	1.570	09/2012	2.605	2.115	2.170
12/2006	2.340	1.700	2.340	12/2009	2.075	1.570	1.865	12/2012	2.345	2.140	2.150
03/2007	2.340	1.790	2.175	03/2010	1.875	1.440	1.440	03/2013	2.600	2.125	2.585
06/2007	2.205	2.015	2.015	06/2010	1.540	1.425	1.510	06/2013	2.615	2.425	2.480
09/2007	2.015	1.520	1.520	09/2010	2.175	1.460	2.175	09/2013	2.600	2.100	2.150
12/2007	2.115	1.490	2.115	12/2010	2.415	1.950	2.275	12/2013	2.400	1.710	2.250

Iowa.   *Source: U.S. Department of Agriculture (USDA)*

FINANCIAL INSTRUMENTS

Current US Interest Rate Outlook

The markets going into 2014 are nervous about the possibility of higher Treasury yields. The Fed in 2014 is expected to slowly end its third quantitative easing program (known as "QE3"), involving the purchase of mortgage securities and long-term Treasury securities. However, the Fed is currently not expected to start raising its federal funds rate from the current target of zero to 0.25% until 2015 or 2016.

Treasury yields are not likely to rise sharply as long as inflation remains under control. The U.S. economy going into 2014 continues to experience disinflationary pressures despite the fact that the U.S. economy has been expanding for nearly five years. The Fed's preferred inflation measure, the core PCE deflator, was at only +1.1% y/y in late 2013, well below the Fed's 2.0% inflation target and only 0.2 points above its record low of +0.9%.

However, long-term Treasury yields cannot remain low forever and will eventually have to rise to more normal levels that reflect a reasonable investor return above expected inflation. Treasury yields are likely to rise in coming years as the U.S. and global economies normalize and global monetary policies return to normal.

However, the return to normalization may be a bumpy process. Indeed, the Fed faces a very tricky task in coming years of removing the more than $3 trillion of excess liquidity that it has injected into the U.S. banking system. The Fed could easily cause a recession if it removes that liquidity too quickly, thus starving the economy of needed liquidity. However, a recession could also ensue if the Fed moves too slowly in withdrawing that liquidity, thus causing an inflation panic and an upward spike in bond yields.

US Interest Rate History

The 1970s to 1990s

U.S. interest rates rose sharply during the period of 1965 to the early 1980s mainly because the Fed let inflation get out of control. The CPI rose sharply in 1973-75 to +11.8%, fell back in 1976-77, but then soared to a peak of +13.6% in 1980. Upward pressure on inflation in the 1970s stemmed from (1) deficit spending for the Vietnam War and President Johnson's Great Society, (2) the end of the Bretton Woods fixed-currency system in 1971, which resulted in the dollar's depreciation, and (3) the Arab oil embargo in 1973.

The Fed should have tightened monetary policy during that time but instead kept interest rates targeted too low and allowed inflation to reach runaway levels. Finally, President Jimmy Carter appointed Paul Volcker as Fed Chairman in 1979. Mr. Volcker used strict monetarist policies to clamp down on reserve and money supply growth, which is the root cause of inflation. The Fed raised

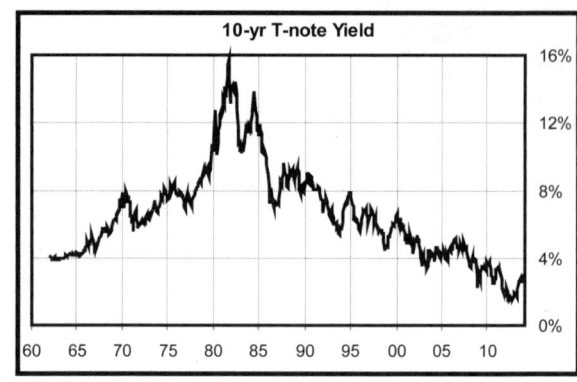

its federal funds rate target as high as 20% in 1980 and again in 1981. The Fed's tight monetary policy caused U.S. interest rates to spike higher and caused a double-dip recession in 1980 (Jan-July) and 1981-82 (July 1981 to Nov 1982).

Throughout the remainder of the 1980s, the 10-year T-note yield moved steadily lower as inflation stabilized in the 4-6% range and as the U.S. economy experienced a long period of expansion. That expansion was interrupted by a recession in 1990-91, which was caused by the first Iraq war and its related oil spike. Yet over the 1982-2003 time frame, the 10-year T-note yield moved steadily lower on the Fed's impressive inflation-fighting effort. U.S. interest rates were able to fall even further in the 1990s as the CPI was able to stabilize at the low average of 2.5-3.0%. The 10-year T-note yield in the 1990s eased from 8% at the end of 1989 to as low as 4.16% by the end of 1998.

Interest Rates During the 2000 Equity Bubble

The latter half of the 1990s was the time of the extraordinary Internet and technology boom. U.S. GDP in the latter half of the 1990s averaged +4.0%, which was significantly stronger than the long-run average of +3.3%. The Fed allowed GDP to run at the high level of +4.0% in the late 1990s because Fed Chairman Greenspan believed that productivity had shifted permanently higher in the late 1990s due to technology improvements.

However, the technology boom, along with low interest rates and speculative Internet fever, produced a massive bubble in the stock market. The Fed by mid-1999 realized that it needed to start taking away the punch bowl and raised the funds rate target from 4.75% in mid-1999 to a 10-year high of 6.5% by mid-2000. The Fed's tighter monetary policy finally popped the stock market bubble in early 2000. The plunge in the stock market that started in 2000, along with the post Y2K technology spending bust, led to a U.S. recession in 2001 (March-November).

In response, the Fed in 2001 slashed its funds rate target from 6.5% to 1.75%, and then cut the funds rate further to 1.00% by July 2003 due to the additional shock to the economy from the al-Qaeda terrorist attack on

September 11, 2001. The war between the U.S. and Iraq in 2003 provided another negative factor for the U.S. economy during that period. The Fed eased monetary policy sharply in order to prevent the possibility of deflation, which the Fed knew had devastated the Japanese economy in the 1990s. The Fed's easy monetary policy, combined with a benign inflation environment, allowed the 10-year T-note yield to fall to a low of 3.07% in June 2003, a level in long-term yields not seen since the 1960s.

By mid-2004, the Fed recognized that the U.S. economy had finally entered a period of sustained expansion and the Fed started to raise the federal funds rate target in 25 basis point increments at consecutive Federal Open Market Committee meetings. The Fed from June 2004 through July 2006 raised the funds rate target by a total of 425 basis points to 5.25%. The U.S. economy continued to perform well in the 2004-05 period despite the Fed's tighter monetary policy and the sharp rise in oil prices that occurred over that timeframe.

2006-13 housing bubble bursts; global crisis ensues; recovery is slow

The Fed's 2-year-long 425-basis-point rate hike finally had an impact in curbing the housing market, which had been in a speculative fever during 2003-06. Home sales started sliding in late 2005 and home prices started falling after mid-2006. In addition, borrowers started to default on sub-prime mortgages where monthly payments adjusted sharply higher once the teaser periods were over. The increasing defaults on sub-prime mortgages caused heavy losses in mortgage-backed securities, producing major losses for banks and hedge funds that held those securities. Bear Stearns in June 2007 had to guarantee two of its hedge funds holding mortgage securities that had become insolvent and BNP Paribas halted investor redemptions from three of its mortgage-related hedge funds in August 2007.

As the scope of the mortgage crisis became clear, the Fed started cutting interest rates to soften the blow. The Fed implemented its first rate cut in September 2007 and cut the funds rate to 2.00% by April 2008. The Bush administration's fiscal stimulus program provided some support for the U.S. economy in the first half of 2008 and the Fed left the funds rate unchanged at 2.00% through September 2008.

However, the crisis then reached epic proportions in September 2008 when Lehman Brothers was forced into bankruptcy by the weight of its bad mortgage portfolio, funding difficulties, and a lack of market confidence. The U.S. and global stock markets plunged and panic emerged among U.S. individual and institutional investors, who started pulling cash out of hedge funds, the stock market, overseas investments, and anything else that had any element of risk.

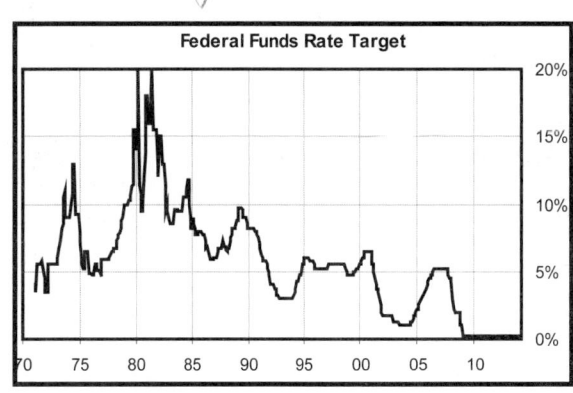

The U.S. Treasury and Federal Reserve were forced into a host of radical measures including (1) pumping huge quantities of cash into the U.S. and global banking systems to keep banks liquid, (2) guaranteeing money market funds, (3) buying commercial paper to keep the market functioning for providing credit to large corporations, and (4) buying mortgage securities to provide capital to the mortgage markets. The Fed in October 2008 cut its funds rate target to 1.00% and in December 2008 cut its funds rate target to the range of zero to 0.25%. The Fed from 2008 through 2013 engaged in three separate security purchase programs (quantitative easing or "QE") totaling more than $3 trillion.

The U.S. economy from December 2007 though June 2009 experienced what has been dubbed the "Great Recession." U.S. GDP fell by –4.1% from peak to trough during the Great Recession, which was by far the worst downturn since the Great Depression.

The U.S. economy began a slow expansion in July 2009. However, GDP growth from mid-2009 through 2013 was anemic at an average of only +2.3%, well below the post-war average of +3.3%. The U.S. faced a number of obstacles over the 2009-13 period that included (1) the worst labor market recovery in post-war history that hurt consumer confidence and spending, (2) the Eurozone sovereign debt crisis that raged from 2010-12, causing global financial market uncertainty and a Eurozone recession, and (3) periodic fiscal battles in Washington that resulted in threats of a Treasury default and a partial government shutdown on October 1-16, 2013.

The 10-year T-note yield remained at low levels in the post-crisis period due to low inflation, weak global economic growth, safe-haven demand, and the Fed's bond-purchase programs. The 10-year T-note yield fell to a record low of 1.38% in July 2012 but then rose to the 2.75% area by late 2013 as the economy gathered some steam and as the Federal Reserve in December 2013 cut its QE3 program by $10 billion to $75 billion per month.

EURODOLLARS, 3-MONTH

EURODOLLARS - IMM
Monthly Selected Futures as of 12/31/2013

Date	Open	High	Low	Close
08/31/13	99.7200	99.7375	99.7150	99.7350
09/30/13	99.7375	99.7481	99.7000	99.7150
10/31/13	99.7150	99.7550	99.6600	99.7500
11/30/13	99.7500	99.7675	99.7450	99.7625
12/31/13	99.7600	99.7625	99.7050	99.7250

MONTHLY SELECTED FUTURES
As of 12/31/2013
Chart High 99.7675 on 11/20/2013
Chart Low 78.0600 on 12/11/1980
CONTRACT SIZE 1,000,000 USD
MIN TICK .005 points
VALUE 12.5 USD / contract
EACH GRID 0.1 points
VALUE 250 USD / contract
DAILY LIMIT None
VALUE
TRADING HOURS
5:00p-4:00p / 7:20a-2:00p CT

Nearby Futures through Last Trading Day using selected contract months: March, June, September and December. Cash (100-rate): 10/1974 to 12/1981; Futures: 12/09/1981 to date.
Shaded areas indicate US recessions.

Annual High, Low and Settle of Eurodollars, 3-Month Futures   In Point of 100%

Year	High	Low	Settle	Year	High	Low	Settle	Year	High	Low	Settle
1972	----	----	----	1986	94.3600	91.7400	93.8900	2000	94.1550	93.0100	94.1100
1973	----	----	----	1987	94.1200	90.1500	92.4400	2001	98.1600	94.1350	98.0250
1974	----	----	----	1988	93.2700	90.4200	90.6200	2002	98.7000	97.3700	98.6800
1975	----	----	----	1989	92.2200	88.7600	91.9800	2003	99.1000	98.6150	98.7750
1976	----	----	----	1990	92.8800	91.0800	92.8000	2004	98.8950	97.0650	97.0950
1977	----	----	----	1991	96.0100	92.5200	95.9600	2005	97.1300	95.1900	95.2250
1978	----	----	----	1992	97.0100	95.0900	96.3600	2006	95.3200	94.3150	94.6800
1979	----	----	----	1993	96.8600	96.3400	96.4900	2007	95.7800	93.9600	95.7650
1980	----	----	----	1994	96.6900	92.7500	92.7700	2008	98.9900	95.7500	98.9400
1981	86.7600	84.6900	85.5800	1995	94.6900	92.7300	94.6800	2009	99.7475	98.5450	99.6450
1982	90.7000	82.8400	90.7000	1996	94.8600	94.0200	94.4400	2010	99.7450	99.1700	99.6350
1983	91.2700	89.0200	89.6500	1997	94.5300	93.9550	94.2250	2011	99.7530	99.2900	99.3550
1984	91.0800	86.6300	90.4800	1998	95.3050	94.2000	95.0450	2012	99.7250	99.3500	99.7000
1985	92.5900	89.2500	92.2500	1999	95.1500	93.8000	93.8350	2013	99.7675	99.5900	99.7250

Futures begin trading 12/09/1981.   *Source: CME Group; Chicago Mercantile Exchange*

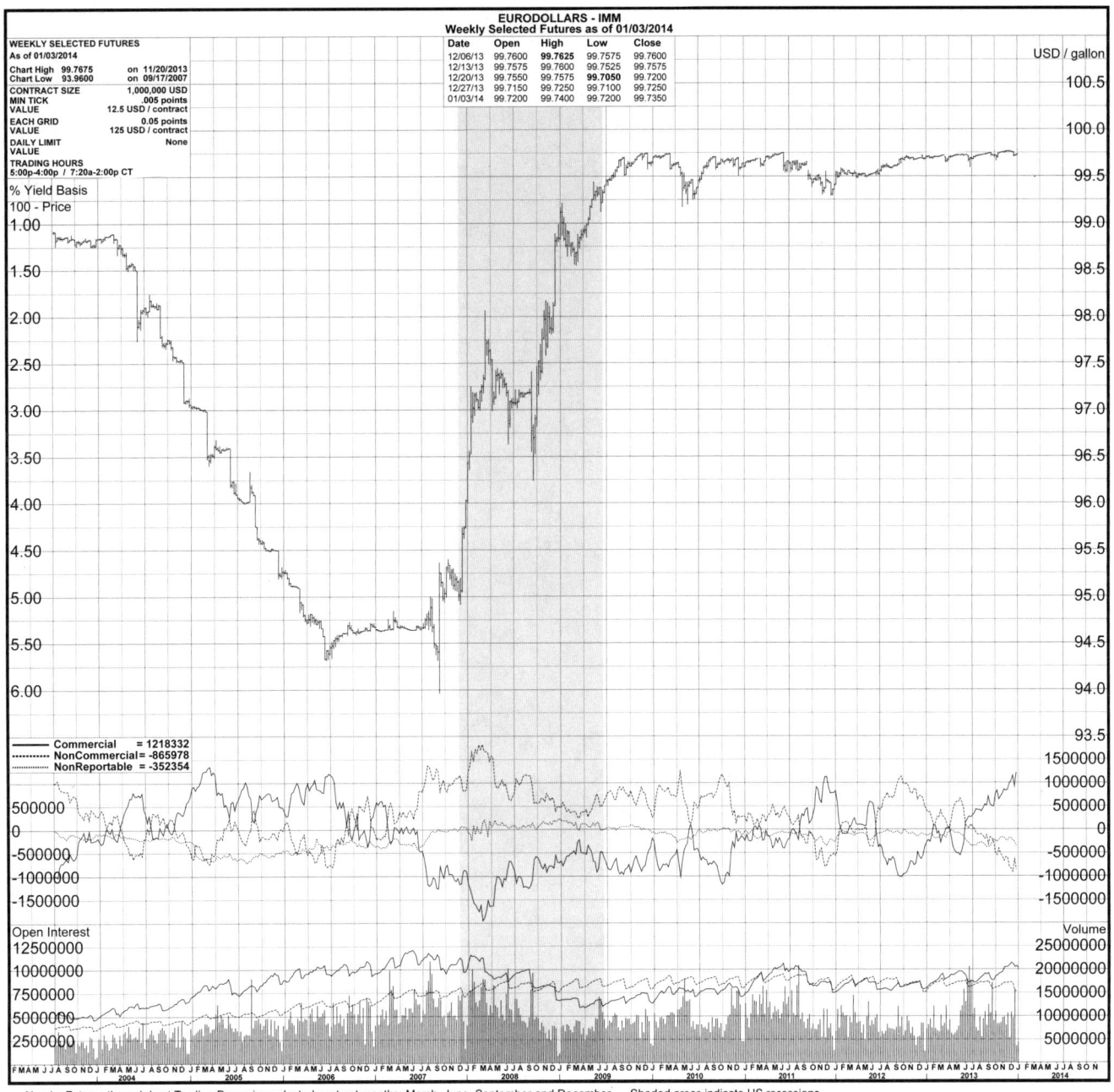

EURODOLLARS - IMM
Weekly Selected Futures as of 01/03/2014

Date	Open	High	Low	Close
12/06/13	99.7600	99.7625	99.7575	99.7600
12/13/13	99.7575	99.7600	99.7525	99.7575
12/20/13	99.7550	99.7575	99.7575	99.7200
12/27/13	99.7150	99.7250	99.7100	99.7250
01/03/14	99.7200	99.7400	99.7200	99.7350

WEEKLY SELECTED FUTURES
As of 01/03/2014

Chart High 99.7675   on 11/20/2013
Chart Low   93.9600   on 09/17/2007
CONTRACT SIZE   1,000,000 USD
MIN TICK   .005 points
VALUE   12.5 USD / contract
EACH GRID   0.05 points
VALUE   125 USD / contract
DAILY LIMIT   None
VALUE
TRADING HOURS
5:00p-4:00p / 7:20a-2:00p CT

% Yield Basis
100 - Price

Commercial = 1218332
NonCommercial= -865978
NonReportable = -352354

Open Interest

USD / gallon

Volume

Nearby Futures through Last Trading Day using selected contract months: March, June, September and December.   Shaded areas indicate US recessions.

Quarterly High, Low and Settle of Eurodollars, 3-Month Futures   In Point of 100%

Quarter	High	Low	Settle	Quarter	High	Low	Settle	Quarter	High	Low	Settle
03/2005	97.1300	96.4000	96.4850	03/2008	98.0650	95.7500	97.7300	03/2011	99.6925	99.5900	99.6400
06/2005	96.6850	96.1400	96.1500	06/2008	97.7400	96.6300	97.0700	06/2011	99.7530	99.5350	99.6550
09/2005	96.3450	95.6100	95.6150	09/2008	97.4100	96.2350	96.5450	09/2011	99.6700	99.4550	99.4700
12/2005	95.6350	95.1900	95.2250	12/2008	98.9900	96.5550	98.9400	12/2011	99.5550	99.2900	99.3550
03/2006	95.3200	94.7800	94.7950	03/2009	99.2150	98.5450	98.9000	03/2012	99.5900	99.3500	99.5300
06/2006	94.8200	94.3150	94.4200	06/2009	99.4425	98.8400	99.3300	06/2012	99.5750	99.4800	99.5200
09/2006	94.7300	94.3250	94.6650	09/2009	99.7050	99.3200	99.6300	09/2012	99.6900	99.5100	99.6800
12/2006	94.7200	94.5800	94.6800	12/2009	99.7475	99.5700	99.6450	12/2012	99.7250	99.6600	99.7000
03/2007	94.8450	94.6200	94.7350	03/2010	99.7450	99.5650	99.6300	03/2013	99.7250	99.6450	99.6700
06/2007	94.7400	94.6350	94.6700	06/2010	99.6500	99.1700	99.3450	06/2013	99.7300	99.5900	99.6850
09/2007	95.3650	93.9600	95.1550	09/2010	99.7100	99.3350	99.6400	09/2013	99.7481	99.6650	99.7150
12/2007	95.7800	94.9100	95.7650	12/2010	99.7000	99.5050	99.6350	12/2013	99.7675	99.6600	99.7250

Source: CME Group; Chicago Mercantile Exchange

EURODOLLARS, 1-MONTH

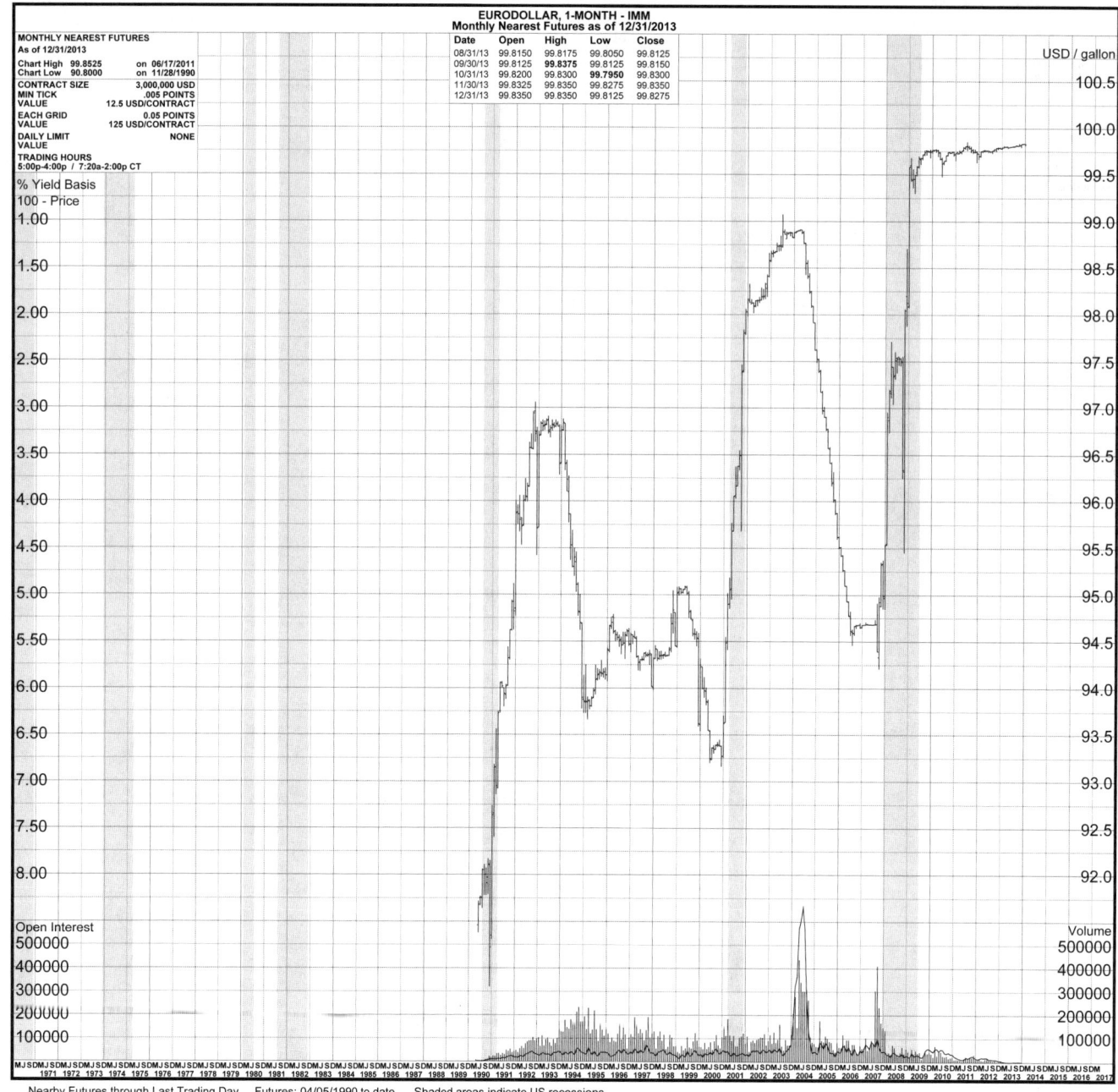

EURODOLLAR, 1-MONTH - IMM
Monthly Nearest Futures as of 12/31/2013

Date	Open	High	Low	Close
08/31/13	99.8150	99.8175	99.8050	99.8125
09/30/13	99.8125	**99.8375**	99.8125	99.8150
10/31/13	99.8200	99.8300	**99.7950**	99.8300
11/30/13	99.8325	99.8350	99.8275	99.8350
12/31/13	99.8350	99.8350	99.8125	99.8275

MONTHLY NEAREST FUTURES
As of 12/31/2013

Chart High 99.8525 on 06/17/2011
Chart Low 90.8000 on 11/28/1990
CONTRACT SIZE 3,000,000 USD
MIN TICK .005 POINTS
VALUE 12.5 USD/CONTRACT
EACH GRID 0.05 POINTS
VALUE 125 USD/CONTRACT
DAILY LIMIT NONE
VALUE
TRADING HOURS
5:00p-4:00p / 7:20a-2:00p CT

Nearby Futures through Last Trading Day. Futures: 04/05/1990 to date. Shaded areas indicate US recessions.

Annual High, Low and Settle of Libor, 1-Month Futures   In Point of 100%

Year	High	Low	Settle	Year	High	Low	Settle	Year	High	Low	Settle
1972	----	----	----	1986	----	----	----	2000	94.2300	93.1600	93.6225
1973	----	----	----	1987	----	----	----	2001	98.1700	93.6300	98.1650
1974	----	----	----	1988	----	----	----	2002	98.6800	98.0150	98.6575
1975	----	----	----	1989	----	----	----	2003	99.0750	98.6125	98.8850
1976	----	----	----	1990	92.7400	90.8000	92.6400	2004	98.9150	97.4850	97.5275
1977	----	----	----	1991	96.0000	92.4000	95.8700	2005	97.5325	95.4975	95.5100
1978	----	----	----	1992	97.0600	95.4200	96.7000	2006	95.5175	94.4600	94.6775
1979	----	----	----	1993	96.9100	96.2800	96.7600	2007	95.5400	94.2075	95.5350
1980	----	----	----	1994	96.8800	93.7300	93.8600	2008	99.5850	95.4500	99.5825
1981	----	----	----	1995	94.4300	93.6600	94.4100	2009	99.7700	99.3000	99.7600
1982	----	----	----	1996	94.7900	94.3100	94.5700	2010	99.7750	99.4775	99.7325
1983	----	----	----	1997	94.6100	93.9800	94.3200	2011	99.8525	99.6300	99.6975
1984	----	----	----	1998	95.0850	94.2900	95.0200	2012	99.7975	99.6900	99.7925
1985	----	----	----	1999	95.0975	93.5375	94.2300	2013	99.8375	99.7850	99.8275

Futures begin trading 04/05/1990.   *Source: CME Group; Chicago Mercantile Exchange*

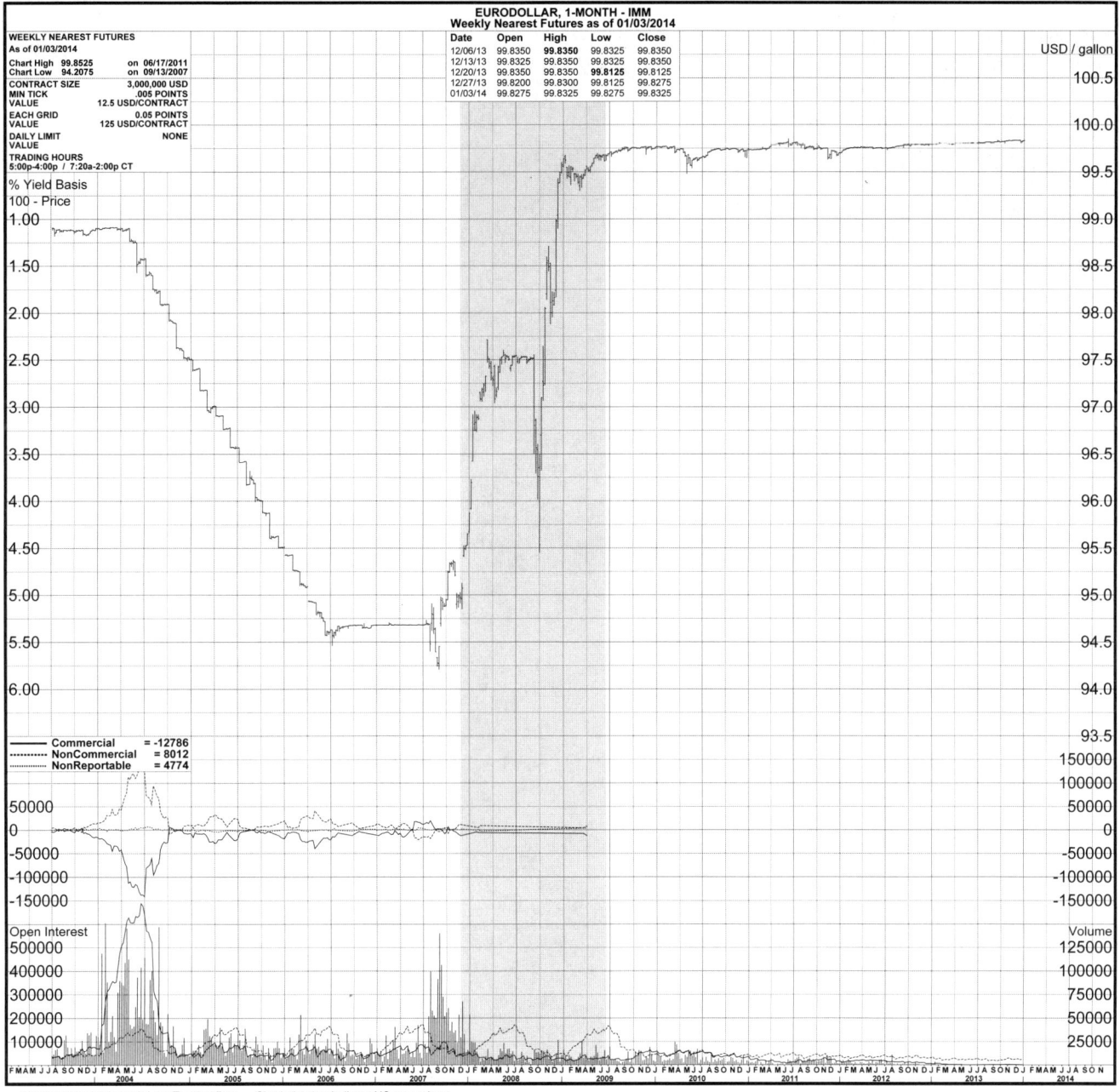

EURODOLLAR, 1-MONTH - IMM
Weekly Nearest Futures as of 01/03/2014

Date	Open	High	Low	Close
12/06/13	99.8350	99.8350	99.8325	99.8350
12/13/13	99.8325	99.8350	99.8325	99.8350
12/20/13	99.8350	99.8350	99.8125	99.8125
12/27/13	99.8200	99.8300	99.8125	99.8275
01/03/14	99.8275	99.8325	99.8275	99.8325

WEEKLY NEAREST FUTURES
As of 01/03/2014

Chart High 99.8525   on 06/17/2011
Chart Low   94.2075   on 09/13/2007
CONTRACT SIZE   3,000,000 USD
MIN TICK   .005 POINTS
VALUE   12.5 USD/CONTRACT
EACH GRID   0.05 POINTS
VALUE   125 USD/CONTRACT
DAILY LIMIT   NONE
VALUE
TRADING HOURS
5:00p-4:00p / 7:20a-2:00p CT

% Yield Basis
100 - Price

Commercial   = -12786
NonCommercial = 8012
NonReportable = 4774

Open Interest

Nearby Futures through Last Trading Day.   Shaded areas indicate US recessions.

Quarterly High, Low and Settle of Libor, 1-Month Futures   In Point of 100%

Quarter	High	Low	Settle	Quarter	High	Low	Settle	Quarter	High	Low	Settle
03/2005	97.5325	96.9350	96.9775	03/2008	97.7150	95.5325	97.4475	03/2011	99.7650	99.7200	99.7575
06/2005	97.0150	96.5675	96.5700	06/2008	97.6025	97.0400	97.5325	06/2011	99.8525	99.7575	99.8075
09/2005	96.5850	95.9900	96.0125	09/2008	97.5550	96.2500	96.3400	09/2011	99.8137	99.7300	99.7450
12/2005	96.0200	95.4975	95.5100	12/2008	99.5850	95.4500	99.5825	12/2011	99.7750	99.6300	99.6975
03/2006	95.5175	95.0950	95.0975	03/2009	99.6800	99.3000	99.4950	03/2012	99.7700	99.6900	99.7625
06/2006	95.1000	94.5650	94.6150	06/2009	99.6975	99.4900	99.6750	06/2012	99.7625	99.7400	99.7500
09/2006	94.6825	94.4600	94.6750	09/2009	99.7650	99.6600	99.7500	09/2012	99.7925	99.7300	99.7875
12/2006	94.7000	94.6425	94.6775	12/2009	99.7700	99.6800	99.7600	12/2012	99.7975	99.7725	99.7925
03/2007	94.7100	94.6775	94.6825	03/2010	99.7750	99.6950	99.7375	03/2013	99.8125	99.7850	99.7950
06/2007	94.6850	94.6775	94.6825	06/2010	99.7450	99.4775	99.6500	06/2013	99.8125	99.7950	99.8050
09/2007	94.9825	94.2075	94.9225	09/2010	99.7450	99.6450	99.7350	09/2013	99.8375	99.8025	99.8150
12/2007	95.5400	94.8500	95.5350	12/2010	99.7500	99.6500	99.7325	12/2013	99.8350	99.7950	99.8275

Source: CME Group; Chicago Mercantile Exchange

FEDERAL FUNDS, 30-DAY

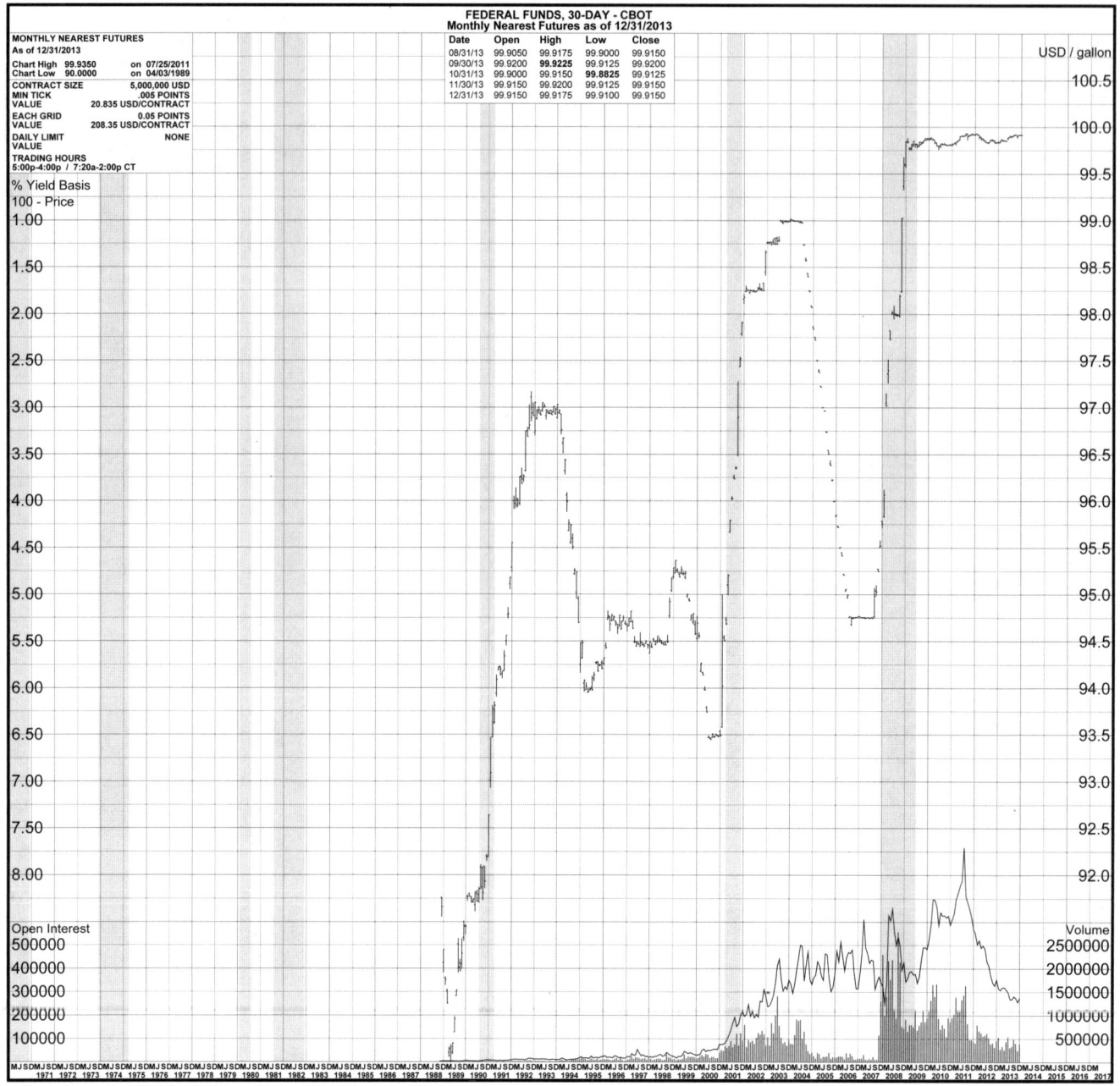

FEDERAL FUNDS, 30-DAY - CBOT
Monthly Nearest Futures as of 12/31/2013

Date	Open	High	Low	Close
08/31/13	99.9050	99.9175	99.9000	99.9150
09/30/13	99.9200	99.9225	99.9125	99.9200
10/31/13	99.9000	99.9150	99.8825	99.9125
11/30/13	99.9150	99.9200	99.9125	99.9150
12/31/13	99.9150	99.9175	99.9100	99.9150

MONTHLY NEAREST FUTURES
As of 12/31/2013

Chart High	99.9350	on 07/25/2011
Chart Low	90.0000	on 04/03/1989
CONTRACT SIZE	5,000,000 USD	
MIN TICK	.005 POINTS	
VALUE	20.835 USD/CONTRACT	
EACH GRID	0.05 POINTS	
VALUE	208.35 USD/CONTRACT	
DAILY LIMIT VALUE	NONE	

TRADING HOURS
5:00p-4:00p / 7:20a-2:00p CT

USD / gallon

Nearby Futures through Last Trading Day.   Futures: 10/06/1988 to date.   Shaded areas indicate US recessions.

Annual High, Low and Settle of Federal Funds, 30-Day Futures   In Point of 100%

Year	High	Low	Settle	Year	High	Low	Settle	Year	High	Low	Settle
1972	----	----	----	1986	----	----	----	2000	94.5950	93.4450	93.4900
1973	----	----	----	1987	----	----	----	2001	98.2100	93.5750	98.1800
1974	----	----	----	1988	91.7900	90.9500	91.2000	2002	98.7750	98.2150	98.7600
1975	----	----	----	1989	91.5100	90.0000	91.4500	2003	99.0200	98.7350	99.0150
1976	----	----	----	1990	92.6400	91.6100	92.6400	2004	99.0100	97.8350	97.8400
1977	----	----	----	1991	95.5600	92.9300	95.5500	2005	97.7600	95.8300	95.8500
1978	----	----	----	1992	97.1700	95.9100	97.0500	2006	95.7350	94.6650	94.7650
1979 8/ Volker	----	----	----	1993	97.0500	96.8700	97.0300	2007	95.7900	94.7400	95.7550
1980	----	----	----	1994	96.9800	94.1600	94.4800	2008	99.8500	95.8250	99.8450
1981	----	----	----	1995	94.5100	93.9500	94.3200	2009	99.8825	99.7525	99.8800
1982	----	----	----	1996	94.8250	94.4150	94.6600	2010	99.8900	99.7575	99.8175
1983	----	----	----	1997	94.8200	94.3650	94.4900	2011	99.9350	99.8050	99.9275
1984	----	----	----	1998	95.2850	94.4300	95.2850	2012	99.9300	99.8250	99.8350
1985	----	----	----	1999	95.3700	94.5100	94.6900	2013	99.9225	99.8350	99.9150

Futures begin trading 10/06/1988.   *Source: CME Group; Chicago Board of Trade*

P 107- 1970 →

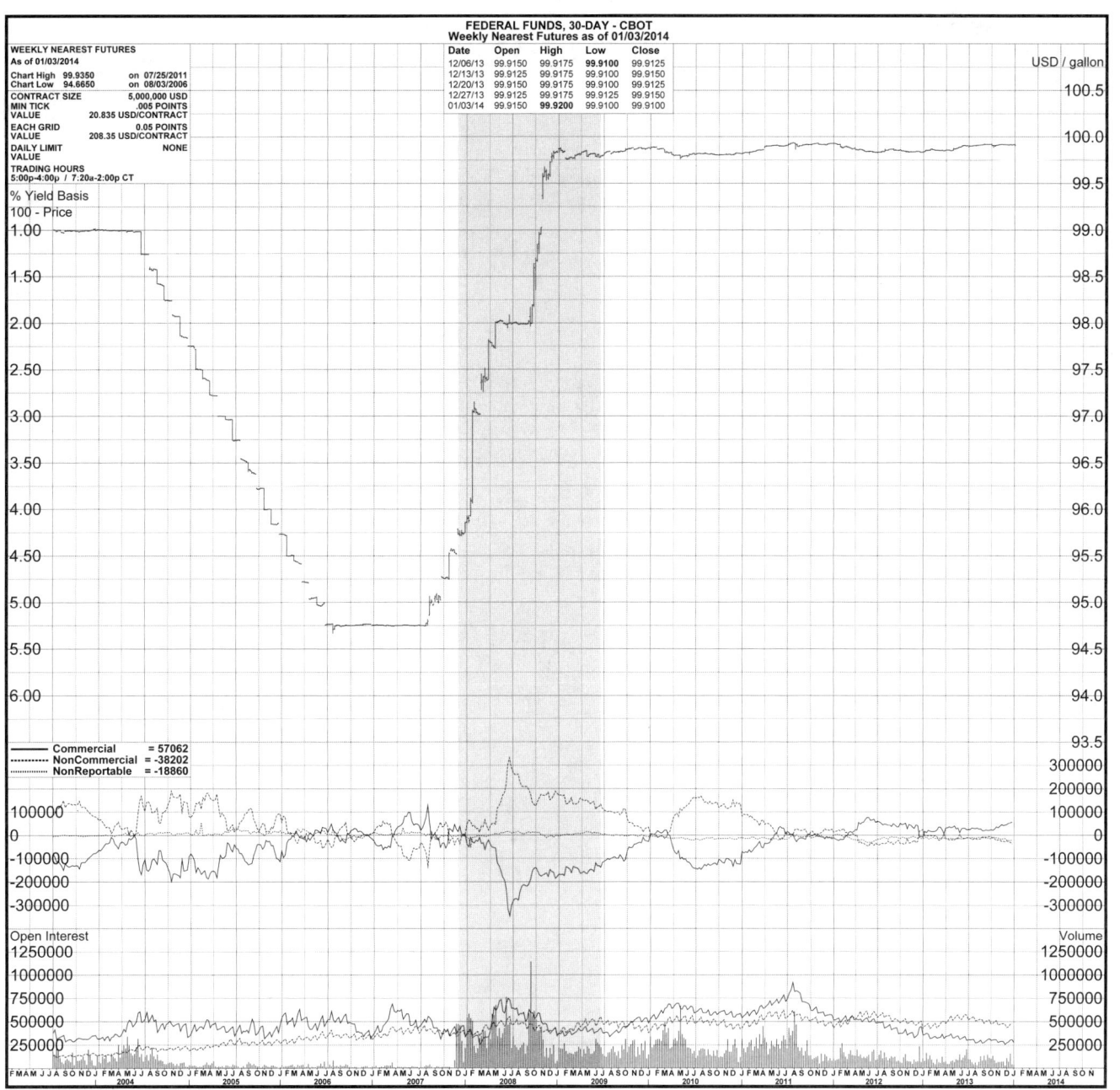

FEDERAL FUNDS, 30-DAY - CBOT
Weekly Nearest Futures as of 01/03/2014

Date	Open	High	Low	Close
12/06/13	99.9150	99.9175	99.9100	99.9125
12/13/13	99.9125	99.9175	99.9100	99.9150
12/20/13	99.9150	99.9175	99.9100	99.9125
12/27/13	99.9125	99.9175	99.9125	99.9150
01/03/14	99.9150	99.9200	99.9100	99.9100

WEEKLY NEAREST FUTURES
As of 01/03/2014

Chart High 99.9350 on 07/25/2011
Chart Low 94.6650 on 08/03/2006
CONTRACT SIZE 5,000,000 USD
MIN TICK VALUE .005 POINTS / 20.835 USD/CONTRACT
EACH GRID VALUE 0.05 POINTS / 208.35 USD/CONTRACT
DAILY LIMIT VALUE NONE
TRADING HOURS 5:00p-4:00p / 7:20a-2:00p CT

% Yield Basis
100 - Price

Commercial = 57062
NonCommercial = -38202
NonReportable = -18860

Nearby Futures through Last Trading Day.   Shaded areas indicate US recessions.

Quarterly High, Low and Settle of Federal Funds, 30-Day Futures   In Point of 100%

Quarter	High	Low	Settle	Quarter	High	Low	Settle	Quarter	High	Low	Settle
03/2005	97.7600	97.3700	97.3750	03/2008	97.5150	95.8250	97.3950	03/2011	99.8625	99.8050	99.8600
06/2005	97.2300	96.9600	96.9650	06/2008	98.0900	97.7250	98.0050	06/2011	99.9100	99.8610	99.9075
09/2005	96.7450	96.3750	96.3800	09/2008	98.2125	97.9650	98.1925	09/2011	99.9350	99.8600	99.9150
12/2005	96.2300	95.8300	95.8500	12/2008	99.8500	98.2300	99.8450	12/2011	99.9300	99.9100	99.9275
03/2006	95.7350	95.4100	95.4150	03/2009	99.8825	99.7525	99.8175	03/2012	99.9300	99.8625	99.8725
06/2006	95.2250	94.9550	94.9950	06/2009	99.8525	99.7750	99.7950	06/2012	99.8800	99.8300	99.8350
09/2006	94.7700	94.6650	94.7500	09/2009	99.8550	99.7900	99.8500	09/2012	99.8725	99.8250	99.8550
12/2006	94.7700	94.7450	94.7650	12/2009	99.8825	99.8550	99.8800	12/2012	99.8600	99.8300	99.8350
03/2007	94.7600	94.7400	94.7450	03/2010	99.8900	99.8225	99.8325	03/2013	99.8700	99.8350	99.8525
06/2007	94.7600	94.7450	94.7500	06/2010	99.8350	99.7575	99.8225	06/2013	99.9100	99.8500	99.9050
09/2007	95.1000	94.7450	95.0250	09/2010	99.8325	99.8025	99.8050	09/2013	99.9225	99.8900	99.9200
12/2007	95.7900	95.2450	95.7550	12/2010	99.8275	99.8000	99.8175	12/2013	99.9200	99.8825	99.9150

Source: CME Group; Chicago Board of Trade

TREASURY NOTES, 2-YEAR

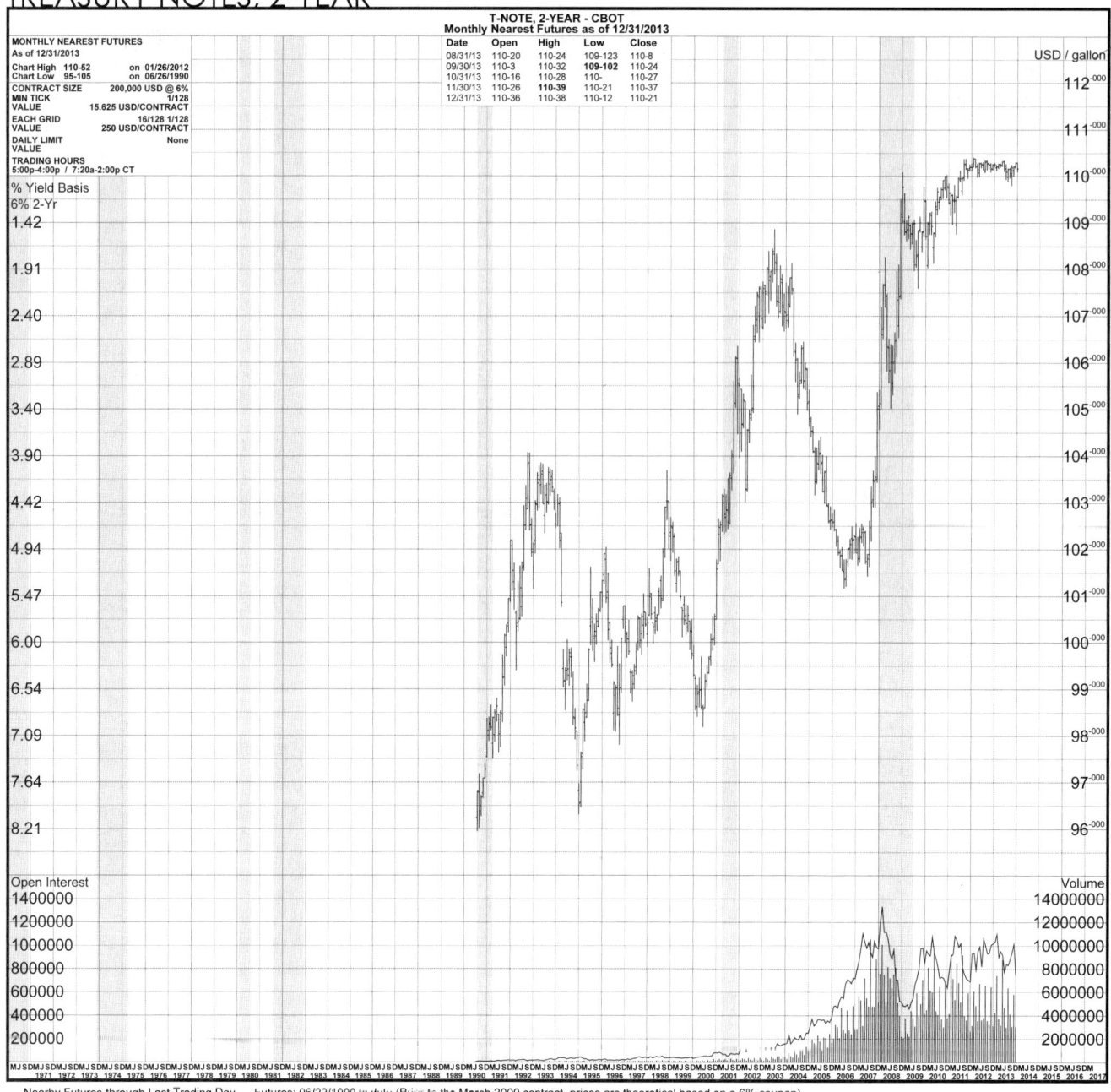

Futures begin trading 06/22/1990.   Source: CME Group; Chicago Board of Trade

T-NOTE, 2-YEAR - CBOT
Monthly Nearest Futures as of 12/31/2013

Date	Open	High	Low	Close
08/31/13	110-20	110-24	109-123	110-8
09/30/13	110-3	110-32	109-102	110-24
10/31/13	110-16	110-28	110-	110-27
11/30/13	110-26	110-39	110-21	110-37
12/31/13	110-36	110-38	110-12	110-21

MONTHLY NEAREST FUTURES
As of 12/31/2013

Chart High	110-52	on 01/26/2012
Chart Low	95-105	on 06/26/1990
CONTRACT SIZE	200,000 USD @ 6%	
MIN TICK	1/128	
VALUE	15.625 USD/CONTRACT	
EACH GRID	16/128 1/128	
VALUE	250 USD/CONTRACT	
DAILY LIMIT VALUE	None	
TRADING HOURS	5:00p-4:00p / 7:20a-2:00p CT	

Nearby Futures through Last Trading Day.   Futures: 06/22/1990 to date (Prior to the March 2000 contract, prices are theoretical based on a 6% coupon)
Shaded areas indicate US recessions.

Annual High, Low and Settle of Treasury Notes, 2-Year Futures   In Nominal Value

Year	High	Low	Settle	Year	High	Low	Settle	Year	High	Low	Settle
1972	----	----	----	1986	----	----	----	2000	101 162/256	98 048/256	101 148/256
1973	----	----	----	1987	----	----	----	2001	106 094/256	101 176/256	104 126/256
1974	----	----	----	1988	----	----	----	2002	107 240/256	103 050/256	107 152/256
1975	----	----	----	1989	----	----	----	2003	108 222/256	106 172/256	107 006/256
1976	----	----	----	1990	98 096/256	95 210/256	98 000/256	2004	108 036/256	104 180/256	104 204/256
1977	----	----	----	1991	102 050/256	97 130/256	102 050/256	2005	104 216/256	102 108/256	102 172/256
1978	----	----	----	1992	104 022/256	99 102/256	102 028/256	2006	102 218/256	101 042/256	101 238/256
1979	----	----	----	1993	103 220/256	101 232/256	102 168/256	2007	105 108/256	101 108/256	105 000/256
1980	----	----	----	1994	103 048/256	96 080/256	96 140/256	2008	110 022/256	105 006/256	109 196/256
1981	----	----	----	1995	101 160/256	96 118/256	101 084/256	2009	109 200/256	107 152/256	108 184/256
1982	----	----	----	1996	102 012/256	97 204/256	100 084/256	2010	110 008/256	108 010/256	109 164/256
1983	----	----	----	1997	101 014/256	98 186/256	100 106/256	2011	110 096/256	108 194/256	110 050/256
1984	----	----	----	1998	103 180/256	99 248/256	102 124/256	2012	110 104/256	109 250/256	110 066/256
1985	----	----	----	1999	102 150/256	99 066/256	99 078/256	2013	110 086/256	109 204/256	110 042/256

MONTHLY CASH
As of 12/31/2013
Chart High 16.950   on 09/08/1981
Chart Low   .160   on 09/19/2011

T-Note Yield, 2-Year Monthly Cash as of 12/31/2013				
Date	Open	High	Low	Close
08/30/13	.350	.420	.300	.390
09/30/13	.430	.520	.330	.330
10/31/13	.330	.400	.310	.310
11/29/13	.330	.340	.280	.280
12/31/13	.300	.420	.280	.380

Constant Maturity Treasury.   Shaded areas indicate US recessions.

Annual High, Low and Settle of Treasury Notes, 2-Year Yield   In Percent

Year	High	Low	Settle	Year	High	Low	Settle	Year	High	Low	Settle
1972	----	----	----	1986	8.380	5.880	6.310	2000	6.947	5.056	5.108
1973	----	----	----	1987	9.430	6.110	7.760	2001	5.108	2.287	3.047
1974	----	----	----	1988	9.229	6.984	9.133	2002	3.753	1.558	1.598
1975	----	----	----	1989	9.929	7.373	7.840	2003	2.140	1.056	1.819
1976	7.260	5.310	5.340	1990	9.075	7.075	7.130	2004	3.138	1.446	3.065
1977	7.260	5.420	7.220	1991	7.231	4.661	4.751	2005	4.502	3.049	4.400
1978	9.980	7.240	9.980	1992	5.915	3.572	4.542	2006	5.275	4.292	4.808
1979	12.630	8.920	11.230	1993	4.658	3.644	4.225	2007	5.128	2.791	3.047
1980	15.360	8.360	13.060	1994	7.768	3.999	7.680	2008	3.114	.604	.764
1981	16.950	12.110	13.630	1995	7.732	5.141	5.150	2009	1.420	.670	1.140
1982	15.180	9.480	9.480	1996	6.517	4.771	5.859	2010	1.180	.330	.610
1983	11.410	9.090	10.850	1997	6.536	5.427	5.617	2011	.870	.160	.250
1984	13.170	9.830	10.020	1998	5.726	3.566	4.511	2012	.410	.210	.250
1985	10.890	7.940	7.980	1999	6.386	4.379	6.218	2013	.520	.200	.380

Source: Federal Reserve Board

TREASURY NOTES, 2-YEAR

Source: CME Group; Chicago Board of Trade

Quarterly High, Low and Settle of Treasury Notes, 2-Year Futures   In Nominal Value

Quarter	High	Low	Settle	Quarter	High	Low	Settle	Quarter	High	Low	Settle
03/2005	104 216/256	103 168/256	103 204/256	03/2008	108 070/256	105 006/256	107 140/256	03/2011	109 210/256	108 246/256	109 122/256
06/2005	104 108/256	103 104/256	104 008/256	06/2008	107 122/256	105 006/256	106 006/256	06/2011	110 032/256	108 194/256	109 244/256
09/2005	104 008/256	102 250/256	103 020/256	09/2008	107 252/256	105 078/256	107 090/256	09/2011	110 096/256	109 152/256	110 042/256
12/2005	103 000/256	102 108/256	102 172/256	12/2008	110 022/256	106 136/256	109 196/256	12/2011	110 070/256	109 244/256	110 050/256
03/2006	102 218/256	101 224/256	101 238/256	03/2009	109 164/256	108 158/256	109 032/256	03/2012	110 104/256	109 250/256	110 038/256
06/2006	102 014/256	101 042/256	101 092/256	06/2009	109 018/256	107 250/256	108 254/256	06/2012	110 078/256	109 252/256	110 036/256
09/2006	102 058/256	101 052/256	102 028/256	09/2009	109 036/256	107 152/256	109 002/256	09/2012	110 090/256	110 020/256	110 062/256
12/2006	102 140/256	101 200/256	101 238/256	12/2009	109 200/256	108 098/256	108 184/256	12/2012	110 074/256	110 022/256	110 066/256
03/2007	102 138/256	101 168/256	102 094/256	03/2010	109 064/256	108 010/256	108 238/256	03/2013	110 072/256	110 030/256	110 064/256
06/2007	102 126/256	101 108/256	101 204/256	06/2010	109 194/256	108 034/256	109 172/256	06/2013	110 086/256	109 238/256	110 024/256
09/2007	103 178/256	101 160/256	103 126/256	09/2010	109 236/256	109 074/256	109 234/256	09/2013	110 064/256	109 204/256	110 048/256
12/2007	105 108/256	102 230/256	105 000/256	12/2010	110 008/256	109 104/256	109 164/256	12/2013	110 078/256	110 000/256	110 042/256

Source: CME Group; Chicago Board of Trade

T-Note Yield, 2-Year
Weekly Cash as of 01/03/2014

Date	Open	High	Low	Close
12/06/13	.300	.300	.280	.300
12/13/13	.300	.340	.300	.340
12/20/13	.340	.370	.320	.370
12/27/13	.380	.420	.380	.400
01/03/14	.390	.410	.380	.410

WEEKLY CASH
As of 01/03/2014
Chart High 5.290   on 06/28/2006
Chart Low .160   on 09/19/2011

Constant Maturity Treasury.   Shaded areas indicate US recessions.

Quarterly High, Low and Settle of Treasury Notes, 2-Year Yield   In Percent

Quarter	High	Low	Settle	Quarter	High	Low	Settle	Quarter	High	Low	Settle
03/2005	3.899	3.049	3.783	03/2008	3.103	1.236	1.614	03/2011	.870	.540	.800
06/2005	3.816	3.418	3.633	06/2008	3.114	1.550	2.616	06/2011	.850	.350	.450
09/2005	4.181	3.567	4.165	09/2008	2.831	1.355	1.968	09/2011	.500	.160	.250
12/2005	4.502	4.149	4.400	12/2008	1.968	.604	.764	12/2011	.320	.220	.250
03/2006	4.841	4.292	4.816	03/2009	1.090	.730	.810	03/2012	.410	.210	.330
06/2006	5.275	4.792	5.150	06/2009	1.420	.830	1.110	06/2012	.360	.250	.330
09/2006	5.250	4.616	4.683	09/2009	1.320	.890	.950	09/2012	.310	.220	.230
12/2006	4.923	4.458	4.808	12/2009	1.140	.670	1.140	12/2012	.320	.230	.250
03/2007	4.991	4.450	4.574	03/2010	1.100	.770	1.020	03/2013	.300	.230	.250
06/2007	5.128	4.558	4.858	06/2010	1.180	.610	.610	06/2013	.430	.200	.360
09/2007	5.009	3.808	3.984	09/2010	.670	.370	.420	09/2013	.520	.300	.330
12/2007	4.285	2.791	3.047	12/2010	.750	.330	.610	12/2013	.420	.280	.380

Source: Federal Reserve Board

TREASURY NOTES, 5-YEAR

T-NOTE, 5-YEAR - CBOT
Monthly Nearest Futures as of 12/31/2013

Date	Open	High	Low	Close
08/31/13	121 25/64	121 42/64	119 53/64	120 37/64
09/30/13	120 20/64	121 54/64	119 19/64	121 43/64
10/31/13	121 4/64	121 61/64	120 42/64	121 44/64
11/30/13	121 39/64	122 11/64	121 6/64	121 51/64
12/31/13	121 46/64	121 50/64	120 16/64	120 23/64

MONTHLY NEAREST FUTURES
As of 12/31/2013
Chart High   125 2/64   on 09/04/2012
Chart Low   86 22/64   on 03/21/1989
CONTRACT SIZE   100,000 USD @ 6%
MIN TICK VALUE   15.625 USD/CONTRACT   1/128
EACH GRID VALUE   32/128 1/128   500 USD/CONTRACT
DAILY LIMIT VALUE   None
TRADING HOURS
5:00p-4:00p / 7:20a-2:00p CT

Nearby Futures through Last Trading Day.   Futures: 05/27/1988 to date (Prior to the March 2000 contract, prices are theoretical based on a 6% coupon)
Shaded areas indicate US recessions.

Annual High, Low and Settle of Treasury Notes, 5-Year Futures   In Nominal Value

Year	High	Low	Settle	Year	High	Low	Settle	Year	High	Low	Settle
1972	----	----	----	1986	----	----	----	2000	103 112/128	96 064/128	103 072/128
1973	----	----	----	1987	----	----	----	2001	110 058/128	102 112/128	105 106/128
1974	----	----	----	1988	91 024/128	87 124/128	88 052/128	2002	114 074/128	103 046/128	113 032/128
1975	----	----	----	1989	94 098/128	86 044/128	93 008/128	2003	117 102/128	110 060/128	111 080/128
1976	----	----	----	1990	93 098/128	88 022/128	93 026/128	2004	115 036/128	107 108/128	109 068/128
1977	----	----	----	1991	100 032/128	91 076/128	100 018/128	2005	110 000/128	105 046/128	106 044/128
1978	----	----	----	1992	102 090/128	94 078/128	99 040/128	2006	106 116/128	102 126/128	105 016/128
1979	----	----	----	1993	106 014/128	99 006/128	103 002/128	2007	111 030/128	103 008/128	110 058/128
1980	----	----	----	1994	104 078/128	92 004/128	92 076/128	2008	122 126/128	109 017/128	120 126/128
1981	----	----	----	1995	102 058/128	92 016/128	102 056/128	2009	120 095/128	113 106/128	115 063/128
1982	----	----	----	1996	103 076/128	95 120/128	99 040/128	2010	122 046/128	113 112/128	118 092/128
1983	----	----	----	1997	101 046/128	96 048/128	100 110/128	2011	124 026/128	116 019/128	123 066/128
1984	----	----	----	1998	107 052/128	100 076/128	105 044/128	2012	125 003/128	121 098/128	124 072/128
1985	----	----	----	1999	105 052/128	98 002/128	98 002/128	2013	124 107/128	119 037/128	120 046/128

Futures begin trading 05/271988.   *Source: CME Group; Chicago Board of Trade*

T-Note Yield, 5-Year
Monthly Cash as of 12/31/2013

Date	Open	High	Low	Close
08/30/13	1.386	1.723	1.337	1.601
09/30/13	1.680	1.848	1.381	1.388
10/31/13	1.409	1.470	1.250	1.315
11/29/13	1.359	1.460	1.289	1.367
12/31/13	1.405	1.755	1.385	1.748

MONTHLY CASH
As of 12/31/2013
Chart High 16.270 on 09/30/1981
Chart Low .541 on 07/24/2012

Constant Maturity Treasury.   Shaded areas indicate US recessions.

Annual High, Low and Settle of Treasury Notes, 5-Year Yield   In Percent

Year	High	Low	Settle	Year	High	Low	Settle	Year	High	Low	Settle
1972	6.320	5.470	6.260	1986	9.000	6.390	6.820	2000	6.834	4.880	4.967
1973	8.130	6.230	6.830	1987	10.110	6.540	8.414	2001	5.108	3.246	4.334
1974	8.790	6.720	7.360	1988	9.244	7.542	9.146	2002	4.877	2.533	2.730
1975	8.560	6.930	7.500	1989	9.761	7.394	7.856	2003	3.617	1.997	3.218
1976	7.820	5.990	6.130	1990	9.137	7.526	7.636	2004	4.101	2.608	3.607
1977	7.580	6.160	7.540	1991	8.082	5.895	5.924	2005	4.578	3.551	4.355
1978	9.350	7.580	9.320	1992	7.186	5.087	6.029	2006	5.263	4.229	4.701
1979	11.500	8.700	10.380	1993	6.073	4.536	5.193	2007	5.241	3.219	3.455
1980	14.120	8.860	12.590	1994	7.904	4.927	7.823	2008	3.744	1.185	1.551
1981	16.270	12.210	13.970	1995	7.935	5.374	5.388	2009	2.991	1.328	2.686
1982	15.020	10.090	10.090	1996	6.917	5.120	6.199	2010	2.757	1.016	2.016
1983	11.950	9.720	11.570	1997	6.899	5.602	5.701	2011	2.415	.771	.830
1984	13.840	10.830	11.080	1998	5.807	3.889	4.542	2012	1.226	.541	.725
1985	11.700	8.480	8.490	1999	6.353	4.387	6.346	2013	1.848	.640	1.748

Source: Federal Researve Board

TREASURY NOTES, 5-YEAR

Source: CME Group; Chicago Board of Trade

Quarterly High, Low and Settle of Treasury Notes, 5-Year Futures   In Nominal Value

Quarter	High	Low	Settle	Quarter	High	Low	Settle	Quarter	High	Low	Settle
03/2005	110 000/128	106 016/128	107 012/128	03/2008	116 048/128	110 008/128	114 030/128	03/2011	119 056/128	116 024/128	117 101/128
06/2005	109 122/128	106 106/128	108 114/128	06/2008	114 051/128	109 017/128	111 000/128	06/2011	121 120/128	116 019/128	120 054/128
09/2005	109 064/128	106 076/128	106 110/128	09/2008	115 063/128	109 101/128	113 088/128	09/2011	124 026/128	118 097/128	123 046/128
12/2005	106 124/128	105 046/128	106 044/128	12/2008	122 126/128	111 030/128	120 126/128	12/2011	123 124/128	121 041/128	123 066/128
03/2006	106 116/128	104 038/128	104 056/128	03/2009	120 095/128	116 049/128	119 034/128	03/2012	124 015/128	121 098/128	122 110/128
06/2006	104 076/128	103 000/128	103 056/128	06/2009	118 118/128	113 106/128	115 099/128	06/2012	124 097/128	122 019/128	124 014/128
09/2006	105 106/128	102 126/128	105 054/128	09/2009	117 048/128	113 106/128	117 021/128	09/2012	125 003/128	123 089/128	124 111/128
12/2006	106 058/128	104 068/128	105 016/128	12/2009	118 084/128	115 013/128	115 063/128	12/2012	124 126/128	123 089/128	124 072/128
03/2007	106 038/128	104 024/128	105 092/128	03/2010	117 034/128	114 008/128	115 126/128	03/2013	124 076/128	123 065/128	124 057/128
06/2007	105 120/128	103 008/128	104 004/128	06/2010	119 030/128	113 112/128	118 125/128	06/2013	124 107/128	120 106/128	121 076/128
09/2007	108 018/128	103 052/128	107 042/128	09/2010	121 106/128	117 119/128	121 064/128	09/2013	121 108/128	119 037/128	121 086/128
12/2007	111 030/128	106 006/128	110 058/128	12/2010	122 046/128	117 099/128	118 092/128	12/2013	122 021/128	120 032/128	120 046/128

T-Note Yield, 5-Year
Weekly Cash as of 01/03/2014

Date	Open	High	Low	Close
12/06/13	1.405	1.545	1.385	1.505
12/13/13	1.481	1.544	1.444	1.532
12/20/13	1.518	1.701	1.470	1.670
12/27/13	1.689	1.755	1.672	1.744
01/03/14	1.719	1.751	1.704	1.727

WEEKLY CASH
As of 01/03/2014
Chart High 5.263 on 06/29/2006
Chart Low .541 on 07/24/2012

Constant Maturity Treasury.   Shaded areas indicate US recessions.

Quarterly High, Low and Settle of Treasury Notes, 5-Year Yield   In Percent

Quarter	High	Low	Settle	Quarter	High	Low	Settle	Quarter	High	Low	Settle
03/2005	4.385	3.559	4.174	03/2008	3.467	2.164	2.467	03/2011	2.415	1.800	2.225
06/2005	4.224	3.551	3.725	06/2008	3.744	2.512	3.341	06/2011	2.352	1.370	1.754
09/2005	4.288	3.735	4.195	09/2008	3.568	2.348	2.986	09/2011	1.846	.771	.965
12/2005	4.578	4.182	4.355	12/2008	3.077	1.185	1.551	12/2011	1.220	.797	.830
03/2006	4.846	4.229	4.814	03/2009	2.117	1.328	1.675	03/2012	1.226	.699	1.043
06/2006	5.263	4.785	5.098	06/2009	2.991	1.636	2.558	06/2012	1.105	.600	.729
09/2006	5.199	4.489	4.587	09/2009	2.869	2.183	2.318	09/2012	.836	.541	.630
12/2006	4.821	4.347	4.701	12/2009	2.760	1.993	2.686	12/2012	.833	.592	.725
03/2007	4.900	4.377	4.537	03/2010	2.693	2.197	2.560	03/2013	.921	.724	.769
06/2007	5.241	4.495	4.936	06/2010	2.757	1.765	1.795	06/2013	1.557	.640	1.385
09/2007	5.110	3.955	4.229	09/2010	1.908	1.225	1.281	09/2013	1.848	1.282	1.388
12/2007	4.463	3.219	3.455	12/2010	2.188	1.016	2.016	12/2013	1.755	1.250	1.748

Source: Federal Researve Board

TREASURY NOTES, 10-YEAR

T-NOTE, 10-YEAR - CBOT
Monthly Nearest Futures as of 12/31/2013

Date	Open	High	Low	Close
08/31/13	126 32/64	126 63/64	124 /64	125 22/64
09/30/13	125 /64	126 59/64	123 21/64	126 25/64
10/31/13	126 27/64	128 4/64	125 34/64	127 23/64
11/30/13	127 15/64	127 58/64	125 46/64	126 41/64
12/31/13	126 32/64	126 38/64	122 49/64	123 3/64

MONTHLY NEAREST FUTURES
As of 12/31/2013

Chart High 135 58/64 on 06/01/2012
Chart Low 60 30/64 on 06/23/1982
CONTRACT SIZE 100,000 USD @ 6%
MIN TICK VALUE 1/64 15.625 USD/CONTRACT
EACH GRID VALUE 32/64 1/64 500 USD/CONTRACT
DAILY LIMIT VALUE None
TRADING HOURS 5:00p-4:00p / 7:20a-2:00p CT

% Yield Basis 6% 10-Yr

Nearby Futures through Last Trading Day. Futures: 05/03/1982 to date (Prior to the March 2000 contract, prices are theoretical based on a 6% coupon)
Shaded areas indicate US recessions.

Annual High, Low and Settle of Treasury Notes, 10-Year Futures   In Nominal Value

Year	High	Low	Settle	Year	High	Low	Settle	Year	High	Low	Settle
1972	----	----	----	1986	95 34/64	79 28/64	91 50/64	2000	105 36/64	93 43/64	104 55/64
1973	----	----	----	1987	93 44/64	74 32/64	82 62/64	2001	112 26/64	102 44/64	105 09/64
1974	----	----	----	1988	87 36/64	79 28/64	81 28/64	2002	116 28/64	101 58/64	115 03/64
1975	----	----	----	1989	90 36/64	79 28/64	88 32/64	2003	121 06/64	109 39/64	112 17/64
1976	----	----	----	1990	88 40/64	80 50/64	87 00/64	2004	117 62/64	107 51/64	111 60/64
1977	----	----	----	1991	94 44/64	84 16/64	94 30/64	2005	114 32/64	107 31/64	109 26/64
1978	----	----	----	1992	98 60/64	87 62/64	94 38/64	2006	110 13/64	104 02/64	107 30/64
1979	----	----	----	1993	106 28/64	93 50/64	102 14/64	2007	115 01/64	104 08/64	113 25/64
1980	----	----	----	1994	104 02/64	85 56/64	88 22/64	2008	130 51/64	111 25/64	125 48/64
1981	----	----	----	1995	103 18/64	87 04/64	102 24/64	2009	127 33/64	114 16/64	115 29/64
1982	77 56/64	60 30/64	76 10/64	1996	104 28/64	91 50/64	97 32/64	2010	128 02/64	114 53/64	120 28/64
1983	77 44/64	67 60/64	70 30/64	1997	101 56/64	92 36/64	101 32/64	2011	132 14/64	117 44/64	131 08/64
1984	72 56/64	61 62/64	71 26/64	1998	112 40/64	100 10/64	106 18/64	2012	135 58/64	128 26/64	132 50/64
1985	82 54/64	68 34/64	82 12/64	1999	108 14/64	95 46/64	95 55/64	2013	133 50/64	122 49/64	123 03/64

Futures begin trading 05/03/1982.   *Source: CME Group; Chicago Board of Trade*

T-Note Yield, 10-Year
Monthly Cash as of 12/31/2013

Date	Open	High	Low	Close
08/30/13	2.601	2.920	2.552	2.749
09/30/13	2.837	2.984	2.599	2.615
10/31/13	2.646	2.757	2.471	2.542
11/29/13	2.589	2.839	2.572	2.741
12/31/13	2.781	3.036	2.759	3.026

MONTHLY CASH
As of 12/31/2013
Chart High 15.840   on 09/30/1981
Chart Low   1.394   on 07/24/2012

Constant Maturity Treasury.   Shaded areas indicate US recessions.

Annual High, Low and Settle of Treasury Notes, 10-Year Yield   In Percent

Year	High	Low	Settle	Year	High	Low	Settle	Year	High	Low	Settle
1972	6.620	5.850	6.410	1986	9.490	6.950	7.230	2000	6.834	4.998	5.102
1973	7.580	6.400	6.900	1987	10.230	7.010	8.830	2001	5.563	4.101	5.033
1974	8.160	6.930	7.400	1988	9.410	8.110	9.133	2002	5.475	3.559	3.818
1975	8.590	7.220	7.760	1989	9.550	7.634	7.917	2003	4.668	3.074	4.257
1976	8.000	6.800	6.810	1990	9.113	7.880	8.063	2004	4.904	3.650	4.216
1977	7.820	6.840	7.780	1991	8.434	6.659	6.701	2005	4.693	3.803	4.395
1978	9.160	7.820	9.150	1992	7.723	6.164	6.701	2006	5.245	4.289	4.710
1979	11.020	8.760	10.330	1993	6.789	5.143	5.790	2007	5.316	3.840	4.035
1980	13.650	9.470	12.430	1994	8.062	5.548	7.820	2008	4.324	2.038	2.244
1981	15.840	12.110	13.980	1995	7.928	5.574	5.581	2009	4.014	2.159	3.843
1982	14.950	10.360	10.360	1996	7.123	5.501	6.418	2010	4.013	2.334	3.305
1983	12.200	10.120	11.820	1997	7.016	5.659	5.725	2011	3.744	1.696	1.871
1984	13.990	11.240	11.550	1998	5.849	4.084	4.654	2012	2.397	1.394	1.756
1985	12.020	8.990	9.000	1999	6.453	4.558	6.440	2013	3.036	1.610	3.026

Source: Federal Researve Board

TREASURY NOTES, 10-YEAR

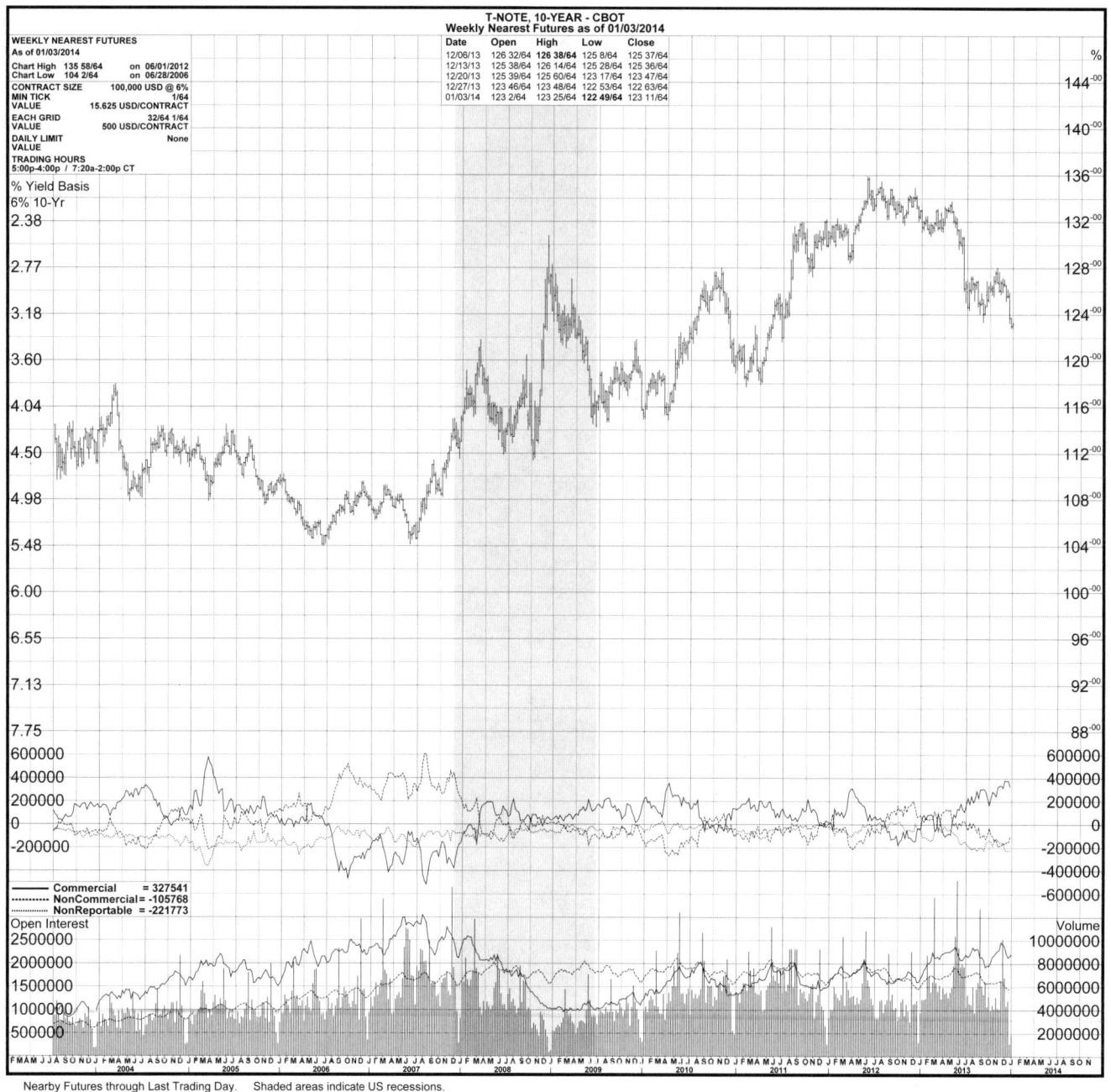

Nearby Futures through Last Trading Day.   Shaded areas indicate US recessions.

Quarterly High, Low and Settle of Treasury Notes, 10-Year Futures   In Nominal Value

Quarter	High	Low	Settle	Quarter	High	Low	Settle	Quarter	High	Low	Settle
03/2005	113 25/64	107 53/64	109 17/64	03/2008	121 52/64	113 04/64	118 61/64	03/2011	123 05/64	117 44/64	119 02/64
06/2005	114 32/64	108 54/64	113 30/64	06/2008	119 06/64	111 56/64	113 59/64	06/2011	125 53/64	117 59/64	122 21/64
09/2005	113 43/64	109 50/64	109 59/64	09/2008	120 33/64	112 54/64	114 40/64	09/2011	131 63/64	121 39/64	130 06/64
12/2005	110 05/64	107 31/64	109 26/64	12/2008	130 51/64	111 25/64	125 48/64	12/2011	132 14/64	127 12/64	131 08/64
03/2006	110 13/64	106 08/64	106 25/64	03/2009	127 33/64	121 05/64	124 05/64	03/2012	132 22/64	128 26/64	129 31/64
06/2006	106 34/64	104 02/64	104 55/64	06/2009	124 36/64	114 16/64	116 17/64	06/2012	135 58/64	128 49/64	133 24/64
09/2006	108 48/64	104 10/64	108 04/64	09/2009	119 56/64	114 42/64	118 21/64	09/2012	135 31/64	132 10/64	133 31/64
12/2006	109 36/64	106 38/64	107 30/64	12/2009	121 55/64	114 57/64	115 29/64	12/2012	134 61/64	131 44/64	132 50/64
03/2007	109 19/64	106 13/64	108 08/64	03/2010	119 11/64	114 62/64	116 16/64	03/2013	133 09/64	130 46/64	131 63/64
06/2007	108 32/64	104 08/64	105 45/64	06/2010	122 54/64	114 53/64	122 35/64	06/2013	133 50/64	125 01/64	126 36/64
09/2007	111 27/64	104 35/64	109 18/64	09/2010	126 56/64	121 29/64	126 03/64	09/2013	127 20/64	123 21/64	126 25/64
12/2007	115 01/64	108 13/64	113 25/64	12/2010	128 02/64	118 57/64	120 28/64	12/2013	128 04/64	122 49/64	123 03/64

Source: CME Group; Chicago Board of Trade

		T-Note Yield, 10-Year Weekly Cash as of 01/03/2014			
Date	Open	High	Low	Close	
12/06/13	2.781	2.932	2.759	2.883	
12/13/13	2.846	2.888	2.792	2.868	
12/20/13	2.848	2.966	2.824	2.887	
12/27/13	2.916	3.019	2.896	3.006	
01/03/14	2.991	3.036	2.967	2.995	

WEEKLY CASH
As of 01/03/2014

Chart High 5.316   on 06/13/2007
Chart Low   1.394   on 07/24/2012

Constant Maturity Treasury.   Shaded areas indicate US recessions.

Quarterly High, Low and Settle of Treasury Notes, 10-Year Yield   In Percent

Quarter	High	Low	Settle	Quarter	High	Low	Settle	Quarter	High	Low	Settle
03/2005	4.693	3.977	4.496	03/2008	4.052	3.281	3.432	03/2011	3.744	3.141	3.454
06/2005	4.541	3.803	3.945	06/2008	4.324	3.430	3.979	06/2011	3.619	2.847	3.158
09/2005	4.435	3.942	4.328	09/2008	4.174	3.250	3.827	09/2011	3.223	1.696	1.924
12/2005	4.682	4.317	4.395	12/2008	4.109	2.038	2.244	12/2011	2.407	1.717	1.871
03/2006	4.884	4.289	4.853	03/2009	3.054	2.159	2.685	03/2012	2.397	1.797	2.216
06/2006	5.245	4.835	5.138	06/2009	4.014	2.634	3.523	06/2012	2.284	1.440	1.659
09/2006	5.241	4.530	4.633	09/2009	3.886	3.265	3.307	09/2012	1.892	1.394	1.637
12/2006	4.848	4.404	4.710	12/2009	3.918	3.106	3.843	12/2012	1.852	1.556	1.756
03/2007	4.906	4.473	4.648	03/2010	3.930	3.537	3.833	03/2013	2.086	1.803	1.852
06/2007	5.316	4.602	5.033	06/2010	4.013	2.947	2.951	06/2013	2.657	1.610	2.478
09/2007	5.201	4.301	4.579	09/2010	3.124	2.419	2.517	09/2013	2.984	2.451	2.615
12/2007	4.719	3.840	4.035	12/2010	3.566	2.334	3.305	12/2013	3.036	2.471	3.026

Source: Federal Researve Board

TREASURY BONDS, 30-YEAR

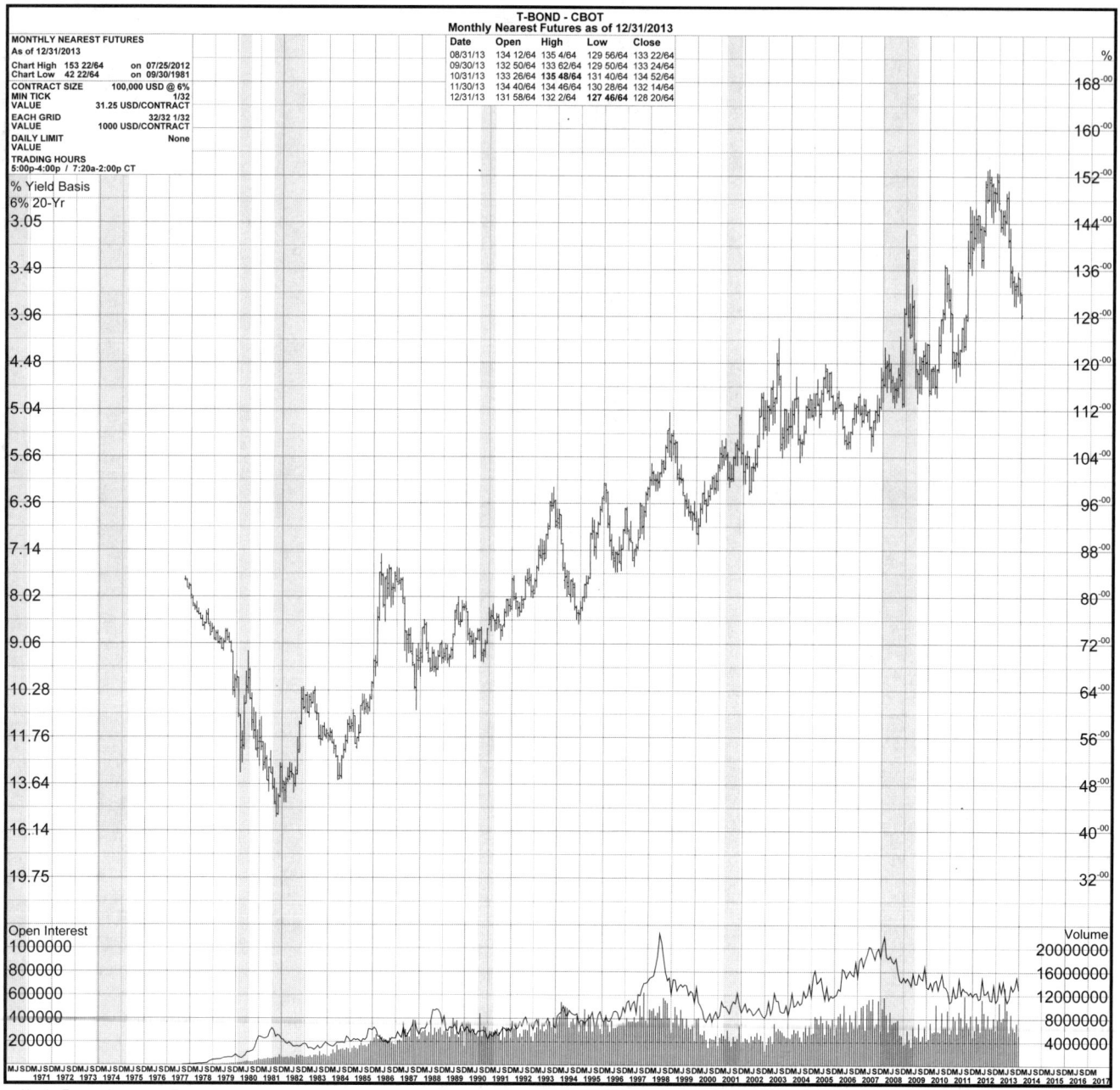

Date	Open	High	Low	Close
08/31/13	134 12/64	135 4/64	129 56/64	133 22/64
09/30/13	132 50/64	133 62/64	129 50/64	133 24/64
10/31/13	133 26/64	135 48/64	131 40/64	134 52/64
11/30/13	134 40/64	134 46/64	130 28/64	132 14/64
12/31/13	131 58/64	132 2/64	127 46/64	128 20/64

MONTHLY NEAREST FUTURES
As of 12/31/2013

Chart High 153 22/64   on 07/25/2012
Chart Low   42 22/64   on 09/30/1981
CONTRACT SIZE   100,000 USD @ 6%
MIN TICK VALUE   31.25 USD/CONTRACT   1/32
EACH GRID VALUE   1000 USD/CONTRACT   32/32 1/32
DAILY LIMIT VALUE   None
TRADING HOURS   5:00p-4:00p / 7:20a-2:00p CT

Nearby Futures through Last Trading Day.   Futures: 08/22/1977 to date (Prior to the March 2000 contract, prices are theoretical based on a 6% coupon)
Shaded areas indicate US recessions.

Annual High, Low and Settle of Treasury Bonds, 30-Year Futures   In Nominal Value

Year	High	Low	Settle	Year	High	Low	Settle	Year	High	Low	Settle
1972	----	----	----	1986	87 12/32	66 11/32	82 17/32	2000	105 23/32	89 00/32	104 20/32
1973	----	----	----	1987	84 29/32	60 18/32	70 11/32	2001	112 19/32	98 24/32	101 17/32
1974	----	----	----	1988	76 04/32	66 11/32	70 09/32	2002	115 04/32	97 16/32	112 22/32
1975	----	----	----	1989	80 01/32	67 31/32	77 28/32	2003	124 12/32	103 27/32	109 10/32
1976	----	----	----	1990	78 06/32	68 26/32	76 03/32	2004	117 26/32	103 02/32	112 16/32
1977	83 19/32	79 17/32	80 07/32	1991	83 06/32	72 16/32	83 04/32	2005	119 30/32	109 00/32	114 06/32
1978	80 02/32	72 17/32	72 26/32	1992	84 30/32	76 16/32	82 24/32	2006	115 13/32	105 11/32	111 14/32
1979	74 16/32	62 21/32	66 08/32	1993	98 26/32	81 19/32	93 12/32	2007	119 12/32	104 31/32	116 12/32
1980	70 23/32	49 28/32	55 25/32	1994	95 02/32	75 09/32	78 02/32	2008	142 30/32	112 14/32	138 02/32
1981	59 15/32	42 11/32	47 09/32	1995	99 17/32	77 19/32	99 13/32	2009	139 18/32	113 04/32	115 12/32
1982	64 20/32	44 25/32	63 03/32	1996	99 15/32	84 07/32	91 22/32	2010	136 31/32	114 06/32	122 04/32
1983	64 20/32	54 15/32	56 08/32	1997	100 21/32	85 06/32	100 01/32	2011	147 00/32	116 26/32	144 26/32
1984	59 17/32	48 19/32	58 09/32	1998	111 21/32	98 02/32	106 09/32	2012	153 11/32	136 12/32	147 16/32
1985	69 11/32	53 30/32	69 00/32	1999	106 31/32	90 25/32	90 30/32	2013	149 21/32	127 23/32	128 10/32

Futures begin trading 08/22/1977.   *Source: CME Group; Chicago Board of Trade*

T-Bond Yield, 30-Year Monthly Cash as of 12/31/2013				
Date	Open	High	Low	Close
08/30/13	3.669	3.929	3.602	3.676
09/30/13	3.754	3.910	3.647	3.686
10/31/13	3.719	3.803	3.565	3.631
11/29/13	3.665	3.938	3.647	3.808
12/31/13	3.843	3.976	3.810	3.964

MONTHLY CASH
As of 12/31/2013
Chart High 15.210   on 10/26/1981
Chart Low 2.452   on 07/25/2012

Constant Maturity Treasury.   Shaded areas indicate US recessions.

Annual High, Low and Settle of Treasury Bonds, 30-Year Yield   In Percent

Year	High	Low	Settle	Year	High	Low	Settle	Year	High	Low	Settle
1972	6.560	5.570	6.340	1986	9.650	7.120	7.490	2000	6.762	5.380	5.457
1973	7.450	6.530	7.010	1987	10.250	7.290	8.950	2001	5.919	4.661	5.472
1974	8.290	7.180	7.620	1988	9.542	8.320	8.995	2002	5.872	4.606	4.783
1975	8.330	7.520	8.050	1989	9.337	7.753	7.973	2003	5.495	4.135	5.068
1976	7.910	7.200	7.200	1990	9.203	7.962	8.240	2004	5.597	4.620	4.822
1977	8.060	7.350	8.030	1991	8.622	7.394	7.396	2005	4.931	4.151	4.547
1978	8.990	8.070	8.960	1992	8.146	7.201	7.403	2006	5.307	4.460	4.818
1979	10.530	8.800	10.110	1993	7.493	5.771	6.341	2007	5.408	4.279	4.459
1980	13.170	9.490	11.980	1994	8.187	6.154	7.883	2008	4.813	2.519	2.691
1981	15.210	11.670	13.650	1995	7.962	5.938	5.956	2009	5.066	2.620	4.641
1982	14.800	10.330	10.430	1996	7.250	5.922	6.639	2010	4.858	3.462	4.362
1983	12.150	10.270	11.870	1997	7.189	5.850	5.915	2011	4.789	2.694	2.889
1984	13.940	11.320	11.540	1998	6.092	4.685	5.092	2012	3.490	2.452	2.952
1985	11.970	9.270	9.270	1999	6.491	5.030	6.479	2013	3.976	2.810	3.964

Source: Federal Researve Board

TREASURY BONDS, 30-YEAR

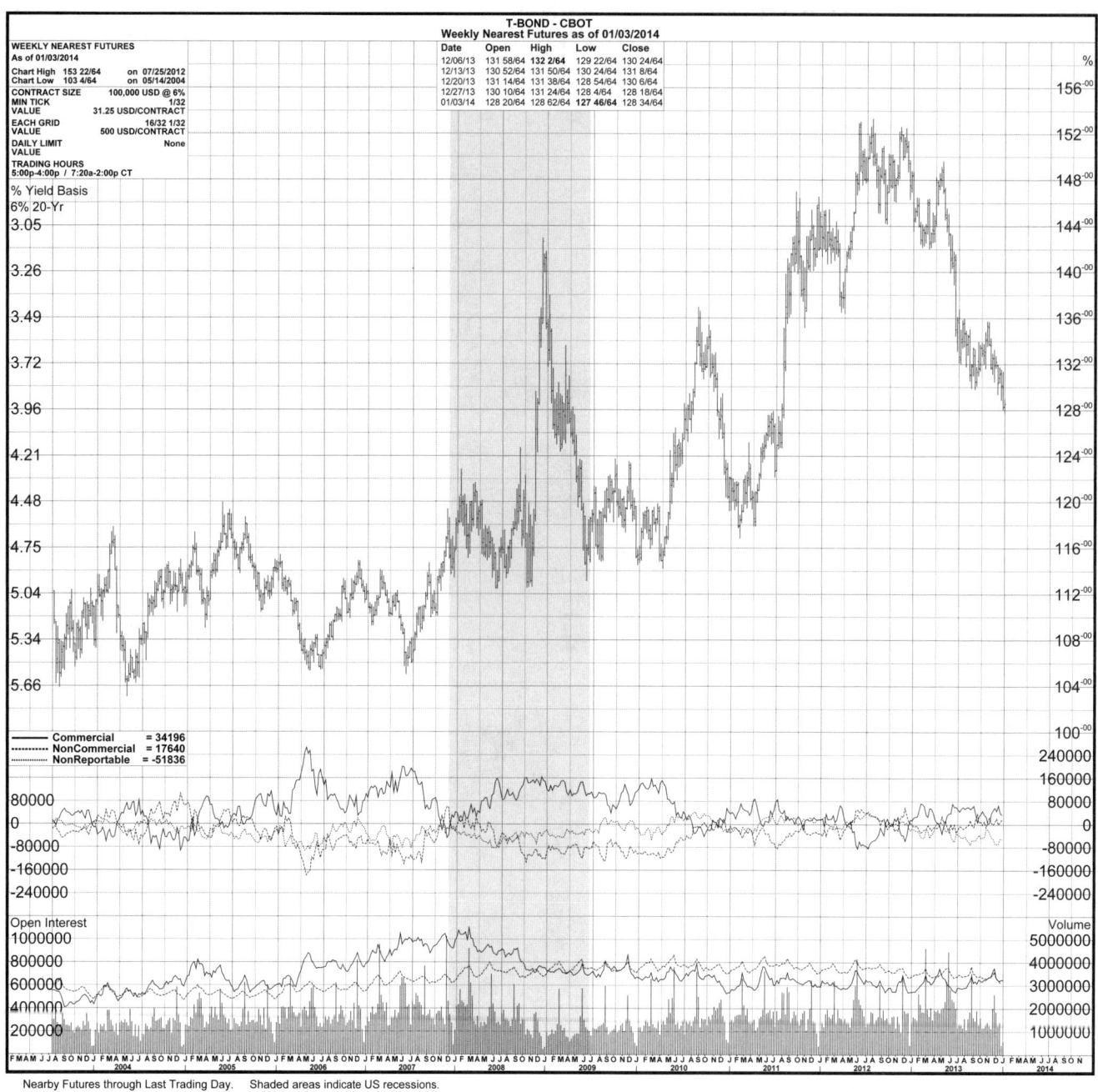

Quarterly High, Low and Settle of Treasury Bonds, 30-Year Futures   In Nominal Value

Quarter	High	Low	Settle	Quarter	High	Low	Settle	Quarter	High	Low	Settle
03/2005	117 12/32	109 00/32	111 12/32	03/2008	122 28/32	115 03/32	118 26/32	03/2011	125 06/32	116 26/32	120 06/32
06/2005	119 30/32	110 25/32	118 24/32	06/2008	120 04/32	112 14/32	115 19/32	06/2011	127 29/32	117 28/32	123 01/32
09/2005	119 04/32	113 24/32	114 13/32	09/2008	124 24/32	113 11/32	117 06/32	09/2011	147 00/32	122 13/32	142 20/32
12/2005	115 00/32	110 12/32	114 06/32	12/2008	142 30/32	112 17/32	138 02/32	12/2011	146 18/32	135 05/32	144 26/32
03/2006	115 13/32	108 26/32	109 05/32	03/2009	139 18/32	124 11/32	129 22/32	03/2012	145 15/32	136 15/32	137 24/32
06/2006	109 14/32	105 11/32	106 21/32	06/2009	130 30/32	113 04/32	118 12/32	06/2012	153 03/32	136 12/32	147 31/32
09/2006	113 11/32	105 14/32	112 13/32	09/2009	122 12/32	114 26/32	121 12/32	09/2012	153 11/32	144 05/32	149 12/32
12/2006	114 29/32	109 27/32	111 14/32	12/2009	123 25/32	114 16/32	115 12/32	12/2012	152 21/32	146 02/32	147 16/32
03/2007	114 04/32	109 06/32	111 08/32	03/2010	119 28/32	114 22/32	116 04/32	03/2013	146 17/32	142 00/32	144 15/32
06/2007	112 10/32	104 31/32	107 24/32	06/2010	127 24/32	114 06/32	127 16/32	06/2013	149 21/32	133 04/32	135 27/32
09/2007	114 23/32	105 31/32	111 11/32	09/2010	136 31/32	125 07/32	133 23/32	09/2013	136 27/32	129 25/32	133 12/32
12/2007	119 12/32	110 02/32	116 12/32	12/2010	135 12/32	119 06/32	122 04/32	12/2013	135 24/32	127 23/32	128 10/32

Source: CME Group; Chicago Board of Trade

T-Bond Yield, 30-Year
Weekly Cash as of 01/03/2014

Date	Open	High	Low	Close
12/06/13	3.843	3.976	3.828	3.917
12/13/13	3.883	3.903	3.827	3.872
12/20/13	3.854	3.953	3.824	3.824
12/27/13	3.835	3.950	3.810	3.943
01/03/14	3.927	3.974	3.896	3.929

WEEKLY CASH
As of 01/03/2014
Chart High 5.597 on 05/14/2004
Chart Low 2.452 on 07/25/2012

Constant Maturity Treasury.   Shaded areas indicate US recessions.

Quarterly High, Low and Settle of Treasury Bonds, 30-Year Yield   In Percent

Quarter	High	Low	Settle	Quarter	High	Low	Settle	Quarter	High	Low	Settle
03/2005	4.931	4.351	4.766	03/2008	4.720	4.102	4.306	03/2011	4.789	4.320	4.508
06/2005	4.825	4.151	4.219	06/2008	4.813	4.275	4.531	06/2011	4.671	4.137	4.382
09/2005	4.618	4.205	4.568	09/2008	4.722	3.895	4.305	09/2011	4.416	2.752	2.921
12/2005	4.879	4.479	4.547	12/2008	4.375	2.519	2.691	12/2011	3.452	2.694	2.889
03/2006	4.921	4.460	4.893	03/2009	3.846	2.620	3.561	03/2012	3.490	2.880	3.345
06/2006	5.307	4.872	5.186	06/2009	5.066	3.494	4.311	06/2012	3.411	2.510	2.763
09/2006	5.292	4.676	4.767	09/2009	4.670	4.017	4.048	09/2012	3.277	2.452	2.834
12/2006	4.976	4.525	4.818	12/2009	4.714	3.888	4.641	12/2012	3.036	2.696	2.952
03/2007	5.021	4.623	4.848	03/2010	4.803	4.486	4.715	03/2013	3.284	2.992	3.104
06/2007	5.408	4.758	5.126	06/2010	4.858	3.908	3.909	06/2013	3.629	2.810	3.497
09/2007	5.291	4.617	4.833	09/2010	4.138	3.462	3.687	09/2013	3.929	3.458	3.686
12/2007	4.928	4.279	4.459	12/2010	4.624	3.637	4.362	12/2013	3.976	3.565	3.964

Source: Federal Reserve Board

STERLING, 3-MONTH

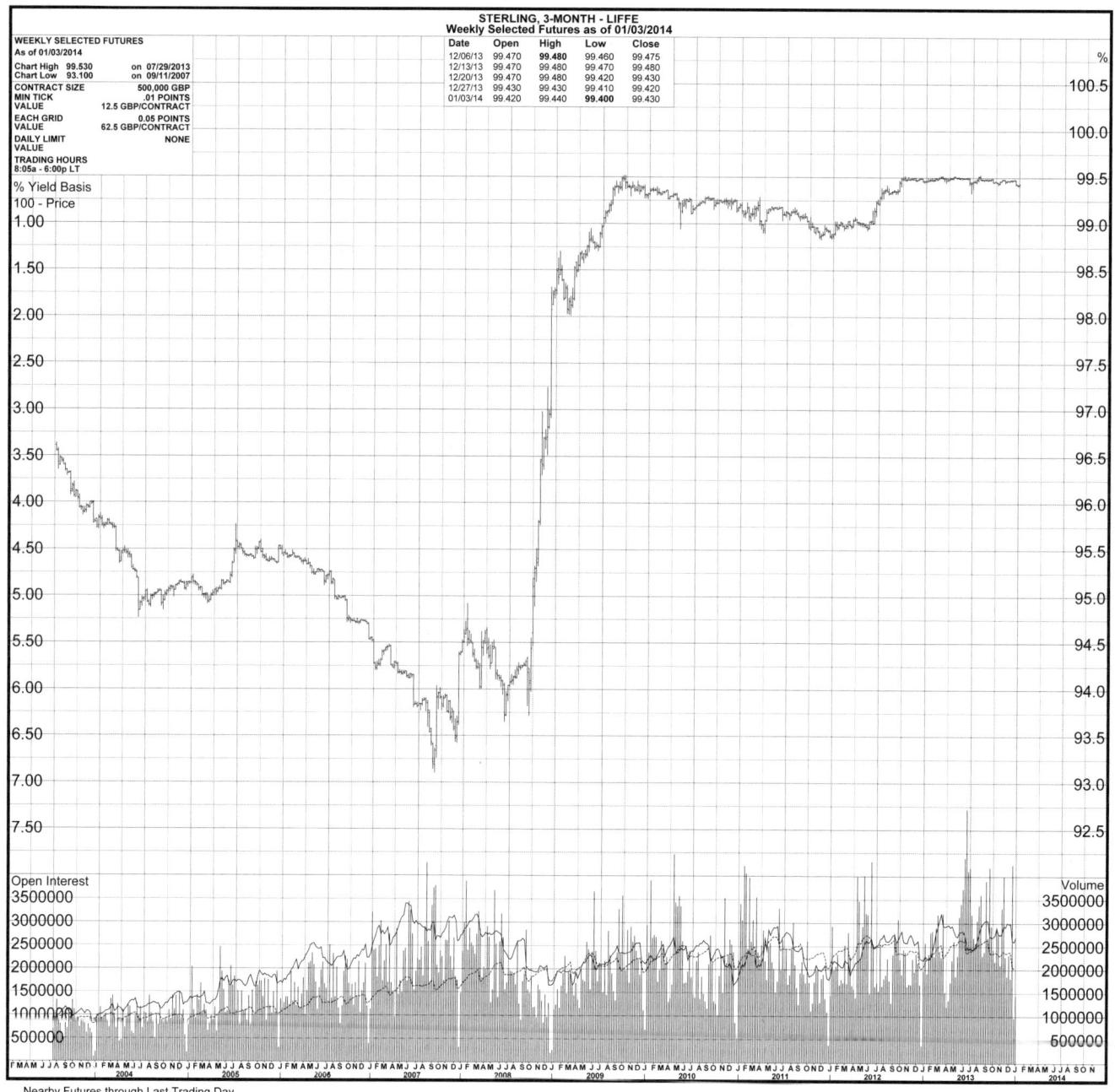

STERLING, 3-MONTH - LIFFE
Weekly Selected Futures as of 01/03/2014

Date	Open	High	Low	Close
12/06/13	99.470	**99.480**	99.460	99.475
12/13/13	99.470	99.480	99.470	99.480
12/20/13	99.470	99.480	99.420	99.430
12/27/13	99.430	99.430	99.410	99.420
01/03/14	99.420	99.440	**99.400**	99.430

WEEKLY SELECTED FUTURES
As of 01/03/2014
Chart High 99.530 on 07/29/2013
Chart Low 93.100 on 09/11/2007
CONTRACT SIZE 500,000 GBP
MIN TICK .01 POINTS
VALUE 12.5 GBP/CONTRACT
EACH GRID 0.05 POINTS
VALUE 62.5 GBP/CONTRACT
DAILY LIMIT NONE
VALUE
TRADING HOURS
8:05a - 6:00p LT

Nearby Futures through Last Trading Day.

Quarterly High, Low and Settle of Sterling, 3-Month Futures   In Point of 100%

Quarter	High	Low	Settle	Quarter	High	Low	Settle	Quarter	High	Low	Settle
03/2005	95.230	94.910	94.990	03/2008	94.920	94.000	94.555	03/2011	99.290	98.930	98.960
06/2005	95.510	94.980	95.500	06/2008	94.660	93.645	93.900	06/2011	99.190	98.900	99.120
09/2005	95.770	95.390	95.500	09/2008	94.350	93.715	94.130	09/2011	99.180	98.950	98.970
12/2005	95.600	95.340	95.500	12/2008	98.320	94.105	98.235	12/2011	99.080	98.830	98.890
03/2006	95.540	95.330	95.370	03/2009	98.705	98.010	98.600	03/2012	99.080	98.840	99.050
06/2006	95.410	95.110	95.210	06/2009	98.950	98.520	98.880	06/2012	99.270	98.930	99.220
09/2006	95.270	94.710	94.770	09/2009	99.520	98.860	99.430	09/2012	99.500	99.210	99.490
12/2006	94.760	94.520	94.550	12/2009	99.460	99.260	99.320	12/2012	99.520	99.440	99.470
03/2007	94.560	94.200	94.230	03/2010	99.400	99.260	99.290	03/2013	99.520	99.440	99.480
06/2007	94.300	93.800	93.840	06/2010	99.330	98.940	99.160	06/2013	99.520	99.330	99.440
09/2007	94.040	93.100	93.960	09/2010	99.300	99.140	99.230	09/2013	99.530	99.380	99.455
12/2007	94.430	93.420	94.420	12/2010	99.280	99.120	99.200	12/2013	99.480	99.410	99.425

Source: Euronext LIFFE

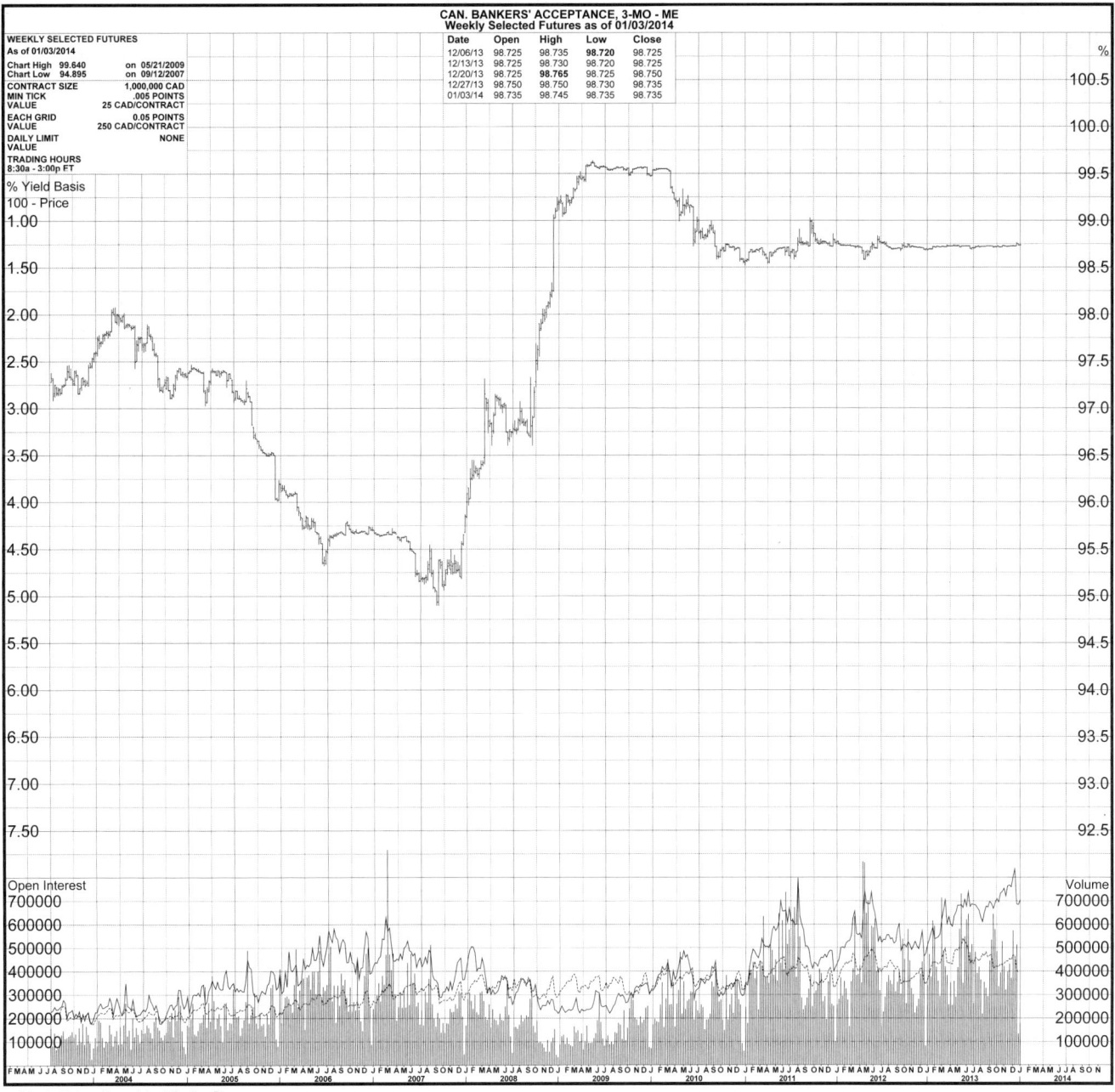

CAN. BANKERS' ACCEPTANCE, 3-MO - ME
Weekly Selected Futures as of 01/03/2014

Date	Open	High	Low	Close
12/06/13	98.725	98.735	98.720	98.725
12/13/13	98.725	98.730	98.720	98.725
12/20/13	98.725	98.735	98.765	98.750
12/27/13	98.750	98.750	98.730	98.735
01/03/14	98.735	98.745	98.735	98.735

WEEKLY SELECTED FUTURES
As of 01/03/2014

Chart High 99.640 on 05/21/2009
Chart Low 94.895 on 09/12/2007
CONTRACT SIZE 1,000,000 CAD
MIN TICK VALUE .005 POINTS / 25 CAD/CONTRACT
EACH GRID VALUE 0.05 POINTS / 250 CAD/CONTRACT
DAILY LIMIT VALUE NONE
TRADING HOURS 8:30a - 3:00p FT

% Yield Basis
100 - Price

Nearby Futures through Last Trading Day.

Quarterly High, Low and Settle of Canadian Bankers' Acceptance   In Point of 100%

Quarter	High	Low	Settle	Quarter	High	Low	Settle	Quarter	High	Low	Settle
03/2005	97.470	97.025	97.160	03/2008	97.315	95.730	97.060	03/2011	98.705	98.520	98.620
06/2005	97.430	97.155	97.320	06/2008	97.150	96.600	96.730	06/2011	98.720	98.535	98.620
09/2005	97.310	96.675	96.695	09/2008	97.330	96.600	96.920	09/2011	99.030	98.580	98.915
12/2005	96.740	96.015	96.015	12/2008	99.245	96.900	99.210	12/2011	98.980	98.720	98.760
03/2006	96.240	95.805	95.840	03/2009	99.510	99.040	99.510	03/2012	98.780	98.700	98.725
06/2006	95.860	95.320	95.380	06/2009	99.640	99.410	99.575	06/2012	98.840	98.575	98.770
09/2006	95.800	95.335	95.750	09/2009	99.585	99.530	99.540	09/2012	98.780	98.670	98.730
12/2006	95.765	95.655	95.705	12/2009	99.570	99.465	99.475	12/2012	98.765	98.675	98.690
03/2007	95.740	95.630	95.670	03/2010	99.555	99.230	99.240	03/2013	98.740	98.675	98.725
06/2007	95.685	95.205	95.235	06/2010	99.340	98.720	98.985	06/2013	98.740	98.685	98.705
09/2007	95.550	94.895	95.360	09/2010	99.040	98.580	98.690	09/2013	98.730	98.695	98.720
12/2007	95.730	95.060	95.700	12/2010	98.750	98.540	98.560	12/2013	98.765	98.710	98.740

Source: Montreal Exchange

131

EIROBOR, 3-MONTH

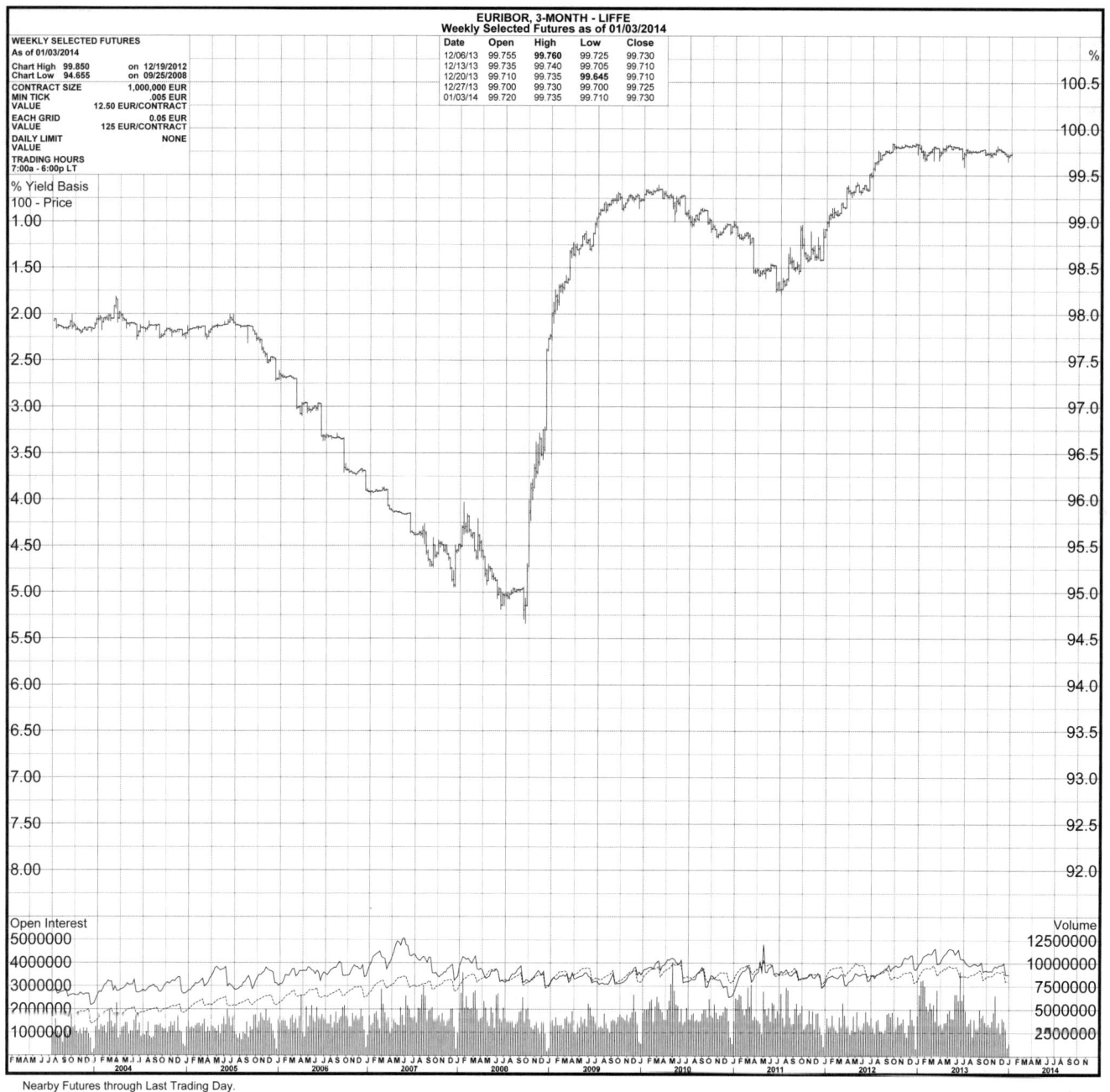

EURIBOR, 3-MONTH - LIFFE
Weekly Selected Futures as of 01/03/2014

Date	Open	High	Low	Close
12/06/13	99.755	**99.760**	99.725	99.730
12/13/13	99.735	99.740	99.705	99.710
12/20/13	99.710	99.735	**99.645**	99.710
12/27/13	99.700	99.730	99.700	99.725
01/03/14	99.720	99.735	99.710	99.730

WEEKLY SELECTED FUTURES
As of 01/03/2014

Chart High 99.850 on 12/19/2012
Chart Low 94.655 on 09/25/2008
CONTRACT SIZE 1,000,000 EUR
MIN TICK .005 EUR
VALUE 12.50 EUR/CONTRACT
EACH GRID 0.05 EUR
VALUE 125 EUR/CONTRACT
DAILY LIMIT NONE
VALUE
TRADING HOURS
7:00a - 6:00p LT

Nearby Futures through Last Trading Day.

Quarterly High, Low and Settle of Euribor, 3-Month Futures   In Points of 100%

Quarter	High	Low	Settle	Quarter	High	Low	Settle	Quarter	High	Low	Settle
03/2005	97.875	97.720	97.790	03/2008	95.970	95.345	95.505	03/2011	98.995	98.435	98.480
06/2005	97.995	97.790	97.945	06/2008	95.510	94.805	94.925	06/2011	98.550	98.235	98.270
09/2005	97.995	97.680	97.785	09/2008	95.090	94.655	94.990	09/2011	98.970	98.210	98.750
12/2005	97.795	97.270	97.295	12/2008	97.785	94.900	97.770	12/2011	98.930	98.560	98.920
03/2006	97.390	96.910	96.925	03/2009	98.755	97.710	98.745	03/2012	99.395	98.900	99.330
06/2006	97.050	96.625	96.680	06/2009	98.990	98.610	98.950	06/2012	99.535	99.260	99.495
09/2006	96.715	96.285	96.320	09/2009	99.320	98.950	99.255	09/2012	99.845	99.470	99.810
12/2006	96.340	96.080	96.085	12/2009	99.305	99.110	99.235	12/2012	99.850	99.720	99.830
03/2007	96.130	95.885	95.890	03/2010	99.395	99.215	99.305	03/2013	99.840	99.650	99.745
06/2007	95.900	95.630	95.640	06/2010	99.330	98.995	99.075	06/2013	99.840	99.585	99.730
09/2007	95.740	95.265	95.395	09/2010	99.150	98.910	98.940	09/2013	99.790	99.705	99.730
12/2007	95.565	95.050	95.470	12/2010	99.010	98.820	98.970	12/2013	99.820	99.645	99.720

Source: Euronext LIFFE

EURO-BUND (FGBL) - EUREX-DE
Weekly Nearest Futures as of 01/03/2014

Date	Open	High	Low	Close
12/06/13	141.57	141.64	139.76	140.00
12/13/13	140.12	140.47	139.94	140.25
12/20/13	140.47	140.59	139.43	139.92
12/27/13	139.77	139.93	138.83	138.96
01/03/14	138.74	139.25	138.68	139.09

WEEKLY NEAREST FUTURES
As of 01/03/2014

Chart High 147.20 on 05/02/2013
Chart Low 109.65 on 06/19/2008
CONTRACT SIZE 100,000 EUR @ 6%
MIN TICK .01 POINTS
VALUE 10 EUR/CONTRACT
EACH GRID 0.2 POINTS
VALUE 200 EUR/CONTRACT
DAILY LIMIT NONE
VALUE
TRADING HOURS
8:00a - 10:00p CET

Nearby Futures through Last Trading Day.

Quarterly High, Low and Settle of Euro-Bund (FGBL) Futures   In Nominal Value

Quarter	High	Low	Settle	Quarter	High	Low	Settle	Quarter	High	Low	Settle
03/2005	120.98	116.89	118.61	03/2008	118.48	112.85	115.98	03/2011	126.52	121.06	121.28
06/2005	123.78	118.51	123.50	06/2008	116.13	109.65	110.57	06/2011	127.57	119.86	125.48
09/2005	124.60	121.16	122.53	09/2008	116.13	109.70	115.07	09/2011	139.19	125.22	136.49
12/2005	122.71	119.03	121.84	12/2008	125.56	113.67	124.84	12/2011	139.58	132.89	139.04
03/2006	122.65	116.85	117.17	03/2009	126.53	121.55	124.43	03/2012	140.52	135.27	138.49
06/2006	117.26	114.55	115.32	06/2009	124.66	117.52	121.08	06/2012	146.89	137.60	140.90
09/2006	118.70	114.65	118.10	09/2009	123.12	119.85	121.88	09/2012	146.26	138.41	141.77
12/2006	118.88	115.96	116.03	12/2009	124.06	120.51	121.19	12/2012	146.17	139.45	145.64
03/2007	116.89	114.62	114.92	03/2010	124.53	120.84	123.35	03/2013	145.87	141.28	145.49
06/2007	115.14	109.66	110.75	06/2010	130.37	122.11	129.39	06/2013	147.20	139.90	141.52
09/2007	114.98	109.75	112.68	09/2010	134.77	127.37	131.43	09/2013	144.37	136.60	140.50
12/2007	115.83	111.54	113.11	12/2010	132.36	123.76	125.31	12/2013	142.32	138.69	139.17

Source: Eurex

JAPANESE GOVERNMENT BOND, 10-YEAR

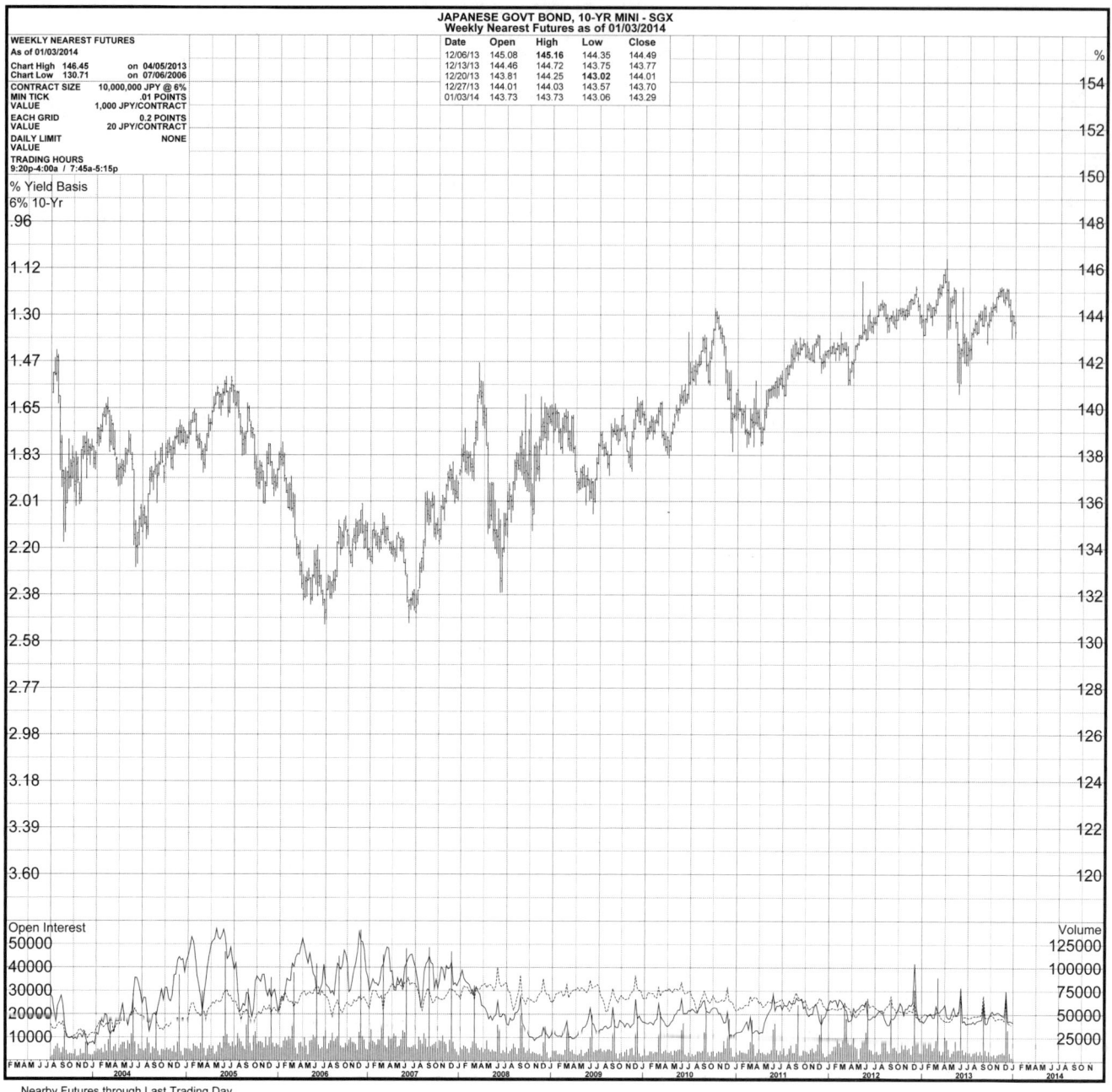

JAPANESE GOVT BOND, 10-YR MINI - SGX
Weekly Nearest Futures as of 01/03/2014

WEEKLY NEAREST FUTURES
As of 01/03/2014

Chart High 146.45	on 04/05/2013	
Chart Low 130.71	on 07/06/2006	
CONTRACT SIZE	10,000,000 JPY @ 6%	
MIN TICK	.01 POINTS	
VALUE	1,000 JPY/CONTRACT	
EACH GRID	0.2 POINTS	
VALUE	20 JPY/CONTRACT	
DAILY LIMIT	NONE	
VALUE		
TRADING HOURS		
9:20p-4:00a / 7:45a-5:15p		

Date	Open	High	Low	Close
12/06/13	145.08	**145.16**	144.35	144.49
12/13/13	144.46	144.72	143.75	143.77
12/20/13	143.81	144.25	**143.02**	144.01
12/27/13	144.01	144.03	143.57	143.70
01/03/14	143.73	143.73	143.06	143.29

% Yield Basis
6% 10-Yr

Nearby Futures through Last Trading Day.

Quarterly High, Low and Settle of Japanese Government Bonds, 10-Year Futures   In Nominal Value

Quarter	High	Low	Settle	Quarter	High	Low	Settle	Quarter	High	Low	Settle
03/2005	139.96	137.22	139.40	03/2008	141.96	136.87	140.46	03/2011	141.20	138.33	139.57
06/2005	141.35	138.95	141.27	06/2008	140.71	132.08	135.24	06/2011	141.64	138.38	141.12
09/2005	141.35	137.36	137.67	09/2008	140.60	134.46	137.32	09/2011	143.07	140.52	142.24
12/2005	138.49	135.90	137.35	12/2008	140.50	134.72	139.75	12/2011	143.19	141.51	142.51
03/2006	138.56	132.81	133.26	03/2009	140.20	137.98	137.99	03/2012	143.30	141.00	141.96
06/2006	134.14	131.50	131.65	06/2009	138.30	135.45	138.20	06/2012	145.46	141.29	143.70
09/2006	135.38	130.71	134.90	09/2009	139.58	137.11	139.32	09/2012	144.68	143.25	144.24
12/2006	135.89	133.18	133.93	12/2009	140.50	137.29	139.73	12/2012	145.26	143.46	143.62
03/2007	135.50	133.30	134.19	03/2010	140.30	138.05	138.09	03/2013	146.00	143.12	145.47
06/2007	134.68	130.76	132.04	06/2010	143.28	137.86	141.62	06/2013	146.45	140.62	142.61
09/2007	136.44	131.16	134.99	09/2010	143.44	140.98	143.40	09/2013	144.49	142.07	144.12
12/2007	137.72	134.15	136.76	12/2010	144.31	138.15	140.61	12/2013	145.24	143.02	143.27

Source: Singapore Exchange

EURO-SWISS, 3-MONTH - LIFFE
Weekly Nearest Futures as of 01/03/2014

Date	Open	High	Low	Close
12/06/13	100.000	100.000	99.980	99.990
12/13/13	99.990	99.990	99.970	99.980
12/20/13	99.980	100.020	99.970	100.010
12/27/13	100.000	100.010	99.990	100.010
01/03/14	100.000	100.010	99.990	99.990

WEEKLY NEAREST FUTURES
As of 01/03/2014

Chart High 100.350 on 08/18/2011
Chart Low 96.850 on 06/17/2008
CONTRACT SIZE 1,000,000 EUR
MIN TICK .005 POINTS
VALUE 12.5 EUR/CONTRACT
EACH GRID 0.02 POINTS
VALUE 50 EUR/CONTRACT
DAILY LIMIT NONE
VALUE
TRADING HOURS
7:30a - 6:00p LT

% Yield Basis
100 - Price

Nearby Futures through Last Trading Day.

Quarterly High, Low and Settle of Euro-Swiss, 3-Month Futures   In Points of 100%

Quarter	High	Low	Settle	Quarter	High	Low	Settle	Quarter	High	Low	Settle
03/2005	99.253	99.150	99.210	03/2008	97.590	97.180	97.230	03/2011	99.860	99.720	99.740
06/2005	99.290	99.180	99.270	06/2008	97.240	96.850	97.100	06/2011	99.860	99.680	99.800
09/2005	99.380	99.080	99.090	09/2008	97.470	97.050	97.220	09/2011	100.350	99.710	100.030
12/2005	99.120	98.690	98.720	12/2008	99.620	97.150	99.530	12/2011	100.060	99.940	100.030
03/2006	98.820	98.410	98.480	03/2009	99.720	99.450	99.670	03/2012	100.040	99.840	99.890
06/2006	98.530	98.140	98.190	06/2009	99.750	99.590	99.640	06/2012	100.070	99.870	99.970
09/2006	98.280	97.940	97.970	09/2009	99.730	99.630	99.720	09/2012	100.040	99.950	100.010
12/2006	98.020	97.720	97.730	12/2009	99.760	99.700	99.730	12/2012	100.070	99.980	100.030
03/2007	97.780	97.510	97.510	03/2010	99.760	99.690	99.720	03/2013	100.040	99.940	100.030
06/2007	97.530	97.020	97.090	06/2010	99.940	99.700	99.830	06/2013	100.040	99.920	99.980
09/2007	97.420	97.060	97.200	09/2010	99.880	99.660	99.810	09/2013	100.000	99.940	99.980
12/2007	97.270	97.090	97.210	12/2010	99.870	99.770	99.840	12/2013	100.100	99.970	100.000

Source: Euronext LIFFE

PRIME RATE AND DISCOUNT RATE

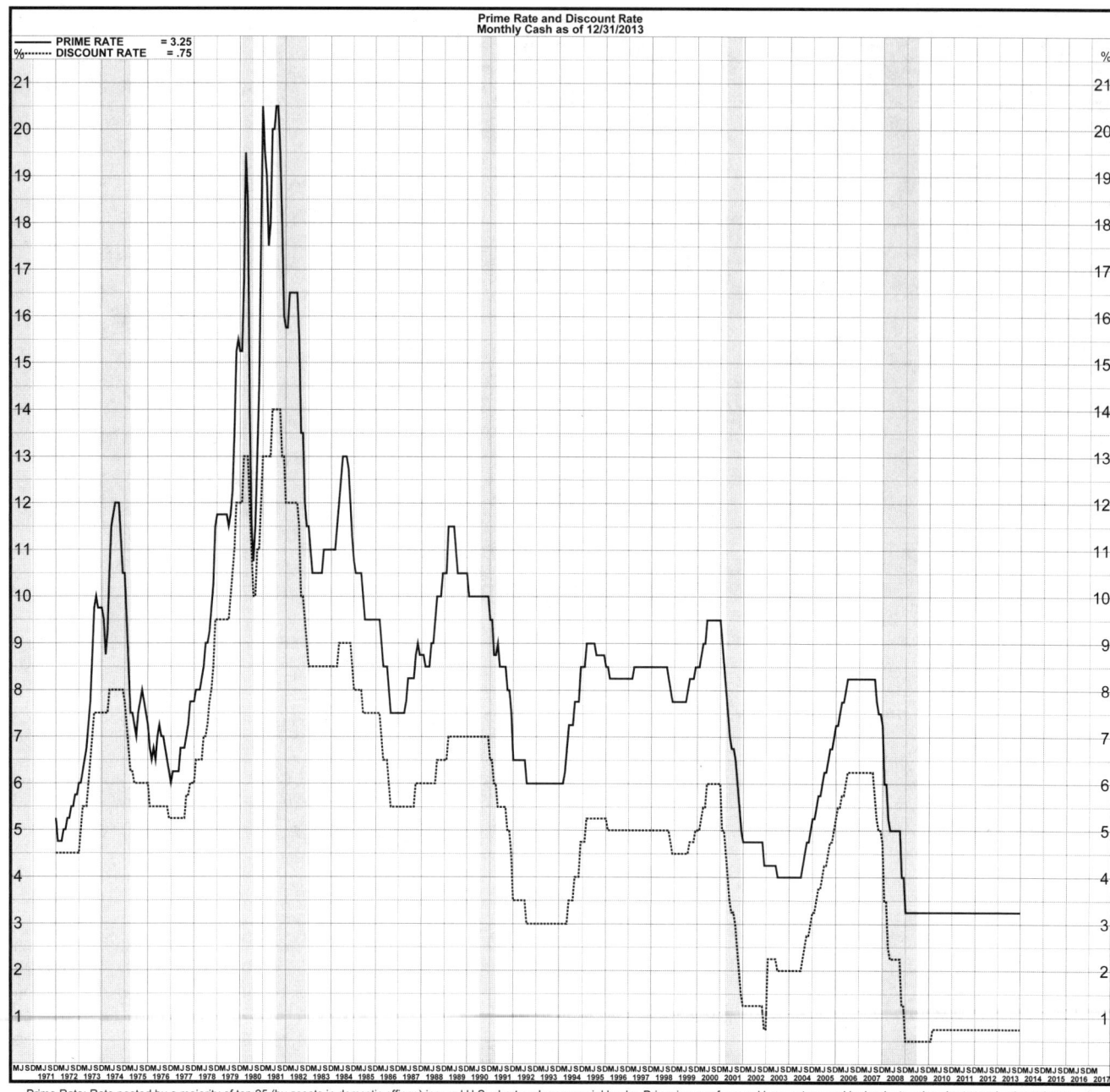

Prime Rate and Discount Rate
Monthly Cash as of 12/31/2013

PRIME RATE = 3.25
% .... DISCOUNT RATE = .75

Prime Rate: Rate posted by a majority of top 25 (by assets in domestic offices) insured U.S.-chartered commercial banks. Prime is one of several base rates used by banks to price short-term business loans.
Discount Rate:The rate charged for discounts made and advances extended under the Federal Reserve's primary credit discount window program, which became effective January 9, 2003. This rate replaces that for adjustment credit, which was discontinued after January 8, 2003.
Shaded areas indicate US recessions.

Annual High, Low and Close of Prime Rate   In Percent

Year	High	Low	Settle	Year	High	Low	Settle	Year	High	Low	Settle
1972	5.75	4.50	5.75	1986	9.50	7.50	7.50	2000	9.50	8.50	9.50
1973	10.00	5.75	9.75	1987	9.25	7.50	8.75	2001	9.50	4.75	4.75
1974	12.00	8.75	10.25	1988	10.50	8.50	10.50	2002	4.75	4.25	4.25
1975	10.00	7.00	7.25	1989	11.50	10.50	10.50	2003	4.25	4.00	4.00
1976	7.25	6.00	6.00	1990	10.50	9.50	9.50	2004	5.25	4.00	5.25
1977	7.75	6.00	7.75	1991	9.50	6.50	6.50	2005	7.25	5.25	7.25
1978	11.75	7.75	11.75	1992	6.50	6.00	6.00	2006	8.25	7.25	8.25
1979	15.75	11.50	15.25	1993	6.00	6.00	6.00	2007	8.25	7.25	7.25
1980	21.50	10.75	20.50	1994	8.50	6.00	8.50	2008	7.25	3.25	3.25
1981	20.50	15.75	15.75	1995	9.00	8.50	8.50	2009	3.25	3.25	3.25
1982	17.00	11.50	11.50	1996	8.50	8.25	8.25	2010	3.25	3.25	3.25
1983	11.50	10.50	11.00	1997	8.50	8.25	8.50	2011	3.25	3.25	3.25
1984	13.00	10.75	10.75	1998	8.50	7.75	7.75	2012	3.25	3.25	3.25
1985	10.75	9.50	9.50	1999	8.50	7.75	8.50	2013	3.25	3.25	3.25

Source: Federal Researve Board

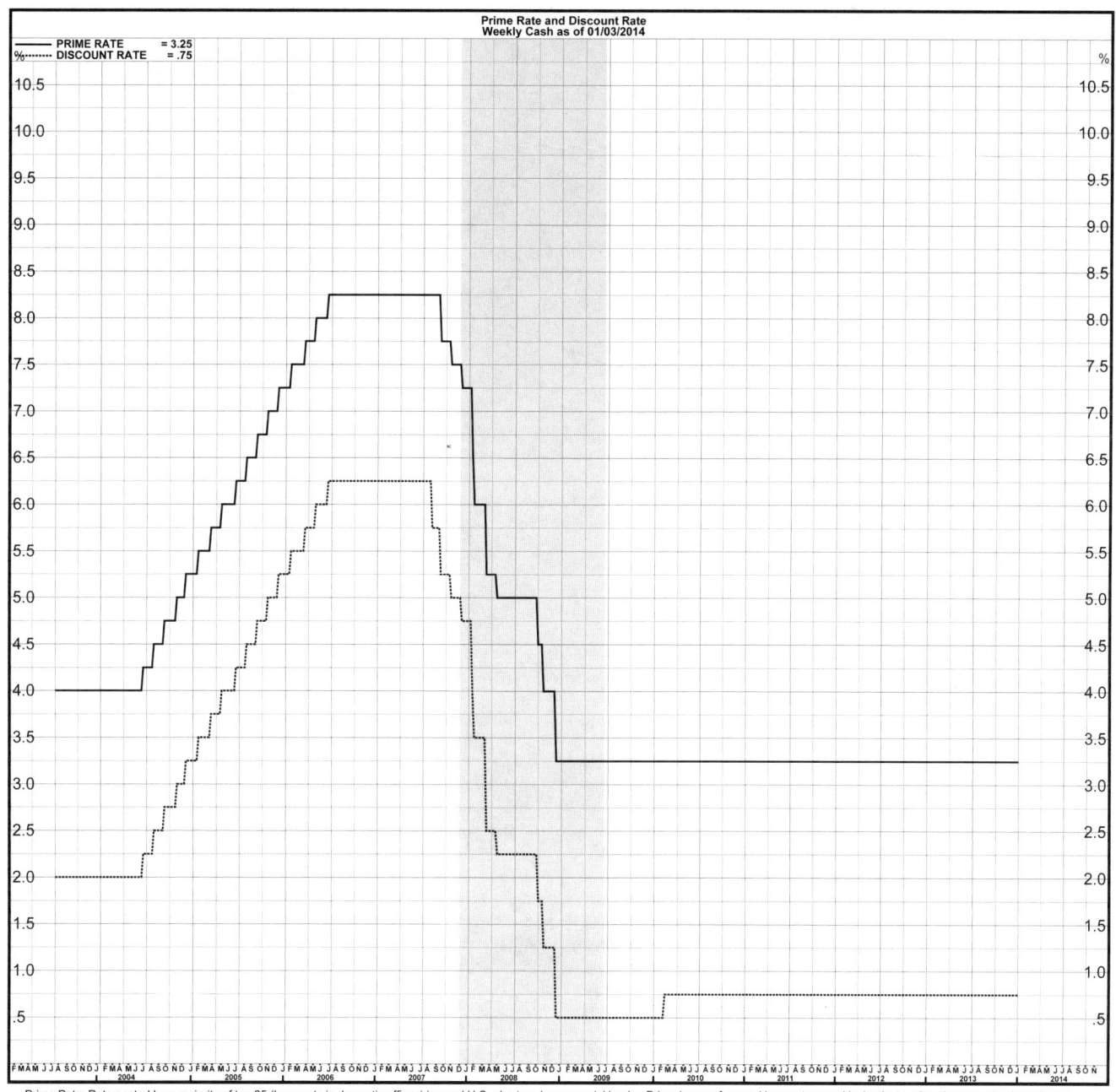

Prime Rate and Discount Rate
Weekly Cash as of 01/03/2014

PRIME RATE = 3.25
% DISCOUNT RATE = .75

Prime Rate: Rate posted by a majority of top 25 (by assets in domestic offices) insured U.S.-chartered commercial banks. Prime is one of several base rates used by banks to price short-term business loans.
Discount Rate: The rate charged for discounts made and advances extended under the Federal Reserve's primary credit discount window program, which became effective January 9, 2003.
Shaded areas indicate US recessions.

Annual High, Low and Close of Discount Rate   In Percent

Year	High	Low	Settle	Year	High	Low	Settle	Year	High	Low	Settle
1972	4.50	4.50	4.50	1986	7.50	5.50	5.50	2000	6.00	5.00	6.00
1973	7.50	5.00	7.50	1987	6.00	5.50	6.00	2001	6.00	1.25	1.25
1974	8.00	7.75	7.75	1988	6.50	6.00	6.50	2002	1.25	0.75	0.75
1975	7.25	6.00	6.00	1989	7.00	6.50	7.00	2003	2.25	0.75	2.00
1976	6.00	5.25	5.25	1990	7.00	6.50	6.50	2004	3.25	2.00	3.25
1977	6.00	5.25	6.00	1991	6.50	3.50	3.50	2005	5.25	3.25	5.25
1978	9.50	6.00	9.50	1992	3.50	3.00	3.00	2006	6.25	5.25	6.25
1979	12.00	9.50	12.00	1993	3.00	3.00	3.00	2007	6.25	4.75	4.75
1980	13.00	10.00	13.00	1994	4.75	3.00	4.75	2008	4.75	0.50	0.50
1981	14.00	12.00	12.00	1995	5.25	4.75	5.25	2009	0.50	0.50	0.50
1982	12.00	8.50	8.50	1996	5.25	5.00	5.00	2010	0.75	0.50	0.75
1983	8.50	8.50	8.50	1997	5.00	5.00	5.00	2011	0.75	0.75	0.75
1984	9.00	8.00	8.00	1998	5.00	4.50	4.50	2012	0.75	0.75	0.75
1985	8.00	7.50	7.50	1999	5.00	4.50	5.00	2013	0.75	0.75	0.75

Source: Federal Reserve Board

CONSUMER PRICE INDEX

CPI for All Urban Consumers: All Items (NSA)
Monthly Cash as of 12/31/2013

MONTHLY CASH
As of 12/31/2013
Chart High 234.149 on 09/30/2013
Chart Low 41.100 on 12/31/1971

Consumer Price Index for All Urban Consumers: All Items (CPIAUCNS)   Shaded areas indicate US recessions.

Annual High, Low and Close of CPI: All Items   In Index Value

Year	High	Low	Settle	Year	High	Low	Settle	Year	High	Low	Settle
1972	42.5	41.1	42.5	1986	110.5	108.6	110.5	2000	174.1	168.8	174.0
1973	46.2	42.6	46.2	1987	115.4	111.2	115.4	2001	178.3	175.1	176.7
1974	51.9	46.6	51.9	1988	120.5	115.7	120.5	2002	181.3	177.1	180.9
1975	55.5	52.1	55.5	1989	126.1	121.1	126.1	2003	185.2	181.7	184.3
1976	58.2	55.6	58.2	1990	133.8	127.4	133.8	2004	191.0	185.2	190.3
1977	62.1	58.5	62.1	1991	137.9	134.6	137.9	2005	199.2	190.7	196.8
1978	67.7	62.5	67.7	1992	142.0	138.1	141.9	2006	203.9	198.3	201.8
1979	76.7	68.3	76.7	1993	145.8	142.6	145.8	2007	210.2	202.4	210.0
1980	86.3	77.8	86.3	1994	149.7	146.2	149.7	2008	220.0	210.2	210.2
1981	94.0	87.0	94.0	1995	153.7	150.3	153.5	2009	216.3	211.1	215.9
1982	98.2	94.3	97.6	1996	158.6	154.4	158.6	2010	219.2	216.7	219.2
1983	101.3	97.8	101.3	1997	161.6	159.1	161.3	2011	226.9	220.2	225.7
1984	105.3	101.9	105.3	1998	164.0	161.6	163.9	2012	231.4	226.7	229.6
1985	109.3	105.5	109.3	1999	168.3	164.3	168.3	2013	234.1	230.3	233.1

Not seasonally adjusted.   *Source: U.S. Department of Labor: Bureau of Labor Statistics*

CPI for All Urban Consumers: All Items (SA)
Monthly Cash as of 12/31/2013

Consumer Price Index for All Urban Consumers: All Items (CPIAUCSL)   Shaded areas indicate US recessions.

Annual High, Low and Close of CPI: All Items   In Index Value

Year	High	Low	Settle	Year	High	Low	Settle	Year	High	Low	Settle
1972	42.5	41.2	42.5	1986	110.8	108.7	110.8	2000	174.6	169.3	174.6
1973	46.3	42.7	46.3	1987	115.6	111.4	115.6	2001	178.1	175.6	177.3
1974	51.9	46.8	51.9	1988	120.7	116.0	120.7	2002	181.6	177.7	181.6
1975	55.6	52.3	55.6	1989	126.3	121.2	126.3	2003	185.0	182.3	185.0
1976	58.4	55.8	58.4	1990	134.2	127.5	134.2	2004	191.2	185.9	191.2
1977	62.3	58.7	62.3	1991	138.2	134.7	138.2	2005	199.1	191.3	197.7
1978	67.9	62.7	67.9	1992	142.3	138.3	142.3	2006	203.8	199.0	202.8
1979	76.9	68.5	76.9	1993	146.3	142.8	146.3	2007	211.7	203.2	211.7
1980	86.4	78.0	86.4	1994	150.1	146.3	150.1	2008	219.2	211.6	211.6
1981	94.1	87.2	94.1	1995	153.9	150.5	153.9	2009	217.2	212.2	217.2
1982	98.1	94.4	97.7	1996	159.1	154.7	159.1	2010	220.2	216.9	220.2
1983	101.4	97.9	101.4	1997	161.8	159.4	161.8	2011	227.0	221.1	227.0
1984	105.5	102.1	105.5	1998	164.4	162.0	164.4	2012	231.6	227.5	231.1
1985	109.5	105.7	109.5	1999	168.8	164.7	168.8	2013	233.9	231.2	233.9

Seasonally adjusted.   *Source: U.S. Department of Labor: Bureau of Labor Statistics*

PRODUCER PRICE INDEX

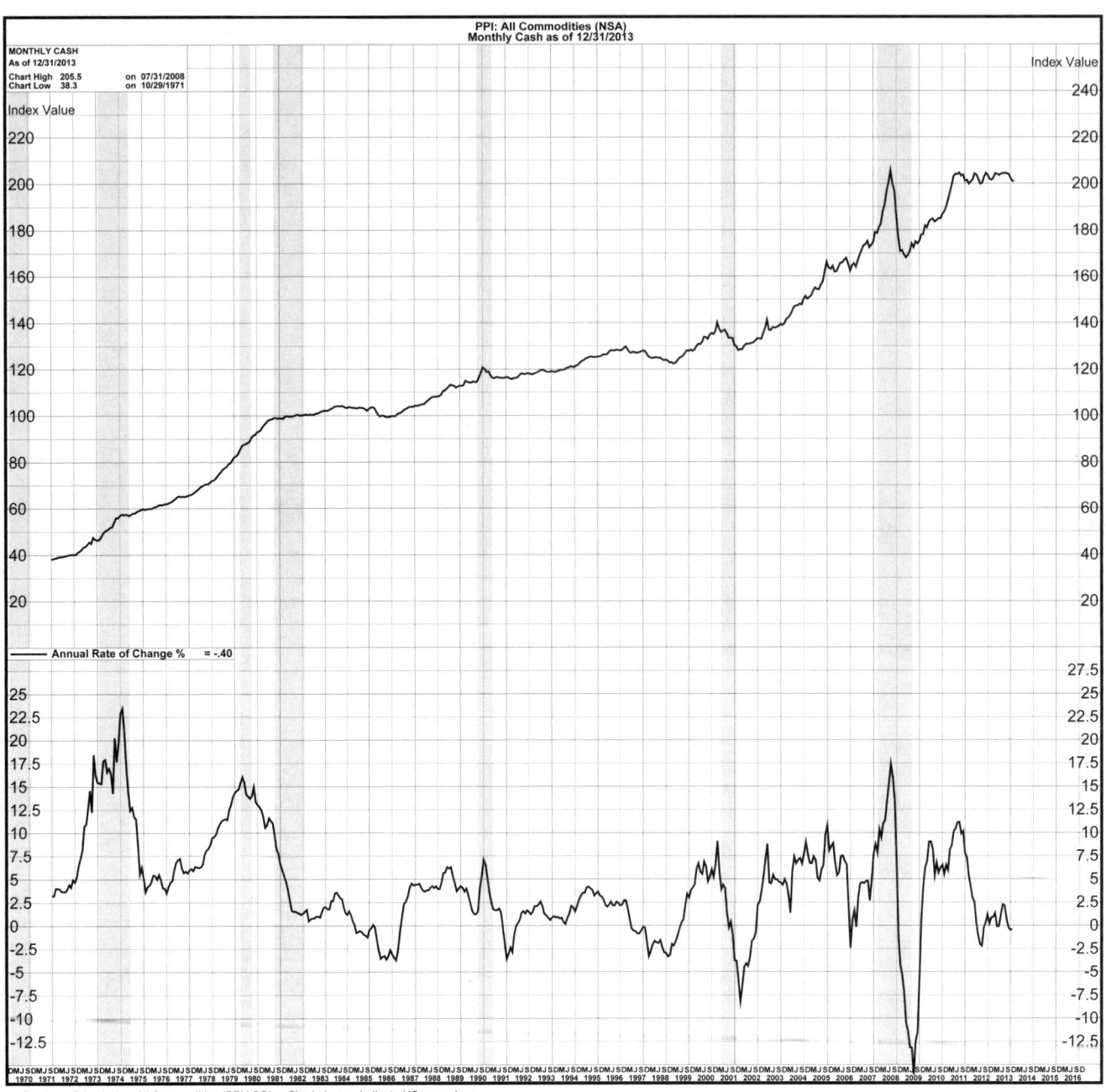

PPI: All Commodities (NSA)
Monthly Cash as of 12/31/2013

MONTHLY CASH
As of 12/31/2013

Chart High 205.5 on 07/31/2008
Chart Low 38.3 on 10/29/1971

Annual Rate of Change %   = -.40

Producer Price Index: All Commodities (PPIACO)   Shaded areas indicate US recessions.

Annual High, Low and Close of PPI: All commodities   In Index Value

Year	High	Low	Settle	Year	High	Low	Settle	Year	High	Low	Settle
1972	41.1	38.8	41.1	1986	103.2	99.3	99.7	2000	136.2	128.3	136.2
1973	47.5	41.6	47.4	1987	104.2	100.5	104.2	2001	140.0	128.1	128.1
1974	57.4	49.0	57.3	1988	109.0	104.6	109.0	2002	133.2	128.4	132.9
1975	59.8	56.9	59.7	1989	113.2	110.5	113.0	2003	141.2	135.3	139.5
1976	62.5	59.9	62.5	1990	120.8	114.1	118.7	2004	151.4	141.4	150.2
1977	66.2	62.8	66.2	1991	119.0	115.9	115.9	2005	166.2	150.9	163.0
1978	72.7	66.8	72.7	1992	118.1	115.6	117.6	2006	167.9	161.9	165.6
1979	83.4	73.8	83.4	1993	119.7	118.0	118.6	2007	179.0	164.0	178.6
1980	93.8	85.2	93.8	1994	121.9	119.1	121.9	2008	205.5	170.9	170.9
1981	99.0	95.2	98.8	1995	125.7	122.9	125.7	2009	178.1	168.1	178.1
1982	100.5	99.6	100.5	1996	129.1	126.2	129.1	2010	189.7	181.0	189.7
1983	102.3	100.2	102.3	1997	129.7	126.8	126.8	2011	204.6	192.7	199.8
1984	104.2	102.9	103.5	1998	125.4	122.8	122.8	2012	204.4	199.8	201.5
1985	103.6	102.1	103.6	1999	128.3	122.3	127.8	2013	204.4	201.0	201.0

Not seasonally adjusted.   *Source: U.S. Department of Labor: Bureau of Labor Statistics*

PPI: Finished Goods (SA)
Monthly Cash as of 12/31/2013

MONTHLY CASH
As of 12/31/2013

Chart High 197.9 on 08/30/2013
Chart Low 41.0 on 01/31/1972

Producer Price Index: Finished Goods (PPIFGS)   Shaded areas indicate US recessions.

Annual High, Low and Close of PPI: Finished Goods   In Index Value

Year	High	Low	Settle	Year	High	Low	Settle	Year	High	Low	Settle
1972	42.7	41.0	42.7	1986	105.5	102.3	103.6	2000	140.5	135.2	140.5
1973	47.6	43.0	47.6	1987	106.2	104.1	105.8	2001	142.2	138.0	138.0
1974	56.4	48.8	56.4	1988	110.0	106.3	110.0	2002	140.0	137.7	139.7
1975	60.1	56.6	60.1	1989	115.5	111.1	115.5	2003	145.3	141.2	145.3
1976	62.4	59.9	62.4	1990	122.6	117.4	122.0	2004	152.1	145.6	151.7
1977	66.7	62.5	66.7	1991	122.6	121.1	122.3	2005	159.9	151.7	159.9
1978	72.8	67.0	72.8	1992	124.2	122.0	124.2	2006	162.1	157.8	161.5
1979	82.2	73.7	82.2	1993	125.7	123.9	124.4	2007	172.3	160.6	171.4
1980	91.8	83.4	91.8	1994	126.6	124.8	126.6	2008	183.9	169.7	169.7
1981	98.3	92.8	98.3	1995	129.3	126.9	129.3	2009	177.1	169.5	177.1
1982	101.8	98.8	101.8	1996	132.9	129.7	132.9	2010	183.7	178.3	183.7
1983	102.3	101.0	102.3	1997	133.0	130.9	131.4	2011	193.6	185.5	193.1
1984	104.0	103.0	104.0	1998	131.3	130.4	131.3	2012	197.2	191.6	195.8
1985	106.0	103.8	106.0	1999	135.2	131.2	135.2	2013	197.9	194.8	197.4

Seasonally adjusted.   Source: U.S. Department of Labor: Bureau of Labor Statistics

U.S. UNEMPLOYMENT RATE

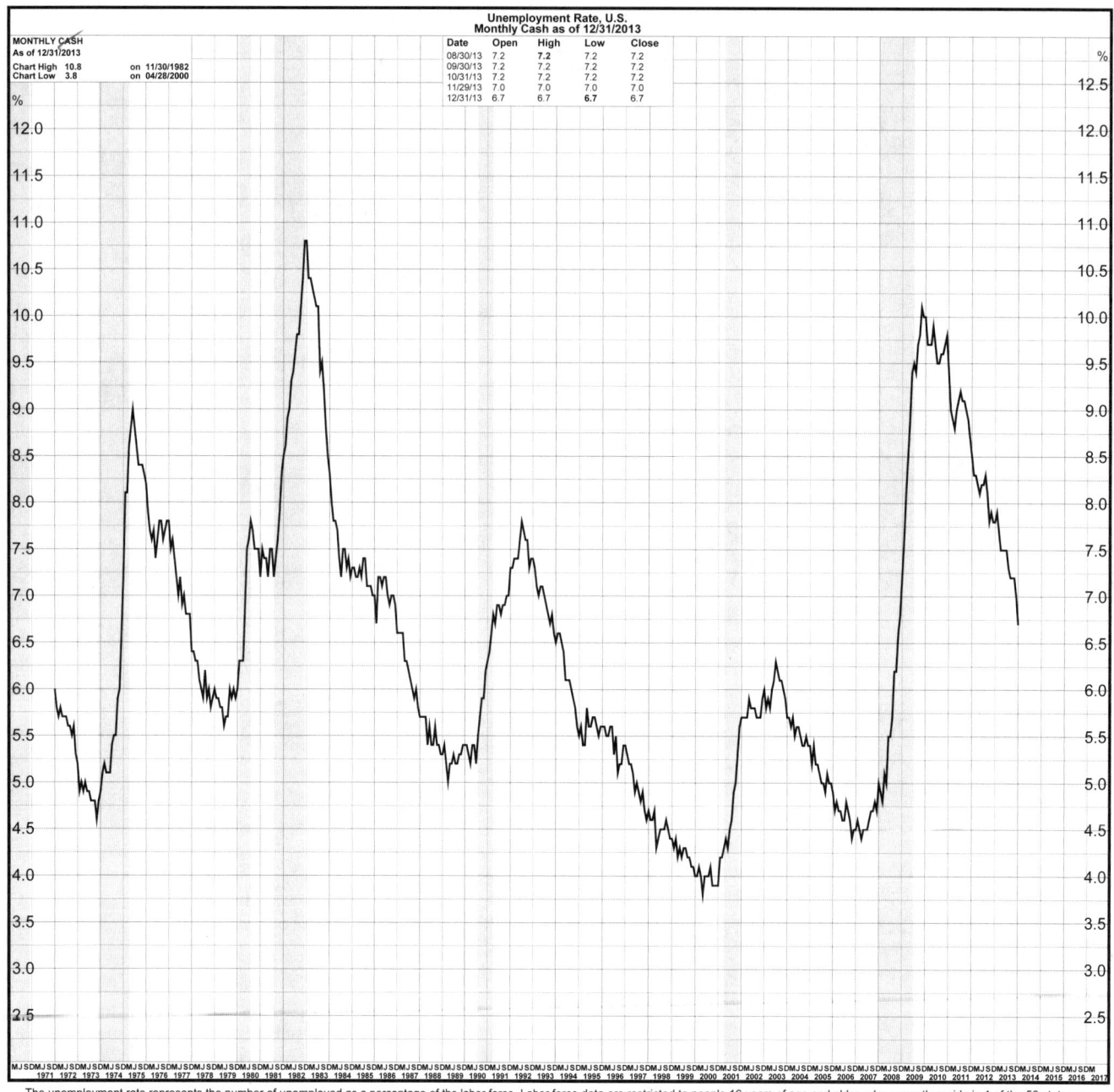

Unemployment Rate, U.S.
Monthly Cash as of 12/31/2013

Date	Open	High	Low	Close
08/30/13	7.2	**7.2**	7.2	7.2
09/30/13	7.2	7.2	7.2	7.2
10/31/13	7.2	7.2	7.2	7.2
11/29/13	7.0	7.0	7.0	7.0
12/31/13	6.7	6.7	**6.7**	6.7

MONTHLY CASH
As of 12/31/2013

Chart High 10.8 on 11/30/1982
Chart Low 3.8 on 04/28/2000

The unemployment rate represents the number of unemployed as a percentage of the labor force. Labor force data are restricted to people 16 years of age and older, who currently reside in 1 of the 50 states or the District of Columbia, who do not reside in institutions (e.g., penal and mental facilities, homes for the aged), and who are not on active duty in the Armed Forces. This rate is also defined as the U-3 measure of labor underutilization.   Shaded areas indicate US recessions.

Annual High, Low and Close of U.S. Unemployment Rate   In Percent

Year	High	Low	Settle	Year	High	Low	Settle	Year	High	Low	Settle
1972	5.8	5.2	5.2	1986	7.2	6.6	6.6	2000	4.1	3.8	3.9
1973	5.0	4.6	4.9	1987	6.6	5.7	5.7	2001	5.7	4.2	5.7
1974	7.2	5.1	7.2	1988	5.7	5.3	5.3	2002	6.0	5.7	6.0
1975	9.0	8.1	8.2	1989	5.4	5.0	5.4	2003	6.3	5.7	5.7
1976	7.9	7.4	7.8	1990	6.3	5.2	6.3	2004	5.7	5.4	5.4
1977	7.6	6.4	6.4	1991	7.3	6.4	7.3	2005	5.4	4.9	4.9
1978	6.4	5.8	6.0	1992	7.8	7.3	7.4	2006	4.8	4.4	4.5
1979	6.0	5.6	6.0	1993	7.3	6.5	6.5	2007	5.0	4.4	5.0
1980	7.8	6.3	7.2	1994	6.6	5.5	5.5	2008	7.2	4.8	7.2
1981	8.5	7.2	8.5	1995	5.8	5.4	5.6	2009	10.1	7.6	10.0
1982	10.8	8.6	10.8	1996	5.6	5.1	5.4	2010	9.9	9.4	9.4
1983	10.4	8.3	8.3	1997	5.3	4.6	4.7	2011	9.2	8.5	8.5
1984	8.0	7.2	7.3	1998	4.7	4.3	4.4	2012	8.3	7.8	7.8
1985	7.4	7.0	7.0	1999	4.4	4.0	4.0	2013	7.9	6.7	6.7

Source: U.S. Department of Labor: Bureau of Labor Statistics

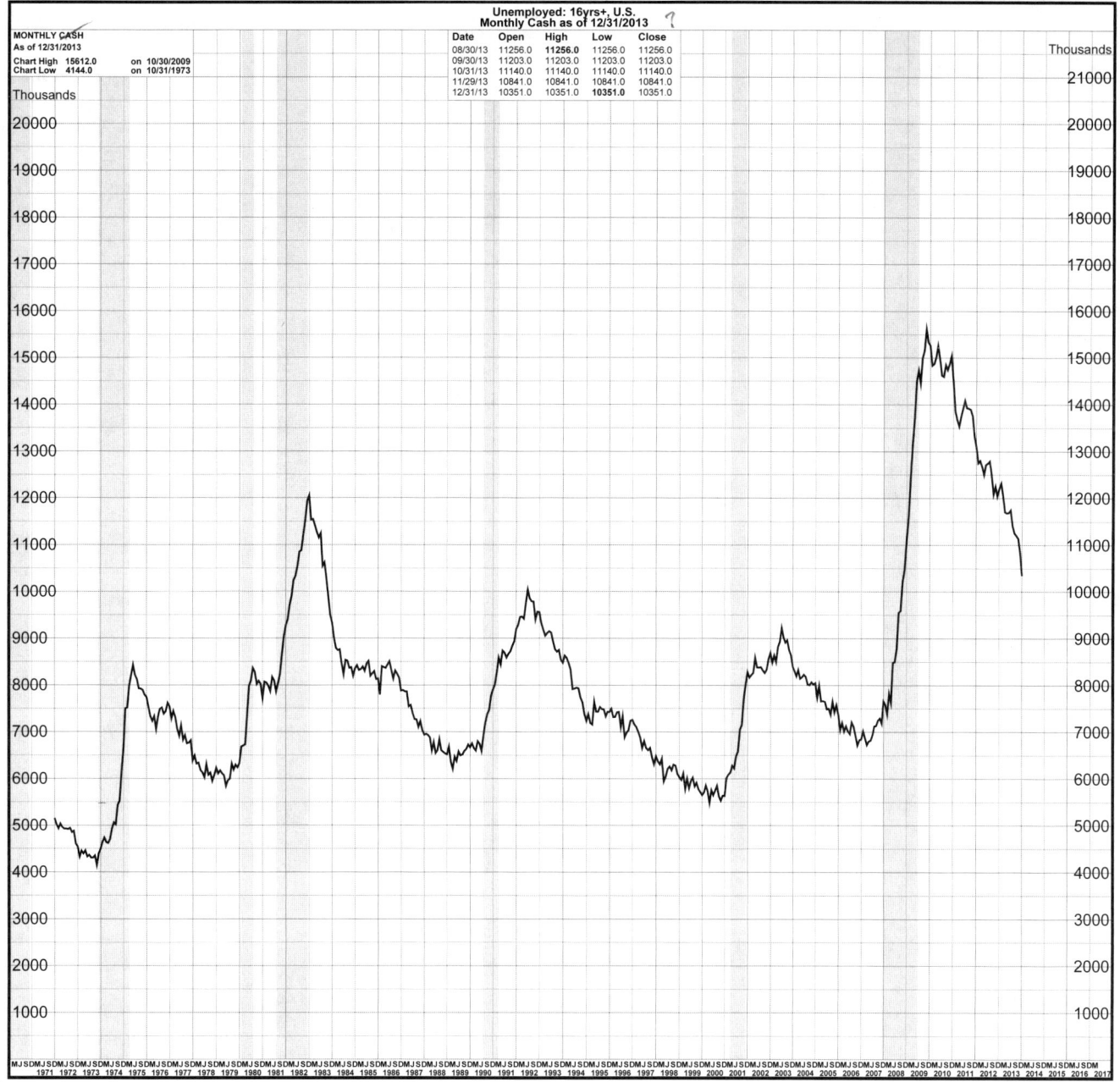

Unemployed: 16yrs+, U.S.
Monthly Cash as of 12/31/2013

Date	Open	High	Low	Close
08/30/13	11256.0	11256.0	11256.0	11256.0
09/30/13	11203.0	11203.0	11203.0	11203.0
10/31/13	11140.0	11140.0	11140.0	11140.0
11/29/13	10841.0	10841.0	10841.0	10841.0
12/31/13	10351.0	10351.0	10351.0	10351.0

MONTHLY CASH
As of 12/31/2013
Chart High 15612.0 on 10/30/2009
Chart Low 4144.0 on 10/31/1973

Persons 16 years of age and older.
The Bureau of Labor Statistics (BLS) announced several revisions to the Household Survey on Friday Feb.7th 2003, with the release of the January 2003 Data. They introduced the Census 2000 population controls (which affect data back to 2000 and cause a break in the data in January 2000), a new seasonal adjustment procedure, and new seasonal factors back to January 1998. Shaded areas indicate US

Annual High, Low and Close of U.S. Unemployed, 16yrs+   In Thousands

Year	High	Low	Settle	Year	High	Low	Settle	Year	High	Low	Settle
1972	5,038	4,543	4,543	1986	8,508	7,795	7,883	2000	5,858	5,481	5,634
1973	4,489	4,144	4,489	1987	7,892	6,936	6,936	2001	8,281	6,017	8,281
1974	6,636	4,618	6,636	1988	6,953	6,518	6,518	2002	8,691	8,165	8,691
1975	8,433	7,501	7,744	1989	6,725	6,205	6,667	2003	9,228	8,399	8,399
1976	7,620	7,053	7,545	1990	7,901	6,590	7,901	2004	8,330	8,005	8,047
1977	7,443	6,386	6,386	1991	9,198	8,015	9,198	2005	7,988	7,367	7,375
1978	6,489	5,947	6,228	1992	10,040	9,283	9,557	2006	7,205	6,715	6,849
1979	6,325	5,840	6,325	1993	9,325	8,477	8,477	2007	7,655	6,724	7,655
1980	8,363	6,683	7,718	1994	8,630	7,230	7,230	2008	11,108	7,381	11,108
1981	9,267	7,863	9,267	1995	7,645	7,153	7,423	2009	15,612	11,616	15,267
1982	12,051	9,397	12,051	1996	7,491	6,882	7,253	2010	15,260	14,485	14,485
1983	11,545	9,331	9,331	1997	7,158	6,308	6,476	2011	14,087	13,097	13,097
1984	9,008	8,198	8,358	1998	6,422	5,941	6,032	2012	12,806	12,042	12,206
1985	8,513	8,128	8,138	1999	6,111	5,653	5,653	2013	12,315	10,351	10,351

Source: U.S. Department of Labor: Bureau of Labor Statistics

U.S. CIVILIAN LABOR FORCE

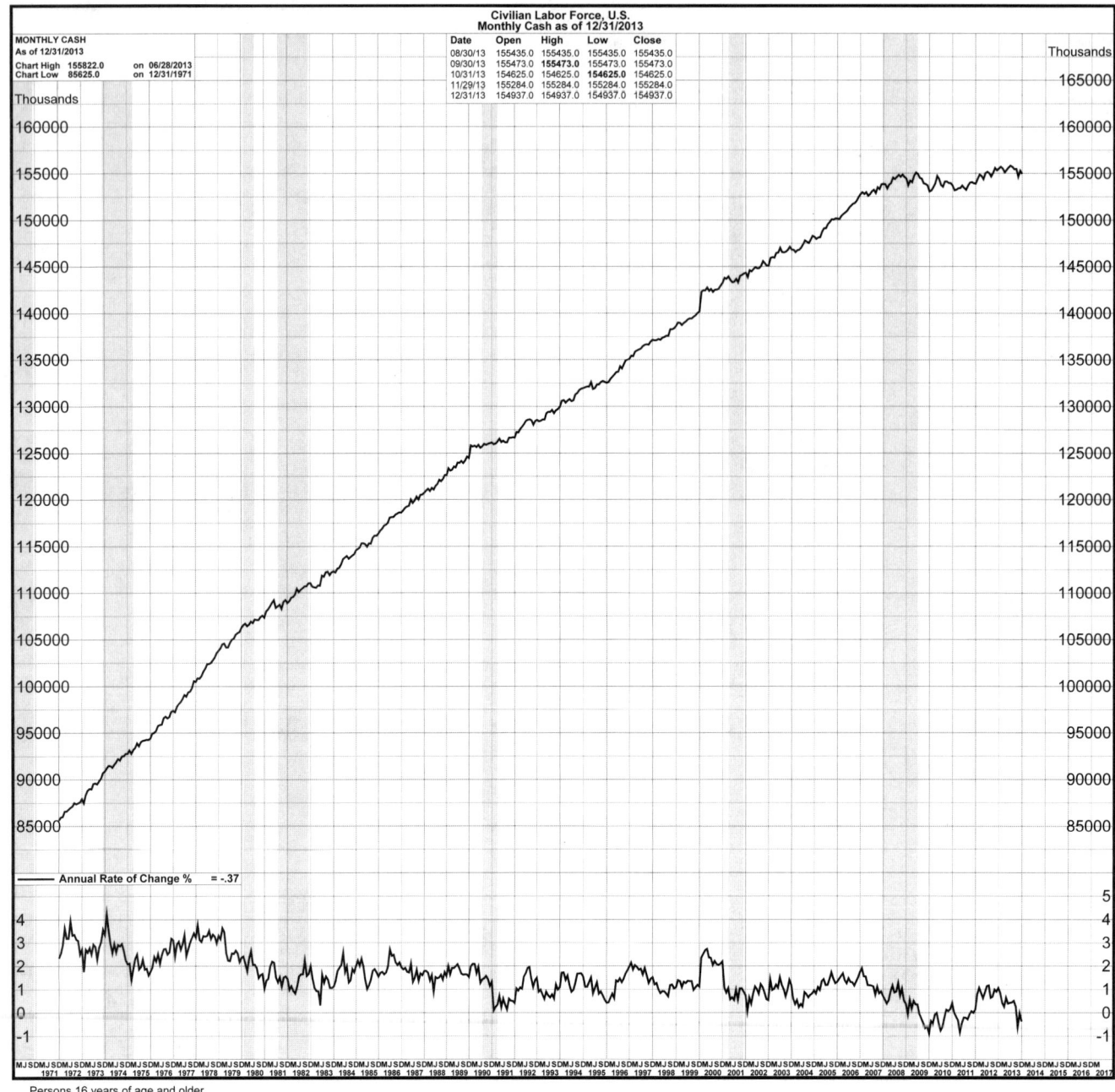

Civilian Labor Force, U.S.
Monthly Cash as of 12/31/2013

MONTHLY CASH
As of 12/31/2013

Chart High 155822.0 on 06/28/2013
Chart Low 85625.0 on 12/31/1971

Thousands

Date	Open	High	Low	Close
08/30/13	155435.0	155435.0	155435.0	155435.0
09/30/13	155473.0	155473.0	155473.0	155473.0
10/31/13	154625.0	154625.0	154625.0	154625.0
11/29/13	155284.0	155284.0	155284.0	155284.0
12/31/13	154937.0	154937.0	154937.0	154937.0

Annual Rate of Change %   = -.37

Persons 16 years of age and older.
The Bureau of Labor Statistics (BLS) announced several revisions to the Household Survey on Friday Feb.7th 2003, with the release of the January 2003 Data. They introduced the Census 2000 population controls (which affect data back to 2000 and cause a break in the data in January 2000), a new seasonal adjustment procedure, and new seasonal factors back to January 1998.   Shaded areas indicate US

Annual High, Low and Close of U.S. Civilian Labor Force   In Thousands

Year	High	Low	Settle	Year	High	Low	Settle	Year	High	Low	Settle
1972	87,943	85,978	87,943	1986	118,634	116,682	118,611	2000	143,248	142,267	143,248
1973	90,890	87,487	90,890	1987	120,729	118,845	120,729	2001	144,324	143,301	144,324
1974	92,780	91,199	92,780	1988	122,637	120,913	122,622	2002	145,573	143,858	145,091
1975	94,409	92,776	94,409	1989	124,637	123,135	124,497	2003	147,109	145,914	146,808
1976	97,348	94,934	97,348	1990	126,142	125,573	126,142	2004	148,313	146,529	148,203
1977	100,576	97,208	100,491	1991	126,701	125,955	126,664	2005	150,183	147,979	150,153
1978	103,809	100,837	103,809	1992	128,613	127,207	128,554	2006	152,775	150,114	152,775
1979	106,258	104,057	106,258	1993	129,941	128,400	129,941	2007	153,866	152,587	153,866
1980	107,568	106,442	107,352	1994	131,951	130,400	131,951	2008	154,878	153,374	154,447
1981	109,236	108,026	108,912	1995	132,716	131,851	132,511	2009	155,081	153,059	153,059
1982	111,083	109,089	111,083	1996	135,113	132,616	135,113	2010	154,715	153,170	153,690
1983	112,327	110,587	112,327	1997	137,155	135,400	137,155	2011	154,057	153,186	153,887
1984	114,581	112,209	114,581	1998	138,634	137,095	138,634	2012	155,576	154,365	155,511
1985	116,354	114,725	116,354	1999	140,177	138,730	140,177	2013	155,822	154,625	154,937

Source: U.S. Department of Labor: Bureau of Labor Statistics

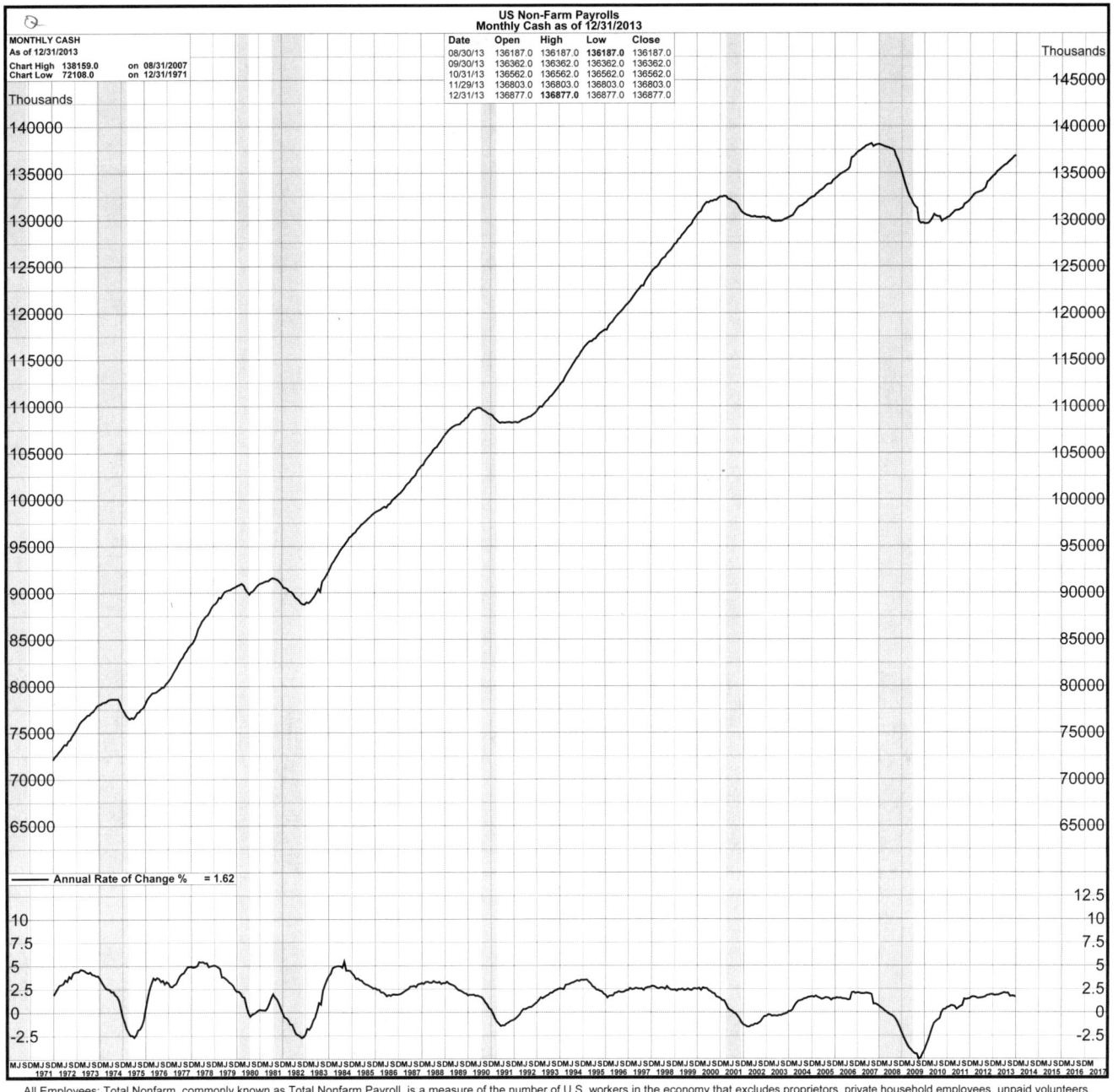

Date	Open	High	Low	Close
08/30/13	136187.0	136187.0	136187.0	136187.0
09/30/13	136362.0	136362.0	136362.0	136362.0
10/31/13	136562.0	136562.0	136562.0	136562.0
11/29/13	136803.0	136803.0	136803.0	136803.0
12/31/13	136877.0	136877.0	136877.0	136877.0

MONTHLY CASH
As of 12/31/2013
Chart High 138159.0 on 08/31/2007
Chart Low 72108.0 on 12/31/1971

Annual Rate of Change % = 1.62

All Employees: Total Nonfarm, commonly known as Total Nonfarm Payroll, is a measure of the number of U.S. workers in the economy that excludes proprietors, private household employees, unpaid volunteers, farm employees, and the unincorporated self-employed.(1) This measure accounts for approximately 80 percent of the workers who contribute to Gross Domestic Product (GDP). Shaded areas indicate US recessions.

Annual High, Low and Close of U.S. Non-Farm Payrolls   In Thousands

Year	High	Low	Settle	Year	High	Low	Settle	Year	High	Low	Settle
1972	75,270	72,445	75,270	1986	100,484	98,710	100,484	2000	132,484	130,781	132,484
1973	78,035	75,620	78,035	1987	103,634	100,655	103,634	2001	132,546	130,705	130,705
1974	78,634	77,657	77,657	1988	106,871	103,728	106,871	2002	130,581	130,161	130,161
1975	78,017	76,463	78,017	1989	108,809	107,133	108,809	2003	130,255	129,827	130,255
1976	80,448	78,506	80,448	1990	109,820	109,118	109,118	2004	132,449	130,372	132,449
1977	84,408	80,692	84,408	1991	108,998	108,203	108,261	2005	134,376	132,471	134,376
1978	88,674	84,595	88,674	1992	109,418	108,242	109,418	2006	137,167	134,530	137,167
1979	90,669	88,811	90,669	1993	112,203	109,725	112,203	2007	138,159	137,329	138,078
1980	90,991	89,832	90,936	1994	116,056	112,473	116,056	2008	138,002	135,074	135,074
1981	91,594	90,884	90,884	1995	118,210	116,377	118,210	2009	134,333	129,588	129,588
1982	90,557	88,756	88,756	1996	121,003	118,192	121,003	2010	130,594	129,602	130,260
1983	92,210	88,903	92,210	1997	124,361	121,232	124,361	2011	132,186	130,328	132,186
1984	96,087	92,657	96,087	1998	127,364	124,629	127,364	2012	134,691	132,461	134,691
1985	98,587	96,353	98,587	1999	130,536	127,477	130,536	2013	136,877	134,839	136,877

Source: U.S. Department of Labor: Bureau of Labor Statistics

U.S. INITIAL JOBLESS CLAIMS

Seasonally Adjusted.   Shaded areas indicate US recessions.

Annual High, Low and Close of U.S. Initial Jobless Claims   In Number

Year	High	Low	Settle	Year	High	Low	Settle	Year	High	Low	Settle
1972	350,000	225,000	225,000	1986	416,000	344,000	345,000	2000	365,000	257,000	352,000
1973	326,000	214,000	300,000	1987	370,000	289,000	315,000	2001	520,000	317,000	421,000
1974	537,000	269,000	537,000	1988	361,000	284,000	304,000	2002	477,000	377,000	410,000
1975	575,000	365,000	391,000	1989	407,000	282,000	358,000	2003	447,000	351,000	351,000
1976	423,000	333,000	380,000	1990	474,000	331,000	454,000	2004	372,000	321,000	346,000
1977	565,000	334,000	364,000	1991	509,000	408,000	441,000	2005	435,000	292,000	292,000
1978	429,000	304,000	358,000	1992	564,000	313,000	341,000	2006	358,000	281,000	325,000
1979	471,000	336,000	428,000	1993	415,000	290,000	341,000	2007	359,000	287,000	337,000
1980	642,000	394,000	399,000	1994	406,000	314,000	319,000	2008	586,000	302,000	491,000
1981	558,000	392,000	495,000	1995	390,000	324,000	359,000	2009	674,000	433,000	433,000
1982	695,000	489,000	534,000	1996	426,000	326,000	357,000	2010	504,000	391,000	410,000
1983	515,000	362,000	372,000	1997	347,000	301,000	303,000	2011	478,000	366,000	375,000
1984	439,000	333,000	379,000	1998	376,000	294,000	331,000	2012	451,000	342,000	367,000
1985	426,000	359,000	390,000	1999	345,000	268,000	286,000	2013	385,000	294,000	345,000

Source: U.S. Department of Labor: Bureau of Labor Statistics

US Initial Jobless Claims
Weekly Cash as of 01/03/2014

WEEKLY CASH
As of 01/03/2014
Chart High 674000.0 on 03/27/2009
Chart Low 281000.0 on 01/13/2006

Date	Open	High	Low	Close
12/06/13	369000.0	369000.0	369000.0	369000.0
12/13/13	380000.0	380000.0	380000.0	380000.0
12/20/13	341000.0	341000.0	341000.0	341000.0
12/27/13	345000.0	345000.0	345000.0	345000.0
01/03/14	330000.0	330000.0	330000.0	330000.0

Seasonally Adjusted.   Shaded areas indicate US recessions.

Quarterly High, Low and Close of U.S. Initial Jobless Claims   In Number

Quarter	High	Low	Settle	Quarter	High	Low	Settle	Quarter	High	Low	Settle
03/2005	352,000	296,000	352,000	03/2008	410,000	302,000	410,000	03/2011	457,000	371,000	392,000
06/2005	351,000	299,000	311,000	06/2008	404,000	345,000	404,000	06/2011	478,000	385,000	432,000
09/2005	435,000	305,000	391,000	09/2008	498,000	348,000	498,000	09/2011	432,000	395,000	405,000
12/2005	391,000	292,000	292,000	12/2008	586,000	463,000	491,000	12/2011	409,000	366,000	375,000
03/2006	319,000	281,000	301,000	03/2009	674,000	470,000	674,000	03/2012	402,000	351,000	367,000
06/2006	344,000	297,000	314,000	06/2009	663,000	605,000	617,000	06/2012	392,000	368,000	376,000
09/2006	334,000	299,000	304,000	09/2009	588,000	524,000	554,000	09/2012	388,000	352,000	369,000
12/2006	358,000	300,000	325,000	12/2009	532,000	433,000	433,000	12/2012	451,000	342,000	367,000
03/2007	359,000	287,000	323,000	03/2010	498,000	433,000	442,000	03/2013	385,000	330,000	385,000
06/2007	343,000	296,000	320,000	06/2010	480,000	446,000	475,000	06/2013	363,000	327,000	344,000
09/2007	337,000	301,000	320,000	09/2010	504,000	427,000	456,000	09/2013	358,000	294,000	308,000
12/2007	357,000	309,000	337,000	12/2010	475,000	391,000	410,000	12/2013	380,000	300,000	345,000

Source: U.S. Department of Labor: Bureau of Labor Statistics

U.S. AVERAGE HOURLY EARNINGS

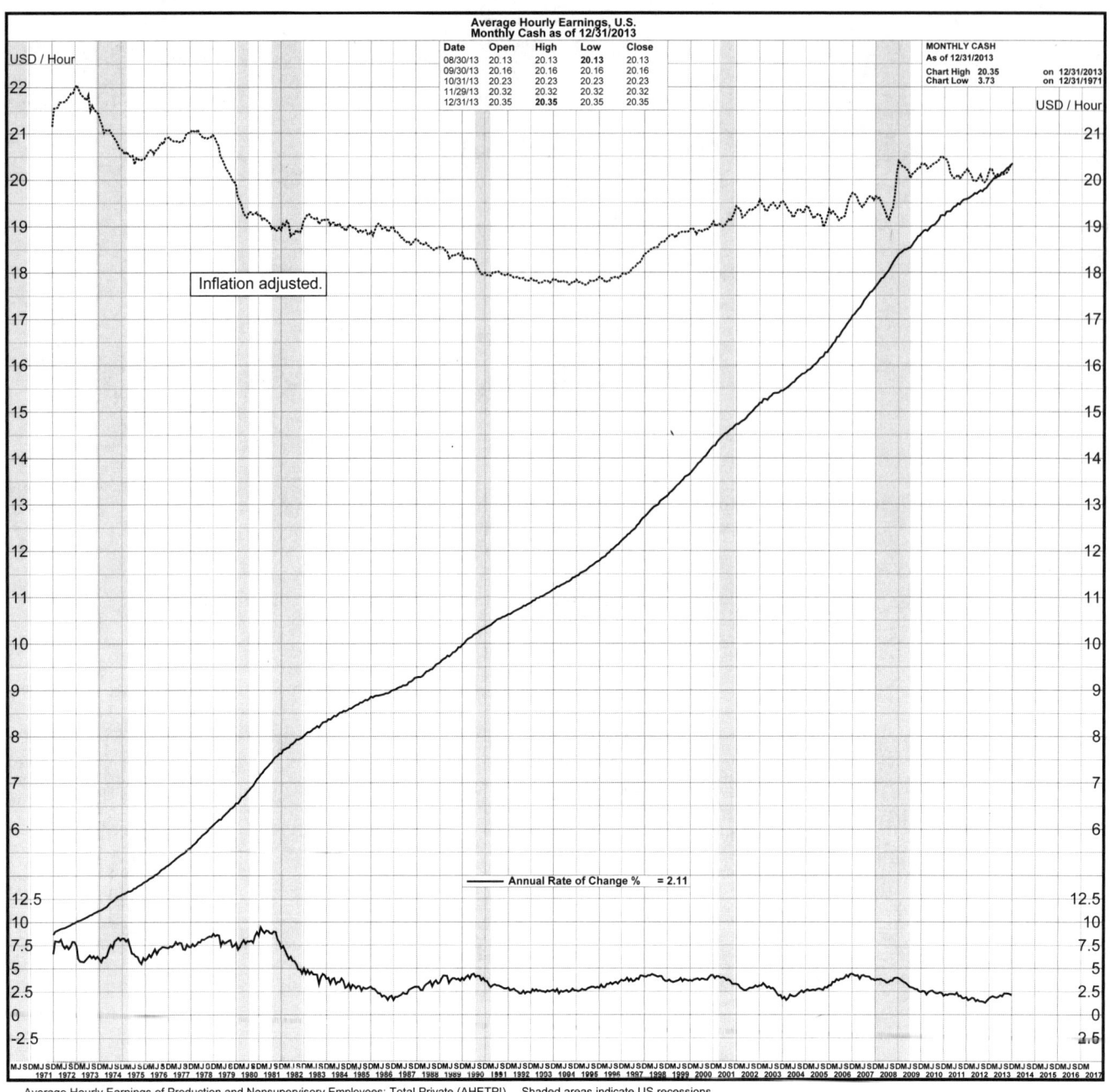

Average Hourly Earnings, U.S.
Monthly Cash as of 12/31/2013

Date	Open	High	Low	Close
08/30/13	20.13	20.13	20.13	20.13
09/30/13	20.16	20.16	20.16	20.16
10/31/13	20.23	20.23	20.23	20.23
11/29/13	20.32	20.32	20.32	20.32
12/31/13	20.35	20.35	20.35	20.35

MONTHLY CASH
As of 12/31/2013

Chart High 20.35 on 12/31/2013
Chart Low 3.73 on 12/31/1971

Inflation adjusted.

Annual Rate of Change % = 2.11

Average Hourly Earnings of Production and Nonsupervisory Employees: Total Private (AHETPI)   Shaded areas indicate US recessions.

Annual High, Low and Close of U.S. Average Hourly Earnings   In Dollars per Hour

Year	High	Low	Settle	Year	High	Low	Settle	Year	High	Low	Settle
1972	4.01	3.80	4.01	1986	9.00	8.84	9.00	2000	14.26	13.73	14.26
1973	4.25	4.03	4.25	1987	9.27	9.01	9.27	2001	14.73	14.27	14.73
1974	4.60	4.26	4.60	1988	9.59	9.28	9.59	2002	15.19	14.73	15.19
1975	4.87	4.61	4.87	1989	9.97	9.64	9.97	2003	15.45	15.19	15.45
1976	5.22	4.89	5.22	1990	10.33	10.00	10.33	2004	15.85	15.48	15.85
1977	5.60	5.25	5.60	1991	10.63	10.36	10.63	2005	16.35	15.90	16.35
1978	6.09	5.65	6.09	1992	10.88	10.63	10.88	2006	17.07	16.40	17.07
1979	6.56	6.13	6.56	1993	11.17	10.92	11.17	2007	17.70	17.10	17.70
1980	7.12	6.56	7.12	1994	11.46	11.19	11.46	2008	18.40	17.75	18.40
1981	7.63	7.18	7.63	1995	11.79	11.47	11.79	2009	18.85	18.43	18.85
1982	8.01	7.71	8.01	1996	12.23	11.84	12.23	2010	19.24	18.90	19.23
1983	8.32	8.05	8.32	1997	12.73	12.27	12.73	2011	19.59	19.31	19.59
1984	8.60	8.36	8.60	1998	13.19	12.77	13.19	2012	19.93	19.61	19.93
1985	8.86	8.60	8.86	1999	13.68	13.25	13.68	2013	20.35	19.98	20.35

Source: U.S. Department of Labor: Bureau of Labor Statistics

ISM MANUFACTURING: PMI COMPOSITE INDEX

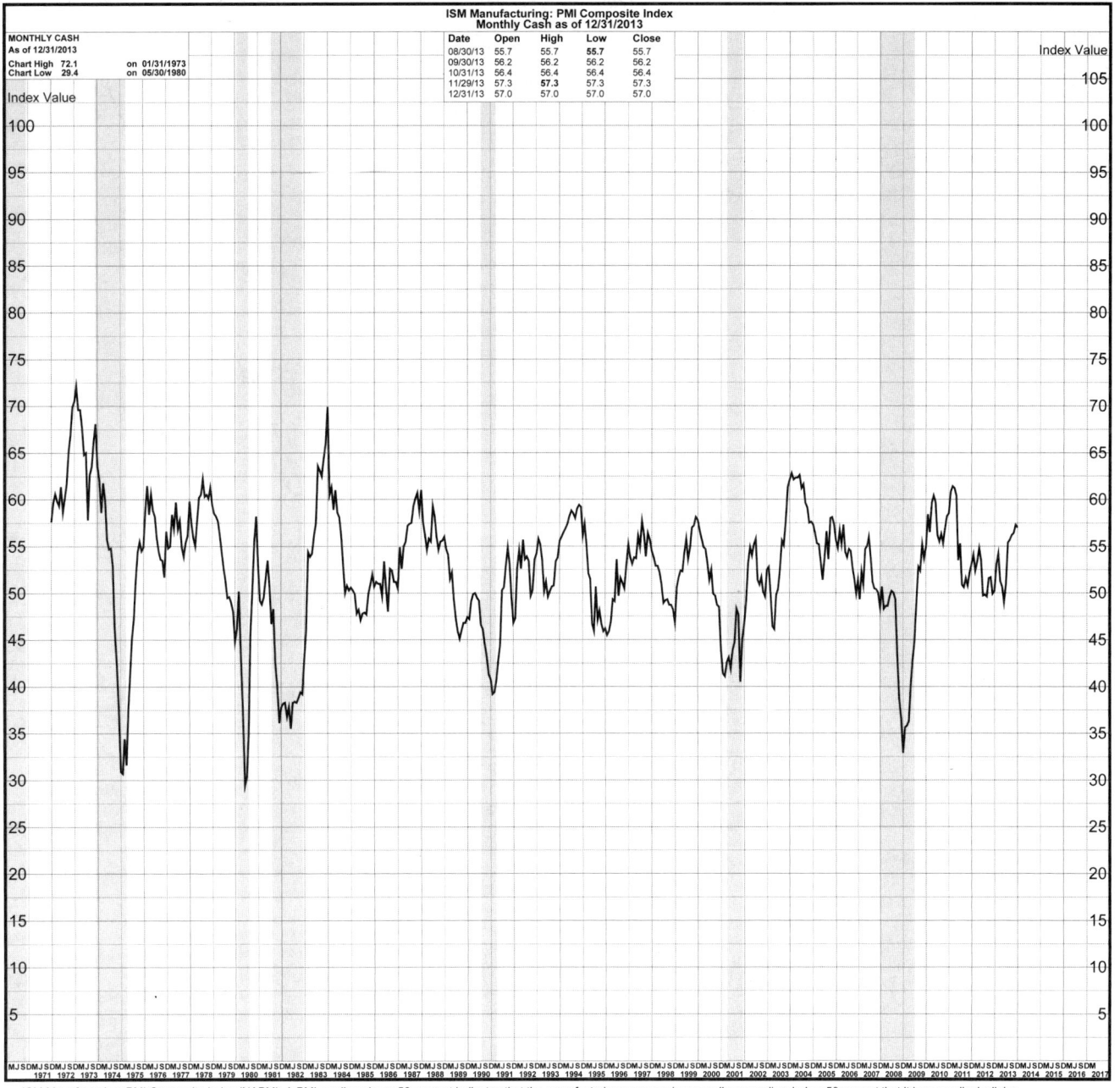

ISM Manufacturing: PMI Composite Index
Monthly Cash as of 12/31/2013

Date	Open	High	Low	Close
08/30/13	55.7	55.7	**55.7**	55.7
09/30/13	56.2	56.2	56.2	56.2
10/31/13	56.4	56.4	56.4	56.4
11/29/13	57.3	**57.3**	57.3	57.3
12/31/13	57.0	57.0	57.0	57.0

MONTHLY CASH
As of 12/31/2013

Chart High 72.1 on 01/31/1973
Chart Low 29.4 on 05/30/1980

Index Value

ISM Manufacturing: PMI Composite Index (NAPM): A PMI reading above 50 percent indicates that the manufacturing economy is generally expanding; below 50 percent that it is generally declining. Shaded areas indicate US recessions.

Annual High, Low and Close of ISM Manufacturing: PMI Index   In Index Value

Year	High	Low	Settle	Year	High	Low	Settle	Year	High	Low	Settle
1972	70.5	58.6	70.5	1986	53.4	48.0	50.5	2000	56.7	43.9	43.9
1973	72.1	57.8	63.6	1987	61.0	52.6	61.0	2001	48.3	40.5	46.7
1974	62.1	30.9	30.9	1988	59.3	54.6	56.0	2002	55.8	49.1	52.5
1975	55.5	30.7	54.9	1989	54.7	45.1	47.4	2003	62.1	46.1	62.1
1976	61.5	51.7	56.6	1990	50.0	40.8	40.8	2004	62.8	57.3	57.3
1977	59.8	53.9	59.8	1991	54.9	39.2	46.8	2005	58.1	51.4	55.6
1978	62.2	55.0	59.4	1992	55.7	47.3	54.2	2006	57.3	49.9	51.4
1979	58.5	44.8	44.8	1993	55.8	49.6	55.6	2007	56.0	48.4	48.4
1980	58.2	29.4	53.0	1994	59.4	56.0	56.1	2008	50.7	32.9	32.9
1981	53.5	36.1	37.8	1995	57.4	45.9	46.2	2009	55.2	35.6	54.9
1982	42.8	35.5	42.8	1996	55.2	45.5	55.2	2010	60.4	55.3	58.5
1983	69.9	46.0	69.9	1997	57.7	53.1	54.5	2011	61.4	50.6	53.1
1984	61.3	50.0	50.6	1998	53.8	46.8	46.8	2012	54.8	49.6	50.2
1985	52.0	47.1	50.7	1999	58.1	50.6	57.8	2013	57.3	49.0	57.0

Source: Institute for Supply Management

U.S. GROSS DOMESTIC PRODUCT

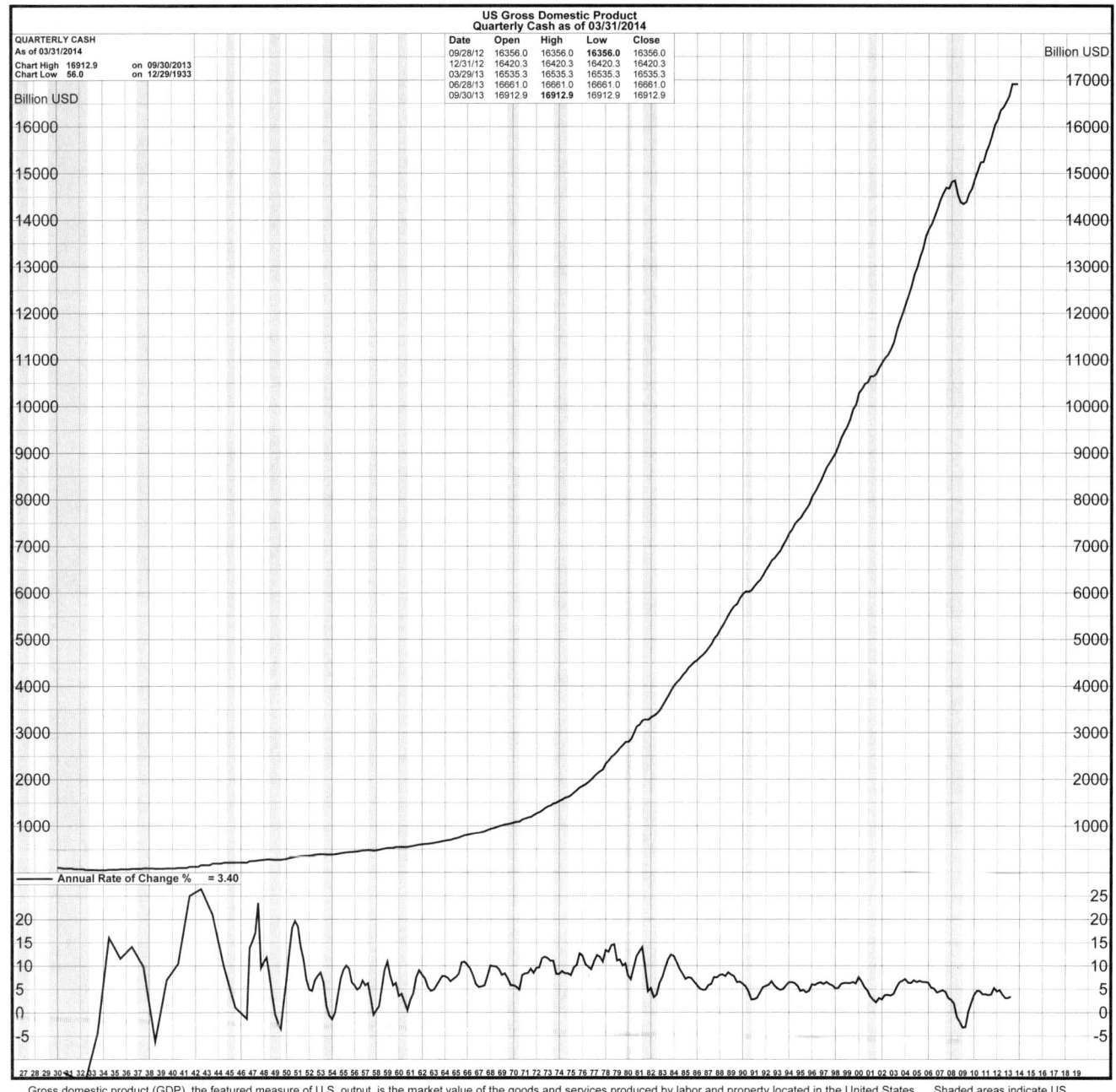

US Gross Domestic Product
Quarterly Cash as of 03/31/2014

Date	Open	High	Low	Close
09/28/12	16356.0	16356.0	16356.0	16356.0
12/31/12	16420.3	16420.3	16420.3	16420.3
03/29/13	16535.3	16535.3	16535.3	16535.3
06/28/13	16661.0	16661.0	16661.0	16661.0
09/30/13	16912.9	**16912.9**	16912.9	16912.9

QUARTERLY CASH
As of 03/31/2014
Chart High 16912.9 on 09/30/2013
Chart Low 56.0 on 12/29/1933

Annual Rate of Change % = 3.40

Gross domestic product (GDP), the featured measure of U.S. output, is the market value of the goods and services produced by labor and property located in the United States.   Shaded areas indicate US recessions.

Annual U.S. Gross Domestic Product   In Billions of Dollars

Year	Close	Year	Close	Year	Close	Year	Close	Year	Close	Year	Close
1930	91.1	1944	211.4	1958	485.0	1972	1,287.0	1986	4,546.1	2000	9,953.6
1931	76.3	1945	213.6	1959	513.2	1973	1,432.3	1987	4,886.3	2001	10,226.3
1932	58.5	1946	210.7	1960	523.6	1974	1,553.4	1988	5,253.7	2002	10,591.1
1933	56.0	1947	260.3	1961	562.5	1975	1,714.6	1989	5,584.3	2003	11,236.0
1934	65.0	1948	280.7	1962	593.3	1976	1,885.3	1990	5,848.8	2004	11,995.2
1935	72.5	1949	271.0	1963	633.5	1977	2,111.6	1991	6,095.8	2005	12,766.1
1936	82.7	1950	313.4	1964	675.6	1978	2,417.0	1992	6,484.3	2006	13,392.3
1937	90.8	1951	348.0	1965	747.5	1979	2,660.5	1993	6,800.2	2007	14,031.2
1938	85.2	1952	371.4	1966	807.1	1980	2,916.9	1994	7,232.2	2008	14,546.7
1939	91.1	1953	375.9	1967	852.8	1981	3,196.4	1995	7,522.5	2009	14,564.1
1940	100.6	1954	389.5	1968	936.3	1982	3,314.4	1996	8,000.4	2010	15,231.7
1941	125.8	1955	426.0	1969	1,004.6	1983	3,690.4	1997	8,471.2	2011	15,818.7
1942	159.1	1956	448.1	1970	1,052.9	1984	4,036.3	1998	8,953.8	2012	16,420.3
1943	192.5	1957	461.5	1971	1,151.7	1985	4,321.8	1999	9,519.5	2013	16,912.9

Source: U.S. Department of Commerce: Bureau of Economic Analysis

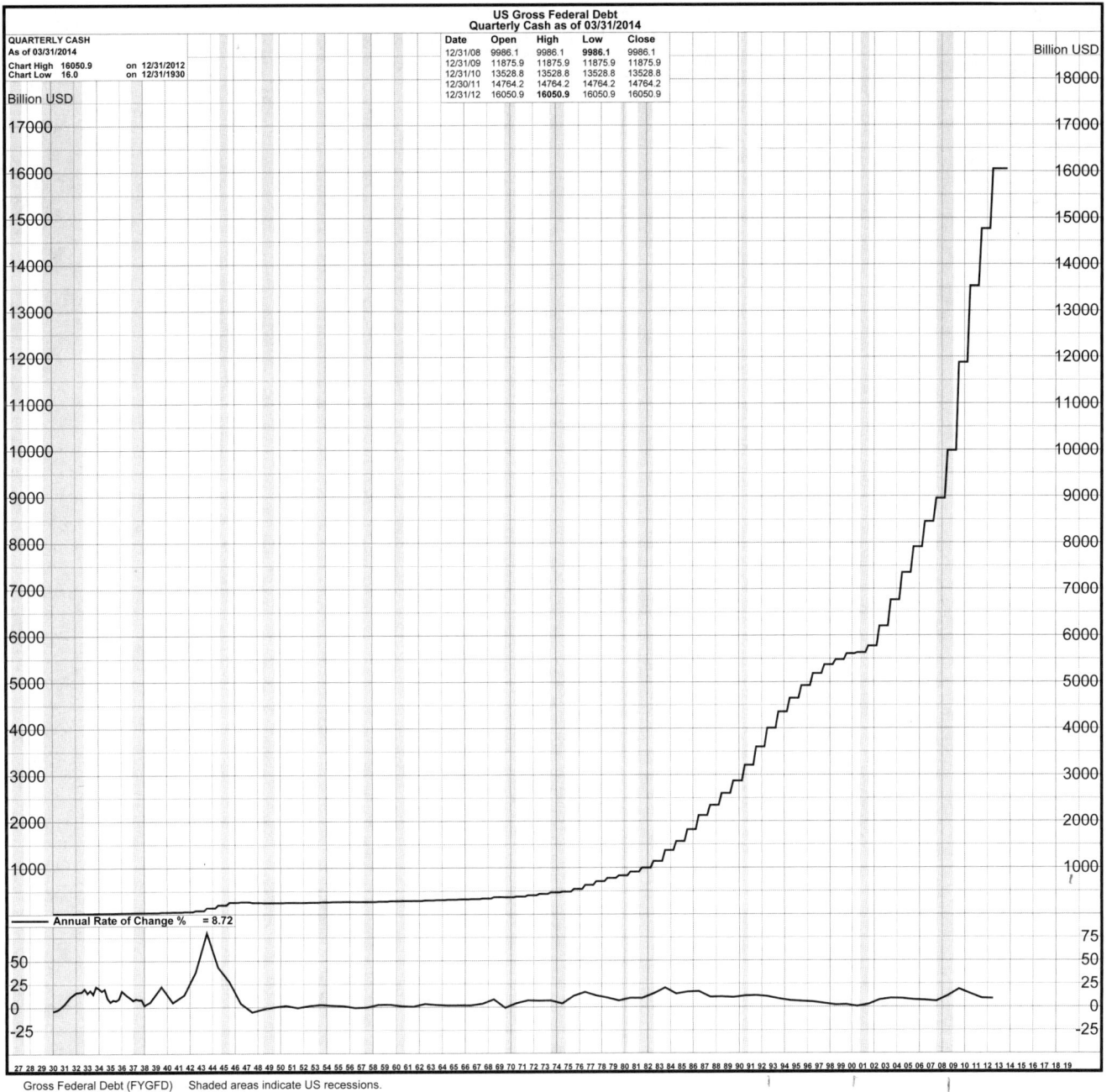

Date	Open	High	Low	Close
12/31/08	9986.1	9986.1	9986.1	9986.1
12/31/09	11875.9	11875.9	11875.9	11875.9
12/31/10	13528.8	13528.8	13528.8	13528.8
12/30/11	14764.2	14764.2	14764.2	14764.2
12/31/12	16050.9	16050.9	16050.9	16050.9

QUARTERLY CASH
As of 03/31/2014

Chart High 16050.9 on 12/31/2012
Chart Low 16.0 on 12/31/1930

Billion USD

Annual Rate of Change % = 8.72

Gross Federal Debt (FYGFD)   Shaded areas indicate US recessions.

FY

Annual U.S. Gross Federal Debt   In Billions of Dollars

Year	Close	Year	Close	Year	Close	Year	Close	Year	Close	Year	Close
1930	16.0	1944	204.1	1958	279.7	1972	435.9	1986	2,120.5	2000	5,628.7
1931	17.8	1945	260.1	1959	287.5	1973	466.3	1987	2,346.0	2001	5,769.9
1932	20.8	1946	271.0	1960	290.5	1974	483.9	1988	2,601.1	2002	6,198.4
1933	23.8	1947	257.1	1961	292.6	1975	541.9	1989	2,867.8	2003	6,760.0
1934	28.5	1948	252.0	1962	302.9	1976	629.0	1990	3,206.3	2004	7,354.7
1935	30.6	1949	252.6	1963	310.3	1977	706.4	1991	3,598.2	2005	7,905.3
1936	34.4	1950	256.9	1964	316.1	1978	776.6	1992	4,001.8	2006	8,451.4
1937	37.3	1951	255.3	1965	322.3	1979	829.5	1993	4,351.0	2007	8,950.7
1938	39.4	1952	259.1	1966	328.5	1980	909.0	1994	4,643.3	2008	9,986.1
1939	48.2	1953	266.0	1967	340.4	1981	994.8	1995	4,920.6	2009	11,875.9
1940	50.7	1954	270.8	1968	368.7	1982	1,137.3	1996	5,181.5	2010	13,528.8
1941	57.5	1955	274.4	1969	365.8	1983	1,371.7	1997	5,369.2	2011	14,764.2
1942	79.2	1956	272.7	1970	380.9	1984	1,564.6	1998	5,478.2	2012	16,050.9
1943	142.6	1957	272.3	1971	408.2	1985	1,817.4	1999	5,605.5	2013	

Source: The White House: Council of Economic Advisors

U.S. FEDERAL SURPLUS OR DEFICIT

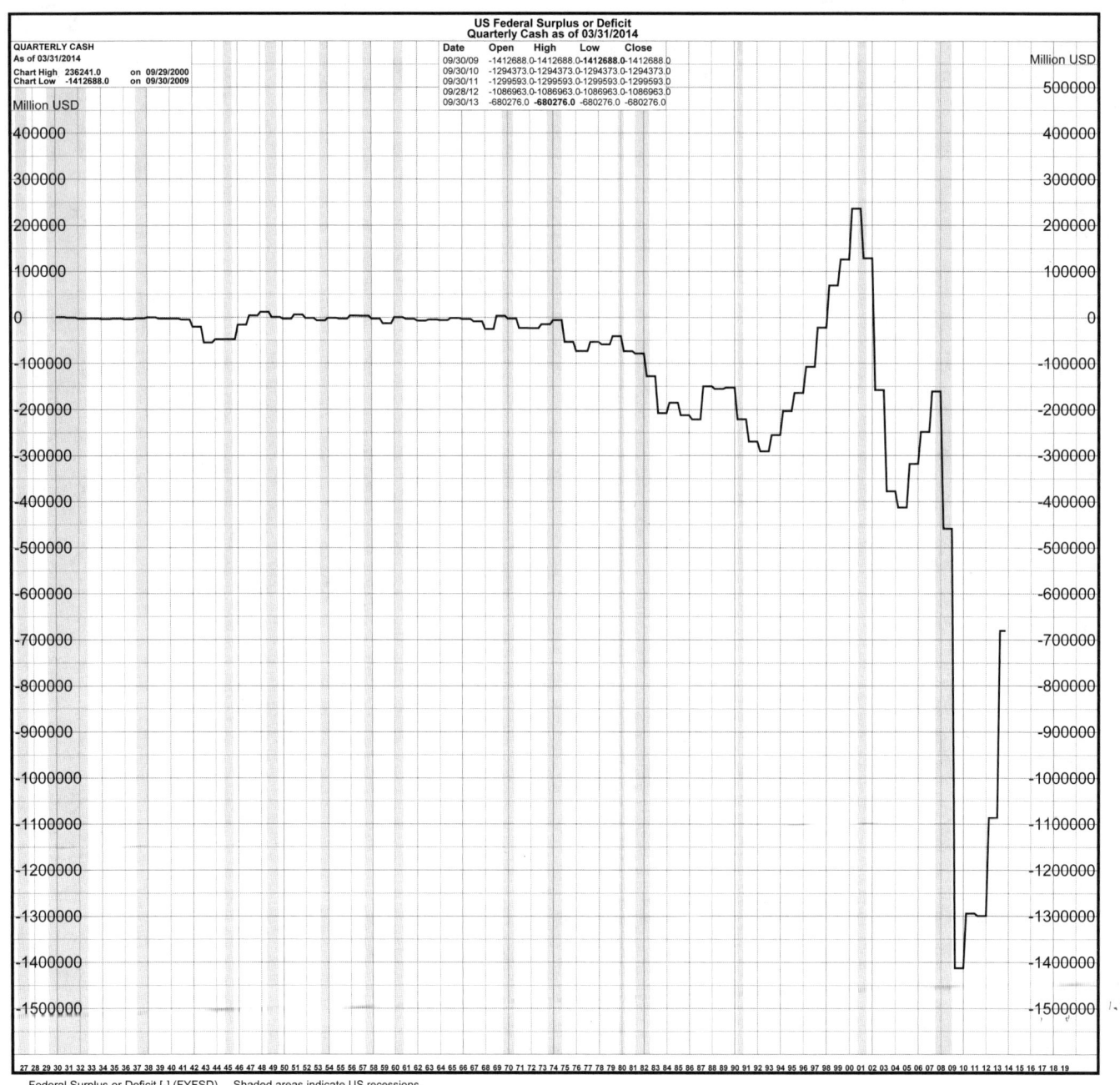

Annual U.S. Federal Surplus or Deficit   In Millions of Dollars

Year	Close	Year	Close	Year	Close	Year	Close	Year	Close	Year	Close
1930	738	1944	-47,557	1958	-2,769	1972	-23,373	1986	-221,227	2000	236,241
1931	-462	1945	-47,553	1959	-12,849	1973	-14,908	1987	-149,730	2001	128,236
1932	-2,735	1946	-15,936	1960	301	1974	-6,135	1988	-155,178	2002	-157,758
1933	-2,602	1947	4,018	1961	-3,335	1975	-53,242	1989	-152,639	2003	-377,585
1934	-3,586	1948	11,796	1962	-7,146	1976	-73,732	1990	-221,036	2004	-412,727
1935	-2,803	1949	580	1963	-4,756	1977	-53,659	1991	-269,238	2005	-318,346
1936	-4,304	1950	-3,119	1964	-5,915	1978	-59,185	1992	-290,321	2006	-248,181
1937	-2,193	1951	6,102	1965	-1,411	1979	-40,726	1993	-255,051	2007	-162,002
1938	-89	1952	-1,519	1966	-3,698	1980	-73,830	1994	-203,186	2008	-458,553
1939	-2,846	1953	-6,493	1967	-8,643	1981	-78,968	1995	-163,952	2009	-1,412,688
1940	-2,920	1954	-1,154	1968	-25,161	1982	-127,977	1996	-107,431	2010	-1,294,373
1941	-4,941	1955	-2,993	1969	3,242	1983	-207,802	1997	-21,884	2011	-1,299,593
1942	-20,503	1956	3,947	1970	-2,842	1984	-185,367	1998	69,270	2012	-1,086,963
1943	-54,554	1957	3,412	1971	-23,033	1985	-212,308	1999	125,610	2013	-680,276

Source: The White House

US Retail Sales Except Autos Monthly Cash as of 12/31/2013				
Date	Open	High	Low	Close
07/31/13	344531.0	344531.0	344531.0	344531.0
08/30/13	344592.0	344592.0	344592.0	344592.0
09/30/13	345916.0	345916.0	345916.0	345916.0
10/31/13	347611.0	347611.0	347611.0	347611.0
11/29/13	349023.0	349023.0	349023.0	349023.0

MONTHLY CASH
As of 12/31/2013
Chart High 349023.0 on 11/29/2013
Chart Low 30298.0 on 01/31/1972

Retail Sales and Food Services Excluding Motor Vehicles and Parts Dealers (RSFSXMV)   Shaded areas indicate US recessions.

Annual High, Low and Close of U.S. Retail Sales, Except Autos   In Millions of Dollars

Year	High	Low	Settle	Year	High	Low	Settle	Year	High	Low	Settle
1972	33,717	30,298	33,717	1986	101,366	97,248	101,366	2000	211,968	200,548	211,968
1973	37,211	34,384	36,928	1987	108,160	101,539	108,160	2001	216,123	211,323	216,123
1974	40,224	37,455	39,428	1988	116,869	107,927	116,869	2002	224,381	217,134	224,381
1975	44,107	40,601	44,107	1989	124,644	117,030	124,644	2003	238,132	225,259	238,132
1976	48,143	44,502	48,143	1990	130,530	125,981	129,765	2004	259,384	241,876	259,384
1977	52,170	47,752	52,170	1991	131,920	128,683	130,476	2005	281,332	261,623	276,667
1978	59,577	51,638	59,577	1992	136,677	130,261	136,677	2006	291,703	283,567	290,265
1979	66,693	59,189	66,693	1993	143,105	136,063	143,105	2007	304,705	290,762	302,353
1980	73,021	67,810	73,021	1994	153,249	142,199	153,249	2008	315,275	279,945	279,945
1981	76,020	73,970	76,020	1995	159,533	152,039	159,533	2009	294,214	282,979	293,791
1982	79,095	75,481	79,095	1996	168,243	157,931	168,243	2010	309,692	295,063	309,692
1983	85,534	78,920	85,408	1997	174,675	168,637	174,675	2011	328,451	311,844	324,955
1984	91,288	87,027	91,146	1998	185,466	175,486	185,466	2012	338,200	327,453	338,200
1985	97,340	91,352	97,340	1999	203,493	185,933	203,493	2013	349,023	338,741	349,023

Source: U.S. Department of Commerece: Census Bureau

U.S. INTERNATIONAL TRADE BALANCE

US International Trade Balance
Monthly Cash as of 12/31/2013

MONTHLY CASH
As of 12/31/2013

Chart High -831.0   on 02/28/1992
Chart Low -68614.0   on 08/31/2006

Million USD

Date	Open	High	Low	Close
07/31/13	-38824.0	.0	-38824.0	-38824.0
08/30/13	-38945.0	.0	-38945.0	-38945.0
09/30/13	-42969.0	.0	-42969.0	-42969.0
10/31/13	-39328.0	.0	-39328.0	-39328.0
11/29/13	-34252.0	.0	-34252.0	-34252.0

Million USD

Trade Balance: Goods and Services, Balance of Payments Basis (BOPGSTB)   Shaded areas indicate US recessions.

Quarterly U.S. Trade Balance, Goods and Services   In Millions of Dollars

Quarter	Close	Quarter	Close	Quarter	Close	Quarter	Close	Quarter	Close	Quarter	Close
03/1996	-7,756	03/1999	-18,424	03/2002	-30,920	03/2005	-54,055	03/2008	-56,964	03/2011	-47,925
06/1996	-7,460	06/1999	-23,502	06/2002	-35,329	06/2005	-59,493	06/2008	-58,689	06/2011	-52,104
09/1996	-10,195	09/1999	-23,527	09/2002	-36,842	09/2005	-65,585	09/2008	-56,559	09/2011	-46,069
12/1996	-10,475	12/1999	-26,367	12/2002	-42,917	12/2005	-65,074	12/2008	-58,036	12/2011	-51,748
03/1997	-8,477	03/2000	-31,732	03/2003	-43,543	03/2006	-62,096	03/2009	-36,582	03/2012	-52,947
06/1997	-7,174	06/2000	-31,279	06/2003	-39,882	06/2006	-64,519	06/2009	-29,130	06/2012	-49,826
09/1997	-9,254	09/2000	-34,474	09/2003	-41,645	09/2006	-64,603	09/2009	-35,281	09/2012	-42,668
12/1997	-11,250	12/2000	-34,154	12/2003	-43,742	12/2006	-60,306	12/2009	-37,132	12/2012	-48,228
03/1998	-12,796	03/2001	-32,700	03/2004	-46,966	03/2007	-62,688	03/2010	-40,148	03/2013	-43,836
06/1998	-13,189	06/2001	-29,498	06/2004	-54,894	06/2007	-59,634	06/2010	-50,130	06/2013	-43,725
09/1998	-14,714	09/2001	-30,782	09/2004	-51,939	09/2007	-56,945	09/2010	-46,759	09/2013	-42,969
12/1998	-14,608	12/2001	-26,679	12/2004	-54,672	12/2007	-57,579	12/2010	-40,454	11/2013	-39,328

Source: U.S. Department of Commerce: Bureau of Economic Analysis

Housing Starts: Total: New Privately Owned Housing Units Started (HOUST)   Shaded areas indicate US recessions.

Annual High, Low and Close of U.S Housing Starts   In Thousands of Units

Year	High	Low	Settle	Year	High	Low	Settle	Year	High	Low	Settle
1972	2,494	2,221	2,366	1986	1,972	1,623	1,833	2000	1,737	1,463	1,532
1973	2,481	1,526	1,526	1987	1,784	1,400	1,400	2001	1,670	1,540	1,568
1974	1,752	975	975	1988	1,573	1,271	1,563	2002	1,829	1,592	1,788
1975	1,360	904	1,321	1989	1,621	1,251	1,251	2003	2,083	1,629	2,057
1976	1,804	1,367	1,804	1990	1,551	969	969	2004	2,062	1,807	2,050
1977	2,142	1,527	2,142	1991	1,103	798	1,079	2005	2,228	1,833	2,002
1978	2,197	1,718	2,044	1992	1,297	1,099	1,227	2006	2,265	1,478	1,629
1979	1,913	1,498	1,498	1993	1,533	1,083	1,533	2007	1,491	1,000	1,000
1980	1,523	927	1,482	1994	1,564	1,272	1,455	2008	1,107	556	556
1981	1,547	837	910	1995	1,461	1,249	1,431	2009	593	479	576
1982	1,372	843	1,303	1996	1,557	1,370	1,370	2010	679	526	526
1983	1,910	1,472	1,688	1997	1,566	1,355	1,566	2011	702	518	697
1984	2,260	1,586	1,612	1998	1,792	1,525	1,792	2012	983	706	983
1985	1,942	1,632	1,942	1999	1,748	1,553	1,708	2013	1,091	835	1,091

Seasonally adjusted.   *Source: U.S. Department of Commerce: Census Bureau*

FOODS & FIBERS

Sugar

Sugar prices during late-2009 and again in late-2010 saw sharp rallies as demand revived after the 2008/09 global recession and as suppliers were caught flat-footed. However, sugar growers then responded to high prices and boosted production. Sugar prices trended lower from late 2011 through 2013 due to four straight years of sugar surpluses and lackluster demand. The International Sugar Organization (ISO) estimated that 2012-13 global sugar production rose by +4.9% to a record 183.7 million metric tons (MMT) and that the sugar surplus in that year reached a record 10.6 MMT. The USDA is forecasting that world sugar ending stocks will rise to a record 43.4 MMT in 2013-14. Another bearish factor is ISO's forecast that Chinese sugar imports in 2013-14 will tumble by −36% y/y to 2.35 MMT as the government phases out sugar stockpiling due to record-high Chinese sugar inventories. Historically, key sugar market events include:

1974 rally—Sugar rallies to a record 66 cents per pound on strong demand, extremely low inventories in 1974, and general commodity market strength tied to inflation and speculation.

1980 rally—Sugar rallies to 45 cents per pound on a drop in sugar production in 1980 and general commodity strength tied to speculation and the spike in US inflation to a record high of 14% in 1980.

1988-90 rally—Sugar rallies to 16 cents per pound as strong demand outpaces production for five consecutive years and as production deficits cause inventories to fall to the lowest levels since 1980-81.

1994 rally—Sugar rallies to the 15 cent per pound area as sugar production dips in 1993-94, causing inventories to drop to low levels in 1994.

1997-99 bear market—Sugar prices fall to 10-year lows after Asian currency crisis causes a sharp drop in demand and sugar inventories reach near-record highs.

2004-05 bull market—Sugar prices soar on strong demand, tight supplies, and the commodity bull market.

2006-2008 correction — Sugar prices correct lower due to increased supplies and weak demand due to the global recession.

Coffee

Coffee prices rallied sharply from mid-2010 through early-2011 as strong demand led to a draw-down in ending stocks to a 13-year low of 25.6 million bags in 2011-12 and a record low of 18.1% in the stocks-to-use ratio. However, coffee prices from early-2011 through 2013 fell sharply as production in 2012-13 rose sharply by +6.4% to 153.3 million bags, thus replenishing inventories. The stocks-to-use ratio improved to 23.8% in 2012-13 and then to 25.2% in 2013-14. Historically, key coffee market events include:

1976-1977 rally—Coffee prices rally to record high of 337.5 cents per pound on a devastating frost in Brazil in 1975 and general commodity market strength.

1979 rally—Coffee prices rally to 230 cents per pound on light frost in Brazil and general commodity price strength.

1981-1985 trading range—Coffee prices trade in a narrow range due to International Coffee Agreement (ICA) quotas.

1985-1986 rally—Coffee prices spike higher to 275 cents per pound on extreme drought in Brazil and a sharp draw-down in inventories.

1989-1993 bear market—Coffee prices fall as ICA quotas end and as ending stocks are near record highs.

1994 rally—Coffee prices spike higher on a severe frost in Brazil.

1997 rally—Coffee prices spike higher on strong demand and steady inventory draw-downs in 1995-97.

1998-2001 bear market—Coffee prices fall on growing world supply.

2002-2006 bull market—Coffee prices more than triple due to strong demand, lagging production due to poor tree tending during bear market, inventory draw-downs, and general commodity strength.

Cocoa

Cocoa prices were generally strong through 2009-11 on improved demand after the global recession. Cocoa prices then rallied to a three-decade high in early 2011 due in part to a political dispute in the Ivory Coast that resulted in a temporary ban on cocoa exports. Cocoa prices fell through the remainder of 2011 on the resumption of Ivory Coast exports. Cocoa prices rallied in the latter half of 2013 mainly due to an increase in demand with 2012-13 grindings up +2.4% at a record high of 4.05 million metric tons. Cocoa prices also saw strength during 2013 as the International Cocoa Organization forecasted a 2012-13 global cocoa deficit of 160,000 metric tons, indicating tightening supplies after two years of surpluses. Historically, key cocoa market events include:

1976-78 rally—Cocoa prices rally sharply on a series of poor crops in the early 1970s which caused the stocks-to-grindings ratio to drop from 35% at the beginning of the 1970s to a record low of 18% in the 1976-77 marketing year. The cocoa market came into the 1970s with poor production capacity because low cocoa prices seen in the 1950s and

1960s caused poor investment in and maintenance of cocoa farms.

1984-92 bear market—Starting in the 1984-85 marketing year, cocoa production grows sharply, causing a big increase in inventories. The stocks-to-grindings ratio reaches a record high of 66% in 1991-92.

1993-98 Brazil production plunges—Brazilian cocoa production is devastated by the fungus "witch's broom," causing annual production to drop by 50% from 305,000 metric tons in 1992-93 to 124,000 MT in 1999-2000.

2001-02 rally—Cocoa prices rally on strong demand and a sharp drop in the ending stocks in the 2000-01 and 2001-02 marketing years.

2004 Ivory Coast ceasefire violation—Cocoa prices rally sharply in November 2004 when Ivory Coast government troops bomb a French peacekeeping force and the French military responds by destroying all the Ivory Coast's military aircraft. The incident causes a temporary disruption of cocoa shipments from the Ivory Coast.

2007-08 rally—Cocoa prices in 2007-08 rallied sharply to a 22-year high of $3,385 per metric ton in July 2008 due to a drop in 2006/07 production and the general commodity bull market

Orange Juice

Orange juice prices have traded in a volatile range in the past few years due to various crop problems in Florida and a sharp drop in U.S. per capita orange juice consumption. The U.S. orange crop is currently being hurt by a bug that causes citrus greening disease. U.S. acreage planted with oranges is now at a record low due to crop damage and urban sprawl. However, Brazil's orange production has surged and is now more than twice that of U.S. production. Historically, key orange market events include:

1980s Florida freezes—Major freezes in Florida in the 1980s (particularly in December 1983 and 1985) destroy one-third of Florida's orange trees and lead to a sharp reduction in Florida and US orange production in 1981 through 1992. Orange juice futures prices spiked higher numerous times during the 1980s.

1988 Brazilian production record—Brazilian orange production surges to a then-record high in 1998-90 and grows further in the 1990s, adding to world supply and curbing orange juice price spikes in 1990s. Brazil's share of world orange production grows to 37% in 2004 from 10% in 1970, while the US share falls to 18% in 2004 from 45% in 1970.

1990s California freezes—Freezes in 1991 and 1998 cause California orange production to plunge by 60% in 1990-91 and 40% in 1998-99 from the 5-year trend.

1992 Florida production surge—Starting in 1992, Florida orange production surges and remains high through most of the rest of the 1990s, leading to generally weak prices.

2003-04 bear market—Orange juice futures prices plunge to a 29-year low on a near-record crop in 2003-04 and the Atkins diet fad which reduced demand for high-carb orange juice.

2004-07 rally—Orange juice futures prices nearly quadruple from 55 cents per pound in mid-2004 to a 3-decade high in March 2007 of 209.50 cents due to a one-third drop in Florida orange production in the 2004-05 and 2005-06 marketing years caused by severe hurricane damage after four hurricanes in 2004 and Hurricane Wilma in 2005.

Cotton

Cotton prices fell to a major low in late-2008 on the global financial crisis and the commodity rout but then recovered in 2009 thanks to short-covering and improved demand. Cotton prices from mid-2010 through early-2011 rallied to a record high on (1) reduced cotton production in Australia, the world's fourth-largest exporter, after the worst floods in 50 years decimated its cotton crop, (2) very strong Chinese demand as China cotton imports for all of 2010 surged +86% y/y to 2.84 MMT, and (3) the tightest level of world ending stocks in nearly two decades in 2009-10 and 2010-11. However, cotton prices then fell sharply later in 2011 and into 2012 as cotton production soared by a total 22% in 2010-11 and 2011-12 to a record of 126.6 million bales, boosting ending stocks to a record high of 89.1 million bales by 2012-13. Historically, key cotton market events include:

1970s price spikes—Cotton prices spike higher along with other US field crops in the 1970s due to inflation and general strength in commodity prices.

1983 and 1988 droughts—Cotton prices in 1983 and again in 1988 spike higher in response to US droughts.

1994-95 rally—Cotton prices rally to their modern day record of $1.172 per pound in April 1996 as a result of strong demand and sharply reduced crops in various Asian producing countries (China, Pakistan, India, Uzbekistan and Turkmenistan) due to dry weather, insect infestation and disease. The rally came despite a record US cotton crop in the 1994-95 marketing year.

2001 bear market—Cotton prices fall sharply in 2001 to 30 cents per pound as the US produces a then-record crop of 20.3 million bales. World ending stocks rise to a near-record high in the 2001-02 marketing year.

COCOA

COCOA - ICE
Quarterly Nearest Futures as of 01/09/2014

Date	Open	High	Low	Close
12/31/12	2500.0	2578.0	2207.0	2236.0
03/29/13	2246.0	2313.0	2046.0	2170.0
06/28/13	2170.0	2418.0	2111.0	2194.0
09/30/13	2203.0	2657.0	2150.0	2640.0
12/31/13	2644.0	2840.0	2561.0	2709.0

QUARTERLY NEAREST FUTURES
As of 01/09/2014

Chart High	5379.2	on 07/18/1977
Chart Low	75.0	on 02/28/1933
CONTRACT SIZE	10 metric tons	
MIN TICK VALUE	1 USD	10 USD / contract
EACH GRID VALUE	40 USD	400 USD / contract
DAILY LIMIT VALUE	None	
TRADING HOURS	4:00a - 2:00p ET	

Nearby Futures through Last Trading Day.   Futures: Data through December 1980 contract converted from cents per pound to dollars per metric ton.

Annual High, Low and Settle of Cocoa Futures   In Dollars per Metric Ton

Year	High	Low	Settle	Year	High	Low	Settle	Year	High	Low	Settle
1930	205	134	134	1944	192	192	192	1958	1,105	816	891
1931	131	88	88	1945	192	192	192	1959	865	597	609
1932	102	82	82	1946	595	192	595	1960	644	484	489
1933	107	75	91	1947	1,179	551	926	1961	586	403	503
1934	122	99	108	1948	1,020	661	667	1962	525	401	454
1935	113	101	109	1949	667	375	592	1963	608	440	572
1936	246	113	246	1950	979	485	755	1964	569	430	477
1937	268	119	119	1951	857	626	716	1965	478	210	473
1938	129	98	100	1952	847	650	714	1966	578	412	553
1939	133	92	128	1953	1,075	645	1,075	1967	633	504	614
1940	130	93	116	1954	1,601	948	1,061	1968	1,032	549	944
1941	188	112	188	1955	1,149	683	711	1969	974	777	786
1942	192	187	192	1956	703	513	560	1970	795	511	620
1943	192	192	192	1957	970	472	871	1971	619	446	455

Futures data begins 07/01/1959.   Data prior to Dec 1980 contract converted from cents per pound.   Data continued on page 160.
Source: ICE Futures U.S.

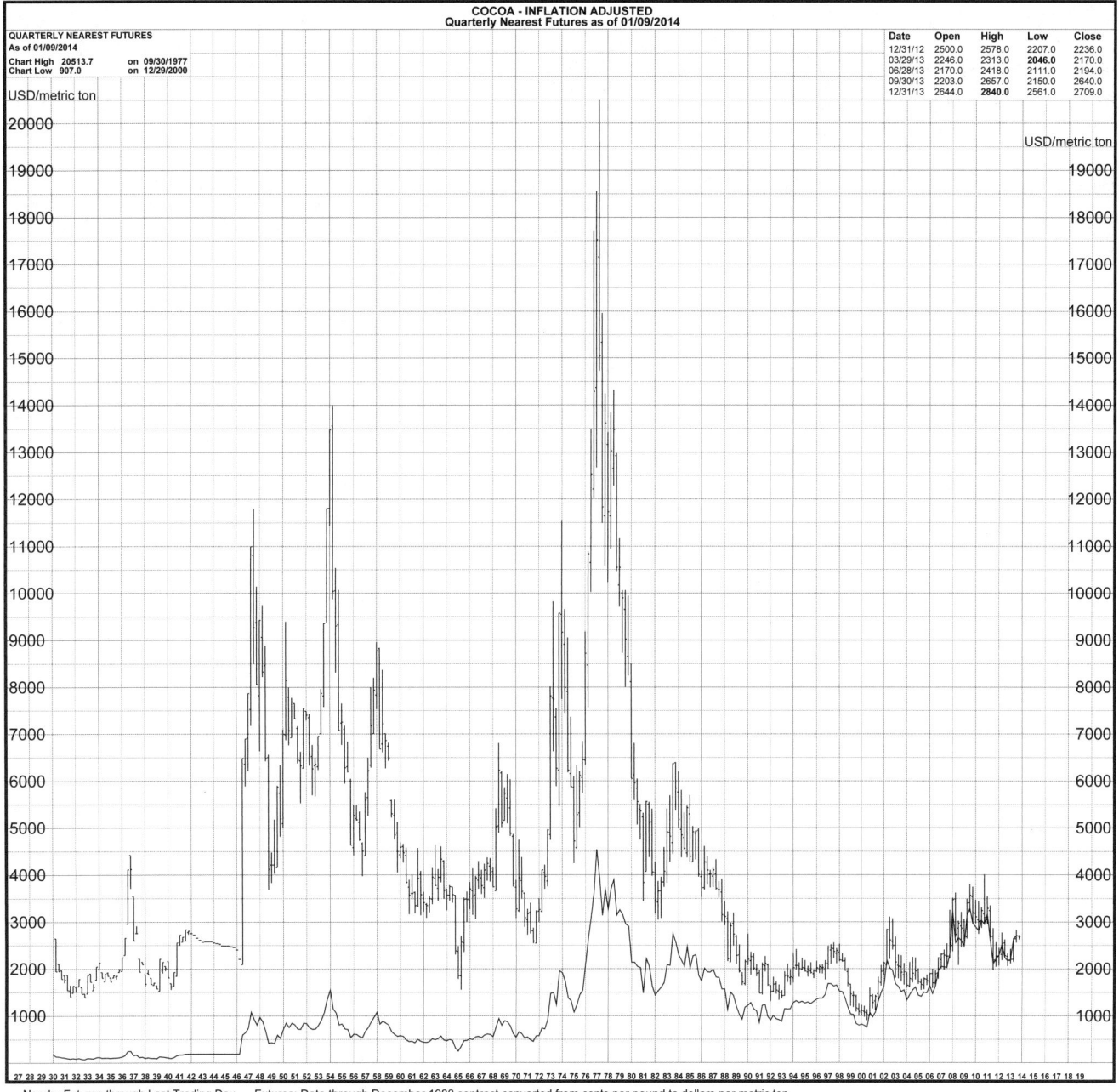

COCOA - INFLATION ADJUSTED
Quarterly Nearest Futures as of 01/09/2014

QUARTERLY NEAREST FUTURES
As of 01/09/2014

Chart High 20513.7 on 09/30/1977
Chart Low 907.0 on 12/29/2000

USD/metric ton

Date	Open	High	Low	Close
12/31/12	2500.0	2578.0	2207.0	2236.0
03/29/13	2246.0	2313.0	2046.0	2170.0
06/28/13	2170.0	2418.0	2111.0	2194.0
09/30/13	2203.0	2657.0	2150.0	2640.0
12/31/13	2644.0	2840.0	2561.0	2709.0

Nearby Futures through Last Trading Day.   Futures: Data through December 1980 contract converted from cents per pound to dollars per metric ton.

Annual High, Low and Settle of Cocoa   In Dollars per Metric Ton

Year	High	Low	Settle	Year	High	Low	Settle	Year	High	Low	Settle
1930	205	134	134	1944	192	192	192	1958	1,105	816	891
1931	131	88	88	1945	192	192	192	1959	865	648	648
1932	102	82	82	1946	595	192	595	1960	672	518	521
1933	107	75	91	1947	1,179	551	926	1961	623	430	538
1934	122	99	108	1948	1,020	661	667	1962	554	430	477
1935	113	101	109	1949	667	375	592	1963	639	466	598
1936	246	113	246	1950	979	485	755	1964	592	472	516
1937	268	119	119	1951	857	626	716	1965	529	251	513
1938	129	98	100	1952	847	650	714	1966	623	463	601
1939	133	92	128	1953	1,075	645	1,075	1967	711	573	692
1940	130	93	116	1954	1,601	948	1,061	1968	1,121	634	1,047
1941	188	112	188	1955	1,149	683	711	1969	1,105	904	909
1942	192	187	192	1956	703	513	560	1970	918	617	708
1943	192	192	192	1957	970	472	871	1971	700	510	510

Ivory Coast.   Data prior to 10/17/1980 converted from cents per pound.   Data continued on page 161.   *Source: ICE Futures U.S.*

COCOA

COCOA - ICE
Monthly Nearest Futures as of 12/31/2013

Date	Open	High	Low	Close
08/31/13	2299.0	2514.0	2278.0	2413.0
09/30/13	2411.0	2657.0	2390.0	2640.0
10/31/13	2644.0	2780.0	2561.0	2677.0
11/30/13	2667.0	2820.0	2568.0	2791.0
12/31/13	2839.0	2840.0	2692.0	2709.0

MONTHLY NEAREST FUTURES
As of 12/31/2013

Chart High 5379.2 on 07/18/1977
Chart Low 446.0 on 12/13/1971
CONTRACT SIZE 10 metric tons
MIN TICK VALUE 10 USD / contract
EACH GRID VALUE 400 USD / contract
DAILY LIMIT VALUE None
TRADING HOURS 4:00a - 2:00p ET

Nearby Futures through Last Trading Day.   Futures: Data through December 1980 contract converted from cents per pound to dollars per metric ton.

Annual High, Low and Settle of Cocoa Futures   In Dollars per Metric Ton

Year	High	Low	Settle	Year	High	Low	Settle	Year	High	Low	Settle
1972	765	453	720	1986	2,315	1,648	1,935	2000	929	674	758
1973	1,896	694	1,237	1987	2,128	1,732	1,814	2001	1,380	752	1,310
1974	2,414	1,116	1,381	1988	1,950	1,103	1,500	2002	2,405	1,260	2,021
1975	1,657	972	1,450	1989	1,670	890	925	2003	2,420	1,360	1,515
1976	3,357	1,371	3,114	1990	1,525	905	1,150	2004	1,830	1,299	1,547
1977	5,379	3,047	3,138	1991	1,337	850	1,245	2005	1,850	1,315	1,504
1978	4,142	2,852	3,897	1992	1,254	785	936	2006	1,732	1,380	1,635
1979	3,869	2,623	2,954	1993	1,310	820	1,144	2007	2,277	1,566	2,035
1980	3,401	1,870	2,050	1994	1,543	1,041	1,280	2008	3,385	1,867	2,665
1981	2,230	1,330	2,054	1995	1,442	1,200	1,258	2009	3,510	2,232	3,289
1982	2,184	1,275	1,603	1996	1,447	1,196	1,374	2010	3,485	2,562	3,035
1983	2,759	1,565	2,755	1997	1,766	1,210	1,630	2011	3,826	1,898	2,109
1984	2,805	1,960	2,052	1998	1,758	1,368	1,379	2012	2,744	2,003	2,236
1985	2,620	1,963	2,298	1999	1,422	782	837	2013	2,840	2,046	2,709

Data prior to Dec 1980 contract converted from cents per pound.   Data continued from page 158.   *Source: ICE Futures U.S.*

Cocoa, Ivory Coast
Monthly Cash as of 12/31/2013

Date	Open	High	Low	Close
08/30/13	2581.0	2765.0	2541.0	2677.0
09/30/13	2711.0	2912.0	2691.0	2894.0
10/31/13	2929.0	3061.0	2905.0	3018.0
11/29/13	2951.0	3087.0	2927.0	3087.0
12/31/13	3088.0	3151.0	3074.0	3090.0

MONTHLY CASH
As of 12/31/2013
Chart High 5732.0 on 09/14/1977
Chart Low 510.0 on 12/10/1971

USD/metric ton

Accra: to 09/1977; Accra: 10/1977 to 09/1980 (avg); Ivory Coast: 10/1980 to date.

Annual High, Low and Settle of Cocoa   In Dollars per Metric Ton

Year	High	Low	Settle	Year	High	Low	Settle	Year	High	Low	Settle
1972	862	518	821	1986	2,597	1,967	2,155	2000	1,106	876	930
1973	2,089	796	1,488	1987	2,377	1,975	2,052	2001	1,596	925	1,565
1974	2,877	1,378	1,786	1988	2,435	1,744	2,317	2002	2,711	1,524	2,336
1975	2,006	1,290	1,709	1989	2,247	1,097	1,128	2003	2,686	1,614	1,763
1976	3,594	1,565	3,456	1990	1,661	1,099	1,348	2004	2,044	1,526	1,770
1977	5,732	3,390	5,512	1991	1,496	1,027	1,413	2005	2,074	1,535	1,714
1978	4,387	3,086	4,101	1992	1,415	1,007	1,154	2006	2,017	1,677	1,898
1979	4,255	3,406	3,417	1993	1,695	1,098	1,499	2007	2,447	1,826	2,414
1980	3,825	2,100	2,285	1994	1,795	1,403	1,582	2008	3,593	2,254	3,060
1981	2,425	1,571	2,246	1995	1,751	1,419	1,419	2009	3,931	2,560	3,764
1982	2,542	1,562	1,832	1996	1,623	1,393	1,534	2010	3,954	3,197	3,485
1983	2,962	1,755	2,962	1997	1,930	1,412	1,802	2011	4,257	2,275	2,359
1984	2,926	2,156	2,215	1998	1,949	1,583	1,583	2012	3,053	2,234	2,539
1985	2,680	2,163	2,580	1999	1,616	988	1,017	2013	3,151	2,390	3,090

Ivory Coast.   Data prior to 10/17/1980 converted from cents per pound.   Data continued from page 159.   *Source: U.S. Department of Agriculture*
(USDA)

COCOA

Quarterly High, Low and Settle of Cocoa Futures — In Dollars per Metric Ton

Quarter	High	Low	Settle	Quarter	High	Low	Settle	Quarter	High	Low	Settle
03/2005	1,850	1,464	1,613	03/2008	2,971	2,028	2,321	03/2011	3,826	2,821	2,952
06/2005	1,669	1,392	1,440	06/2008	3,280	2,217	3,245	06/2011	3,424	2,851	3,170
09/2005	1,519	1,316	1,413	09/2008	3,385	2,510	2,558	09/2011	3,249	2,587	2,608
12/2005	1,525	1,315	1,504	12/2008	2,718	1,867	2,665	12/2011	2,767	1,898	2,109
03/2006	1,600	1,410	1,489	03/2009	2,919	2,232	2,605	03/2012	2,519	2,003	2,219
06/2006	1,650	1,410	1,646	06/2009	2,823	2,262	2,487	06/2012	2,396	2,026	2,289
09/2006	1,732	1,380	1,472	09/2009	3,219	2,442	3,140	09/2012	2,744	2,159	2,516
12/2006	1,694	1,396	1,635	12/2009	3,510	2,967	3,289	12/2012	2,578	2,207	2,236
03/2007	1,969	1,566	1,953	03/2010	3,485	2,761	2,969	03/2013	2,313	2,046	2,170
06/2007	2,074	1,790	2,054	06/2010	3,234	2,767	2,894	06/2013	2,418	2,111	2,194
09/2007	2,143	1,763	2,036	09/2010	3,210	2,562	2,814	09/2013	2,657	2,150	2,640
12/2007	2,277	1,810	2,035	12/2010	3,100	2,691	3,035	12/2013	2,840	2,561	2,709

Source: ICE Futures U.S.

Cocoa, Ivory Coast
Weekly Cash as of 01/03/2014

Date	Open	High	Low	Close
12/06/13	3088.0	3103.0	3088.0	3103.0
12/13/13	3103.0	3103.0	3074.0	3074.0
12/20/13	3074.0	3074.0	3074.0	3074.0
12/27/13	3149.0	3151.0	3149.0	3151.0
01/03/14	3078.0	3153.0	3078.0	3153.0

WEEKLY CASH
As of 01/03/2014
Chart High 4257.0 on 03/04/2011
Chart Low 1526.0 on 05/17/2004
USD/metric ton

USD/metric ton

Ivory Coast.

Quarterly High, Low and Settle of Cocoa   In Dollars per Metric Ton

Quarter	High	Low	Settle	Quarter	High	Low	Settle	Quarter	High	Low	Settle
03/2005	2,074	1,679	1,832	03/2008	3,232	2,354	2,614	03/2011	4,257	3,336	3,842
06/2005	1,801	1,605	1,652	06/2008	3,499	2,523	3,499	06/2011	3,910	3,303	3,364
09/2005	1,774	1,535	1,614	09/2008	3,593	2,853	3,059	09/2011	3,518	2,898	2,898
12/2005	1,714	1,536	1,714	12/2008	3,060	2,254	3,060	12/2011	3,038	2,275	2,359
03/2006	1,828	1,677	1,757	03/2009	3,200	2,560	2,977	03/2012	2,815	2,234	2,549
06/2006	1,914	1,686	1,914	06/2009	3,159	2,600	2,828	06/2012	2,698	2,398	2,636
09/2006	2,017	1,713	1,760	09/2009	3,573	2,790	3,518	09/2012	3,053	2,541	2,898
12/2006	1,949	1,683	1,898	12/2009	3,931	3,381	3,764	12/2012	2,891	2,539	2,539
03/2007	2,241	1,826	2,241	03/2010	3,954	3,412	3,429	03/2013	2,573	2,390	2,435
06/2007	2,375	2,086	2,375	06/2010	3,787	3,387	3,713	06/2013	2,629	2,409	2,425
09/2007	2,422	2,112	2,356	09/2010	3,740	3,197	3,319	09/2013	2,912	2,432	2,894
12/2007	2,447	2,138	2,414	12/2010	3,485	3,219	3,485	12/2013	3,151	2,905	3,090

Ivory Coast.   Source: U.S. Department of Agriculture (USDA)

COCOA #7

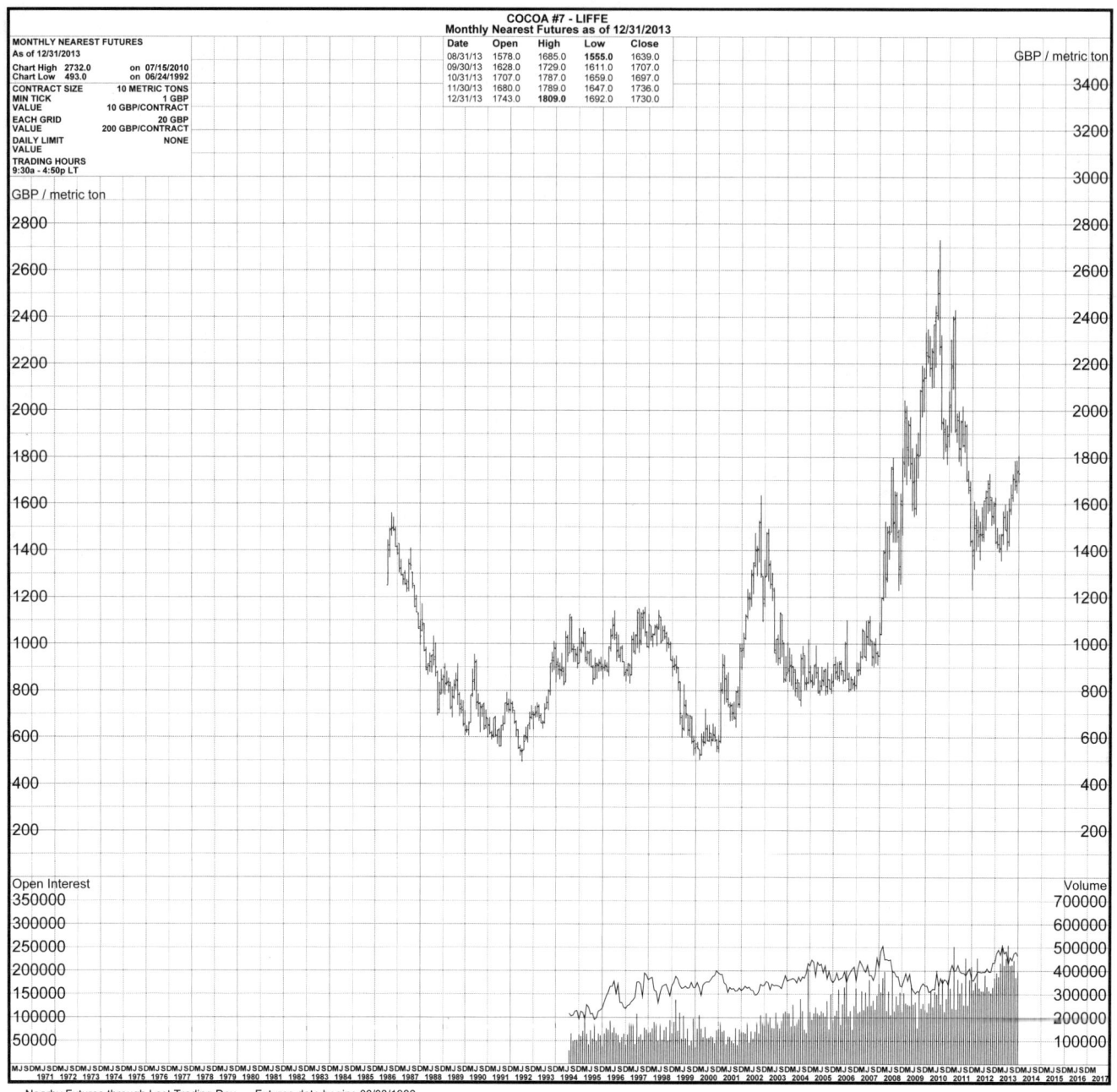

COCOA #7 - LIFFE
Monthly Nearest Futures as of 12/31/2013

Date	Open	High	Low	Close
08/31/13	1578.0	1685.0	**1555.0**	1639.0
09/30/13	1628.0	1729.0	1611.0	1707.0
10/31/13	1707.0	1787.0	1659.0	1697.0
11/30/13	1680.0	1789.0	1647.0	1736.0
12/31/13	1743.0	**1809.0**	1692.0	1730.0

MONTHLY NEAREST FUTURES
As of 12/31/2013

Chart High	2732.0	on 07/15/2010
Chart Low	493.0	on 06/24/1992
CONTRACT SIZE	10 METRIC TONS	
MIN TICK VALUE	1 GBP 10 GBP/CONTRACT	
EACH GRID VALUE	20 GBP 200 GBP/CONTRACT	
DAILY LIMIT VALUE	NONE	
TRADING HOURS	9:30a - 4:50p LT	

Nearby Futures through Last Trading Day.   Futures data begins 06/03/1986.

Annual High, Low and Settle of Cocoa #7 Futures   In Pounds per Metric Ton

Year	High	Low	Settle	Year	High	Low	Settle	Year	High	Low	Settle
1972	----	----	----	1986	1,560	1,236	1,386	2000	723	503	582
1973	----	----	----	1987	1,427	993	1,030	2001	1,001	574	973
1974	----	----	----	1988	1,170	690	857	2002	1,636	941	1,287
1975	----	----	----	1989	915	605	627	2003	1,493	835	893
1976	----	----	----	1990	955	598	651	2004	1,021	733	844
1977	----	----	----	1991	793	558	745	2005	994	780	911
1978	----	----	----	1992	753	493	693	2006	1,102	795	888
1979	----	----	----	1993	1,011	635	910	2007	1,121	864	1,043
1980	----	----	----	1994	1,124	821	975	2008	1,840	1,041	1,781
1981	----	----	----	1995	1,068	825	899	2009	2,337	1,545	2,250
1982	----	----	----	1996	1,142	838	890	2010	2,732	1,770	2,017
1983	----	----	----	1997	1,158	830	1,082	2011	2,433	1,232	1,380
1984	----	----	----	1998	1,144	860	902	2012	1,730	1,321	1,435
1985	----	----	----	1999	950	521	571	2013	1,809	1,357	1,730

Futures data begins 06/03/1986.   *Source: Euronext LIFFE*

COCOA #7 - LIFFE
Weekly Nearest Futures as of 01/03/2014

Date	Open	High	Low	Close
12/06/13	1743.0	1763.0	1698.0	1742.0
12/13/13	1732.0	1777.0	1692.0	1767.0
12/20/13	1752.0	1800.0	1747.0	1798.0
12/27/13	1798.0	1809.0	1758.0	1760.0
01/03/14	1752.0	1762.0	1676.0	1730.0

WEEKLY NEAREST FUTURES
As of 01/03/2014

Chart High 2732.0 on 07/15/2010
Chart Low 733.0 on 07/06/2004
CONTRACT SIZE 10 METRIC TONS
MIN TICK 1 GBP
VALUE 10 GBP/CONTRACT
EACH GRID 20 GBP
VALUE 200 GBP/CONTRACT
DAILY LIMIT NONE
VALUE
TRADING HOURS
9:30a - 4:50p LT

Nearby Futures through Last Trading Day.

Quarterly High, Low and Settle of Cocoa #7 Futures   In Pounds per Metric Ton

Quarter	High	Low	Settle	Quarter	High	Low	Settle	Quarter	High	Low	Settle
03/2005	994	812	877	03/2008	1,525	1,041	1,284	03/2011	2,433	1,907	1,915
06/2005	903	780	846	06/2008	1,760	1,266	1,758	06/2011	1,997	1,765	1,954
09/2005	922	780	848	09/2008	1,800	1,435	1,480	09/2011	2,020	1,697	1,699
12/2005	914	787	911	12/2008	1,840	1,228	1,781	12/2011	1,745	1,232	1,380
03/2006	947	840	914	03/2009	2,045	1,681	1,940	03/2012	1,612	1,321	1,462
06/2006	1,010	830	1,001	06/2009	1,974	1,545	1,581	06/2012	1,616	1,360	1,614
09/2006	1,102	795	849	09/2009	2,090	1,554	2,085	09/2012	1,730	1,488	1,631
12/2006	923	800	888	12/2009	2,337	1,973	2,250	12/2012	1,631	1,430	1,435
03/2007	1,066	864	1,059	03/2010	2,350	2,096	2,255	03/2013	1,499	1,357	1,467
06/2007	1,103	928	1,091	06/2010	2,608	2,100	2,503	06/2013	1,601	1,404	1,440
09/2007	1,121	901	1,000	09/2010	2,732	1,793	1,910	09/2013	1,729	1,420	1,707
12/2007	1,092	909	1,043	12/2010	2,083	1,770	2,017	12/2013	1,809	1,647	1,730

Source: Euronext LIFFE

COFFEE

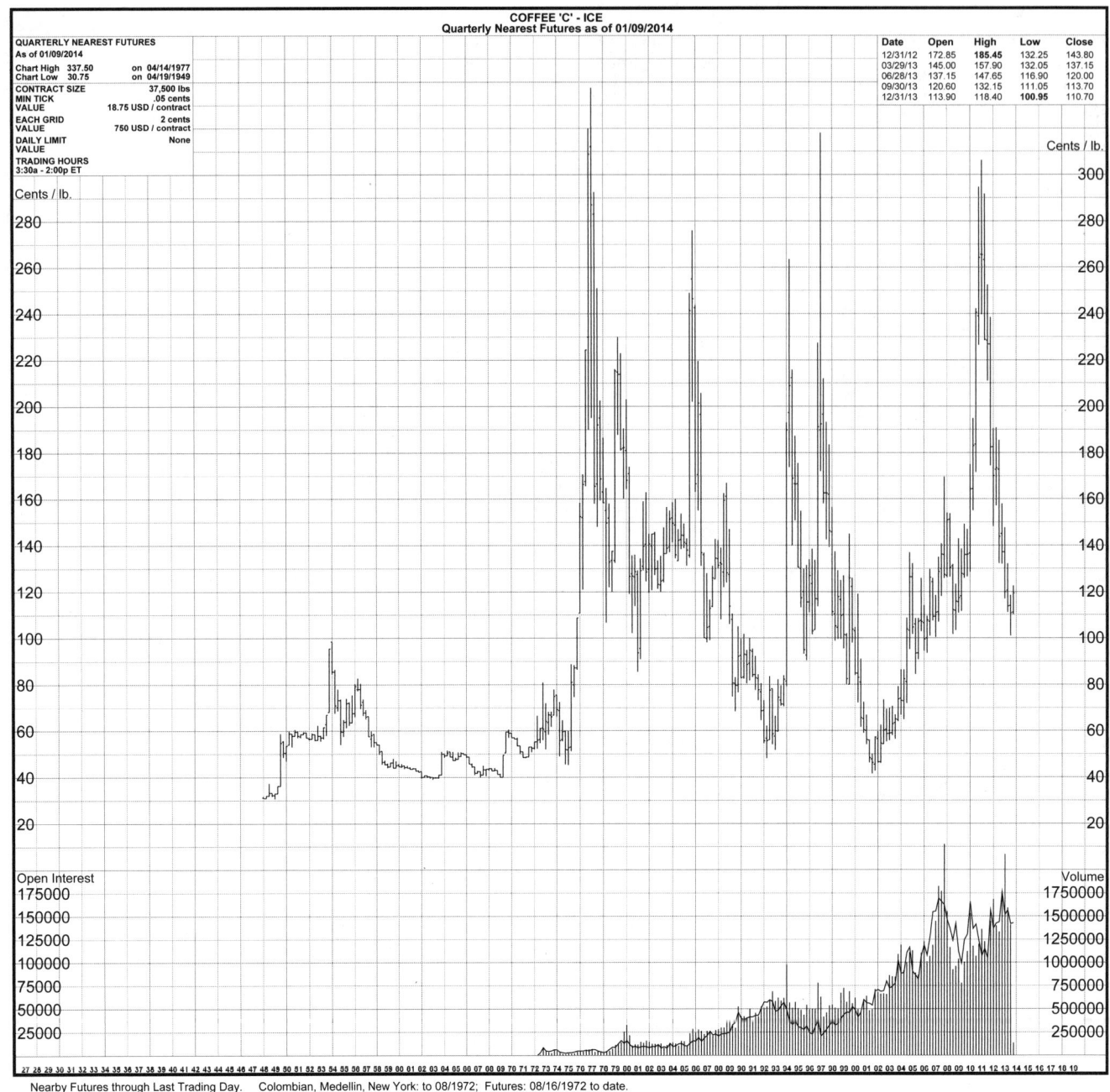

Nearby Futures through Last Trading Day.   Colombian, Medellin, New York: to 08/1972; Futures: 08/16/1972 to date.

Annual High, Low and Settle of Coffee   In Cents per Pound

Year	High	Low	Settle	Year	High	Low	Settle	Year	High	Low	Settle
1930	----	----	----	1944	----	----	----	1958	58.75	45.50	46.50
1931	----	----	----	1945	----	----	----	1959	48.00	44.00	44.00
1932	----	----	----	1946	----	----	----	1960	47.00	43.62	44.25
1933	----	----	----	1947	----	----	----	1961	45.00	42.75	42.75
1934	----	----	----	1948	37.35	31.00	33.25	1962	43.00	39.50	40.25
1935	----	----	----	1949	58.75	30.75	54.75	1963	41.00	39.00	41.00
1936	----	----	----	1950	59.75	47.00	57.75	1964	51.50	41.00	48.75
1937	----	----	----	1951	60.50	57.00	59.25	1965	51.00	47.25	50.25
1938	----	----	----	1952	59.25	55.75	56.00	1966	50.25	44.25	44.50
1939	----	----	----	1953	66.87	55.50	66.87	1967	45.00	40.00	43.25
1940	----	----	----	1954	98.50	67.50	73.25	1968	44.00	40.50	43.00
1941	----	----	----	1955	74.00	54.00	63.50	1969	59.50	40.00	59.50
1942	----	----	----	1956	82.75	63.50	71.25	1970	60.50	53.50	53.50
1943	----	----	----	1957	73.75	53.00	58.00	1971	53.50	48.25	53.00

Colombian, NY.   Data continued on page 168.   *Source: ICE Futures U.S.*

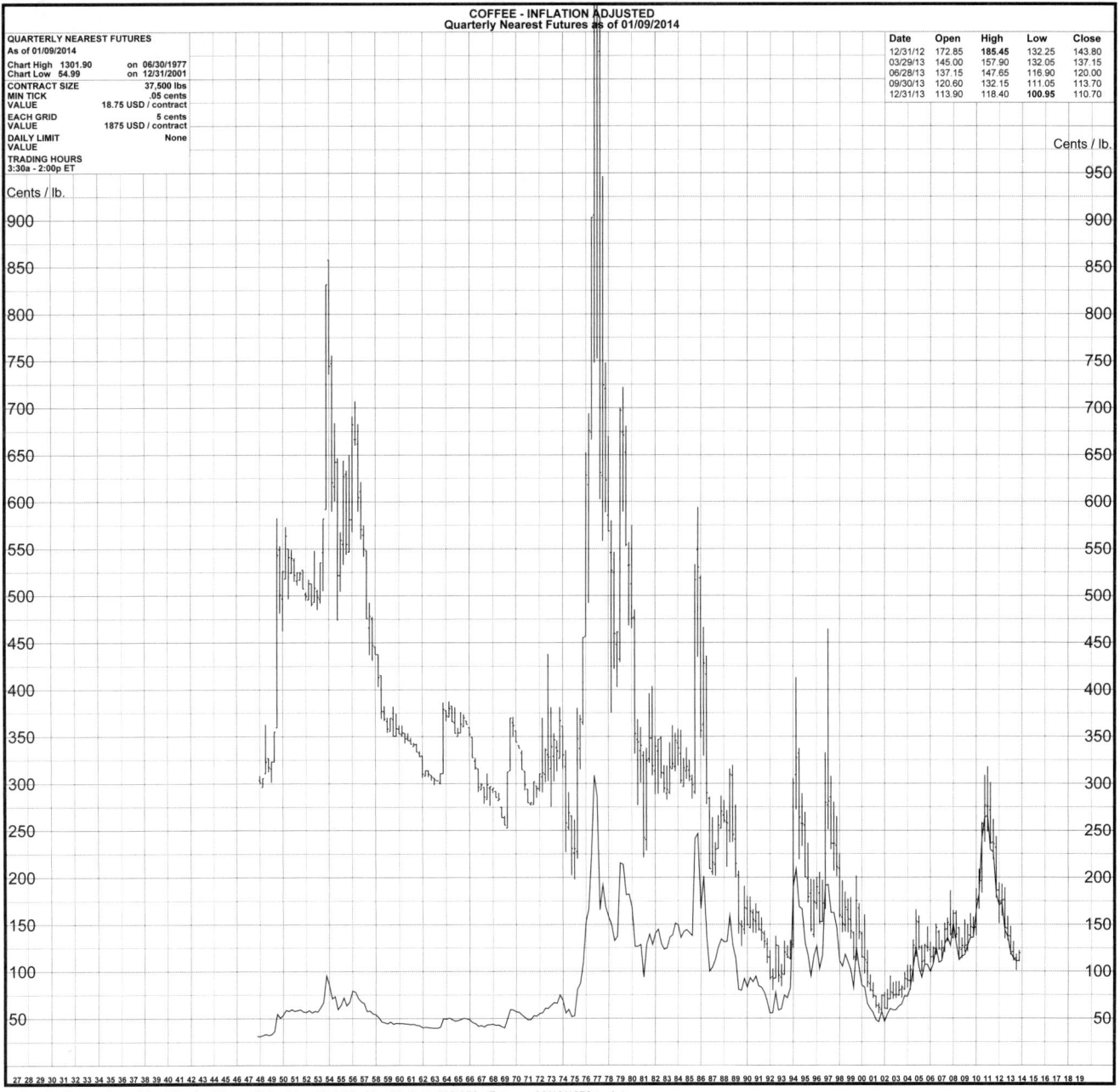

COFFEE - INFLATION ADJUSTED
Quarterly Nearest Futures as of 01/09/2014

QUARTERLY NEAREST FUTURES
As of 01/09/2014

Chart High	1301.90	on 06/30/1977
Chart Low	54.99	on 12/31/2001
CONTRACT SIZE	37,500 lbs	
MIN TICK	.05 cents	
VALUE	18.75 USD / contract	
EACH GRID	5 cents	
VALUE	1875 USD / contract	
DAILY LIMIT	None	
VALUE		
TRADING HOURS		
3:30a - 2:00p ET		

Date	Open	High	Low	Close
12/31/12	172.85	185.45	132.25	143.80
03/29/13	145.00	157.90	132.05	137.15
06/28/13	137.15	147.65	116.90	120.00
09/30/13	120.60	132.15	111.05	113.70
12/31/13	113.90	118.40	100.95	110.70

Cents / lb.

Nearby Futures through Last Trading Day.   Colombian, Medellin, New York: to 08/1972;   Futures: 08/16/1972 to date.

Annual High, Low and Settle of Coffee   In Cents per Pound

Year	High	Low	Settle	Year	High	Low	Settle	Year	High	Low	Settle
1930	----	----	----	1944	----	----	----	1958	58.75	45.50	46.50
1931	----	----	----	1945	----	----	----	1959	48.00	44.00	44.00
1932	----	----	----	1946	----	----	----	1960	47.00	43.62	44.25
1933	----	----	----	1947	----	----	----	1961	45.00	42.75	42.75
1934	----	----	----	1948	37.35	31.00	33.25	1962	43.00	39.50	40.25
1935	----	----	----	1949	58.75	30.75	54.75	1963	41.00	39.00	41.00
1936	----	----	----	1950	59.75	47.00	57.75	1964	51.50	41.00	48.75
1937	----	----	----	1951	60.50	57.00	59.25	1965	51.00	47.25	50.25
1938	----	----	----	1952	59.25	55.75	56.00	1966	50.25	44.25	44.50
1939	----	----	----	1953	66.87	55.50	66.87	1967	45.00	40.00	43.25
1940	----	----	----	1954	98.50	67.50	73.25	1968	44.00	40.50	43.00
1941	----	----	----	1955	74.00	54.00	63.50	1969	59.50	40.00	59.50
1942	----	----	----	1956	82.75	63.50	71.25	1970	60.50	53.50	53.50
1943	----	----	----	1957	73.75	53.00	58.00	1971	53.50	48.25	53.00

Colombian, NY.   Data continued on page 169.   *Source: ICE Futures U.S.*

COFFEE

	COFFEE 'C' - ICE				
Monthly Nearest Futures as of 12/31/2013					
Date	Open	High	Low	Close	
08/31/13	118.75	124.60	112.00	112.10	
09/30/13	113.00	119.20	111.05	113.70	
10/31/13	113.90	117.95	105.25	105.40	
11/30/13	105.40	111.85	100.95	110.25	
12/31/13	109.80	118.40	105.40	110.70	

MONTHLY NEAREST FUTURES
As of 12/31/2013

Chart High 337.50 on 04/14/1977
Chart Low 41.50 on 12/04/2001

Cents / lb.

CONTRACT SIZE 37,500 lbs
MIN TICK .05 cents
VALUE 18.75 USD / contract
EACH GRID 2 cents
VALUE 750 USD / contract
DAILY LIMIT None
VALUE
TRADING HOURS
3:30a - 2:00p ET

Nearby Futures through Last Trading Day.   Colombian, Medellin, New York: to 08/1972; Futures: 08/16/1972 to date.

Annual High, Low and Settle of Coffee 'C' Futures   In Cents per Pound

Year	High	Low	Settle	Year	High	Low	Settle	Year	High	Low	Settle
1972	61.25	52.25	60.90	1986	276.00	131.20	136.83	2000	126.00	61.55	65.55
1973	81.00	52.00	66.00	1987	136.90	98.10	125.96	2001	72.50	41.50	46.20
1974	77.90	49.00	59.62	1988	162.50	108.00	159.34	2002	73.50	42.70	60.20
1975	88.75	45.25	87.22	1989	166.90	68.30	79.57	2003	70.75	55.30	64.95
1976	224.50	86.40	224.45	1990	105.00	76.60	88.65	2004	108.70	64.00	103.75
1977	337.50	148.00	192.03	1991	100.00	73.25	77.70	2005	137.00	84.45	107.10
1978	202.50	106.60	132.88	1992	83.55	48.10	77.55	2006	129.75	93.50	126.20
1979	230.05	120.00	181.56	1993	82.20	51.70	71.55	2007	140.80	100.35	136.20
1980	203.00	102.10	126.80	1994	263.50	70.55	168.85	2008	169.60	101.60	112.05
1981	159.00	85.50	139.71	1995	187.25	93.15	94.90	2009	149.20	103.30	135.95
1982	162.90	119.50	129.83	1996	138.50	90.40	116.90	2010	242.25	126.55	240.50
1983	156.50	120.10	138.79	1997	318.00	113.60	162.45	2011	306.25	210.95	226.85
1984	160.00	133.20	142.25	1998	183.50	98.75	117.75	2012	238.50	132.25	143.80
1985	249.00	131.25	241.29	1999	145.00	80.00	125.90	2013	157.90	100.95	110.70

Futures begin trading 08/16/1972.   Data continued from page 166.   *Source: ICE Futures U.S.*

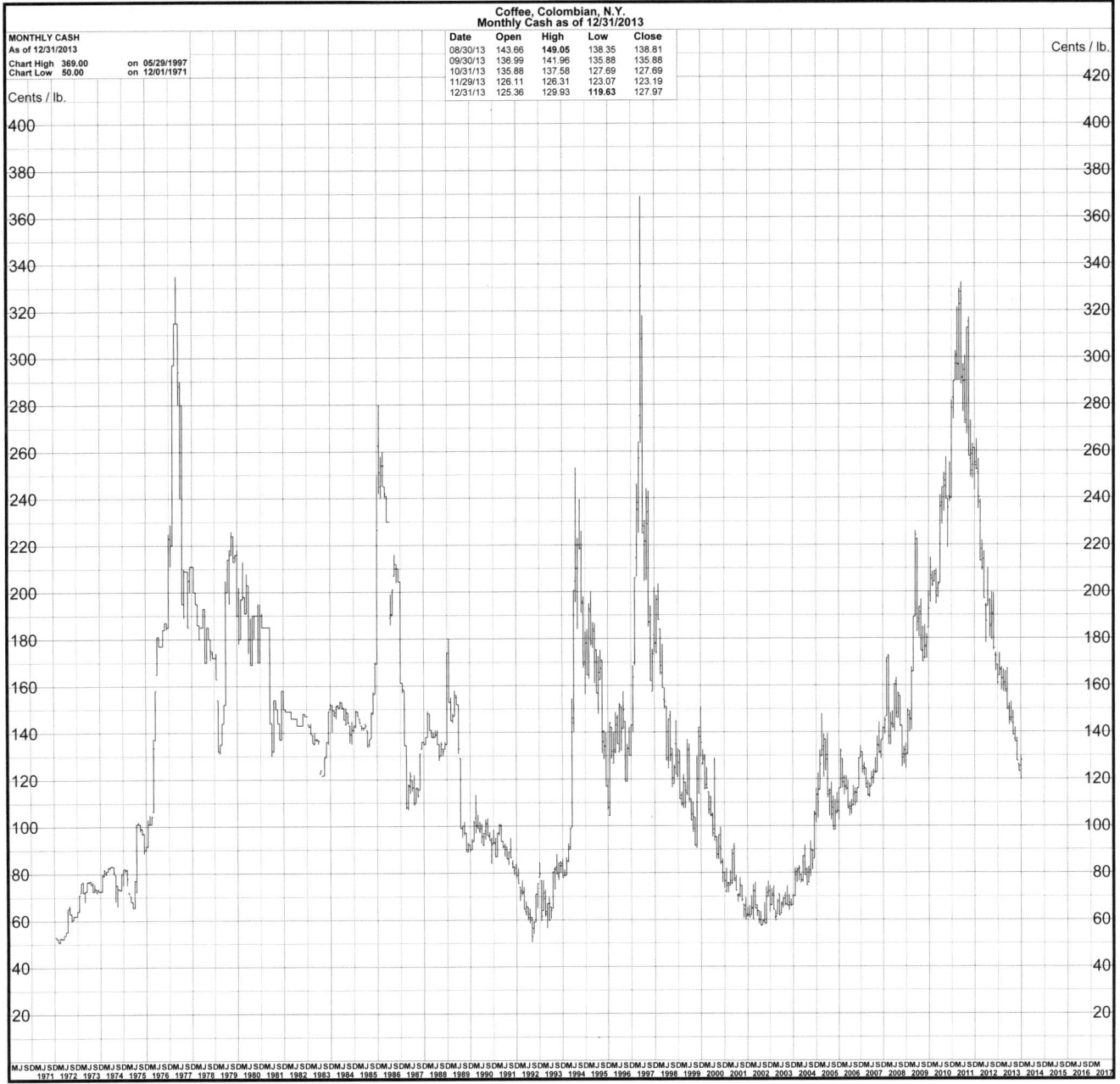

	Coffee, Colombian, N.Y. Monthly Cash as of 12/31/2013			
Date	Open	High	Low	Close
08/30/13	143.66	149.05	138.35	138.81
09/30/13	136.99	141.96	135.88	135.88
10/31/13	135.88	137.58	127.69	127.69
11/29/13	126.11	126.31	123.07	123.19
12/31/13	125.36	129.93	119.63	127.97

MONTHLY CASH
As of 12/31/2013
Chart High 369.00 on 05/29/1997
Chart Low 50.00 on 12/01/1971
Cents / lb.

Colombian Medellin, New York: to 12/1977; Colombian, New York: 01/1978 to date.

Annual High, Low and Settle of Coffee   In Cents per Pound

Year	High	Low	Settle	Year	High	Low	Settle	Year	High	Low	Settle
1972	66.50	50.75	64.00	1986	280.00	161.25	161.25	2000	132.50	73.50	76.50
1973	77.00	64.00	72.50	1987	161.25	107.00	135.00	2001	92.50	60.00	62.00
1974	83.50	66.00	82.00	1988	174.00	128.00	174.00	2002	76.50	57.50	66.25
1975	102.00	65.50	91.50	1989	180.00	89.00	90.00	2003	74.50	59.50	70.00
1976	225.00	91.50	223.00	1990	113.50	84.00	93.00	2004	116.00	70.00	113.25
1977	335.00	185.00	211.00	1991	101.00	78.00	79.00	2005	147.75	98.00	115.98
1978	211.00	170.00	172.00	1992	84.50	50.50	79.50	2006	134.12	104.15	131.32
1979	226.00	131.00	190.00	1993	88.00	56.50	78.00	2007	144.14	112.07	141.48
1980	213.00	169.00	190.00	1994	253.00	78.50	178.00	2008	172.75	124.35	130.55
1981	191.00	130.00	150.00	1995	200.00	107.00	108.00	2009	225.97	130.55	192.46
1982	150.00	143.00	147.00	1996	157.50	104.50	143.00	2010	281.54	194.51	278.19
1983	152.50	121.50	151.75	1997	369.00	140.00	178.00	2011	332.07	243.23	255.00
1984	153.50	135.05	143.00	1998	203.50	116.50	127.00	2012	265.05	160.38	161.02
1985	249.50	134.00	226.50	1999	151.00	90.75	135.50	2013	173.77	119.63	127.97

Colombian, NY.   Data continued from page 167.   *Source: U.S. Department of Agriculture (USDA)*

COFFEE

Source: ICE Futures U.S.

COFFEE 'C' - ICE
Weekly Nearest Futures as of 01/03/2014

Date	Open	High	Low	Close
12/06/13	109.80	110.50	105.40	105.80
12/13/13	106.30	114.50	105.50	114.50
12/20/13	115.35	116.70	113.10	115.30
12/27/13	115.00	118.40	114.05	116.35
01/03/14	116.35	117.45	110.20	116.35

Quarterly High, Low and Settle of Coffee 'C' Futures   In Cents per Pound

Quarter	High	Low	Settle	Quarter	High	Low	Settle	Quarter	High	Low	Settle
03/2005	137.00	95.10	126.40	03/2008	169.60	125.85	127.40	03/2011	294.70	226.50	264.15
06/2005	132.25	101.70	104.65	06/2008	154.05	126.20	150.90	06/2011	306.25	239.65	265.35
09/2005	108.50	84.45	93.45	09/2008	153.75	126.45	130.45	09/2011	291.75	228.50	228.90
12/2005	108.50	90.75	107.10	12/2008	131.90	101.60	112.05	12/2011	252.50	210.95	226.85
03/2006	125.90	102.80	107.00	03/2009	123.40	103.30	115.75	03/2012	238.50	174.45	182.45
06/2006	113.90	94.50	99.50	06/2009	142.90	110.80	117.30	06/2012	190.45	148.20	170.10
09/2006	109.50	93.50	107.65	09/2009	138.60	111.50	127.80	09/2012	190.85	157.10	173.50
12/2006	129.75	100.90	126.20	12/2009	149.20	125.90	135.95	12/2012	185.45	132.25	143.80
03/2007	125.90	107.45	109.25	03/2010	146.95	126.55	136.15	03/2013	157.90	132.05	137.15
06/2007	118.40	100.35	111.00	06/2010	175.00	128.60	164.20	06/2013	147.65	116.90	120.00
09/2007	135.00	106.90	128.65	09/2010	194.85	155.00	183.05	09/2013	132.15	111.05	113.70
12/2007	140.80	118.00	136.20	12/2010	242.25	171.60	240.50	12/2013	118.40	100.95	110.70

Coffee, Colombian, N.Y.
Weekly Cash as of 01/03/2014

Date	Open	High	Low	Close
12/06/13	125.36	125.36	119.89	119.89
12/13/13	120.09	124.63	119.63	124.63
12/20/13	128.52	129.93	128.29	128.72
12/27/13	129.27	129.62	128.17	129.62
01/03/14	127.97	131.75	126.80	131.75

WEEKLY CASH
As of 01/03/2014
Chart High 332.07 on 05/03/2011
Chart Low 59.50 on 03/28/2003

Colombian, New York.

Quarterly High, Low and Settle of Coffee   In Cents per Pound

Quarter	High	Low	Settle	Quarter	High	Low	Settle	Quarter	High	Low	Settle
03/2005	147.75	103.25	132.25	03/2008	172.75	134.60	138.02	03/2011	321.41	273.50	296.88
06/2005	139.50	112.00	113.25	06/2008	160.67	134.60	160.40	06/2011	332.07	276.58	289.62
09/2005	118.75	98.00	99.76	09/2008	163.29	142.21	142.75	09/2011	317.09	257.78	257.78
12/2005	115.98	98.11	115.98	12/2008	142.45	124.35	130.55	12/2011	273.01	243.23	255.00
03/2006	132.73	113.17	116.90	03/2009	167.73	130.55	165.76	03/2012	265.05	212.88	213.12
06/2006	121.30	104.15	107.03	06/2009	225.97	165.76	186.87	06/2012	221.85	178.06	187.33
09/2006	117.19	104.93	113.95	09/2009	196.54	170.07	170.07	09/2012	209.96	179.25	190.61
12/2006	134.12	109.78	131.32	12/2009	200.01	171.10	192.46	12/2012	199.46	160.38	161.02
03/2007	131.32	115.95	117.84	03/2010	214.53	195.23	208.62	03/2013	173.77	157.16	161.04
06/2007	123.03	112.07	120.06	06/2010	241.18	194.51	236.25	06/2013	167.35	142.84	145.92
09/2007	138.13	117.69	134.45	09/2010	257.42	228.65	240.35	09/2013	153.00	135.88	135.88
12/2007	144.14	128.58	141.48	12/2010	281.54	218.65	278.19	12/2013	137.58	119.63	127.97

Colombian, NY.   *Source: U.S. Department of Agriculture (USDA)*

COFFEE, ROBUSTA

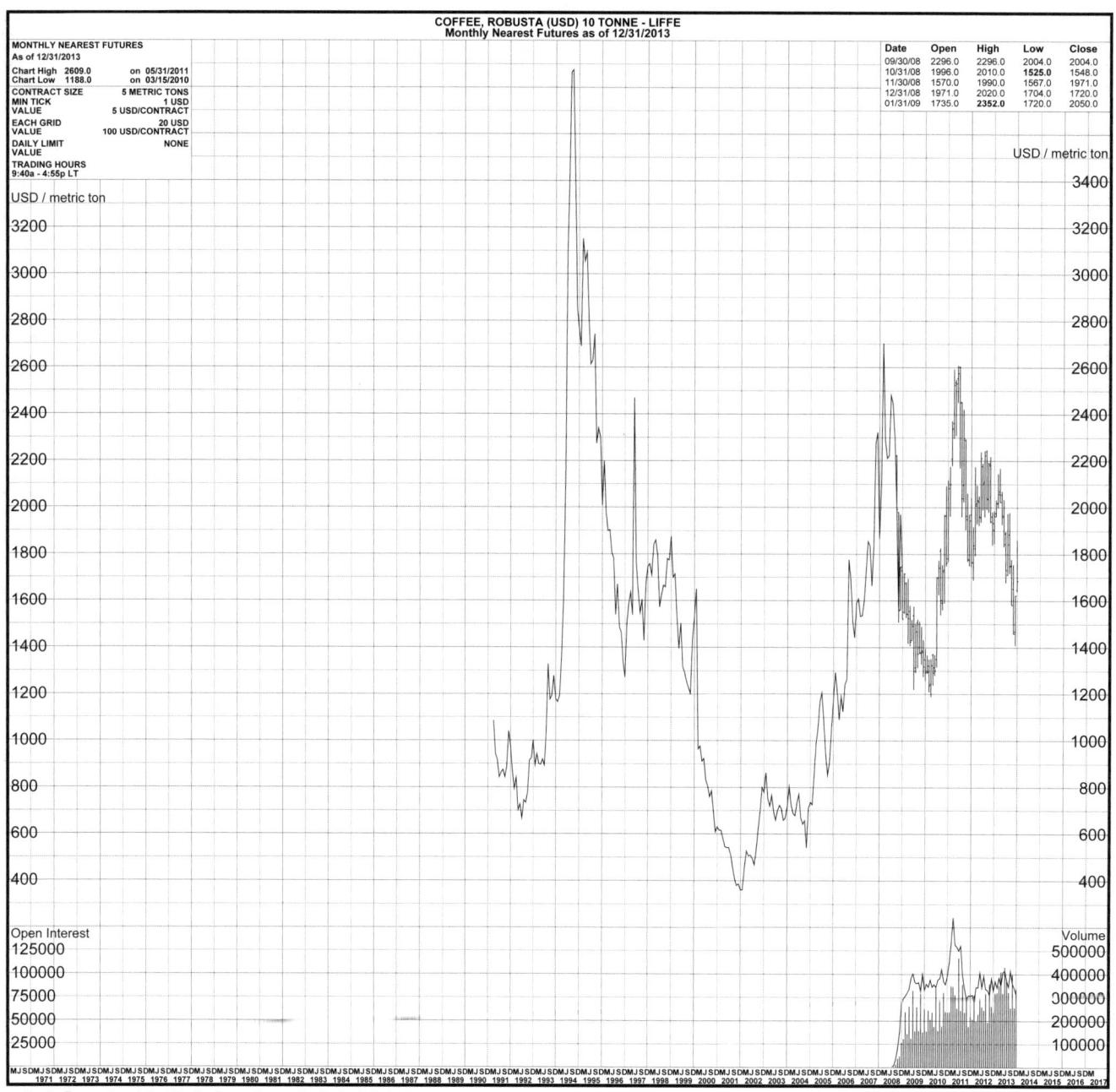

COFFEE, ROBUSTA (USD) 10 TONNE - LIFFE
Monthly Nearest Futures as of 12/31/2013

Date	Open	High	Low	Close
09/30/08	2296.0	2296.0	2004.0	2004.0
10/31/08	1996.0	2010.0	1525.0	1548.0
11/30/08	1570.0	1990.0	1567.0	1971.0
12/31/08	1971.0	2020.0	1704.0	1720.0
01/31/09	1735.0	2352.0	1720.0	2050.0

MONTHLY NEAREST FUTURES
As of 12/31/2013

Chart High 2609.0 on 05/31/2011
Chart Low 1188.0 on 03/15/2010
CONTRACT SIZE 5 METRIC TONS
MIN TICK 1 USD
VALUE 5 USD/CONTRACT
EACH GRID 20 USD
VALUE 100 USD/CONTRACT
DAILY LIMIT NONE
VALUE
TRADING HOURS
9:40a - 4:55p LT

Nearby Futures through Last Trading Day.   Futures data begins 03/01/1991; ends 01/30/2009.   Futures data begins 08/01/2008.

Annual High, Low and Settle of Coffee, Robusta Futures   In Dollars per Metric Ton

Year	High	Low	Settle	Year	High	Low	Settle	Year	High	Low	Settle
1986	----	----	----	2000	1,751	543	630	2000	----	----	----
1987	----	----	----	2001	685	345	361	2001	----	----	----
1988	----	----	----	2002	830	350	780	2002	----	----	----
1989	----	----	----	2003	896	645	720	2003	----	----	----
1990	----	----	----	2004	879	530	737	2004	----	----	----
1991	1,140	830	977	2005	1,306	689	1,171	2005	----	----	----
1992	1,060	653	1,001	2006	2,063	1,068	1,590	2006	----	----	----
1993	1,400	809	1,178	2007	2,495	1,444	1,866	2007	----	----	----
1994	4,287	1,145	2,765	2008	2,805	1,525	1,720	2008	2,340	1,508	1,522
1995	3,385	1,964	2,008	2009	2,352	1,720	2,050	2009	1,718	1,219	1,294
1996	2,200	1,250	1,272	2010	----	----	----	2010	2,116	1,188	2,082
1997	2,580	1,225	1,747	2011	----	----	----	2011	2,609	1,747	1,766
1998	2,280	1,510	1,875	2012	----	----	----	2012	2,248	1,688	1,963
1999	1,885	1,160	1,535	2013	----	----	----	2013	2,168	1,409	1,685

Futures data begins 03/01/1991; ends 01/30/2009.   Futures data begins 08/01/2008.   *Source: Euronext LIFFE*

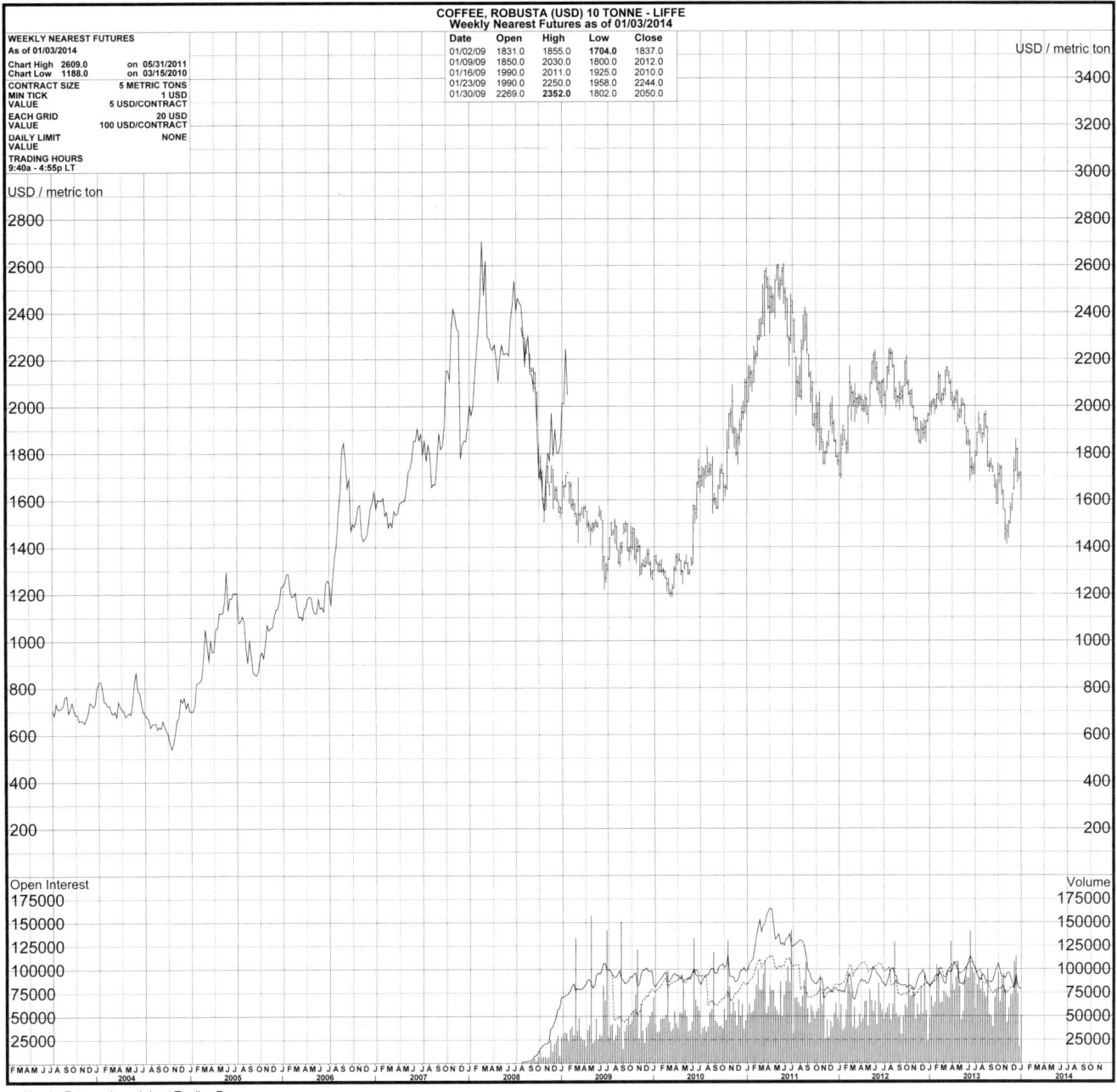

COFFEE, ROBUSTA (USD) 10 TONNE - LIFFE
Weekly Nearest Futures as of 01/03/2014

Date	Open	High	Low	Close
01/02/09	1831.0	1855.0	**1704.0**	1837.0
01/09/09	1850.0	2030.0	1800.0	2012.0
01/16/09	1990.0	2011.0	1925.0	2010.0
01/23/09	1990.0	2250.0	1958.0	2244.0
01/30/09	2269.0	**2352.0**	1802.0	2050.0

WEEKLY NEAREST FUTURES
As of 01/03/2014
Chart High 2609.0 on 05/31/2011
Chart Low 1188.0 on 03/15/2010
CONTRACT SIZE 5 METRIC TONS
MIN TICK 1 USD
VALUE 5 USD/CONTRACT
EACH GRID 20 USD
VALUE 100 USD/CONTRACT
DAILY LIMIT NONE
VALUE
TRADING HOURS
9:40a - 4:55p LT

Nearby Futures through Last Trading Day.

Quarterly High, Low and Settle of Coffee, Robusta Futures   In Dollars per Metric Ton

Quarter	High	Low	Settle	Quarter	High	Low	Settle	Quarter	High	Low	Settle
03/2007	1,680	1,444	1,536	03/2008	----	----	----	03/2011	2,593	1,962	2,525
06/2007	1,928	1,510	1,855	06/2008	----	----	----	06/2011	2,609	2,169	2,453
09/2007	1,985	1,640	1,831	09/2008	2,340	1,992	1,992	09/2011	2,454	1,905	1,964
12/2007	2,495	1,711	1,866	12/2008	1,980	1,508	1,522	12/2011	2,061	1,747	1,766
03/2008	2,805	1,860	2,288	03/2009	1,718	1,417	1,524	03/2012	2,174	1,688	2,031
06/2008	2,496	2,080	2,480	06/2009	1,579	1,219	1,299	06/2012	2,239	1,923	2,103
09/2008	2,599	2,004	2,004	09/2009	1,520	1,292	1,375	09/2012	2,248	1,960	2,188
12/2008	2,020	1,525	1,720	12/2009	1,489	1,258	1,294	12/2012	2,218	1,839	1,963
01/2009	2,352	1,720	2,050	03/2010	1,367	1,188	1,324	03/2013	2,168	1,960	2,023
06/2009	----	----	----	06/2010	1,702	1,239	1,699	06/2013	2,069	1,677	1,731
09/2009	----	----	----	09/2010	1,827	1,539	1,726	09/2013	1,979	1,582	1,582
12/2009	----	----	----	12/2010	2,116	1,590	2,082	12/2013	1,860	1,409	1,685

Futures data ends 01/30/2009.   Futures data begins 08/01/2008.   *Source: Euronext LIFFE*

ORANGE JUICE

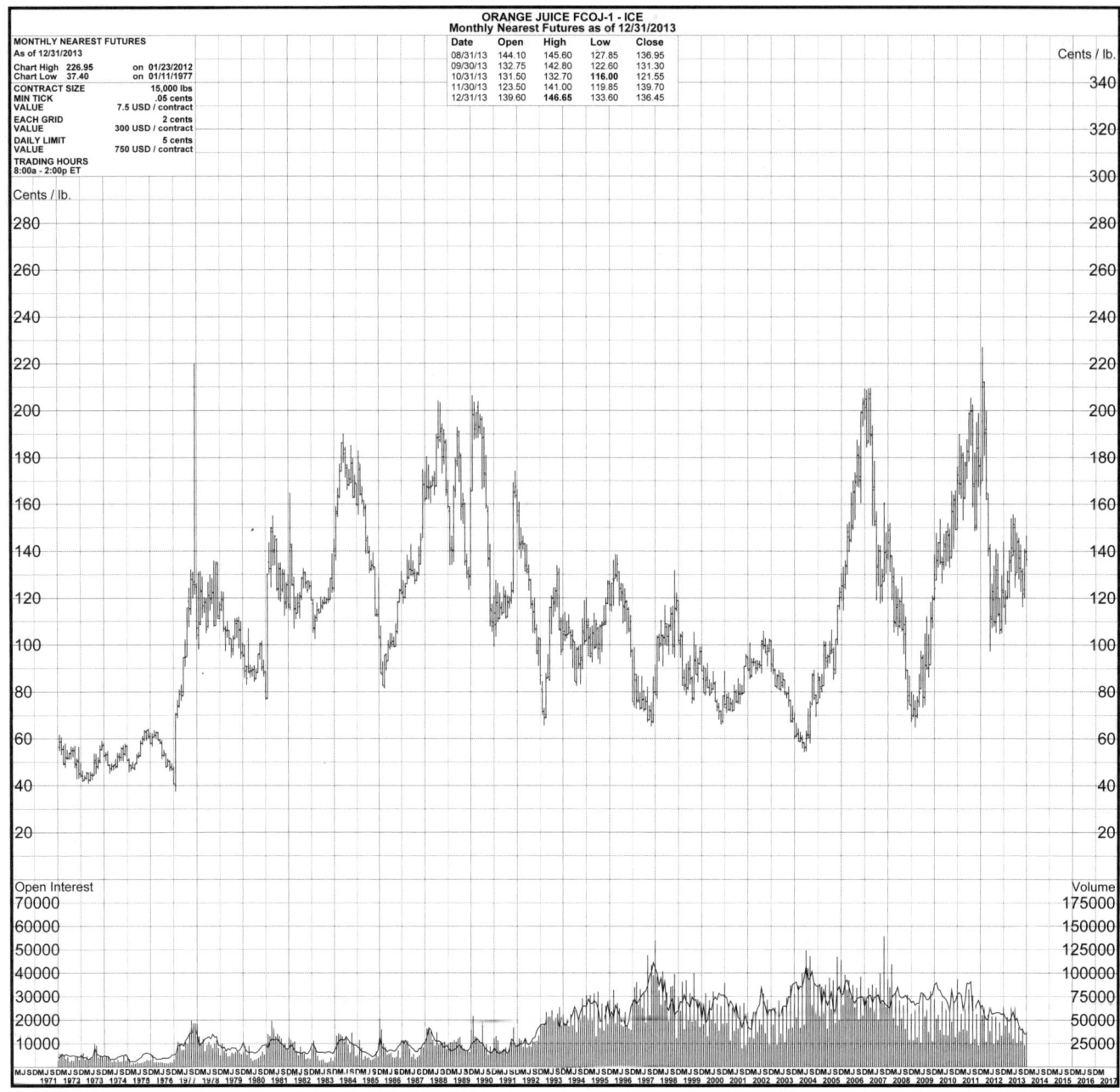

Nearby Futures through Last Trading Day. Futures: 02/01/1967 to date.

Annual High, Low and Settle of Orange Juice Futures   In Cents per Pound

Year	High	Low	Settle	Year	High	Low	Settle	Year	High	Low	Settle
1972	61.80	42.75	44.35	1986	131.50	81.45	122.00	2000	92.25	66.15	74.60
1973	59.10	40.85	52.60	1987	175.00	117.50	161.95	2001	96.20	70.80	89.10
1974	57.85	45.10	50.75	1988	204.25	158.00	158.95	2002	106.00	85.40	91.75
1975	64.35	45.60	58.00	1989	193.10	123.30	165.65	2003	98.50	60.05	60.75
1976	63.65	40.50	40.80	1990	206.50	99.00	113.50	2004	89.40	54.20	86.10
1977	220.00	37.40	107.10	1991	174.25	103.50	155.15	2005	130.80	77.00	125.20
1978	136.00	98.00	115.05	1992	161.00	83.00	87.00	2006	209.40	114.50	201.25
1979	122.95	93.95	95.75	1993	134.00	65.45	104.40	2007	209.50	117.50	143.60
1980	107.00	76.75	77.40	1994	119.90	82.50	107.30	2008	152.00	67.10	68.55
1981	155.10	76.90	117.20	1995	127.60	91.75	117.00	2009	138.50	64.60	124.00
1982	164.85	106.75	118.90	1996	138.75	75.60	75.65	2010	175.95	126.05	172.35
1983	145.25	102.50	140.90	1997	99.00	65.00	80.00	2011	205.50	148.50	169.00
1984	190.00	136.00	159.95	1998	131.95	77.00	101.80	2012	226.95	97.10	116.05
1985	183.00	102.60	103.50	1999	105.75	74.80	88.95	2013	155.75	108.60	136.45

Futures begin trading 02/01/1967.   *Source: ICE Futures U.S.*

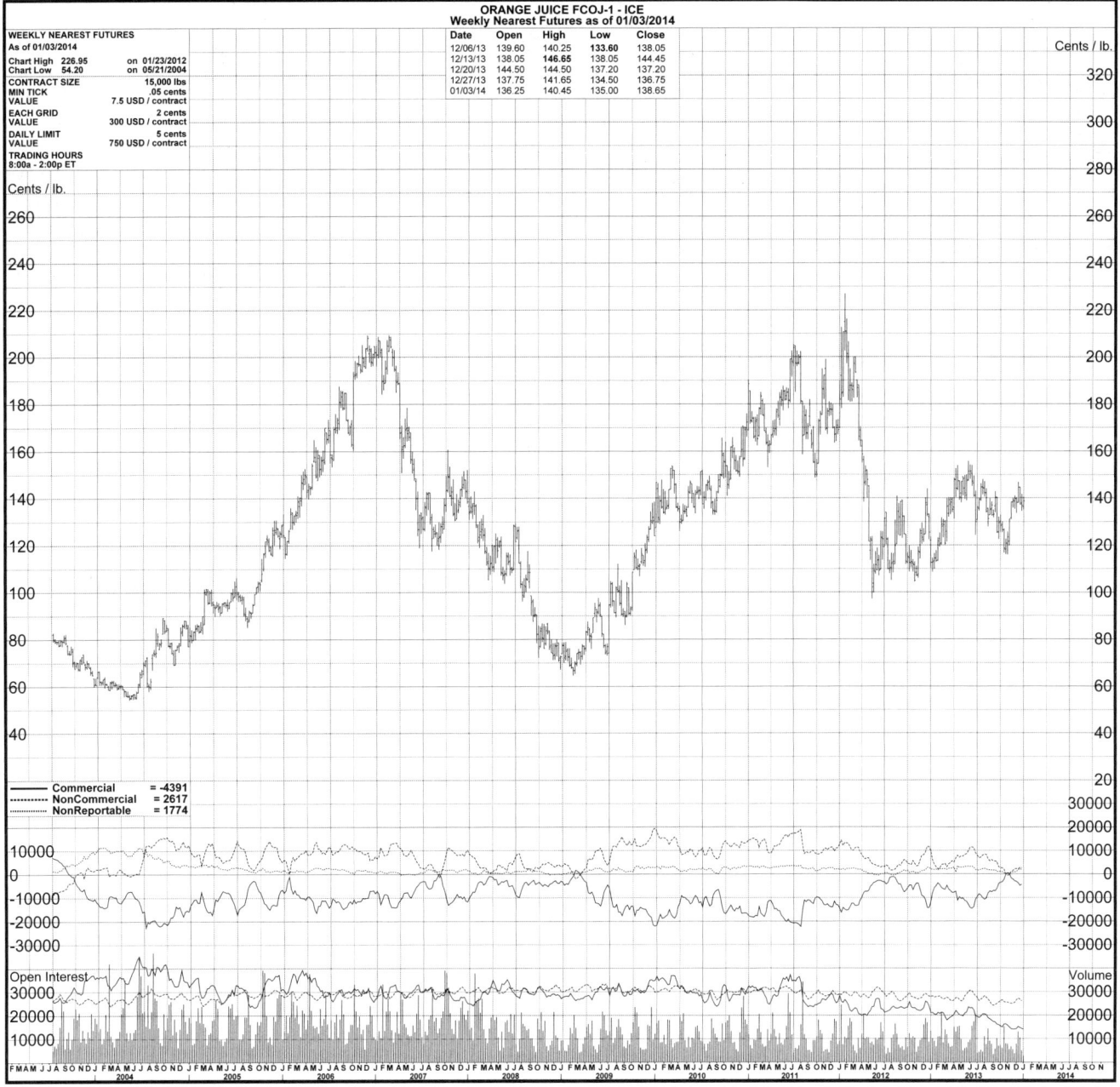

ORANGE JUICE FCOJ-1 - ICE
Weekly Nearest Futures as of 01/03/2014

Date	Open	High	Low	Close
12/06/13	139.60	140.25	133.60	138.05
12/13/13	138.05	146.65	138.05	144.45
12/20/13	144.50	144.50	137.20	137.20
12/27/13	137.75	141.65	134.50	136.75
01/03/14	136.25	140.45	135.00	138.65

WEEKLY NEAREST FUTURES
As of 01/03/2014

Chart High 226.95 on 01/23/2012
Chart Low 54.20 on 05/21/2004
CONTRACT SIZE 15,000 lbs
MIN TICK .05 cents
VALUE 7.5 USD / contract
EACH GRID 2 cents
VALUE 300 USD / contract
DAILY LIMIT 5 cents
VALUE 750 USD / contract
TRADING HOURS
8:00a - 2:00p ET

Commercial = -4391
NonCommercial = 2617
NonReportable = 1774

Nearby Futures through Last Trading Day.

Quarterly High, Low and Settle of Orange Juice Futures   In Cents per Pound

Quarter	High	Low	Settle	Quarter	High	Low	Settle	Quarter	High	Low	Settle
03/2005	101.70	77.00	99.55	03/2008	152.00	105.25	109.65	03/2011	190.00	153.10	162.80
06/2005	101.70	89.85	96.35	06/2008	125.10	103.75	118.35	06/2011	199.10	162.20	198.60
09/2005	106.50	85.10	102.30	09/2008	129.30	85.20	89.20	09/2011	205.50	148.50	150.00
12/2005	130.80	100.20	125.20	12/2008	89.40	67.10	68.55	12/2011	199.00	148.85	169.00
03/2006	151.50	114.50	148.15	03/2009	78.90	64.60	76.30	03/2012	226.95	161.75	164.50
06/2006	170.00	139.70	165.05	06/2009	97.55	73.10	77.50	06/2012	164.60	97.10	122.65
09/2006	187.60	153.25	170.30	09/2009	112.15	74.05	91.50	09/2012	140.95	105.15	113.15
12/2006	209.40	160.35	201.25	12/2009	138.50	91.50	124.00	12/2012	144.00	104.50	116.05
03/2007	209.50	184.20	189.25	03/2010	153.65	127.50	135.30	03/2013	140.30	108.60	135.15
06/2007	193.60	118.85	133.00	06/2010	148.50	126.05	148.25	06/2013	155.75	124.30	129.90
09/2007	142.80	117.50	129.10	09/2010	165.70	132.90	156.95	09/2013	147.95	122.60	131.30
12/2007	160.80	127.00	143.60	12/2010	175.95	140.90	172.35	12/2013	146.65	116.00	136.45

Source: ICE Futures U.S.

SUGAR

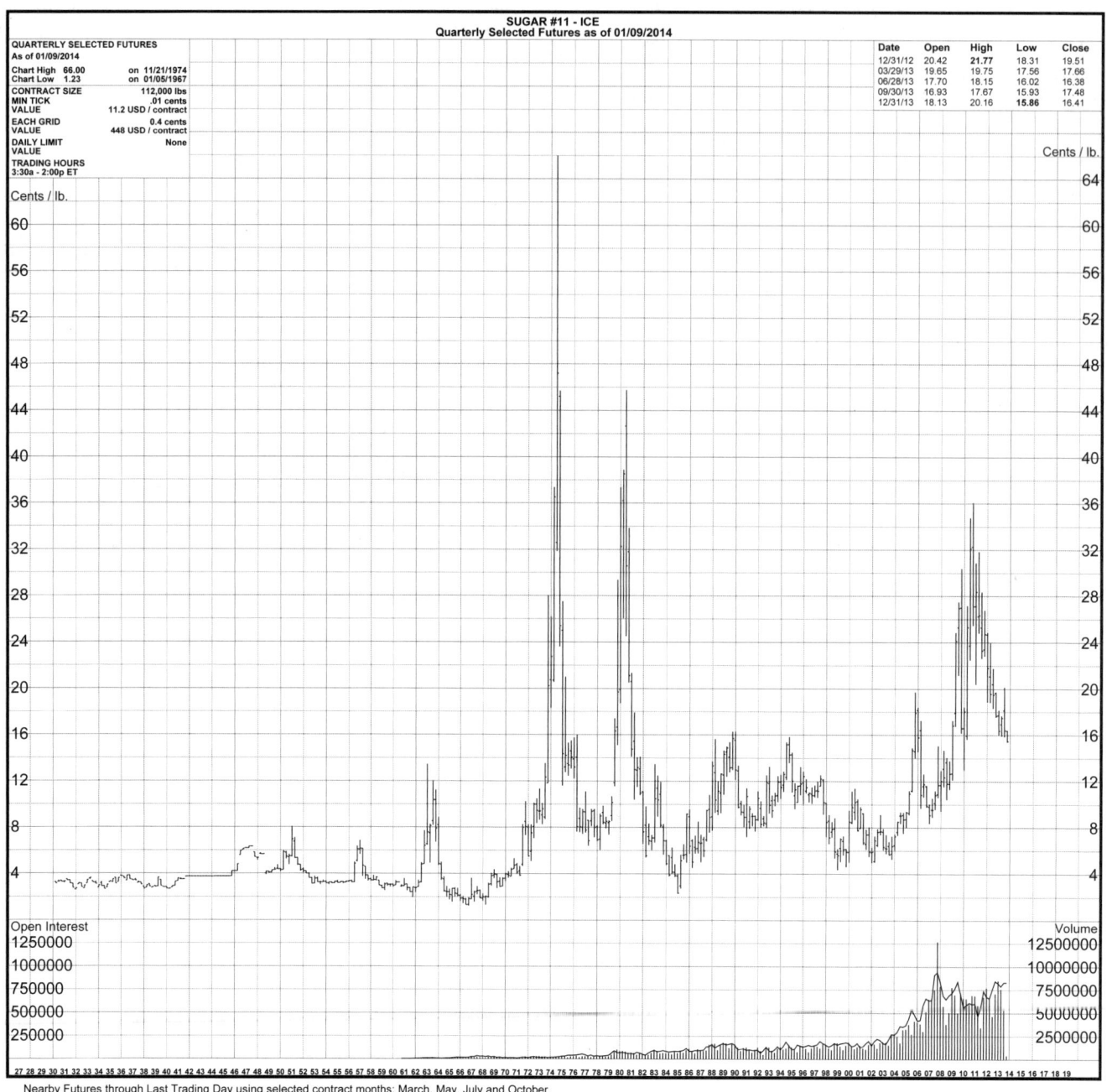

SUGAR #11 - ICE
Quarterly Selected Futures as of 01/09/2014

QUARTERLY SELECTED FUTURES
As of 01/09/2014

Chart High	66.00	on 11/21/1974
Chart Low	1.23	on 01/05/1967
CONTRACT SIZE	112,000 lbs	
MIN TICK	.01 cents	
VALUE	11.2 USD / contract	
EACH GRID	0.4 cents	
VALUE	448 USD / contract	
DAILY LIMIT VALUE	None	
TRADING HOURS	3:30a - 2:00p ET	

Date	Open	High	Low	Close
12/31/12	20.42	21.77	18.31	19.51
03/29/13	19.65	19.75	17.56	17.66
06/28/13	17.70	18.15	16.02	16.38
09/30/13	16.93	17.67	15.93	17.48
12/31/13	18.13	20.16	15.86	16.41

Nearby Futures through Last Trading Day using selected contract months: March, May, July and October.

Annual High, Low and Settle of Sugar #11 Futures   In Cents per Pound

Year	High	Low	Settle	Year	High	Low	Settle	Year	High	Low	Settle
1930	3.70	3.14	3.29	1944	3.75	3.74	3.75	1958	3.85	3.35	3.67
1931	3.49	3.14	3.14	1945	3.75	3.75	3.75	1959	3.40	2.55	3.05
1932	3.16	2.59	2.83	1946	5.94	3.76	5.94	1960	3.40	2.85	3.25
1933	3.62	2.72	3.23	1947	6.32	6.02	6.32	1961	3.58	2.41	2.41
1934	3.32	2.67	2.67	1948	5.82	5.14	5.67	1962	4.95	1.95	4.80
1935	3.62	2.79	3.13	1949	4.50	3.90	4.33	1963	13.45	4.83	10.37
1936	3.82	3.27	3.82	1950	5.95	4.15	5.45	1964	11.24	2.42	2.50
1937	3.83	3.18	3.24	1951	8.05	4.70	4.77	1965	2.91	1.56	2.30
1938	3.21	2.69	2.88	1952	4.75	3.62	3.62	1966	2.76	1.32	1.32
1939	3.65	2.77	2.93	1953	3.77	3.05	3.25	1967	3.63	1.23	2.52
1940	2.91	2.64	2.91	1954	3.43	3.05	3.17	1968	3.20	1.31	3.08
1941	3.60	2.93	3.50	1955	3.41	3.13	3.23	1969	4.36	2.74	2.88
1942	3.74	3.72	3.74	1956	5.00	3.22	4.85	1970	4.48	2.92	4.36
1943	3.74	3.74	3.74	1957	6.85	3.50	3.85	1971	8.25	3.79	7.99

Futures data begins 01/04/1961.   Contract months: March, May, July, October.   Data continued on page 178.   *Source: ICE Futures U.S.*

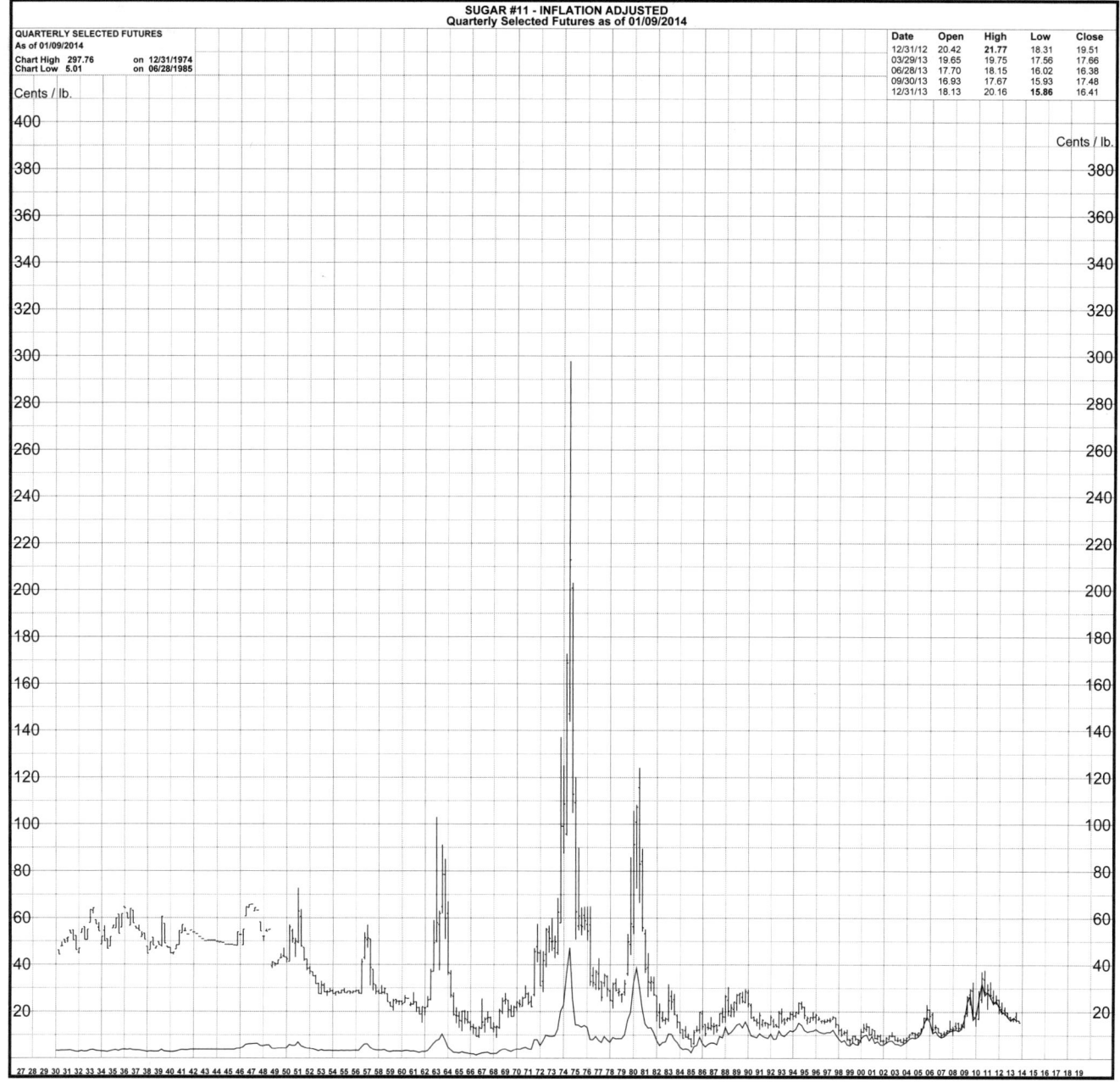

SUGAR #11 - INFLATION ADJUSTED
Quarterly Selected Futures as of 01/09/2014

QUARTERLY SELECTED FUTURES
As of 01/09/2014

Chart High 297.76 on 12/31/1974
Chart Low 5.01 on 06/28/1985

Cents / lb.

Date	Open	High	Low	Close
12/31/12	20.42	21.77	18.31	19.51
03/29/13	19.65	19.75	17.56	17.66
06/28/13	17.70	18.15	16.02	16.38
09/30/13	16.93	17.67	15.93	17.48
12/31/13	18.13	20.16	15.86	16.41

Nearby Futures through Last Trading Day using selected contract months: March, May, July and October.

Annual High, Low and Settle of Sugar   In Cents per Pound

Year	High	Low	Settle	Year	High	Low	Settle	Year	High	Low	Settle
1930	3.70	3.14	3.29	1944	3.75	3.74	3.75	1958	3.85	3.35	3.67
1931	3.49	3.14	3.14	1945	3.75	3.75	3.75	1959	3.40	2.55	3.05
1932	3.16	2.59	2.83	1946	5.94	3.76	5.94	1960	3.40	2.85	3.25
1933	3.62	2.72	3.23	1947	6.32	6.02	6.32	1961	3.42	2.43	2.43
1934	3.32	2.67	2.67	1948	5.82	5.14	5.67	1962	4.75	2.05	4.75
1935	3.62	2.79	3.13	1949	4.50	3.90	4.33	1963	12.60	4.80	10.25
1936	3.82	3.27	3.82	1950	5.95	4.15	5.45	1964	11.18	2.53	2.53
1937	3.83	3.18	3.24	1951	8.05	4.70	4.77	1965	2.91	1.60	2.10
1938	3.21	2.69	2.88	1952	4.75	3.62	3.62	1966	2.60	1.34	1.34
1939	3.65	2.77	2.93	1953	3.77	3.05	3.25	1967	3.10	1.23	2.30
1940	2.91	2.64	2.91	1954	3.43	3.05	3.17	1968	2.95	1.37	2.95
1941	3.60	2.93	3.50	1955	3.41	3.13	3.23	1969	4.08	2.70	2.80
1942	3.74	3.72	3.74	1956	5.00	3.22	4.85	1970	4.25	2.80	4.25
1943	3.74	3.74	3.74	1957	6.85	3.50	3.85	1971	7.50	3.90	7.50

World Raw #11, NY.   Data continued on page 179.   Source: ICE Futures U.S.

SUGAR

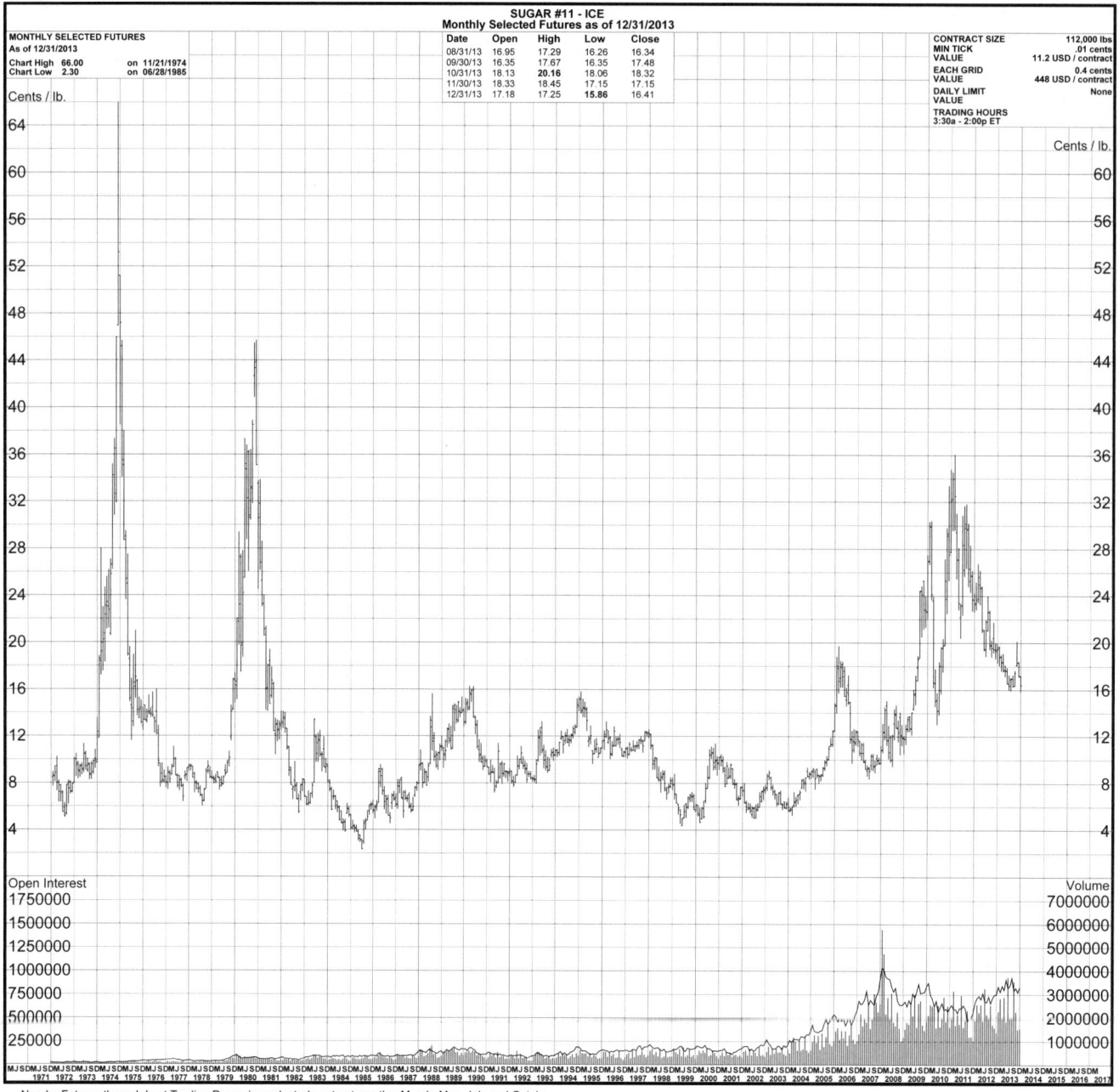

SUGAR #11 - ICE
Monthly Selected Futures as of 12/31/2013

MONTHLY SELECTED FUTURES
As of 12/31/2013
Chart High 66.00   on 11/21/1974
Chart Low 2.30   on 06/28/1985

Date	Open	High	Low	Close
08/31/13	16.95	17.29	16.26	16.34
09/30/13	16.35	17.67	16.35	17.48
10/31/13	18.13	20.16	18.06	18.32
11/30/13	18.33	18.45	17.15	17.15
12/31/13	17.18	17.25	15.86	16.41

CONTRACT SIZE 112,000 lbs
MIN TICK .01 cents
VALUE 11.2 USD / contract
EACH GRID 0.4 cents
VALUE 448 USD / contract
DAILY LIMIT VALUE None
TRADING HOURS 3:30a - 2:00p ET

Nearby Futures through Last Trading Day using selected contract months: March, May, July and October.

Annual High, Low and Settle of Sugar #11 Futures   In Cents per Pound

Year	High	Low	Settle	Year	High	Low	Settle	Year	High	Low	Settle
1972	10.25	5.08	10.00	1986	9.58	4.52	6.16	2000	11.40	4.62	10.20
1973	13.53	8.25	12.33	1987	9.55	5.00	9.49	2001	10.49	6.11	7.39
1974	66.00	11.83	47.20	1988	15.64	7.56	11.15	2002	8.05	4.97	7.61
1975	45.70	11.60	13.37	1989	15.38	9.26	13.16	2003	9.13	5.66	5.67
1976	16.00	7.58	8.03	1990	16.28	9.08	9.37	2004	9.37	5.27	9.04
1977	11.10	6.40	9.40	1991	11.40	7.18	9.00	2005	14.89	7.50	14.68
1978	9.88	6.05	8.43	1992	11.14	7.66	8.41	2006	19.73	9.70	11.75
1979	17.40	7.37	16.31	1993	13.26	7.96	10.77	2007	11.66	8.36	10.82
1980	45.75	15.10	30.58	1994	15.38	10.23	15.17	2008	15.07	9.44	11.81
1981	33.85	10.41	13.18	1995	15.83	9.62	11.60	2009	27.49	11.32	26.95
1982	14.10	5.40	6.85	1996	13.25	10.05	11.00	2010	34.77	13.00	32.12
1983	13.47	6.05	8.18	1997	12.55	10.10	12.22	2011	36.08	20.40	23.30
1984	8.29	3.79	4.16	1998	12.22	6.60	7.86	2012	26.78	18.31	19.51
1985	6.56	2.30	5.62	1999	8.82	4.36	6.12	2013	20.16	15.86	16.41

Contract months: March, May, July, October.   Data continued fom page 176.   *Source: ICE Futures U.S.*

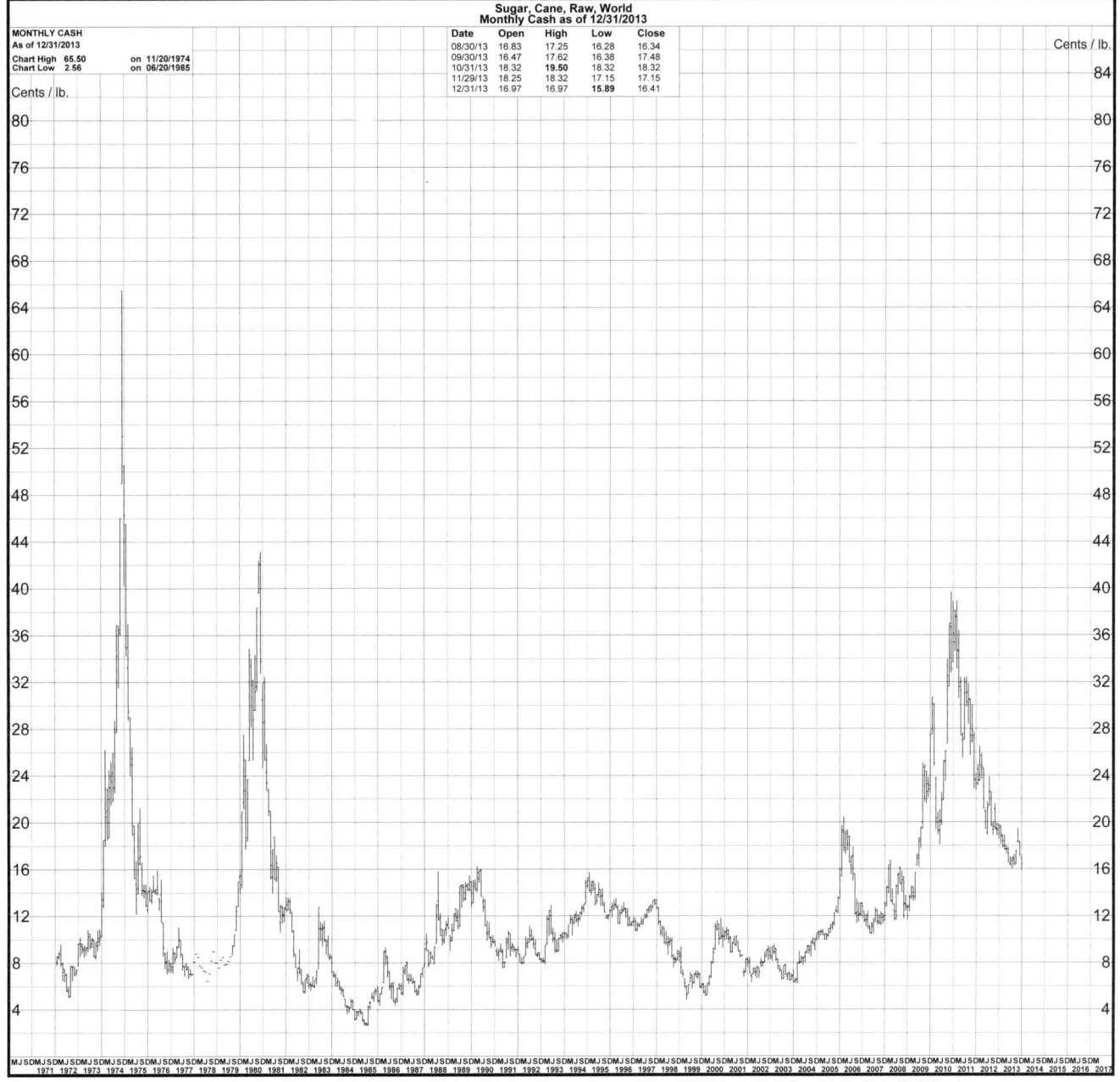

	Sugar, Cane, Raw, World Monthly Cash as of 12/31/2013				
Date	Open	High	Low	Close	
08/30/13	16.83	17.25	16.28	16.34	
09/30/13	16.47	17.62	16.38	17.48	
10/31/13	18.32	19.50	18.32	18.32	
11/29/13	18.25	18.32	17.15	17.15	
12/31/13	16.97	16.97	15.89	16.41	

MONTHLY CASH
As of 12/31/2013

Chart High 65.50 on 11/20/1974
Chart Low 2.56 on 06/20/1985

World Raw #8, New York: to 12/1970; World Raw #11, New York: 01/1971 to 10/1977; World Raw #11, New York: 11/1977 to 07/1979 (avg); World Raw #11, New York: 08/1979 to date.

Annual High, Low and Settle of Sugar   In Cents per Pound

Year	High	Low	Settle	Year	High	Low	Settle	Year	High	Low	Settle
1972	9.65	5.10	9.65	1986	9.31	4.34	5.43	2000	11.84	5.17	10.64
1973	14.00	8.35	13.40	1987	9.21	5.19	9.21	2001	10.99	6.76	7.96
1974	65.50	12.70	46.30	1988	15.83	7.61	10.93	2002	9.43	6.30	8.42
1975	45.50	12.15	14.15	1989	15.49	9.03	13.14	2003	9.60	6.33	6.35
1976	15.90	7.05	7.45	1990	16.25	9.24	9.42	2004	10.49	6.22	10.45
1977	11.75	6.69	11.75	1991	10.72	7.58	9.04	2005	16.03	9.89	15.98
1978	15.17	12.63	14.25	1992	11.16	7.85	8.23	2006	20.46	11.36	12.80
1979	15.91	8.69	15.47	1993	12.93	7.85	10.52	2007	13.22	10.41	13.02
1980	43.13	14.38	28.55	1994	15.29	10.04	15.02	2008	16.70	11.54	12.75
1981	32.43	10.56	12.96	1995	15.74	11.66	12.48	2009	27.76	12.36	27.45
1982	13.60	5.37	6.20	1996	13.53	11.04	11.82	2010	39.65	18.07	36.15
1983	12.75	5.64	7.23	1997	13.46	10.66	12.70	2011	38.91	22.75	23.30
1984	7.25	3.08	3.16	1998	12.70	7.56	8.54	2012	26.50	18.54	19.51
1985	5.90	2.56	4.75	1999	9.33	4.79	6.13	2013	19.69	15.89	16.41

World Raw #11, NY.   Data continued fom page 177.   *Source: U.S. Department of Agriculture (USDA)*

SUGAR

SUGAR #11 - ICE
Weekly Selected Futures as of 01/03/2014

Date	Open	High	Low	Close
12/06/13	17.18	17.25	16.55	16.59
12/13/13	16.55	16.84	16.22	16.27
12/20/13	16.32	16.48	15.86	16.45
12/27/13	16.48	16.49	16.20	16.43
01/03/14	16.40	16.58	16.06	16.08

WEEKLY SELECTED FUTURES
As of 01/03/2014

Chart High 36.08	on 02/02/2011
Chart Low 5.27	on 02/12/2004
CONTRACT SIZE	112,000 lbs
MIN TICK	.01 cents
VALUE	11.2 USD / contract
EACH GRID	0.2 cents
VALUE	224 USD / contract
DAILY LIMIT VALUE	None
TRADING HOURS	
3:30a - 2:00p ET	

Commercial = -28659
NonCommercial = 33967
NonReportable = -5308

Nearby Futures through Last Trading Day using selected contract months: March, May, July and October.

Quarterly High, Low and Settle of Sugar #11 Futures   In Cents per Pound

Quarter	High	Low	Settle	Quarter	High	Low	Settle	Quarter	High	Low	Settle
03/2005	9.33	7.50	8.70	03/2008	15.07	10.62	11.69	03/2011	36.08	25.47	27.11
06/2005	9.42	8.02	9.34	06/2008	12.94	9.44	12.04	06/2011	30.88	20.40	28.36
09/2005	11.20	9.10	10.95	09/2008	14.69	11.55	12.36	09/2011	31.85	24.80	26.34
12/2005	14.89	11.12	14.68	12/2008	14.07	10.44	11.81	12/2011	28.35	22.62	23.30
03/2006	19.73	14.00	17.90	03/2009	13.77	11.32	12.67	03/2012	26.78	22.82	24.71
06/2006	18.39	14.57	15.79	06/2009	17.25	12.13	16.81	06/2012	24.86	18.86	21.81
09/2006	17.25	9.70	10.85	09/2009	24.85	16.75	24.12	09/2012	24.00	18.81	19.58
12/2006	12.65	10.66	11.75	12/2009	27.49	21.18	26.95	12/2012	21.77	18.31	19.51
03/2007	11.66	9.79	9.88	03/2010	30.40	16.17	16.59	03/2013	19.75	17.56	17.66
06/2007	10.06	8.36	9.07	06/2010	18.40	13.00	18.03	06/2013	18.15	16.02	16.38
09/2007	10.56	8.90	9.56	09/2010	27.17	15.64	25.30	09/2013	17.67	15.93	17.48
12/2007	11.19	9.59	10.82	12/2010	34.77	22.49	32.12	12/2013	20.16	15.86	16.41

Contract months: March, May, July, October.   *Source: ICE Futures U.S.*

Sugar, Cane, Raw, World
Weekly Cash as of 01/03/2014

Date	Open	High	Low	Close
12/06/13	16.97	**16.97**	16.59	16.59
12/13/13	16.55	16.62	16.27	16.27
12/20/13	16.27	16.45	**15.89**	16.45
12/27/13	16.23	16.43	16.21	16.43
01/03/14	16.38	16.41	16.08	16.08

WEEKLY CASH
As of 01/03/2014

Chart High 39.65   on 11/09/2010
Chart Low   6.22   on 02/09/2004

Cents / lb.

World Raw #11, New York.

Quarterly High, Low and Settle of Sugar   In Cents per Pound

Quarter	High	Low	Settle	Quarter	High	Low	Settle	Quarter	High	Low	Settle
03/2005	10.86	9.98	10.55	03/2008	16.70	12.83	13.23	03/2011	38.91	30.56	31.58
06/2005	10.88	9.89	10.88	06/2008	14.68	11.54	14.51	06/2011	32.38	25.47	31.05
09/2005	12.26	10.55	12.26	09/2008	16.13	13.76	15.05	09/2011	32.41	25.69	27.40
12/2005	16.03	12.23	15.98	12/2008	15.32	11.63	12.75	12/2011	30.04	22.75	23.30
03/2006	20.46	15.39	19.02	03/2009	14.51	12.36	13.52	03/2012	26.50	23.13	24.71
06/2006	19.28	15.52	17.05	06/2009	18.67	13.34	18.35	06/2012	24.58	18.90	21.21
09/2006	17.91	11.36	12.31	09/2009	25.02	17.73	24.85	09/2012	23.92	18.87	19.58
12/2006	13.14	11.46	12.80	12/2009	27.76	21.62	27.45	12/2012	21.60	18.54	19.51
03/2007	12.44	10.89	11.03	03/2010	30.64	19.36	20.34	03/2013	19.69	17.66	17.66
06/2007	11.77	10.41	11.73	06/2010	22.55	18.07	21.88	06/2013	18.03	16.21	16.38
09/2007	12.72	11.23	11.83	09/2010	33.93	21.94	32.51	09/2013	17.62	16.00	17.48
12/2007	13.22	11.19	13.02	12/2010	39.65	31.62	36.15	12/2013	19.50	15.89	16.41

World Raw #11, NY.   *Source: U.S. Department of Agriculture (USDA)*

SUGAR, WHITE

SUGAR, WHITE #5 - LIFFE
Monthly Selected Futures as of 12/31/2013

Date	Open	High	Low	Close
08/31/13	490.60	508.20	472.90	477.90
09/30/13	477.30	500.20	474.90	486.10
10/31/13	485.40	529.40	482.10	483.30
11/30/13	483.50	491.50	445.70	464.00
12/31/13	459.40	462.00	432.10	449.00

MONTHLY SELECTED FUTURES
As of 12/31/2013
Chart High 890.10 on 07/13/2011
Chart Low 158.50 on 04/28/1999
CONTRACT SIZE 50 METRIC TONS
MIN TICK .1 USD
VALUE 5 USD/CONTRACT
EACH GRID 5 USD
VALUE 250 USD/CONTRACT
DAILY LIMIT NONE
VALUE
TRADING HOURS
9:45a - 6:20p LT

USD / metric ton

Nearby Futures through Last Trading Day. Futures data begins 04/11/1990.

Annual High, Low and Settle of Sugar, White Futures In Dollars per Metric Ton

Year	High	Low	Settle	Year	High	Low	Settle	Year	High	Low	Settle
1972	----	----	----	1986	----	----	----	2000	285	164	248
1973	----	----	----	1987	----	----	----	2001	284	203	240
1974	----	----	----	1988	----	----	----	2002	260	173	208
1975	----	----	----	1989	----	----	----	2003	251	173	185
1976	----	----	----	1990	458	287	297	2004	260	181	259
1977	----	----	----	1991	330	260	276	2005	355	238	355
1978	----	----	----	1992	305	245	249	2006	499	337	343
1979	----	----	----	1993	315	245	285	2007	360	258	315
1980	----	----	----	1994	422	284	411	2008	425	294	318
1981	----	----	----	1995	429	305	354	2009	711	321	710
1982	----	----	----	1996	429	295	309	2010	836	421	778
1983	----	----	----	1997	345	293	309	2011	890	572	602
1984	----	----	----	1998	308	207	240	2012	675	495	524
1985	----	----	----	1999	256	159	176	2013	544	432	449

Futures data begins 04/11/1990. *Source: Euronext LIFFE*

SUGAR, WHITE #5 - LIFFE
Weekly Selected Futures as of 01/03/2014

Date	Open	High	Low	Close
12/06/13	459.40	**462.00**	446.20	448.70
12/13/13	448.50	453.90	442.10	443.90
12/20/13	444.70	448.50	**432.10**	446.50
12/27/13	446.50	448.10	440.90	447.00
01/03/14	447.00	450.00	440.00	440.40

WEEKLY SELECTED FUTURES
As of 01/03/2014

Chart High 890.10 on 07/13/2011
Chart Low 182.00 on 01/16/2004
CONTRACT SIZE 50 METRIC TONS
MIN TICK .1 USD
VALUE 5 USD/CONTRACT
EACH GRID 5 USD
VALUE 250 USD/CONTRACT
DAILY LIMIT NONE
VALUE
TRADING HOURS
9:45a - 6:20p LT

Nearby Futures through Last Trading Day.

Quarterly High, Low and Settle of Sugar, White Futures   In Dollars per Metric Ton

Quarter	High	Low	Settle	Quarter	High	Low	Settle	Quarter	High	Low	Settle
03/2005	276	249	254	03/2008	400	311	335	03/2011	857	664	712
06/2005	297	238	280	06/2008	390	317	384	06/2011	770	572	739
09/2005	324	276	298	09/2008	425	345	380	09/2011	890	618	663
12/2005	355	271	355	12/2008	388	294	318	12/2011	735	593	602
03/2006	481	338	472	03/2009	414	321	393	03/2012	675	597	644
06/2006	497	436	466	06/2009	464	353	459	06/2012	644	548	611
09/2006	499	360	378	09/2009	618	430	618	09/2012	664	545	575
12/2006	431	337	343	12/2009	711	546	710	12/2012	602	495	524
03/2007	355	319	332	03/2010	767	463	504	03/2013	544	481	503
06/2007	360	298	321	06/2010	558	421	529	06/2013	525	470	502
09/2007	331	258	280	09/2010	648	512	617	09/2013	508	458	486
12/2007	321	268	315	12/2010	836	597	778	12/2013	529	432	449

Source: Euronext LIFFE

COTTON

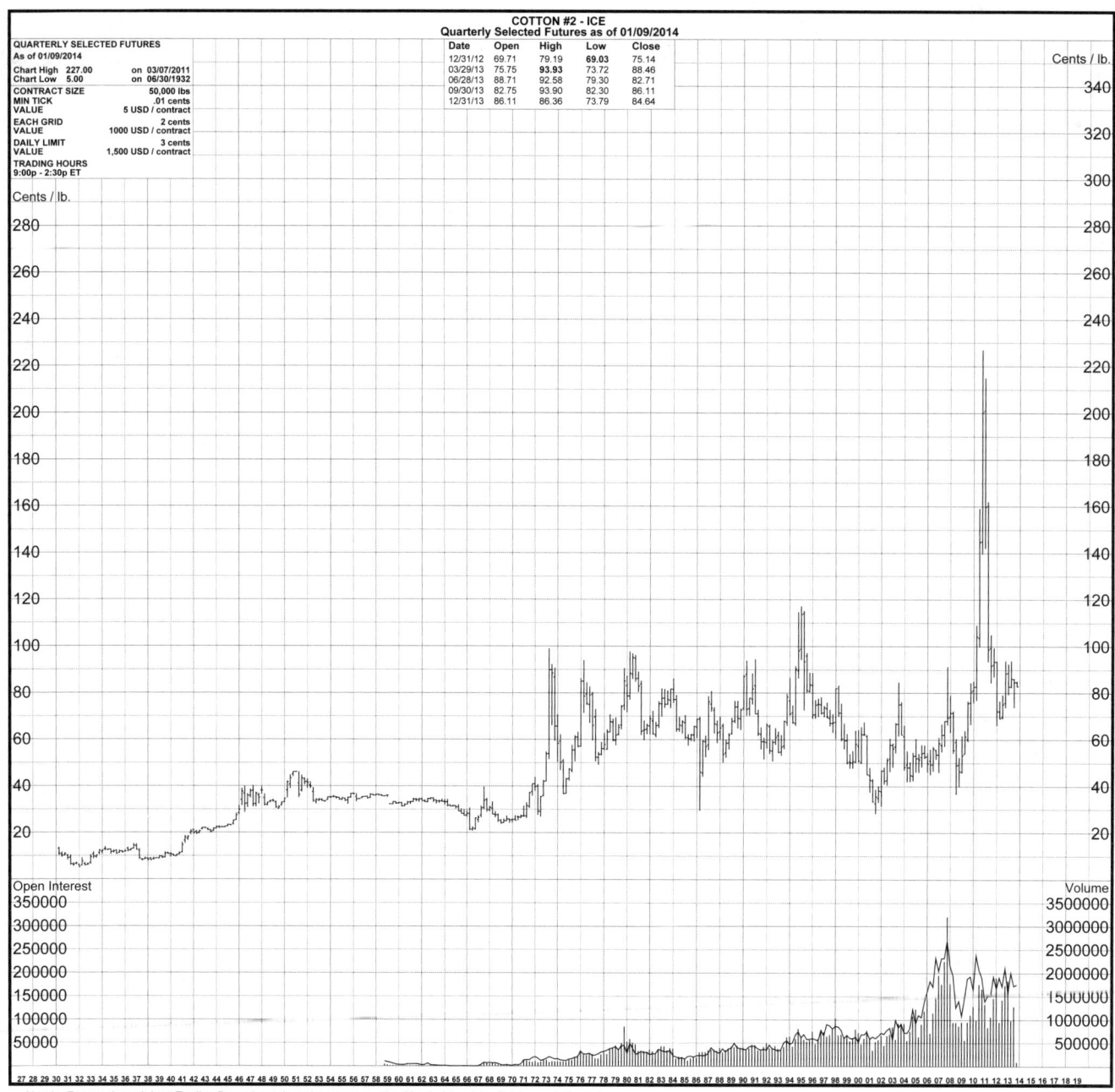

Nearby Futures through Last Trading Day using selected contract months: March, May, July, October and December.

Annual High, Low and Settle of Cotton #2 Futures   In Cents per Pound

Year	High	Low	Settle	Year	High	Low	Settle	Year	High	Low	Settle
1930	16.56	9.55	9.55	1944	21.64	20.17	21.55	1958	33.35	32.95	32.95
1931	10.54	5.97	5.99	1945	24.51	21.59	24.51	1959	33.31	29.92	33.21
1932	7.55	5.13	5.85	1946	36.88	24.71	32.38	1960	33.20	31.12	32.12
1933	10.67	5.99	10.05	1947	37.52	31.56	35.79	1961	34.84	31.98	34.12
1934	13.36	11.09	12.94	1948	37.55	31.18	32.17	1962	34.93	32.95	34.64
1935	12.89	10.76	12.02	1949	32.97	29.61	30.30	1963	35.10	32.50	33.60
1936	13.30	11.66	13.17	1950	42.59	31.03	42.59	1964	34.50	31.15	31.43
1937	14.77	8.26	8.58	1951	45.23	34.97	42.23	1965	32.10	28.25	28.25
1938	9.34	8.41	8.74	1952	41.88	33.09	33.09	1966	30.75	20.80	21.80
1939	10.56	8.79	10.56	1953	33.41	32.49	32.63	1967	39.70	21.20	33.95
1940	10.80	9.38	9.86	1954	34.94	33.21	34.94	1968	34.79	26.45	27.67
1941	17.26	10.10	17.26	1955	34.05	32.93	33.70	1969	28.19	23.75	25.75
1942	20.23	18.57	19.67	1956	35.52	31.94	32.02	1970	27.41	24.08	26.58
1943	21.20	19.68	19.68	1957	33.40	31.96	33.40	1971	37.46	26.15	37.20

Futures data begins 07/01/1959.   Data continued on page 186.   *Source: ICE Futures U.S.*

COTTON #2 - INFLATION ADJUSTED
Quarterly Selected Futures as of 01/09/2014

QUARTERLY SELECTED FUTURES
As of 01/09/2014

Chart High 512.85   on 09/28/1973
Chart Low   37.37   on 12/31/2001

Cents / lb.

Date	Open	High	Low	Close
12/31/12	69.71	79.19	69.03	75.14
03/29/13	75.75	93.93	73.72	88.46
06/28/13	88.71	92.58	79.30	82.71
09/30/13	82.75	93.90	82.30	86.11
12/31/13	86.11	86.36	73.79	84.64

Nearby Futures through Last Trading Day using selected contract months: March, May, July and October.

Annual High, Low and Settle of Cotton   In Cents per Pound

Year	High	Low	Settle	Year	High	Low	Settle	Year	High	Low	Settle
1930	16.56	9.55	9.55	1944	21.64	20.17	21.55	1958	33.35	32.95	32.95
1931	10.54	5.97	5.99	1945	24.51	21.59	24.51	1959	33.06	29.92	30.09
1932	7.55	5.13	5.85	1946	36.88	24.71	32.38	1960	30.59	28.57	28.57
1933	10.67	5.99	10.05	1947	37.52	31.56	35.79	1961	32.35	28.60	32.34
1934	13.36	11.09	12.94	1948	37.55	31.18	32.17	1962	32.93	31.77	31.89
1935	12.89	10.76	12.02	1949	32.97	29.61	30.30	1963	32.83	31.80	31.84
1936	13.30	11.66	13.17	1950	42.59	31.03	42.59	1964	32.05	29.23	29.23
1937	14.77	8.26	8.58	1951	45.23	34.97	42.23	1965	29.57	28.12	28.12
1938	9.34	8.41	8.74	1952	41.88	33.09	33.09	1966	28.13	20.17	20.17
1939	10.56	8.79	10.56	1953	33.41	32.49	32.63	1967	35.44	19.94	34.09
1940	10.80	9.38	9.86	1954	34.94	33.21	34.94	1968	34.01	26.22	26.25
1941	17.26	10.10	17.26	1955	34.05	32.93	33.70	1969	26.25	24.83	24.83
1942	20.23	18.57	19.67	1956	35.52	31.94	32.02	1970	25.99	24.46	24.53
1943	21.20	19.68	19.68	1957	33.40	31.96	33.40	1971	33.67	24.58	33.67

1-1/16" 7-Market average.   Data continued on page 187.   *Source: ICE Futures U.S.*

COTTON

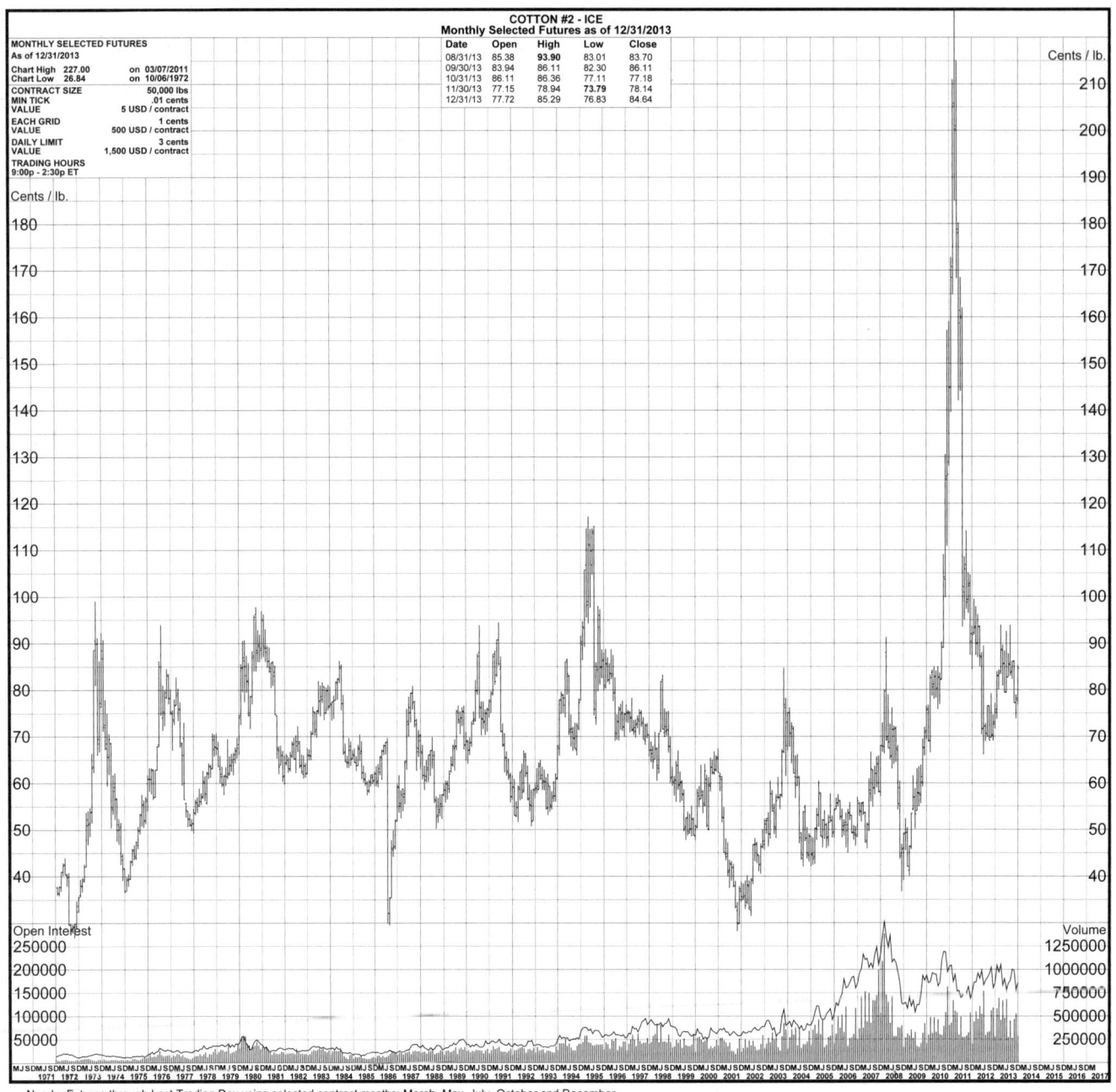

COTTON #2 - ICE
Monthly Selected Futures as of 12/31/2013

Date	Open	High	Low	Close
08/31/13	85.38	93.90	83.01	83.70
09/30/13	83.94	86.11	82.30	86.11
10/31/13	86.11	86.36	77.11	77.18
11/30/13	77.15	78.94	73.79	78.14
12/31/13	77.72	85.29	76.83	84.64

MONTHLY SELECTED FUTURES
As of 12/31/2013

Chart High	227.00	on 03/07/2011
Chart Low	26.84	on 10/06/1972
CONTRACT SIZE	50,000 lbs	
MIN TICK	.01 cents	
VALUE	5 USD / contract	
EACH GRID	1 cents	
VALUE	500 USD / contract	
DAILY LIMIT	3 cents	
VALUE	1,500 USD / contract	
TRADING HOURS		
9:00p - 2:30p ET		

Nearby Futures through Last Trading Day using selected contract months: March, May, July, October and December.

Annual High, Low and Settle of Cotton #2 Futures   In Cents per Pound

Year	High	Low	Settle	Year	High	Low	Settle	Year	High	Low	Settle
1972	43.98	26.84	35.50	1986	69.70	29.50	59.28	2000	67.50	49.80	62.28
1973	99.00	35.60	88.50	1987	80.90	52.50	66.76	2001	62.20	28.20	35.59
1974	90.79	36.53	36.80	1988	69.85	50.20	58.49	2002	52.25	31.47	51.16
1975	61.75	36.85	60.87	1989	76.60	55.85	69.07	2003	84.80	46.30	75.07
1976	93.95	56.50	75.20	1990	93.90	64.15	77.80	2004	76.18	42.00	44.77
1977	82.75	49.10	53.69	1991	94.45	55.85	59.17	2005	60.50	42.40	54.19
1978	70.73	53.19	67.57	1992	67.00	50.68	58.86	2006	57.65	45.00	56.19
1979	74.70	57.50	74.06	1993	68.18	53.10	67.88	2007	68.10	45.94	68.01
1980	97.77	71.60	95.12	1994	91.60	65.90	90.35	2008	91.38	36.70	49.02
1981	96.20	59.67	64.27	1995	117.20	72.50	81.05	2009	76.58	40.01	75.60
1982	72.24	61.00	65.92	1996	88.80	69.00	75.15	2010	159.12	66.55	144.81
1983	81.95	64.90	77.11	1997	78.25	65.75	67.07	2011	227.00	84.35	91.80
1984	86.25	63.30	66.17	1998	83.30	59.45	60.36	2012	99.47	66.10	75.14
1985	70.45	57.40	62.06	1999	67.00	47.75	50.74	2013	93.93	73.72	84.64

Data continued from page 184.   *Source: ICE Futures U.S.*

Cotton, 1-1/16", 7 Market Avg
Monthly Cash as of 12/31/2013

MONTHLY CASH
As of 12/31/2013

Chart High 209.60 on 03/07/2011
Chart Low   25.94 on 08/01/1986

Cents / lb.

Date	Open	High	Low	Close
08/30/13	81.84	89.14	79.86	80.04
09/30/13	79.37	83.83	79.00	83.83
10/31/13	82.67	83.55	74.66	74.66
11/29/13	74.16	75.68	73.49	75.68
12/31/13	74.94	81.40	74.94	81.28

1-1/16", 7-Market: to 02/1967 (avg); 1-1/16", 7-Market: 03/1967 to date.

Annual High, Low and Settle of Cotton   In Cents per Pound

Year	High	Low	Settle	Year	High	Low	Settle	Year	High	Low	Settle
1972	39.69	27.08	32.81	1986	67.48	25.94	57.60	2000	66.27	47.84	57.70
1973	86.08	33.05	85.27	1987	77.17	53.18	62.48	2001	58.22	25.94	31.10
1974	84.98	34.93	34.93	1988	64.96	50.05	54.71	2002	48.48	28.44	47.83
1975	56.93	35.39	56.48	1989	71.19	52.91	64.41	2003	77.66	45.56	69.09
1976	86.84	53.43	71.87	1990	80.67	60.69	71.29	2004	69.99	40.87	42.67
1977	78.26	47.02	49.62	1991	87.82	53.39	53.55	2005	53.20	40.39	50.49
1978	67.57	49.27	63.47	1992	62.02	47.11	52.11	2006	53.25	44.34	51.46
1979	68.33	56.46	68.33	1993	63.34	51.48	63.34	2007	61.86	42.84	61.86
1980	92.96	67.54	88.37	1994	87.07	62.74	87.07	2008	79.16	36.93	45.44
1981	88.72	53.51	56.65	1995	113.84	78.99	79.86	2009	69.43	37.13	69.04
1982	66.04	56.40	59.68	1996	86.48	68.00	71.43	2010	152.76	61.19	134.42
1983	74.84	59.33	71.61	1997	73.71	62.73	63.84	2011	209.60	81.94	87.57
1984	81.61	59.17	60.31	1998	77.79	57.06	57.19	2012	91.94	60.71	70.92
1985	63.50	55.34	58.60	1999	59.70	45.94	47.53	2013	89.14	70.49	81.28

1-1/16" 7-Market average.   Data continued from page 185.   *Source: U.S. Department of Agriculture (USDA)*

COTTON

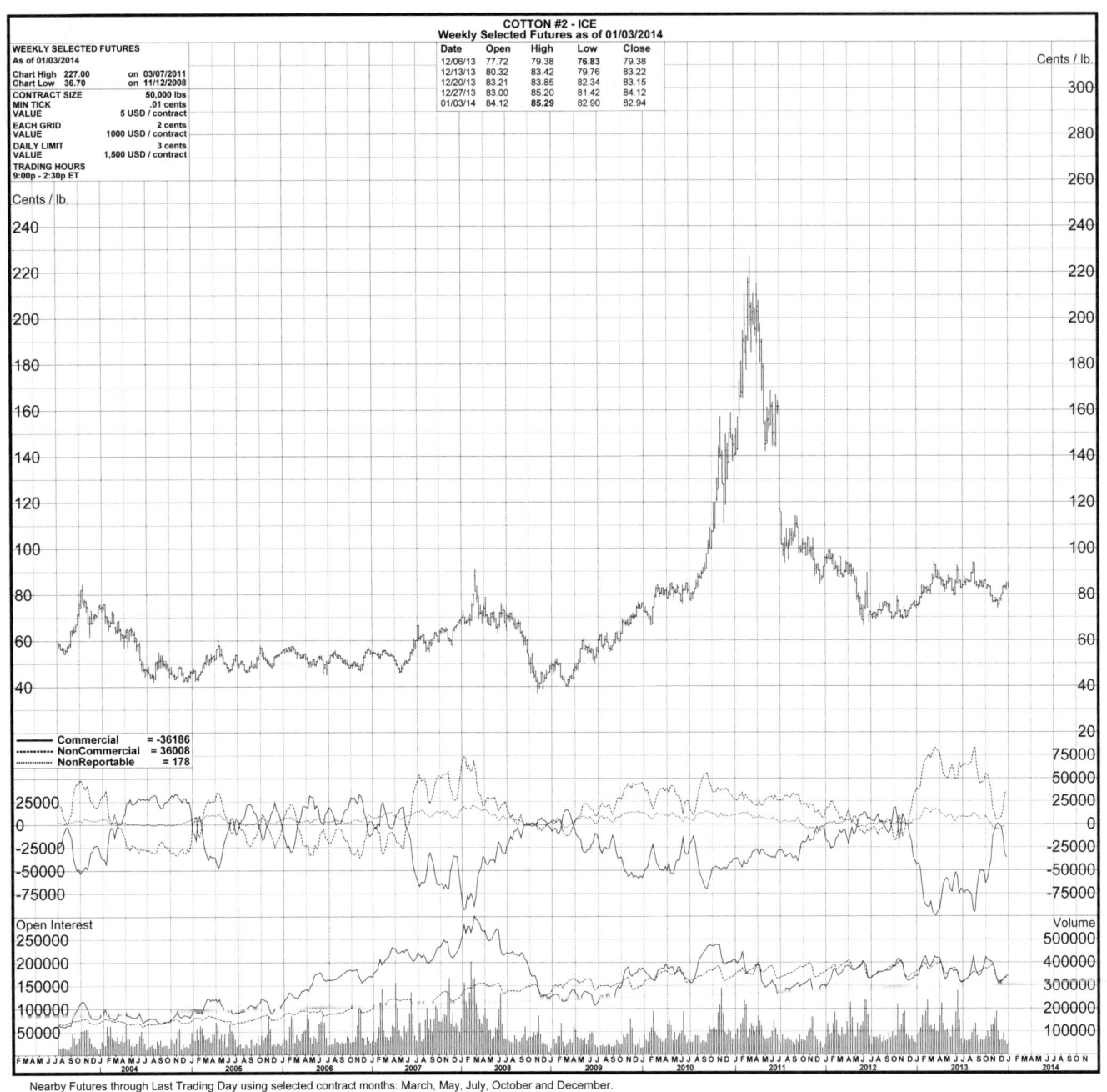

COTTON #2 - ICE
Weekly Selected Futures as of 01/03/2014

Date	Open	High	Low	Close
12/06/13	77.72	79.38	**76.83**	79.38
12/13/13	80.32	83.42	79.76	83.22
12/20/13	83.21	83.85	82.34	83.15
12/27/13	83.00	85.20	81.42	84.12
01/03/14	84.12	**85.29**	82.90	82.94

WEEKLY SELECTED FUTURES
As of 01/03/2014

Chart High 227.00 on 03/07/2011
Chart Low 36.70 on 11/12/2008

CONTRACT SIZE	50,000 lbs
MIN TICK VALUE	.01 cents 5 USD / contract
EACH GRID VALUE	2 cents 1000 USD / contract
DAILY LIMIT VALUE	3 cents 1,500 USD / contract
TRADING HOURS	9:00p - 2:30p ET

Commercial = -36186
NonCommercial = 36008
NonReportable = 178

Nearby Futures through Last Trading Day using selected contract months: March, May, July, October and December.

Quarterly High, Low and Settle of Cotton #2 Futures In Cents per Pound

Quarter	High	Low	Settle	Quarter	High	Low	Settle	Quarter	High	Low	Settle
03/2005	54.60	42.40	53.03	03/2008	91.38	66.35	69.34	03/2011	227.00	139.61	200.23
06/2005	60.50	46.10	52.00	06/2008	78.95	63.10	71.40	06/2011	215.06	142.06	159.79
09/2005	54.10	46.00	51.50	09/2008	72.28	54.25	55.50	09/2011	162.05	93.50	98.71
12/2005	57.80	48.25	54.19	12/2008	60.50	36.70	49.02	12/2011	105.05	84.35	91.80
03/2006	57.65	52.02	52.65	03/2009	52.40	40.01	46.47	03/2012	99.47	87.00	93.52
06/2006	54.45	46.12	49.75	06/2009	61.67	45.81	53.30	06/2012	93.80	66.10	72.16
09/2006	55.90	45.00	49.30	09/2009	63.91	54.00	61.34	09/2012	76.56	68.95	69.15
12/2006	57.05	46.50	56.19	12/2009	76.58	59.26	75.60	12/2012	79.19	69.03	75.14
03/2007	55.95	51.65	53.57	03/2010	84.32	66.55	80.55	03/2013	93.93	73.72	88.46
06/2007	61.00	45.94	58.50	06/2010	85.10	75.80	82.60	06/2013	92.58	79.30	82.71
09/2007	66.70	54.81	62.05	09/2010	109.10	76.83	104.18	09/2013	93.90	82.30	86.11
12/2007	68.10	57.20	68.01	12/2010	159.12	99.78	144.81	12/2013	86.36	73.79	84.64

Source: ICE Futures U.S.

WEEKLY CASH
As of 01/03/2014

Chart High 209.60   on 03/07/2011
Chart Low   36.93   on 11/12/2008

Cents / lb.

Cotton, 1-1/16", 7 Market Avg
Weekly Cash as of 01/03/2014

Date	Open	High	Low	Close
12/06/13	74.94	77.19	74.94	77.19
12/13/13	77.15	79.91	77.15	79.91
12/20/13	80.09	80.09	79.61	79.96
12/27/13	79.03	81.01	79.03	81.01
01/03/14	81.40	81.40	79.56	79.56

7-Market Average.

Quarterly High, Low and Settle of Cotton   In Cents per Pound

Quarter	High	Low	Settle	Quarter	High	Low	Settle	Quarter	High	Low	Settle
03/2005	49.97	40.39	49.02	03/2008	79.16	61.41	61.92	03/2011	209.60	133.96	195.38
06/2005	52.30	43.28	50.23	06/2008	67.98	56.58	65.77	06/2011	203.37	131.42	131.42
09/2005	51.06	43.46	48.94	09/2008	64.38	52.36	52.36	09/2011	129.58	94.42	95.64
12/2005	53.20	47.89	50.49	12/2008	53.60	36.93	45.44	12/2011	101.87	81.94	87.57
03/2006	53.25	48.84	49.32	03/2009	47.76	37.13	41.55	03/2012	91.94	80.53	86.51
06/2006	50.41	46.01	47.14	06/2009	55.17	41.39	50.16	06/2012	86.09	60.71	67.55
09/2006	49.63	45.68	45.68	09/2009	58.94	50.98	57.53	09/2012	72.59	64.36	65.43
12/2006	51.97	44.34	51.46	12/2009	69.43	55.90	69.04	12/2012	72.97	65.11	70.92
03/2007	50.53	47.93	49.09	03/2010	76.01	61.19	74.21	03/2013	87.25	70.49	83.29
06/2007	55.64	42.84	55.64	06/2010	78.43	71.65	76.15	06/2013	87.55	75.01	81.26
09/2007	60.67	50.34	59.39	09/2010	100.10	74.47	97.51	09/2013	89.14	79.00	83.83
12/2007	61.86	57.25	61.86	12/2010	152.76	93.45	134.42	12/2013	83.55	73.49	81.28

1-1/16" 7-Market average.   *Source: U.S. Department of Agriculture (USDA)*

LUMBER

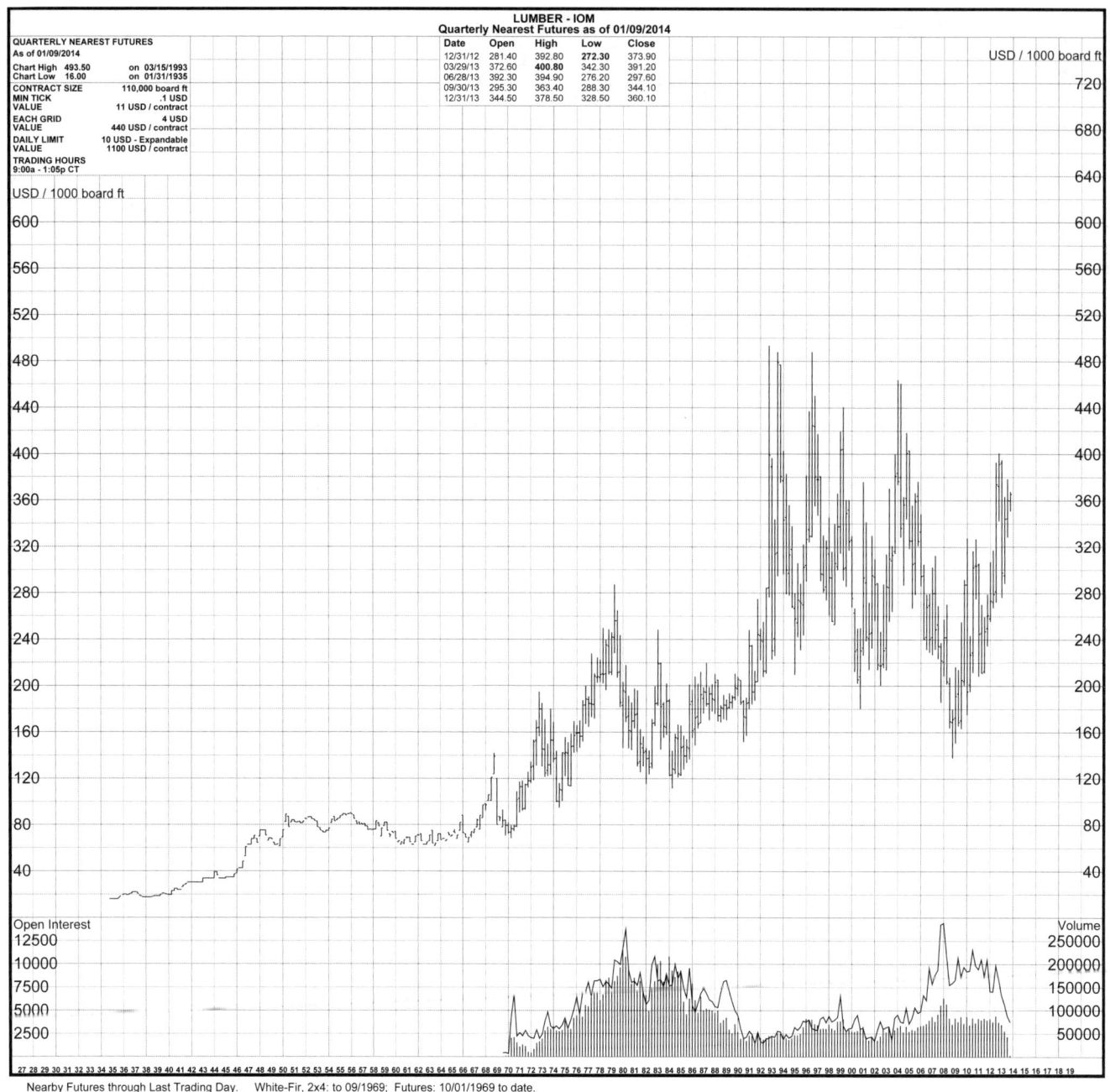

LUMBER - IOM
Quarterly Nearest Futures as of 01/09/2014

Date	Open	High	Low	Close
12/31/12	281.40	392.80	272.30	373.90
03/29/13	372.60	400.80	342.30	391.20
06/28/13	392.30	394.90	276.20	297.60
09/30/13	295.30	363.40	288.30	344.10
12/31/13	344.50	378.50	328.50	360.10

QUARTERLY NEAREST FUTURES
As of 01/09/2014
Chart High 493.50 on 03/15/1993
Chart Low 16.00 on 01/31/1935
CONTRACT SIZE 110,000 board ft
MIN TICK .1 USD
VALUE 11 USD / contract
EACH GRID 4 USD
VALUE 440 USD / contract
DAILY LIMIT 10 USD - Expandable
VALUE 1100 USD / contract
TRADING HOURS
9:00a - 1:05p CT

USD / 1000 board ft

Nearby Futures through Last Trading Day.   White-Fir, 2x4: to 09/1969; Futures: 10/01/1969 to date.

Annual High, Low and Settle of Lumber   In Dollars per 1,000 Board Feet

Year	High	Low	Settle	Year	High	Low	Settle	Year	High	Low	Settle
1930	----	----	----	1944	39.20	33.81	33.81	1958	83.20	75.59	78.66
1931	----	----	----	1945	34.79	33.81	34.79	1959	82.00	69.00	71.00
1932	----	----	----	1946	48.31	34.79	48.31	1960	74.00	63.00	65.00
1933	----	----	----	1947	70.59	52.74	70.59	1961	69.00	63.00	63.00
1934	----	----	----	1948	75.24	64.35	70.79	1962	72.00	63.00	63.00
1935	16.00	16.00	16.00	1949	68.31	62.72	63.21	1963	75.00	62.00	64.00
1936	20.29	18.13	20.29	1950	88.95	61.48	78.09	1964	72.00	66.00	67.00
1937	22.05	18.50	18.50	1951	83.94	81.37	81.37	1965	76.00	68.00	71.00
1938	18.01	17.64	18.01	1952	86.58	81.51	84.95	1966	88.00	65.00	69.00
1939	21.07	18.42	21.07	1953	84.67	73.12	73.41	1967	88.00	69.00	88.00
1940	24.99	19.60	24.99	1954	86.85	73.40	83.05	1968	121.00	86.00	121.00
1941	29.20	24.01	29.20	1955	89.32	83.97	88.10	1969	142.00	78.00	83.50
1942	30.38	30.38	30.38	1956	89.92	80.65	80.65	1970	84.00	68.25	78.70
1943	33.81	30.38	33.81	1957	81.99	75.61	75.61	1971	118.20	78.00	114.60

Spruce-Pine-Fir 2x4.   Data continued on page 192.   *Source: CME Group; Chicago Mercantile Exchange*

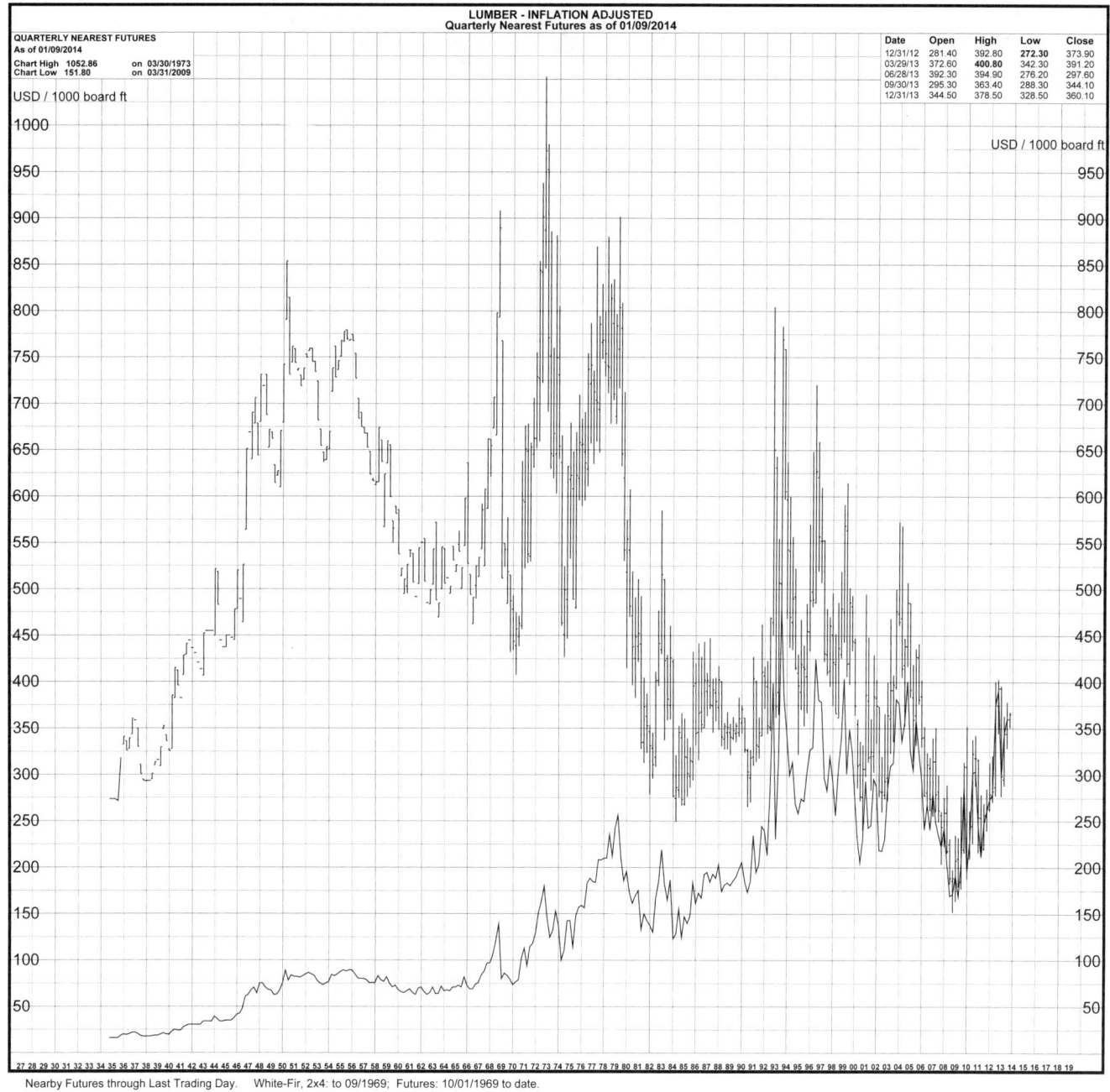

LUMBER - INFLATION ADJUSTED
Quarterly Nearest Futures as of 01/09/2014

QUARTERLY NEAREST FUTURES
As of 01/09/2014

Chart High 1052.86   on 03/30/1973
Chart Low   151.80   on 03/31/2009

USD / 1000 board ft

Date	Open	High	Low	Close
12/31/12	281.40	392.80	272.30	373.90
03/29/13	372.60	400.80	342.30	391.20
06/28/13	392.30	394.90	276.20	297.60
09/30/13	295.30	363.40	288.30	344.10
12/31/13	344.50	378.50	328.50	360.10

Nearby Futures through Last Trading Day.   White-Fir, 2x4: to 09/1969; Futures: 10/01/1969 to date.

Annual High, Low and Settle of Lumber   In Dollars per 1,000 Board Feet

Year	High	Low	Settle	Year	High	Low	Settle	Year	High	Low	Settle
1930	----	----	----	1944	39.20	33.81	33.81	1958	83.20	75.59	78.66
1931	----	----	----	1945	34.79	33.81	34.79	1959	82.00	69.00	71.00
1932	----	----	----	1946	48.31	34.79	48.31	1960	74.00	63.00	65.00
1933	----	----	----	1947	70.59	52.74	70.59	1961	69.00	63.00	63.00
1934	----	----	----	1948	75.24	64.35	70.79	1962	72.00	63.00	63.00
1935	16.00	16.00	16.00	1949	68.31	62.72	63.21	1963	75.00	62.00	64.00
1936	20.29	18.13	20.29	1950	88.95	61.48	78.09	1964	72.00	66.00	67.00
1937	22.05	18.50	18.50	1951	83.94	81.37	81.37	1965	76.00	68.00	71.00
1938	18.01	17.64	18.01	1952	86.58	81.51	84.95	1966	88.00	65.00	69.00
1939	21.07	18.42	21.07	1953	84.67	73.12	73.41	1967	88.00	69.00	88.00
1940	24.99	19.60	24.99	1954	86.85	73.40	83.05	1968	121.00	86.00	121.00
1941	29.20	24.01	29.20	1955	89.32	83.97	88.10	1969	142.00	80.00	80.00
1942	30.38	30.38	30.38	1956	89.92	80.65	80.65	1970	83.00	76.00	79.00
1943	33.81	30.38	33.81	1957	81.99	75.61	75.61	1971	121.00	89.00	114.00

Spruce-Pine-Fir 2x4.   Data continued on page 193.   *Source: CME Group; Chicago Mercantile Exchange*

LUMBER

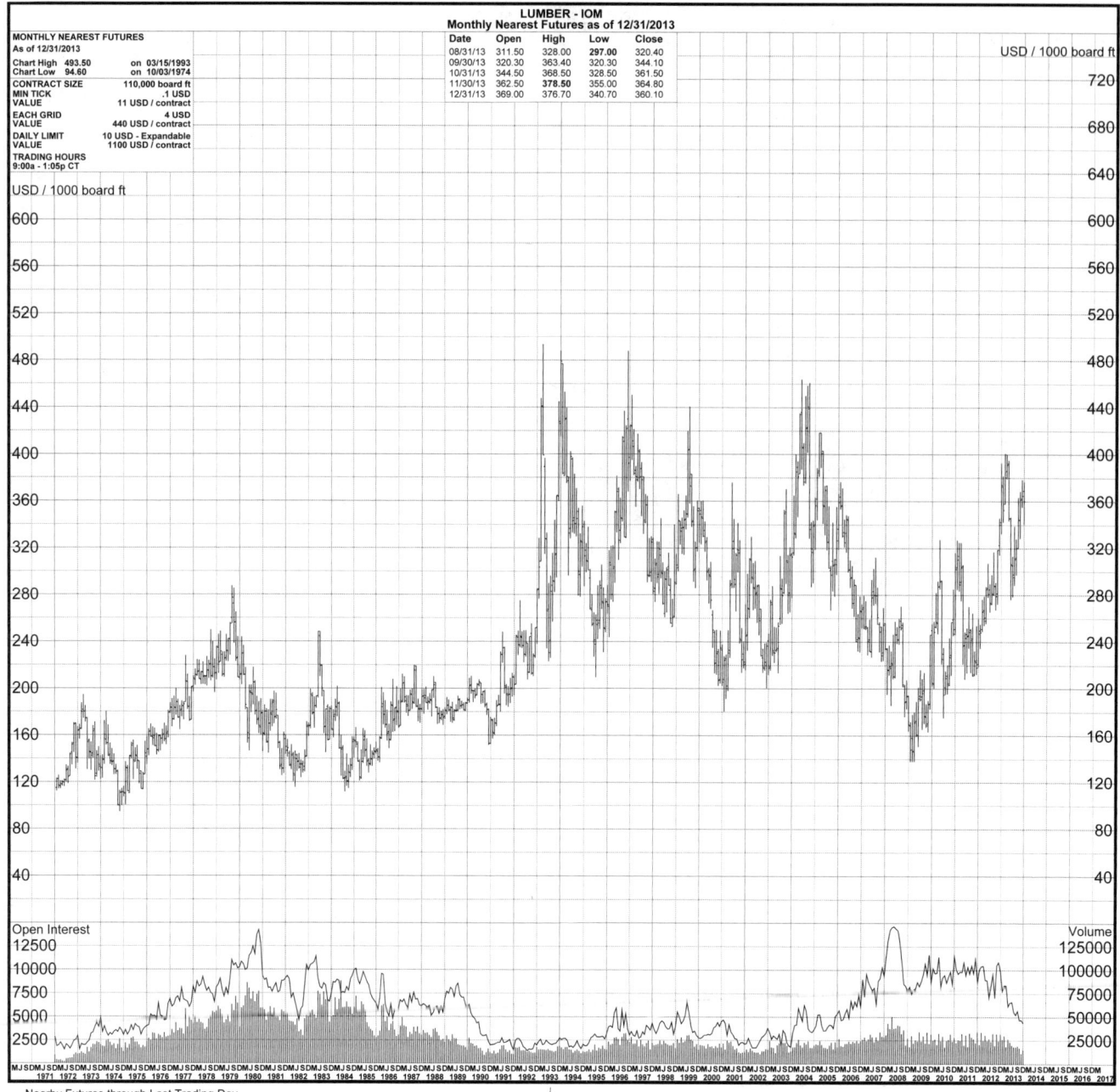

LUMBER - IOM
Monthly Nearest Futures as of 12/31/2013

Date	Open	High	Low	Close
08/31/13	311.50	328.00	**297.00**	320.40
09/30/13	320.30	363.40	320.30	344.10
10/31/13	344.50	368.50	328.50	361.50
11/30/13	362.50	**378.50**	355.00	364.80
12/31/13	369.00	376.70	340.70	360.10

MONTHLY NEAREST FUTURES
As of 12/31/2013

Chart High	493.50	on 03/15/1993
Chart Low	94.60	on 10/03/1974
CONTRACT SIZE	110,000 board ft	
MIN TICK	.1 USD	
VALUE	11 USD / contract	
EACH GRID	4 USD	
VALUE	440 USD / contract	
DAILY LIMIT	10 USD - Expandable	
VALUE	1100 USD / contract	
TRADING HOURS		
9:00a - 1:05p CT		

USD / 1000 board ft

Nearby Futures through Last Trading Day.

Annual High, Low and Settle of Lumber Futures In Dollars per 1,000 Board Feet

Year	High	Low	Settle	Year	High	Low	Settle	Year	High	Low	Settle
1972	170.30	112.30	163.60	1986	207.90	136.60	167.10	2000	360.50	202.10	205.50
1973	194.70	121.50	131.80	1987	219.70	168.00	192.90	2001	376.00	180.40	245.10
1974	180.00	94.60	110.60	1988	210.30	168.50	181.20	2002	329.80	200.50	217.70
1975	158.70	100.50	147.52	1989	193.50	170.30	189.90	2003	370.40	213.50	312.60
1976	187.50	142.20	183.20	1990	210.70	151.60	173.30	2004	464.00	286.70	356.40
1977	228.00	164.60	208.40	1991	248.30	157.00	203.50	2005	418.50	267.00	359.00
1978	249.90	196.20	235.30	1992	284.70	203.50	284.10	2006	376.40	231.30	268.00
1979	287.30	207.10	211.50	1993	493.50	223.00	479.00	2007	312.30	223.50	234.50
1980	243.80	146.00	161.40	1994	477.00	278.00	313.20	2008	270.30	163.70	169.40
1981	197.60	125.50	149.90	1995	337.90	209.60	271.50	2009	255.20	137.90	205.00
1982	171.40	115.50	167.50	1996	488.00	243.70	424.70	2010	327.50	175.20	302.00
1983	248.50	145.00	165.00	1997	450.50	280.60	282.90	2011	326.90	208.10	247.10
1984	201.90	111.70	155.40	1998	345.40	253.00	305.60	2012	392.80	234.60	373.90
1985	166.50	121.10	147.20	1999	440.80	285.60	349.00	2013	400.80	276.20	360.10

Futures begin trading 10/01/1969.   Data continued from page 190.   *Source: CME Group; Chicago Mercantile Exchange*

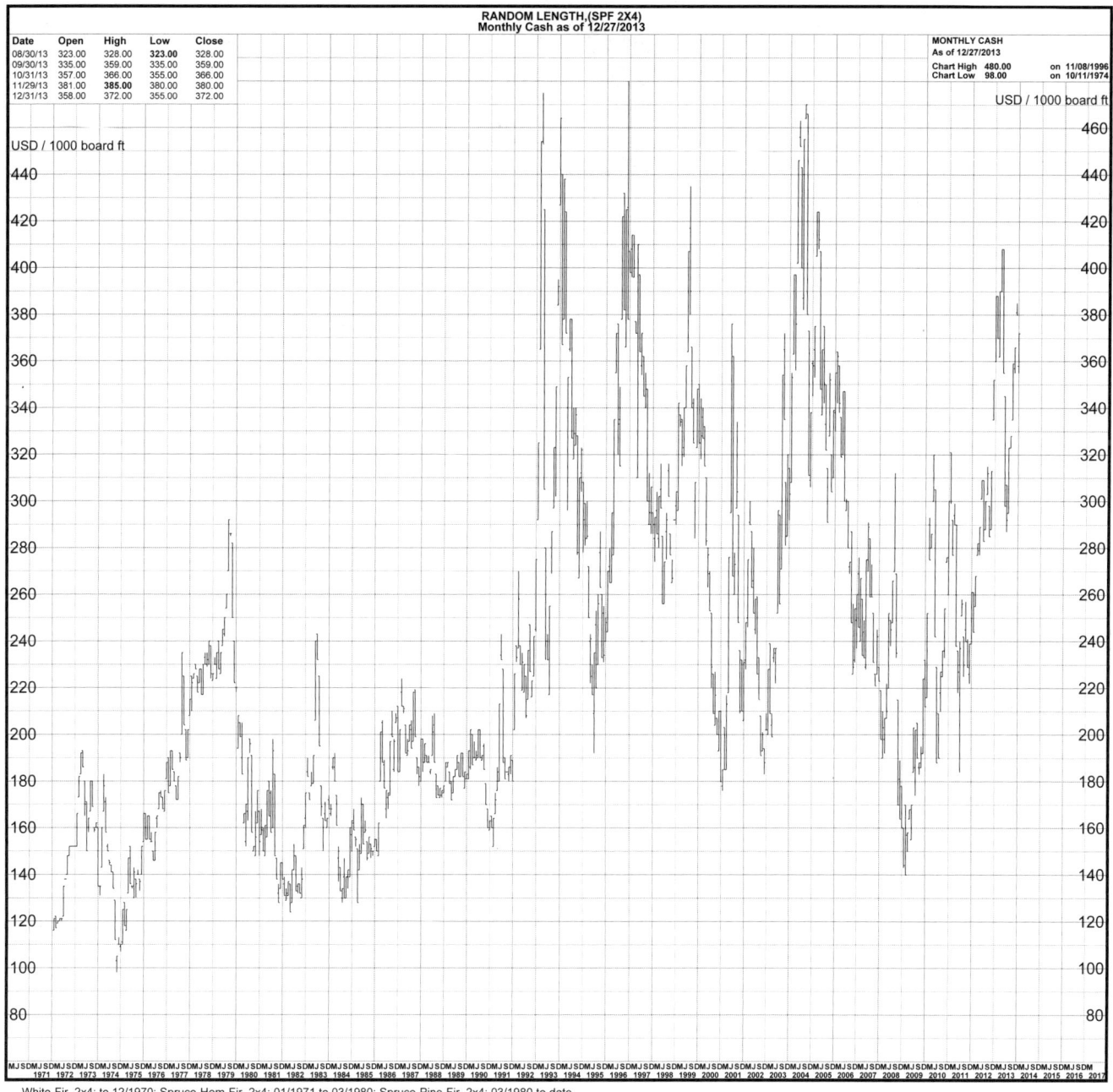

RANDOM LENGTH,(SPF 2X4)
Monthly Cash as of 12/27/2013

Date	Open	High	Low	Close
08/30/13	323.00	328.00	**323.00**	328.00
09/30/13	335.00	359.00	335.00	359.00
10/31/13	357.00	366.00	355.00	366.00
11/29/13	381.00	**385.00**	380.00	380.00
12/31/13	358.00	372.00	355.00	372.00

MONTHLY CASH
As of 12/27/2013

Chart High 480.00 on 11/08/1996
Chart Low   98.00   on 10/11/1974

USD / 1000 board ft

White-Fir, 2x4: to 12/1970; Spruce-Hem-Fir, 2x4: 01/1971 to 03/1980; Spruce-Pine-Fir, 2x4: 03/1980 to date.

Annual High, Low and Settle of Lumber   In Dollars per 1,000 Board Feet

Year	High	Low	Settle	Year	High	Low	Settle	Year	High	Low	Settle
1972	152.00	116.00	152.00	1986	212.00	148.00	184.00	2000	344.00	180.00	180.00
1973	193.00	135.00	135.00	1987	224.00	178.00	198.00	2001	376.00	176.00	231.00
1974	183.00	98.00	110.00	1988	209.00	173.00	178.00	2002	300.00	183.00	202.00
1975	166.00	110.00	166.00	1989	192.00	172.00	183.00	2003	372.00	199.00	303.00
1976	188.00	146.00	188.00	1990	202.00	159.00	163.00	2004	470.00	306.00	358.00
1977	235.00	172.00	215.00	1991	243.00	152.00	180.00	2005	424.00	291.00	355.00
1978	240.00	210.00	226.00	1992	275.00	202.00	275.00	2006	364.00	226.00	260.00
1979	292.00	218.00	220.00	1993	475.00	217.00	464.00	2007	291.00	221.00	223.00
1980	208.00	148.00	154.00	1994	440.00	267.00	292.00	2008	312.00	160.00	160.00
1981	198.00	128.00	138.00	1995	300.00	192.00	248.00	2009	232.00	140.00	212.00
1982	175.00	124.00	175.00	1996	480.00	244.00	398.00	2010	320.00	188.00	300.00
1983	243.00	150.00	168.00	1997	414.00	286.00	290.00	2011	321.00	184.00	261.00
1984	192.00	128.00	163.00	1998	316.00	256.00	304.00	2012	388.00	244.00	388.00
1985	173.00	128.00	155.00	1999	435.00	284.00	325.00	2013	408.00	287.00	372.00

Spruce-Pine-Fir 2x4.   Data continued from page 191.   *Source: U.S. Department of Agriculture (USDA)*

LUMBER

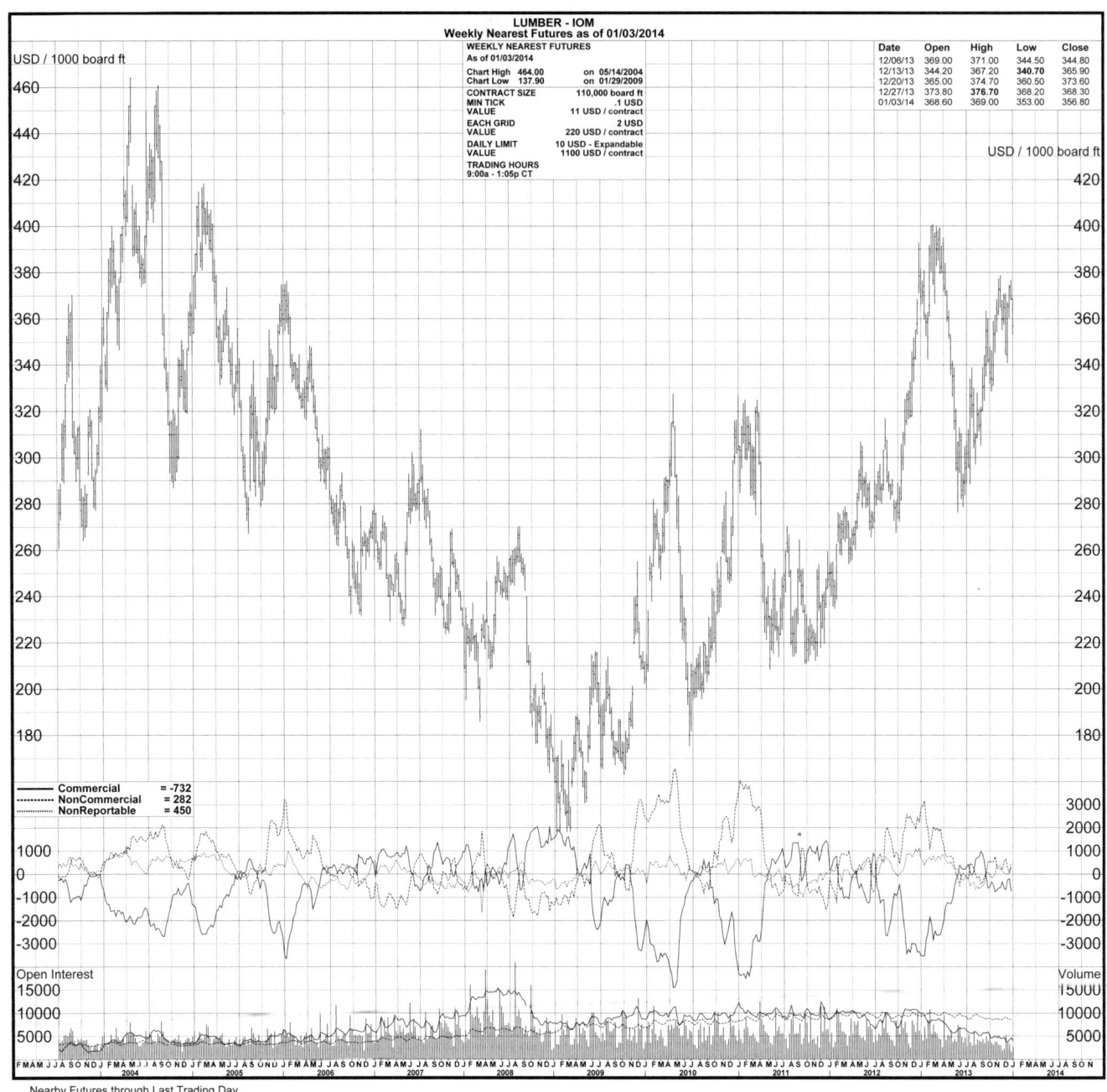

LUMBER - IOM
Weekly Nearest Futures as of 01/03/2014

WEEKLY NEAREST FUTURES
As of 01/03/2014

Chart High 464.00 on 05/14/2004
Chart Low 137.90 on 01/29/2009
CONTRACT SIZE 110,000 board ft
MIN TICK .1 USD
VALUE 11 USD / contract
EACH GRID 2 USD
VALUE 220 USD / contract
DAILY LIMIT 10 USD - Expandable
VALUE 1100 USD / contract
TRADING HOURS
9:00a - 1:05p CT

Date	Open	High	Low	Close
12/06/13	369.00	371.00	344.50	344.80
12/13/13	344.20	367.20	340.70	365.90
12/20/13	365.00	374.70	360.50	373.60
12/27/13	373.80	376.70	368.20	368.30
01/03/14	368.60	369.00	353.00	356.80

Commercial = -732
NonCommercial = 282
NonReportable = 450

Nearby Futures through Last Trading Day.

Quarterly High, Low and Settle of Lumber Futures   In Dollars per 1,000 Board Feet

Quarter	High	Low	Settle	Quarter	High	Low	Settle	Quarter	High	Low	Settle
03/2005	418.50	344.00	400.70	03/2008	237.30	185.70	222.10	03/2011	326.90	275.00	303.40
06/2005	402.90	318.50	325.30	06/2008	257.50	208.30	242.00	06/2011	305.70	208.10	244.90
09/2005	355.80	267.00	304.90	09/2008	270.30	201.50	203.50	09/2011	270.20	211.10	211.10
12/2005	366.50	278.70	359.00	12/2008	207.40	163.70	169.40	12/2011	259.60	211.20	247.10
03/2006	376.40	320.90	324.90	03/2009	179.80	137.90	171.30	03/2012	279.00	234.60	260.90
06/2006	348.40	286.10	294.50	06/2009	216.30	150.70	191.00	06/2012	307.00	255.70	273.40
09/2006	304.80	240.10	240.60	09/2009	214.00	165.30	168.70	09/2012	317.00	267.40	279.00
12/2006	279.00	231.30	268.00	12/2009	255.20	163.00	205.00	12/2012	392.80	272.30	373.90
03/2007	279.50	229.00	240.50	03/2010	291.70	200.40	287.20	03/2013	400.80	342.30	391.20
06/2007	302.30	227.00	279.80	06/2010	327.50	175.20	195.00	06/2013	394.90	276.20	297.60
09/2007	312.30	231.50	248.70	09/2010	243.50	195.00	227.00	09/2013	363.40	288.30	344.10
12/2007	269.10	223.50	234.50	12/2010	316.40	211.30	302.00	12/2013	378.50	328.50	360.10

Source: CME Group; Chicago Mercantile Exchange

Date	Open	High	Low	Close
12/06/13	358.00	358.00	358.00	358.00
12/13/13	355.00	355.00	355.00	355.00
12/20/13	372.00	372.00	372.00	372.00
12/27/13	372.00	372.00	372.00	372.00
01/03/14	372.00	372.00	372.00	372.00

WEEKLY CASH
As of 01/03/2014

Chart High 470.00 on 08/27/2004
Chart Low 140.00 on 02/27/2009

USD / 1000 board ft

Spruce-Pine-Fir, 2x4

Quarterly High, Low and Settle of Lumber   In Dollars per 1,000 Board Feet

Quarter	High	Low	Settle	Quarter	High	Low	Settle	Quarter	High	Low	Settle
03/2005	424.00	353.00	412.00	03/2008	219.00	190.00	207.00	03/2011	321.00	277.00	290.00
06/2005	407.00	337.00	350.00	06/2008	252.00	207.00	245.00	06/2011	290.00	184.00	237.00
09/2005	355.00	291.00	352.00	09/2008	312.00	233.00	235.00	09/2011	258.00	225.00	240.00
12/2005	355.00	304.00	355.00	12/2008	215.00	160.00	160.00	12/2011	261.00	222.00	261.00
03/2006	364.00	319.00	319.00	03/2009	170.00	140.00	158.00	03/2012	282.00	244.00	282.00
06/2006	347.00	296.00	300.00	06/2009	203.00	155.00	203.00	06/2012	309.00	277.00	283.00
09/2006	300.00	248.00	248.00	09/2009	205.00	174.00	188.00	09/2012	315.00	285.00	285.00
12/2006	260.00	226.00	260.00	12/2009	232.00	186.00	212.00	12/2012	388.00	288.00	388.00
03/2007	276.00	234.00	234.00	03/2010	293.00	216.00	286.00	03/2013	408.00	362.00	408.00
06/2007	291.00	228.00	289.00	06/2010	320.00	188.00	188.00	06/2013	408.00	287.00	292.00
09/2007	284.00	231.00	231.00	09/2010	236.00	190.00	236.00	09/2013	359.00	295.00	359.00
12/2007	245.00	221.00	223.00	12/2010	300.00	233.00	300.00	12/2013	385.00	355.00	372.00

Spruce-Pine-Fir 2x4.   *Source: U.S. Department of Agriculture (USDA)*

GRAINS & OILSEEDS

Grain and Oilseed Outlook

The long-term outlook for grain and oilseed prices is mildly bullish due to expectations for steady global economic growth, long-term population growth, the increasing food needs of the world's underdeveloped countries, and biofuel demand.

The United Nations predicts that the world's population will grow by a net 2.5 billion persons by 2050. Not only will there be more mouths to feed, but the need for food will grow as the world's poor slowly make more money and can afford more food and meat. A larger proportion of the world's grain supply will go towards feeding cattle, hogs and poultry to produce the higher-value proteins that a wealthier world will demand.

Still, the global supply of grain and oilseeds should largely meet increased demand due to steadily improving yields and the use of more land for farming. The result is that long-term grain and oilseed prices should rise in order to offset inflation and induce suppliers to meet increased long-term demand.

A big wildcard for long-term grain and oilseed prices is climate change. Climate change could cause volatility in grain and oilseed prices if climate change causes an increase in damaging storms and droughts. Yet there may be a partially offsetting effect if warmer climates produce more arable land and longer growing seasons in the northern-most and southern-most regions of the world.

Demand for corn by ethanol producers was a big driver for corn prices during 2006 through 2012. U.S. ethanol producers currently use as much as 35-40% of the U.S. corn crop to produce ethanol, although about 30% of that corn is returned to the corn feed market by the ethanol industry's production of distiller dried grains.

The biofuel industry's demand for corn, however, may have peaked in 2012. The Environmental Protection Agency (EPA) in late 2013 proposed cutting the 2014 mandate for corn-based ethanol usage to 13.0 billion gallons from 13.8 billion gallons in 2012. The EPA proposed that cut in part because ethanol usage in the U.S. has already reached nearly 10%, which is referred to as the "blend wall." It will be difficult for ethanol usage to exceed the 10% blend wall because of the low availability of pumps that can dispense E15 (15% ethanol, 85%) gasoline) and E85 (85% ethanol, 15% gasoline). Moreover, overall U.S. fuel usage is declining due to higher vehicle fuel economy standards and the advent of electric hybrids and other alternative energy vehicles.

The U.S. corn industry is therefore not likely to see any further big increase in demand from the ethanol industry. Moreover, government regulators are now more interested in promoting advanced biofuels that are made from non-food feedstocks such as cellulosic ethanol.

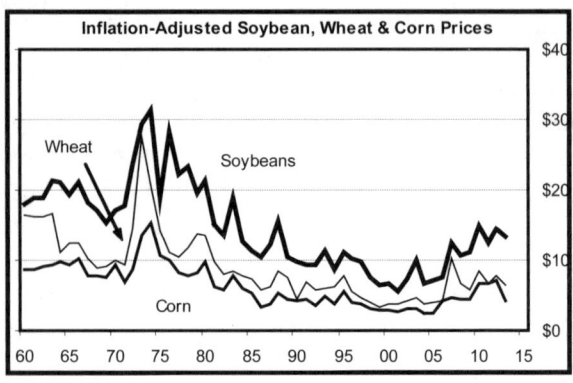

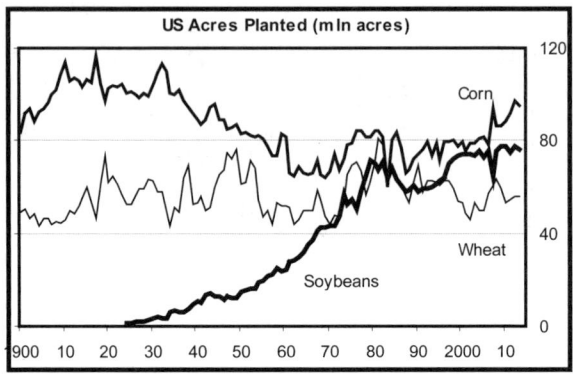

Long-term US acreage planting trends

The nearby chart of U.S. planting trends, which incorporates data from the *CRB Commodity Yearbook* shows how corn a century ago in 1900 was the dominant crop in the U.S., with corn acreage almost twice that of wheat acreage. Acres planted with wheat have fluctuated in a wide range but have moved basically sideways in the past 100 years and current wheat planting acreage in the U.S. isn't much different than it was back in 1900.

The most striking feature of the chart is the rise in the popularity of soybeans in the 1930s and 1940s, and particularly after World War II. In fact, U.S. farmland planted with soybeans is now only mildly below that of corn. Corn acres fell from 1930 through the 1970s to accommodate the higher acres planted with soybeans.

Soybeans after World War II became known as the "Miracle Bean." Soybean prices were higher than corn prices and soybeans were generally easier to grow. Demand for soybeans surged due in part to the high protein content in soybeans. Soybean meal, with its high protein content, could be used as a super-charger for animal feed. Soybean oil found very strong demand since it is nearly tasteless and colorless and is ideal for use in processed foods. Soybean oil is now used to produce biodiesel vehicle fuel as well.

Grain & Soybean Price History

Grain and soybean prices during the 1950s and 1960s were undoubtedly considered by farmers at the time to be volatile as prices were buffeted by the usual fluctuations in supply due mainly to the weather. The U.S. government tried to support and stabilize prices in order to support U.S. farmers. However, by modern standards of volatility, grain and soybean prices during the 1950s and 1960s were remarkably stable. That stability ended in the early 1970s, however, when grain and soybean prices soared to levels that were unimaginable at the time.

In theory, the volatility of grain and soybean prices should be trending lower. The rise of South America as a major producer now provides a counter-cyclical harvest supply during the winter season in the Northern Hemisphere and also diversifies world production from a weather standpoint. Yet a quick look at the charts shows that grain and soybean prices are now even more volatile than they were back in the 1980s and 1990s.

1972 Soviet grain purchases and inflation

Starting in the summer of 1972, grain and soybean prices started to rally sharply. Soybean prices nearly quadrupled from $3.50 per bushel to a then-record high of $12.90 per bushel (nearest-futures) in early 1973. Corn prices more than tripled from $1.20 per bushel in mid 1972 to nearly $4 in 1973. Wheat prices more than tripled to as high as $6 per bushel from about $1.60 in mid-1972.

The main factor driving that rally was the Soviet Union's secret purchase of 24 million metric tons of wheat, corn, soybeans and soybean meal during the summer of 1972. The Soviets were forced to make the purchases because of domestic shortages caused by poor crops in the Soviet Union starting in 1970. When the Soviet purchases came to light in late 1972 and early 1973, grain and soybean prices soared. Soybean inventories were so depleted that President Nixon had to impose an embargo on soy meal exports so that the U.S. would have enough soy meal for its own needs.

Prices were also boosted in the first half of the 1970s by the general surge in inflation seen in response to the Federal Reserve's expansionary monetary policy and the surge in crude oil prices caused by the Arab oil embargo in October 1973. U.S. inflation soared to 11% in 1975.

The surge in grain and soybean prices in 1972-73 caused the U.S. government to drop its former policy of trying to restrict production in order to support prices. Instead, the U.S. government adopted policies encouraging U.S. farmers to plant as much acreage as they could to meet demand. In addition, Brazil during the early 1970s quickly ramped up its soybean production to take advantage of high prices. Brazilian soybean production soared by roughly six-fold from about 2 million metric tons in 1970-71 to 12.5 million metric tons just 6 years later in 1976-77. This

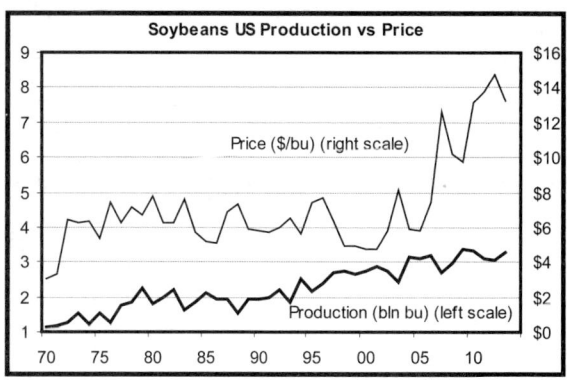

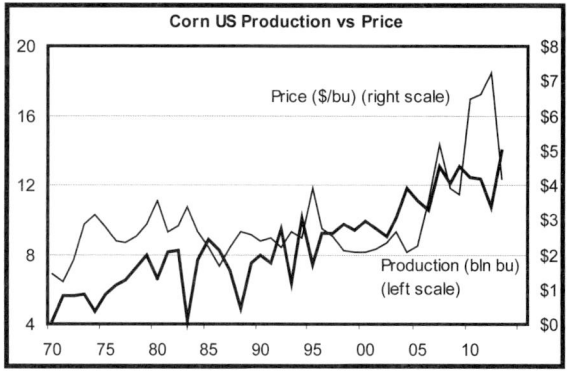

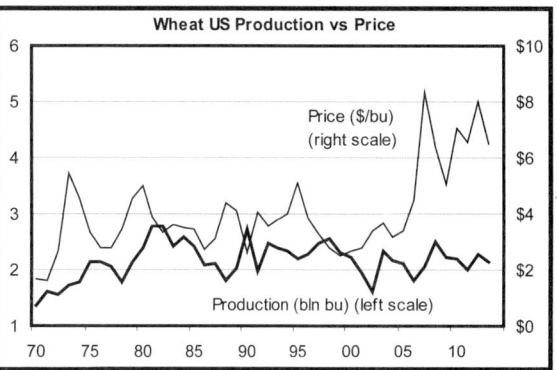

burst of world production created a production surplus of grain and soybeans, which led to extremely volatile prices through the 1970s.

1979 Soviet Grain Embargo

The Soviet Union in the latter half of 1979 entered the market again to make huge purchases of US grain and soybeans, thus pushing prices higher. However, in January 1980, President Carter announced a grain embargo against the Soviet Union in retaliation for its invasion of Afghanistan. The US government was able to prevent a melt-down in prices in response to the embargo by placing the canceled Soviet grain purchases into government loan and reserve programs. The restrictions that kept those inventories locked in loan and reserve programs were so tight that the inventories were not available on the open market when a drought occurred during the summer of 1980. The drought, combined with restricted inventories, resulted in a sharp rally in grain and soybean prices in the first three quarters of 1980. Prices then fell sharply in late 1980 and into 1981-82 after the drought eased and large crops were harvested in 1981 and 1982. There was also the continued overhang from large government inventories. The plunge in grain and soybean prices in 1981-82 caused a farm recession tied to low prices and the buildup of debt that occurred in the 1970s as farmers expanded output.

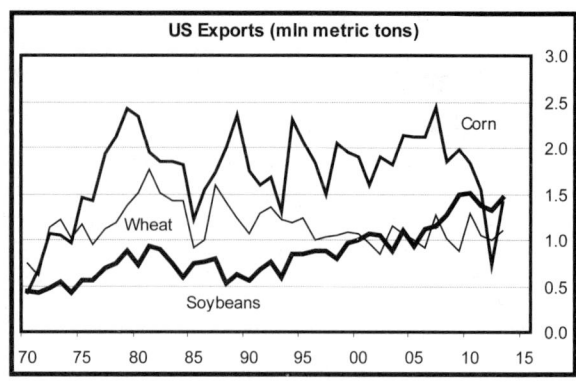

1983 PIK program and drought

In order to allow huge US government inventories of grain and soybeans caused by the Soviet grain embargo to be worked down, the US government created the "PIK" program (payment-in-kind) where the government paid farmers in grain for not planting crops. However, this program took acreage out of production just as a severe drought hit during the summer of 1983, caused by El Nino conditions in the Pacific. The combination of the PIK program and the severe drought caused grain and soybean prices to soar in 1983.

Grain and soybean prices then fell sharply in 1984-86 as US production returned to normal and as the PIK grain that was paid to farmers came onto the market. This caused the return of the recessionary conditions for farmers that started in the early 1980s. There were widespread bankruptcies in the agriculture industry during the mid-1980s. The first Farm Aid concert was organized in 1985 by Willie Nelson, Neil Young and John Mellencamp in an effort to help American farmers during those recessionary times (see www.FarmAid.org).

1988 Drought

Grain and soybean prices soared during spring-1988 as a severe winter drought extended into spring. However, rain in July eased conditions and improved yields, and prices quickly dropped back to more normal levels.

1993 Midwestern Flood

Grain and soybean prices were subdued in 1991-92 with generally favorable weather and large crops in 1992. However, the Midwest was swamped with rain in 1993 in a "500-year flood" that destroyed a significant part of Midwestern crops, thus leading to a moderate rally in grain and soybean prices in 1993.

1996-97 demand-driven rally

Grain and soybean prices rallied in 1995-97 mainly because of strong demand by China, which in 1995 became a net importer, rather than an exporter, of corn. China also became a big buyer of vegetable oils and wheat.

1998-2000 bear market

US crops were relatively large during 1997-2002, which led to relatively high inventories and depressed prices in that time frame.

2003-04 spike on poor weather and low inventories

Inventory levels were already headed downward in 2000-02 when a spell of hot and dry weather hit in 2003. The US soybean crop in 2003 was the smallest in seven years. Demand remained relatively strong, however, driving inventories to extremely low levels that produced the sharp rally in late 2003 and early-2004. Corn showed a smaller rally in 2003-04 since corn escaped from the hot and dry weather and the 2003-04 crop was large at 10.1 billion bushels.

2004-05 large crops produce subdued prices

The summer of 2004 saw ideal growing conditions with plenty of rain and cool temperatures. The result was record crops for soybeans and corn, and a large wheat crop as well. Crop sizes were large again in 2005 despite drought conditions in the Central Midwest. The result was a buildup in inventories into 2005 with a record carry-over in soybeans and a 12-year high carry-over in corn. The high production and carry-overs resulted in depressed soybean and corn prices in 2004 and 2005. At the time, there were great concerns about soybean rust disease which first reached the US in late 2004 (see www.usda.gov/soybeanrust). Fortunately, soybean rust turned out to be a minor problem during the summer of 2005 and did not cause significant yield losses.

2006-08 rally

Corn, wheat and soybean prices soared starting in 2006 mainly because ethanol demand suddenly became a major factor in driving corn prices higher. The strong demand for corn, in fact, led to a sharp 34% decline in

2006-07 U.S. ending stocks to a 3-year low of 1.304 billion bushels. Ethanol producers scrambled to buy cash corn during fall 2006 and winter 2007 in order to ensure they could keep their ethanol plants running at full capacity.

As a result of the rally in corn prices to the $4 per bushel area by winter 2007, U.S. farmers sharply boosted their corn planting in spring 2007 by 19.4% to a then-record 93.5 million acres in the spring of 2007. The huge number of acres planted with corn during spring 2007, combined with favorable weather during summer 2007, led to a big +24% increase in the 2007-08 corn crop to a then-record 13.1 billion bushels. The 2007 corn crop was large enough to meet the increased demand of ethanol producers and corn prices therefore eased to the low-$3 per bushel area by summer 2007. In fact, the U.S. ending stocks in 2007-08 rose +24.5% to 1.624 billion bushels, higher than the 5-year average of 1.59 billion bushels.

Corn, soybean and wheat prices in early 2008 extended their rallies to record highs thanks in part to speculative fever for commodities. Wheat on a nearest-futures basis posted a record high of $13.3450 per bushel in February 2008. Corn hit its then-record high of $7.65 per bushel four months later in June 2008. Soybeans finally posted their then-record high of $16.63 per bushel in July 2008.

2008 plunge

After posting record highs earlier in 2008, corn, soybean and wheat prices went into an all-out plunge in late 2008. From the 2008 record highs to the lows established in December 2008, corn plunged by an overall -62%, soybeans by -53%, and wheat by -65%. Grain and wheat prices had already sold off sharply even before the banking crisis emerged in mid-September 2008 with the bankruptcy of Lehman Brothers. The weather during the summer of 2008 was favorable and crop sizes were relatively large, leading to downward price pressure. Corn prices were also hurt by a sharp drop in ethanol production, which became unprofitable in late 2008 and early 2009 when gasoline prices fell sharply and took ethanol prices lower as well.

2009-2011

After the 2008 plunge, corn, soybean and wheat prices moved sideways during 2009 and the first half of 2010. In mid-2010, wheat prices soared due to the worst drought in Russia since record-keeping began more than 130 years ago. Corn and soybeans saw carry-over support from the wheat rally and were also supported by strong Chinese demand for U.S. corn and soybean exports.

The 2011 planting season in the U.S. got off to a slow start due to heavy rain and flooding during the spring. However, weather was generally favorable during the summer and there were good-sized crops. Corn and soybean prices saw some strength during the winter of 2011/12 due to a drought in South America that hurt the South

American corn and soybean crops. This was the second consecutive drought during the South American growing season, which helped tighten global corn and soybean inventories.

Summer 2012 drought → 2016 | > 2017

The weather in spring 2012 started out on a favorable note and farmers were able to get into the fields to plant their crops early. However, a severe drought appeared by June and lasted throughout the summer. Corn and soybean conditions later in the summer were as bad as they were during the 1988 "drought of the century." The drought by September turned out to be the worst since 1956 and the fifth worst in U.S. recorded history going back to 1895, affecting 57.2% of the lower 48 states, according to NOAA. The drought did not have much effect on the 2012 spring wheat crop, however, since the drought did not extend up in the northern reaches of the U.S. where most spring wheat is grown.

The drought caused U.S. corn production in 2012-13 to drop sharply by -12.8% to 10.78 billion bushels. U.S. 2012-13 ending stocks plunged by -54% to 661 million bushels, causing the stocks-to-use ratio to drop to 5.9%, the tightest in nearly two decades.

U.S. soybean production during 2012-13 fell by -1.9% to 3.03 billion bushels while ending stocks fell by -20% to a 10-year low of 141 million bushels.

2013 record crops

Corn and soybean prices then weakened in late-2012 and early 2013 thanks to reduced demand and record crops in Brazil and Argentina. Prices then plunged through mid-2013 after heavy spring rains replenished soil moisture in the U.S.. The heavy spring rains delayed planting but that turned out not to be a problem. The weather was very favorable early in the summer and there were bumper crops despite some dryness late in the season.

U.S. corn production in 2013-14 rose by +30% y/y to a record high of 13.989 billion bushels in 2013-14 and corn ending stocks rose sharply to 1.79 billion bushels from 661 million bushels in 2012-13, according to preliminary figures. U.S. soybean production in 2013-14 rose by +7.4% y/y to a near-record high of 3.258 billion bushels. However, 2013-14 U.S. soybean ending stocks rose to only 150 million bushels from 141 million bushels in 2012-13 due to very strong Chinese demand for U.S. soybean exports.

Corn prices saw further weakness in late 2013 when the EPA announced a cut in the corn-based ethanol mandate in the Renewable Fuel Standard to 13.0 billion gallons for 2014 from 13.8 billion gallons in 2013. The market expects that ethanol mandate cut to reduce corn demand from U.S. ethanol producers in 2014.

CORN

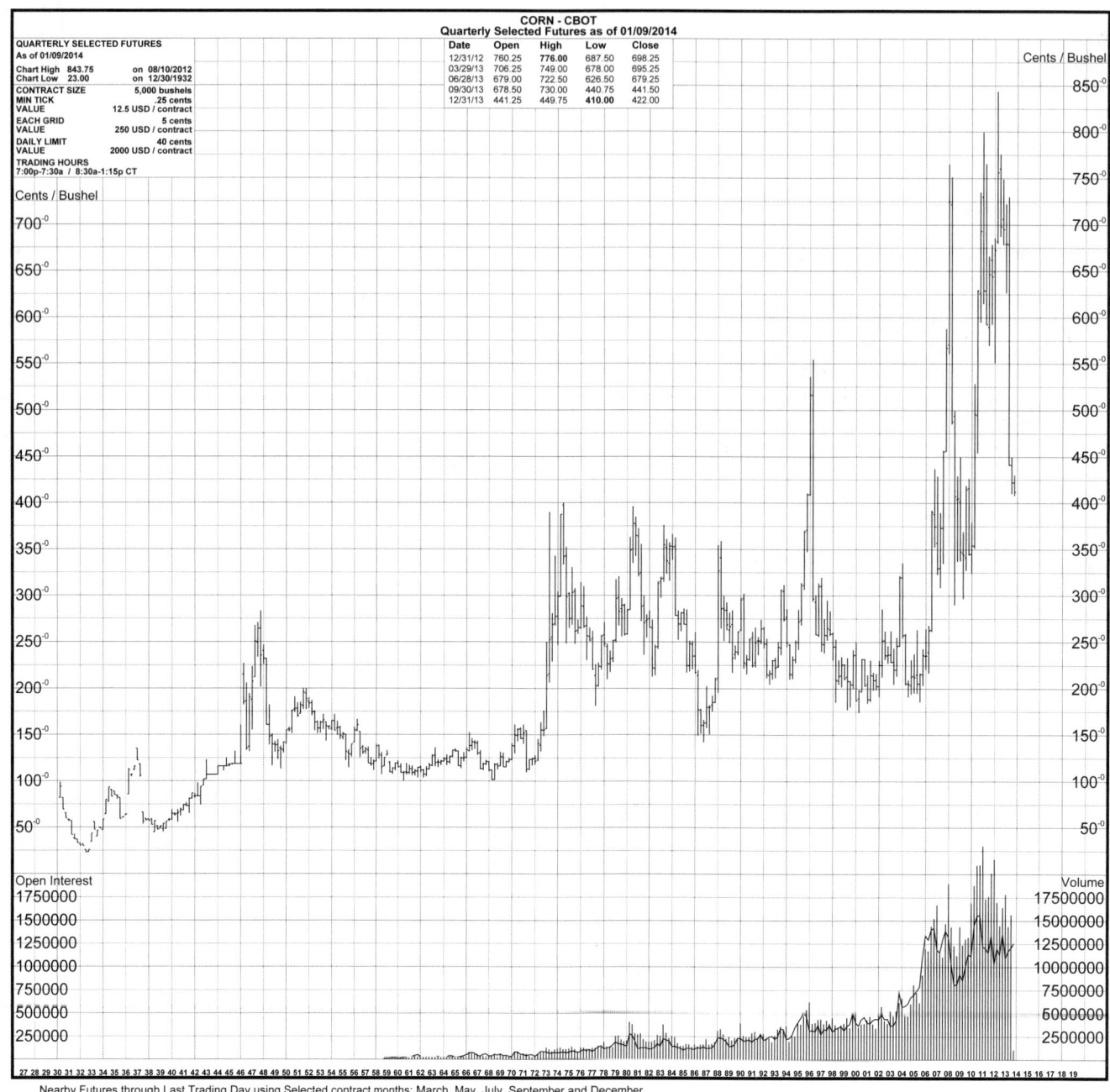

Nearby Futures through Last Trading Day using Selected contract months: March, May, July, September and December.

Annual High, Low and Settle of Corn Futures In Cents per Bushel

Year	High	Low	Settle	Year	High	Low	Settle	Year	High	Low	Settle
1930	98.88	69.50	69.50	1944	116.00	107.00	116.00	1958	140.25	107.25	115.50
1931	65.38	37.13	37.13	1945	132.25	115.50	118.50	1959	133.25	107.38	113.88
1932	37.00	23.00	23.00	1946	227.00	118.50	135.25	1960	122.00	100.25	109.38
1933	55.88	23.13	46.50	1947	271.00	131.75	264.00	1961	119.13	105.75	110.75
1934	93.25	47.25	93.25	1948	283.38	139.00	147.88	1962	116.25	103.50	112.75
1935	90.75	59.00	59.00	1949	150.50	113.00	134.25	1963	136.00	112.25	120.13
1936	113.50	60.75	107.25	1950	176.25	130.25	176.00	1964	128.50	117.00	126.38
1937	135.00	53.38	56.13	1951	200.13	168.63	195.75	1965	135.25	113.75	124.88
1938	59.25	44.75	57.00	1952	199.63	154.25	163.13	1966	152.38	121.00	142.00
1939	56.25	45.00	56.25	1953	171.88	143.00	159.00	1967	144.00	111.63	118.38
1940	69.50	55.50	65.50	1954	171.75	149.38	157.38	1968	122.75	101.25	117.88
1941	82.00	62.00	81.00	1955	159.13	114.50	128.75	1969	131.50	112.50	121.13
1942	98.25	74.50	94.00	1956	166.50	125.63	135.00	1970	160.75	120.13	155.50
1943	123.00	95.25	107.00	1957	138.38	116.13	118.13	1971	160.75	109.50	123.38

Futures data begins 07/01/1959. Data continued on page 202. *Source: CME Group; Chicago Board of Trade*

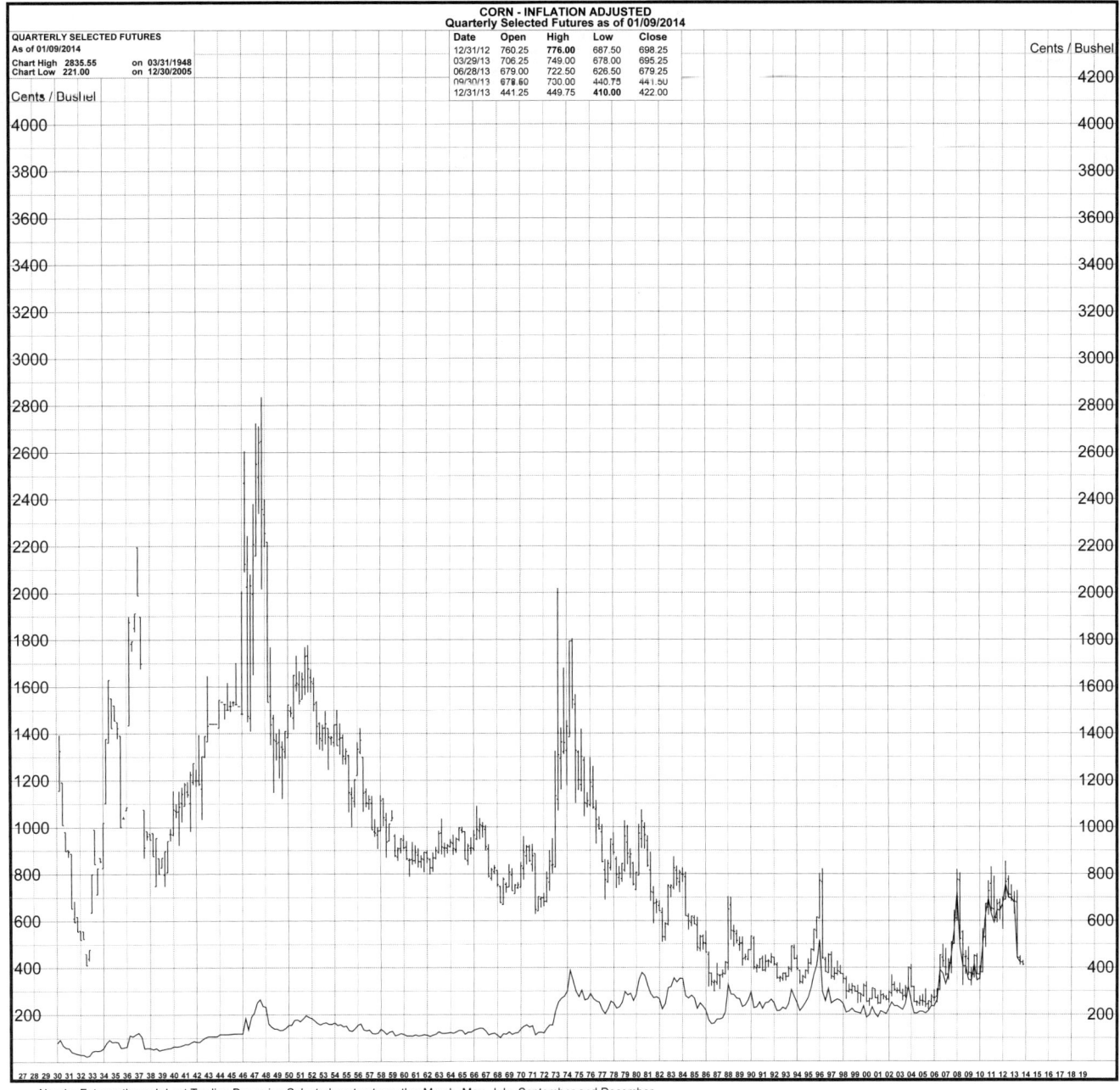

CORN - INFLATION ADJUSTED
Quarterly Selected Futures as of 01/09/2014

Date	Open	High	Low	Close
12/31/12	760.25	**776.00**	687.50	698.25
03/29/13	706.25	749.00	678.00	695.25
06/28/13	679.00	722.50	626.50	679.25
09/30/13	678.60	730.00	440.75	441.50
12/31/13	441.25	449.75	**410.00**	422.00

QUARTERLY SELECTED FUTURES
As of 01/09/2014

Chart High 2835.55 on 03/31/1948
Chart Low 221.00 on 12/30/2005

Cents / Bushel

Nearby Futures through Last Trading Day using Selected contract months: March, May, July, September and December.

Annual High, Low and Settle of Corn — In Cents per Bushel

Year	High	Low	Settle	Year	High	Low	Settle	Year	High	Low	Settle
1930	98.88	69.50	69.50	1944	116.00	107.00	116.00	1958	140.25	107.25	115.50
1931	65.38	37.13	37.13	1945	132.25	115.50	118.50	1959	133.25	108.75	116.00
1932	37.00	23.00	23.00	1946	227.00	118.50	135.25	1960	125.00	94.50	110.50
1933	55.88	23.13	46.50	1947	271.00	131.75	264.00	1961	119.00	104.75	111.50
1934	93.25	47.25	93.25	1948	283.38	139.00	147.88	1962	119.25	108.00	117.00
1935	90.75	59.00	59.00	1949	150.50	113.00	134.25	1963	138.50	116.00	124.50
1936	113.50	60.75	107.25	1950	176.25	130.25	176.00	1964	130.50	115.00	129.50
1937	135.00	53.38	56.13	1951	200.13	168.63	195.75	1965	139.00	114.50	126.50
1938	59.25	44.75	57.00	1952	199.63	154.25	163.13	1966	153.50	125.50	144.00
1939	56.25	45.00	56.25	1953	171.88	143.00	159.00	1967	145.00	106.50	113.50
1940	69.50	55.50	65.50	1954	171.75	149.38	157.38	1968	121.50	103.00	119.00
1941	82.00	62.00	81.00	1955	159.13	114.50	128.75	1969	135.25	115.00	122.25
1942	98.25	74.50	94.00	1956	166.50	125.63	135.00	1970	159.88	121.50	157.50
1943	123.00	95.25	107.00	1957	138.38	116.13	118.13	1971	163.75	102.50	122.25

Chicago #3 Yellow through 12/1939; Chicago #2 Yellow 01/02/1940 to date. Data continued on page 203. *Source: U.S. Department of Agriculture*

CORN

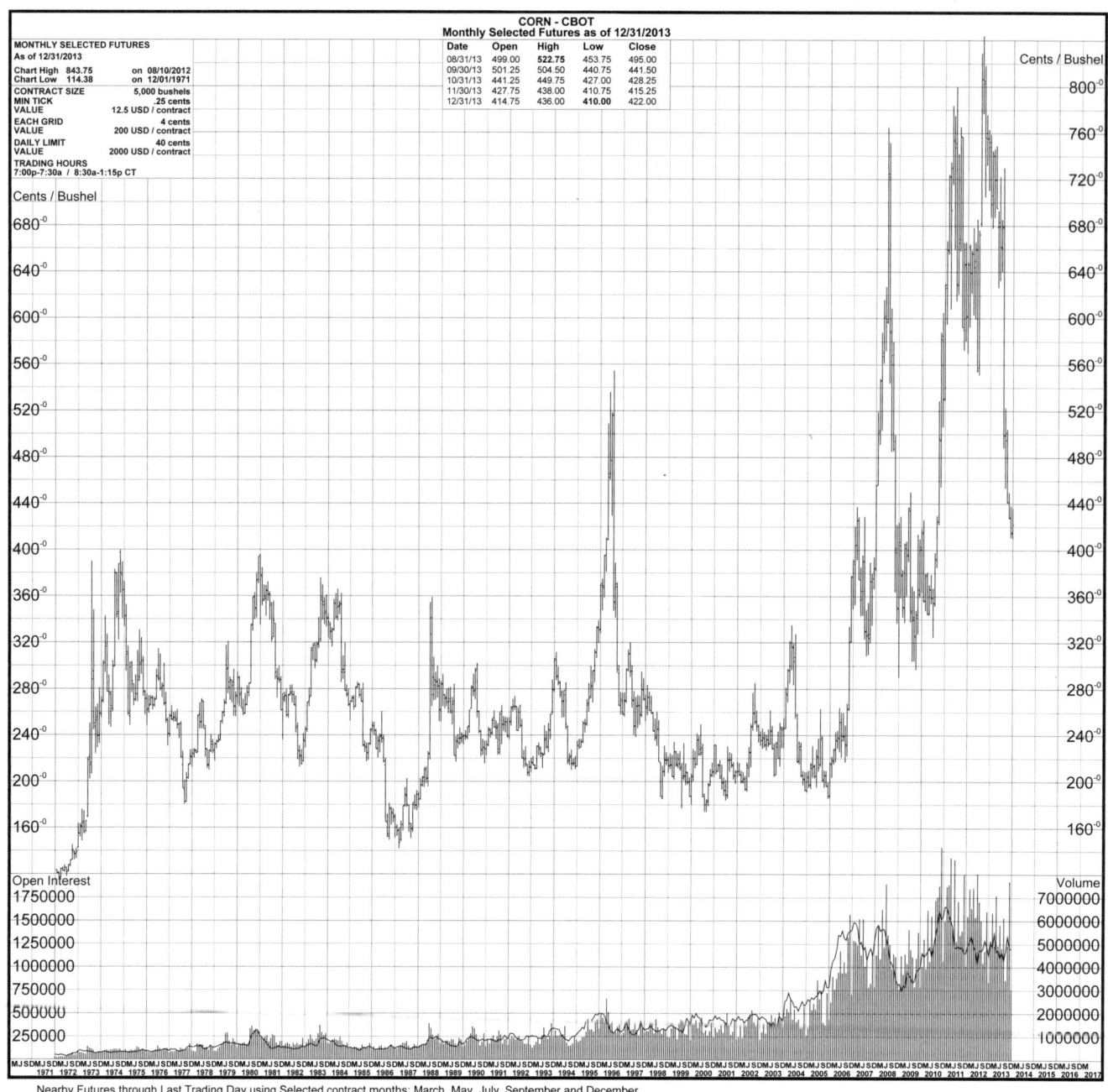

CORN - CBOT
Monthly Selected Futures as of 12/31/2013

Date	Open	High	Low	Close
08/31/13	499.00	522.75	453.75	495.00
09/30/13	501.25	504.50	440.75	441.50
10/31/13	441.25	449.75	427.00	428.25
11/30/13	427.75	438.00	410.75	415.25
12/31/13	414.75	436.00	410.00	422.00

MONTHLY SELECTED FUTURES
As of 12/31/2013

Chart High 843.75 on 08/10/2012
Chart Low 114.38 on 12/01/1971
CONTRACT SIZE 5,000 bushels
MIN TICK .25 cents
VALUE 12.5 USD / contract
EACH GRID 4 cents
VALUE 200 USD / contract
DAILY LIMIT 40 cents
VALUE 2000 USD / contract
TRADING HOURS
7:00p-7:30a / 8:30a-1:15p CT

Nearby Futures through Last Trading Day using Selected contract months: March, May, July, September and December.

Annual High, Low and Settle of Corn Futures   In Cents per Bushel

Year	High	Low	Settle	Year	High	Low	Settle	Year	High	Low	Settle
1972	163.50	116.87	155.00	1986	260.50	149.25	160.00	2000	249.50	174.00	231.75
1973	390.00	148.50	268.75	1987	202.75	142.00	184.75	2001	232.00	184.00	209.00
1974	400.00	246.50	342.00	1988	359.00	184.25	284.50	2002	285.50	191.50	235.75
1975	352.50	247.75	261.50	1989	292.75	217.00	239.75	2003	262.00	204.50	246.00
1976	314.50	230.50	256.50	1990	302.25	215.50	231.75	2004	335.25	191.00	204.75
1977	265.50	180.75	223.75	1991	266.00	223.00	251.50	2005	263.25	185.75	215.75
1978	271.50	209.75	231.75	1992	274.00	204.50	216.50	2006	392.00	203.50	390.25
1979	320.75	228.00	289.50	1993	306.75	210.00	306.00	2007	457.00	308.50	455.50
1980	396.00	256.50	378.00	1994	311.75	210.00	231.00	2008	765.00	290.00	407.00
1981	384.75	236.00	270.50	1995	370.50	227.75	369.25	2009	450.00	296.75	414.50
1982	283.50	212.50	244.75	1996	554.50	257.75	258.25	2010	630.00	324.50	629.00
1983	376.00	242.25	337.25	1997	320.00	238.25	265.00	2011	799.75	570.00	646.50
1984	366.00	252.25	269.25	1998	283.50	185.00	213.50	2012	843.75	551.00	698.25
1985	286.00	217.00	248.25	1999	234.25	177.00	204.50	2013	749.00	410.00	422.00

Data continued from page 200.   *Source: CME Group; Chicago Board of Trade*

MONTHLY CASH
As of 12/31/2013

Chart High 864.50   on 07/20/2012
Chart Low 115.50   on 12/01/1971

Cents / Bushel

Date	Open	High	Low	Close
08/30/13	602.50	**684.25**	585.25	662.00
09/30/13	605.25	605.25	450.50	450.50
10/31/13	450.00	451.38	424.75	424.75
11/29/13	423.75	437.75	**417.00**	424.25
12/31/13	430.75	437.75	418.50	418.50

Corn, #2 Yellow, Chicago
Monthly Cash as of 12/31/2013

#2 yellow, Chicago: to 03/1982; #2 yellow, Chicago: 03/1982 to date.

Annual High, Low and Settle of Corn   In Cents per Bushel

Year	High	Low	Settle	Year	High	Low	Settle	Year	High	Low	Settle
1972	165.50	120.00	156.25	1986	265.00	143.00	160.00	2000	243.75	161.75	222.25
1973	340.00	153.00	266.50	1987	199.75	141.25	183.25	2001	227.25	183.50	205.00
1974	396.50	253.50	341.75	1988	327.50	189.50	277.50	2002	292.50	196.75	240.75
1975	347.75	247.75	255.50	1989	285.50	228.25	237.25	2003	265.75	219.75	249.00
1976	313.75	223.25	251.75	1990	297.25	214.50	237.75	2004	331.50	189.50	202.75
1977	262.75	172.25	220.25	1991	268.25	230.00	256.50	2005	256.00	179.00	205.75
1978	270.25	209.50	228.75	1992	282.75	208.00	219.00	2006	380.25	199.00	380.25
1979	312.50	225.50	271.00	1993	311.00	210.00	311.00	2007	449.75	302.00	448.50
1980	369.00	230.25	362.00	1994	311.75	204.75	236.00	2008	732.75	287.25	388.00
1981	365.75	242.00	251.50	1995	369.25	233.50	369.25	2009	449.50	316.00	386.50
1982	284.00	204.00	242.75	1996	558.50	266.50	268.25	2010	610.00	327.00	604.00
1983	383.75	240.75	335.25	1997	313.25	245.25	269.00	2011	792.00	582.50	651.50
1984	370.25	259.25	275.25	1998	287.75	182.25	213.25	2012	864.50	597.50	709.75
1985	291.75	221.75	254.25	1999	230.50	173.75	204.50	2013	764.00	417.00	418.50

Chicago #2 Yellow.   Data continued from page 201.   *Source: U.S. Department of Agriculture (USDA)*

CORN

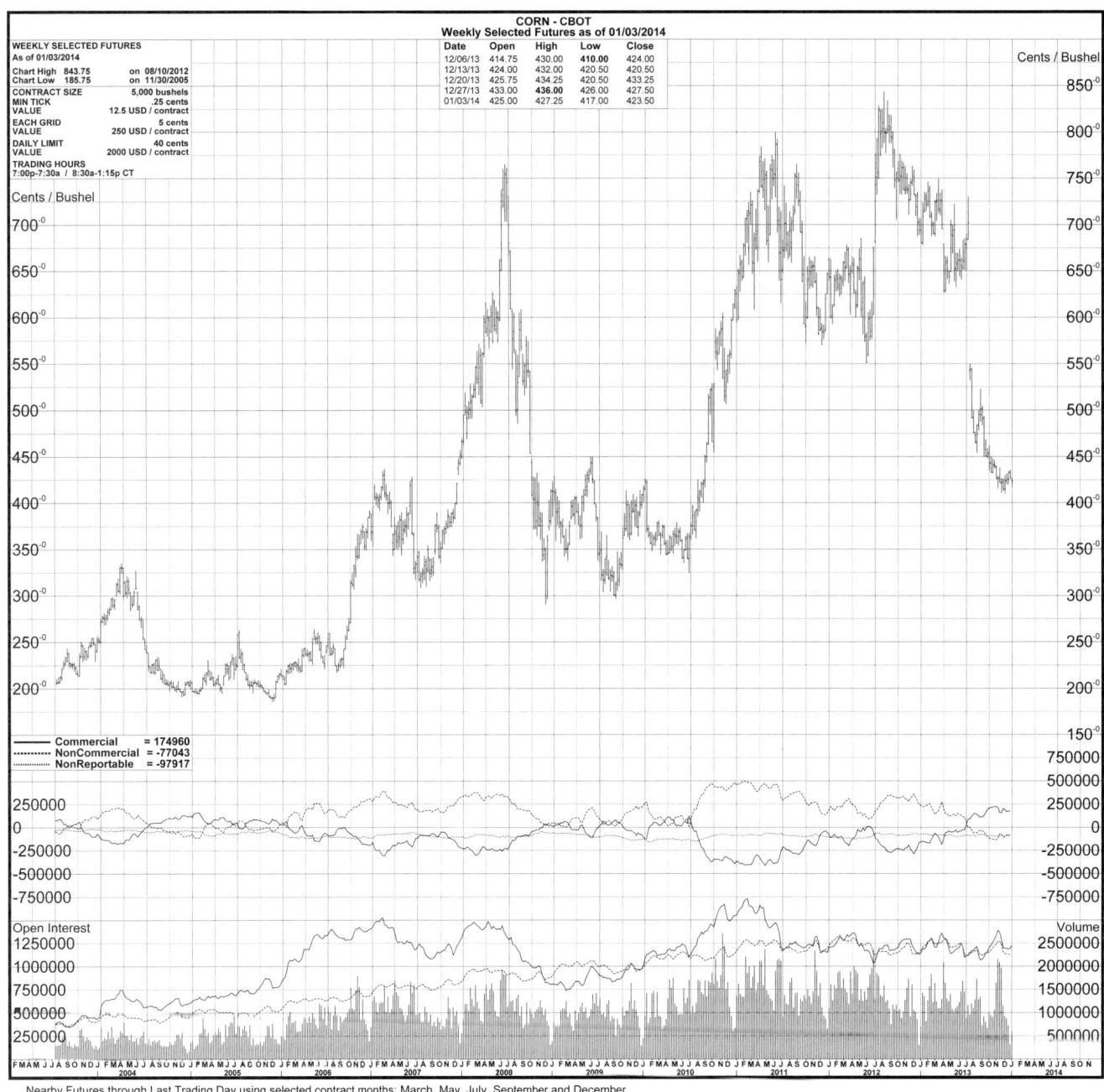

CORN - CBOT
Weekly Selected Futures as of 01/03/2014

Date	Open	High	Low	Close
12/06/13	414.75	430.00	**410.00**	424.00
12/13/13	424.00	432.00	420.50	420.50
12/20/13	425.75	434.25	420.50	433.25
12/27/13	433.00	**436.00**	426.00	427.50
01/03/14	425.00	427.25	417.00	423.50

WEEKLY SELECTED FUTURES
As of 01/03/2014

Chart High 843.75 on 08/10/2012
Chart Low   185.75 on 11/30/2005
CONTRACT SIZE   5,000 bushels
MIN TICK   .25 cents
VALUE   12.5 USD / contract
EACH GRID   5 cents
VALUE   250 USD / contract
DAILY LIMIT   40 cents
VALUE   2000 USD / contract
TRADING HOURS
7:00p-7:30a / 8:30a-1:15p CT

Commercial   = 174960
NonCommercial = -77043
NonReportable = -97917

Open Interest

Nearby Futures through Last Trading Day using selected contract months: March, May, July, September and December.

Quarterly High, Low and Settle of Corn Futures   In Cents per Bushel

Quarter	High	Low	Settle	Quarter	High	Low	Settle	Quarter	High	Low	Settle
03/2005	231.00	194.00	213.00	03/2008	588.00	456.00	567.25	03/2011	735.00	595.00	693.25
06/2005	237.50	195.25	212.25	06/2008	765.00	561.25	724.75	06/2011	799.75	615.00	629.00
09/2005	263.25	195.00	205.50	09/2008	751.50	485.25	487.50	09/2011	765.50	592.50	592.50
12/2005	217.00	185.75	215.75	12/2008	500.00	290.00	407.00	12/2011	666.00	570.00	646.50
03/2006	243.00	203.50	236.00	03/2009	429.00	337.25	404.75	03/2012	678.50	592.50	644.00
06/2006	264.25	221.00	235.50	06/2009	450.00	337.75	347.75	06/2012	685.75	551.00	672.50
09/2006	268.00	216.75	262.50	09/2009	369.00	296.75	344.00	09/2012	843.75	679.75	756.25
12/2006	392.00	261.50	390.25	12/2009	418.75	327.50	414.50	12/2012	776.00	687.50	698.25
03/2007	437.25	352.50	374.50	03/2010	426.25	344.00	345.00	03/2013	749.00	678.00	695.25
06/2007	428.75	323.00	329.50	06/2010	379.00	324.50	354.25	06/2013	722.50	626.50	679.25
09/2007	389.50	308.50	373.00	09/2010	528.75	351.50	495.75	09/2013	730.00	440.75	441.50
12/2007	457.00	335.00	455.50	12/2010	630.00	454.25	629.00	12/2013	449.75	410.00	422.00

Source: CME Group; Chicago Board of Trade

Corn, #2 Yellow, Chicago
Weekly Cash as of 01/03/2014

Date	Open	High	Low	Close
12/06/13	430.75	434.50	430.75	432.25
12/13/13	436.50	437.75	425.50	425.50
12/20/13	423.25	429.25	422.50	429.25
12/27/13	430.25	430.50	422.75	424.00
01/03/14	420.00	424.00	418.50	424.00

WEEKLY CASH
As of 01/03/2014

Chart High 864.50 on 07/20/2012
Chart Low 179.00 on 10/28/2005

Cents / Bushel

#2 yellow, Chicago.

Quarterly High, Low and Settle of Corn   In Cents per Bushel

Quarter	High	Low	Settle	Quarter	High	Low	Settle	Quarter	High	Low	Settle
06/2005	234.75	205.50	216.25	03/2008	562.25	455.50	562.25	03/2011	718.75	583.00	681.25
09/2005	256.00	191.75	196.50	06/2008	732.75	570.25	702.75	06/2011	792.00	641.00	641.00
12/2005	206.25	179.00	205.75	09/2008	726.00	468.50	468.50	09/2011	763.50	582.50	582.50
03/2006	220.00	199.00	220.00	12/2008	465.00	287.25	388.00	12/2011	670.50	589.00	651.50
06/2006	250.00	220.50	235.50	03/2009	412.50	350.50	408.75	03/2012	690.00	601.50	667.00
09/2006	260.25	206.75	257.50	06/2009	449.50	361.75	361.75	06/2012	694.50	597.50	688.50
12/2006	380.25	251.00	380.25	09/2009	376.00	316.00	350.00	09/2012	864.50	692.25	767.25
03/2007	422.00	351.50	368.50	12/2009	401.75	339.50	386.50	12/2012	793.25	705.50	709.75
06/2007	424.00	333.50	333.50	03/2010	404.50	344.00	344.00	03/2013	764.00	701.25	722.25
09/2007	376.50	302.00	360.00	06/2010	376.25	327.00	356.25	06/2013	746.25	652.00	672.25
12/2007	449.75	330.25	448.50	09/2010	494.75	352.75	465.75	09/2013	703.25	450.50	450.50
12/2002	266.00	237.75	240.75	12/2010	610.00	435.75	604.00	12/2013	451.38	417.00	418.50

Chicago #2 Yellow.   *Source: U.S. Department of Agriculture (USDA)*

OATS

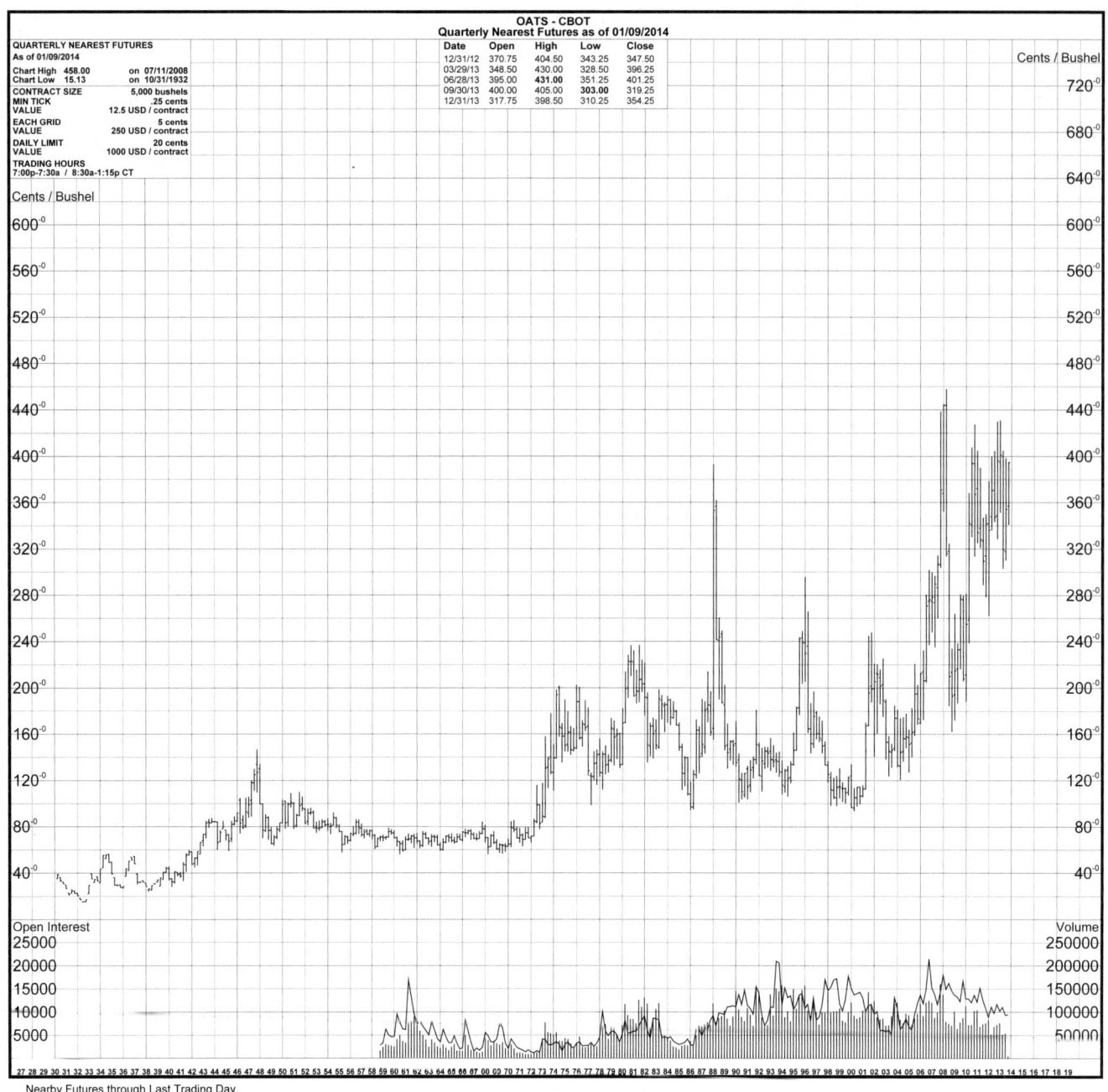

OATS - CBOT
Quarterly Nearest Futures as of 01/09/2014

Date	Open	High	Low	Close
12/31/12	370.75	404.50	343.25	347.50
03/29/13	348.50	430.00	328.50	396.25
06/28/13	395.00	431.00	351.25	401.25
09/30/13	400.00	405.00	303.00	319.25
12/31/13	317.75	398.50	310.25	354.25

QUARTERLY NEAREST FUTURES
As of 01/09/2014
Chart High 458.00 on 07/11/2008
Chart Low 15.13 on 10/31/1932
CONTRACT SIZE 5,000 bushels
MIN TICK .25 cents
VALUE 12.5 USD / contract
EACH GRID 5 cents
VALUE 250 USD / contract
DAILY LIMIT 20 cents
VALUE 1000 USD / contract
TRADING HOURS
7:00p-7:30a / 8:30a-1:15p CT

Nearby Futures through Last Trading Day.

Annual High, Low and Settle of Oats Futures   In Cents per Bushel

Year	High	Low	Settle	Year	High	Low	Settle	Year	High	Low	Settle
1930	44.75	32.50	33.63	1944	87.75	60.00	75.00	1958	77.50	60.50	69.38
1931	32.38	20.75	24.75	1945	85.00	59.00	82.00	1959	81.75	67.25	75.63
1932	24.63	15.13	15.38	1946	105.00	74.00	79.00	1960	77.75	56.00	64.88
1933	39.25	15.13	34.63	1947	130.00	79.00	125.00	1961	74.00	58.50	71.75
1934	55.75	31.75	55.75	1948	146.75	70.00	88.13	1962	76.00	61.13	73.63
1935	56.25	29.00	29.25	1949	89.13	63.25	77.63	1963	75.38	62.38	70.75
1936	50.38	26.63	50.38	1950	103.25	75.13	99.50	1964	73.00	59.00	71.63
1937	54.38	30.25	32.38	1951	110.00	78.00	98.38	1965	74.25	65.13	70.88
1938	33.50	24.00	29.25	1952	106.25	81.25	92.50	1966	78.00	67.13	76.13
1939	40.75	28.75	40.75	1953	94.25	74.50	84.25	1967	77.75	67.75	73.88
1940	45.75	28.00	41.25	1954	92.50	73.25	88.00	1968	84.38	56.00	72.13
1941	57.00	33.00	55.50	1955	88.50	57.50	71.50	1969	75.88	56.50	63.63
1942	59.75	44.75	58.50	1956	86.50	65.00	84.00	1970	85.75	58.00	77.25
1943	87.00	56.50	83.25	1957	86.50	69.63	73.25	1971	80.00	62.75	74.50

Chicago, #2 White.   Futures data begins 07/01/1959.   Data continued on page 208.   *Source: CME Group; Chicago Board of Trade*

OATS - INFLATION ADJUSTED
Quarterly Nearest Futures as of 01/09/2014

Date	Open	High	Low	Close
12/31/12	370.75	404.50	343.25	347.50
03/29/13	348.50	430.00	328.50	396.25
06/28/13	395.00	431.00	351.25	401.25
09/30/13	400.00	405.00	303.00	319.25
12/31/13	317.75	398.50	310.25	354.25

QUARTERLY NEAREST FUTURES
As of 01/09/2014

Chart High 1468.43   on 03/31/1948
Chart Low   126.04   on 09/29/2000

Cents / Bushel

Nearby Futures through Last Trading Day.

Annual High, Low and Settle of Oats   In Cents per Bushel

Year	High	Low	Settle	Year	High	Low	Settle	Year	High	Low	Settle
1930	----	----	----	1944	82.00	60.50	70.63	1958	66.50	59.13	63.38
1931	----	----	----	1945	78.25	59.00	76.13	1959	72.13	63.13	71.50
1932	----	----	----	1946	84.50	75.38	81.25	1960	71.75	60.25	61.63
1933	----	----	----	1947	126.13	79.75	126.13	1961	72.00	59.63	72.00
1934	----	----	----	1948	136.63	70.25	80.88	1962	72.00	61.38	72.00
1935	----	----	----	1949	78.25	62.50	74.75	1963	70.38	63.25	68.25
1936	52.63	39.50	52.63	1950	91.75	74.13	91.75	1964	69.75	62.00	69.75
1937	54.38	29.00	29.38	1951	99.75	77.75	99.75	1965	70.25	64.25	67.25
1938	31.25	24.25	28.75	1952	96.38	83.13	87.25	1966	75.25	67.88	74.63
1939	37.00	27.25	37.00	1953	84.88	73.00	79.13	1967	74.63	67.25	70.13
1940	40.50	25.63	34.75	1954	82.50	69.88	78.00	1968	76.25	60.38	67.00
1941	51.38	33.25	51.38	1955	77.13	57.88	65.75	1969	70.38	59.50	65.63
1942	55.63	44.25	52.75	1956	78.00	63.25	77.38	1970	73.88	63.50	72.25
1943	80.25	57.38	80.25	1957	77.88	64.00	65.50	1971	77.50	61.75	68.00

Minneapolis #2 Milling.   Data continued on page 209.   *Source: U.S. Department of Agriculture*

OATS

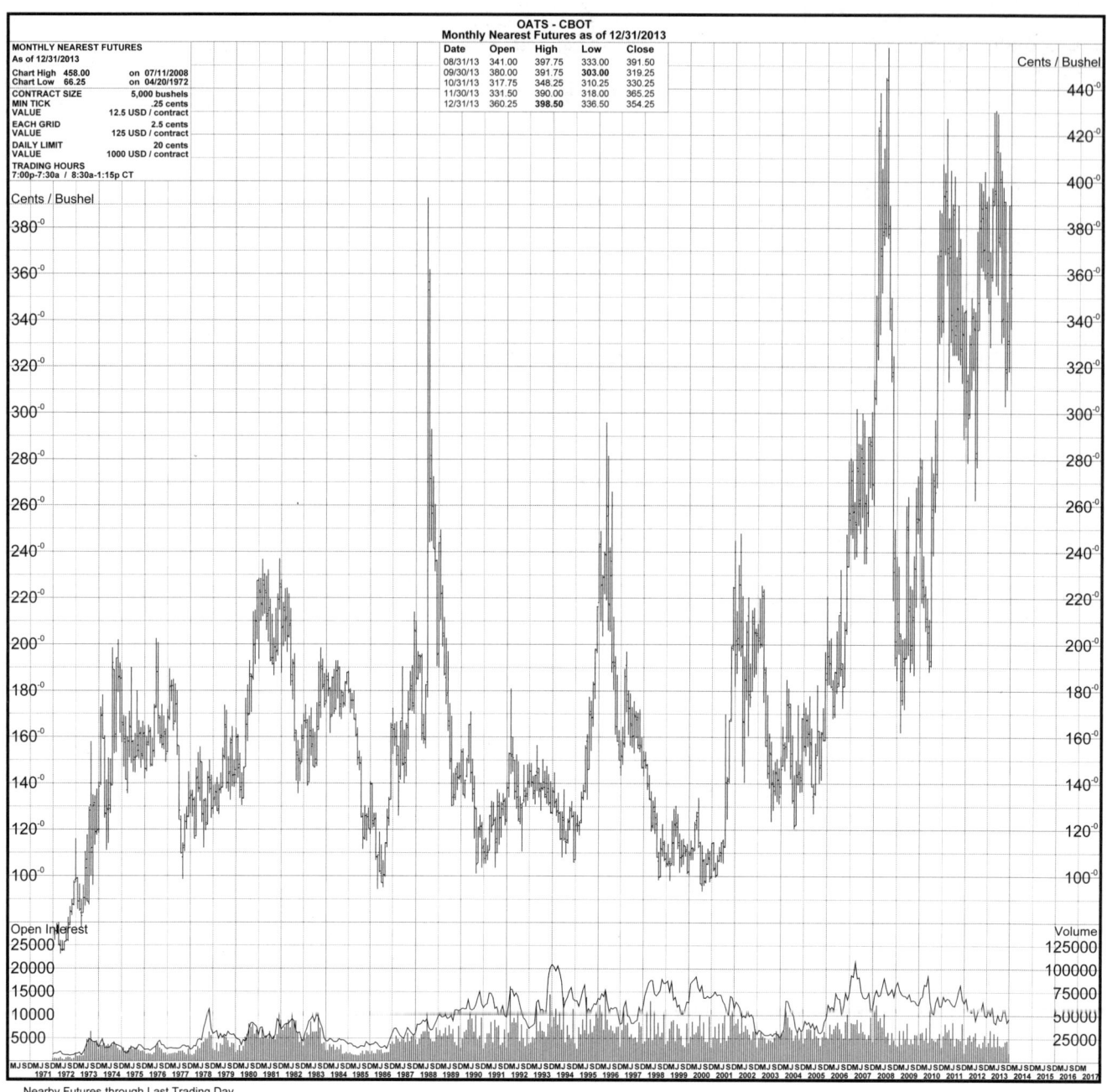

OATS - CBOT Monthly Nearest Futures as of 12/31/2013				
Date	Open	High	Low	Close
08/31/13	341.00	397.75	333.00	391.50
09/30/13	380.00	391.75	303.00	319.25
10/31/13	317.75	348.25	310.25	330.25
11/30/13	331.50	390.00	318.00	365.25
12/31/13	360.25	398.50	336.50	354.25

MONTHLY NEAREST FUTURES
As of 12/31/2013
Chart High 458.00 on 07/11/2008
Chart Low 66.25 on 04/20/1972
CONTRACT SIZE 5,000 bushels
MIN TICK .25 cents
VALUE 12.5 USD / contract
EACH GRID 2.5 cents
VALUE 125 USD / contract
DAILY LIMIT 20 cents
VALUE 1000 USD / contract
TRADING HOURS
7:00p-7:30a / 8:30a-1:15p CT

Nearby Futures through Last Trading Day.

Annual High, Low and Settle of Oats Futures   In Cents per Bushel

Year	High	Low	Settle	Year	High	Low	Settle	Year	High	Low	Settle
1972	116.00	66.25	98.75	1986	172.50	94.25	163.25	2000	134.00	93.50	114.25
1973	158.00	77.75	138.50	1987	214.00	126.00	185.50	2001	245.00	99.50	195.75
1974	202.00	111.00	166.00	1988	393.00	155.00	243.75	2002	248.00	140.50	201.75
1975	190.00	135.50	146.25	1989	249.50	130.25	153.50	2003	225.50	123.50	146.25
1976	202.50	145.00	168.50	1990	171.00	101.00	110.25	2004	185.00	120.50	156.25
1977	189.50	98.50	134.50	1991	140.50	103.50	138.00	2005	220.75	127.00	195.00
1978	155.75	112.00	133.00	1992	181.00	110.50	145.25	2006	280.75	168.00	271.00
1979	173.75	126.50	159.75	1993	156.50	126.75	136.75	2007	314.50	235.00	306.75
1980	228.50	130.50	223.00	1994	144.75	106.00	121.75	2008	458.00	184.50	210.00
1981	237.00	186.50	207.00	1995	243.75	117.50	242.25	2009	281.00	162.00	277.00
1982	224.25	135.50	166.75	1996	296.00	143.50	152.00	2010	407.75	188.25	394.00
1983	198.50	138.75	186.00	1997	197.00	143.25	149.75	2011	427.50	288.75	309.50
1984	193.00	161.50	180.25	1998	153.75	98.25	105.50	2012	404.50	262.25	347.50
1985	181.00	111.50	139.50	1999	130.50	98.00	109.25	2013	431.00	303.00	354.25

Data continued from page 206.   Source: CME Group; Chicago Board of Trade

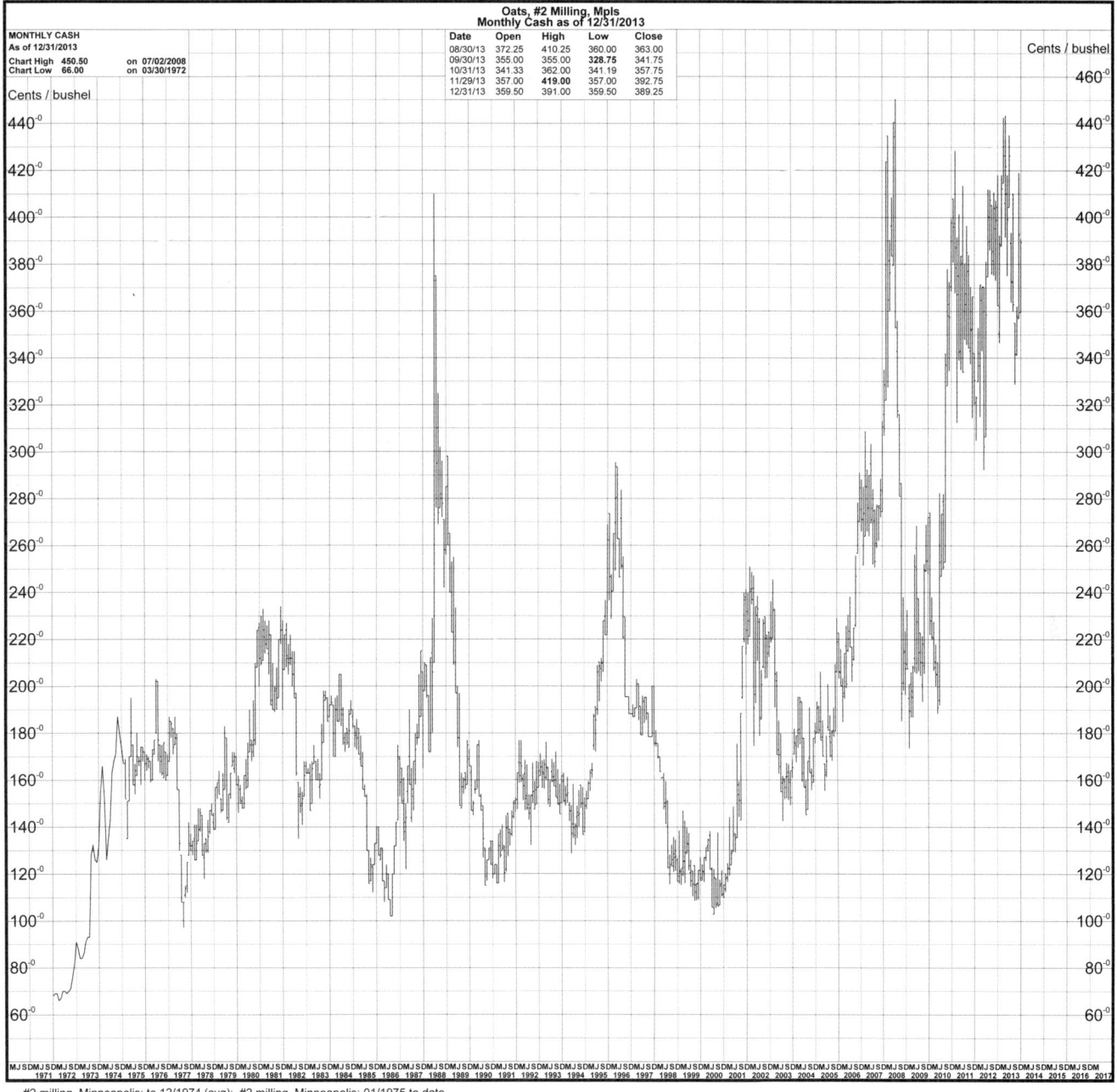

Oats, #2 Milling, Mpls
Monthly Cash as of 12/31/2013

MONTHLY CASH
As of 12/31/2013

Chart High 450.50 on 07/02/2008
Chart Low 66.00 on 03/30/1972

Cents / bushel

Date	Open	High	Low	Close
08/30/13	372.25	410.25	360.00	363.00
09/30/13	355.00	355.00	328.75	341.75
10/31/13	341.33	362.00	341.19	357.75
11/29/13	357.00	419.00	357.00	392.75
12/31/13	359.50	391.00	359.50	389.25

#2 milling, Minneapolis: to 12/1974 (avg); #2 milling, Minneapolis: 01/1975 to date.

Annual High, Low and Settle of Oats   In Cents per Bushel

Year	High	Low	Settle	Year	High	Low	Settle	Year	High	Low	Settle
1972	91.00	66.00	91.00	1986	175.00	102.00	159.00	2000	138.25	102.75	115.25
1973	132.00	84.00	132.00	1987	215.00	122.00	198.00	2001	241.50	112.25	223.75
1974	187.00	126.00	174.00	1988	410.00	172.00	285.00	2002	251.00	174.50	216.75
1975	195.00	135.00	167.00	1989	298.00	148.00	166.00	2003	245.50	142.50	165.25
1976	203.00	159.00	168.00	1990	177.00	115.00	120.00	2004	195.50	145.25	179.75
1977	187.00	97.00	132.00	1991	152.50	116.00	151.50	2005	229.00	155.50	219.00
1978	150.00	118.00	139.00	1992	177.00	132.25	163.75	2006	291.25	184.75	284.50
1979	183.00	139.00	158.00	1993	176.25	145.50	161.75	2007	313.00	250.75	310.75
1980	227.00	146.00	212.00	1994	163.00	128.75	149.00	2008	450.50	185.00	207.50
1981	234.00	189.00	207.00	1995	268.75	147.50	262.25	2009	272.00	173.50	272.00
1982	227.00	135.00	163.00	1996	295.50	188.25	188.25	2010	399.50	188.25	397.75
1983	198.00	147.00	192.00	1997	203.00	174.50	175.50	2011	428.50	312.50	330.50
1984	205.00	170.00	183.00	1998	181.25	115.50	116.75	2012	418.00	292.25	362.50
1985	186.00	112.00	140.00	1999	147.00	108.50	118.25	2013	443.50	328.75	389.25

Minneapolis #2 Milling.   Data continued from page 207.   *Source: U.S. Department of Agriculture (USDA)*

OATS

OATS - CBOT					
Weekly Nearest Futures as of 01/03/2014					
Date	Open	High	Low	Close	
12/06/13	360.25	369.00	359.00	366.00	
12/13/13	370.50	398.50	366.00	398.50	
12/20/13	336.50	355.25	336.50	348.75	
12/27/13	348.25	358.00	346.00	356.00	
01/03/14	353.75	357.50	340.75	344.25	

Nearby Futures through Last Trading Day.

Quarterly High, Low and Settle of Oats Futures   In Cents per Bushel

Quarter	High	Low	Settle	Quarter	High	Low	Settle	Quarter	High	Low	Settle
03/2005	178.00	148.00	157.75	03/2008	438.50	303.75	371.25	03/2011	427.50	313.50	367.25
06/2005	164.00	127.00	151.25	06/2008	445.00	352.00	444.00	06/2011	405.00	325.00	334.00
09/2005	182.75	140.00	161.50	09/2008	458.00	313.50	316.00	09/2011	390.00	321.00	328.00
12/2005	220.75	158.50	195.00	12/2008	324.75	184.50	210.00	12/2011	347.00	288.75	309.50
03/2006	203.00	168.00	173.50	03/2009	234.00	162.00	193.00	03/2012	350.00	278.50	341.25
06/2006	213.00	168.50	212.75	06/2009	264.00	172.00	214.75	06/2012	378.75	262.25	336.00
09/2006	232.50	172.50	206.25	09/2009	238.50	186.75	233.00	09/2012	400.00	336.00	370.50
12/2006	280.75	204.50	271.00	12/2009	281.00	216.25	277.00	12/2012	404.50	343.25	347.50
03/2007	302.00	237.00	276.50	03/2010	280.25	205.75	208.00	03/2013	430.00	328.50	396.25
06/2007	300.00	248.00	278.50	06/2010	281.50	188.25	255.00	06/2013	431.00	351.25	401.25
09/2007	297.00	235.00	289.75	09/2010	368.50	238.50	342.00	09/2013	405.00	303.00	319.25
12/2007	314.50	260.00	306.75	12/2010	407.75	330.25	394.00	12/2013	398.50	310.25	354.25

Source: CME Group; Chicago Board of Trade

Oats, #2 Milling, Mpls
Weekly Cash as of 01/03/2014

Date	Open	High	Low	Close
12/06/13	359.50	373.00	359.50	373.00
12/13/13	377.25	386.75	375.00	375.00
12/20/13	380.50	389.75	380.50	383.75
12/27/13	386.75	391.00	386.75	391.00
01/03/14	388.75	389.25	379.25	379.25

WEEKLY CASH
As of 01/03/2014

Chart High 450.50   on 07/02/2008
Chart Low   142.50   on 07/22/2003

Cents / bushel

#2 milling, Minneapolis.

Quarterly High, Low and Settle of Oats   In Cents per Bushel

Quarter	High	Low	Settle	Quarter	High	Low	Settle	Quarter	High	Low	Settle
03/2005	206.25	177.00	177.00	03/2008	434.75	307.00	364.75	03/2011	428.50	312.50	367.25
06/2005	185.50	155.50	168.00	06/2008	440.50	360.00	440.50	06/2011	413.50	334.00	334.00
09/2005	201.00	168.25	180.50	09/2008	450.50	281.00	281.00	09/2011	396.50	344.50	344.50
12/2005	229.00	178.75	219.00	12/2008	286.50	185.00	207.50	12/2011	370.50	314.50	330.50
03/2006	222.75	184.75	195.75	03/2009	232.50	173.50	198.00	03/2012	371.25	305.00	371.25
06/2006	230.50	194.75	220.25	06/2009	268.50	186.75	227.50	06/2012	381.25	292.25	358.50
09/2006	238.25	202.00	224.75	09/2009	237.50	193.50	218.00	09/2012	412.00	374.75	385.50
12/2006	291.25	225.25	284.50	12/2009	272.00	205.50	272.00	12/2012	418.00	362.50	362.50
03/2007	308.75	251.50	285.00	03/2010	274.00	206.75	208.00	03/2013	442.50	346.50	426.25
06/2007	303.50	264.00	271.00	06/2010	282.50	188.25	253.00	06/2013	443.50	375.00	426.25
09/2007	284.00	250.75	277.25	09/2010	342.00	247.00	337.00	09/2013	410.25	328.75	341.75
12/2007	313.00	262.00	310.75	12/2010	399.50	328.25	397.75	12/2013	419.00	341.19	389.25

Minneapolis #2 Milling.   *Source: U.S. Department of Agriculture (USDA)*

RICE

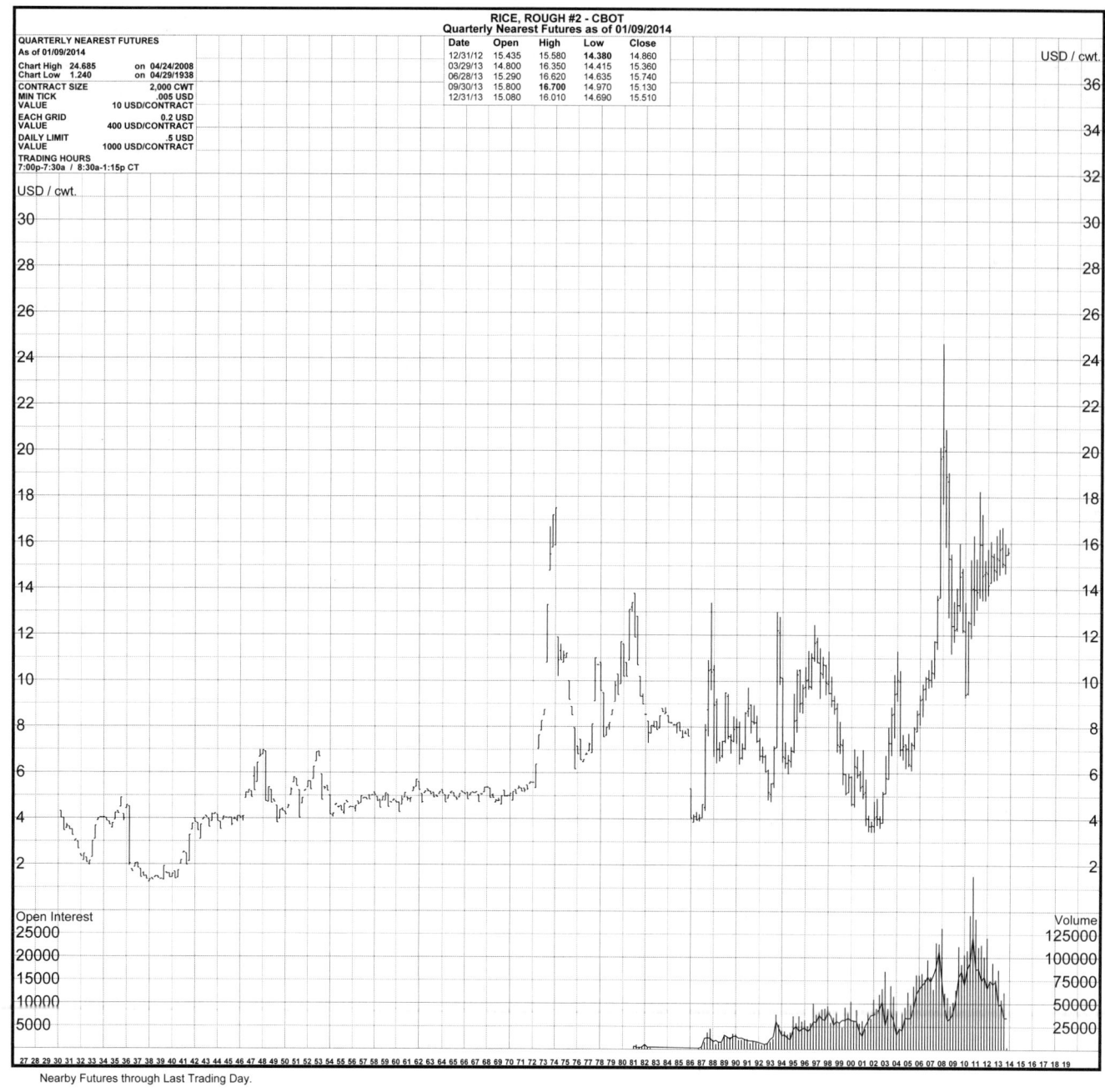

RICE, ROUGH #2 - CBOT
Quarterly Nearest Futures as of 01/09/2014

QUARTERLY NEAREST FUTURES
As of 01/09/2014

Chart High 24.685 on 04/24/2008
Chart Low 1.240 on 04/29/1938
CONTRACT SIZE 2,000 CWT
MIN TICK .005 USD
VALUE 10 USD/CONTRACT
EACH GRID 0.2 USD
VALUE 400 USD/CONTRACT
DAILY LIMIT .5 USD
VALUE 1000 USD/CONTRACT
TRADING HOURS
7:00p-7:30a / 8:30a-1:15p CT

Date	Open	High	Low	Close
12/31/12	15.435	15.580	**14.380**	14.860
03/29/13	14.800	16.350	14.415	15.360
06/28/13	15.290	16.620	14.635	15.740
09/30/13	15.800	**16.700**	14.970	15.130
12/31/13	15.080	16.010	14.690	15.510

Nearby Futures through Last Trading Day.

Annual High, Low and Settle of Rice   In Dollars per Cwt.

Year	High	Low	Settle	Year	High	Low	Settle	Year	High	Low	Settle
1930	4.56	3.46	3.46	1944	4.24	3.53	4.07	1958	5.14	4.48	4.48
1931	3.75	3.00	3.06	1945	4.04	3.67	3.96	1959	5.11	4.52	4.71
1932	2.97	2.08	2.08	1946	5.13	3.84	5.13	1960	4.98	4.30	4.83
1933	3.99	1.95	3.99	1947	6.42	4.93	6.42	1961	5.39	4.71	5.33
1934	4.03	3.72	3.72	1948	6.98	4.73	5.36	1962	5.70	4.68	5.19
1935	4.90	3.56	4.90	1949	5.24	3.82	4.37	1963	5.28	4.94	4.96
1936	4.57	1.69	1.69	1950	5.33	4.19	5.26	1964	5.25	4.72	5.02
1937	2.06	1.44	1.48	1951	5.81	4.03	4.90	1965	5.18	4.81	5.09
1938	1.50	1.24	1.48	1952	6.25	5.20	6.25	1966	5.20	4.86	5.12
1939	1.92	1.31	1.60	1953	6.91	4.82	5.34	1967	5.18	4.74	5.08
1940	1.74	1.38	1.74	1954	5.42	4.06	4.64	1968	5.37	4.92	4.92
1941	3.27	1.98	3.27	1955	4.77	4.19	4.71	1969	5.23	4.63	4.98
1942	3.98	3.10	3.72	1956	4.75	4.29	4.65	1970	5.26	4.80	5.09
1943	4.22	3.62	4.18	1957	5.04	4.68	4.84	1971	5.46	5.15	5.30

Louisiana #2 Long grain.   Data continued on page 214.   *Source: U.S. Department of Agriculture*

RICE

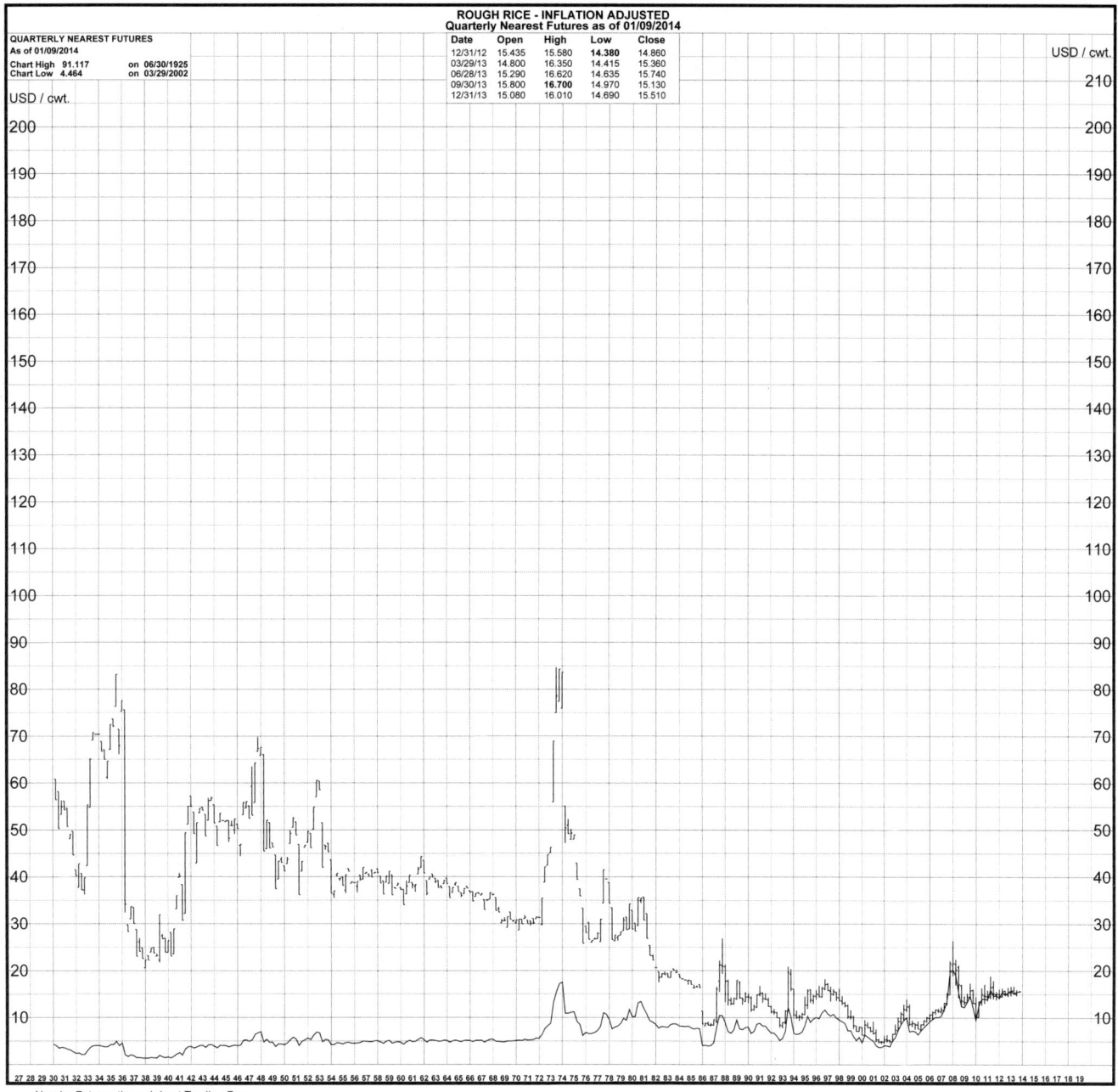

ROUGH RICE - INFLATION ADJUSTED
Quarterly Nearest Futures as of 01/09/2014

Date	Open	High	Low	Close
12/31/12	15.435	15.580	14.380	14.860
03/29/13	14.800	16.350	14.415	15.360
06/28/13	15.290	16.620	14.635	15.740
09/30/13	15.800	16.700	14.970	15.130
12/31/13	15.080	16.010	14.690	15.510

QUARTERLY NEAREST FUTURES
As of 01/09/2014
Chart High 91.117 on 06/30/1925
Chart Low 4.464 on 03/29/2002
USD / cwt.

Nearby Futures through Last Trading Day.

Annual High, Low and Settle of Rice   In Dollars per Cwt.

Year	High	Low	Settle	Year	High	Low	Settle	Year	High	Low	Settle
1930	4.56	3.46	3.46	1944	4.24	3.53	4.07	1958	5.14	4.48	4.48
1931	3.75	3.00	3.06	1945	4.04	3.67	3.96	1959	5.11	4.52	4.71
1932	2.97	2.08	2.08	1946	5.13	3.84	5.13	1960	4.98	4.30	4.83
1933	3.99	1.95	3.99	1947	6.42	4.93	6.42	1961	5.39	4.71	5.33
1934	4.03	3.72	3.72	1948	6.98	4.73	5.36	1962	5.70	4.68	5.19
1935	4.90	3.56	4.90	1949	5.24	3.82	4.37	1963	5.28	4.94	4.96
1936	4.57	1.69	1.69	1950	5.33	4.19	5.26	1964	5.25	4.72	5.02
1937	2.06	1.44	1.48	1951	5.81	4.03	4.90	1965	5.18	4.81	5.09
1938	1.50	1.24	1.48	1952	6.25	5.20	6.25	1966	5.20	4.86	5.12
1939	1.92	1.31	1.60	1953	6.91	4.82	5.34	1967	5.18	4.74	5.08
1940	1.74	1.38	1.74	1954	5.42	4.06	4.64	1968	5.37	4.92	4.92
1941	3.27	1.98	3.27	1955	4.77	4.19	4.71	1969	5.23	4.63	4.98
1942	3.98	3.10	3.72	1956	4.75	4.29	4.65	1970	5.26	4.80	5.09
1943	4.22	3.62	4.18	1957	5.04	4.68	4.84	1971	5.46	5.15	5.30

Louisiana #2 Long grain.   Data continued on page 215.   Source: U.S. Department of Agriculture

213

RICE

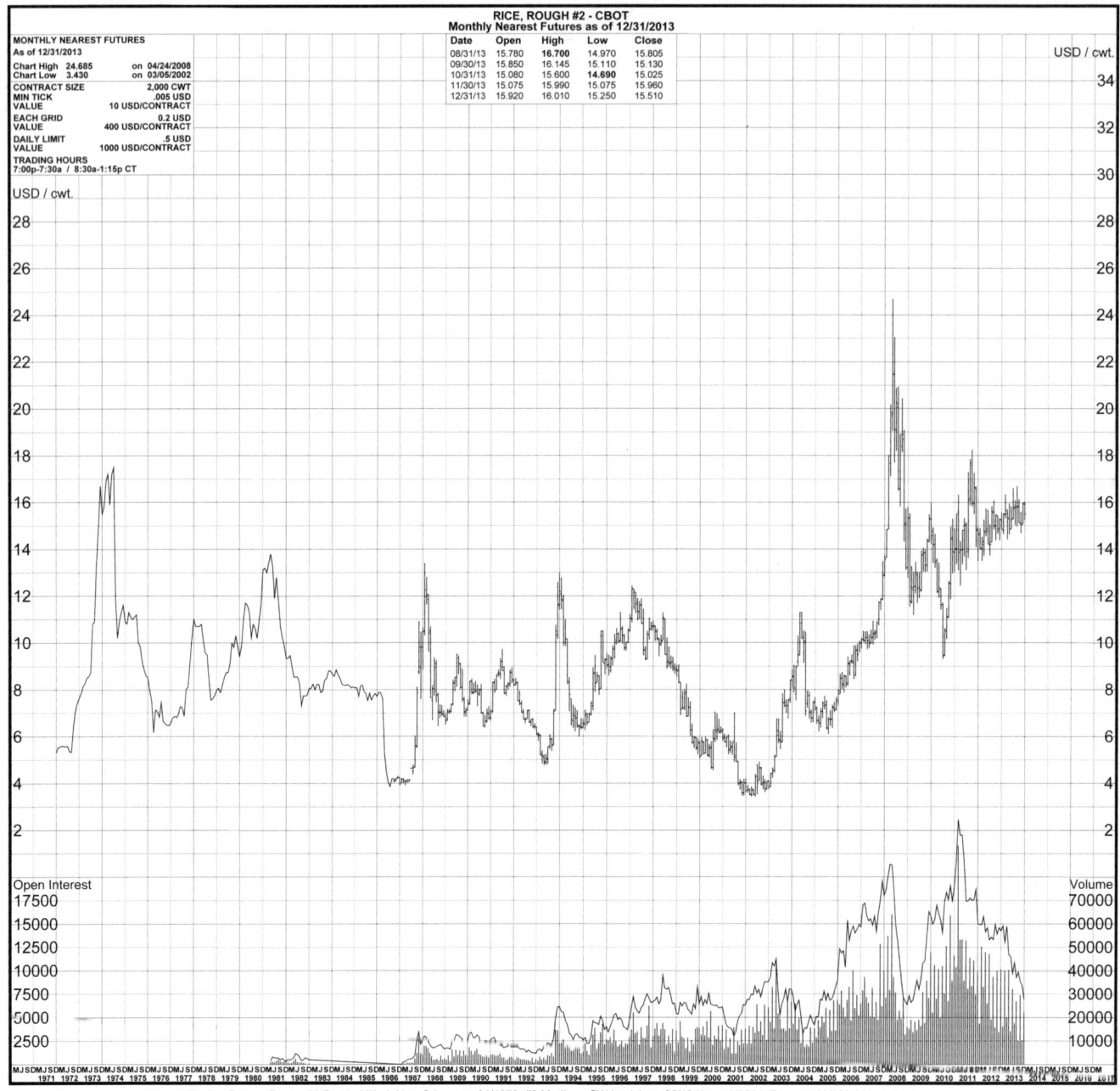

RICE, ROUGH #2 - CBOT
Monthly Nearest Futures as of 12/31/2013

Date	Open	High	Low	Close
08/31/13	15.780	**16.700**	14.970	15.805
09/30/13	15.850	16.145	15.110	15.130
10/31/13	15.080	15.600	**14.690**	15.025
11/30/13	15.075	15.990	15.075	15.960
12/31/13	15.920	16.010	15.250	15.510

MONTHLY NEAREST FUTURES
As of 12/31/2013

Chart High 24.685	on 04/24/2008
Chart Low 3.430	on 03/05/2002
CONTRACT SIZE	2,000 CWT
MIN TICK	.005 USD
VALUE	10 USD/CONTRACT
EACH GRID	0.2 USD
VALUE	400 USD/CONTRACT
DAILY LIMIT	.5 USD
VALUE	1000 USD/CONTRACT

TRADING HOURS
7:00p-7:30a / 8:30a-1:15p CT

USD / cwt.

Nearby Futures through Last Trading Day.   Fancy, #2 Zenith, Milled, New Orleans to 04/1972; #2 Medium, SW Louisiana 05/1972 to 12/2004; Futures: 08/20/1986 to date.

Annual High, Low and Settle of Rice, Rough Futures   In Dollars per Cwt.

Year	High	Low	Settle	Year	High	Low	Settle	Year	High	Low	Settle
1972	7.64	5.34	7.64	1986	4.320	3.905	3.950	2000	7.060	4.540	5.920
1973	16.70	7.84	15.50	1987	10.920	3.900	10.460	2001	7.030	3.460	3.690
1974	17.50	10.20	10.90	1988	13.400	6.430	6.670	2002	4.920	3.430	3.850
1975	11.30	8.51	8.51	1989	9.520	6.670	7.430	2003	8.880	3.840	8.540
1976	7.95	6.17	6.57	1990	8.470	6.380	7.070	2004	11.320	6.580	7.180
1977	11.00	6.79	11.00	1991	9.730	7.020	8.190	2005	8.030	6.110	7.935
1978	10.80	7.56	7.98	1992	8.500	6.050	6.070	2006	10.220	7.820	10.130
1979	10.30	7.87	9.41	1993	13.000	4.760	12.200	2007	13.740	9.715	13.550
1980	13.10	9.88	13.10	1994	12.795	5.970	6.570	2008	24.685	12.770	15.340
1981	13.80	9.34	9.34	1995	10.520	6.260	9.030	2009	15.985	11.195	14.565
1982	9.46	7.31	8.06	1996	11.330	8.600	11.030	2010	15.300	9.300	13.995
1983	8.80	7.88	8.66	1997	12.450	9.250	10.720	2011	18.255	12.440	14.605
1984	8.85	8.08	8.08	1998	11.300	8.560	8.790	2012	16.090	13.500	14.860
1985	8.20	7.54	7.71	1999	9.070	5.060	5.140	2013	16.700	14.415	15.510

Futures begin trading 08/20/1986.   Data continued from page 212.   *Source: CME Group; Chicago Board of Trade*

Rice, Rough #2, Long, LA
Monthly Cash as of 12/27/2013

MONTHLY CASH
As of 12/27/2013

Chart High 19.750 on 04/11/2008
Chart Low 3.490 on 07/31/1987

USD / cwt.

Date	Open	High	Low	Close
08/30/13	15.750	15.750	15.100	15.100
09/30/13	15.250	15.250	15.250	15.250
10/31/13	15.250	15.250	15.250	15.250
11/29/13	15.250	15.250	15.110	15.110
12/31/13	15.110	15.110	15.110	15.110

Fancy, #2 Zenith, Milled, New Orleans to 04/1972; #2 Medium, SW Louisiana 05/1972 to 12/2004; Milled, #2 Long grain, Louisiana 01/03/2005 to date.

Annual High, Low and Settle of Rice   In Dollars per Cwt.

Year	High	Low	Settle	Year	High	Low	Settle	Year	High	Low	Settle
1972	7.64	5.34	7.64	1986	7.90	3.74	3.74	2000	5.98	5.53	5.69
1973	16.70	7.84	15.50	1987	7.64	3.49	7.64	2001	5.86	4.07	4.07
1974	17.50	10.20	10.90	1988	9.37	6.68	6.68	2002	4.30	3.69	4.13
1975	11.30	8.51	8.51	1989	7.59	6.58	7.05	2003	7.57	4.24	7.57
1976	7.95	6.17	6.57	1990	7.57	6.02	6.13	2004	9.37	7.36	7.37
1977	11.00	6.79	11.00	1991	7.98	6.39	7.98	2005	8.03	6.06	7.72
1978	10.80	7.56	7.98	1992	7.97	6.39	6.39	2006	10.59	7.78	10.55
1979	10.30	7.87	9.41	1993	8.91	4.92	8.91	2007	12.35	9.83	12.35
1980	13.10	9.88	13.10	1994	10.20	6.47	6.56	2008	19.75	12.35	14.81
1981	13.80	9.34	9.34	1995	9.36	6.64	9.36	2009	15.43	11.51	13.89
1982	9.46	7.31	8.06	1996	10.10	9.10	9.82	2010	13.89	9.26	12.75
1983	8.80	7.88	8.66	1997	10.30	9.77	9.77	2011	14.82	10.90	13.38
1984	8.85	8.08	8.08	1998	9.75	9.01	9.10	2012	14.60	12.23	14.55
1985	8.20	7.54	7.71	1999	9.09	5.91	6.01	2013	16.10	14.85	15.11

Louisiana #2 Long grain.   Data continued from page 213.   *Source: U.S. Department of Agriculture (USDA)*

RICE

RICE, ROUGH #2 - CBOT Weekly Nearest Futures as of 01/03/2014				
Date	Open	High	Low	Close
12/06/13	15.920	**16.010**	15.450	15.545
12/13/13	15.545	15.645	15.415	15.545
12/20/13	15.625	15.680	**15.250**	15.500
12/27/13	15.415	15.520	15.365	15.450
01/03/14	15.400	15.830	15.295	15.760

WEEKLY NEAREST FUTURES
As of 01/03/2014
Chart High 24.685 on 04/24/2008
Chart Low 6.110 on 07/07/2005
CONTRACT SIZE 2,000 CWT
MIN TICK .005 USD
VALUE 10 USD/CONTRACT
EACH GRID 0.2 USD
VALUE 400 USD/CONTRACT
DAILY LIMIT .5 USD
VALUE 1000 USD/CONTRACT
TRADING HOURS
7:00p-7:30a / 8:30a-1:15p CT

Commercial = 203
NonCommercial = -534
NonReportable = 331

Nearby Futures through Last Trading Day.

Quarterly High, Low and Settle of Rice, Rough   In Dollars per Cwt.

Quarter	High	Low	Settle	Quarter	High	Low	Settle	Quarter	High	Low	Settle
03/2005	7.280	6.210	7.070	03/2008	20.175	13.630	19.690	03/2011	16.335	12.440	13.985
06/2005	7.740	6.300	6.400	06/2008	24.685	17.700	20.210	06/2011	15.330	13.100	13.885
09/2005	7.360	6.110	7.260	09/2008	20.950	15.830	18.895	09/2011	18.255	13.620	15.950
12/2005	8.030	7.050	7.935	12/2008	19.080	12.770	15.340	12/2011	17.260	13.505	14.605
03/2006	8.750	7.820	8.560	03/2009	15.540	11.195	12.410	03/2012	15.270	13.500	14.765
06/2006	9.410	8.090	9.200	06/2009	13.470	11.710	12.230	06/2012	15.755	13.725	14.190
09/2006	9.890	8.460	9.665	09/2009	14.060	12.190	13.315	09/2012	16.090	14.300	15.475
12/2006	10.220	9.200	10.130	12/2009	15.985	13.050	14.565	12/2012	15.580	14.380	14.860
03/2007	10.520	9.715	10.080	03/2010	14.930	12.125	12.215	03/2013	16.350	14.415	15.360
06/2007	10.950	9.760	10.390	06/2010	13.435	9.300	9.430	06/2013	16.620	14.635	15.740
09/2007	11.770	10.130	11.730	09/2010	12.640	9.430	12.565	09/2013	16.700	14.970	15.130
12/2007	13.740	11.390	13.550	12/2010	15.300	11.870	13.995	12/2013	16.010	14.690	15.510

Source: CME Group; Chicago Board of Trade

Rice, Rough #2, Long, LA Weekly Cash as of 01/03/2014				
Date	Open	High	Low	Close
12/06/13	15.110	15.110	15.110	15.110
12/13/13	15.110	15.110	15.110	15.110
12/20/13	15.110	15.110	15.110	15.110
12/27/13	15.110	15.110	15.110	15.110
01/03/14	15.110	15.110	15.110	15.110

WEEKLY CASH
As of 01/03/2014
Chart High 19.750 on 04/11/2008
Chart Low 4.240 on 02/28/2003

USD / cwt.

Milled, #2 Long grain, Louisiana.

Quarterly High, Low and Settle of Rice   In Dollars per Cwt.

Quarter	High	Low	Settle	Quarter	High	Low	Settle	Quarter	High	Low	Settle
03/2005	8.03	6.98	6.98	03/2008	18.52	12.35	18.52	03/2011	12.75	11.52	11.52
06/2005	7.25	6.73	6.73	06/2008	19.75	15.43	17.28	06/2011	12.14	10.90	12.14
09/2005	6.73	6.06	6.29	09/2008	17.90	16.33	17.90	09/2011	14.82	12.76	14.03
12/2005	7.72	6.45	7.72	12/2008	17.90	14.20	14.81	12/2011	14.03	13.00	13.38
03/2006	8.58	7.78	8.58	03/2009	15.43	12.35	12.56	03/2012	13.38	12.23	12.24
06/2006	9.11	8.58	9.04	06/2009	12.96	11.51	11.73	06/2012	14.01	12.24	14.01
09/2006	10.49	8.95	10.49	09/2009	12.65	11.73	12.35	09/2012	14.25	13.69	14.25
12/2006	10.59	10.37	10.55	12/2009	13.90	12.04	13.89	12/2012	14.60	14.50	14.55
03/2007	10.55	10.01	10.01	03/2010	13.89	11.88	11.88	03/2013	16.10	14.85	15.80
06/2007	10.01	9.83	9.88	06/2010	12.06	10.80	10.80	06/2013	15.80	15.80	15.80
09/2007	10.67	9.88	10.67	09/2010	10.90	9.26	10.90	09/2013	15.80	15.10	15.25
12/2007	12.35	11.11	12.35	12/2010	13.58	10.90	12.75	12/2013	15.25	15.11	15.11

Louisiana #2 Long grain.   *Source: U.S. Department of Agriculture (USDA)*

WHEAT, CHICAGO

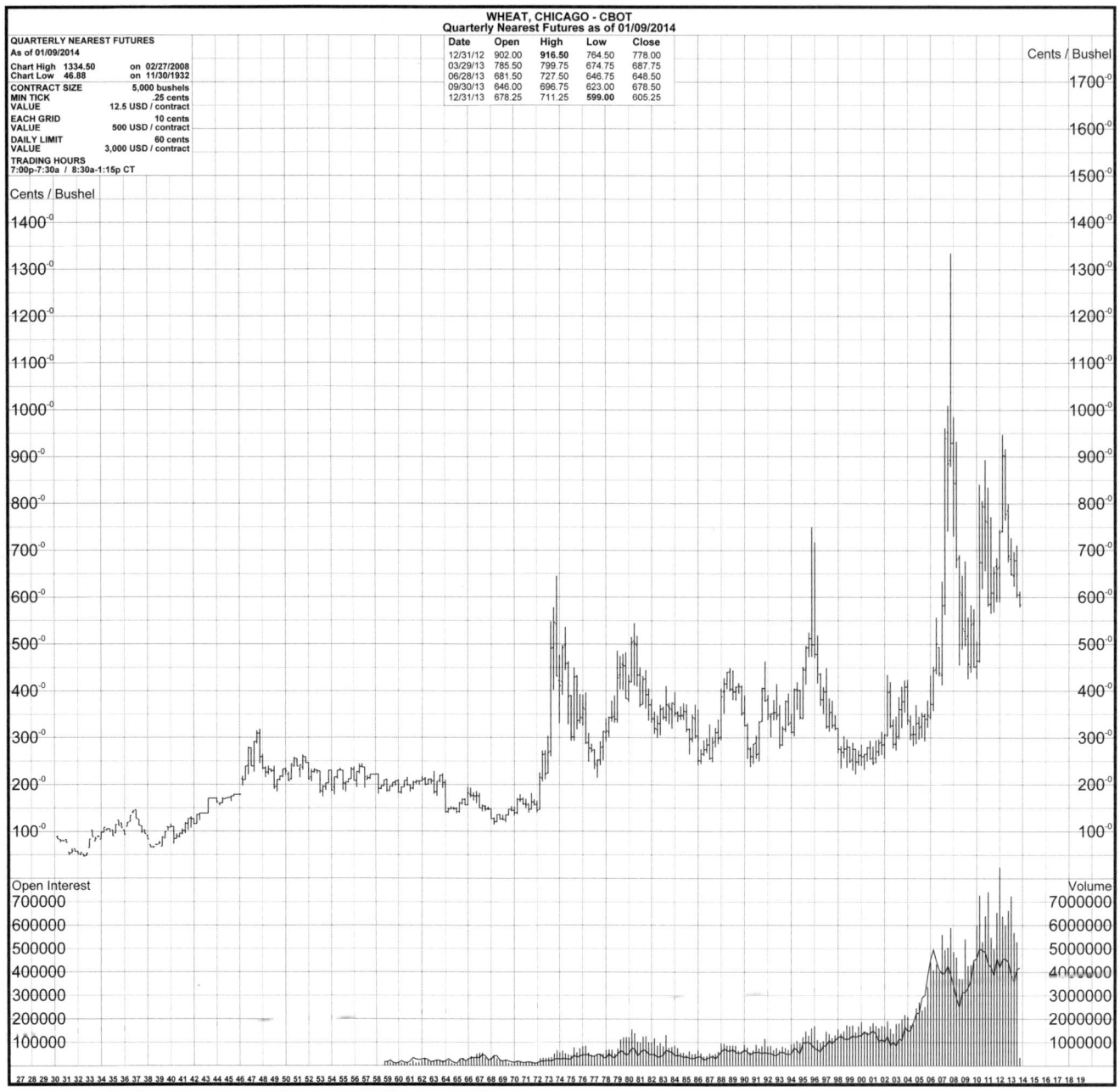

WHEAT, CHICAGO - CBOT
Quarterly Nearest Futures as of 01/09/2014

Date	Open	High	Low	Close
12/31/12	902.00	916.50	764.50	778.00
03/29/13	785.50	799.75	674.75	687.75
06/28/13	681.50	727.50	646.75	648.50
09/30/13	646.00	696.75	623.00	678.50
12/31/13	678.25	711.25	599.00	605.25

Nearby Futures through Last Trading Day.   #2 red, Chicago: to 06/1959; Futures: 07/1959 to date.

Annual High, Low and Settle of Wheat Futures   In Cents per Bushel

Year	High	Low	Settle	Year	High	Low	Settle	Year	High	Low	Settle
1930	123.75	76.63	79.75	1944	172.38	155.25	169.50	1958	222.00	179.75	197.50
1931	82.75	49.38	58.00	1945	180.00	164.25	179.00	1959	212.00	184.00	204.25
1932	62.63	46.88	46.88	1946	239.00	179.00	239.00	1960	211.00	180.00	208.63
1933	102.88	48.25	83.88	1947	315.00	221.00	309.00	1961	215.75	184.63	207.25
1934	109.13	83.00	105.88	1948	318.50	215.00	232.25	1962	217.00	198.50	211.13
1935	124.00	90.00	113.00	1949	239.50	184.75	217.75	1963	228.63	176.00	219.50
1936	134.00	93.00	134.00	1950	244.50	207.00	243.75	1964	224.00	138.75	149.88
1937	146.00	96.00	99.00	1951	263.50	214.75	259.00	1965	170.75	138.00	168.63
1938	103.00	64.00	67.00	1952	259.00	206.50	230.75	1966	195.00	156.25	175.75
1939	99.00	68.00	99.00	1953	230.75	174.00	202.75	1967	186.25	142.38	147.88
1940	116.00	73.00	89.00	1954	230.00	178.25	230.00	1968	153.25	114.25	135.50
1941	127.50	86.25	127.50	1955	235.00	184.00	211.75	1969	148.25	119.50	147.38
1942	138.75	107.00	138.75	1956	244.50	194.00	238.00	1970	179.38	133.25	168.50
1943	170.50	138.75	170.50	1957	245.00	192.50	221.50	1971	182.00	139.75	163.13

Futures data begins 07/01/1959.   Data continued on page 220.   *Source: CME Group; Chicago Board of Trade*

WHEAT - INFLATION ADJUSTED
Quarterly Nearest Futures as of 01/09/2014

Date	Open	High	Low	Close
12/31/12	902.00	916.50	764.50	778.00
03/29/13	785.50	799.75	674.75	687.75
06/28/13	681.50	727.50	646.75	648.50
09/30/13	646.00	696.75	623.00	678.50
12/31/13	678.25	711.25	599.00	605.25

QUARTERLY NEAREST FUTURES
As of 01/09/2014

Chart High 3187.03 on 03/31/1948
Chart Low 309.56 on 12/31/1999

Cents / Bushel

Nearby Futures through Last Trading Day.   #2 red, Chicago: to 06/1959; Futures: 07/1959 to date.

Annual High, Low and Settle of Wheat   In Cents per Bushel

Year	High	Low	Settle	Year	High	Low	Settle	Year	High	Low	Settle
1930	123.75	76.63	79.75	1944	172.38	155.25	169.50	1958	222.00	179.75	197.50
1931	82.75	49.38	58.00	1945	180.00	164.25	179.00	1959	212.00	184.00	203.25
1932	62.63	46.88	46.88	1946	239.00	179.00	239.00	1960	211.75	183.00	211.75
1933	102.88	48.25	83.88	1947	315.00	221.00	309.00	1961	215.00	186.00	208.25
1934	109.13	83.00	105.88	1948	318.50	215.00	232.25	1962	219.38	198.63	213.75
1935	124.00	90.00	113.00	1949	239.50	184.75	217.75	1963	228.63	179.00	222.13
1936	134.00	93.00	134.00	1950	244.50	207.00	243.75	1964	225.75	140.75	153.00
1937	146.00	96.00	99.00	1951	263.50	214.75	259.00	1965	173.50	141.88	169.50
1938	103.00	64.00	67.00	1952	259.00	206.50	230.75	1966	194.00	159.00	176.00
1939	99.00	68.00	99.00	1953	230.75	174.00	202.75	1967	187.75	142.50	145.00
1940	116.00	73.00	89.00	1954	230.00	178.25	230.00	1968	153.88	115.63	138.38
1941	127.50	86.25	127.50	1955	235.00	184.00	211.75	1969	151.00	124.63	150.50
1942	138.75	107.00	138.75	1956	244.50	194.00	238.00	1970	181.88	139.25	174.50
1943	170.50	138.75	170.50	1957	245.00	192.50	221.50	1971	181.75	140.00	170.00

Chicago #2 Soft Red.   Data continued on page 221.   *Source: U.S. Department of Agriculture*

WHEAT, CHICAGO

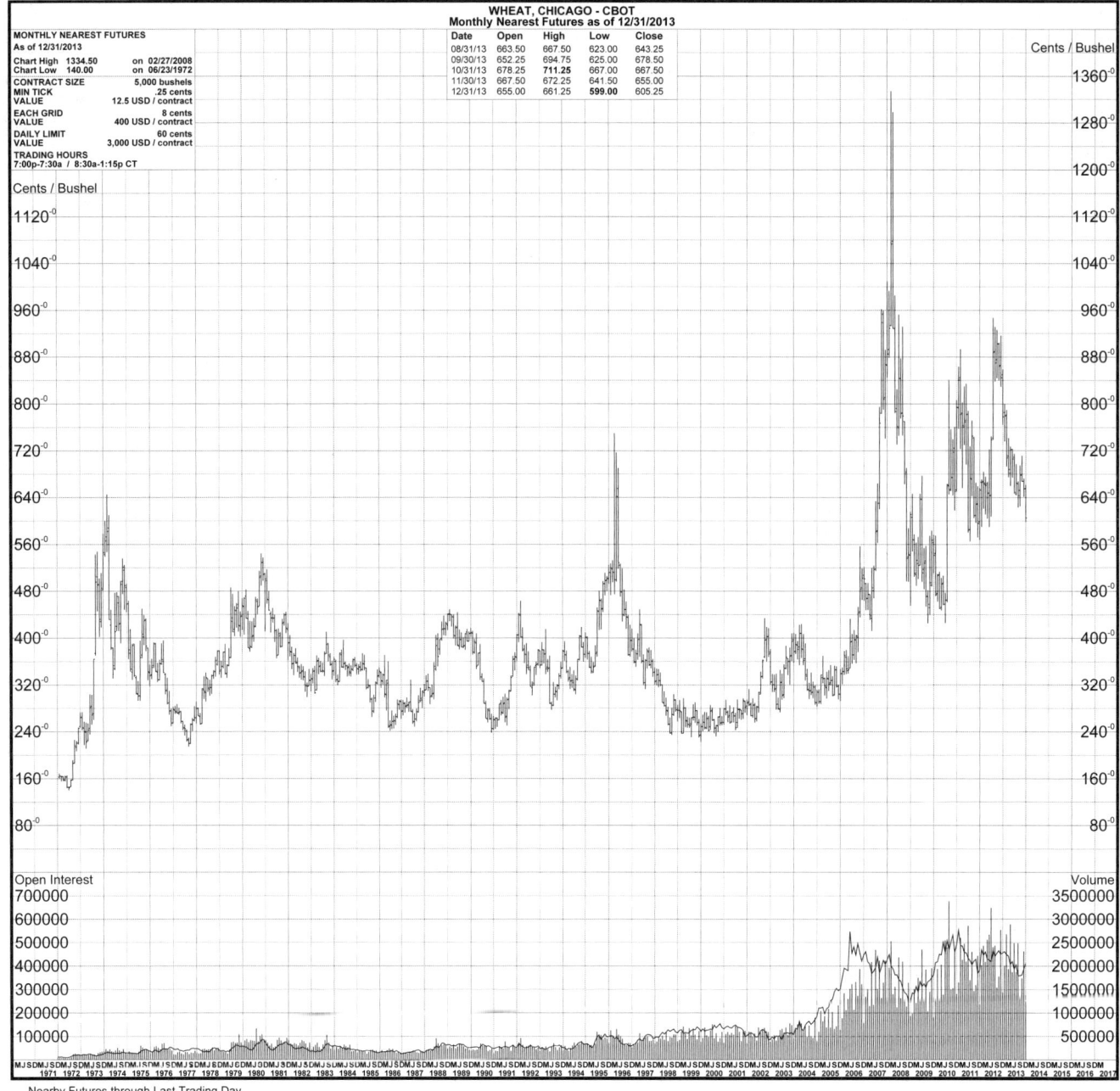

WHEAT, CHICAGO - CBOT
Monthly Nearest Futures as of 12/31/2013

Date	Open	High	Low	Close
08/31/13	663.50	667.50	623.00	643.25
09/30/13	652.25	694.75	625.00	678.50
10/31/13	678.25	711.25	667.00	667.50
11/30/13	667.50	672.25	641.50	655.00
12/31/13	655.00	661.25	**599.00**	605.25

MONTHLY NEAREST FUTURES
As of 12/31/2013

Chart High	1334.50	on 02/27/2008
Chart Low	140.00	on 06/23/1972
CONTRACT SIZE	5,000 bushels	
MIN TICK VALUE	.25 cents / 12.5 USD / contract	
EACH GRID VALUE	8 cents / 400 USD / contract	
DAILY LIMIT VALUE	60 cents / 3,000 USD / contract	
TRADING HOURS	7:00p-7:30a / 8:30a-1:15p CT	

Nearby Futures through Last Trading Day.

Annual High, Low and Settle of Wheat Futures   In Cents per Bushel

Year	High	Low	Settle	Year	High	Low	Settle	Year	High	Low	Settle
1972	272.75	140.00	264.00	1986	371.00	241.50	274.50	2000	285.50	232.00	279.50
1973	578.00	211.00	546.00	1987	329.00	248.00	310.75	2001	297.00	242.50	289.00
1974	645.00	331.00	458.00	1988	441.50	286.50	440.00	2002	434.00	255.50	325.00
1975	463.50	293.00	335.75	1989	449.00	379.50	409.25	2003	409.00	273.00	377.00
1976	396.00	249.00	277.50	1990	412.00	238.00	260.50	2004	424.00	282.50	307.50
1977	292.00	214.25	279.25	1991	407.00	244.50	404.75	2005	370.00	287.00	339.25
1978	378.75	251.75	343.25	1992	463.25	301.50	353.75	2006	557.00	321.50	501.00
1979	486.00	332.00	454.25	1993	415.00	277.00	378.25	2007	1,009.50	412.00	885.00
1980	544.50	376.50	501.00	1994	418.75	303.50	401.50	2008	1,334.50	455.00	610.75
1981	517.50	362.00	391.50	1995	525.00	339.50	512.25	2009	677.00	425.25	541.50
1982	405.00	299.25	330.75	1996	750.00	368.00	381.25	2010	841.00	425.50	794.25
1983	410.50	305.00	363.50	1997	449.00	313.00	325.75	2011	893.25	565.25	652.75
1984	397.00	319.50	347.75	1998	348.00	234.50	276.25	2012	947.25	589.75	778.00
1985	374.00	264.50	343.25	1999	297.00	222.50	248.50	2013	799.75	599.00	605.25

Data continued from page 218.   *Source: CME Group; Chicago Board of Trade*

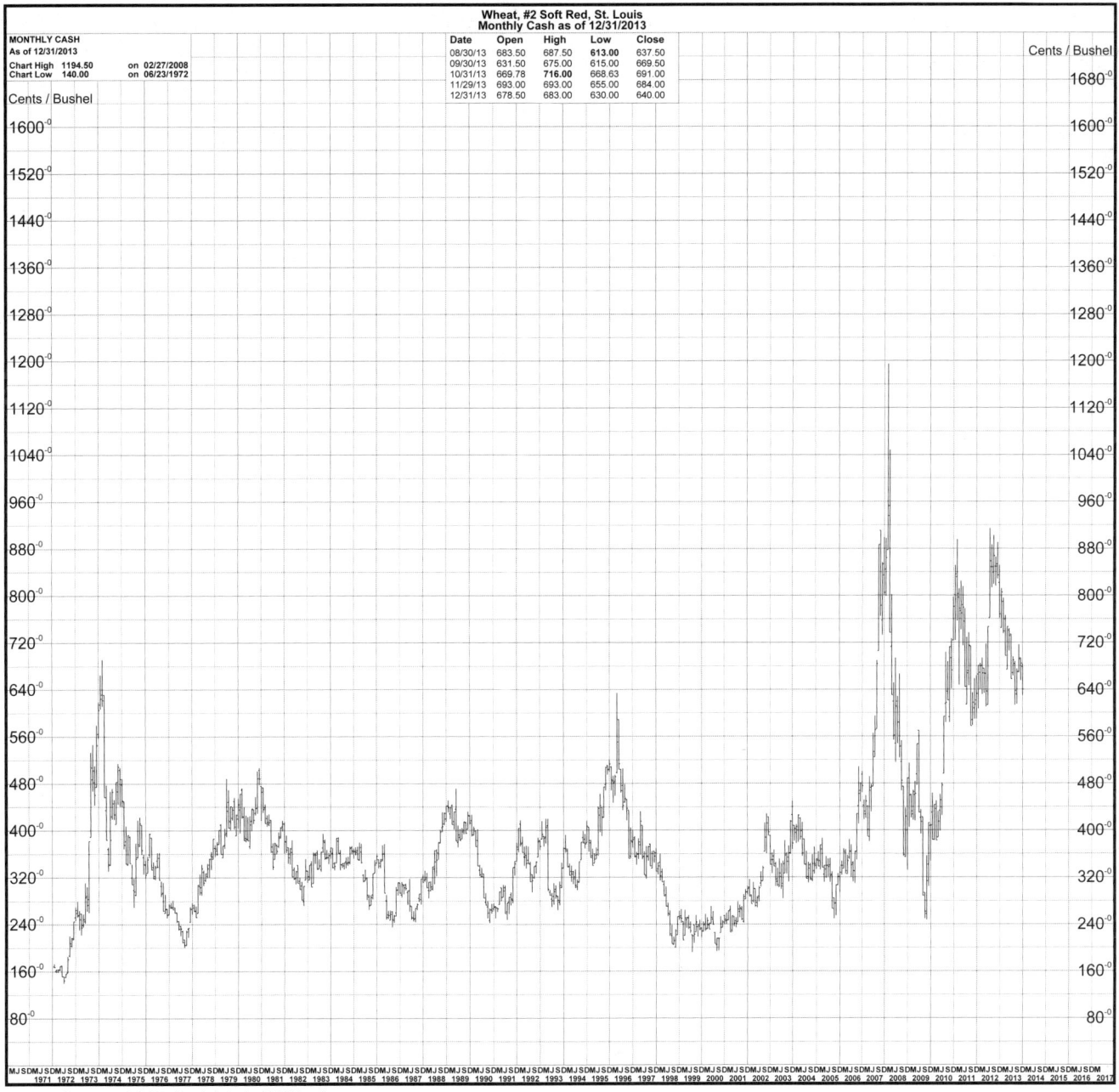

Wheat, #2 Soft Red, St. Louis
Monthly Cash as of 12/31/2013

Date	Open	High	Low	Close
08/30/13	683.50	687.50	613.00	637.50
09/30/13	631.50	675.00	615.00	669.50
10/31/13	669.78	716.00	668.63	691.00
11/29/13	693.00	693.00	655.00	684.00
12/31/13	678.50	683.00	630.00	640.00

MONTHLY CASH
As of 12/31/2013
Chart High 1194.50 on 02/27/2008
Chart Low 140.00 on 06/23/1972
Cents / Bushel

#2 red, Chicago: to 04/1982; #2 red, St Louis: 04/1982 to date.

Annual High, Low and Settle of Wheat   In Cents per Bushel

Year	High	Low	Settle	Year	High	Low	Settle	Year	High	Low	Settle
1972	270.00	140.00	264.25	1986	377.00	234.50	293.50	2000	270.50	193.50	248.00
1973	618.50	222.00	605.00	1987	325.00	243.50	312.00	2001	304.50	226.50	300.50
1974	691.50	330.50	450.50	1988	441.50	284.50	441.50	2002	428.50	268.50	341.50
1975	449.75	269.50	324.75	1989	471.50	371.00	412.50	2003	450.00	283.50	377.50
1976	395.25	250.75	272.50	1990	426.50	242.50	269.00	2004	426.50	310.50	350.50
1977	281.25	201.00	273.00	1991	378.50	248.00	371.50	2005	386.50	249.50	327.50
1978	386.00	252.00	369.25	1992	417.00	294.50	372.50	2006	508.50	309.50	475.50
1979	488.75	353.50	444.25	1993	419.50	264.00	369.00	2007	910.50	380.50	804.50
1980	507.00	369.00	466.00	1994	416.00	298.00	407.00	2008	1,194.50	331.50	488.50
1981	473.50	333.50	381.50	1995	520.00	340.00	513.00	2009	569.50	247.50	408.00
1982	392.00	272.00	322.00	1996	634.50	352.00	384.00	2010	797.50	382.50	780.50
1983	394.50	304.00	370.50	1997	432.50	317.00	330.00	2011	895.50	577.50	632.50
1984	388.50	332.50	365.00	1998	359.50	200.50	251.00	2012	914.50	606.50	768.00
1985	379.50	265.00	356.50	1999	265.50	192.00	228.50	2013	812.00	613.00	640.00

Chicago #2 Red through 04/29/1982, St. Louis #2 Red 04/30/1982 to date.   Data continued from page 219.   *Source: U.S. Department of Agriculture (USDA)*

WHEAT, CHICAGO

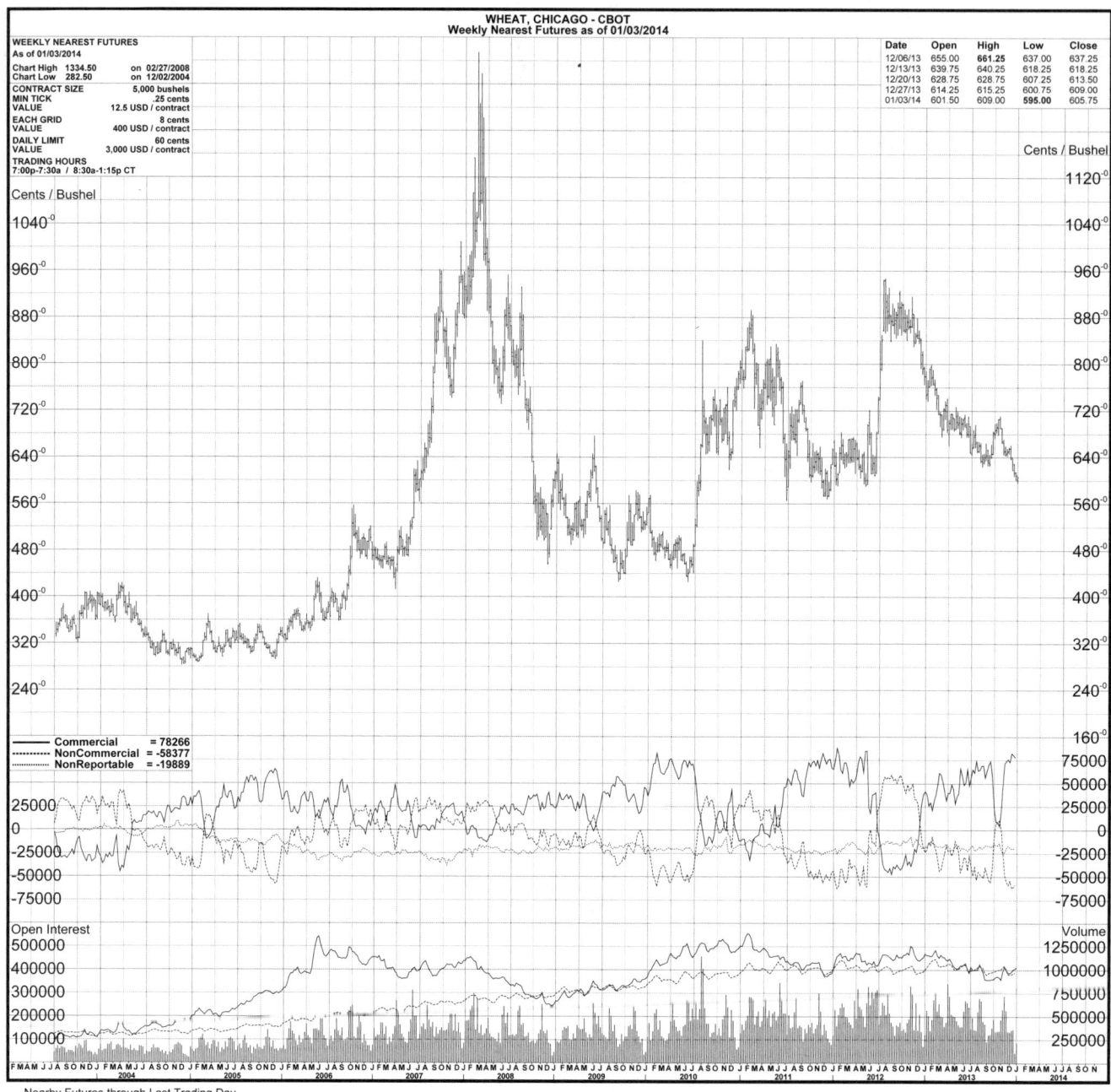

WHEAT, CHICAGO - CBOT
Weekly Nearest Futures as of 01/03/2014

WEEKLY NEAREST FUTURES
As of 01/03/2014

Chart High	1334.50	on 02/27/2008
Chart Low	282.50	on 12/02/2004
CONTRACT SIZE	5,000 bushels	
MIN TICK	.25 cents	
VALUE	12.5 USD / contract	
EACH GRID	8 cents	
VALUE	400 USD / contract	
DAILY LIMIT	60 cents	
VALUE	3,000 USD / contract	
TRADING HOURS		
7:00p-7:30a / 8:30a-1:15p CT		

Date	Open	High	Low	Close
12/06/13	655.00	661.25	637.00	637.25
12/13/13	639.75	640.25	618.25	618.25
12/20/13	628.75	628.75	607.25	613.50
12/27/13	614.25	615.25	600.75	609.00
01/03/14	601.50	609.00	595.00	605.75

Commercial = 78266
NonCommercial = -58377
NonReportable = -19889

Nearby Futures through Last Trading Day.

Quarterly High, Low and Settle of Wheat Futures   In Cents per Bushel

Quarter	High	Low	Settle	Quarter	High	Low	Settle	Quarter	High	Low	Settle
03/2005	370.00	287.00	331.00	03/2008	1,334.50	878.50	929.00	03/2011	893.25	656.00	763.25
06/2005	345.50	296.50	321.50	06/2008	985.50	730.50	843.50	06/2011	834.50	580.25	584.75
09/2005	354.00	300.75	346.25	09/2008	932.25	662.50	680.00	09/2011	771.50	565.25	609.25
12/2005	352.00	292.50	339.25	12/2008	690.25	455.00	610.75	12/2011	665.25	567.75	652.75
03/2006	380.00	321.50	347.75	03/2009	646.25	489.00	532.75	03/2012	683.75	590.00	660.75
06/2006	433.00	339.50	371.50	06/2009	677.00	495.75	511.25	06/2012	744.75	589.75	739.00
09/2006	453.00	357.25	443.00	09/2009	557.50	425.25	457.50	09/2012	947.25	739.00	902.50
12/2006	557.00	435.25	501.00	12/2009	583.50	439.25	541.50	12/2012	916.50	764.50	778.00
03/2007	494.00	431.00	438.00	03/2010	575.00	450.00	450.50	03/2013	799.75	674.75	687.75
06/2007	633.75	412.00	582.00	06/2010	506.25	425.50	464.75	06/2013	727.50	646.75	648.50
09/2007	961.75	562.50	939.00	09/2010	841.00	461.00	674.00	09/2013	696.75	623.00	678.50
12/2007	1,009.50	740.75	885.00	12/2010	806.25	617.75	794.25	12/2013	711.25	599.00	605.25

Source: CME Group; Chicago Board of Trade

Wheat, #2 Soft Red, St. Louis Weekly Cash as of 01/03/2014				
Date	Open	High	Low	Close
12/06/13	678.50	**683.00**	677.00	681.00
12/13/13	681.00	681.00	658.00	658.00
12/20/13	652.00	652.00	635.00	643.00
12/27/13	639.00	639.00	635.00	639.00
01/03/14	630.00	640.00	**630.00**	640.00

WEEKLY CASH
As of 01/03/2014

Chart High 1194.50 on 02/27/2008
Chart Low 247.50 on 10/05/2009

Cents / Bushel

#2 red, St Louis.

Quarterly High, Low and Settle of Wheat   In Cents per Bushel

Quarter	High	Low	Settle	Quarter	High	Low	Settle	Quarter	High	Low	Settle
03/2005	386.50	332.50	336.50	03/2008	1,194.50	736.50	736.50	03/2011	895.50	647.50	777.50
06/2005	355.50	311.50	337.50	06/2008	801.50	515.50	610.50	06/2011	825.00	644.50	644.50
09/2005	352.50	249.50	275.50	09/2008	666.50	467.50	484.50	09/2011	736.50	577.50	577.50
12/2005	337.50	254.50	327.50	12/2008	488.50	331.50	488.50	12/2011	663.50	578.50	632.50
03/2006	368.50	323.50	330.50	03/2009	514.50	404.50	465.50	03/2012	693.50	606.50	667.50
06/2006	384.50	320.50	340.50	06/2009	569.50	416.50	430.50	06/2012	746.50	610.00	746.50
09/2006	428.00	309.50	428.00	09/2009	435.50	249.50	261.50	09/2012	914.50	761.50	867.50
12/2006	508.50	410.50	475.50	12/2009	412.50	247.50	408.00	12/2012	890.50	761.50	768.00
03/2007	459.50	388.50	400.50	03/2010	463.50	382.50	382.50	03/2013	812.00	697.00	697.00
06/2007	565.50	380.50	533.50	06/2010	480.50	387.50	476.50	06/2013	746.50	657.50	657.50
09/2007	886.50	524.50	886.50	09/2010	703.50	496.50	621.50	09/2013	695.50	613.00	669.50
12/2007	910.50	732.50	804.50	12/2010	797.50	583.50	780.50	12/2013	716.00	630.00	640.00

St. Louis #2 Soft Red.   *Source: U.S. Department of Agriculture (USDA)*

WHEAT, KANSAS CITY

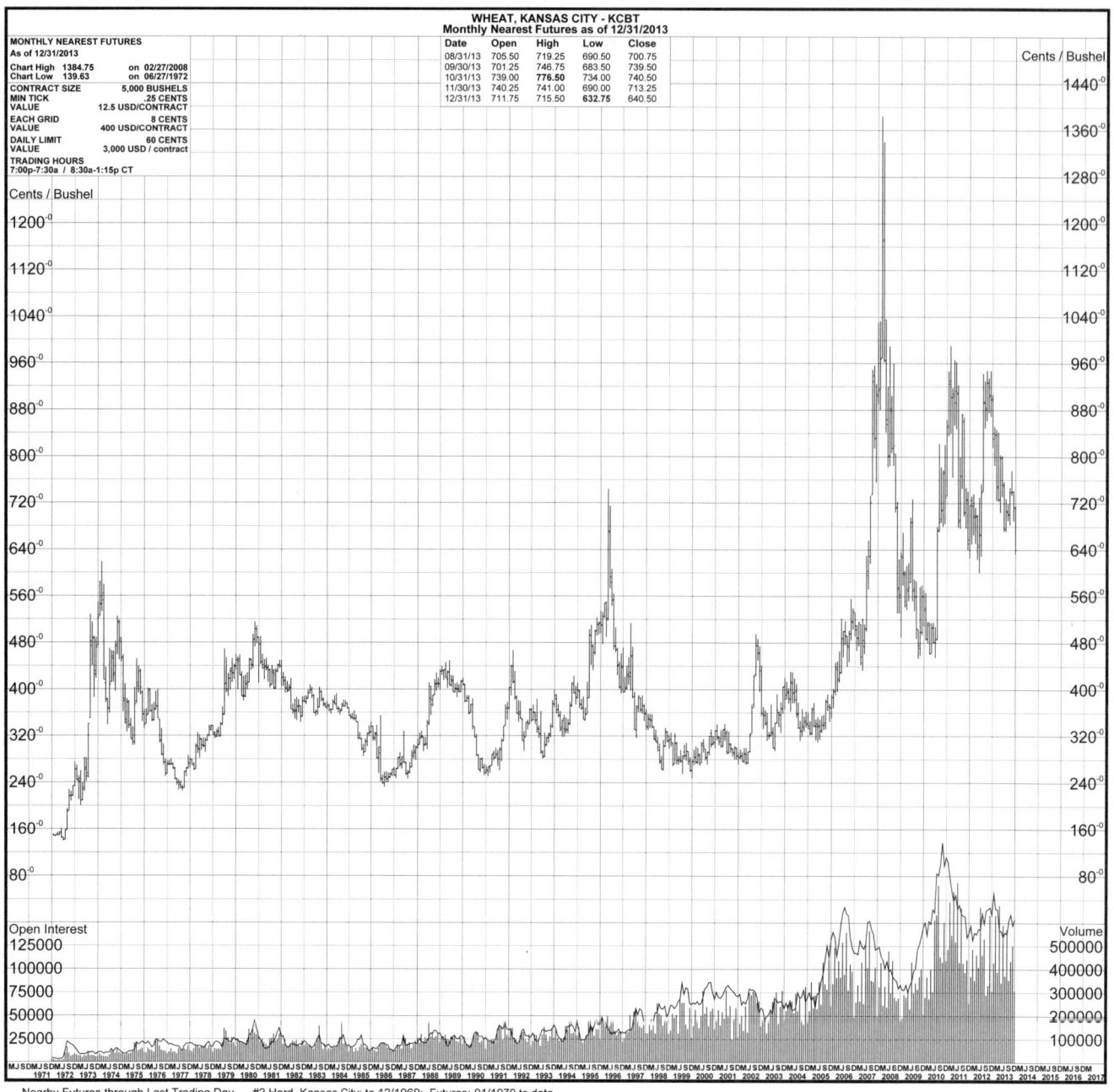

Source: Kansas City Board of Trade

Annual High, Low and Settle of Wheat   In Cents per Bushel

Year	High	Low	Settle	Year	High	Low	Settle	Year	High	Low	Settle
1972	275.00	139.63	262.25	1986	354.75	232.50	252.00	2000	331.50	270.00	330.00
1973	550.00	200.00	523.00	1987	328.00	246.50	303.75	2001	340.00	271.50	284.00
1974	619.00	338.50	452.50	1988	433.50	293.50	431.00	2002	495.00	271.25	359.75
1975	459.00	303.25	338.50	1989	449.50	386.25	408.50	2003	420.50	294.50	384.75
1976	402.00	250.00	272.00	1990	409.50	252.25	261.00	2004	431.00	312.00	338.00
1977	286.75	225.00	278.25	1991	404.00	250.25	402.75	2005	392.50	309.50	387.00
1978	338.00	260.50	321.00	1992	467.00	294.00	347.25	2006	556.00	368.00	509.75
1979	469.00	315.00	450.00	1993	399.00	281.00	389.25	2007	1,029.25	433.00	913.50
1980	515.50	380.00	477.25	1994	423.25	318.00	399.00	2008	1,384.75	489.75	630.00
1981	490.50	400.50	419.50	1995	535.00	346.50	509.50	2009	727.25	453.50	536.25
1982	428.75	342.50	378.25	1996	744.00	393.00	395.25	2010	863.50	454.75	851.00
1983	407.75	353.00	372.75	1997	514.00	317.00	335.50	2011	990.50	625.75	717.00
1984	393.00	354.00	354.00	1998	358.00	262.00	314.00	2012	948.00	601.00	831.00
1985	363.00	284.50	336.00	1999	326.00	248.00	276.25	2013	852.00	632.75	640.50

Source: Kansas City Board of Trade

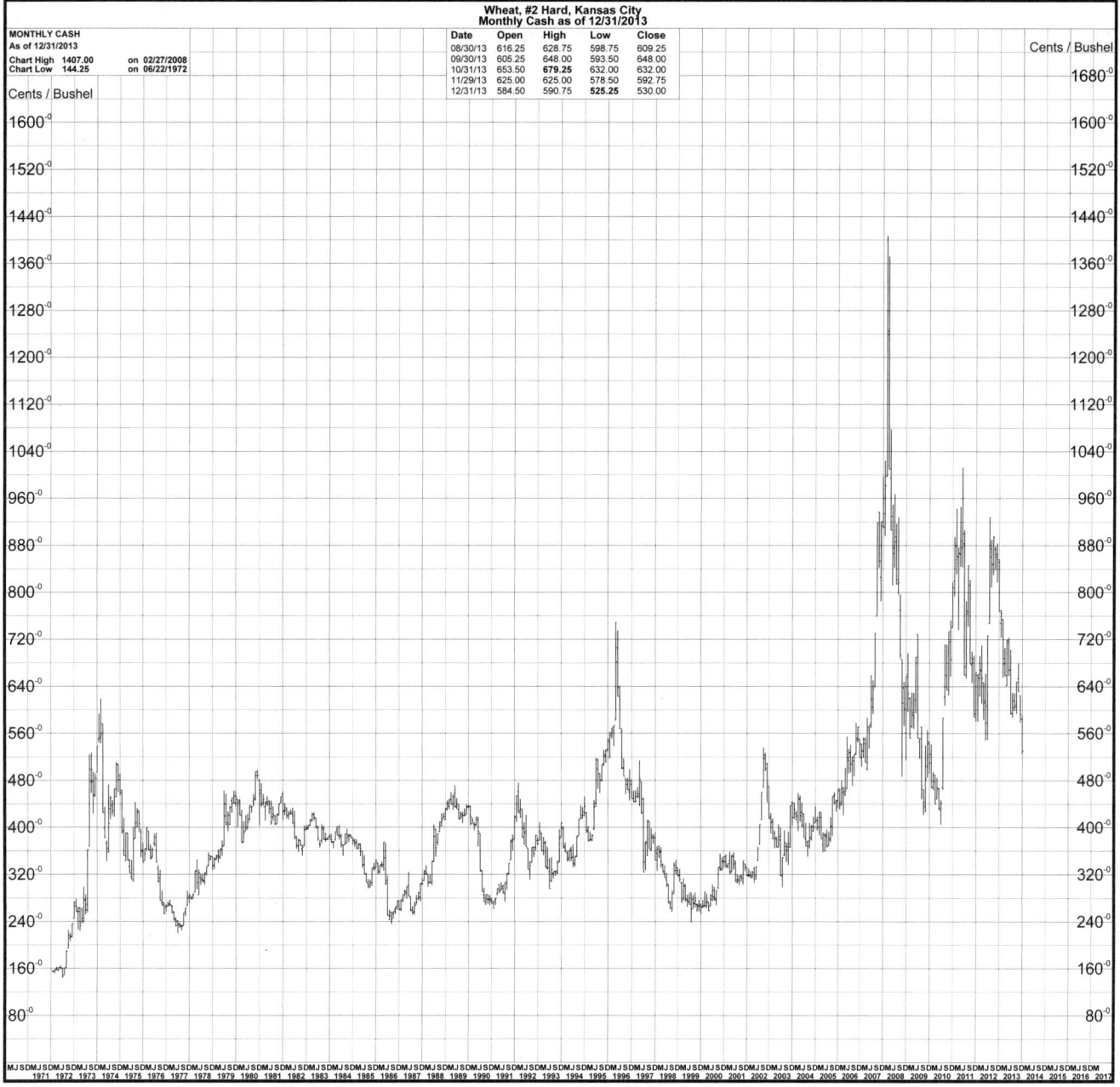

Wheat, #2 Hard, Kansas City
Monthly Cash as of 12/31/2013

MONTHLY CASH
As of 12/31/2013
Chart High 1407.00 on 02/27/2008
Chart Low   144.25   on 06/22/1972

Cents / Bushel

Date	Open	High	Low	Close
08/30/13	616.25	628.75	598.75	609.25
09/30/13	605.25	648.00	593.50	648.00
10/31/13	653.50	679.25	632.00	632.00
11/29/13	625.00	625.00	578.50	592.75
12/31/13	584.50	590.75	525.25	530.00

#2 hard, Kansas City.

Annual High, Low and Settle of Wheat   In Cents per Bushel

Year	High	Low	Settle	Year	High	Low	Settle	Year	High	Low	Settle
1972	274.00	144.25	272.25	1986	374.50	235.50	260.00	2000	355.00	258.25	350.50
1973	537.50	223.63	537.50	1987	324.00	251.50	304.25	2001	358.50	302.00	318.50
1974	618.50	342.50	458.75	1988	432.75	299.00	431.50	2002	536.25	305.50	415.25
1975	463.25	308.25	340.50	1989	471.50	406.50	435.50	2003	444.00	298.00	417.25
1976	398.50	252.00	266.50	1990	436.75	267.75	270.50	2004	458.75	350.25	412.00
1977	292.50	219.75	283.75	1991	420.00	261.00	419.00	2005	465.75	358.00	462.50
1978	357.50	277.50	334.50	1992	476.50	310.88	372.00	2006	578.00	421.00	541.75
1979	463.00	328.50	452.50	1993	409.00	296.00	407.00	2007	998.00	496.75	911.50
1980	498.00	373.50	458.00	1994	453.00	332.00	436.00	2008	1,407.00	486.50	657.00
1981	475.00	404.25	427.00	1995	551.00	376.50	549.00	2009	729.00	421.50	510.25
1982	441.50	351.50	398.75	1996	750.00	445.50	449.75	2010	817.50	405.00	808.00
1983	426.00	365.25	384.25	1997	514.00	324.00	345.00	2011	1,013.00	580.50	664.00
1984	404.00	351.50	378.50	1998	369.00	257.75	317.50	2012	929.00	548.00	768.00
1985	380.50	296.00	343.75	1999	329.25	238.75	265.75	2013	770.75	525.25	530.00

Kansas City #2 Hard Winter   Source: U.S. Department of Agriculture (USDA)

WHEAT, KANSAS CITY

WHEAT, KANSAS CITY - KCBT
Weekly Nearest Futures as of 01/03/2014

Date	Open	High	Low	Close
12/06/13	711.75	**715.50**	702.00	705.25
12/13/13	705.00	706.00	657.00	657.00
12/20/13	672.00	672.50	651.00	657.00
12/27/13	656.50	658.50	638.50	644.25
01/03/14	636.00	644.00	**630.25**	642.50

WEEKLY NEAREST FUTURES
As of 01/03/2014

Chart High 1384.75 on 02/27/2008
Chart Low 309.50 on 05/16/2005
CONTRACT SIZE 5,000 BUSHELS
MIN TICK .25 CENTS
VALUE 12.5 USD/CONTRACT
EACH GRID 8 CENTS
VALUE 400 USD/CONTRACT
DAILY LIMIT 60 CENTS
VALUE 3,000 USD / contract
TRADING HOURS
7:00p-7:30a / 8:30a-1:15p CT

Commercial = -277
NonCommercial = 10915
NonReportable = -10638

Nearby Futures through Last Trading Day.

Quarterly High, Low and Settle of Wheat Futures   In Cents per Bushel

Quarter	High	Low	Settle	Quarter	High	Low	Settle	Quarter	High	Low	Settle
03/2005	378.00	322.00	338.00	03/2008	1,384.75	880.75	965.00	03/2011	990.50	765.00	908.00
06/2005	352.50	309.50	328.00	06/2008	1,036.25	782.00	883.00	06/2011	966.00	679.25	688.75
09/2005	384.00	326.50	380.25	09/2008	960.00	704.50	712.00	09/2011	874.50	677.00	704.00
12/2005	392.50	345.00	387.00	12/2008	722.75	489.75	630.00	12/2011	746.75	625.75	717.00
03/2006	449.00	368.00	418.50	03/2009	670.00	537.00	573.25	03/2012	735.75	650.25	697.50
06/2006	522.50	413.00	499.75	06/2009	727.25	552.00	569.75	06/2012	753.00	601.00	738.50
09/2006	518.00	440.25	496.00	09/2009	590.00	453.50	476.50	09/2012	948.00	740.75	927.50
12/2006	556.00	485.00	509.75	12/2009	579.75	458.50	536.25	12/2012	947.00	815.75	831.00
03/2007	516.00	442.25	456.50	03/2010	566.25	461.00	461.75	03/2013	852.00	723.25	726.75
06/2007	630.25	433.00	596.50	06/2010	515.50	454.75	486.00	06/2013	803.50	671.75	676.75
09/2007	949.50	573.00	929.25	09/2010	822.75	486.00	707.75	09/2013	746.75	671.75	739.50
12/2007	1,029.25	755.50	913.50	12/2010	863.50	680.25	851.00	12/2013	776.50	632.75	640.50

Source: Kansas City Board of Trade

Wheat, #2 Hard, Kansas City Weekly Cash as of 01/03/2014				
Date	Open	High	Low	Close
12/06/13	584.50	590.75	584.50	584.75
12/13/13	583.00	583.00	536.50	536.50
12/20/13	536.50	550.00	536.50	546.75
12/27/13	538.00	538.00	533.75	533.75
01/03/14	525.25	532.00	520.75	532.00

WEEKLY CASH
As of 01/03/2014
Chart High 1407.00 on 02/27/2008
Chart Low 298.00 on 07/08/2003

Cents / Bushel

#2 hard, Kansas City.

Quarterly High, Low and Settle of Wheat   In Cents per Bushel

Quarter	High	Low	Settle	Quarter	High	Low	Settle	Quarter	High	Low	Settle
03/2005	426.50	380.50	380.50	03/2008	1,407.00	896.00	1,009.50	03/2011	943.00	736.00	867.00
06/2005	396.75	358.00	367.00	06/2008	1,078.00	812.25	895.00	06/2011	1,013.00	659.75	659.75
09/2005	452.75	368.50	452.75	09/2008	928.00	687.50	694.00	09/2011	846.00	654.00	679.00
12/2005	465.75	427.00	462.50	12/2008	686.00	486.50	657.00	12/2011	700.00	580.50	664.00
03/2006	480.50	421.00	460.50	03/2009	697.00	552.00	595.25	03/2012	710.50	580.00	654.50
06/2006	554.50	453.25	526.75	06/2009	729.00	551.75	551.75	06/2012	726.50	548.00	726.50
09/2006	541.00	470.50	524.00	09/2009	571.00	421.50	443.50	09/2012	929.00	747.50	894.50
12/2006	578.00	518.50	541.75	12/2009	566.00	426.50	510.25	12/2012	884.00	768.00	768.00
03/2007	553.50	503.50	511.00	03/2010	542.00	440.75	440.75	03/2013	770.75	655.50	658.75
06/2007	659.50	496.75	618.50	06/2010	485.25	405.00	442.00	06/2013	723.25	593.25	593.25
09/2007	918.75	593.00	918.75	09/2010	712.00	464.25	634.75	09/2013	648.00	587.25	648.00
12/2007	998.00	784.50	911.50	12/2010	817.50	626.25	808.00	12/2013	679.25	525.25	530.00

Kansas City #2 Hard Winter   *Source: U.S. Department of Agriculture (USDA)*

WHEAT, MINNEAPOLIS

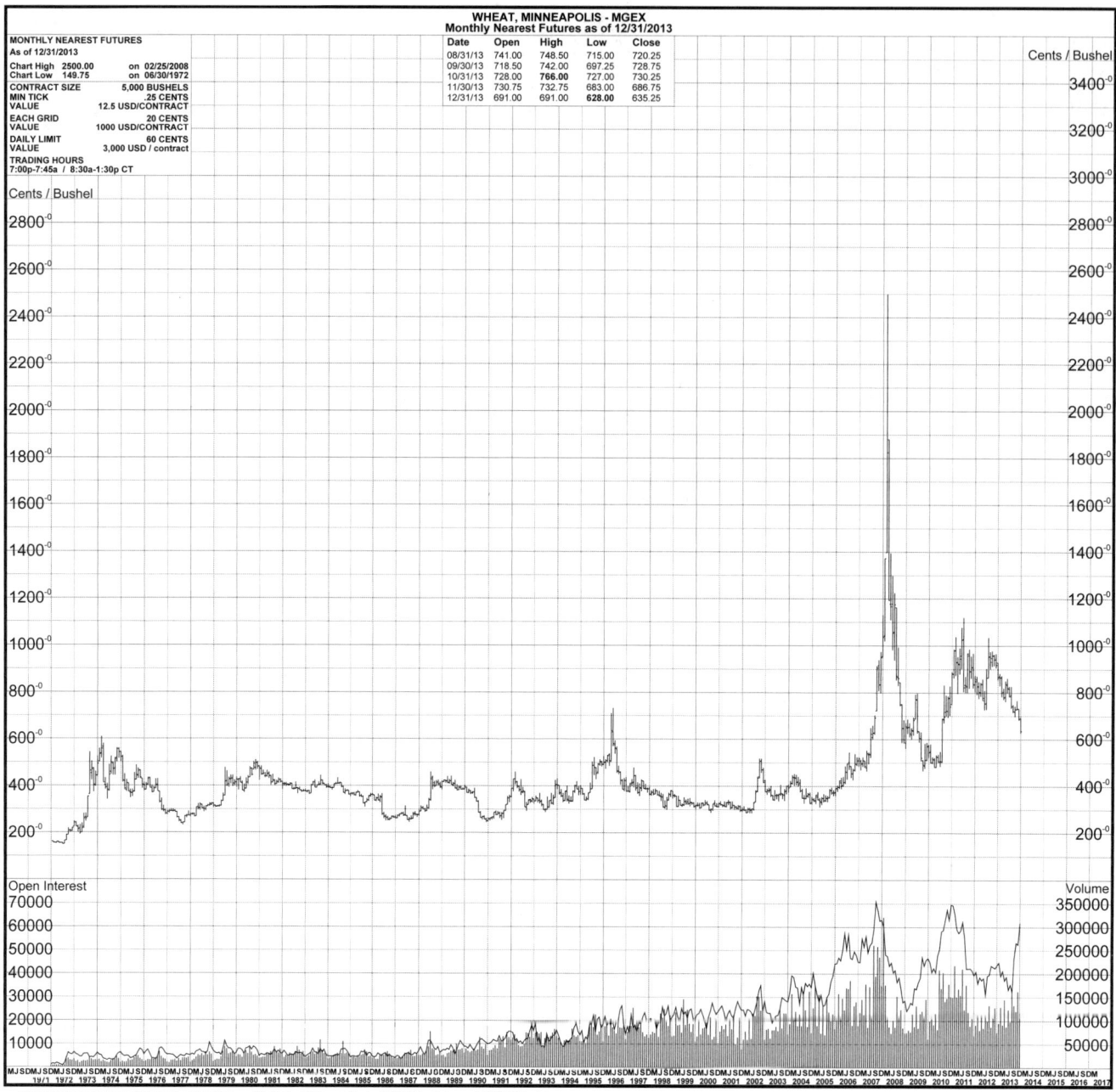

WHEAT, MINNEAPOLIS - MGEX
Monthly Nearest Futures as of 12/31/2013

Date	Open	High	Low	Close
08/31/13	741.00	748.50	715.00	720.25
09/30/13	718.50	742.00	697.25	728.75
10/31/13	728.00	766.00	727.00	730.25
11/30/13	730.75	732.75	683.00	686.75
12/31/13	691.00	691.00	628.00	635.25

MONTHLY NEAREST FUTURES
As of 12/31/2013

Chart High 2500.00 on 02/25/2008
Chart Low 149.75 on 06/30/1972
CONTRACT SIZE 5,000 BUSHELS
MIN TICK .25 CENTS
VALUE 12.5 USD/CONTRACT
EACH GRID 20 CENTS
VALUE 1000 USD/CONTRACT
DAILY LIMIT 60 CENTS
VALUE 3,000 USD / contract
TRADING HOURS
7:00p-7:45a / 8:30a-1:30p CT

Nearby Futures through Last Trading Day.   #1 Dark, Minneapolis: to 12/1969; Futures: 01/1970 to date.

Annual High, Low and Settle of Wheat Futures   In Cents per Bushel

Year	High	Low	Settle	Year	High	Low	Settle	Year	High	Low	Settle
1972	249.00	149.75	243.50	1986	367.00	251.00	262.75	2000	341.00	286.50	327.25
1973	543.50	191.50	493.00	1987	315.00	245.00	290.75	2001	336.25	290.00	300.00
1974	609.00	342.00	522.00	1988	460.00	288.50	417.00	2002	518.00	285.00	377.25
1975	528.00	348.00	383.00	1989	442.25	379.50	393.50	2003	408.00	338.00	393.75
1976	435.00	276.00	289.25	1990	395.00	245.00	259.50	2004	449.50	325.00	346.00
1977	301.00	232.50	278.00	1991	390.00	252.25	389.00	2005	395.00	310.50	392.00
1978	327.00	267.75	314.50	1992	460.00	292.75	335.75	2006	545.00	377.50	518.50
1979	477.25	306.75	425.00	1993	430.00	287.75	403.50	2007	1,130.00	464.00	1,036.25
1980	510.00	370.50	472.00	1994	419.50	324.00	390.00	2008	2,500.00	561.00	654.75
1981	484.00	383.00	406.50	1995	527.00	336.50	499.50	2009	797.25	465.50	545.00
1982	415.75	366.00	375.00	1996	732.00	377.50	377.75	2010	889.25	481.50	881.50
1983	444.00	363.00	394.25	1997	478.50	357.00	364.00	2011	1,120.00	797.25	849.50
1984	434.00	353.50	367.00	1998	389.00	299.00	359.25	2012	1,035.00	726.00	865.50
1985	380.25	309.75	360.50	1999	366.00	303.00	318.00	2013	882.25	628.00	635.25

Source: Minneapolis Grain Exchange

Wheat, Spring 14% Protein, Mpls.
Monthly Cash as of 12/31/2013

Date	Open	High	Low	Close
08/30/13	824.75	877.75	793.25	877.75
09/30/13	880.00	880.00	781.25	826.25
10/31/13	827.05	894.50	827.00	890.25
11/29/13	886.50	886.50	824.25	849.25
12/31/13	845.00	938.50	826.75	862.75

MONTHLY CASH
As of 12/31/2013
Chart High 2255.75 on 02/26/2008
Chart Low 146.00 on 06/30/1972

#1 dark, Minneapolis: to 12/1978; #1 dark, 14% protein, Minneapolis: 01/1979 to date.

Annual High, Low and Settle of Wheat   In Cents per Bushel

Year	High	Low	Settle	Year	High	Low	Settle	Year	High	Low	Settle
1972	241.50	146.00	241.50	1986	440.00	279.00	297.75	2000	400.00	297.50	384.75
1973	537.00	207.25	508.00	1987	344.00	276.25	310.75	2001	400.00	342.00	352.50
1974	616.00	354.00	503.00	1988	474.00	308.50	438.00	2002	549.00	345.00	422.25
1975	497.50	328.50	339.00	1989	464.75	400.00	423.50	2003	475.50	374.50	436.25
1976	399.00	262.50	274.25	1990	430.00	273.50	283.50	2004	513.00	388.75	473.50
1977	291.88	214.00	271.00	1991	428.00	276.50	428.00	2005	536.50	421.75	504.50
1978	339.25	262.50	312.50	1992	486.25	337.50	385.75	2006	616.00	465.25	550.88
1979	479.50	305.13	412.88	1993	582.25	360.25	546.00	2007	1,180.50	504.75	1,111.25
1980	494.50	373.00	465.75	1994	561.25	374.25	432.50	2008	2,255.75	682.25	767.25
1981	484.50	395.75	414.38	1995	587.00	389.25	587.00	2009	852.00	564.50	680.00
1982	437.63	365.00	377.00	1996	751.75	430.50	441.75	2010	1,048.25	602.25	1,037.00
1983	450.75	373.50	417.13	1997	503.75	406.50	406.50	2011	1,458.50	916.25	992.00
1984	445.75	345.75	391.00	1998	448.50	325.50	390.38	2012	1,089.00	882.50	950.50
1985	425.00	346.75	420.50	1999	408.00	329.00	365.50	2013	966.50	781.25	862.75

Minneapolis #1 Dark 15% through 12/1978, Minneapolis #1 Dark 14% 01/1979 to date.   *Source: Minneapolis Grain Exchange*

WHEAT, MINNEAPOLIS

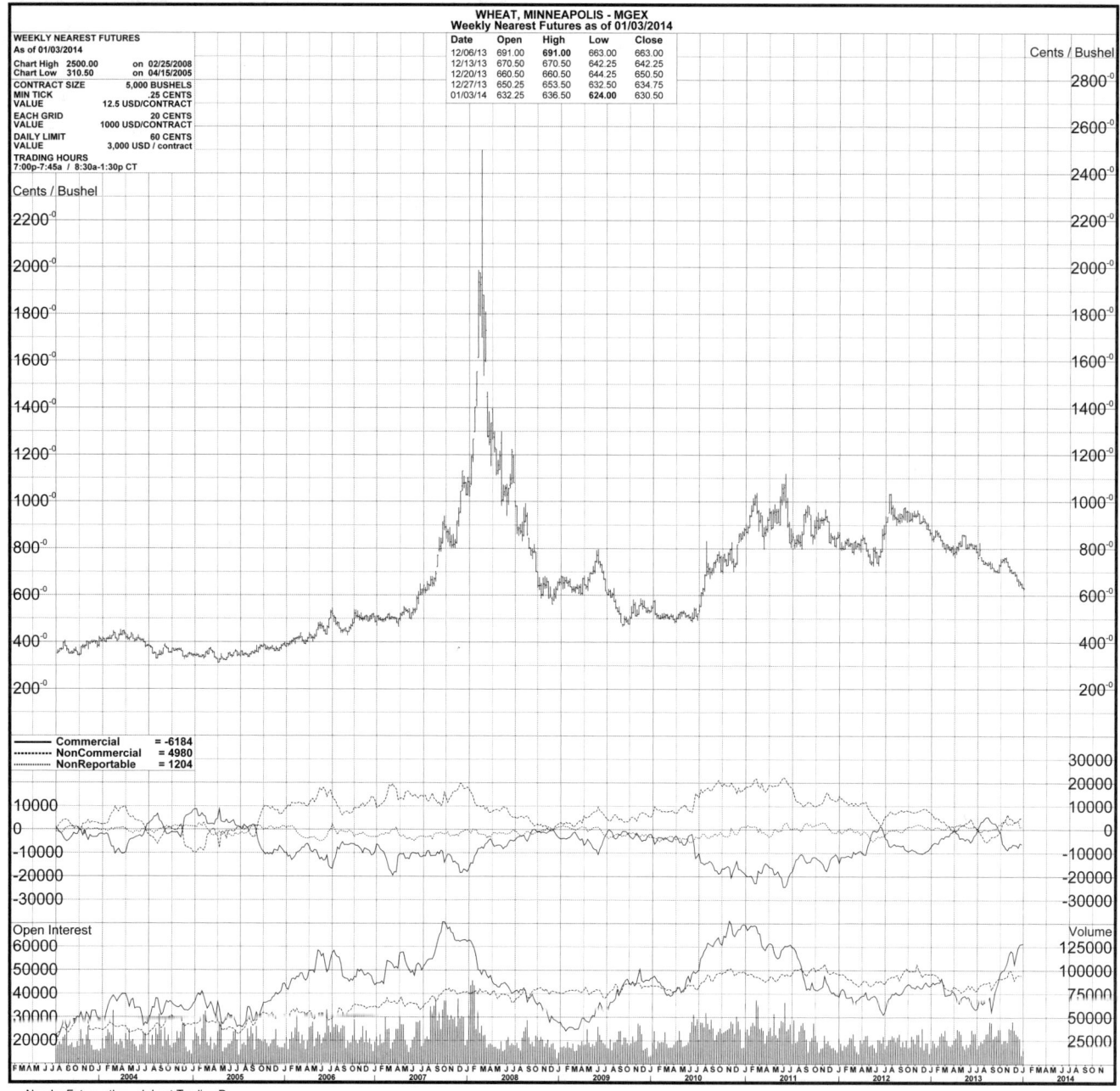

WHEAT, MINNEAPOLIS - MGEX
Weekly Nearest Futures as of 01/03/2014

Date	Open	High	Low	Close
12/06/13	691.00	691.00	663.00	663.00
12/13/13	670.50	670.50	642.25	642.25
12/20/13	660.50	660.50	644.25	650.50
12/27/13	650.25	653.50	632.50	634.75
01/03/14	632.25	636.50	624.00	630.50

WEEKLY NEAREST FUTURES
As of 01/03/2014

Chart High	2500.00	on 02/25/2008
Chart Low	310.50	on 04/15/2005
CONTRACT SIZE	5,000 BUSHELS	
MIN TICK		.25 CENTS
VALUE		12.5 USD/CONTRACT
EACH GRID		20 CENTS
VALUE		1000 USD/CONTRACT
DAILY LIMIT		60 CENTS
VALUE	3,000 USD / contract	
TRADING HOURS		
7:00p-7:45a / 8:30a-1:30p CT		

Commercial = -6184
NonCommercial = 4980
NonReportable = 1204

Nearby Futures through Last Trading Day.

Quarterly High, Low and Settle of Wheat Futures   In Cents per Bushel

Quarter	High	Low	Settle	Quarter	High	Low	Settle	Quarter	High	Low	Settle
03/2005	376.00	326.00	343.75	03/2008	2,500.00	1,019.50	1,194.00	03/2011	1,038.50	797.25	923.75
06/2005	367.50	310.50	339.00	06/2008	1,395.00	938.00	1,175.00	06/2011	1,120.00	804.50	823.25
09/2005	389.00	333.25	383.00	09/2008	1,162.25	743.00	746.75	09/2011	985.75	798.50	892.25
12/2005	395.00	359.00	392.00	12/2008	750.00	561.00	654.75	12/2011	968.00	805.00	849.50
03/2006	438.00	377.50	404.25	03/2009	685.75	600.00	639.25	03/2012	870.75	775.25	837.50
06/2006	498.00	400.00	496.00	06/2009	797.25	617.75	636.00	06/2012	903.25	726.00	864.00
09/2006	545.00	426.50	468.75	09/2009	634.00	465.50	491.75	09/2012	1,035.00	864.00	958.50
12/2006	538.00	465.00	518.50	12/2009	587.00	477.00	545.00	12/2012	966.25	855.00	865.50
03/2007	524.00	469.00	485.00	03/2010	580.25	481.50	482.00	03/2013	882.25	771.25	780.25
06/2007	649.00	464.00	623.00	06/2010	548.75	482.25	507.00	06/2013	861.75	761.25	785.00
09/2007	914.25	600.00	905.75	09/2010	833.00	503.00	721.00	09/2013	827.00	697.25	728.75
12/2007	1,130.00	799.50	1,036.25	12/2010	889.25	693.75	881.50	12/2013	766.00	628.00	635.25

Source: Minneapolis Grain Exchange

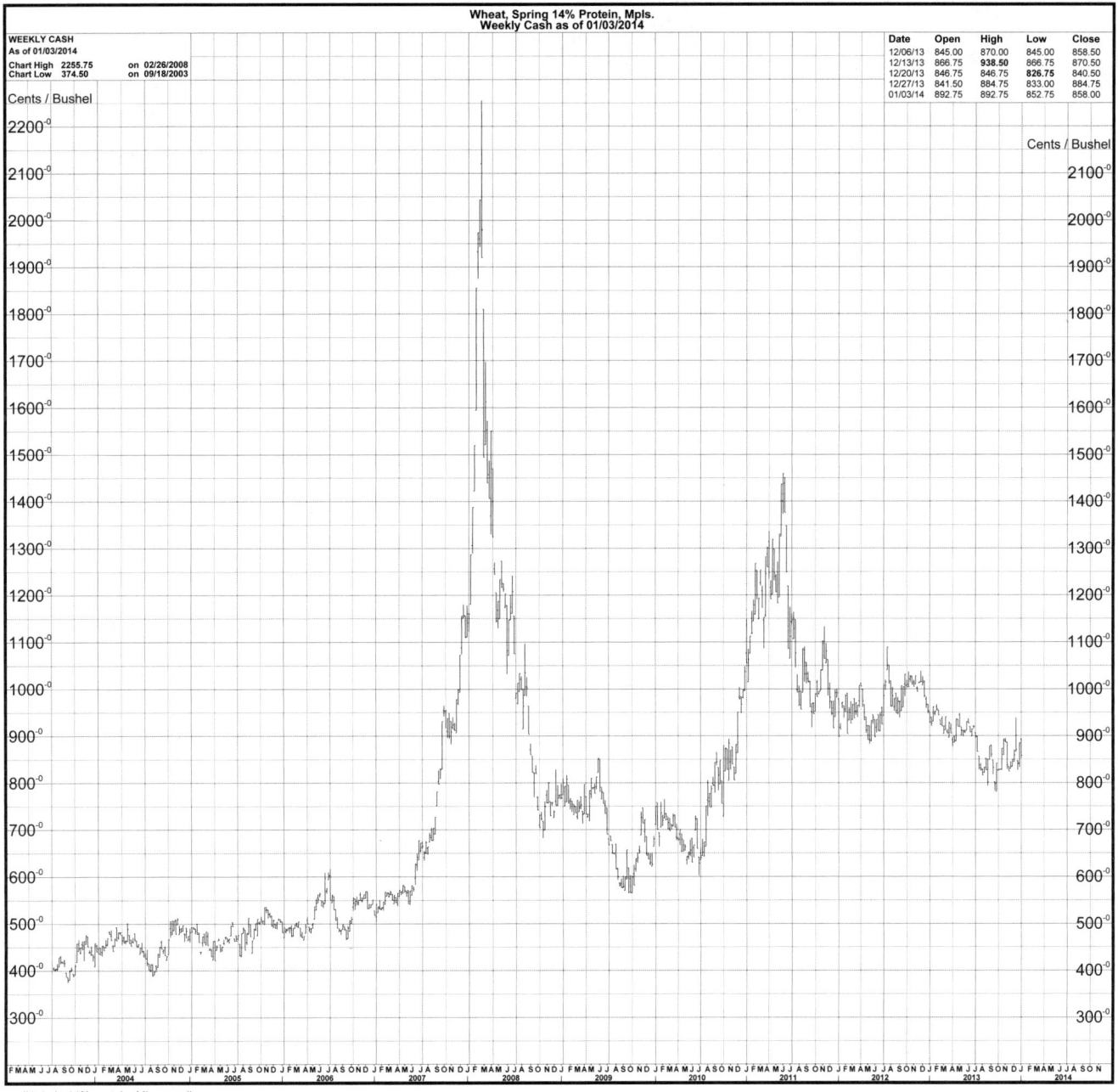

Wheat, Spring 14% Protein, Mpls.
Weekly Cash as of 01/03/2014

WEEKLY CASH
As of 01/03/2014
Chart High   2255.75   on 02/26/2008
Chart Low   374.50   on 09/18/2003

Cents / Bushel

Date	Open	High	Low	Close
12/06/13	845.00	870.00	845.00	858.50
12/13/13	866.75	938.50	866.75	870.50
12/20/13	846.75	846.75	826.75	840.50
12/27/13	841.50	884.75	833.00	884.75
01/03/14	892.75	892.75	852.75	858.00

#1 dark, 14% protein, Minneapolis.

Quarterly High, Low and Settle of Wheat   In Cents per Bushel

Quarter	High	Low	Settle	Quarter	High	Low	Settle	Quarter	High	Low	Settle
03/2005	500.75	434.75	438.75	03/2008	2,255.75	1,122.50	1,369.00	03/2011	1,303.25	1,015.25	1,283.75
06/2005	503.50	421.75	464.50	06/2008	1,550.75	1,032.00	1,155.50	06/2011	1,458.50	1,065.25	1,127.50
09/2005	513.25	430.25	510.50	09/2008	1,138.50	769.25	771.75	09/2011	1,164.00	917.50	946.50
12/2005	536.50	488.00	504.50	12/2008	828.75	682.25	767.25	12/2011	1,133.00	916.25	992.00
03/2006	504.75	465.50	473.25	03/2009	816.50	712.50	756.75	03/2012	1,007.50	898.50	1,007.50
06/2006	609.00	479.50	575.50	06/2009	852.00	716.25	716.25	06/2012	1,012.75	882.50	924.50
09/2006	616.00	465.25	506.25	09/2009	723.50	564.50	589.25	09/2012	1,089.00	938.25	1,031.00
12/2006	568.50	501.00	550.88	12/2009	746.75	565.50	680.00	12/2012	1,038.75	947.25	950.50
03/2007	570.75	504.75	545.00	03/2010	765.25	663.25	677.00	03/2013	966.50	896.25	905.25
06/2007	677.00	537.50	677.00	06/2010	730.50	602.25	622.25	06/2013	947.75	876.50	920.00
09/2007	930.75	634.50	930.75	09/2010	863.75	628.50	793.50	09/2013	906.50	781.25	826.25
12/2007	1,180.50	882.50	1,111.25	12/2010	1,048.25	728.25	1,037.00	12/2013	938.50	824.25	862.75

Minneapolis #1 Dark 14% .   Source: U.S. Department of Agriculture (USDA)

CANOLA

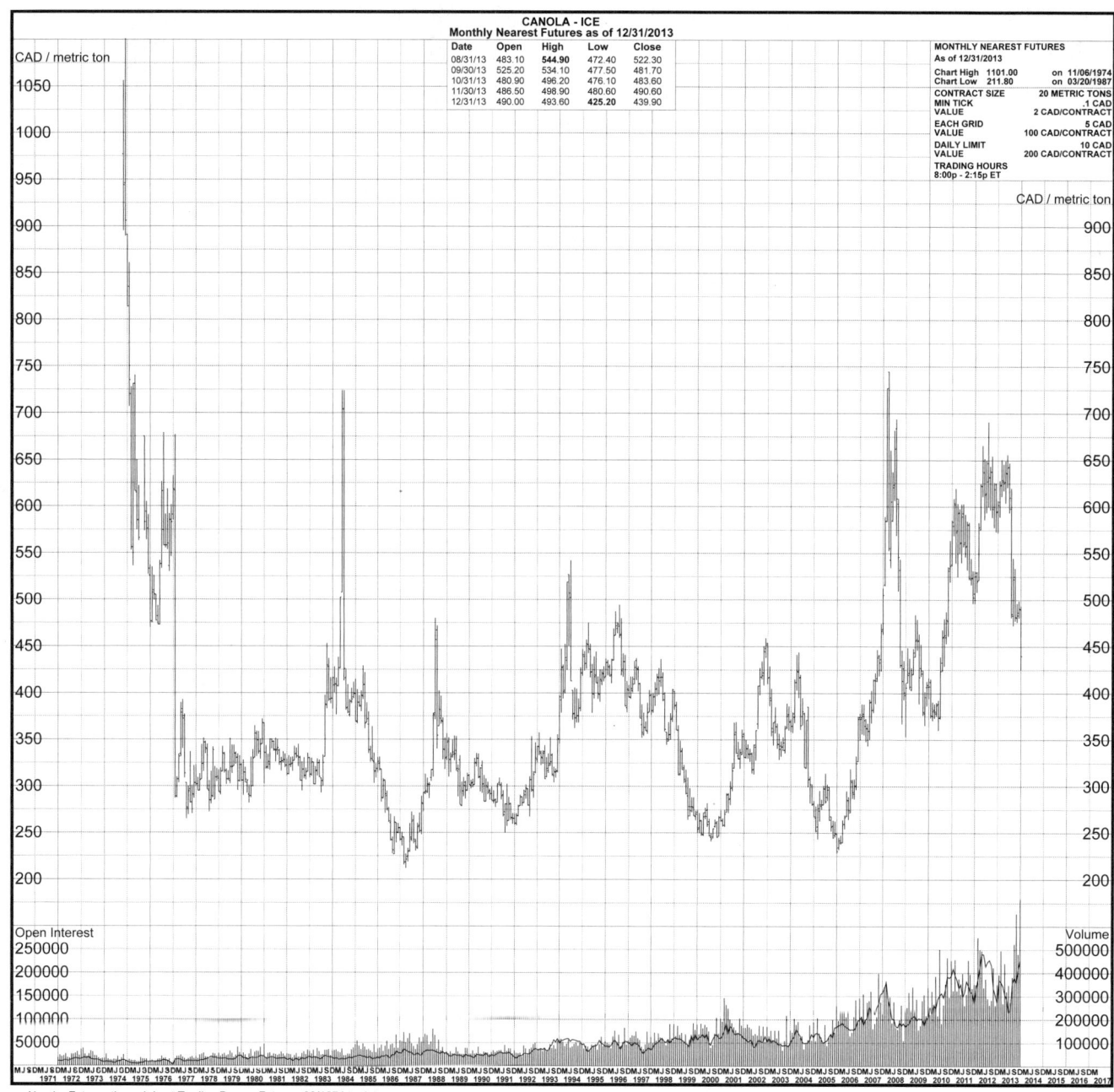

CANOLA - ICE
Monthly Nearest Futures as of 12/31/2013

Date	Open	High	Low	Close
08/31/13	483.10	**544.90**	472.40	522.30
09/30/13	525.20	534.10	477.50	481.70
10/31/13	480.90	496.20	476.10	483.60
11/30/13	486.50	498.90	480.60	490.60
12/31/13	490.00	493.60	**425.20**	439.90

MONTHLY NEAREST FUTURES
As of 12/31/2013

Chart High	1101.00	on 11/06/1974
Chart Low	211.80	on 03/20/1987
CONTRACT SIZE		20 METRIC TONS
MIN TICK		.1 CAD
VALUE		2 CAD/CONTRACT
EACH GRID		5 CAD
VALUE		100 CAD/CONTRACT
DAILY LIMIT		10 CAD
VALUE		200 CAD/CONTRACT
TRADING HOURS		
8:00p - 2:15p ET		

Nearby Futures through Last Trading Day.   Futures: 09/1974 to date.

Annual High, Low and Settle of Canola Futures   In CAD per Metric Ton

Year	High	Low	Settle	Year	High	Low	Settle	Year	High	Low	Settle
1972	----	----	----	1986	331.50	226.90	242.70	2000	282.20	241.00	263.30
1973	----	----	----	1987	293.20	211.80	292.60	2001	369.00	256.60	331.00
1974	1,101.00	777.60	814.00	1988	480.00	287.00	346.70	2002	459.00	313.00	416.60
1975	861.00	470.00	476.40	1989	354.00	278.50	301.60	2003	428.90	328.50	364.50
1976	679.00	472.40	618.00	1990	335.40	283.50	285.00	2004	444.00	267.00	267.50
1977	677.00	265.00	302.00	1991	309.00	250.00	260.00	2005	314.00	228.00	230.10
1978	351.50	272.50	294.00	1992	353.60	257.80	342.70	2006	378.00	231.90	372.00
1979	351.00	290.50	306.00	1993	398.00	304.00	395.90	2007	512.20	343.10	505.00
1980	372.00	282.00	335.70	1994	542.20	362.20	441.00	2008	744.50	353.10	406.10
1981	351.20	311.00	313.00	1995	475.50	378.50	432.50	2009	484.10	365.20	407.20
1982	345.00	295.00	312.30	1996	494.50	379.10	396.00	2010	585.40	360.00	583.80
1983	453.00	292.80	416.10	1997	437.50	352.00	380.90	2011	619.50	496.10	525.80
1984	724.00	368.90	369.30	1998	436.50	344.50	386.20	2012	691.10	508.10	601.80
1985	429.20	303.10	326.30	1999	390.70	250.00	254.00	2013	656.20	425.20	439.90

Futures data begins 04/30/1974.   *Source: ICE Futures Canada*

CANOLA - ICE
Weekly Nearest Futures as of 01/03/2014

Date	Open	High	Low	Close
12/06/13	490.00	493.60	471.10	471.90
12/13/13	472.30	475.00	438.40	439.90
12/20/13	439.90	447.40	439.60	443.60
12/27/13	444.70	444.70	427.30	427.60
01/03/14	425.20	440.70	425.20	433.10

WEEKLY NEAREST FUTURES
As of 01/03/2014

Chart High 744.50 on 03/03/2008
Chart Low 228.00 on 12/30/2005

CONTRACT SIZE	20 METRIC TONS
MIN TICK	.1 CAD
VALUE	2 CAD/CONTRACT
EACH GRID VALUE	80 CAD/CONTRACT
DAILY LIMIT	10 CAD
VALUE	200 CAD/CONTRACT

TRADING HOURS
8:00p - 2:15p ET

CAD / metric ton

Nearby Futures through Last Trading Day.

Quarterly High, Low and Settle of Canola Futures   In CAD per Metric Ton

Quarter	High	Low	Settle	Quarter	High	Low	Settle	Quarter	High	Low	Settle
03/2005	295.50	243.20	280.90	03/2008	744.50	514.80	555.30	03/2011	619.50	525.00	593.30
06/2005	314.00	275.50	283.90	06/2008	681.80	534.60	662.30	06/2011	603.00	540.00	560.20
09/2005	302.30	251.80	256.50	09/2008	693.90	427.60	430.10	09/2011	591.80	522.00	523.80
12/2005	263.40	228.00	230.10	12/2008	446.10	353.10	406.10	12/2011	544.60	496.10	525.80
03/2006	263.80	231.90	259.60	03/2009	448.70	403.00	420.40	03/2012	624.50	508.10	622.50
06/2006	295.00	254.20	274.30	06/2009	484.10	420.40	456.00	06/2012	665.90	586.10	627.10
09/2006	318.80	272.20	300.10	09/2009	463.50	376.10	379.60	09/2012	691.10	588.60	597.70
12/2006	378.00	296.50	372.00	12/2009	416.40	365.20	407.20	12/2012	626.00	572.20	601.80
03/2007	388.00	347.80	362.40	03/2010	415.40	370.40	380.00	03/2013	650.80	589.00	625.50
06/2007	403.00	343.10	381.70	06/2010	438.90	360.00	423.80	06/2013	656.20	593.60	609.80
09/2007	446.70	378.90	438.10	09/2010	487.30	423.50	478.40	09/2013	619.60	472.40	481.70
12/2007	512.20	418.40	505.00	12/2010	585.40	461.00	583.80	12/2013	498.90	425.20	439.90

Source: ICE Futures Canada

SOYBEANS

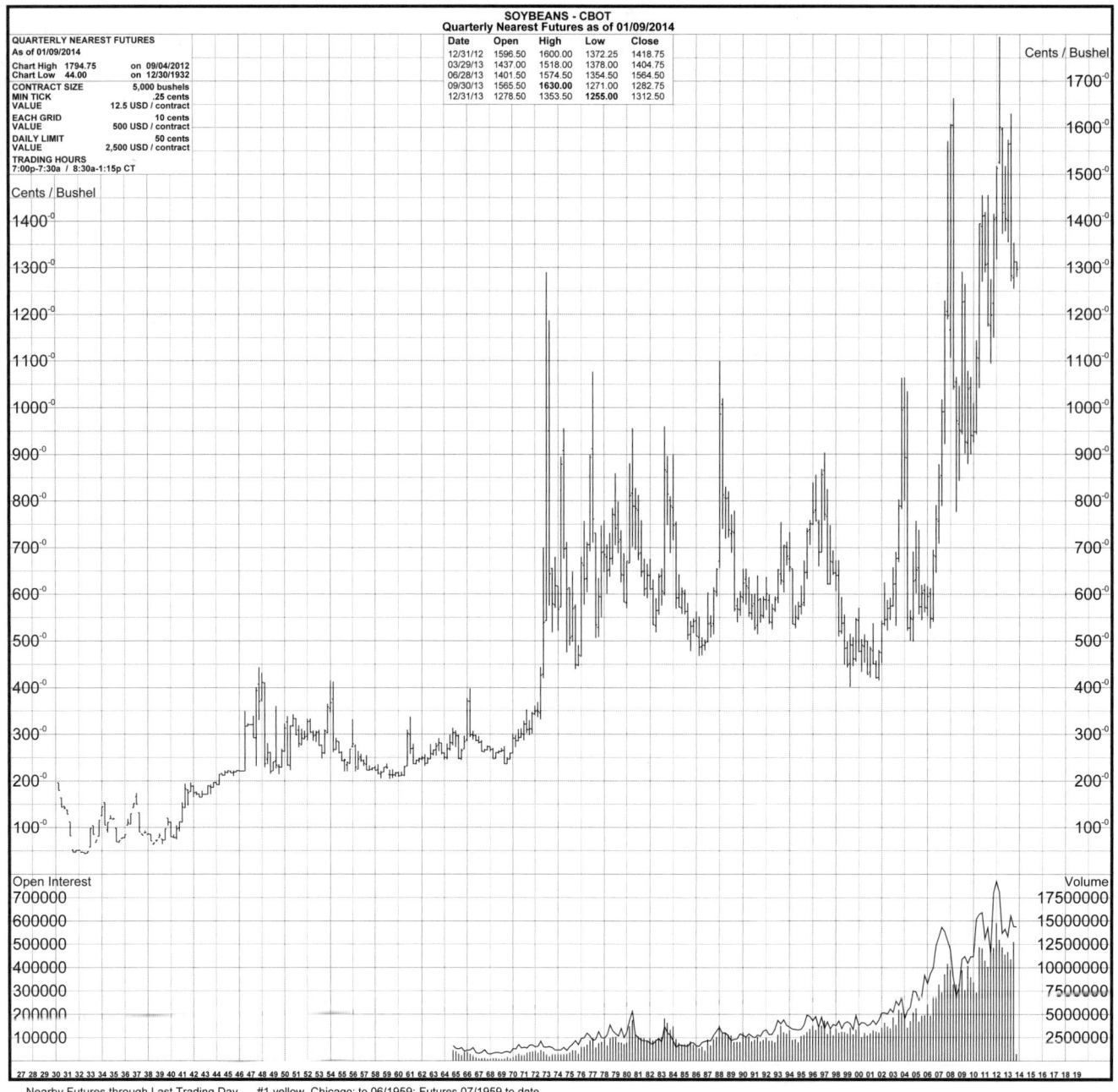

SOYBEANS - CBOT
Quarterly Nearest Futures as of 01/09/2014

Date	Open	High	Low	Close
12/31/12	1596.50	1600.00	1372.25	1418.75
03/29/13	1437.00	1518.00	1378.00	1404.75
06/28/13	1401.50	1574.50	1354.50	1564.50
09/30/13	1565.50	1630.00	1271.00	1282.75
12/31/13	1278.50	1353.50	1255.00	1312.50

QUARTERLY NEAREST FUTURES
As of 01/09/2014

Chart High 1794.75 on 09/04/2012
Chart Low 44.00 on 12/30/1932
CONTRACT SIZE 5,000 bushels
MIN TICK .25 cents
VALUE 12.5 USD / contract
EACH GRID 10 cents
VALUE 500 USD / contract
DAILY LIMIT 50 cents
VALUE 2,500 USD / contract
TRADING HOURS
7:00p-7:30a / 8:30a-1:15p CT

Nearby Futures through Last Trading Day.   #1 yellow, Chicago: to 06/1959; Futures 07/1959 to date.

Annual High, Low and Settle of Soybean Futures   In Cents per Bushel

Year	High	Low	Settle	Year	High	Low	Settle	Year	High	Low	Settle
1930	216.00	144.00	144.00	1944	216.00	186.00	212.00	1958	235.50	205.25	217.50
1931	146.00	47.00	47.00	1945	222.00	210.00	219.00	1959	237.00	204.13	212.38
1932	52.00	44.00	44.00	1946	349.00	219.00	317.00	1960	232.00	208.75	230.13
1933	104.00	45.00	73.00	1947	401.25	231.50	394.00	1956	331.50	220.00	246.50
1934	154.00	81.00	111.00	1948	443.75	228.75	259.88	1957	257.50	222.50	223.50
1935	127.00	68.00	72.00	1949	360.00	214.25	229.63	1958	235.50	205.25	217.50
1936	130.00	76.00	130.00	1950	338.25	222.63	316.75	1959	237.00	204.13	212.38
1937	174.00	83.00	83.00	1951	342.13	271.63	291.00	1960	232.00	208.75	230.13
1938	93.00	63.00	67.00	1952	333.00	285.38	296.13	1961	337.00	231.50	243.63
1939	97.00	64.00	97.00	1953	309.75	247.75	306.50	1962	257.00	232.00	246.88
1940	120.50	74.25	96.50	1954	415.75	261.00	285.00	1963	291.50	246.38	281.25
1941	194.00	91.25	174.50	1955	284.00	220.00	239.50	1964	298.50	245.50	281.63
1942	196.50	165.25	165.25	1956	331.50	220.00	246.50	1965	313.50	244.50	264.75
1943	192.00	165.25	186.00	1957	257.50	222.50	223.50	1966	398.00	268.00	296.50

Futures data begins 07/01/1959.   Data continued on page 236.   Source: CME Group; Chicago Board of Trade

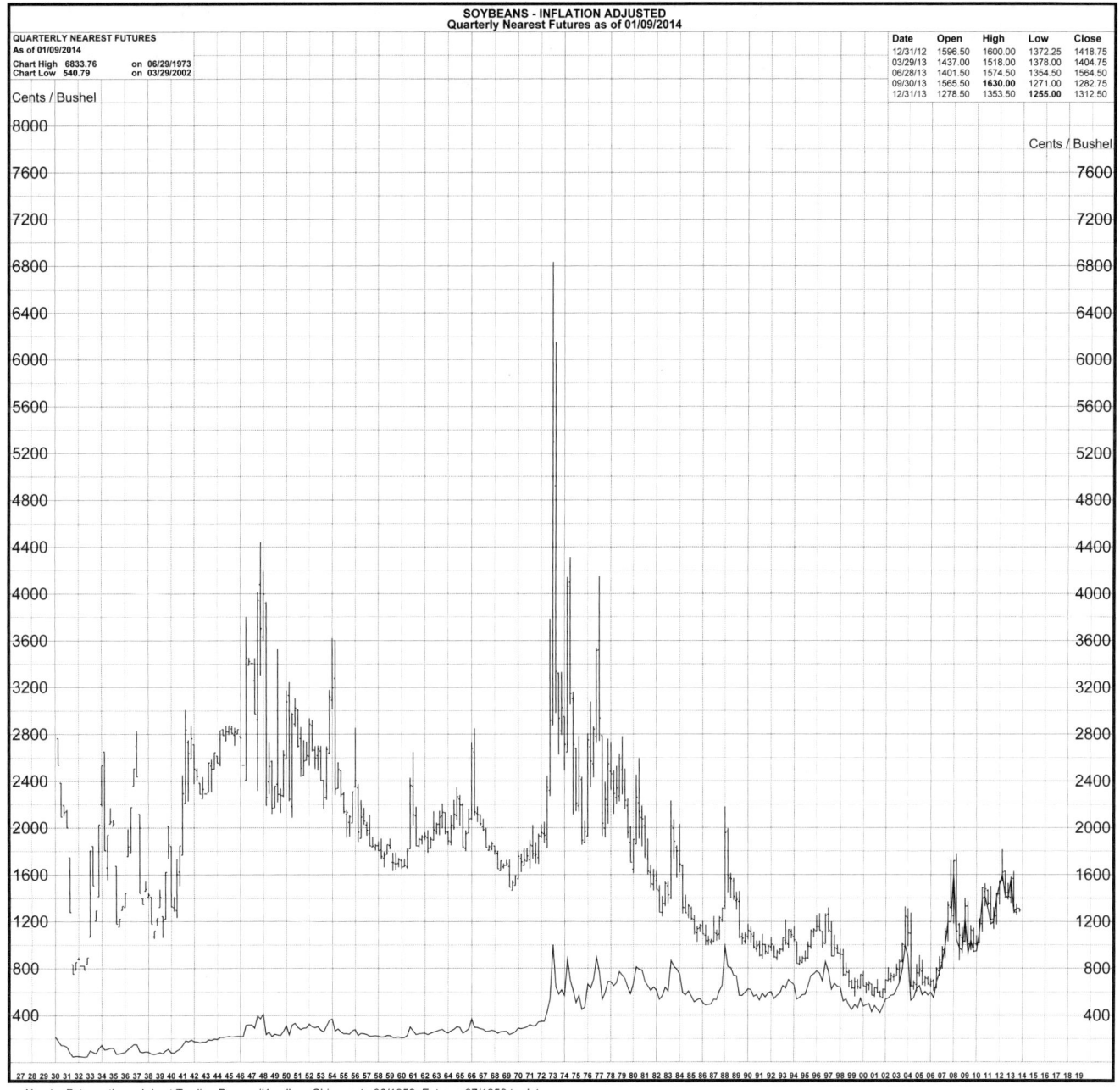

SOYBEANS - INFLATION ADJUSTED
Quarterly Nearest Futures as of 01/09/2014

QUARTERLY NEAREST FUTURES
As of 01/09/2014

Chart High 6833.76 on 06/29/1973
Chart Low 540.79 on 03/29/2002

Cents / Bushel

Date	Open	High	Low	Close
12/31/12	1596.50	1600.00	1372.25	1418.75
03/29/13	1437.00	1518.00	1378.00	1404.75
06/28/13	1401.50	1574.50	1354.50	1564.50
09/30/13	1565.50	1630.00	1271.00	1282.75
12/31/13	1278.50	1353.50	1255.00	1312.50

Nearby Futures through Last Trading Day.   #1 yellow, Chicago: to 06/1959; Futures 07/1959 to date.

Annual High, Low and Settle of Soybeans   In Cents per Bushel

Year	High	Low	Settle	Year	High	Low	Settle	Year	High	Low	Settle
1930	216.00	144.00	144.00	1944	216.00	186.00	212.00	1958	235.50	205.25	217.50
1931	146.00	47.00	47.00	1945	222.00	210.00	219.00	1959	237.00	207.00	215.00
1932	52.00	44.00	44.00	1946	349.00	219.00	317.00	1960	233.00	206.00	233.00
1933	104.00	45.00	73.00	1947	401.25	231.50	394.00	1961	334.00	232.00	246.00
1934	154.00	81.00	111.00	1948	443.75	228.75	259.88	1962	257.00	236.00	253.00
1935	127.00	68.00	72.00	1949	360.00	214.25	229.63	1963	293.00	254.00	284.00
1936	130.00	76.00	130.00	1950	338.25	222.63	316.75	1964	296.00	250.00	283.00
1937	174.00	83.00	83.00	1951	342.13	271.63	291.00	1965	311.25	246.00	267.00
1938	93.00	63.00	67.00	1952	333.00	285.38	296.13	1966	397.88	271.88	298.00
1939	97.00	64.00	97.00	1953	309.75	247.75	306.50	1967	298.38	257.00	265.63
1940	120.50	74.25	96.50	1954	415.75	261.00	285.00	1968	276.63	243.88	262.00
1941	194.00	91.25	174.50	1955	284.00	220.00	239.50	1969	274.25	233.25	248.63
1942	196.50	165.25	165.25	1956	331.50	220.00	246.50	1970	306.00	248.25	290.00
1943	192.00	165.25	186.00	1957	257.50	222.50	223.50	1971	350.00	287.25	309.25

Chicago #2 Yellow through 12/1956, Chicago #1 Yellow 01/1957 to 03/26/1982   Data continued on page 237.
Source: CME Group; Chicago Board of Trade

SOYBEANS

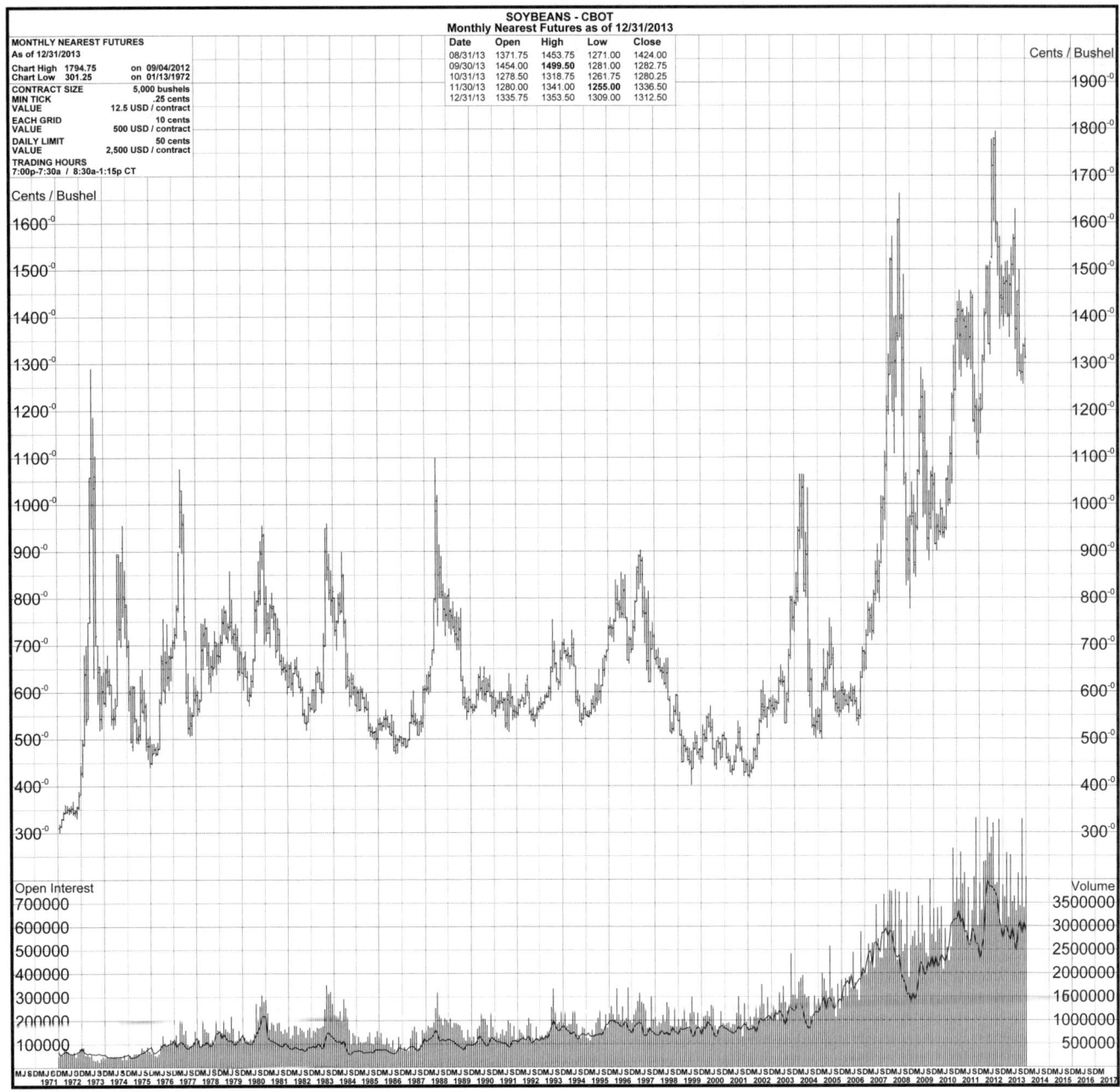

SOYBEANS - CBOT
Monthly Nearest Futures as of 12/31/2013

MONTHLY NEAREST FUTURES
As of 12/31/2013

Date	Open	High	Low	Close
08/31/13	1371.75	1453.75	1271.00	1424.00
09/30/13	1454.00	1499.50	1281.00	1282.75
10/31/13	1278.50	1318.75	1261.75	1280.25
11/30/13	1280.00	1341.00	1255.00	1336.50
12/31/13	1335.75	1353.50	1309.00	1312.50

Chart High 1794.75 on 09/04/2012
Chart Low 301.25 on 01/13/1972
CONTRACT SIZE 5,000 bushels
MIN TICK .25 cents
VALUE 12.5 USD / contract
EACH GRID 10 cents
VALUE 500 USD / contract
DAILY LIMIT 50 cents
VALUE 2,500 USD / contract
TRADING HOURS
7:00p-7:30a / 8:30a-1:15p CT

Cents / Bushel

Open Interest / Volume

Nearby Futures through Last Trading Day.

Annual High, Low and Settle of Soybean Futures   In Cents per Bushel

Year	High	Low	Settle	Year	High	Low	Settle	Year	High	Low	Settle
1972	444.00	301.25	426.25	1986	563.00	467.50	490.75	2000	570.50	433.50	499.50
1973	1,290.00	420.00	579.00	1987	614.50	479.50	607.00	2001	538.00	419.50	421.00
1974	956.00	521.00	697.00	1988	1,099.50	594.50	804.75	2002	625.00	415.50	569.50
1975	712.00	439.50	448.75	1989	820.50	540.00	568.00	2003	803.50	532.00	789.00
1976	757.00	446.00	706.50	1990	655.00	552.00	559.75	2004	1,064.00	501.00	547.75
1977	1,076.50	506.00	594.75	1991	640.00	514.00	554.75	2005	757.50	498.50	602.00
1978	758.00	550.25	676.50	1992	637.00	524.50	568.75	2006	695.75	526.50	683.50
1979	859.00	625.00	641.25	1993	755.00	561.75	704.25	2007	1,230.00	645.50	1,199.00
1980	956.00	569.50	788.75	1994	732.50	526.75	550.75	2008	1,663.00	776.25	972.25
1981	827.50	596.00	610.50	1995	741.75	544.50	735.25	2009	1,291.25	843.00	1,039.75
1982	675.50	518.00	564.50	1996	856.00	659.75	690.50	2010	1,394.50	900.00	1,393.75
1983	960.00	555.50	814.50	1997	903.50	620.00	670.50	2011	1,456.00	1,094.25	1,198.50
1984	899.00	568.50	572.25	1998	694.00	509.25	537.75	2012	1,794.75	1,150.00	1,418.75
1985	614.00	478.00	531.25	1999	556.50	401.50	461.75	2013	1,630.00	1,255.00	1,312.50

Data continued from page 234.   *Source: CME Group; Chicago Board of Trade*

MONTHLY CASH
As of 12/31/2013

Chart High 1790.00 on 07/20/2012
Chart Low 299.63 on 12/01/1971

Cents / Bushel

Soybeans, #1 Yellow, Central, IL
Monthly Cash as of 12/31/2013

Date	Open	High	Low	Close
08/30/13	1332.50	1516.00	1303.00	1484.50
09/30/13	1515.50	1515.50	1265.00	1265.00
10/31/13	1263.54	1294.00	1260.00	1263.50
11/29/13	1251.00	1321.00	1248.00	1312.50
12/31/13	1313.50	1340.50	1303.50	1303.50

#1 yellow, Chicago: to 03/1982; #1 yellow, Central IL: 03/1982 to date.

Annual High, Low and Settle of Soybeans   In Cents per Bushel

Year	High	Low	Settle	Year	High	Low	Settle	Year	High	Low	Settle
1972	431.88	301.63	421.25	1986	537.50	454.00	475.50	2000	541.50	429.50	487.50
1973	1,228.75	419.88	575.63	1987	590.50	463.50	587.50	2001	520.00	398.50	413.63
1974	931.00	513.00	694.63	1988	1,004.00	581.50	789.00	2002	594.00	410.00	560.63
1975	705.63	440.25	445.88	1989	802.50	528.50	561.50	2003	782.63	533.63	779.00
1976	727.63	436.88	701.63	1990	641.00	548.00	557.00	2004	1,040.63	480.00	540.63
1977	1,046.25	482.63	587.00	1991	625.50	518.00	551.50	2005	733.63	497.00	588.00
1978	734.63	543.63	672.63	1992	619.50	511.50	555.50	2006	660.00	504.50	652.50
1979	853.00	607.88	616.25	1993	719.00	553.00	696.50	2007	1,180.50	632.00	1,158.00
1980	905.00	563.00	770.88	1994	723.50	500.00	545.50	2008	1,618.50	759.50	958.00
1981	800.88	601.88	605.50	1995	728.50	539.00	725.50	2009	1,259.50	834.50	1,021.50
1982	648.50	483.50	551.00	1996	835.00	657.50	688.00	2010	1,350.50	887.00	1,341.50
1983	925.50	547.50	809.50	1997	882.50	609.00	666.00	2011	1,439.50	1,080.00	1,182.50
1984	881.00	550.00	571.50	1998	685.00	488.00	526.00	2012	1,790.00	1,135.00	1,420.50
1985	605.50	479.50	523.00	1999	542.00	387.50	447.50	2013	1,610.00	1,248.00	1,303.50

Chicago #1 Yellow to 03/26/1982, Central Illinois #1 Yellow 03/29/1982 to date.   Data continued from page 235.
Source: U.S. Department of Agriculture (USDA)

SOYBEANS

SOYBEANS - CBOT
Weekly Nearest Futures as of 01/03/2014

Date	Open	High	Low	Close
12/06/13	1335.75	1346.00	1311.25	1325.50
12/13/13	1324.75	1353.50	1312.25	1327.50
12/20/13	1328.00	1351.00	1315.75	1339.00
12/27/13	1343.50	1347.00	1316.75	1331.50
01/03/14	1320.00	1331.00	1280.25	1289.25

WEEKLY NEAREST FUTURES
As of 01/03/2014

Chart High 1794.75   on 09/04/2012
Chart Low   498.50   on 02/04/2005
CONTRACT SIZE   5,000 bushels
MIN TICK   .25 cents
VALUE   12.5 USD / contract
EACH GRID   10 cents
VALUE   500 USD / contract
DAILY LIMIT   50 cents
VALUE   2,500 USD / contract
TRADING HOURS
7:00p-7:30a / 8:30a-1:15p CT

Commercial   = -144934
NonCommercial = 175774
NonReportable = -30840

Nearby Futures through Last Trading Day.

Quarterly High, Low and Settle of Soybean Futures   In Cents per Bushel

Quarter	High	Low	Settle	Quarter	High	Low	Settle	Quarter	High	Low	Settle
03/2005	691.75	498.50	627.50	03/2008	1,571.00	1,189.50	1,197.25	03/2011	1,455.75	1,270.00	1,410.25
06/2005	757.50	602.00	651.75	06/2008	1,607.25	1,106.50	1,605.00	06/2011	1,419.50	1,290.00	1,306.25
09/2005	738.00	556.50	573.25	09/2008	1,663.00	1,039.00	1,045.00	09/2011	1,456.00	1,174.00	1,179.00
12/2005	619.50	544.25	602.00	12/2008	1,066.00	776.25	972.25	12/2011	1,275.75	1,094.25	1,198.50
03/2006	622.00	561.00	571.50	03/2009	1,046.50	843.00	952.00	03/2012	1,416.00	1,150.00	1,403.00
06/2006	617.00	553.25	594.75	06/2009	1,291.25	943.00	1,226.25	06/2012	1,517.75	1,317.50	1,512.75
09/2006	613.00	526.50	547.50	09/2009	1,265.50	901.50	927.00	09/2012	1,794.75	1,522.50	1,601.00
12/2006	695.75	540.50	683.50	12/2009	1,078.50	878.75	1,039.75	12/2012	1,600.00	1,372.25	1,418.75
03/2007	791.00	645.50	761.25	03/2010	1,065.50	900.00	941.00	03/2013	1,518.00	1,378.00	1,404.75
06/2007	878.50	708.50	850.00	06/2010	1,009.50	926.00	948.50	06/2013	1,574.50	1,354.50	1,564.50
09/2007	1,017.75	789.00	991.25	09/2010	1,144.00	943.25	1,106.75	09/2013	1,630.00	1,271.00	1,282.75
12/2007	1,230.00	922.00	1,199.00	12/2010	1,394.50	1,042.00	1,393.75	12/2013	1,353.50	1,255.00	1,312.50

Source: CME Group; Chicago Board of Trade

Soybeans, #1 Yellow, Central, IL
Weekly Cash as of 01/03/2014

Date	Open	High	Low	Close
12/06/13	1313.50	1325.50	1313.50	1318.00
12/13/13	1337.00	1337.00	1319.50	1322.00
12/20/13	1332.00	1340.50	1319.00	1323.00
12/27/13	1321.00	1326.00	1310.00	1325.50
01/03/14	1320.00	1320.00	1281.00	1281.50

WEEKLY CASH
As of 01/03/2014
Chart High 1790.00 on 07/20/2012
Chart Low 480.00 on 10/13/2004

Cents / Bushel

#1 yellow, Central IL.

Quarterly High, Low and Settle of Soybeans   In Cents per Bushel

Quarter	High	Low	Settle	Quarter	High	Low	Settle	Quarter	High	Low	Settle
03/2005	654.00	497.00	605.00	03/2008	1,487.50	1,126.50	1,132.50	03/2011	1,419.00	1,206.00	1,381.50
06/2005	733.63	589.63	642.63	06/2008	1,565.00	1,146.00	1,565.00	06/2011	1,408.50	1,300.50	1,303.00
09/2005	717.00	525.00	537.63	09/2008	1,618.50	979.00	979.00	09/2011	1,439.50	1,175.00	1,175.00
12/2005	598.63	515.00	588.00	12/2008	987.00	759.50	958.00	12/2011	1,242.50	1,080.00	1,182.50
03/2006	605.63	539.00	547.00	03/2009	1,010.50	834.50	940.00	03/2012	1,383.00	1,135.00	1,383.00
06/2006	580.50	529.50	567.50	06/2009	1,259.50	939.50	1,170.00	06/2012	1,500.00	1,330.50	1,500.00
09/2006	577.00	504.50	515.50	09/2009	1,207.00	912.00	915.50	09/2012	1,790.00	1,506.50	1,588.50
12/2006	660.00	507.50	652.50	12/2009	1,042.00	872.50	1,021.50	12/2012	1,558.50	1,371.00	1,420.50
03/2007	750.50	632.00	717.00	03/2010	1,033.50	887.00	917.00	03/2013	1,502.50	1,376.00	1,420.00
06/2007	807.50	677.50	802.00	06/2010	981.50	911.50	940.00	06/2013	1,565.50	1,381.00	1,565.50
09/2007	950.00	739.00	933.50	09/2010	1,091.00	943.50	1,067.50	09/2013	1,610.00	1,265.00	1,265.00
12/2007	1,180.50	868.50	1,158.00	12/2010	1,350.50	1,015.50	1,341.50	12/2013	1,340.50	1,248.00	1,303.50

Central Illinois #1 Yellow .   *Source: U.S. Department of Agriculture (USDA)*

SOYBEAN MEAL

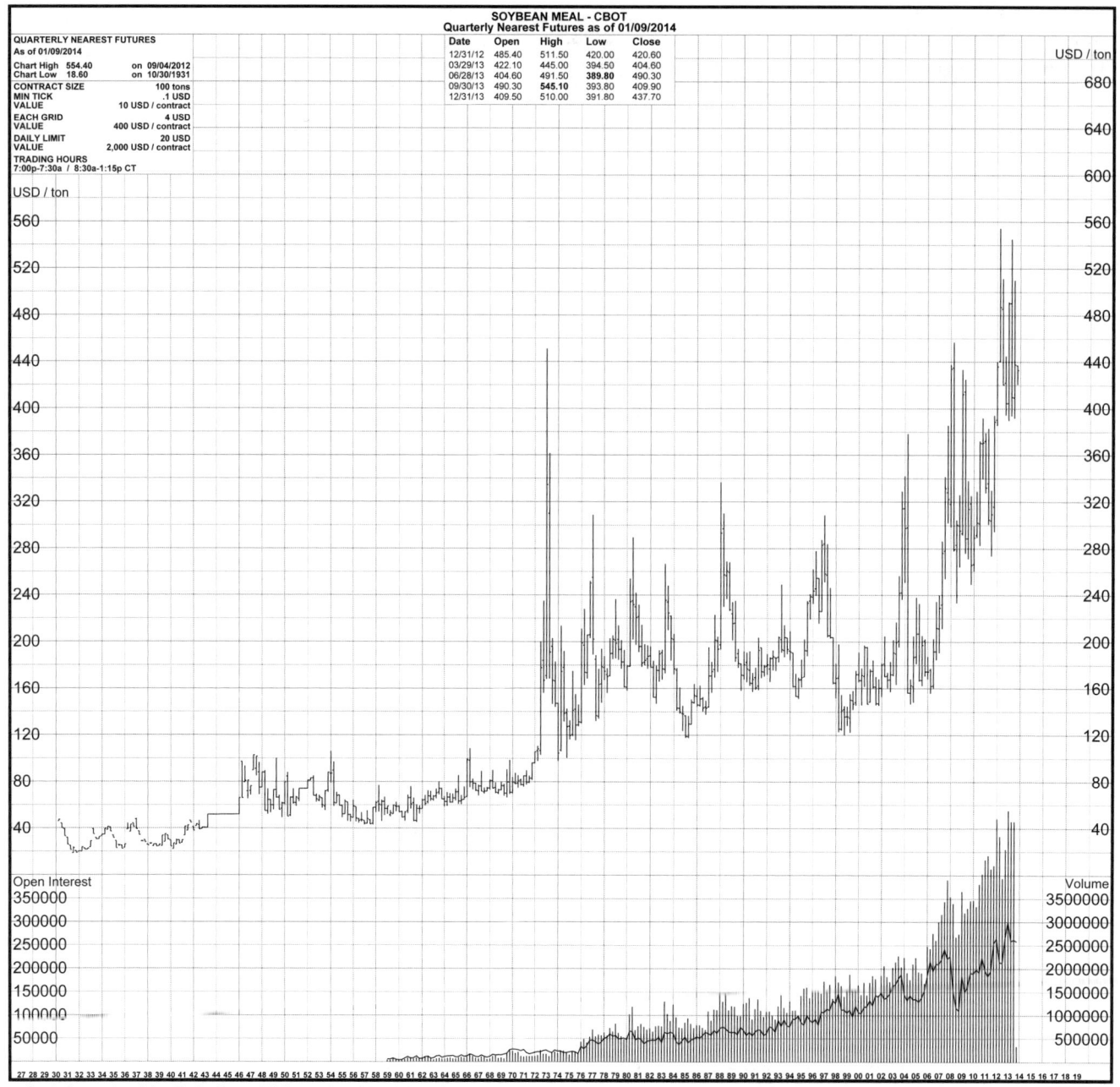

SOYBEAN MEAL - CBOT
Quarterly Nearest Futures as of 01/09/2014

QUARTERLY NEAREST FUTURES
As of 01/09/2014

Chart High 554.40 on 09/04/2012
Chart Low 18.60 on 10/30/1931
CONTRACT SIZE 100 tons
MIN TICK .1 USD
VALUE 10 USD / contract
EACH GRID 4 USD
VALUE 400 USD / contract
DAILY LIMIT 20 USD
VALUE 2,000 USD / contract
TRADING HOURS
7:00p-7:30a / 8:30a-1:15p CT

Date	Open	High	Low	Close
12/31/12	485.40	511.50	420.00	420.60
03/29/13	422.10	445.00	394.50	404.60
06/28/13	404.60	491.50	389.80	490.30
09/30/13	490.30	545.10	393.80	409.90
12/31/13	409.50	510.00	391.80	437.70

Nearby Futures through Last Trading Day.   48% Protein, Central IL: to 06/1959; Futures (44% protein): to 09/1992; Futures (48% protein): 09/1992 to date.

Annual High, Low and Settle of Soybean Meal Futures   In Dollars per Ton

Year	High	Low	Settle	Year	High	Low	Settle	Year	High	Low	Settle
1930	51.80	40.00	40.00	1944	52.00	51.90	52.00	1958	77.00	43.00	63.00
1931	39.30	18.60	23.00	1945	52.00	52.00	52.00	1959	67.00	49.00	59.90
1932	23.70	18.75	21.70	1946	97.00	52.00	80.70	1960	62.75	46.15	53.75
1933	39.20	21.70	30.50	1947	102.70	65.40	101.50	1961	76.00	45.05	56.90
1934	41.20	30.60	41.20	1948	96.50	52.00	64.50	1962	72.50	52.30	67.80
1935	40.70	22.85	25.50	1949	100.00	53.50	56.00	1963	80.00	63.50	74.20
1936	44.30	22.30	43.00	1950	88.00	49.00	66.50	1964	74.60	58.85	62.40
1937	48.35	28.80	28.80	1951	74.00	59.00	74.00	1965	85.50	60.70	64.55
1938	30.00	24.40	26.20	1952	85.00	68.00	68.00	1966	108.50	64.75	78.65
1939	34.95	24.45	34.95	1953	72.50	55.50	72.00	1967	89.00	68.10	71.90
1940	33.90	22.25	29.60	1954	106.00	59.00	68.00	1968	90.00	70.05	70.90
1941	42.50	26.60	42.50	1955	68.50	46.00	51.50	1969	90.50	66.50	79.70
1942	46.60	37.90	39.00	1956	64.50	44.50	46.50	1970	98.50	69.50	80.60
1943	51.90	39.35	51.90	1957	55.00	43.00	43.50	1971	89.70	75.70	83.00

Futures data begins 07/01/1959.   44% protein.   Data continued on page 242.   *Source: CME Group; Chicago Board of Trade*

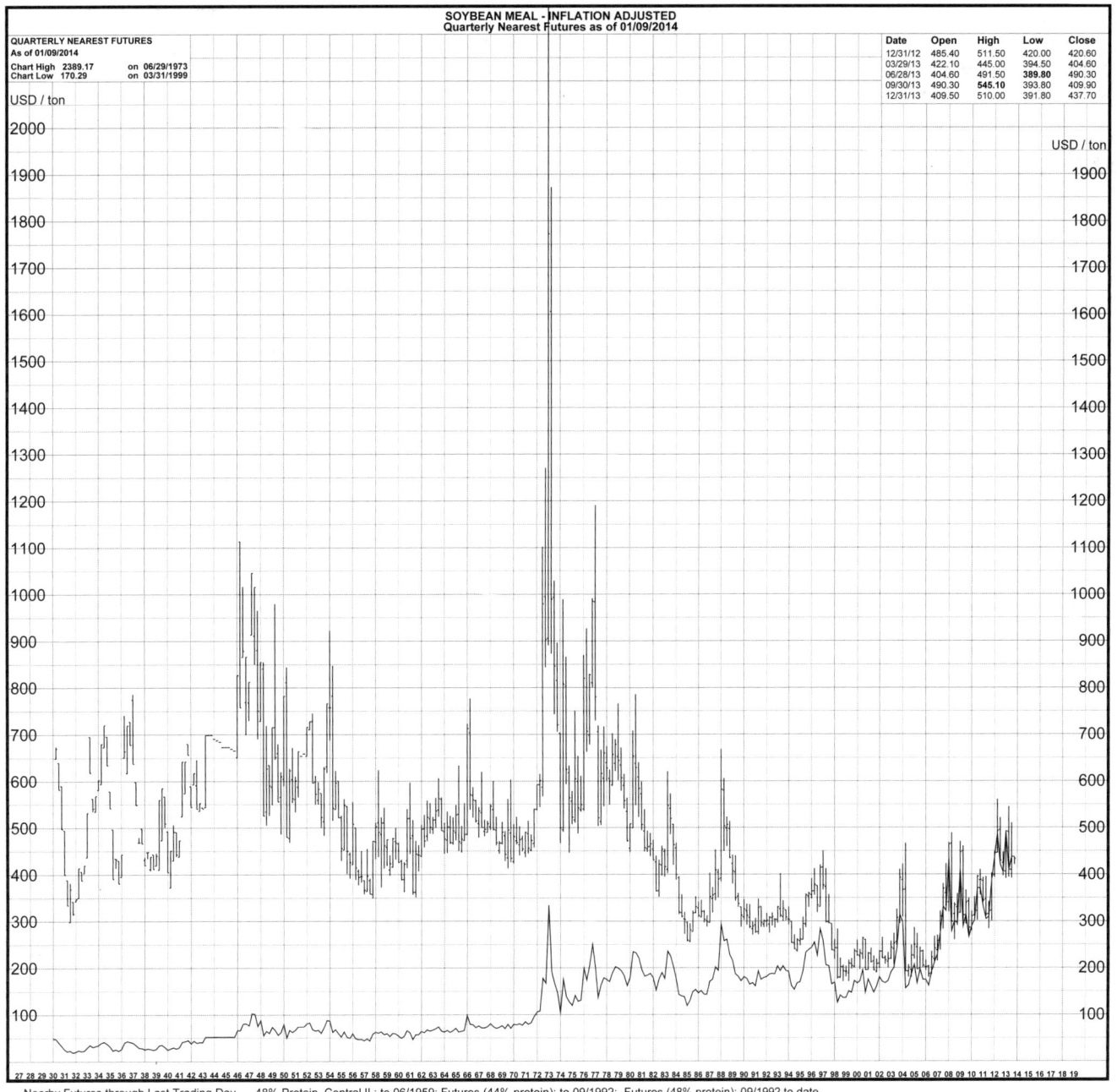

SOYBEAN MEAL - INFLATION ADJUSTED
Quarterly Nearest Futures as of 01/09/2014

QUARTERLY NEAREST FUTURES
As of 01/09/2014

Chart High 2389.17 on 06/29/1973
Chart Low   170.29   on 03/31/1999

USD / ton

Date	Open	High	Low	Close
12/31/12	485.40	511.50	420.00	420.60
03/29/13	422.10	445.00	394.50	404.60
06/28/13	404.60	491.50	389.80	490.30
09/30/13	490.30	545.10	393.80	409.90
12/31/13	409.50	510.00	391.80	437.70

Nearby Futures through Last Trading Day.   48% Protein, Central IL: to 06/1959; Futures (44% protein): to 09/1992; Futures (48% protein): 09/1992 to date.

Annual High, Low and Settle of Soybean Meal   In Dollars per Ton

Year	High	Low	Settle	Year	High	Low	Settle	Year	High	Low	Settle
1930	51.80	40.00	40.00	1944	52.00	51.90	52.00	1958	77.00	43.00	63.00
1931	39.30	18.60	23.00	1945	52.00	52.00	52.00	1959	67.00	49.00	60.50
1932	23.70	18.75	21.70	1946	97.00	52.00	80.70	1960	63.50	43.00	54.00
1933	39.20	21.70	30.50	1947	102.70	65.40	101.50	1961	80.00	50.50	59.50
1934	41.20	30.60	41.20	1948	96.50	52.00	64.50	1962	80.50	57.00	72.00
1935	40.70	22.85	25.50	1949	100.00	53.50	56.00	1963	81.50	66.00	79.00
1936	44.30	22.30	43.00	1950	88.00	49.00	66.50	1964	78.00	61.50	66.00
1937	48.35	28.80	28.80	1951	74.00	59.00	74.00	1965	102.50	65.50	72.50
1938	30.00	24.40	26.20	1952	85.00	68.00	68.00	1966	107.00	69.50	86.00
1939	34.95	24.45	34.95	1953	72.50	55.50	72.00	1967	87.50	69.50	73.00
1940	33.90	22.25	29.60	1954	106.00	59.00	68.00	1968	90.00	70.00	70.50
1941	42.50	26.60	42.50	1955	68.50	46.00	51.50	1969	92.00	67.00	87.00
1942	46.60	37.90	39.00	1956	64.50	44.50	46.50	1970	98.00	68.50	79.50
1943	51.90	39.35	51.90	1957	55.00	43.00	43.50	1971	86.00	71.50	82.00

Central Illinois 44% Protein.   Data continued on page 243.   *Source: CME Group; Chicago Board of Trade*

SOYBEAN MEAL

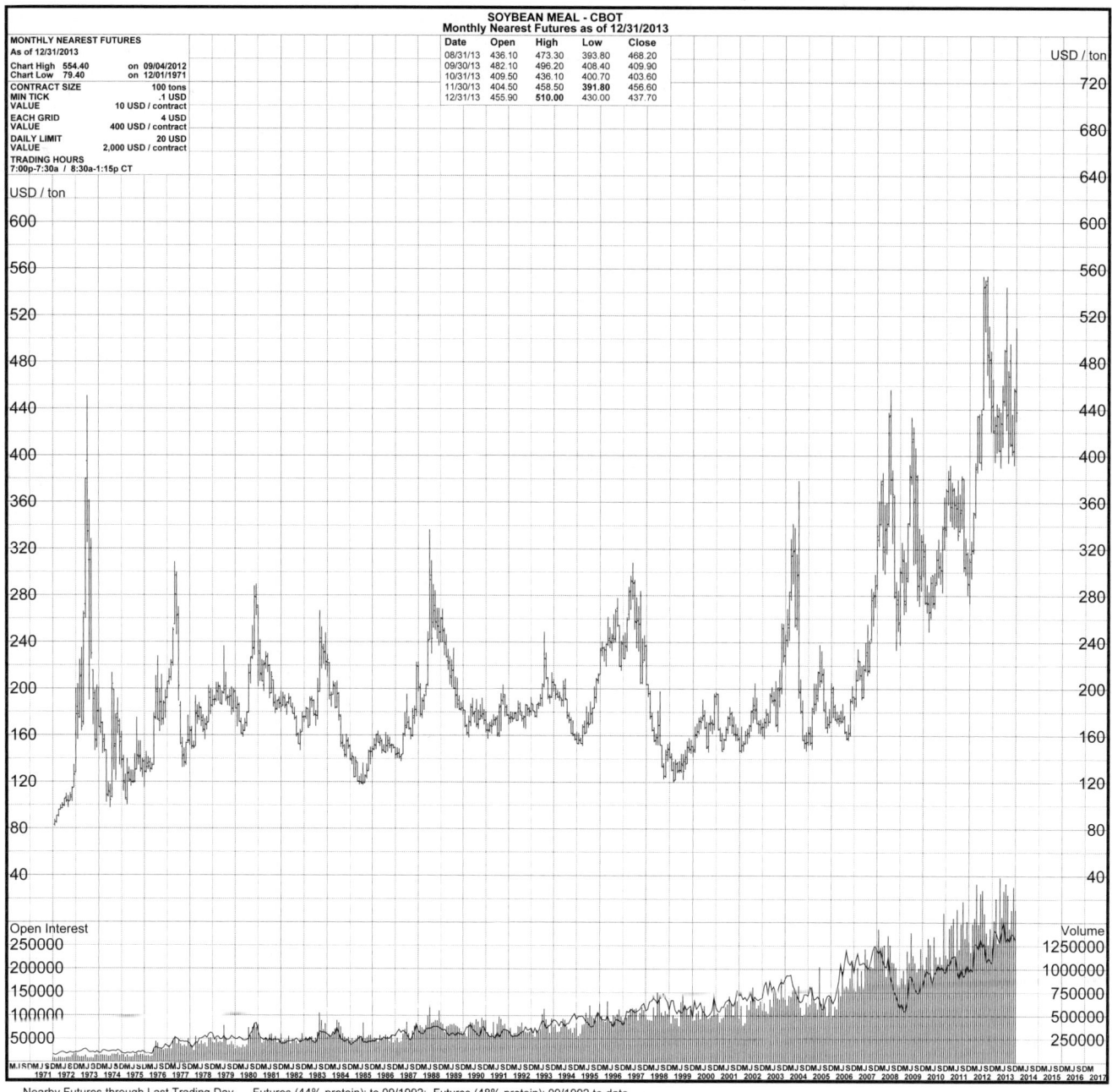

SOYBEAN MEAL - CBOT
Monthly Nearest Futures as of 12/31/2013

MONTHLY NEAREST FUTURES
As of 12/31/2013

Chart High 554.40 on 09/04/2012
Chart Low 79.40 on 12/01/1971

CONTRACT SIZE	100 tons
MIN TICK	.1 USD
VALUE	10 USD / contract
EACH GRID VALUE	4 USD / 400 USD / contract
DAILY LIMIT VALUE	20 USD / 2,000 USD / contract

TRADING HOURS
7:00p-7:30a / 8:30a-1:15p CT

Date	Open	High	Low	Close
08/31/13	436.10	473.30	393.80	468.20
09/30/13	482.10	496.20	408.40	409.90
10/31/13	409.50	436.10	400.70	403.60
11/30/13	404.50	458.50	391.80	456.60
12/31/13	455.90	510.00	430.00	437.70

Nearby Futures through Last Trading Day.   Futures (44% protein): to 09/1992; Futures (48% protein): 09/1992 to date.

Annual High, Low and Settle of Soybean Meal Futures   In Dollars per Ton

Year	High	Low	Settle	Year	High	Low	Settle	Year	High	Low	Settle
1972	200.00	81.45	177.75	1986	163.90	140.10	143.30	2000	197.20	145.50	195.40
1973	451.00	146.50	167.00	1987	223.20	137.50	201.50	2001	196.00	145.80	147.10
1974	213.70	97.76	138.50	1988	336.50	174.30	260.50	2002	205.00	145.40	167.30
1975	175.00	100.50	128.40	1989	268.40	177.80	181.60	2003	256.50	157.10	241.90
1976	228.00	127.50	205.70	1990	192.00	158.00	164.50	2004	378.50	146.60	162.60
1977	308.70	132.00	163.40	1991	203.70	157.00	174.70	2005	238.00	148.10	197.30
1978	203.00	147.60	189.90	1992	192.80	165.50	187.40	2006	202.80	155.80	191.90
1979	236.50	177.00	182.80	1993	249.00	175.20	203.80	2007	341.50	184.70	331.50
1980	289.50	158.10	231.80	1994	209.00	153.00	153.20	2008	456.80	233.30	300.50
1981	242.00	178.50	184.20	1995	235.00	151.10	233.20	2009	433.40	264.00	313.90
1982	197.00	146.80	175.60	1996	278.00	215.70	226.30	2010	372.00	249.20	370.30
1983	267.00	166.00	224.70	1997	308.50	203.00	203.80	2011	392.00	273.50	309.40
1984	222.50	138.50	139.60	1998	204.00	122.80	141.10	2012	554.40	294.50	420.60
1985	150.50	117.50	148.20	1999	158.00	120.00	146.70	2013	545.10	389.80	437.70

44% protein through September 1992 contract, 48% protein October 1992 contract to date.   Data continued from page 240.
Source: CME Group; Chicago Board of Trade

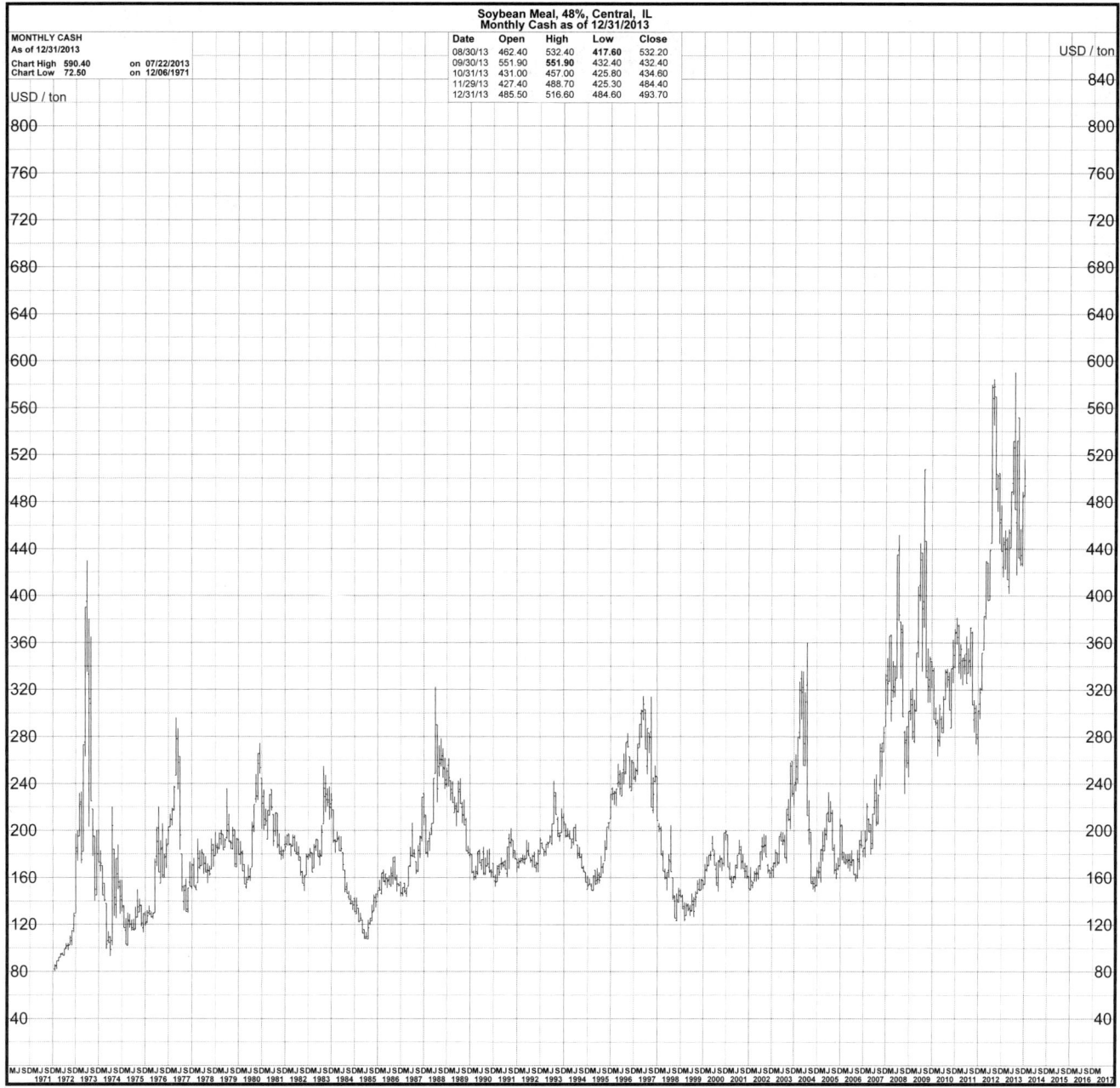

	Soybean Meal, 48%, Central, IL Monthly Cash as of 12/31/2013				
Date	Open	High	Low	Close
08/30/13	462.40	532.40	417.60	532.20
09/30/13	551.90	551.90	432.40	432.40
10/31/13	431.00	457.00	425.80	434.60
11/29/13	427.40	488.70	425.30	484.40
12/31/13	485.50	516.60	484.60	493.70

MONTHLY CASH
As of 12/31/2013

Chart High 590.40 on 07/22/2013
Chart Low 72.50 on 12/06/1971

USD / ton

48% Protein, Central IL: to 11/1992; 44% Protein, Central IL: 11/1992 to date.

Annual High, Low and Settle of Soybean Meal   In Dollars per Ton

Year	High	Low	Settle	Year	High	Low	Settle	Year	High	Low	Settle
1972	197.00	80.50	185.00	1986	178.00	144.00	147.00	2000	200.00	148.00	199.00
1973	430.00	140.00	173.00	1987	231.50	143.50	211.50	2001	196.50	150.50	150.50
1974	220.00	93.00	135.00	1988	322.50	177.00	250.50	2002	197.00	149.50	166.50
1975	150.00	102.00	121.00	1989	261.50	177.00	180.00	2003	259.00	160.00	239.00
1976	220.00	121.00	203.00	1990	186.25	157.50	160.50	2004	360.00	148.00	165.60
1977	296.00	130.00	170.50	1991	202.00	152.00	172.50	2005	232.90	155.70	203.80
1978	198.50	149.50	187.00	1992	194.00	164.50	192.00	2006	204.70	156.60	184.90
1979	236.00	169.00	179.50	1993	242.50	178.00	207.00	2007	333.70	177.20	328.50
1980	274.50	150.50	223.00	1994	205.50	150.00	153.00	2008	452.00	231.50	301.50
1981	235.00	175.00	186.00	1995	231.00	149.00	231.00	2009	507.50	274.80	336.40
1982	197.00	148.50	179.75	1996	283.00	221.00	244.00	2010	371.60	263.30	368.40
1983	255.00	164.50	226.00	1997	314.50	208.50	208.50	2011	381.60	264.40	301.90
1984	217.50	131.00	131.00	1998	206.25	123.00	143.50	2012	584.60	295.00	438.10
1985	149.00	107.50	149.00	1999	159.00	123.00	154.25	2013	590.40	401.80	493.70

Central Illinois 44% Protein through 11/16/1992, Central Illinois 48% Protein 11/17/1992 to date.   Data continued from page 241.
Source: U.S. Department of Agriculture (USDA)

SOYBEAN MEAL

Nearby Futures through Last Trading Day.

Quarterly High, Low and Settle of Soybean Meal Futures   In Dollars per Ton

Quarter	High	Low	Settle	Quarter	High	Low	Settle	Quarter	High	Low	Settle
03/2005	205.00	148.10	187.00	03/2008	385.70	302.00	322.30	03/2011	392.00	339.70	370.70
06/2005	238.00	181.30	207.00	06/2008	437.50	298.50	434.00	06/2011	379.30	327.70	332.20
09/2005	232.80	166.20	167.20	09/2008	456.80	278.00	279.40	09/2011	383.10	300.80	304.70
12/2005	205.40	162.30	197.30	12/2008	304.50	233.30	300.50	12/2011	329.90	273.50	309.40
03/2006	202.50	170.50	174.60	03/2009	326.00	264.00	295.30	03/2012	394.30	294.50	388.70
06/2006	187.50	168.10	174.60	06/2009	433.40	291.80	412.30	06/2012	439.90	385.60	436.00
09/2006	177.50	155.80	161.90	09/2009	425.00	276.00	288.70	09/2012	554.40	439.90	487.00
12/2006	202.80	160.20	191.90	12/2009	338.10	271.00	313.90	12/2012	511.50	420.00	420.60
03/2007	234.60	184.70	211.80	03/2010	325.20	249.20	265.80	03/2013	445.00	394.50	404.60
06/2007	240.00	190.80	229.20	06/2010	299.50	260.50	289.40	06/2013	491.50	389.80	490.30
09/2007	286.50	211.40	276.30	09/2010	329.00	289.40	302.10	09/2013	545.10	393.80	409.90
12/2007	341.50	254.00	331.50	12/2010	372.00	282.70	370.30	12/2013	510.00	391.80	437.70

48% protein .   *Source: CME Group; Chicago Board of Trade*

WEEKLY CASH
As of 01/03/2014

Chart High 590.40 on 07/22/2013
Chart Low 148.00 on 11/05/2004

USD / ton

Soybean Meal, 48%, Central, IL
Weekly Cash as of 01/03/2014

Date	Open	High	Low	Close
12/06/13	485.50	490.30	484.60	490.30
12/13/13	502.10	502.10	491.10	493.60
12/20/13	500.00	516.60	500.00	516.60
12/27/13	502.70	505.90	499.50	504.20
01/03/14	506.30	506.30	462.10	462.10

44% Protein, Central IL.

Quarterly High, Low and Settle of Soybean Meal   In Dollars per Ton

Quarter	High	Low	Settle	Quarter	High	Low	Settle	Quarter	High	Low	Settle
03/2005	199.20	155.70	187.00	03/2008	366.70	292.80	310.30	03/2011	381.60	329.30	354.70
06/2005	232.90	182.70	207.50	06/2008	435.00	313.20	435.00	06/2011	365.80	324.20	325.70
09/2005	225.20	163.20	166.40	09/2008	452.00	296.90	296.90	09/2011	373.10	307.10	307.10
12/2005	210.30	158.80	203.80	12/2008	301.50	231.50	301.50	12/2011	311.50	264.40	301.90
03/2006	204.70	171.60	175.10	03/2009	321.80	274.80	302.80	03/2012	382.70	295.00	382.70
06/2006	183.40	165.30	174.60	06/2009	445.00	301.80	430.80	06/2012	439.00	380.30	439.00
09/2006	183.80	156.60	175.65	09/2009	507.50	330.10	336.20	09/2012	584.60	445.00	503.50
12/2006	199.50	166.70	184.90	12/2009	355.30	309.10	336.40	12/2012	504.30	438.10	438.10
03/2007	223.60	177.20	198.80	03/2010	338.90	263.30	277.30	03/2013	456.00	414.10	414.10
06/2007	244.30	179.70	225.70	06/2010	314.80	271.70	311.90	06/2013	531.80	401.80	531.80
09/2007	274.30	203.90	267.50	09/2010	338.10	302.90	302.90	09/2013	590.40	417.60	432.40
12/2007	333.70	246.00	328.50	12/2010	371.60	287.40	368.40	12/2013	516.60	425.30	493.70

48% protein .   Source: U.S. Department of Agriculture (USDA)

SOYBEAN OIL

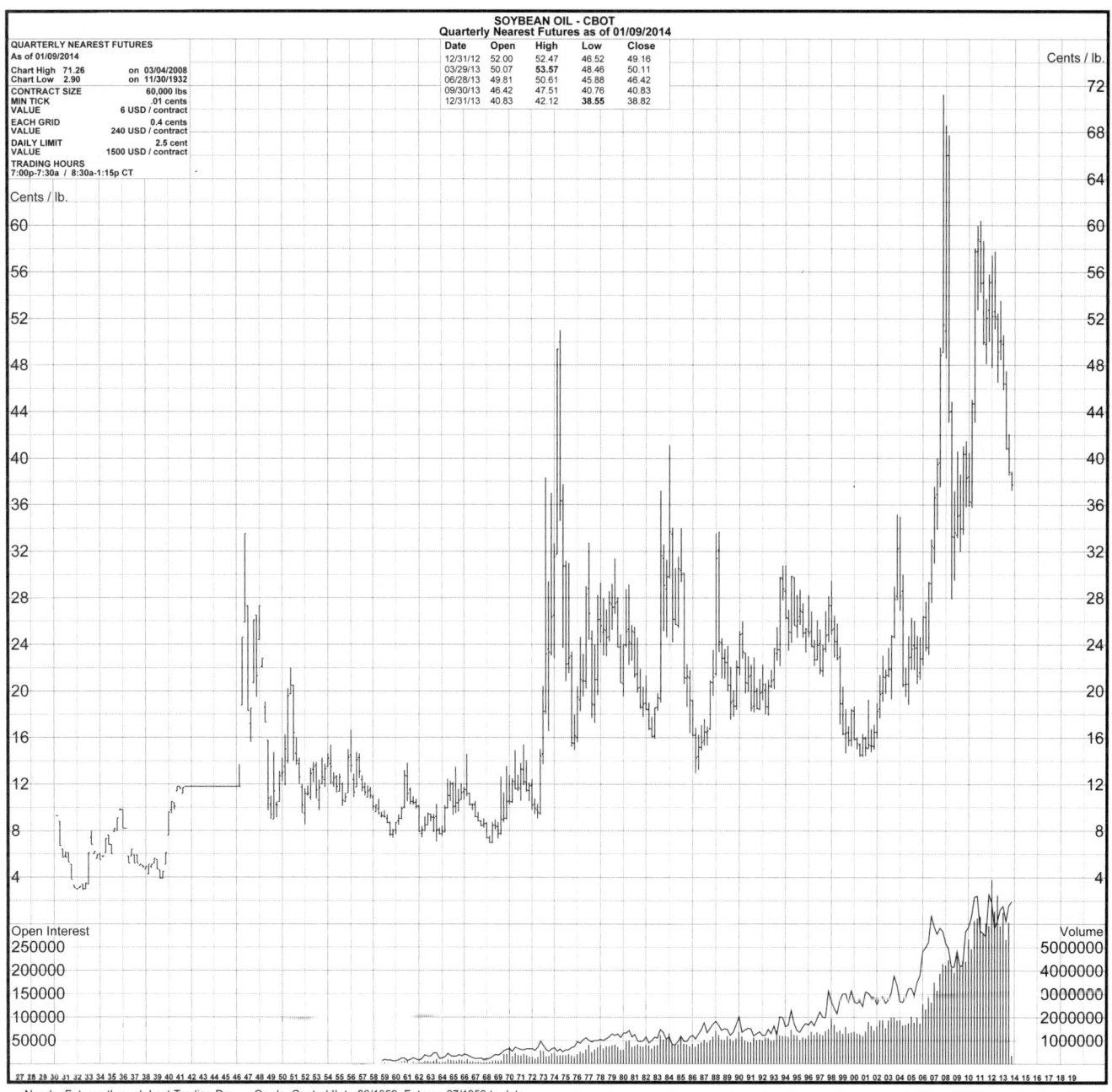

SOYBEAN OIL - CBOT
Quarterly Nearest Futures as of 01/09/2014

Date	Open	High	Low	Close
12/31/12	52.00	52.47	46.52	49.16
03/29/13	50.07	53.57	48.46	50.11
06/28/13	49.81	50.61	45.88	46.42
09/30/13	46.42	47.51	40.76	40.83
12/31/13	40.83	42.12	38.55	38.82

QUARTERLY NEAREST FUTURES
As of 01/09/2014
Chart High 71.26 on 03/04/2008
Chart Low 2.90 on 11/30/1932
CONTRACT SIZE 60,000 lbs
MIN TICK VALUE 6 USD / contract .01 cents
EACH GRID VALUE 240 USD / contract 0.4 cents
DAILY LIMIT VALUE 1500 USD / contract 2.5 cent
TRADING HOURS 7:00p-7:30a / 8:30a-1:15p CT

Nearby Futures through Last Trading Day.   Crude, Central IL to 06/1959; Futures 07/1959 to date.

Annual High, Low and Settle of Soybean Oil Futures   In Cents per Pound

Year	High	Low	Settle	Year	High	Low	Settle	Year	High	Low	Settle
1930	9.30	6.70	6.70	1944	11.80	11.80	11.80	1958	11.75	9.38	9.50
1931	6.40	3.80	3.80	1945	11.80	11.80	11.80	1959	9.40	7.51	7.66
1932	3.40	2.90	3.00	1946	24.60	11.80	24.60	1960	10.07	7.37	9.92
1933	8.00	3.00	6.20	1947	33.50	15.60	26.10	1961	13.85	9.93	10.43
1934	7.30	5.50	7.30	1948	27.30	17.30	17.30	1962	10.73	7.40	8.48
1935	9.10	6.00	9.10	1949	15.75	9.00	10.20	1963	10.30	7.05	8.06
1936	9.90	5.20	5.20	1950	20.25	10.50	19.60	1964	12.46	7.51	11.03
1937	6.40	5.00	5.10	1951	22.00	12.00	12.60	1965	13.50	9.36	10.61
1938	5.10	4.20	5.10	1952	13.38	8.50	12.90	1966	14.58	10.17	10.26
1939	5.60	3.90	4.50	1953	14.25	9.75	12.60	1967	10.55	8.37	8.44
1940	10.50	5.10	10.10	1954	15.38	11.75	12.50	1968	9.04	6.91	8.45
1941	11.80	11.20	11.80	1955	12.88	10.13	10.90	1969	12.65	7.32	9.05
1942	11.80	11.80	11.80	1956	16.63	10.88	14.10	1970	14.90	8.95	11.62
1943	11.80	11.80	11.80	1957	14.63	10.88	11.40	1971	15.40	10.57	11.47

Futures data begins 07/01/1959.   Data continued on page 248.   *Source: CME Group; Chicago Board of Trade*

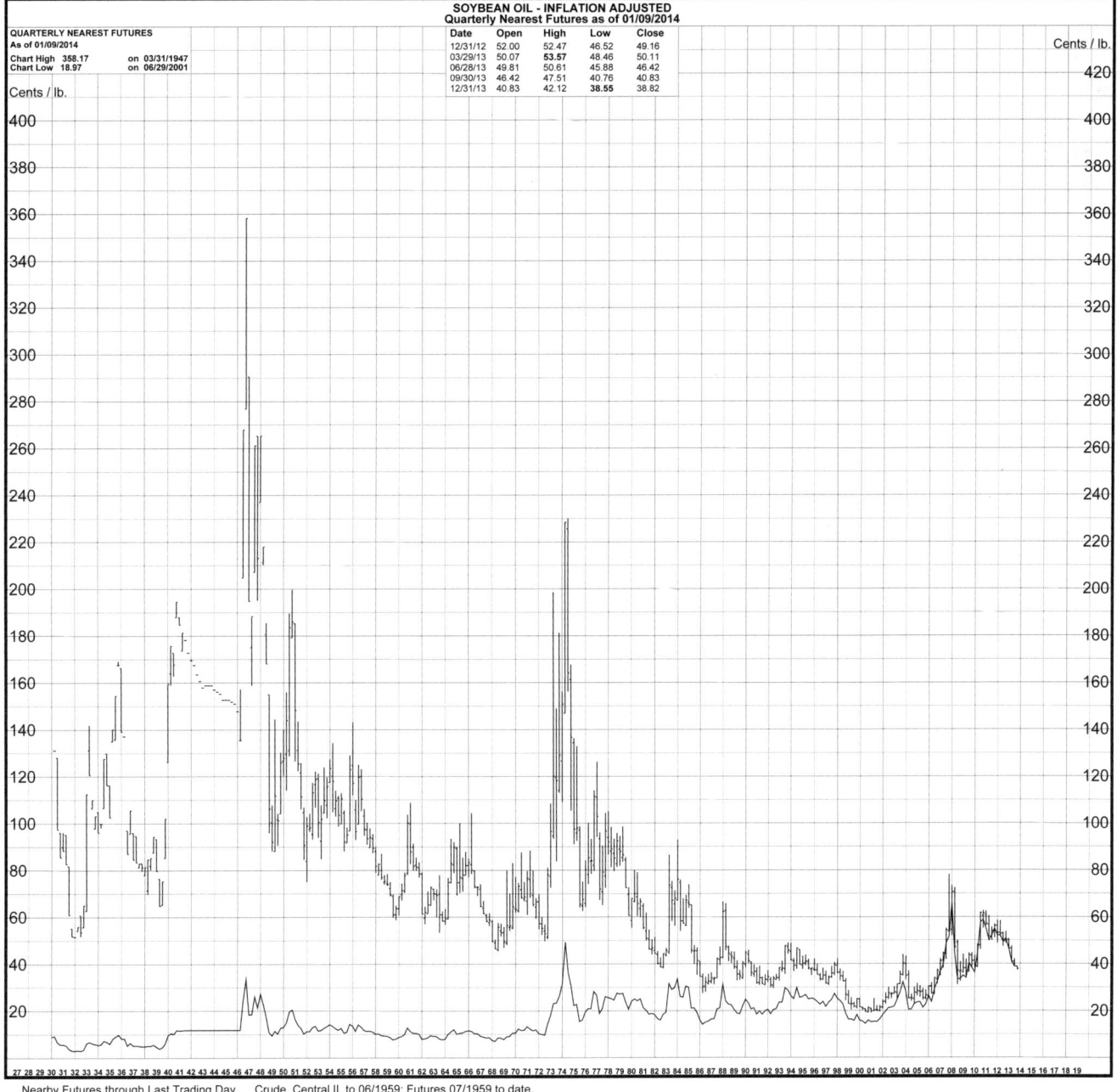

SOYBEAN OIL - INFLATION ADJUSTED
Quarterly Nearest Futures as of 01/09/2014

Date	Open	High	Low	Close
12/31/12	52.00	52.47	46.52	49.16
03/29/13	50.07	53.57	48.46	50.11
06/28/13	49.81	50.61	45.88	46.42
09/30/13	46.42	47.51	40.76	40.83
12/31/13	40.83	42.12	38.55	38.82

QUARTERLY NEAREST FUTURES
As of 01/09/2014
Chart High 358.17 on 03/31/1947
Chart Low 18.97 on 06/29/2001

Cents / lb.

Nearby Futures through Last Trading Day.   Crude, Central IL to 06/1959; Futures 07/1959 to date.

Annual High, Low and Settle of Soybean Oil   In Cents per Pound

Year	High	Low	Settle	Year	High	Low	Settle	Year	High	Low	Settle
1930	9.30	6.70	6.70	1944	11.80	11.80	11.80	1958	11.75	9.38	9.50
1931	6.40	3.80	3.80	1945	11.80	11.80	11.80	1959	9.75	7.63	7.80
1932	3.40	2.90	3.00	1946	24.60	11.80	24.60	1960	10.90	7.50	10.90
1933	8.00	3.00	6.20	1947	33.50	15.60	26.10	1961	13.75	10.00	10.37
1934	7.30	5.50	7.30	1948	27.30	17.30	17.30	1962	10.63	7.50	8.60
1935	9.10	6.00	9.10	1949	15.75	9.00	10.20	1963	10.25	7.75	8.30
1936	9.90	5.20	5.20	1950	20.25	10.50	19.60	1964	12.82	7.75	12.00
1937	6.40	5.00	5.10	1951	22.00	12.00	12.60	1965	12.67	9.68	10.91
1938	5.10	4.20	5.10	1952	13.38	8.50	12.90	1966	14.64	10.34	10.38
1939	5.60	3.90	4.50	1953	14.25	9.75	12.60	1967	10.49	8.51	8.64
1940	10.50	5.10	10.10	1954	15.38	11.75	12.50	1968	9.31	7.08	8.65
1941	11.80	11.20	11.80	1955	12.88	10.13	10.90	1969	11.73	7.61	9.36
1942	11.80	11.80	11.80	1956	16.63	10.88	14.10	1970	15.25	9.26	11.76
1943	11.80	11.80	11.80	1957	14.63	10.88	11.40	1971	15.38	10.79	11.47

Decatur, Illinois.   Data continued on page 249.   Source: CME Group; Chicago Board of Trade

SOYBEAN OIL

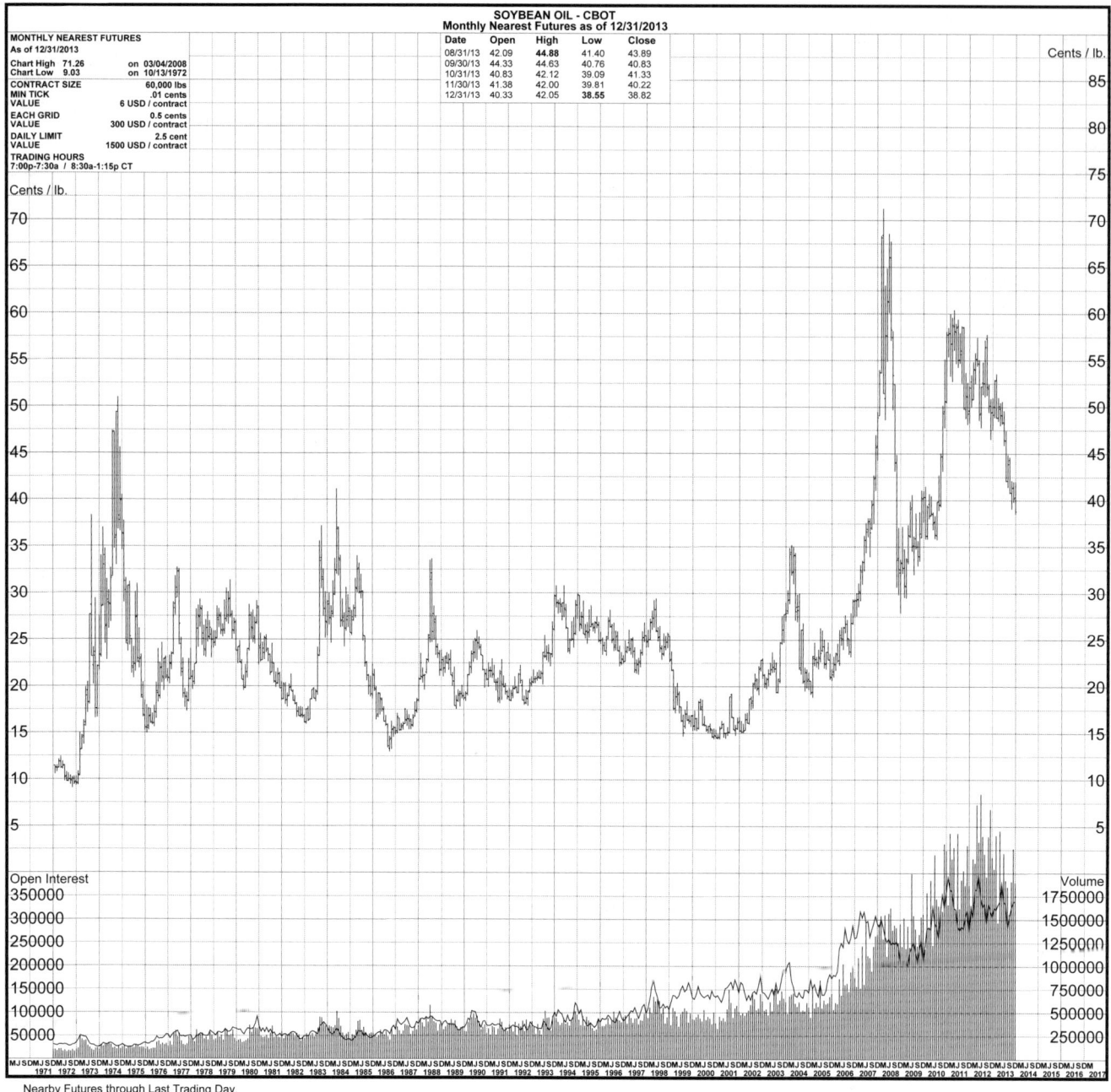

SOYBEAN OIL - CBOT
Monthly Nearest Futures as of 12/31/2013

Date	Open	High	Low	Close
08/31/13	42.09	**44.88**	41.40	43.89
09/30/13	44.33	44.63	40.76	40.83
10/31/13	40.83	42.12	39.09	41.33
11/30/13	41.38	42.00	39.81	40.22
12/31/13	40.33	42.05	**38.55**	38.82

MONTHLY NEAREST FUTURES
As of 12/31/2013

Chart High 71.26 on 03/04/2008
Chart Low 9.03 on 10/13/1972
CONTRACT SIZE 60,000 lbs
MIN TICK .01 cents
VALUE 6 USD / contract
EACH GRID 0.5 cents
VALUE 300 USD / contract
DAILY LIMIT 2.5 cent
VALUE 1500 USD / contract
TRADING HOURS
7:00p-7:30a / 8:30a-1:15p CT

Nearby Futures through Last Trading Day.

Annual High, Low and Settle of Soybean Oil Futures   In Cents per Pound

Year	High	Low	Settle	Year	High	Low	Settle	Year	High	Low	Settle
1972	12.43	9.03	9.60	1986	21.82	12.95	15.18	2000	18.70	14.36	14.53
1973	38.33	9.36	23.35	1987	20.95	14.90	20.77	2001	19.26	14.35	15.27
1974	51.00	22.80	36.35	1988	33.70	19.57	22.82	2002	23.08	14.99	21.24
1975	37.75	15.20	15.55	1989	23.90	17.54	18.70	2003	29.00	19.30	27.87
1976	24.65	14.92	20.90	1990	26.00	18.37	20.74	2004	35.18	19.50	20.61
1977	32.75	17.27	20.99	1991	23.00	18.15	18.50	2005	26.31	18.82	21.30
1978	29.30	19.63	24.60	1992	22.29	17.89	20.47	2006	29.40	21.00	29.26
1979	31.40	23.75	23.78	1993	29.80	20.17	29.71	2007	49.51	27.58	48.85
1980	29.15	19.53	24.25	1994	30.82	23.48	29.83	2008	71.26	27.90	33.29
1981	25.68	18.45	18.59	1995	29.75	24.57	24.97	2009	41.08	29.50	40.35
1982	21.32	16.08	16.08	1996	28.23	22.16	22.71	2010	58.05	35.75	57.74
1983	37.20	15.91	29.07	1997	26.87	21.25	24.79	2011	60.40	48.11	52.09
1984	41.15	24.21	25.72	1998	29.46	22.65	22.83	2012	57.78	46.52	49.16
1985	34.00	18.63	21.26	1999	23.80	14.65	15.75	2013	53.57	38.55	38.82

Data continued from page 246.   *Source: CME Group; Chicago Board of Trade*

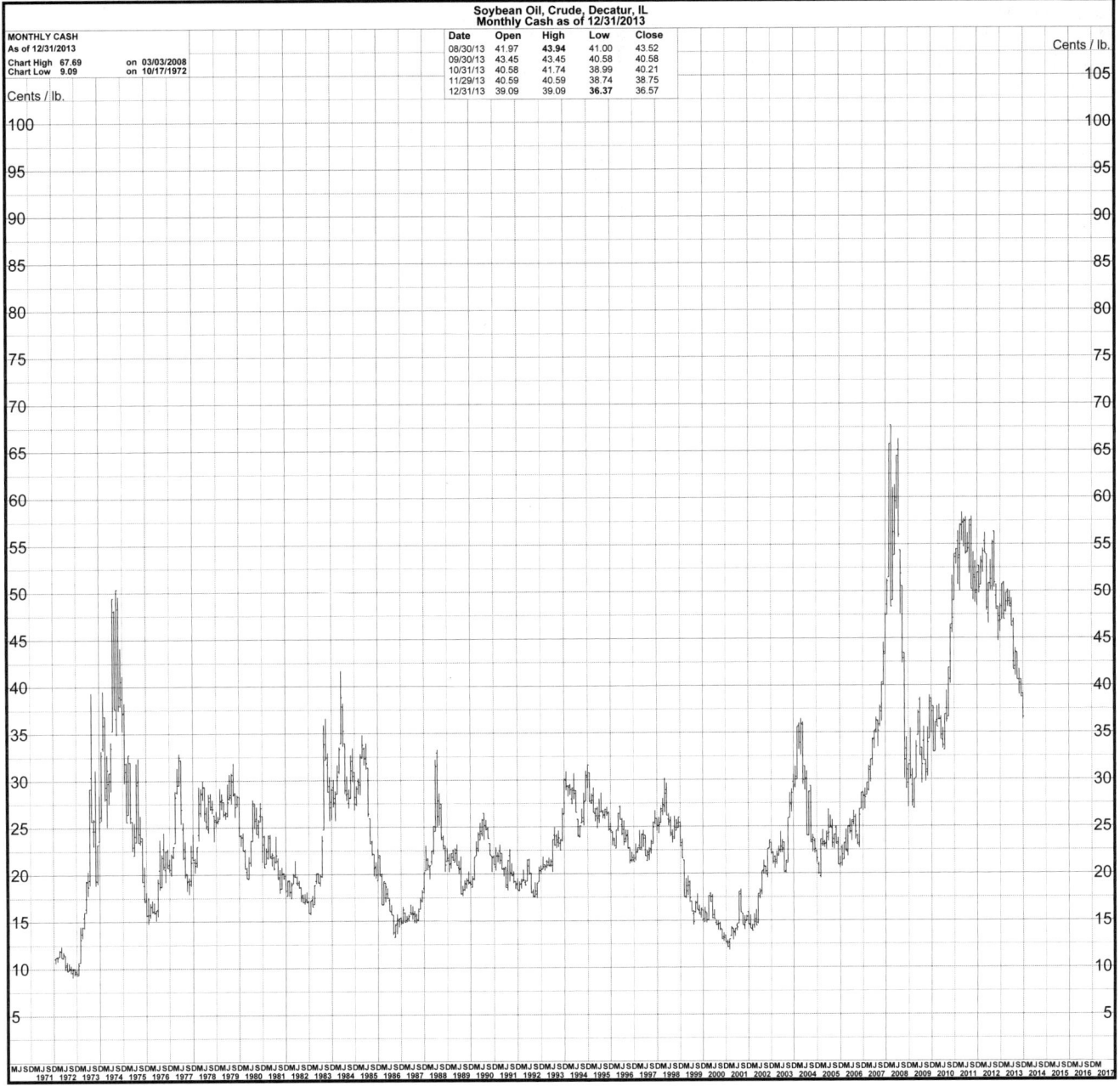

MONTHLY CASH
As of 12/31/2013

Chart High 67.69 on 03/03/2008
Chart Low 9.09 on 10/17/1972

Cents / lb.

Soybean Oil, Crude, Decatur, IL Monthly Cash as of 12/31/2013				
Date	Open	High	Low	Close
08/30/13	41.97	43.94	41.00	43.52
09/30/13	43.45	43.45	40.58	40.58
10/31/13	40.58	41.74	38.99	40.21
11/29/13	40.59	40.59	38.74	38.75
12/31/13	39.09	39.09	36.37	36.57

Crude, Central IL.

Annual High, Low and Settle of Soybean Oil   In Cents per Pound

Year	High	Low	Settle	Year	High	Low	Settle	Year	High	Low	Settle
1972	12.39	9.09	9.54	1986	22.02	13.27	14.88	2000	17.94	12.65	12.66
1973	39.35	9.35	25.68	1987	20.20	14.76	20.17	2001	18.35	11.83	14.62
1974	50.37	25.10	37.13	1988	33.25	19.45	21.69	2002	23.52	13.85	22.12
1975	38.25	15.65	15.65	1989	23.18	17.65	18.93	2003	30.52	20.05	29.25
1976	24.45	14.73	20.55	1990	26.46	18.60	21.01	2004	36.45	21.05	21.59
1977	32.87	17.90	21.59	1991	23.13	18.25	18.30	2005	26.83	19.49	21.05
1978	29.97	20.19	25.57	1992	21.60	17.42	20.47	2006	28.61	20.71	28.26
1979	31.85	24.10	24.10	1993	30.07	20.20	30.07	2007	47.68	26.82	47.47
1980	27.93	19.52	23.20	1994	31.57	23.85	31.57	2008	67.69	27.05	31.56
1981	24.26	18.00	18.27	1995	30.75	24.38	24.56	2009	38.96	26.88	37.17
1982	21.48	15.88	15.88	1996	27.25	21.06	21.25	2010	53.97	32.90	53.61
1983	36.60	15.73	29.01	1997	26.72	21.32	25.04	2011	58.40	48.40	51.97
1984	41.68	25.67	28.22	1998	30.18	22.84	22.93	2012	56.32	44.68	46.86
1985	34.83	19.34	21.79	1999	23.67	14.53	15.15	2013	50.99	36.37	36.57

Decatur, Illinois Crude.   Data continued from page 247.   *Source: U.S. Department of Agriculture (USDA)*

SOYBEAN OIL

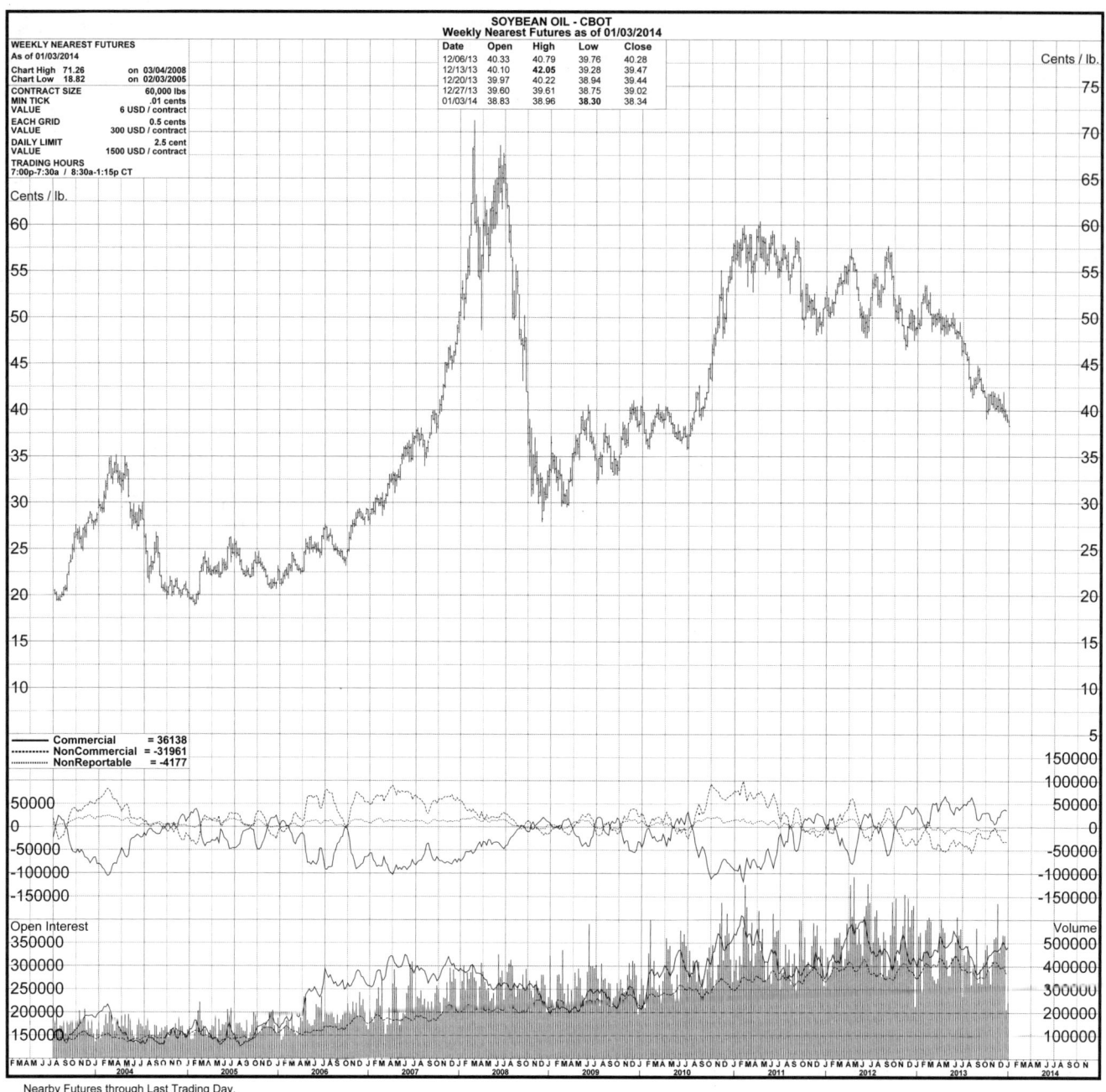

SOYBEAN OIL - CBOT
Weekly Nearest Futures as of 01/03/2014

Date	Open	High	Low	Close
12/06/13	40.33	40.79	39.76	40.28
12/13/13	40.10	**42.05**	39.28	39.47
12/20/13	39.97	40.22	38.94	39.44
12/27/13	39.60	39.61	38.75	39.02
01/03/14	38.83	38.96	**38.30**	38.34

WEEKLY NEAREST FUTURES
As of 01/03/2014

Chart High 71.26 on 03/04/2008
Chart Low 18.82 on 02/03/2005
CONTRACT SIZE 60,000 lbs
MIN TICK .01 cents
VALUE 6 USD / contract
EACH GRID 0.5 cents
VALUE 300 USD / contract
DAILY LIMIT 2.5 cent
VALUE 1500 USD / contract
TRADING HOURS
7:00p-7:30a / 8:30a-1:15p CT

Commercial = 36138
NonCommercial = -31961
NonReportable = -4177

Nearby Futures through Last Trading Day.

Quarterly High, Low and Settle of Soybean Oil Futures   In Cents per Pound

Quarter	High	Low	Settle	Quarter	High	Low	Settle	Quarter	High	Low	Settle
03/2005	24.75	18.82	22.90	03/2008	71.26	49.10	51.48	03/2011	59.96	52.73	58.78
06/2005	26.31	21.86	23.61	06/2008	68.59	48.60	66.04	06/2011	60.40	54.25	55.04
09/2005	26.05	21.85	23.72	09/2008	67.77	43.10	44.00	09/2011	58.68	49.77	49.95
12/2005	24.77	20.62	21.30	12/2008	44.88	27.90	33.29	12/2011	53.70	48.11	52.09
03/2006	24.65	21.00	22.79	03/2009	37.20	29.50	33.62	03/2012	55.82	50.02	55.10
06/2006	26.45	22.25	26.36	06/2009	40.60	33.17	35.02	06/2012	57.45	47.76	52.21
09/2006	27.68	23.45	23.77	09/2009	38.63	32.00	33.97	09/2012	57.78	51.11	52.18
12/2006	29.40	23.15	29.26	12/2009	41.08	33.45	40.35	12/2012	52.47	46.52	49.16
03/2007	33.07	27.58	32.48	03/2010	41.50	35.80	38.31	03/2013	53.57	48.46	50.11
06/2007	37.57	30.98	36.63	06/2010	40.48	35.86	36.28	06/2013	50.61	45.88	46.42
09/2007	40.00	33.91	39.49	09/2010	45.06	35.75	44.70	09/2013	47.51	40.76	40.83
12/2007	49.51	37.53	48.85	12/2010	58.05	43.10	57.74	12/2013	42.12	38.55	38.82

Source: CME Group; Chicago Board of Trade

Soybean Oil, Crude, Decatur, IL
Weekly Cash as of 01/03/2014

Date	Open	High	Low	Close
12/06/13	39.09	39.09	38.27	38.41
12/13/13	38.18	38.53	37.96	37.96
12/20/13	37.88	37.88	36.81	37.19
12/27/13	37.03	37.03	36.62	36.77
01/03/14	36.37	36.57	35.98	35.98

WEEKLY CASH
As of 01/03/2014
Chart High 67.69 on 03/03/2008
Chart Low 19.49 on 02/03/2005

Cents / lb.

Crude.

Quarterly High, Low and Settle of Soybean Oil   In Cents per Pound

Quarter	High	Low	Settle	Quarter	High	Low	Settle	Quarter	High	Low	Settle
03/2005	24.62	19.49	23.28	03/2008	67.69	47.43	48.35	03/2011	57.08	49.96	57.08
06/2005	26.83	22.55	24.29	06/2008	64.45	49.02	64.41	06/2011	58.40	53.91	54.04
09/2005	26.19	22.59	24.10	09/2008	66.24	42.35	42.87	09/2011	57.97	50.20	50.20
12/2005	24.99	20.59	21.05	12/2008	43.43	27.05	31.56	12/2011	54.17	48.40	51.97
03/2006	24.66	20.71	22.42	03/2009	35.42	26.88	29.99	03/2012	54.56	49.75	54.25
06/2006	25.77	21.82	25.61	06/2009	38.70	30.12	32.52	06/2012	56.23	46.55	50.84
09/2006	26.69	23.01	23.15	09/2009	35.58	29.55	30.72	09/2012	56.32	50.02	50.93
12/2006	28.61	22.66	28.26	12/2009	38.96	30.28	37.17	12/2012	50.73	44.68	46.86
03/2007	31.47	26.82	30.98	03/2010	37.77	32.90	35.56	03/2013	50.99	46.92	48.86
06/2007	35.13	29.69	35.13	06/2010	37.92	33.25	33.60	06/2013	50.16	46.25	46.25
09/2007	37.84	33.42	37.61	09/2010	41.85	33.09	41.85	09/2013	47.06	40.58	40.58
12/2007	47.68	36.15	47.47	12/2010	53.97	40.17	53.61	12/2013	41.74	36.37	36.57

Decatur, Illinois Crude.   *Source: U.S. Department of Agriculture (USDA)*

INDICES - COMMODITIES

Current Outlook

Commodity prices trended lower during 2011-13 due to generally weak global economic growth, slower commodity demand from China, disinflationary pressures, and reduced speculative fervor for commodities. Yet, the Continuous Commodity Index (CCI) remained in the general bull market that began in 2001. The downward corrections seen in 2008 and 2011/13 look much less severe when looking at the CCI on an inflation-adjusted basis (see nearby chart).

Commodity prices come into 2014 in a lull but the long-term outlook for commodity prices continues to be generally bullish. The main drivers of economic growth and commodity demand in coming years will continue to be rising living standards in the developing world and the United Nations' projection for a 2.5 billion person increase in the world's population through 2050. As the world economy normalizes in coming years, then commodity demand should start to grow more quickly, thus boosting commodity prices.

1970s Commodity Bull Market

The second-largest commodity bull market in post-war history was the +146.7% rally in the CCI seen in 1971-74. That rally was driven by a sharp increase in inflation and related weakness in the dollar. As the nearby table shows, the average U.S. inflation rate during that bull market was a lofty +4.9% and the dollar fell by an average of -7.5% per year. Inflation at the time stemmed from the Federal Reserve's overly easy monetary policy. The weak dollar stemmed from inflation and the fact that the dollar was adjusting downward after the Bretton Woods agreement broke down and currencies started floating.

In addition to inflation and a weak dollar, there were supply/demand factors in particular markets that helped drive the 1971-74 commodity bull market. Grain and soybean prices soared during that time largely because of huge Soviet grain and soybean purchases in 1972 and 1973. The 1971-74 bull market was also driven in its latter stages by the October 1973 Arab Oil Embargo, which caused oil prices to triple, thus pushing the CCI higher.

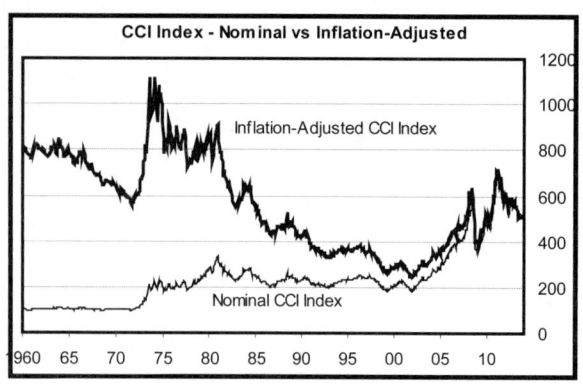

1977-80 Bull Market

After the CCI peaked in 1974, commodity prices moved sideways later in the 1970s as inflation and demand were undercut by the severe U.S. recession seen in 1973-75. After the recession, however, commodity prices staged the third largest bull market in post-war history of +82.8% during 1977-80. Inflation was the key driver behind that rally. The U.S. average annual CPI during that commodity bull market averaged an extraordinarily high +10.2%. The dollar was also weak during that time with an average annual -5.2% decline in the dollar index.

1980-2001 Bear Market

Fed Chairman Paul Volcker started to crack down on inflation in 1979, causing the double-dip recession in 1980 and 1981-82. Commodity prices were forced lower in the early-1980s by the double-dip recessions and the downward trend in inflation. Commodity prices were also pushed lower by the sharp rally in the dollar seen from 1980 until the 1985 Plaza Accord. Crude oil prices trended downward from 1981-85 and then plunged to $10 per barrel in March 1986, also undercutting the commodity indexes in the early to mid-1980s.

Although the CCI was volatile in the 1980s and 1990s, the general trend was downward. On an inflation-adjusted basis (see chart on previous page), it is easy to

Commodity Bull Markets Ranked by Percentage Gain in Continuous Commodity Index (1960-2013)

Bull Market Period	--------- Low ---------		--------- High ---------		Percent Rally	Rally Duration (months)	Avg CPI (yr-yr%)	Avg Dollar Index (yr/yr%)	Correlation CRB-CPI	Correlation CRB-DXY
2001-13	Oct-01	182.83	Apr-11	691.09	278.0%	84	2.3%	-2.5%	0.93	-0.80
1971-74	Oct-71	96.40	Feb-74	237.80	146.7%	28	4.9%	-7.5%	0.97	-0.79
1977-80	Aug-77	184.70	Nov-80	337.60	82.8%	39	10.2%	-5.2%	0.97	-0.93
1986-88	Jul-86	196.16	Jun-88	272.19	38.8%	23	3.2%	-13.3%	0.89	-0.68
1992-96	Aug-92	198.17	Apy-86	263.79	33.1%	44	2.8%	-0.6%	0.96	-0.32

Note: Data is current through December 31, 2013. Source: Commodity Research Bureau

see that commodity prices in reality were in a serious bear market from 1980 until 2001. The main reasons for that commodity bear market included (1) the success of global central banks in taming inflation, and (2) greatly expanded supply in nearly all commodity markets due to improved technology and new producers such as Brazil coming into the markets.

2001-13 Bull Market

Commodity prices hit a post-war low in inflation-adjusted terms in October 2001. Commodity prices were depressed in 2001 due to the post-bubble plunge in the U.S. stock market, the U.S. recession in 2001, and a U.S. inflation rate that fell sharply through 2001 (i.e., from +3.7% in Jan-2001 to +1.1% by mid-2002).

However, commodity prices bottomed out in October 2001 as the Federal Reserve was in the process of slashing interest rates to revive the economy and prevent a an extremely damaging deflationary episode such as the one Japan experienced in the last two decades. The Fed's easier monetary policy, combined with a sharp -33% plunge in the dollar index during 2002-04, were the main factors that drove the 2002-04 stage of the commodity bull market. The nearby chart illustrates the very strong negative correlation of -0.94 seen between the dollar index and the CCI over the 2002-04 period.

The commodity rally continued in 2005 but for different reasons. In 2005, the dollar started to recover because of the Fed's tighter monetary policy. Yet the CCI rallied even in the face of the stronger dollar because of strong demand in key commodity markets, driven in large part by China. China, with its truly massive scale of development, drove the prices of many commodities higher, particularly energy prices, metals prices, and construction materials prices.

The commodity rally then kicked into high gear again in the latter half of 2007 when the Fed was forced into easing due to the fact that Wall Street firms started experiencing big losses on their mortgage portfolios. From August 2007 through the then-record high in July 2008, the CCI soared by +48.7%. That rally was driven by the Fed's interest rate cuts, the decline in the dollar over that period, and speculative fever.

The CCI in the latter half of 2008 went into a steep downside correction where it fell by -47.6% and retraced 68% of the 2001-08 rally. The correction was over fairly quickly and the CCI in 2009 began a new bull leg that culminated in the record high of 691.09 posted in April 2011. That rally was driven by the slow recovery in the global economy and by the Fed's extraordinarily easy monetary policy that injected a huge amount of liquidity into the financial system.

The CCI then trended lower during the remainder of

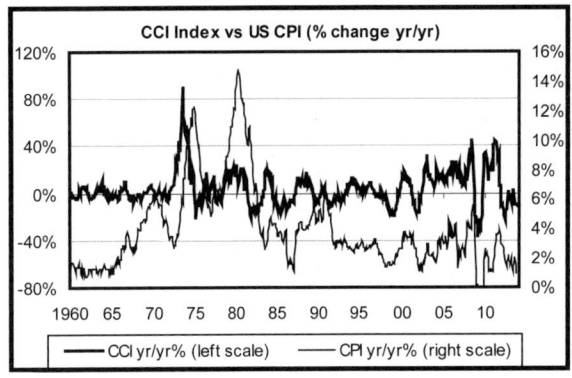

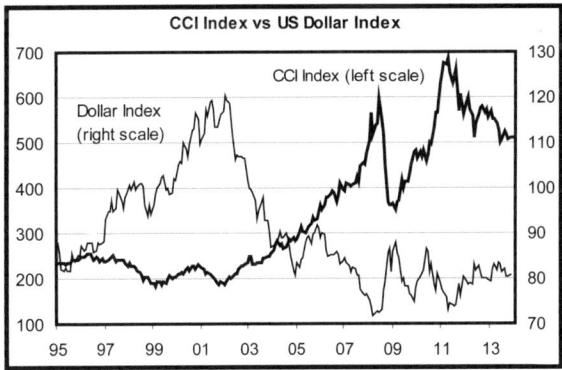

2011 and through 2012-13. The CCI fell by a total of -28% over the time to post a 3-year low of 499.99 in June 2013. Commodity prices moved lower during 2011-13 due to weak global economic growth, deflationary pressures, and long liquidation pressures.

Many investors had anticipated hyperinflation from the Fed's injection of $3 trillion of liquidity into the banking system and investors bought commodities and gold for protection. However, the economy instead saw disinflation and by late 2013 the Fed's preferred inflation measure, the core PCE deflator, had fallen to a near-record low of +1.1% y/y. The disinflation trend, combined with the lack of any fresh global financial crisis, caused long liquidation pressures in the commodity markets, particularly in gold and silver.

Commodity prices also cooled in 2011-13 due to slower economic growth in China. China's real GDP growth accelerated to a peak of +10.4% in 2010 thanks to China's 2008-09 stimulus measures. However, Chinese GDP then slid to +7.5% by 2013 and the markets are looking for Chinese GDP to remain stable near +7.5% over the next few years. Chinese authorities clamped down on building and on excess production capacity, thus reducing commodity demand.

CRB SPOT INDEX

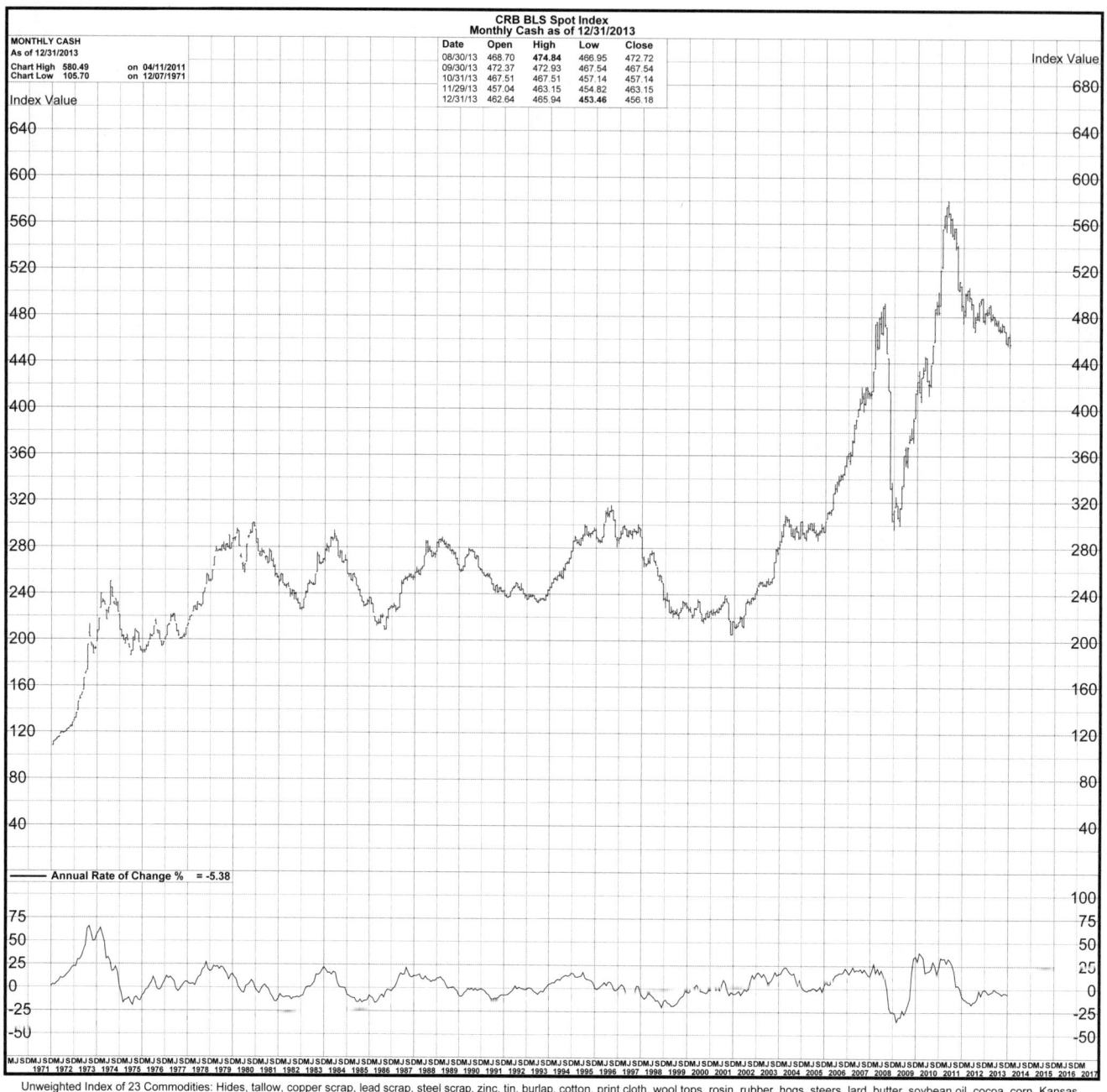

CRB BLS Spot Index
Monthly Cash as of 12/31/2013

Date	Open	High	Low	Close
08/30/13	468.70	474.84	466.95	472.72
09/30/13	472.37	472.93	467.54	467.54
10/31/13	467.51	467.51	457.14	457.14
11/29/13	457.04	463.15	454.82	463.15
12/31/13	462.64	465.94	453.46	456.18

MONTHLY CASH
As of 12/31/2013
Chart High 580.49 on 04/11/2011
Chart Low 105.70 on 12/07/1971

Annual Rate of Change % = -5.38

Unweighted Index of 23 Commodities: Hides, tallow, copper scrap, lead scrap, steel scrap, zinc, tin, burlap, cotton, print cloth, wool tops, rosin, rubber, hogs, steers, lard, butter, soybean oil, cocoa, corn, Kansas City wheat, Minneapolis wheat, and sugar.

Annual High, Low and Settle of CRB Spot Index   Index Value

Year	High	Low	Settle	Year	High	Low	Settle	Year	High	Low	Settle
1972	131.60	108.20	131.60	1986	236.00	208.40	228.33	2000	236.22	215.29	223.99
1973	213.10	131.90	206.00	1987	258.68	223.77	258.21	2001	239.10	205.62	212.10
1974	249.90	207.30	207.90	1988	286.12	255.73	284.35	2002	246.42	211.20	244.31
1975	208.40	186.10	188.30	1989	289.18	260.60	260.60	2003	287.25	246.84	283.58
1976	217.30	188.70	201.90	1990	279.24	257.93	258.13	2004	309.10	285.36	292.97
1977	221.90	200.20	213.20	1991	258.78	238.24	238.24	2005	303.27	286.50	303.27
1978	256.50	216.20	250.30	1992	250.00	234.98	235.27	2006	362.51	305.89	362.35
1979	289.80	251.50	286.90	1993	246.55	232.09	245.44	2007	419.46	352.81	413.40
1980	300.90	257.40	283.50	1994	286.32	245.33	285.98	2008	492.28	296.35	312.98
1981	286.80	246.20	250.00	1995	300.48	282.34	289.10	2009	424.18	299.71	424.18
1982	256.80	225.20	227.40	1996	317.00	280.81	288.22	2010	520.33	406.46	520.33
1983	278.40	226.60	277.80	1997	300.77	271.81	271.81	2011	580.49	474.46	481.80
1984	294.80	257.20	257.20	1998	278.23	228.66	235.22	2012	505.76	467.51	482.10
1985	257.70	228.30	236.70	1999	241.97	218.71	227.25	2013	490.58	453.46	456.18

1967=100.   Index data begins 01/07/1947.   *Source: Commodity Research Bureau*

CRB BLS Spot Index
Weekly Cash as of 01/03/2014

Date	Open	High	Low	Close
12/06/13	462.64	462.64	461.84	462.22
12/13/13	461.24	465.94	460.76	460.76
12/20/13	460.45	460.48	453.46	454.64
12/27/13	455.80	456.66	455.54	456.66
01/03/14	455.98	456.18	455.35	455.35

WEEKLY CASH
As of 01/03/2014
Chart High 580.49 on 04/11/2011
Chart Low 246.98 on 05/05/2003

Annual Rate of Change % = -5.66

Unweighted Index of 23 Commodities: Hides, tallow, copper scrap, lead scrap, steel scrap, zinc, tin, burlap, cotton, print cloth, wool tops, rosin, rubber, hogs, steers, lard, butter, soybean oil, cocoa, corn, Kansas City wheat, Minneapolis wheat, and sugar.

Quarterly High, Low and Settle of CRB Spot Index   Index Value

Quarter	High	Low	Settle	Quarter	High	Low	Settle	Quarter	High	Low	Settle
03/2005	301.81	286.82	298.11	03/2008	470.66	415.74	450.32	03/2011	575.42	522.04	575.04
06/2005	302.83	294.15	294.15	06/2008	478.21	449.02	476.69	06/2011	580.49	549.42	550.85
09/2005	296.40	286.50	294.61	09/2008	481.00	412.62	412.62	09/2011	557.08	503.94	503.94
12/2005	303.27	293.64	303.27	12/2008	415.85	296.35	312.98	12/2011	511.20	474.46	481.80
03/2006	313.87	305.89	313.17	03/2009	325.06	299.71	315.22	03/2012	505.76	480.68	497.36
06/2006	337.92	313.85	337.92	06/2009	368.09	314.88	354.50	06/2012	496.97	467.51	475.81
09/2006	344.51	334.16	344.05	09/2009	384.45	349.94	375.47	09/2012	496.23	476.68	496.19
12/2006	362.51	343.26	362.35	12/2009	424.18	371.09	424.18	12/2012	496.88	474.11	482.10
03/2007	387.64	352.81	386.91	03/2010	436.97	406.46	431.44	03/2013	490.58	476.23	479.96
06/2007	410.20	383.96	405.20	06/2010	446.18	411.73	421.68	06/2013	480.88	468.28	468.28
09/2007	419.46	397.97	417.74	09/2010	487.26	419.87	487.26	09/2013	474.84	466.39	467.54
12/2007	419.37	409.44	413.40	12/2010	520.33	481.65	520.33	12/2013	467.51	453.46	456.18

1967=100.   *Source: Commodity Research Bureau*

CRB SPOT METALS SUB-INDEX

Unweighted Index of 5 Commodities: Copper scrap, lead scrap, steel scrap, tin, and zinc.

Annual High, Low and Settle of CRB Metals Sub-Index   Index Value

Year	High	Low	Settle	Year	High	Low	Settle	Year	High	Low	Settle
1972	117.90	105.70	116.00	1986	211.98	177.30	211.98	2000	264.00	211.82	214.03
1973	206.20	118.30	198.50	1987	296.72	206.71	296.72	2001	214.63	168.65	172.45
1974	279.00	196.10	196.10	1988	342.43	264.83	342.43	2002	195.23	171.46	184.50
1975	205.70	161.20	171.10	1989	367.15	292.78	296.49	2003	276.69	193.76	276.69
1976	227.70	172.00	197.80	1990	335.30	282.81	283.16	2004	367.73	275.47	357.69
1977	233.90	195.70	211.70	1991	285.85	238.11	248.51	2005	442.86	346.21	440.85
1978	278.00	211.50	267.30	1992	295.04	240.36	248.79	2006	701.71	440.78	693.88
1979	341.20	275.60	322.00	1993	260.68	214.08	236.27	2007	923.58	652.98	811.85
1980	346.00	257.60	288.30	1994	310.10	233.68	310.10	2008	1,050.21	372.80	390.88
1981	314.20	256.20	264.20	1995	322.03	292.37	300.57	2009	809.18	395.83	809.14
1982	270.80	188.80	202.30	1996	314.72	285.88	289.90	2010	1,006.24	685.92	1,006.24
1983	256.00	204.10	250.40	1997	329.13	268.60	269.78	2011	1,121.70	829.58	837.77
1984	259.00	214.70	216.90	1998	276.33	214.38	218.51	2012	973.91	778.16	918.72
1985	226.50	199.40	207.70	1999	261.60	210.36	261.60	2013	945.58	821.88	935.24

1967=100.   Index data begins 01/07/1947.   *Source: Commodity Research Bureau*

256

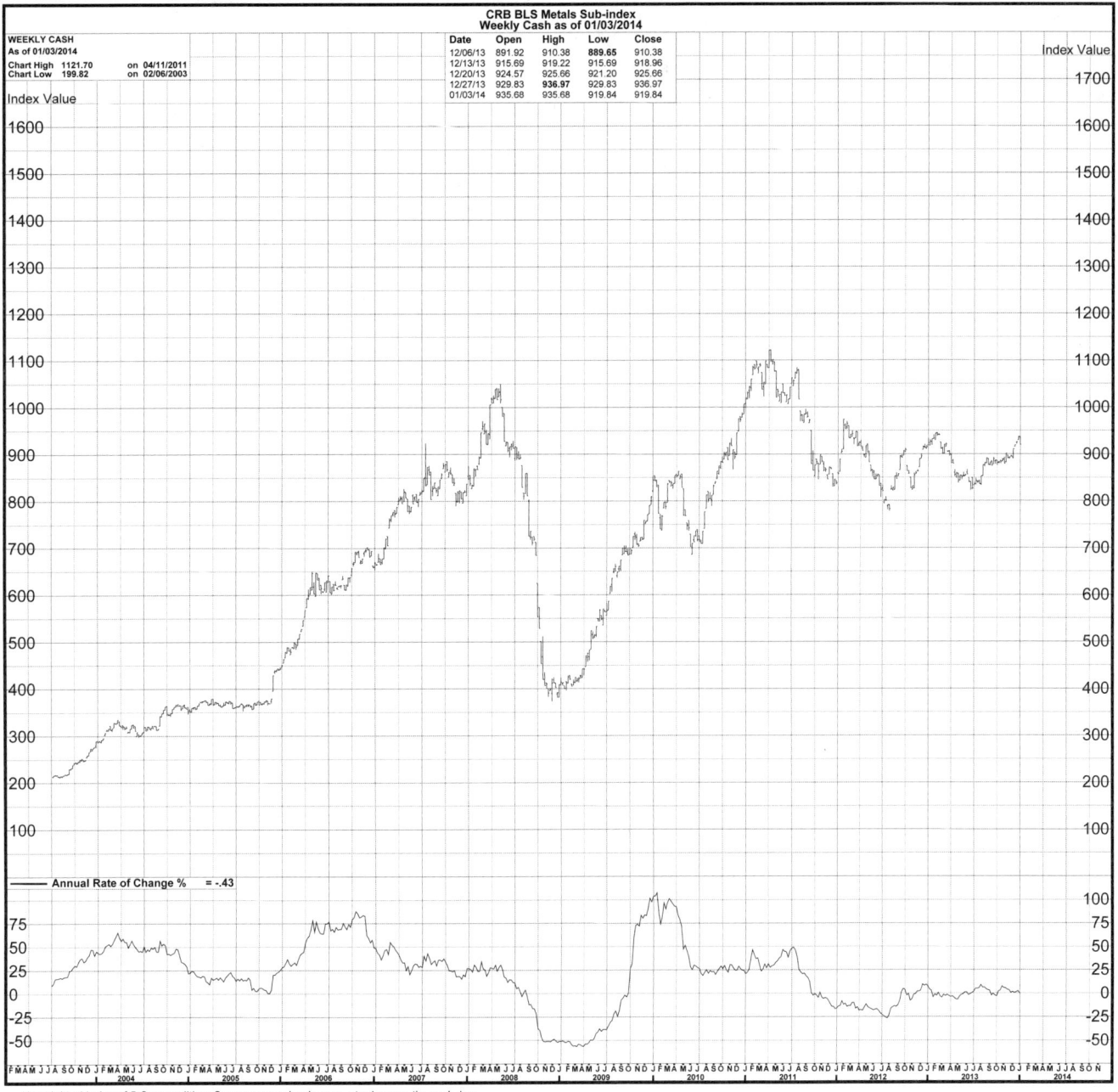

Date	Open	High	Low	Close
12/06/13	891.92	910.38	**889.65**	910.38
12/13/13	915.69	919.22	915.69	918.96
12/20/13	924.57	925.66	921.20	925.66
12/27/13	929.83	**936.97**	929.83	936.97
01/03/14	935.68	935.68	919.84	919.84

CRB BLS Metals Sub-index
Weekly Cash as of 01/03/2014

WEEKLY CASH
As of 01/03/2014
Chart High 1121.70 on 04/11/2011
Chart Low 199.82 on 02/06/2003

Annual Rate of Change % = -.43

Unweighted Index of 5 Commodities: Copper scrap, lead scrap, steel scrap, tin, and zinc.

Quarterly High, Low and Settle of CRB Metals Sub-Index   Index Value

Quarter	High	Low	Settle	Quarter	High	Low	Settle	Quarter	High	Low	Settle
03/2005	376.26	346.21	369.95	03/2008	931.12	775.75	909.03	03/2011	1,097.92	997.16	1,086.27
06/2005	378.72	361.01	361.42	06/2008	964.75	806.75	829.25	06/2011	1,121.70	1,007.00	1,040.42
09/2005	370.53	352.78	366.01	09/2008	839.01	673.00	673.00	09/2011	1,084.34	864.30	864.36
12/2005	442.86	365.67	440.85	12/2008	702.51	372.80	390.88	12/2011	897.78	829.58	837.77
03/2006	527.52	440.78	527.52	03/2009	429.75	395.83	429.25	03/2012	973.91	855.19	925.16
06/2006	649.98	533.91	627.15	06/2009	569.88	428.72	565.75	06/2012	929.20	807.21	823.38
09/2006	642.24	602.43	636.97	09/2009	705.18	556.11	699.12	09/2012	906.71	778.16	906.71
12/2006	701.71	627.20	693.88	12/2009	809.18	684.69	809.14	12/2012	920.68	823.56	918.72
03/2007	780.95	652.98	773.13	03/2010	853.44	737.73	848.60	03/2013	945.58	895.51	899.58
06/2007	826.50	773.63	804.51	06/2010	862.75	685.92	716.91	06/2013	898.12	821.88	826.46
09/2007	923.58	803.98	856.92	09/2010	876.81	708.92	876.81	09/2013	892.87	832.87	885.64
12/2007	884.98	789.82	811.85	12/2010	1,006.24	866.48	1,006.24	12/2013	936.97	875.33	935.24

1967=100.   *Source: Commodity Research Bureau*

CRB SPOT TEXTILES SUB-INDEX

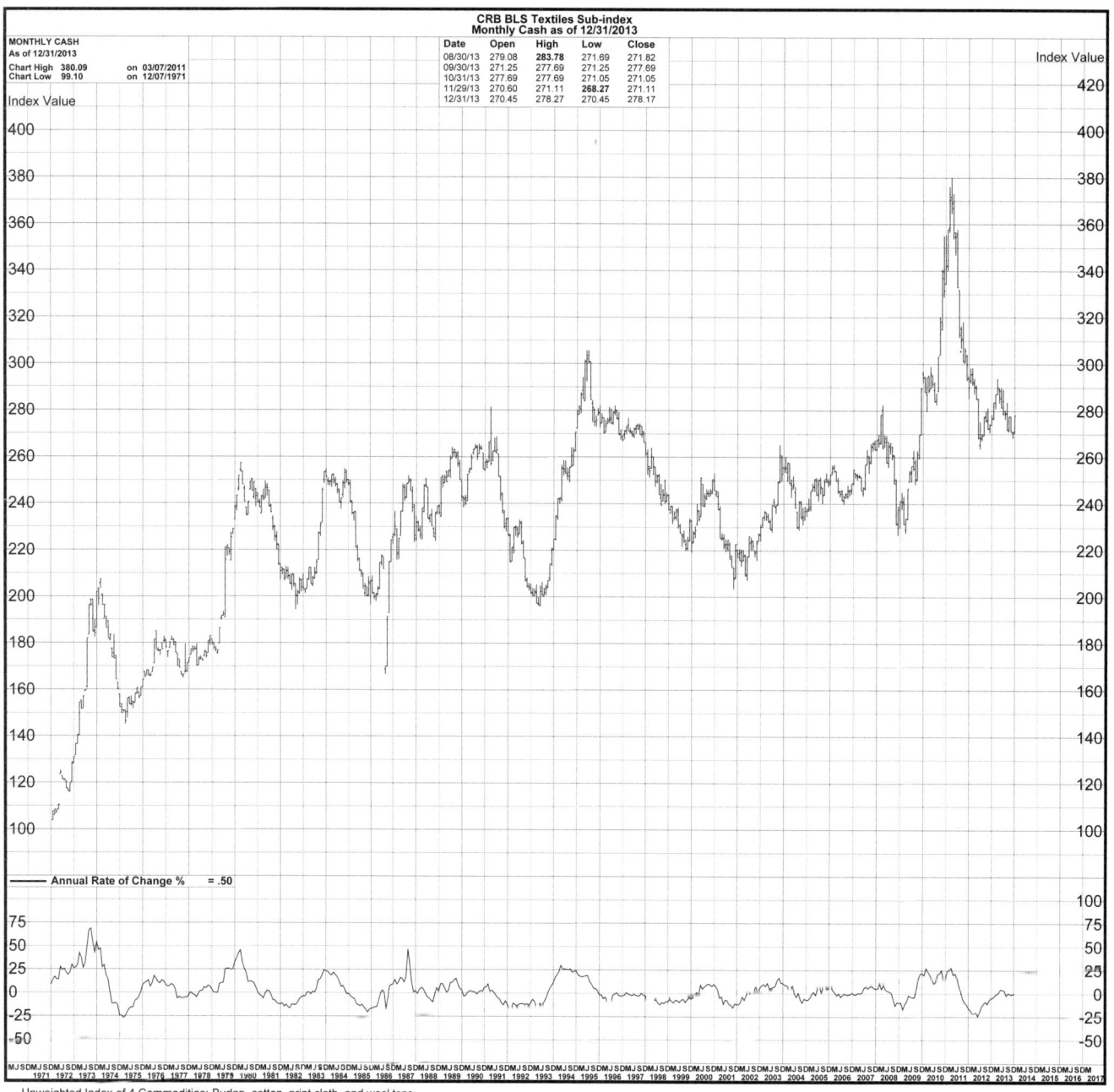

Date	Open	High	Low	Close
08/30/13	279.08	**283.78**	271.69	271.82
09/30/13	271.25	277.69	271.25	277.69
10/31/13	277.69	277.69	271.05	271.05
11/29/13	270.60	271.11	**268.27**	271.11
12/31/13	270.45	278.27	270.45	278.17

CRB BLS Textiles Sub-index
Monthly Cash as of 12/31/2013

MONTHLY CASH
As of 12/31/2013

Chart High 380.09 on 03/07/2011
Chart Low 99.10 on 12/07/1971

Unweighted Index of 4 Commodities: Burlap, cotton, print cloth, and wool tops.

Annual High, Low and Settle of CRB Textiles Sub-Index   Index Value

Year	High	Low	Settle	Year	High	Low	Settle	Year	High	Low	Settle
1972	130.90	103.80	130.90	1986	227.00	166.70	226.56	2000	253.02	223.32	245.74
1973	201.90	131.70	201.90	1987	251.88	215.72	231.79	2001	245.85	203.36	217.41
1974	207.30	152.50	152.50	1988	250.80	223.80	235.99	2002	230.93	207.01	230.15
1975	164.30	145.00	164.30	1989	264.16	234.03	243.02	2003	265.16	227.81	255.19
1976	185.00	165.20	178.20	1990	265.70	238.25	257.64	2004	260.19	228.68	237.87
1977	182.90	165.00	173.50	1991	281.41	226.23	226.23	2005	253.23	237.00	252.48
1978	182.90	170.20	179.40	1992	233.04	200.93	201.77	2006	256.89	239.76	254.40
1979	238.90	175.00	238.00	1993	224.69	195.96	224.69	2007	267.49	243.34	267.49
1980	257.30	234.70	240.40	1994	279.67	224.16	279.67	2008	282.52	226.60	241.27
1981	249.50	207.00	211.00	1995	305.73	272.62	274.31	2009	297.06	227.57	294.00
1982	213.00	194.30	203.90	1996	282.16	266.83	267.43	2010	355.52	279.71	342.07
1983	254.90	201.30	251.20	1997	276.78	260.32	261.54	2011	380.09	285.33	290.15
1984	254.90	237.50	248.50	1998	264.02	237.33	237.47	2012	298.50	263.64	276.79
1985	249.80	196.70	206.70	1999	239.23	219.16	223.75	2013	293.88	268.27	278.17

1967=100.   Index data begins 01/07/1947.   *Source: Commodity Research Bureau*

CRB BLS Textiles Sub-index
Weekly Cash as of 01/03/2014

Date	Open	High	Low	Close
12/06/13	270.45	273.75	270.45	273.75
12/13/13	273.71	277.42	273.71	277.42
12/20/13	277.57	277.57	276.82	277.03
12/27/13	276.22	277.94	276.22	277.94
01/03/14	278.27	278.27	276.68	276.68

WEEKLY CASH
As of 01/03/2014

Chart High 380.09 on 03/07/2011
Chart Low 226.60 on 11/12/2008

Unweighted Index of 4 Commodities: Burlap, cotton, print cloth, and wool tops.

Quarterly High, Low and Settle of CRB Textiles Sub-Index   Index Value

Quarter	High	Low	Settle	Quarter	High	Low	Settle	Quarter	High	Low	Settle
03/2005	248.89	237.00	247.37	03/2008	282.52	263.80	263.80	03/2011	380.09	340.24	369.14
06/2005	251.27	241.21	250.35	06/2008	269.60	255.64	264.64	06/2011	373.24	333.09	333.09
09/2005	251.38	240.04	249.45	09/2008	265.97	248.82	248.82	09/2011	331.92	300.90	301.50
12/2005	253.23	247.39	252.48	12/2008	250.67	226.60	241.27	12/2011	307.09	285.33	290.15
03/2006	256.89	249.93	249.93	03/2009	245.03	227.57	233.74	03/2012	298.50	287.28	290.48
06/2006	251.30	241.44	241.62	06/2009	256.23	233.52	256.23	06/2012	291.21	263.64	268.02
09/2006	247.98	239.76	245.89	09/2009	262.92	248.31	261.22	09/2012	280.04	267.13	275.63
12/2006	255.03	243.37	254.40	12/2009	297.06	259.35	294.00	12/2012	281.41	270.56	276.79
03/2007	253.39	250.27	251.77	03/2010	295.07	279.71	288.75	03/2013	293.88	276.36	290.10
06/2007	256.84	243.34	256.84	06/2010	298.96	284.05	284.05	06/2013	289.83	278.31	279.01
09/2007	265.74	253.00	264.41	09/2010	320.22	282.47	318.13	09/2013	283.78	271.25	277.69
12/2007	267.49	262.70	267.49	12/2010	355.52	314.76	342.07	12/2013	278.27	268.27	278.17

1967=100.   *Source: Commodity Research Bureau*

CRB SPOT RAW INDUSTRIALS SUB-INDEX

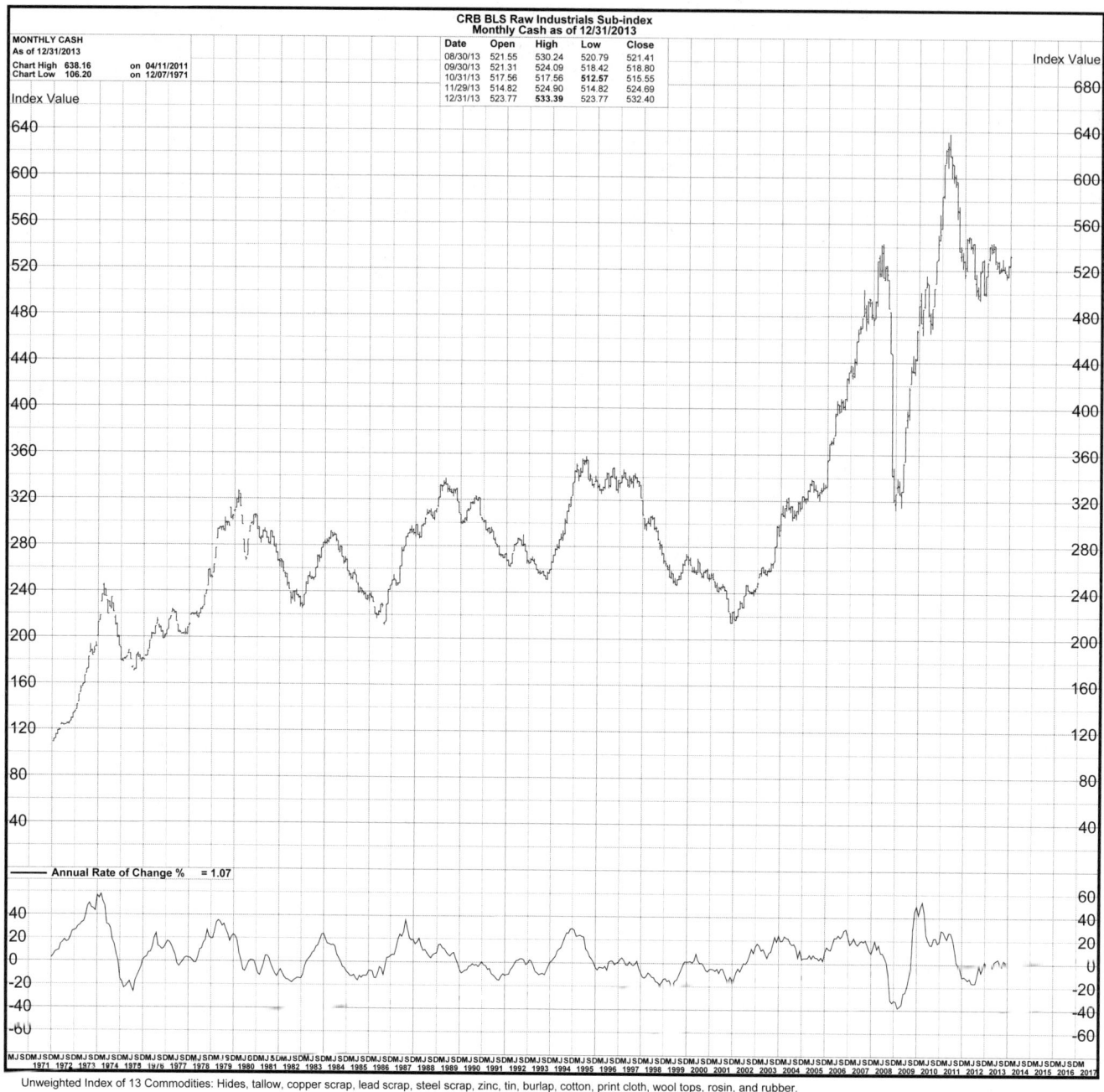

Unweighted Index of 13 Commodities: Hides, tallow, copper scrap, lead scrap, steel scrap, zinc, tin, burlap, cotton, print cloth, wool tops, rosin, and rubber.

Annual High, Low and Settle of CRB Raw Industrials Sub-Index   Index Value

Year	High	Low	Settle	Year	High	Low	Settle	Year	High	Low	Settle
1972	135.60	109.00	135.60	1986	249.98	211.00	249.76	2000	270.87	250.46	255.81
1973	212.30	137.10	212.30	1987	297.81	245.21	297.81	2001	257.51	214.16	217.33
1974	245.60	179.20	179.20	1988	321.14	286.05	321.14	2002	249.48	216.70	248.56
1975	188.30	170.70	180.30	1989	338.54	298.99	300.40	2003	309.07	253.85	309.07
1976	216.30	183.10	205.40	1990	322.85	299.31	301.21	2004	324.30	302.90	321.50
1977	224.20	202.10	211.10	1991	302.16	267.25	267.25	2005	355.19	318.08	354.65
1978	258.60	216.30	251.90	1992	290.01	261.96	265.22	2006	437.28	355.77	437.28
1979	311.70	255.60	309.80	1993	271.13	250.72	266.50	2007	503.45	426.12	476.99
1980	326.90	266.40	293.50	1994	345.12	265.81	345.12	2008	543.15	312.28	326.50
1981	295.20	260.90	265.80	1995	357.98	330.29	332.15	2009	489.44	314.53	489.44
1982	267.50	224.90	226.90	1996	348.08	325.50	334.92	2010	583.81	463.53	583.81
1983	284.50	227.60	281.60	1997	346.84	306.88	307.52	2011	638.16	513.49	516.47
1984	292.00	258.00	258.00	1998	307.26	263.49	265.32	2012	549.26	494.02	526.75
1985	259.10	231.00	237.60	1999	274.15	246.90	268.88	2013	544.01	512.57	532.40

1967=100.   Index data begins 01/07/1947.   *Source: Commodity Research Bureau*

CRB BLS Raw Industrials Sub-index
Weekly Cash as of 01/03/2014

Date	Open	High	Low	Close
12/06/13	523.77	526.99	**523.77**	526.99
12/13/13	528.15	530.36	528.15	530.36
12/20/13	531.40	531.40	529.78	530.37
12/27/13	530.81	**533.39**	530.81	533.39
01/03/14	532.55	532.55	528.14	528.14

WEEKLY CASH
As of 01/03/2014

Chart High 638.16 on 04/11/2011
Chart Low 254.97 on 02/06/2003

Annual Rate of Change % = -.18

Unweighted Index of 13 Commodities: Hides, tallow, copper scrap, lead scrap, steel scrap, zinc, tin, burlap, cotton, print cloth, wool tops, rosin, and rubber.

Quarterly High, Low and Settle of CRB Raw Industrials Sub-Index Index Value

Quarter	High	Low	Settle	Quarter	High	Low	Settle	Quarter	High	Low	Settle
03/2005	335.63	318.08	335.00	03/2008	523.88	473.27	510.00	03/2011	631.33	582.54	627.00
06/2005	338.83	327.95	329.32	06/2008	525.71	491.89	502.04	06/2011	638.16	596.02	601.64
09/2005	332.03	320.49	328.75	09/2008	504.18	440.96	440.96	09/2011	603.54	536.65	536.65
12/2005	355.19	329.50	354.65	12/2008	447.60	312.28	326.50	12/2011	540.96	513.49	516.47
03/2006	375.00	355.77	374.92	03/2009	339.66	314.53	328.75	03/2012	549.26	519.82	540.71
06/2006	407.33	376.77	402.91	06/2009	398.77	328.54	394.18	06/2012	543.56	498.52	502.60
09/2006	408.99	397.68	408.80	09/2009	446.61	390.83	432.40	09/2012	528.54	494.02	528.54
12/2006	437.28	406.89	437.28	12/2009	489.44	429.38	489.44	12/2012	529.97	498.51	526.75
03/2007	458.44	426.12	458.39	03/2010	504.37	463.53	504.13	03/2013	544.01	529.08	539.57
06/2007	478.68	458.32	478.26	06/2010	515.50	465.05	474.13	06/2013	541.43	517.82	518.93
09/2007	503.45	467.65	492.58	09/2010	528.31	469.38	528.31	09/2013	530.24	518.42	518.80
12/2007	495.46	472.14	476.99	12/2010	583.81	528.98	583.81	12/2013	533.39	512.57	532.40

1967=100.   *Source: Commodity Research Bureau*

CRB SPOT FOODSTUFFS SUB-INDEX

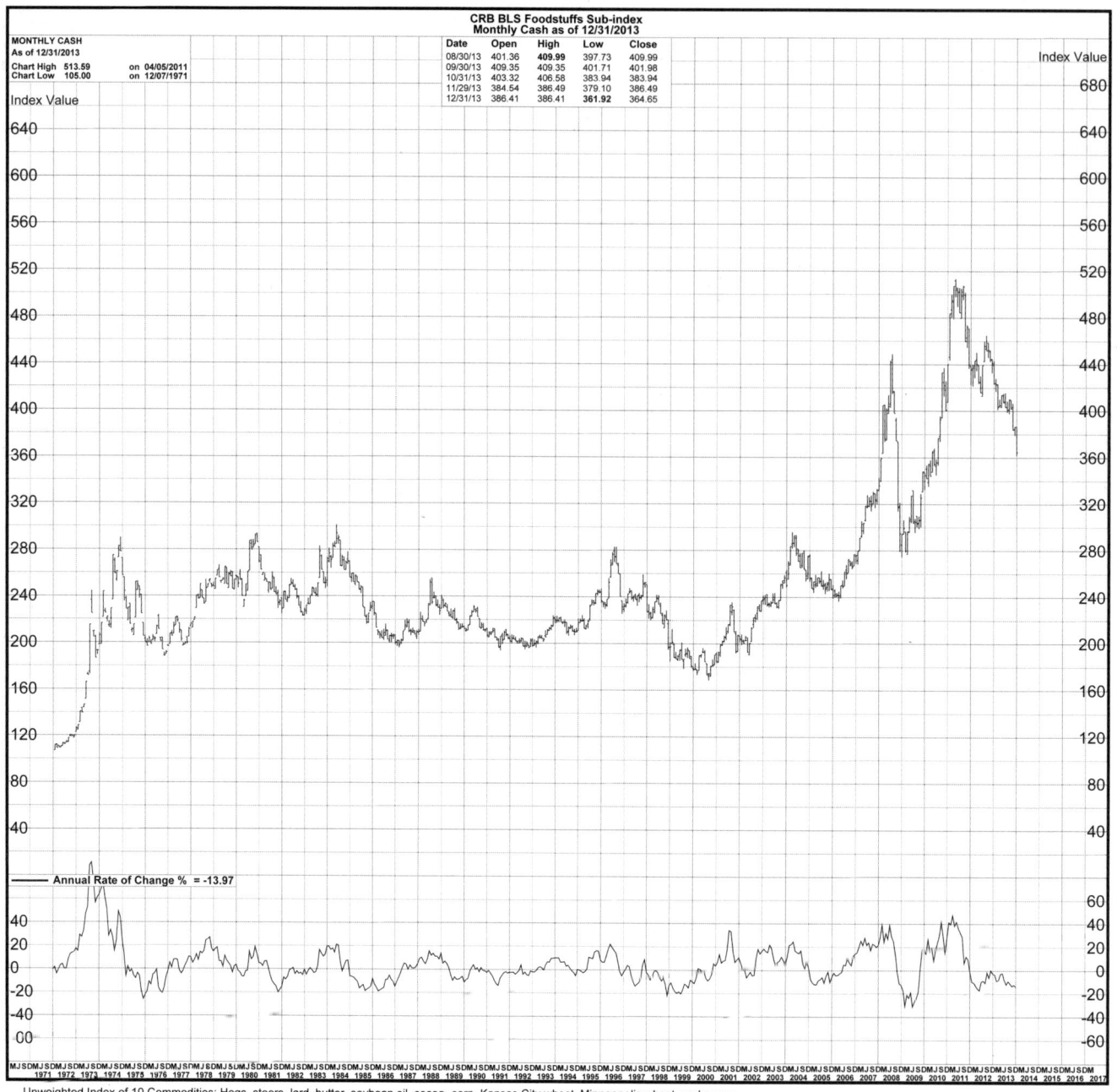

MONTHLY CASH
As of 12/31/2013
Chart High 513.59 on 04/05/2011
Chart Low 105.00 on 12/07/1971

Index Value

CRB BLS Foodstuffs Sub-index Monthly Cash as of 12/31/2013				
Date	Open	High	Low	Close
08/30/13	401.36	409.99	397.73	409.99
09/30/13	409.35	409.35	401.71	401.98
10/31/13	403.32	406.58	383.94	383.94
11/29/13	384.54	386.49	379.10	386.49
12/31/13	386.41	386.41	361.92	364.65

Annual Rate of Change % = -13.97

Unweighted Index of 10 Commodities: Hogs, steers, lard, butter, soybean oil, cocoa, corn, Kansas City wheat, Minneapolis wheat, and sugar.

Annual High, Low and Settle of CRB Foodstuffs Sub-Index   Index Value

Year	High	Low	Settle	Year	High	Low	Settle	Year	High	Low	Settle
1972	127.10	107.00	126.00	1986	235.00	198.48	200.41	2000	196.59	168.61	184.74
1973	244.40	124.70	206.00	1987	220.83	195.92	209.95	2001	235.78	183.96	204.61
1974	290.00	198.30	257.50	1988	255.28	209.71	238.33	2002	241.87	190.17	238.10
1975	255.80	200.30	200.30	1989	237.54	210.98	212.06	2003	263.46	230.27	250.24
1976	223.60	188.10	196.70	1990	232.42	205.33	206.39	2004	295.90	253.41	255.97
1977	222.00	196.90	216.10	1991	212.87	193.61	201.64	2005	262.61	239.08	241.73
1978	254.50	212.50	247.90	1992	207.45	194.55	197.72	2006	276.91	236.45	275.99
1979	266.70	245.20	256.70	1993	223.90	196.11	217.76	2007	342.76	268.39	335.94
1980	293.50	230.30	269.50	1994	223.58	206.53	217.82	2008	449.04	274.44	294.20
1981	274.90	224.60	228.80	1995	246.80	212.23	236.39	2009	348.17	277.11	344.70
1982	255.30	222.80	228.00	1996	283.18	225.39	231.83	2010	440.27	335.27	440.27
1983	283.10	224.00	272.00	1997	259.21	227.26	227.26	2011	513.59	422.79	435.45
1984	301.40	255.90	255.90	1998	242.06	184.37	197.52	2012	465.00	412.96	423.87
1985	260.00	215.90	235.20	1999	212.74	176.76	178.10	2013	428.13	361.92	364.65

1967=100.   Index data begins 01/07/1947.   *Source: Commodity Research Bureau*

CRB BLS Foodstuffs Sub-index
Weekly Cash as of 01/03/2014

Date	Open	High	Low	Close
12/06/13	386.41	**386.41**	382.16	382.16
12/13/13	378.97	386.37	375.73	375.73
12/20/13	374.06	374.68	361.92	363.64
12/27/13	365.47	365.47	363.54	364.61
01/03/14	364.11	367.26	364.11	367.26

WEEKLY CASH
As of 01/03/2014
Chart High 513.59 on 04/05/2011
Chart Low 230.27 on 08/04/2003

Annual Rate of Change % = -13.06

Unweighted Index of 10 Commodities: Hogs, steers, lard, butter, soybean oil, cocoa, corn, Kansas City wheat, Minneapolis wheat, and sugar.

Quarterly High, Low and Settle of CRB Foodstuffs Sub-Index   Index Value

Quarter	High	Low	Settle	Quarter	High	Low	Settle	Quarter	High	Low	Settle
03/2005	259.37	243.81	251.68	03/2008	405.44	339.26	375.92	03/2011	507.10	443.74	507.10
06/2005	262.61	249.40	249.67	06/2008	443.40	374.98	441.97	06/2011	513.59	484.58	484.58
09/2005	255.10	242.91	251.27	09/2008	449.04	374.58	374.58	09/2011	507.68	459.83	459.83
12/2005	260.53	239.08	241.73	12/2008	373.62	274.44	294.20	12/2011	473.93	422.79	435.45
03/2006	247.00	236.45	241.30	03/2009	306.59	277.11	296.43	03/2012	450.46	421.49	440.46
06/2006	261.89	239.29	261.89	06/2009	331.99	295.62	303.90	06/2012	439.56	412.96	439.28
09/2006	272.61	255.65	267.98	09/2009	310.06	295.47	305.96	09/2012	465.00	442.91	452.57
12/2006	276.91	264.24	275.99	12/2009	348.17	300.35	344.70	12/2012	452.35	423.14	423.87
03/2007	305.67	268.39	302.65	03/2010	357.92	335.27	344.27	03/2013	428.13	401.22	404.98
06/2007	327.94	294.49	318.66	06/2010	368.10	345.05	355.73	06/2013	415.89	403.15	403.40
09/2007	330.98	313.99	328.99	09/2010	433.20	353.38	433.20	09/2013	409.99	397.73	401.98
12/2007	342.76	316.85	335.94	12/2010	440.27	399.88	440.27	12/2013	406.58	361.92	364.65

1967=100.   *Source: Commodity Research Bureau*

CRB SPOT FATS & OILS SUB-INDEX

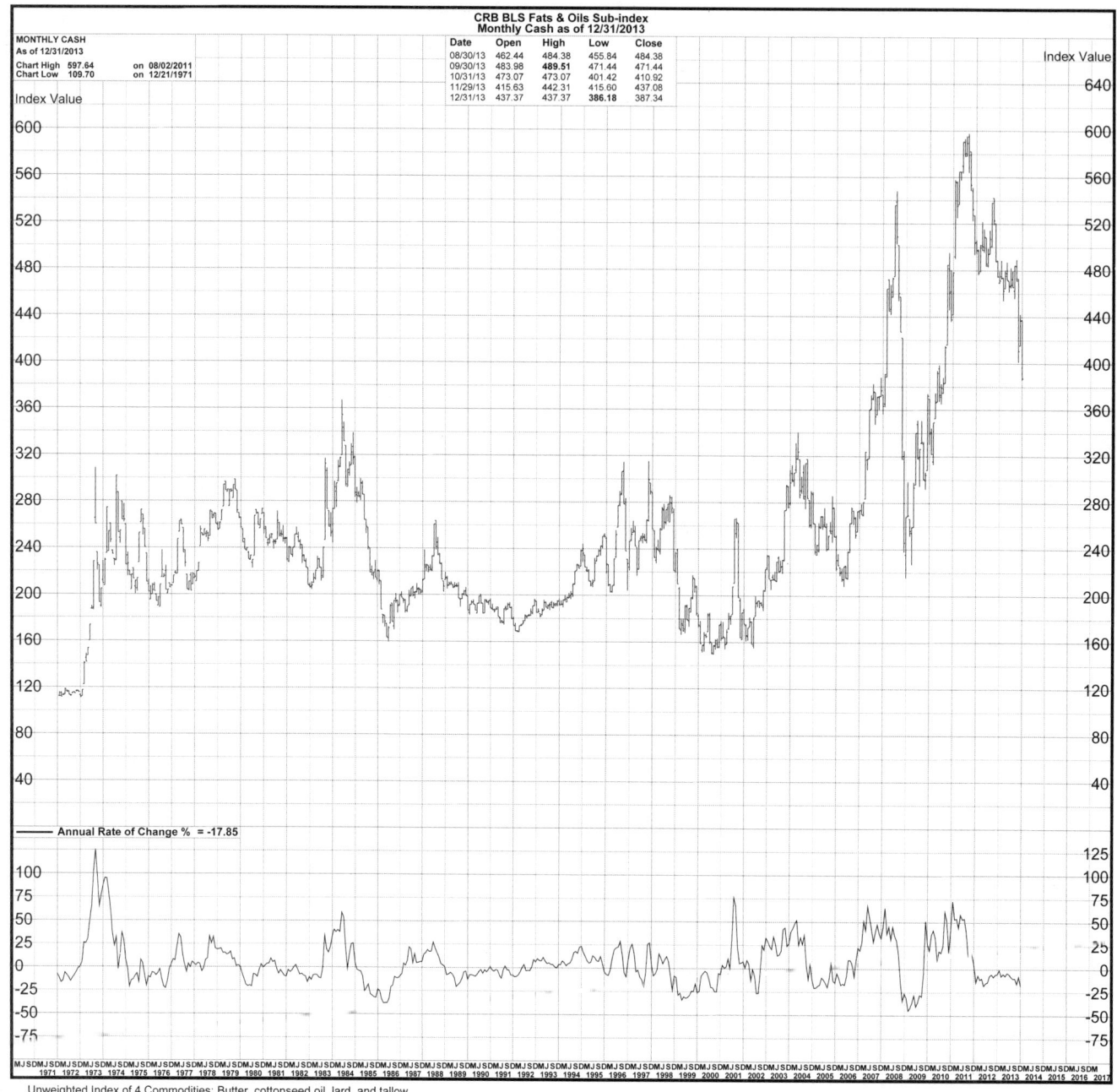

CRB BLS Fats & Oils Sub-index
Monthly Cash as of 12/31/2013

Date	Open	High	Low	Close
08/30/13	462.44	484.38	455.84	484.38
09/30/13	483.98	489.51	471.44	471.44
10/31/13	473.07	473.07	401.42	410.92
11/29/13	415.63	442.31	415.60	437.08
12/31/13	437.37	437.37	386.18	387.34

MONTHLY CASH
As of 12/31/2013
Chart High 597.64 on 08/02/2011
Chart Low 109.70 on 12/21/1971

Annual Rate of Change % = -17.85

Unweighted Index of 4 Commodities: Butter, cottonseed oil, lard, and tallow.

Annual High, Low and Settle of CRB Fats & Oils Sub-Index   Index Value

Year	High	Low	Settle	Year	High	Low	Settle	Year	High	Low	Settle
1972	118.90	111.40	111.40	1986	220.80	159.60	199.79	2000	185.48	149.78	163.62
1973	308.50	112.00	209.10	1987	213.46	184.32	212.54	2001	266.74	154.27	175.82
1974	301.70	207.40	225.30	1988	263.51	202.43	214.70	2002	235.00	155.22	234.00
1975	272.20	200.40	202.10	1989	215.92	186.81	186.81	2003	308.13	205.23	297.20
1976	237.80	188.90	207.40	1990	200.23	182.74	188.67	2004	340.45	258.58	262.55
1977	263.70	202.90	214.80	1991	193.72	173.80	173.80	2005	285.99	221.76	223.41
1978	271.70	211.00	255.20	1992	196.60	168.16	184.97	2006	276.40	208.14	273.93
1979	298.40	256.00	257.40	1993	196.81	180.94	191.71	2007	387.96	269.31	363.44
1980	273.20	222.50	255.90	1994	244.05	189.45	236.17	2008	548.03	215.59	268.03
1981	271.30	228.70	229.90	1995	253.28	206.82	226.68	2009	374.14	227.00	339.74
1982	257.70	205.70	205.70	1996	314.46	202.26	246.42	2010	495.40	313.19	478.28
1983	317.00	204.10	273.40	1997	315.23	216.70	257.08	2011	597.64	490.22	497.68
1984	366.90	273.20	287.10	1998	285.99	220.04	236.01	2012	542.38	469.41	471.49
1985	299.50	210.70	220.20	1999	240.47	166.42	174.78	2013	489.51	386.18	387.34

1967=100.   Index data begins 01/07/1947.   *Source: Commodity Research Bureau*

CRB BLS Fats & Oils Sub-index
Weekly Cash as of 01/03/2014

WEEKLY CASH
As of 01/03/2014

Chart High 597.64   on 08/02/2011
Chart Low   205.23   on 02/12/2003

Index Value

Date	Open	High	Low	Close
12/06/13	437.37	437.37	430.55	432.79
12/13/13	433.12	434.11	424.66	424.66
12/20/13	422.33	422.33	392.22	393.91
12/27/13	394.57	394.57	390.76	390.76
01/03/14	386.18	388.11	386.18	388.11

Annual Rate of Change % = -18.40

Unweighted Index of 4 Commodities: Butter, cottonseed oil, lard, and tallow.

Quarterly High, Low and Settle of CRB Fats & Oils Sub-Index   Index Value

Quarter	High	Low	Settle	Quarter	High	Low	Settle	Quarter	High	Low	Settle
03/2005	262.77	235.02	259.41	03/2008	472.43	362.89	444.98	03/2011	564.86	490.22	564.86
06/2005	275.71	257.33	259.68	06/2008	535.78	441.80	535.78	06/2011	593.15	557.41	580.86
09/2005	263.95	238.50	254.11	09/2008	548.03	427.09	427.09	09/2011	597.64	548.71	553.28
12/2005	285.99	221.76	223.41	12/2008	421.94	215.59	268.03	12/2011	551.09	493.59	497.68
03/2006	236.20	212.44	214.38	03/2009	298.43	227.00	259.17	03/2012	521.80	476.47	500.79
06/2006	238.42	208.14	238.00	06/2009	351.06	259.45	318.28	06/2012	515.66	483.19	494.03
09/2006	276.40	237.56	266.85	09/2009	350.79	294.38	300.42	09/2012	542.38	494.57	522.96
12/2006	273.93	249.59	273.93	12/2009	374.14	291.95	339.74	12/2012	520.51	469.41	471.49
03/2007	323.87	269.31	323.87	03/2010	374.71	313.19	366.66	03/2013	488.72	453.94	475.59
06/2007	372.96	308.46	369.51	06/2010	398.63	365.25	379.09	06/2013	487.33	461.28	467.61
09/2007	382.52	347.36	371.21	09/2010	484.72	374.52	484.72	09/2013	489.51	455.84	471.44
12/2007	387.96	356.30	363.44	12/2010	495.40	435.94	478.28	12/2013	473.07	386.18	387.34

1967=100.   *Source: Commodity Research Bureau*

CRB SPOT LIVESTOCK SUB-INDEX

CRB BLS Livestock Sub-index Monthly Cash as of 12/31/2013				
Date	Open	High	Low	Close
08/30/13	639.21	639.21	623.75	637.12
09/30/13	638.55	645.28	619.06	619.06
10/31/13	620.77	620.77	560.42	567.92
11/29/13	574.97	605.12	569.25	605.12
12/31/13	606.27	606.27	542.95	547.76

MONTHLY CASH
As of 12/31/2013
Chart High 662.52 on 08/08/2011
Chart Low 114.10 on 12/14/1971

Annual Rate of Change % = -8.66

Unweighted Index of 5 Commodities: Hides, hogs, lard, steers, and tallow.

Annual High, Low and Settle of CRB Livestock Sub-Index   Index Value

Year	High	Low	Settle	Year	High	Low	Settle	Year	High	Low	Settle
1972	163.40	120.10	163.10	1986	276.80	217.30	268.07	2000	272.11	234.91	265.51
1973	336.50	161.10	224.60	1987	307.91	261.46	280.14	2001	348.32	244.00	257.21
1974	263.50	190.10	192.80	1988	319.70	257.00	285.74	2002	320.63	243.62	317.79
1975	264.80	185.10	210.00	1989	298.22	269.53	286.98	2003	400.83	301.67	365.87
1976	232.40	198.70	223.90	1990	310.15	275.28	292.73	2004	407.25	343.74	365.02
1977	256.20	216.50	234.40	1991	294.48	248.50	248.62	2005	390.12	322.62	326.62
1978	308.20	239.10	305.10	1992	296.91	247.91	286.64	2006	395.37	304.32	378.58
1979	380.50	290.00	300.30	1993	307.55	272.74	274.28	2007	468.30	372.22	402.56
1980	302.50	223.10	281.00	1994	321.75	276.72	319.33	2008	565.98	267.14	310.84
1981	295.00	259.80	264.20	1995	329.83	296.14	307.44	2009	416.68	268.02	407.63
1982	313.60	250.90	254.40	1996	399.67	292.73	363.01	2010	530.36	392.36	528.00
1983	323.90	250.20	303.10	1997	369.22	306.09	306.09	2011	662.52	533.39	575.35
1984	366.40	302.90	308.20	1998	320.31	201.75	232.28	2012	627.75	569.29	599.67
1985	310.60	245.10	271.10	1999	297.13	206.26	265.72	2013	646.63	542.95	547.76

1967=100.   Index data begins 01/07/1947.   *Source: Commodity Research Bureau*

266

Date	Open	High	Low	Close
12/06/13	606.27	**606.27**	585.79	585.79
12/13/13	582.61	585.42	579.81	579.81
12/20/13	577.68	581.80	544.67	545.87
12/27/13	545.87	546.15	**542.95**	545.77
01/03/14	548.12	552.00	547.76	552.00

Unweighted Index of 5 Commodities: Hides, hogs, lard, steers, and tallow.

Quarterly High, Low and Settle of CRB Livestock Sub-Index   Index Value

Quarter	High	Low	Settle	Quarter	High	Low	Settle	Quarter	High	Low	Settle
03/2005	369.79	333.63	363.04	03/2008	476.50	401.49	472.74	03/2011	622.33	533.39	622.33
06/2005	390.12	339.00	339.00	06/2008	549.60	460.62	549.56	06/2011	653.14	610.47	649.51
09/2005	358.65	322.62	347.21	09/2008	565.98	480.46	481.44	09/2011	662.52	616.89	638.73
12/2005	377.54	326.62	326.62	12/2008	477.40	267.14	310.84	12/2011	644.13	567.96	575.35
03/2006	337.79	311.11	313.84	03/2009	344.90	268.02	301.04	03/2012	626.84	569.85	594.73
06/2006	358.88	304.32	354.16	06/2009	379.67	300.94	360.44	06/2012	627.75	590.77	613.05
09/2006	395.37	353.32	380.75	09/2009	404.14	342.51	350.58	09/2012	618.70	575.07	587.93
12/2006	392.44	349.29	378.58	12/2009	416.68	345.76	407.63	12/2012	600.81	569.29	599.67
03/2007	429.22	372.22	429.22	03/2010	461.31	392.36	456.10	03/2013	613.89	573.33	586.31
06/2007	468.30	418.96	454.81	06/2010	507.51	456.64	472.64	06/2013	635.84	592.69	630.28
09/2007	466.94	435.38	445.91	09/2010	527.12	456.53	527.12	09/2013	646.63	619.06	619.06
12/2007	447.17	402.56	402.56	12/2010	530.36	465.13	528.00	12/2013	620.77	542.95	547.76

1967=100.   *Source: Commodity Research Bureau*

S&P GOLDMAN SACHS COMMODITY INDEX

S&P Goldman Sachs Commodity Index
Monthly Cash as of 12/31/2013

Date	Open	High	Low	Close
08/30/13	638.99	675.44	623.15	657.05
09/30/13	657.44	664.81	628.27	632.40
10/31/13	632.44	644.09	620.01	622.52
11/29/13	622.54	626.75	604.63	620.12
12/31/13	620.74	642.59	618.40	632.29

MONTHLY CASH
As of 12/31/2013
Chart High 893.86 on 07/03/2008
Chart Low 108.67 on 12/08/1971

Annual Rate of Change % = -2.21

Standard & Poor's GSCI is a registered trademark of Standard & Poor's Financial Services LLC ("S&P"), a subsidiary of The McGraw-Hill Companies, Inc.
Currently the S&P GSCI includes 24 commodity nearby futures contracts.

Annual High, Low and Settle of S&P Goldman Sachs Commodity Index   Index Value

Year	High	Low	Settle	Year	High	Low	Settle	Year	High	Low	Settle
1972	147.16	110.50	147.14	1986	193.08	144.33	159.27	2000	265.93	187.73	246.92
1973	234.93	144.31	218.73	1987	180.86	152.89	164.33	2001	250.40	160.12	169.15
1974	308.10	185.44	264.03	1988	184.41	159.39	184.41	2002	246.53	161.72	235.15
1975	264.03	179.07	183.46	1989	207.25	176.33	207.25	2003	284.61	211.63	260.54
1976	199.06	147.92	158.10	1990	270.41	181.56	219.97	2004	374.89	254.74	310.47
1977	176.66	137.03	159.33	1991	228.35	174.43	176.92	2005	478.08	301.32	431.72
1978	199.85	153.97	193.07	1992	196.04	171.70	181.01	2006	512.36	405.22	433.94
1979	239.61	189.20	237.81	1993	191.62	161.38	163.55	2007	623.63	389.81	610.17
1980	302.21	212.05	268.69	1994	185.01	163.41	180.84	2008	893.86	307.84	349.04
1981	274.33	199.09	201.65	1995	208.02	171.19	203.44	2009	529.46	305.59	524.62
1982	225.07	194.93	201.46	1996	229.87	182.66	215.26	2010	633.77	458.56	631.83
1983	221.08	195.05	216.14	1997	231.82	169.69	175.62	2011	762.22	572.92	644.91
1984	219.40	190.55	195.53	1998	177.62	127.94	133.02	2012	717.45	555.56	646.58
1985	202.14	172.26	196.04	1999	199.61	129.38	194.54	2013	681.70	596.36	632.29

12/31/1969=100.   Index data begins 12/31/1969.   *Source: CME Group; Chicago Mercantile Exchange*

S&P GOLDMAN SACHS COMMODITY INDEX

S&P Goldman Sachs Commodity Index
Weekly Cash as of 01/03/2014

Date	Open	High	Low	Close
12/06/13	620.74	634.34	618.40	631.94
12/13/13	632.31	633.62	622.11	623.59
12/20/13	623.95	637.12	622.95	637.10
12/27/13	637.03	642.59	634.89	640.67
01/03/14	640.60	641.90	614.09	614.43

WEEKLY CASH
As of 01/03/2014

Chart High 893.86 on 07/03/2008
Chart Low 211.63 on 04/29/2003

Index Value

Annual Rate of Change % = -4.99

Standard & Poor's GSCI is a registered trademark of Standard & Poor's Financial Services LLC ("S&P"), a subsidiary of The McGraw-Hill Companies, Inc.
Currently the S&P GSCI includes 24 commodity nearby futures contracts.

Quarterly High, Low and Settle of S&P Goldman Sachs Commodity Index   Index Value

Quarter	High	Low	Settle	Quarter	High	Low	Settle	Quarter	High	Low	Settle
03/2005	389.43	301.32	383.87	03/2008	722.65	575.83	668.91	03/2011	731.72	613.60	725.62
06/2005	400.58	337.98	380.05	06/2008	882.81	655.70	862.81	06/2011	762.22	635.27	668.85
09/2005	478.08	381.05	469.56	09/2008	893.86	588.48	622.24	09/2011	704.70	583.68	591.00
12/2005	472.38	405.91	431.72	12/2008	634.35	307.84	349.04	12/2011	674.10	572.92	644.91
03/2006	459.94	405.22	442.52	03/2009	383.84	305.59	358.53	03/2012	717.45	647.66	688.71
06/2006	500.53	438.71	484.68	06/2009	480.19	347.24	450.22	06/2012	702.09	555.56	599.44
09/2006	512.36	412.53	428.05	09/2009	481.22	398.37	462.75	09/2012	699.13	590.42	665.73
12/2006	465.28	406.37	433.94	12/2009	529.46	447.71	524.62	12/2012	674.77	622.45	646.58
03/2007	472.42	389.81	468.11	03/2010	550.38	468.44	530.16	03/2013	681.70	637.89	655.05
06/2007	499.11	456.86	489.15	06/2010	555.73	458.56	495.18	06/2013	655.95	596.36	611.30
09/2007	555.07	472.40	546.13	09/2010	547.01	478.84	546.06	09/2013	675.44	609.29	632.40
12/2007	623.63	526.36	610.17	12/2010	633.77	544.91	631.83	12/2013	644.09	604.63	632.29

12/31/1969=100.   *Source: CME Group; Chicago Mercantile Exchange*

DOW JONES-UBS COMMODITY INDEX

DOW JONES-UBS FUTURES
Monthly Cash as of 12/31/2013

Date	Open	High	Low	Close
08/30/13	126.890	**133.620**	123.600	130.440
09/30/13	130.440	132.010	126.630	127.110
10/31/13	127.110	129.110	125.190	125.220
11/29/13	125.220	125.450	**122.000**	124.210
12/31/13	124.210	127.980	123.440	125.750

MONTHLY CASH
As of 12/31/2013
Chart High 238.521 on 07/03/2008
Chart Low 33.426 on 12/01/1971
Index Value

Index Value

Annual Rate of Change % = -9.58

Dow Jones-UBS Commodity Index is a trademark of Dow Jones and UBS AG.
10/03/1933 to 12/31/1981 (1924-26=100) Adjusted; 01/02/1982 to 12/31/1998 (1974=100) Adjusted; 01/04/1999 to date (12/31/1990=100)

Annual High, Low and Settle of Dow Jones-UBS Commodity Index   Index Value

Year	High	Low	Settle	Year	High	Low	Settle	Year	High	Low	Settle
1972	43.60	33.93	43.51	1986	88.30	71.09	74.02	2000	116.09	90.75	114.61
1973	75.76	43.22	75.56	1987	87.46	72.11	86.45	2001	115.55	87.41	89.03
1974	102.00	67.83	84.22	1988	93.52	83.30	93.08	2002	112.78	87.37	111.25
1975	82.80	57.11	67.87	1989	93.75	81.75	82.67	2003	137.45	107.38	135.27
1976	87.87	67.70	86.63	1990	86.80	79.11	81.64	2004	159.96	136.55	145.60
1977	103.13	74.10	78.31	1991	83.84	76.16	76.77	2005	180.94	139.98	171.15
1978	94.37	77.25	90.43	1992	78.88	73.06	78.29	2006	188.11	154.64	166.51
1979	103.83	86.89	99.74	1993	91.25	76.59	91.25	2007	186.93	154.71	184.96
1980	119.10	98.30	109.58	1994	102.97	86.00	99.27	2008	238.52	105.88	117.24
1981	111.44	84.16	86.28	1995	100.17	93.38	93.55	2009	141.19	101.48	139.18
1982	90.15	74.74	89.13	1996	101.49	90.74	94.80	2010	162.56	121.19	162.39
1983	98.63	88.88	91.59	1997	106.89	90.08	90.08	2011	175.67	136.16	140.68
1984	93.87	78.85	79.70	1998	93.50	76.28	78.18	2012	152.71	126.22	139.07
1985	85.20	71.57	85.20	1999	93.15	74.24	92.27	2013	143.67	122.00	125.75

10/03/1933 to 12/31/1981 (1924-26=100) Adjusted; 01/02/1982 to 12/31/1998 (1974=100) Adjusted; 01/04/1999 to date (12/31/1990=100)
Source: CME Group; Chicago Mercantile Exchange

DOW JONES-UBS FUTURES
Weekly Cash as of 01/03/2014

WEEKLY CASH
As of 01/03/2014

Chart High 238.521 on 07/03/2008
Chart Low 101.479 on 02/20/2009

Index Value

Date	Open	High	Low	Close
12/06/13	124.210	125.880	**123.440**	125.380
12/13/13	125.380	127.230	125.380	126.110
12/20/13	126.110	127.730	125.580	127.580
12/27/13	127.580	**127.980**	127.190	127.610
01/03/14	127.610	127.830	124.660	124.900

— Annual Rate of Change % = -9.32

Dow Jones-UBS Commodity Index is a trademark of Dow Jones and UBS AG.   12/31/1990=100

Quarterly High, Low and Settle of Dow Jones-UBS Commodity Index   Index Value

Quarter	High	Low	Settle	Quarter	High	Low	Settle	Quarter	High	Low	Settle
03/2005	166.19	139.98	162.09	03/2008	220.57	181.06	201.60	03/2011	170.53	157.35	169.55
06/2005	163.28	145.73	152.89	06/2008	236.07	197.03	233.03	06/2011	175.67	153.84	158.13
09/2005	180.32	153.26	178.25	09/2008	238.52	166.78	167.78	09/2011	166.53	140.11	140.20
12/2005	180.94	162.05	171.15	12/2008	169.61	105.88	117.24	12/2011	151.34	136.16	140.68
03/2006	175.34	157.87	165.19	03/2009	123.79	101.48	109.78	03/2012	149.66	139.77	141.90
06/2006	188.11	164.39	173.24	06/2009	131.59	106.82	122.54	06/2012	144.06	126.22	135.42
09/2006	181.37	155.35	159.96	09/2009	133.10	112.60	127.68	09/2012	152.71	134.67	148.50
12/2006	175.58	154.64	166.51	12/2009	141.19	122.78	139.18	12/2012	149.90	138.21	139.07
03/2007	174.62	154.71	171.96	03/2010	145.11	125.56	132.15	03/2013	143.67	135.37	137.47
06/2007	177.10	167.43	169.67	06/2010	137.36	121.19	125.74	06/2013	137.10	124.43	124.46
09/2007	180.38	160.16	178.25	09/2010	140.69	123.40	140.29	09/2013	133.62	123.60	127.11
12/2007	186.93	171.88	184.96	12/2010	162.56	138.00	162.39	12/2013	129.11	122.00	125.75

12/31/1969=100.   *Source: CME Group; Chicago Mercantile Exchange*

INDICES - EQUITIES

Current U.S. Stock Market Outlook

The stock market enters 2014 near the top of a long bull market that started in early-2009 at the bottom of the financial crisis. The stock market in early 2014 is mildly stretched to the upside on valuation, which means that further stock market gains are likely to be more grudging. The slow improvement in the global economy is clearly a positive factor for stocks in early 2014 as is continued extraordinarily easy monetary policy in the U.S., Europe, and Japan.

However, the stock market faces some potentially large obstacles including the fact that the Fed during 2014 is expected to progressively end its third quantitative easing move and that the Fed by 2015 is expected to start raising interest rates. The stock market faces a tricky period that depends heavily on how deft the Fed is in slowly returning to a normal monetary policy.

U.S. Stock Market History

The nearby chart of the Dow Jones Industrial Average (DJIA) going back to 1900 shows the major phases for the U.S. stock market. U.S. stocks moved sideways in a volatile range during the 1900-1920 period. U.S. stocks rallied sharply during the Roaring Twenties, but then plunged in 1929-1932 during the Great Depression. U.S. stocks recovered later in the 1930s but then moved sideways during World War II. After World War II, the U.S. stock market entered a long-term uptrend, with sharp corrections in the 1970s and more recently in 2000-02 and 2008-09. The nearby chart of the S&P 500 of the post-World War II period shows how poorly investors did in U.S. stocks during the 1970s and early 1980s on an inflation-adjusted basis when stagflation prevailed in the U.S..

The main lesson from these long-term charts is that stock investors tend to fare very well during periods of stable U.S. economic growth and low inflation but that they fare very poorly during periods of stagflation such as in the 1970s or during financial crises such as the Great Depression or the 2008-09 banking crisis. The charts also show that the stock market occasionally goes through bubble periods, such as during the Roaring Twenties and in the late-1990s, which later prompt painful corrections.

1929 Stock Market Crash   — 47.9% > total − 90% (1932)
                                (1929)

During the period from 1900 to 1920, the Dow Jones Industrial Average (DJIA) traded in a wide and volatile range. Several times during this period the DJIA fell by about 40% (e.g., in 1902-04, 1906-08, and 1910-15), but always rallied back within about two years.

40%
3 X

After World War I ended in 1918, the U.S. stock market traded in a volatile range for several years but finally started to gather a head of steam after bottoming out in 1921. In fact, the DJIA from its low of 67.11 in 1921 more than quintupled over the following eight years to a record

1925 US low % to bail out UK or churchill gold dival

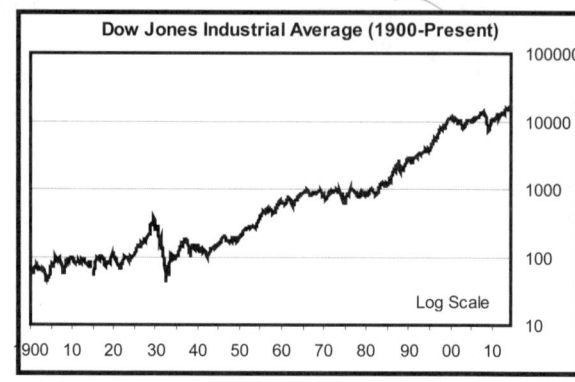

Dow Jones Industrial Average (1900-Present)
Log Scale

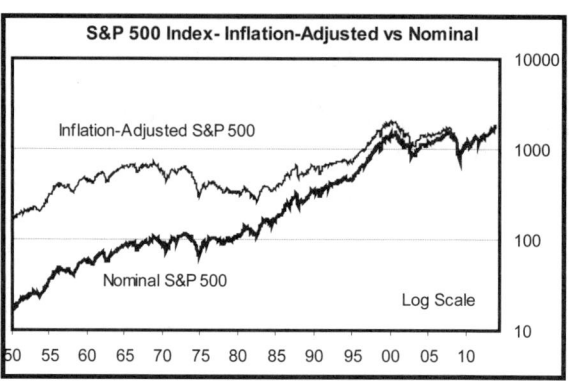

S&P 500 Index- Inflation-Adjusted vs Nominal
Inflation-Adjusted S&P 500
Nominal S&P 500
Log Scale

high of 381.17 in September 1929. The Roaring Twenties was a time of great optimism with World War I in the past and with American industrial activity and productivity rapidly expanding.

However, the 1929 Stock Market Crash brought the Roaring Twenties to an abrupt halt. The DJIA in just two days (October 28-29) plunged by an overall -23.6%. In the following two months, the DJIA continued lower for an overall sell-off of -47.9% from the peak. After a modest recovery in early 1930, the plunge resumed later in the year and the DJIA continued its plunge for another two years until finally bottoming in 1932 with a total loss of -90% from the 1929 peak. The 1929 Stock Market Crash helped set off the Great Depression, which of course, resulted in mass unemployment and poverty across America.

There were a variety of reasons for the 1929 Stock Market Crash including (1) rampant speculation during the 1920s and the use of excessive margin (up to 90%) to buy stocks, (2) overvaluation of stocks, particularly highly-levered public utility stocks and investment trusts, and (3) the Smoot-Hawley trade tariff bill which was passed in the midst of the crash and which would cause a plunge in world trade. + Fed - low % to bail out UK
                                                                    — secret function of UK peg b/ 1930!
                                                                    — reduce money supply by 1/3

After the 1929-32 crash, the U.S. stock market rallied through most of the rest of the 1930s as America slowly Gov't came out of the Depression and as the economy began to expand again. However, the DJIA would not exceed its 1929 peak until 2-1/2 decades later in November 1954.

Post-World War II Bull Market—1948 to 1973 + 675%

The post-war period was a golden age for the U.S. stock market. Stocks rallied sharply from 1949 to about 1966 as American business expanded its industrial base and profits. Moreover, macroeconomic conditions were very favorable with low inflation and low interest rates. The S&P 500 index rallied by a total of +675% from 15.51 at the end of World War II in August 1946 to the stock market peak of 102.24 seen in January 1973. That amounted to an average annual gain of +7.7%.

However, the stock market ran into trouble and turned sideways in the late-1960s on an inflation-adjusted basis as the U.S. began to run a budget deficit in order to fund the Vietnam War and President Johnson's Great Society social programs. The Federal Reserve monetized that deficit spending to keep interest rates low, thus allowing inflation to move higher. The U.S. CPI, which averaged only +1.2% in the first-half of the 1960s, started rising in 1966 and by the end of 1969 it was over +6.0%.

1973-75 Bear Market −(48%

U.S. macroeconomic conditions in the early 1970s deteriorated due to increased inflation, rising interest rates, and a decline in the dollar after the breakdown of the Bretton Woods agreement (which fixed the world's major currencies after World War II). The U.S. economy and stock market were then hit with a major shock from the Arab Oil Embargo in October 1973, which was retaliation against the U.S. for supporting Israel during the Yom Kippur War.

Crude oil prices (West Texas Intermediate oil) nearly tripled from $3.56 per barrel in July 1973 to $10.11 by early 1974. Crude oil prices then continued to rise steadily through the remainder of the 1970s, rising by another 50% to $15 per barrel by the end of 1978. The oil price shock caused inflation to soar from under +4.0% in 1972 to a peak of +12.3% two years later in 1974. The U.S. experienced a long and grinding recession from November 1973 to March 1975.

The U.S. stock market saw a serious bear market in 1973-74 due to the oil price shock and the U.S. economic recession. The S&P 500 fell by a total of -48% during the 1973-74 bear market, from a high of 120.24 in January 1973 to the low of 62.28 in October 1974.

While the S&P 500 rose in the latter half of the 1970s on a nominal basis and recovered most of the losses seen in 1974-75, the earlier chart of the inflation-adjusted S&P 500 shows that the U.S. stock market on an inflation-adjusted basis actually continued to grind lower through the latter half of the 1970s. Stock investors did poorly over that time frame due to high inflation and continued damage from high oil prices to the U.S. economy and to corporate profits.

The U.S. stock market then received another oil shock in 1980. Oil prices in 1979-80 more than doubled from $15 a barrel at the beginning of 1979 to a peak of $39.59 in June 1980 (which equates to about $112 a barrel in current dollars). That spike was caused by a near shutdown of Iranian oil production due to the Iranian revolution against the Shah of Iran.

Also during that time, Paul Volcker took over as Federal Reserve Chairman in August 1979 and started cracking down on the money supply to tame inflation. The Fed drove the federal funds rate as high as 20% in March 1980 and then again to 20% in May 1981. The combination of the oil and interest rate shocks caused double dip recessions in 1980 (Jan-July) and again in 1981-82 (July-81 to Nov-82).

The S&P 500 dropped by a total of -17% in Feb-March 1980, but then rallied through the remainder of 1980 as the U.S. recession turned out to be short. However, the S&P 500 then saw another bear market in 1981-82 totaling -27% (from 140.52 in Nov 1980 to 102.42 in Aug 1982) because of continued high oil prices and interest rates and the second phase of the double-dip recession.

1982 Bull Market Begins

Another golden age for the U.S. stock market finally began in 1982 after the Federal Reserve got inflation under control and U.S. interest rates started to fall. The devastating 1970s were finally over. The 10-year T-note yield, which peaked at about 16% in late 1981, moved lower through most of the 1980s and fell to 8% by 1990. The S&P 500 rallied sharply by a total of 229% from 1982 through 1987 (i.e., from a 102.42 low in August 1982 to a high of 336.77 in August 1987).

The infamous 1987 stock market crash then occurred on October 19, 1987, when the S&P 500 fell by -20.5% in a single day. The 1987 stock market crash of -20.5% was just slightly less than the 1929 Stock Market Crash of -23.6%, which was spread over two days (October 28-29, 1929).

The 1987 stock market crash was caused by a number of factors including (1) overvaluation in the stock market after the S&P 500 had rallied by 39% from the beginning of the year through the peak in August 1987, (2) the Fed's 150 basis point hike in the funds rate target to 7.50% in September 1987 from 6.00% in March 1987, and (3) suspicion that program trading and portfolio insurance worsened the slide due to sell stops and automated selling. The 1987 stock market crash was a global event as stock markets around the world also plunged (UK -26.4%, Germany -9.3%, Japan -14.9%, Canada -22.5%, Australia -41.8%, Hong Kong -45.8%).

While the situation looked dire at the time, Fed Chairman Alan Greenspan, who had been on the job for only two months, quickly stepped in to calm the markets. The Fed flooded the financial system with liquidity to prevent any banking system defaults. In addition, U.S. corporations also helped to stem the panic by announcing large stock buyback programs to show that they thought the sell-off was overdone and that their stocks were trading at unreasonably cheap levels.

The U.S. stock market after the 1987 stock market crash stabilized at its lower level very quickly. Within just two months the correction was over and the stock market was headed higher again. There was surprisingly little damage to the U.S. economy despite the huge loss in shareholder and household wealth that had just occurred. In less than two years, the S&P 500 had regained all of the losses seen during the 1987 stock market crash. While a momentous event at the time, the 1987 stock market crash is now just a blip in the overall 1982-2000 bull market.

The S&P 500 in July-October 1990 saw a brief 3-month downdraft of -20.3% due to America's first war against Iraq, which caused another oil price spike and a U.S. recession from July 1990 to March 1991. However, the S&P 500 was able to regain those losses within just four months.

The U.S. stock market in the first half of the 1990s benefited as the Federal Reserve continued to cut interest rates in response to an improved inflation situation. The S&P 500 rallied by a total of 64% from the low of 294.51 seen in October 1990 to the high of 482.85 seen in January 1994. Inflation fell from an average of 5% in 1989-90 to an average of 3% in 1992-96. That allowed the Fed to cut the federal funds rate target from 9.75% in early 1989 to 3.00% by the end of 1992 and the funds rate remained at 3.00% into early 1994. The 10-year T-note yield fell sharply over that period from 9% in 1990 to the 6-8% range during the 1994-97 period. U.S. GDP averaged strong growth of +3.6% in 1992-94. S&P 500 annual profit growth during the 1992-94 period was very strong at an average +14.3%.

Bubble Market develops in the late-1990s.

In the second-half of the 1990s, the U.S. stock market entered an accelerated bull market that took the market to new record highs. The S&P 500 rallied by a total of +238% from the beginning of 1995 to the then-record high of 1552.87 posted in March 2000. The S&P 500 in the second half of the 1990s (1995-99) showed an average annual gain of an eye-popping +26.3% (+34.1% in 1995, +20.3% in 1996, +31.0% in 1997, +26.7% in 1998, +19.5% in 1999).

The late-1990s was a time of great optimism stemming from the technology and Internet boom, a structural increase in productivity, low interest rates, and low inflation-adjusted crude oil prices. The U.S. economy performed very well in the latter half of the 1990s, averaging +4.0% annual GDP growth. Furthermore, average annual earnings growth for the S&P 500 companies during 1995-2000 was very strong at +12.6%, far exceeding the long-term average of +7.5%, as seen on the nearby chart.

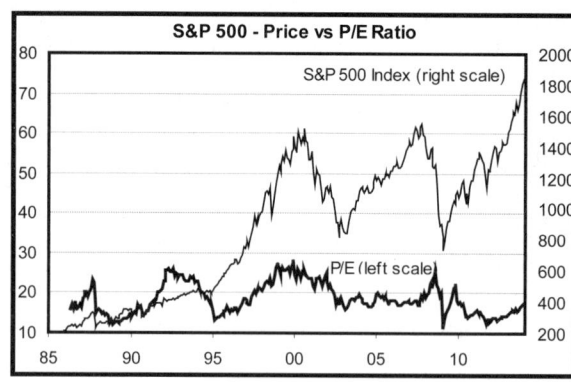

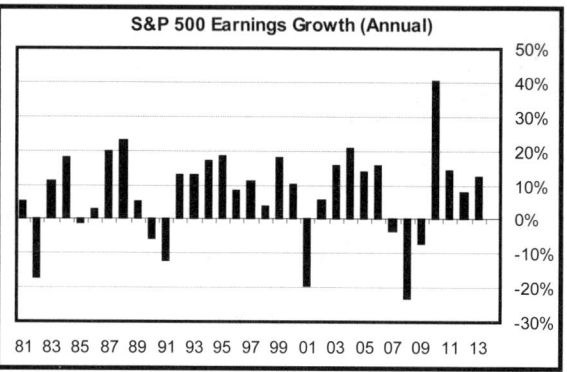

In addition, foreign investors piled into the U.S. stock market in the latter half of the 1990s, helping to drive stock prices even higher. Specifically, foreign ownership of U.S. equities more than tripled from about $500 billion in 1995 to $1.6 trillion in 1999. Foreign investors accounted for 10% of the ownership of all U.S. equities in 1999, up 4 percentage points from 6% in 1995.

However, speculative fever eventually drove technology stock prices too high during the 1995-2000 stock boom. The bubble in technology stocks is best demonstrated by the Nasdaq Composite index during the 1995-2000 period, which rose nearly seven-fold from 751.96 at the beginning of 1995 to the peak of 5,132.52 in March 2000.

As early as 1996, Fed Chairman Greenspan realized that an equity bubble might be developing. Mr. Greenspan, in a now-famous speech delivered on December 15, 1996, asked the question about how the Fed can know when "irrational exuberance" has "unduly escalated asset values."

By early 2000, stock market valuations had become extreme. The Nasdaq Composite was trading at a price/earnings ratio of about 150, meaning that investors were willing to pay $150 for each dollar of current earnings in technology stocks. The price/earnings ratio for the S&P

500 based on forward-looking earnings was trading at 26 in March 2000, which was far above the average P/E ratio of 18 seen in the pre-bubble 1985-95 period.

Equity bubble bursts, causing 2000-02 bear market

The U.S. stock market reached its peak in March 2000 and subsequently started its descent into the 2000-02 bear market. A variety of factors finally caught up with the stock market. Technology spending started slowing in early 2000 since corporations had already made their technology investments ahead of Y2K on fears of massive disruptions when the year 2000 began (which fortunately never occurred). In addition, the Fed raised its funds rate target by 175 basis points from 4.75% in mid-1999 to 6.50% in mid-2000. The U.S. economy also started to stumble in the latter half of 2000, with GDP falling -0.5% in Q3-2000. After the equity bubble burst, household wealth plunged and consumer and business confidence was severely damaged. A full-blown, though short, recession emerged from March to November 2001.

To make things worse, the S&P 500 index fell by -13.5% in the two weeks after the September 11, 2001, terrorist attack on the World Trade Center and the Pentagon. However, the S&P 500 more than regained its losses within a month as confidence returned.

The U.S. stock market finally bottomed out in October 2002. At the bottom of the bear market, the S&P 500 was down by a total of -50.5%, and the Nasdaq Composite was down by a total of -78.4%, from their record highs posted in March 2000.

2002-07 bull market

In October 2002, the U.S. stock market finally turned higher as the Fed's extraordinarily easy monetary policy started to stimulate asset prices, including home prices and the equity market. Moreover, U.S. consumer spending held up well and pulled the rest of the U.S. economy through the soft period seen in 2001-03. By the end of 2003, GDP growth had recovered and averaged a strong +3.5% in 2004-05.

Since the U.S. had escaped deflation and the U.S. economy was on the mend, the Fed in June 2004 started raising its funds rate target in 25 basis point increments at successive FOMC meetings. Over the 2-year period from June 2004 to June 2006, the Fed raised the funds rate target from 1% to a peak of 5.25%. The U.S. economy was resilient enough to absorb the Fed's slow tightening process and the U.S. economy performed well from 2003-05. The U.S. economy was also able to absorb the shock of crude oil prices more than doubling in price from $30 per barrel in late 2003 to a high of $70.85 in August 2005. The 2002-06 stock market rally was driven largely by a surge in

corporate earnings. U.S. corporations were able to produce double-digit annual earnings growth averaging +17.3% per year in 2003-05.

2008-09 financial crisis and bear market

The U.S. stock market started to run into trouble in mid-2007 when the sub-prime mortgage crisis emerged and two Bear Stearns hedge funds became insolvent in June 2007. In addition, BNP Paribas froze redemptions from three of its mortgage security hedge funds in August 2007. The U.S. economy started to weaken in mid to late 2007. The Fed responded by starting to cut interest rates in September 2007. The S&P 500 was able to make a last run to a record high of 1576.09 in October 2007, but the stock market then sank for the rest of 2007.

The year 2008 was tumultuous for the stock market. The stock market moved lower in early 2008 as the housing market crisis became worse with increased foreclosures, falling home prices, and huge losses for banks and hedge funds holding mortgage securities. The crisis finally reached epic proportions in mid-September 2008 when Lehman Brothers was forced to declare bankruptcy. The S&P 500 then went into a terrifying decline during September-November 2008, falling by a total of 42% from the August close to the 11-1/2 year low of 741.02 posted in November 2008. The 2008 plunge completely erased the 2002/06 bull market and left the S&P 500 back to where it was in 1997.

2009-2013 bull market

After bottoming out in March 2009, the S&P 500 began a long and nearly uninterrupted bull market totaling 172% that continued into late 2013. That rally was driven by the economic recovery that started in July 2009, near-zero short-term interest rates, and the Fed's extraordinary steps to inject a total of $3 trillion of excess into the banking system through late 2013.

Despite that rally, stock market valuation levels remained at reasonable levels because of a solid recovery in earnings during 2009-13. Corporate profits in fact recovered by a total of $1.1 trillion from a 7-year low of $1.0 trillion in Q4-2008 to $2.1 trillion in Q3-2013. The growth in corporate profits allowed stock prices to move higher without causing a large rise in the price/earnings ratio. The forward P/E ratio for the S&P 500 was mostly in the range of 12-14 in 2010-12, although it rose to 16 by late 2013.

DOW JONES INDUSTRIALS

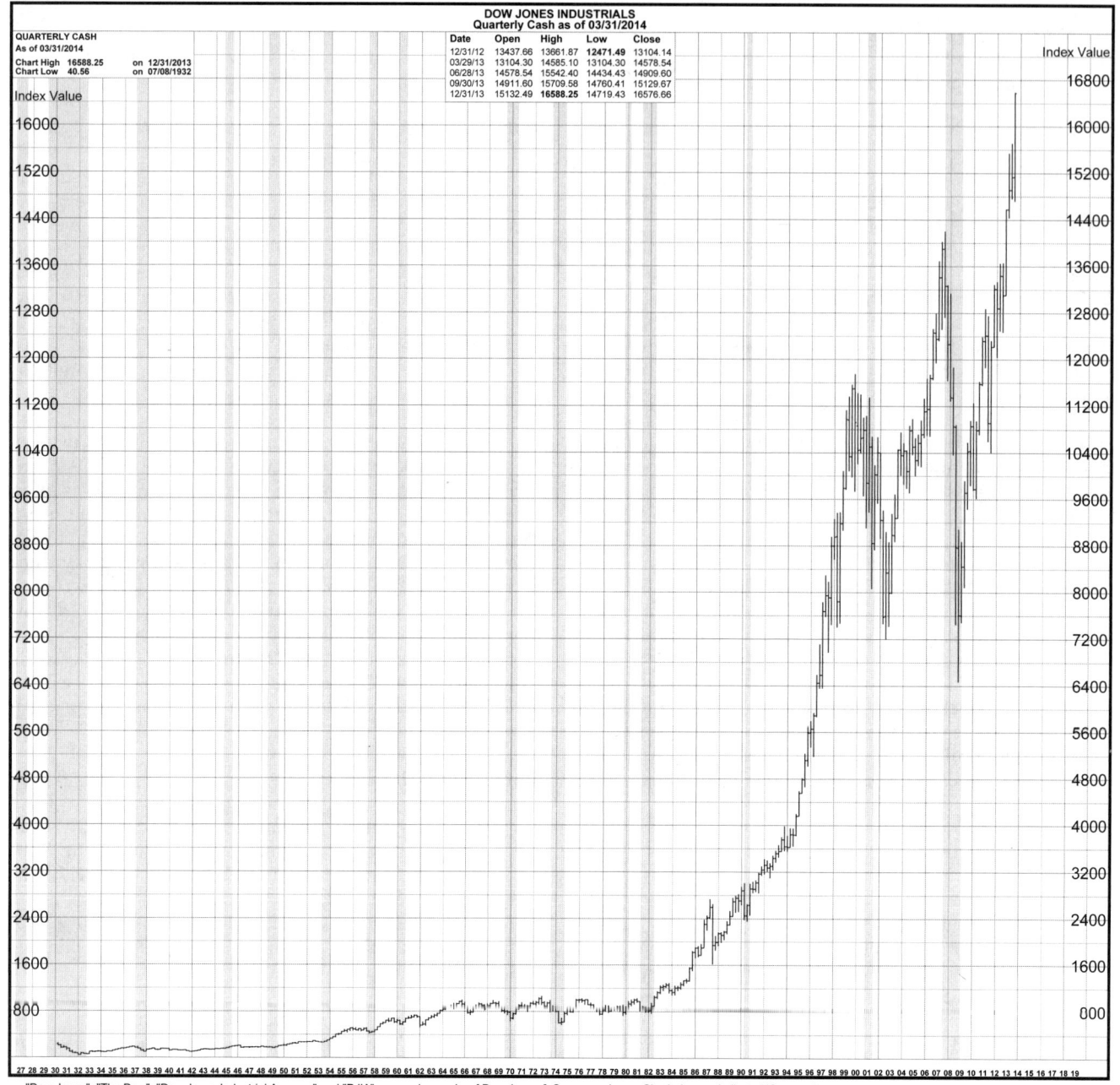

DOW JONES INDUSTRIALS
Quarterly Cash as of 03/31/2014

QUARTERLY CASH
As of 03/31/2014

Chart High 16588.25   on 12/31/2013
Chart Low   40.56   on 07/08/1932

Index Value

Date	Open	High	Low	Close
12/31/12	13437.66	13661.87	12471.49	13104.14
03/29/13	13104.30	14585.10	13104.30	14578.54
06/28/13	14578.54	15542.40	14434.43	14909.60
09/30/13	14911.60	15709.58	14760.41	15129.67
12/31/13	15132.49	16588.25	14719.43	16576.66

"Dow Jones", "The Dow", "Dow Jones Industrial Average" and "DJIA" are service marks of Dow Jones & Company, Inc.   Shaded areas indicate US recessions.

Annual High, Low and Settle of Dow Jones Industrials Index   In Index Value

Year	High	Low	Settle	Year	High	Low	Settle	Year	High	Low	Settle
1888	88.10	75.28	86.48	1902	68.44	59.57	64.29	1916	110.15	86.42	95.00
1889	73.26	70.72	72.17	1903	67.70	42.15	49.11	1917	99.18	65.95	74.38
1890	78.38	58.10	61.96	1904	73.23	46.46	70.05	1918	89.07	73.38	82.20
1891	73.25	61.50	72.88	1905	96.56	68.76	96.56	1919	119.62	79.35	107.23
1892	75.68	66.86	68.10	1906	103.00	85.18	94.35	1920	108.85	66.75	71.95
1893	70.87	43.47	51.35	1907	96.37	53.00	58.75	1921	81.50	63.90	80.80
1894	57.60	50.73	51.06	1908	88.38	58.62	86.15	1922	102.76	78.59	98.17
1895	63.77	48.56	52.23	1909	100.53	79.91	99.05	1923	105.38	85.91	95.52
1896	56.79	41.82	51.33	1910	98.34	73.62	81.41	1924	120.51	88.33	120.51
1897	55.82	39.13	49.41	1911	87.06	72.94	80.58	1925	159.39	115.00	156.66
1898	60.97	42.00	60.52	1912	94.15	80.19	87.87	1926	166.14	135.20	157.20
1899	77.61	58.27	66.08	1913	88.57	72.11	78.78	1927	200.93	152.73	200.70
1900	71.04	52.96	70.71	1914	83.43	53.17	54.58	1928	301.61	191.80	300.00
1901	78.26	61.52	64.56	1915	99.21	54.22	99.15	1929	386.10	195.35	248.48

Data continued on page 277.   *Source: New York Stock Exchange*

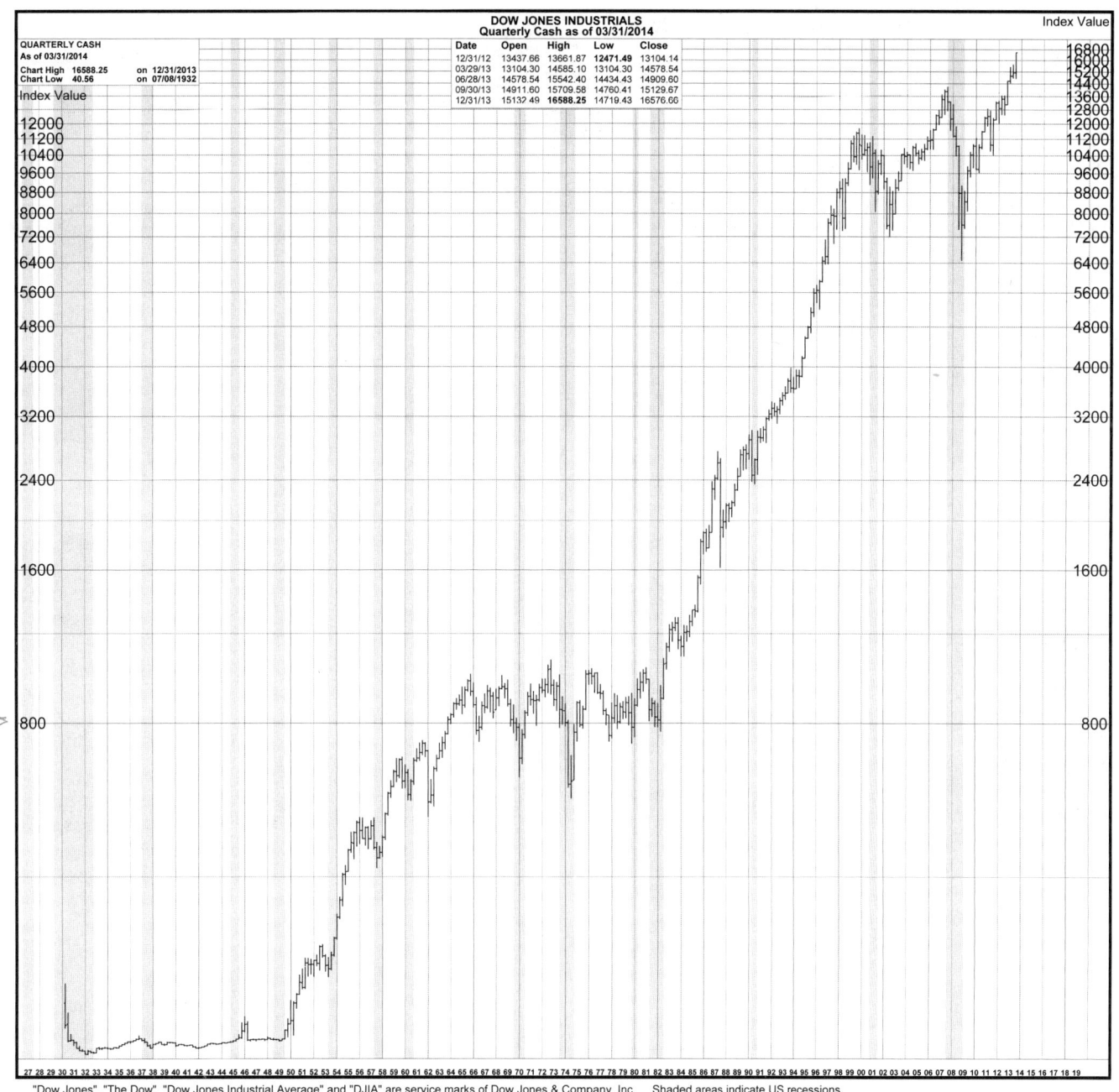

DOW JONES INDUSTRIALS
Quarterly Cash as of 03/31/2014

Date	Open	High	Low	Close
12/31/12	13437.66	13661.87	12471.49	13104.14
03/29/13	13104.30	14585.10	13104.30	14578.54
06/28/13	14578.54	15542.40	14434.43	14909.60
09/30/13	14911.60	15709.58	14760.41	15129.67
12/31/13	15132.49	16588.25	14719.43	16576.66

QUARTERLY CASH
As of 03/31/2014

Chart High 16588.25 on 12/31/2013
Chart Low 40.56 on 07/08/1932

Annual High, Low and Settle of Dow Jones Industrials Index   In Index Value

Year	High	Low	Settle	Year	High	Low	Settle	Year	High	Low	Settle
1930	297.25	154.45	164.58	1944	152.75	134.10	151.93	1958	587.44	434.04	583.65
1931	196.96	71.79	77.90	1945	196.59	150.53	192.91	1959	683.90	571.73	679.36
1932	89.87	40.56	60.26	1946	213.36	160.49	177.20	1960	688.21	564.23	615.89
1933	110.53	49.68	98.67	1947	187.66	161.38	181.16	1961	741.30	606.09	731.14
1934	111.93	84.58	104.04	1948	194.49	164.07	177.30	1962	734.38	524.55	652.10
1935	149.42	95.95	144.13	1949	200.91	160.62	200.52	1963	773.07	643.57	762.95
1936	186.39	141.53	179.90	1950	236.63	193.94	235.42	1964	897.00	760.34	874.13
1937	195.59	112.54	120.85	1951	277.51	234.93	269.23	1965	976.61	832.74	969.26
1938	158.90	97.46	154.36	1952	293.50	254.70	291.90	1966	1,001.11	735.74	785.69
1939	157.77	120.04	149.99	1953	295.03	254.36	280.90	1967	951.57	776.16	905.11
1940	153.29	110.41	131.13	1954	407.17	278.91	404.39	1968	994.65	817.61	943.75
1941	134.27	105.52	110.96	1955	490.75	385.65	488.40	1969	974.92	764.45	800.36
1942	120.19	92.69	119.40	1956	524.37	458.21	499.47	1970	848.23	627.46	838.92
1943	146.41	118.84	135.89	1957	523.11	416.15	435.69	1971	958.12	790.67	890.20

Data continued from page 276 and continued on page 278.   *Source: New York Stock Exchange*

"Dow Jones", "The Dow", "Dow Jones Industrial Average" and "DJIA" are service marks of Dow Jones & Company, Inc.   Shaded areas indicate US recessions.

DOW JONES INDUSTRIALS

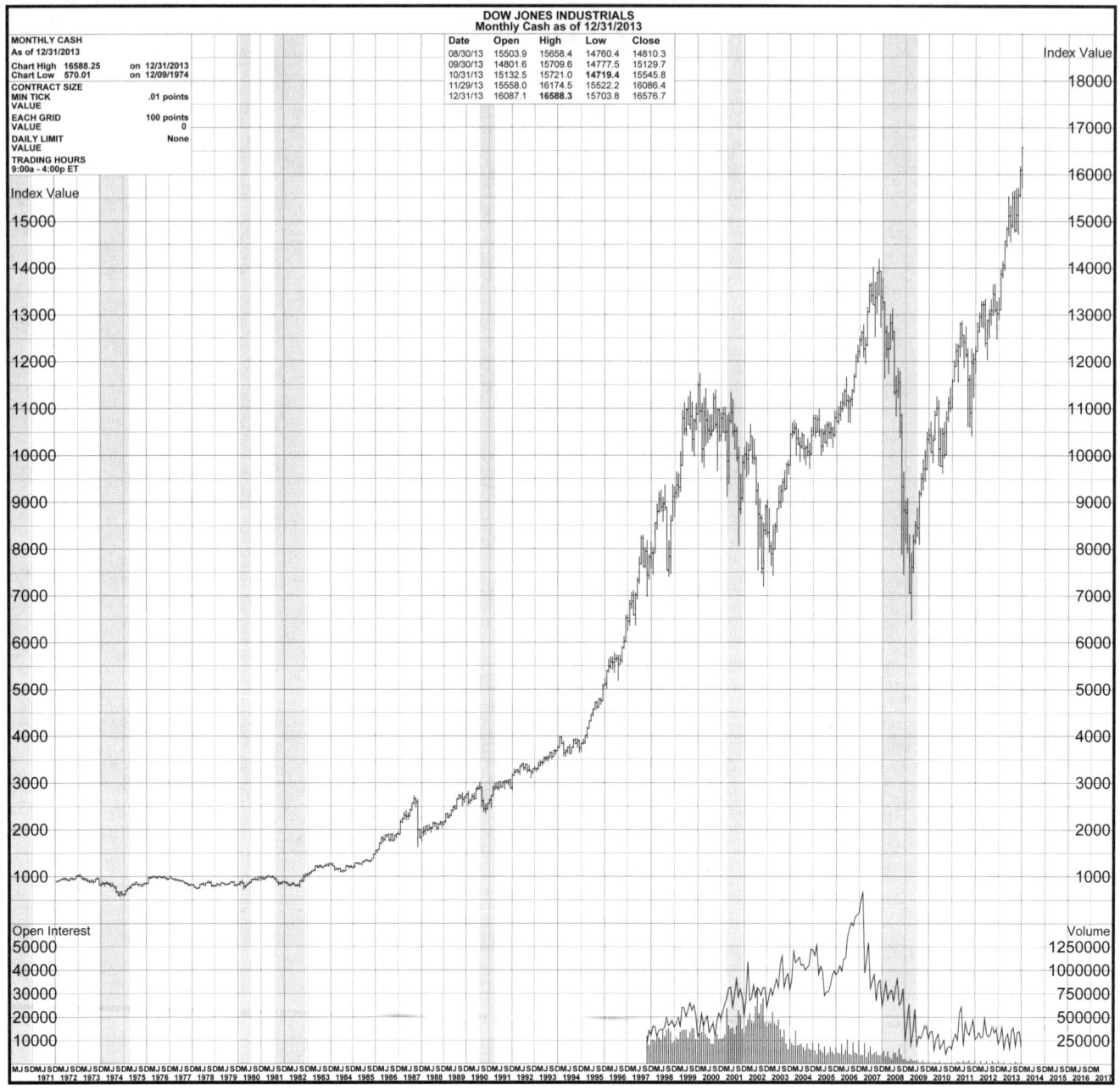

Annual High, Low and Settle of Dow Jones Industrials Index   In Index Value

Year	High	Low	Settle	Year	High	Low	Settle	Year	High	Low	Settle
1972	1,042.44	882.75	1,020.02	1986	1,961.47	1,497.71	1,895.11	2000	11,750.28	9,654.64	10,786.85
1973	1,067.20	783.56	850.86	1987	2,736.61	1,616.21	1,938.82	2001	11,350.05	8,062.34	10,021.50
1974	904.02	570.01	616.24	1988	2,188.04	1,850.96	2,168.57	2002	10,673.10	7,197.49	8,341.63
1975	888.85	619.13	852.41	1989	2,795.97	2,131.79	2,753.20	2003	10,462.44	7,416.64	10,453.92
1976	1,026.26	848.63	1,004.65	1990	3,010.64	2,354.21	2,633.66	2004	10,868.07	9,708.40	10,783.01
1977	1,007.81	792.79	831.17	1991	3,188.05	2,457.67	3,168.83	2005	10,984.46	10,000.46	10,717.50
1978	917.27	736.75	805.01	1992	3,422.01	3,095.80	3,301.11	2006	12,529.88	10,661.15	12,463.15
1979	904.86	792.24	838.74	1993	3,799.92	3,231.96	3,754.09	2007	14,198.10	11,939.61	13,264.82
1980	1,009.39	729.95	963.98	1994	3,985.69	3,552.48	3,834.44	2008	13,279.54	7,449.38	8,776.39
1981	1,030.98	807.45	875.00	1995	5,235.62	3,817.28	5,117.12	2009	10,580.33	6,469.95	10,428.05
1982	1,074.32	769.98	1,046.54	1996	6,589.53	5,014.52	6,448.27	2010	11,625.00	9,614.32	11,577.51
1983	1,291.67	1,020.24	1,258.63	1997	8,299.49	6,352.82	7,908.25	2011	12,876.00	10,404.49	12,217.56
1984	1,291.87	1,082.05	1,211.57	1998	9,380.20	7,400.30	9,181.43	2012	13,661.87	12,035.09	13,104.14
1985	1,563.76	1,180.99	1,546.67	1999	11,568.77	9,063.26	11,497.12	2013	16,588.25	13,104.30	16,576.66

Data continued from page 277.   Source: New York Stock Exchange

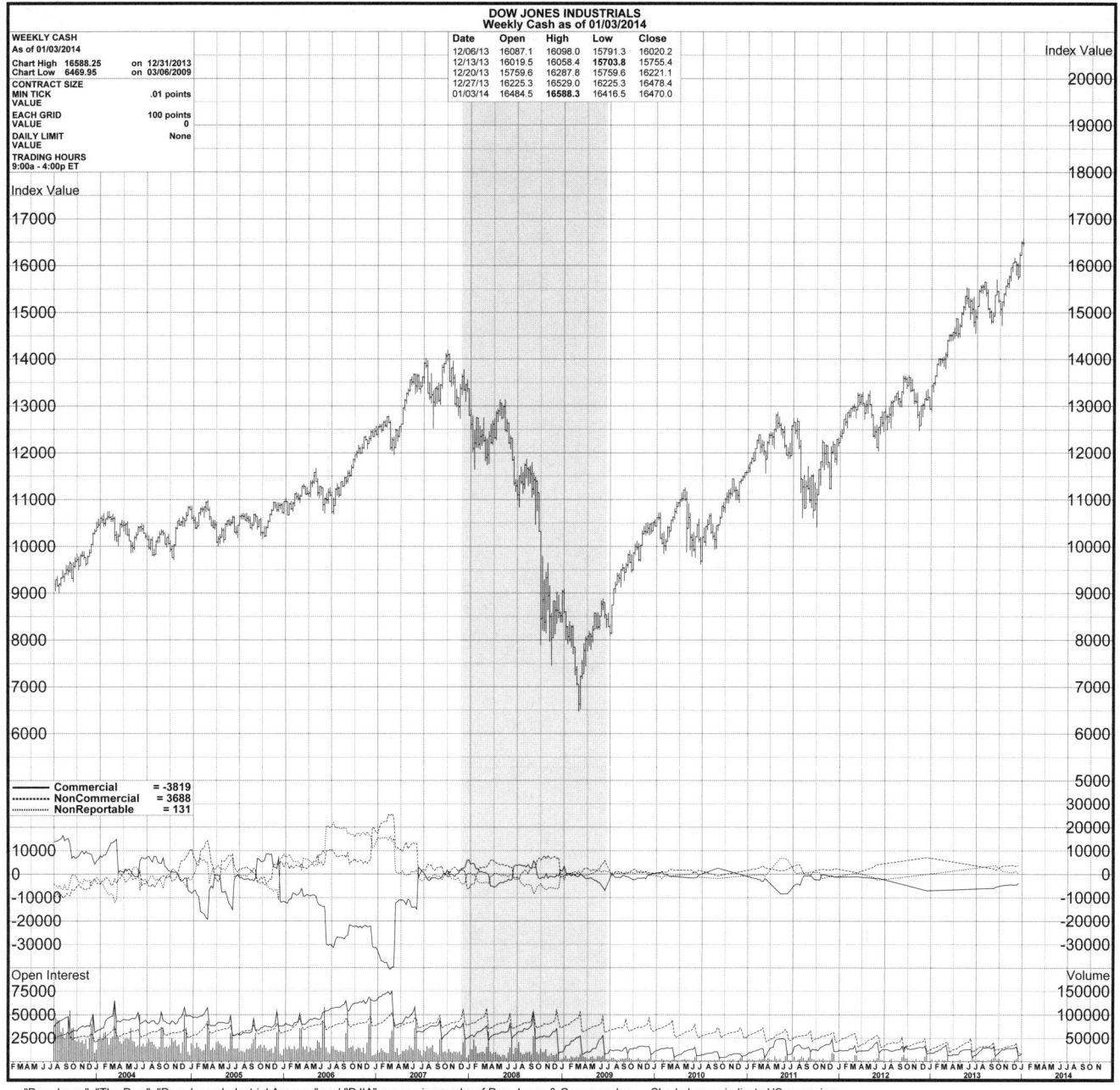

DOW JONES INDUSTRIALS
Weekly Cash as of 01/03/2014

Date	Open	High	Low	Close
12/06/13	16087.1	16098.0	15791.3	16020.2
12/13/13	16019.5	16058.4	15703.8	15755.4
12/20/13	15759.6	16287.8	15759.6	16221.1
12/27/13	16225.3	16529.0	16225.3	16478.4
01/03/14	16484.5	16588.3	16416.5	16470.0

WEEKLY CASH
As of 01/03/2014

Chart High 16588.25 on 12/31/2013
Chart Low 6469.95 on 03/06/2009

CONTRACT SIZE
MIN TICK VALUE .01 points
EACH GRID VALUE 100 points
0
DAILY LIMIT VALUE None
TRADING HOURS
9:00a - 4:00p ET

Commercial = -3819
NonCommercial = 3688
NonReportable = 131

"Dow Jones", "The Dow", "Dow Jones Industrial Average" and "DJIA" are service marks of Dow Jones & Company, Inc.   Shaded areas indicate US recessions.

Quarterly High, Low and Settle of Dow Jones Industrials Index   In Index Value

Quarter	High	Low	Settle	Quarter	High	Low	Settle	Quarter	High	Low	Settle
03/2005	10,984.46	10,368.61	10,503.76	03/2008	13,279.54	11,634.82	12,262.89	03/2011	12,391.29	11,555.48	12,319.73
06/2005	10,656.29	10,000.46	10,274.97	06/2008	13,136.69	11,287.56	11,350.01	06/2011	12,876.00	11,862.53	12,414.34
09/2005	10,719.41	10,175.40	10,568.70	09/2008	11,867.11	10,365.45	10,850.66	09/2011	12,753.89	10,597.14	10,913.38
12/2005	10,959.79	10,156.46	10,717.50	12/2008	10,882.52	7,449.38	8,776.39	12/2011	12,328.47	10,404.49	12,217.56
03/2006	11,334.96	10,661.15	11,109.32	03/2009	9,088.06	6,469.95	7,608.92	03/2012	13,289.08	12,221.19	13,212.04
06/2006	11,670.19	10,698.85	11,150.22	06/2009	8,877.93	7,483.87	8,447.00	06/2012	13,338.66	12,035.09	12,880.09
09/2006	11,741.99	10,683.32	11,679.07	09/2009	9,917.99	8,087.19	9,712.28	09/2012	13,653.24	12,492.25	13,437.13
12/2006	12,529.88	11,653.06	12,463.15	12/2009	10,580.33	9,430.08	10,428.05	12/2012	13,661.87	12,471.49	13,104.14
03/2007	12,795.93	11,939.61	12,354.35	03/2010	10,955.48	9,835.09	10,856.63	03/2013	14,585.10	13,104.30	14,578.54
06/2007	13,692.00	12,324.28	13,408.62	06/2010	11,258.01	9,753.84	9,774.02	06/2013	15,542.40	14,434.43	14,909.60
09/2007	14,021.95	12,517.94	13,895.63	09/2010	10,948.88	9,614.32	10,788.05	09/2013	15,709.58	14,760.41	15,129.67
12/2007	14,198.10	12,724.09	13,264.82	12/2010	11,625.00	10,711.12	11,577.51	12/2013	16,588.25	14,719.43	16,576.66

Source: New York Stock Exchange

DOW JONES TRANSPORTS

DOW JONES TRANSPORTS
Monthly Cash as of 12/31/2013

Date	Open	High	Low	Close
08/30/13	6472.87	6686.86	6237.14	6249.88
09/30/13	6260.13	6754.81	6239.90	6582.43
10/31/13	6588.32	7064.67	6401.51	6975.18
11/29/13	6985.76	7273.81	6935.70	7235.69
12/31/13	7240.49	7410.25	7036.12	7400.57

MONTHLY CASH
As of 12/31/2013
Chart High 7410.25 on 12/31/2013
Chart Low 124.30 on 10/04/1974

"Dow Jones", "The Dow", "Dow Jones Industrial Average" and "DJIA" are service marks of Dow Jones & Company, Inc.   Shaded areas indicate US recessions.

Annual High, Low and Settle of Dow Jones Transports Index   In Index Value

Year	High	Low	Settle	Year	High	Low	Settle	Year	High	Low	Settle
1972	278.27	210.19	227.17	1986	876.32	677.20	807.17	2000	3,017.18	2,260.78	2,946.60
1973	231.66	150.38	196.19	1987	1,104.19	653.86	747.86	2001	3,157.44	1,942.01	2,639.99
1974	204.89	124.30	143.44	1988	966.63	732.43	960.92	2002	3,050.98	2,008.31	2,309.96
1975	177.07	143.23	172.65	1989	1,540.54	946.14	1,177.81	2003	3,038.15	1,918.12	3,007.05
1976	238.06	172.07	237.03	1990	1,216.06	812.68	910.23	2004	3,823.96	2,743.46	3,798.05
1977	247.91	197.46	217.18	1991	1,358.55	887.37	1,358.00	2005	4,306.09	3,348.36	4,196.03
1978	264.95	198.19	206.56	1992	1,472.53	1,202.67	1,449.23	2006	5,013.67	4,059.87	4,560.20
1979	273.42	201.56	252.39	1993	1,789.47	1,441.18	1,762.32	2007	5,487.05	4,346.39	4,570.55
1980	430.18	229.79	398.10	1994	1,874.87	1,353.96	1,455.03	2008	5,536.57	2,909.29	3,537.15
1981	451.93	326.18	380.30	1995	2,105.19	1,443.62	1,981.00	2009	4,213.61	2,134.21	4,099.63
1982	468.90	288.97	448.38	1996	2,336.43	1,858.88	2,255.67	2010	5,123.52	3,742.01	5,106.75
1983	613.14	434.24	596.69	1997	3,372.42	2,203.27	3,256.50	2011	5,627.85	3,950.66	5,019.69
1984	615.19	439.61	557.68	1998	3,701.42	2,282.18	3,149.31	2012	5,390.11	4,795.28	5,306.77
1985	729.17	550.04	708.33	1999	3,797.05	2,778.56	2,977.20	2013	7,410.25	5,307.64	7,400.57

Source: New York Stock Exchange

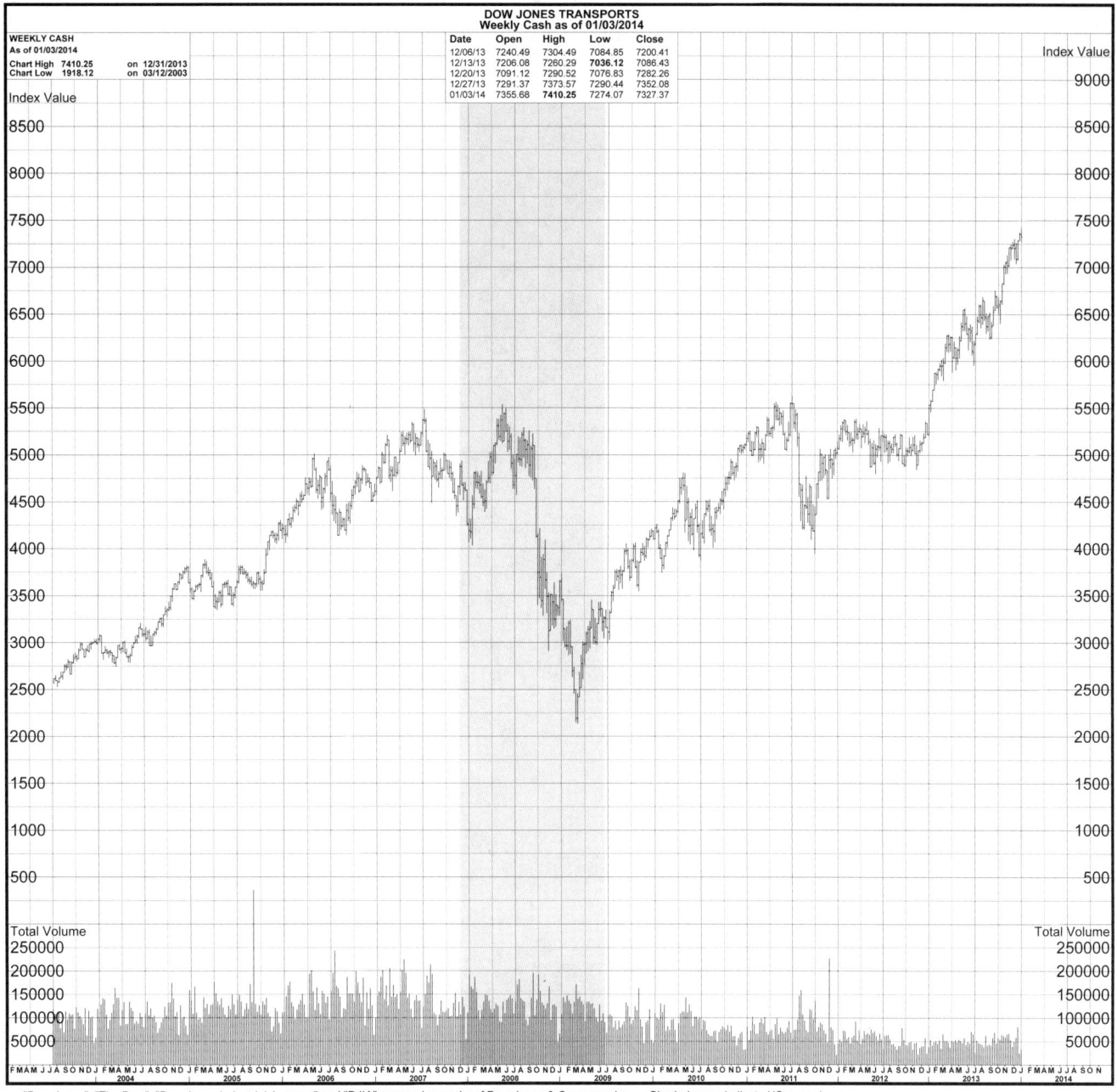

DOW JONES TRANSPORTS
Weekly Cash as of 01/03/2014

Date	Open	High	Low	Close
12/06/13	7240.49	7304.49	7084.85	7200.41
12/13/13	7206.08	7260.29	**7036.12**	7086.43
12/20/13	7091.12	7290.52	7076.83	7282.26
12/27/13	7291.37	7373.57	7290.44	7352.08
01/03/14	7355.68	**7410.25**	7274.07	7327.37

WEEKLY CASH
As of 01/03/2014
Chart High 7410.25 on 12/31/2013
Chart Low 1918.12 on 03/12/2003

Index Value

"Dow Jones", "The Dow", "Dow Jones Industrial Average" and "DJIA" are service marks of Dow Jones & Company, Inc.   Shaded areas indicate US recessions.

Quarterly High, Low and Settle of Dow Jones Transports Index   In Index Value

Quarter	High	Low	Settle	Quarter	High	Low	Settle	Quarter	High	Low	Settle
03/2005	3,889.97	3,454.74	3,715.97	03/2008	4,932.57	4,032.88	4,783.88	03/2011	5,328.39	4,906.63	5,299.89
06/2005	3,758.59	3,348.36	3,487.76	06/2008	5,536.57	4,779.33	4,948.03	06/2011	5,565.78	5,043.21	5,423.82
09/2005	3,821.96	3,473.33	3,740.55	09/2008	5,293.41	4,440.80	4,616.01	09/2011	5,627.85	4,095.81	4,189.37
12/2005	4,306.09	3,550.55	4,196.03	12/2008	4,623.59	2,909.29	3,537.15	12/2011	5,077.36	3,950.66	5,019.69
03/2006	4,615.83	4,059.87	4,568.00	03/2009	3,737.01	2,134.21	2,684.08	03/2012	5,390.11	5,003.63	5,253.16
06/2006	5,013.67	4,410.16	4,928.89	06/2009	3,458.23	2,621.70	3,234.56	06/2012	5,361.06	4,795.28	5,209.18
09/2006	4,975.56	4,134.72	4,453.46	09/2009	4,055.58	2,988.88	3,799.84	09/2012	5,265.80	4,870.74	4,892.62
12/2006	4,891.05	4,416.02	4,560.20	12/2009	4,213.61	3,546.48	4,099.63	12/2012	5,358.30	4,838.10	5,306.77
03/2007	5,211.42	4,564.56	4,810.70	03/2010	4,439.24	3,742.01	4,374.62	03/2013	6,291.65	5,307.64	6,255.33
06/2007	5,348.47	4,785.80	5,098.88	06/2010	4,812.87	3,983.18	4,007.84	06/2013	6,568.41	5,878.12	6,173.86
09/2007	5,487.05	4,486.60	4,836.32	09/2010	4,614.00	3,872.64	4,522.32	09/2013	6,754.81	6,170.31	6,582.43
12/2007	5,023.46	4,346.39	4,570.55	12/2010	5,123.52	4,417.93	5,106.75	12/2013	7,410.25	6,401.51	7,400.57

Source: New York Stock Exchange

DOW JONES UTILITIES

Within the chart:

DOW JONES UTILITIES
Monthly Cash as of 12/31/2013

Date	Open	High	Low	Close
08/30/13	505.22	509.49	474.13	477.87
09/30/13	479.61	497.98	467.93	482.29
10/31/13	482.38	509.30	476.97	499.87
11/29/13	500.49	510.49	485.57	487.13
12/31/13	487.13	491.57	476.05	490.57

MONTHLY CASH
As of 12/31/2013
Chart High 555.71   on 01/08/2008
Chart Low   57.10   on 09/16/1974

Annual High, Low and Settle of Dow Jones Utilities Index   In Index Value

Year	High	Low	Settle	Year	High	Low	Settle	Year	High	Low	Settle
1972	125.32	104.58	119.50	1986	219.75	168.09	205.84	2000	418.25	272.37	412.16
1973	121.45	83.81	89.37	1987	231.06	160.38	175.08	2001	412.48	270.26	293.94
1974	95.83	57.10	68.76	1988	190.02	166.25	186.28	2002	313.25	162.52	215.18
1975	88.19	69.53	83.65	1989	236.29	181.37	235.04	2003	267.90	186.54	266.90
1976	108.64	83.53	108.38	1990	236.23	188.76	209.70	2004	337.79	259.08	334.95
1977	119.09	104.23	111.28	1991	226.15	195.05	226.15	2005	438.74	323.79	405.11
1978	111.84	96.04	98.24	1992	226.02	200.23	221.02	2006	462.88	380.97	456.77
1979	110.86	97.70	106.60	1993	257.59	215.82	229.30	2007	555.07	443.78	532.53
1980	118.69	95.23	114.42	1994	229.77	172.03	181.52	2008	555.71	294.30	370.76
1981	119.42	99.75	109.02	1995	226.66	180.79	225.40	2009	408.57	288.66	398.01
1982	124.17	102.21	119.46	1996	239.59	202.84	232.53	2010	413.75	346.95	404.99
1983	141.14	119.37	131.89	1997	273.44	207.80	273.07	2011	467.64	381.99	464.68
1984	150.13	119.56	149.36	1998	322.21	260.51	312.30	2012	499.82	435.57	453.09
1985	174.96	146.03	174.70	1999	336.03	268.59	283.36	2013	537.86	453.29	490.57

Source: New York Stock Exchange

DOW JONES UTILITIES
Weekly Cash as of 01/03/2014

WEEKLY CASH
As of 01/03/2014

Chart High 555.71 on 01/08/2008
Chart Low 186.54 on 02/13/2003

Index Value

Date	Open	High	Low	Close
12/06/13	487.13	491.30	482.72	490.29
12/13/13	489.99	489.99	476.75	477.81
12/20/13	478.63	490.81	476.05	488.34
12/27/13	489.03	491.08	484.96	487.94
01/03/14	487.82	491.57	479.05	481.40

Index Value

"Dow Jones", "The Dow", "Dow Jones Industrial Average" and "DJIA" are service marks of Dow Jones & Company, Inc.   Shaded areas indicate US recessions.

Quarterly High, Low and Settle of Dow Jones Utilities Index   In Index Value

Quarter	High	Low	Settle	Quarter	High	Low	Settle	Quarter	High	Low	Settle
03/2005	363.82	323.79	358.33	03/2008	555.71	466.74	479.00	03/2011	422.43	394.11	413.06
06/2005	389.28	349.25	386.59	06/2008	530.57	479.61	520.85	06/2011	441.86	405.98	433.48
09/2005	434.91	379.53	432.38	09/2008	527.28	420.25	428.45	09/2011	449.09	381.99	433.38
12/2005	438.74	378.95	405.11	12/2008	431.65	294.30	370.76	12/2011	467.64	411.54	464.68
03/2006	427.50	388.79	389.01	03/2009	388.86	288.66	329.37	03/2012	466.79	441.88	458.93
06/2006	416.65	380.97	413.95	06/2009	360.58	324.39	357.81	06/2012	486.39	448.92	481.36
09/2006	443.49	411.81	428.40	09/2009	385.91	342.02	377.23	09/2012	499.82	466.37	475.75
12/2006	462.88	426.84	456.77	12/2009	408.57	359.33	398.01	12/2012	487.58	435.57	453.09
03/2007	505.15	443.78	500.18	03/2010	403.95	361.50	378.82	03/2013	508.79	453.29	508.40
06/2007	537.12	484.38	498.17	06/2010	393.89	346.95	357.74	06/2013	537.86	462.66	485.90
09/2007	521.32	460.68	501.54	09/2010	402.40	353.53	398.23	09/2013	510.43	467.93	482.29
12/2007	555.07	493.41	532.53	12/2010	413.75	387.88	404.99	12/2013	510.49	476.05	490.57

Source: New York Stock Exchange

CBOE VOLATILITY INDEX (VIX)

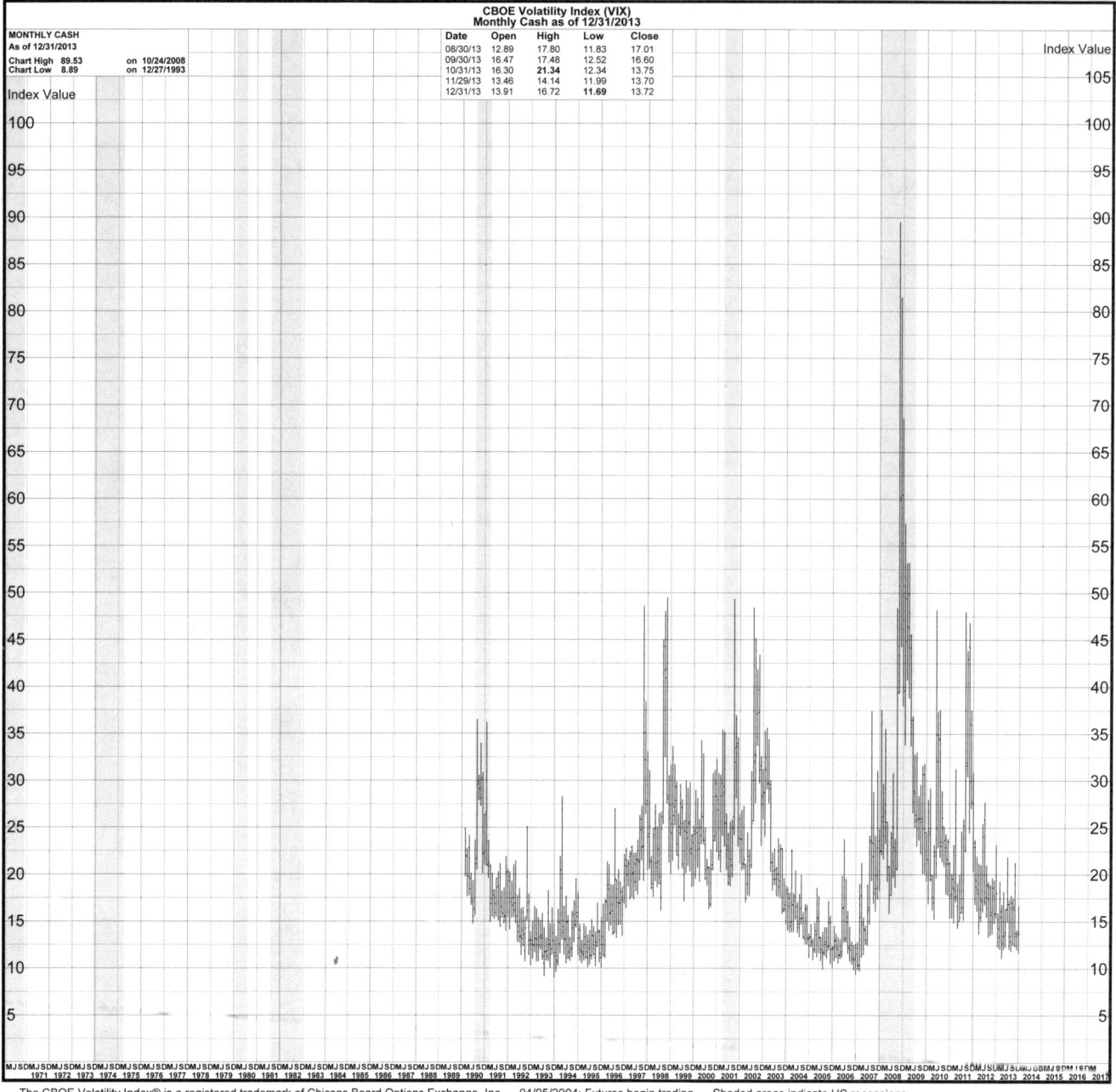

CBOE Volatility Index (VIX) Monthly Cash as of 12/31/2013				
Date	Open	High	Low	Close
08/30/13	12.89	17.80	11.83	17.01
09/30/13	16.47	17.48	12.52	16.60
10/31/13	16.30	21.34	12.34	13.75
11/29/13	13.46	14.14	11.99	13.70
12/31/13	13.91	16.72	11.69	13.72

MONTHLY CASH
As of 12/31/2013

Chart High 89.53 on 10/24/2008
Chart Low 8.89 on 12/27/1993

The CBOE Volatility Index® is a registered trademark of Chicago Board Options Exchange, Inc.   04/05/2004: Futures begin trading.   Shaded areas indicate US recessions.

Annual High, Low and Settle of CBOE Volatility Index (VIX)   In Index Value

Year	High	Low	Settle	Year	High	Low	Settle	Year	High	Low	Settle
1972	----	----	----	1986	28.41	15.75	18.71	2000	41.53	18.06	30.23
1973	----	----	----	1987 >	172.79	10.43	39.45	2001	57.31	20.26	23.22
1974	----	----	----	1988	52.60	15.22	18.53	2002	56.74	18.87	32.03
1975	----	----	----	1989	51.71	11.60	17.39	2003	41.16	14.83	18.31
1976	----	----	----	1990	40.01	15.51	23.55	2004	22.67	11.14	13.29
1977	----	----	----	1991	38.21	12.16	20.17	2005	18.59	9.88	12.07
1978	----	----	----	1992	27.28	11.89	13.55	2006	23.81	8.60	11.56
1979	----	----	----	1993	18.00	8.86	11.46	2007	37.50	9.70	22.50
1980	----	----	----	1994	25.31	9.25	13.44	2008 ⌐	89.53	15.82	40.00
1981	----	----	----	1995	18.27	10.41	13.89	2009	57.36	19.25	21.68
1982	----	----	----	1996	28.45	12.66	21.67	2010	48.20	15.23	17.75
1983	----	----	----	1997	55.48	13.24	24.89	2011	48.00	14.27	23.40
1984	----	----	----	1998	60.63	16.73	25.41	2012	27.73	13.30	18.02
1985	----	----	----	1999	36.79	17.70	26.71	2013	21.91	11.05	13.72

Index data begins 01/02/1990.   *Source: Chicago Board of Options Exchange*

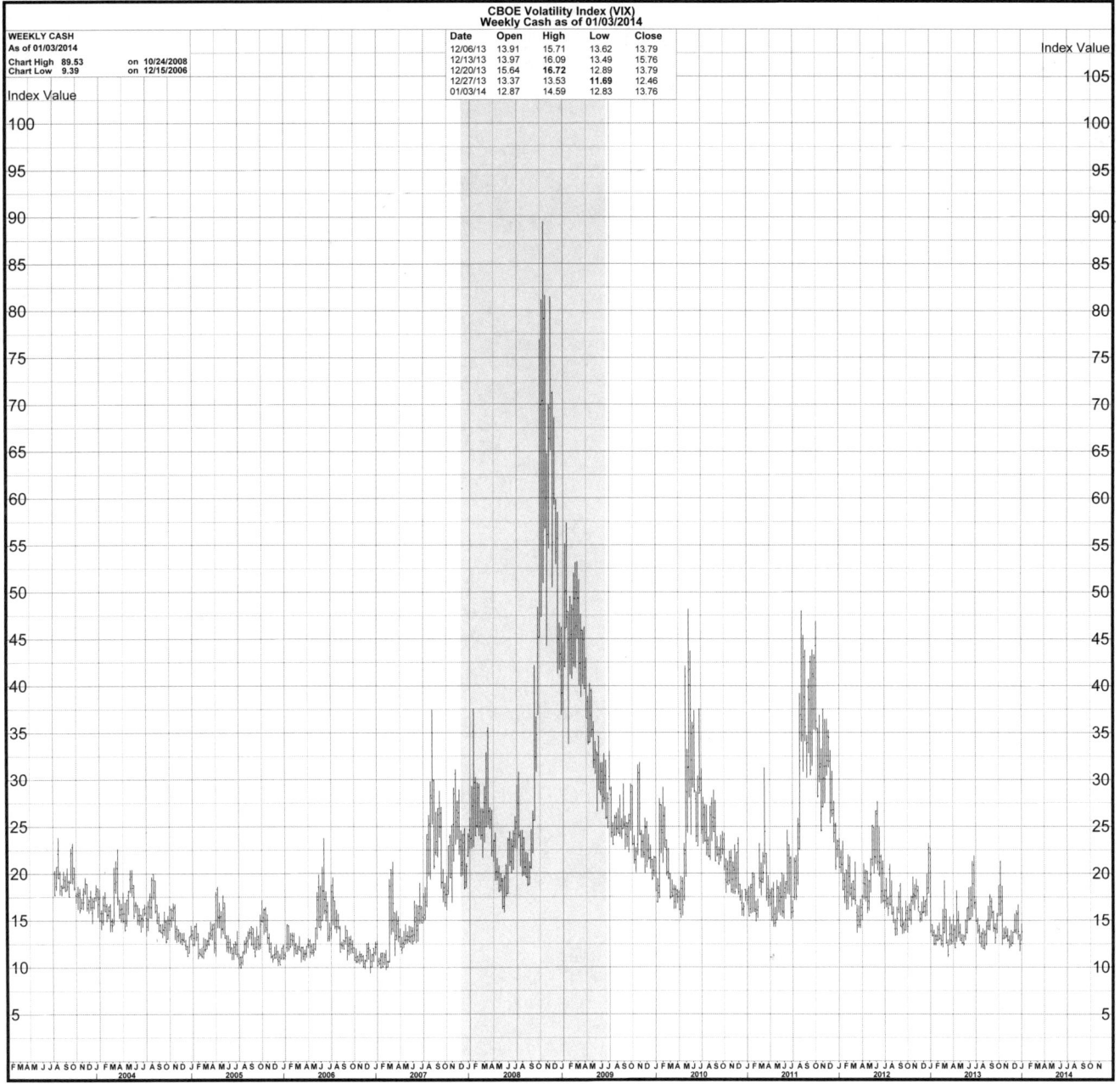

		CBOE Volatility Index (VIX) Weekly Cash as of 01/03/2014			
Date	**Open**	**High**	**Low**	**Close**	
12/06/13	13.91	15.71	13.62	13.79	
12/13/13	13.97	16.09	13.49	15.76	
12/20/13	15.64	16.72	12.89	13.79	
12/27/13	13.37	13.53	11.69	12.46	
01/03/14	12.87	14.59	12.83	13.76	

WEEKLY CASH
As of 01/03/2014
Chart High 89.53 on 10/24/2008
Chart Low 9.39 on 12/15/2006

The CBOE Volatility Index® is a registered trademark of Chicago Board Options Exchange, Inc. 04/05/2004: Futures begin trading. Shaded areas indicate US recessions.

Quarterly High, Low and Settle of CBOE Volatility Index (VIX) In Index Value

Quarter	High	Low	Settle	Quarter	High	Low	Settle	Quarter	High	Low	Settle
03/2005	14.89	10.90	14.02	03/2008	37.57	21.64	25.61	03/2011	31.28	14.86	17.74
06/2005	18.59	10.78	12.04	06/2008	25.61	15.82	23.95	06/2011	24.65	14.27	16.52
09/2005	14.41	9.88	11.92	09/2008	48.40	18.64	39.39	09/2011	48.00	15.12	42.96
12/2005	16.47	10.15	12.07	12/2008	89.53	37.96	40.00	12/2011	46.88	20.34	23.40
03/2006	14.56	10.53	11.39	03/2009	57.36	33.76	44.14	03/2012	23.73	13.66	15.50
06/2006	23.81	11.02	13.08	06/2009	45.60	25.02	26.35	06/2012	27.73	15.02	17.08
09/2006	19.58	10.74	11.98	09/2009	33.05	22.19	25.61	09/2012	21.00	13.30	15.73
12/2006	12.91	8.60	11.56	12/2009	31.84	19.25	21.68	12/2012	23.23	13.67	18.02
03/2007	21.25	9.70	14.64	03/2010	29.22	16.17	17.59	03/2013	19.27	11.05	12.70
06/2007	18.98	11.46	16.23	06/2010	48.20	15.23	34.54	06/2013	21.91	11.99	16.86
09/2007	37.50	14.67	18.00	09/2010	37.58	20.85	23.70	09/2013	17.80	11.83	16.60
12/2007	31.09	16.08	22.50	12/2010	24.34	15.40	17.75	12/2013	21.34	11.69	13.72

Source: Chicago Board of Options Exchange

NASDAQ 100 INDEX

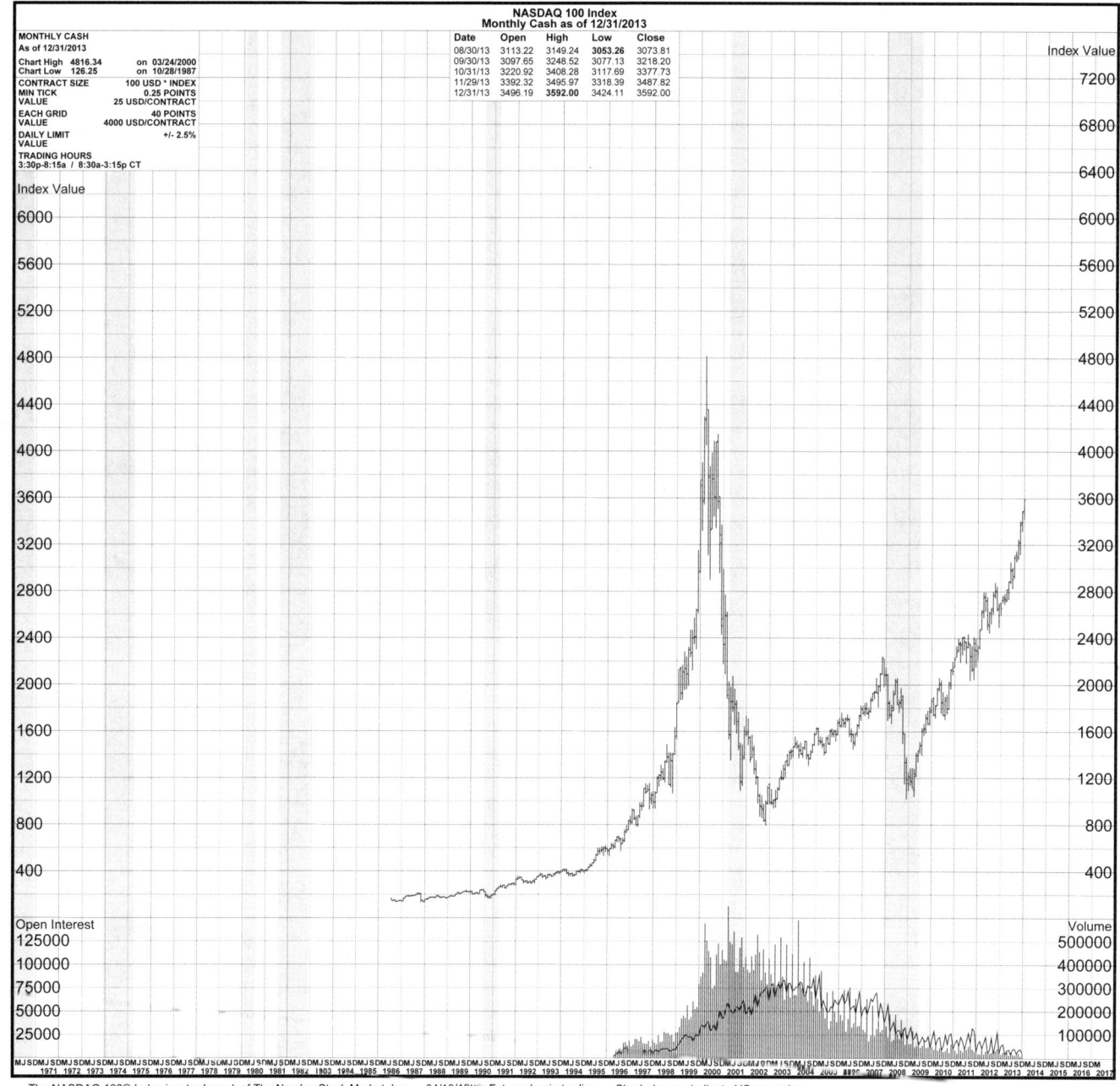

MONTHLY CASH
As of 12/31/2013

Chart High 4816.34 on 03/24/2000
Chart Low 126.25 on 10/28/1987

CONTRACT SIZE	100 USD * INDEX
MIN TICK	0.25 POINTS
VALUE	25 USD/CONTRACT
EACH GRID	40 POINTS
VALUE	4000 USD/CONTRACT
DAILY LIMIT	+/- 2.5%
VALUE	

TRADING HOURS
3:30p-8:15a / 8:30a-3:15p CT

NASDAQ 100 Index
Monthly Cash as of 12/31/2013

Date	Open	High	Low	Close
08/30/13	3113.22	3149.24	3053.26	3073.81
09/30/13	3097.65	3248.52	3077.13	3218.20
10/31/13	3220.92	3408.28	3117.69	3377.73
11/29/13	3392.32	3495.97	3318.39	3487.82
12/31/13	3496.19	3592.00	3424.11	3592.00

The NASDAQ 100® Index is a trademark of The Nasdaq Stock Market, Inc.   04/10/1996: Futures begin trading.   Shaded areas indicate US recessions.

Annual High, Low and Settle of NASDAQ 100 Index   In Index Value

Year	High	Low	Settle	Year	High	Low	Settle	Year	High	Low	Settle
1972	----	----	----	1986	164.55	133.28	141.41	2000	4,816.34	2,174.76	2,341.70
1973	----	----	----	1987	214.03	126.25	156.25	2001	2,771.63	1,088.96	1,577.05
1974	----	----	----	1988	192.77	151.57	177.41	2002	1,710.23	795.25	984.36
1975	----	----	----	1989	238.85	172.95	223.84	2003	1,474.24	938.52	1,467.92
1976	----	----	----	1990	246.82	162.55	200.53	2004	1,635.70	1,302.03	1,621.12
1977	----	----	----	1991	332.67	190.90	330.70	2005	1,716.65	1,394.49	1,645.20
1978	----	----	----	1992	363.20	287.67	360.19	2006	1,824.21	1,446.77	1,756.90
1979	----	----	----	1993	401.81	326.56	398.28	2007	2,239.23	1,710.97	2,084.93
1980	----	----	----	1994	418.99	350.03	404.27	2008	2,094.22	1,018.86	1,211.65
1981	----	----	----	1995	623.53	394.59	576.23	2009	1,882.58	1,040.41	1,860.31
1982	----	----	----	1996	873.00	526.80	821.36	2010	2,238.92	1,700.04	2,217.86
1983	----	----	----	1997	1,153.89	779.17	990.80	2011	2,438.44	2,034.92	2,277.83
1984	----	----	----	1998	1,848.36	933.01	1,836.03	2012	2,878.38	2,307.56	2,660.93
1985	----	----	----	1999	3,750.41	1,838.65	3,707.83	2013	3,592.00	2,689.83	3,592.00

Index data begins 06/19/1986.   *Source: NASDAQ*

286

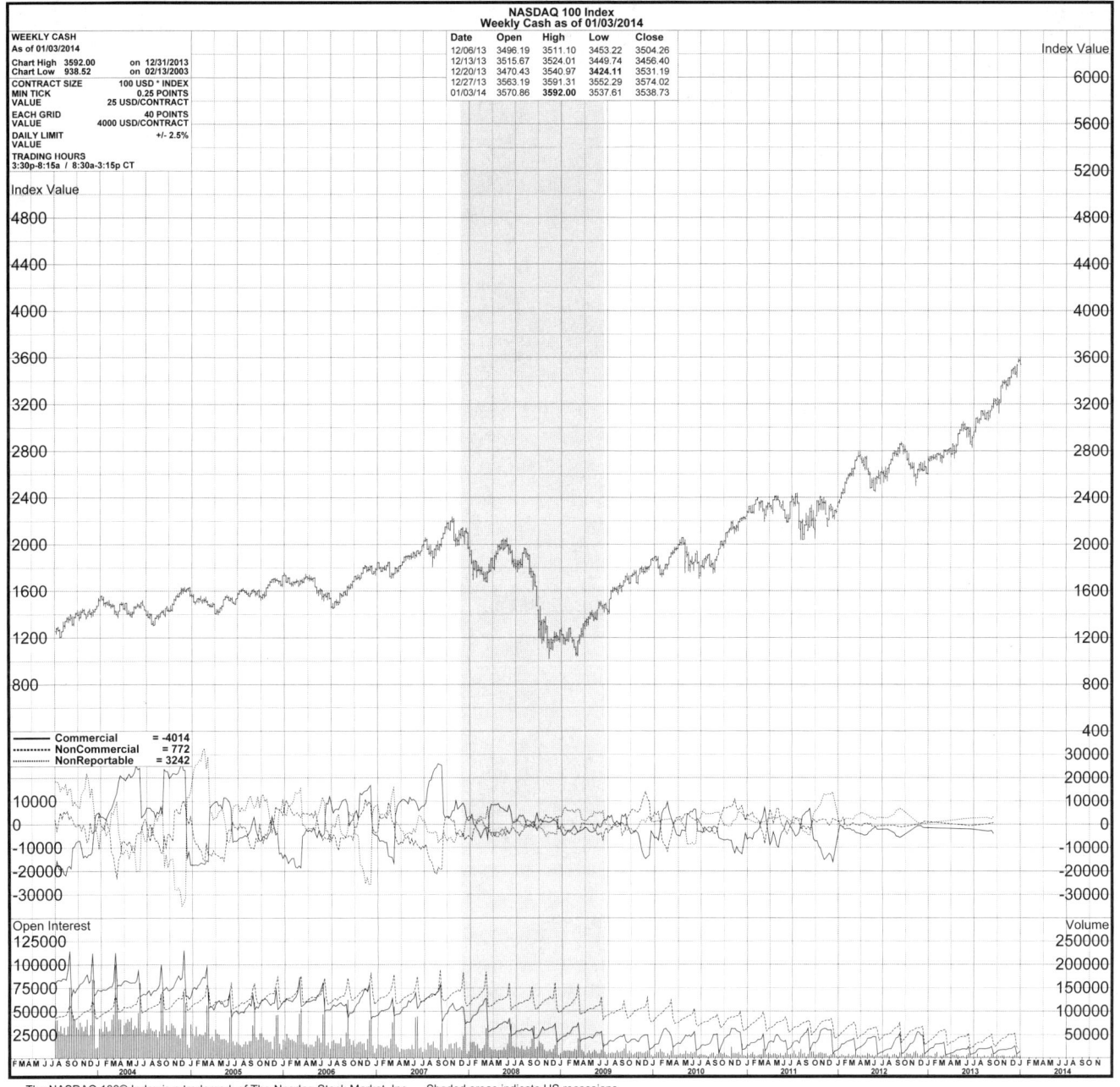

NASDAQ 100 Index
Weekly Cash as of 01/03/2014

Date	Open	High	Low	Close
12/06/13	3496.19	3511.10	3453.22	3504.26
12/13/13	3515.67	3524.01	3449.74	3456.40
12/20/13	3470.43	3540.97	3424.11	3531.19
12/27/13	3563.19	3591.31	3552.29	3574.02
01/03/14	3570.86	3592.00	3537.61	3538.73

WEEKLY CASH
As of 01/03/2014

Chart High 3592.00 on 12/31/2013
Chart Low 938.52 on 02/13/2003

CONTRACT SIZE	100 USD * INDEX
MIN TICK	0.25 POINTS
VALUE	25 USD/CONTRACT
EACH GRID	40 POINTS
VALUE	4000 USD/CONTRACT
DAILY LIMIT	+/- 2.5%
VALUE	

TRADING HOURS
3:30p-8:15a / 8:30a-3:15p CT

Commercial = -4014
NonCommercial = 772
NonReportable = 3242

The NASDAQ 100® Index is a trademark of The Nasdaq Stock Market, Inc.   Shaded areas indicate US recessions.

Quarterly High, Low and Settle of NASDAQ 100 Index   In Index Value

Quarter	High	Low	Settle	Quarter	High	Low	Settle	Quarter	High	Low	Settle
03/2005	1,635.45	1,458.26	1,482.53	03/2008	2,094.22	1,668.57	1,781.93	03/2011	2,403.52	2,188.92	2,338.99
06/2005	1,568.96	1,394.49	1,493.52	06/2008	2,055.82	1,776.60	1,837.09	06/2011	2,417.83	2,180.94	2,325.07
09/2005	1,628.57	1,484.46	1,601.66	09/2008	1,973.56	1,496.15	1,584.60	09/2011	2,438.44	2,034.92	2,139.18
12/2005	1,716.65	1,515.75	1,645.20	12/2008	1,584.26	1,018.86	1,211.65	12/2011	2,412.52	2,042.90	2,277.83
03/2006	1,761.46	1,633.71	1,703.66	03/2009	1,286.90	1,040.41	1,237.01	03/2012	2,794.00	2,307.56	2,755.27
06/2006	1,750.23	1,511.53	1,575.23	06/2009	1,511.94	1,211.60	1,477.25	06/2012	2,795.35	2,443.92	2,615.72
09/2006	1,666.03	1,446.77	1,654.13	09/2009	1,754.54	1,394.87	1,718.99	09/2012	2,878.38	2,522.89	2,799.19
12/2006	1,824.21	1,623.07	1,756.90	12/2009	1,882.58	1,652.44	1,860.31	12/2012	2,845.97	2,494.38	2,660.93
03/2007	1,851.47	1,710.97	1,772.36	03/2010	1,976.38	1,712.89	1,958.34	03/2013	2,820.67	2,689.83	2,818.69
06/2007	1,948.58	1,761.65	1,934.10	06/2010	2,059.42	1,734.90	1,739.14	06/2013	3,053.51	2,730.97	2,909.60
09/2007	2,101.96	1,805.66	2,091.11	09/2010	2,029.65	1,700.04	1,998.04	09/2013	3,248.52	2,913.48	3,218.20
12/2007	2,239.23	1,980.18	2,084.93	12/2010	2,238.92	1,963.68	2,217.86	12/2013	3,592.00	3,117.69	3,592.00

Source: NASDAQ

NASDAQ COMPOSITE INDEX

NASDAQ Composite Index
Monthly Cash as of 12/31/2013

MONTHLY CASH
As of 12/31/2013

Chart High 5132.52 on 03/10/2000
Chart Low 54.87 on 10/03/1974

Index Value

Date	Open	High	Low	Close
08/30/13	3654.18	3694.19	3573.57	3589.87
09/30/13	3622.64	3798.76	3593.62	3771.48
10/31/13	3774.18	3966.71	3650.03	3919.71
11/29/13	3932.45	4069.70	3855.07	4059.89
12/31/13	4065.66	4177.73	3981.22	4176.59

Shaded areas indicate US recessions.

Annual High, Low and Settle of NASDAQ Composite Index   In Index Value

Year	High	Low	Settle	Year	High	Low	Settle	Year	High	Low	Settle
1972	----	----	----	1986	411.30	322.10	348.80	2000	5,132.52	2,288.16	2,470.52
1973	----	----	----	1987	456.30	288.50	330.50	2001	2,892.36	1,387.06	1,950.40
1974	----	----	----	1988	397.50	329.00	381.40	2002	2,098.88	1,108.49	1,335.51
1975	----	----	----	1989	487.50	376.90	454.80	2003	2,015.23	1,253.22	2,003.37
1976	----	----	----	1990	470.30	323.00	373.80	2004	2,185.56	1,750.82	2,175.44
1977	----	----	----	1991	586.35	353.00	586.34	2005	2,278.16	1,889.91	2,205.32
1978	----	----	----	1992	676.95	545.95	676.95	2006	2,470.95	2,012.78	2,415.29
1979	----	----	----	1993	791.20	644.71	776.80	2007	2,861.51	2,331.57	2,652.28
1980	----	----	----	1994	804.43	690.95	751.96	2008	2,661.50	1,295.48	1,577.03
1981	----	----	----	1995	1,074.85	740.47	1,052.13	2009	2,295.80	1,265.52	2,269.14
1982	----	----	----	1996	1,328.45	977.79	1,291.03	2010	2,675.26	2,061.13	2,652.87
1983	----	----	----	1997	1,748.62	1,194.39	1,570.35	2011	2,887.75	2,298.89	2,605.15
1984	252.30	237.70	247.10	1998	2,200.63	1,357.09	2,192.69	2012	3,196.93	2,627.23	3,019.51
1985	325.60	245.80	324.90	1999	4,090.61	2,193.13	4,069.31	2013	4,177.73	3,076.60	4,176.59

Index data begins 10/11/1984.   Source: NASDAQ

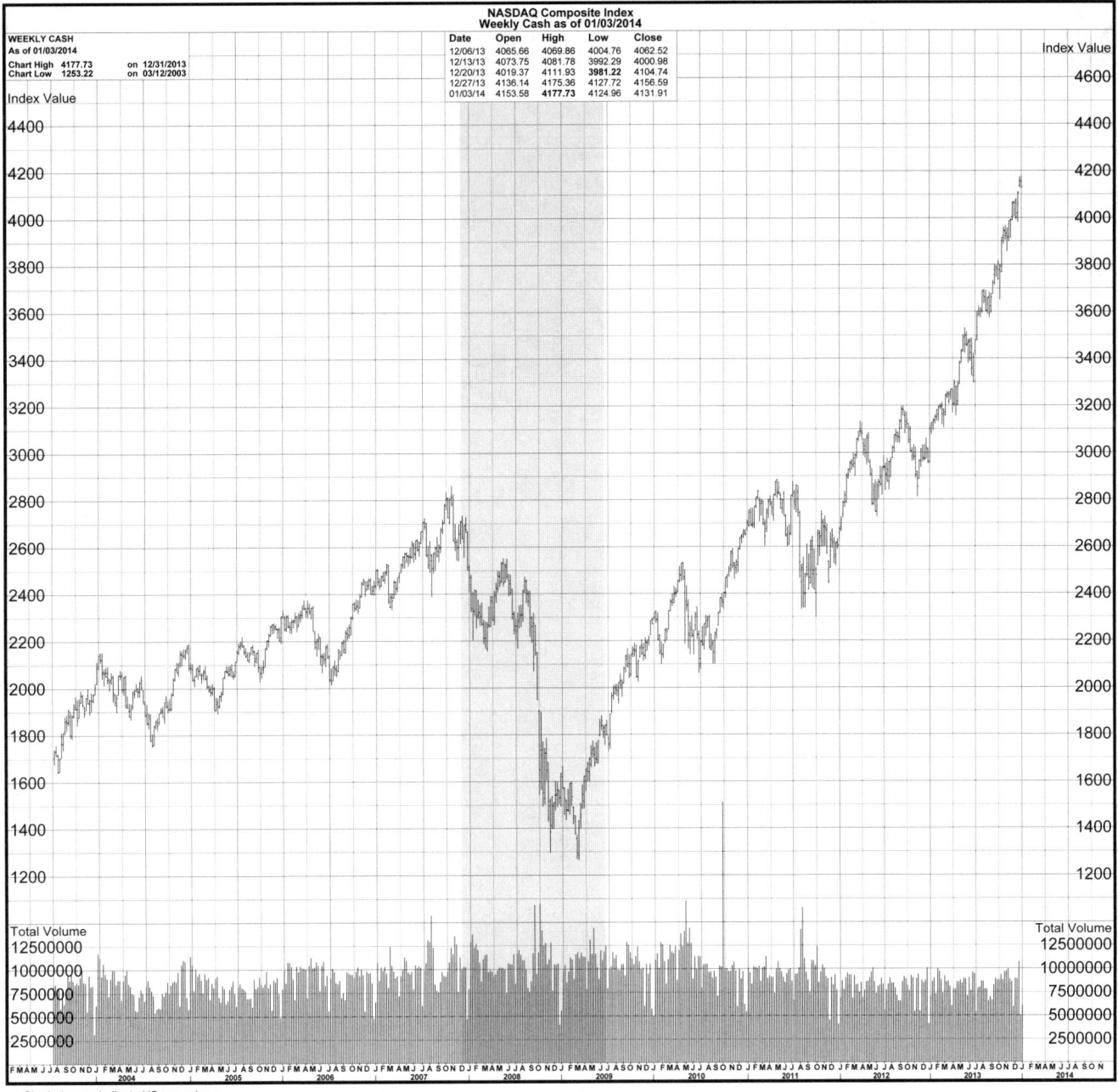

NASDAQ Composite Index
Weekly Cash as of 01/03/2014

WEEKLY CASH
As of 01/03/2014

Chart High 4177.73 on 12/31/2013
Chart Low 1253.22 on 03/12/2003

Index Value

Date	Open	High	Low	Close
12/06/13	4065.66	4069.86	4004.76	4062.52
12/13/13	4073.75	4081.78	3992.29	4000.98
12/20/13	4019.37	4111.93	3981.22	4104.74
12/27/13	4136.14	4175.36	4127.72	4156.59
01/03/14	4153.58	4177.73	4124.96	4131.91

Shaded areas indicate US recessions.

Quarterly High, Low and Settle of NASDAQ Composite Index   In Index Value

Quarter	High	Low	Settle	Quarter	High	Low	Settle	Quarter	High	Low	Settle
03/2005	2,191.60	1,968.58	1,999.23	03/2008	2,661.50	2,155.42	2,279.10	03/2011	2,840.51	2,603.50	2,781.07
06/2005	2,106.57	1,889.91	2,056.96	06/2008	2,551.47	2,266.29	2,292.98	06/2011	2,887.75	2,599.86	2,773.52
09/2005	2,219.91	2,050.30	2,151.69	09/2008	2,473.20	1,983.73	2,082.33	09/2011	2,878.94	2,331.65	2,415.40
12/2005	2,278.16	2,025.95	2,205.32	12/2008	2,083.20	1,295.48	1,577.03	12/2011	2,753.37	2,298.89	2,605.15
03/2006	2,353.13	2,189.91	2,339.79	03/2009	1,665.63	1,265.52	1,528.59	03/2012	3,134.17	2,627.23	3,091.57
06/2006	2,375.54	2,065.11	2,172.09	06/2009	1,879.92	1,498.54	1,835.04	06/2012	3,128.25	2,726.68	2,935.05
09/2006	2,273.30	2,012.78	2,258.43	09/2009	2,167.70	1,727.05	2,122.42	09/2012	3,196.93	2,837.72	3,116.23
12/2006	2,470.95	2,224.21	2,415.29	12/2009	2,295.80	2,024.27	2,269.14	12/2012	3,171.46	2,810.80	3,019.51
03/2007	2,531.42	2,331.57	2,421.63	03/2010	2,432.25	2,100.17	2,397.96	03/2013	3,270.30	3,076.60	3,267.52
06/2007	2,634.60	2,409.04	2,603.23	06/2010	2,535.28	2,105.26	2,109.24	06/2013	3,532.04	3,154.96	3,403.25
09/2007	2,724.74	2,386.69	2,701.50	09/2010	2,400.06	2,061.13	2,368.62	09/2013	3,798.76	3,415.23	3,771.48
12/2007	2,861.51	2,539.81	2,652.28	12/2010	2,675.26	2,332.46	2,652.87	12/2013	4,177.73	3,650.03	4,176.59

Source: NASDAQ

S&P 500 INDEX

S&P 500 INDEX Quarterly Cash as of 03/31/2014				
Date	Open	High	Low	Close
12/31/12	1440.90	1470.96	1343.35	1426.19
03/29/13	1426.19	1570.28	1426.19	1569.19
06/28/13	1568.77	1687.18	1536.03	1606.28
09/30/13	1609.78	1729.86	1604.57	1681.55
12/31/13	1682.41	1849.44	1646.47	1848.36

QUARTERLY CASH
As of 03/31/2014
Chart High 1849.44 on 12/31/2013
Chart Low 4.40 on 06/01/1932

The S&P 500® Index is a trademark of The McGraw-Hill Companies, Inc.   Shaded areas indicate US recessions.

Annual High, Low and Settle of S&P 500 Index   In Index Value

Year	High	Low	Settle	Year	High	Low	Settle	Year	High	Low	Settle
1888	----	----	----	1902	----	----	----	1916	----	----	----
1889	----	----	----	1903	----	----	----	1917	----	----	----
1890	----	----	----	1904	----	----	----	1918	----	----	----
1891	----	----	----	1905	----	----	----	1919	----	----	----
1892	----	----	----	1906	----	----	----	1920	----	----	----
1893	----	----	----	1907	----	----	----	1921	----	----	----
1894	----	----	----	1908	----	----	----	1922	----	----	----
1895	----	----	----	1909	----	----	----	1923	----	----	----
1896	----	----	----	1910	----	----	----	1924	----	----	----
1897	----	----	----	1911	----	----	----	1925	----	----	----
1898	----	----	----	1912	----	----	----	1926	----	----	----
1899	----	----	----	1913	----	----	----	1927	----	----	----
1900	----	----	----	1914	----	----	----	1928	24.28	16.97	24.20
1901	----	----	----	1915	----	----	----	1929	31.83	17.66	21.45

Index data begins 01/03/1928.   Data continued on page 291.   *Source: CME Group; Chicago Mercantile Exchange*

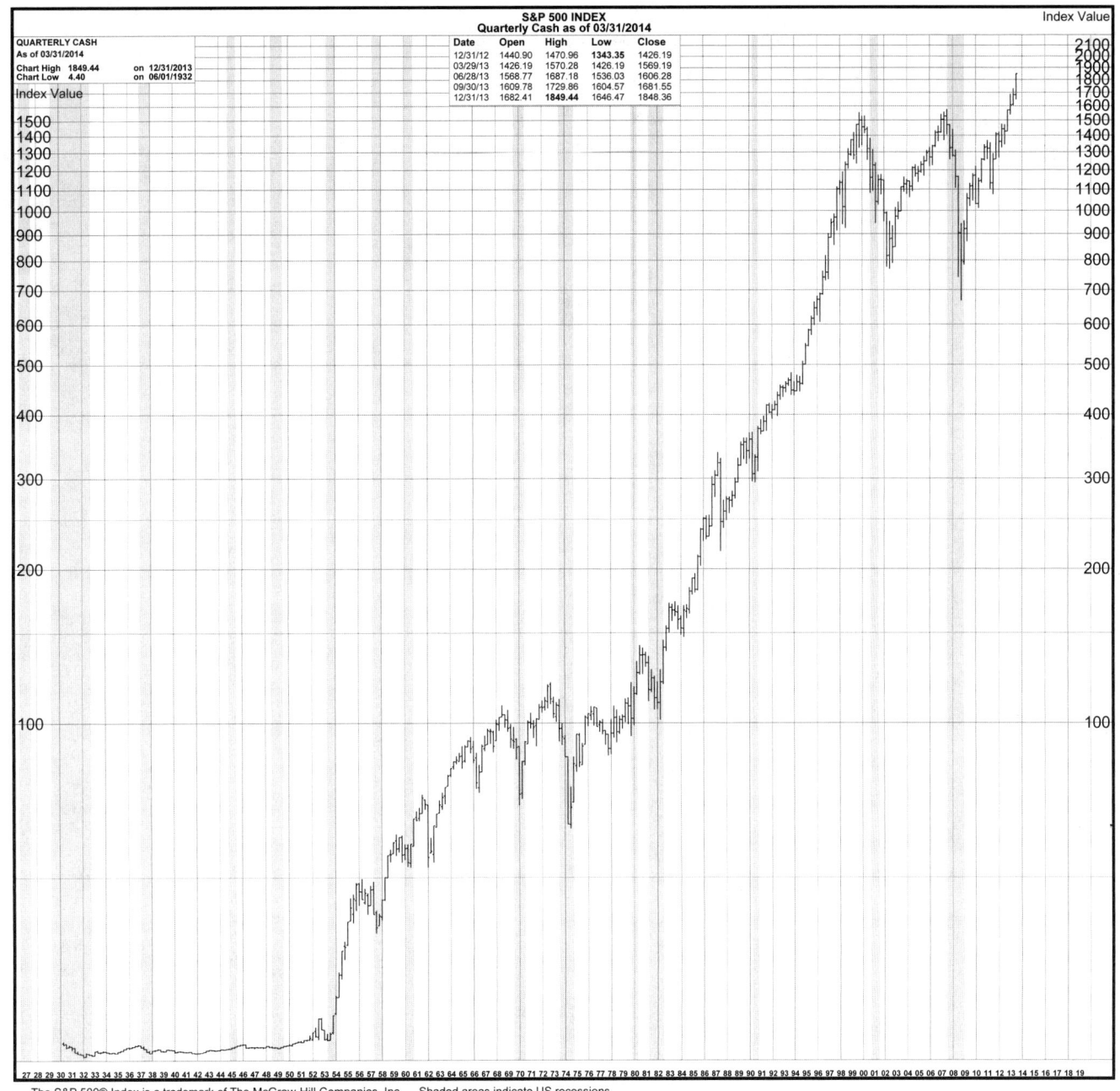

Date	Open	High	Low	Close
12/31/12	1440.90	1470.96	1343.35	1426.19
03/29/13	1426.19	1570.28	1426.19	1569.19
06/28/13	1568.77	1687.18	1536.03	1606.28
09/30/13	1609.78	1729.86	1604.57	1681.55
12/31/13	1682.41	1849.44	1646.47	1848.36

QUARTERLY CASH
As of 03/31/2014

Chart High 1849.44 on 12/31/2013
Chart Low 4.40 on 06/01/1932

The S&P 500® Index is a trademark of The McGraw-Hill Companies, Inc.   Shaded areas indicate US recessions.

Annual High, Low and Settle of S&P 500 Index   In Index Value

Year	High	Low	Settle	Year	High	Low	Settle	Year	High	Low	Settle
1930	25.92	14.44	15.34	1944	13.28	11.60	13.28	1958	55.21	40.33	55.21
1931	18.17	7.72	8.12	1945	17.67	13.21	17.36	1959	60.71	53.58	59.89
1932	9.31	4.40	6.92	1946	19.25	14.12	15.30	1960	60.39	52.30	58.11
1933	12.20	5.56	9.97	1947	16.14	13.74	15.30	1961	72.64	57.57	71.55
1934	11.82	8.36	9.47	1948	17.06	13.84	15.20	1962	71.13	52.32	63.10
1935	13.46	8.06	13.43	1949	16.79	13.55	16.79	1963	75.02	62.69	75.02
1936	17.69	13.40	17.18	1950	20.43	16.66	20.43	1964	86.28	75.43	84.75
1937	18.67	10.17	10.55	1951	23.83	20.69	23.73	1965	92.63	81.60	92.43
1938	13.79	8.50	13.14	1952	26.59	23.09	26.57	1966	94.06	73.20	80.33
1939	13.23	10.31	12.46	1953	26.66	22.71	24.81	1967	97.59	80.38	96.47
1940	12.77	9.09	10.58	1954	35.98	24.80	35.98	1968	108.37	87.72	103.86
1941	10.86	8.38	8.69	1955	46.41	34.58	45.48	1969	106.16	89.20	92.06
1942	9.77	7.47	9.77	1956	49.74	43.11	46.67	1970	93.46	69.29	92.00
1943	12.64	9.88	11.67	1957	49.13	38.98	39.99	1971	104.77	90.16	101.95

Index data begins 01/03/1928.   Data continued from page 290 and continued on page 292.   *Source: CME Group; Chicago Mercantile Exchange*

S&P 500 INDEX

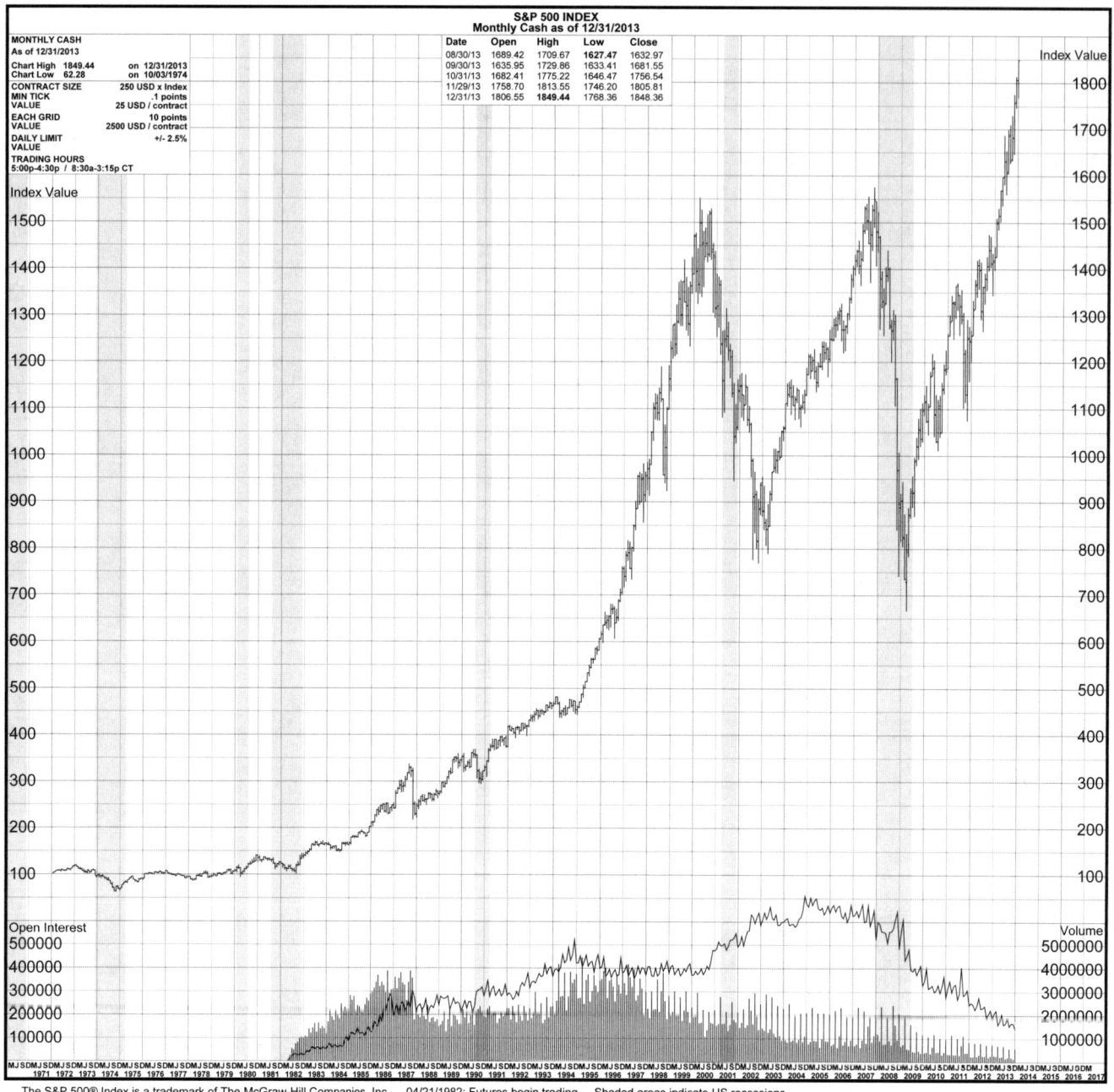

	S&P 500 INDEX Monthly Cash as of 12/31/2013				
Date	**Open**	**High**	**Low**	**Close**	
08/30/13	1689.42	1709.67	1627.47	1632.97	
09/30/13	1635.95	1729.86	1633.41	1681.55	
10/31/13	1682.41	1775.22	1646.47	1756.54	
11/29/13	1758.70	1813.55	1746.20	1805.81	
12/31/13	1806.55	1849.44	1768.36	1848.36	

MONTHLY CASH
As of 12/31/2013

Chart High	1849.44	on 12/31/2013
Chart Low	62.28	on 10/03/1974
CONTRACT SIZE	250 USD x Index	
MIN TICK VALUE	.1 points 25 USD / contract	
EACH GRID VALUE	10 points 2500 USD / contract	
DAILY LIMIT VALUE	+/- 2.5%	
TRADING HOURS	5:00p-4:30p / 8:30a-3:15p CT	

The S&P 500® Index is a trademark of The McGraw-Hill Companies, Inc.   04/21/1982: Futures begin trading.   Shaded areas indicate US recessions.

Annual High, Low and Settle of S&P 500 Index   In Index Value

Year	High	Low	Settle	Year	High	Low	Settle	Year	High	Low	Settle
1972	119.12	101.67	118.05	1986	254.86	202.60	242.16	2000	1,552.87	1,254.07	1,320.28
1973	120.24	92.16	97.55	1987	337.89	216.47	247.09	2001	1,383.37	944.75	1,148.08
1974	99.80	62.28	68.56	1988	283.77	240.17	277.72	2002	1,176.97	768.63	879.82
1975	95.61	70.04	90.19	1989	360.44	273.81	353.40	2003	1,112.56	788.90	1,111.92
1976	107.83	90.90	107.46	1990	369.78	294.51	330.23	2004	1,217.33	1,060.72	1,211.92
1977	107.00	90.71	95.10	1991	418.32	309.35	417.09	2005	1,275.80	1,136.22	1,248.29
1978	108.05	86.45	96.11	1992	442.65	392.41	435.71	2006	1,431.81	1,219.29	1,418.30
1979	112.16	95.22	107.94	1993	471.29	426.88	466.45	2007	1,576.09	1,363.98	1,468.36
1980	141.96	94.24	135.76	1994	482.85	435.86	459.27	2008	1,471.77	741.02	903.25
1981	140.32	110.19	122.55	1995	622.88	457.20	615.93	2009	1,130.38	666.79	1,115.10
1982	145.33	101.44	140.64	1996	762.12	597.29	740.74	2010	1,262.60	1,010.91	1,257.64
1983	172.65	138.08	164.93	1997	986.25	729.55	970.43	2011	1,370.58	1,074.77	1,257.60
1984	170.41	147.26	167.24	1998	1,244.93	912.83	1,229.23	2012	1,474.51	1,258.86	1,426.19
1985	213.08	163.36	211.28	1999	1,473.10	1,206.59	1,469.25	2013	1,849.44	1,426.19	1,848.36

Data continued from page 291.   *Source: CME Group; Chicago Mercantile Exchange*

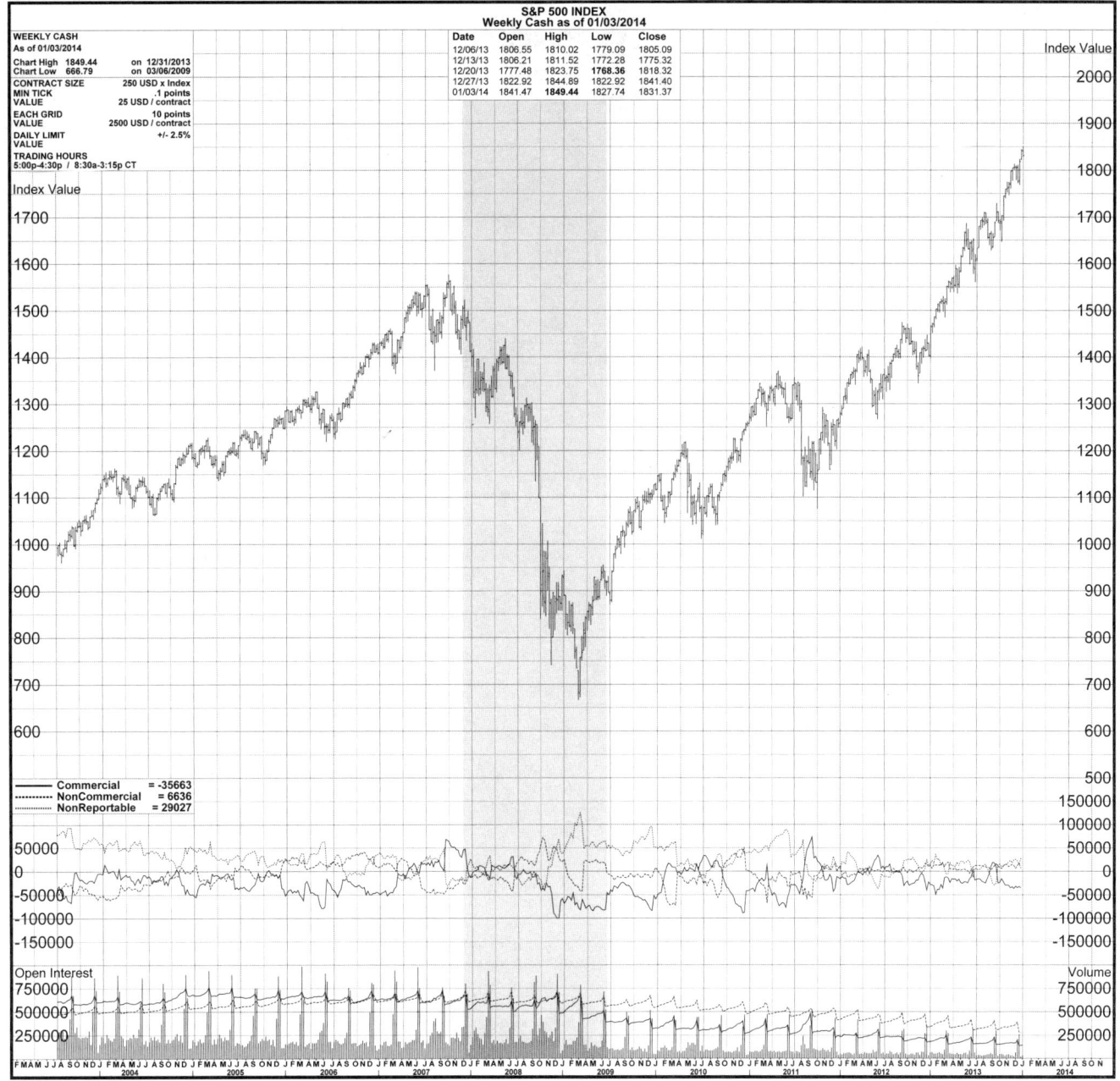

S&P 500 INDEX
Weekly Cash as of 01/03/2014

Date	Open	High	Low	Close
12/06/13	1806.55	1810.02	1779.09	1805.09
12/13/13	1806.21	1811.52	1772.28	1775.32
12/20/13	1777.48	1823.75	1768.36	1818.32
12/27/13	1822.92	1844.89	1822.92	1841.40
01/03/14	1841.47	1849.44	1827.74	1831.37

WEEKLY CASH
As of 01/03/2014

Chart High 1849.44 on 12/31/2013
Chart Low   666.79   on 03/06/2009
CONTRACT SIZE   250 USD x Index
MIN TICK   .1 points
VALUE   25 USD / contract
EACH GRID   10 points
VALUE   2500 USD / contract
DAILY LIMIT   +/- 2.5%
VALUE
TRADING HOURS
5:00p-4:30p / 8:30a-3:15p CT

Commercial   = -35663
NonCommercial = 6636
NonReportable = 29027

The S&P 500® Index is a trademark of The McGraw-Hill Companies, Inc.   Shaded areas indicate US recessions.

Quarterly High, Low and Settle of S&P 500 Index   In Index Value

Quarter	High	Low	Settle	Quarter	High	Low	Settle	Quarter	High	Low	Settle
03/2005	1,229.11	1,163.69	1,180.59	03/2008	1,471.77	1,256.98	1,322.70	03/2011	1,344.07	1,250.11	1,325.83
06/2005	1,219.59	1,136.22	1,191.33	06/2008	1,440.24	1,272.00	1,280.00	06/2011	1,370.58	1,258.07	1,320.64
09/2005	1,245.86	1,183.55	1,228.81	09/2008	1,313.15	1,106.39	1,166.36	09/2011	1,356.48	1,101.54	1,131.42
12/2005	1,275.80	1,168.20	1,248.29	12/2008	1,167.03	741.02	903.25	12/2011	1,292.66	1,074.77	1,257.60
03/2006	1,310.88	1,245.74	1,294.82	03/2009	943.85	666.79	797.87	03/2012	1,419.15	1,258.86	1,408.47
06/2006	1,326.70	1,219.29	1,270.20	06/2009	956.23	783.32	919.32	06/2012	1,422.38	1,266.74	1,362.16
09/2006	1,340.28	1,224.54	1,335.85	09/2009	1,080.15	869.32	1,057.08	09/2012	1,474.51	1,325.41	1,440.67
12/2006	1,431.81	1,327.10	1,418.30	12/2009	1,130.38	1,019.95	1,115.10	12/2012	1,470.96	1,343.35	1,426.19
03/2007	1,461.57	1,363.98	1,420.86	03/2010	1,180.69	1,044.50	1,169.43	03/2013	1,570.28	1,426.19	1,569.19
06/2007	1,540.56	1,416.37	1,503.35	06/2010	1,219.80	1,028.33	1,030.71	06/2013	1,687.18	1,536.03	1,606.28
09/2007	1,555.90	1,370.60	1,526.75	09/2010	1,157.16	1,010.91	1,141.20	09/2013	1,729.86	1,604.57	1,681.55
12/2007	1,576.09	1,406.10	1,468.36	12/2010	1,262.60	1,131.87	1,257.64	12/2013	1,849.44	1,646.47	1,848.36

Source: CME Group; Chicago Mercantile Exchange

S&P MIDCAP 400 INDEX

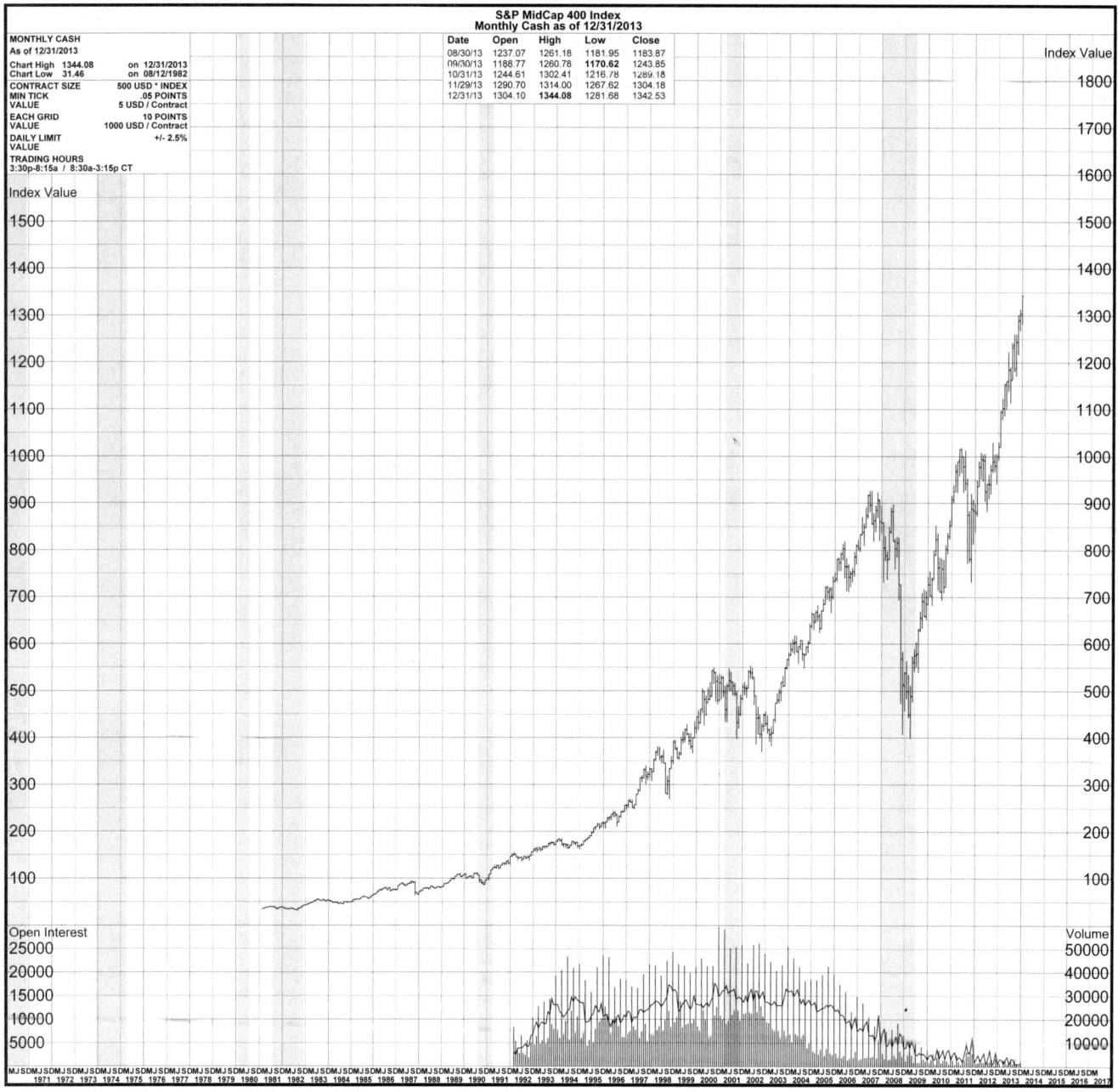

S&P MidCap 400 Index
Monthly Cash as of 12/31/2013

Date	Open	High	Low	Close
08/30/13	1237.07	1261.18	1181.95	1183.87
09/30/13	1188.77	1260.78	1170.62	1243.85
10/31/13	1244.61	1302.41	1216.78	1289.18
11/29/13	1290.70	1314.00	1267.62	1304.18
12/31/13	1304.10	1344.08	1281.68	1342.53

MONTHLY CASH
As of 12/31/2013
Chart High 1344.08 on 12/31/2013
Chart Low 31.46 on 08/12/1982
CONTRACT SIZE 500 USD * INDEX
MIN TICK .05 POINTS
VALUE 5 USD / Contract
EACH GRID 10 POINTS
VALUE 1000 USD / Contract
DAILY LIMIT +/- 2.5%
VALUE
TRADING HOURS
3:30p-8:15a / 8:30a-3:15p CT

The S&P MidCap 400® Index is a trademark of The McGraw-Hill Companies, Inc.   02/13/1992: Futures begin trading.   Shaded areas indicate US recessions.

Annual High, Low and Settle of S&P 400 MidCap Index   In Index Value

Year	High	Low	Settle	Year	High	Low	Settle	Year	High	Low	Settle
1972	----	----	----	1986	80.76	64.52	74.34	2000	549.63	415.98	516.76
1973	----	----	----	1987	93.91	63.13	70.74	2001	547.51	397.54	508.31
1974	----	----	----	1988	83.11	70.75	82.78	2002	554.01	370.83	429.79
1975	----	----	----	1989	110.82	81.95	108.78	2003	581.92	381.82	576.01
1976	----	----	----	1990	112.88	85.39	100.00	2004	666.99	548.29	663.31
1977	----	----	----	1991	146.59	95.16	146.59	2005	752.00	623.57	738.05
1978	----	----	----	1992	160.58	135.12	160.56	2006	822.03	710.53	804.37
1979	----	----	----	1993	179.44	155.02	179.38	2007	926.67	796.64	858.20
1980	----	----	----	1994	184.95	161.55	169.44	2008	897.37	406.45	538.28
1981	40.32	33.64	37.67	1995	220.73	167.93	217.84	2009	743.15	397.97	726.67
1982	43.56	31.46	43.56	1996	259.29	206.34	255.58	2010	916.18	681.91	907.25
1983	55.96	43.30	52.50	1997	340.40	247.27	333.37	2011	1,018.65	731.62	879.16
1984	53.56	44.37	50.63	1998	392.31	268.66	392.31	2012	1,030.17	872.77	1,020.43
1985	66.02	49.67	65.98	1999	445.10	352.35	444.67	2013	1,344.08	1,020.43	1,342.53

Index data begins 01/02/1981.   *Source: CME Group; Chicago Mercantile Exchange*

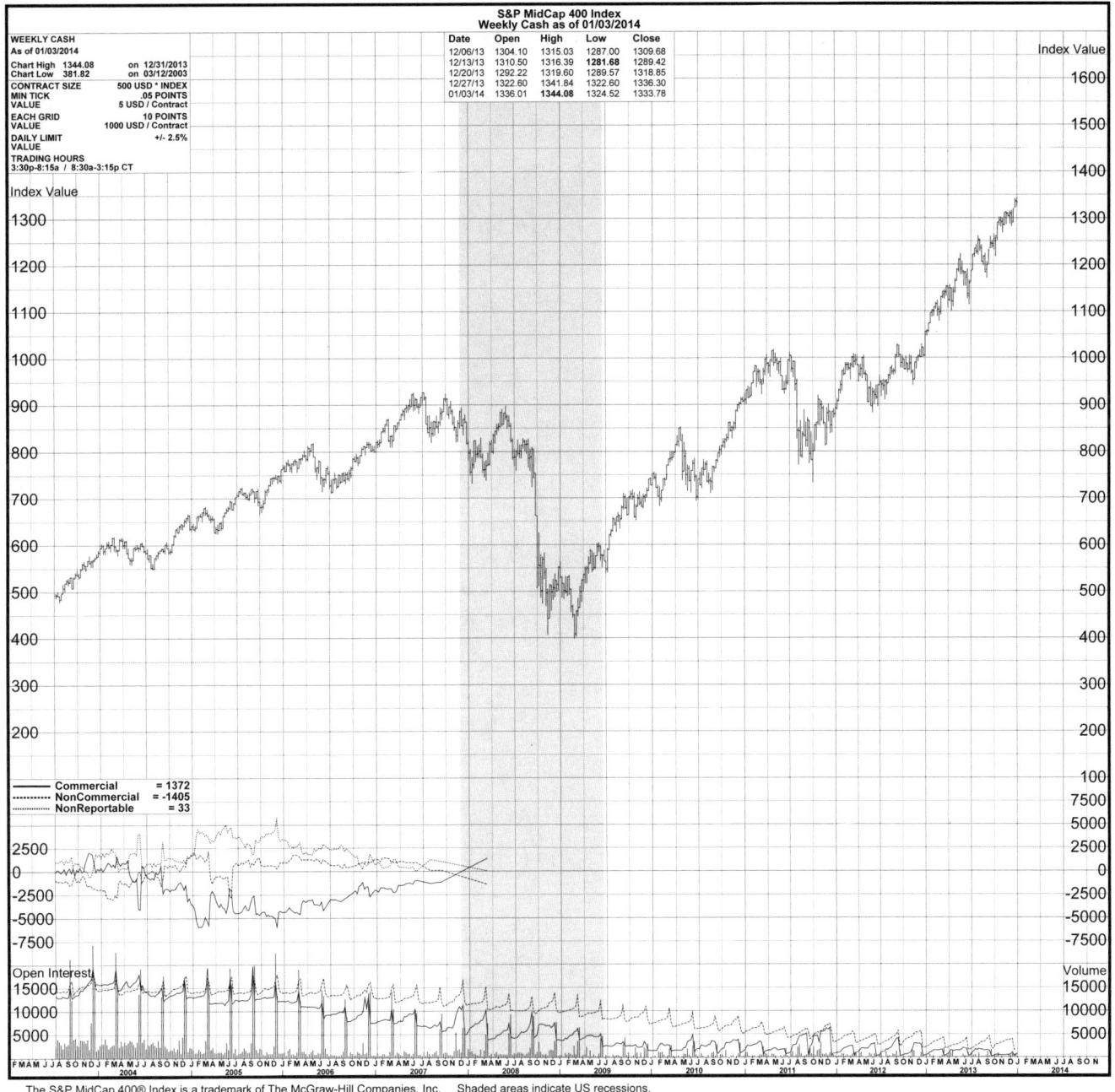

S&P MidCap 400 Index
Weekly Cash as of 01/03/2014

Date	Open	High	Low	Close
12/06/13	1304.10	1315.03	1287.00	1309.68
12/13/13	1310.50	1316.39	1281.68	1289.42
12/20/13	1292.22	1319.60	1289.57	1318.85
12/27/13	1322.60	1341.84	1322.60	1336.30
01/03/14	1336.01	1344.08	1324.52	1333.78

WEEKLY CASH
As of 01/03/2014
Chart High 1344.08 on 12/31/2013
Chart Low 381.82 on 03/12/2003
CONTRACT SIZE 500 USD * INDEX
MIN TICK .05 POINTS
VALUE 5 USD / Contract
EACH GRID 10 POINTS
VALUE 1000 USD / Contract
DAILY LIMIT +/- 2.5%
VALUE
TRADING HOURS
3:30p-8:15a / 8:30a-3:15p CT

Commercial = 1372
NonCommercial = -1405
NonReportable = 33

The S&P MidCap 400® Index is a trademark of The McGraw-Hill Companies, Inc.   Shaded areas indicate US recessions.

Quarterly High, Low and Settle of S&P 400 MidCap Index   In Index Value

Quarter	High	Low	Settle	Quarter	High	Low	Settle	Quarter	High	Low	Settle
03/2005	683.36	629.29	658.87	03/2008	859.43	731.29	779.51	03/2011	989.62	900.84	989.05
06/2005	695.91	623.57	684.94	06/2008	897.37	779.47	818.99	06/2011	1,018.65	922.54	978.64
09/2005	725.02	685.08	716.33	09/2008	828.09	694.10	727.29	09/2011	1,013.34	770.58	781.26
12/2005	752.00	665.23	738.05	12/2008	727.29	406.45	538.28	12/2011	920.24	731.62	879.16
03/2006	795.50	732.57	792.11	03/2009	563.87	397.97	489.00	03/2012	1,008.68	872.77	994.30
06/2006	818.87	713.09	764.87	06/2009	604.26	476.41	578.14	06/2012	1,006.14	882.01	941.64
09/2006	770.44	710.53	754.25	09/2009	710.20	539.04	691.02	09/2012	1,030.00	909.43	989.02
12/2006	822.03	744.09	804.37	12/2009	743.15	651.79	726.67	12/2012	1,030.17	940.92	1,020.43
03/2007	870.89	796.64	848.47	03/2010	800.73	681.91	789.90	03/2013	1,154.66	1,020.43	1,153.68
06/2007	925.90	847.63	895.51	06/2010	852.90	710.71	711.73	06/2013	1,223.37	1,101.03	1,160.82
09/2007	926.67	818.78	885.06	09/2010	811.70	692.75	802.10	09/2013	1,261.18	1,163.34	1,243.85
12/2007	924.07	820.06	858.20	12/2010	916.18	791.00	907.25	12/2013	1,344.08	1,216.78	1,342.53

Source: CME Group; Chicago Mercantile Exchange

S&P 100 INDEX

S&P 100 Index (OEX)
Monthly Cash as of 12/31/2013

Date	Open	High	Low	Close
08/30/13	756.57	765.70	728.63	730.92
09/30/13	731.54	772.02	730.80	748.12
10/31/13	748.51	791.52	733.05	783.39
11/29/13	784.33	809.86	780.31	806.36
12/31/13	806.87	824.21	788.08	823.81

MONTHLY CASH
As of 12/31/2013
Chart High 846.19 on 03/24/2000
Chart Low 46.35 on 03/06/1978

The S&P 100® Index is a trademark of The McGraw-Hill Companies, Inc.   Shaded areas indicate US recessions.

Annual High, Low and Settle of S&P 100 Index   In Index Value

Year	High	Low	Settle	Year	High	Low	Settle	Year	High	Low	Settle
1972	----	----	----	1986	121.49	97.91	115.54	2000	846.19	656.67	686.45
1973	----	----	----	1987	167.02	105.85	119.13	2001	725.07	480.02	584.28
1974	----	----	----	1988	134.12	115.06	131.93	2002	600.80	384.96	444.75
1975	----	----	----	1989	167.62	129.83	164.68	2003	550.90	400.24	550.78
1976	59.41	50.00	58.23	1990	175.95	139.67	155.24	2004	578.13	518.67	575.29
1977	57.92	48.76	51.03	1991	193.87	145.42	192.78	2005	586.81	542.77	570.00
1978	58.04	46.35	52.99	1992	202.18	181.69	198.32	2006	665.95	559.02	660.41
1979	58.19	52.39	55.53	1993	217.44	193.65	214.73	2007	734.51	624.81	685.65
1980	71.01	51.03	68.83	1994	223.60	201.17	214.32	2008	687.47	361.32	431.54
1981	70.58	56.13	59.77	1995	299.18	212.94	292.96	2009	520.48	317.37	514.09
1982	72.79	51.66	71.09	1996	369.87	285.16	359.99	2010	568.25	459.29	565.90
1983	87.33	69.78	83.06	1997	474.99	355.11	459.94	2011	611.06	488.67	570.79
1984	85.00	72.92	82.54	1998	615.90	431.76	604.03	2012	677.02	570.79	646.61
1985	104.09	80.30	103.00	1999	798.38	598.01	792.83	2013	824.21	646.61	823.81

Index data begins 01/02/1976.   *Source: Chicago Board of Options Exchange*

S&P 100 Index (OEX)
Weekly Cash as of 01/03/2014

Date	Open	High	Low	Close
12/06/13	806.87	807.89	795.42	805.75
12/13/13	805.99	808.77	790.35	791.56
12/20/13	792.05	812.58	788.08	809.74
12/27/13	811.92	822.95	811.92	821.25
01/03/14	821.16	824.21	815.42	816.47

WEEKLY CASH
As of 01/03/2014
Chart High 824.21   on 12/31/2013
Chart Low   317.37   on 03/06/2009

The S&P 100® Index is a trademark of The McGraw-Hill Companies, Inc.   Shaded areas indicate US recessions.

Quarterly High, Low and Settle of S&P 100 Index   In Index Value

Quarter	High	Low	Settle	Quarter	High	Low	Settle	Quarter	High	Low	Settle
03/2005	586.81	555.05	561.86	03/2008	687.47	583.64	613.71	03/2011	602.77	559.23	592.72
06/2005	574.37	542.88	558.07	06/2008	658.72	577.27	581.09	06/2011	611.06	561.57	587.31
09/2005	578.22	553.50	566.80	09/2008	608.81	515.52	543.49	09/2011	603.39	499.30	513.37
12/2005	584.33	542.77	570.00	12/2008	548.43	361.32	431.54	12/2011	580.67	488.67	570.79
03/2006	596.28	568.37	587.75	03/2009	447.86	317.37	377.35	03/2012	645.52	570.79	640.68
06/2006	604.06	559.02	579.56	06/2009	444.47	370.92	429.66	06/2012	646.76	579.26	623.82
09/2006	622.12	562.88	620.03	09/2009	499.01	408.76	488.35	09/2012	676.65	609.03	663.80
12/2006	665.95	617.71	660.41	12/2009	520.48	472.75	514.09	12/2012	677.02	611.25	646.61
03/2007	671.47	624.81	649.89	03/2010	541.09	481.80	534.90	03/2013	705.08	646.61	704.57
06/2007	707.76	647.12	692.77	06/2010	554.78	466.52	467.65	06/2013	757.61	692.75	720.62
09/2007	720.26	640.50	714.49	09/2010	521.83	459.29	514.65	09/2013	772.02	720.52	748.12
12/2007	734.51	657.14	685.65	12/2010	568.25	511.35	565.90	12/2013	824.21	733.05	823.81

Source: Chicago Board of Options Exchange

RUSSELL 2000 INDEX

Russell 2000 Index, Mini
Monthly Cash as of 12/31/2013

Date	Open	High	Low	Close
08/30/13	1051.23	1063.52	1009.46	1010.90
09/30/13	1010.90	1082.00	1009.00	1073.79
10/31/13	1073.77	1123.26	1037.85	1100.15
11/29/13	1099.09	1147.00	1079.08	1142.89
12/31/13	1142.30	1167.96	1099.67	1163.64

MONTHLY CASH
As of 12/31/2013
Chart High 1167.96 on 12/26/2013
Chart Low 40.52 on 12/29/1978
CONTRACT SIZE 100 USD * INDEX
MIN TICK .05 POINTS
VALUE 25 USD/CONTRACT
EACH GRID 10 POINTS
VALUE 5000 USD/CONTRACT
DAILY LIMIT NONE
VALUE
TRADING HOURS
6:00p - 4:00p ET

Shaded areas indicate US recessions.

Annual High, Low and Settle of Russell 2000 Index   In Index Value

Year	High	Low	Settle	Year	High	Low	Settle	Year	High	Low	Settle
1972	----	----	----	1986	155.30	128.23	135.00	2000	614.16	440.76	483.53
1973	----	----	----	1987	174.44	106.07	120.42	2001	519.89	373.62	488.50
1974	----	----	----	1988	152.08	120.43	147.37	2002	523.79	324.90	383.09
1975	----	----	----	1989	180.95	146.33	168.30	2003	566.74	343.06	556.91
1976	----	----	----	1990	171.08	118.45	132.20	2004	656.11	515.90	651.57
1977	----	----	----	1991	189.93	124.52	189.91	2005	693.63	570.03	673.22
1978	40.52	40.52	40.52	1992	221.01	183.40	221.01	2006	801.01	666.58	787.66
1979	55.91	40.81	55.91	1993	260.41	216.43	258.59	2007	856.48	734.38	766.03
1980	77.70	45.36	74.80	1994	271.08	233.89	250.36	2008	768.47	371.26	499.45
1981	85.16	65.37	73.67	1995	316.98	246.38	315.97	2009	635.99	342.57	625.39
1982	91.01	60.33	88.90	1996	364.96	299.45	362.61	2010	793.28	580.49	783.65
1983	126.99	88.29	112.27	1997	466.21	335.18	437.02	2011	868.57	601.71	740.92
1984	116.69	93.95	101.49	1998	492.28	303.87	421.97	2012	868.50	729.75	849.35
1985	129.87	101.21	129.87	1999	504.75	381.96	504.75	2013	1,167.96	849.33	1,163.64

Index data begins 12/29/1978.   *Source: IntercontinentalExchange (ICE)*

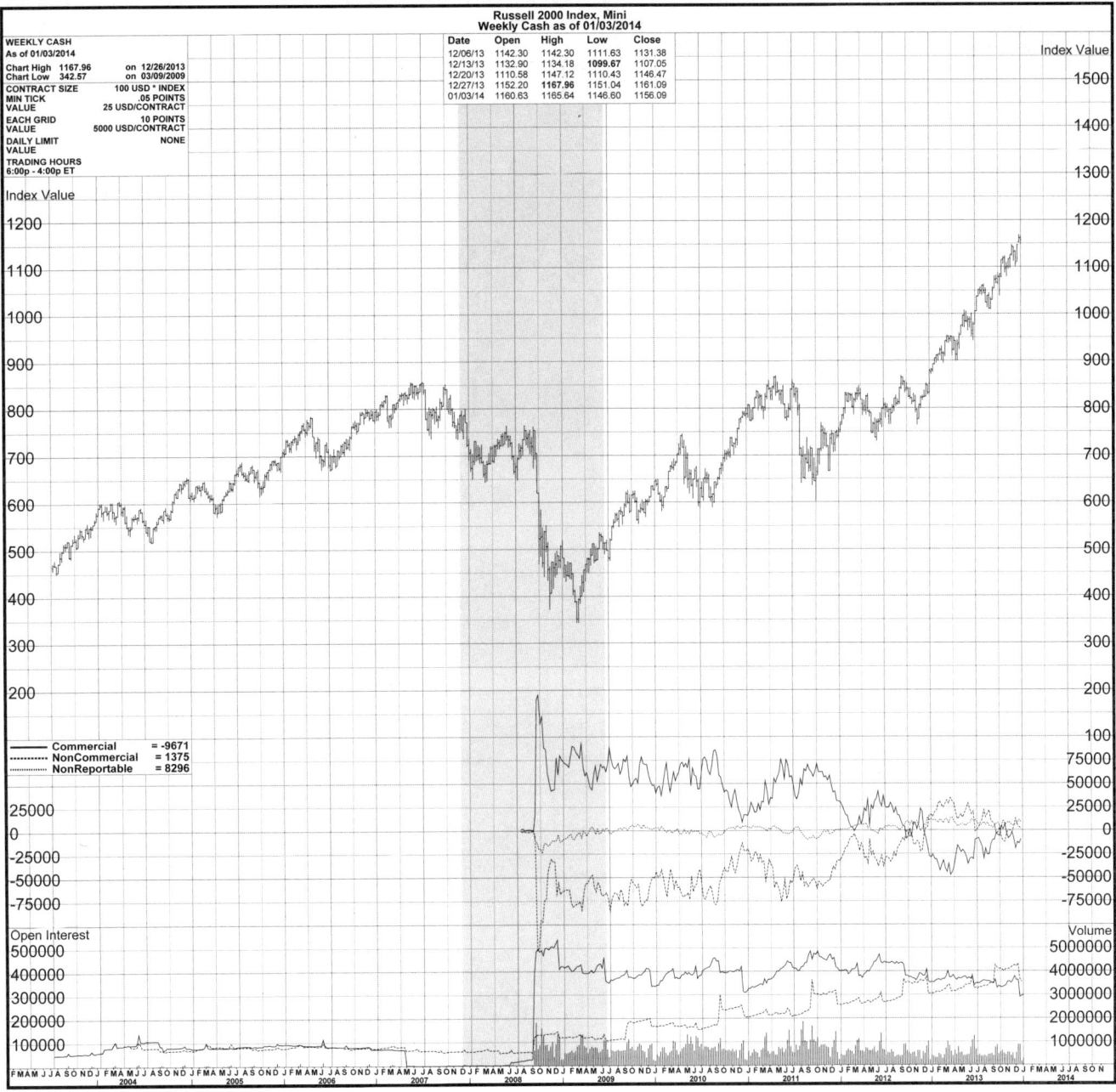

Russell 2000 Index, Mini
Weekly Cash as of 01/03/2014

Date	Open	High	Low	Close
12/06/13	1142.30	1142.30	1111.63	1131.38
12/13/13	1132.90	1134.18	1099.67	1107.05
12/20/13	1110.58	1147.12	1110.43	1146.47
12/27/13	1152.20	1167.96	1151.04	1161.09
01/03/14	1160.63	1165.64	1146.60	1156.09

WEEKLY CASH
As of 01/03/2014
Chart High 1167.96 on 12/26/2013
Chart Low 342.57 on 03/09/2009
CONTRACT SIZE 100 USD * INDEX
MIN TICK .05 POINTS
VALUE 25 USD/CONTRACT
EACH GRID 10 POINTS
VALUE 5000 USD/CONTRACT
DAILY LIMIT NONE
VALUE
TRADING HOURS
6:00p - 4:00p ET

Commercial = -9671
NonCommercial = 1375
NonReportable = 8296

Shaded areas indicate US recessions.

Quarterly High, Low and Settle of Russell 2000 Index   In Index Value

Quarter	High	Low	Settle	Quarter	High	Low	Settle	Quarter	High	Low	Settle
03/2005	654.30	603.75	615.07	03/2008	768.47	643.29	687.97	03/2011	843.73	771.71	843.55
06/2005	648.16	570.03	639.66	06/2008	763.27	684.89	689.66	06/2011	868.57	772.62	827.43
09/2005	688.51	638.93	667.80	09/2008	764.38	647.37	679.58	09/2011	860.37	634.71	644.16
12/2005	693.63	614.76	673.22	12/2008	676.21	371.26	499.45	12/2011	769.46	601.71	740.92
03/2006	767.17	666.58	765.14	03/2009	519.18	342.57	422.75	03/2012	847.92	736.78	830.30
06/2006	784.62	669.88	724.58	06/2009	535.85	412.77	508.28	06/2012	841.06	729.75	798.49
09/2006	738.17	668.58	725.59	09/2009	625.31	473.54	604.28	09/2012	868.50	765.05	837.45
12/2006	801.01	712.16	787.66	12/2009	635.99	553.32	625.39	12/2012	853.57	763.55	849.35
03/2007	830.02	760.06	800.71	03/2010	693.32	580.49	678.64	03/2013	954.00	849.33	951.54
06/2007	856.42	798.17	833.70	06/2010	745.95	607.30	609.49	06/2013	1,008.23	898.40	977.48
09/2007	856.48	735.95	805.45	09/2010	684.61	587.60	676.14	09/2013	1,082.00	977.46	1,073.79
12/2007	852.07	734.38	766.03	12/2010	793.28	665.99	783.65	12/2013	1,167.96	1,037.85	1,163.64

Source: IntercontinentalExchange (ICE)

VALUE LINE INDEX

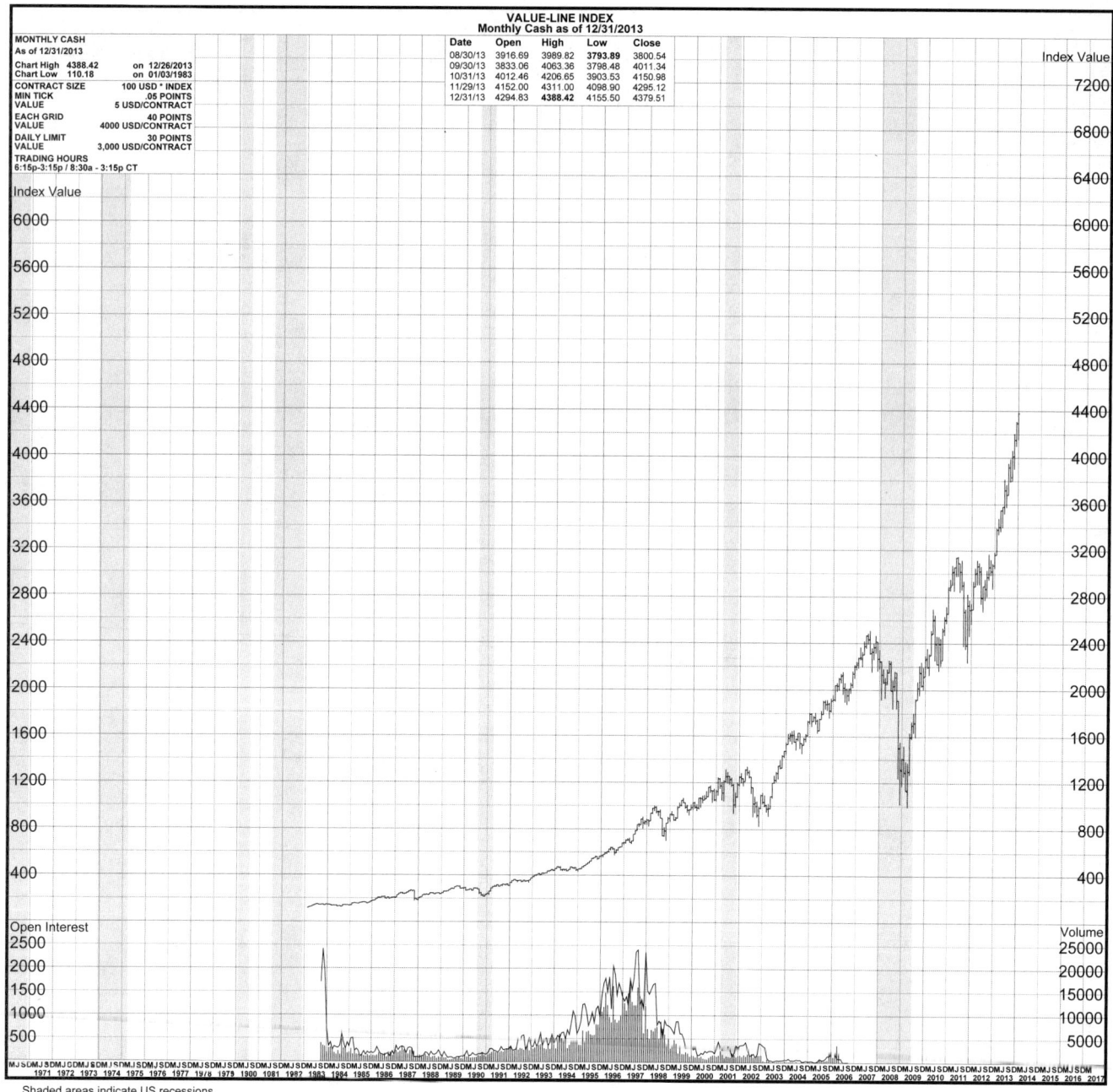

VALUE-LINE INDEX
Monthly Cash as of 12/31/2013

Date	Open	High	Low	Close
08/30/13	3916.69	3989.82	3793.89	3800.54
09/30/13	3833.06	4063.36	3798.48	4011.34
10/31/13	4012.46	4206.65	3903.53	4150.98
11/29/13	4152.00	4311.00	4098.90	4295.12
12/31/13	4294.83	**4388.42**	4155.50	4379.51

MONTHLY CASH
As of 12/31/2013

Chart High 4388.42 on 12/26/2013
Chart Low 110.18 on 01/03/1983
CONTRACT SIZE 100 USD * INDEX
MIN TICK .05 POINTS
VALUE 5 USD/CONTRACT
EACH GRID .40 POINTS
VALUE 4000 USD/CONTRACT
DAILY LIMIT 30 POINTS
VALUE 3,000 USD/CONTRACT
TRADING HOURS
6:15p-3:15p / 8:30a - 3:15p CT

Shaded areas indicate US recessions.

Annual High, Low and Settle of Value-Line Index   In Index Value

Year	High	Low	Settle	Year	High	Low	Settle	Year	High	Low	Settle
1972	----	----	----	1986	213.82	176.68	203.14	2000	1,176.20	956.69	1,124.76
1973	----	----	----	1987	271.17	176.93	200.08	2001	1,311.09	934.49	1,247.13
1974	----	----	----	1988	248.56	201.85	245.51	2002	1,337.54	824.77	1,033.75
1975	----	----	----	1989	307.55	243.68	290.15	2003	1,545.05	910.60	1,530.52
1976	----	----	----	1990	294.88	215.35	241.52	2004	1,803.83	1,448.33	1,794.19
1977	----	----	----	1991	335.32	229.57	335.30	2005	1,955.17	1,627.84	1,916.74
1978	----	----	----	1992	386.10	331.76	386.09	2006	2,243.69	1,874.87	2,216.74
1979	----	----	----	1993	456.15	382.19	455.88	2007	2,509.12	2,152.63	2,245.58
1980	----	----	----	1994	476.76	431.10	452.53	2008	2,255.21	1,016.04	1,404.78
1981	----	----	----	1995	571.20	450.32	569.91	2009	2,293.87	992.45	2,259.45
1982	----	----	----	1996	686.65	552.31	682.62	2010	2,888.95	2,126.98	2,865.39
1983	150.23	110.18	144.10	1997	906.20	670.94	876.84	2011	3,149.52	2,235.13	2,695.60
1984	148.69	124.60	140.18	1998	999.91	699.44	927.84	2012	3,187.27	2,675.38	3,164.70
1985	179.66	139.19	179.66	1999	1,067.98	871.42	1,025.80	2013	4,388.42	3,164.54	4,379.51

Index data begins 01/03/1983.   *Source: Kansas City Board of Trade*

VALUE-LINE INDEX
Weekly Cash as of 01/03/2014

WEEKLY CASH
As of 01/03/2014

Chart High	4388.42 on 12/26/2013
Chart Low	910.60 on 03/12/2003
CONTRACT SIZE	100 USD * INDEX
MIN TICK	.05 POINTS
VALUE	5 USD/CONTRACT
EACH GRID	20 POINTS
VALUE	2000 USD/CONTRACT
DAILY LIMIT	30 POINTS
VALUE	3,000 USD/CONTRACT
TRADING HOURS	
6:15p-3:15p / 8:30a - 3:15p CT	

Date	Open	High	Low	Close
12/06/13	4294.83	4294.83	4206.58	4247.93
12/13/13	4253.27	4262.89	4155.50	4177.88
12/20/13	4193.06	4299.22	4185.49	4297.88
12/27/13	4314.63	4388.42	4314.41	4358.89
01/03/14	4357.58	4384.57	4337.13	4349.49

Shaded areas indicate US recessions.

Quarterly High, Low and Settle of Value-Line Index   In Index Value

Quarter	High	Low	Settle	Quarter	High	Low	Settle	Quarter	High	Low	Settle
03/2005	1,805.50	1,684.89	1,735.57	03/2008	2,249.29	1,916.18	2,050.82	03/2011	3,072.86	2,852.02	3,056.73
06/2005	1,822.31	1,627.84	1,791.95	06/2008	2,255.21	1,994.58	1,994.64	06/2011	3,149.52	2,842.40	3,018.37
09/2005	1,915.54	1,788.90	1,879.39	09/2008	2,159.79	1,839.15	1,908.30	09/2011	3,117.11	2,351.88	2,385.05
12/2005	1,955.17	1,757.86	1,916.74	12/2008	1,909.39	1,016.04	1,404.78	12/2011	2,827.49	2,235.13	2,695.60
03/2006	2,105.37	1,903.40	2,095.25	03/2009	1,517.86	992.45	1,296.92	03/2012	3,117.85	2,694.92	3,066.24
06/2006	2,156.12	1,894.76	2,003.89	06/2009	1,802.57	1,269.46	1,714.53	06/2012	3,096.20	2,675.38	2,894.52
09/2006	2,064.40	1,874.87	2,044.67	09/2009	2,210.49	1,592.67	2,149.38	09/2012	3,171.84	2,774.66	3,058.03
12/2006	2,243.69	2,019.11	2,216.74	12/2009	2,293.87	2,005.36	2,259.45	12/2012	3,187.27	2,871.82	3,164.70
03/2007	2,366.25	2,185.89	2,303.00	03/2010	2,511.13	2,126.98	2,477.96	03/2013	3,552.33	3,164.54	3,548.79
06/2007	2,487.03	2,301.00	2,431.47	06/2010	2,697.44	2,218.05	2,222.27	06/2013	3,815.16	3,397.58	3,680.93
09/2007	2,509.12	2,152.63	2,365.37	09/2010	2,535.81	2,163.11	2,504.79	09/2013	4,063.36	3,680.79	4,011.34
12/2007	2,467.61	2,161.83	2,245.58	12/2010	2,888.95	2,471.86	2,865.39	12/2013	4,388.42	3,903.53	4,379.51

Source: Kansas City Board of Trade

DAX INDEX

DAX® is <u>Deutsche</u> Börse's <u>blue chip index</u> for the German stock market. It comprises the <u>30</u> largest and most actively traded German companies.   Shaded areas indicate German recessions.

Annual High, Low and Settle of DAX Index   In Index Value

Year	High	Low	Settle	Year	High	Low	Settle	Year	High	Low	Settle
1972	596.90	471.20	536.40	1986	1,586.00	1,248.60	1,432.30	2000	8,136.16	6,110.26	6,433.61
1973	581.00	386.30	396.30	1987	1,570.30	945.90	1,000.00	2001	6,795.14	3,539.18	5,160.10
1974	436.40	372.30	401.80	1988	1,343.84	931.18	1,327.87	2002	5,467.31	2,519.30	2,892.63
1975	566.20	411.20	563.20	1989	1,805.01	1,268.69	1,790.37	2003	3,996.28	2,188.75	3,965.16
1976	593.80	486.70	509.00	1990	1,976.43	1,320.43	1,398.23	2004	4,272.18	3,618.58	4,256.08
1977	567.60	491.40	549.30	1991	1,728.30	1,311.82	1,577.90	2005	5,469.96	4,157.51	5,408.26
1978	611.70	525.00	575.10	1992	1,814.64	1,413.68	1,545.05	2006	5,993.90	5,290.49	5,970.08
1979	593.30	492.20	497.80	1993	2,284.56	1,514.31	2,266.68	2007	8,151.57	6,444.70	8,067.32
1980	535.20	473.90	480.90	1994	2,282.60	1,953.23	2,106.58	2008	8,100.64	4,014.60	4,810.20
1981	548.20	468.30	490.40	1995	2,320.22	1,893.63	2,253.88	2009	6,026.69	3,588.89	5,957.43
1982	554.60	476.60	552.80	1996	2,914.61	2,271.40	2,888.69	2010	7,087.84	5,434.34	6,914.19
1983	777.00	530.00	774.00	1997	4,459.89	2,833.78	4,249.69	2011	7,600.41	4,965.80	5,898.35
1984	820.90	692.70	820.90	1998	6,217.83	3,833.71	5,002.39	2012	7,682.90	5,900.18	7,612.39
1985	1,366.20	820.30	1,366.20	1999	6,992.92	4,605.27	6,958.14	2013	9,594.35	7,418.36	9,552.16

Index data begins 10/01/1959.   *Source: Eurex*

DAX Index (FDAX)
Weekly Cash as of 01/03/2014

Date	Open	High	Low	Close
12/06/13	9413.0	9424.8	9069.8	9172.4
12/13/13	9218.8	9225.5	**8984.3**	9006.5
12/20/13	9004.6	9413.1	8997.8	9400.2
12/27/13	9436.5	9589.4	9427.5	9589.4
01/03/14	9586.5	**9620.9**	9368.0	9435.2

WEEKLY CASH
As of 01/03/2014
Chart High 9620.9 on 01/02/2014
Chart Low 2188.8 on 03/12/2003

DAX® is Deutsche Börse's blue chip index for the German stock market. It comprises the 30 largest and most actively traded German companies.   Shaded areas indicate German recessions.

Quarterly High, Low and Settle of DAX Index   In Index Value

Quarter	High	Low	Settle	Quarter	High	Low	Settle	Quarter	High	Low	Settle
03/2005	4,435.31	4,160.83	4,348.77	03/2008	8,100.64	6,167.82	6,534.97	03/2011	7,441.82	6,495.80	7,041.31
06/2005	4,637.34	4,157.51	4,586.28	06/2008	7,231.86	6,308.24	6,418.32	06/2011	7,600.41	6,991.62	7,376.24
09/2005	5,061.84	4,444.94	5,044.12	09/2008	6,626.70	5,658.20	5,831.02	09/2011	7,523.53	4,965.80	5,502.02
12/2005	5,469.96	4,762.75	5,408.26	12/2008	5,876.93	4,014.60	4,810.20	12/2011	6,430.60	5,125.44	5,898.35
03/2006	5,993.90	5,290.49	5,970.08	03/2009	5,111.02	3,588.89	4,084.76	03/2012	7,194.33	5,900.18	6,946.83
06/2006	6,162.37	5,243.71	5,683.31	06/2009	5,177.59	3,997.46	4,808.64	06/2012	7,081.06	5,914.43	6,416.28
09/2006	6,031.55	5,365.06	6,004.33	09/2009	5,760.83	4,524.01	5,675.16	09/2012	7,478.53	6,324.53	7,216.15
12/2006	6,629.33	5,944.57	6,596.92	12/2009	6,026.69	5,312.64	5,957.43	12/2012	7,682.90	6,950.53	7,612.39
03/2007	7,040.20	6,444.70	6,917.03	03/2010	6,203.50	5,434.34	6,153.55	03/2013	8,074.47	7,537.29	7,795.31
06/2007	8,131.73	6,891.80	8,007.32	06/2010	6,341.52	5,607.68	5,965.52	06/2013	8,557.86	7,418.36	7,959.22
09/2007	8,151.57	7,190.36	7,861.51	09/2010	6,386.97	5,809.37	6,229.02	09/2013	8,770.10	7,730.37	8,594.40
12/2007	8,117.79	7,444.62	8,067.32	12/2010	7,087.84	6,116.35	6,914.19	12/2013	9,594.35	8,489.62	9,552.16

Source: Eurex

CAC-40 INDEX

	CAC 40 Index Monthly Cash as of 12/31/2013			
Date	Open	High	Low	Close
08/30/13	3998.0	4123.9	3933.8	3933.8
09/30/13	3975.3	4227.2	3927.6	4143.4
10/31/13	4150.0	4309.9	4105.7	4299.9
11/29/13	4302.7	4356.3	4211.8	4295.2
12/31/13	4296.4	4309.3	4051.3	4296.0

MONTHLY CASH
As of 12/31/2013
Chart High 6944.8 on 09/04/2000
Chart Low 1425.3 on 01/15/1991

The CAC 40® is a free float market capitalization weighted index that reflects the performance of the 40 largest and most actively traded shares listed on Euronext Paris, and is the most widely used indicator of the Paris stock market. Shaded areas indicate French recessions.

Annual High, Low and Settle of CAC-40 Index   In Index Value

Year	High	Low	Settle	Year	High	Low	Settle	Year	High	Low	Settle
1972	----	----	----	1986	----	----	----	1995	2,025.15	1,711.80	1,871.97
1973	----	----	----	1987	----	----	----	1996	2,358.65	1,873.14	2,315.73
1974	----	----	----	1988	----	----	----	1997	3,114.00	2,251.53	2,998.91
1975	----	----	----	1989	2,005.92	1,751.33	2,001.08	1998	4,404.94	2,809.73	3,942.66
1976	----	----	----	1990	2,141.13	1,472.59	1,517.93	1999	5,979.54	3,845.77	5,958.32
1977	----	----	----	1991	1,897.26	1,425.26	1,765.66	2000	6,944.77	5,388.85	5,926.42
1978	----	----	----	1992	2,080.80	1,577.74	1,857.78	2001	5,999.18	3,463.07	4,624.58
1979	----	----	----	1993	2,289.48	1,755.90	2,268.22	2002	4,720.04	2,612.03	3,063.91
1980	----	----	----	1994	2,360.98	1,796.82	1,881.15	2003	3,566.76	2,401.15	3,557.90
1981	----	----	----	1995	2,025.15	1,711.80	1,871.97	2004	3,856.01	3,452.41	3,821.16
1982	----	----	----	1996	2,358.65	1,873.14	2,315.73	2005	4,780.05	3,804.92	4,715.23
1983	----	----	----	1997	3,114.00	2,251.53	2,998.91	2006	5,553.86	4,564.69	5,541.76
1984	----	----	----	1998	4,404.94	2,809.73	3,942.66	2007	6,168.15	5,217.70	5,627.25
1985	----	----	----	1999	5,979.54	3,845.77	5,958.32	2008	5,665.94	2,838.50	3,217.97

Index data begins 10/27/1989.   *Source: Euronext Paris*

CAC 40 Index
Weekly Cash as of 01/03/2014

Date	Open	High	Low	Close
12/06/13	4296.4	4309.3	4082.1	4129.4
12/13/13	4142.9	4144.8	4053.4	4059.7
12/20/13	4052.0	4200.3	4051.3	4193.8
12/27/13	4201.6	4279.3	4188.0	4277.7
01/03/14	4282.4	4312.6	4226.7	4247.7

WEEKLY CASH
As of 01/03/2014
Chart High 6168.2 on 06/01/2007
Chart Low 2401.2 on 03/12/2003

The CAC 40® is a free float market capitalization weighted index that reflects the performance of the 40 largest and most actively traded shares listed on Euronext Paris, and is the most widely used indicator of the Paris stock market. Shaded areas indicate French recessions.

Quarterly High, Low and Settle of CAC-40 Index   In Index Value

Quarter	High	Low	Settle	Quarter	High	Low	Settle	Quarter	High	Low	Settle
03/2005	4,108.00	3,804.92	4,067.78	03/2008	5,665.94	4,416.71	4,707.07	03/2011	4,169.87	3,694.52	3,989.18
06/2005	4,254.80	3,882.42	4,229.35	06/2008	5,142.10	4,348.31	4,434.85	06/2011	4,137.97	3,742.31	3,982.21
09/2005	4,620.85	4,089.27	4,600.02	09/2008	4,558.56	3,844.63	4,032.10	09/2011	4,023.59	2,693.21	2,981.96
12/2005	4,780.05	4,288.15	4,715.23	12/2008	4,112.24	2,838.50	3,217.97	12/2011	3,411.22	2,793.22	3,159.81
03/2006	5,247.31	4,719.33	5,220.85	03/2009	3,426.04	2,465.46	2,807.34	03/2012	3,600.48	3,114.45	3,423.81
06/2006	5,329.16	4,564.69	4,965.96	06/2009	3,399.59	2,741.27	3,140.44	06/2012	3,473.20	2,922.26	3,196.65
09/2006	5,285.34	4,710.61	5,250.01	09/2009	3,856.67	2,957.83	3,795.41	09/2012	3,588.02	3,065.47	3,354.82
12/2006	5,553.86	5,196.07	5,541.76	12/2009	3,976.92	3,549.65	3,936.33	12/2012	3,684.16	3,341.52	3,641.07
03/2007	5,771.69	5,295.58	5,634.16	03/2010	4,088.18	3,545.91	3,974.01	03/2013	3,871.58	3,600.81	3,731.42
06/2007	6,168.15	5,620.70	6,054.93	06/2010	4,086.00	3,291.05	3,442.89	06/2013	4,072.24	3,575.17	3,738.91
09/2007	6,156.16	5,217.70	5,715.69	09/2010	3,824.98	3,321.35	3,715.18	09/2013	4,227.21	3,668.77	4,143.44
12/2007	5,882.07	5,358.76	5,627.25	12/2010	3,961.70	3,592.55	3,804.78	12/2013	4,356.28	4,051.25	4,295.95

Source: Euronext Paris

FTSE 100 INDEX

Date	Open	High	Low	Close
08/30/13	6621.1	6696.6	6386.7	6412.9
09/30/13	6412.9	6659.1	6412.9	6462.2
10/31/13	6462.2	6819.9	6316.9	6731.4
11/29/13	6731.4	6780.1	6614.0	6650.6
12/31/13	6650.6	6768.4	6422.2	6749.1

The FTSE 100 Index covers 100 of the largest companies traded on the LSE.   Shaded areas indicate United Kingdom recessions.

Annual High, Low and Settle of FTSE 100 Index   In Index Value

Year	High	Low	Settle	Year	High	Low	Settle	Year	High	Low	Settle
1972	----	----	----	1986	1,721.7	1,365.7	1,679.0	2000	6,900.2	5,915.2	6,222.5
1973	----	----	----	1987	2,449.1	1,515.0	1,712.7	2001	6,360.3	4,219.8	5,217.4
1974	----	----	----	1988	1,892.2	1,687.5	1,793.1	2002	5,362.3	3,609.9	3,940.4
1975	----	----	----	1989	2,435.7	1,782.4	2,422.7	2003	4,491.8	3,277.5	4,476.9
1976	----	----	----	1990	2,479.4	1,974.1	2,143.5	2004	4,826.2	4,283.0	4,814.3
1977	----	----	----	1991	2,683.7	2,052.3	2,493.1	2005	5,647.2	4,765.4	5,618.8
1978	----	----	----	1992	2,848.9	2,260.9	2,846.5	2006	6,271.4	5,467.4	6,220.8
1979	----	----	----	1993	3,480.8	2,727.6	3,418.4	2007	6,754.1	5,821.7	6,456.9
1980	----	----	----	1994	3,539.2	2,844.7	3,065.5	2008	6,534.7	3,665.2	4,434.2
1981	----	----	----	1995	3,690.6	2,949.4	3,689.3	2009	5,445.2	3,460.7	5,412.9
1982	----	----	----	1996	4,123.2	3,612.6	4,118.5	2010	6,021.5	4,790.0	5,899.9
1983	----	----	----	1997	5,367.3	4,036.9	5,135.5	2011	6,105.8	4,791.0	5,572.3
1984	1,231.3	978.7	1,231.2	1998	6,183.7	4,599.2	5,882.6	2012	5,997.0	5,229.8	5,897.8
1985	1,460.7	1,199.6	1,412.6	1999	6,950.6	5,697.7	6,930.2	2013	6,875.6	5,897.8	6,749.1

Index data begins 04/02/1984.   *Source: Euronext Liffe*

FTSE 100 INDEX
Weekly Cash as of 01/03/2014

Date	Open	High	Low	Close
12/06/13	6650.6	6657.4	6479.7	6552.0
12/13/13	6552.0	6571.9	6433.5	6440.0
12/20/13	6440.0	6616.8	6422.2	6606.6
12/27/13	6606.6	6754.1	6606.2	6750.9
01/03/14	6750.9	6768.4	6699.3	6730.7

WEEKLY CASH
As of 01/03/2014

Chart High 6875.6   on 05/22/2013
Chart Low   3277.5   on 03/12/2003

The FTSE 100 Index covers 100 of the largest companies traded on the LSE.   Shaded areas indicate United Kingdom recessions.

Quarterly High, Low and Settle of FTSE 100 Index   In Index Value

Quarter	High	Low	Settle	Quarter	High	Low	Settle	Quarter	High	Low	Settle
03/2005	5,077.8	4,765.4	4,894.4	03/2008	6,534.7	5,338.7	5,702.1	03/2011	6,105.8	5,594.3	5,938.7
06/2005	5,138.2	4,773.7	5,113.2	06/2008	6,377.0	5,470.9	5,625.9	06/2011	6,103.7	5,644.4	5,945.7
09/2005	5,508.4	5,022.1	5,477.7	09/2008	5,649.1	4,671.0	4,902.5	09/2011	6,084.1	4,791.0	5,128.5
12/2005	5,647.2	5,130.9	5,618.8	12/2008	5,052.0	3,665.2	4,434.2	12/2011	5,747.3	4,868.6	5,572.3
03/2006	6,047.0	5,618.8	5,964.6	03/2009	4,675.7	3,460.7	3,926.1	03/2012	5,989.1	5,572.3	5,768.5
06/2006	6,137.1	5,467.4	5,833.4	06/2009	4,520.8	3,838.2	4,249.2	06/2012	5,890.2	5,229.8	5,571.2
09/2006	6,002.9	5,654.6	5,960.8	09/2009	5,190.0	4,096.1	5,133.9	09/2012	5,932.6	5,478.0	5,742.1
12/2006	6,271.4	5,897.3	6,220.8	12/2009	5,445.2	4,955.0	5,412.9	12/2012	5,997.0	5,605.6	5,897.8
03/2007	6,451.4	5,999.8	6,308.0	03/2010	5,742.8	5,033.0	5,679.6	03/2013	6,534.0	5,897.8	6,411.7
06/2007	6,751.3	6,293.9	6,607.9	06/2010	5,833.7	4,898.5	4,916.9	06/2013	6,875.6	6,023.4	6,215.5
09/2007	6,754.1	5,821.7	6,466.8	09/2010	5,650.3	4,790.0	5,548.6	09/2013	6,696.6	6,185.2	6,462.2
12/2007	6,751.7	6,026.9	6,456.9	12/2010	6,021.5	5,519.2	5,899.9	12/2013	6,819.9	6,316.9	6,749.1

Source: Euronext Liffe

HANG SENG INDEX

HANG SENG INDEX
Monthly Cash as of 12/31/2013

MONTHLY CASH
As of 12/31/2013

Chart High	31958.4	on 10/30/2007
Chart Low	1645.0	on 04/11/1986

Index Value

Date	Open	High	Low	Close
08/30/13	22025.8	22696.0	21465.7	21731.4
09/30/13	21948.7	23554.3	21948.7	22859.9
10/31/13	22997.2	23534.7	22640.2	23206.4
11/29/13	23208.8	24014.8	22463.4	23881.3
12/31/13	23936.2	24111.6	22713.7	23306.4

The Hang Seng Index is a freefloat-adjusted market capitalization-weighted stock market index in Hong Kong. The Index was created by Hong Kong banker Stanley Kwan in 1969.

Annual High, Low and Settle of Hang Seng Index   In Index Value

Year	High	Low	Settle	Year	High	Low	Settle	Year	High	Low	Settle
1972	----	----	----	1986	2,543.00	1,645.00	2,524.00	2000	18,397.57	13,596.63	15,095.53
1973	----	----	----	1987	3,968.00	1,876.00	2,302.00	2001	16,274.67	8,894.36	11,397.21
1974	----	----	----	1988	2,774.00	2,199.00	2,687.00	2002	12,021.72	8,772.48	9,321.29
1975	----	----	----	1989	3,329.00	2,022.00	2,836.00	2003	12,740.50	8,331.87	12,575.94
1976	----	----	----	1990	3,559.00	2,697.00	3,024.00	2004	14,339.06	10,917.65	14,230.14
1977	----	----	----	1991	4,309.00	2,970.00	4,297.00	2005	15,508.57	13,320.53	14,876.43
1978	----	----	----	1992	6,470.00	4,284.00	5,512.00	2006	20,049.03	14,843.97	19,964.72
1979	----	----	----	1993	11,959.00	5,431.00	11,888.00	2007	31,958.41	18,659.23	27,812.65
1980	----	----	----	1994	12,599.00	7,670.00	8,191.00	2008	27,853.60	10,676.29	14,387.48
1981	----	----	----	1995	10,073.00	6,890.00	10,073.00	2009	23,099.57	11,344.58	21,872.50
1982	----	----	----	1996	13,744.00	10,070.00	13,451.00	2010	24,988.57	18,971.52	23,035.45
1983	----	----	----	1997	16,820.00	8,775.00	10,722.00	2011	24,468.64	16,170.35	18,434.39
1984	----	----	----	1998	11,926.00	6,544.00	10,048.58	2012	22,718.83	18,056.40	22,656.92
1985	----	----	----	1999	17,138.11	9,000.24	16,962.10	2013	24,111.55	19,426.36	23,306.39

Index data begins 04/11/1986.   *Source: Hong Kong Futures Exchange*

HANG SENG INDEX
Weekly Cash as of 01/03/2014

WEEKLY CASH
As of 01/03/2014

Chart High 31958.4   on 10/30/2007
Chart Low   8331.9   on 04/25/2003

Date	Open	High	Low	Close
12/06/13	23936.2	24111.6	23563.2	23743.1
12/13/13	23970.0	23970.0	23017.3	23246.0
12/20/13	23138.3	23404.5	22713.7	22812.2
12/27/13	22946.6	23283.3	22862.9	23243.2
01/03/14	23353.5	23469.3	22782.4	22817.3

The Hang Seng Index is a freefloat-adjusted market capitalization-weighted stock market index in Hong Kong. The Index was created by Hong Kong banker Stanley Kwan in 1969.

Quarterly High, Low and Settle of Hang Seng Index   In Index Value

Quarter	High	Low	Settle	Quarter	High	Low	Settle	Quarter	High	Low	Settle
03/2005	14,272.54	13,320.53	13,516.88	03/2008	27,853.60	20,572.92	22,849.20	03/2011	24,434.40	22,123.26	23,527.52
06/2005	14,365.05	13,337.44	14,201.06	06/2008	26,387.37	21,773.67	22,102.01	06/2011	24,468.64	21,508.77	22,398.10
09/2005	15,508.57	13,920.87	15,428.52	09/2008	23,369.05	16,283.72	18,016.21	09/2011	22,835.03	16,999.54	17,592.41
12/2005	15,493.00	14,189.47	14,876.43	12/2008	18,285.68	10,676.29	14,387.48	12/2011	20,272.38	16,170.35	18,434.39
03/2006	15,999.31	14,843.97	15,805.04	03/2009	15,763.55	11,344.58	13,576.02	03/2012	21,760.34	18,302.84	20,555.58
06/2006	17,328.43	15,204.86	16,267.62	06/2009	19,161.97	13,411.79	18,378.73	06/2012	21,385.30	18,056.40	19,441.46
09/2006	17,683.45	15,948.76	17,543.05	09/2009	21,929.79	17,185.96	20,955.25	09/2012	20,895.61	18,710.59	20,840.38
12/2006	20,049.03	17,428.10	19,964.72	12/2009	23,099.57	20,305.06	21,872.50	12/2012	22,718.83	20,767.36	22,656.92
03/2007	20,971.46	18,659.23	19,800.93	03/2010	22,671.92	19,423.05	21,239.35	03/2013	23,944.74	21,975.90	22,299.63
06/2007	22,085.59	19,672.94	21,772.73	06/2010	22,388.77	18,971.52	20,128.99	06/2013	23,512.42	19,426.36	20,803.29
09/2007	27,254.97	19,386.72	27,142.47	09/2010	22,439.19	19,777.83	22,358.17	09/2013	23,554.34	20,119.56	22,859.86
12/2007	31,958.41	25,861.73	27,812.65	12/2010	24,988.57	22,392.67	23,035.45	12/2013	24,111.55	22,463.40	23,306.39

Source: Hong Kong Futures Exchange

NIKKEI 225 INDEX

NIKKEI 225 Index
Monthly Cash as of 12/30/2013

MONTHLY CASH
As of 12/30/2013
Chart High 38957.00 on 12/29/1989
Chart Low 2714.00 on 12/31/1971
Index Value

Date	Open	High	Low	Close
08/30/13	13674.50	14466.16	**13188.14**	13388.86
09/30/13	13438.07	14817.50	13407.53	14455.80
10/31/13	14517.98	14799.28	13748.94	14327.94
11/29/13	14403.07	15729.09	14026.17	15661.87
12/31/13	15659.74	**16320.22**	15112.54	16291.31

The Nikkei Stock Average is owned by and proprietary to Nihon Keisai Shimbun.   Shaded areas indicate Japan recessions.

Annual High, Low and Settle of Nikkei 225 Index   In Index Value

Year	High	Low	Settle	Year	High	Low	Settle	Year	High	Low	Settle
1972	5,208.00	2,857.00	5,208.00	1986	18,988.00	12,881.00	18,820.00	2000	20,833.21	13,182.51	13,785.69
1973	5,226.00	4,307.00	4,307.00	1987	26,646.00	18,525.00	21,564.00	2001	14,556.11	9,382.95	10,542.62
1974	4,773.00	3,595.00	3,817.00	1988	30,264.00	21,148.00	30,159.00	2002	12,081.43	8,197.22	8,578.95
1975	4,533.00	3,886.00	4,359.00	1989	38,957.00	30,082.00	38,915.00	2003	11,238.63	7,603.76	10,676.64
1976	4,991.00	4,507.00	4,991.00	1990	38,950.00	19,781.00	23,848.00	2004	12,195.66	10,299.43	11,488.76
1977	5,264.00	4,866.00	4,866.00	1991	27,270.00	21,123.00	22,983.00	2005	16,445.56	10,770.58	16,111.43
1978	6,002.00	5,112.00	6,002.00	1992	23,801.00	14,194.00	16,924.00	2006	17,563.37	14,045.53	17,225.83
1979	6,591.00	6,073.00	6,569.00	1993	21,281.00	15,671.00	17,417.00	2007	18,300.39	14,669.85	15,307.78
1980	7,165.00	6,556.00	7,116.00	1994	21,573.00	17,242.00	19,723.00	2008	15,156.66	6,994.90	8,859.56
1981	7,867.00	7,150.00	7,682.00	1995	20,023.00	14,295.00	19,868.00	2009	10,767.00	7,021.28	10,546.44
1982	8,026.00	6,849.00	8,016.00	1996	22,750.70	18,819.92	19,361.00	2010	11,408.17	8,796.45	10,228.92
1983	9,893.00	7,803.00	9,893.00	1997	20,910.79	14,488.21	15,258.74	2011	10,891.60	8,135.79	8,455.35
1984	11,577.00	9,703.00	11,542.00	1998	17,352.95	12,787.90	13,842.17	2012	10,433.63	8,238.96	10,395.18
1985	13,128.00	11,558.00	13,083.00	1999	19,036.08	13,122.61	18,934.34	2013	16,320.22	10,398.61	16,291.31

Index data begins 05/1949.   *Source: Singapore Exchange*

NIKKEI 225 Index Weekly Cash as of 12/30/2013				
Date	Open	High	Low	Close
12/06/13	15659.74	15794.15	15112.54	15299.86
12/13/13	15556.60	15650.21	15251.45	15403.11
12/20/13	15408.35	15891.82	15146.13	15870.42
12/27/13	15955.90	16232.69	15849.00	16178.94
12/30/13	16269.22	16320.22	16182.71	16291.31

WEEKLY CASH
As of 12/30/2013
Chart High 18300.39 on 02/26/2007
Chart Low 6994.90 on 10/28/2008

The Nikkei Stock Average is owned by and proprietary to Nihon Keisai Shimbun.   Shaded areas indicate Japan recessions.

Quarterly High, Low and Settle of Nikkei 225 Index   In Index Value

Quarter	High	Low	Settle	Quarter	High	Low	Settle	Quarter	High	Low	Settle
03/2005	11,975.46	11,212.63	11,668.95	03/2008	15,156.66	11,691.00	12,525.54	03/2011	10,891.60	8,227.63	9,755.10
06/2005	11,911.90	10,770.58	11,584.01	06/2008	14,601.27	12,521.84	13,481.38	06/2011	10,017.47	9,318.62	9,816.09
09/2005	13,678.44	11,540.93	13,574.30	09/2008	13,603.31	11,160.83	11,259.86	09/2011	10,207.91	8,359.70	8,700.29
12/2005	16,445.56	12,996.29	16,111.43	12/2008	11,456.64	6,994.90	8,859.56	12/2011	9,152.39	8,135.79	8,455.35
03/2006	17,125.64	15,059.52	17,059.66	03/2009	9,325.35	7,021.28	8,109.53	03/2012	10,255.15	8,349.33	10,083.56
06/2006	17,563.37	14,045.53	15,505.18	06/2009	10,170.82	8,084.62	9,958.44	06/2012	10,190.35	8,238.96	9,006.78
09/2006	16,414.94	14,437.24	16,127.58	09/2009	10,767.00	9,050.33	10,133.23	09/2012	9,288.53	8,328.02	8,870.16
12/2006	17,301.69	15,615.56	17,225.83	12/2009	10,707.51	9,076.41	10,546.44	12/2012	10,433.63	8,488.14	10,395.18
03/2007	18,300.39	16,532.91	17,287.65	03/2010	11,147.62	9,867.39	11,089.94	03/2013	12,650.26	10,398.61	12,397.91
06/2007	18,297.00	16,999.05	18,138.36	06/2010	11,408.17	9,347.07	9,382.64	06/2013	15,942.60	11,805.78	13,677.32
09/2007	18,295.27	15,262.10	16,785.69	09/2010	9,807.36	8,796.45	9,369.35	09/2013	14,953.29	13,188.14	14,455.80
12/2007	17,488.97	14,669.85	15,307.78	12/2010	10,394.22	9,123.62	10,228.92	12/2013	16,320.22	13,748.94	16,291.31

Source: Singapore Exchange

SPI 200 INDEX

ASX SPI 200 INDEX
Monthly Cash as of 12/31/2013

Date	Open	High	Low	Close
08/30/13	5062.0	5168.2	**5007.9**	5135.0
09/30/13	5127.1	5314.3	5115.1	5218.9
10/31/13	5218.1	**5457.3**	5118.9	5425.5
11/29/13	5419.8	5439.2	5284.9	5320.1
12/31/13	5322.2	5367.4	5028.2	5352.2

MONTHLY CASH
As of 12/31/2013

Chart High 6851.5 on 11/01/2007
Chart Low 173.5 on 09/30/1974

The ASX200™ is a trademark of ASX Operations Pty Limited, a member of the ASX Group.   Shaded areas indicate Australia recessions.

Annual High, Low and Settle of ASX SPI 200 Index   In Index Value

Year	High	Low	Settle	Year	High	Low	Settle	Year	High	Low	Settle
1972	431.9	331.1	408.6	1986	1,473.2	1,010.8	1,473.2	2000	3,343.7	2,883.0	3,154.7
1973	429.9	287.2	297.5	1987	2,312.4	1,149.3	1,318.8	2001	3,425.2	2,828.0	3,359.9
1974	362.1	173.5	201.6	1988	1,657.6	1,169.6	1,487.2	2002	3,443.9	2,842.6	2,975.5
1975	299.3	195.8	299.3	1989	1,786.6	1,411.9	1,649.8	2003	3,317.5	2,666.3	3,299.8
1976	353.0	273.5	291.4	1990	1,713.7	1,266.5	1,280.7	2004	4,055.0	3,252.9	4,050.6
1977	322.4	283.5	322.3	1991	1,697.7	1,199.8	1,651.4	2005	4,775.8	3,926.6	4,763.4
1978	382.9	298.0	366.1	1992	1,688.9	1,355.6	1,549.9	2006	5,684.4	4,751.1	5,669.9
1979	472.8	369.1	458.9	1993	2,173.6	1,487.4	2,173.6	2007	6,851.5	5,483.3	6,339.8
1980	746.2	509.1	713.5	1994	2,350.1	1,814.5	1,912.7	2008	6,385.7	3,217.5	3,722.3
1981	737.4	545.8	595.5	1995	2,237.4	1,817.2	2,203.0	2009	4,895.3	3,073.1	4,870.6
1982	595.5	443.1	485.4	1996	2,426.5	2,092.4	2,424.6	2010	5,025.1	4,175.7	4,745.2
1983	775.3	487.9	775.3	1997	2,797.3	2,210.0	2,616.5	2011	4,976.4	3,765.9	4,056.6
1984	787.9	646.3	726.1	1998	2,893.7	2,386.7	2,813.4	2012	4,688.6	3,985.0	4,648.9
1985	1,052.1	715.2	1,003.8	1999	3,156.9	2,771.1	3,152.5	2013	5,457.3	4,632.3	5,352.2

Index data begins 07/1936.   *Source: Australian Securities Exchange*

ASX SPI 200 INDEX
Weekly Cash as of 01/03/2014

WEEKLY CASH
As of 01/03/2014
Chart High 6851.5   on 11/01/2007
Chart Low   2666.3   on 03/13/2003

Index Value

Date	Open	High	Low	Close
12/06/13	5322.2	5332.7	5154.6	5186.0
12/13/13	5195.3	5207.6	5028.2	5098.4
12/20/13	5090.5	5265.2	5059.7	5265.2
12/27/13	5262.9	5365.3	5257.4	5324.1
01/03/14	5332.9	5383.4	5325.8	5350.1

The ASX200™ is a trademark of ASX Operations Pty Limited, a member of the ASX Group.   Shaded areas indicate Australia recessions.

Quarterly High, Low and Settle of ASX SPI 200 Index   In Index Value

Quarter	High	Low	Settle	Quarter	High	Low	Settle	Quarter	High	Low	Settle
03/2005	4,266.9	4,026.1	4,109.9	03/2008	6,385.7	5,039.6	5,355.7	03/2011	4,944.4	4,477.4	4,837.9
06/2005	4,321.7	3,926.6	4,277.5	06/2008	5,980.8	5,144.7	5,215.3	06/2011	4,976.4	4,451.7	4,608.0
09/2005	4,679.1	4,213.6	4,641.2	09/2008	5,231.9	4,527.4	4,600.5	09/2011	4,657.4	3,765.9	4,008.6
12/2005	4,775.8	4,311.1	4,763.4	12/2008	4,832.5	3,217.5	3,722.3	12/2011	4,417.6	3,840.2	4,056.6
03/2006	5,139.5	4,751.1	5,129.7	03/2009	3,817.9	3,073.1	3,582.1	03/2012	4,361.1	4,069.1	4,335.2
06/2006	5,406.7	4,758.3	5,073.9	06/2009	4,079.4	3,550.9	3,954.9	06/2012	4,448.5	3,985.0	4,094.6
09/2006	5,164.2	4,899.9	5,154.1	09/2009	4,767.9	3,709.2	4,743.6	09/2012	4,421.0	4,062.3	4,387.0
12/2006	5,684.4	5,113.9	5,669.9	12/2009	4,895.3	4,502.5	4,870.6	12/2012	4,688.6	4,334.3	4,648.9
03/2007	6,052.1	5,499.0	5,995.0	03/2010	4,955.1	4,464.9	4,875.5	03/2013	5,163.5	4,648.9	4,966.5
06/2007	6,409.2	5,915.8	6,274.9	06/2010	5,025.1	4,175.7	4,301.5	06/2013	5,249.6	4,632.3	4,802.6
09/2007	6,594.4	5,483.3	6,567.8	09/2010	4,698.0	4,182.3	4,582.9	09/2013	5,314.3	4,702.7	5,218.9
12/2007	6,851.5	6,105.1	6,339.8	12/2010	4,815.0	4,551.2	4,745.2	12/2013	5,457.3	5,028.2	5,352.2

Source: Australian Securities Exchange

LIVESTOCK & MEATS

Cattle

Cattle prices in 2002-03 rallied sharply due to strong U.S. domestic demand, strong export demand for high-quality grain-fed U.S. beef, and the declining trend seen in the size of the U.S. cattle herd since 1996 (and more generally since 1975). However, cattle prices then plunged in December 2003 and early 2004 after a dairy cow in Washington state was found to have Mad Cow disease. That led to more than 50 countries suspending U.S. beef imports, including Japan which is the most important export destination for U.S. beef. U.S. beef exports plunged to near zero in a matter of days, causing cattle prices to plunge. However, cattle prices quickly recovered in 2004-05 due to continued strong U.S. domestic demand and the relatively quick action by producers to reduce supplies.

Cattle prices in early 2006 plunged due to (1) high slaughter numbers and increased cattle weights, (2) price competition tied to huge poultry inventories which resulted from bird flu overseas, and (3) virtually non-existent U.S. beef exports due to the continued overseas bans on U.S. beef. Cattle prices then rallied in the second half of 2006 and remained strong through mid-2008 when cattle prices were boosted by the big commodity bull market. Cattle prices were also boosted in early 2007 as U.S. beef exports to Asia resumed.

Cattle prices in the latter half of 2008 fell sharply and remained weak through 2009 due to (1) the general plunge in commodity prices, (2) the 2008/09 financial crisis, which made it more difficult and expensive for cattle feeder lots to finance herds, and (3) the global recession which reduced demand for beef and encouraged switching to less expensive proteins.

Cattle prices rallied sharply from 2010-12 due to (1) improved beef demand with the economic recovery that started in mid-2009, and (2) the doubling of corn prices from 2010-11 that increased feed costs and encouraged cattle producers to slash herd sizes. Cattle prices were also boosted starting in 2011 when U.S. cattle exports finally recovered to an 11-year high in 2011 and U.S. beef exports rose to a record high.

Cattle prices during 2012 rallied sharply as corn prices surged on the severe summer 2012 drought, which caused cattle producers to reduce their herd sizes to reduce feed costs. The drought also decimated hay and grazing land, causing ranchers to slash their herds. The number of cattle on feed in 2012 fell sharply by -6.2% to 22.342 million head.

Cattle prices remained strong in 2013 despite a sharp drop in corn prices due to tight supplies. U.S. cattle on feed in 2013 hovered near a 10-year low and U.S. beef production in 2013 fell -1.2% to an 8-year low of 25.59 billion pounds. Also, U.S. beef exports in 2013 were strong at 24.6 billion pounds.

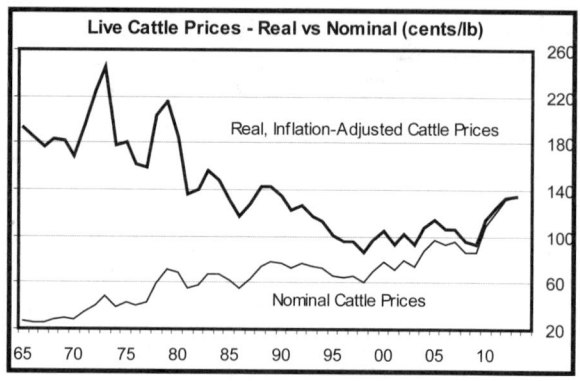

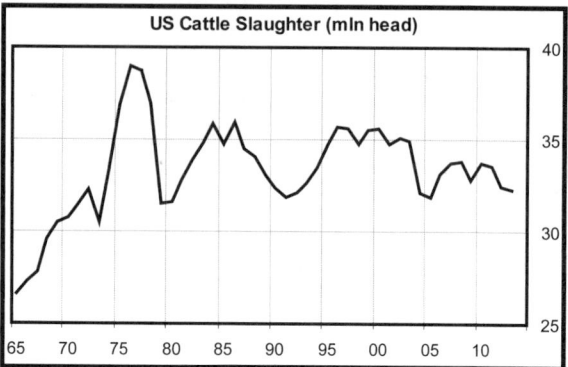

Cattle Market Events

1975—US cattle numbers peak—Cattle herd numbers in the US peak at 132 million head, having nearly doubled from 1940, but then enter a steady downtrend to current levels near 95 million.

1985—US per-capita beef consumption peaks—US per-capita beef consumption peaks in 1985 at 79.3 pounds per year but then falls sharply in the 1990s (due to health concerns about eating beef) and finally stabilizes near 66 pounds.

1989—World cattle numbers peak—World cattle numbers grow steadily in the 1980s but then peak in 1989 at 1.10 billion head, and then trend lower to 1.02 billion in 2005.

2001—Brazil cattle herd soars—Brazil cattle herd numbers, which were stable near 150 million head in the 1990s, surge starting in 2001 to 170 million by 2005, as Brazil puts more emphasis on meat production and the export of higher-value agriculture products.

May 2003—First case of Mad Cow disease (BSE) is found in Canada, prompting the US to suspend the import of Canadian cattle.

December 2003—First case of BSE is found in the US in a Canadian-born dairy cow in Washington state. More than 50 countries suspend US beef exports.

China to 2017 >?

Hogs

Lean hog prices showed more than the usual volatility starting in the mid-1990s. There were major declines to 3-decade lows in 1998 and again in 2002. The plunge in hog prices in 1998 was caused by an overexpansion of pork production in 1996-97 when prices were high. That expansion caused an industry disaster in 1998 when hog prices plunged and many smaller hog farmers were forced out of business. In addition, Asian demand for pork was reduced in late-1997 and 1998 by the Asian financial crisis. Hog prices recovered in 2000-01 but then plunged again in 2002 as U.S. hog farmers again overproduced and caused another pork glut.

Hog prices in 2003 and 2004 recovered as the U.S. economy improved after the 2001 recession and as U.S. hog exports were strong starting in 2002. In addition, herd sizes and slaughter rates were relatively low during that period. Hog prices faded in 2005 and early 2006 on adequate hog supplies supply and competition from poultry, which was cheap due to a glut of domestic poultry inventories tied to bird flu in Asia. Yet bird flu and mad cow disease sparked stronger demand in Asia for U.S. pork as consumers avoided poultry and beef.

Lean hog futures prices surged to a then-record high of 90 cents/lb in August 2008 as hog prices were caught up in the commodity bull market frenzy. Hog prices then fell sharply in late 2008 on the general commodity market melt-down and the financial crisis that emerged in September 2008. Hog prices rallied sharply from late-2009 through 2011 due to the surge in corn and feed prices, which led to smaller herd sizes and tighter supplies. Hog prices found support from mid-2012 through early-2013 due to the 2012 U.S. summer drought, which caused corn and feed prices to surge. The sharp drop in corn prices in 2013 helped push hog prices lower as reduced feed costs encouraged producers to build herd sizes and supply.

The long-term outlook for the pork market is favorable, according to the USDA's "Agricultural Baseline Projections to 2022." Domestic demand for pork should grow at a slightly higher rate than the U.S. population since the USDA is expecting U.S. per-capita pork consumption to improve by more than 2 pounds over the next decade from 47.0 pounds per year in 2013. The USDA is projecting steady growth in U.S. pork exports of about +1.4% per year, driven by increased global demand for meat and the efficiency of U.S. pork production facilities. The USDA expects U.S. annual pork production to grow by an average +1.3% from 2013-22, driven by lower feed costs and productivity gains in the breeding herd and increased slaughter weights. The USDA expects carcass weights to improve by an average +0.5% per year from 57.9 pounds in 2013 to 62.0 pounds by 2022. The USDA is expecting hog prices on the farm to rise by an average of +1.1% per year during 2013-22, from 63.47 cents per pound in 2012 to 70.22 cents by 2022.

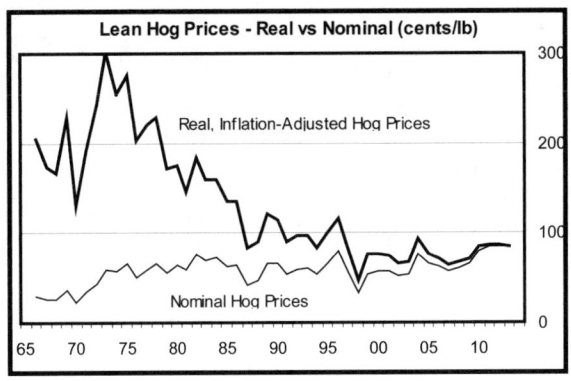

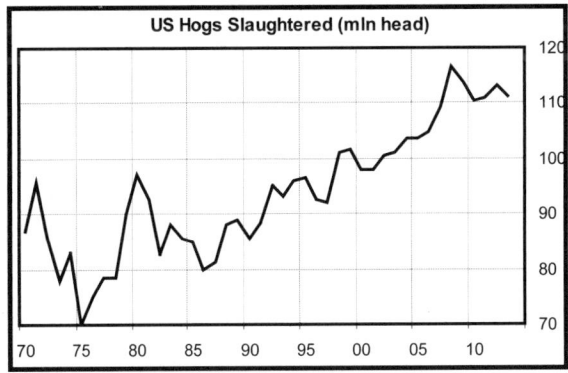

Hog Market Events

1970s—Hog prices rally—Hog prices rallied sharply in the early-1970s due to high inflation and a general rise in commodity prices. Hog prices in 1975 reached an inflation-adjusted record high close of 257 cents per pound (2006 dollars) due to tight supplies caused by a sharp drop in pork production in the first half of the 1970s. On an inflation-adjusted basis, hog prices are currently only about one-fourth of the record high of 257 cents per pound posted in 1975.

1980s—Lower pork production supports prices—In 1980, the number of US hogs slaughtered reached a then-record high of 97.2 million head, causing hog prices to plunge to 37 cents per pound. However, the number of hogs slaughtered then fell sharply by -4.8% in 1981 then and by -10.4% in 1982, leading to a sharp rally in pork prices to the all-time record high of 91.80 cents per pound in August 1982.

1990s—Pork exports surge in the 1990s—Between 1994 and 1998, the volume of US pork exports tripled due to efficient new plants, genetics, and the penetration of the Japanese market. In 1995, US pork exports exceeded imports for the first time in post-war history. US pork exports now account for more than 12% of production, versus 1% of production in the late 1980s.

1998—Hog prices drop to 30-year lows—Due to a severe production glut, hog prices in 1998 fell to levels not seen since the early-1970s and inflation-adjusted prices fall to levels not seen since the Depression.

CATTLE, FEEDER

CATTLE, FEEDER - CME
Quarterly Nearest Futures as of 01/09/2014

Date	Open	High	Low	Close
12/31/12	143.650	154.750	142.500	151.400
03/29/13	151.900	153.600	134.525	135.525
06/28/13	144.050	150.775	131.500	149.450
09/30/13	149.900	164.900	149.550	164.100
12/31/13	163.775	168.475	162.750	166.700

QUARTERLY NEAREST FUTURES
As of 01/09/2014
Chart High 169.400 on 01/09/2014
Chart Low 25.375 on 03/03/1975
CONTRACT SIZE 50,000 lbs
MIN TICK .025 cents
VALUE 12.5 USD / contract
EACH GRID 1 cents
VALUE 500 USD / contract
DAILY LIMIT 3 cents
VALUE 1,500 USD / contract
TRADING HOURS
5:00p-4:00p / 9:05a-1:00p CT

Nearby Futures through Last Trading Day.   Oklahoma City: 01/1970 to 11/1971; Futures: 11/30/1971 to date.

Annual High, Low and Settle of Feeder Cattle Futures   In Cents per Pound

Year	High	Low	Settle	Year	High	Low	Settle	Year	High	Low	Settle
1972	47.750	36.475	47.400	1986	68.300	52.000	60.725	2000	92.200	82.050	91.500
1973	71.200	47.250	54.000	1987	80.200	60.725	76.875	2001	92.750	81.400	86.025
1974	59.750	26.800	30.100	1988	84.550	69.150	84.150	2002	86.200	72.525	83.800
1975	41.650	25.375	38.650	1989	85.600	75.150	84.850	2003	110.170	73.950	78.925
1976	48.250	32.675	39.525	1990	90.350	79.650	89.400	2004	118.700	79.800	101.800
1977	45.500	36.800	44.100	1991	91.100	75.700	78.050	2005	119.750	97.800	115.250
1978	76.900	44.300	74.675	1992	86.750	74.700	86.625	2006	119.350	95.500	99.600
1979	95.150	71.950	82.700	1993	89.500	81.000	83.050	2007	120.200	92.100	105.100
1980	87.600	65.475	73.450	1994	84.000	71.250	76.225	2008	116.500	85.450	94.050
1981	75.700	57.250	57.350	1995	76.900	60.450	61.025	2009	104.925	87.600	95.850
1982	74.900	58.000	66.525	1996	68.250	46.150	67.525	2010	122.475	95.175	121.875
1983	74.450	55.500	69.225	1997	83.400	66.250	75.875	2011	149.850	120.500	146.350
1984	72.000	61.950	71.200	1998	79.050	65.450	69.175	2012	161.500	133.000	151.400
1985	74.750	56.500	65.450	1999	85.850	68.450	85.350	2013	168.475	131.500	166.700

Futures begin trading 11/30/1971.   *Source: CME Group; Chicago Mercantile Exchange*

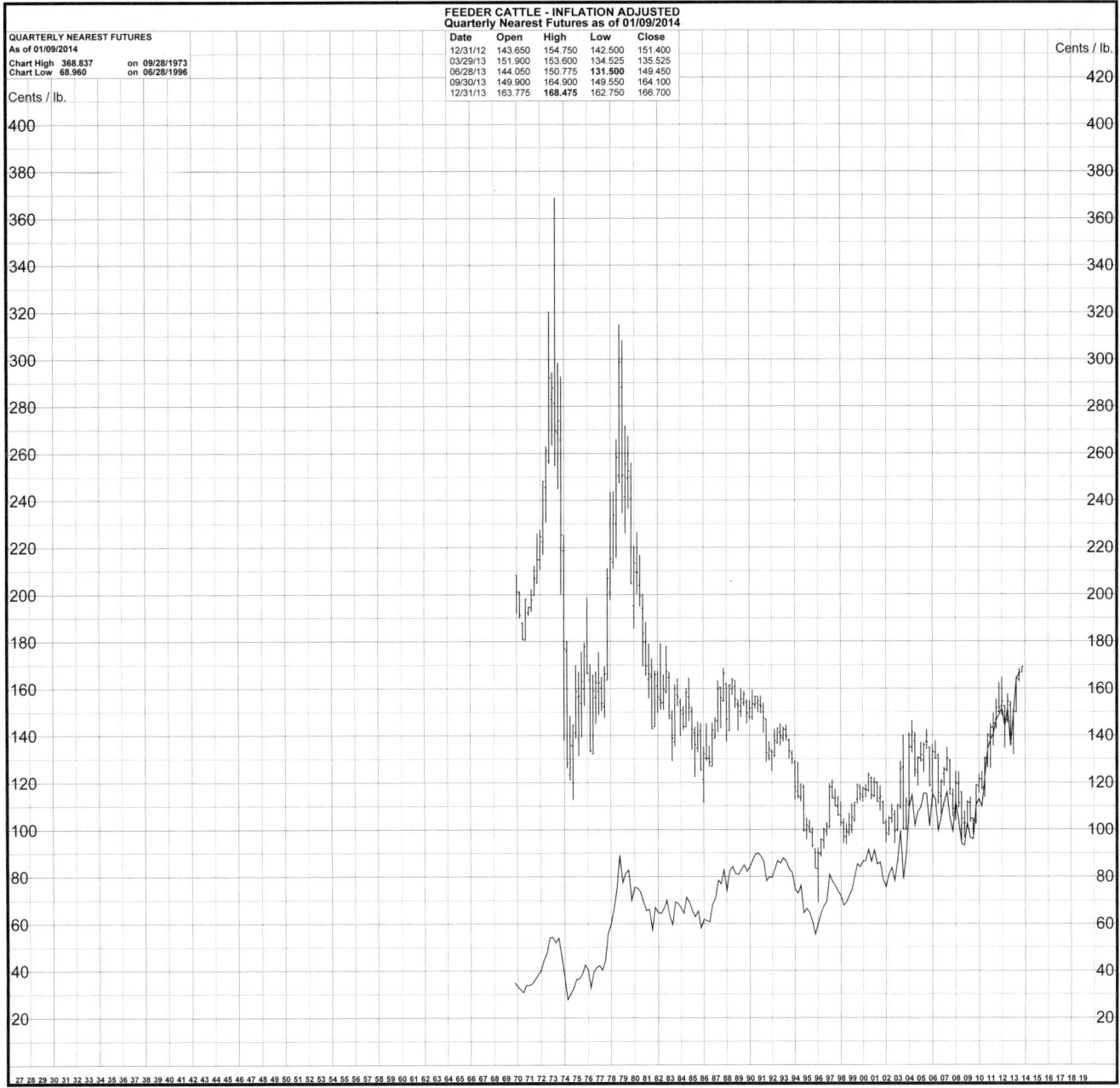

FEEDER CATTLE - INFLATION ADJUSTED
Quarterly Nearest Futures as of 01/09/2014

Date	Open	High	Low	Close
12/31/12	143.650	154.750	142.500	151.400
03/29/13	151.900	153.600	134.525	135.525
06/28/13	144.050	150.775	131.500	149.450
09/30/13	149.900	164.900	149.550	164.100
12/31/13	163.775	168.475	162.750	166.700

QUARTERLY NEAREST FUTURES
As of 01/09/2014

Chart High 368.837 on 09/28/1973
Chart Low 68.960 on 06/28/1996

Cents / lb.

Nearby Futures through Last Trading Day.   Oklahoma City: 01/1970 to 11/1971; Futures: 11/30/1971 to date.

Annual High, Low and Settle of Feeder Cattle   In Cents per Pound

Year	High	Low	Settle	Year	High	Low	Settle	Year	High	Low	Settle
1972	44.81	37.35	44.81	1986	69.15	58.00	65.50	2000	106.88	89.50	98.88
1973	65.40	45.31	47.50	1987	88.75	65.50	82.00	2001	109.88	83.63	95.31
1974	52.25	26.50	26.50	1988	95.75	78.90	91.25	2002	96.06	81.00	89.25
1975	41.20	24.75	39.50	1989	96.40	84.50	90.25	2003	112.25	75.00	75.70
1976	46.20	34.25	35.75	1990	102.13	88.00	100.50	2004	128.50	73.63	113.19
1977	43.50	35.45	42.75	1991	105.25	86.00	86.00	2005	131.80	108.00	122.63
1978	76.25	42.75	76.25	1992	94.75	83.75	90.63	2006	131.75	97.68	97.96
1979	97.75	75.50	85.75	1993	102.50	89.00	91.25	2007	119.29	94.10	104.13
1980	90.00	68.00	75.00	1994	95.00	76.13	82.63	2008	113.61	88.58	92.93
1981	75.13	59.00	59.50	1995	85.75	62.63	64.13	2009	101.61	90.81	93.30
1982	70.50	59.50	65.00	1996	69.63	54.25	68.75	2010	123.47	94.38	123.47
1983	74.50	59.75	65.00	1997	93.75	68.75	85.37	2011	145.31	122.44	144.20
1984	71.75	62.00	70.00	1998	90.88	68.88	74.75	2012	159.19	134.18	146.88
1985	74.50	60.38	65.00	1999	97.00	75.63	95.75	2013	168.32	130.81	166.31

Oklahoma City.   *Source: CME Group; Chicago Mercantile Exchange*

CATTLE, FEEDER

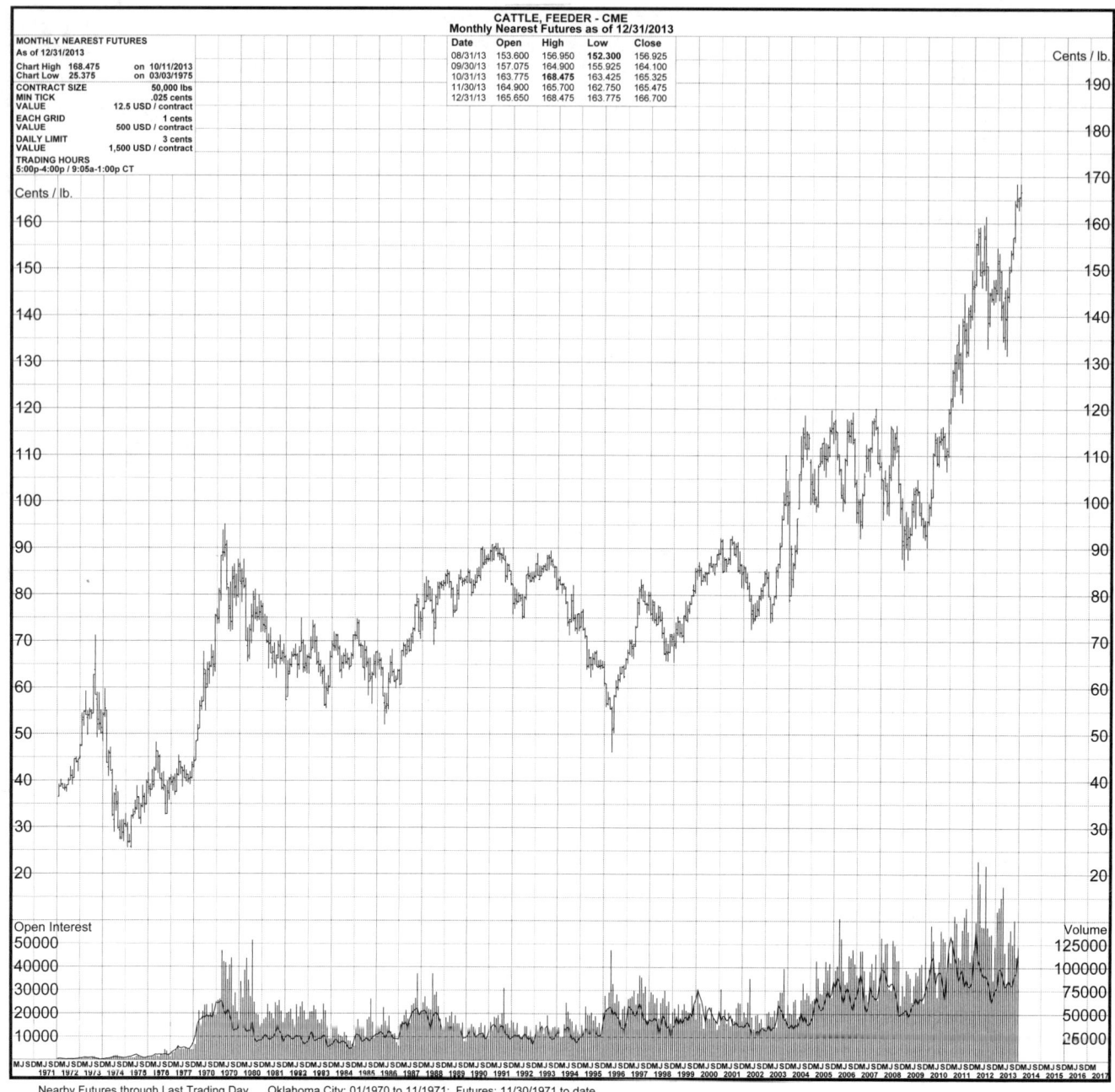

CATTLE, FEEDER - CME
Monthly Nearest Futures as of 12/31/2013

Date	Open	High	Low	Close
08/31/13	153.600	156.950	**152.300**	156.925
09/30/13	157.075	164.900	155.925	164.100
10/31/13	163.775	**168.475**	163.425	165.325
11/30/13	164.900	165.700	162.750	165.475
12/31/13	165.650	168.475	163.775	166.700

MONTHLY NEAREST FUTURES
As of 12/31/2013
Chart High 168.475 on 10/11/2013
Chart Low 25.375 on 03/03/1975
CONTRACT SIZE 50,000 lbs
MIN TICK .025 cents
VALUE 12.5 USD / contract
EACH GRID 1 cents
VALUE 500 USD / contract
DAILY LIMIT 3 cents
VALUE 1,500 USD / contract
TRADING HOURS
5:00p-4:00p / 9:05a-1:00p CT

Nearby Futures through Last Trading Day.   Oklahoma City: 01/1970 to 11/1971; Futures: 11/30/1971 to date.

Annual High, Low and Settle of Feeder Cattle Futures   In Cents per Pound

Year	High	Low	Settle	Year	High	Low	Settle	Year	High	Low	Settle
1972	47.750	36.475	47.400	1986	68.300	52.000	60.725	2000	92.200	82.050	91.500
1973	71.200	47.250	54.000	1987	80.200	60.725	76.875	2001	92.750	81.400	86.025
1974	59.750	26.800	30.100	1988	84.550	69.150	84.150	2002	86.200	72.525	83.800
1975	41.650	25.375	38.650	1989	85.600	75.150	84.850	2003	110.170	73.950	78.925
1976	48.250	32.675	39.525	1990	90.350	79.650	89.400	2004	118.700	79.800	101.800
1977	45.500	36.800	44.100	1991	91.100	75.700	78.050	2005	119.750	97.800	115.250
1978	76.900	44.300	74.675	1992	86.750	74.700	86.625	2006	119.350	95.500	99.600
1979	95.150	71.950	82.700	1993	89.500	81.000	83.050	2007	120.200	92.100	105.100
1980	87.600	65.475	73.450	1994	84.000	71.250	76.225	2008	116.500	85.450	94.050
1981	75.700	57.250	57.350	1995	76.900	60.450	61.025	2009	104.925	87.600	95.850
1982	74.900	58.000	66.525	1996	68.250	46.150	67.525	2010	122.475	95.175	121.875
1983	74.450	55.500	69.225	1997	83.400	66.250	75.875	2011	149.850	120.500	146.350
1984	72.000	61.950	71.200	1998	79.050	65.450	69.175	2012	161.500	133.000	151.400
1985	74.750	56.500	65.450	1999	85.850	68.450	85.350	2013	168.475	131.500	166.700

Futures begin trading 11/30/1971.   *Source: CME Group; Chicago Mercantile Exchange*

Cattle, Oklahoma City Avg
Monthly Cash as of 12/31/2013

Date	Open	High	Low	Close
08/30/13	149.010	155.630	**149.010**	155.320
09/30/13	156.100	159.630	155.930	159.630
10/31/13	159.920	165.390	159.920	165.390
11/29/13	165.110	165.500	164.520	164.630
12/31/13	165.880	**168.320**	164.140	166.310

MONTHLY CASH
As of 12/31/2013
Chart High 168.320 on 12/13/2013
Chart Low 24.750 on 01/31/1975

Cents / lb.

Oklahoma City: 01/1970 to date.

Annual High, Low and Settle of Feeder Cattle   In Cents per Pound

Year	High	Low	Settle	Year	High	Low	Settle	Year	High	Low	Settle
1972	44.81	37.35	44.81	1986	69.15	58.00	65.50	2000	106.88	89.50	98.88
1973	65.40	45.31	47.50	1987	88.75	65.50	82.00	2001	109.88	83.63	95.31
1974	52.25	26.50	26.50	1988	95.75	78.90	91.25	2002	96.06	81.00	89.25
1975	41.20	24.75	39.50	1989	96.40	84.50	90.25	2003	112.25	75.00	75.70
1976	46.20	34.25	35.75	1990	102.13	88.00	100.50	2004	128.50	73.63	113.19
1977	43.50	35.45	42.75	1991	105.25	86.00	86.00	2005	131.80	108.00	122.63
1978	76.25	42.75	76.25	1992	94.75	83.75	90.63	2006	131.75	97.68	97.96
1979	97.75	75.50	85.75	1993	102.50	89.00	91.25	2007	119.29	94.10	104.13
1980	90.00	68.00	75.00	1994	95.00	76.13	82.63	2008	113.61	88.58	92.93
1981	75.13	59.00	59.50	1995	85.75	62.63	64.13	2009	101.61	90.81	93.30
1982	70.50	59.50	65.00	1996	69.63	54.25	68.75	2010	123.47	94.38	123.47
1983	74.50	59.75	65.00	1997	93.75	68.75	85.37	2011	145.31	122.44	144.20
1984	71.75	62.00	70.00	1998	90.88	68.88	74.75	2012	159.19	134.18	146.88
1985	74.50	60.38	65.00	1999	97.00	75.63	95.75	2013	168.32	130.81	166.31

Oklahoma City.   *Source: CME Group; Chicago Mercantile Exchange*

CATTLE, FEEDER

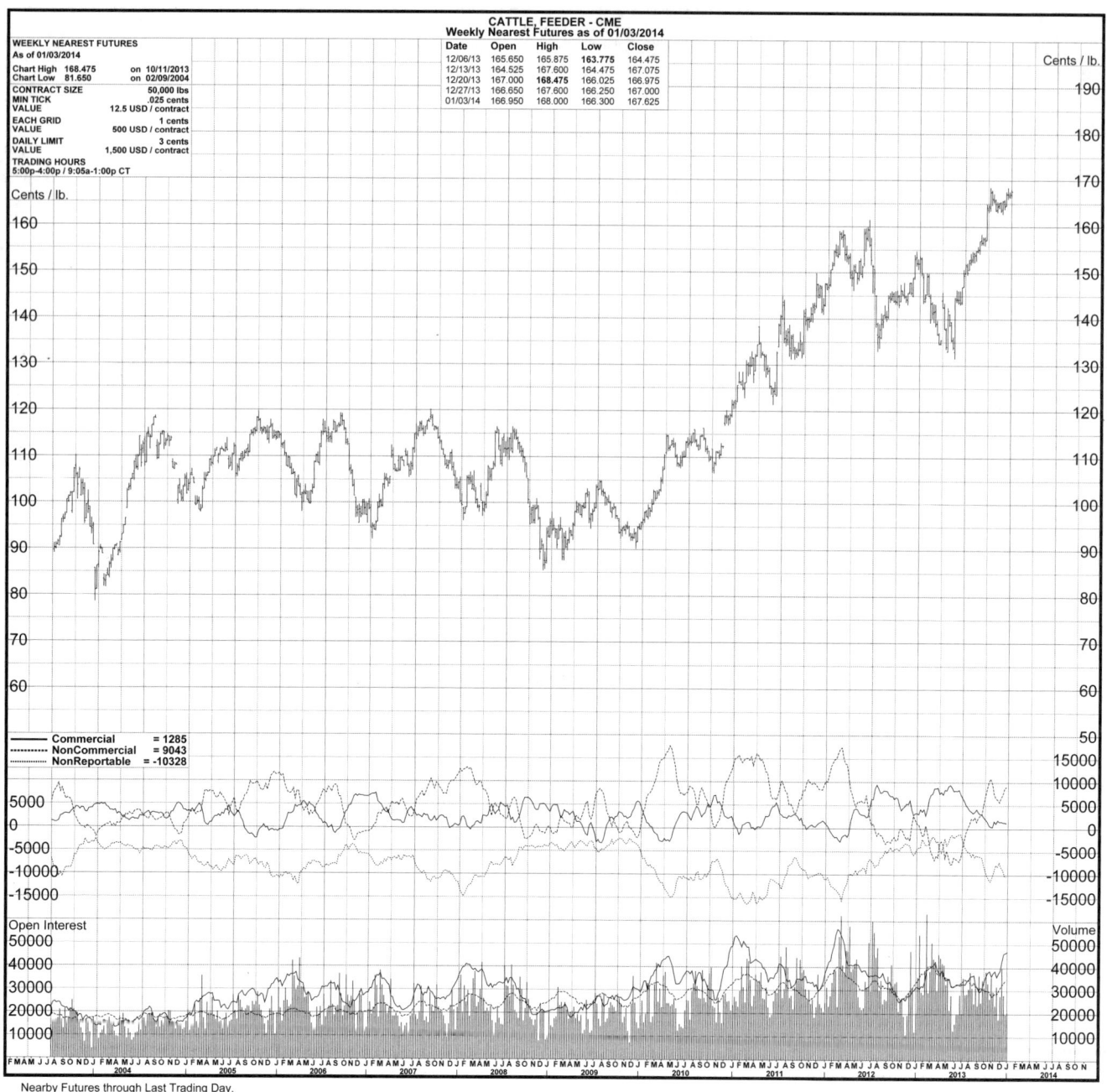

Source: CME Group; Chicago Mercantile Exchange

Quarterly High, Low and Settle of Feeder Cattle Futures In Cents per Pound

Quarter	High	Low	Settle	Quarter	High	Low	Settle	Quarter	High	Low	Settle
03/2005	108.100	97.800	107.675	03/2008	107.000	96.150	99.300	03/2011	134.050	120.500	134.025
06/2005	113.920	106.850	109.425	06/2008	116.500	97.100	111.875	06/2011	139.675	121.375	138.075
09/2005	116.200	105.400	115.425	09/2008	116.500	102.000	104.000	09/2011	144.900	131.250	140.525
12/2005	119.750	112.600	115.250	12/2008	104.200	85.450	94.050	12/2011	149.850	137.500	146.350
03/2006	115.100	100.800	101.475	03/2009	98.050	87.600	93.175	03/2012	159.250	146.550	148.825
06/2006	117.920	98.000	115.200	06/2009	103.425	92.925	102.825	06/2012	161.500	145.575	151.450
09/2006	119.350	112.450	112.900	09/2009	104.925	95.050	96.500	09/2012	150.825	133.000	143.800
12/2006	113.800	95.500	99.600	12/2009	96.750	90.175	95.850	12/2012	154.750	142.500	151.400
03/2007	106.370	92.100	105.590	03/2010	110.700	95.175	110.425	03/2013	153.600	134.525	135.525
06/2007	112.500	105.500	111.550	06/2010	114.950	107.625	113.050	06/2013	150.775	131.500	149.450
09/2007	120.200	110.700	116.040	09/2010	116.300	109.025	109.925	09/2013	164.900	149.550	164.100
12/2007	116.400	102.850	105.100	12/2010	122.475	106.550	121.875	12/2013	168.475	162.750	166.700

Source: CME Group; Chicago Mercantile Exchange

Cattle, Oklahoma City Avg
Weekly Cash as of 01/03/2014

Date	Open	High	Low	Close
12/06/13	165.880	166.530	165.220	165.790
12/13/13	165.750	168.320	165.750	168.320
12/20/13	167.620	167.620	166.530	166.530
12/27/13	165.730	165.730	164.140	164.670
01/03/14	164.670	169.470	164.670	169.470

WEEKLY CASH
As of 01/03/2014
Chart High 169.470 on 01/03/2014
Chart Low 73.630 on 01/09/2004
Cents / lb.

Oklahoma City.

Quarterly High, Low and Settle of Feeder Cattle   In Cents per Pound

Quarter	High	Low	Settle	Quarter	High	Low	Settle	Quarter	High	Low	Settle
03/2005	126.13	108.00	118.75	03/2008	103.99	97.16	99.31	03/2011	134.43	122.44	134.43
06/2005	131.80	120.50	125.25	06/2008	110.32	98.43	108.92	06/2011	136.14	122.71	134.02
09/2005	129.13	115.13	120.88	09/2008	113.61	106.17	106.17	09/2011	139.44	131.12	133.42
12/2005	125.81	118.25	122.63	12/2008	105.62	88.58	92.93	12/2011	145.31	134.66	144.20
03/2006	131.75	116.19	117.38	03/2009	96.59	90.81	93.79	03/2012	159.19	145.90	153.93
06/2006	129.06	115.13	129.06	06/2009	100.52	94.57	98.44	06/2012	155.14	147.28	147.66
09/2006	129.06	113.67	115.77	09/2009	101.61	95.49	95.49	09/2012	149.14	134.18	143.05
12/2006	115.44	97.68	97.96	12/2009	95.36	92.16	93.30	12/2012	148.51	142.92	146.88
03/2007	106.09	94.10	106.09	03/2010	107.43	94.38	107.43	03/2013	151.08	133.58	134.94
06/2007	109.43	106.23	108.52	06/2010	114.10	107.66	111.48	06/2013	140.27	130.81	137.73
09/2007	119.29	108.81	116.40	09/2010	115.04	109.72	110.03	09/2013	159.63	139.22	159.63
12/2007	116.42	102.79	104.13	12/2010	123.47	107.48	123.47	12/2013	168.32	159.92	166.31

Oklahoma City.   *Source: CME Group; Chicago Mercantile Exchange*

321

CATTLE, LIVE

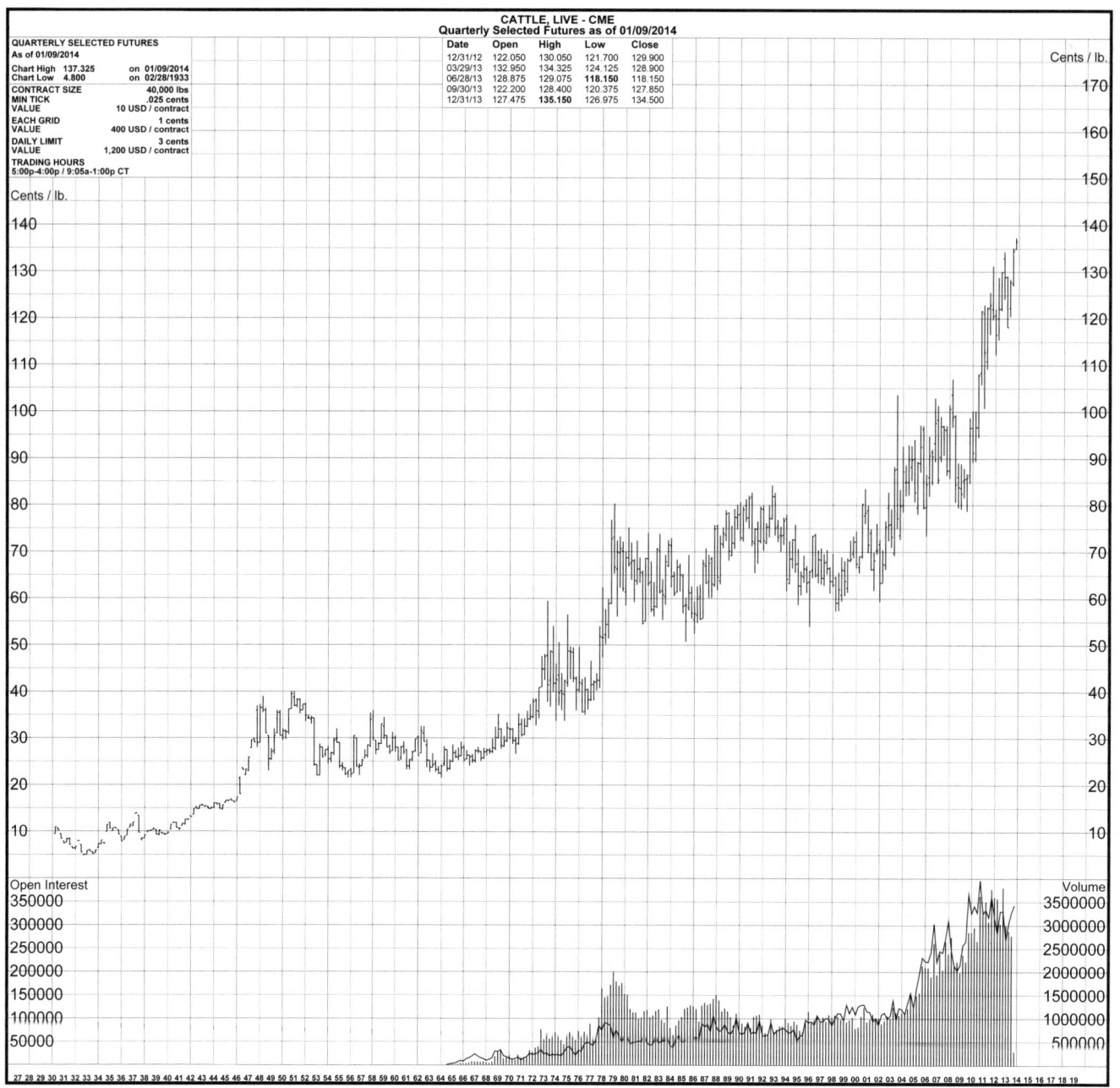

CATTLE, LIVE - CME
Quarterly Selected Futures as of 01/09/2014

Date	Open	High	Low	Close
12/31/12	122.050	130.050	121.700	129.900
03/29/13	132.950	134.325	124.125	128.900
06/28/13	128.875	129.075	118.150	118.150
09/30/13	122.200	128.400	120.375	127.850
12/31/13	127.475	135.150	126.975	134.500

QUARTERLY SELECTED FUTURES
As of 01/09/2014

Chart High	137.325	on 01/09/2014
Chart Low	4.800	on 02/28/1933
CONTRACT SIZE	40,000 lbs	
MIN TICK	.025 cents	
VALUE	10 USD / contract	
EACH GRID VALUE	1 cents 400 USD / contract	
DAILY LIMIT VALUE	3 cents 1,200 USD / contract	
TRADING HOURS	5:00p-4:00p / 9:05a-1:00p CT	

Nearby Futures through Last Trading Day using Selected contract months: February, April, June, August, October and December.   Good, Chicago: to 11/1964; Futures: 11/30/1964 to date.

Annual High, Low and Settle of Live Cattle Futures   In Cents per Pound

Year	High	Low	Settle	Year	High	Low	Settle	Year	High	Low	Settle
1930	12.62	9.42	10.17	1944	16.07	14.81	14.87	1958	36.00	26.50	28.75
1931	9.43	7.11	7.11	1945	16.91	14.71	16.59	1959	34.50	26.50	27.00
1932	7.91	5.44	5.44	1946	23.64	16.14	23.19	1960	31.25	25.25	28.00
1933	6.01	4.80	5.17	1947	29.82	21.94	29.08	1961	29.25	23.25	27.00
1934	8.06	5.35	7.41	1948	39.00	28.00	31.00	1962	32.50	26.25	29.25
1935	11.91	9.90	10.62	1949	36.00	23.00	35.50	1963	29.75	22.75	23.25
1936	10.38	7.80	10.38	1950	36.25	29.50	36.25	1964	28.25	21.50	23.450
1937	13.97	9.69	9.69	1951	40.00	35.25	36.00	1965	28.600	23.200	26.225
1938	10.16	7.91	10.16	1952	37.50	33.00	34.25	1966	29.200	24.100	25.950
1939	10.64	9.03	9.44	1953	34.25	22.00	26.00	1967	28.100	24.675	25.700
1940	12.06	9.08	11.85	1954	30.00	24.50	29.50	1968	29.850	25.525	27.925
1941	12.57	10.23	12.57	1955	32.00	22.00	22.25	1969	35.250	27.400	29.300
1942	15.30	12.39	14.85	1956	30.50	21.50	24.00	1970	33.350	26.600	28.725
1943	15.71	14.84	14.87	1957	28.50	22.00	28.50	1971	35.900	28.550	34.200

Futures begin trading 11/30/1964.   Data continued on page 324.   *Source: CME Group; Chicago Mercantile Exchange*

LIVE CATTLE - INFLATION ADJUSTED
Quarterly Selected Futures as of 01/09/2014

Date	Open	High	Low	Close
12/31/12	122.050	130.050	121.700	129.900
03/29/13	132.950	134.325	124.125	128.900
06/28/13	128.875	129.075	118.150	118.150
09/30/13	122.200	128.400	120.375	127.850
12/31/13	127.475	135.150	126.975	134.500

QUARTERLY SELECTED FUTURES
As of 01/09/2014
Chart High 372.727 on 09/30/1948
Chart Low 77.247 on 06/28/2002

Cents / lb.

Nearby Futures through Last Trading Day using Selected contract months: February, April, June, August, October and December.   Good, Chicago: to 11/1964; Futures: 11/30/1964 to date.

Annual High, Low and Settle of Live Cattle   In Cents per Pound

Year	High	Low	Settle	Year	High	Low	Settle	Year	High	Low	Settle
1930	12.62	9.42	10.17	1944	16.07	14.81	14.87	1958	36.00	26.50	28.75
1931	9.43	7.11	7.11	1945	16.91	14.71	16.59	1959	34.50	26.50	27.00
1932	7.91	5.44	5.44	1946	23.64	16.14	23.19	1960	31.25	25.25	28.00
1933	6.01	4.80	5.17	1947	29.82	21.94	29.08	1961	29.25	23.25	27.00
1934	8.06	5.35	7.41	1948	39.00	28.00	31.00	1962	32.50	26.25	29.25
1935	11.91	9.90	10.62	1949	36.00	23.00	35.50	1963	29.75	22.75	23.25
1936	10.38	7.80	10.38	1950	36.25	29.50	36.25	1964	28.25	21.50	25.50
1937	13.97	9.69	9.69	1951	40.00	35.25	36.00	1965	30.00	25.00	27.00
1938	10.16	7.91	10.16	1952	37.50	33.00	34.25	1966	32.00	24.50	25.25
1939	10.64	9.03	9.44	1953	34.25	22.00	26.00	1967	29.25	25.00	28.00
1940	12.06	9.08	11.85	1954	30.00	24.50	29.50	1968	29.75	26.50	29.15
1941	12.57	10.23	12.57	1955	32.00	22.00	22.25	1969	35.25	28.15	28.15
1942	15.30	12.39	14.85	1956	30.50	21.50	24.00	1970	32.75	27.00	28.00
1943	15.71	14.84	14.87	1957	28.50	22.00	28.50	1971	34.65	28.10	34.60

Chicago: All Grades to 12/1947; Good 01/1948 to 12/1964; Choice 01/1965 to 07/1971.   Data continued on page 325.
Source: CME Group; Chicago Mercantile Exchange

CATTLE, LIVE

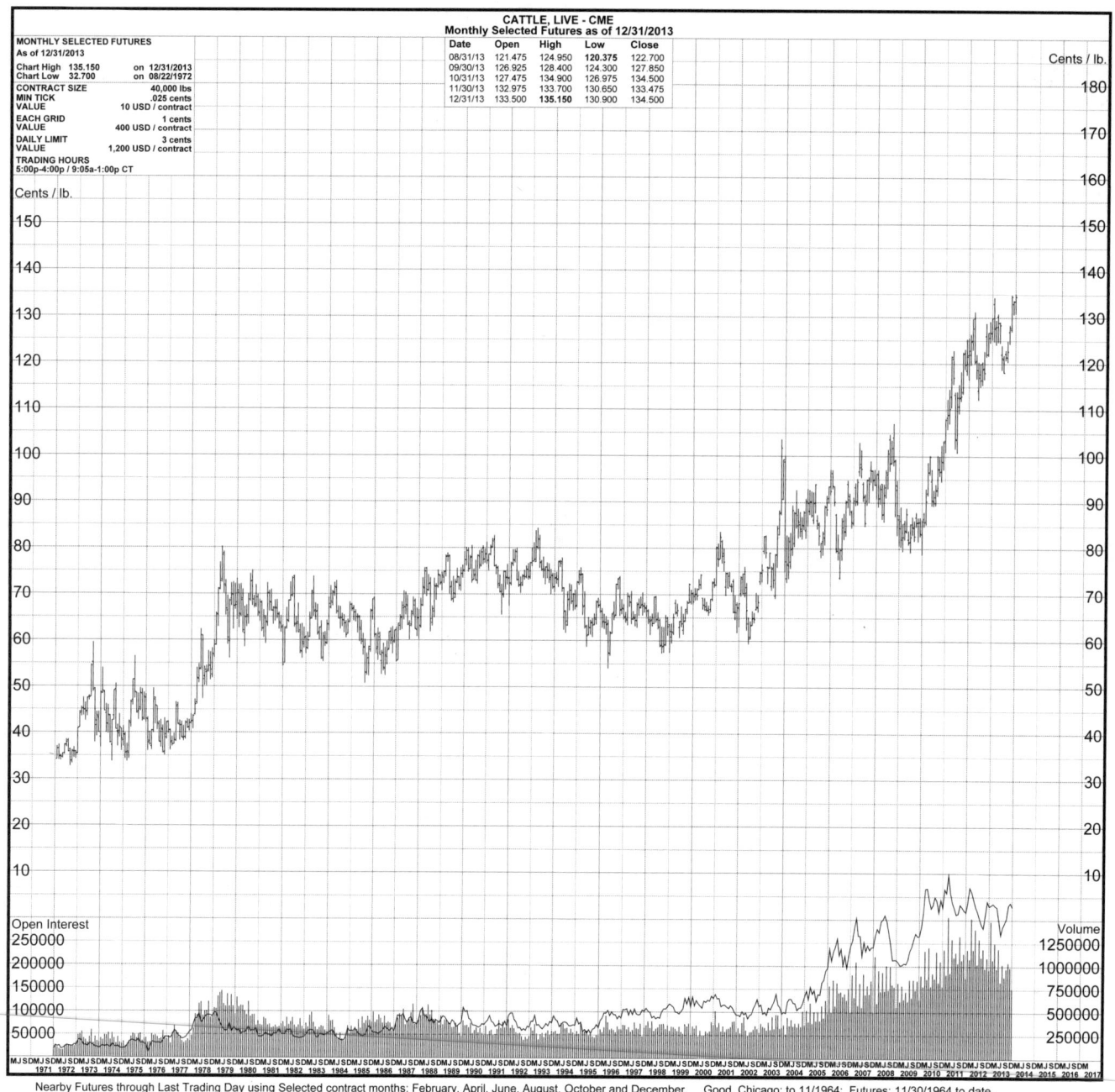

CATTLE, LIVE - CME
Monthly Selected Futures as of 12/31/2013

Date	Open	High	Low	Close
08/31/13	121.475	124.950	120.375	122.700
09/30/13	126.925	128.400	124.300	127.850
10/31/13	127.475	134.900	126.975	134.500
11/30/13	132.975	133.700	130.650	133.475
12/31/13	133.500	135.150	130.900	134.500

MONTHLY SELECTED FUTURES
As of 12/31/2013

Chart High 135.150 on 12/31/2013
Chart Low 32.700 on 08/22/1972
CONTRACT SIZE 40,000 lbs
MIN TICK .025 cents
VALUE 10 USD / contract
EACH GRID 1 cents
VALUE 400 USD / contract
DAILY LIMIT 3 cents
VALUE 1,200 USD / contract
TRADING HOURS
5:00p-4:00p / 9:05a-1:00p CT

Nearby Futures through Last Trading Day using Selected contract months: February, April, June, August, October and December.   Good, Chicago: to 11/1964; Futures: 11/30/1964 to date.

Annual High, Low and Settle of Live Cattle Futures   In Cents per Pound

Year	High	Low	Settle	Year	High	Low	Settle	Year	High	Low	Settle
1972	40.900	32.700	40.875	1986	62.975	52.425	55.525	2000	80.400	65.525	80.225
1973	59.500	36.750	48.600	1987	70.725	55.700	63.125	2001	83.600	61.750	68.175
1974	54.000	33.750	39.550	1988	75.750	61.825	73.950	2002	76.650	59.350	75.350
1975	56.500	33.750	42.925	1989	79.150	68.150	77.375	2003	103.600	69.175	77.200
1976	49.600	35.100	40.400	1990	81.250	72.225	77.200	2004	92.950	72.650	89.850
1977	46.600	36.150	42.375	1991	82.700	65.500	72.400	2005	97.125	78.050	92.450
1978	62.350	40.725	58.925	1992	80.000	70.250	77.125	2006	97.050	73.450	90.425
1979	80.250	56.050	70.675	1993	84.300	70.000	73.450	2007	102.920	84.750	96.250
1980	75.125	58.500	68.075	1994	77.925	61.650	72.675	2008	107.050	80.625	84.475
1981	72.400	54.375	54.650	1995	75.825	58.650	66.425	2009	89.100	78.700	86.000
1982	74.000	55.100	58.325	1996	73.950	54.000	64.975	2010	108.150	84.750	107.900
1983	73.825	55.350	67.850	1997	70.800	62.800	66.450	2011	125.575	100.750	122.900
1984	72.875	60.500	66.675	1998	69.725	57.300	62.000	2012	131.250	112.225	129.900
1985	69.350	50.725	61.150	1999	72.450	59.450	68.475	2013	135.150	118.150	134.500

Data continued from page 322.   *Source: CME Group; Chicago Mercantile Exchange*

Cattle, Choice Avg. TX/OK Monthly Cash as of 12/31/2013				
Date	Open	High	Low	Close
08/30/13	122.000	124.530	119.000	124.530
09/30/13	124.530	125.960	122.900	125.960
10/31/13	125.360	132.410	125.360	132.000
11/29/13	132.940	132.940	130.530	132.220
12/31/13	134.000	134.000	130.000	133.580

MONTHLY CASH
As of 12/31/2013
Chart High 134.000 on 12/02/2013
Chart Low 32.400 on 11/20/1972

Cents / lb.

Good, Chicago: to 12/1964; Choice, Chicago: 01/1965 to 07/1971; Choice, Omaha: 08/1971 to 08/1987; Average, Texas-Oklahoma: 08/1987 to date.

Annual High, Low and Settle of Live Cattle   In Cents per Pound

Year	High	Low	Settle	Year	High	Low	Settle	Year	High	Low	Settle
1972	39.00	32.40	37.50	1981	70.81	57.75	58.19	1995	75.00	60.00	65.00
1973	56.40	37.00	42.10	1982	74.75	55.50	59.75	1996	73.00	54.50	66.00
1974	49.50	35.00	36.90	1983	69.25	58.25	66.12	1997	70.00	61.00	66.00
1975	54.00	33.90	44.45	1984	70.00	60.40	65.88	1998	67.00	56.00	60.25
1976	46.50	34.40	39.10	1985	65.90	49.75	63.00	1999	70.87	60.00	68.00
1977	44.10	36.50	43.40	1986	63.75	53.10	59.12	2000	78.00	64.00	78.00
1978	61.50	43.30	55.55	1987	73.00	58.00	65.75	2001	81.55	60.03	64.21
1979	77.75	55.70	67.00	1988	77.75	65.25	74.75	2002	74.46	60.00	74.00
1980	73.95	60.00	63.62	1989	80.00	69.00	79.75	2003	111.43	72.76	75.22
1981	70.81	57.75	58.19	1990	82.25	74.00	81.00	2004	91.38	73.86	87.35
1982	74.75	55.50	59.75	1991	81.75	64.00	70.75	2005	96.76	77.50	93.34
1983	69.25	58.25	66.12	1992	79.75	71.00	78.25	2006	96.56	78.00	87.43
1984	70.00	60.40	65.88	1993	84.75	69.50	70.50	2007	100.00	83.27	92.92
1985	65.90	49.75	63.00	1994	77.25	60.25	71.00	2008	101.59	83.20	85.36

Chicago: Omaha: Choice to 08/1987; Texas/Oklahoma Average 09/1987 to date.   Data continued from page 323.
Source: CME Group; Chicago Mercantile Exchange

CATTLE, LIVE

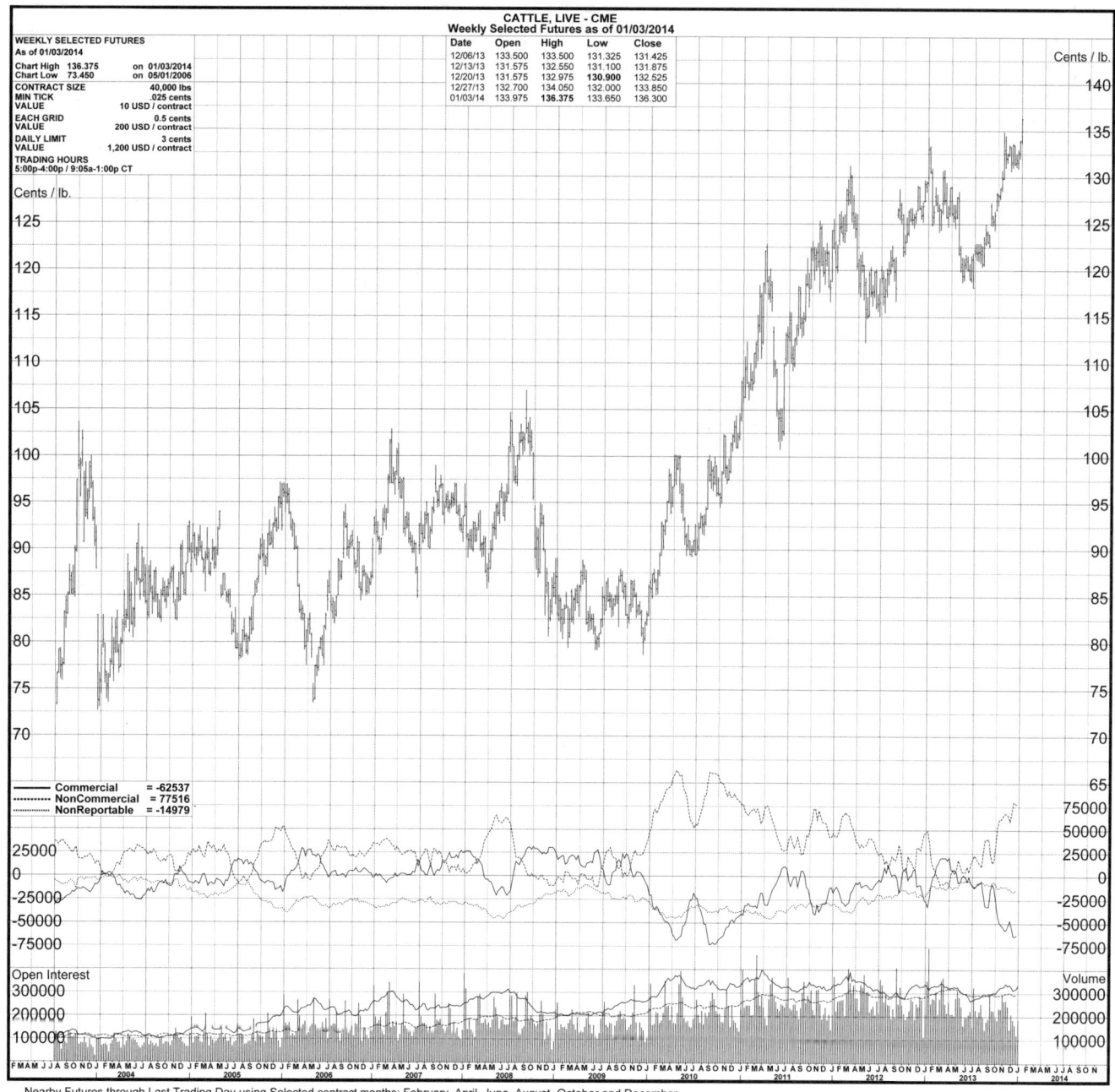

CATTLE, LIVE - CME
Weekly Selected Futures as of 01/03/2014

Date	Open	High	Low	Close
12/06/13	133.500	133.500	131.325	131.425
12/13/13	131.575	132.550	131.100	131.875
12/20/13	131.575	132.975	130.900	132.525
12/27/13	132.700	134.050	132.000	133.850
01/03/14	133.975	136.375	133.650	136.300

WEEKLY SELECTED FUTURES
As of 01/03/2014

Chart High 136.375 on 01/03/2014
Chart Low 73.450 on 05/01/2006
CONTRACT SIZE 40,000 lbs
MIN TICK .025 cents
VALUE 10 USD / contract
EACH GRID 0.5 cents
VALUE 200 USD / contract
DAILY LIMIT 3 cents
VALUE 1,200 USD / contract
TRADING HOURS
5:00p-4:00p / 9:05a-1:00p CT

Commercial = -62537
NonCommercial = 77516
NonReportable = -14979

Nearby Futures through Last Trading Day using Selected contract months: February, April, June, August, October and December.

Quarterly High, Low and Settle of Live Cattle Futures   In Cents per Pound

Quarter	High	Low	Settle	Quarter	High	Low	Settle	Quarter	High	Low	Settle
03/2005	92.750	85.350	89.825	03/2008	97.050	86.400	87.425	03/2011	121.700	105.800	121.550
06/2005	94.050	80.700	82.775	06/2008	101.500	85.775	100.600	06/2011	122.875	100.750	112.750
09/2005	89.400	78.050	89.125	09/2008	107.050	96.750	98.900	09/2011	122.500	109.200	122.150
12/2005	97.125	87.150	92.450	12/2008	99.375	80.625	84.475	12/2011	125.575	116.575	122.900
03/2006	97.050	79.150	79.500	03/2009	89.100	79.425	83.925	03/2012	131.250	119.750	120.450
06/2006	86.650	73.450	84.550	06/2009	88.900	79.175	82.525	06/2012	122.050	112.225	116.550
09/2006	94.800	81.950	90.650	09/2009	87.925	81.650	85.600	09/2012	128.775	115.425	122.075
12/2006	92.000	84.425	90.425	12/2009	86.800	78.700	86.000	12/2012	130.050	121.700	129.900
03/2007	102.920	89.350	97.600	03/2010	98.700	84.750	96.550	03/2013	134.325	124.125	128.900
06/2007	101.350	84.750	85.500	06/2010	100.200	89.250	91.250	06/2013	129.075	118.150	118.150
09/2007	99.000	89.400	96.950	09/2010	100.200	89.400	96.700	09/2013	128.400	120.375	127.850
12/2007	97.150	90.750	96.250	12/2010	108.150	94.500	107.900	12/2013	135.150	126.975	134.500

Source: CME Group; Chicago Mercantile Exchange

Cattle, Choice Avg, TX/OK
Weekly Cash as of 01/03/2014

Date	Open	High	Low	Close
12/06/13	134.000	134.000	131.990	131.990
12/13/13	131.000	131.000	131.000	131.000
12/20/13	130.810	130.810	130.000	130.230
12/27/13	130.230	130.230	130.230	130.230
01/03/14	133.580	137.290	133.580	137.290

WEEKLY CASH
As of 01/03/2014
Chart High 137.290 on 01/03/2014
Chart Low 72.760 on 06/20/2003

Texas-Oklahoma.

Quarterly High, Low and Settle of Live Cattle   In Cents per Pound

Quarter	High	Low	Settle	Quarter	High	Low	Settle	Quarter	High	Low	Settle
03/2005	94.75	84.00	94.69	03/2008	94.99	87.44	87.44	03/2011	120.62	104.00	120.62
06/2005	94.01	80.00	80.00	06/2008	98.91	85.50	98.91	06/2011	123.06	104.00	112.02
09/2005	87.02	77.50	87.01	09/2008	101.59	94.00	98.00	09/2011	119.50	107.00	116.03
12/2005	96.76	86.50	93.34	12/2008	98.00	83.20	85.36	12/2011	125.87	118.44	125.87
03/2006	96.56	84.03	84.03	03/2009	86.45	79.63	82.50	03/2012	130.27	120.65	125.16
06/2006	83.48	78.00	83.08	06/2009	89.32	80.60	81.95	06/2012	125.00	115.71	115.90
09/2006	90.89	79.00	87.54	09/2009	85.00	80.96	84.50	09/2012	127.06	112.89	122.46
12/2006	91.37	84.50	87.43	12/2009	88.00	78.87	84.54	12/2012	128.00	122.46	127.05
03/2007	98.64	85.59	95.41	03/2010	96.90	83.58	95.00	03/2013	128.51	122.08	125.12
06/2007	100.00	83.27	84.90	06/2010	100.36	90.00	90.00	06/2013	128.63	119.00	119.00
09/2007	94.86	86.92	92.10	09/2010	100.00	90.88	96.97	09/2013	125.96	119.00	125.96
12/2007	96.04	89.50	92.92	12/2010	106.35	94.99	106.35	12/2013	134.00	125.36	133.58

Omaha: Texas/Oklahoma Average.   *Source: CME Group; Chicago Mercantile Exchange*

HOGS, LEAN

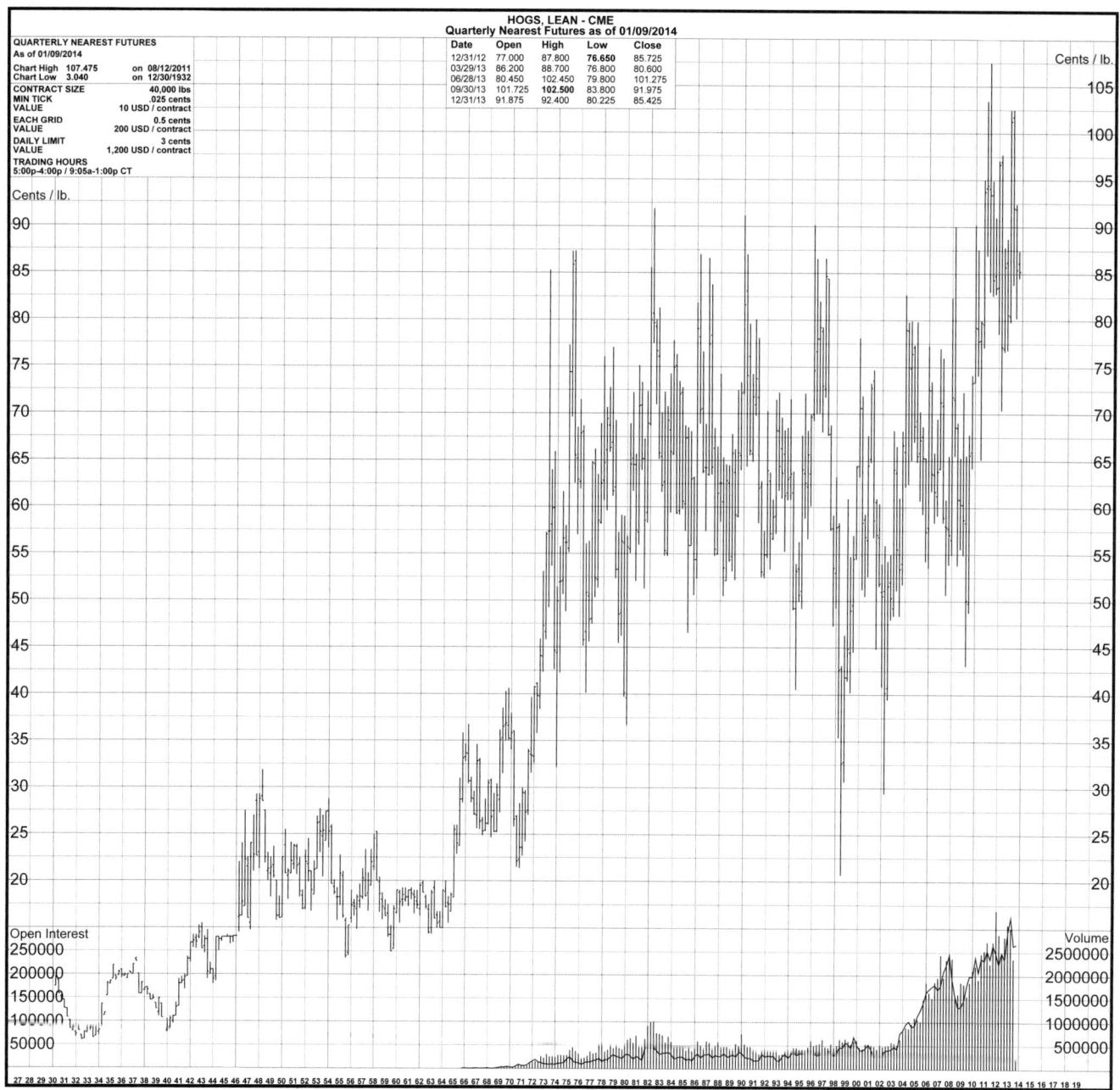

Futures begin trading 02/28/1966.   Data through December 1996 contract; "Live Hogs" / .74; adjusted to correspond to "Lean Hogs".   Data continued on page 330.   Source: CME Group; Chicago Mercantile Exchange

HOGS, LEAN - CME
Quarterly Nearest Futures as of 01/09/2014

Date	Open	High	Low	Close
12/31/12	77.000	87.800	76.650	85.725
03/29/13	86.200	88.700	76.800	80.600
06/28/13	80.450	102.450	79.800	101.275
09/30/13	101.725	102.500	83.800	91.975
12/31/13	91.875	92.400	80.225	85.425

QUARTERLY NEAREST FUTURES
As of 01/09/2014

Chart High 107.475 on 08/12/2011
Chart Low 3.040 on 12/30/1932
CONTRACT SIZE 40,000 lbs
MIN TICK .025 cents
VALUE 10 USD / contract
EACH GRID VALUE 0.5 cents 200 USD / contract
DAILY LIMIT 3 cents VALUE 1,200 USD / contract
TRADING HOURS 5:00p-4:00p / 9:05a-1:00p CT

Nearby Futures through Last Trading Day.   Top, Chicago: to 02/1966; Futures: 02/28/1966 to date (Data through December 1996 contract are for Live Hogs / .74)

Annual High, Low and Settle of Lean Hogs Futures   In Cents per Pound

Year	High	Low	Settle	Year	High	Low	Settle	Year	High	Low	Settle
1930	10.67	7.92	7.92	1944	14.00	9.00	13.75	1958	25.25	16.63	18.60
1931	7.65	4.20	4.20	1945	14.25	13.25	14.00	1959	18.75	12.50	12.50
1932	4.58	3.04	3.04	1946	24.00	13.40	17.75	1960	19.25	12.75	18.50
1933	4.51	3.12	3.25	1947	27.50	14.75	22.75	1961	19.25	16.50	18.25
1934	6.82	3.41	5.89	1948	31.85	21.25	22.50	1962	20.00	16.25	17.25
1935	10.95	7.70	9.57	1949	23.65	15.75	16.25	1963	20.00	14.35	15.50
1936	10.47	9.48	9.96	1950	25.50	16.00	21.00	1964	20.00	15.00	17.50
1937	11.77	7.90	7.90	1951	24.10	18.25	18.85	1965	31.00	16.75	28.70
1938	9.12	7.24	7.24	1952	24.50	16.75	19.00	1966	36.757	15.50	28.851
1939	7.77	5.38	5.38	1953	27.70	18.50	25.35	1967	34.595	24.865	25.338
1940	5.60	3.85	5.50	1954	28.75	18.50	18.75	1968	30.912	24.662	25.270
1941	10.00	5.55	9.70	1955	22.75	11.75	12.00	1969	40.270	25.203	36.892
1942	14.25	9.75	13.50	1956	19.00	12.00	18.25	1970	40.608	21.486	22.128
1943	15.50	9.50	10.25	1957	23.35	16.75	20.00	1971	34.088	21.351	33.851

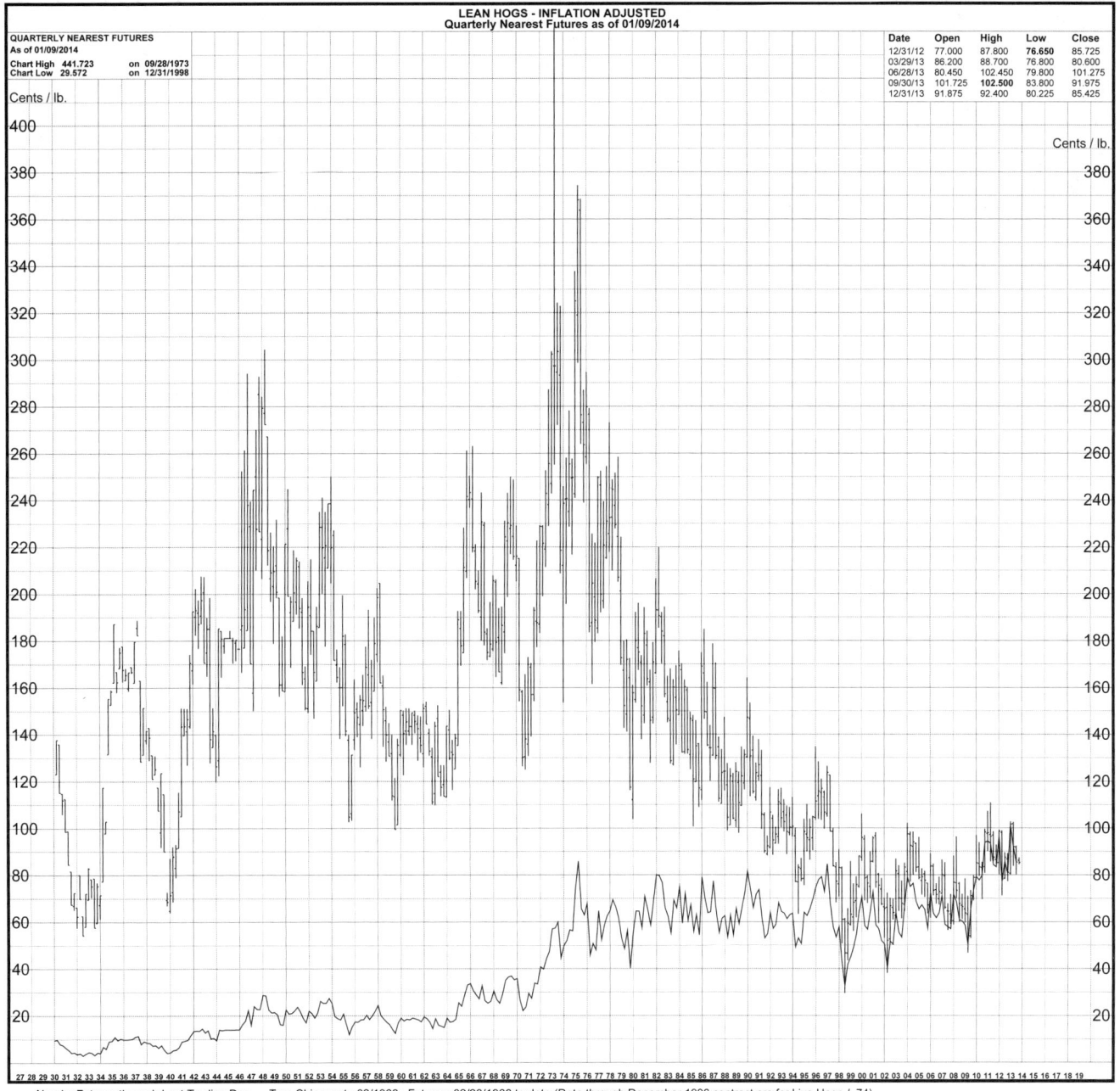

LEAN HOGS - INFLATION ADJUSTED
Quarterly Nearest Futures as of 01/09/2014

QUARTERLY NEAREST FUTURES
As of 01/09/2014

Chart High 441.723   on 09/28/1973
Chart Low   29.572   on 12/31/1998

Cents / lb.

Date	Open	High	Low	Close
12/31/12	77.000	87.800	76.650	85.725
03/29/13	86.200	88.700	76.800	80.600
06/28/13	80.450	102.450	79.800	101.275
09/30/13	101.725	102.500	83.800	91.975
12/31/13	91.875	92.400	80.225	85.425

Nearby Futures through Last Trading Day.   Top, Chicago: to 02/1966; Futures: 02/28/1966 to date (Data through December 1996 contract are for Live Hogs / .74)

Annual High, Low and Settle of Lean Hogs   In Cents per Pound

Year	High	Low	Settle	Year	High	Low	Settle	Year	High	Low	Settle
1930	10.67	7.92	7.92	1944	14.00	9.00	13.75	1958	25.25	16.63	18.60
1931	7.65	4.20	4.20	1945	14.25	13.25	14.00	1959	18.75	12.50	12.50
1932	4.58	3.04	3.04	1946	24.00	13.40	17.75	1960	19.25	12.75	18.50
1933	4.51	3.12	3.25	1947	27.50	14.75	22.75	1961	19.25	16.50	18.25
1934	6.82	3.41	5.89	1948	31.85	21.25	22.50	1962	20.00	16.25	17.25
1935	10.95	7.70	9.57	1949	23.65	15.75	16.25	1963	20.00	14.35	15.50
1936	10.47	9.48	9.96	1950	25.50	16.00	21.00	1964	20.00	15.00	17.50
1937	11.77	7.90	7.90	1951	24.10	18.25	18.85	1965	31.00	16.75	28.70
1938	9.12	7.24	7.24	1952	24.50	16.75	19.00	1966	30.50	21.00	22.00
1939	7.77	5.38	5.38	1953	27.70	18.50	25.35	1967	25.85	18.50	19.25
1940	5.60	3.85	5.50	1954	28.75	18.50	18.75	1968	24.00	19.00	21.50
1941	10.00	5.55	9.70	1955	22.75	11.75	12.00	1969	30.00	20.75	29.00
1942	14.25	9.75	13.50	1956	19.00	12.00	18.25	1970	29.15	14.75	15.75
1943	15.50	9.50	10.25	1957	23.35	16.75	20.00	1971	22.80	15.15	22.25

Chicago: Top.   Data continued on page 331.   *Source: CME Group; Chicago Mercantile Exchange*

HOGS, LEAN

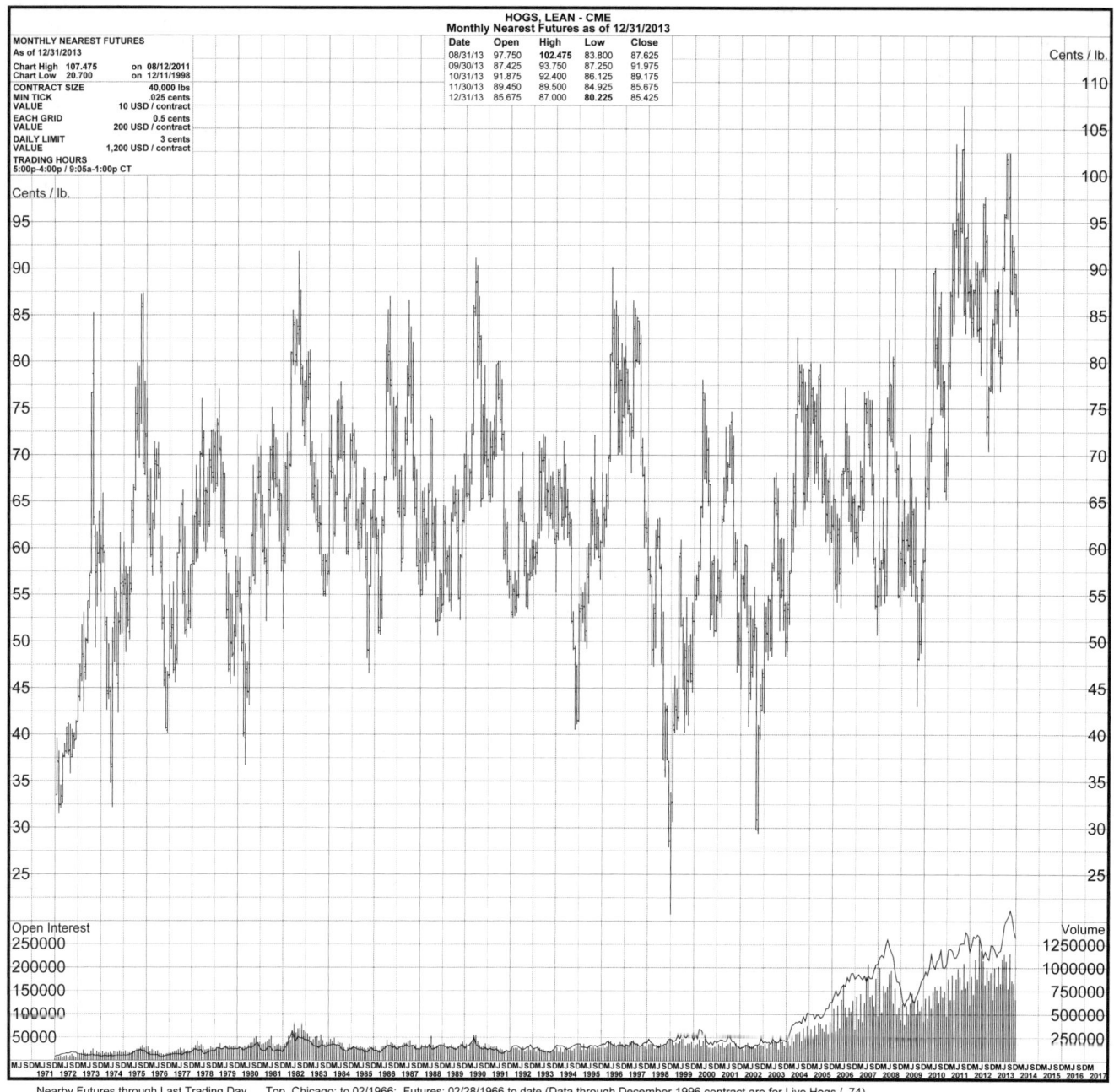

Date	Open	High	Low	Close
08/31/13	97.750	102.475	83.800	87.625
09/30/13	87.425	93.750	87.250	91.975
10/31/13	91.875	92.400	86.125	89.175
11/30/13	89.450	89.500	84.925	85.675
12/31/13	85.675	87.000	80.225	85.425

MONTHLY NEAREST FUTURES
As of 12/31/2013

Chart High	107.475	on 08/12/2011
Chart Low	20.700	on 12/11/1998
CONTRACT SIZE	40,000 lbs	
MIN TICK	.025 cents	
VALUE	10 USD / contract	
EACH GRID	0.5 cents	
VALUE	200 USD / contract	
DAILY LIMIT	3 cents	
VALUE	1,200 USD / contract	

TRADING HOURS
5:00p-4:00p / 9:05a-1:00p CT

Nearby Futures through Last Trading Day.   Top, Chicago: to 02/1966; Futures: 02/28/1966 to date (Data through December 1996 contract are for Live Hogs / .74)

Annual High, Low and Settle of Lean Hogs Futures   In Cents per Pound

Year	High	Low	Settle	Year	High	Low	Settle	Year	High	Low	Settle
1972	45.878	31.554	44.054	1986	87.027	50.608	63.851	2000	78.100	50.500	56.825
1973	85.270	42.331	59.865	1987	86.622	54.797	55.507	2001	74.700	44.850	57.050
1974	65.912	32.162	56.622	1988	74.257	50.541	62.872	2002	60.425	29.400	51.600
1975	87.365	48.784	65.507	1989	72.534	52.230	65.811	2003	68.200	48.000	53.425
1976	71.453	40.135	50.845	1990	91.149	63.986	66.047	2004	82.700	51.750	76.400
1977	66.216	45.574	58.547	1991	80.068	52.568	53.108	2005	79.850	59.275	65.275
1978	76.047	58.176	66.351	1992	70.270	52.466	58.953	2006	77.250	53.550	61.700
1979	77.061	45.439	56.318	1993	72.264	55.270	61.284	2007	76.975	50.650	57.875
1980	72.230	36.689	64.527	1994	71.554	40.507	53.176	2008	90.000	53.800	60.875
1981	75.135	51.284	58.581	1995	72.162	49.189	65.642	2009	72.300	43.050	65.600
1982	91.892	58.311	76.689	1996	90.169	60.135	79.225	2010	90.175	64.200	79.750
1983	81.284	54.764	69.257	1997	86.600	57.550	57.700	2011	107.475	77.100	84.300
1984	77.804	59.189	72.061	1998	63.275	20.700	32.650	2012	97.725	70.375	85.725
1985	72.770	46.554	63.007	1999	60.925	30.650	54.500	2013	102.500	76.800	85.425

Data through December 1996 contract; "Live Hogs" / .74; adjusted to correspond to "Lean Hogs".   Data continued from page 328.
Source: CME Group; Chicago Mercantile Exchange

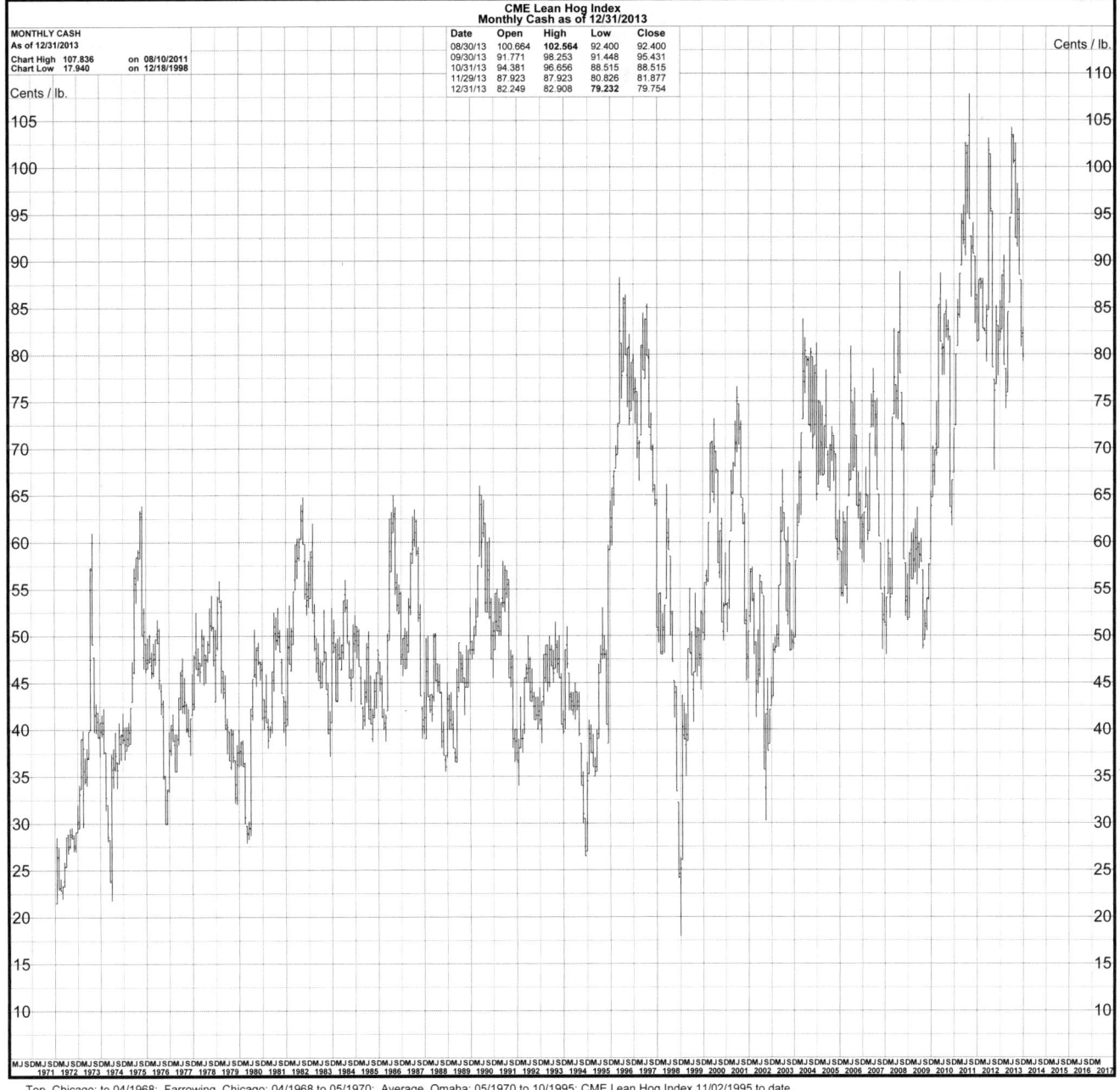

CME Lean Hog Index
Monthly Cash as of 12/31/2013

Date	Open	High	Low	Close
08/30/13	100.664	102.564	92.400	92.400
09/30/13	91.771	98.253	91.448	95.431
10/31/13	94.381	96.656	88.515	88.515
11/29/13	87.923	87.923	80.826	81.877
12/31/13	82.249	82.908	79.232	79.754

MONTHLY CASH
As of 12/31/2013

Chart High 107.836 on 08/10/2011
Chart Low 17.940   on 12/18/1998

Cents / lb.

Top, Chicago: to 04/1968; Farrowing, Chicago: 04/1968 to 05/1970; Average, Omaha: 05/1970 to 10/1995; CME Lean Hog Index 11/02/1995 to date.

Annual High, Low and Settle of Lean Hogs   In Cents per Pound

Year	High	Low	Settle	Year	High	Low	Settle	Year	High	Low	Settle
1972	32.00	21.50	30.20	1986	65.00	38.70	47.75	2000	70.31	46.24	50.94
1973	61.00	29.50	40.75	1987	63.50	39.00	41.25	2001	74.24	41.83	49.57
1974	42.30	21.75	38.95	1988	50.30	35.50	43.25	2002	57.24	25.66	40.46
1975	63.90	36.80	46.50	1989	53.00	36.50	49.35	2003	66.46	41.39	48.53
1976	51.75	29.95	37.85	1990	66.00	45.50	50.50	2004	83.21	49.00	66.14
1977	47.70	35.55	42.80	1991	58.00	36.50	36.70	2005	78.82	55.14	57.26
1978	54.35	42.20	48.00	1992	50.00	34.00	41.00	2006	81.21	50.23	59.10
1979	55.90	32.00	37.50	1993	51.50	38.50	39.75	2007	77.84	44.79	47.03
1980	50.70	27.85	41.25	1994	51.00	26.50	34.50	2008	88.85	47.97	51.66
1981	53.00	38.00	40.40	1995	53.00	35.00	43.00	2009	65.42	48.56	63.84
1982	64.80	40.40	55.50	1996	65.00	40.00	55.00	2010	88.71	61.71	72.06
1983	62.00	37.10	49.25	1997	62.00	34.00	34.00	2011	107.84	72.39	81.39
1984	56.00	43.00	49.50	1998	47.00	10.00	17.25	2012	103.08	67.63	82.39
1985	51.00	38.65	48.00	1999	52.22	24.48	45.53	2013	104.23	74.21	79.75

Chicago: Top to 03/1968; Farrowing 04/1968 to 05/1970; Omaha: Average 06/1970 to 10/1995; CME Lean Hog Index 11/1995 to date.   Data continued
from page 329.   *Source: CME Group; Chicago Mercantile Exchange*

HOGS, LEAN

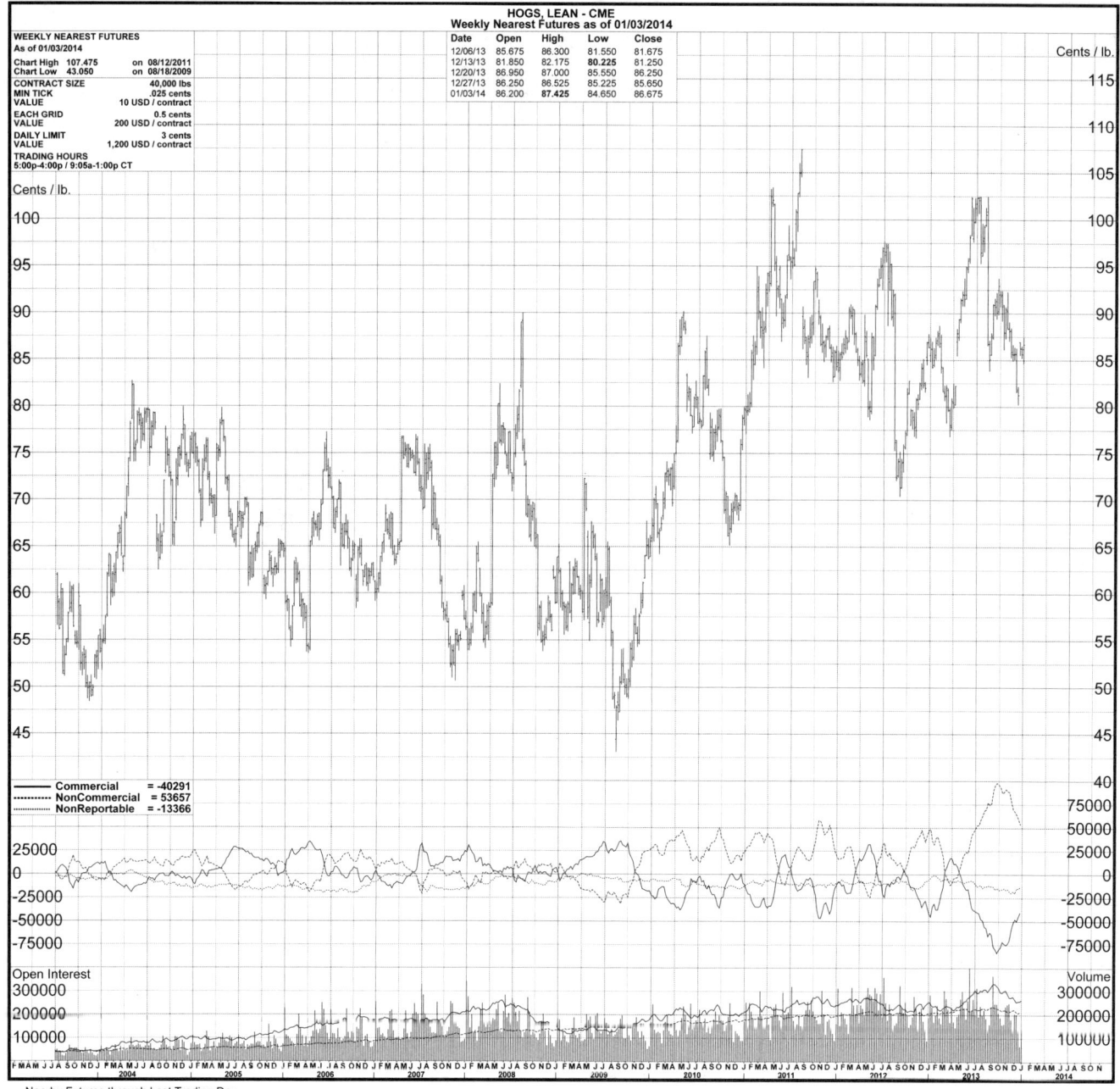

Source: CME Group; Chicago Mercantile Exchange

Quarterly High, Low and Settle of Lean Hogs Futures   In Cents per Pound

Quarter	High	Low	Settle	Quarter	High	Low	Settle	Quarter	High	Low	Settle
03/2005	77.350	67.000	68.700	03/2008	65.500	53.875	57.075	03/2011	95.000	77.100	93.725
06/2005	79.850	64.850	65.525	06/2008	82.400	54.950	71.775	06/2011	103.425	86.925	94.400
09/2005	70.225	60.725	67.200	09/2008	90.000	65.500	68.575	09/2011	107.475	83.050	93.375
12/2005	68.650	59.275	65.275	12/2008	69.050	53.800	60.875	12/2011	94.900	82.625	84.300
03/2006	65.325	54.225	57.350	03/2009	65.300	55.550	60.350	03/2012	90.975	82.775	83.425
06/2006	77.250	53.550	72.550	06/2009	72.300	54.900	58.675	06/2012	97.050	78.575	96.625
09/2006	73.475	61.725	63.625	09/2009	65.550	43.050	50.075	09/2012	97.725	70.375	77.175
12/2006	65.850	58.350	61.700	12/2009	67.775	48.775	65.600	12/2012	87.800	76.650	85.725
03/2007	69.450	59.100	63.850	03/2010	74.150	64.200	73.325	03/2013	88.700	76.800	80.600
06/2007	76.975	64.100	71.225	06/2010	90.175	73.400	79.225	06/2013	102.450	79.800	101.275
09/2007	75.975	58.350	58.900	09/2010	87.575	74.100	77.775	09/2013	102.500	83.800	91.975
12/2007	60.850	50.650	57.875	12/2010	80.000	65.150	79.750	12/2013	92.400	80.225	85.425

Source: CME Group; Chicago Mercantile Exchange

WEEKLY CASH
As of 01/03/2014

Chart High 107.836 on 08/10/2011
Chart Low 47.524 on 01/20/2003

Cents / lb.

CME Lean Hog Index Weekly Cash as of 01/03/2014				
Date	Open	High	Low	Close
12/06/13	82.249	82.908	81.979	81.979
12/13/13	81.692	81.692	80.943	80.943
12/20/13	80.772	80.772	79.732	79.732
12/27/13	79.469	79.523	79.232	79.523
01/03/14	79.664	80.313	79.664	80.313

CME Lean Hog Index.

Quarterly High, Low and Settle of Lean Hogs   In Cents per Pound

Quarter	High	Low	Settle	Quarter	High	Low	Settle	Quarter	High	Low	Settle
03/2005	76.89	64.23	65.89	03/2008	59.96	46.06	54.16	03/2011	88.61	72.39	88.61
06/2005	78.82	63.69	63.72	06/2008	83.78	52.43	71.53	06/2011	102.61	89.49	102.24
09/2005	73.05	62.22	68.24	09/2008	88.77	65.76	71.03	09/2011	107.84	86.11	91.30
12/2005	68.28	55.14	57.26	12/2008	72.63	51.66	51.66	12/2011	94.09	81.39	81.39
03/2006	63.33	50.27	53.79	03/2009	61.41	51.87	58.00	03/2012	88.14	81.51	82.78
06/2006	81.21	50.23	70.25	06/2009	63.70	55.39	58.65	06/2012	103.08	79.17	101.76
09/2006	76.49	60.79	61.52	09/2009	60.38	48.56	51.24	09/2012	101.37	67.63	76.12
12/2006	67.30	54.62	59.10	12/2009	65.42	50.52	63.84	12/2012	85.74	76.80	82.39
03/2007	66.12	54.30	59.50	03/2010	75.00	64.73	69.49	03/2013	90.59	74.21	75.56
06/2007	77.84	60.54	72.10	06/2010	88.71	70.04	80.77	06/2013	104.23	75.94	103.38
09/2007	76.77	57.25	57.93	09/2010	85.82	77.79	82.66	09/2013	103.46	91.45	95.43
12/2007	58.15	44.79	47.03	12/2010	81.92	61.71	72.06	12/2013	96.66	79.23	79.75

Iowa/S. Minn.   *Source: CME Group; Chicago Mercantile Exchange*

PORK BELLIES

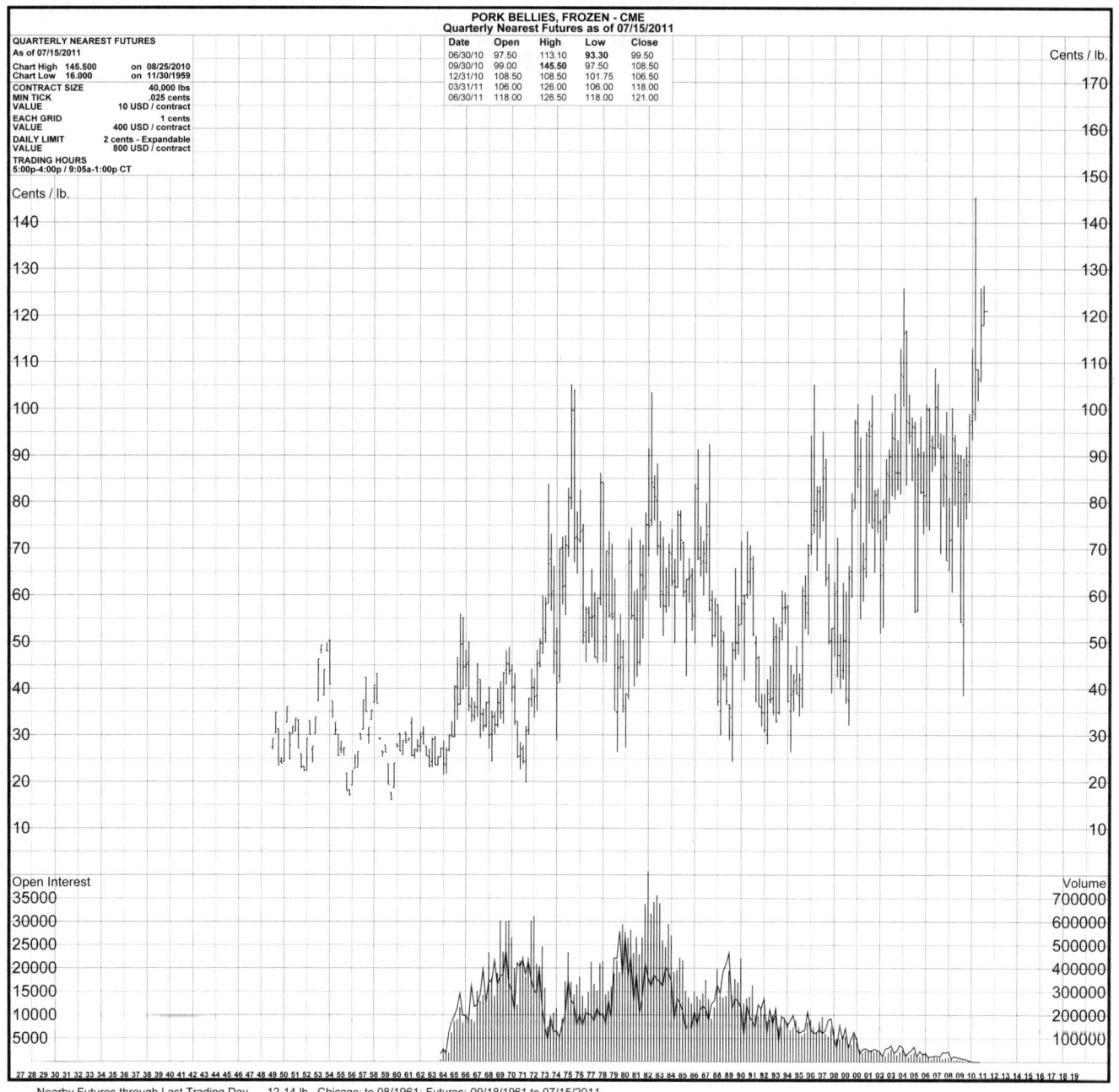

PORK BELLIES, FROZEN - CME
Quarterly Nearest Futures as of 07/15/2011

Date	Open	High	Low	Close
06/30/10	97.50	113.10	93.30	99.50
09/30/10	99.00	145.50	97.50	108.50
12/31/10	108.50	108.50	101.75	106.50
03/31/11	106.00	126.00	106.00	118.00
06/30/11	118.00	126.50	118.00	121.00

QUARTERLY NEAREST FUTURES
As of 07/15/2011

Chart High	145.500	on 08/25/2010
Chart Low	16.000	on 11/30/1959
CONTRACT SIZE		40,000 lbs
MIN TICK		.025 cents
VALUE		10 USD / contract
EACH GRID VALUE		1 cents
		400 USD / contract
DAILY LIMIT		2 cents - Expandable
VALUE		800 USD / contract
TRADING HOURS		
5:00p-4:00p / 9:05a-1:00p CT		

Nearby Futures through Last Trading Day.   12-14 lb., Chicago: to 08/1961; Futures: 09/18/1961 to 07/15/2011.

Annual High, Low and Settle of Pork Belly Futures   In Cents per Pound

Year	High	Low	Settle	Year	High	Low	Settle	Year	High	Low	Settle
1930	----	----	----	1944	----	----	----	1958	43.13	28.88	29.25
1931	----	----	----	1945	----	----	----	1959	27.75	16.00	16.13
1932	----	----	----	1946	----	----	----	1960	30.25	18.63	28.75
1933	----	----	----	1947	----	----	----	1961	23.75	24.975	26.750
1934	----	----	----	1948	----	----	----	1962	31.750	25.500	25.500
1935	----	----	----	1949	34.75	23.50	23.50	1963	29.700	23.000	25.250
1936	----	----	----	1950	36.00	23.88	27.75	1964	30.000	21.425	29.750
1937	----	----	----	1951	33.50	22.75	23.13	1965	56.000	29.425	49.400
1938	----	----	----	1952	33.00	22.25	27.50	1966	55.250	32.650	34.250
1939	----	----	----	1953	49.25	30.25	44.00	1967	45.450	29.250	31.850
1940	----	----	----	1954	50.25	30.00	31.00	1968	40.400	24.225	32.200
1941	----	----	----	1955	30.00	18.00	18.00	1969	48.100	31.550	45.400
1942	----	----	----	1956	26.38	17.00	26.38	1970	48.875	25.100	25.375
1943	----	----	----	1957	42.38	28.00	31.50	1971	37.950	19.750	37.900

Futures begin trading 09/18/1961.   Data continued on page 336.   *Source: CME Group; Chicago Mercantile Exchange*

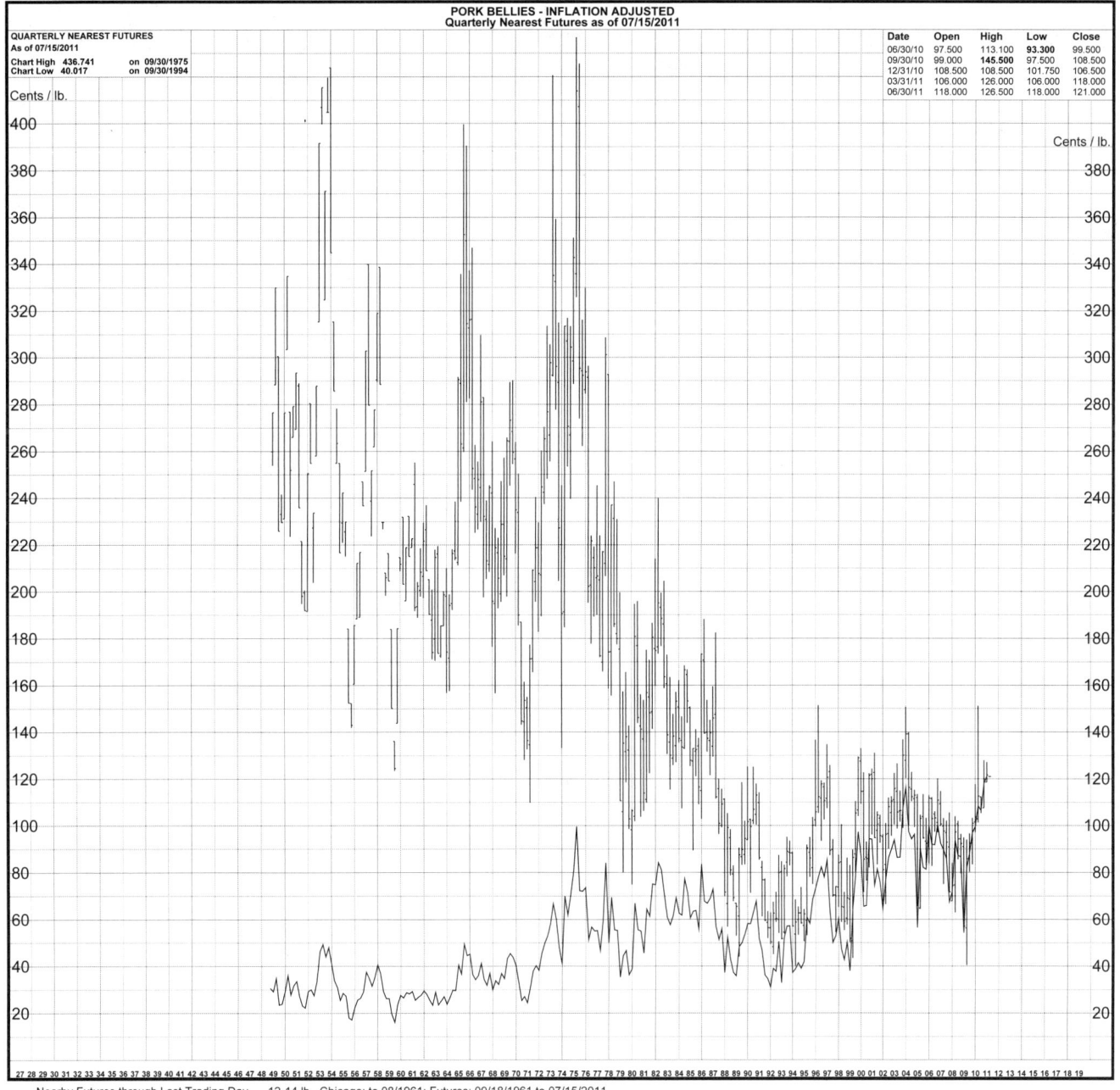

PORK BELLIES - INFLATION ADJUSTED
Quarterly Nearest Futures as of 07/15/2011

QUARTERLY NEAREST FUTURES
As of 07/15/2011
Chart High 436.741   on 09/30/1975
Chart Low   40.017   on 09/30/1994

Date	Open	High	Low	Close
06/30/10	97.500	113.100	93.300	99.500
09/30/10	99.000	145.500	97.500	108.500
12/31/10	108.500	108.500	101.750	106.500
03/31/11	106.000	126.000	106.000	118.000
06/30/11	118.000	126.500	118.000	121.000

Nearby Futures through Last Trading Day.   12-14 lb., Chicago: to 08/1961; Futures: 09/18/1961 to 07/15/2011.

Annual High, Low and Settle of Pork Bellies   In Cents per Pound

Year	High	Low	Settle	Year	High	Low	Settle	Year	High	Low	Settle
1930	----	----	----	1944	----	----	----	1958	43.13	28.88	29.25
1931	----	----	----	1945	----	----	----	1959	27.75	16.00	16.13
1932	----	----	----	1946	----	----	----	1960	30.25	18.63	28.75
1933	----	----	----	1947	----	----	----	1961	35.88	24.25	24.25
1934	----	----	----	1948	----	----	----	1962	31.25	23.75	23.75
1935	----	----	----	1949	34.75	23.50	23.50	1963	30.50	20.50	24.50
1936	----	----	----	1950	36.00	23.88	27.75	1964	28.00	20.50	27.00
1937	----	----	----	1951	33.50	22.75	23.13	1965	55.00	27.25	49.50
1938	----	----	----	1952	33.00	22.25	27.50	1966	53.00	32.00	33.50
1939	----	----	----	1953	49.25	30.25	44.00	1967	46.50	26.50	29.00
1940	----	----	----	1954	50.25	30.00	31.00	1968	37.00	25.25	29.50
1941	----	----	----	1955	30.00	18.00	18.00	1969	46.00	28.00	45.00
1942	----	----	----	1956	26.38	17.00	26.38	1970	46.00	21.00	21.50
1943	----	----	----	1957	42.38	28.00	31.50	1971	30.00	19.00	30.00

Chicago: 12-14 lb.   Data continued on page 337.   *Source: CME Group; Chicago Mercantile Exchange*

PORK BELLIES

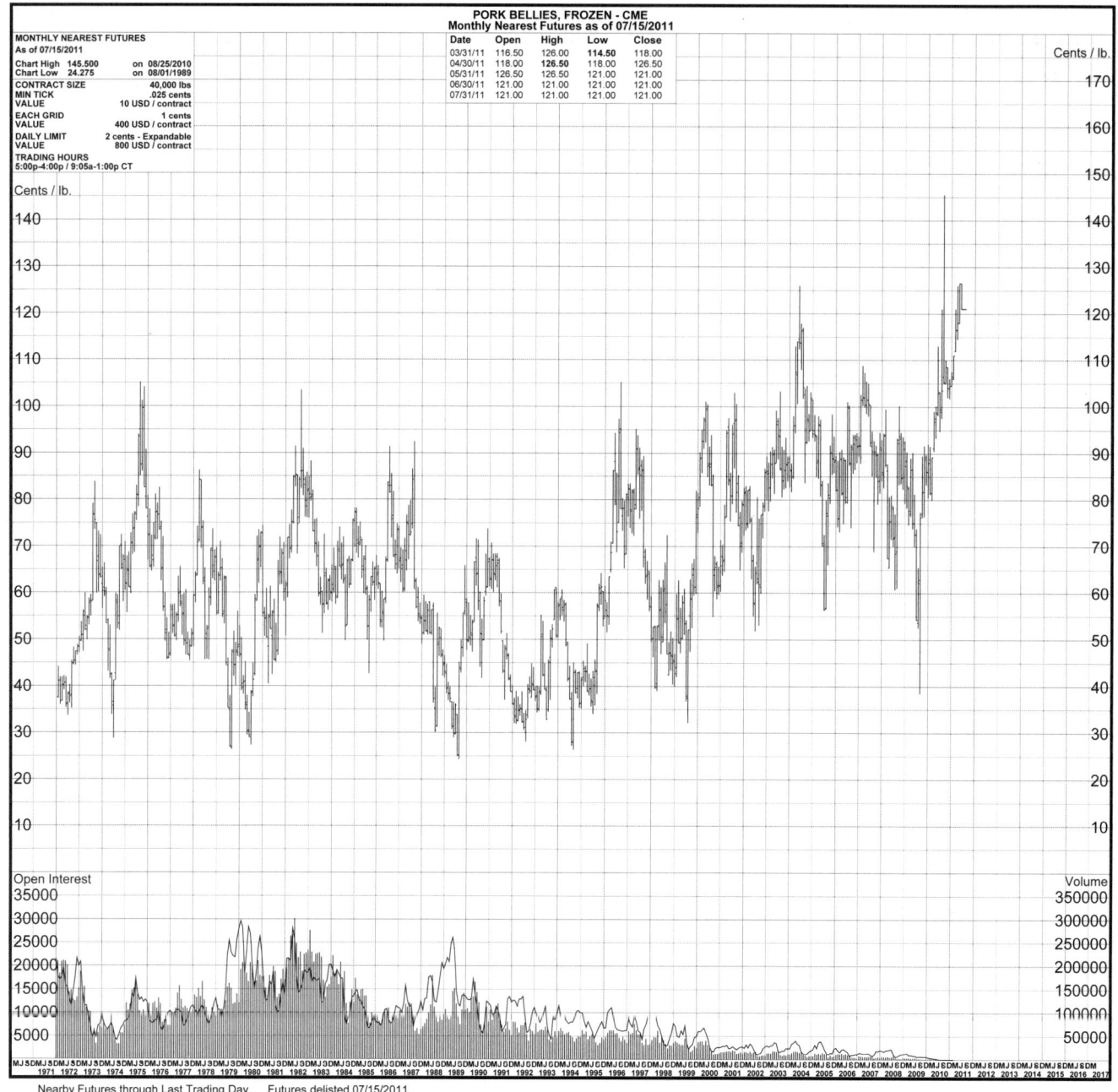

PORK BELLIES, FROZEN - CME
Monthly Nearest Futures as of 07/15/2011

Date	Open	High	Low	Close
03/31/11	116.50	126.00	**114.50**	118.00
04/30/11	118.00	**126.50**	118.00	126.50
05/31/11	126.50	126.50	121.00	121.00
06/30/11	121.00	121.00	121.00	121.00
07/31/11	121.00	121.00	121.00	121.00

MONTHLY NEAREST FUTURES
As of 07/15/2011

Chart High	145.500	on 08/25/2010
Chart Low	24.275	on 08/01/1989
CONTRACT SIZE		40,000 lbs
MIN TICK		.025 cents
VALUE		10 USD / contract
EACH GRID		1 cents
VALUE		400 USD / contract
DAILY LIMIT		2 cents - Expandable
VALUE		800 USD / contract
TRADING HOURS		
5:00p-4:00p / 9:05a-1:00p CT		

Nearby Futures through Last Trading Day.   Futures delisted 07/15/2011.

Annual High, Low and Settle of Pork Belly Futures   In Cents per Pound

Year	High	Low	Settle	Year	High	Low	Settle	Year	High	Low	Settle
1972	50.650	33.600	49.700	1986	91.400	49.650	66.850	2000	101.100	54.875	65.875
1973	83.800	47.350	60.300	1987	92.500	49.000	51.325	2001	103.000	63.775	81.425
1974	72.500	28.750	61.900	1988	59.450	30.050	43.050	2002	89.350	51.825	86.200
1975	105.100	55.650	72.250	1989	65.900	24.275	49.900	2003	103.300	77.600	86.475
1976	82.550	45.600	56.850	1990	73.800	41.725	63.100	2004	126.000	81.700	94.250
1977	65.650	45.400	59.400	1991	70.750	36.075	36.225	2005	98.400	56.300	82.150
1978	86.250	45.600	55.550	1992	44.875	28.050	37.750	2006	101.050	73.125	91.775
1979	71.050	26.350	46.650	1993	61.150	32.700	57.150	2007	108.800	68.900	85.975
1980	74.500	27.300	55.575	1994	60.700	26.350	41.375	2008	100.225	60.700	87.375
1981	71.950	40.450	61.375	1995	64.300	34.000	58.275	2009	92.000	38.500	88.000
1982	103.500	58.850	81.100	1996	105.250	51.500	82.350	2010	145.500	80.000	106.500
1983	88.300	51.250	61.725	1997	95.200	49.500	50.025	2011	126.500	106.000	121.000
1984	78.200	49.700	77.300	1998	72.475	39.000	42.750	2012	----	----	----
1985	78.200	42.650	63.825	1999	81.950	32.100	78.150	2013	----	----	----

Data continued from page 334.   Futures delisted 07/15/2011.   *Source: CME Group; Chicago Mercantile Exchange*

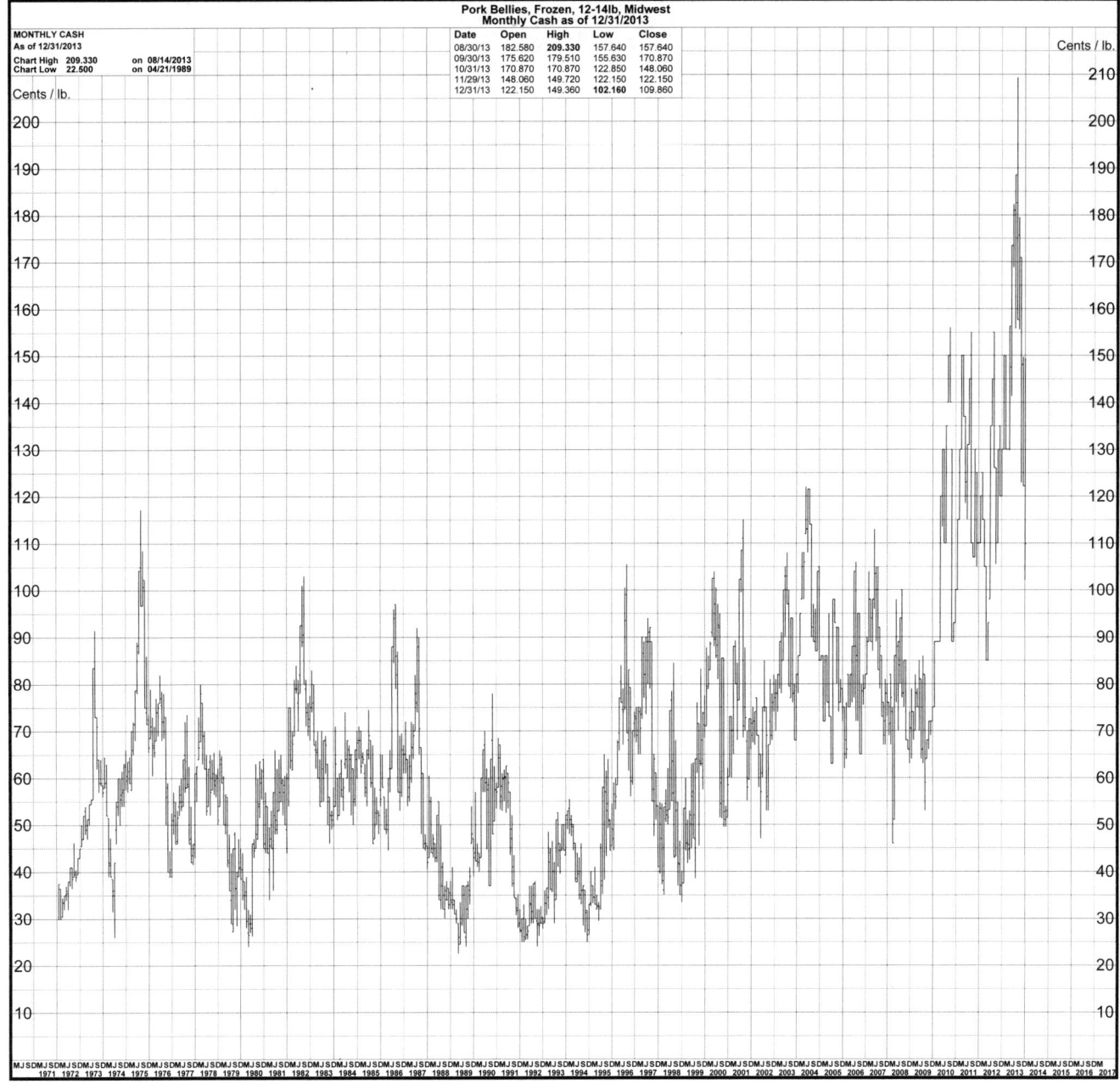

Pork Bellies, Frozen, 12-14lb, Midwest
Monthly Cash as of 12/31/2013

MONTHLY CASH
As of 12/31/2013

Chart High 209.330 on 08/14/2013
Chart Low 22.500 on 04/21/1989

Cents / lb.

Date	Open	High	Low	Close
08/30/13	182.580	209.330	157.640	157.640
09/30/13	175.620	179.510	155.630	170.870
10/31/13	170.870	170.870	122.850	148.060
11/29/13	148.060	149.720	122.150	122.150
12/31/13	122.150	149.360	102.160	109.860

12-14 lb., Chicago: to 10/1975; 12-14 lb., Midwest: 10/1975 to date.

Annual High, Low and Settle of Pork Bellies In Cents per Pound

Year	High	Low	Settle	Year	High	Low	Settle	Year	High	Low	Settle
1972	46.25	30.00	45.00	1986	97.00	44.50	65.00	2000	104.00	49.50	58.50
1973	91.50	45.50	57.00	1987	92.00	40.50	42.00	2001	115.00	55.13	69.00
1974	66.00	26.00	59.50	1988	60.50	30.00	34.00	2002	85.00	47.00	78.00
1975	117.25	57.00	66.50	1989	54.00	22.50	43.00	2003	108.00	68.00	82.00
1976	82.00	39.00	50.00	1990	78.00	37.00	57.00	2004	122.00	78.00	85.00
1977	73.50	41.50	61.00	1991	68.50	27.00	27.50	2005	98.00	63.00	75.00
1978	80.00	50.00	51.00	1992	38.00	24.00	29.00	2006	106.00	62.00	82.00
1979	66.00	27.25	38.50	1993	52.50	29.00	52.00	2007	113.00	67.00	76.00
1980	64.00	24.00	45.00	1994	55.50	25.00	33.00	2008	100.00	46.00	70.50
1981	66.00	34.00	60.00	1995	65.00	29.50	49.00	2009	86.00	53.00	75.00
1982	103.00	54.00	75.00	1996	105.50	44.50	73.00	2010	156.00	75.00	100.00
1983	83.00	46.00	54.00	1997	94.00	41.00	41.00	2011	155.00	100.00	110.00
1984	74.00	50.00	67.50	1998	84.50	33.50	37.50	2012	155.00	85.00	130.00
1985	74.50	46.00	55.50	1999	83.25	37.50	71.00	2013	209.33	102.16	109.86

Chicago: 12-14 lb. to 09/1975; Midwest: 12-14 lb. 10/1975 to date   Data continued from page 335.   *Source: CME Group; Chicago Mercantile Exchange*

PORK BELLIES

PORK BELLIES, FROZEN - CME
Weekly Nearest Futures as of 07/15/2011

Date	Open	High	Low	Close
06/17/11	121.00	121.00	121.00	121.00
06/24/11	121.00	121.00	121.00	121.00
07/01/11	121.00	121.00	121.00	121.00
07/08/11	121.00	121.00	121.00	121.00
07/15/11	121.00	121.00	121.00	121.00

WEEKLY NEAREST FUTURES
As of 07/15/2011

Chart High 145.500 on 08/25/2010
Chart Low 38.500 on 08/14/2009
CONTRACT SIZE 40,000 lbs
MIN TICK .025 cents
VALUE 10 USD / contract
EACH GRID 1 cents
VALUE 400 USD / contract
DAILY LIMIT 2 cents - Expandable
VALUE 800 USD / contract
TRADING HOURS
5:00p-4:00p / 9:05a-1:00p CT

Commercial = -79
NonCommercial = -100
NonReportable = 179

Nearby Futures through Last Trading Day.   Futures delisted 07/15/2011.

Quarterly High, Low and Settle of Pork Belly Futures   In Cents per Pound

Quarter	High	Low	Settle	Quarter	High	Low	Settle	Quarter	High	Low	Settle
03/2005	98.250	84.600	96.250	03/2008	99.500	67.500	67.500	03/2011	126.000	106.000	118.000
06/2005	97.300	56.300	56.500	06/2008	81.000	65.500	71.800	06/2011	126.500	118.000	121.000
09/2005	91.750	56.500	90.275	09/2008	100.225	60.700	93.750	09/2011	121.000	121.000	121.000
12/2005	98.400	81.800	82.150	12/2008	94.500	79.300	87.375	12/2011	----	----	----
03/2006	90.900	73.125	81.350	03/2009	90.375	74.650	86.550	03/2012	----	----	----
06/2006	101.050	74.950	99.975	06/2009	90.250	54.250	54.300	06/2012	----	----	----
09/2006	100.350	74.000	92.025	09/2009	89.475	38.500	81.700	09/2012	----	----	----
12/2006	94.400	86.575	91.775	12/2009	92.000	76.400	88.000	12/2012	----	----	----
03/2007	108.800	87.900	100.400	03/2010	99.000	80.000	96.800	03/2013	----	----	----
06/2007	105.450	91.600	92.400	06/2010	113.100	93.300	99.500	06/2013	----	----	----
09/2007	94.800	68.900	89.675	09/2010	145.500	97.500	108.500	09/2013	----	----	----
12/2007	94.500	79.050	85.975	12/2010	108.500	101.750	106.500	12/2013	----	----	----

Futures delisted 07/15/2011.   *Source: CME Group; Chicago Mercantile Exchange*

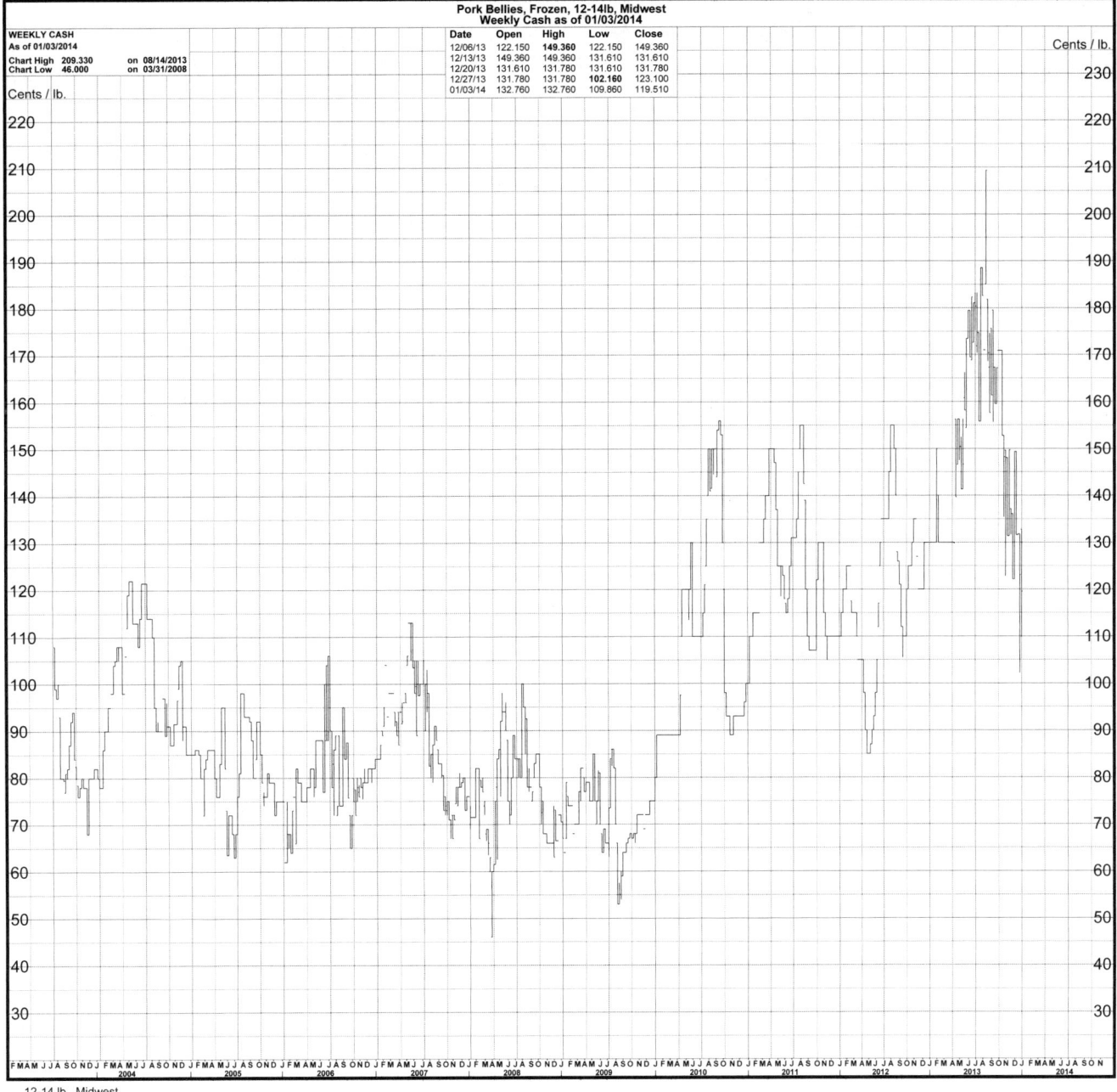

		Pork Bellies, Frozen, 12-14lb, Midwest			
		Weekly Cash as of 01/03/2014			
Date	Open	High	Low	Close	
12/06/13	122.150	149.360	122.150	149.360	
12/13/13	149.360	149.360	131.610	131.610	
12/20/13	131.610	131.780	131.610	131.780	
12/27/13	131.780	131.780	102.160	123.100	
01/03/14	132.760	132.760	109.860	119.510	

WEEKLY CASH
As of 01/03/2014
Chart High 209.330 on 08/14/2013
Chart Low   46.000   on 03/31/2008

Cents / lb.

12-14 lb., Midwest.

Quarterly High, Low and Settle of Pork Bellies   In Cents per Pound

Quarter	High	Low	Settle	Quarter	High	Low	Settle	Quarter	High	Low	Settle
03/2005	86.00	72.00	86.00	03/2008	82.00	46.00	46.00	03/2011	150.00	100.00	150.00
06/2005	95.00	63.00	63.00	06/2008	98.00	51.00	89.00	06/2011	150.00	115.00	131.00
09/2005	98.00	63.00	92.00	09/2008	100.00	75.00	85.00	09/2011	155.00	107.00	107.00
12/2005	92.00	72.00	75.00	12/2008	85.00	63.00	70.50	12/2011	130.00	105.00	110.00
03/2006	82.00	62.00	75.00	03/2009	82.00	64.00	78.00	03/2012	125.00	105.00	105.00
06/2006	104.00	75.00	104.00	06/2009	85.00	64.00	66.00	06/2012	135.00	85.00	135.00
09/2006	106.00	65.00	65.00	09/2009	86.00	53.00	68.00	09/2012	155.00	105.50	110.00
12/2006	82.00	65.00	82.00	12/2009	75.00	66.00	75.00	12/2012	135.00	110.00	130.00
03/2007	104.00	82.00	89.00	03/2010	89.00	75.00	89.00	03/2013	150.00	130.00	130.00
06/2007	113.00	87.00	100.00	06/2010	130.00	89.00	110.00	06/2013	182.28	129.83	181.02
09/2007	105.00	73.00	73.00	09/2010	156.00	110.00	140.00	09/2013	209.33	155.63	170.87
12/2007	81.00	67.00	76.00	12/2010	130.00	89.00	100.00	12/2013	170.87	102.16	109.86

Midwest: 12-14 lb.   *Source: CME Group; Chicago Mercantile Exchange*

HIDES

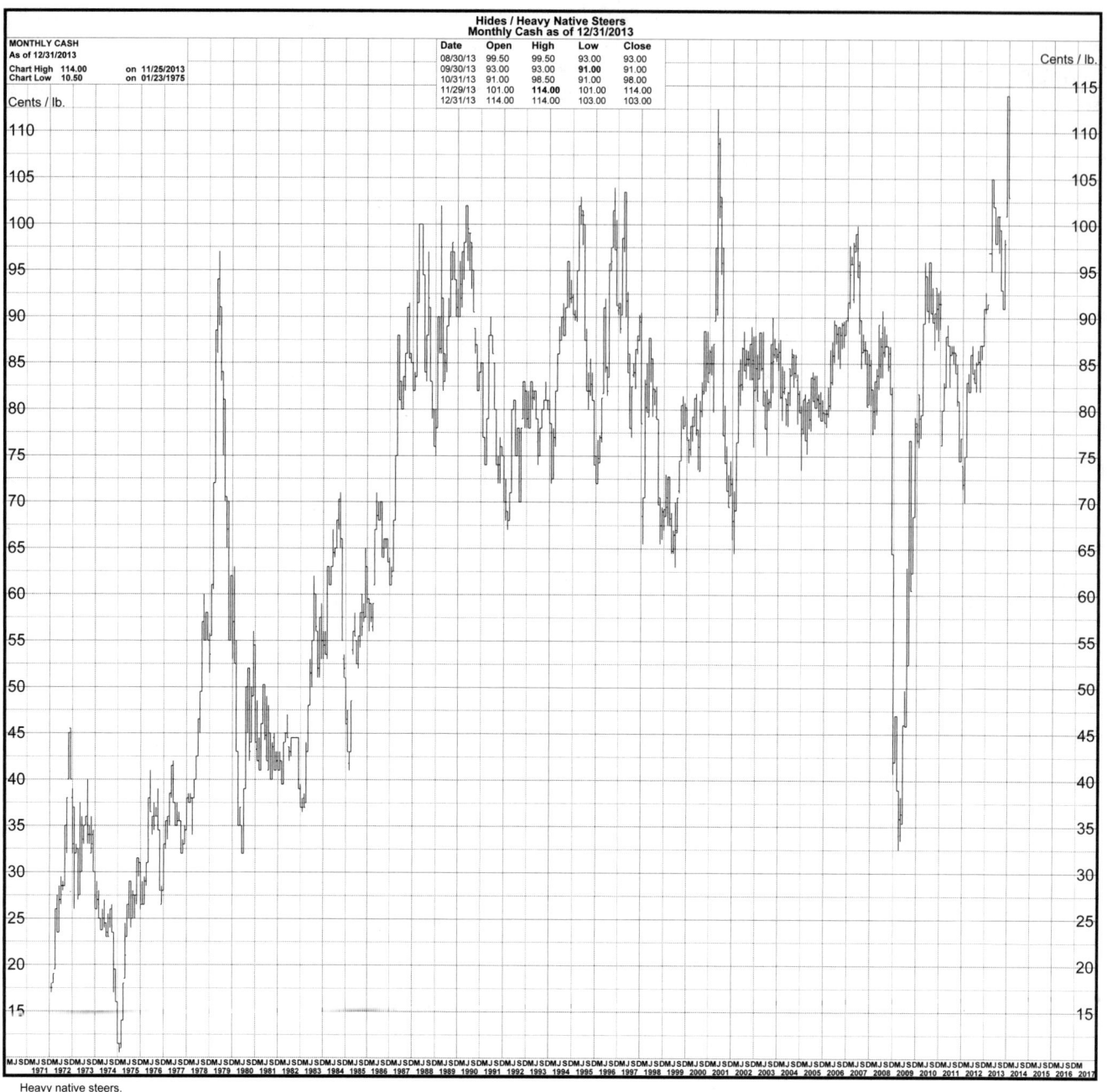

Hides / Heavy Native Steers Monthly Cash as of 12/31/2013				
Date	Open	High	Low	Close
08/30/13	99.50	99.50	93.00	93.00
09/30/13	93.00	93.00	91.00	91.00
10/31/13	91.00	98.50	91.00	98.00
11/29/13	101.00	114.00	101.00	114.00
12/31/13	114.00	114.00	103.00	103.00

MONTHLY CASH
As of 12/31/2013
Chart High 114.00   on 11/25/2013
Chart Low 10.50   on 01/23/1975

Heavy native steers.

Annual High, Low and Settle of Hides   In Cents per Pound

Year	High	Low	Settle	Year	High	Low	Settle	Year	High	Low	Settle
1972	45.50	17.00	33.00	1986	71.00	56.00	61.00	2000	88.50	73.37	86.25
1973	40.00	26.00	26.00	1987	91.50	61.00	82.00	2001	112.50	66.00	68.00
1974	29.00	11.50	11.50	1988	100.00	75.00	78.00	2002	89.00	64.50	84.50
1975	31.50	10.50	26.50	1989	102.00	78.00	90.00	2003	90.00	75.13	86.25
1976	41.00	26.50	33.00	1990	102.00	82.00	85.00	2004	87.63	73.50	78.00
1977	42.00	32.00	38.00	1991	90.00	70.00	70.00	2005	84.13	75.25	78.63
1978	60.00	34.00	53.50	1992	83.00	67.00	79.00	2006	91.63	78.13	91.63
1979	97.00	53.00	57.00	1993	83.00	74.00	78.50	2007	99.88	80.38	82.25
1980	63.00	32.00	44.00	1994	96.00	72.00	90.25	2008	90.75	40.75	42.00
1981	50.25	40.00	41.00	1995	103.00	72.00	72.00	2009	79.25	32.50	76.75
1982	47.00	37.00	37.00	1996	104.00	72.00	91.00	2010	96.00	76.00	91.50
1983	62.00	36.50	54.50	1997	103.50	77.00	78.50	2011	89.25	71.50	72.00
1984	71.00	46.00	46.00	1998	87.75	65.50	69.25	2012	92.75	70.00	91.00
1985	65.00	41.00	59.50	1999	81.50	63.00	77.00	2013	114.00	91.00	103.00

Heavy Native Steers.   *Source: U.S. Department of Agriculture*

Hides / Heavy Native Steers Weekly Cash as of 01/03/2014				
Date	Open	High	Low	Close
12/06/13	114.00	114.00	104.00	104.00
12/13/13	104.00	104.00	103.00	104.00
12/20/13	104.00	104.00	103.00	103.00
12/27/13	103.00	103.00	103.00	103.00
01/03/14	103.00	103.00	103.00	103.00

WEEKLY CASH
As of 01/03/2014
Chart High 114.00 on 11/25/2013
Chart Low 32.50 on 03/13/2009

Cents / lb.

Heavy native steers.

Quarterly High, Low and Settle of Hides   In Cents per Pound

Quarter	High	Low	Settle	Quarter	High	Low	Settle	Quarter	High	Low	Settle
03/2005	81.75	75.25	80.88	03/2008	84.50	77.38	83.75	03/2011	88.00	76.25	88.00
06/2005	84.13	77.75	81.00	06/2008	90.75	82.25	86.25	06/2011	89.25	82.50	86.25
09/2005	83.75	79.25	80.75	09/2008	89.13	84.25	84.75	09/2011	87.00	80.50	81.00
12/2005	82.00	78.63	78.63	12/2008	86.88	40.75	42.00	12/2011	81.00	71.50	72.00
03/2006	86.50	78.13	83.00	03/2009	47.00	32.50	35.88	03/2012	84.00	70.00	82.00
06/2006	89.75	82.75	88.25	06/2009	49.75	33.50	45.88	06/2012	87.00	82.00	83.00
09/2006	89.50	84.50	89.25	09/2009	76.75	45.88	60.50	09/2012	87.00	82.00	87.00
12/2006	91.63	86.75	91.63	12/2009	79.25	62.38	76.75	12/2012	92.75	85.50	91.00
03/2007	98.13	91.00	97.75	03/2010	89.38	76.00	89.38	03/2013	105.00	91.00	105.00
06/2007	99.88	88.25	89.75	06/2010	96.00	89.38	96.00	06/2013	105.00	98.00	101.00
09/2007	89.75	84.50	86.50	09/2010	96.00	86.50	90.50	09/2013	101.00	91.00	91.00
12/2007	86.50	80.38	82.25	12/2010	93.25	87.50	91.50	12/2013	114.00	91.00	103.00

Heavy Native Steers.   *Source: U.S. Department of Agriculture*

TALLOW

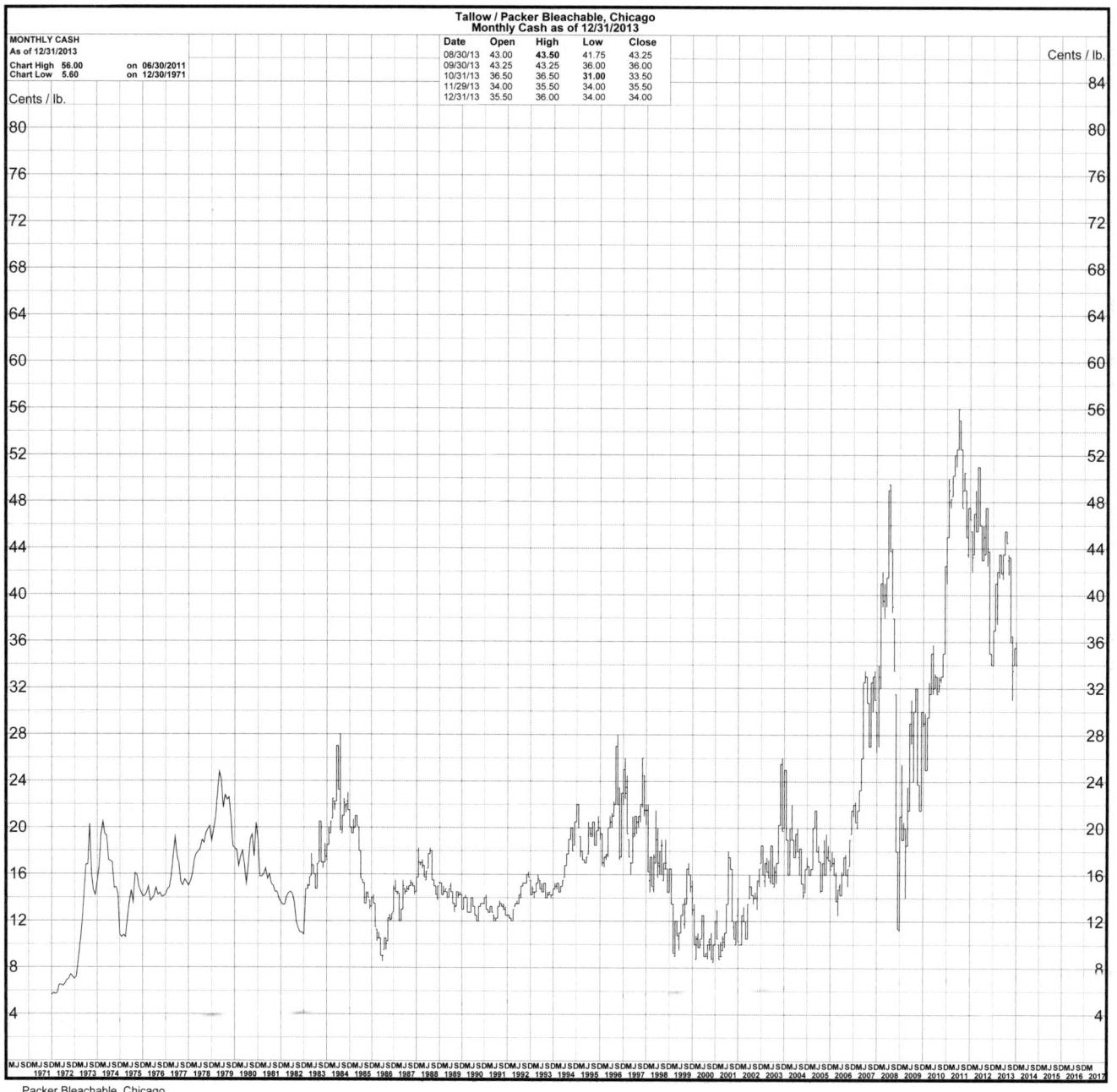

Tallow / Packer Bleachable, Chicago
Monthly Cash as of 12/31/2013

MONTHLY CASH
As of 12/31/2013

Chart High 56.00   on 06/30/2011
Chart Low   5.60   on 12/30/1971

Cents / lb.

Date	Open	High	Low	Close
08/30/13	43.00	43.50	41.75	43.25
09/30/13	43.25	43.25	36.00	36.00
10/31/13	36.50	36.50	31.00	33.50
11/29/13	34.00	35.50	34.00	35.50
12/31/13	35.50	36.00	34.00	34.00

Packer Bleachable, Chicago.

Annual High, Low and Settle of Tallow   In Cents per Pound

Year	High	Low	Settle	Year	High	Low	Settle	Year	High	Low	Settle
1972	7.40	5.70	7.00	1986	15.00	8.50	14.75	2000	13.50	8.50	12.00
1973	20.30	7.20	15.40	1987	15.75	12.00	15.75	2001	18.00	8.75	10.25
1974	20.50	10.80	10.80	1988	18.25	13.75	15.25	2002	18.50	10.00	18.50
1975	16.10	10.60	14.10	1989	15.25	12.75	13.00	2003	26.00	15.00	25.00
1976	14.95	13.69	14.25	1990	14.25	12.00	14.00	2004	25.00	14.00	16.75
1977	19.15	14.70	15.00	1991	14.25	12.00	12.50	2005	21.50	14.50	16.50
1978	20.12	15.38	18.83	1992	16.25	12.00	14.25	2006	22.00	12.50	22.00
1979	24.80	18.20	18.20	1993	16.00	14.00	14.75	2007	33.50	20.00	28.00
1980	20.40	15.20	19.00	1994	22.00	14.50	22.00	2008	49.50	11.25	21.00
1981	16.50	13.60	13.60	1995	22.00	17.00	19.50	2009	32.00	14.00	29.00
1982	14.50	10.80	10.80	1996	28.00	16.63	25.00	2010	45.00	25.00	45.00
1983	20.50	14.00	18.50	1997	26.00	16.00	21.50	2011	56.00	43.25	46.50
1984	28.00	18.50	20.00	1998	22.00	14.50	16.50	2012	51.00	34.00	37.00
1985	21.00	13.00	14.00	1999	17.00	9.00	13.00	2013	45.50	31.00	34.00

Packer Bleachable, Chicago.   *Source: U.S. Department of Agriculture*

Tallow / Packer Bleachable, Chicago
Weekly Cash as of 01/03/2014

WEEKLY CASH
As of 01/03/2014

Chart High 56.00   on 06/30/2011
Chart Low   11.25   on 12/01/2008

Cents / lb.

Date	Open	High	Low	Close
12/06/13	35.50	**36.00**	35.50	36.00
12/13/13	36.00	36.00	35.38	35.38
12/20/13	35.13	35.13	34.63	34.63
12/27/13	34.63	34.63	34.63	34.63
01/03/14	34.00	34.00	**34.00**	34.00

Cents / lb.

Packer Bleachable, Chicago.

Quarterly High, Low and Settle of Tallow   In Cents per Pound

Quarter	High	Low	Settle	Quarter	High	Low	Settle	Quarter	High	Low	Settle
03/2005	20.00	16.00	20.00	03/2008	42.00	27.00	39.50	03/2011	50.25	45.00	50.25
06/2005	21.50	17.13	17.13	06/2008	49.00	38.00	49.00	06/2011	56.00	50.25	56.00
09/2005	19.00	14.50	16.00	09/2008	49.50	33.50	33.50	09/2011	55.00	47.50	50.50
12/2005	19.50	16.00	16.50	12/2008	31.50	11.25	21.00	12/2011	49.00	43.25	46.50
03/2006	18.00	13.75	13.75	03/2009	25.50	14.00	18.50	03/2012	49.00	42.00	45.50
06/2006	16.25	12.50	16.00	06/2009	31.00	18.50	28.00	06/2012	51.00	43.00	43.00
09/2006	17.75	15.00	16.50	09/2009	32.00	23.75	23.75	09/2012	47.50	42.50	43.75
12/2006	22.00	16.75	22.00	12/2009	30.00	21.50	29.00	12/2012	43.75	34.00	37.00
03/2007	23.25	20.00	23.25	03/2010	32.50	25.00	31.50	03/2013	43.50	37.00	43.50
06/2007	33.50	23.25	33.00	06/2010	35.75	31.50	33.00	06/2013	45.50	41.38	45.50
09/2007	33.00	27.00	32.50	09/2010	33.00	31.50	33.00	09/2013	45.50	36.00	36.00
12/2007	33.50	26.50	28.00	12/2010	45.00	33.00	45.00	12/2013	36.50	31.00	34.00

Packer Bleachable, Chicago.   *Source: U.S. Department of Agriculture*

METALS

Gold

Gold and Silver—Current Outlook

Gold and silver prices sold off sharply in 2012 and 2013 as speculators bailed out of long positions taken in the immediate aftermath of the 2008/09 global financial crisis. Many investors had expected the massive liquidity injections by the world's major central banks to cause hyperinflation and a big increase in precious metals prices. Instead, inflation in the industrialized world remains remarkably low due to continued deflationary pressures from the "Great Recession" in 2007/09. In late 2013, the Fed's preferred inflation measure, the core PCE deflator, was at +1.1% y/y, only 0.2 points above its record low.

Gold and silver prices are likely to remain under wraps as long as inflation remains low. However, there is still the possibility of a serious inflation outbreak in coming years if the Fed's $3 trillion in excess liquidity starts to get traction in stimulating lending and economic growth. It remains to be seen whether the Fed will withdraw that liquidity on a timely basis in coming years in order to prevent an inflation outbreak that would be highly bullish for gold and silver.

Gold prices during Bretton Woods (1945-71)

During the Bretton Woods period of 1945-1971, gold was fixed at about $35 per ounce. Bretton Woods was the global currency management system that fixed global currencies in terms of the dollar and also fixed gold in terms of the dollar at $35 per ounce. However, President Nixon on August 15, 1971 announced that the U.S. government would no longer convert dollars into gold. That was the end of the Bretton Woods system and currency rates and gold prices have since floated freely.

Gold soars in the 1970s

After Bretton Woods broke down and gold started to trade freely, gold prices started to rally sharply. Gold prices were driven higher mainly by the sharp inflation pressures that emerged from (1) deficit spending for President Johnson's Great Society and the Vietnam war in the 1960s and early 1970s, (2) the oil price spike in 1973 caused by the Arab oil embargo, and (3) monetary mismanagement by the Federal Reserve. The Fed refused to raise interest rates fast enough to curb inflation, trying to avoid a recession. But in the end, the Fed did more harm than good by waiting to curb inflation.

U.S. inflation finally peaked at +14.8% yr/yr in March 1980 shortly after Paul Volcker took over from G. William Miller as Fed Chairman and started clamping down on the money supply. By no coincidence, gold peaked at roughly the same time in January 1980 at $850 (London PM gold fix) and then started a steep descent.

Gold moves lower during the 1980s and 1990s

Fed Chairman Volcker's stiff monetarist medicine took a toll on both the U.S. economy and gold prices. The U.S. economy experienced a double-dip recession in 1980 and 1981-82. Gold sold off sharply during that time as the double-dip recessions caused inflation to fall and undercut demand for gold. Gold was also undercut in the first half of the 1980s by the sharp rally in the dollar.

During the latter-half of the 1980s and the first half of the 1990s, gold was relatively stable and traded in the range of $300-500 per ounce. However, gold on an inflation-adjusted basis moved steadily lower from the early 1980s all the way until 2001. On an inflation-adjusted basis (in 2013 dollars), gold fell from the peak of $2,549 in January 1980, to $634 in 1990, and then to a 35-year low of $342 in 2001.

Gold was also pressured from about 1990 through 2007 by heavy selling by central banks. Central banks started selling gold due to increased trust in paper currencies and the high cost of holding gold reserves. In fact, according to the World Gold Council, the world's central banks as a whole slashed their ownership of gold by 22% from a peak of 38,347 metric tons in 1965 to a post-war low of 29,963 metric tons in 2007. During the disinflationary 1980s and 1990s, the heavy selling by central banks forced gold prices lower. However, some central banks since 2007 have been building their gold reserves and total central bank gold holdings in 2013 of 31,925 metric tons were up by 6% from the 2007 low.

The plunge in inflation-adjusted gold prices from 1980 through 2001 demoralized gold investors, and more importantly, mining companies. Gold mining almost doubled during the 1980s, but was then largely stagnant after 1990. Mining companies refused to invest the large amount of capital needed to open new mines because of low prices and rising mining expenses. By the time demand started to re-emerge in 2001, mining companies were caught flat-footed without the ability to boost supply to take advantage of higher prices. However, gold companies since 2008 boosted their mining production by 25% in order to take advantage of the surge in gold prices.

2001-11 bull market

Gold prices rallied by 653% from 2001 through 2011, i.e., from $255.00 per ounce in early 2001 to a record high of $1920.8 in September 2011. However, that record high of $1920.8 in nominal terms was actually still well below the inflation-adjusted record high of $2,549 that was posted in January 1980 (in current 2013 dollars).

The early stage of the 2001-11 gold rally was driven in part by the -41% plunge in the dollar index from 2001-2007. The weaker dollar increased the value of gold that is priced in terms of depreciated dollars. However, the dollar index during 2009-13 traded sideways in a choppy range and ceased to have much of a bullish influence on gold prices.

The gold rally kicked into high gear following the 2008/09 global financial crisis when the world's major central banks started injecting massive quantities of liquidity into the world financial system. The Fed and the Bank of Japan even resorted to "quantitative easing," which involved buying bonds and permanently increasing the country's money supply. Before the 2008/09 global financial crisis, it would have been unthinkable that the Fed would have engaged in bond-buying, which had previously been associated in history with desperate central banks and hyperinflation.

After peaking in March 2011, gold prices went into a steep decline, falling by -39% to a 3-year low of $1179.4 in early 2013 and correcting 44.5% of the 2001-11 bull market. The 20012-13 sell-off was caused mainly by heavy long liquidation pressure as many investors gave up on expecting hyperinflation any time soon. Core inflation in the U.S. declined even though the Fed in September 2012 started its third quantitative easing program and continued that program into 2014. Yet many investors are holding onto their long gold positions as they wait patiently to see whether the Fed's $3 trillion liquidity injection during 2008-13 will eventually cause a major inflation panic.

Silver

Silver, like gold, has been a store of value and a medium of exchange for thousands of years. However, silver has more importance as a metal for use in photography and industrial applications. Data from the Silver Institute for 2012 shows that 50% of silver usage (of 1,048 million ounces) goes to industrial applications (466 million ounces) and photography (58 million ounces). Silver therefore trades not only as a precious metal, but also as an industrial metal. The strength of the world economy and industrial demand is therefore an important demand driver for silver prices.

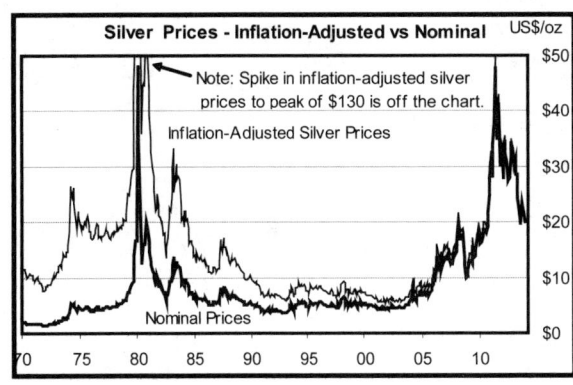

Silver prices in January 1980 posted what at the time was a record high of $48.00 per ounce (NY daily close), which was equivalent to $144 per ounce in current dollars. Silver was driven to that record high in 1980 by the same inflation-driven fundamentals that caused the surge in gold prices. Silver was also pushed to that high by Nelson Bunker Hunt's infamous attempt to corner the silver market. The Hunt family and a group of wealthy Arabs in 1973 started amassing more than 200 million ounces of silver, amounting to about one-half of the world's deliverable supply. However, the silver market then crashed when the New York Metals Exchange changed its trading rules and the Federal Reserve intervened. Nelson Bunker Hunt eventually filed for bankruptcy and was convicted of manipulating the markets.

Silver prices traded on a generally depressed note in the 1980s and 1990s due to the Federal Reserve's successful anti-inflation policy and a steady increase in silver mining output. Starting in 2004, however, silver became caught up in the general commodity bull market. Silver futures prices in fact rallied by +1,141% from the low of $4.015 per ounce in November 2001 to the record high of $49.82 posted in April 2011. That record silver high in nominal terms of $49.82, however, was far short of the inflation-adjusted record high of $144 that was posted back in 1980.

The 2001-11 silver rally was driven by investor safe-haven demand for silver, industrial silver demand from rapidly-developing countries such as China, and fears about hyperinflation stemming from the extraordinarily easy monetary policies by the world's key central banks.

Silver prices during 2012-13 plunged, however, as hyperinflation failed to appear and speculators were forced to bail out of the long positions taken during the worst of the financial crisis. Silver futures prices fell from the record high by 63.5% to a 3-year low of $18.185 in June 2013, retracing 69% of the 2001-11 bull market. However, silver prices in 2013 were still near $19 per ounce and were far above the levels near $7 seen in 2005 before the U.S. housing market started to collapse. Many investors are still holding silver as a hedge against the possibility of another financial crisis or an inflation panic.

ALUMINUM

LME ALUMINIUM - 3-MO
Monthly Cash as of 12/31/2013

Date	Open	High	Low	Close
08/30/13	1805.00	**1949.00**	1773.30	1813.50
09/30/13	1819.00	1860.00	1775.50	1845.00
10/31/13	1845.00	1905.80	1809.00	1859.00
11/29/13	1865.00	1877.00	1741.30	1755.00
12/31/13	1747.80	1839.00	**1736.30**	1800.00

MONTHLY CASH
As of 12/31/2013
Chart High 3380.20 on 07/11/2008
Chart Low 932.00 on 06/17/1982
CONTRACT SIZE 25 METRIC TONS
MIN TICK 1 USD
VALUE 25 USD/CONTRACT
EACH GRID 20 USD
VALUE 500 USD/CONTRACT
DAILY LIMIT NONE
VALUE
TRADING HOURS

3-month Forward.

Annual High, Low and Settle of Aluminium   In USD per Metric Ton

Year	High	Low	Settle	Year	High	Low	Settle	Year	High	Low	Settle
1972	----	----	----	1986	1,241.0	1,115.0	1,157.7	2000	1,752.0	1,428.0	1,554.0
1973	----	----	----	1987	1,930.0	1,157.1	1,892.0	2001	1,649.0	1,255.0	1,355.0
1974	----	----	----	1988	3,200.0	1,830.0	2,475.0	2002	1,465.0	1,289.0	1,350.0
1975	----	----	----	1989	2,540.0	1,587.0	1,630.0	2003	1,607.0	1,324.0	1,600.0
1976	----	----	----	1990	2,138.0	1,405.0	1,568.0	2004	1,972.0	1,558.0	1,958.0
1977	----	----	----	1991	1,605.0	1,097.0	1,150.0	2005	2,289.5	1,681.0	2,288.4
1978	----	----	----	1992	1,370.5	1,124.0	1,259.5	2006	3,310.0	2,220.0	2,803.2
1979	----	----	----	1993	1,267.0	1,037.0	1,124.0	2007	2,932.0	2,375.0	2,402.8
1980	2,230.0	1,445.2	1,508.7	1994	2,005.0	1,124.0	1,981.0	2008	3,380.2	1,430.5	1,540.0
1981	1,605.4	1,079.2	1,181.6	1995	2,194.0	1,640.0	1,706.0	2009	2,305.0	1,279.0	2,230.0
1982	1,193.2	932.0	1,029.0	1996	1,699.0	1,309.0	1,546.0	2010	2,500.0	1,828.0	2,470.0
1983	1,711.8	1,035.2	1,621.9	1997	1,770.0	1,514.0	1,552.0	2011	2,803.0	1,955.8	2,020.0
1984	1,623.9	1,010.6	1,074.3	1998	1,546.0	1,237.0	1,245.0	2012	2,361.5	1,827.3	2,073.0
1985	1,162.6	961.9	1,129.7	1999	1,651.0	1,158.0	1,650.0	2013	2,184.0	1,736.3	1,800.0

3-month Forward.   *Source: London Metal Exchange*

WEEKLY CASH
As of 01/03/2014

Chart High	3380.20	on 07/11/2008
Chart Low	1279.00	on 02/24/2009
CONTRACT SIZE	25 METRIC TONS	
MIN TICK VALUE	1 USD	
VALUE	25 USD/CONTRACT	
EACH GRID VALUE	10 USD	
VALUE	250 USD/CONTRACT	
DAILY LIMIT VALUE	NONE	
TRADING HOURS		

Date	Open	High	Low	Close
12/06/13	1747.80	1784.30	1736.30	1779.00
12/13/13	1774.00	1824.00	1769.80	1799.00
12/20/13	1800.50	1809.00	1771.30	1785.00
12/27/13	1786.80	1814.00	1755.00	1810.00
01/03/14	1808.25	1839.00	1772.00	1772.50

USD / metric ton

3-month Forward.

Quarterly High, Low and Settle of Aluminium   In USD per Metric Ton

Quarter	High	Low	Settle	Quarter	High	Low	Settle	Quarter	High	Low	Settle
03/2005	2,015.0	1,782.0	1,970.0	03/2008	3,255.0	2,377.0	2,990.0	03/2011	2,656.0	2,360.0	2,648.0
06/2005	1,990.0	1,700.0	1,719.5	06/2008	3,169.0	2,828.0	3,120.3	06/2011	2,803.0	2,465.0	2,531.9
09/2005	1,951.0	1,681.0	1,851.0	09/2008	3,380.2	2,404.9	2,425.0	09/2011	2,675.3	2,155.0	2,157.0
12/2005	2,289.5	1,843.8	2,288.4	12/2008	2,450.0	1,430.5	1,540.0	12/2011	2,295.0	1,955.8	2,020.0
03/2006	2,678.2	2,220.0	2,435.0	03/2009	1,648.0	1,279.0	1,395.0	03/2012	2,361.5	2,016.0	2,126.0
06/2006	3,310.0	2,413.0	2,620.0	06/2009	1,701.0	1,350.0	1,629.0	06/2012	2,144.0	1,832.3	1,911.0
09/2006	2,710.0	2,405.0	2,575.0	09/2009	2,115.0	1,545.0	1,891.0	09/2012	2,200.0	1,827.3	2,112.0
12/2006	2,875.0	2,440.8	2,803.2	12/2009	2,305.0	1,776.0	2,230.0	12/2012	2,212.0	1,887.0	2,073.0
03/2007	2,905.0	2,550.0	2,780.0	03/2010	2,394.0	1,967.5	2,323.3	03/2013	2,184.0	1,900.0	1,904.0
06/2007	2,932.0	2,657.8	2,725.0	06/2010	2,494.0	1,828.0	1,969.0	06/2013	1,981.0	1,758.0	1,773.0
09/2007	2,870.0	2,375.0	2,512.8	09/2010	2,354.0	1,921.8	2,351.0	09/2013	1,949.0	1,768.0	1,845.0
12/2007	2,661.0	2,376.0	2,402.8	12/2010	2,500.0	2,185.0	2,470.0	12/2013	1,905.8	1,736.3	1,800.0

3-month Forward.   *Source: London Metal Exchange*

COPPER

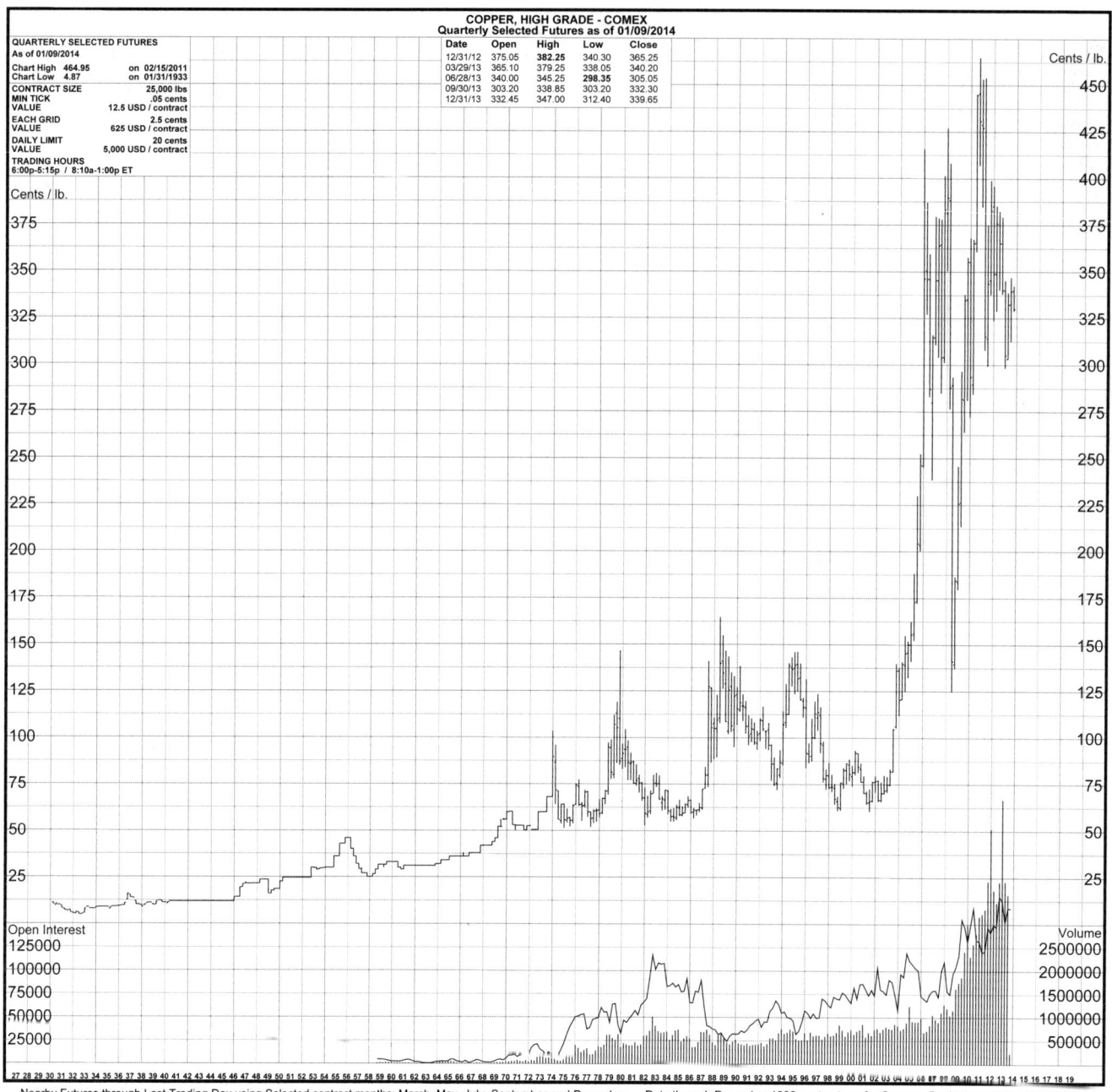

COPPER, HIGH GRADE - COMEX
Quarterly Selected Futures as of 01/09/2014

Date	Open	High	Low	Close
12/31/12	375.05	**382.25**	340.30	365.25
03/29/13	365.10	379.25	338.05	340.20
06/28/13	340.00	345.25	**298.35**	305.05
09/30/13	303.20	338.85	303.20	332.30
12/31/13	332.45	347.00	312.40	339.65

QUARTERLY SELECTED FUTURES
As of 01/09/2014

Chart High	464.95	on 02/15/2011
Chart Low	4.87	on 01/31/1933
CONTRACT SIZE	25,000 lbs	
MIN TICK	.05 cents	
VALUE	12.5 USD / contract	
EACH GRID	2.5 cents	
VALUE	625 USD / contract	
DAILY LIMIT	20 cents	
VALUE	5,000 USD / contract	
TRADING HOURS		
6:00p-5:15p / 8:10a-1:00p ET		

Nearby Futures through Last Trading Day using Selected contract months: March, May, July, September and December.   Data through December 1988 contract are for Copper. Beginning with the March 1989 contract data are for "High Grade" Copper.

Annual High, Low and Settle of High-Grade Copper Futures   In Cents per Pound

Year	High	Low	Settle	Year	High	Low	Settle	Year	High	Low	Settle
1930	17.87	9.70	10.49	1944	11.87	11.87	11.87	1958	29.00	25.00	29.00
1931	10.02	6.67	6.72	1945	11.87	11.87	11.87	1959	35.35	27.44	31.68
1932	7.21	4.91	4.91	1946	19.37	11.87	19.37	1960	35.00	27.50	27.71
1933	8.87	4.87	8.00	1947	22.19	19.45	21.37	1961	32.60	26.67	30.21
1934	8.87	7.87	8.87	1948	23.50	21.50	23.50	1962	31.05	27.95	28.77
1935	9.12	7.87	9.12	1949	23.50	16.00	18.50	1963	30.59	28.67	30.50
1936	10.89	9.12	10.89	1950	24.50	18.50	24.50	1964	61.80	30.40	36.95
1937	15.87	10.11	10.11	1951	24.50	24.50	24.50	1965	60.85	36.25	57.25
1938	11.12	8.87	11.12	1952	24.50	24.50	24.50	1966	82.75	46.25	53.90
1939	12.37	9.87	12.37	1953	30.00	24.50	29.50	1967	64.90	41.40	56.50
1940	12.09	10.69	11.87	1954	30.00	29.50	30.00	1968	76.30	43.30	50.80
1941	11.87	11.87	11.87	1955	43.00	30.00	43.00	1969	76.40	50.50	72.75
1942	11.87	11.87	11.87	1956	46.00	36.00	36.00	1970	78.00	45.05	48.90
1943	11.87	11.87	11.87	1957	36.00	27.00	27.00	1971	58.70	44.05	48.75

Futures data begins 07/01/1959.   Data continued on page 350.   *CME Group; New York Mercantile Exchange*

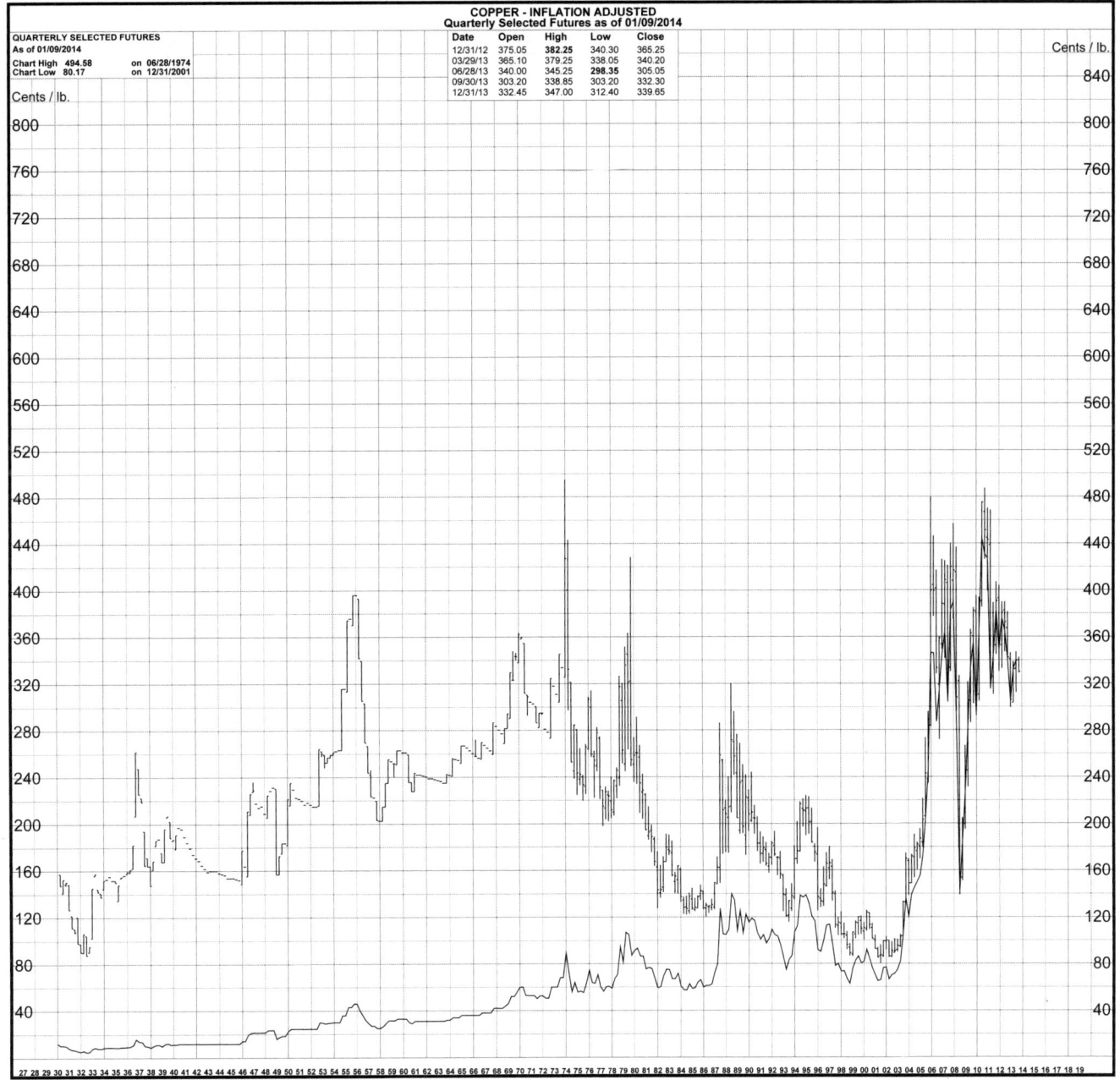

COPPER - INFLATION ADJUSTED
Quarterly Selected Futures as of 01/09/2014

Date	Open	High	Low	Close
12/31/12	375.05	382.25	340.30	365.25
03/29/13	365.10	379.25	338.05	340.20
06/28/13	340.00	345.25	298.35	305.05
09/30/13	303.20	338.85	303.20	332.30
12/31/13	332.45	347.00	312.40	339.65

QUARTERLY SELECTED FUTURES
As of 01/09/2014

Chart High   494.58   on 06/28/1974
Chart Low   80.17   on 12/31/2001

Cents / lb.

Nearby Futures through Last Trading Day using Selected contract months: March, May, July, September and December.   Data through December 1988 contract are for Copper. Beginning with the March 1989 contract data are for "High Grade" Copper.

Annual High, Low and Settle of Copper   In Cents per Pound

Year	High	Low	Settle	Year	High	Low	Settle	Year	High	Low	Settle
1930	17.87	9.70	10.49	1944	11.87	11.87	11.87	1958	29.00	25.00	29.00
1931	10.02	6.67	6.72	1945	11.87	11.87	11.87	1959	33.00	29.00	33.00
1932	7.21	4.91	4.91	1946	19.37	11.87	19.37	1960	33.00	30.00	30.00
1933	8.87	4.87	8.00	1947	22.19	19.45	21.37	1961	31.00	29.00	31.00
1934	8.87	7.87	8.87	1948	23.50	21.50	23.50	1962	31.00	31.00	31.00
1935	9.12	7.87	9.12	1949	23.50	16.00	18.50	1963	31.00	31.00	31.00
1936	10.89	9.12	10.89	1950	24.50	18.50	24.50	1964	34.00	31.00	34.00
1937	15.87	10.11	10.11	1951	24.50	24.50	24.50	1965	36.00	34.00	36.00
1938	11.12	8.87	11.12	1952	24.50	24.50	24.50	1966	38.00	36.00	36.00
1939	12.37	9.87	12.37	1953	30.00	24.50	29.50	1967	38.00	36.00	38.00
1940	12.09	10.69	11.87	1954	30.00	29.50	30.00	1968	42.00	38.00	42.00
1941	11.87	11.87	11.87	1955	43.00	30.00	43.00	1969	56.00	42.00	52.00
1942	11.87	11.87	11.87	1956	46.00	36.00	36.00	1970	60.25	53.00	53.00
1943	11.87	11.87	11.87	1957	36.00	27.00	27.00	1971	53.00	50.00	50.25

New York: Pig Ingots 01/1910 to 10/1986.   Data continued on page 351.   *CME Group; New York Mercantile Exchange*

COPPER

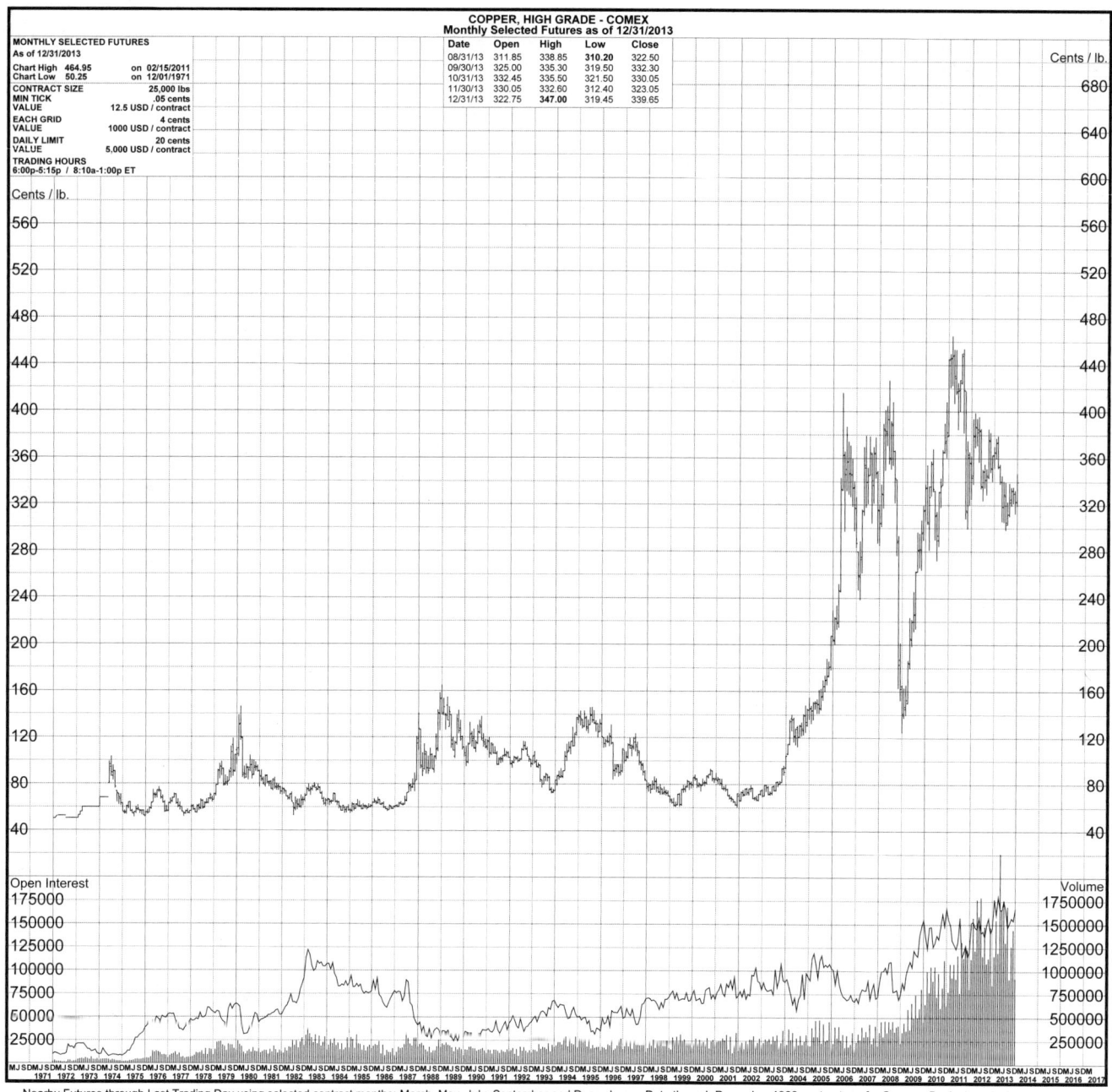

COPPER, HIGH GRADE - COMEX
Monthly Selected Futures as of 12/31/2013

Date	Open	High	Low	Close
08/31/13	311.85	338.85	310.20	322.50
09/30/13	325.00	335.50	319.50	332.30
10/31/13	332.45	335.50	321.50	330.05
11/30/13	330.05	332.60	312.40	323.05
12/31/13	322.75	347.00	319.45	339.65

MONTHLY SELECTED FUTURES
As of 12/31/2013

Chart High 464.95 on 02/15/2011
Chart Low 50.25 on 12/01/1971
CONTRACT SIZE 25,000 lbs
MIN TICK .05 cents
VALUE 12.5 USD / contract
EACH GRID 4 cents
VALUE 1000 USD / contract
DAILY LIMIT 20 cents
VALUE 5,000 USD / contract
TRADING HOURS
6:00p-5:15p / 8:10a-1:00p ET

Nearby Futures through Last Trading Day using selected contract months: March, May, July, September and December.   Data through December 1988 contract are for Copper. Beginning with the March 1989 contract data are for "High Grade" Copper.

Annual High, Low and Settle of High-Grade Copper Futures   In Cents per Pound

Year	High	Low	Settle	Year	High	Low	Settle	Year	High	Low	Settle
1972	53.40	45.85	50.25	1986	68.55	56.60	61.15	2000	93.40	74.10	84.30
1973	109.90	49.85	84.80	1987	141.00	60.05	127.40	2001	86.40	60.50	65.90
1974	140.70	53.20	53.60	1988	164.75	86.50	139.75	2002	79.45	65.65	70.25
1975	63.20	51.30	55.30	1989	154.75	101.95	106.40	2003	105.10	70.00	104.55
1976	77.30	53.80	63.20	1990	138.40	95.00	116.85	2004	155.00	105.40	145.25
1977	71.80	51.90	60.30	1991	119.70	96.05	97.55	2005	229.90	132.35	204.20
1978	71.75	54.70	71.05	1992	116.70	93.70	103.60	2006	416.00	200.25	287.10
1979	119.00	69.25	105.20	1993	108.00	72.00	83.30	2007	379.50	238.50	304.10
1980	146.50	77.05	86.55	1994	140.00	78.50	138.60	2008	427.00	124.75	141.00
1981	91.70	70.40	75.70	1995	146.10	120.00	120.55	2009	337.90	137.15	334.65
1982	76.10	52.80	69.65	1996	131.40	83.90	100.25	2010	445.20	272.00	444.70
1983	80.90	60.75	67.00	1997	123.60	76.10	78.10	2011	464.95	299.40	343.60
1984	71.80	54.90	57.20	1998	86.70	64.40	67.20	2012	398.95	323.80	365.25
1985	66.55	55.70	64.15	1999	86.40	60.90	86.30	2013	379.25	298.35	339.65

Data through December 1988 contract "Old Copper", January 1989 contract to date "High-Grade Copper".   Data continued from page 348.
CME Group; New York Mercantile Exchange

MONTHLY CASH
As of 12/31/2013

Chart High 462.30   on 02/14/2011
Chart Low 50.25   on 12/01/1971

Cents / lb.

Copper, Scrap #2 Wire, NY Monthly Cash as of 12/31/2013				
Date	Open	High	Low	Close
08/30/13	316.40	336.45	316.40	322.50
09/30/13	329.65	335.00	320.70	332.10
10/31/13	327.20	332.85	322.15	329.45
11/29/13	329.35	329.35	315.35	323.05
12/31/13	321.75	347.00	320.10	344.15

Scrap No. 2 Wire

Annual High, Low and Settle of Copper   In Cents per Pound

Year	High	Low	Settle	Year	High	Low	Settle	Year	High	Low	Settle
1972	52.52	50.25	50.50	1986	70.50	60.00	63.25	2000	92.85	74.20	84.65
1973	68.10	50.50	68.10	1987	150.00	62.50	150.00	2001	86.70	60.40	65.30
1974	85.60	68.00	68.60	1988	168.00	93.50	156.75	2002	78.35	65.30	69.70
1975	68.60	60.60	63.60	1989	163.00	102.75	109.00	2003	104.30	70.90	104.30
1976	74.00	63.60	65.00	1990	138.65	99.12	120.00	2004	154.25	106.25	148.70
1977	74.00	60.00	63.00	1991	122.00	100.25	101.25	2005	228.00	139.50	216.15
1978	72.00	60.00	71.25	1992	120.00	97.44	105.50	2006	407.55	213.00	285.40
1979	107.00	71.25	103.00	1993	110.50	79.00	86.00	2007	377.20	240.45	303.05
1980	138.00	79.25	86.25	1994	143.00	84.50	143.00	2008	407.75	124.75	139.50
1981	89.00	78.00	78.00	1995	149.00	121.00	126.00	2009	332.75	138.10	332.75
1982	79.00	63.00	72.00	1996	130.00	87.00	103.00	2010	443.95	277.25	443.95
1983	84.00	65.00	68.00	1997	122.00	77.00	77.00	2011	462.30	305.45	343.15
1984	76.00	60.00	63.00	1998	86.00	65.00	66.00	2012	397.45	328.35	364.10
1985	71.00	61.00	66.50	1999	88.00	61.00	85.25	2013	377.55	302.60	344.15

New York: Pig Ingots to 10/1986; Midwest: Pig Ingots 11/1986 to date.   Data continued from page 349.   *CME Group; New York Mercantile Exchange*

COPPER

CME Group; New York Mercantile Exchange

COPPER, HIGH GRADE - COMEX
Weekly Selected Futures as of 01/03/2014

Date	Open	High	Low	Close
12/06/13	322.75	329.05	319.45	326.95
12/13/13	326.10	335.70	325.95	335.20
12/20/13	336.00	337.85	332.00	334.80
12/27/13	334.70	347.00	334.40	347.00
01/03/14	338.30	342.45	334.55	335.50

WEEKLY SELECTED FUTURES
As of 01/03/2014

Chart High	464.95	on 02/15/2011
Chart Low	106.70	on 01/15/2004
CONTRACT SIZE	25,000 lbs	
MIN TICK VALUE	.05 cents 12.5 USD / contract	
EACH GRID VALUE	4 cents 1000 USD / contract	
DAILY LIMIT VALUE	20 cents 5,000 USD / contract	
TRADING HOURS	6:00p-5:15p / 8:10a-1:00p ET	

Commercial = -984
NonCommercial = 4735
NonReportable = -3751

Nearby Futures through Last Trading Day using selected contract months: March, May, July, September and December.

Quarterly High, Low and Settle of High-Grade Copper Futures   In Cents per Pound

Quarter	High	Low	Settle	Quarter	High	Low	Settle	Quarter	High	Low	Settle
03/2005	152.00	132.35	150.25	03/2008	401.55	301.20	383.10	03/2011	464.95	407.00	430.75
06/2005	162.50	141.00	155.35	06/2008	427.00	350.65	389.55	06/2011	453.30	384.60	427.20
09/2005	188.20	152.35	172.75	09/2008	408.25	276.50	287.90	09/2011	454.00	308.00	315.20
12/2005	229.90	172.25	204.20	12/2008	293.45	124.75	141.00	12/2011	375.00	299.40	343.60
03/2006	252.35	200.25	246.30	03/2009	186.45	137.15	184.45	03/2012	398.95	337.80	382.50
06/2006	416.00	245.30	346.25	06/2009	245.75	179.60	225.80	06/2012	395.80	323.80	349.00
09/2006	387.00	327.00	346.05	09/2009	296.60	213.45	281.90	09/2012	385.20	328.85	375.80
12/2006	359.50	283.00	287.10	12/2009	337.90	264.00	334.65	12/2012	382.25	340.30	365.25
03/2007	316.00	238.50	314.60	03/2010	357.75	281.10	355.35	03/2013	379.25	338.05	340.20
06/2007	379.50	310.75	345.35	06/2010	368.00	272.00	293.60	06/2013	345.25	298.35	305.05
09/2007	378.70	304.10	364.00	09/2010	367.35	284.45	365.15	09/2013	338.85	303.20	332.30
12/2007	378.00	285.00	304.10	12/2010	445.20	360.65	444.70	12/2013	347.00	312.40	339.65

CME Group; New York Mercantile Exchange

Copper, Scrap #2 Wire, NY
Weekly Cash as of 01/03/2014

Date	Open	High	Low	Close
12/06/13	321.75	327.15	320.10	326.95
12/13/13	329.55	335.20	329.55	335.20
12/20/13	337.60	337.60	334.05	334.80
12/27/13	335.05	347.00	335.05	347.00
01/03/14	342.05	344.15	340.60	340.60

WEEKLY CASH
As of 01/03/2014
Chart High 462.30 on 02/14/2011
Chart Low 70.90 on 04/03/2003
Cents / lb.

Scrap No. 2 Wire

Quarterly High, Low and Settle of Copper   In Cents per Pound

Quarter	High	Low	Settle	Quarter	High	Low	Settle	Quarter	High	Low	Settle
03/2005	152.35	139.50	151.05	03/2008	398.95	305.05	386.35	03/2011	462.30	412.50	430.00
06/2005	168.95	143.35	155.35	06/2008	402.80	353.25	387.50	06/2011	449.50	390.20	427.20
09/2005	187.65	153.65	180.15	09/2008	407.75	288.80	288.80	09/2011	447.40	314.50	314.50
12/2005	228.00	183.40	216.15	12/2008	279.70	124.75	139.50	12/2011	370.20	305.45	343.15
03/2006	250.35	213.00	248.80	03/2009	184.95	138.10	183.90	03/2012	397.45	341.25	382.40
06/2006	407.55	257.35	346.25	06/2009	243.80	184.55	225.80	06/2012	391.85	328.35	349.00
09/2006	382.95	331.65	345.90	09/2009	293.45	214.80	280.90	09/2012	385.15	329.25	377.30
12/2006	356.00	283.00	285.40	12/2009	332.75	267.15	332.75	12/2012	380.70	344.30	364.10
03/2007	314.35	240.45	314.35	03/2010	355.50	285.40	354.60	03/2013	377.55	339.50	339.50
06/2007	377.20	317.40	345.35	06/2010	362.60	277.25	293.60	06/2013	343.80	302.60	305.05
09/2007	375.40	312.95	363.05	09/2010	365.65	286.50	364.60	09/2013	336.45	304.10	332.10
12/2007	374.95	287.00	303.05	12/2010	443.95	365.75	443.95	12/2013	347.00	315.35	344.15

Midwest: Pig Ingots.   *CME Group; New York Mercantile Exchange*

COPPER

3-month Forward.

Annual High, Low and Settle of Copper In USD per Metric Ton

Year	High	Low	Settle	Year	High	Low	Settle	Year	High	Low	Settle
1972	----	----	----	1986	1,500.0	1,313.0	1,369.0	2000	2,036.0	1,639.0	1,833.0
1973	----	----	----	1987	2,750.0	1,356.0	2,750.0	2001	1,845.0	1,336.0	1,483.0
1974	----	----	----	1988	3,200.0	1,995.0	3,125.0	2002	1,719.0	1,440.0	1,560.0
1975	----	----	----	1989	3,280.0	2,353.0	2,400.0	2003	2,303.0	1,557.0	2,301.0
1976	----	----	----	1990	2,980.0	2,197.0	2,610.0	2004	3,179.5	2,307.0	3,150.0
1977	1,579.0	1,154.0	1,309.0	1991	2,640.0	2,160.0	2,193.0	2005	4,518.0	2,875.0	4,395.0
1978	1,620.0	1,210.0	1,604.0	1992	2,570.0	2,119.0	2,310.3	2006	8,800.0	4,330.0	6,324.9
1979	2,466.0	1,546.0	2,242.0	1993	2,392.0	1,613.0	1,785.0	2007	8,335.0	5,250.0	6,695.0
1980	3,181.0	1,856.0	1,949.0	1994	3,030.0	1,736.0	3,023.0	2008	8,940.0	2,817.3	3,090.0
1981	2,041.0	1,630.0	1,727.0	1995	3,072.0	2,650.0	2,657.0	2009	7,423.8	3,025.0	7,375.0
1982	1,713.0	1,250.0	1,538.0	1996	2,710.0	1,745.0	2,127.0	2010	9,687.0	6,037.5	9,600.0
1983	1,847.0	1,387.0	1,464.0	1997	2,608.0	1,720.0	1,747.0	2011	10,190.0	6,635.0	7,600.0
1984	1,603.0	1,274.0	1,318.0	1998	1,905.0	1,466.0	1,485.0	2012	8,765.0	7,219.5	7,931.0
1985	1,535.0	1,305.0	1,426.0	1999	1,890.0	1,376.0	1,880.5	2013	8,346.0	6,602.0	7,360.0

3-month Forward. *Source: London Metal Exchange*

LME COPPER - 3-MO
Weekly Cash as of 01/03/2014

Date	Open	High	Low	Close
12/06/13	7041.00	7140.50	6938.00	7122.00
12/13/13	7110.00	7265.30	7087.00	7255.00
12/20/13	7237.00	7300.00	7176.00	7238.00
12/27/13	7244.00	7415.50	7227.00	7382.00
01/03/14	7381.50	7460.00	7312.00	7315.00

WEEKLY CASH
As of 01/03/2014
Chart High 10190.00 on 02/15/2011
Chart Low 1571.00 on 04/24/2003
CONTRACT SIZE 25 METRIC TONS
MIN TICK VALUE .5 USD
EACH GRID VALUE 12.5 USD/CONTRACT
50 USD
1250 USD/CONTRACT
DAILY LIMIT VALUE NONE
TRADING HOURS

3-month Forward.

Quarterly High, Low and Settle of Copper   In USD per Metric Ton

Quarter	High	Low	Settle	Quarter	High	Low	Settle	Quarter	High	Low	Settle
03/2005	3,308.0	2,875.0	3,288.0	03/2008	8,820.0	6,675.0	8,390.0	03/2011	10,190.0	8,944.5	9,428.0
06/2005	3,435.0	2,960.0	3,319.0	06/2008	8,880.0	7,760.0	8,560.0	06/2011	9,944.8	8,504.5	9,430.0
09/2005	3,835.0	3,188.0	3,769.5	09/2008	8,940.0	6,170.0	6,360.0	09/2011	9,905.0	6,800.0	7,018.5
12/2005	4,518.0	3,750.0	4,395.0	12/2008	6,530.0	2,817.3	3,090.0	12/2011	8,280.0	6,635.0	7,600.0
03/2006	5,510.3	4,330.0	5,385.0	03/2009	4,168.0	3,025.0	4,084.0	03/2012	8,765.0	7,445.0	8,445.0
06/2006	8,800.0	5,390.0	7,320.0	06/2009	5,388.0	3,960.8	4,970.3	06/2012	8,702.8	7,219.5	7,685.0
09/2006	8,210.0	7,000.0	7,590.0	09/2009	6,549.0	4,710.0	6,179.5	09/2012	8,422.0	7,280.0	8,205.0
12/2006	7,890.0	6,250.0	6,324.9	12/2009	7,423.8	5,810.0	7,375.0	12/2012	8,379.8	7,506.0	7,931.0
03/2007	6,935.0	5,250.0	6,875.0	03/2010	7,878.0	6,225.0	7,819.8	03/2013	8,346.0	7,486.3	7,540.0
06/2007	8,335.0	6,807.0	7,560.2	06/2010	8,043.8	6,037.5	6,522.0	06/2013	7,645.3	6,602.0	6,750.0
09/2007	8,212.0	6,730.0	8,030.0	09/2010	8,075.0	6,318.0	8,014.0	09/2013	7,420.0	6,671.8	7,302.0
12/2007	8,315.0	6,317.0	6,695.0	12/2010	9,687.0	7,920.0	9,600.0	12/2013	7,415.5	6,910.0	7,360.0

3-month Forward.   *Source: London Metal Exchange*

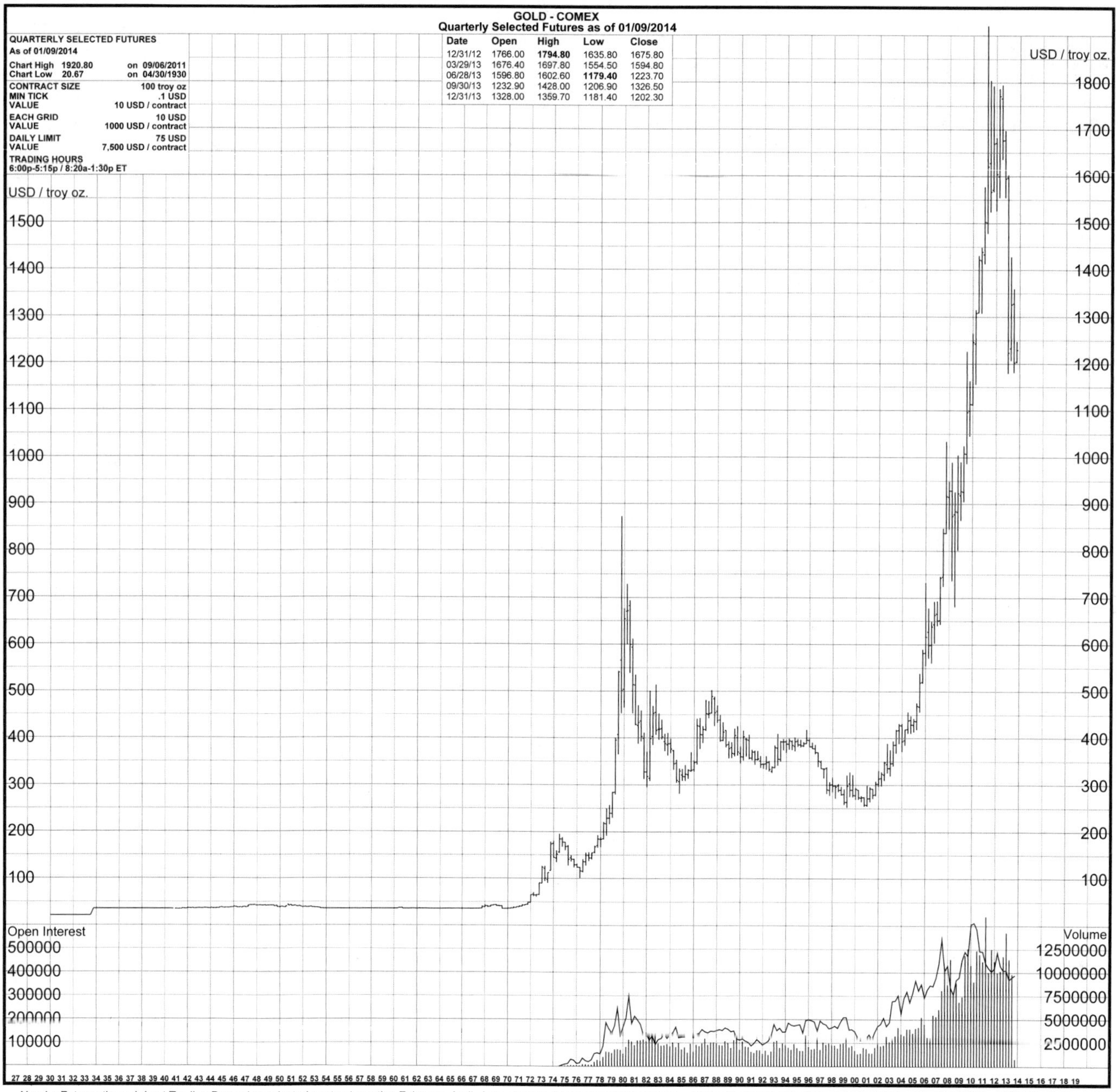
GOLD - COMEX
Quarterly Selected Futures as of 01/09/2014
QUARTERLY SELECTED FUTURES
As of 01/09/2014
Chart High 1920.80 on 09/06/2011
Chart Low 20.67 on 04/30/1930
CONTRACT SIZE 100 troy oz
MIN TICK .1 USD
VALUE 10 USD / contract
EACH GRID 10 USD
VALUE 1000 USD / contract
DAILY LIMIT 75 USD
VALUE 7,500 USD / contract
TRADING HOURS
6:00p-5:15p / 8:20a-1:30p ET
Date Open High Low Close
12/31/12 1766.00 1794.80 1635.80 1675.80
03/29/13 1676.40 1697.80 1554.50 1594.80
06/28/13 1596.80 1602.60 1179.40 1223.70
09/30/13 1232.90 1428.00 1206.90 1326.50
12/31/13 1328.00 1359.70 1181.40 1202.30
USD / troy oz.
1800
1700
1600
1500
1400
1300
1200
1100
1000
900
800
700
600
500
400
300
200
100
Open Interest
500000
400000
300000
200000
100000
Volume
12500000
10000000
7500000
5000000
2500000
27 28 29 30 31 32 33 34 35 36 37 38 39 40 41 42 43 44 45 46 47 48 49 50 51 52 53 54 55 56 57 58 59 60 61 62 63 64 65 66 67 68 69 70 71 72 73 74 75 76 77 78 79 80 81 82 83 84 85 86 87 88 89 90 91 92 93 94 95 96 97 98 99 00 01 02 03 04 05 06 07 08 09 10 11 12 13 14 15 16 17 18 19

Nearby Futures through Last Trading Day using selected contract months: February, April, June, August, October and December. Black Market: to 02/1968; Handy and Harman: 03/1968 to 12/1974; Futures: 12/31/1974 to date.

Annual High, Low and Settle of Gold In USD per Troy Ounce

Year	High	Low	Settle	Year	High	Low	Settle	Year	High	Low	Settle
1930	20.67	20.67	20.67	1944	36.75	36.00	36.25	1958	35.25	35.25	35.25
1931	20.67	20.67	20.67	1945	38.25	36.25	37.25	1959	35.25	35.25	35.25
1932	20.67	20.67	20.67	1946	39.50	37.75	38.25	1960	36.50	35.20	36.50
1933	20.67	20.67	20.67	1947	43.25	37.50	43.00	1961	36.50	35.15	35.50
1934	35.00	35.00	35.00	1948	43.25	41.50	42.00	1962	35.50	35.20	35.45
1935	35.00	35.00	35.00	1949	42.50	40.50	40.50	1963	35.42	35.25	35.25
1936	35.00	35.00	35.00	1950	41.50	36.50	40.25	1964	35.35	35.25	35.35
1937	35.00	35.00	35.00	1951	44.00	40.00	40.00	1965	35.50	35.28	35.50
1938	35.00	35.00	35.00	1952	40.75	38.15	38.70	1966	35.50	35.30	35.40
1939	35.00	35.00	35.00	1953	39.25	35.25	35.50	1967	35.50	35.27	35.50
1940	35.00	35.00	35.00	1954	35.50	35.25	35.25	1968	43.25	35.85	42.05
1941	35.50	34.25	35.50	1955	35.25	35.15	35.15	1969	44.05	35.20	35.45
1942	36.25	35.00	35.50	1956	35.20	35.15	35.20	1970	39.30	34.95	37.65
1943	36.50	35.50	36.50	1957	35.25	35.15	35.25	1971	44.25	37.70	43.85

U.S. Government price control to 12/1940; Black Market 01/1941 to 02/1968; Handy and Harman 03/1968 to 05/1990. Data continued on page 358.
CME Group; New York Mercantile Exchange

GOLD

QUARTERLY SELECTED FUTURES
As of 01/09/2014

Chart High 2551.96 on 03/31/1980
Chart Low 212.05 on 09/30/1970

USD / troy oz.

Date	Open	High	Low	Close
12/31/12	1766.00	1794.80	1635.80	1675.80
03/29/13	1676.40	1697.80	1554.50	1594.80
06/28/13	1596.80	1602.60	1179.40	1223.70
09/30/13	1232.90	1428.00	1206.90	1326.50
12/31/13	1328.00	1359.70	1181.40	1202.30

USD / troy oz.

Nearby Futures through Last Trading Day using selected contract months: February, April, June, August, October and December. Black Market: to 02/1968; Handy and Harman: 03/1968 to 12/1974; Futures: 12/31/1974 to date.

Annual High, Low and Settle of Gold   In USD per Troy Ounce

Year	High	Low	Settle	Year	High	Low	Settle	Year	High	Low	Settle
1930	20.67	20.67	20.67	1944	36.75	36.00	36.25	1958	35.25	35.25	35.25
1931	20.67	20.67	20.67	1945	38.25	36.25	37.25	1959	35.25	35.25	35.25
1932	20.67	20.67	20.67	1946	39.50	37.75	38.25	1960	36.50	35.20	36.50
1933	20.67	20.67	20.67	1947	43.25	37.50	43.00	1961	36.50	35.15	35.50
1934	35.00	35.00	35.00	1948	43.25	41.50	42.00	1962	35.50	35.20	35.45
1935	35.00	35.00	35.00	1949	42.50	40.50	40.50	1963	35.42	35.25	35.25
1936	35.00	35.00	35.00	1950	41.50	36.50	40.25	1964	35.35	35.25	35.35
1937	35.00	35.00	35.00	1951	44.00	40.00	40.00	1965	35.50	35.28	35.50
1938	35.00	35.00	35.00	1952	40.75	38.15	38.70	1966	35.50	35.30	35.40
1939	35.00	35.00	35.00	1953	39.25	35.25	35.50	1967	35.50	35.27	35.50
1940	35.00	35.00	35.00	1954	35.50	35.25	35.25	1968	43.25	35.85	42.05
1941	35.50	34.25	35.50	1955	35.25	35.15	35.15	1969	44.05	35.20	35.45
1942	36.25	35.00	35.50	1956	35.20	35.15	35.20	1970	39.30	34.95	37.65
1943	36.50	35.50	36.50	1957	35.25	35.15	35.25	1971	44.25	37.70	43.85

U.S. Government price control to 12/1940; Black Market 01/1941 to 02/1968; Handy and Harman 03/1968 to 05/1990. Data continued on page 359.
CME Group; New York Mercantile Exchange

GOLD

Futures

GOLD - COMEX
Monthly Selected Futures as of 12/31/2013

Date	Open	High	Low	Close
08/31/13	1323.00	**1428.00**	1274.00	1395.80
09/30/13	1392.20	1415.60	1281.80	1326.50
10/31/13	1328.00	1359.70	1254.10	1323.70
11/30/13	1323.10	1327.30	1225.70	1250.60
12/31/13	1251.40	1267.00	**1181.40**	1202.30

MONTHLY SELECTED FUTURES
As of 12/31/2013
Chart High 1920.80 on 09/06/2011
Chart Low 43.05 on 12/17/1971
CONTRACT SIZE 100 troy oz
MIN TICK .1 USD
VALUE 10 USD / contract
EACH GRID 10 USD
VALUE 1000 USD / contract
DAILY LIMIT 75 USD
VALUE 7,500 USD / contract
TRADING HOURS
6:00p-5:15p / 8:20a-1:30p ET

Nearby Futures through Last Trading Day using selected contract months: February, April, June, August, October and December.   Handy and Harman: to 12/1974; Futures: 12/31/1974 to date.

Annual High, Low and Settle of Gold Futures   In USD per Troy Ounce

Year	High	Low	Settle	Year	High	Low	Settle	Year	High	Low	Settle
1972	70.30	44.30	65.20	1986	443.00	328.00	406.90	2000	322.00	264.40	273.60
1973	126.45	64.20	112.30	1987	502.30	389.00	488.90	2001	298.60	255.00	279.00
1974	195.50	116.80	183.90	1988	488.50	391.80	412.30	2002	350.80	277.20	348.20
1975	187.50	127.40	141.00	1989	419.70	356.50	405.20	2003	418.40	319.30	416.10
1976	141.50	101.00	135.70	1990	425.00	346.00	396.20	2004	456.50	371.30	438.40
1977	169.90	127.50	167.50	1991	406.90	343.00	355.20	2005	538.50	410.10	518.90
1978	249.40	165.50	229.00	1992	361.50	328.90	333.10	2006	732.00	517.60	638.00
1979	543.00	216.60	541.00	1993	409.00	325.80	391.90	2007	848.00	603.00	838.00
1980	873.00	453.00	599.50	1994	398.60	369.10	384.40	2008	1,033.90	681.00	884.30
1981	612.00	387.50	402.80	1995	401.00	372.00	388.10	2009	1,226.40	801.50	1,096.20
1982	501.00	294.70	453.00	1996	417.50	366.00	369.20	2010	1,431.10	1,045.20	1,421.40
1983	514.00	372.00	388.00	1997	369.40	281.50	289.90	2011	1,920.80	1,307.70	1,566.80
1984	410.50	304.70	309.70	1998	315.60	271.60	289.20	2012	1,794.80	1,526.70	1,675.80
1985	342.20	281.20	331.10	1999	327.50	252.50	289.60	2013	1,697.80	1,179.40	1,202.30

Futures begin trading 12/31/1974.   Data continued from page 356.   *CME Group; New York Mercantile Exchange*

MONTHLY CASH
As of 12/31/2013
Chart High 1920.18 on 09/06/2011
Chart Low 43.05 on 12/17/1971

USD / troy oz.

USD / troy oz.

Gold Composite Monthly Cash as of 12/31/2013				
Date	Open	High	Low	Close
08/30/13	1324.47	**1433.49**	1272.90	1394.47
09/30/13	1392.20	1416.20	1291.68	1328.60
10/31/13	1328.60	1361.61	1251.71	1322.75
11/29/13	1322.80	1327.32	1227.67	1251.26
12/31/13	1251.14	1267.71	**1182.60**	1205.24

MJSDMJSDMJSDMJSDMJSDMJSDMJSDMJSDMJSDMJSDMJSDMJSDMJSDMJSDMJSDMJSDMJSDMJSDMJSDMJSDMJSDMJSDMJSDMJSDMJSDMJSDMJSDMJSDMJSDMJSDMJSDMJSDMJSDMJSDMJSDMJSDMJSDMJSDMJSDMJSDMJSDMJSDMJSDMJSDM
1971 1972 1973 1974 1975 1976 1977 1978 1979 1980 1981 1982 1983 1984 1985 1986 1987 1988 1989 1990 1991 1992 1993 1994 1995 1996 1997 1998 1999 2000 2001 2002 2003 2004 2005 2006 2007 2008 2009 2010 2011 2012 2013 2014 2015 2016 2017

Handy and Harman: to 06/1990; 24-HR Composite: 06/1990 to date.

Annual High, Low and Settle of Gold   In USD per Troy Ounce

Year	High	Low	Settle	Year	High	Low	Settle	Year	High	Low	Settle
1972	70.30	44.30	65.20	1986	438.35	326.55	397.00	2000	319.00	262.62	271.90
1973	126.45	64.20	112.30	1987	499.75	390.00	484.05	2001	296.00	254.35	278.95
1974	195.50	116.80	186.75	1988	483.90	395.30	410.90	2002	354.25	277.05	348.05
1975	185.50	128.90	140.35	1989	415.50	355.75	402.90	2003	417.75	319.15	415.65
1976	139.20	102.20	134.75	1990	423.75	345.85	394.00	2004	456.87	371.70	438.44
1977	168.10	130.10	164.96	1991	410.00	342.80	354.00	2005	541.00	410.40	517.03
1978	242.75	165.95	226.00	1992	361.00	328.80	333.10	2006	730.40	511.96	636.60
1979	515.50	217.10	512.00	1993	408.90	325.50	390.20	2007	845.90	602.34	833.60
1980	850.00	481.50	586.00	1994	398.00	369.50	382.70	2008	1,032.80	682.75	881.70
1981	599.25	391.25	401.00	1995	397.75	371.20	386.85	2009	1,226.40	802.55	1,096.47
1982	481.00	296.75	456.90	1996	417.90	366.30	367.45	2010	1,430.63	1,044.80	1,420.68
1983	509.25	374.25	381.50	1997	368.15	282.00	288.80	2011	1,920.18	1,308.11	1,563.48
1984	405.85	307.50	308.30	1998	314.70	271.50	288.00	2012	1,795.78	1,527.52	1,675.21
1985	341.15	284.25	329.70	1999	337.50	252.00	287.50	2013	1,695.99	1,180.64	1,205.24

Black Market to 02/1968; Handy and Harman 03/1968 to 05/1990; Composite 06/1990 to date.   Data continued from page 357.
CME Group; New York Mercantile Exchange

GOLD

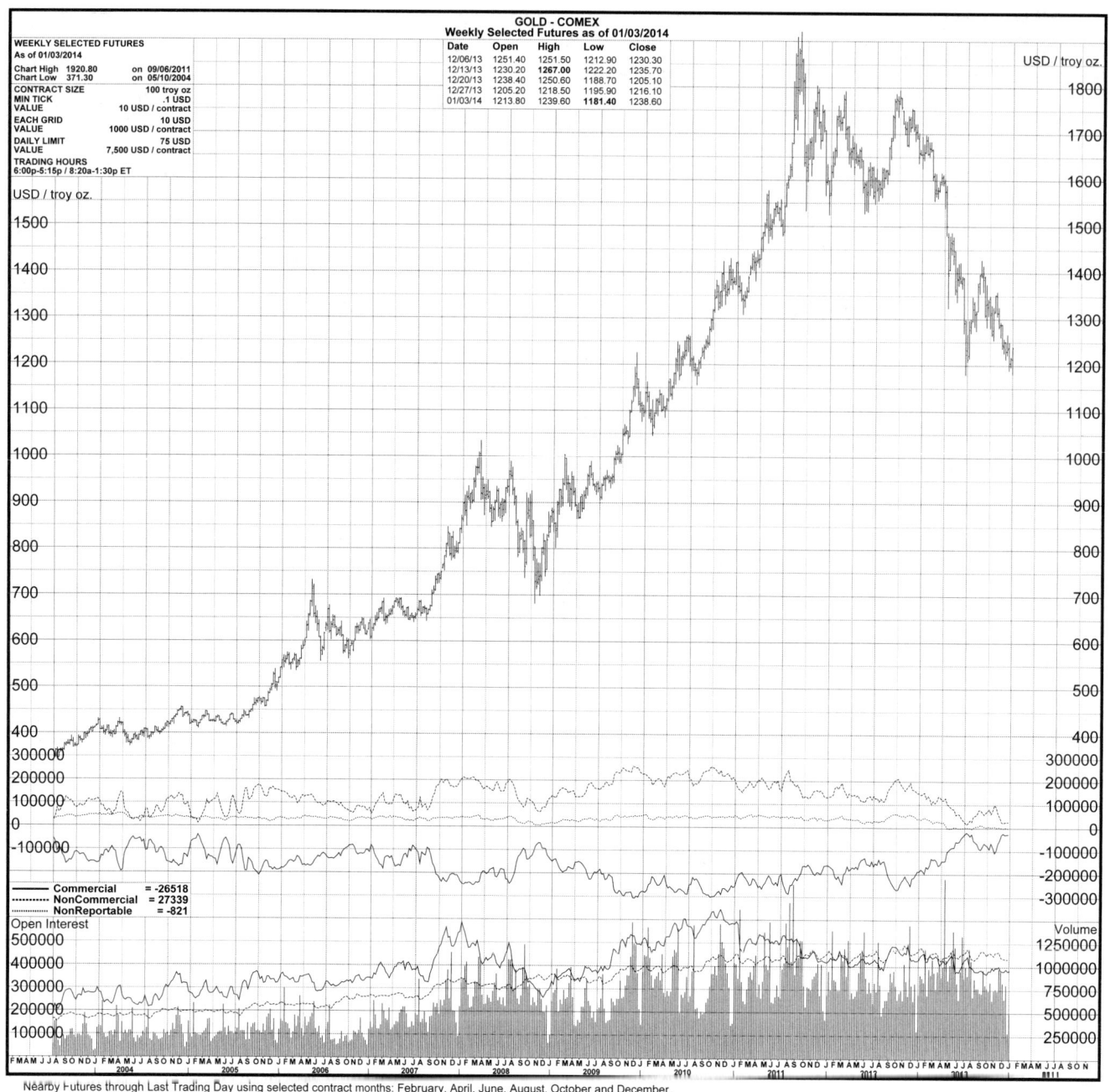

GOLD - COMEX				
Weekly Selected Futures as of 01/03/2014				
Date	Open	High	Low	Close
12/06/13	1251.40	1251.50	1212.90	1230.30
12/13/13	1230.20	1267.00	1222.20	1235.70
12/20/13	1238.40	1250.60	1188.70	1205.10
12/27/13	1205.20	1218.50	1195.90	1216.10
01/03/14	1213.80	1239.60	1181.40	1238.60

WEEKLY SELECTED FUTURES
As of 01/03/2014

Chart High 1920.80 on 09/06/2011
Chart Low 371.30 on 05/10/2004
CONTRACT SIZE 100 troy oz
MIN TICK .1 USD
VALUE 10 USD / contract
EACH GRID 10 USD
VALUE 1000 USD / contract
DAILY LIMIT 75 USD
VALUE 7,500 USD / contract
TRADING HOURS
6:00p-5:15p / 8:20a-1:30p ET

Commercial = -26518
NonCommercial = 27339
NonReportable = -821

Open Interest

Volume

Nearby Futures through Last Trading Day using selected contract months: February, April, June, August, October and December.

Quarterly High, Low and Settle of Gold Futures   In USD per Troy Ounce

Quarter	High	Low	Settle	Quarter	High	Low	Settle	Quarter	High	Low	Settle
03/2005	448.00	410.10	428.70	03/2008	1,033.90	837.50	916.20	03/2011	1,448.60	1,307.70	1,438.90
06/2005	442.50	413.20	437.10	06/2008	948.70	846.40	928.30	06/2011	1,577.40	1,413.00	1,502.80
09/2005	475.70	418.20	469.00	09/2008	989.60	736.40	874.20	09/2011	1,920.80	1,478.30	1,620.40
12/2005	538.50	456.10	518.90	12/2008	925.70	681.00	884.30	12/2011	1,804.40	1,523.90	1,566.80
03/2006	589.60	517.60	581.80	03/2009	1,004.90	801.50	922.60	03/2012	1,792.70	1,566.80	1,669.30
06/2006	732.00	555.00	616.00	06/2009	990.30	865.00	927.40	06/2012	1,682.80	1,526.70	1,604.20
09/2006	677.50	571.00	598.60	09/2009	1,024.70	904.80	1,008.00	09/2012	1,787.00	1,554.40	1,771.10
12/2006	649.50	560.50	638.00	12/2009	1,226.40	986.80	1,096.20	12/2012	1,794.80	1,635.80	1,675.80
03/2007	692.50	603.00	663.00	03/2010	1,163.00	1,045.20	1,113.30	03/2013	1,697.80	1,554.50	1,594.80
06/2007	693.30	640.00	650.90	06/2010	1,264.80	1,111.30	1,245.90	06/2013	1,602.60	1,179.40	1,223.70
09/2007	745.70	642.90	742.80	09/2010	1,315.20	1,155.60	1,307.80	09/2013	1,428.00	1,206.90	1,326.50
12/2007	848.00	724.30	838.00	12/2010	1,431.10	1,309.00	1,421.40	12/2013	1,359.70	1,181.40	1,202.30

CME Group; New York Mercantile Exchange

Gold Composite
Weekly Cash as of 01/03/2014

Date	Open	High	Low	Close
12/06/13	1251.14	1251.31	1211.66	1228.75
12/13/13	1230.04	1267.71	1220.65	1238.40
12/20/13	1238.25	1251.86	1186.84	1202.88
12/27/13	1202.70	1218.83	1192.70	1213.04
01/03/14	1214.20	1240.11	1182.60	1237.58

WEEKLY CASH
As of 01/03/2014
Chart High 1920.18 on 09/06/2011
Chart Low 319.15 on 04/07/2003
USD / troy oz.

24-HR Composite.

Quarterly High, Low and Settle of Gold   In USD per Troy Ounce

Quarter	High	Low	Settle	Quarter	High	Low	Settle	Quarter	High	Low	Settle
03/2005	447.05	410.40	428.55	03/2008	1,032.80	834.95	916.95	03/2011	1,447.28	1,308.11	1,431.89
06/2005	443.70	413.85	435.30	06/2008	952.76	846.27	925.59	06/2011	1,575.11	1,412.82	1,499.93
09/2005	475.50	418.25	469.35	09/2008	988.02	736.55	870.85	09/2011	1,920.18	1,478.65	1,623.37
12/2005	541.00	455.50	517.03	12/2008	932.11	682.75	881.70	12/2011	1,802.69	1,522.53	1,563.48
03/2006	589.51	511.96	582.95	03/2009	1,006.43	802.55	918.82	03/2012	1,790.28	1,557.17	1,667.92
06/2006	730.40	542.27	616.00	06/2009	989.77	859.85	926.60	06/2012	1,683.27	1,527.52	1,597.37
09/2006	676.41	570.94	598.93	09/2009	1,024.22	905.09	1,007.75	09/2012	1,787.04	1,555.06	1,772.18
12/2006	649.96	559.30	636.60	12/2009	1,226.40	986.98	1,096.47	12/2012	1,795.78	1,635.56	1,675.21
03/2007	688.73	602.34	663.74	03/2010	1,161.75	1,044.80	1,113.20	03/2013	1,695.99	1,555.06	1,598.85
06/2007	694.19	639.48	649.50	06/2010	1,265.03	1,111.94	1,242.58	06/2013	1,603.72	1,180.64	1,234.26
09/2007	745.92	642.25	743.00	09/2010	1,315.74	1,155.90	1,308.31	09/2013	1,433.49	1,208.20	1,328.60
12/2007	845.90	721.22	833.60	12/2010	1,430.63	1,306.55	1,420.68	12/2013	1,361.61	1,182.60	1,205.24

Composite.   *CME Group; New York Mercantile Exchange*

LEAD

					LME LEAD - 3-MO		
					Monthly Cash as of 12/31/2013		
MONTHLY CASH				Date	Open	High	Low	Close
As of 12/31/2013				08/30/13	2067.00	**2295.00**	2065.50	2152.00
Chart High 3890.20 on 10/10/2007			09/30/13	2162.00	2189.00	**2037.80**	2117.00
Chart Low 346.10 on 03/18/1985			10/31/13	2106.00	2218.00	2042.00	2184.00
CONTRACT SIZE 25 METRIC TONS			11/29/13	2178.30	2211.30	2063.00	2080.00
MIN TICK .5 USD			12/31/13	2070.00	2289.00	2057.50	2219.00

3-month Forward.

Annual High, Low and Settle of Lead   In USD per Metric Ton

Year	High	Low	Settle	Year	High	Low	Settle	Year	High	Low	Settle
1972	----	----	----	1986	480.6	371.1	462.4	2000	517.0	415.0	484.0
1973	----	----	----	1987	684.1	438.8	656.9	2001	523.0	441.0	497.0
1974	----	----	----	1988	731.9	588.0	700.8	2002	530.0	409.0	436.0
1975	----	----	----	1989	743.0	584.5	707.0	2003	727.0	435.0	724.0
1976	----	----	----	1990	935.0	624.0	633.0	2004	1,019.0	651.0	1,004.0
1977	762.9	530.9	697.8	1991	643.0	509.0	560.0	2005	1,125.0	812.0	1,051.0
1978	867.4	540.7	843.4	1992	684.0	459.0	463.0	2006	1,785.0	924.8	1,665.2
1979	1,417.5	838.0	1,094.5	1993	499.0	365.0	488.0	2007	3,890.2	1,505.0	2,550.0
1980	1,190.6	719.2	768.3	1994	703.0	435.0	673.0	2008	3,480.0	850.0	999.0
1981	929.1	647.6	721.1	1995	742.0	523.0	714.0	2009	2,525.5	957.0	2,432.0
1982	719.1	445.1	487.4	1996	861.0	666.5	700.0	2010	2,690.0	1,535.0	2,550.0
1983	514.7	403.6	436.2	1997	731.0	525.0	564.0	2011	2,904.0	1,772.3	2,035.0
1984	522.8	378.6	378.6	1998	603.0	466.0	474.0	2012	2,347.8	1,742.0	2,330.0
1985	423.4	346.1	391.6	1999	562.0	460.0	495.5	2013	2,499.0	1,938.0	2,219.0

3-month Forward.   *Source: London Metal Exchange*

	LME LEAD - 3-MO				
	Weekly Cash as of 01/03/2014				
Date	Open	High	Low	Close
12/06/13	2070.00	2103.00	2057.50	2093.50
12/13/13	2092.00	2162.80	2085.00	2150.00
12/20/13	2151.00	2218.00	2147.00	2216.00
12/27/13	2208.00	2289.00	2199.50	2287.00
01/03/14	2283.00	2289.00	2170.00	2176.00

3-month Forward.

Quarterly High, Low and Settle of Lead   In USD per Metric Ton

Quarter	High	Low	Settle	Quarter	High	Low	Settle	Quarter	High	Low	Settle
03/2005	991.0	867.0	989.0	03/2008	3,480.0	2,405.0	2,790.0	03/2011	2,747.0	2,325.0	2,695.0
06/2005	996.0	880.0	880.0	06/2008	3,000.0	1,745.0	1,780.0	06/2011	2,904.0	2,200.0	2,684.0
09/2005	970.0	812.0	938.0	09/2008	2,293.8	1,531.0	1,835.0	09/2011	2,779.0	1,800.0	1,985.0
12/2005	1,125.0	923.9	1,051.0	12/2008	1,873.0	850.0	999.0	12/2011	2,167.5	1,772.3	2,035.0
03/2006	1,435.0	1,049.0	1,175.0	03/2009	1,380.0	957.0	1,275.0	03/2012	2,329.0	1,950.0	2,042.0
06/2006	1,360.0	924.8	1,015.0	06/2009	1,833.5	1,219.8	1,693.0	06/2012	2,200.0	1,742.0	1,861.0
09/2006	1,410.5	995.0	1,380.0	09/2009	2,517.3	1,548.0	2,280.0	09/2012	2,325.0	1,818.0	2,280.0
12/2006	1,785.0	1,340.0	1,665.2	12/2009	2,525.5	2,070.0	2,432.0	12/2012	2,347.8	1,979.0	2,330.0
03/2007	1,975.2	1,505.0	1,920.0	03/2010	2,690.0	1,911.0	2,154.3	03/2013	2,499.0	2,093.0	2,112.0
06/2007	2,725.0	1,905.0	2,657.9	06/2010	2,400.0	1,535.0	1,749.5	06/2013	2,259.3	1,938.0	2,051.0
09/2007	3,520.0	2,670.0	3,400.0	09/2010	2,321.0	1,697.5	2,278.0	09/2013	2,295.0	2,000.0	2,117.0
12/2007	3,890.2	2,371.0	2,550.0	12/2010	2,650.0	2,150.0	2,550.0	12/2013	2,289.0	2,042.0	2,219.0

3-month Forward.   *Source: London Metal Exchange*

NICKEL

3-month Forward.

Annual High, Low and Settle of Nickel   In USD per Metric Ton

Year	High	Low	Settle	Year	High	Low	Settle	Year	High	Low	Settle
1972	----	----	----	1986	4,356	3,541	3,568	2000	10,450	6,610	6,830
1973	----	----	----	1987	9,039	3,484	8,995	2001	7,450	4,320	5,575
1974	----	----	----	1988	19,000	7,154	16,800	2002	7,760	5,470	7,130
1975	----	----	----	1989	18,900	7,850	8,000	2003	16,900	7,140	16,500
1976	----	----	----	1990	11,350	5,800	8,300	2004	17,700	10,400	14,875
1977	----	----	----	1991	9,350	7,050	7,215	2005	16,901	11,480	13,500
1978	----	----	----	1992	8,245	5,320	6,020	2006	34,950	13,300	33,326
1979	7,748	5,748	6,302	1993	6,440	4,030	5,305	2007	51,800	24,800	26,100
1980	7,404	6,057	6,477	1994	9,400	5,240	8,975	2008	35,150	8,850	11,700
1981	6,701	5,051	5,647	1995	10,500	6,770	8,010	2009	21,325	9,250	18,525
1982	5,962	3,219	3,906	1996	8,850	6,360	6,465	2010	27,595	16,975	24,750
1983	5,313	3,665	4,842	1997	8,320	5,920	6,070	2011	29,425	16,550	18,710
1984	5,168	4,701	4,825	1998	6,080	3,775	4,170	2012	22,150	15,236	17,060
1985	5,602	4,000	4,131	1999	8,515	3,940	8,500	2013	18,770	13,205	13,900

3-month Forward.   *Source: London Metal Exchange*

LME NICKEL - 3-MO.
Weekly Cash as of 01/03/2014

Date	Open	High	Low	Close
12/06/13	13501.00	13918.00	**13382.00**	13760.00
12/13/13	13788.00	14227.00	13735.00	14100.00
12/20/13	14055.00	14451.00	13970.00	14420.00
12/27/13	14450.00	**14479.00**	14108.00	14200.00
01/03/14	14186.00	14300.00	13792.00	13845.00

WEEKLY CASH
As of 01/03/2014

Chart High	51800.00	on 05/09/2007
Chart Low	7690.00	on 03/27/2003
CONTRACT SIZE	6 METRIC TONS	
MIN TICK VALUE	1 USD 6 USD/CONTRACT	
EACH GRID VALUE	250 USD 1500 USD/CONTRACT	
DAILY LIMIT VALUE	NONE	
TRADING HOURS		

USD / metric ton

3-month Forward.

Quarterly High, Low and Settle of Nickel   In USD per Metric Ton

Quarter	High	Low	Settle	Quarter	High	Low	Settle	Quarter	High	Low	Settle
03/2005	16,350	13,700	15,900	03/2008	35,150	26,250	29,755	03/2011	29,425	23,822	26,095
06/2005	16,901	14,325	14,590	06/2008	30,325	21,355	21,905	06/2011	27,950	21,337	23,425
09/2005	15,450	12,825	13,500	09/2008	22,599	15,588	15,850	09/2011	25,195	16,800	17,600
12/2005	14,451	11,480	13,500	12/2008	16,400	8,850	11,700	12/2011	20,300	16,550	18,710
03/2006	15,802	13,300	15,200	03/2009	13,550	9,250	9,800	03/2012	22,150	17,125	17,825
06/2006	23,050	15,150	21,050	06/2009	16,100	9,625	15,411	06/2012	18,800	15,980	16,730
09/2006	29,950	21,400	29,300	09/2009	21,325	14,120	17,800	09/2012	18,675	15,236	18,475
12/2006	34,950	28,000	33,326	12/2009	19,750	15,720	18,525	12/2012	18,920	15,758	17,060
03/2007	48,500	30,000	44,800	03/2010	25,085	16,975	25,050	03/2013	18,770	16,372	16,660
06/2007	51,800	35,350	36,200	06/2010	27,595	17,375	19,650	06/2013	16,660	13,525	13,710
09/2007	37,500	24,800	30,501	09/2010	23,570	18,401	23,400	09/2013	15,001	13,205	13,955
12/2007	34,250	25,177	26,100	12/2010	25,200	20,450	24,750	12/2013	14,880	13,274	13,900

3-month Forward.   *Source: London Metal Exchange*

PALLADIUM

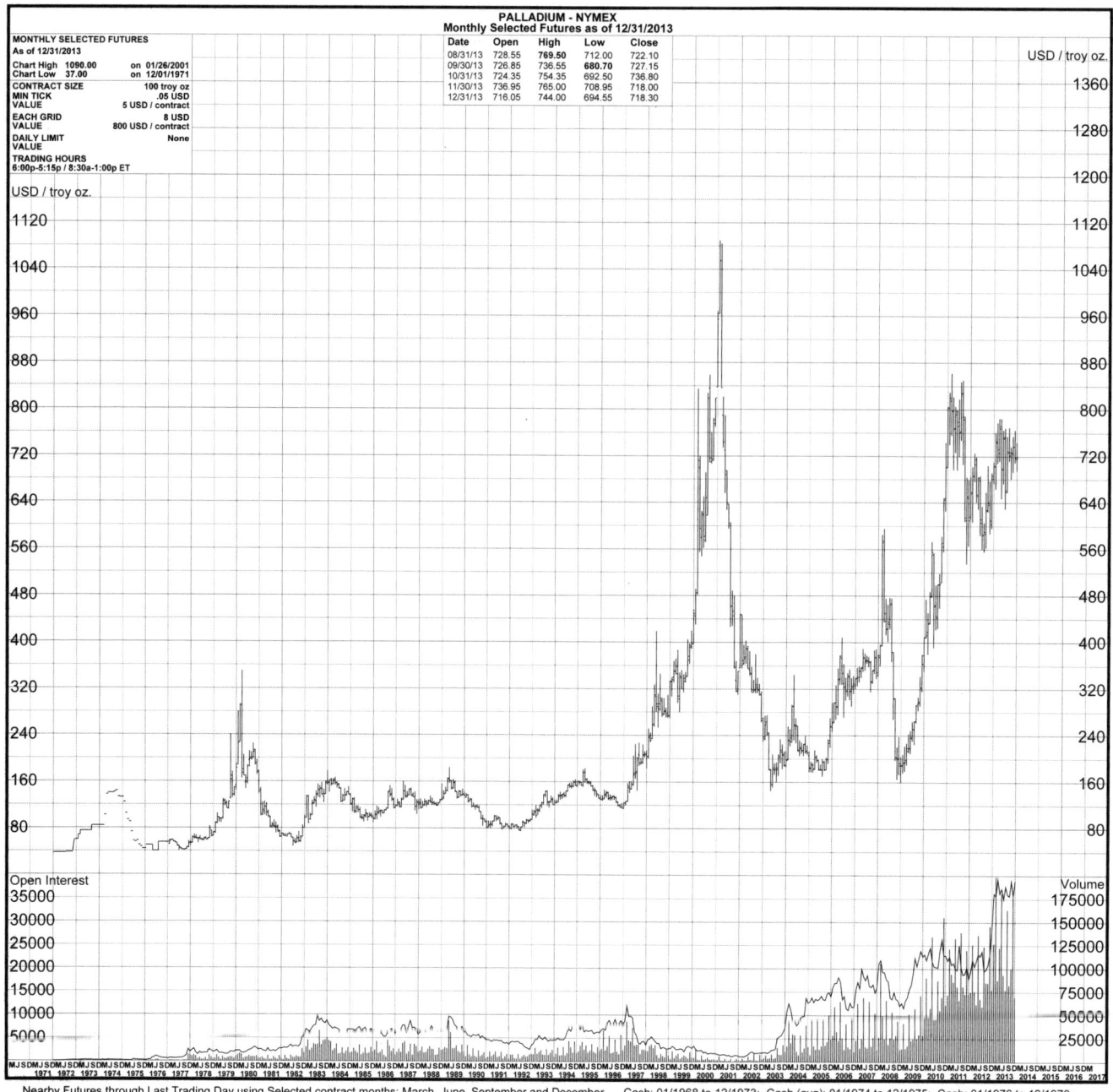

PALLADIUM - NYMEX
Monthly Selected Futures as of 12/31/2013

Date	Open	High	Low	Close
08/31/13	728.55	**769.50**	712.00	722.10
09/30/13	726.85	736.55	**680.70**	727.15
10/31/13	724.35	754.35	692.50	736.80
11/30/13	736.95	765.00	708.95	**718.00**
12/31/13	716.05	744.00	694.55	718.30

MONTHLY SELECTED FUTURES
As of 12/31/2013

Chart High 1090.00 on 01/26/2001
Chart Low 37.00 on 12/01/1971
CONTRACT SIZE 100 troy oz
MIN TICK .05 USD
VALUE
EACH TICK 5 USD / contract
VALUE
EACH GRID 8 USD
VALUE 800 USD / contract
DAILY LIMIT None
VALUE
TRADING HOURS
6:00p-5:15p / 8:30a-1:00p ET

Nearby Futures through Last Trading Day using Selected contract months: March, June, September and December. Cash: 01/1968 to 12/1973; Cash (avg): 01/1974 to 12/1975; Cash: 01/1976 to 12/1976;
Futures: 01/1977 to date.

Annual High, Low and Settle of Palladium Futures   In USD per Troy Ounce

Year	High	Low	Settle	Year	High	Low	Settle	Year	High	Low	Settle
1972	60.00	37.00	60.00	1986	153.00	94.00	118.30	2000	975.00	430.20	954.45
1973	84.00	60.00	84.00	1987	160.00	103.65	123.60	2001	1,090.00	310.00	448.00
1974	143.80	84.00	132.50	1988	155.95	113.00	129.00	2002	447.00	229.70	238.00
1975	124.32	44.00	44.00	1989	184.00	129.25	135.50	2003	275.00	145.00	197.50
1976	55.00	40.00	55.00	1990	139.90	80.55	81.25	2004	344.70	177.75	185.25
1977	59.80	40.10	53.50	1991	102.50	77.50	80.65	2005	297.10	170.20	261.50
1978	83.35	52.40	72.50	1992	112.00	74.50	104.45	2006	409.00	262.00	338.50
1979	240.50	70.10	182.50	1993	145.00	98.00	124.35	2007	389.50	315.20	378.20
1980	350.00	139.00	142.25	1994	164.00	122.50	160.25	2008	595.10	160.00	188.70
1981	149.00	63.00	69.30	1995	182.90	128.80	129.65	2009	410.00	176.10	408.85
1982	102.00	48.00	97.50	1996	147.00	114.50	124.05	2010	804.90	380.05	803.30
1983	178.00	88.00	157.45	1997	227.60	120.25	203.15	2011	862.00	535.00	656.15
1984	166.75	120.00	121.50	1998	419.00	200.00	332.15	2012	725.85	555.90	703.35
1985	132.00	89.75	95.40	1999	456.95	280.00	449.20	2013	785.00	629.40	718.30

Futures data begins 01/03/1977.   *CME Group; New York Mercantile Exchange*

Date	Open	High	Low	Close
08/30/13	730.00	763.00	717.00	718.00
09/30/13	710.00	731.00	679.00	720.00
10/31/13	716.00	750.00	690.00	734.00
11/29/13	737.00	761.00	707.00	716.00
12/31/13	715.00	739.00	690.00	712.00

Industrial, Engelhard
Monthly Cash as of 12/31/2013

MONTHLY CASH
As of 12/31/2013
Chart High 1100.00 on 01/26/2001
Chart Low 37.00 on 12/01/1971
USD / troy oz.

Engelhard.

Annual High, Low and Settle of Palladium   In USD per Troy Ounce

Year	High	Low	Settle	Year	High	Low	Settle	Year	High	Low	Settle
1972	60.00	37.00	60.00	1986	142.30	101.83	118.15	2000	985.00	437.00	965.00
1973	84.00	60.00	84.00	1987	148.50	106.50	125.50	2001	1,100.00	319.00	446.00
1974	143.80	84.00	132.50	1988	146.00	114.25	133.00	2002	439.00	225.00	237.00
1975	124.32	44.00	44.00	1989	181.50	131.00	135.50	2003	273.00	150.00	196.00
1976	55.00	40.00	55.00	1990	138.00	82.75	82.75	2004	340.00	180.00	186.00
1977	55.00	55.00	55.00	1991	102.50	79.00	81.00	2005	297.00	174.00	255.00
1978	80.00	55.00	80.00	1992	114.00	78.50	107.00	2006	407.00	263.00	330.00
1979	120.00	80.00	120.00	1993	145.00	100.00	124.00	2007	383.00	322.00	370.00
1980	225.00	120.00	225.00	1994	163.00	124.00	158.00	2008	585.00	167.00	185.00
1981	225.00	110.00	110.00	1995	179.00	130.00	130.00	2009	406.00	182.00	406.00
1982	110.00	110.00	110.00	1996	146.00	117.00	123.00	2010	797.00	385.00	794.00
1983	160.69	99.55	160.69	1997	246.00	122.00	207.00	2011	855.00	533.00	647.00
1984	161.10	135.83	136.72	1998	417.00	205.00	338.00	2012	715.00	558.00	700.00
1985	127.88	94.50	94.50	1999	466.00	293.00	466.00	2013	780.00	630.00	712.00

CME Group; New York Mercantile Exchange

PALLADIUM

PALLADIUM - NYMEX
Weekly Selected Futures as of 01/03/2014

Date	Open	High	Low	Close
12/06/13	716.05	737.80	709.20	735.45
12/13/13	734.55	744.00	715.75	715.75
12/20/13	715.90	715.90	695.30	697.85
12/27/13	694.75	711.05	694.55	711.05
01/03/14	711.90	733.65	706.60	731.20

WEEKLY SELECTED FUTURES
As of 01/03/2014

Chart High	862.00	on 02/22/2011
Chart Low	160.00	on 12/05/2008
CONTRACT SIZE		100 troy oz
MIN TICK		.05 USD
VALUE	5 USD / contract	
EACH GRID		10 USD
VALUE	1000 USD / contract	
DAILY LIMIT		None
VALUE		

TRADING HOURS
6:00p-5:15p / 8:30a-1:00p ET

Commercial = -18151
NonCommercial = 17185
NonReportable = 966

Nearby Futures through Last Trading Day using selected contract months: March, June, September and December.

Quarterly High, Low and Settle of Palladium Futures   In USD per Troy Ounce

Quarter	High	Low	Settle	Quarter	High	Low	Settle	Quarter	High	Low	Settle
03/2005	215.00	177.00	203.55	03/2008	595.10	360.10	450.20	03/2011	862.00	696.00	767.90
06/2005	207.00	180.50	181.95	06/2008	476.85	401.50	464.75	06/2011	818.05	695.75	760.65
09/2005	202.70	170.20	199.80	09/2008	475.90	197.50	202.70	09/2011	850.20	608.00	614.55
12/2005	297.10	192.10	261.50	12/2008	238.30	160.00	188.70	12/2011	684.65	535.00	656.15
03/2006	355.80	262.00	336.80	03/2009	227.00	176.10	218.80	03/2012	725.85	607.00	654.10
06/2006	409.00	271.00	323.50	06/2009	264.00	209.10	250.95	06/2012	686.20	560.60	584.55
09/2006	354.05	301.00	316.40	09/2009	306.70	225.10	299.20	09/2012	704.30	555.90	640.80
12/2006	343.10	290.10	338.50	12/2009	410.00	290.85	408.85	12/2012	710.80	586.95	703.35
03/2007	358.90	325.20	357.25	03/2010	487.50	380.05	479.95	03/2013	785.00	663.20	768.25
06/2007	389.50	350.20	368.50	06/2010	573.60	391.20	444.40	06/2013	784.80	629.40	660.70
09/2007	375.80	315.20	351.95	09/2010	582.65	424.00	571.25	09/2013	769.50	658.25	727.15
12/2007	389.00	338.00	378.20	12/2010	804.90	556.10	803.30	12/2013	765.00	692.50	718.30

CME Group; New York Mercantile Exchange

Industrial, Engelhard
Weekly Cash as of 01/03/2014

Date	Open	High	Low	Close
12/06/13	715.00	732.00	707.00	731.00
12/13/13	733.00	**739.00**	711.00	713.00
12/20/13	714.00	714.00	693.00	696.00
12/27/13	698.00	708.00	**690.00**	708.00
01/03/14	706.00	729.00	706.00	722.00

WEEKLY CASH
As of 01/03/2014
Chart High 855.00 on 02/21/2011
Chart Low 150.00 on 04/25/2003
CONTRACT SIZE 100 troy oz
MIN TICK .05 USD
VALUE 5 USD / contract
EACH GRID 5 USD
VALUE 500 USD / contract
DAILY LIMIT None
VALUE
TRADING HOURS
6:00p-5:15p / 8:30a-1:00p ET

USD / troy oz.

Engelhard.

Quarterly High, Low and Settle of Palladium   In USD per Troy Ounce

Quarter	High	Low	Settle	Quarter	High	Low	Settle	Quarter	High	Low	Settle
03/2005	211.00	180.00	202.00	03/2008	585.00	368.00	447.00	03/2011	855.00	681.00	757.00
06/2005	205.00	184.00	185.00	06/2008	480.00	408.00	472.00	06/2011	811.00	692.00	750.00
09/2005	203.00	174.00	196.00	09/2008	468.00	204.00	204.00	09/2011	841.00	601.00	604.00
12/2005	297.00	194.00	255.00	12/2008	235.00	167.00	185.00	12/2011	680.00	533.00	647.00
03/2006	349.00	263.00	332.00	03/2009	223.00	182.00	215.00	03/2012	715.00	610.00	648.00
06/2006	407.00	286.00	317.00	06/2009	262.00	215.00	249.00	06/2012	676.00	560.00	583.00
09/2006	351.00	306.00	318.00	09/2009	303.00	230.00	295.00	09/2012	690.00	558.00	634.00
12/2006	335.00	297.00	330.00	12/2009	406.00	292.00	406.00	12/2012	704.00	586.00	700.00
03/2007	357.00	331.00	355.00	03/2010	483.00	385.00	479.00	03/2013	780.00	667.00	767.00
06/2007	383.00	353.00	368.00	06/2010	570.00	398.00	446.00	06/2013	778.00	630.00	655.00
09/2007	373.00	322.00	347.00	09/2010	578.00	425.00	565.00	09/2013	763.00	679.00	720.00
12/2007	382.00	346.00	370.00	12/2010	797.00	554.00	794.00	12/2013	761.00	690.00	712.00

CME Group; New York Mercantile Exchange

PLATINUM

Nearby Futures through Last Trading Day using selected contract months: January, April, July and October.   Cash (avg): to 09/1967; Cash: 10/1967 to 03/1968; Futures: 03/1968 to date.

Annual High, Low and Settle of Platinum Futures   In USD per Troy Ounce

Year	High	Low	Settle	Year	High	Low	Settle	Year	High	Low	Settle
1972	161.60	96.00	141.70	1986	682.00	334.00	470.70	2000	800.00	408.00	609.60
1973	188.80	134.60	160.10	1987	658.50	469.00	500.60	2001	641.10	406.00	493.00
1974	293.50	159.50	159.50	1988	630.00	439.50	516.60	2002	610.50	445.20	604.40
1975	179.50	137.00	146.90	1989	566.20	466.20	487.30	2003	847.70	590.00	811.30
1976	184.50	135.00	149.50	1990	536.90	387.50	408.70	2004	954.00	756.00	863.70
1977	186.90	144.20	186.40	1991	421.50	330.00	338.70	2005	1,026.00	843.20	973.00
1978	390.00	183.00	349.00	1992	400.00	330.00	354.10	2006	1,347.00	972.00	1,139.30
1979	730.00	337.00	692.60	1993	427.50	335.50	394.90	2007	1,551.50	1,109.00	1,528.40
1980	1,045.00	465.00	578.00	1994	435.40	379.00	414.70	2008	2,308.80	761.80	936.20
1981	599.00	365.50	373.20	1995	463.00	397.00	398.20	2009	1,514.80	914.00	1,460.00
1982	409.00	238.00	383.10	1996	436.90	369.00	369.30	2010	1,811.80	1,446.20	1,773.30
1983	502.00	375.00	390.50	1997	473.80	339.50	370.80	2011	1,918.50	1,347.00	1,399.70
1984	417.50	285.50	287.70	1998	440.00	332.00	364.50	2012	1;739.00	1,382.00	1,538.70
1985	359.80	236.00	340.30	1999	435.00	341.00	430.20	2013	1,744.50	1,295.40	1,371.10

Futures begin trading 03/04/1968.   *CME Group; New York Mercantile Exchange*

	Free Market Monthly Cash as of 12/31/2013			
Date	Open	High	Low	Close
08/30/13	1436.00	1551.00	1414.00	1518.00
09/30/13	1517.00	1535.00	1398.00	1401.00
10/31/13	1381.00	1477.00	1356.00	1446.00
11/29/13	1449.00	1467.00	1348.00	1359.00
12/31/13	1362.00	1395.00	1316.00	1369.00

MONTHLY CASH
As of 12/31/2013
Chart High 2275.00 on 03/04/2008
Chart Low 120.00 on 12/01/1971
USD / troy oz.

Free Market.

Annual High, Low and Settle of Platinum   In USD per Troy Ounce

Year	High	Low	Settle	Year	High	Low	Settle	Year	High	Low	Settle
1972	130.00	120.00	130.00	1986	675.50	341.30	477.50	2000	622.00	405.00	619.00
1973	158.00	130.00	158.00	1987	632.00	461.00	500.00	2001	637.00	415.00	480.00
1974	190.00	158.00	190.00	1988	623.50	446.00	520.50	2002	602.00	453.00	598.00
1975	190.00	155.00	155.00	1989	563.75	470.00	488.50	2003	840.00	603.00	813.00
1976	175.00	155.00	162.00	1990	532.00	391.50	411.75	2004	936.00	767.00	861.00
1977	180.00	162.00	180.00	1991	423.00	333.00	338.25	2005	1,004.00	844.00	965.00
1978	300.00	180.00	280.00	1992	391.00	332.75	353.50	2006	1,360.00	982.00	1,120.00
1979	350.00	280.00	350.00	1993	422.00	338.25	394.00	2007	1,547.00	1,122.00	1,528.00
1980	420.00	350.00	420.00	1994	425.50	378.00	417.00	2008	2,275.00	760.00	912.00
1981	475.00	420.00	475.00	1995	461.50	398.25	398.25	2009	1,505.00	916.00	1,467.00
1982	475.00	475.00	475.00	1996	431.50	367.00	369.50	2010	1,806.00	1,451.00	1,766.00
1983	475.00	475.00	475.00	1997	497.00	342.50	363.00	2011	1,910.00	1,368.00	1,395.00
1984	475.00	475.00	475.00	1998	429.00	334.25	360.25	2012	1,720.00	1,380.00	1,536.00
1985	475.00	276.75	340.30	1999	457.00	342.00	443.00	2013	1,731.00	1,300.00	1,369.00

Free Market.   *CME Group; New York Mercantile Exchange*

PLATINUM

PLATINUM - NYMEX
Weekly Selected Futures as of 01/03/2014

Date	Open	High	Low	Close
12/06/13	1362.80	1378.20	1335.50	1356.30
12/13/13	1356.90	1400.30	1354.90	1362.90
12/20/13	1363.40	1367.00	1311.70	1332.20
12/27/13	1330.60	1382.20	1324.20	1376.00
01/03/14	1377.00	1414.40	1349.00	1411.50

WEEKLY SELECTED FUTURES
As of 01/03/2014

Chart High 2308.80 on 03/04/2008
Chart Low 756.00 on 04/29/2004

CONTRACT SIZE 50 troy oz
MIN TICK .1 USD
VALUE 5 USD / contract
EACH GRID 20 USD
VALUE 1000 USD / contract
DAILY LIMIT None to 50 USD
VALUE 1,250 USD / contract
TRADING HOURS
6:00p-5:15p / 8:20a-1:05p ET

Commercial = -22285
NonCommercial = 21155
NonReportable = 1130

Nearby Futures through Last Trading Day using selected contract months: January, April, July and October.

Quarterly High, Low and Settle of Platinum Futures   In USD per Troy Ounce

Quarter	High	Low	Settle	Quarter	High	Low	Settle	Quarter	High	Low	Settle
03/2005	950.00	843.20	870.60	03/2008	2,308.80	1,523.60	2,024.40	03/2011	1,869.00	1,658.00	1,779.30
06/2005	905.00	846.50	883.50	06/2008	2,234.90	1,835.00	2,069.50	06/2011	1,889.50	1,666.20	1,724.80
09/2005	938.50	860.30	930.30	09/2008	2,089.60	995.20	1,015.10	09/2011	1,918.50	1,475.30	1,519.40
12/2005	1,026.00	914.50	973.00	12/2008	1,045.00	761.80	936.20	12/2011	1,676.40	1,347.00	1,399.70
03/2006	1,095.00	972.00	1,059.40	03/2009	1,167.40	914.00	1,120.80	03/2012	1,739.00	1,388.70	1,638.30
06/2006	1,347.00	1,065.00	1,246.70	06/2009	1,301.90	1,075.00	1,176.70	06/2012	1,658.30	1,382.00	1,449.10
09/2006	1,287.90	1,124.00	1,141.20	09/2009	1,356.30	1,090.00	1,295.60	09/2012	1,716.50	1,382.30	1,665.30
12/2006	1,289.00	1,059.60	1,139.30	12/2009	1,514.80	1,270.30	1,460.00	12/2012	1,731.20	1,515.30	1,538.70
03/2007	1,269.90	1,109.00	1,248.30	03/2010	1,646.60	1,452.00	1,639.80	03/2013	1,744.50	1,536.60	1,571.20
06/2007	1,353.80	1,240.00	1,279.00	06/2010	1,755.00	1,446.20	1,530.90	06/2013	1,601.30	1,295.40	1,336.90
09/2007	1,395.50	1,226.50	1,395.20	09/2010	1,659.90	1,491.10	1,652.00	09/2013	1,558.00	1,324.40	1,408.10
12/2007	1,551.50	1,350.00	1,528.40	12/2010	1,811.80	1,628.00	1,773.30	12/2013	1,481.30	1,311.70	1,371.10

CME Group; New York Mercantile Exchange

Free Market
Weekly Cash as of 01/03/2014

Date	Open	High	Low	Close
12/06/13	1362.00	1368.00	1337.00	1356.00
12/13/13	1356.00	1395.00	1354.00	1359.00
12/20/13	1359.00	1359.00	**1316.00**	1331.00
12/27/13	1332.00	1373.00	1322.00	1373.00
01/03/14	1356.00	**1413.00**	1356.00	1408.00

WEEKLY CASH
As of 01/03/2014
Chart High 2275.00 on 03/04/2008
Chart Low 603.00 on 04/30/2003
CONTRACT SIZE 50 troy oz
MIN TICK .1 USD
VALUE 5 USD / contract
EACH GRID 10 USD
VALUE 500 USD / contract
DAILY LIMIT None to 50 USD
VALUE 1,250 USD / contract
TRADING HOURS
6:00p-5:15p / 8:20a-1:05p ET

Free Market.

Quarterly High, Low and Settle of Platinum   In USD per Troy Ounce

Quarter	High	Low	Settle	Quarter	High	Low	Settle	Quarter	High	Low	Settle
03/2005	877.00	844.00	864.00	03/2008	2,275.00	1,534.00	2,044.00	03/2011	1,863.00	1,656.00	1,764.00
06/2005	900.00	856.00	884.00	06/2008	2,185.00	1,880.00	2,069.00	06/2011	1,880.00	1,663.00	1,722.00
09/2005	930.00	860.00	929.00	09/2008	2,080.00	1,010.00	1,010.00	09/2011	1,910.00	1,480.00	1,520.00
12/2005	1,004.00	914.00	965.00	12/2008	1,036.00	760.00	912.00	12/2011	1,668.00	1,368.00	1,395.00
03/2006	1,084.00	982.00	1,076.00	03/2009	1,160.00	916.00	1,122.00	03/2012	1,720.00	1,399.00	1,634.00
06/2006	1,335.00	1,070.00	1,232.00	06/2009	1,275.00	1,080.00	1,177.00	06/2012	1,646.00	1,385.00	1,385.00
09/2006	1,282.00	1,130.00	1,145.00	09/2009	1,346.00	1,092.00	1,297.00	09/2012	1,702.00	1,380.00	1,657.00
12/2006	1,360.00	1,055.00	1,120.00	12/2009	1,505.00	1,267.00	1,467.00	12/2012	1,715.00	1,518.00	1,536.00
03/2007	1,251.00	1,122.00	1,248.00	03/2010	1,650.00	1,457.00	1,643.00	03/2013	1,731.00	1,552.00	1,569.00
06/2007	1,338.00	1,238.00	1,276.00	06/2010	1,753.00	1,451.00	1,533.00	06/2013	1,589.00	1,300.00	1,337.00
09/2007	1,384.00	1,244.00	1,384.00	09/2010	1,659.00	1,491.00	1,657.00	09/2013	1,551.00	1,323.00	1,401.00
12/2007	1,547.00	1,356.00	1,528.00	12/2010	1,806.00	1,630.00	1,766.00	12/2013	1,477.00	1,316.00	1,369.00

CME Group; New York Mercantile Exchange

SILVER

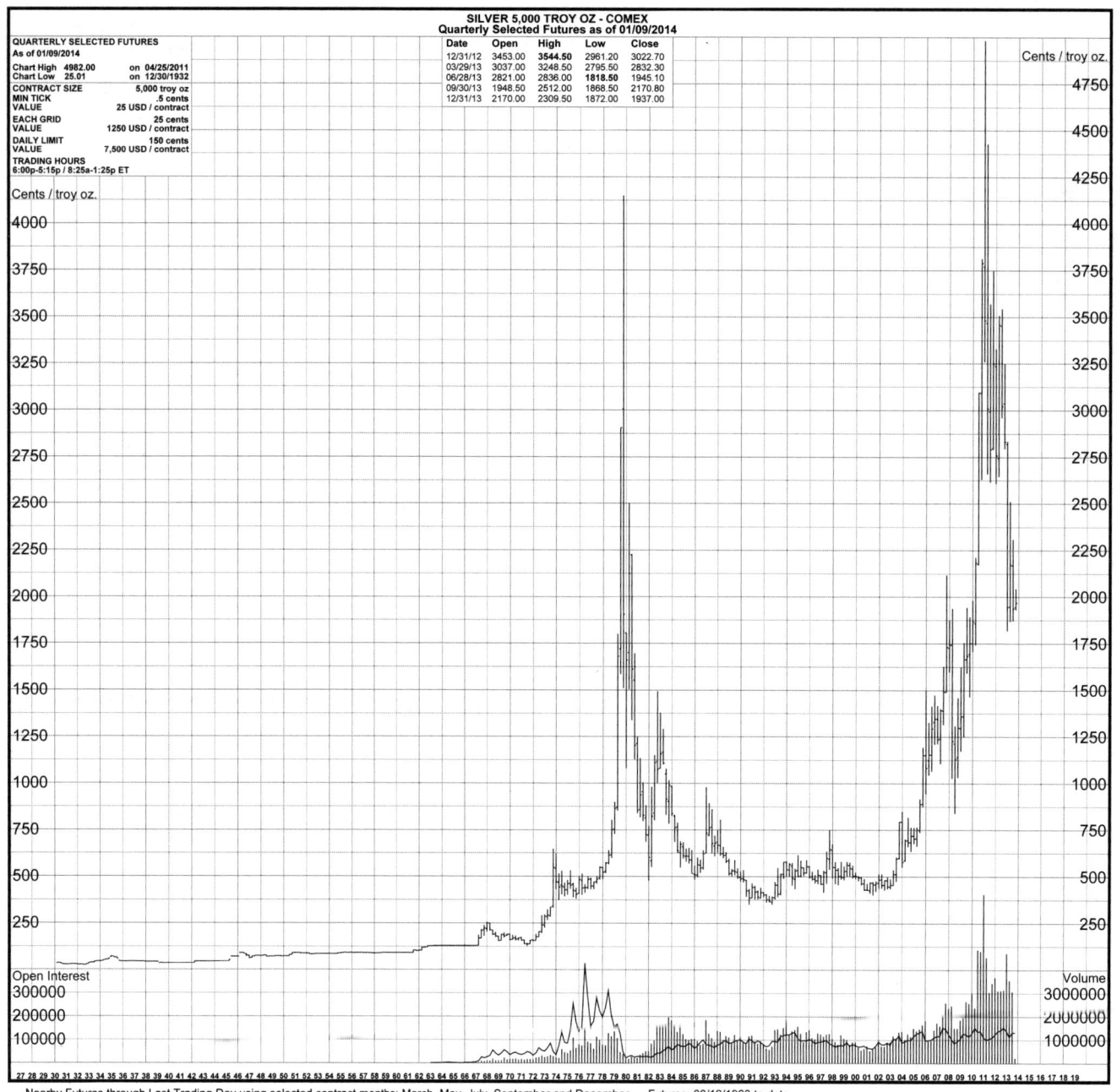

Date	Open	High	Low	Close
12/31/12	3453.00	3544.50	2961.20	3022.70
03/29/13	3037.00	3248.50	2795.50	2832.30
06/28/13	2821.00	2836.00	1818.50	1945.10
09/30/13	1948.50	2512.00	1868.50	2170.80
12/31/13	2170.00	2309.50	1872.00	1937.00

QUARTERLY SELECTED FUTURES
As of 01/09/2014

Chart High 4982.00 on 04/25/2011
Chart Low 25.01 on 12/30/1932
CONTRACT SIZE 5,000 troy oz
MIN TICK .5 cents
VALUE 25 USD / contract
EACH GRID 25 cents
VALUE 1250 USD / contract
DAILY LIMIT 150 cents
VALUE 7,500 USD / contract
TRADING HOURS
6:00p-5:15p / 8:25a-1:25p ET

Nearby Futures through Last Trading Day using selected contract months: March, May, July, September and December. Futures: 06/12/1963 to date.

Annual High, Low and Settle of Silver Futures   In Cents per Troy Ounce

Year	High	Low	Settle	Year	High	Low	Settle	Year	High	Low	Settle
1930	45.00	32.63	32.63	1944	44.75	44.75	44.75	1958	90.38	88.63	89.88
1931	32.22	26.77	30.12	1945	70.75	44.75	70.75	1959	91.63	89.88	91.38
1932	30.14	25.01	25.01	1946	90.12	70.75	86.73	1960	91.50	91.38	91.38
1933	43.55	25.40	43.55	1947	86.25	59.75	74.63	1961	104.75	91.38	104.75
1934	54.39	44.19	54.39	1948	77.50	70.00	70.00	1962	122.00	101.00	120.50
1935	74.36	54.42	58.42	1949	73.25	70.00	73.25	1963	129.50	121.00	129.50
1936	47.25	44.75	45.35	1950	80.00	71.75	80.00	1964	129.30	129.30	129.30
1937	45.46	43.81	43.81	1951	90.16	80.00	88.00	1965	129.30	129.30	129.30
1938	44.75	42.75	42.75	1952	88.00	82.75	83.25	1966	129.30	129.30	129.30
1939	42.75	34.75	34.96	1953	85.25	83.25	85.25	1967	217.00	129.30	210.00
1940	34.95	34.75	34.75	1954	85.25	85.25	85.25	1968	256.50	181.00	190.00
1941	35.12	34.75	35.12	1955	92.00	85.25	90.50	1969	202.50	154.00	180.00
1942	44.75	35.12	44.75	1956	91.63	90.00	91.38	1970	193.00	157.00	163.50
1943	44.75	44.75	44.75	1957	91.38	89.63	89.63	1971	175.20	128.80	138.00

Futures begin trading 06/12/1963.   Data continued on page 376.   *CME Group; New York Mercantile Exchange*

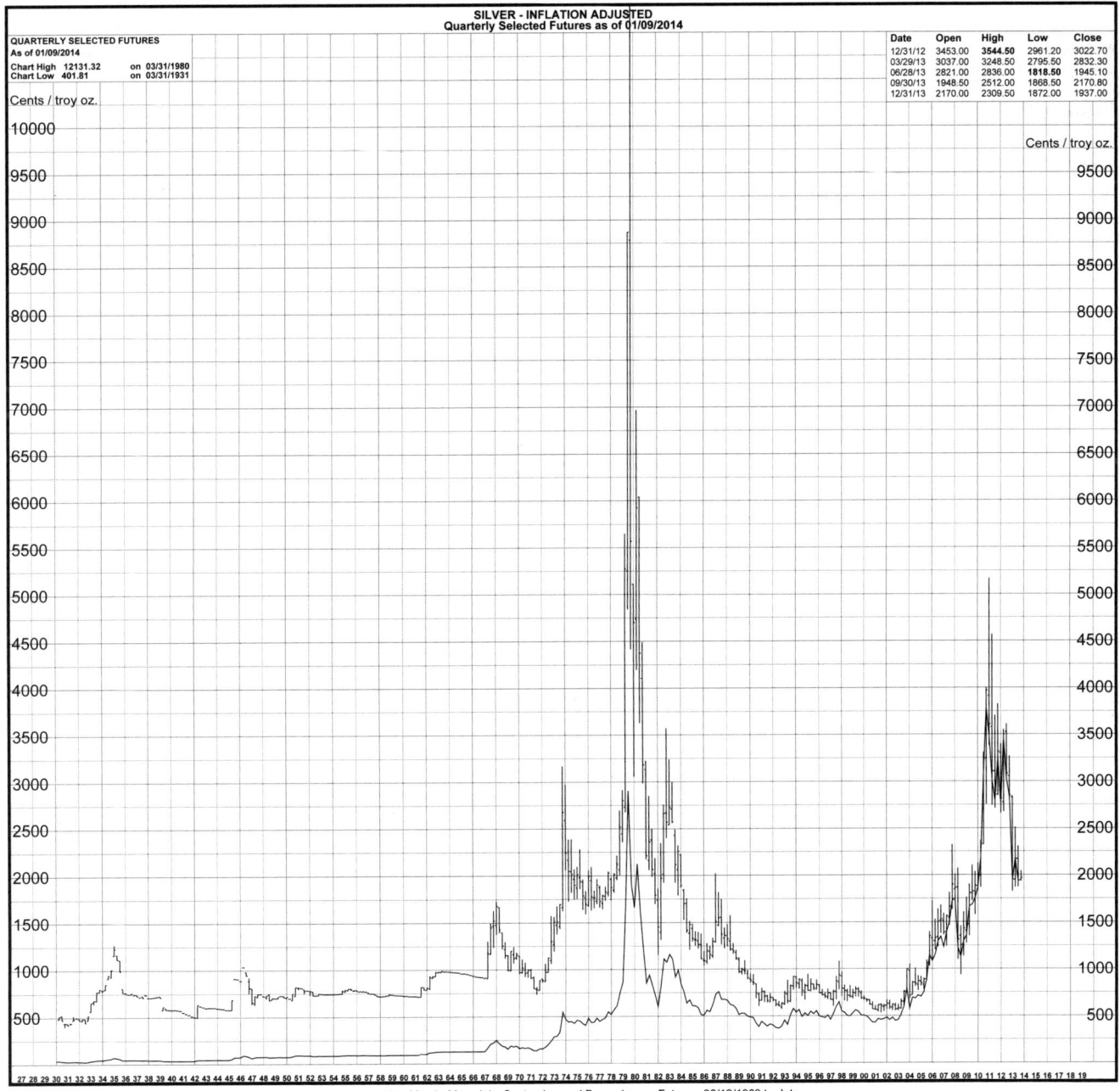

SILVER - INFLATION ADJUSTED
Quarterly Selected Futures as of 01/09/2014

QUARTERLY SELECTED FUTURES
As of 01/09/2014
Chart High 12131.32 on 03/31/1980
Chart Low 401.81 on 03/31/1931

Cents / troy oz.

Date	Open	High	Low	Close
12/31/12	3453.00	3544.50	2961.20	3022.70
03/29/13	3037.00	3248.50	2795.50	2832.30
06/28/13	2821.00	2836.00	1818.50	1945.10
09/30/13	1948.50	2512.00	1868.50	2170.80
12/31/13	2170.00	2309.50	1872.00	1937.00

Nearby Futures through Last Trading Day using selected contract months: March, May, July, September and December.   Futures: 06/12/1963 to date.

Annual High, Low and Settle of Silver   In Cents per Troy Ounce

Year	High	Low	Settle	Year	High	Low	Settle	Year	High	Low	Settle
1930	45.00	32.63	32.63	1944	44.75	44.75	44.75	1958	90.38	88.63	89.88
1931	32.22	26.77	30.12	1945	70.75	44.75	70.75	1959	91.63	89.88	91.38
1932	30.14	25.01	25.01	1946	90.12	70.75	86.73	1960	91.50	91.38	91.38
1933	43.55	25.40	43.55	1947	86.25	59.75	74.63	1961	104.75	91.38	104.75
1934	54.39	44.19	54.39	1948	77.50	70.00	70.00	1962	122.00	101.00	120.50
1935	74.36	54.42	58.42	1949	73.25	70.00	73.25	1963	129.30	121.00	129.30
1936	47.25	44.75	45.35	1950	80.00	71.75	80.00	1964	129.30	129.30	129.30
1937	45.46	43.81	43.81	1951	90.16	80.00	88.00	1965	129.30	129.30	129.30
1938	44.75	42.75	42.75	1952	88.00	82.75	83.25	1966	129.30	129.30	129.30
1939	42.75	34.75	34.96	1953	85.25	83.25	85.25	1967	217.00	129.30	210.00
1940	34.95	34.75	34.75	1954	85.25	85.25	85.25	1968	256.50	181.00	190.00
1941	35.12	34.75	35.12	1955	92.00	85.25	90.50	1969	202.50	154.00	180.00
1942	44.75	35.12	44.75	1956	91.63	90.00	91.38	1970	193.00	157.00	163.50
1943	44.75	44.75	44.75	1957	91.38	89.63	89.63	1971	175.20	128.80	138.00

Data continued on page 377.   *CME Group; New York Mercantile Exchange*

SILVER

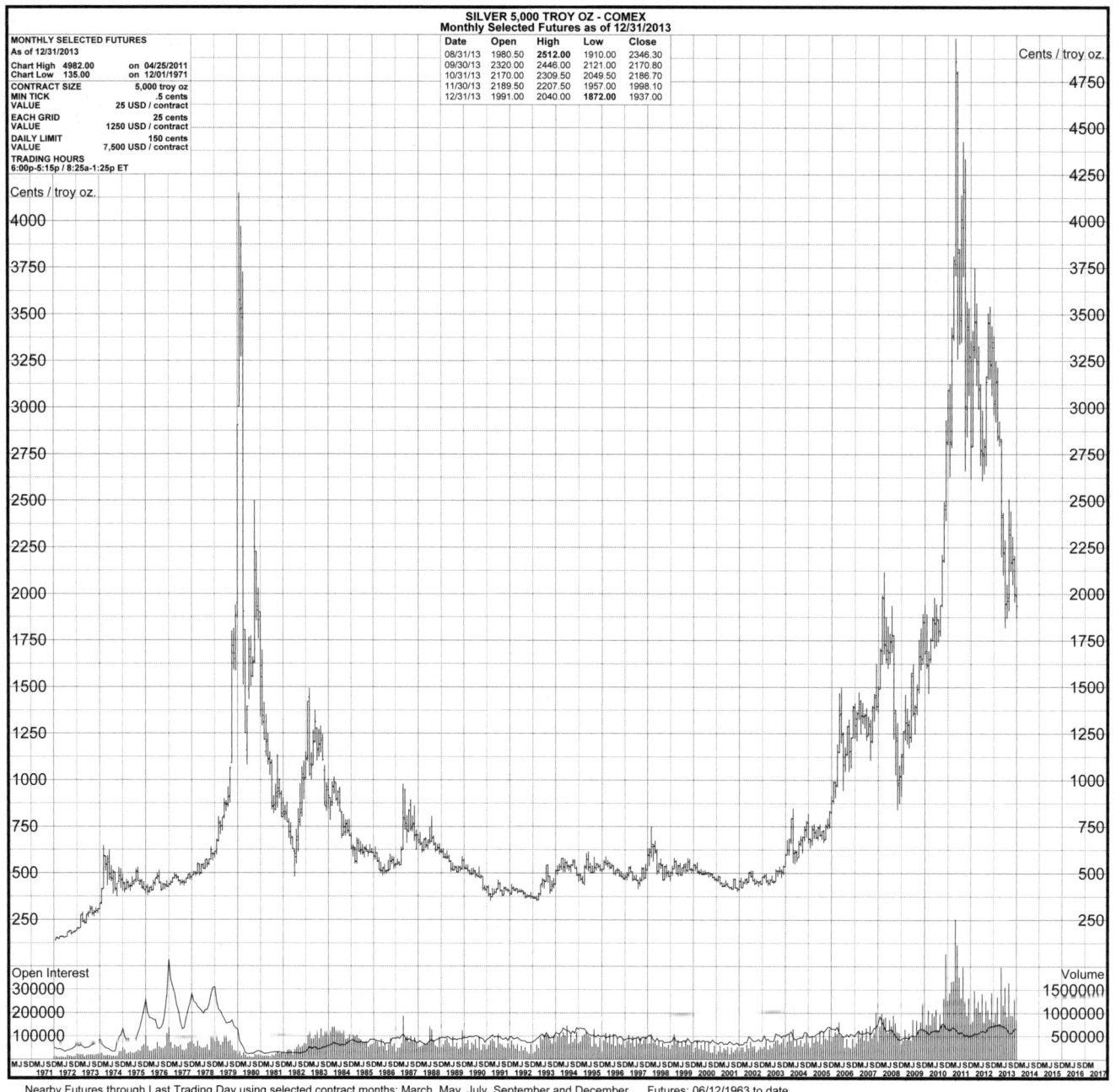

SILVER 5,000 TROY OZ - COMEX
Monthly Selected Futures as of 12/31/2013

Date	Open	High	Low	Close
08/31/13	1980.50	2512.00	1910.00	2346.30
09/30/13	2320.00	2446.00	2121.00	2170.80
10/31/13	2170.00	2309.50	2049.50	2186.70
11/30/13	2189.50	2207.50	1957.00	1998.10
12/31/13	1991.00	2040.00	1872.00	1937.00

MONTHLY SELECTED FUTURES
As of 12/31/2013
Chart High 4982.00 on 04/25/2011
Chart Low 135.00 on 12/01/1971
CONTRACT SIZE 5,000 troy oz
MIN TICK .5 cents
VALUE 25 USD / contract
EACH GRID 25 cents
VALUE 1250 USD / contract
DAILY LIMIT 150 cents
VALUE 7,500 USD / contract
TRADING HOURS
6:00p-5:15p / 8:25a-1:25p ET

Nearby Futures through Last Trading Day using selected contract months: March, May, July, September and December.   Futures: 06/12/1963 to date.

Annual High, Low and Settle of Silver Futures   In Cents per Troy Ounce

Year	High	Low	Settle	Year	High	Low	Settle	Year	High	Low	Settle
1967	230.25	128.80	226.00	1981	1,697.00	797.00	829.00	1995	616.00	434.00	520.70
1968	259.00	184.00	198.20	1982	1,150.00	478.00	1,110.00	1996	589.00	464.00	479.00
1969	206.90	151.00	184.10	1983	1,493.00	832.00	915.50	1997	635.00	415.50	598.80
1970	195.00	152.10	166.00	1984	1,017.00	624.50	638.00	1998	750.00	456.00	502.00
1971	177.20	128.20	138.40	1985	689.00	548.00	590.50	1999	581.00	482.00	545.30
1972	205.50	138.70	204.70	1986	642.00	485.00	546.00	2000	560.00	455.00	463.50
1973	331.30	195.40	329.70	1987	979.50	536.50	677.00	2001	488.00	401.50	458.80
1974	643.00	326.10	447.00	1988	806.00	598.00	613.00	2002	515.00	421.00	481.20
1975	532.00	388.00	423.60	1989	631.00	502.00	527.30	2003	605.00	434.60	596.50
1976	515.00	380.00	439.00	1990	544.50	393.00	424.70	2004	850.00	549.50	683.70
1977	500.00	430.50	484.90	1991	464.00	350.50	391.20	2005	917.00	635.00	889.00
1978	640.00	482.20	613.70	1992	441.00	362.00	369.00	2006	1,497.00	876.00	1,293.50
1979	2,905.00	598.00	2,905.00	1993	547.00	351.00	511.70	2007	1,627.50	1,106.00	1,492.00
1980	4,150.00	1,080.00	1,612.00	1994	582.00	453.00	491.70	2008	2,118.50	840.00	1,129.50

Data continued from page 374.   *CME Group; New York Mercantile Exchange*

Silver Composite
Monthly Cash as of 12/31/2013

Date	Open	High	Low	Close
08/30/13	1981.40	**2509.80**	1914.20	2346.20
09/30/13	2405.00	2447.50	2119.60	2166.40
10/31/13	2166.40	2307.00	2049.80	2188.80
11/29/13	2191.00	2205.30	1958.00	1997.50
12/31/13	1994.00	2047.40	**1872.30**	1944.70

MONTHLY CASH
As of 12/31/2013
Chart High 4975.20 on 04/25/2011
Chart Low 135.00 on 12/01/1971

Gold / Silver Ratio

Annual High, Low and Settle of Silver   In Cents per Troy Ounce

Year	High	Low	Settle	Year	High	Low	Settle	Year	High	Low	Settle
1972	204.80	138.70	204.20	1986	619.50	487.00	536.50	2000	551.00	455.00	457.00
1973	328.40	196.20	328.40	1987	1,020.00	536.00	669.50	2001	484.00	404.00	462.00
1974	670.00	327.00	437.00	1988	799.00	601.00	602.00	2002	515.00	423.00	478.00
1975	522.50	391.00	416.50	1989	617.00	501.50	518.00	2003	601.00	434.00	594.00
1976	510.00	381.50	437.50	1990	539.00	392.00	422.00	2004	845.00	545.50	682.28
1977	496.00	430.00	478.00	1991	463.00	352.00	390.00	2005	926.94	632.60	881.60
1978	629.60	482.90	607.40	1992	439.00	363.00	368.00	2006	1,521.30	869.40	1,289.50
1979	2,800.00	596.10	2,800.00	1993	551.00	353.00	510.00	2007	1,621.20	1,106.19	1,479.42
1980	4,800.00	1,080.00	1,565.00	1994	585.00	454.00	488.00	2008	2,134.90	845.76	1,137.45
1981	1,645.00	795.00	825.00	1995	613.00	436.00	518.00	2009	1,945.40	1,034.76	1,687.30
1982	1,121.00	488.50	1,090.00	1996	587.00	468.00	477.00	2010	3,091.40	1,463.45	3,084.60
1983	1,474.50	834.00	895.00	1997	638.00	418.00	593.00	2011	4,975.20	2,604.60	2,771.40
1984	1,003.50	626.00	636.00	1998	787.00	462.00	502.00	2012	3,743.00	2,613.30	3,029.30
1985	673.50	557.00	583.00	1999	582.00	482.00	540.00	2013	3,245.40	1,820.10	1,944.70

Handy and Harman: to 05/1990; Composite: 06/1990 to date.   Data continued from page 375.   *CME Group; New York Mercantile Exchange*

SILVER

SILVER 5,000 TROY OZ - COMEX
Weekly Selected Futures as of 01/03/2014

Date	Open	High	Low	Close
12/06/13	1991.00	1991.00	1898.00	1946.50
12/13/13	1946.50	2040.00	1940.20	1955.90
12/20/13	1950.00	2020.00	1910.00	1941.80
12/27/13	1943.00	2001.30	1935.00	2001.30
01/03/14	2008.00	2044.00	1872.00	2021.10

WEEKLY SELECTED FUTURES
As of 01/03/2014

Chart High 4982.00 on 04/25/2011
Chart Low 549.50 on 05/10/2004
CONTRACT SIZE 5,000 troy oz
MIN TICK .5 cents
VALUE 25 USD / contract
EACH GRID 40 cents
VALUE 2000 USD / contract
DAILY LIMIT 150 cents
VALUE 7,500 USD / contract
TRADING HOURS
6:00p-5:15p / 8:25a-1:25p ET

Commercial = -19686
NonCommercial = 12098
NonReportable = 7588

Nearby Futures through Last Trading Day using selected contract months: March, May, July, September and December.

Quarterly High, Low and Settle of Silver Futures   In Cents per Troy Ounce

Quarter	High	Low	Settle	Quarter	High	Low	Settle	Quarter	High	Low	Settle
03/2005	764.00	635.00	718.00	03/2008	2,118.50	1,491.00	1,731.00	03/2011	3,813.00	2,630.00	3,788.80
06/2005	763.00	677.00	702.80	06/2008	1,877.00	1,599.50	1,742.00	06/2011	4,982.00	3,259.50	3,481.20
09/2005	764.50	663.00	751.20	09/2008	1,937.50	1,028.00	1,227.50	09/2011	4,427.50	2,658.50	3,008.30
12/2005	917.00	736.00	889.00	12/2008	1,308.00	840.00	1,129.50	12/2011	3,570.00	2,614.50	2,791.50
03/2006	1,194.00	876.00	1,152.00	03/2009	1,460.00	1,032.00	1,298.50	03/2012	3,748.00	2,790.50	3,248.40
06/2006	1,497.00	945.00	1,083.30	06/2009	1,625.00	1,172.50	1,357.40	06/2012	3,329.50	2,607.00	2,758.00
09/2006	1,326.00	1,045.00	1,154.00	09/2009	1,755.50	1,248.00	1,665.80	09/2012	3,509.00	2,644.50	3,457.70
12/2006	1,414.00	1,065.00	1,293.50	12/2009	1,943.00	1,592.00	1,684.50	12/2012	3,544.50	2,961.20	3,022.70
03/2007	1,474.50	1,209.50	1,345.00	03/2010	1,892.50	1,465.00	1,752.60	03/2013	3,248.50	2,795.50	2,832.30
06/2007	1,417.00	1,212.50	1,235.30	06/2010	1,980.00	1,709.00	1,867.10	06/2013	2,836.00	1,818.50	1,945.10
09/2007	1,400.00	1,106.00	1,392.00	09/2010	2,212.50	1,742.30	2,182.10	09/2013	2,512.00	1,868.50	2,170.80
12/2007	1,627.50	1,315.00	1,492.00	12/2010	3,097.50	2,172.50	3,093.70	12/2013	2,309.50	1,872.00	1,937.00

CME Group; New York Mercantile Exchange

378

Silver Composite
Weekly Cash as of 01/03/2014

Date	Open	High	Low	Close
12/06/13	1994.00	1996.00	1888.30	1947.50
12/13/13	1948.00	2047.40	1928.90	1968.90
12/20/13	1965.50	2029.20	1911.90	1937.30
12/27/13	1938.00	2010.40	1927.10	2004.40
01/03/14	2006.00	2041.80	1872.30	2012.10

WEEKLY CASH
As of 01/03/2014
Chart High 4975.20 on 04/25/2011
Chart Low 434.00 on 03/21/2003

Cents / troy oz.

24-HR Composite.

Quarterly High, Low and Settle of Silver   In Cents per Troy Ounce

Quarter	High	Low	Settle	Quarter	High	Low	Settle	Quarter	High	Low	Settle
03/2005	764.08	632.60	715.53	03/2008	2,134.90	1,480.10	1,722.60	03/2011	3,814.10	2,638.90	3,764.30
06/2005	761.00	676.60	704.40	06/2008	1,876.86	1,599.10	1,741.50	06/2011	4,975.20	3,231.80	3,465.60
09/2005	759.60	664.40	745.40	09/2008	1,947.50	1,026.50	1,201.70	09/2011	4,416.70	2,604.60	2,989.70
12/2005	926.94	731.50	881.60	12/2008	1,298.77	845.76	1,137.45	12/2011	3,564.70	2,615.10	2,771.40
03/2006	1,192.50	869.40	1,150.70	03/2009	1,463.65	1,034.76	1,295.60	03/2012	3,743.00	2,772.20	3,221.30
06/2006	1,521.30	947.60	1,106.60	06/2009	1,623.70	1,182.28	1,359.20	06/2012	3,326.10	2,613.30	2,742.20
09/2006	1,327.60	1,044.60	1,145.70	09/2009	1,766.40	1,245.70	1,665.75	09/2012	3,514.60	2,647.00	3,445.30
12/2006	1,417.82	1,058.60	1,289.50	12/2009	1,945.40	1,589.55	1,687.30	12/2012	3,534.80	2,960.10	3,029.30
03/2007	1,474.40	1,205.56	1,337.40	03/2010	1,889.60	1,463.45	1,749.00	03/2013	3,245.40	2,794.60	2,845.59
06/2007	1,414.50	1,212.80	1,237.60	06/2010	1,981.00	1,708.90	1,861.00	06/2013	2,836.60	1,820.10	1,965.60
09/2007	1,385.40	1,106.19	1,374.60	09/2010	2,207.00	1,735.00	2,175.00	09/2013	2,509.80	1,869.60	2,166.40
12/2007	1,621.20	1,309.00	1,479.42	12/2010	3,091.40	2,172.50	3,084.60	12/2013	2,307.00	1,872.30	1,944.70

Composite.   *CME Group; New York Mercantile Exchange*

TIN

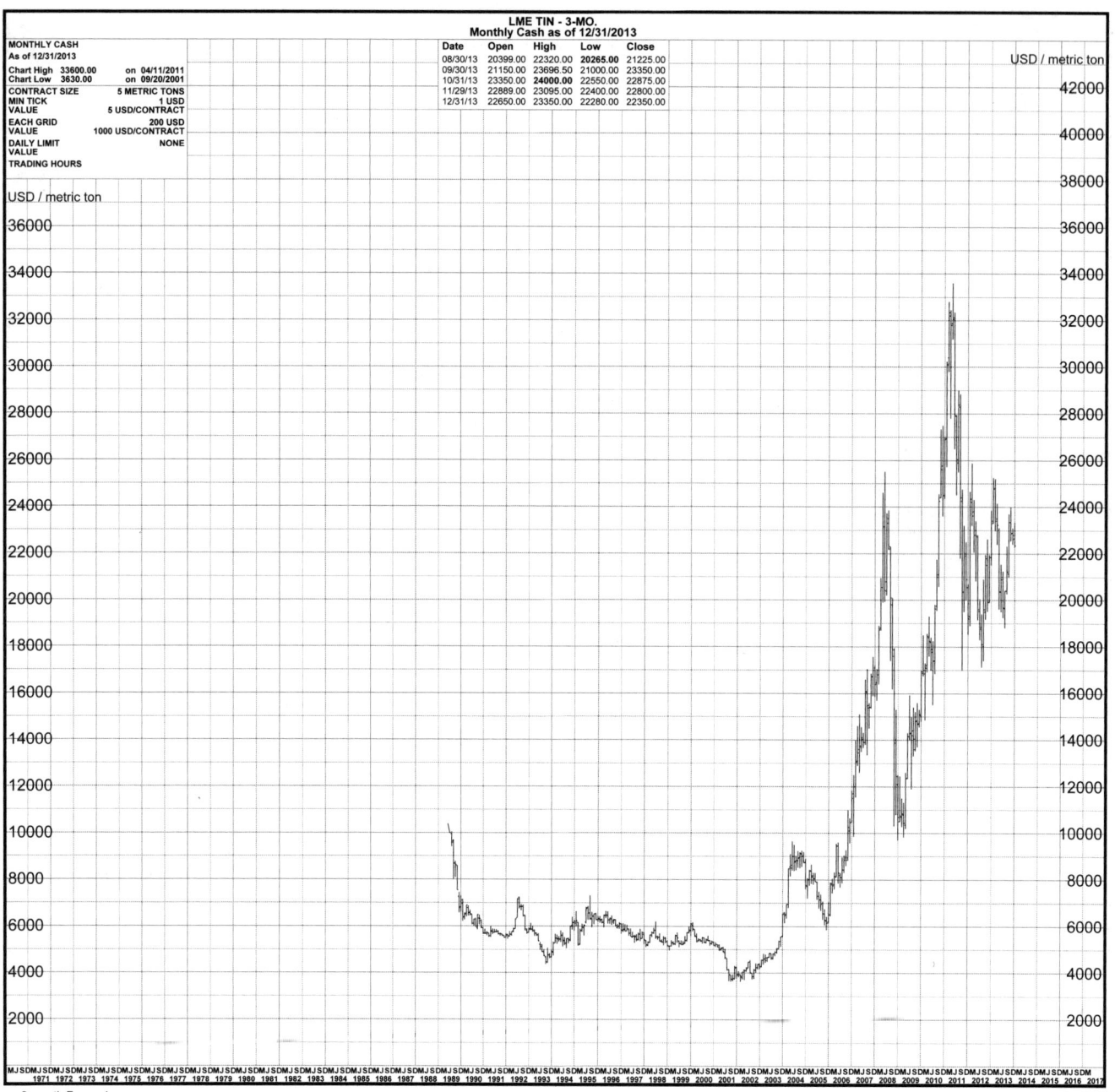

LME TIN - 3-MO.
Monthly Cash as of 12/31/2013

Date	Open	High	Low	Close
08/30/13	20399.00	22320.00	20265.00	21225.00
09/30/13	21150.00	23696.50	21000.00	23350.00
10/31/13	23350.00	24000.00	22550.00	22875.00
11/29/13	22889.00	23095.00	22400.00	22800.00
12/31/13	22650.00	23350.00	22280.00	22350.00

MONTHLY CASH
As of 12/31/2013
Chart High 33600.00 on 04/11/2011
Chart Low 3630.00 on 09/20/2001
CONTRACT SIZE 5 METRIC TONS
MIN TICK 1 USD
VALUE 5 USD/CONTRACT
EACH GRID 200 USD
VALUE 1000 USD/CONTRACT
DAILY LIMIT NONE
VALUE
TRADING HOURS

USD / metric ton

3-month Forward.

Annual High, Low and Settle of Tin   In USD per Metric Ton

Year	High	Low	Settle	Year	High	Low	Settle	Year	High	Low	Settle
1972	----	----	----	1986	----	----	----	2000	6,175	5,160	5,180
1973	----	----	----	1987	----	----	----	2001	5,320	3,630	3,940
1974	----	----	----	1988	----	----	----	2002	4,550	3,630	4,280
1975	----	----	----	1989	10,440	6,570	7,100	2003	6,570	4,260	6,525
1976	----	----	----	1990	7,150	5,650	5,705	2004	9,650	6,150	7,765
1977	----	----	----	1991	5,990	5,500	5,605	2005	8,650	5,850	6,500
1978	----	----	----	1992	7,250	5,447	5,850	2006	11,850	6,450	11,510
1979	----	----	----	1993	6,130	4,360	4,900	2007	17,575	9,849	16,400
1980	----	----	----	1994	6,400	4,730	6,210	2008	25,500	9,700	10,700
1981	----	----	----	1995	7,310	5,170	6,325	2009	17,000	9,825	16,950
1982	----	----	----	1996	6,650	5,680	5,840	2010	27,500	14,850	26,900
1983	----	----	----	1997	6,130	5,235	5,420	2011	33,600	17,000	19,200
1984	----	----	----	1998	6,210	5,100	5,170	2012	25,880	17,125	23,400
1985	----	----	----	1999	6,150	4,960	6,100	2013	25,250	18,809	22,350

3-month Forward.   *Source: London Metal Exchange*

Date	Open	High	Low	Close
12/06/13	22650.00	23250.00	22400.00	23150.00
12/13/13	23240.00	23350.00	22303.00	22750.00
12/20/13	22800.00	23145.00	22651.00	22950.00
12/27/13	22950.00	23000.00	22700.00	22850.00
01/03/14	22849.00	22850.00	21300.00	21500.00

3-month Forward.

Quarterly High, Low and Settle of Tin   In USD per Metric Ton

Quarter	High	Low	Settle	Quarter	High	Low	Settle	Quarter	High	Low	Settle
03/2005	8,650	7,200	8,125	03/2008	20,950	15,700	20,550	03/2011	32,799	25,725	31,800
06/2005	8,300	7,150	7,300	06/2008	25,500	19,900	23,305	06/2011	33,600	24,510	26,050
09/2005	7,500	6,300	6,555	09/2008	23,850	16,190	17,600	09/2011	29,000	17,000	20,350
12/2005	7,050	5,850	6,500	12/2008	17,950	9,700	10,700	12/2011	23,200	18,525	19,200
03/2006	8,325	6,450	8,150	03/2009	12,450	9,825	10,435	03/2012	25,880	18,900	22,800
06/2006	9,602	7,675	8,100	06/2009	15,925	10,195	14,275	06/2012	23,400	18,300	18,775
09/2006	9,275	7,860	8,850	09/2009	15,400	11,900	14,800	09/2012	21,948	17,125	21,800
12/2006	11,850	8,825	11,510	12/2009	17,000	13,700	16,950	12/2012	23,847	19,511	23,400
03/2007	14,600	9,849	13,450	03/2010	18,565	14,850	18,450	03/2013	25,250	22,391	23,230
06/2007	15,100	12,600	13,900	06/2010	19,300	15,500	17,400	06/2013	23,100	19,250	19,675
09/2007	17,050	13,348	15,400	09/2010	24,550	16,850	24,250	09/2013	23,697	18,809	23,350
12/2007	17,575	15,350	16,400	12/2010	27,500	23,602	26,900	12/2013	24,000	22,280	22,350

3-month Forward.   *Source: London Metal Exchange*

ZINC

LME SHG ZINC - 3-MO.
Monthly Cash as of 12/31/2013

Date	Open	High	Low	Close
08/30/13	1845.30	2009.00	1833.30	1905.00
09/30/13	1907.30	1930.00	1855.00	1918.00
10/31/13	1917.00	1980.00	1861.00	1952.00
11/29/13	1953.00	1967.00	1863.00	1887.00
12/31/13	1880.50	2108.00	1870.00	2055.00

MONTHLY CASH
As of 12/31/2013
Chart High 4580.00 on 11/10/2006
Chart Low 468.50 on 02/22/1978
CONTRACT SIZE 25 METRIC TONS
MIN TICK .5 USD
VALUE 12.5 USD/CONTRACT
EACH GRID 20 USD
VALUE 500 USD/CONTRACT
DAILY LIMIT NONE
VALUE
TRADING HOURS

USD / metric ton

3-month Forward.

Annual High, Low and Settle of Zinc   In USD per Metric Ton

Year	High	Low	Settle	Year	High	Low	Settle	Year	High	Low	Settle
1972	----	----	----	1986	890.4	601.4	794.3	2000	1,235.0	1,042.0	1,042.0
1973	----	----	----	1987	916.2	711.3	787.8	2001	1,081.0	745.0	787.0
1974	----	----	----	1988	1,575.0	771.0	1,555.0	2002	874.5	738.0	767.0
1975	----	----	----	1989	1,975.0	1,275.0	1,292.0	2003	1,023.0	757.0	1,017.0
1976	----	----	----	1990	1,750.0	1,220.0	1,257.0	2004	1,262.0	950.0	1,246.0
1977	771.6	507.2	559.6	1991	1,273.0	989.0	1,115.0	2005	1,925.0	1,160.0	1,909.0
1978	775.2	468.5	726.3	1992	1,397.0	1,032.0	1,081.0	2006	4,580.0	1,877.0	4,205.7
1979	848.3	641.0	759.1	1993	1,134.0	873.5	1,030.0	2007	4,270.0	2,135.0	2,360.0
1980	956.4	670.5	828.6	1994	1,214.0	918.0	1,162.0	2008	2,900.0	1,038.0	1,215.0
1981	1,054.5	746.1	903.3	1995	1,239.0	963.0	1,024.0	2009	2,615.0	1,070.0	2,560.0
1982	895.0	667.9	690.0	1996	1,118.0	1,000.5	1,060.0	2010	2,736.0	1,577.0	2,454.0
1983	918.5	680.3	914.6	1997	1,674.0	1,054.5	1,107.0	2011	2,599.8	1,718.5	1,845.0
1984	1,049.3	740.2	782.7	1998	1,185.0	923.0	934.0	2012	2,220.0	1,745.0	2,080.0
1985	905.2	574.8	708.7	1999	1,245.0	914.0	1,245.0	2013	2,230.0	1,740.0	2,055.0

3-month Forward.   *Source: London Metal Exchange*

LME SHG ZINC - 3-MO. Weekly Cash as of 01/03/2014				
Date	Open	High	Low	Close
12/06/13	1880.50	1912.00	1870.00	1905.00
12/13/13	1900.00	1978.80	1899.80	1978.00
12/20/13	1972.50	2045.00	1969.50	2040.00
12/27/13	2039.00	2108.00	2032.00	2089.00
01/03/14	2087.00	2103.00	2025.00	2026.00

WEEKLY CASH As of 01/03/2014

Chart High 4580.00 on 11/10/2006
Chart Low 757.00 on 04/23/2003
CONTRACT SIZE 25 METRIC TONS
MIN TICK .5 USD
VALUE 12.5 USD/CONTRACT
EACH GRID 20 USD
VALUE 500 USD/CONTRACT
DAILY LIMIT NONE
VALUE
TRADING HOURS

3-month Forward.

Quarterly High, Low and Settle of Zinc   In USD per Metric Ton

Quarter	High	Low	Settle	Quarter	High	Low	Settle	Quarter	High	Low	Settle
03/2005	1,450.0	1,160.0	1,375.0	03/2008	2,900.0	2,150.0	2,320.0	03/2011	2,599.8	2,220.0	2,362.0
06/2005	1,392.0	1,215.0	1,230.0	06/2008	2,420.0	1,850.0	1,940.0	06/2011	2,555.0	2,048.0	2,364.9
09/2005	1,460.2	1,170.0	1,420.0	09/2008	2,120.0	1,605.0	1,680.0	09/2011	2,539.5	1,821.0	1,860.0
12/2005	1,925.0	1,399.0	1,909.0	12/2008	1,699.0	1,038.0	1,215.0	12/2011	2,112.0	1,718.5	1,845.0
03/2006	2,705.0	1,877.0	2,655.0	03/2009	1,365.0	1,070.0	1,328.0	03/2012	2,220.0	1,824.0	2,000.0
06/2006	4,000.0	2,620.0	3,220.0	06/2009	1,720.3	1,281.5	1,546.0	06/2012	2,073.8	1,745.0	1,877.0
09/2006	3,740.0	3,065.0	3,344.9	09/2009	2,015.0	1,440.0	1,950.0	09/2012	2,153.8	1,779.0	2,096.0
12/2006	4,580.0	3,260.0	4,205.7	12/2009	2,615.0	1,855.0	2,560.0	12/2012	2,134.0	1,812.5	2,080.0
03/2007	4,270.0	2,990.0	3,255.2	03/2010	2,736.0	1,935.0	2,370.0	03/2013	2,230.0	1,875.0	1,897.0
06/2007	4,170.5	3,119.9	3,350.2	06/2010	2,550.0	1,577.0	1,782.0	06/2013	1,970.0	1,811.8	1,853.0
09/2007	3,780.0	2,680.0	3,045.0	09/2010	2,284.8	1,736.5	2,195.0	09/2013	2,009.0	1,740.0	1,918.0
12/2007	3,205.0	2,135.0	2,360.0	12/2010	2,638.8	2,019.5	2,454.0	12/2013	2,108.0	1,861.0	2,055.0

3-month Forward.   *Source: London Metal Exchange*